Tenth Edition

Wrightsman's
Psychology
and the Legal System

Kirk Heilbrun
Drexel University

Edie Greene
University of Colorado Springs

Amy Bradfield Douglass
Bates College

Cengage

Australia • Brazil • Canada • Mexico • Singapore • United Kingdom • United States

Wrightsman's Psychology and the Legal System, Tenth Edition

Kirk Heilbrun, Edie Greene and Amy Bradfield Douglass

SVP, Product: Erin Joyner

VP, Product: Thais Alencar

Portfolio Product Director: Laura Ross

Portfolio Product Manager: Marta Healey-Gerth

Product Assistant: Fantasia Mejia

Content Manager: Sangeetha Vijay, Lumina Datamatics Ltd.

Digital Project Manager: Scott Diggins

VP, Product Marketing: Jason Sakos

Director, Product Marketing: Neena Bali

Product Marketing Manager: Chris Walz

Content Acquisition Analyst: Deanna Ettinger

Production Service: Lumina Datamatics Ltd.

Designer: Sara Greenwood

Cover Image Source: ET-ARTWORKS/Getty Images

Interior Image: Lightspring/Shutterstock.com

For product information and technology assistance, contact us at **Cengage Customer & Sales Support, 1-800-354-9706 or support.cengage.com**.

For permission to use material from this text or product, submit all requests online at **www.copyright.com**.

Library of Congress Control Number: 2022922040

ISBN: 978-0-357-79746-4

Cengage
200 Pier 4 Boulevard
Boston, MA 02210
USA

Cengage is a leading provider of customized learning solutions with employees residing in nearly 40 different countries and sales in more than 125 countries around the world. Find your local representative at **www.cengage.com.**

To learn more about Cengage platforms and services, register or access your online learning solution, or purchase materials for your course, visit **www.cengage.com**.

Notice to the Reader

Publisher does not warrant or guarantee any of the products described herein or perform any independent analysis in connection with any of the product information contained herein. Publisher does not assume, and expressly disclaims, any obligation to obtain and include information other than that provided to it by the manufacturer. The reader is expressly warned to consider and adopt all safety precautions that might be indicated by the activities described herein and to avoid all potential hazards. By following the instructions contained herein, the reader willingly assumes all risks in connection with such instructions. The publisher makes no representations or warranties of any kind, including but not limited to, the warranties of fitness for particular purpose or merchantability, nor are any such representations implied with respect to the material set forth herein, and the publisher takes no responsibility with respect to such material. The publisher shall not be liable for any special, consequential, or exemplary damages resulting, in whole or part, from the readers' use of, or reliance upon, this material.

Printed in the United States of America
Print Number: 01   Print Year: 2023

Dedication
To the importance of facts, evidence, and critical thinking
in psychology and law and beyond.

Brief Contents

Contents

Chapter 9

Alternatives to Traditional Criminal Prosecution and Civil Litigation   170

Chapter 10

Forensic Assessment in Juvenile and Criminal Cases   186

Preface

This is the 10th edition of *Psychology and the Legal System.* Its authors have continued to present the material by striving to be incisive, rigorous, and accessible—values in place since the 1st edition, solely authored by Lawrence Wrightsman more than three decades ago. Professor Wrightsman's name is included in the title to honor his many contributions to this book and to the field of psychology and law. In this edition, Kirk Heilbrun and Edie Greene are joined by a third author, Amy Bradfield Douglass.

We continue to believe that the law is inherently psychological. It is made by people with varying desires and ambitions, interpreted by individuals with different (sometimes contradictory) perspectives, and experienced—either directly or indirectly—by all of us. Both psychology and the law are about motivation and behavior. Indeed, for centuries the legal system has been a powerful influence on people's everyday activities. From the Supreme Court's 1954 school desegregation decision to its 2014 case concerning application of the death penalty to people with intellectual disabilities, and with the Court's composition transitioning considerably during the Trump presidency, the legal system continues to have considerable impact on individual lives.

As we move further into the 21st century, we find it ever more useful to describe the law from the perspective of psychology, a behavioral science that also has a significant applied component. We are not alone. In fact, matters of law and psychology are often cited in the media. Whether they involve concerns about excessive use of force by police, partisanship in judicial elections, the impact of trauma on human behavior, the role of extremist ideology and beliefs in fostering violence, or the status of a government-guided healthcare plan, headlines and lead stories are often about some aspect of psychology and law. Although this attention appears to cater to an almost insatiable curiosity about crime and other types of legal disputes, it also promotes some ambivalence about the law. Many citizens are suspicious of the police, but police are still the first responders in a crisis. Juries are sometimes criticized for their decisions, but many litigants would prefer to have their cases decided by juries rather than judges. Citizens value their constitutionally protected rights, but also demand security in a post-9/11 era. The experience of a global pandemic and a more intensive focus on social justice in a society that often appears extraordinarily polarized have affected how these issues are perceived. This 10th edition explores these tensions as well as many other captivating and controversial issues that arise at the crossroads of psychology and the law.

The primary audiences for *Psychology and the Legal System* are students taking a course in psychology and the law, forensic psychology, or the criminal justice system, and others who seek to learn more about the legally relevant science and practice of psychology. This book (and its individual chapters) may also be used as a supplement in psychology courses that emphasize applied psychology, social issues, or policy analysis. In addition, it covers a number of topics relevant to law school courses that introduce law students to social science research findings and applications.

We have attempted to find the right mix of psychology and legal analysis in the text. The book's emphasis remains on psychological science and practice, but we also summarize the legal history of many key topics and present the current status of relevant legal theories and court decisions. Specific recent topics that are covered in some detail in this edition include assessing the risk of terrorist acts based on ideologies and affiliations, the increase in mass shootings, sexual harassment in the workplace, the expectations for police in the larger context of racial mistrust, and how psychology has contributed to criminal profiling.

We continue to focus on the psychological dimensions of several topics that remain important in contemporary society, just as they were important when previous editions of this text were written. These include how attributions about the causes of behavior affect judgments of offenders and victims, lawyers' and judges' use of intuitive cognitive mechanisms to evaluate cases and make decisions, the association between beliefs about procedural fairness and people's willingness to obey the law, clinicians' assessments of competence in various domains, and racial influences on police, jury, and judicial decision making. As in previous editions, we have updated each of these topics using the best available scientific evidence published since our most recent edition went to press.

New Features and Revisions

We have made the following major changes from the last edition:

- For the first time in 15 years, we welcome a new author to our team. Amy Bradfield Douglass brings expertise in eyewitness testimony, jury decision making, social influence in legal judgments, and social psychology to the current team of a clinical psychologist and a cognitive psychologist.

- We strived to make *Psychology and the Legal System* more user friendly by providing current examples to illustrate the material in a straightforward and accessible way.
- We provided several new real-world examples in boxes ("The Case of…"). These summaries describe scenarios and cases that illustrate or explain an important legal concept or psychological principle covered in the chapter. Readers will be familiar with many recent examples including the killing of George Floyd, partisan allegiances that arose in the Kyle Rittenhouse case, publicity surrounding the Parkland High School shooting, the case of antigovernment protestors Ammon and Ryan Bundy, and the sexual assault trial of Bill Cosby. We also feature the historic cases of Ernest Miranda, Clarence Gideon, John Hinckley, Ted Bundy, the McMartin Preschool child sexual abuse scandal, and others. A few cases are either fictional (such as Dexter Morgan from the popular television series *Dexter*) or composites, but still highly applicable to the chapter material.
- We updated examples of the themes, introduced in Chapter 1, that infuse a psychological analysis of the law. These include the rights of individuals versus the common good; equality versus discretion as ideals that can guide the legal system; discovering the truth or resolving conflicts as the goals that the legal system strives to accomplish; and science versus the law as a source of legal decisions. The COVID pandemic is featured in our coverage of diversion and court processes and its effects are mentioned several times throughout the text.
- This edition includes a thorough, authoritative revision of every chapter in light of research and professional literature published since the last edition. Highlights include the following:
- Chapter 1 provides an overview of the field and details the many roles that psychologists can play in the legal system.
- Chapter 2 includes new coverage of the conservative super-majority on the U.S. Supreme Court and how partisan judicial appointments might influence the perceived legitimacy of the Court.
- Chapter 3 focuses on criminal offending. Recent statistics on different kinds of offending are reviewed, some of which are at odds with the public perception that crime is constantly increasing. Theories of why crimes are committed—sociological, biological, psychological, and social-psychological—are presented. We take the strongest aspects of each to present an integrated theory of criminal behavior.
- Chapter 4, on the psychology of police, includes new material on domestic violent extremism and policing, the excessive use of force in police encounters with minority

citizens, and training in crisis interventions with citizens experiencing mental illness.
- Chapter 5 updates scientific studies on the variables that affect eyewitness memory and that have led to reforms in police procedures in cases involving eyewitness identifications.
- Chapter 6 covers the psychology of victims of crime and violence. It updates research on the experiences of victims of hate crimes, PTSD that stems from victimization, the dynamics of intimate partner violence, and the increased recognition of sexual harassment as a societal problem.
- Chapter 7, on the evaluation of criminal suspects, describes how interrogation procedures are being reformed in light of psychological research on social influence factors, concerns about false confessions by adults as well as juveniles, and the "cumulative disadvantage framework" that explains how and why innocence can lead to confessing.
- Chapter 8 describes important new research on psychological factors inherent in plea bargaining, the manner by which the vast majority of criminal cases are resolved.
- Chapter 9 updates coverage of community-based alternatives to standard prosecution, including problem-solving courts designed to address homelessness, mental illness, and trauma.
- Chapter 10 describes updates on forensic assessment in criminal cases, and Chapter 11 does the same for civil cases.
- Chapter 12 describes, among other pretrial topics, the complexity of jury selection in a location saturated with publicity about the crime. The case of the Parkland school shooter serves as an example. The chapter also addresses racial bias in jury selection and the relevance of prospective jurors' online activities.
- Chapter 13 expands the discussion of juries in the previous chapter to cover jurors' cognitive processes and the dynamics of juries' group decision making.
- Chapter 14 updates data on mass incarceration and public opinion about the death penalty and describes new studies on judges' sentencing practices.
- Chapter 15 covers new studies related to juvenile and adult corrections.
- The appendices for this book are now available online at www.cengage.com/psychology/greene. They include the Ethical Principles of Psychologists and Code of Conduct as well as the Specialty Guidelines for Forensic Psychologists, both of which provide ethical guidance for practice and research in forensic psychology. They also include the Bill of Rights, which describes the amendments to the United States Constitution.

For assistance in preparing this edition, we thank Colin Grover, Abby DeVeuve, and Sangeetha Vijayanand. Each was extremely helpful in writing the 10th edition of Psychology and the Legal System.

About the Authors

Anna Heilbrun

Kirk Heilbrun is currently Professor, Department of Psychological and Brain Sciences, Drexel University. He received his doctorate in clinical psychology in 1980 from the University of Texas at Austin, and completed postdoctoral fellowship training from 1981 to 1982 in psychology and criminal justice at Florida State University. His current research focuses on juvenile and adult offenders, legal decision making, and forensic evaluation associated with such decision-making, as well as reentry and the diversion of individuals with behavioral health problems from standard prosecution. He is the author of a number of articles on forensic assessment, violence risk assessment and risk communication, and the diversion and treatment of mentally disordered offenders. In addition to serving as co-author for the 6th through the 10th editions of *Psychology and the Legal System*, he has published thirteen other books on topics including forensic mental health assessment, juvenile delinquency, violence risk assessment, the Sequential Intercept Model, evaluating juvenile transfer, forensic ethics, and university-state collaboration. His practice interests also center around forensic assessment, and he directs a clinic within the department in this area, as well as a reentry project for the assessment and treatment of individuals returning to the community from federal prison. He is board certified in Clinical Psychology and in Forensic Psychology by the American Board of Professional Psychology, and has previously served as president of both the American Psychology-Law Psychology/APA Division 41, and the American Board of Forensic Psychology. He received the 2004 Distinguished Contributions to Forensic Psychology award and the 2008 Beth Clark Distinguished Service award from the American Academy of Forensic Psychology, and the 2016 Distinguished Contributions to Psychology and Law award from the American Psychology-Law Society. In his free time, he enjoys biking into work and playing padel (Google it).

Rebecca Siegel

Edie Greene is Emerita Professor of Psychology at the University of Colorado Colorado Springs where she served on the faculty for 35 years. She earned her Ph.D. in cognitive psychology and law at the University of Washington in 1983. She has been a fellow in Law and Psychology at Harvard Law School and a Visiting Scholar at John Jay College of Criminal Justice and Victoria University of Wellington (New Zealand). She has obtained several federally funded grants to support her research on legal decision making, eyewitness memory, and psycholegal aspects of aging. Greene received a college-wide award for Outstanding Research and Creative Works, a university-wide award for Excellence in Research, and the Chancellor's Award for Distinguished Faculty. She has been invited to lecture at the National Judicial College and at continuing legal education programs nationwide. She consults with lawyers on various trial-related issues including jury selection, trial strategies, and jury decisions, and has, on numerous occasions, testified as an expert witness on jury behavior and eyewitness memory. In addition to serving as coauthor of the 5th through the 10th editions of *Psychology and the Legal System*, Greene is author of a number of articles, columns, and book chapters on jury decision making, trial reforms, witness memory, elder law issues, and teaching in psychology and law; co-signer on several *amicus* briefs presented to the U.S. Supreme Court; and co-author of an additional three books. She served as President of the American Psychology-Law Society/APA Division 41 and received their Award for Outstanding Teaching and Mentoring. She lives in the foothills of the Rocky Mountains where she hikes, bikes, and skis.

Luke Douglass

Amy Bradfield Douglass is professor of psychology at Bates College in Lewiston, Maine, where she has also served as department chair and division chair for social sciences. She earned her undergraduate degree from Williams College in 1996 and her Ph.D. in social psychology from Iowa State University in 2001. Since receiving her Ph.D., she has been on the faculty at Bates College. For six years Dr. Douglass served as an associate editor for Law & Human Behavior, the flagship journal for the American Psychology - Law Society. She is currently the secretary/treasurer for the Society for Applied Research in Memory & Cognition. Dr. Douglass conducts research on eyewitness memory and identification decisions. Her work has been supported by the National Science Foundation and Australian Research Council and featured in multiple court decisions. She has been an affiliated research fellow at Flinders University in Adelaide, Australia. Most recently, she was awarded a Fulbright U.S. Scholar grant to conduct research on eyewitness memory in Japan. Dr. Douglass lives in Maine with her husband, twin daughters and very spoiled black Labrador.

Chapter 1

Psychology and the Law: Choices and Roles

Orienting Questions

1. Why do we have laws and what is the psychological approach to studying law?

2. What choices are reflected in the psychological approach to the law?

3. How do laws reflect the contrast between due process and crime control in the criminal justice system?

4. What are five roles that psychologists may play in the legal system and what does each entail?

Consider the following stories, all of which are relevant to psychology and law:

- In a case that elevated debate about police shootings of Black citizens, racial bias, and no-knock warrants, Louisville police with such a warrant entered an apartment in March 2020 seeking to arrest Kenneth Walker. Officers later said they had announced themselves; Mr. Walker contended that he did not hear this and thought they were intruders. He fired one shot, striking one of the officers in the leg. Police responded by firing 32 shots in return. Mr. Walker was not hit, but his girlfriend Breonna Taylor was struck six times and killed. Later in 2020, the City of Louisville agreed to pay Taylor's family $12 million and to reform police practices. This killing, along with other highly publicized deaths of Black individuals in the course of encounters with police, contributed to the protests of Black Lives Matter and other organizations prominent in 2020–2021.

- The question of whether vaccination for COVID-19 should be mandatory—required by law and policy—has been a thorny one for a country affected, like the rest of the world, by a global pandemic. The arguments for and against mandatory vaccination must necessarily incorporate scientific evidence, legal rights, and societal values. But this debate became a political flashpoint in certain ways that were not anticipated. This includes individuals who decline vaccinations citing beliefs that are inconsistent with scientific evidence, and seem much more influenced by ideology.

- A federal reentry court in Philadelphia focuses on providing a range of services to individuals returning to the community following incarceration in federal prison. This requires collaboration among federal judges, the U.S. Attorney, the Federal Defender, parole and probation staff, and a number of service-providers who offer pro bono contributions. This is a good example of a problem-solving court, identifying individuals at risk for reoffending and providing them with support, structure, and encouragement for responsible living. People who successfully complete the program have lower rates of reoffending than individuals who are not in this program.

These stories illustrate a few of the many psycholegal topics that we consider in this book including police-community relations and discrimination, the motivations of offenders and victims, the impact of eyewitness accounts, the importance of confessions and some reasons why false confessions are given, the discretion in judges' sentencing decisions and jury decisions, traditional and alternative criminal justice processing, the role of science in public health policy, and public perceptions of security and law enforcement officials. They show the real flesh and blood of some of the many psychological issues that arise in the law.

The Importance of Laws

These examples also illustrate the pervasiveness of the law in our society. But how does the law work? This book will help you understand how the legal system operates by applying psychological concepts, theories, methods, and empirical evidence to its study.

Laws as Human Creations

Laws are everywhere. They affect everything from birth to death. Laws regulate our private lives and our public actions. Laws dictate how long we must stay in school, how fast we can drive, when (and, to some extent, whom) we can marry, and whether we are allowed to play our car stereos at full blast or let our boisterous dog romp through the neighbors' yards and gardens. Given that the body of laws has such a widespread impact, we might expect that the law is a part of nature, that it was originally discovered by a set of archaeologists or explorers.

But our laws are not chiseled in stone. Rather, laws are human creations that evolve out of the needs for order and consistency. To be responsive to a constantly changing society, our laws must also change. As some become outdated, others take their place. For example, before there were shootings on school grounds, no laws forbade the presence of weapons in schools. But after a generation of deadly incidents, laws that banned weapons from school property have been widely established. Such laws can make school settings more secure. They can also have unintended harmful consequences, as when zero-tolerance policies result in the expulsion of a child who forgot to remove his Cub Scout pocket knife from his backpack before leaving for school. When this sort of overreaching occurs, ideally there will be changes in the policy that simultaneously protect children and avoid unnecessarily harsh reactions in cases with little risk of harm to others.

Another example of the law as sometimes subject to social and political influence involves the topic of abortion. The United States Supreme Court held, in *Roe v. Wade* (1973), that the U.S. Constitution protects the right of a pregnant woman to choose to have an abortion based on a right to privacy associated with the Fourteenth Amendment. But there remains wide variability across states on abortion-related considerations such as hospital requirements, gestational limits, partial-birth abortions, public funding and private insurance, healthcare provider refusal, waiting periods, mandated counseling, and parental involvement (https://www.guttmacher.org/state-policy/explore/overview -abortion-laws). The U.S. Supreme Court overturned *Roe* in 2022, opening the door for states to implement laws that impose new restrictions.

Laws Help Resolve Conflict and Protect the Public

Many standards of acceptable behavior—not purposely touching strangers on elevators, for example—seem universally supported. But in some situations, people have differences of opinion about what is considered appropriate, and disagreements result. When this occurs, society must have ways to resolve the disagreements. Thus, societies develop laws and regulations to function as conflict resolution mechanisms. Customs and rules of conduct evolve partly to deal with the conflict between one person's impulses and desires and other people's rights. Similarly, laws are developed to manage and resolve those conflicts that cannot be prevented.

Public safety is always an important consideration in a civilized society. In earlier times, before laws were established to deter and punish unacceptable behavior, people "took the law" into their own hands, acting as vigilantes to secure the peace and impose punishment on offenders. Now, in the United States and most other nations, all governmental entities—federal, state, county, borough, municipality, and even some neighborhoods—have enacted laws to protect the public. But individual rights must also be considered here. How far can legislatures and police go in making and enforcing, respectively, laws designed to quell civil unrest and protest?

The Changing of Laws

The basic raw material for the construction and the revision of laws is human experience. As our experiences and opportunities change, laws must be developed, interpreted, reinterpreted, and modified to keep up with these rapid changes in our lives. The framers of the U.S. Constitution, and even legislators of more recent times, could not have anticipated how laws have changed and will continue to change. They probably never contemplated the possibility that advances in neuroscience, for example, would affect how police investigate cases, attorneys represent their clients, and juries and judges make decisions. But as we describe in Chapter 7, brain imaging technology is now used to detect brain injuries and assess pain in those involved in accidents, determine mental state and capacity for rational thought in individuals involved in the justice system, and detect lies and deception in those under interrogation. Although the correspondence between brain activity and behavior is far from clear at this point, neuroimaging will undoubtedly raise thorny questions for the legal system. New rules, policies, and laws will have to be created to address them.

Similarly, no one could have anticipated how DNA testing would change laws involving criminal investigations. Legislatures have passed statutes that mandate the collection of DNA samples from millions of Americans, including those who have simply been arrested and are awaiting trial. Some of these individuals have objected to having their DNA collected and catalogued. Law enforcement officials assert that widespread testing will help them solve more crimes and exonerate people who were wrongly convicted. (We describe the role of DNA analysis in the exoneration of convicted individuals in Chapter 5.)

Legislators must now consider what, if any, restrictions should be placed on online activities. (Cyber-law, virtually nonexistent 40 years ago, has become an important subfield in the law.) For example, individuals have been convicted of sexually abusing minors after they sexted nude and seminude pictures, and drivers have been ticketed for looking at their phones when stopped at red lights, thereby violating their states' hands-free requirements. Should laws regulate these activities? Many believe that these laws protect the dignity and safety of the public; others claim that they interfere with constitutionally protected speech and privacy rights. But most people would agree that vast changes in society have necessitated far-reaching adjustments in the law.

The invention of the automobile produced several new adversaries, including pedestrians versus drivers, and hence new laws. Car accidents—even minor ones—cause conflicts over basic rights. Consider a driver whose car strikes and injures a pedestrian. Does this driver have a legal responsibility to report the incident to the police? Yes. But doesn't this requirement violate the Fifth Amendment to the U.S. Constitution, which safeguards each of us against self-incrimination, against being a witness in conflict with our own legal interests?

Shortly after automobiles became popular in the first two decades of the twentieth century, a man named Edward Rosenheimer was charged with violating the newly implemented reporting laws. He did not contest the charge that he had caused an accident that injured another person, but he claimed that the law requiring him to report it to the police was unconstitutional because it forced him to incriminate himself. Therefore, he argued, this particular law should be removed from the books, and he should be freed of the charge of leaving the scene of an accident. Surprisingly, a New York judge agreed and released him from custody.

But authorities in New York were unhappy with a decision that permitted a person who had caused an injury to avoid being apprehended, so they appealed the decision to a higher court, the New York Court of Appeals. This court, recognizing that the Constitution and the recent law clashed with each other, ruled in favor of the state and overturned the previous decision. This appeals court concluded that rights to "constitutional privilege"—that is, to avoid self-incrimination—must give way to the competing principle of the right of injured persons to seek redress for their sufferings (Post, 1963).

This historical example underscores how the law is an evolving human creation, designed to arbitrate between values in opposition to each other. Before the advent of automobiles, hit-and-run accidents seldom occurred. Before the invention of smartphones, texting at stoplights (or worse, while driving) or sexting never occurred. However, once cars and smartphones became a part of society, new laws were enacted to regulate their use, and courts have determined that most of these new laws are constitutional. The widespread availability of driverless vehicles will raise new questions about rights and responsibilities with which the law will have to grapple. Psychological research can be relevant to these questions by assessing, for example, whether navigating using newly developed technology while driving is sufficiently distracting to merit regulation—just as glancing at a GPS or text message on a phone might have been in 2020.

The Psychological Study of Law

Laws and legal systems are studied by several traditional disciplines other than psychology. For example, anthropologists compare laws (and mechanisms for instituting and altering laws) in different societies and relate them to other characteristics of these societies. They may be interested in how frequently women are sexually assaulted in different types of societies and in the relationship between sexual assault and other factors, such as the extent of separation of the sexes during childhood or the degree to which males dominate females.

Sociologists, in contrast, usually study a specific society and examine its institutions (e.g., the family, the church, or the subculture) to determine their role in developing adherence to the law. The sociologist might study the role that socioeconomic status plays in criminal behavior. This approach tries to predict and explain social behavior by focusing on groups of people rather than on individuals.

A psychological approach to the law focuses on the individual as the unit of analysis. Individuals are seen as ultimately responsible for their own conduct and as contributing causes and consequences. Psychology examines the thoughts and actions of individuals—an individual involved in minor or more serious criminal offending, police officer, victim, juror, expert witness, defense attorney, prosecutor, judge, defendant, correctional officer, and parole officer, for example—involved in the legal system. Psychology assumes that characteristics of these participants affect how the system operates, and it also recognizes that the law, in turn, can affect individuals' characteristics and behavior (Melton et al., 2018). By *characteristics*, we mean these persons' abilities, perspectives, values, and experiences—all the factors that influence their behavior. These characteristics affect whether a defendant and his attorney decide to plea bargain or go to trial. They influence whether a Hispanic juror will be more sympathetic toward a Hispanic defendant than toward a non-Hispanic defendant. They affect whether a jury with many parents might be more sympathetic to a defendant who is a parent. They help determine whether a justice-involved youth will fare better in the juvenile system or the criminal (adult) system.

But the behavior of participants in the legal system is not just a result of their personal qualities. The setting in which they operate matters as well. Kurt Lewin, a founder of social psychology, proposed that behavior is a function of both the person and the environment. Qualities of the external environment and pressures from the situation affect an individual's behavior. A prosecuting attorney may recommend a harsher sentence for a convicted felon if the case has been highly publicized, the community is outraged over the crime, and the prosecutor is running for reelection. A juror holding out for a guilty verdict may yield if all the other jurors passionately proclaim the defendant's innocence. A justice-involved youth may desist from criminal behavior if their gang affiliations are severed. A Black youth stopped by police officers may respond differently depending on how the officers behave—but also depending on their experience with prior stops by police. The social environment affects legally relevant choices and conduct.

This book concentrates on the behavior of participants in the legal system. As the examples at the beginning of this chapter indicate, as citizens we are all active participants in the system. This is true even if we do not work in occupations directly related to the administration of justice. We all face daily choices that are affected by the law—whether to speed through a school zone because we are late to work, whether to report the person who removes someone else's laptop from a table at the library, or how to vote on a proposal to strengthen environmental protections. Hence, this book will also consider the influences on our conceptions of justice and the moral dilemmas we all face.

We pay particular attention to the role of psychology in the criminal and civil justice systems and to the central participants in those settings: defendants and witnesses, civil and criminal lawyers, judges and juries, convicts and parole boards. We also focus on the activities of **forensic psychologists** who generate and communicate information to answer specific legal questions or to help resolve legal disputes (Melton et al., 2018). Most forensic psychologists are trained as clinical psychologists, whose specialty involves the psychological evaluation and treatment of others. Forensic psychologists are often asked to evaluate a person and then prepare a report for a court, and sometimes provide expert testimony in a hearing or trial. For example, as we explain in Chapter 10, they may evaluate adult criminal defendants or children involved with the juvenile justice system and offer the court information relevant to determining whether the defendant has a mental disorder that prevents her from going to trial, what the defendant's mental state was at the time of the offense, or what treatment might be appropriate for a particular defendant. Psychologists can also play other roles in the legal system. We describe these roles later in the chapter.

Basic Choices in the Psychological Study of the Law

Just as each of us has to make decisions about personal values, society must decide which values it wants its laws to reflect. Choices lead to conflict, and often the resulting dilemmas are difficult to resolve. Should the laws uphold the rights of specific individuals or protect society in general? Should each of us be able to impose our preferences on others, or must we be attentive to other people's needs? You may have pondered this question during the COVID-19 pandemic while walking into a store indicating that masks were strongly recommended but optional. Should that store have dispensed with the "optional" and simply required masks? Should the store have recognized that masks are aggravating even for those who wear them, and that the risk of contracting COVID-19 was reduced by widely available vaccinations? Or what about the airline passenger who loudly and repeatedly asserts that they don't have to wear a mask after consuming three drinks, and threatens anyone who tries to compel them to wear one? What about the person who does not take precautions, is hospitalized with COVID, and uses a bed that is not available to another person whose illness was not a function of their choices? The law struggles with this fact: rights desirable for some individuals may be problematic for others.

Consider as well the question about whether to wear a seat belt. People who opt not to use seat belts in a car are making a seemingly personal choice. Perhaps they don't like the way the belt feels. Perhaps they like having freedom to move around the car. But that choice puts them at greater risk for death or serious injury in an accident, and accidents involve costs to society, including lost wages, higher insurance premiums, and disability payments to the injured person and that person's dependents. So the good of society can be adversely affected by the split-second decision of individuals as they step into their cars.

This tension between individual rights and the common good is one example of the basic choices that pervade the psychological study of the law. There are others. In this chapter, we highlight four basic choices inherent in laws and that apply to each of us in the United States, Canada, and many other countries. Each choice creates a dilemma and has psychological implications. No decision about these choices will be completely satisfactory because no decision can simultaneously attain two incompatible goals—such as individual rights and societal rights—both of which we value. These four choices (and the tension inherent in their competing values) are so basic that they surface repeatedly throughout this book, as they did with different examples in earlier editions. They unify many of the research findings, policy decisions, and judicial holdings that are discussed in subsequent chapters.

The First Choice: Rights of Individuals Versus the Common Good

Consider the following:

- Payton Gendron, an 18-year-old White male, entered a Buffalo, NY supermarket on May 14, 2022 wearing tactical gear (including plated armor) and carrying an assault rifle. He shot and killed ten people and wounded another three before surrendering to police. Eleven of these thirteen individuals were Black. Judging both from his statements after the attack and the race of most of his victims, Gendron appeared to be targeting Black individuals. He reportedly streamed the attack live and posted a 180-page document describing his reasons for this horrific attack; he was subsequently charged with a hate crime. About a year earlier, in June 2021, it was reported that he had made a statement while in high school that pertained to his desire to kill others, resulting in his being taken for a mental health evaluation under applicable New York State law. The results of this evaluation will undoubtedly be scrutinized as Gendron is prosecuted. But events like this raise questions about how carefully individuals should be evaluated and their liberty restricted (rights of the individual) versus how important it is to protect the public from a small number of individuals who make serious threats and subsequently carry them out (safety of the community, a form of the common good)

  (https://www.cnn.com/2022/05/15/us/payton-gendron-buffalo-shooting-suspect-what-we-know/index.html).

- Gay and lesbian troops have served openly in the U.S. military since 2011, as have transgender troops since 2016. In July 2017, President Trump tweeted that transgender people would be barred from enlisting and active-duty transgender personnel would be subject to expulsion. This declaration raised the prospect that opportunities for transgender individuals to serve in the military would be effectively eliminated. According to Trump, the military must be focused on winning and cannot be burdened with the "tremendous medical costs and disruption" of transgender service members. Transgender advocates quickly denounced this communication, claiming that it imposed one set of standards on transgender troops and another set on everyone else, and politicians from both parties stated that anyone who is willing to fight for their country should be welcomed into the military. As of 2022, Army policy was to allow transgender individuals to serve (https://www.army.mil/standto/archive/2021/06/25/). Who is right?

- COVID-19 resulted in a global pandemic, the effects of which began to be experienced in the United States in early 2020. The introduction of vaccines for this virus in December 2020 followed an intensive research effort and for a short time appeared to present an opportunity to bring it under control and allow a return to some semblance of pre-pandemic life. But there was active opposition to taking this vaccine on the part of some. There had also been opposition to public health efforts such as social distancing and masking prior to the introduction of the vaccine. Much of this opposition seemed in reaction to laws or policies mandating the use of vaccines, and cited justifications ranging from liberty to bodily integrity to political opposition to the perceived values of those supporting use of vaccinations. Those favoring mandatory vaccination cited the documented effectiveness of vaccines in reducing both transmission and (particularly) hospitalization and fatalities, especially in the elderly and people with pre-existing medical conditions. Which position do you favor?

Values in Conflict. The preceding vignettes share a common theme. On the one hand, individuals possess rights, and one function of the law is to ensure that these rights are protected. The United States is perhaps the most individualistic society in the world. People can deviate from the norm, or make their own choices, to a greater degree in the United States than virtually anywhere else. Freedom and personal autonomy are two of our most deeply desired values; "the right to liberty" is a key phrase in the U.S. Constitution.

On the other hand, our society also has expectations. People need to feel secure. They need to believe that potential lawbreakers are discouraged from breaking laws because they

Many openly gay individuals serve in the military.

know they will be punished. All of us have rights to a peaceful, safe existence. Likewise, society claims a vested interest in restricting those who take risks that may result in harm to themselves and others, or who demand excessive resources, because these actions can create burdens on individuals and on society. The tension between individual rights and the collective good is presented in the situation we describe in Box 1.1.

It is clear that two sets of rights and two goals for the law are often in conflict. The tension between the rights of the individual and the constraints that may be placed on the individual for the collective good is always present. It has factored prominently into various U.S. Supreme Court decisions since the 1960s with respect to the rights of criminal suspects and defendants versus the rights of crime victims and the power of the police.

In the 1960s, the Supreme Court established a number of principles that provided or expanded explicit rights for those suspected of breaking the law. The *Miranda* rule guaranteeing the right to remain silent (detailed in Chapter 7) was established in 1966. About the same time, the courts required that criminal defendants, in all cases in which incarceration was possible, have the right to an attorney, even if they cannot afford to pay for one. These and other rights were established in an effort to redress a perceived imbalance between a lowly defendant and a powerful government.

But many of these rights were trimmed in subsequent years when courts frequently ruled in favor of the police. For example, in 1996, the Supreme Court ruled that the police can properly stop a motorist whom they believe has violated traffic laws even if their ulterior motive is to investigate the possibility of illegal drug dealing (*Whren v. United States,* 1996). In 2012, the Court ruled that jail officials can strip search petty offenders even if there is no suspicion they are concealing weapons or contraband (*Florence v. Board of Chosen Freeholders,* 2012).

Two Models of the Criminal Justice System. The
conflict between the rights of individuals and the rights of

society is related to a distinction between two models of the criminal justice system. This distinction is between the due process model and the crime control model (Packer, 1964). The values underlying each of these models are legitimate, and the goal of our society is to achieve a balance between them. But because different priorities are important to each model, there is constant tension between them.

The **due process model**, favored in the 1960s, places primary value on the protection of citizens, including criminal suspects, from possible abuses by the police and the law enforcement system generally. It assumes the innocence of suspects and requires that they be treated fairly (receive "due process") by the criminal justice system. It subscribes to the maxim that 'it is better that ten guilty persons shall go free than that one innocent person should suffer.' Thus the due process model emphasizes the rights of individuals, especially those suspected of crimes, over the temptation by society to assume suspects are guilty even before a trial.

In contrast, the **crime control model**, favored in the 1990s, seeks the apprehension and punishment of law-breakers. It emphasizes the efficient detection of suspects and the effective prosecution of defendants, to help ensure that criminal activity is being contained or reduced. The crime control model is exemplified by a statement by former Attorney General of the United States William Barr, with respect to career criminals. He noted that the goal is "incapacitation through incarceration" (Barr, 1992)—that is, removing them permanently from circulation.

When the crime control model is dominant in society, laws are passed that in other times would be seen as unacceptable violations of individual rights. A 2017 Texas law known as a "show me your papers law" prohibits local authorities from limiting the ability of law enforcement or court personnel to demand proof of a person's immigration status and report it to federal officials. Texas Governor Greg Abbott asserted that the law protects public safety. But opponents contend that it erodes public trust and actually makes communities and neighborhoods less safe. Laws like this raise complicated questions about the rights of individuals to be free from police scrutiny and the obligation of the government to provide safety and security to its citizens.

Vestiges of the crime control model still linger in the United States, substantially more than in Canada, Europe, or Australia. This is true despite the drop in the crime rates in recent years, followed by some increases during the 2020–21 period. As we describe in Chapter 14, the United States still incarcerates a higher percentage of its citizens than any other developed nation.

The recession of 2007–2009 changed some aspects of public policy toward crime, tightening federal and state budgets. Certain "tough-on-crime" policies were also strengthened, which expanded prison but did little to prevent repeat offending by released inmates (Dvoskin et al., 2011). However, some new programs were effective in reducing repeat

Box 1.1

The "Unite the Right" Rally in Charlottesville and the Speech Rights of White Supremacists

The First Amendment to the U.S. Constitution protects the freedom of speech so long as it does not include threats, fighting words, perjury and a few other types of speech. Even racially offensive speech is protected, as the Supreme Court noted in *Matal v. Tam* (2017). According to Justice Samuel Alito, who wrote the opinion in the case, "Speech that demeans on the basis of race, ethnicity, gender, religion, age, disability, or any other similar ground is hateful; but the proudest boast of our free speech jurisprudence is that we protect the freedom to express 'the thought that we hate'."

Those protections came into sharp relief in 2017 after White nationalists held a rally in Charlottesville, Virginia, that turned deadly. Charlottesville officials initially denied organizers' request for a permit to protest the removal of a statue of Confederate General Robert E. Lee from a city park. But after a lawsuit was filed by the American Civil Liberties Union (A.C.L.U.)—an organization whose work has included defending the speech rights of neo-Nazis—and a federal judge ruled against the city, rally organizers received their permit. The protest escalated into a brawl as White nationalists, some carrying clubs and assault weapons, clashed with counter-protestors, and a car attack injured 19 and killed one of the counter-protestors.

The A.C.L.U. has long maintained that its advocacy of free speech for White supremacists serves to protect the First Amendment rights of all Americans by confronting vile and detestable ideas head-on, rather than by suppressing them (Goldstein, 2017). But the freedom of speech does not extend to speech that is "directed to inciting imminent lawless action and is likely to incite or produce such action" (*Brandenburg v. Ohio,* 1969) and some contend that support from the A.C.L.U. actually encourages such actions. (The A.C.L.U. has vowed to review closely requests from White supremacist groups to assess the potential for violence and has stated that it will refuse to represent groups who protest with guns.)

White nationalists clash with counter-protesters at the Unite the Right rally in Charlottesville, VA.

This episode raises difficult questions for the future: Will local officials be tempted to thwart extremist groups who wish to hold rallies and protests in their communities? Will doing so further embolden White nationalists who have risen in prominence in recent years? Is openly carrying a gun, allowed in 45 states, a form of free speech? (This discussion shows that it may be impossible, in open carry states, to disentangle First Amendment free speech rights and the Second Amendment right to keep and bear arms.) Even more fundamentally, how does one strike a balance between the right to free expression of speech—including hate-filled speech intended to intimidate and threaten—and the right of the community to be protected from speech that promotes "lawless action"?

Critical Thought Question: What two values are in conflict in this incident?

offending. Crime rates in Texas dropped after the state began investing in treatment programs for parolees. The prison population in Mississippi was reduced substantially after it allowed inmates to earn time off their sentences by participating in educational and re-entry programs. Other proven alternatives included providing employment counseling and substance abuse and mental health treatment for inmates, problem-solving courts, and diverting offenders from the criminal justice system and into community-based treatment programs. We describe many of these alternatives in Chapter 9.

The COVID-19 pandemic and the Black Lives Matter movement provided other important influences on the political and social climate in the United States beginning in 2020. It remains to be seen whether increases in certain kinds of violent crime, observed in 2020 and 2021, will drop again as the country is no longer locked down—or whether these increases will be more stable. But the increased emphasis on fairness and social justice, reflected in protests following the highly publicized killing of minority citizens in the course of police encounters, will very likely remain a priority for many in the United States for years to come.

The Second Choice: Equality Versus Discretion

Imagine two defendants in 2022, each charged in federal court with drug trafficking offenses. For the purposes of this example, we can make the cases similar in terms of seriousness, defendant age, prior history of offending—everything except race. One of the defendants is Black, the other White. In *United States v. Booker* (2005), the Supreme Court held nearly two decades ago that the Federal Sentencing Guidelines (which structure the assignment of criminal sentencing following conviction for federal crimes, as shown in https://www.ussc.gov/guidelines) are discretionary rather than mandatory. This decision increased the amount of discretion that could be exercised in this context, aptly illustrating that equality and discretion are sometimes at odds with one another. The *Booker* decision meant that federal judges subsequently had the option to "depart downward" in their sentences, assigning a sentence that was outside the length specified in a complex matrix in the Guidelines. In our example with the two defendants, the attorney for each files a motion for a downward departure. Each defendant receives a psychological evaluation focusing on domains such as risk of reoffending, rehabilitation needs, likely response to interventions, and other aspects of their character and lives. The Black defendant receives a substantially longer sentence than the White offender.

This example illustrates the second choice in the psychological study of the law: the choice between equality and discretion. In one respect, given the very substantial similarities between these two defendants (except for their race), we would hope that the sentences would also be very similar. We would be troubled if there was evidence that this sentencing discrepancy was attributable to racial bias. While the legal world can never be as clear as one can make it in hypothetical examples, there is evidence of a troubling trend in sentencing: sentence lengths in federal court have been decreasing across all categories of crime, but are decreasing much faster for White than for Black defendants (Klein, 2016).

What should be the underlying principle guiding the response to persons accused of violating the law? Again, we find that two equally desirable values—equality and discretion—are often incompatible and hence create conflict. The principle of **equality** means that all people who commit the same crime or misdeed should receive the same consequences. But blind adherence to equality can lead to unfairness in situations in which the particular characteristics of offender, victim, or offense matter. For example, most people would think differently about punishing someone who killed randomly, ruthlessly, and without remorse, and someone else who killed a loved one suffering from a painful and terminal illness. In this example, discretion is called for. **Discretion** in the legal system involves considering the circumstances of certain offenders and offenses to determine the appropriate consequences for wrongdoing. Psychology provides concepts through which this conflict can be studied and better understood.

The Principle of Equality. Fundamental to our legal system is the assumption advanced by the founders of the American republic that "all men are created equal." In fact, the "equal protection clause" of the Fourteenth Amendment states that no state shall "deny to any person within its jurisdiction the equal protection of the laws." This statement is frequently interpreted to mean that all people should be treated equally and that no one should receive special treatment by the courts simply because they are rich, influential, or otherwise advantaged. We cherish the belief that in the United States, politically powerful or affluent people are brought before the courts and, if guilty, convicted and punished just like anyone else who commits similar offenses. Consider the example of Elizabeth Holmes, who dropped out of Stanford at the age of 19 to found Theranos, a blood-testing start-up company that at one time was valued at $9 billion. But the technology did not work, the cover-up was substantial, and the company was forced to close. Her conduct led to massive investor losses, and she was subsequently convicted of fraud in federal court (https://www.businessinsider.com/theranos-founder-ceo-elizabeth-holmes-life-story-bio-2018-4).

But the value of equality before the law is not always implemented. In the last three decades, Americans have witnessed a series of incidents that—at least on the surface—seemed to indicate unequal treatment of citizens by the legal system. A common practice among police and state patrols in the United States is *profiling*—viewing certain characteristics as indicators of criminal behavior. Black and Latino motorists have filed numerous lawsuits over the practice of profiling, alleging that the police, in an effort to seize illegal drugs and weapons or to find undocumented immigrants, apply a "race-based profile" to stop and search them more frequently than White drivers. In addition, there is evidence that police speak more disrespectfully to Black motorists, decreasing the potential for trust (Camp et al., 2021). Said former Michigan Congressman John Conyers, Jr., "There are virtually no

Elizabeth Holmes, wealthy CEO of a biotech firm, who was convicted of defrauding her investors.

Black males—including Congressmen, actors, athletes, and office workers—who have not been stopped at one time or another for … driving while Black" (Barovick, 1998).

The issue is not limited to driving. It affects people when they shop, eat in restaurants, travel in trains and airplanes, hail a cab, and walk through their neighborhoods. New York City police officers stopped approximately four million people between 2004 and 2012, questioning all, and frisking and arresting some. But police department statistics show that the stops were not race-neutral. African Americans accounted for 52% of the stops, and Latinos for 31%, despite constituting 23% and 29% of the city's population, respectively. According to columnist Bob Herbert, "[T]he people getting stopped and frisked are mostly young, and most of them are black or brown and poor … If the police officers were treating white middle-class or wealthy individuals this way, the movers and shakers in this town would be apoplectic" (Herbert, 2010). Moreover, New York City police were less likely to find weapons or contraband on Black and Latino suspects than on White suspects (Gelman et al., 2007), and "stop and frisk" may create two distinct kinds of harm: adverse emotional and psychological reactions among those stopped, and interference with the capacity of law enforcement officers to effectively investigate crime (Bandes et al., 2019).

Since police agencies have gathered statistics on the racial makeup of people targeted for traffic stops, border inspections, and other routine searches, and these disparities have come to light, some courts have ruled that a person's appearance may not be the basis for such stops. Psychologists also have a part to play, gathering data on the psychological consequences to victims of racial profiling, improving police training so that cultural and racial awareness is enhanced, and examining how decision makers form implicit judgments of others on the basis of race.

In keeping with the laudable goal of equality under the law, the U.S. Supreme Court has occasionally applied a **principle of proportionality** to its analysis of cases involving criminal sentencing. This principle means that the punishment should be consistently related to the magnitude of the offense. More serious wrongdoing should earn more severe penalties. If a relatively minor crime leads to a harsh punishment, then the fundamental value of proportionality and hence, equality, has been violated.

The principle of proportionality has influenced the way that juvenile offenders are sentenced. Recognizing that impulsiveness and psychosocial immaturity render juveniles less culpable *and* more likely to be rehabilitated than adult offenders, the U.S. Supreme Court has, in the quest for equality, overturned harsh sentences for juvenile offenders. As we describe in Chapter 14, individuals who commit murder before the age of 18 cannot be subjected to the death penalty (*Roper v. Simmons,* 2005) nor automatically sentenced to life without the possibility of parole *(Miller v. Alabama,* 2012). The Court has determined that because juveniles sentenced to life in prison would spend more years and a larger percentage of their lives behind bars, that sentence is disproportionately harsh and not equal to a life sentence received by adults. We describe the case that led to that ruling in Box 1.2.

The *Miller* ruling was expanded in a 2016 decision in which the Court said that *Miller* should be applied retroactively (*Montgomery v. Louisiana,* 2016). This meant that those sentenced to mandatory life sentences as teenagers would be resentenced or paroled. The prospect of resentencing thousands of people serving life sentences posed challenging questions for psychology and the courts. Whereas psychological research ably provided to the Court information about normative development (i.e., that adolescence is distinguished by immaturity and thus, lessened culpability), different sources of data were needed when deciding how each individual should be resentenced. Courts could focus on the developmental status of individuals around the time of the original sentencing and decide how to interpret such retrospective data. Courts could also decide whether information about the individual's current rehabilitation status, including mental health issues, was relevant. Psychologists played an important role in assisting the courts to incorporate relevant developmental and clinical data on the individuals considered for resentencing (Grisso & Kavanaugh, 2016).

The Value of Discretion. Although equality often remains an overriding principle, society also believes that in certain circumstances, discretion is appropriate. Discretion refers to judgments about the circumstances of certain offenses that lead to appropriate *variations* in how the system responds to these offenses. It acknowledges that rigid application of the law can lead to injustices.

Many professionals in the legal system have the opportunity to exercise discretion, and most do so regularly. Police officers show discretion when they decide not to arrest someone who has technically broken the law. They show discretion when they calculate the level of fines for speeding. (Incidentally, saying "I'm sorry" actually results in lower fines, according to Day and Ross, 2011!) Prosecutors exercise discretion when they decide which of many arrested individuals to charge and for what particular crime. Juries exercise discretion in not convicting defendants who killed under circumstances that may have justified their actions (e.g., self-defense or heat of passion). Prison officials have discretion to reward "good behavior," grant furloughs, and move incarcerated individuals to more and less confining conditions. Probation officers and parole boards make discretionary recommendations based on the circumstances and characteristics of individual offenders.

Parole boards also have the opportunity to exercise discretion when they decide whether to commute a death sentence to life imprisonment (a process called granting clemency) or to allow an execution to proceed as planned. The Texas Board of Pardons and Parole faced that decision in the case of Melissa Lucio, although her execution was halted by a Texas appeals court rather than by the Parole Board. She had been convicted

Box 1.2

The Case of Evan Miller: Mandatory Life Without Parole Sentences for Juvenile Offenders Are Excessive Punishment

On July 15, 2003, 52-year-old Cole Cannon knocked on the door of his neighbor's trailer in the small town of Speake, Alabama, asking for some food. That trailer belonged to the family of 14-year-old Evan Miller, an active drug user being raised in an extremely abusive family and experiencing mental health problems. After Cannon had eaten, Miller and a friend accompanied him back to his trailer, intending to get him drunk and rob him. The three played drinking games and smoked marijuana, and when Cannon passed out, Miller began hitting him, first with his fists and then with a baseball bat. The friends then set fire to Cannon's trailer, where he died of smoke inhalation.

Miller was charged with murder in the course of arson and was tried as an adult, subject to all the penalties of adult felons. After he was convicted, the judge imposed a mandatory sentence of life without parole. Miller's appeal focused on his immature judgment and lack of moral sense. His attorneys argued that such a severe sentence was a form of cruel and unusual punishment, banned by the Eighth Amendment.

The case was eventually decided by the U.S. Supreme Court. Among the documents that justices considered was a brief submitted by the American Psychological Association summarizing research relevant to adolescent development. It concluded that a) adolescents are less mature than adults in ways that make them less culpable and b) it is not possible to predict with any reliability whether a particular juvenile offender is likely to reoffend violently (APA, 2012). In her majority decision, Justice Elena Kagan acknowledged that youths are different than adults, given their "diminished culpability and heightened capacity for change." She concluded that laws which mandate life sentences, when applied to juvenile offenders, are unconstitutional. Miller's case was referred back to the courts in Alabama for reconsideration of his life sentence.

Critical Thought Question: According to the Supreme Court, why does a sentence of life without parole constitute cruel and unusual punishment when applied to a juvenile offender?

of murdering her two-year-old daughter, but many had come to doubt her guilt despite the conviction. This case, described in Box 1.3, raises important questions about both discretion and the possibility of error in the criminal justice system.

Discretion may be most obvious in the sentences administered by judges to convicted criminals. In many cases, judges are able to consider the particular circumstances of the defendant and of the crime itself when they determine the sentence. It would seem that this use of discretion is good. Yet as we describe in Chapter 14 and discussed earlier in this chapter, it can also lead to sentencing disparity, the tendency for judges to administer a variety of penalties for the same crime. Such disparities may occur because state laws typically determine sentencing options, so convicted individuals sentenced in one state may receive different sanctions than those who commit the same offense in another state.

Earlier in this chapter we observed that post-*Booker* sentencing in federal court has decreased in length more for White than Black defendants. Such disparity is apparent in other evidence as well. In a 2018 report to the United Nations, The Sentencing Project indicated that Black and Brown Americans are more likely than White Americans to be arrested, convicted, and receive long prison sentences. Incarceration is 5.9 times more likely for Black individuals and 3.1 times more likely for Latino individuals, relative to White defendants (The Sentencing Project, 2018).

One explanation for this disparity is racial bias, whereby police officers, prosecutors, jurors, and judges use an individual's race as a basis for judging their behavior. Race-based stereotypes affect beliefs about offenders' culpability and dangerousness, as well as perceptions of the likelihood of reoffending (Spohn, 2015). Sometimes bias and stereotyping is explicit and intentional, and other times it is implicit and unintentional. Implicit bias is especially concerning, since people are unaware that they are being influenced by race; for example, they may get a "bad feeling" from a Latino defendant (Kovera, 2019). But once these biases occur, they can act as a filter for interpreting and using other information about the offender and the circumstances. Fortunately, some studies have shown that once decision makers are made aware of the potential for racial bias, they can largely avoid it (Pearson et al., 2009).

A subtler, more insidious form of race-based judgments may also be prevalent in the justice system, however. Social psychological research has shown that individuals of the same race may be stereotyped and discriminated against to different degrees, depending how "typical" of their group they appear. Individuals receive longer sentences when they have more Afrocentric facial features (Blair et al., 2004) and darker skin tones (Viglione et al., 2011). Even more troubling, in death penalty cases involving White victims, the likelihood of a Black defendant being sentenced to death is

Box 1.3

The Case of Melissa Lucio and a Parole Board's Discretion

Melissa Lucio was convicted of murdering her two-year-old daughter and sentenced to death in Cameron County (TX) in 2008. But her execution was halted in April 2022 by the Texas Court of Criminal Appeals. This decision came only minutes before the Texas Board of Pardons and Paroles was to vote on whether to recommend to Governor Greg Abbott that the execution be deferred.

Why did the appellate court intervene? There had been growing concern about whether Lucio had been falsely convicted in 2008; although the jury in her trial decided that her daughter's fatal head injury had been caused by abuse, a growing number of individuals (including some of the jurors in her trial) were now considering that it might have resulted from an accidental fall. Trial court evidence included Lucio's confession, which may have resulted from prolonged police interrogation. In addition, the trial did not include expert evidence about the conditions under which false confessions can occur. (Such false confessions are discussed later in Chapter 7).

It would indeed have been tragic if Melissa Lucio were innocent and had been executed. The appellate court sent her case back to the trial court for reconsideration of the evidence, so her conviction may yet be affirmed. The Board of Pardons and Paroles, which had the discretion to recommend to the Governor that her execution be deferred, did not need to make that decision in this case. But in other instances, their decisions in such cases are critical for defendants facing execution.

Melissa Lucio was sentenced to death in 2008.

Critical Thought Question: Explain why the Texas Board of Pardons and Paroles, if they had faced this decision, might not have recommended in Ms. Lucio's favor.

influenced by whether he has a stereotypically Black appearance (Eberhardt et al., 2006).

To counteract sentencing disparity, many states implemented what is known as **determinate sentencing**: the offense determines the sentence, and judges and parole commissions have little discretion. But judges have been frustrated by the severe limitations on their discretion imposed by determinate sentencing. One federal judge who resigned his appointment in protest said, "It's an unfair system that has been dehumanized. There are rarely two cases that are identical. Judges should always have discretion. That's why we're judges. But now we're being made to be robots."

The pendulum has now swung away from determinate sentencing and toward allowing judges more discretion. Permitting judges more leeway to consider factors such as

the defendant's background, motivations for committing the crime, and any psychological disorders may strike a balance between the uniformity that determinate sentencing imposed and the judicial discretion that many judges prefer. This was discussed earlier in this chapter. Both determinate sentencing (more consistent with equal protection) and judicial discretion (more consistent with flexibility stemming from the features of individual cases) have their advantages—and well illustrate the parameters of "equality versus discretion" conflict.

The Third Choice: To Discover the Truth or to Resolve Conflicts

What is the purpose of a court hearing or a trial? Your first reaction may be "To find out the truth, of course!"

Jerry Sandusky

Determining the truth means learning the facts of a dispute, including events, intentions, actions, and outcomes. All this assumes that "what really happened" between two parties can be determined.

Finding out the truth is desirable goal. It may also be aspirational and is sometimes simply impossible. The truth often lies somewhere between competing versions of an event. Because it is difficult for even well-meaning people to ascertain the true facts in certain cases, some observers have proposed that the real purpose of a hearing or trial is to provide social stability by resolving conflict. Supreme Court Justice Louis Brandeis once wrote that "it is more important that the applicable rule of law be settled than [that] it be settled right" (*Burnet v. Coronado Oil and Gas Co.*, 1932). This is a shift away from viewing the legal system's purpose as doing justice toward viewing its goal as "creating a sense that justice is being done" (Miller & Boster, 1977, p. 34).

Because truth is elusive, the most important priority of a hearing or a trial may be to provide a setting in which all interested parties have their "day in court." Justice replaces truth as the predominant goal. In fact, attorneys representing the opposing parties in a case do not necessarily seek "the truth." Nor do they represent themselves as "objective." They reflect a different value—the importance of giving their side the best representation possible, within the limits of the law. (The Code of Ethics of the American Bar Association even instructs attorneys to defend their clients "zealously.") Because lawyers believe the purpose of a hearing or trial is to win disputes, they present arguments supporting their client's perspective and back up their arguments with the best available evidence.

One argument in favor of the adversary system, in which a different attorney represents each party, is that it encourages the attorneys to discover and introduce all evidence that might induce the judge or jury to react favorably to their client's case. When both sides believe that they have had the chance to voice their case fully and their witnesses have revealed all the relevant facts, participants are more likely to feel they have been treated fairly by the system, and the system is more likely to be considered an effective one. This is an important part of a theory known as **procedural justice**, a concept presented in Chapter 2.

"Conflict resolution" and "truth," as goals, are not always incompatible. When all participants in a legal dispute are able to raise concerns and provide supporting documentation, the goal of learning the truth becomes more attainable. But frequently there is tension between these goals, and in some instances, the satisfactory resolution of a conflict may be socially and morally preferable to discovering an objectively established truth. Yet resolving conflict in a hurried manner can have a downside, as illustrated by the experience of Jerry Sandusky.

Sandusky was an assistant football coach at Penn State for about 15 years. In November 2011, reports surfaced that led to his being charged with 52 counts of the sexual abuse of children for acts allegedly occurring between 1994 and 2009. He was tried in June 2012 and convicted of 45 counts of sexual abuse of children, and sentenced to 30–60 years in state prison. This is not a comment about the accuracy of that conviction—but 7 months is very fast to investigate, charge, and convict an individual at trial in a case of this complexity. Because Sandusky's crimes were facilitated by his access to youth as part of his coaching position in a very prominent football program, the consequences of the Sandusky case for Penn State were catastrophic. Amidst the enormous public pressure to convict Sandusky, was 7 months sufficient? Sandusky's appeals have found no traction, suggesting that the evidence was gathered and considered with sufficient care to pass legal muster. But it is easy to imagine how a process this fast, in a case this complex, could have increased the potential for error.

Truth Versus Conflict Resolution in Plea Bargaining and Settlement Negotiations. The legal system is a massive bureaucracy, and in every bureaucracy, there is a temptation to value pragmatic efficiency rather than correct or just outcomes. The heavy reliance on plea bargaining is often criticized because it appears to give priority to conflict resolution over truth seeking. As we describe in Chapter 8, between 90% and 95% of defendants never go to trial; they accept the offer of the prosecutor and plead guilty to a lesser charge. Even some innocent persons plea-bargain after being convinced that the evidence against them is overwhelming. Indeed, plea bargaining is an integral part of the criminal justice system. The state benefits by avoiding the expense and trouble of a trial and the possibility of an acquittal, and by obtaining the testimony of the accused person against others involved in the crime. The defendant benefits by receiving some kind of reduction in the sentence imposed. In addition to these pragmatic benefits, justice is furthered by a system that rewards a show of remorse (which usually accompanies a guilty plea) and enables the prosecutor and defense counsel, together with the judge, to negotiate a resolution appropriate to the degree of wrong-doing (Kamisar et al., 1999). Nonetheless, plea bargaining reveals that the goal of maintaining stability and efficiency in the system is achieved at some cost. That cost is the public's opportunity to determine the complete truth.

The civil justice system uses a procedure similar to plea bargaining to resolve about 90% of the conflicts between a plaintiff and a defendant. **Settlement negotiation** involves a sometimes lengthy pretrial process of give-and-take, offer-and-demand that ends when a plaintiff agrees to accept what a defendant is willing to offer (typically, money) to end their legal disagreement. It also favors the goal of conflict resolution at the expense of determining what *really* happened.

For example, in 2013, settlement negotiations led to an agreement between the National Football League (N.F.L.) and thousands of former players who suffered concussive injuries on the gridiron. Players alleged that the N.F.L. was responsible for the rules and regulations of the game and that it concealed information on the potential consequences of repetitive head injuries. They settled for $765 million, including $75 million for baseline medical exams for nearly 20,000 former players. The negotiated settlement avoided lengthy and expensive litigation, enabled many players to seek the medical attention they needed, and, according to one football commentator, "saved the game" (Spencer, 2013).

Additional Thoughts on Conflict Resolution. Despite the traditional prominence of adversarial procedures to resolve disputes, many legal problems are actually handled in a non-adversarial manner. Throughout the book we present situations in which people work together in a cooperative way to settle their differences and reach a resolution that is acceptable to all.

Many divorcing couples opt to collaborate rather than contend with each other as they end their marriage. In situations where parents have failed to nurture their children, family court judges temporarily remove children from their homes and provide extensive counseling, education, and other social service interventions to parents, hoping eventually to restore the family unit. In some jurisdictions, people arrested for certain kinds of crimes are given the opportunity to have their cases resolved in problem-solving courts that focus on treating underlying problems such as substance abuse, severe mental illness, or veterans' difficulties adjusting to civilian life rather than simply punishing the offender. In lawsuits in which plaintiffs are injured due to defendants' negligence and the parties attempt to negotiate a settlement rather than go to trial, these negotiations offer an opportunity for defendants to apologize to plaintiffs. Research shows that apologies advance settlement negotiations (Robbennolt, 2013) and reduce plaintiffs' inclinations to sue (Greene, 2008). They also affect the bottom line: In medical malpractice cases, apologies reduce the average payout by $32,000 (Ho & Liu, 2011).

What these situations have in common is that they do not operate in a zero-sum fashion in which one party wins and another loses. Rather, they attempt to maximize positive outcomes for all concerned, with the objective of keeping the dispute from escalating further and involving more formal adjudication proceedings.

The idea that the law is a social force with consequences for people's well-being is an approach termed **therapeutic jurisprudence**. Reform-minded lawyers, jurists, and legal scholars advocate for legal procedures and institutions that facilitate therapeutic ends. They ask how the law can be applied or reformed to enhance individuals' welfare. Therapeutic jurisprudence has been applied in nearly all areas of the law including criminal law, family law, employment law, probate, health care, workers' compensation, and labor arbitration.

The Fourth Choice: Science Versus the Law as a Source of Decisions

When one discipline (in our case, psychology) seeks to understand another (the law), a dilemma is likely to arise because each approaches knowledge in a different way. When asked, "How do you know whether that decision is the right one?" each relies on different methods, even though both share the goal of understanding human experience.

As you read this book you will learn that in many cases the U.S. Supreme Court and other courts have considered data and conclusions presented by psychologists and other social scientists. In some of these, the American Psychological Association (APA) prepared a written document, called an *amicus curiae* ("friend of the court") **brief**, for consideration by an appellate court (consider Gilfoyle & Dvoskin, 2017). Such *amicus curiae* briefs provide the courts with information from psychological science and practice relevant to the issues in a particular case. In many of its decisions (including *Miller v. Alabama*, presented earlier in this chapter), the Supreme Court incorporated input from the *amicus curiae* brief, although in other cases it disregarded the social science data altogether. Justices may have different reasons for disregarding scientific data, of course—some philosophical, some

The justices of the U.S. Supreme Court.

procedural, some reflecting skepticism—so it is perhaps not surprising that some Supreme Court opinions appear strongly influenced by scientific thinking and data while others do not.

In addition to employing different procedures, each profession may use idiosyncratic or unique concepts to describe the same phenomenon. An attorney and a social scientist will observe the same event from different perspectives. Neither is necessarily more accurate than the other and their differences are the result of exposure to and training in different points of view. The following subsections illustrate such differences in more detail (Robbennolt & Davidson, 2011).

Law Relies on Precedents; Psychology Relies on Scientific Methods. In contrast to the law, psychology is generally committed to the idea that there is an objective world of experience that can be understood by adherence to the rules of science—systematic testing of hypotheses by observation and experimental methodology. As a scientist, the psychologist should be committed to a public, impersonal, objective pursuit of truth, relying on methods that can be repeated by others and interpreting results by using predetermined standards. Although this traditional view of psychology's approach to truth has been criticized for failing to capture the complexity of human experience accurately or without bias, it still represents the values and methods in which more senior psychologists were trained. (It also represents the authors' beliefs that the scientific method and the research skills of psychologists are the most essential and reliable tools available for examining the many important legal questions we address throughout the book.)

By contrast, when they establish new laws, legal experts rely heavily on **precedents**—rulings in previous cases (as well as the Constitution and the statutes) for guidance. **Case law**—the law made by judges ruling in individual cases—is very influential; statutes and constitutional safeguards do not apply to every new situation, so past cases often serve as precedents for deciding current ones. The principle of *stare decisis* ("let the decision stand," reflecting the importance of abiding by previous decisions) is also important in this process. Judges typically are reluctant to make decisions that contradict earlier ones, as the history of the Supreme Court's school desegregation cases indicates.

When the U.S. Supreme Court decided unanimously in 1954, in *Brown v. Board of Education*, that public school segregation was contrary to the notion of equality for all, many reports claimed that it "supplanted" or even "overturned" a ruling in the 1896 case of *Plessy v. Ferguson*. But intermediate decisions by the Court permitted this seemingly abrupt change to evolve gradually. A brief history of rulings that led up to the *Brown v. Board of Education* decision illustrates this phenomenon, and the way that the law proceeds from case to case.

We begin with the state of Louisiana's dispute with Homer Plessy. During a train trip in Louisiana in the 1890s, Plessy sat down in a railroad car labeled "Whites Only." Plessy's ancestry was mostly White, but he had one Black great-grandparent. Therefore, according to the laws of Louisiana at that time,

Plessy was considered Black (or *colored*, the term used then). Plessy refused to move to a car designated for "colored" passengers, as a recently passed state law required. He took his claim to court, but a New Orleans judge ruled that, contrary to Plessy's argument, the statute that segregated railroad cars by race did not violate the Fourteenth Amendment to the Constitution. In other words, it did not fail to give Plessy "equal protection under the law." Plessy persisted in his appeal, and eventually, in 1896, the U.S. Supreme Court upheld the decision of the judge and the lower courts. Judge Henry Billings Brown, speaking for the majority faction of the Supreme Court, declared that laws that had established separate facilities for the races did not necessarily imply that one race was inferior to the other.

Although this opinion was a far cry from the 1954 *Brown* decision, which highlighted the detrimental effects of segregation on the personality development of Black children, cases decided between *Plessy* and *Brown* would foreshadow the Court's eventual leanings. One case was brought by George McLaurin, the first Black student admitted to the University of Oklahoma's Graduate School of Education. Although McLaurin was allowed to enroll, he was segregated from all his classmates. His desk was separated from all the others by a rail, to which the sign "Reserved for Colored" was attached. He was given a separate desk at the library and was required to eat by himself in the cafeteria. In the 1950 case of *McLaurin v. Oklahoma State Regents*, the U.S. Supreme Court ruled unanimously that these procedures denied McLaurin the right to equal protection of the law. The Court concluded that such restrictions would "impair and inhibit his ability to study, to engage in discussion and exchange of views with other students." But the Court did not strike down *Plessy v. Ferguson* in this decision.

With a more liberal Court in the 1950s, however, there was enough momentum to reverse *Plessy v. Ferguson*. Chief Justice Earl Warren liked to ask, "What is fair?" (We find this a compelling question about race even 70 years later.) Justice Warren spearheaded the unanimous decision that finally overturned the idea that separate facilities can be "equal." He wrote that separating Black children "from others of similar age and qualifications solely because of their race generates a feeling of inferiority as to their status in the community that may affect their hearts and minds in a way unlikely to ever be undone" (*Brown v. Board of Education*, 1954).

The school desegregation cases show that lawyers have historically reasoned from case to case. They locate cases that are similar to the one at hand and then base their arguments on the rulings from these legal precedents. Psychologists, on the other hand, value the scientific method, rely on experimental and evaluation studies, and prefer to gather data that describe large numbers of people.

Some commentators have suggested that society would be better served by a legal profession that was less resistant to objective, rigorous, and scientific evidence, however (Greiner & Matthews, 2016). They extol the virtues of using scientific research designs such as **randomized controlled trials (RCT)** to accumulate knowledge about what works in the legal system and what does not. We note very few examples of such studies in law. There are easily understood reasons why this is so; to conduct an RCT in a legal setting, the investigator must convince decision-makers to randomly assign participants to an experimental condition involving an intervention that is not yet established. Judges, parole boards, and prison wardens are understandably reluctant to agree to this. One possible parameter of RCTs in legal contexts involves using a "treatment as usual" control group and comparing that to an experimental group that includes treatment as usual *plus* other components. Doing so can help investigators to convince reluctant decision-makers that nobody is likely to be put at greater risk of harm by this—including citizens who could be victims of future crime if the outcome involved reoffending.

Law Deals with Absolutes; Psychology Deals with Probabilities. Legal questions often require an "either–or" response: A person is either fit or unfit to be a parent; a person was either insane or not insane when they committed a particular act (Melton et al., 2018). Psychologists are less comfortable reasoning in absolutes. They prefer to think in terms of probabilities (e.g., that a defendant's delusional thinking *could* indicate a psychiatric disorder, that a White eyewitness to a crime is *more likely to* misidentify a Black perpetrator than a White perpetrator). Although the law looks to psychologists for "either–or" answers (e.g., "Is the defendant competent to stand trial?" and "Was the defendant insane at the time of the crime?"), psychologists usually prefer to answer in terms of likelihoods or quantified "maybes." Lawyers may have difficulty with such probabilistic responses because they need a final resolution to a dispute.

Law Supports Contrasting Views of Reality; Psychology Seeks One Refined View of Reality. Judges and jurors must decide which of the two conceptions of the truth is more acceptable in light of conflicting facts. Attorneys assemble all the facts that support their side and argue forcefully that their version of the facts is the correct one. Although this procedure is similar to some scientific activities (a psychologist may do a study that compares predictions from two theories), the psychologist is trained to be objective and open to all perspectives and types of data. The psychologist's ultimate goal is to integrate or assimilate conflicting findings into one refined view of the truth, rather than choosing between alternative views.

Some observers have likened this difference between psychology and law to the difference between scaling a mountain and fighting in a boxing match. As psychologists gain a clearer understanding of a topic (e.g., the causes of elder abuse), they scale a figurative mountain, at the top of which lies true and complete understanding. Although they may never actually reach this pinnacle of knowledge, psychologists highly value the accumulation of data, the development of psychological theory, and the quest for "truth." By contrast, lawyers are less interested in ascertaining the objective truth about a topic and are more concerned with winning against their adversary, resolving a dispute, or, more recently, enhancing the laws' effect on all parties.

Such distinctions only scratch the surface of the differences between law and psychology. In Chapter 2 we consider differing notions of justice in the two fields, and in subsequent chapters we will discuss the implications of these differences. As with the previous choices, selecting one domain over the other does not always yield a satisfactory resolution. The use of both perspectives moves us closer to an adequate understanding than does relying only on one. For example, using a psychological principle such as attribution of responsibility—a judgment of who is responsible for a particular outcome in a particular situation—can explain why some people decide to sue and others do not (Robbennolt & Hans, 2016). Both psychologists and lawyers should remain aware of the limits of their own perspective and realize that both viewpoints are essential for a fuller understanding of complex behavioral issues in the law.

But the contrast in knowledge-generating procedures does raise difficult procedural questions. What roles should the psychologist play in the legal system? What ethical concerns are associated with psychologists' involvement in the legal system? These and other basic questions are among the areas discussed in this book.

Psychologists' Roles in the Law

Most courses in psychology portray only two roles for psychologists: those of the scientist who conducts basic research about the causes and consequences of behavior, and the applied psychologist (usually a clinical psychologist) who tries to understand and assist individuals or groups in improving behavioral health. The possibilities are more elaborate, however, when the psychologist is involved in the legal system. We describe five distinct roles for psychologists in the legal system: basic scientist, applied scientist, policy evaluator, forensic evaluator, and consultant. The work inherent in these roles ranges from isolated academic research in psychology that may be relevant to law, on one end, to active collaboration with people who work in the legal system, on the other end.

As you will see, the five roles vary in several respects. But whatever the role, it includes standards about what is acceptable and unacceptable behavior. Professionals often develop explicit statements of ethical standards of behavior. For psychologists, those principles and standards (called the *Ethical Principles of Psychologists and Code of Conduct*) have been published by the American Psychological Association (2017). They describe a series of broad principles followed by a more specific set of standards. Adherence to the standards is mandatory for psychologists. Among the many topics they cover is when psychologists should terminate treatment and how to do so.

Making the right ethical choice can be complicated. Sometimes, certain standards (e.g., confidentiality in therapy) may conflict with other obligations (e.g., the legal obligation to prevent harm to third parties inflicted by

Box 1.4

The Case of Tatiana Tarasoff: Duty to Warn, Duty to Protect

Few legal decisions have had as much impact on the practice of psychotherapy as the now-famous case of *Tarasoff v. Regents of the University of California*. The decision focuses on the duties required of psychotherapists whose clients threaten violence to identifiable others.

Prosenjit Poddar was a graduate student at the University of California who became infatuated with Tatiana Tarasoff. Poddar was inexperienced in romantic relationships and was confused about Tatiana's on-again–off-again behavior; she was friendly toward him one day but avoided him completely the next night. After Poddar became a client of a psychologist at the university counseling center, he confided that he intended to kill a girl who had rebuffed him. The psychologist told his supervisor of this threat and then called the campus police, requesting that they detain Poddar. They did so but soon released him, believing his promise that he would stay away from Tatiana, who was out of the country at the time. Poddar didn't keep his promise. Two months later, he went to Tatiana's home and stabbed her to death. (He was eventually convicted of murder, but this conviction was overturned on the basis of inadequate jury instructions. He returned to India.)

Tatiana Tarasoff's parents sued the university, the psychologists, and the campus police for failing to warn them or their daughter about Poddar's threats. The California Supreme Court ruled in the parents' favor by deciding that the university had been negligent. The first *Tarasoff* decision (1974) established a duty on psychotherapists to warn the victims of therapy patients when the therapist "knows or should have known" that the patient presented a threat to that victim. The court established a standard that therapists have a duty to use "reasonable care" to protect identifiable potential victims from clients in psychotherapy who threaten violence. A second *Tarasoff* decision in 1976 broadened this duty to include the protection of third parties from patient violence. Courts in several other states have extended this duty to the protection of property and the protection of all foreseeable victims, not just identifiable ones.

The *Tarasoff* case still governs psychologists' conduct in multiple states. Many psychologists feel caught in a no-win situation: They can be held responsible for their clients' violence if they do not warn potential victims, but they can also be held responsible for breaching their clients' confidentiality if they do.

Critical Thought Question: Why is it necessary to specify explicitly what psychologists must do if they hear a client threaten to harm a person or property?

therapy patients). This conflict was apparent in the controversial *Tarasoff* decision by the Supreme Court of California, described in Box 1.4.

In the following sections, we describe the various roles that psychologists assume in relation to the legal system and the ethical issues that arise in each context. A footnote on psychologists' relationship to the law: Students often wonder how they can become involved in this field as basic scientists, applied scientists, policy evaluators, forensic evaluators, or consultants. What career paths should one pursue, and what professional opportunities exist at the ends of those trails? How might a developmental psychologist, a cognitive neuropsychologist, or a clinician (for example) interact with the legal system? The website of the American Psychology-Law Society (a division of the APA) has practical and career-related advice for practitioners, educators, researchers, and students (https://ap-ls.org). Those undertaking careers in psychology and law should also familiarize themselves with the ethical requirements pertaining to their professions.

The Psychologist as a Basic Scientist of the Law

A basic scientist pursues knowledge for its own sake. Basic scientists study a phenomenon for the satisfaction of understanding it and contributing to scientific advances in the area. They do not necessarily seek to apply their research findings, and do not prioritize whether the knowledge they generate will be used to resolve real-world problems. Yet often their results can address important practical issues, including some that arise in the law. For example, though not specifically conducted for use in the courtroom, laboratory research on visual perception can help us understand the accuracy of eyewitness testimony about a crime or accident. Psychologists who test different theories of memory promote a better understanding of whether repression can cause long-term forgetting of traumatic events. Basic research on the relationship between social attitudes and behavior can clarify why people obey or disobey the law. Research in personality psychology can help to show what kind of person will become a follower in a terrorist group and what kind of person will be a leader. Studies of adolescents' brain development may be relevant to their decisions about whether to commit crimes. Finally, research can assess whether forensic psychologists' attitudes about the causes of crime affect their professional evaluations of criminal defendants.

The Ethics of the Basic Scientist. Like all scientists, psychologists who do basic research must adhere to standards of conduct in how they undertake and report their studies. In practical terms, this means that they cannot fabricate or forge data, plagiarize, or present a skewed selection of the data to hide observations that do not fit their conclusions. They must treat research participants in an ethical manner. (All institutions that receive federal research funding must have review boards that evaluate the way scientists treat human and animal subjects. Even research projects that are not funded by federal grants must be approved by such boards, often called "institutional review boards" or IRBs.) Basic researchers sometimes have a conflict of interest when faced with competing concerns such as honestly reporting their research findings versus obtaining grant funding or publishing studies. In these situations, they should learn to recognize and be honest about potential conflicts of interest and communicate them to interested parties before undertaking the research.

The Psychologist as an Applied Scientist in the Law

An **applied scientist** is dedicated to generating and applying knowledge to solve real-life problems. Most of the public's awareness of a psychologist's work reflects this role, whether this awareness comes from reading blog posts and tweets or watching an expert witness in a fictional crime show. Indeed, an important role for psychologists who are interested in applying the findings of their profession involves serving as an expert witness in a legislative hearing or in a courtroom.

Juries, judges, and legislators cannot be well versed in every topic from abscesses to zinfandel wine. An **expert witness** is someone who possesses specialized knowledge about a subject, knowledge that the average person does not have. Psychologists may testify as expert witnesses during a trial based on their knowledge, experience, and training regarding psychological issues. The expert's task is to assist jurors and judges by providing an opinion based on this specialized knowledge.

Either side, as part of its presentation of the evidence, may ask the judge to allow expert witnesses to testify. The judge must be convinced that the testimony is of a kind that requires specialized knowledge, skill, or experience and that it will help promote better legal decision making. (When psychologists testify concerning a particular individual based on the results of a forensic evaluation, they take on a different role, one we describe later in this chapter.)

The psychological topics that call for scientific expertise are almost limitless. As expert witnesses, psychologists have been called on to testify in many types of cases. For example, expert testimony may be useful in understanding:

- Employee discrimination through selection and promotion procedures

- The effects of posting warning signs or safety instructions on potentially dangerous equipment

- The factors that may cause a suspect to make a false confession

- The influence of human development on the accuracy of children's testimony

- The effects of suggestive questions on children's memory of alleged abuse

The Ethics of the Applied Scientist/Expert Witness. The psychologist as expert witness represents a profession that values objectivity and accuracy in its procedures. Even though expert witnesses are usually retained and paid by one side, they are responsible for reporting all their conclusions, regardless of whether these favor the side paying them. It violates the ethical standards of both psychologists and lawyers for expert witnesses to accept payment that is contingent on the outcome of the case.

But achieving objectivity is not easy. When testifying as experts, psychologists have an ethical responsibility to be honest and open with the court about their opinions. Yet they may be tempted to sympathize with the side that has employed them. Is it possible to increase experts' objectivity? One commentator has proposed using "blinded" experts selected by an intermediary and hired to review the case without knowing which side has requested an opinion (Robertson, 2010). When blinded experts were pitted against traditional experts in a study examining mock jurors' decisions, the former were perceived as more credible and persuasive than the latter (Robertson & Yokum, 2011). Other investigators have observed that psychological experts are subject to cognitive biases, including confirmation bias (deciding prematurely and valuing evidence supporting that decision and discounting evidence that is not supportive), availability bias (emphasizing particularly vivid cases that are easily recalled, or "available"), and blind-spot bias (believing that others are subject to biases but you are not) (Neal et al., 2018).

Another ethical dilemma arises whenever the adversary system forces an expert to make absolute "either–or" judgments. Has the pretrial publicity caused potential jurors to be biased against the defendant? In a custody case stemming from a divorce, which parent would be better for the child to live with? Does the evaluation of a defendant indicate that she is mentally ill? In all of these situations, the law requires the psychologist to reach a firm conclusion on the witness stand, regardless of ambiguity in the evidence (Melton et al., 2018). This is an example of the absolute versus probabilistic judgment differences we described earlier in the chapter.

Admissibility of Expert Testimony. In order to maximize the likelihood that expert testimony is based on legitimate scientific knowledge and to exclude "junk science," lawmakers have developed criteria for judges to use when determining whether to allow an "expert" to testify. Each state and the federal government have their own criteria for determining admissibility.

In federal courts and over half of the states, these criteria are informed by a two-prong test developed by the U.S. Supreme Court in a highly influential case, *Daubert v. Merrell Dow Pharmaceuticals, Inc.* (1993). First, the trial judge must determine whether the testimony is relevant and if relevant, whether it is based on reliable and valid science. In essence, judges function as "gatekeepers" who must evaluate potential expert testimony by the standards of science.

Judges have disallowed expert psychological testimony as irrelevant. Consider the case of Pedro Gil. Gil dropped a bucket of plaster over the wall of a Manhattan rooftop; it dropped seven stories to the ground and hit and killed a police officer standing on the street below. Gil claimed that he expected the bucket to drop unceremoniously onto an unoccupied street directly below him, rather than to continue forward as it fell and land on the street where the police officer was positioned. To support his naive belief that objects drop straight down, Gil's attorneys attempted to introduce the testimony of a cognitive psychologist with expertise in intuitive physics. The expert planned to testify that people commonly misunderstand physical laws but the trial judge did not let him testify, claiming that intuitive physics was irrelevant to the issues under contention. The jury convicted Gil of second-degree manslaughter.

Judges have also disallowed expert testimony as unreliable. Richard Coons, a Texas psychiatrist, testified in death penalty trials that he developed his own methodology to determine whether a defendant poses a risk of future dangerousness. (Prior to sentencing a defendant to death, juries in Texas must agree that there is a probability that they pose a continuing threat to society.) Coons considers an offender's criminal history, attitudes toward violence, and conscience, yet he could not show that these factors have been validated by any research or that his predictions are accurate. After an appellate court deemed Coons' testimony unreliable, over-ruling a trial court judge who had admitted the expert testimony, a defense attorney quipped, "It's overdue."

One clear implication of the *Daubert* decision is that judges must become savvy consumers of science if they are to decide which opinions qualify as "scientific." Since the *Daubert* case, the admissibility of expert evidence has become an important pretrial issue and judges need to scrutinize the reasoning and methodology underlying experts' opinions (Chlistunoff, 2016). They have the option to appoint neutral experts to help them decide whether to admit disputed scientific evidence (Domitrovich, 2016). Perhaps they should do so more often, as evidence suggests that judges are not keeping "junk science" out of the courtroom very effectively (Neal et al., 2020).

The Psychologist as a Policy Evaluator in the Law

In addition to their knowledge of substantive problems, psychologists have methodological skills that they use in assessing or evaluating how well an intervention has worked. Psychologists and other social scientists have been asked so frequently to conduct evaluation studies that a separate subfield called policy evaluation, or evaluation research, has emerged. The **policy evaluator** provides data to answer questions such as "I have instituted a policy; how do I know whether it was effective?" Or "I want to make a change in our organization's procedures, but before I do, how do I design it so I will be able to determine later whether it worked?"

Psychologists working as policy evaluators might be asked whether changing the laws for teen drivers by restricting the number of passengers they can carry will reduce traffic accidents, whether the chemical castration of released rapists will reduce the rate of sexual violence, or whether changing from automobile patrols to foot patrols will improve relations between police and the community. The methodological skills of a psychologist as policy evaluator are essential in assessing existing programs and policies and designing innovations so that their effects can be tested.

As an example, psychologists have been involved in evaluating policies and programs intended to help children prepare to testify in court. In one program, nearly two hundred 4- to 17-year-olds attended Kids' Court School in Las Vegas a week or two before their scheduled testimony. Psychologists measured their court-related anxiety before and after an intervention that consisted of education about legal proceedings, stress inoculation, and a mock trial. As predicted, anticipatory anxiety decreased from pre-test to post-test, suggesting that the program can serve as a model for reducing court-related stress in child witnesses (Nathanson & Saywitz, 2015).

The Ethics of the Policy Evaluator. The psychologist who evaluates the impact of proposed or existing legislation and court or correctional procedures faces ethical responsibilities similar to those of the expert witness. The standard rules of scientific procedure apply, but because of the source of employment and payment, there are pressures to interpret results of evaluation studies in a certain way.

Consider, for example, a large state criminal justice system that wants to improve its parole process. Officials know that when released into society, heavy drug users are likely to commit further crimes to maintain their drug habit, and are therefore likely to return to prison. Accordingly, the system seeks to introduce and evaluate an innovative halfway house program for individuals on parole with a history of narcotics addiction. It hires a policy evaluator to design a study and evaluate the effects of this innovation. The state system provides funding to carry out the study, and officials are sincerely committed to its goals. Assume the psychologist concludes that the halfway house does not significantly reduce drug use by parolees. The authorities are disappointed and may even challenge the integrity of the policy evaluator. Yet, as scientists, program evaluators must "call 'em like they see 'em," regardless of the desirability of the outcome.

Even if the program is successful, the policy evaluator faces other ethical dilemmas. To assess such an innovative program, the researcher might conduct a randomized controlled trial that entails denying some parolees access to the program and placing them in a "treatment as usual" control group. The ethical dilemma becomes more critical when some potentially lifesaving innovation is being evaluated. But often it is only through such research methods that a potentially helpful new program can be convincingly demonstrated to be effective.

The Psychologist as a Forensic Evaluator in Litigation

In addition to evaluating policies and programs, psychologists may be asked to evaluate individuals involved in civil and criminal cases, to report their findings to a judge, and on occasion, to testify about the results in court. Forensic evaluators assess matters such as:

- The competence of a defendant to proceed with adjudication of charges (often called "competence to stand trial," although most criminal charges are adjudicated through plea bargaining rather than trial)

- The mental state of a defendant at the time of an alleged offense (often called "sanity at the time of the offense")

- The degree of emotional or brain damage suffered by a victim in an accident

- The effects on a child of alternative custody arrangements after divorce

- The risk of future violent or other criminal behavior

- The prospects for a convicted defendant's rehabilitation in prison or on probation

There are two ways that mental health professionals become involved in litigation as **forensic evaluators**: they are either court-appointed, or hired by one of the parties involved in the litigation (defense, prosecution, or plaintiff). Serving in the court-appointed role involves receiving an order from the judge authorizing the mental health professional to evaluate a given individual for a specific purpose. The judge may also specify additional considerations such as how the results are to be communicated. There is typically an expectation that the resulting forensic evaluation will be considered by the judge without being introduced by either side.

Forensic evaluators employed by one of the parties involved in the litigation have a different expectation: That particular party may control when (and whether) the forensic assessment findings are actually introduced as evidence in the case. Some referrals for forensic assessment come from

attorneys who authorize the evaluations without resorting to any kind of court authority. (This kind of right is usually reserved for the defense in a criminal prosecution; the prosecutor cannot request a **forensic mental health assessment** unless it is approved by the court—and therefore known to the defense.) These tasks will be discussed in much more detail in Chapters 10 and 11 of this book. They are also described in detail elsewhere (e.g., Heilbrun et al., 2009; Melton et al., 2018).

The Ethics of the Forensic Evaluator. The ethical considerations associated with the role of forensic evaluator are fairly formal and specifically described in several documents. In addition to the ethical principles disseminated by the APA, two other sets of ethical guidelines affect the practice of forensic evaluators. Neither is "enforceable" in the sense that the APA *Ethical Principles of Psychologists and Code of Conduct* is. Nonetheless, both serve as important sources of authority, and may affect the judgments of courts regarding the admissibility and weight of forensic assessment evidence. These two documents are the *Specialty Guidelines for Forensic Psychologists* (APA, 2013) and the *Guidelines for Child Custody Evaluations in Family Law Proceedings* (APA, 2010).

Across these three documents, there is substantial emphasis on providing evaluations that (1) are clear in their purpose; (2) are conducted by individuals who are competent by virtue of their education, training, and experience; (3) are respectful of appropriate relationships (and avoid multiple relationships, such as both forensic evaluator and therapist, in the same case); (4) provide the appropriate level of confidentiality consistent with circumstances and the applicable legal privilege; (5) use methods and procedures that are accurate, current, and consistent with science and standards of practice; and (6) communicated appropriately.

Like other expert witnesses, forensic evaluators have an obligation to be objective in their assessments and reporting, yet may be tempted to favor the side that has retained them. This concern is illustrated by a study of how independent forensic psychologists, retained by opposing attorneys, evaluated a description of the same individual. Despite using a standardized diagnostic test for psychopathy, the psychologists tended to rate the individual in a manner favorable to the side that retained them (Murrie et al., 2013). This sympathy may not even be conscious; instead, the psychologist may reach conclusions that are motivated by subtle partisan allegiance to the retaining attorney. For this reason, adherence to relevant ethical standards is very important, as is consideration of the motivations for discounting factual evidence (Hornsey, 2020).

The Psychologist as a Consultant in Litigation

The final role for psychologists in the law is that of consultant. The field of **trial consulting** provides one example of this role for psychologists working in the legal arena. Social scientists who began this work in the 1970s used so-called scientific jury selection procedures (further described in Chapter 12) to assist defense lawyers in highly politicized trials resulting from antiwar activities in the United States. Since then, these techniques have been refined and expanded. The national media devoted extensive coverage to the use of trial consultants in the celebrity-status trials of Martha Stewart and Bill Cosby, and such consultants are often used in such high-visibility trials. The long-running CBS series, *Bull*, presented a highly fictionalized portrayal of a trial consultant.

Today the field of trial consulting is a booming business and involves far more than jury selection. Trial consultants also conduct community attitude surveys to document extensive pretrial publicity or to introduce findings as evidence in trials involving discrimination or trademark violation claims (Posey, 2015). They test the effectiveness of demonstrative evidence (Richter & Humke, 2011), provide guidance to attorneys seeking damage awards (Bornstein & Greene, 2011a), and prepare witnesses to testify (Stinson & Cutler, 2011). They have even evaluated the pros and cons of virtual trials (Gordon, 2022).

There is no expectation of impartiality in any of these roles as there would be for psychologists acting as basic scientists, applied scientists, policy evaluators, or forensic evaluators. Nor is there an expectation that the consultant must present information in a balanced way. However, the psychologist must still provide the attorney with good information in order to promote more effective performance in litigation. How the attorney decides to use such information is within that attorney's discretion.

Critics have argued that these techniques essentially rig the jury (Kressel & Kressel, 2002) and create a perception that psychologists can manipulate the trial process (Strier, 2011). But at least in the realm of jury selection, it is difficult to determine whether scientific jury selection is more effective than traditional jury selection. Cases that employ scientific jury selection techniques differ in many ways from cases that

do not, and "success" is hard to define (Lieberman, 2011). (Does a low damage award or conviction on a less serious charge connote success? Perhaps.) Consultants suggest that they are simply borrowing techniques commonly used in politics and advertising and bringing them into the courtroom. Politicians hire people to help them project a better image, and advertisers try to enhance the ways that retailers connect with consumers. Shouldn't lawyers be able to do the same? Consultants also argue that in an adversarial system, attorneys should be able to use every tool available to them.

The Ethics of the Consultant in Litigation. As we noted earlier, when the psychologist becomes a consultant for one side in the selection of jurors, there may be ethical questions. Just how far should the selection procedures go? Should jurors have to answer consultants' intrusive questions about their private lives? Should consultants be able to sculpt the jury to their clients' advantage? Do these techniques simply constitute the latest tools in the attorney's arsenal of trial tactics? Or do they bias the proceedings and jeopardize the willingness of citizens to participate in the process? These questions deal with fairness, and scientific jury selection may conflict with the way some people interpret the intent of the law.

But consider that rival attorneys—whether they employ trial consultants or not—always try to select jurors who will sympathize with their version of the facts. Since the adversarial system permits attorneys from each side to eliminate some prospective jurors, it does not seem unethical for psychologists to assist these attorneys, as long as their advocacy is consistent with the law and the administration of justice.

When psychologists become trial consultants, they also subscribe to the ethical code of the attorneys, who, after all, are in charge of the trial preparation (Stolle & Studebaker, 2011). Trial consultants who are members of the American Society of Trial Consultants must adhere to the Code of Ethical Principles, Professional Standards, and Practice Guidelines developed by that organization (ASTC, 2017).

Summary

1. **Why do we have laws and what is the psychological approach to studying law?** Laws are human creations whose major purposes are the resolution of conflict and the protection of society. As society has changed, new conflicts surfaced, leading to expansion and revision of the legal system. A psychological approach focuses on individuals as agents within a legal system, asking how their internal qualities (personality, values, abilities, and experiences) and their environments, including the law itself, affect their behavior.

2. **What choices are reflected in the psychological approach to the law?** Several basic choices must be made between pairs of options in the psychological study of the law. These options are often irreconcilable because each is attractive, but both usually cannot be attained at the same time. The choices are (1) whether the goal of law is achieving personal freedom or ensuring the common good, (2) whether equality or discretion should be the standard for our legal policies, (3) whether the purpose of a legal inquiry is

to discover the truth or to provide a means of conflict resolution, and (4) whether it is better to apply the methods of law or those of science for making decisions.

3. **How do laws reflect the contrast between the due process model and the crime control model of the criminal justice system?** The decade of the 1960s represented an era in which due process concerns were paramount and court decisions tended to favor rights of the individuals, particularly those suspected of crimes, over the power of the police and law enforcement. Since then, the crime control model, which seeks to contain or reduce criminal activity, has been favored by many. But some of the harsh policies and penalties consistent with this perspective have resulted in large increases in prison populations and little reduction in rates of reoffending. The 2007–2009 recession caused legislators and judges to consider community-based alternatives that control crime more effectively. The trend toward lower incarceration and greater community-based correctional interventions has continued for the last decade.

4. **What are five roles that psychologists may play in the legal system and what does each entail?** Five possible roles are identified in this chapter: the psychologist as (1) a basic scientist, interested in knowledge related to psychology and law for its own sake; (2) an applied scientist who seeks to apply basic research knowledge to a particular problem in the legal system; a psychologist serving as an expert witness on a scientific question is an applied scientist in the law; (3) a policy evaluator who capitalizes on methodological skills to design and conduct research that assesses the effects of policies and program changes in the legal system; (4) a forensic evaluator who is either appointed by the court or retained at the request of one of the parties in the litigation to perform a psychological evaluation of an individual related to a legal question; and (5) a consultant who works on behalf of a party or position in litigation. Each role entails its own set of ethical dilemmas.

Key Terms

amicus curiae brief

applied scientist

basic scientist

case law

crime control model

determinate sentencing

discretion

due process model

equality

expert witness

forensic evaluator

forensic mental health assessment

forensic psychologists

implicit bias

policy evaluator

precedents

principle of proportionality

procedural justice

racial bias

randomized controlled trials

sentencing disparity

settlement negotiation

stare decisis

therapeutic jurisprudence

trial consulting

Chapter 2

The Legal System: Issues, Structure, and Players

Orienting Questions

1. What is the difference between the adversarial and inquisitorial systems of justice?
2. How do notions of morality and legality differ?
3. How do different models of justice explain people's level of satisfaction with the legal system?
4. What is commonsense justice?
5. How are judges selected and how do their demographic characteristics and ideologies influence their decisions?
6. How does the experience of law school affect its students?
7. What factors explain lawyers' overconfidence and how can it be remedied?

To understand how and why psychologists interact with the law, one needs a basic understanding of how the legal system operates. Accordingly, in this chapter, we focus on the legal system itself. We describe the nature of the adversarial system and psychological aspects of legality, morality, and justice. We discuss courts and examine the roles of judges and lawyers. An understanding of the workings of the legal system will help clarify why psychologists are interested in studying and assisting judges, lawyers, and ordinary citizens involved in the law.

The Adversarial System

Criminal cases concern conduct that is prohibited by law, and civil cases concern disputes between private parties. In both instances, American legal procedures involve an **adversarial system** of justice. Exhibits, evidence, and witnesses are assembled on behalf of one side or the other to convince the fact finder—judge or jury—that their side's viewpoint is the correct one. During a trial, the choice of what evidence to present is within the discretion of those involved in the litigation and their attorneys. Judges rarely call witnesses or introduce evidence on their own.

The adversarial system is derived from English common law. This approach contrasts with the **inquisitorial system** used in Europe (but not in Great Britain), in which the judge has more control over the proceedings. Lind (1982) described the procedure in France as follows: "The questioning of witnesses is conducted almost exclusively by the presiding judge. The judge interrogates the disputing parties and witnesses…Although the parties probably have partisan attorneys present at the trial, it is evident that control over the presentation of evidence and arguments is firmly in the hands of the judge" (p. 14). In the inquisitorial system, the two sides do not have separate witnesses; the witnesses testify for the judge's benefit, and the opposing parties are not allowed to prepare the witnesses before the trial.

Is one system inherently superior? In fact, no: there are pros and cons to each. The adversarial model allows disputants freedom to "call the shots" but has been criticized for promoting a competitive atmosphere that can distort the truth. Relevant research confirms that having an adversarial mindset tends to lead to skewed judgments that are self-serving and self-affirming. This so-called **myside bias** (Stanovich et al., 2013) manifests itself in a favorable impression of oneself and unfavorable perceptions of one's adversary. It also affects the ways that people perceive and evaluate the disputed situation itself, leading them to believe a version of the facts that supports their own positions. In the end, these behaviors can escalate, rather than resolve, conflicts and defeat the adversaries' stated interests.

Consider a situation in which mediators or negotiators try to resolve a dispute. Having a myside bias can cause them to overestimate the strengths of their case and their chances of prevailing, to view their positions as more just than those of their opponents, and to fail to consider their counterparts' perspective, all of which leads them to distrust and disfavor proposals offered by their counterparts and forego solutions that could benefit both sides. In one study, research participants assigned to an adversarial role in a labor dispute skewed a wide range of judgments in their favor, including the inferences they drew from the facts and the impressions they held of themselves and their counterparts. Participants assigned to a non-adversarial role made less extreme judgments of the facts and viewed their counterparts' judgments as less biased (Simon et al., 2020).

So although an adversarial perspective allows disputing parties to build and present a case as they wish, it can also compromise their evaluation of the facts and relevant laws. The implications are wide-ranging and include concerns about whether law enforcement agencies can conduct truly neutral investigations, whether lawyers can objectively counsel their clients about the appropriateness of accepting plea bargains and settling civil disputes, and whether even the most cautious expert witnesses can remain impartial. According to law professor Christopher Slobogin (2014), it is highly likely that the skewed judgments that flow from an adversarial process contribute to wrongful convictions, wrongful acquittals, and wrongful punishments alike.

Can inquisitorial procedures result in more objective justice? Maybe. According to Thibaut and Walker (1978), inquisitorial procedures seem optimized to produce more truthful outcomes because they involve a neutral third party who gathers the relevant evidence without influence from the parties with a stake in the dispute. Some research (O'Brien, 2009; Sevier, 2014) supports their position. In the study by Sevier, participants read details (including the verdict) of a dog-bite case, presented in either an adversarial manner where the litigants found their own scientific experts and prepared them for trial or an inquisitorial manner where the judge appointed expert witnesses who worked independently of the litigants. Compared to the adversarial framework, inquisitorial procedures resulted in verdicts that were deemed accurate, but not necessarily just. Overall then, adversarial systems seem to provide the *perception of* justice but may lack accuracy, whereas inquisitorial systems seem to provide the *perception of* accuracy but may lack justice.

So the search for justice and truth apparently depends on the legal procedures in play. But in addition to justice and truth, one should also consider the tensions between what is legal (or illegal) and what is moral (or immoral). Another equally important consideration is how differing notions of legality and morality—a result of our current culture wars—factor into the equation.

Legality Versus Morality

Laws are designed to regulate the behavior of individuals—to specify precisely what conduct is illegal. But do laws always correspond to people's sense of right and wrong? Moreover, how can the legal system reconcile differing beliefs about what is right and wrong?

Consider first the case of Lester Zygmanik. Lester was charged with murdering his brother George after George demanded that Lester kill him. A motorcycle accident a few days earlier had left George, age 26, paralyzed from the neck down. He saw a future with nothing but pain, suffering, and invalidism; as he lay in agony, he insisted that his younger brother Lester, age 23, swear he would not let him continue in such a desperate state. (Other family members later verified that this had been George's wish.) So Lester slipped into his brother's hospital room and shot him in the head with a 20-gauge shotgun. Dropping the gun by the bed, he then turned himself in. There was no question about the cause of death; later, on the witness stand during his murder trial, Lester told the jury that he had done it as an act of love for his brother.

The prosecutor believed that Lester's actions met every one of the elements that the law required for his guilt to be proved. First, there was premeditation, or a plan to kill. Second, there was deliberation (as defined in the New Jersey criminal code—"the weighing of the 'pros' and 'cons' of that plan"). Third, there was willfulness ("the intentional carrying out of that plan"). Lester had even sawed off the shotgun before hiding it under his coat, and he had packed the shells with candle wax, which compacted the explosion and made it more deadly. Lester forthrightly admitted to his lawyer: "I gave it a lot of thought. You don't know how much thinking I did on it. I had to do something I knew that would definitely put him away" (Mitchell, 1976, p. vii).

If you had been a juror in this trial, how would you have voted? College students usually split just about evenly between verdicts of "guilty of first-degree murder" and "not guilty." Those who vote guilty believe it is their duty to consider the evidence and apply the law. Certainly, this was an act of murder, they say, regardless of Lester's good intentions. But those who vote not guilty often feel that it is appropriate, on occasion, to disregard the law when mitigating circumstances are present or when community standards argue for forgiveness.

Both reactions are reasonable, and they illustrate important differences between judgments based on black-letter law and those based on one's conscience or personal sentiments about a given situation. By "black-letter law" (sometimes referred to as the *law on the books*), we mean the law as set down by our founding fathers in the Constitution, as written by legislators, and as interpreted by judges. According to the black-letter law, Lester Zygmanik was guilty. But there is another way to judge his actions—by focusing on his altruistic motives and his desire to help his brother, rather than to harm him.

As Lester Zygmanik's trial began, the prosecutor was confident that Lester would be found guilty because the jury was predominantly tough, conservative, and blue-collar. But after deliberating for fewer than three hours, they found the defendant not guilty. The jurors focused, apparently, on the relationship between Lester and his brother, and they concluded that Lester had been overcome by grief, love, and selflessness. Their decision implicitly acknowledged that moral considerations such as the commitment to care for others were more important to their decision than the strict guidelines of the law.

Obviously, the Lester Zygmanik trial is not the only one in which defendants claimed their act was merciful. Helping terminally ill patients to commit suicide (so-called assisted suicide) is usually justified by the "offender" as an act of compassion or mercy, ending the "victim's" pain and suffering. In fact, physician-suicide is now legal in 10 states and the District of Columbia and is supported by a large majority of Americans (Brenan, 2018). Many people would be loath to call the "perpetrators" of these acts criminals, and proponents of assisted suicide often hail them as heroes.

Mercy killings and assisted suicides are examples of euthanasia, the act of ending an individual's life for reasons that are considered merciful. They illustrate the often tragic differences between what an individual feels is morally right or just, and what the law describes as an illegal act to avoid. Should someone who voluntarily, willfully, and with premeditation assists in killing another human *always* be punished? Or should that person, in some circumstances, be treated with compassion and forgiveness? Many people can imagine circumstances in which individuals who have technically broken the law should be excused. The topic of euthanasia highlights the tension between legality and people's perceptions of what is moral, ethical, and just.

Citizens' Sense of Legality and Morality

We might assume at first that what is defined as "legal" and what is judged to be "morally right" would be synonymous. But in the Zygmanik case, what the jury considered to be a moral action and what the system considered the proper legal resolution were inconsistent. Legislators and scholars have argued for centuries about whether the law should be consistent with citizens' sense of morality. But in fact, inconsistencies abound. For example, in many cultures, prostitution is condemned as immoral, yet it is legal in parts of Nevada and in many European and South American countries as well as in Australia and New Zealand. Acts of civil disobedience, whether performed six decades ago in racially segregated buses in Montgomery, Alabama, or more recently to protest COVID-19 mask mandates, are applauded by those who consider some laws and policies to be morally indefensible.

Psychologists have conducted studies that illustrate the differences between citizens' sense of morality and justice, on the one hand, and the legal system's set of formal rules and laws, on the other. At first glance, it may seem nearly impossible to study people's views about the legitimacy of formal laws because there are so many variations in laws and so many different penalties for violating those laws. (Criminal penalties are decided on a state-by-state basis in the United States, so there could be 50 different penalties for the same crime.) Fortunately, though, a large majority of states base their criminal laws on the Model Penal Code drafted by the influential American Law Institute in the 1960s. Thus we can ask whether the principles embodied in the Model Penal Code are compatible with citizens' intuitions about justice and legality. Do people tend to agree with the Model Penal Code or does their sense of right and wrong diverge from this black-letter law? One set of relevant studies examined the category of attempted crimes and the important role that intention plays in these cases.

Attempted Crimes and the Concept of Intention in Law and Psychology. Consider this fundamental question of criminal law: How should attempted (but not completed) crimes be punished? An attempt may be unsuccessful because the perpetrator tries to commit a crime but fails (e.g., shoots but misses) or because the attempt is interrupted or abandoned (e.g., robbers are about to enter a bank with guns drawn when they encounter a police officer inside).

The Model Penal Code says that attempts should be punished in the same way as completed crimes. If the offender's conduct strongly corroborates their criminal intention—showing that they not only thought about the crime but actually tried to accomplish it—the Model Penal Code decrees that they should be punished to the same degree as the successful offender. Focusing on the central role of intent, the Model Penal Code assigns the same penalty to attempted crimes as completed crimes. Thus, the pickpocket who thrusts a hand into another person's pocket, only to find it empty, is just as guilty (and just as deserving of punishment) as the pickpocket who makes off with a fat wallet. Regardless of the outcome of this act, the pickpocket tried to steal—and so, by definition, a crime was committed. A similar situation arose in the interesting case of *People v. Taylor* (1992), described in Box 2.1.

According to the Model Penal Code, an offender who tries but fails is just as culpable as an offender who tries and succeeds. But do ordinary people think about intent and attempted crimes this way? Do they think that *trying* to break into a store is as serious as *actually* breaking into the store?

Psychologist John Darley and his colleagues asked respondents to read short scenarios that described people who had taken one or more steps toward committing either robbery or murder and to assign punishment to those people (Darley et al., 1996). They found that people's intuitions differed in predictable ways from the position of the Model Penal Code. In situations where the person depicted in the scenario had taken only preliminary action (e.g., examining the store they planned to burgle or telling a friend about the plan), few respondents thought the person was guilty of any offense, and punishments were generally mild. Yet, according to the Model Penal Code, this person is just as guilty as one who actually completed the burglary. When the scenario described a person who had reached the point of "dangerous proximity" to the crime, punishments increased, but they still were only half as severe as those assigned to the person who actually completed the crime. Apparently people do not accept the view that intent to commit an act is the moral equivalent of actually doing it. Their notions about criminality and the need for punishment were more nuanced, less "black and white" than what the Model Penal Code prescribed.

Box 2.1

The Case of the Duped Would-Be Offender

In March, 1987, George Taylor forced his way into a woman's apartment in New York City and made sexual advances while threatening her with a knife. Fearful of the knife, the victim tried to convince Taylor that he could be her boyfriend, that he didn't need to impose himself in this way, and that he could come to her house anytime. Taylor relented, walked into an adjacent room, and took off the surgical gloves he had been wearing, saying he was not going to need these anymore. The victim then persuaded Taylor to accompany her to a liquor store to buy a bottle to celebrate getting to know each other. But as they were leaving the apartment she ducked back inside, locked the door, and called the police.

Despite arguing that he voluntarily and completely abandoned any intention of carrying out a crime, Taylor was convicted of attempted rape. The appellate court pointed out that in a parallel situation, if a person shoots at an intended victim and misses, he has no defense to the charge of attempted murder because his poor aim, rather than his lack of criminal intent, allowed the victim to live. Following that logic, the court ruled that it was the victim's escape, rather than Taylor abandoning his criminal intention, that prevented the rape.

Critical Thought Question

Did the jury that convicted Taylor and the appellate court that upheld his conviction follow the rule of the Model Penal Code? Do you think jurors should be asked to peer into an offender's minds and guess what they were thinking at the time of an attempted but incomplete act? How far along in executing a crime must offenders go in order to be guilty of a crime that they did not complete?

Factors That Influence Beliefs About Legality and Morality. Psychology's focus on mental states reflects more nuances and less clear-cut distinctions than those of black-letter law. Psychology considers a spectrum of behavior, ranging from accidents, to behavior influenced by stress, peer pressure, or immature judgment, to actions that are deliberate and carefully planned.

Even this continuum may oversimplify variations in intention because it minimizes the importance of environmental and cultural influences that affect people differently. The social context in which behavior occurs can strongly influence a person's intention to behave in certain ways. In some contexts, it can be very hard for an individual to conceive of behavioral options. Therefore, one person's ability to intend a given behavior might be much more limited than that of another person who has more behavioral alternatives.

How people assign causes to the behavior of others is yet another factor that affects judgments of what is legal and what is moral. A well-established theory in social psychology, **attribution theory**, allows us to understand how people explain others' behavior, including their intentions. According to the theory, attributions tend to vary along three dimensions: *internality*—whether we explain the cause of an event as due to something internal to a person or to something that exists in the environment; *stability*—whether we assess the cause of a behavior as enduring or merely temporary; and *globalness*—whether we see the cause as specific to a limited situation or applicable to all situations. An individual who makes internal, stable, global attributions about an act of misconduct ("They are so evil that they don't care what anyone thinks or feels about them") will judge an offender as more culpable and more deserving of punishment than a person who offers external, unstable, specific explanations for the same act ("As a result of hanging out with a rough crowd, they were in the wrong place at the wrong time").

When making inferences about what caused another person's behavior—especially behavior that has negative consequences—we tend to attribute the cause to stable factors that are internal to the person. That is, we are inclined to believe that others are predisposed to act the way they do. But when our own actions lead to negative outcomes, we are more likely to blame the external environment for the outcome, suggesting an unstable cause for our behavior that will probably change in the future.

In assessing how people think about legality and morality, we must also consider divergent beliefs based on political ideology. Former U.S. Supreme Court Justice Oliver Wendell Holmes once wrote, "[The] first requirement of a sound body of law is that it should correspond with the actual feelings and demands of the community" (1881, pp. 41–42). This quote implies that the feelings and demands of a community are undifferentiated and monolithic, like a large obelisk or column fabricated from a single piece of marble. But people's beliefs about legality and morality, particularly in this time of heightened political polarization, are anything but uniform. Although culture wars have been a constant feature of American history (Hunter, 1991), recent acts of political violence—the storming of the U.S. Capitol on January 6, 2021 is a vivid example—have become more commonplace, and sizeable factions in and out of government now embrace violent speech and violent resistance toward authority.

Political partisanship and polarization are concerning because they reduce the likelihood of any shared understanding about what is legal and what is right. Jonathan Haidt and his colleagues found that political liberals and political conservatives base their moral beliefs on different sets of underlying principles: the former are more concerned about harm, care, fairness, and reciprocity, while conservatives are equally concerned about ingroup loyalty, respect for authority, purity, and sanctity. This may explain why it is hard to understand how ethical people could hold beliefs so profoundly different from our own (Graham et al., 2009).

People who hold divergent views about acceptable behavior in a democratic society will find little common ground in the legal arena. What to some people seem like reasonable laws—those that regulate behavior "appropriately"—will be rejected as fundamentally unjust and illegitimate by others. So while there was once general agreement that violent speech and acts, for example, should be condemned and punished, a sizeable faction of the American populace now endorse those tactics as legitimate political tools (Lerer & Herndon, 2021). This partisan divide is at the core of different views on the events of August 25, 2020 when 17-year-old Kyle Rittenhouse drove from his home in Antioch, Illinois to Kenosha, Wisconsin. There, Rittenhouse fatally shot two men and wounded a third who were protesting a police shooting they believed to be racially motivated. We describe the case in Box 2.2.

Consequences of Citizen–Code Disagreements. Does it matter if laws do not comport with people's sense of right and wrong, however divergent they may be? Can people simply ignore laws they believe to be immoral? Indeed, we can find many examples of situations in which people opt not to obey laws and legal authority. When parents fail to make child support payments or when people violate restraining orders, it is often because they do not accept the legitimacy of a judge's decision. When people use illegal drugs or cheat on their income tax returns, it is often because they do not believe that the laws regulating these behaviors are just or morally right. During the era of prohibition in the United States, when alcohol consumption was outlawed, honest citizens became "criminals," entire illicit industries were created, and gang membership and gang-related violence increased significantly.

But there may be more significant and more general consequences of discrepancies between citizens' sense of morality and the legal system's sense of legality. For the law to have any authority, it must be consistent with people's shared sense of morality. When that consistency is lacking, citizens may feel alienated from authority and become less likely to comply with laws they perceive as illegitimate (Carlsmith & Darley, 2008). Initial disagreement with one law can lead to contempt for the legal system as a whole, including the police who enforce laws and the judges who punish wrongdoers. If the law criminalizes behaviors that people do not think are immoral, it begins to lose its legitimacy.

What Is Justice?

More than 2,000 years ago, at the beginning of the *Republic*, Socrates posed this question and we continue to ponder it today. Definitions of justice have changed throughout history. In the Old Testament and in Homer's *The Iliad*, justice meant something like revenge. By the time of the Golden Age of Athens in the fifth century B.C.E., the concept of justice came to be less about vengeance and more about achievement of the well-being of individuals (Solomon, 1990). The development of Christianity and Islam accentuated a conception of justice within religious traditions of morality. As a result,

Box 2.2

The Case of Kyle Rittenhouse and Partisan Notions of Legality

Just months after the killing of George Floyd in Minneapolis, cellphone video captured another police shooting, this time in Kenosha, Wisconsin, that led to a series of nightly protests in that city. The demonstrations resulted in looting, arson, and property damage and prompted a group of citizens to organize themselves as self-styled paramilitaries, most of them armed with military-style weapons and sporting tactical gear. They vowed to assist the police and National Guard in protecting Kenosha. Kyle Rittenhouse, 17 years old, was a member of that group. On the third night of civil unrest, he walked among the unruly crowd wielding a military-style semiautomatic rifle that had been purchased for him by a friend and claiming to be a medic. Shortly before midnight, after being chased into a parking lot and lunged at by an unarmed man named Joseph Rosenbaum, Rittenhouse turned and fired four shots, hitting Rosenbaum in the head and killing him. As he fled others in pursuit, Rittenhouse fell to the ground and shot two more people, killing one and wounding another.

The six criminal counts against Rittenhouse carried a maximum sentence of life in prison. But after the shootings, discussion of the Rittenhouse case on social media and elsewhere began to veer in different directions: to politically conservative people he became a cause célèbre who, according to his lawyer, was exercising his "patriotic and civic duty to serve Kenosha during a destructive insurrection." Murals in Colorado applauded his actions and his mother received a standing ovation at a Wisconsin Republican party event. Those sentiments garnered close to $2 million in online fundraising. But others pointed out that Rittenhouse, a minor, was possessing a weapon illegally, that he had no business patrolling the streets of Kenosha with a rifle, and no medical training to back up his offer

Kyle Rittenhouse prior to firing shots at the Kenosha, Wisconsin protest.

to help the wounded. They viewed the incident as vigilante justice gone terribly awry.

At his trial, Rittenhouse claimed that he acted in self-defense, and was acquitted on all counts. The verdicts did little to quell the divide among the country's partisan political factions, with politically conservative people celebrating the acquittals as a victory for the right to self-defense, while politically liberal people condemned it as a miscarriage of justice (Medina & Epstein, 2021).

Critical Thought Question

How might the partisan politics surrounding this case have affected the presentation of evidence in the courtroom and the deliberations of jurors? What are some of the consequences for rendering justice when people have starkly different beliefs about what is morally and legally acceptable public conduct?

---

people began to view instances of social injustice (e.g., the suffering of the poor and the oppressed) as issues of concern, along with offenses against one's person or one's family (Solomon, 1990). Today, concerns about social injustices and movements for social justice (e.g., Black Lives Matter, #MeToo) are front and center in many people's lives.

Distributive and Procedural Justice

Our discussion so far has assessed perceptions of legitimacy in the *outcomes* of legal disputes, such as whether the would-be pickpocket who came up empty-handed should be punished as severely as the one who got the loot. This focus on the fairness of the outcome in a legal dispute is the main concern of **distributive justice** models. According to the principles of distributive justice, a person will be more accepting of decisions and more likely to believe that disputes have been resolved appropriately if the outcomes seem just (or if

the outcomes—in the same sense as salaries or promotions—seem distributed equitably, hence the term *distributive justice*).

A series of classic studies in psychology and law showed that although distributive justice theories were correct, there was clearly more to the story. This work, conducted by a psychologist and a law professor, suggests that disputants' perceptions of the fairness of the *procedures* are vitally important to the sense that "justice" was done (Thibaut & Walker, 1975). Such an orientation leads us to think of justice not only as punishment for wrongdoing, but also as a process by which people receive what they deserve or are due. **Procedural justice** models suggest that if individuals view the procedures of dispute resolution or decision-making as fair, then they will view the outcome as just, regardless of whether it favors them or not. According to this perspective, one might ask whether, in a dispute with an insurance company over an accident claim, the injured party was treated fairly or unfairly.

Generally, individuals perceive a decision-making process as fair to the extent that they believe they have a voice in how the process unfolds, are treated with dignity and respect during the process, and trust that authorities in charge of the process are motivated by concerns about fairness (Sydeman et al., 1997). A full opportunity to state one's viewpoint and to participate actively and personally in the decision makes a strong contribution to an assessment of fairness, probably because it allows people to feel that they retain some control over their affairs (Ebreo et al., 1996).

Procedural fairness is an important consideration in the resolution of child custody and child support disputes. When family court judges use fair procedures, they are more successful in creating post-divorce situations in which both fathers and mothers are involved in their children's lives and take responsibility for financial and emotional support (Bryan, 2005). This is true regardless of the outcome. Thus, fathers, who often lose child custody hearings, are more likely to maintain contact with their children into the future if they believe that the hearing was fair.

These findings also apply in the public's real-world interactions with police officers and judges. Neither group is likely to generate warm feelings in the community if they give people less than what those people feel they deserve, or limit people's abilities to act as they wish. Do citizens have a better view of police officers and judges (and, by extension, of the entire legal system) if they perceive that they are being treated fairly? Will this make them more likely to cooperate with legal authorities and comply with the law?

To answer these questions, Tom Tyler and Yuen Huo (2002) interviewed individuals in Oakland and Los Angeles who had a recent experience with a police officer or a judge. The researchers asked about the fairness of the outcomes of those encounters, as well as about the fairness of the procedures that were used to achieve the outcomes. They also measured people's trust in the motives of a particular authority figure by asking participants whether they felt that their views had been considered and whether the authority cared about their concerns.

As one might expect, the favorability of the outcomes shaped participants' responses to this encounter. We feel better about situations and people when we get what we want from those situations and those individuals. But importantly, the willingness to accept the decision of a police officer or judge was strongly influenced by perceptions of procedural fairness and trustworthiness: When people perceived that police officers and judges were treating them fairly and when they trusted the motives of these officials, they were more likely to accept their decisions and directives.

But is fair and respectful treatment by police officers sufficient to engender trust in the law? Newer studies paint a somewhat more nuanced picture. They suggest that people are concerned not only with *how* police officers behave when exercising power, but also *what* power is being used *when* and *where* (Trickner et al., 2018). The police have significant discretion over how they administer their duties, including what laws they opt to enforce and in what circumstances

they enforce them. But when police act in ways that seem inequitable, intrusive, or unjust—for example, by using stop-and-frisk procedures and surveillance technology primarily on people of color—those people feel harassed and stigmatized. Thus, whether the citizen-officer interaction was respectful is not enough. A more complete picture of how police-citizen interactions shape beliefs about the law's legitimacy must also include attention to whether police overstepped the bounds of their authority.

Perceived fairness also has long-term effects on people's willingness to obey the law. Tyler and Jackson (2014) surveyed 1,600 people who mirrored the demographics of the American population about their views of the police, courts, and the law, and about their public behaviors. They found, unsurprisingly, that the risk of being caught and punished affected compliance with the law, but so did people's views about the legitimacy of the police and the courts. If people thought these authorities were legitimate—a crucial component of procedural justice—they were more willing to obey laws regarding both minor crimes like speeding and littering, and serious crimes like theft. The police themselves are affected by perceptions of procedural fairness: those who believe their departments have fair procedures and decision making are likely to obey their supervisors, be psychologically and emotionally grounded, and trust the communities they police (Trinkner et al., 2016).

The principles and consequences of procedural fairness extend well beyond the confines of a police station or courthouse. How adults, particularly parents, resolve conflicts that inevitably arise in a family influences the behavior of children. One team of researchers asked middle-school students to describe how a recent conflict or disagreement with their parents was resolved: "Did your parents treat you with respect? Were they equally fair to everyone involved?" The students also described mild forms of aggressive behavior—bullying—they had directed at other students. Analyzing these two sets of responses, the researchers determined that higher perceived levels of procedural fairness at home were

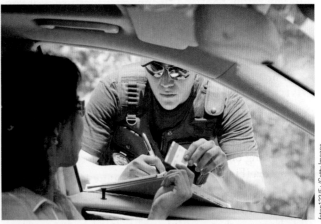

Citizens are more likely to obey laws when they think that police use fair procedures.

associated with lower frequencies of bullying behavior at school (Brubacher et al., 2009).

Commonsense Justice: Everyday Intuitions About Fairness

Another approach to the study of justice—one closely aligned with the analysis of citizens' agreement with the criminal code—concerns the intuitions that average people hold about culpability, fairness, and justice. Norman Finkel examined the relationship between the black-letter law and what he calls commonsense justice—ordinary citizens' basic notions of what is just and fair. Finkel's work has much to say about inconsistencies between the law and public sentiment in the types of cases we have examined in this chapter—assisted suicide and euthanasia—as well as in cases involving self-defense, the insanity defense, the death penalty, and felony murder (Finkel, 1995). Commonsense justice is also reflected in cases in which a jury refuses to convict a defendant who is legally guilty of the crime charged—the phenomenon known as jury nullification.

According to Finkel and others who have pondered commonsense justice (e.g., Miller et al., 2015), there is evidence that the black-letter law on the books may be at odds with community sentiment. This work is an important contribution to the field of law because it explains *how* people's sentiments depart from legal concepts and procedures. There are three identifiable discrepancies.

1. *The commonsense context is typically wider than the law's.* Ordinary people tend to consider the big picture: Their assessment of the event in question extends backward and forward in time (including, for example, a defendant's conduct prior to the incident and behavior after the crime), whereas the law allows consideration of a more limited set of circumstances. For example, in an acquaintance rape case or other case in which the victim and defendant knew each other, jurors would be likely to consider the history of the individuals, both together and apart. Is the incident one in a series of troublesome encounters in a tumultuous relationship? Have these events been alleged by other partners?

   Although people contemplate the wider context of the story, the law freezes the frame at the time of a wrongful act and then zooms in on that relatively finite moment. Reasoning that this narrower perspective will result in a cleaner and more precise judgment, the law determines culpability on the basis of actions and intentions within this narrow window. But people would rather learn about the big picture; for many, viewing only the last act does little to reveal the entire drama (Finkel & Groscup, 1997).

2. *Commonsense perspectives on the actions of a defendant and victim are more subjective than the law allows.* In disputes that involve people with a prior history, observers tend to construct a story about what happened and why. They do this by stepping into the shoes of the disputants and viewing the events through their eyes. The stories they construct typically describe hidden motives and desires gleaned from past conduct. But this perspective can result in judgments based on changing and inconsistent sentiments rather than discernible and objective facts.

3. *Observers take a proportional approach to punishment, whereas the law asks them to consider the defendant in isolation.* Imagine a situation in which an armed robber enters a convenience store while an accomplice stands guard outside the store. Further imagine that things go awry—the robber ends up shooting the cashier, and the cashier dies. The robber has certainly committed a crime, but what about the accomplice?

   According to the felony-murder doctrine (which applies in about half the states), the accomplice should be considered independently from the robber and, in fact, is as culpable as the triggerman. Yet this egalitarian approach seems to contradict the notion of proportional justice, in which a defendant's actions and intentions are assessed in comparison to others and more culpable defendants are dealt with more severely. People easily make distinctions among types of crimes and criminals, and they usually want more severe punishment for those they find most blameworthy.

It is now understood that community sentiments affect laws and policies in many aspects of our everyday lives, including same-sex marriage and divorce (Barth & Huffman, 2015), campus-related violence and safety (Campbell, 2015), the use of social media (Kwiatkowski & Miller, 2015) and child custody (Sigillo, 2015). In each instance, there are legitimate debates about the extent to which commonly held beliefs—community sentiments—*should* influence the laws and policies that govern our behavior.

Courts

We now turn to the reality of resolving legal disputes and the structures that society has developed for doing so. Disputes that reach the legal system are often, though not always, resolved in court. But new community-based alternatives to standard prosecutions are increasingly used. Diversion to an alternative system may occur during one's first encounter with a police officer, or when the case is referred to any of several "problem-solving courts" (also called specialty courts). Rather than focusing on punishment for wrongdoing, as traditional courts tend to do, problem-solving courts deal with the underlying reasons that individuals commit crimes in the first place.

Consider an offender with serious mental health issues. Many such individuals have weak support systems, little access to mental health care, and comorbid conditions. Rather than involving the courts to order evaluations and hospitalizations, diversion into a treatment program under court supervision reduces costs and lessens the probability of further interactions with the criminal justice system

U.S. Supreme Court building.

(Hoge & Bonnie, 2021). In addition to mental health courts, problem-solving courts include drug court, homeless court, and veterans' court (addressing issues of drug abuse, homelessness, and exposure to trauma, respectively), among others.

Different kinds of courts have been created to handle specific legal issues but in nearly all instances, courts are expected to follow legal **precedents**, decisions made in previous cases that serve as authority for subsequent cases involving similar facts. Because we cover various court cases relevant to psychology throughout this book, an understanding of the structure of both the traditional and alternative court system will be helpful. In the next section we describe the traditional court system. Chapter 9 describes community-based alternatives, including specialty courts, in detail.

State Courts

Although there are 50 different state court systems in the United States, they all typically include "lower" courts, trial courts, and appellate courts. Lower courts have jurisdiction over specific matters such as probate of wills (proving that a will was properly signed), administration of estates (supervising the payment of the deceased person's debts and the distribution of their assets), small claims, and traffic offenses. Family courts handle cases involving divorce, child custody, and child dependency. Juvenile courts deal with legal questions concerning delinquency and juvenile offenders. Both family courts and juvenile courts tend to focus on helping people rather than punishing them. In fact, juvenile courts have functioned for many years to protect children from the rough-and-tumble world of adult criminal courts and to resolve cases in a supportive, non-adversarial way.

Trial courts typically decide any case that concerns a violation of state laws. Most criminal cases (e.g., those involving drunken driving, armed robbery, and sexual assault) are tried in state trial courts. Prominent recent examples of trial courts in action come from the spate of prosecutions of police officers for assaulting or killing Black citizens.

State court systems also include one or more courts of appeal, similar to the federal appellate courts, and a state

supreme court. Like the United States Supreme Court, state supreme courts review only those cases deemed to be especially important or controversial. Published opinions are found in bound volumes called Reporters, and all opinions are accessible online.

Federal Courts

Federal courts have jurisdiction over cases arising under the Constitution or laws of the United States but typically do not have jurisdiction over cases arising under state law, unless the plaintiff and defendant in a civil case are from different states. Federal courts include trial courts, appellate courts, and the U.S. Supreme Court. When Congress passes a law regarding federal crime (e.g., the statute making identity theft a federal crime), the effect is to increase the caseload of the federal courts. Immigration courts, in particular, have experienced exponential growth in caseloads over the past decade as a result of migrant families and unaccompanied minors crossing the southern border of the U.S. and of the former President Donald Trump administration's policy separating children from their parents at the border. Hundreds of thousands of immigrants wait for years to have their cases heard. Federal courts have also been deluged recently with voting rights cases and cases alleging partisan gerrymandering in elections redistricting.

Federal trial courts are called United States District Courts. There is at least one district in every state; some states (California, for example) have several districts.

The federal appellate courts are called the United States Courts of Appeals. There are 13 federal courts of appeals, divided into geographical "circuits." In population, the largest circuit is the Ninth Circuit, which includes California, and the smallest is the First Circuit, which includes only a few New England states. Appeals are assigned to three-judge panels. The three judges examine the record (documents that the lawyers believe the judges need in order to decide the case), read the briefs (the lawyers' written arguments—in actuality, rarely brief), and listen to the oral argument (the lawyers' debate about the case) before voting. The panel decides the case by majority vote, and one of the judges writes an opinion explaining why the court decided as it did. Like state court opinions, these opinions are published in bound volumes called Reporters, which can be accessed online.

The U.S. Supreme Court

Nine justices make up the United States Supreme Court. The Supreme Court has the authority to review all federal appellate court decisions as well as state supreme court decisions that involve constitutional or federal law issues. But the Supreme Court reexamines only a small percentage of the cases it is asked to consider—cases that the justices view as most significant. A case involving a constitutional issue, namely, whether using racial preferences in undergraduate admissions violated the Equal Protection Clause of the Fourteenth Amendment, was both legally and psychologically significant. We describe it in Box 2.3.

Box 2.3

The Case of Abigail Fisher and the Consideration of Race in Undergraduate Admissions

Abigail Fisher, a White student, was denied admission to the University of Texas in 2008. She and other applicants challenged the university's use of racial preferences in undergraduate admissions decisions. After winding its way through various federal courts, the case was heard by the U.S. Supreme Court (*Fisher v. University of Texas*, 2016). Fisher's core argument was that the university's admissions system disadvantaged her and other White applicants in violation of the Equal Protection Clause of the Fourteenth Amendment ("…nor shall any States deny to any person within its jurisdiction the equal protection of the laws").

This was not the first instance in which the Supreme Court considered race-based admissions decisions. A landmark legal precedent is *Grutter v. Bollinger* (2003), in which the Court reasoned that considering race as a means to achieve a diverse student body serves a compelling state interest, so long as the school also considers other ways that an applicant might contribute to a diverse learning environment and the diversity goal can be expressed in concrete terms. In her petition to the Supreme Court, Fisher contended that the "University of Texas had never been clear about precisely why it needs to use racial preferences."

Psychological research studies have generally shown educational benefits of diversity for all students alike. In campuses that lack diversity, underrepresented students experience feelings of distinctiveness and negative stereotypes that impair their academic performance (Rosenthal & Crisp, 2006). In addition, these environments perpetuate implicit racial biases and discriminatory behavior that disrupt educational achievement (Richeson et al., 2005). Increasing diversity reduces these effects.

In 2016, the Supreme Court ruled in favor of the University of Texas, reasoning that it had indeed articulated the precise goals of ending stereotypes, promoting interracial cohesion, and preparing students to participate in modern workplaces. A diverse student body, it reasoned, furthers these goals.

Critical Thought Question:

Have you directly experienced any ways in which diversity, or lack of diversity, among students at your school has affected the learning environment and cultural climate?

Justices of the Supreme Court, like other federal judges, are appointed by the president and confirmed by the Senate. They are granted a lifelong tenure to allow them to be impartial, not influenced by the whims of political or legislative interests. In theory, their nominations are also expected to be above the fray of partisanship, and throughout most of the Court's history, that was true. But since 2010, all justices nominated by Democratic presidents have been ideologically to the left of those nominated by Republican presidents (Devins & Baum, 2016). Never before has the linkage between political party and ideology been so strong. This is likely a result of the partisan divide in American politics in which party leaders who select and confirm nominees have very divergent beliefs. (Prime examples are the contentious confirmation processes of Justices Brett Kavanaugh in 2018, Amy Coney Barrett in 2020, and Ketanji Brown Jackson in 2022.) Into the foreseeable future then, any Court with five Republican-nominated Justices will reach very different decisions than a Court with five Democratic-nominated Justices (Devins & Baum), raising serious doubts about the Court's neutrality.

Players in the Legal System: Judges

Most of us can easily conjure the image of a black-robed judge presiding over a hushed courtroom, approving plea bargains, determining what evidence will be admitted into a trial, and sentencing offenders to lengthy prison terms. To litigants—plaintiffs, defendants, prosecutors, and defense attorneys—and indeed, even to the general public, the proclamations of a judge demand deference and, in most instances, respect. Their words are often the "last words" in a legal dispute. Until the early 2000s, we knew relatively little about how judges make decisions, the extent to which their judgments are influenced by personality, attitudes, or past experiences, and how those decisions are constrained by various rules and roles. But psychologists have expressed increasing interest in judicial decision making (Vidmar, 2011). Thus, we are gradually beginning to understand how these robe-cloaked jurists think and how various structural features of the justice system influence their thoughts. One such feature is the means by which judges are selected to serve. A subsidiary concern, to which we have already alluded, is whether they can be truly independent of other branches of government.

How Are Judges Selected?

The majority of state court judges face elections. Typically, the governor makes an initial appointment and the judge is then retained (or not) in a popular election. If retained, judges serve a number of years, after which they again run for retention. Supporters claim that this system makes judges accountable to the public and that a judge who makes unpopular decisions can be removed from the bench.

But like other elections, some judicial races have been hotly contested over the years, with special interest groups and political parties pouring millions of dollars into advertising to elect judges of a certain persuasion. Alabama leads the nation in this regard: Between 2000 and 2009, appellate judges alone took in $206 million in campaign contributions, some from lawyers whose cases they would later decide. Furthermore, lower court judges in Alabama are able to contribute to the campaigns of appellate justices who may be in position to uphold their decisions (Sample et al., 2010). The Alabama State Bar Association considers none of this unethical. But it raises the specter of "politicians in robes," a term coined by former Supreme Court Justice Sandra Day O'Connor.

Although the due process clause of the Fourteenth Amendment requires judges to avoid even the appearance of bias, campaign contributions from political parties and interest groups increase the chances that judges will favor litigants who align with those interests (Kang & Shepherd, 2011). Also, according to one study, judges tend to become more punitive when up for re-election. Using sentencing data from more than 22,000 criminal cases in the 1990s, Huber and Gordon (2004) found that judges added more than 2,700 years of additional prison time in aggravated assault, rape, and robbery cases when they were standing for election.

We discussed judicial independence—the insulation of judges from politics and the court of public opinion—in the context of Supreme Court appointments. In theory, *all* judges should be shielded from the sometimes-fickle inclinations of politicians and the public. But there have been many attempts to oust state court judges who made politically unpopular decisions. One such attempt occurred in 2010 when three Iowa Supreme Court judges were up for retention. Despite having favorable performance evaluations, all were unseated after a group called Iowa for Freedom waged a million-dollar campaign urging voters to remove them. Why? Because the year before, the Iowa Supreme Court decided unanimously that denying marriage licenses to same-sex couples violated the state constitution. Iowa for Freedom argued that the decision ignored the will of voters (Rogers & Guillon, 2019).

Fortunately, most judges aspire to stay above the fray of politics. But increasing politicization of judicial elections is concerning because many forces, including recall efforts, threaten judges' independence from the whims of public opinion. There is no easy resolution to the issues of judicial selection and independence. Perhaps the balance between public accountability and judicial independence can be achieved by a system that combines merit appointments with retention elections in which voters are provided with an evaluation of the judge's entire tenure in office by a nonpartisan commission. Such a system is in place in more than a dozen states.

Influences on Judicial Judgments

There are at least two schools of thought about whether judges' rulings are influenced solely by the facts of a case and the applicable laws, or whether **extralegal factors** play a role. **Legal formalism** is the perspective that judges apply legal rulings to the facts of a case in a careful, rational, mechanical way, and pay little heed to political or social influences on, or implications of, their judgments. This perspective is exemplified by Supreme Court Justice Clarence Thomas's assertion that "There are right and wrong answers to legal questions" (Thomas, 1996). In contrast, **legal realism** holds that judges' decisions are influenced by a variety of psychological, social, and political factors, and that judges indeed are concerned about the real-world ramifications of their decisions.

One caricature of legal realism is that judges are influenced by very personal matters, such as when they last ate. In fact, there is some empirical support of this idea: in their study of successive parole decisions by experienced judges, Danziger, Levav, and Avnaim-Pesso (2011) found that the percentage of favorable rulings dropped from approximately 65% to nearly zero as a morning or afternoon courtroom session wore on, but that the percentage of favorable rulings rose again to about 65% after the judge had taken a food break!

Food matters aside, one might ask whether trial judges, as human beings, reflect on their own experiences, assumptions, and biases when reaching decisions from the bench, especially when the choice involves some leeway (e.g., deciding whether to allow evidence in a trial or on a sentence length). Might they have biases for or against certain groups—gay and lesbian parents, rappers, or older adults, for example—that affect the way they process evidence and make decisions? Do judges who have been prosecutors maintain their sympathy with the government's evidence in criminal trials? Conversely, do judges who were once defense attorneys tend to favor criminal defendants?

One commentator has compared judges to baseball umpires, proposing that although judges' decisions are constrained by procedural rules and precedents, there is still opportunity for personal discretion (Quinn, 1996). This would suggest that the life experiences of judges who are female or members of racial or sexual minorities might predispose them to make decisions that differ from those of their White, male, heterosexual counterparts.

Although women make up more than half of the U.S. populace, until recently federal judges were almost exclusively male. Racial minorities and openly gay individuals are also vastly underrepresented on the federal bench. One reason for the lack of diversity is the life tenure of federal judges, meaning that new judges are appointed only when current judges retire, resign, or die. This imbalance began to change during the presidencies of Jimmy Carter and Bill Clinton and since 2022, four women have served simultaneously as justices of the U.S. Supreme Court. (Former Supreme Court Justice Ruth Bader Ginsburg famously stated that there would be enough women on the Supreme Court when there were nine.)

In fact, decisions rendered by judges who are female or members of racial minorities do differ in predictable ways from those issued by White men, but typically only when gender or race is a salient feature of the case (Harris & Sen, 2019). As Rachlinski and Wistrich (2017) state, "When it comes to the effect of demographics on judicial decision making, it is personal" (p. 7).

The powerful forces associated with years of legal education and practice also influence judicial judgments. Legal socialization broadens attorneys' knowledge base and usually increases their respect for precedents and legal compliance. Because judges have typically practiced law for many years before assuming the bench, most understand that personal inclinations cannot dominate their decision making but rather, that they must rule consistently with prior decisions and statutory guidelines (Vidmar, 2011). If they deviate radically from previous decisions, their rulings will be overturned on appeal. All those years of legal socialization confer another benefit on judges by reducing the influence of political commitments on their decisions (Kahan et al., 2016). In fact, across 25 experiments involving 2,200 judges, Rachlinski, Wistrich, and Guthrie (2017) showed that a judge's political leanings had only minimal effect on how they decided a range of cases. This finding certainly challenges the belief that judges are "politicians in robes."

Even though judicial decisions are not strongly influenced by political beliefs, other factors, including life experiences, demographics, and attitudes, can predispose judges to decide in particular ways, at least in some kinds of cases. This challenges the legal formalists' belief that judges dispassionately consider the relevant laws, precedents, and constitutional principles, and that judicial bias has no part in decision making. Indeed, most social scientists now reject the legal formalism model and instead favor the legal realism perspective.

How Do Judges Decide?

Psychologists have a ready explanation for why judges' attitudes and values affect their decisions: When people, including judges, have opinions about desired outcomes, those goals direct how they seek out and weigh empirical evidence. Information congruent with a particular goal is disproportionately attended to and valued, while incongruent evidence is dismissed. This process, called **motivated reasoning,** is typically outside of one's awareness, but functions as a powerful determinant of how people evaluate information and reach conclusions about the law (Kahan et al., 2012; Kunda, 1990). Judges apparently use a variety of techniques to rationalize their decisions: strategically interpreting legal standards and finessing how they apply the relevant law, among them (Liu & Li, 2019).

Also relevant to judges' decision making, cognitive psychologists have proposed various two-process models of human judgment. Though the details vary, all the models distinguish between **intuitive processes** that occur spontaneously, often without careful thought or effort, and **deliberative processes** that involve mental effort, concentration, motivation, and the application of learned rules. The former is sometimes referred to as System 1 and the latter, System 2 (Kahneman, 2011). Motivated reasoning is implicated in both because end goals can unconsciously steer both intuitive and deliberative evaluations of evidence.

A team of law professors has used a two-process model to explain trial judges' decision making and, in particular, to assess how emotions can influence their judgments (Wistrich et al., 2015). They claim that although judges try to make decisions by relying on facts, evidence, and legal rules rather than personal biases or emotions, because they are ordinary people (who happen to wear robes), judges tend, like all of us, to favor intuitive reactions over careful deliberate responses. And though quick judgments can be overridden by complex, deliberative thoughts, judges must expend the effort to do so.

To demonstrate the effect of emotions on judicial decisions, the researchers exposed 500 judges to a hypothetical case involving illegal immigration, among the most contentious social issues of our time. Judges were told they were deciding the case of a Peruvian citizen who had purchased a forged U.S. entry visa and pasted it into his genuine passport. The question was whether doing so constituted forgery of an identification document. If they answered yes, the defendant would almost certainly be convicted of a crime and sentenced to prison prior to deportation. If they answered no, he would be immediately deported. There were two versions: half the judges learned that the defendant was hired by a drug cartel to sneak into the U.S. illegally to kill someone stealing their profits, and the other half learned that he was a father trying to earn money to pay for a liver transplant for his critically ill nine-year-old daughter. Despite deciding a pure question of law ("does pasting a forged visa into a genuine document constitute forging an identification card?") about defendants who had performed identical acts, judges' sympathies intervened and they responded differently to the two defendants. Only 44% who read about the father ruled that he had committed forgery, compared with 60% who read about the drug cartel's assassin.

The same team of law professors has shown that judges use intuitive and emotional decision processes to respond to suggested damage awards, descriptions of litigants' conduct, and inadmissible evidence (Guthrie et al., 2001; Wistrich et al., 2005). They have even shown that administrative judges, who handle massive numbers of disputes related to environmental safety, labor relations, civil rights violations, and regulatory compliance, and who have vast subject matter expertise, fall victim to the same snap judgments informed by intuitions and emotions (Guthrie et al., 2009). So despite Supreme Court Justice Elena Kagan's assertion, during her confirmation hearing, that judges' emotions play no role in determining the law (she stated "it's law all the way down"), these findings show that judges do not make decisions based entirely on the law alone. Researchers have been able to reduce decision-making biases by warning people about bias, providing post-decision feedback, and coaching (Sellier et al., 2019), and some forward-thinking judges have availed themselves of training to overcome implicit biases.

Players in the Legal System: Lawyers

Lawyers are plentiful in the United States. The American Bar Association (ABA) reported that in 2020 there were more than 1,300,000 attorneys in the U.S., or roughly one per every 250 citizens. This means that "every weekday morning [more than a million] chairs throughout the nation await indentation behind a lawyer's desk" (Kiser, 2010, p. 13).

Lawyers' Work Settings

The legal field permeates the American economy. The work of lawyers influences everything from "automobile design to pharmaceutical research, from kindergarten field trip waivers to Fortune 500 companies' earnings guidance" (Kiser, 2010, pp. 11–12). Given this vast array of legal services, it is not surprising that lawyers work in a wide variety of settings.

The most likely place to find a lawyer is in private practice, working either independently in a solo practice or as part of a larger team in a law firm. Lawyers who work in law firms attend to the needs of the firm's clients. Some of them specialize (e.g., in labor law or intellectual property), and others are generalists, trying to handle most of their clients' legal matters. Some lawyers work for corporations and have only one client—their corporate employer.

Many lawyers work for the government on the federal, state, or local level. Like attorneys for corporations, government lawyers have only one client: the governmental unit for which they work. Prosecutors are government lawyers responsible for prosecuting individuals charged with crimes. Federal prosecutors (called U.S. Attorneys) are appointed by the president and prosecute people for violating federal laws. The head prosecutors for cities and counties, typically called States' Attorneys or district attorneys, are elected, often in partisan elections. They prosecute individuals who have allegedly violated the criminal law in cities, counties, or states.

Because many people accused of crime cannot afford to hire a lawyer, criminal defendants are typically represented by public defenders who are also government employees. The history of public defenders dates from the 1963 case of *Gideon v. Wainwright*, in which the Supreme Court held that the State of Florida was obligated to pay for a lawyer for Clarence Earl Gideon, whose story is detailed in Box 2.4.

States responded to the Gideon case by appointing and paying lawyers to represent indigent defendants on a case-by-case basis and by establishing public defender programs, with lawyers hired by the state to represent those who cannot afford to hire them. Public defenders know the law, the system, and the other players in the system (the judge, the prosecutor, the probation officer), and though they have large caseloads, they often obtain excellent results for their clients.

Occasionally one reads of a public defender or appointed attorney who goes far beyond what can reasonably be expected of someone who is overworked and underpaid. Abbe Smith, now a law professor at Georgetown University, has written a book about her experience in representing Patsy Kelly Jarrett over a span of 25 years (Smith, 2008). Smith first met Jarrett in 1980, three years after Jarrett, driver of a getaway car, was convicted of felony murder and sentenced to life imprisonment in New York. Convinced that Jarrett (whose conviction was based on eyewitness testimony) was innocent, Smith agreed to represent her and

became a tireless advocate over the next 25 years, trying to secure Jarrett's freedom. Jarrett's conviction was eventually overturned and she was pardoned by former New York Governor Andrew Cuomo in 2016.

Law Schools and Legal Education

American lawyers of the eighteenth and nineteenth centuries typically learned to practice law through the apprentice method: An enterprising young man (the first female lawyer graduated in 1869) would attach himself to an attorney for a period of time, until both he and the lawyer were satisfied that he was ready to be "admitted to the bar." He would then be questioned, often superficially, by a judge or lawyer and pronounced fit to practice (Stevens, 1983).

Powerful forces shaped legal education as we know it today. States began to require those aspiring to be lawyers to pass meaningful examinations. Influenced by the ABA, the states also gradually increased the educational requirements for taking these exams, first requiring some college, then some law school, and finally graduation from an accredited law school.

In addition to providing enhanced knowledge and skills to prospective attorneys, law schools have helped to diversify the profession in recent years. Whereas only 3.5% of law students in 1960 were women, their numbers have increased significantly since then and women now constitute a solid majority on most law school campuses. As a result, the percentage of women practicing law in the U.S. has also increased: from 31% in 2010 to 38% in 2020 (Smith, 2021). The percentage of Hispanic students in law schools has also increased, nearly doubling between 1999 and 2019. Hispanic individuals now account for 13% of law school students (Kuris, 2020).

Legal education focuses on fostering analytic skills and deepening one's knowledge of the law, and though largely successful in that regard, those are but a subset of skills required for effective lawyering. Consider the many other tasks undertaken by attorneys: questioning and interviewing, persuading and communicating, resolving conflicts, collaborating, planning and managing, and acting in ethically responsible ways. Despite the extensive research by psychologists on these interpersonal aspects of advocacy, most law schools pay scant attention to developing these competences. Two law school professors trained in social sciences—Jean Sternlight and Jennifer Robbennolt—have provided various models of incorporating psychology into law school curricula (Sternlight & Robbennolt, 2015).

A law school education can sometimes take a toll on students' well-being. Studies show that attending law school tends to undermine students' values, motivation, and mental health. Researchers examined behavioral health issues in a sample of approximately 100 students at a Midwestern law school who completed various questionnaires regarding their psychological functioning and alcohol use (Reed et al., 2016). Overall, students showed relatively high levels of psychological distress: 13% had scores that placed them above

Box 2.4

The Case of Clarence Gideon, His Famous Pauper's Plea, and the Right to an Attorney

Clarence Earl Gideon

At age 51, Clarence Earl Gideon was tried for breaking into a pool hall and stealing money from a cigarette machine and a jukebox. At his trial, Gideon asked the judge to appoint an attorney to defend him because he had no money to pay for one. The judge, following the laws in Florida, refused.

Gideon did not have a lawyer during his trial. Though no stranger to a courtroom, having been convicted on four previous occasions, he lost this case as well. Eventually, from his prison cell, Gideon filed a pauper's appeal to the U.S. Supreme Court. His contention, laboriously written in pencil and misspelled, was that the U.S. Constitution guaranteed the right of every defendant in a criminal trial to have the services of a lawyer. Gideon's effort was a long shot; well over 1,500 paupers' appeals are filed each term, and the Supreme Court agrees to consider only about 3% of them.

Furthermore, 20 years earlier, in the case of *Betts v. Brady* (1942), the Supreme Court had rejected the very proposition that Gideon was making by holding that poor defendants had a right to free counsel only under "special circumstances" (e.g., if the defendant was very young, illiterate, or mentally ill). Yet, ever since its adoption, the doctrine of *Betts v. Brady* had been criticized as inconsistent and unjust. The folly of requiring poor people to represent themselves is exemplified by Gideon's cross-examination of the most important witness for the prosecution:

Q. Do you know positively I was carrying a pint of wine?
A. Yes.
Q. How do you know that?
A. Because I seen it in your hand. (Lewis, 1964)

When Gideon's case was argued before the Supreme Court in January 1963, he was represented by Abe Fortas, a Washington attorney later appointed to the Supreme Court. Fortas argued that it was impossible for defendants to have a fair trial unless they were represented by a lawyer. He also observed that the "special circumstances" rule was very hard to apply fairly.

Later that year, the Supreme Court ruled unanimously that Gideon had the right to be represented by an attorney, even if he could not afford one. As Justice Hugo Black put it, "[that] the government hires lawyers to prosecute and [that] defendants who have the money hire lawyers to defend are the strongest indications of the widespread belief that lawyers in criminal cases are necessities, not luxuries" (*Gideon v. Wainwright*, 1963, p. 344). Nearly two years after he was sentenced, Clarence Gideon was given a new trial. With the help of a free court-appointed attorney, he was acquitted. The simple handwritten petition of a financially modest man had forever changed the procedures of criminal trials.

Critical Thought Question

(1) What are some important functions performed by a defense attorney that a defendant such as Clarence Gideon could not provide in his own case? (2) How might this change if Mr. Gideon had been middle class and college educated? (3) What if Mr. Gideon had been a criminal attorney himself? (Why is there an old saying among lawyers that "the attorney who represents himself has a fool for a client?")?

"normal" for anxiety, as did 11% on measures of stress and 10% on measures of depression. First year students showed the most distress, consistent with the adage that "the first year will scare you to death, the second year will work you to death, and the third year will bore you to death."

These symptoms have been attributed to law schools' excessive workload, intimidating teaching practices, competitive grading systems, status-seeking job placement services, and lack of concern about personal feelings, values, or subjective well-being (Reed & Bornstein, 2013). Changes in motivation that occur over the course of one's law school career can explain some of the dysfunction (perhaps especially among "bored to death" third year students!). Particularly relevant is the **self-determination theory of optimal motivation** (Deci & Ryan, 2000), which describes situational and personality factors that cause positive and negative motivation and, eventually, changes in subjective well-being. Sheldon and Krieger (2004) found that the increase in mental health symptoms in the first year of law school was correlated with a decrease in **intrinsic motivation** (engaging in an activity because it is interesting and enjoyable). Over the course of that year, students moved from pursuing their professional goals for reasons of interest and enjoyment (i.e., because of their intrinsic motivation) to pursuing goals that would please and impress others (i.e., for reasons of **extrinsic motivation**). In other words, they felt less self-determined at the end of the year than they had at the beginning. Importantly, students who perceived that faculty supported their autonomy showed fewer declines in psychological well-being in the first year of law school and had higher grades in the third year (Sheldon & Krieger, 2007).

How Do Lawyers Make Professional Decisions?

Although there is relatively little systematic information about how lawyers undertake and perform their work, we are beginning to have a clearer picture of how they make decisions, particularly when the decisions are related to litigation (e.g., whether to pursue a case on behalf of a client who is eager to sue, or to settle a case or go to trial) (Reed, 2020).

An attorney's decision to settle a lawsuit by agreeing on a resolution prior to trial is especially important because delays and unnecessary trials can consume time and resources of the litigants, court officials, and lawyers themselves. On the other hand, premature settlement may compromise the quality of the agreement. Andrew Wistrich and Jeffrey Rachlinski, researchers whose studies of judges' decisions we described earlier, have also evaluated how lawyers make decisions, including how they think about settlements (Wistrich & Rachlinski, 2013). They claim that, like a tennis racket's sweet spot, there is a temporal sweet spot for settling a lawsuit. They ask whether lawyers can find that sweet spot, and if not, why not.

To assess the quality of lawyers' reasoning, they presented short vignettes and asked lawyers to assume various roles.

In one study, lawyers learned that a plaintiff would recover $200,000 if successful in a lawsuit that had a 50% chance of success. The incentive for settling was to avoid $50,000 in litigation expenses each side would incur if the case did not settle. Half of the lawyers were assigned to represent the plaintiff and the other half to represent the defendant and each received a "take it or leave it" offer. The question for the lawyers was whether to advise their client to accept the offer.

Using this methodology, Wistrich and Rachlinski (2013) determined that lawyers, like judges, rely on intuitive cognitive mechanisms rather than deliberative processes to evaluate cases. As a result, they take chances on trials that are not worth taking, seek information that supports their misguided choices and avoid information that would be useful—the so-called **confirmation bias**, and continue to invest resources even when it would be advantageous to cut their losses—the so-called **sunk-cost fallacy**. Taken together, these intuitive reasoning processes lead to significant wasteful litigation.

But there's more. Lawyers are also overly confident of their abilities, including their ability to predict and produce successful case outcomes (Goodman-Delahunty et al., 2010). When lawyers are deciding whether to take on a new client or settle a case, they have to make predictions about case outcomes months and years in advance of those outcomes. These are **probabilistic estimates**, in the sense that the correct answer is not yet known. Like all of us, lawyers make more optimistic predictions about events in the distant future than in the near future (Gilovich et al., 1993) and over time—including hours of strategizing, preparing arguments and locating witnesses—they become increasingly confident that their predicted outcomes are attainable (Trope & Liberman, 2003). As the adage goes, they miss the forest for the trees. And oftentimes, they get little to no feedback on the accuracy of their decisions.

The skewed way that people in adversarial roles draw inferences from the facts—what we referred to earlier as the myside bias—can lead lawyers to be overly optimistic. Compounding the problem is that an adversarial mindset leads to favorable impressions of one's own side and a naive belief in one's objectivity (Simon et al., 2020).

How can lawyers improve their ability to assess the likelihood of future outcomes? A seemingly simple way to gain insight is to discuss the case with peers—other lawyers—who are less invested in the outcome (Jacobson et al., 2011). In a variety of situations that involve probabilistic estimates, both novices and experts profit from the opinion of just one other person, even though they continue to give more weight to their own opinions than to the opinions of others. Attorneys would also benefit from Daniel Kahneman's (2011) advice to "think slow," allowing them to avoid snap judgments, consider alternatives, and examine the bases for their decisions.

Summary

1. **What is the difference between the adversarial and inquisitorial models of trials?** The trial process in the United States and several other countries is called the adversarial model because all the witnesses, evidence, and exhibits are presented by one side or the other. In contrast, in the inquisitorial model used in much of Europe, the judge does nearly all questioning of witnesses. Although the adversarial model has been criticized for instigating undesirable competition, distorting the presentation of evidence, and leading to inaccurate results, it has been judged to be fairer than the inquisitorial model.`

2. **How do notions of morality and legality differ?** What is considered moral is not always what is ruled legal, and vice versa. When determining right and wrong, some people rely on the law almost entirely, but many people have internalized principles of morality that may be inconsistent with the laws. Notions of what is legal and what is moral have become more partisan in recent years.

3. **How do different models of justice explain people's level of satisfaction with the legal system?** According to the distributive justice model, people's acceptance of a legal decision is related to whether they think the outcome, or decision, is fair. According to the procedural justice model, fairness in the procedures is a more important determinant of satisfaction. When people think they were treated fairly, they are more accepting of legal outcomes.

4. **What is commonsense justice?** Commonsense justice reflects the basic notions of everyday citizens about what is just and fair. In contrast to black-letter law, commonsense justice emphasizes the overall context in which an act occurs, the subjective intent of the person committing the act, and a desire to make the legal consequences of the act proportionate to the perceived culpability of the actor.

5. **How are judges selected and how do their demographic characteristics and ideologies influence their decisions?** Federal judges are appointed for life. Many state court judges are appointed and then run on their records in retention elections. Judges' demographic characteristics tend to influence their decisions but only in cases where their gender or race is salient. Although the experiences of law school and years of work as a lawyer are powerful socializing forces, judges' attitudes also tend to influence judgments.

6. **How does the experience of law school affect its students?** A law school education enhances one's analytic skills and knowledge base. Law school populations have become more diverse as the numbers of women and ethnic minority students have both increased in recent years. On the other hand, attending law school tends to undermine students' values, motivation, and psychological health because it reduces their intrinsic motivation and sense of self-determination.

7. **What factors explain lawyers' overconfidence and how can it be remedied?** Lawyers, particularly trial lawyers, are overconfident about their chances of future success because they rarely get useful feedback about their decisions and because their adversarial roles make them susceptible to certain cognitive biases in interpreting the facts and predicting outcomes. Discussing a case with just one other attorney and engaging in deliberative thought processes can lead to more accurate predictions about future results.

Key Terms

adversarial system
attribution theory
black-letter law
commonsense justice
confirmation bias
deliberative processes
distributive justice

diversion
euthanasia
extralegal factors
extrinsic motivation
inquisitorial system
intention
intrinsic motivation

intuitive processes
legal formalism
legal realism
motivated reasoning
myside bias
precedent
probabilistic estimates

procedural justice
self-determination theory of
   optimal motivation
sunk-cost fallacy

Chapter 3

Understanding Crime

Orienting Questions

1. Theories of crime can be grouped into four categories. What are they?

2. Among sociological explanations of crime, how does the subcultural explanation differ from the structural explanation?

3. What is emphasized in biological theories of crime?

4. What psychological factors have been advanced to explain crime?

5. How do social–psychological theories view crime?

6. What are the four major categories of influence on crime described in this chapter?

Offending in the United States

Crime is a serious problem in our society. How often are crimes committed? What are the important influences to consider in understanding such offending? Questions about the causes of crime are the concern of **criminology**, which is the study of crime and criminal behavior. The patterns of thinking and behavior associated with criminal offending are also the focus of **forensic psychology** and **correctional psychology**. The process of influencing others to commit crime has been discussed in **social psychology**. In addition, there are **sociological** and **biological theories of crime**. But no single discipline offers a compelling and widely accepted explanation for criminal offending, so we also discuss theories and explanations that integrate the perspectives of different disciplines. These include two important theories for explaining and classifying crime: **Risk-Need-Responsivity** and the **Good Lives Model**. In this chapter, we discuss those theories and other explanations of crime, beginning with a review of the historical predecessors of twenty-first-century criminology. We also provide an overview of non-violent offending (against property), violent offending (against persons), and very serious offenses—including school violence and workplace violence.

Several changes in certain aspects of crime have been seen during recent years. One involves a heightened scrutiny of police conduct with respect to encounters with and arrests of individuals of color. (This is also discussed in the next chapter on policing.) The perceptions that Black citizens, such as George Floyd and Breonna Taylor, were victims of excessive police force led to public demonstrations protesting racism and police misconduct. The storming of the U.S. Capitol on January 6, 2021 by a crowd of individuals intent on stopping the certification of election results, observed in real time by live media scrutiny, led to the arrests and prosecutions of hundreds of individuals. There is a First Amendment right in the United States to speak and assemble in order to protest: "Congress shall make no law abridging the freedom of speech…or the right of the people peaceably to assemble…" In this chapter, we discuss the question of what such rights allow—and when behavior becomes illegal. Another consideration involves the increase in domestic groups advocating violence with the goal of suppressing rights and opportunities of citizens of color. The increase of so-called "domestic violent extremists" (DVE) is another topic addressed in this chapter.

Non-Violent Offending

Property crime in the United States, comprising burglary, theft, and motor vehicle theft, decreased between 2014 and 2018, becoming less frequent in each subsequent year during this period and decreasing by a total of 15%. Burglary decreased even more, falling in frequency a total of 30% during this time (Bureau of Justice Statistics, 2020). The property crimes committed by youthful offenders (ages 12–17) showed an even more striking change between 2015 and 2019, with a 43% decrease—and a 67% decrease for the period 2010–2019 (OJJDP, 2020).

Violent Offending

Rates of serious crime—typically considered to be offenses such as homicide, attempted homicide, sexual assault, armed robbery, and other offenses against persons that cause death or great harm—have been steadily declining in the United States until 2020. This may sound odd, given the barrage of information on social media and the Internet seemingly to the contrary, but it is consistent with both victimization studies and official police statistics. According to the National Crime Victimization Survey (Bureau of Justice Statistics, 2016), the rate of violent crime dropped sharply between 1993 and 2001, and has continued to decrease (but more slowly, with year-to-year variations) since 2002, with these variations including slight rises in recent years. Between 2014 and 2016, the violent crime rate rose 7%, but then fell 5% from 2016 to 2018 for a small overall increase from 2014 to 2018 (Bureau of Justice Statistics, 2020). There was variation across different kinds of crime, however, with the rate of rape increasing every year between 2014 and 2018 (and increasing a total of 15% over this period) and the rate of assault increasing about 7% over this time, but the rate of robbery dropping 14% from 2014 to 2018. There were 3,249 more murders in the U.S. in 2016 than in 2014, but 1,199 fewer murders in 2018 than in 2016. Breaking this down according to race, the murder rate of White persons in the U.S. rose 19% from 2014 to 2016 and fell 8% from 2016 to 2018, while the murder rate of Black persons in the U.S. rose 22% from 2014 to 2016 and fell 9% from 2016 to 2018. Overall, the murder rate in 2018 of Black persons in the U.S. was 6.6 times that of White persons and 13.8 times that of Asians or Pacific Islanders (Bureau of Justice Statistics, 2020). In general, with some minor discrepancies, there was a substantial decrease in the rates of murder and other violent crime over the nearly three decades prior to 2020.

This general decrease in serious crime from 1990 to 2019 changed in 2020, with an increase in murder of around 29% during that year and an increase of 5% in serious crime more broadly (https://www.nytimes.com/2021/11/15/us/homicides-america.html). The one obvious difference between 2020 and the preceding decades was the presence of COVID-19, with personal disputes involving those in the home escalating. It remains to be seen whether this increased rate will remain stable, continue to increase, or drop to pre-pandemic levels when the virus no longer affects life so substantially.

The involvement of youthful offenders in serious violent crime, while historically substantial, has also continued to decrease. The number of serious violent offenses committed by youth ages 12–17 declined by 40% from 2010 to 2019, with decreases in murder and non-negligent manslaughter (15%), robbery (41%), and aggravated assault (40%) (OJJDP, 2020). Considering homicide in particular, we note that the decrease was less striking than for other violent offenses committed by youth. It remains to be seen whether serious crimes committed by juveniles in 2020 will have increased just as adult crime has—and whether this increased frequency will remain, or revert to the pattern of the last decade in the years to follow.

What should we make of recent national crime statistics? First, the falling frequency of property crime is noteworthy. The statistics on violent crime during 2014–2018 showed some minor divergence with the years-long trend of dropping violent crime rates, largely driven by increases in rates of sexual and non-sexual assault. There was an increase in violent offending generally in 2020, however, including a substantial increase in homicide. So the news is mixed: violent offending increased in 2020, interrupting a years-long trend of falling violent crime rates in the U.S.

Are these changes consistent with why Americans' concern about crime remains high? Almost certainly not. Such concern has remained stable during times of rising and falling crime rates. What seems far more likely is that concern about crime remains stable because the information available to most citizens—on cable news, social media, and even in fictionalized accounts of crime (TV crime shows, movies)—makes the risk of victimization seem higher than it actually is. Among the array of cognitive biases that affect perceptions and decisions (Kahneman, 2011), the most influential in this respect might be the *availability* heuristic. People rely on information that is most easily accessible, whether that is a news account of a mass shooting or a re-posted tweet. Awareness of specific crimes is increased by the rapid, widespread access facilitated by the Internet. Crime coverage invokes people's fascination and fear: "if it bleeds, it leads."

Consider these examples:

- In May 2021, hooded shooters fired into a crowd in a Miami-area club using assault rifles and handguns, killing three and wounding 20.
- Also in May 2021, a 57-year-old individual named Samuel Cassidy killed 10 co-workers at the maintenance yard where he worked in San Jose, California before killing himself.

These are two examples of crimes, often involving powerful weapons, that result in the deaths of multiple individuals. Various websites archiving such events (see, e.g., gunviolencearchive.org) describe a large number of cases like these.

School Violence

Public perception is fueled by the high visibility and rapid dissemination of information about high-profile fatal events on social media, including:

- In February 2018, a former student at Marjory Stoneman Douglas High School in Parkland, Florida, Nikolas Cruz (19) entered the school and killed 17 students, wounding another 17. Although he had a history of disciplinary problems, this individual did not present a clear motive for harming students.
- In November 2021, a 15-year-old student at Oxford High School in Oakland County, Michigan, Ethan Crumbley, shot and killed 4 students in the school. The local prosecutor charged his parents, James and Jennifer, with involuntary manslaughter, alleging that they ignored numerous warning signs that their son was considering harming other students—and even bought him a gun as a present.

These events are not representative of most school shootings. Most involve a very small number of individuals, and fatalities are rare. Nonetheless, the phrase "school shooting" is associated with events like those at Columbine, Sandy Hook, Marjory Stoneman Douglas, Uvalde and Oxford—another example of the availability heuristic that leads to the mistaken conclusion that mass killings are more frequent in schools than they are.

Regardless of how frequent or destructive they are, though, school shootings are extraordinarily tragic. In addition to the trauma experienced by survivors, there are other kinds of harm to schools and students where a shooting has occurred, including decreased enrollments and lower standardized test scores among remaining students (Beland & Kim, 2016).

Part of the public's fear about any kind of crime is increased when they perceive it is occurring in traditionally safe environments. In the past three decades, crime in the workplace and violence in our schools have caused great national concern. In some respects, this concern is misplaced. Student deaths from homicide or suicide rarely occur in school, and rarely involve more than a single victim, while about 98% of homicides and 99.7% of suicides involving youth 5–18 years old occurred away from school in 2017–2018 (National Center for Education Statistics, 2021). According to the School-Associated Violent Death Study (Centers for Disease Control and Prevention, 2018):

- 90% of school-related homicides from 1994 to 2016 involved a single victim, with many of the characteristics of such events paralleling the factors associated with youth homicide in the community (e.g., urban setting, victims disproportionately male and Black, Indigenous, and other People of Color)
- when there are multiple victims, 95% of these events involve firearms, which predominantly come from the perpetrator's home or a friend or relative's home
- the number of homicides of youth between the ages of 5 and 18 was lower in 2015–2015 (N = 18) than it was in 1992–1993 (N = 34) for deaths occurring on school grounds

High-profile shootings also occur on college campuses. Seung-Hui Cho was a child of South Korean immigrants who moved to the United States in 1992. In his earlier school days, he was often so uncommunicative that he would not even respond when his teacher took the roll. Cho enrolled at Virginia Tech and on April 16, 2007, at 7:15 A.M., shot and killed two students in a campus dormitory. Later that morning, he took the two handguns and ammunition he had obtained off campus and went from room to room in Norris Hall, a building on campus. Police responded quickly to an emergency call placed at 9:43 A.M., but by the time they were able to break into the building (Cho had chained several doors shut), Cho and 30 students and faculty members were dead.

School shooting fatalities in particular cause experts, parents, teachers, and youth themselves to try to understand what motivates such shootings and what can be done to prevent them. Are school environments to blame? Is the ready availability of guns one explanation? Are those who carry out such shootings mentally ill or severely emotionally disturbed? Were they driven by violent music and gory video games? Did their parents fail to support and supervise them adequately?

Although homicides at school remain very rare, they attract a great deal of speculation about the motives of the shooters when they do occur (Cornell, 2006). Some evidence indicates that we can identify some characteristics that are often seen in boys responsible for school killings (Rowhani-Rahbar & Moe, 2019; Verlinden et al., 2000). Such boys tend to be more experienced with guns, socially isolated, preoccupied with violence (media, music, Internet, video games), teased due to their physical appearance, angry brooders, perpetrators and/or victims of bullying, seeking revenge, and with a plan for their aggression that was often communicated to others prior to the event.

But it is clear that the characteristics such as these do not allow us to "profile" school shooters, as there is considerable variability among those who are involved in serious school violence (Vosskuil et al., 2004). Why? For example,

we might think that being bullied, having an interest in violent themes, having a grievance, and experiencing difficulty in coping with significant loss would be sufficient to create a profile like this. But such a profile would identify a high percentage of school-aged adolescents who would never go on to commit a school shooting.

So how can we make schools safer without unnecessarily targeting those who would not seriously threaten their classmates? A number of reforms and programs have been attempted: requiring school uniforms, beefing up security measures, offering violence prevention programs, and restricting access to violent movies, among others. One promising approach involves reducing the influences that are commonly seen in school shootings—particularly bullying—while being attentive to particular interest in violent themes, and the experience of loss and **trauma**, among students. Providing a school environment that greatly reduces bullying while offering safe and effective help for students experiencing loss would assist far more students than attempting (often mistakenly) to identify potential school shooters.

There are two other steps that have the potential for reducing the risk of school shootings. The first is communication. Better communication between students and school administrators is important in identifying the planning surrounding school violence and weapons (Mulvey & Cauffman, 2001). For example, there is such a program in Colorado—the Safe2Tell program—that allows teachers, students, and parents to anonymously report concerns or threats about their safety or that of others (see https://safe2tell.org/how-it-works). A second step involves a careful **threat assessment** using a multidisciplinary team. This team would respond to any identified threat by carefully considering the nature of the threat, the risk posed by the individual, and the needed response to reduce the risk of harmful action (Cornell & Sheras, 2006). This allows a graduated response depending upon the seriousness of the harm and the likelihood that the threat will be carried out, with the most serious threats treated proportionally. Threat assessment has been refined by organizations such as the U.S. Secret Service in their work with threats of violence toward those they protect (such as the U.S. president and vice president and their families) and modified for use in other settings such as schools and colleges.

Additional research on secondary school and campus shootings (Borum et al., 2010; Cornell, 2020; Heilbrun et al., 2009) underscores several important points:

- The most prevalent problem with aggression in education settings is not shootings. In school contexts, it is bullying; on college campuses, it is more likely to be date rape and hazing. Much of this aggression is unreported and hence underestimated by official records.

- Most of those who make implied or direct threats will not go on to commit serious violence. Threatening communications are made for a variety of reasons, including angry disputes, fear, jealousy, and ideology.

Seung-Hui Cho

- It is more effective to appraise the seriousness of threats and respond proportionately than to attempt to predict who will carry out the most serious acts of violence in school settings.

- "Zero tolerance" policies are ineffective and have the potential to stigmatize and harm a variety of mistakenly identified individuals.

Workplace Violence

Violence in the workplace involves harm threatened or deliberately inflicted on one or more individuals where they work. It may also include harassment, intimidation, or deliberately disruptive behavior. It may come from another employee, but also includes acts perpetrated in the workplace setting by those who are not employees. For example, an estranged spouse or a former employee who seeks specific targets would be included in our discussion of workplace violence. A categorization of workplace violence by the National Institute for Occupational Safety and Health provides four descriptions of such behavior: criminal intent, customer/client, worker-worker, and personal relationship (see https://wwwn.cdc.gov/WPVHC/Nurses/Course/Slide/Unit1_5).

Much of the attention to such violence is centered around acts that result in fatal injuries. But non-fatal workplace violence is far more frequent. In 2018, for example, the Bureau of Labor Statistics documented a total of 20,790 workers who were harmed by violence deliberately inflicted by others—but who did not die as a result, although (by definition) they needed at least a day off work. Most of those harmed were female (71%), with about 2/3 between the ages of 25 and 54 and nearly 3/4 (73%) working in the healthcare and social assistance sectors. Fatal injuries as a result of workplace violence, by contrast, were far less frequent, with a total of 453 occurring in 2018. Unlike non-fatal injuries, the great majority of those killed by workplace violence were male (82%), with 20% working in sales and related activities and another 19% in protective service activities. These figures may considerably underestimate the overall number of acts that may be threats or intimidation, particularly when they are not reported or the victim is not physically harmed.

What are the broader trends in workplace violence in the United States? A review of workplace violence events between 1993 and 2009 (Office of Justice Programs, 2011) provides context for certain relevant statistics. Among the highlights reported in this review:

- There was a substantial decline in non-fatal workplace violence from 1993 to 2002 (62%), followed by another 35% decline from 2002 to 2009.

- The workplace is less likely to have serious violent events than the world away from work; people are victimized by violent crimes more than 3 times as often when they are not at work.

- The highest rates of harm from non-fatal workplace violence were experienced by law enforcement officers, security guards, and bartenders. The greatest proportion of these acts were committed by strangers (not known to the victim).

There are several parallels between workplace violence and the other kinds of crime and school violence that we have discussed thus far in this chapter. First, its frequency has decreased steadily over the last 20 years. Second, much of what is recorded as violence in the workplace is actually a form of violent crime more generally, committed by strangers in the course of criminal acts such as robbery. In this respect, workplace violence trends have more closely paralleled criminal offending in general (which has largely decreased in frequency over two decades) than school violence, which has remained stable in frequency although relatively rare overall. Third, firearms are rarely used when there are non-fatal injuries, but commonly used in workplace fatalities.

Thus far in this chapter we have considered crime in general, violence in schools, and violence in the workplace. In none of these have there been noteworthy increases in frequency during the last decade. Yet there remains the perception that our society has become riskier—a perception that is at odds with the data. Are social media, cable news, and the availability heuristic combining to mislead our perceptions? Or are they accurate in some respects? Let us now consider one domain in which harm to others has become more frequent: mass killings.

Mass Killings

It might seem that mass killings (defined as the killing or attempted killing of four or more individuals) in public places (rather than private homes) are increasingly frequent. Is this supported by evidence?

Considering the number of mass killings each year during the period from 1982 to 2021 (see, e.g., https://www.statista.com/statistics/811487/number-of-mass-shootings-in-the-us/) provides the following context. Fortunately, these events are very rare. Between 1982 and 2011, for instance, the number of mass killings per year in the United States ranged from 0 to 5. In 2012, the number increased to 7, and continued to increase in 2017 (11 events), 2018 (12 events), and 2019 (10 events). The number dropped dramatically in 2020 (2 events), a decrease almost certainly attributable to the drastic changes in people's lives during the COVID-19 pandemic.

We can draw several conclusions from this information. Mass shootings, horrific and tragic as they are, are exceedingly rare. Nevertheless, these data are troubling. Unlike other crime—general offending, school violence, workplace violence—that has largely remained stable or decreased during the last decade, mass killings are increasing in frequency. They are also very destructive events when they do occur, with a disproportionately large impact on people's fears relative to the frequency of the events.

For several reasons, it is difficult to learn about the characteristics, motivation, and influences on individuals who commit mass killings. Those perpetrating them often commit suicide or are killed by responding law enforcement officers. It may be that some of the same influences that affect violent crime generally—substance use, weapon availability, family dysfunction, unemployment, emotional volatility—exert some influence on such individuals. It may also be that wanting to die, wishing to become famous, seeking revenge for real or perceived slights, airing grievances, and other distinctive influences are at work. For reasons we discussed in the previous section on school shootings, it will probably never be feasible to "profile" such individuals or predict such events with accuracy. But as we learn more about such rare but highly destructive tragedies, it may be possible to better prepare for them.

Highly publicized acts of violence at school or in the workplace threaten fundamental assumptions about personal security and the safety of our children and fellow citizens—and can have a major effect on how individuals feel about their quality of life. For these reasons, policymakers and social scientists must pay particular attention to workplace and school violence, although neighborhood violence also continues to be a priority.

Why Does Crime Happen?

Behavioral scientists argue that to ease the crime problem, we must first understand its causes. Why does crime happen? What motivates people to commit illegal acts? Bad genes? Inadequate parents? Failed schooling? Twisted impulses? Harsh environments? Trauma and abuse? Delinquent friends? Social disadvantage? Criminal thinking? Entitlement? Drug addiction? Easy access to weapons? Some combination of these factors? Can crime be predicted from knowing about a person's early life? Or are many people capable of crime under the wrong circumstances? Are some crimes, like those of the fictional Dexter Morgan (see Box 3.1), so extreme that they defy scientific explanation, or can behavioral scientists make sense of them?

Box 3.1

The Case of Dexter Morgan: A Fictional Psychopath?

Dexter Morgan is playful, handsome, and has a wonderfully ironic sense of humor. He is the fictional star of novels (*Dearly Devoted Dexter, Darkly Dreaming Dexter, Dexter in the Dark*) and two television series ("Dexter" and "Dexter: New Blood"). To his co-workers and fiancée, he is the blood-splatter analyst for the Miami Police Department. Privately, however, he is a selective serial killer who is guided by an internal companion whom he calls "the Dark Passenger." Dexter's adoptive father, a Miami cop, taught him to present himself as "normal"—and to kill only those who deserve it, according to a strict set of rules designed to avoid detection.

Can a fictional character such as Dexter tell us anything about reality? Are there real-life, nonfictional Dexter Morgans out there? Perhaps not, but reading about and watching Dexter can illustrate genuine phenomena. Engaging in a heinous act, such as the killing of neighborhood pets, and needing to be taught to act "as if" one feels certain emotions are associated with the personality disorder of psychopathy. Dexter's character might meet some of the criteria for this disorder, but does he

Michael Hall plays Dexter Morgan.

qualify as a psychopath? Would a real measure of this disorder (the Hare Psychopathy Checklist-Revised, or PCL-R; Hare, 2003) classify the fictional Dexter as a psychopath? Let's consider how some of the PCL-R items might apply.

PCL-R Item	Dexter
Glibness/superficial charm	• Flirts with women to keep up appearances. • Talks his way out of difficult situations easily.
Pathological lying	• Lies often, but presumably for self-preservation rather than without any understandable motivation.

PCL-R Item	Dexter
Conning/manipulative	• Able to obtain files from clerks with flirting and donuts. • Plans his killings carefully, using ruses and cons to capture and subdue his victims.
Lack of remorse or guilt	• Does not describe feeling these things for his victims. • Does not feel remorse or guilt for anything he does with co-workers or his wife or her children, although he feigns these emotions to fit in.
Callous/lack of empathy	• Shows no empathy for his victims.
Promiscuous sexual behavior	• No. He describes himself as disinterested in all aspects of sexuality, including both physical and emotional intimacy.
Need for stimulation/proneness to boredom	• Describes this as a hunger for killing, which he must satisfy periodically. • Has a professional position involving the inspection of highly stimulating phenomena (homicide crime scenes). • In other respects, however, he is not a great stimulation seeker, nor does he portray himself as easily bored.
Parasitic lifestyle	• No. He has a steady job and does not rely on others for assistance.
Poor behavioral controls	• No. He is careful and calculating, the antithesis of an impulsive offender.
Irresponsibility	• No. He is gainfully employed and does his job well. • He is committed to his wife and her family, although not attracted to the intimacy. • He uses both his job and his relationships as a cover for his self-designated role as the protector of society from serial killers.
Early behavior problems	• Showed behavior that could have resulted in arrest (e.g., killing neighborhood pets, taping up and threatening a classmate).
Criminal versatility	• No. He is a "specialist" whose offending is limited to abducting and killing his victims.

In some respects, the fictional Dexter Morgan (Phillips, 2006) is quite similar to those who have the personality disorder of psychopathy. These similarities are most apparent in his superficial emotions and lack of the capacity for deep emotional attachments. But Dexter does not possess some of the other characteristics and much of the history that are core elements of psychopathy. We might conclude that Dexter Morgan is a charming fictional character who can portray what it's like to have difficulty feeling deep emotions—but it's not clear whether he would be classified suffering from psychopathy.

Critical Thought Question

Dexter Morgan is obviously very disturbed. Why would he not be classified as a psychopath?

Theories of Crime as Explanations of Criminal Behavior

Theories of crime are as old as crime itself. Aristotle claimed that "poverty is the parent of revolution and crime." But most ancient explanations of crime took a religious tone; crime was either equivalent to or due to sin, a view that was popular throughout the Middle Ages and lives on today in many religious belief systems.

In the seventeenth century, Sir Francis Bacon argued that "opportunity makes a thief." During the 1700s, philosophers and social critics such as Voltaire and Rousseau emphasized concepts such as free will, hedonism, and flaws in the social contract to explain criminal conduct. These principles ultimately grew into the **classical school of criminology**.

The two leading proponents of classical criminology were the Italian intellectual Cesare Beccaria and the British philosopher Jeremy Bentham, who believed that lawbreaking occurred when people freely chose to behave wrongly when faced with a choice between right and wrong. People chose crime when they believed that the gains from crime outweighed the losses it entailed. Classical theorists were interested in reforming the harsh administration of justice in post-Renaissance Europe, and they believed that punishment of criminals should be commensurate with the crimes committed—that punishment should fit the crime. (This is seen in contemporary thinking about **proportionality in sentencing**.)

Classical theory influenced several principles of justice in Western societies (e.g., the U.S. Constitution's Eighth Amendment ban against "cruel and unusual punishment"). It still exerts an important effect on modern correctional philosophy.

Modern theories of crime developed from the **positivist school of criminology**. Rather than focusing on individuals' free will, positivists emphasized factors that they believed determined criminal behavior. They sought to understand crime through the scientific method and the analysis of empirical data. Some stressed sociological factors, whereas others preferred biological, psychological, or environmental explanations.

An early positivist was Adolphe Quetelet, a Belgian statistician who studied crime data and concluded that crime occurred more often in certain geographic areas and under specific social conditions. Lombroso (1876) and Garofalo (1914), other theorists who relied on scientific data, emphasized the physical characteristics of criminals and proposed a strong biological predisposition to crime. Although the early positivists considered themselves scientists, their methods were crude by current standards and led to conclusions that are not taken seriously today. Positivists believed that punishment should fit the criminal rather than the crime. This position foreshadowed rehabilitation as a correctional priority and the indeterminate sentence—from 6 to 10 years, for example—as a means for achieving it.

Most modern theories of criminal behavior—including those of biology, genetics, psychology, sociology, economics, anthropology, and religion—are a legacy of the positivist tradition. The validity of these theories varies greatly. Most can account reasonably well for certain types of crime, but none explains all forms of criminality—and some explain very few. Empirical data, rational analyses, moral values, and political ideologies all play a role in shaping preferences for the leading theories in criminology.

For the most part, criminologists have concentrated on those crimes that frighten the average citizen—violent acts (e.g., robbery, rape, assault, and murder) or aggressive behavior against property (e.g., burglary, theft, and arson). Certainly many other kinds of legally prohibited conduct—identity theft, computer hacking, and business fraud, for example—can cause great damage to individuals and society. (Consider the ransomware attacks in which an organization's computer system is frozen until a ransom is paid.) However, the major focus of criminologists historically has been on violent crime (e.g., homicide, sexual assault, armed robbery) and property crime (e.g., burglary, auto theft). As our lives are increasingly influenced by communications technology, it is likely that society's view of crime will expand accordingly.

Most theories of crime have focused on men. This may be reasonable, given that about three-quarters of all those arrested are male, and that almost 85% of violent crimes are committed by men. However, the factors that influence female criminal offending deserve attention, at least in part because crime by females has increased greatly in the last four decades. Between 1980 and 2014, the number of women in jails, and in state and federal prisons nationwide, increased by 700% (The Sentencing Project, 2016, 2020). These numbers grew from 1980 (26,378) to 1990 (81,023) to 2000 (164,221), with additional substantial growth in 2010 (205,190) and a slight leveling off in 2014 (215,332). This total rose to 222,455 in 2019. Considered by race and ethnicity, the rate of incarceration for Black women has been declining since 2000, while the rate for White and Latinx women has increased. Nonetheless the incarceration rate for Black women (83 per 100,000) in 2019 was still 1.7 times higher than the rate for White women (48 per 100,000), with Latina women incarcerated at an intermediate rate (63 per 100,000) (The Sentencing Project, 2020).

In 2019, there were 1.2 million women under correctional supervision. The vast majority of these women were on probation (885,000) (The Sentencing Project, 2020). Despite increases in violent criminal behavior, women are still most often arrested for larceny and theft. Such arrests often involve collaborating with a male partner. One implication of this pattern is that explanations of female crime need to carefully consider the role of coercion, especially as it is exerted in close relationships.

There are four contemporary theories that attempt to explain criminal offending. We group these theories as sociological, biological, psychological, and social–psychological. There are important distinctions among them.

Crime may appear to result from an individual's experience with their environment. This belief is explained through **sociological theories**, which maintain that crime results from broad social or cultural forces that are external to any specific individual; exist prior to any criminal act; and emerge from social class, political, ecological, or physical structures affecting large groups of people. Contemporary sociological theories of crime and delinquency focus on *strain* (adjustment associated with pursuing societal goals), *social control* (deviance developing in reaction to societal standards and the absence of social bonds such as attachment, commitment, involvement, and belief), *opportunity* (crime committed due to absence of certain opportunities but availability of others), *conflict* (focusing on power, with attention to rebellion, class conflict, and the philosophy of Marxism), and *developmental life course* (understanding crime over the life span, including onset, continuation, and desistance) (Zembrowski, 2011).

Alternatively, criminal behavior may appear to result from an individual's biological characteristics. **Biological theories of crime** stress genetic influences, neuropsychological abnormalities, and biochemical irregularities. But as we shall see, there is little empirical evidence that either sociological or biological theories independently predict criminal behavior. Instead, current theories of crime incorporate a combination of environmental and biological factors to understand the causes of offending behaviors.

Some **psychological theories** emphasize that crime results from personality attributes that are distinctively possessed by the individual involved in offending. For example, some psychological approaches have focused on patterns of thinking—particularly with respect to recognized risk factors such as pro-criminal attitudes or certain kinds of personality disorders. Others focus on intellectual functioning or cognitive and social development (Moore, 2011).

Social–psychological theories (Arrigo, 2006) bridge the gap between the environmentalism of sociology and the individualism of psychological or biological theories. Social–psychological theories propose that criminal behavior is learned, but they differ from sociological and psychological theories regarding *what* is learned and *how* it is learned.

Sociological Theories of Crime

Sociological theories may be divided into **structural** and **subcultural explanations**. Structural theories emphasize that dysfunctional social arrangements (e.g., inadequate schooling, economic adversity, or community disorganization) thwart people's efforts toward legitimate attainments and result in their breaking the law. Subcultural theories hold that crime originates when various groups of people endorse cultural values that clash with the dominant, conventional rules of society. In this view, crime is the product of a subculture's deviation from the accepted norms that underlie the criminal law.

Structural Explanations. A key concept of structural approaches is that certain groups of people suffer fundamental inequalities in opportunities to achieve the goals valued by society. Differential opportunity (Cloward & Ohlin, 1960) is one example of a **structural explanation** of crime. This theory can be traced to Émile Durkheim's ideas about the need to maintain moral bonds between individuals in society. Durkheim thought that life without moral or social obligations becomes intolerable and results in **anomie**, a feeling of normlessness that often precedes suicide and crime. One implication of anomie theory was that thwarted aspirations pressure individuals to deviate from social norms.

According to Cloward and Ohlin (1960), people in lower socioeconomic subcultures usually want to succeed through legal means, but society denies them legitimate opportunities to do so. For example, consider a person with limited means from Nicaragua who immigrates to the United States because of a sincere desire to make a better life for their family. This person faces cultural and language differences, financial hardships, and limited access to the resources that are crucial for upward mobility. It remains more difficult for poor people to obtain an advanced education, despite advances in the practice of need-blind admissions and need-based tuition adjustments that are now offered by some U.S. universities. In addition, crowding in large cities makes class distinctions more apparent.

This theory maintains that when legal means of goal achievement are blocked, intense frustration results—and crime is more likely to ensue. Youthful crime, especially in gangs, is one consequence of this sequence. The theory of differential opportunity assumes that people who grow up in crowded, impoverished, deteriorating neighborhoods endorse goals related to health, property, and safety. Thus, crime becomes an illicit means to understandable ends.

Contemporary sociological research on structural explanations for crime particularly focuses on the role of the neighborhood in leading to crime and violence. Consider the experience of growing up in a disadvantaged neighborhood with higher levels of crime and violence, fewer job opportunities, under-resourced schools, and other challenges, compared to growing up in a neighborhood with more resources, greater safety, and higher incomes. Research has identified a relationship between neighborhood-level variables and child maltreatment (Coulton et al., 1995), crime (Sampson & Groves, 1989), school drop-out (Brooks-Gunn et al., 1993), delinquent and risky behavior (Wikstrom & Loeber, 2000), community violence and early child behavior problems (Linares et al., 2001), and exposure to neighborhood violence and aggression (Forster et al., 2015).

Some (e.g., Garbarino, 1995) have pointed out the similarity of living in neighborhoods with frequent violence to that of a war zone. Youth can show symptoms related to trauma, even post-traumatic stress disorder (PTSD) (particularly hyperarousal) even if their exposure to gun violence is indirect—rather than observing it, they nonetheless hear about it and learn about the deaths of family members or friends (Luthar & Goldstein, 2004).

Subcultural Explanations. The subcultural version of the sociological theory maintains that a conflict between norms held by different groups causes criminal behavior. This conflict arises when various groups endorse subcultural norms, pressuring their members to deviate from the norms underlying the criminal law (Nietzel, 1979). Gangs, for example, enforce behavioral norms about how to behave. For many youths, a gang replaces the young person's parents as the main source of norms, even when parents attempt to instill their own values.

Like structural theories of crime, subcultural explanations have not demonstrated a strong theoretical or empirical basis. Questions remain: How do cultural standards originate? How are they transmitted from one generation to the next? How do they control the behavior of any one individual? The most troublesome concept is the main one—subculture. Some critics reject the assumption that different socioeconomic groups embrace radically different values.

Biological Theories of Crime

Biological theories of crime search for genetic vulnerabilities, neuropsychological abnormalities, or biochemical irregularities that predispose people to criminal behavior. These dispositions, biological theorists believe, are then translated into specific criminal behavior through environments and social interactions. Research on biological theories commonly focuses on twin and adoption studies to distinguish genetic from environmental factors.

In twin studies, the researcher compares the **concordance rate** (the percentage of pairs of twins sharing the behavior of interest) for **monozygotic twins** (identical twins) and **dizygotic twins** (commonly called fraternal twins). If the monozygotic concordance rate is significantly higher, the investigator concludes that the behavior in question is genetically influenced, because monozygotic twins are genetically identical whereas dizygotic pairs share, on average, only 50% of their genetic material.

In a major Swedish study using twin ($N = 36,877$ pairs), adoptee-parent ($N = 5,068$ pairs), adoptee-sibling ($N = 10,610$ pairs), and sibling ($N = 1,521,066$ pairs) designs, the heritability ratings (the extent to which genes are responsible for variations between individuals, ranging between 0 and 1.0) for violent offending were .40 to .50 (Frisell et al., 2012). Such evidence suggests that inherited tendencies may play a crucial role in causing crime. However, studies that distinguish between crimes against property and violent crimes against persons have found that although heredity and environment play important roles in both types of crime, the influence of heredity is higher for aggressive types of antisocial behavior (e.g., assaults, robberies, and sexual offenses) than for nonaggressive crimes such as drug taking, shoplifting, and truancy (Eley, 1997).

The larger pattern of results in this area was considered in a meta-analysis of 51 twin and adoption studies addressing the genetic and environmental influences on antisocial behavior. The investigators (Rhee & Waldman, 2002) described moderate proportions of variance due to shared genetic influences and somewhat larger effects of environmental influences.

Potential influence of a "genome-wide polygenic score" (an aggregated estimate of the effect of different genetic variants) on educational attainment, and subsequently on crime and antisocial behavior, was considered by researchers (Wertz et al., 2018) using two birth cohorts followed prospectively. Education polygenic scores were modestly associated with criminal offending, suggesting that the genetic influence on educational performance indirectly affects offending risk, as poor educational performance is itself a risk factor for criminal offending. Among the observed outcomes showing such modest association were poorer self-control, academic problems, and truancy, as well as a life-course-persistent pattern of antisocial conduct. This study was particularly interesting for two reasons. First, it used molecular-genetic advances as part of its methodology. Second, it incorporated other theories of crime—particularly psychological theories discussed later in this chapter—and integrated them with biological theories.

An interesting possibility regarding a biological contributor to offending was first raised by a 1993 study (Brunner et al., 1993). Studying individuals who had committed offenses, the investigators noted that some participants had both borderline intellectual deficiency and impaired control of impulsive aggression. These individuals showed a complete absence of activity of a certain enzyme (monoamine oxidase type A, or MAO-A), which affects important neurotransmitters. This absence resulted from a mutation on the X chromosome in the gene coding for MAO-A.

The MAO-A mutation was dubbed the "warrior gene" in a 2004 review in the journal *Science*, and that name continues to be used (with the unfortunate consequence of possibly exaggerating the influence of the mutation). The MAO-A allele (an alternative form of a mutated gene) occurs in apes, monkeys, and humans; some have suggested that it had a common ancestor 25 million years ago and was favored by natural selection (Horgan, 2011).

Without replication, the initial finding—involving a small number of affected individuals—would not have had implications for the broader scientific and legal fields (Appelbaum, 2005). But a second study with a large cohort (1,037 individuals followed since birth in Dunedin, New Zealand) replicated and extended these findings (Caspi et al., 2002). The investigators considered both the levels of MAO-A and the history of maltreatment between the ages of 3 and 11 on rates of offending. Using multiple measures of antisocial behavior, they reported that the 12% of participants who had both low MAO-A and maltreatment accounted for 44% of the total convictions for violent offenses, with 85% of individuals with both low MAO-A and maltreatment later showing some form of antisocial behavior.

What is the current status of this discovery? In a detailed review, Buades-Rotger and Gallardo-Pujol (2014) conclude that there is converging evidence indicating that the low MAO-A mutation contributes to antisocial behavior when combined with a history of childhood abuse. They describe several implications of this conclusion: (1) incorporating genetic data into current violence risk assessment procedures could make them more accurate; (2) genetic data could be used to detect individuals at a greater risk of having the mutation; and (3) genetic data could also help in comparing the impact of specific treatments, including psychological and pharmacological.

Consistent with the effects of childhood abuse combined with a biological influence on criminal behavior, researchers (Goh et al., 2021) compared 33 individuals convicted as adults of homicide with 75 others who had not committed any offense and were otherwise healthy. They reported that those convicted of homicide were both higher in childhood trauma scores and lower in plasma oxytocin levels, consistent with the hypothesis that dysfunction of the oxytocinergic system may be linked with high levels of aggression.

Certainly there are cautionary notes to be sounded. Using terms such as "warrior gene" or "oxytocinergic system dysfunction" may suggest a direct or causal influence on violent behavior that is not supported by the research. One should not conclude that having this genetic mutation or this dysfunction (combined with childhood abuse) means that one will behave violently. Nor should one conclude that not having the mutation-abuse constellation means that one will not. Rather, the combination of childhood abuse with a biological marker appears to be a risk factor that exerts some influence, although violence is a behavior that has multiple causes and influences. Also, the genetic condition may be seen with different frequency across different racial and ethnic groups. Investigators (e.g., Lea & Chambers, 2007) have identified rates of MAO-A mutation as occurring in Maori men (56%), Caucasians (34%), Hispanics (29%), Africans (59%), and Chinese (77%), raising the question of whether some would use race or culture as a proxy for violence risk. This would be wrong for at least two reasons. First, risk should be an individualized determination rather than one that relies only on influences such as one's racial or ethnic group—and it is objectionable to use race on the grounds of fairness and equal protection as well. Second, the empirical data do not indicate that any single risk factor—including the MAO-A mutation or oxytocinergic dysfunction—has a compelling influence on violence risk. The picture is more complex and multi-determined than that. Nonetheless, the combination of childhood adversity with a certain biological marker appears to be potentially promising for future investigators of criminal aggression.

Genetic and Biological Influences on Crime: Promising Possibilities.

If genetic or biological factors do influence crime, the important question has always been: what influences what? There is a lengthy list of likely candidates (Brennan & Raine, 1997), but five possibilities are emphasized:

1. *Low MAO-A in combination with a history of maltreatment.* As we have noted, evidence may help to explain how a combination of an adverse experience (child maltreatment) and a biological risk factor (low MAO-A) could increase impulsivity and propensity to antisocial behavior.

2. *Neuropsychological abnormalities.* High rates of abnormal electroencephalogram (EEG) patterns have been reported in prison populations and in youth who have committed violent offenses. These EEG irregularities may indicate neurological deficits that result in poor impulse control and impaired judgment. Studies of violent offenders have shown slow-wave EEG patterns indicating underarousal (Milstein, 1988). Although a high percentage of persons in the general population also have EEG abnormalities, rates of EEG abnormalities are somewhat higher in impulsive delinquent youth (Yoshi, Ishiwara, & Tani, 2008) and impulsive adult offenders (Zukov et al., 2008).

   More promising results have been reported concerning abnormalities in four subcortical regions of the brain—the amygdala, hippocampus, thalamus, and midbrain—specifically in the right hemisphere of the brain, which has been linked to the experience of negative emotions. In one study (Raine et al., 1998), brain scans of a group of homicide offenders showed that, compared with normal controls, the offenders experienced excessive activity in these four subcortical

structures. Excessive subcortical activity may underlie a more aggressive temperament that could, in turn, predispose an individual to violent behavior.

A review of the neuropsychological literature also supports a relationship between deficits in the prefrontal cortex, a region of the brain responsible for planning, monitoring, and controlling behavior, and antisocial behavior (see Raine, 2002). Damage to the prefrontal cortex may predispose individuals to criminal behavior in one of several ways. Patients with impairment in this region of the brain have decreased reasoning abilities that may lead to impulsive decision-making in risky situations (Bechara et al., 1997). In addition, prefrontal impairment is associated with decreased levels of arousal, and individuals may engage in stimulation-seeking and antisocial behaviors to compensate for these arousal deficits (Raine et al., 2000). Impairments in the prefrontal cortex may help to explain why offenders, on average, have about an 8- to 10-point lower IQ (intelligence quotient) than nonoffenders and are less able to (1) postpone impulsive actions, (2) use effective problem-solving strategies (Lynam et al., 1993), and (3) achieve academic success in schools as a route to socially approved attainments (Binder, 1988).

Low IQ is among the most stable of risk factors for conduct disorder and delinquency (Murray & Farrington, 2010). In one longitudinal study of 411 London boys, a low IQ at ages 8–10 was linked to persistent criminality and more convictions for violent crimes up to age 32 (Farrington, 1995). In a comparison of intelligence of juvenile offenders within different racial/ethnic groups (Black, Hispanic, and White; Trivedi, 2011), White violent offenders had lower Performance IQ scores than White non-violent offenders. Overall, however, gender, ethnicity, and lower IQ scores also seem to be related in a complex way, indicating the need for further investigation.

3. *Autonomic nervous system differences.* The autonomic nervous system (ANS) carries information between the brain and all organs of the body. Because of these connections, emotions are associated with changes in the ANS. In fact, we can "see" the effects of emotional arousal on such ANS responses as heart rate, skin conductance, respiration, and blood pressure. Some who commit criminal offenses—particularly those whose offending is most chronic—are thought to differ from those who do not in that they show chronically low levels of autonomic arousal and weaker physiological reactions to stimulation (see Patrick, 2008, discussed in detail in the next section). These differences, which might also involve hormonal irregularities (see the next section), could cause this group of offenders to have (1) difficulty learning how to inhibit behavior likely to lead to punishment and (2) a high need for extra stimulation that they gratify through aggressive thrill seeking. These difficulties are also considered an important

predisposing factor by some social–psychological theorists, discussed later.

4. *Physiological differences.* Among the physiological factors that may be associated with offending are (1) abnormally high levels of testosterone, (2) increased secretion of insulin, and (3) lower levels of serotonin (Booij et al., 2010). One study using animal models provides support for the role of these physiological variables in aggressive behavior. Researchers found that rats with increased production of testosterone and lower levels of serotonin exhibited more aggressive behaviors; these rats displayed an increased number of attacks and inflicted a greater number of wounds on other rats compared to rats with lower testosterone and higher serotonin levels (Toot et al., 2004). Such findings may be helpful in understanding the biological contributions to human aggression as well.

A major review of psychophysiological studies of aggression and violence (Patrick, 2008) identified other physiological correlates of persistent aggressive behavior: (1) low baseline heart rate, (2) greater autonomic reactivity to stressful or aversive stimuli, (3) enhanced EEG slow-wave activity, (4) reduced brain potential response, and (5) dysfunction in cortical and limbic brain regions that influence emotional regulation. One of the proposed explanations for these findings was impairment in emotional regulation circuits in the brain that would otherwise inhibit impulsive aggression.

5. *Personality and temperament differences.* Some dimensions of personality are highly heritable, and thus can be discussed within the scope of genetic influence on behavior. Some heritable dimensions are further related to antisocial behavior. Individuals with personalities marked by undercontrol, unfriendliness, irritability, low empathy, callous unemotionality, and a tendency to become easily frustrated are at greater risk for antisocial conduct (McLoughlin et al., 2010). We discuss some of these characteristics more fully in the next section on psychological theories of crime.

Psychological Theories of Crime

Psychological explanations of crime emphasize individual differences in the way people think or feel about their behavior. These differences, which can take the form of subtle variations or more extreme personality disturbances, might make some people more prone to criminal behavior by increasing their anger, weakening their attachments to others, or enhancing their desire to take risks and seek thrills.

Criminal Thinking Patterns. A systematic and scientifically validated approach to investigating the role of offender thinking has been undertaken by Glenn Walters, who for many years served as a psychologist with the Federal Bureau of Prisons. He developed the Psychological Inventory of Criminal Thinking Styles (PICTS), an 80-item self-report inventory that measures cognitive patterns that are supportive of offending. Data from both male and female offenders, as well as meta-analyses, indicate that the PICTS is reliable, correlated with previous offending, and modestly predictive of future adjustment and release outcome (Walters, 2002; Walters & Mandell, 2007). A similar measure (the Measure of Offending Thinking Styles–Revised) was developed as well, also focusing on offender thinking styles, and following a comparable pattern of appropriate scientific development and validation (Mandracchia & Morgan, 2011). Several other additional measures of such thinking styles have also been developed (Kroner & Morgan, 2014). This general approach, involving the appraisal of thinking styles and cognitive "errors" among offenders, has added significantly to our current ability to assess offender risk and rehabilitation needs.

Personality-Based Explanations. Many personality-based explanations for criminal offending in the last three decades have focused on the construct of **psychopathy**, which we discuss in this section. Historically, however, a number of theories of personality have been offered to help understand offending. A prominent example is Costa and McCrae's five-factor model (**Neuroticism**, **Extraversion**, Openness to Experience, Agreeableness, and Conscientiousness; McCrae & Costa, 1990). According to a meta-analysis (Miller & Lynam, 2001), those who were low on Agreeableness or low on Conscientiousness were more likely to be involved in antisocial behavior. The other dimensions were less important—suggesting that general personality theory has identified two domains (agreeableness and conscientiousness) that are important to understanding criminal offending. Other research (Wilcox et al., 2014) considered how agreeableness and conscientiousness interacted with opportunity to commit crime in affecting adolescent offending, with opportunity less likely to lead to offending when individuals were agreeable and conscientious. This is consistent with the relationship between certain personality styles (neurotics and aggressives, as measured by the Jesness Inventory; Jesness, 1996) and criminal recidivism among those in U.S. federal prison facilities over a period of 10–12 years (Listwan et al., 2006).

There is some evidence, therefore, of a relationship between personality variables generally and criminal offending. Such variables have included agreeableness, conscientiousness, and aggressiveness. But it is the personality disorder of psychopathy, to which we now turn, that has been particularly associated with crime and other kinds of antisocial behavior.

Psychopathy. The construct of *psychopathy* has a long history. This term is used to describe individuals who engage in frequent, repetitive antisocial activity for which they feel little or no remorse. Such persons appear chronically deceitful and manipulative; they seem to have a nearly total lack of conscience that propels them into repeated conflict with society, often from a very early age. They are superficial, arrogant, and do not seem to learn from experience; they lack empathy and loyalty to individuals, groups, or society (Hare & Neumann, 2008). They are also described as selfish, callous, and irresponsible; they tend to blame others or to offer plausible rationalizations for their behavior.

The closest diagnosis within the *Diagnostic and Statistical Manual-5* (DSM-5; American Psychiatric Association, 2013) is **antisocial personality disorder**. The disorders of psychopathy and antisocial personality disorder are similar in their emphasis on chronic antisocial behavior, but they differ in the role of personal characteristics, which are important in psychopathy but are less emphasized among the diagnostic criteria for antisocial personality disorder. About 80% of psychopathic individuals are men, and their acts sometimes are well publicized. We give an example in Box 3.2.

Box 3.2

The Case of Ted Bundy: A Real-Life Psychopath

Born in 1946, Theodore Robert Bundy seemed destined for a charmed life; he was intelligent, attractive, and articulate (Holmes & DeBurger, 1988). A Boy Scout as a youth and then an honor student and psychology major at the University of Washington, he was at one time a work-study student at the Seattle Crisis Clinic. Later he became assistant to the chairman of the Washington State Republican Party. It is probably around this time that he claimed his first victim, a college-age woman who was viciously attacked while sleeping, left alive but brain damaged.

From 1974 through 1978, Bundy stalked, attacked, killed, and then sexually assaulted as many as 36 victims in Washington, Oregon, Utah, Colorado, and Florida. Apparently, some of the women were taken off guard when the good-looking, casual Bundy approached, seeming helpless: walking with crutches, or having an apparent broken arm. He usually choked them to death and then sexually abused and mutilated them before disposing of their bodies in remote areas (Nordheimer, 1989).

Maintaining a charming façade is characteristic of many people with psychopathy; acquaintances often describe them (as they did Bundy) as "fascinating," "charismatic," and "compassionate." Beneath his superficial charm, though, Bundy was deceitful and dangerous. Embarrassed because he was an illegitimate child and his mother was poor, he constantly sought, as a youth, to give the impression of being an upper-class kid. He wore fake mustaches and used makeup to change his appearance. He faked a British accent and stole cars in high school to help maintain his image. He constantly sought out the company of attractive women, not because he was genuinely interested in them but because he wanted people to notice and admire him.

At his trial for the murder of two Chi Omega sorority sisters in their bedrooms at Florida State University, he served as his own attorney. (Bundy had attended two law schools, although he did not graduate from either.) He was convicted; he was also found guilty of the kidnapping, murder, and mutilation of a Lake City, Florida, girl who was 12 years old. Bundy was sentenced to death.

Shortly before he was executed on January 24, 1989, Bundy gave a television interview to evangelist James Dobson in which he blamed his problems on pornography. He said, "Those of us who are … so much influenced by violence in the media, in particular pornographic violence, are not some

Serial killer Ted Bundy

kind of inherent monsters. We are your husbands, and we grew up in regular families" (quoted by Lamar, 1989, p. 34).

Bundy claimed that he spent his formative years with a grandfather who had an insatiable craving for pornography. He told Dr. Dobson, "People will accuse me of being self-serving but I am just telling you how I feel. Through God's help, I have been able to come to the point where I, much too late, but better late than never, feel the hurt and the pain that I am responsible for" (quoted by Kleinberg, 1989, p. 5A).

The tape of Bundy's last interview, produced by Dobson and titled "Fatal Addiction," was widely disseminated, especially by those who seek to eliminate all pornography. But Bundy's claim that pornography was the "fuel for his fantasies" should be viewed skeptically. In none of his previous interviews, including extensive conversations in 1986 with Dorothy Lewis, a psychiatrist he had come to trust, did he ever cite "a pornographic preamble to his grotesqueries" (Nobile, 1989, p. 41).

Critical Thought Question

How would Dexter Morgan, a "fictional psychopath," compare with Ted Bundy, who was apparently the real thing?

Psychopathy, as measured by the Hare Psychopathy Checklist (PCL) (Hare, 2003) and its various iterations and revisions (the Hare Psychopathy Checklist-Revised [PCL-R], the Hare Psychopathy Checklist-Screening Version, the Hare Psychopathy Checklist-Youth Version, and the Hare Psychopathy Checklist-Revised-Second Edition), has been well established as a risk factor for offending and for violent offending. Perhaps the best demonstration of this relationship comes from a meta-analysis (Leistico et al., 2008). The authors integrated 95 nonoverlapping studies ($N = 15,826$ participants) to summarize the relation between the various Hare Psychopathy Checklists and antisocial conduct. Their results indicated that higher PCL total scores were moderately associated with greater antisocial conduct. These results depended on the setting from which the participants were drawn. PCL scores were more strongly associated with offending in the community than with serious misconduct in correctional facilities and secure hospitals.

There are many theories about what causes psychopathic behavior. One view is that psychopathic individuals experience cortical immaturity that makes it difficult for them to inhibit behavior. Hare himself has proposed that psychopathic individuals may have a deficiency in the left hemisphere of their brains that impairs executive function, the ability to plan and regulate behavior carefully (Moffitt & Lynam, 1994). Considerable research supports a strong relationship between antisocial behavior and impaired executive functioning (Morgan & Lilienfeld, 2000).

Compared to normal controls, psychopaths experience less anxiety after experiencing aversive stimulation, and show relatively low cortical arousal in the resting state as well. This low autonomic arousal generates a high need for stimulation. Consequently, psychopathic individuals prefer novel situations and tend to pay less attention to many other stimuli, thereby being less influenced by them. This is consistent with stimulation-seeking theory (Quay, 1965), which suggests that the thrill-seeking and disruptive behavior of psychopathic individuals serves to increase sensory input and arousal to a more tolerable level. As a result of such thrill seeking, the individual with psychopathy seems "immune" to many social cues that govern behavior.

Another popular historical explanation for psychopathy involves being raised in a dysfunctional family (Loeber & Stouthamer-Loeber, 1986). Two parental patterns that might foster psychopathy were cited by Buss (1966). The first is having parents who are cold and distant. The child who imitates these parents develops an unfeeling, detached interpersonal style that conveys a superficial appearance of social involvement but lacks the empathy required for stable, satisfying relationships. The second pattern involves having parents who are inconsistent in their use of rewards and punishments, making it difficult for the child to imitate a stable role model and develop a consistent self-identity. A child in this situation learns to avoid blame and punishment but fails to learn the finer differences between appropriate and less appropriate behavior.

Limitations of Psychopathy in Explaining Offending. The major drawback of psychopathy as an explanation for crime is that it describes only a small percentage of offenders. It might be tempting to classify most who commit crime as psychopathic and explain their offending with that classification. But most of those who commit criminal acts—even most of those who are convicted and incarcerated—are not psychopathic. One study found that only about 25% of a correctional sample could be classified as psychopathic, and this percentage was even smaller for women than for men (Salekin et al., 2001).

In addition, there is controversy about using the PCL and other versions of the instrument as diagnostic tools on which legal decisions are based. Although the PCL-R has an excellent inter-rater reliability when carried out in accordance with instructions (indicating that two raters using the PCL-R would tend to reach the same conclusion), a lack of training and possible biases on the part of the clinician may contribute to disparities in scores. There is evidence, for example, that "allegiance bias" (a tendency to favor the side retaining the evaluator) may have a substantial effect on scoring the PCL-R and reporting the results (Murrie et al., 2013). Of course, allegiance bias does not only affect the PCL-R—other commonly used risk assessment measures are also influenced by allegiance bias—but it is important to note that even measures that are psychometrically sound and accepted in the field can be influenced in this way.

In addition, some legal questions are not well informed by PCL-R results. In cases involving capital punishment, for example, a question can arise at sentencing as to whether a convicted individual is likely to harm others in the future. If that individual were in the community, there is good empirical evidence that a high score on the PCL-R (above 30 out of a possible 40, for example) would justify a conclusion of higher risk. But that individual has been convicted of murder and will be incarcerated, probably for life. In a correctional facility context, the PCL-R does not distinguish well between those who will be violent toward others and those who will not, and hence is not useful to inform the appraisal of future violence risk in prison (DeMatteo et al., 2020a; see also Olver et al., 2020 and DeMatteo et al., 2020b for a spirited debate on this point).

Furthermore, because the PCL depends partly on self-report, the information obtained may be inaccurate. As a safeguard against potentially erroneous information, the evaluator must have access to collateral information to compare with information obtained from the examinee. Because the number of judicial decisions that rely on the PCL-R is considerable, the ongoing training efforts for this measure are particularly important.

Yet another criticism of the use of these psychopathy assessment instruments in criminal proceedings revolves around their use in cases involving adolescent and female offenders. Although some evidence suggests that these instruments can be successfully used with female offenders (Nicholls et al., 2005; Vitale & Newman, 2001) and male adolescents (Corrado et al., 2004; Marsee et al., 2005), other evidence is more mixed. For example, one component of psychopathy (deficient affective experience) was related to aggression in female juveniles, but when victimization experience was taken into account, such deficient emotional range no longer showed an impact (Odgers et al., 2005). It appears that while psychopathy may have some applications with women (Kreis & Cooke, 2012) and adolescents, there are important gender and developmental differences, respectively, that must be considered (Verona & Vitale, 2018). These psychopathy assessment tools offer a valuable way of assessing personal characteristics and history that are related to criminal offending by some offenders. But there are other contributors as well. These include social influences, to which we now turn.

Social–Psychological Theories of Crime

Social–psychological explanations view crime as being learned through social interaction. Sometimes called social-process theories in order to draw attention to the processes by which an individual becomes a criminal, social–psychological theories fall into two subcategories: control theories and direct learning theories. **Control theory** assumes that people will behave antisocially unless they learn, through a combination of inner controls and external constraints on behavior, not to offend. **Learning theory** stresses how individuals directly acquire specific criminal behaviors through different forms of learning.

Control Theories. Control theories assume that people will behave antisocially unless they are trained not to by others (Conger, 1980). Young people are bonded to society at several levels. They differ in (1) the degree to which they are affected by the opinions and expectations of others, (2) the payoffs they receive for conventional behavior, and (3) the extent to which they subscribe to the prevailing norms. Some people never form emotional bonds with significant others, so they never internalize necessary controls over antisocial behavior.

The "general theory of crime" (Gottfredson & Hirschi, 1990) is an example of a control theory, although it modifies the focus of social bonding as a protective influence in favor of emphasizing the primary role of personal self-control. Such self-control, as described in this theory, is developed in childhood through social learning occurring in the family and other parts of the individual's social environment. The combination of impulsivity and poor self-control with limited social bonds and opportunity for crime is thought to yield antisocial behavior (Siegel & McCormick, 2006). Supporting research is seen in the relationship between low self-control and violent behavior with youth (Baron, 2003; Piquero, 2005), although self-control was not the only variable associated with crime (younger age and offending history were also prominent). Lower levels of self-control have also been associated with gang violence (Chapple & Hope, 2003).

Reckless (1967) proposed that it is largely external containment (i.e., social pressure and institutionalized rules) that controls crime. If a society is well integrated, has well-defined limits on behavior, encourages family discipline and supervision, and provides reinforcers for positive accomplishments, crime will be contained. But if these external controls weaken, control of crime must depend on internal restraints, mainly an individual's conscience. This is an "in-between" view, neither rigidly environmental nor entirely disposition-based. Containment accounts for the law-abiding individual in a high-crime environment. But this theory explains only a part of criminal behavior. It does not apply to crimes within groups that are organized around their commitment to deviant behavior. Greater emphasis on heredity as a version of **containment theory** (Eysenck, 1964) suggested that certain individuals are predisposed to criminal offending because of their genes, but are still influenced by socialization as they grow up. Particular influences are considered under **operant learning** (responses that are followed by rewards are strengthened, whereas responses followed by aversive events are weakened) and **classical conditioning** (development of conscience conditioned through repeated, close pairings of a child's undesirable behaviors with the prompt punishment of these behaviors). As discussed earlier in this chapter, there is some evidence for a genetic contribution to individuals' predispositions to antisocial behavior— but this is subject to the influence of socialization, much like Eysenck was describing in more general terms nearly 60 years ago. But what are the socialization influences more specifically? We turn to that question now.

Learning Theories. Learning theory focuses on how criminal behavior is learned. For example, Sutherland and Cressey (1974) proposed various explanations of criminal behavior, including the following:

1. Criminal behavior is learned through interaction with other persons in a process of communication.
2. When criminal behavior is learned, the learning includes (a) techniques of committing the crime, which are sometimes very complicated but at other times simple, and (b) the specific direction of motives, drives, rationalizations, and attitudes.
3. A person becomes delinquent because there are more examples favorable to violating the law than unfavorable to violating the law.

Sutherland's theory has been translated into the language of operant learning theory as developed by B. F. Skinner. According to **differential association reinforcement theory** (Akers et al., 1996), criminal behavior is acquired through operant conditioning and modeling. A person behaves criminally when reinforcement for such behavior is more frequent than punishment. Families, peer groups, and schools control most sources of reinforcement and punishment and expose people to many behavioral models (Akers et al., 1996).

Such theory attempts to explain crime in places where it would not necessarily be expected (e.g., among those who criminally offend but grew up in relatively resource-rich environments). But it has difficulty explaining impulsive violence, and it does not explain why certain individuals, even in the same family, have the different associations they do. Why are some people more likely than others to form criminal associations?

Social Learning Theory/Social Cognitive Theory. One answer comes from social learning theory. (The name of this theory was subsequently changed to "social cognitive theory" to reflect the enhanced emphasis on thinking.) Social cognitive theory acknowledges the importance of differential reinforcement for developing new behaviors, but it assigns more importance to cognitive factors and to observational or vicarious learning. Its chief proponent, Albert Bandura (1986), observed that "most human behavior is learned by observation through modeling" (p. 47). Learning through modeling is more efficient than learning through differential reinforcement. Complex behaviors such as speech and driving a car require models from which to learn. In all likelihood, so does crime. Observational learning depends on (1) *attention* to the important features of modeled behavior; (2) *retention* of these features in memory to guide later performance; (3) *reproduction* of the observed behaviors; and (4) *reinforcement* of performed behaviors, which determines whether they will be performed again. Bandura applied social learning theory to criminal behavior in three social contexts.

1. *Familial influences.* Familial aggression assumes many forms, from child abuse at one extreme to aggressive parental attitudes and language at the other. It is in the arena of discipline, however, where children are exposed most often to vivid examples of coercion and aggression as a preferred style for resolving conflicts and asserting desires.

2. *Subcultural influences.* Some environments and subcultures provide context that supports aggression and an abundance of rewards for their most combative members. "The highest rates of aggressive behavior are found in environments where aggressive models abound and where aggressiveness is regarded as a highly valued attribute" (Bandura, 1976, p. 207).

3. *Symbolic models.* The influence of symbolic models on aggression has been attributed to the mass media, particularly the Internet and television.

Consider how social learning theory might apply to contemporary thinking about crime. The leading theory describing risk factors and needs (deficits which, when improved, reduce the risk of offending) is Risk-Need-Responsivity (RNR; Bonta & Andrews, 2017). This theory, supported by a good deal of research, includes *family* and *antisocial peers* among the major needs areas for offenders—just as Bandura describes family and subcultural influences, above. Another leading theory of offender appraisal, the Good Lives Model (Ward & Brown, 2004), suggests that the risk of crime is reduced by intervening to help individuals improve the overall quality of their lives. This would go beyond focusing on risk factors to include strengths and broader quality of life indicators.

Social learning theory can also help to explain the influence of trauma and adverse experience on children's subsequent risk of criminal offending. Trauma (events that involve life-threatening, physically destructive, or sexually assaultive events) and adverse experience (less severe but more frequent exposure to aggression and antisocial behavior) increase the risk that children and youth will be involved in offending, particularly when they co-occur with other risk factors such as family, education, and antisocial peer problems. It is also important to observe, however, that most maltreated children do not go on to be involved in crime (Zelechoski, 2016).

Regarding symbolic models, a number of studies have investigated the effects of televised violence on viewers, especially children. One longitudinal study, conducted over a 15-year period, suggests that there are significant long-term effects from watching violent television in childhood (Huesmann et al., 2003). Results from this study revealed a significant relationship between watching violence on television as children and aggressive behavior in adulthood. This pattern held for male and female participants, although the types of aggressive behavior differed. Males engaged in more overt aggression (e.g., domestic violence, physical fights), whereas women engaged in more indirect aggression (e.g., traffic violations). Women who watched violent television as children were also four times more likely than other women to be victims of domestic violence. Furthermore, the study found that early exposure to violence on television significantly predicted aggression in adulthood regardless of the level of aggression the individual displayed in childhood.

Researchers also hypothesized that viewing television violence in childhood can lead to other potentially harmful effects. For instance, children may become desensitized to the effects of violence (e.g., may care less about others' feelings) or experience a heightened fear of victimization. Children younger than eight years may be especially vulnerable to the effects of viewing violence because of their cognitive limitations in distinguishing fantasy and cartoon violence from reality. Of more recent interest is the question of whether movies and video games, which often feature much more graphic depictions of violence than those allowed on TV, exert stronger modeling effects on aggression. We describe a relevant case in Box 3.3.

A review by a task force of the American Psychological Association on violent media (2015) drew a number of conclusions from the existing scientific evidence:

- There is a consistent relationship between the use of violent video games, increases in aggression (behavior, thinking, and emotion), and decreases in prosocial behavior and empathy.

- These are more than temporary effects. They occur in short-term laboratory studies and longer-term longitudinal observations.

Box 3.3

The Case of "Teenage Amusement," a Murder, and a Video Game

A 2006 report from the National Coalition for the Homeless noted a disturbing trend: there were 122 attacks and 20 murders of homeless people in 2005, several of them by teenage perpetrators. According to the Coalition's executive director Michael Stoops, "It's disturbing to know that young people would literally kick someone when they're already down on their luck. We recognize that this isn't every teenager, but for some this passes as amusement."

Three teenage perpetrators from Milwaukee—16-year-old Luis Oyola, 17-year-old Andrew Ihrcke, and 15-year-old Nathan Moore—claimed that killing Rex Baum was never part of their plan. But the trio, who had been drinking with Baum at his campsite, suddenly began punching and kicking the 49-year-old man and then hurled anything they could find—rocks, bricks, even a barbeque grill, at the hapless victim. After smearing him with feces, cutting him, and bragging about their actions, they were arrested. One of the teens told police that killing "the bum" reminded him of playing the violent video game "Bumfights," which depicts homeless people pummeling each other to make a few bucks.

Critical Thought Question
What are your hypotheses about the influences on the three adolescents who attacked and killed Rex Baum?

- These effects remain when other influences are statistically controlled, but thus far only a small number of studies has been conducted on this question.

- Higher amounts of gaming experience are associated with higher levels of aggression and other problematic outcomes.

- Most of the research has been conducted on individuals between age 14 and young adulthood. Also, limited research is available on gender, race, ethnicity, or culture as influences—so conclusions are limited on the question of how these factors influence the relationship between violent video game exposure and adverse outcomes.

Social cognitive theory also points to several environmental cues that increase antisocial behavior. These "instigators" signal when it might be rewarding to behave antisocially (rather than risky to do so). One instigator, already mentioned, is *models*: observing others and modeling their behavior can influence some, particularly when they have been frustrated or see the aggression as justified. A second (related) instigator is *prior aversive treatment*. People often treat others the way they have been treated. A third

is *incentive inducements*, which includes the anticipated rewards of misbehavior. Habitual offenders often overestimate their chances of succeeding in criminal acts and ignore the consequences of failing. A fourth is *instructions*, particularly from one in authority. Milgram's famous (1963) study demonstrating widespread willingness to follow orders to inflict "pain" on another person is a good illustration. Although not a common feature of offending, this kind of influence may play a role in some hate crimes, in which the perpetrator believes they are doing the will of a religious or patriotic fanatic. It may also be illustrated by the reactions of some to President Trump's "fight like hell" speech to followers on January 6, 2021 prior to the storming of the United States Capitol. A fifth is *delusions and hallucinations*: individuals occasionally respond aggressively to false beliefs or hallucinated commands that stem from severe mental illness. Finally, there is a strong, positive association between crime and *alcohol or drug use*, especially for violent crime (see https://www.niaaa.nih.gov/publications/brochures-and-fact-sheets/alcohol-facts-and-statistics). By depressing a person's responsiveness to other cues that could inhibit impulsive or aggressive behavior, alcohol often leads to an increase in antisocial behavior even though it is not a stimulant. Drug use, by virtue of its cost and deviant status, also acts as a catalyst to or amplifier of criminality, especially property crime.

According to social learning theorists, people also regulate their behavior through self-reinforcement. Individuals who derive pleasure, pride, revenge, or self-worth from an ability to harm or "con" others find criminal behavior gratifying, while those who find it leads to self-criticism and self-contempt are less likely to continue it. Self-reinforcement, as well as the reactions of others, thus plays an important part in behavioral regulation.

People can also learn to exempt themselves from their own conscience after behaving antisocially. These tactics of "self-exoneration" assume many forms: minimizing the seriousness of one's acts by pointing to more serious offenses by others, justifying aggression by appealing to higher values, displacing the responsibility for misbehavior onto a higher authority, blaming victims for their misfortune, diffusing responsibility for wrongdoing, dehumanizing victims so that they are stripped of sympathetic qualities, and underestimating the damage inflicted by one's actions. This is part of what has been called "criminal thinking," which is a major risk factor for offending (Bonta & Andrews, 2017).

The major strength of social learning theory is that it explains how specific patterns of criminal offending are developed by individuals. A second strength is that the theory applies to a wide range of crimes. The major limitation of social learning theory is that little empirical evidence indicates that real-life crime is learned according to behavioral principles. Most of the data come from laboratory research where the experimental setting cannot replicate the legal and social sanctions that actual offenders must risk incurring. A second problem is that the theory does not explain why some people fall prey to "bad" learning experiences and others resist them. Learning might be a necessary ingredient for criminality, but probably not a sufficient one. Individual differences in the way people respond to reinforcement need to be considered. The theory we review next does so.

Multiple-Component Learning Theory. Some theorists have integrated several learning processes into comprehensive, learning-based explanations of criminality (e.g., Feldman, 1977). The most influential and controversial multiple-component learning theory is Wilson and Herrnstein's (1985) book *Crime and Human Nature*. Wilson and Herrnstein begin by observing that criminal and noncriminal behavior have both gains and losses. Gains from committing crime include revenge, excitement, and peer approval. Gains associated with not committing crime include avoiding punishment and having a clear conscience. Whether a crime is committed depends, in part, on the net ratio of gains and losses for criminal and noncriminal behavior. If the ratio for committing a crime exceeds the ratio for not committing it, the likelihood of the crime being committed increases.

Wilson and Herrnstein argued that several individual differences influence these ratios and determine whether an individual is likely to commit a crime. Like Eysenck, they proposed that individuals differ in the ease with which they learn to associate, through classical conditioning, negative emotions with misbehaviors and positive emotions with proper behaviors. These conditioned responses are the building blocks of a strong conscience that enhances the gains of not offending and the losses associated with crime.

Another important factor is what Wilson and Herrnstein called *time discounting*. All reinforcers lose strength as they become more removed from a behavior, but people differ in their ability to delay gratification and obtain reinforcement from potential long-term gains. More impulsive persons have greater difficulty deriving benefits from distant reinforcers. Time discounting is important for understanding crime because the gains associated with crime (e.g., revenge, money) accrue immediately, whereas the losses from such behavior (e.g., punishment) occur later, if at all. Thus, for impulsive persons, the ratio of gains to losses shifts in a direction that favors criminal behavior.

Another major component in Wilson and Herrnstein's theory is a set of constitutional factors, including sex, intelligence, variations in physiological arousal, and impulsivity, all of which combine to make some persons more attracted to wrongdoing and less deterred by the potential aversive consequences of crime.

Of several social factors linked to criminal behavior, Wilson and Herrnstein believe that family influences and early school experiences are the most important. Families that foster (1) *attachment* of children to their parents; (2) *longer time horizons*, where children consider the distant consequences of their behavior; and (3) *strong consciences* about misbehavior will go far in reducing the risk of criminal offending as children mature.

Research on parenting practices and the quality of the parent–child relationship underscores the relevance of familial interaction to childhood delinquency. Family has long been recognized as a crucial contributor to the development of juvenile offending (see https://www.ebpsociety.org/blog/education/378-root-causes-of-juvenile-delinquency) and is the basis for empirically supported intervention programs to reduce the risk of juvenile offending (see discussion in Chapter 15). Children raised in families that are unstable or abusive have less capacity to develop problem-solving skills (Derzon, 2010). Those with greater adverse childhood experience, including different forms of abuse and neglect, tend to have poorer outcomes (socially, vocationally, and healthwise) as adults (Baglivio et al., 2014). Families may face challenges related to housing, food insecurity, neighborhood crime, poverty, and the absence of caretakers. Considering all this, it should not be surprising that an individual's family is quite important in development across a wide range of outcomes—including juvenile and criminal involvement.

Biological factors can interact with family problems and early school experiences to further increase the risks of poorly controlled behavior. Not only are impulsive, poorly socialized children with intellectual limitations more directly at risk for criminality, but their interactions with schools that do not facilitate educational success can further discourage them from embracing social norms. Consistent with this part of the theory is a long line of research studies showing that children officially diagnosed with early conduct problems and/or attention deficit/hyperactivity disorder face a heightened likelihood of becoming adult offenders (Slobogin & Fondacoro, 2011).

Because they took hereditary and biological factors seriously, Wilson and Herrnstein have been criticized for overemphasis on genetic influence. But their theory restores psychological factors (some heritable, some not) and family interaction variables to a place of importance in criminology, which for decades was dominated by sociological concepts.

Social Labeling Theory. The most extreme version of a social–psychological theory of crime is the social labeling perspective, a different approach to learning. Its basic assumption is that society assigns labels to certain acts, which leads to the perception of deviance. Deviance is not simply based on the act itself, but also on society's reactions. Social labeling theory makes a distinction between primary deviance, or the individual's actual behavior, and secondary deviance, or society's reaction to the offending behavior (Lemert, 1972). With regard to primary deviance, offenders often rationalize their behavior as a temporary mistake, or they perceive it as part of a socially acceptable role (Lilly et al., 1989). Whether or not that self-assessment is accurate, secondary deviance serves to brand them with a more permanent "criminal" stigma.

One illustration of social labeling is the allegation that police use racial profiling as a basis for making a disproportionate number of traffic stops of minority motorists, particularly African Americans. Police officials have sometimes justified such practice as a tool for catching drug traffickers, but arresting motorists for "driving while Black" as a pretext for additional criminal investigations clearly raises the risk of harmful and inappropriate labeling, to say nothing of its discriminatory impact. The outcry over racial profiling has resulted in a call for federal legislation that would prohibit the practice and has led to litigation. This is also the kind of behavior that leads Black citizens to perceive that they are being singled out unfairly, with sometimes fatal consequences, leading to protests such as "Black Lives Matter." Such behavior also erodes the trust between citizens and police that is so important for citizens to feel safe and police to perceive that they can do their jobs effectively. The main point of **social labeling theory** is that the stigma of being branded as a crime risk can create a self-fulfilling prophecy (Merton, 1968). Even those formerly incarcerated individuals who seek to live responsibly may face stigma and bias from prospective employers and their families. Frustrated in their efforts to make good, they may adopt this label and "live up to" its negative connotations by engaging in further lawbreaking (Irwin, 1970). For example, individuals returning to the community after release from prison may need particular help with housing, employment, and family if they are to avoid becoming discouraged by stigma and negative expectations. There is evidence that the impact of social labeling is most observable in those already disadvantaged, such as children having a parent who has been involved in the criminal justice system (Besemer et al., 2017).

The social labeling approach raises our awareness about the difficulties offenders face in returning to society. It reminds us that some individuals involved in criminal behavior (e.g., those who live in high-crime neighborhoods where the police patrol often) are more likely to be inaccurately perceived to present a risk for offending—and their encounters with the police may create other problems. But the social labeling approach does not explain most criminal behavior. Nor is it favored as a primary explanation for criminal offending in contemporary society. Primary deviance (i.e., a law violation in the first place) usually has to occur before secondary deviance takes its toll, and many who break the law have been involved in offending well before ever being apprehended. Behavioral differences between people exist and persist, whatever we call them.

Integration of Theories of Crime

Where do all these theories leave us? Do any of them offer a convincing explanation of crime? Do they suggest how we should intervene to prevent or reduce crime? We do not presently have a single, comprehensive, convincing theory of crime. But knowledge about the contributors to crime has accumulated and now provides certain well-supported explanations for how repeated, violent criminality develops. Many serious offenders are extraordinarily versatile, with careers that include violent behavior, property offenses, vandalism, and substance abuse.

One implication of the discussion in this section is that individuals travel several causal pathways to different kinds of offending. No single variable causes all crime, just as no one agent causes all fevers or all upset stomachs. However, several causal factors are associated reliably with many types of criminality. Any one of these factors may sometimes be a sufficient explanation for some type of criminal behavior, but more often they act in combination to produce criminality. Our attempt to integrate these various factors (see Figure 3.1) emphasizes four contributors to crime that occur in a developmental sequence.

Our model emphasizes what we believe are the variables best supported by criminological research as causal factors in crime:

1. *Antecedent conditions.* Chances of repeated offending are increased by biological, psychological, and environmental antecedents that make it easier for certain individuals to learn to behave criminally and easier for this learning to occur in specific settings. The leading candidates for biological risk are genetic inheritance, neurochemical abnormalities, brain dysfunction, and autonomic nervous system irregularities.

    Psychological variables enhancing risk of offending include poor social skills; lower verbal intelligence; personality traits of irritability, impulsiveness, callousness, meanness, and low empathy; and deficiencies in inner restraint (or conscience). These can result in attitudes, thinking, and motivations that encourage antisocial behavior—and also render individuals less susceptible to negative consequences for misconduct. These psychological factors may accompany biological risks or may convey their own independent vulnerability to crime.

    Finally, certain environments provide opportunities and temptations for crime and help translate biological or psychological predispositions toward criminal behavior into stronger antisocial tendencies. Such environments function this way because of social impoverishment and disorganization, fundamental economic inequalities, a tradition of tolerating (or even encouraging) crime, social dissension and strife, and an abundance of inviting targets and easy victims of crime. Such environments promote offending in those who have a propensity toward crime (Wikstrom et al., 2010).

    Within family environments, high levels of mental disorders, criminality, parental absenteeism, and substance abuse also lead to more violence. These links may be forged through any of several factors: genetic influence, modeling, growing anger in the larger context of harsh living conditions, disturbed attachments with parents, or lax or overly punitive discipline that does not teach children and youth how to control behavior effectively. Research suggests that early exposure to harsh family living conditions can aggravate some of the biological factors that contribute to aggression, such as a child's physical and emotional reactions to threat (Farrington, 2019; Zelechoski, 2016).

Figure 3.1 An Integrated Model for Explaining Repeated Crime

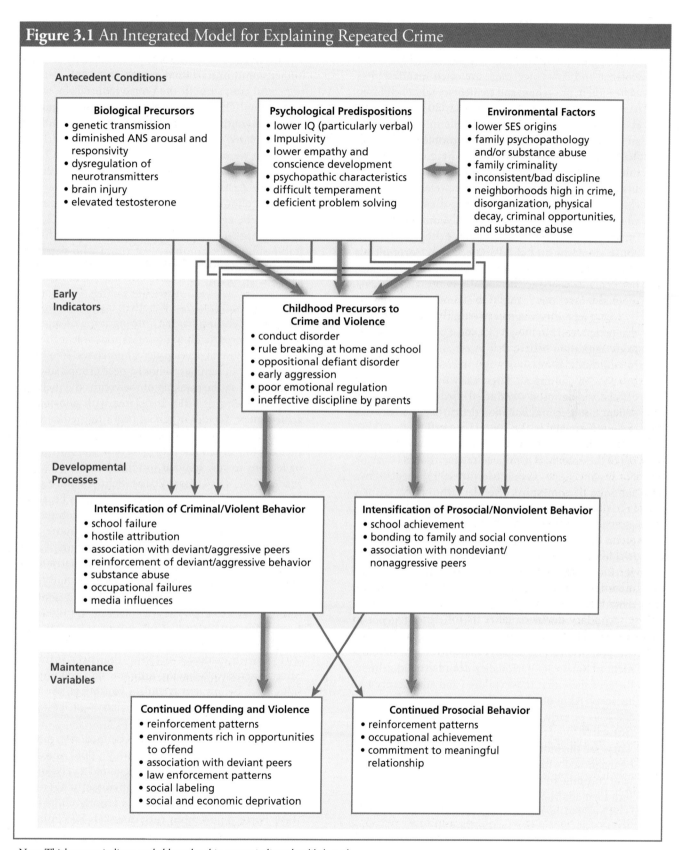

Note: Thick arrows indicate probable paths; thin arrows indicate less likely paths.

2. *Early indicators.* Repetitive antisocial conduct can be stable over time. Aggressive children often grow up to be aggressive adults, and the precedents for adult violence and substance abuse are often manifested as aggression in pre-school and elementary school children (Asendorpf et al., 2008; Farrington, 2019; Temcheff et al., 2008). Although tests can identify youth who are at elevated risk for behavioral problems, it is difficult to predict whether these individuals will continue to commit violent acts as adults. Relatively few at-risk youth commit serious, violent offenses as adults (Mulvey, 2011), but many display major long-term adjustment problems. For instance, youth identified as "at risk" in childhood may experience drug and alcohol abuse, domestic and child abuse, divorce or multiple relationships, employment problems, mental health problems, dependence on social services, and involvement in less-serious crimes (Obiakor et al., 1997).

Many repetitively aggressive adults began to exhibit that pattern early in life. In fact, most psychologists who study aggression believe that severe antisocial behavior in adulthood is nearly always preceded by antisocial behavior in childhood. These early indicators include officially diagnosed conduct disorder, oppositional defiant disorder, and attention deficit/hyperactivity disorder (Goldstein et al., 2006; Temcheff et al., 2008). Developmental models have enhanced our understanding of the onset and maintenance of antisocial behavior. For instance, one model (Moffitt, 1993) suggests two subtypes of adolescent offenders: those who display behavioral problems later in adolescence and desist in early adulthood (adolescent-limited), and the smaller group who display conduct-disordered behaviors earlier in adolescence that persist into adulthood (lifecourse persistent). Adolescent offenders in the latter group are more likely to develop antisocial personality disorder than those in the former group.

Another model suggests that early emergence of conduct-disordered behavior that is displayed across multiple and diverse settings may predict the development of antisocial personality disorder in adulthood. Reviews show that most children and adolescents who are involved in offending stop sometime in their teenage years or early 20s, but some persist into adulthood (Russell & Odgers, 2016; Woolard & Fountain, 2016). These are the individuals who are much more likely to be diagnosed with antisocial personality disorder, and who continue to be at risk for criminal offending well into their adulthood.

The "Pathways to Desistance" study (Mulvey, 2011) followed 1,354 serious juvenile offenders over a seven-year period. They reported that about 9% of youth continued in serious offending; 15% reduced their level of offending but continued, and the remainder desisted. They also indicated that quality services, longer community-based supervision, and fair and respectful contact with the police reduced the risk of reoffending. This is consistent with other longitudinal studies of youth showing that aggression in childhood was associated with adult offending, particularly for boys who were risk takers, had lower verbal IQ, and had larger and disrupted families (Farrington, 2019). In a New Zealand cohort followed from birth, 11% of males followed a trajectory of persistent aggression between the ages of 7 and 15 (Odgers et al., 2008). Among high-risk and all-offender samples, highly stable subgroups composed of those who persist in offending have been identified (Connell et al., 2012; Miller et al., 2010).

3. *Developmental processes.* Whether early indicators of criminal offending harden into patterns of repeated adult crime or soften into prosocial non-violent conduct depends on several developmental processes. These processes occur in families, schools, peer groups, and the media—and in the thinking of the youths themselves.

Delinquency is often associated with poor school achievement. Grades in school begin to predict delinquency around age 15. As adolescent youth fall further behind in school, they have fewer opportunities or reasons to stay bonded to school and to strive for academic success (Hoge, 2016). School failure seems to narrow the options for prosocial behavior because it decreases the chances of employability and job success.

Modeling and peer pressure also promote antisocial behavior in children and adolescents. Crime increases when peers support it, as is sometimes the case in the juvenile justice system itself when, through its placement of youth, those with limited experience with justice involvement are placed with others who have a longer history of offending. This has been termed the "contagion effect" (Dishion & Tipsord, 2011), with evidence showing that peer influence affects aggressive behavior, drug use, and delinquency. The more delinquent friends a youth has, the more likely they are to behave antisocially—at least until age 20 (Monahan et al., 2009).

Modeling influences can also be mediated through the media. One investigator (Murray, 2008) noted that 50 years of research strongly suggested a relationship between TV violence and the increase in aggressive attitudes, values, and behaviors among children. A Task Force report from the American Psychological Association (APA, 2015) suggests a similar relationship between violent video games and aggression. These changes may be mediated by neurological changes in children who view frequent TV violence or engage in frequent violent gaming. It is, of course, difficult to know whether there is a causal relationship between such TV, gaming, and other media violence and aggressive behavior. What makes this even more difficult is that most of the studies in this area are surveys, rather than controlled experiments. But other investigators (Glymour et al., 2008) considered these difficulties and concluded, in light of the existing evidence, that there is probably a causal relationship between exposure to TV violence and subsequent adult aggression, consistent with the conclusions about violent gaming and subsequent aggressive attitudes and behavior (APA, 2015). Despite the growing evidence of this linkage, it is not clear that U.S. courts will intervene to reduce the violence on television or in gaming. For instance, the U.S. Supreme Court overturned a California law banning the sale of violent video games to children on First Amendment grounds, protecting the free speech rights of video game makers (*Brown v. Entertainment Merchants Association*, 2011). This meant that more violent video games would be readily available to youth, perhaps leading occasionally to tragic outcomes (refer to Box 3.3). However, the Court's decision reflected the greater weight of First Amendment considerations on the decision about banning such games.

Another intensifier of aggression is alcohol and substance abuse (Bonta & Andrews, 2017; Snyder & Sickmund, 2006). Numerous influences could account for the tendency for substance abuse to lead to more crime. Alcohol is a depressant, so it might suppress the ability of certain areas of the brain to inhibit behavior effectively. The more time a youth spends abusing drugs and alcohol, the less time they have for prosocial, academic activities. Substance abuse typically results in more associations with deviant peers, thereby increasing the opportunities for antisocial behavior to be reinforced. Repeated substance abuse during adolescence can reduce youths' options for prosocial behavior. These limits, in turn, increase the reinforcing potential of antisocial conduct.

Unfortunately, these developmental processes tend to compound one another. The impulsive, lower-IQ child is more likely to struggle in school. Those who drop out of school increasingly associate with antisocial peers. Parents who fail to appropriately discipline their children when they misbehave may also show less concern about their children's Internet access and video gaming. Finally, early conduct and academic problems are strongly related to later substance abuse. At-risk youth have multiple influences that can interact to push them toward offending.

4. *Maintenance factors.* Violent offending can become an entrenched way of life when one or more of the following maintenance factors are in place. First, the short-run positive payoffs for offending are stronger and more probable than the long-term risks of apprehension and punishment. Second, the person lives in environments that are rich in opportunities for offending and low in the chances of being detected. Third, as a result of the inevitable arrests and incarcerations that repeat offenders experience, their associations with aggressive peers increase, just as contacts with law-abiding citizens decrease. Fourth, as a longer-term consequence of earlier estrangements from conventional norms and values, delinquents begin to feel growing resentment and indifference for social rules. These maintenance factors do not cause crime so much as solidify it. Once they are established, the battle is often already lost, because criminal conduct has become a part of a person's identity.

One implication of our integrative model is that preventing crime might be a better way of fighting the "crime problem" than rehabilitating offenders. Certainly, with the help of treatment programs that strengthen their social skills, build better cognitive controls, model prosocial behavior, and reinforce law-abiding conduct, some people can "turn around" a life of violent offending (Heilbrun et al., 2016). But however promising the rates of "success" in correctional rehabilitation might become, it is still likely that some who are arrested and incarcerated will continue to offend throughout their lives.

This should not be surprising. After a protracted history of learning antisocial behavior, rejecting prosocial behavior, and facing obstacles to legitimate opportunity, individuals who repeatedly offend will not be easily influenced by interventions to change offending behavior. That is why prevention becomes so important. If most at-risk youth can be reliably identified, we can then intervene in multiple areas—with individuals, families, schools, peer groups, and neighborhoods—to interrupt those processes that eventually lead youth into antisocial lifestyles. Brought about by adverse environments and the decisions of youth themselves, these processes include experimenting with alcohol and drugs, learning from violent media and subcultures, dropping out of school, failing at legitimate employment, and associating with others who break the law. These are the pathways to deviance that must be blocked early—before they become too well traveled—if meaningful change is to occur.

Summary

1. **Theories of crime can be grouped into four categories. What are they?** The most common theories can be classified into four groups: sociological, biological, psychological, and social–psychological. The "integrated theory" presented in this chapter draws upon the best-supported elements of each.

2. **Among sociological explanations of crime, how does the subcultural explanation differ from the structural explanation?** The structural explanation for crime emphasizes chronic barriers to conventional success that certain people face; these barriers include cultural and language differences, financial hardships, and limited access to resources needed for responsible functioning in society. In contrast, the subcultural explanation proposes that certain groups, such as gangs, adhere to norms that conflict with the values of others in society and encourage criminal conduct.

3. **What is emphasized in biological theories of crime?** Both genetic and physiological factors are emphasized in biological explanations of criminal behavior. Hereditary factors influence criminal behavior, but the mechanisms through which this influence is exerted are unclear. The most likely candidates involve neurotransmitters, such as serotonin, and certain subcortical and cortical brain structures, particularly the prefrontal cortex, which is responsible for monitoring behavioral inhibition, planning, and decision-making. A more specific prospect involves a mutation on the X chromosome in the gene coding for MAO-A, in combination with maltreatment as a child. Promising research on genetic predisposition to offending has focused on certain risk factors, such as educational performance, which may in turn increase the risk of criminal offending when they are problematic.

4. **What psychological factors have been advanced to explain crime?** Psychological theories of criminal behavior emphasize criminal thinking patterns or a personality disorder such as psychopathy.

5. **How do social–psychological theories view crime?** Social–psychological theories view criminal behavior as a learned response resulting from classical conditioning, reinforcement, observation or modeling, and social labeling.

6. **What are the four major categories of influence on crime described in this chapter?** Antecedent conditions, early indicators, developmental processes, and maintenance factors. Each of these categories can contain influences from the disciplines of sociology, biology, psychology, and social psychology. This can explain why the most promising approach to understanding and addressing crime presently involves drawing upon all four disciplines, looking for ways in which their influences can interact, and considering them in this kind of functional categorization.

Key Terms

adverse experience

anomie

antisocial personality disorder

biological theories of crime

classical conditioning

classical school of criminology

concordance rate

containment theory

control theory

correctional psychology

criminology

differential association reinforcement theory

dizygotic twins

executive function

extraversion

forensic psychology

Good Lives Model

learning theory

monozygotic twins

neuroticism

operant learning

positivist school of criminology

primary deviance

proportionality in sentencing

psychological theories (of crime)

psychopathy

racial profiling

Risk-Need-Responsivity

secondary deviance

social cognitive theory

social labeling theory

social learning theory

social–psychological theory (of crime)

sociological theories (of crime)

stimulation-seeking theory

structural explanations

subcultural explanations

threat assessment

trauma

vicarious learning

Chapter 4

Psychology of Police

Orienting Questions

1. What is the role of the police in our society?

2. What procedures are used to select police?

3. How has the training of police officers expanded into new areas?

4. What are the respective explanations for police conduct associated with the "bad apples" and "systemic racism" positions?

5. Describe the different activities of the police. Is law enforcement central?

6. What stressors do the police face?

7. What is the relationship between the police and the communities they serve?

8. What is the future of policing in the United States in the twenty-first century?

Psychology of Police

In any survey of public concerns, "crime" is usually near the top. This ranking stems from the nature of crime in our country, as well as from the fear that crime typically instills. As discussed in Chapter 3, crime in the United States had been decreasing for the last two decades prior to 2020, which saw an increase in violent crime and particularly in homicide. While the larger trend toward a lower crime rate is encouraging (and at odds with the frequently cited view that crime in the United States is constantly increasing), the annual economic impact of crime (whether measured in lost cash, damaged property, medical expenses, emotional trauma, or lost income due to injuries) amounts to billions of dollars.

In addition, the year 2020 witnessed a powerful focus on social justice that was greatly influenced by police encounters with citizens in which Black and other individuals of color were killed. The combination of a global pandemic that greatly limited in-person interactions and extensive attention in social media with press coverage and other reactions to fatal police-citizen encounters created a toxic environment in which minority (and other) citizens felt angry and afraid—and police felt under siege. Although there were a number of these fatal encounters, the most stark,

inexplicable, and infuriating involved the killing of George Floyd by Minneapolis police office Derek Chauvin. The murder was documented by smartphone videos taken by observers as Officer Chauvin kneeled on Mr. Floyd's neck for nine minutes. The case is described in Box 4.1.

How would we describe the police force in the U.S. at present? We can consider the number of fatal encounters with police experienced by BIPOC citizens. We can use analytic tools to better understand whether this was an anomaly, part of a trend, or something else. But there is little doubt that the *perception* of police conduct in 2020 was highly polarized. Many BIPOC citizens openly expressed fear and outrage. "Black Lives Matter" protests occurred following several police shootings. Minneapolis police had been prepared for major demonstrations if Officer Chauvin had been acquitted. He was not—he was convicted on second and third degree murder as well as manslaughter charges—but many anticipated a more limited conviction or even acquittal, the clear evidence documenting police misconduct in the video notwithstanding.

In this context, we approach the current chapter. Effective policing, always difficult, has become far more difficult in the 2020s. The mistrust between many in the BIPOC community

---

Box 4.1

The Case of George Floyd: Death of a Black Man in a Police Encounter

Minneapolis police were called by a store clerk on May 25, 2020 at about 8 P.M. to investigate the clerk's claim that George Floyd had used a counterfeit $20 bill to buy cigarettes. Four police officers—Derek Chauvin, Tou Thao, Alexander Kueng, and Thomas Lane—responded to the call. They reported that Floyd "appeared to be under the influence" and resisted these officers after he got out of his car, as ordered. This report did not indicate what occurred between the time he "resisted" and when he "appeared to be in medical distress," prompting officers to call for an ambulance. But the intervening events were documented by a bystander with a cell phone who recorded one of the officers, Derek Chauvin, kneeling on Mr. Floyd's neck while two other officers restrained his legs and the fourth kept onlookers back. Chauvin continued to kneel on his neck for nine and a half minutes, even as Mr. Floyd pleaded that he could not breathe (and after one officer could not find a pulse about six minutes into this "restraint"). Mr. Floyd was pronounced dead that night. Viewing this video was horrifying and excruciating, but it was key evidence in the subsequent trial and conviction of Derek Chauvin for second degree murder, third degree murder, and second degree manslaughter.

George Floyd restrained by Minneapolis police.

The other three officers were convicted of violating Mr. Floyd's civil rights by failing to intervene and to provide aid in time to prevent his death. (All four resigned shortly following this event.) (https://www.nytimes.com/article/George-floyd.htm).

Critical Thought Question

When, in your opinion, is physical force in the course of an arrest excessive? When does it become criminal?

and those who provide policing services is tangible. Whether police misconduct exemplified by Derek Chauvin is deeply systemic or more limited, there are strong and ongoing demands for change. In this chapter, we identify areas that might be usefully reformed and describe the arguments for such reform. One of the key questions is whether police misconduct is attributable to a small minority of "bad apples"—officers who are brutal, corrupt, racist, or whatever else might drive their misconduct, but a small minority of officers within a larger pool of those who perform effectively—or whether racial discrimination and other adverse influences are so deeply embedded in policing systems that focusing only on individual bad actors will be insufficient. This question will be discussed in more detail in this chapter.

Police are responsible for a complex set of tasks in the criminal justice system. They are the officials in the criminal justice system with whom citizens have the most contact. The police must recognize and directly respond to criminal activities, and we expect them to keep our streets safe and our homes secure. They stand for public order, their visibility and authority heightened by the uniforms they wear, the weapons they carry, and the special powers they are given. This visibility makes the police convenient targets for the public's frustrations with the criminal justice system at all times, but particularly when there has been an event involving the death of a citizen. Police are both trusted by many and mistrusted by many others—trusted because they are the first response to citizen-reported emergencies but, especially for many BIPOC individuals, mistrusted for escalating certain encounters (e.g., traffic stops) unnecessarily and increasing the risk of harm to those stopped. Consequently, some seek protection at all costs; others resist police intrusion and seek to avoid them. The balance of expectations between what police should and should not do may be shifting, but it will be extremely challenging to satisfy both sides. Some have suggested, for example, that traffic stops (with greater potential for escalation) be reduced or eliminated to reduce the risk of harm to citizens for relatively minor reasons. The counter-argument is that traffic stops in many instances lead to arrests for more serious offenses such as auto theft, driving while impaired, and possession of drugs with intent to distribute.

To be effective at their jobs, officers must have some combination of physical strength, perceptiveness, social awareness, and good judgment. They need to make quick decisions about all sorts of human behavior, often under very stressful conditions. They should know the law and have at least some familiarity with the social sciences. Despite the complexity of these demands, police are often overworked, underappreciated, and heavily criticized. These factors, along with the job pressures they face, the crime they investigate, and the isolated conditions in which they often work, can take a toll on their judgment and make some officers susceptible to corruption and abuse of power.

When we consider the police from a psychological perspective, we encounter various dilemmas. Law enforcement in a democratic society must strike a balance: protecting citizens through crime prevention and investigation while simultaneously respecting constitutional rights. Police officers investigate crime, but they must also make arrests and promote an image of stability in society. Operating within this balance can be very difficult, particularly when domestic violent extremism, cybercrime, street protests, and other challenges are added to the traditional kinds of criminal offending. But when this balance is not achieved, both effective crime control and protection of civil liberties and criminal rights can suffer. When police are perceived as treating citizens of racial, ethnic, or cultural minority status unfairly, then public trust is eroded—making it more difficult for both citizens and police to achieve the balance in which rights are respected but crime is prevented and offenders apprehended.

Another conflict arises when social scientists question the validity of techniques that the police often use, such as lineup identifications and lie detector tests, to investigate crime. Last, but of great importance to the police, is the dilemma of equality versus discretion. Related to the issue of trust and fairness, this dilemma raises important questions. Should all suspects be treated the same way or should police be able to exercise discretion in how they handle illegal activity? When should an arrest be made, and when should only a warning be issued? How much force can legitimately be used in an arrest? When does the exercise of Constitutional rights such as assembly and free speech cross the line into criminal conduct? These and other questions are discussed in this chapter.

Racial Bias in Policing

Questions involving the nature and extent of possible racial bias in policing have taken on a special urgency since the 1990s as a result of highly publicized cases in which police officers had brutally beaten suspects in their custody, or used lethal force in encountering a suspect. Many of these cases involved White officers attacking Black citizens, raising the possibility that racial bias was a motive. When present, is such bias better explained by the presence of a few officers with certain beliefs and attitudes? Is it more systemic, with the influences of how police officers are trained and supervised within their system the better way of accounting for racial bias? We discuss this briefly in this section, and at other times throughout this chapter.

Highly publicized deaths of African American citizens (mostly men) in the course of police encounters during the last decade have fueled the perception that minorities are disproportionately targeted by police. Alton Sterling in Baton Rouge, Philando Castile in Minnesota, Freddie Gray in Baltimore, Eric Garner in New York, Daunte Wright and George Floyd in Minneapolis, Breonna Taylor in Louisville, Rayshard Brooks in Atlanta, and Daniel Prude in Rochester all died in encounters with police. The widespread availability of smartphones allowing observers to video encounters and post these videos immediately on social media has meant that there is often widespread awareness of a citizen fatality within a short time. What is the evidence that minority citizens are disproportionately targeted by police and much more likely to be the victims of lethal violence?

This is not a simple question. For example, according to the Washington Post, 50% of the fatal police shootings in 2014 involved White victims and 26% involved Black victims. Between 2014 and 2020, at least 7,680 citizens reportedly died as a result of encounters with the police, with 25% of them Black—a percentage that is substantially higher than the proportion of Black citizens in the United States (https://interactive.aljazeera.com). Both would suggest that Black citizens are disproportionately the victims of fatal encounters with police. But Roland Fryer, a Harvard economist, conducted a study of 1,000 police shootings from 10 large police departments in California, Florida, and Texas (Fryer, 2019). He also studied police use of nonlethal force, and considered racial differences in both. Blacks and Hispanics were more than 50% more likely than Whites to experience some form of nonlethal force in interactions with police, a difference that could not be fully accounted for by controls for context and civilian behavior. For officer-involved shootings, however, Fryer reported no racial differences (either in the raw data or when contextual factors were considered). He concluded that some police officers have a "preference for discrimination," but this does not extend to disproportionate officer shootings of minority citizens.

So what does this evidence mean? Are police encounters with minority citizens consistently carried out without discrimination? (No.) Are most of those killed in police-involved shootings minority citizens? (No.) Is there discrimination by police that increases the number of nonlethal force events in their encounters with minority citizens? (Fryer's data support this conclusion, although the more meaningful comparison would be the percentage of legitimate criminal suspects who are stopped for good cause, rather than the percentage of a certain minority group in the general population.)

A related consideration is whether police are *perceived* to disproportionately target BIPOC individuals in cases culminating in lethal violence. The information that is widely available—certain shootings involving a Black man and a White officer for example, for which there is body camera video or observer video posted on social media—is likely to factor disproportionately into this perception. According to the cognitive bias lens termed the *availability heuristic* (Kahneman, 2011), our perception of such bias is influenced strongly by the most prominent instances available in our memory.

Selection of Police Officers

One purpose of this chapter is to examine the police officer from a psychological perspective. How are police officers selected? Do the selection criteria work? Do police officers share certain personality characteristics? How are the police trained, and does training improve their performance on the job? Can the police officer's image in the community be improved?

Certainly there is much evidence, both from scientific studies and the accounts of individuals, that racial discrimination continues to be a very real problem in the United States and in police departments nationwide. Police officers, as the public face of law enforcement, must pursue the challenging combination of keeping the public's trust while preventing crime and apprehending offenders. Are certain police officers more inclined to use unnecessary force? If so, can they be identified in advance and screened out of police work?

Psychological evaluation of police personnel began in 1916 when Lewis Terman, the Stanford University psychologist who revised Alfred Binet's intelligence scales to produce the Stanford-Binet intelligence test, tested the intelligence of 30 applicants for police and firefighter jobs in San Jose, California. Terman (1917) found that the average IQ among these applicants was 84 and recommended that no one with an IQ below 80 be accepted for these jobs. A few years later, L. L. Thurstone tested the intelligence of 358 Detroit policemen, using the Army Alpha Intelligence Examination. Like Terman, he reported below-average IQ scores, and he also found that police of higher ranks scored lower than entry-level patrolmen.

Throughout the years, psychologists continued to assess police candidates, although in a way that was often unsystematic and poorly evaluated. In 1955, only 14 American cities with populations greater than 100,000 formally tested police candidates; by 1965, only 27% of local police agencies reported some psychological evaluation of applicants (Ostrov, 1986). In the 1960s and 1970s, the period when police psychology became an established specialty, several national commissions recommended formal psychological assessment of police personnel in all departments. By the mid-1980s, 11 states required psychological screening of police candidates, and more than 50% of the country's departments psychologically screened beginning police

Early in encounter between police officer and a citizen.

officers (Benner, 1986). By the 1990s, formal assessment of police candidates had become routine, due in part to attempts by municipal governments to prevent or defeat lawsuits claiming that they were liable for dangerous or improper conduct by their police employees. This has continued into the 2000s (Corey & Zelig, 2020).

Psychological evaluation of police applicants can focus on selecting candidates who appear most psychologically fit—or on eliminating individuals who appear least suited for police work. Most selection methods are developed to screen out inappropriate candidates, because it is very difficult to agree on the "ideal" police profile. Despite concerns about the validity of psychological evaluations in police selection, some (Bartol & Bartol, 2006) believe that psychological screening is useful in the selection process and should be included. However, the current standards for screening may not be sufficient. Psychological tests are currently used to assess levels of psychopathology that may interfere with officers' abilities to perform their duties rather than focusing on specific skills or capacities that are directly relevant to police work (Detrick & Chibnall, 2008; Detrick et al., 2001).

In general, the courts have upheld the legality of psychological screening of police candidates as long as the evaluation and testing involved do not violate the provisions of various civil rights acts or the Americans with Disabilities Act and are in compliance with federal guidelines. If it were your task to select police officers from a pool of applicants, what psychological qualities would you look for? Your answers would probably reflect your values, as well as your impression of what police officers do. Among the psychological characteristics usually cited in such a list are the following:

- *Incorruptible*: A police officer should be of high moral character. Reports of officers taking bribes or framing innocent suspects are especially disturbing, because the police officer should treat all citizens fairly within the rules of law.

- *Well adjusted*: A police officer should be able to carry out the stressful duties of the job without becoming seriously and continuously affected by the stress. Officers are always in the public view. They need to be thick-skinned enough to operate without defensiveness, yet they must be attentive to the needs of others. They also need to cope with the dangers of their jobs, including the constant awareness that injury or death could occur at any time.

- *People oriented*: A police officer's major duty is service to others. An officer needs to have a genuine interest in people and compassion for them. Part of this orientation involves showing respect for all citizens, and the absence of bias toward minority individuals. For example, the Mobile, Alabama police department publishes online a set of "mutual respect guidelines" for citizens and police officers that includes "treat all citizens with respect," "address adults as 'ma'am' or 'sir,'" and "explain the reason for the interaction" (https://www.mobilepd.org/youth/mutual-respect-guidelines/).

- *Free of overly emotional reactions*: Although a certain caution and suspicion may be useful on the job, the police officer should be free of impulsive, overly aggressive reactions and other responses in which emotions overcome the discipline imposed by training. Restraint is essential because officers are trained to take an active stance in crime detection and are even encouraged by their superiors to be wary of what is happening around them (Barber et al., 2009).

- *Dedicated*: Officers should be committed to their jobs, and not be inclined toward frequent lateness or absenteeism or have personal problems that interfere with this commitment in an ongoing way.

- *Disciplined*: Police officers should be team players, able to function effectively within a chain of command. This includes the ability to give orders to supervisees and accept orders from superior officers.

- *Logical*: Police officers should be able to examine a crime scene and develop hypotheses about what happened and what characteristics might be present in the person who committed the offense.

Keep these characteristics in mind as we discuss particular approaches to evaluating police candidates. To what extent can each of these characteristics be accurately assessed? There are several reported purposes for evaluating police candidates. Generally it is important to focus on *functional capacities*—those characteristics that are specifically related to effective police work (Corey & Zelig, 2020). These might include reliability, capacity for communication and regulation of emotion, and responsibility. Psychological evaluation seeks both to identify promising candidates and to screen out those with specific problems that would interfere with their effective functioning as police officers.

The selection of police officer candidates can involve up to 10 steps: (1) application/prescreening, (2) entrance exam (focusing on reading, writing, problem-solving, judgment, and memory), (3) simulated scenario and verbal response, (4) physical fitness, (5) background investigation, (6) drug testing, (7) psychological testing, (8) polygraph, (9) oral interview, and (10) medical exam (International Association of Chiefs of Police [IACP], 2016). Consulting psychologists can provide parts of the entrance exam, simulated scenario, psychological testing, and oral interview. More specifically, psychologists may conduct or participate in an interview, observe candidates' responses to simulated scenarios, and provide testing. How much emphasis different psychologists place on these procedures depends on several factors, including their professional background and training, the resources available for the evaluation, and the focus of the assessment (e.g., different strategies will be used for assessing mental disorders than for predicting what type of person will do best in which kind of position; various police departments will use somewhat different approaches to personnel selection).

The Interview

Personal interviews are the most widely employed tool, despite evidence that interviews are subject to distortion, low reliability, and questionable validity. The extent to which an interview yields the same information on different occasions or with different interviewers (*reliability*) and the degree to which that information is accurately related to important job performance criteria (*validity*) have not been clearly established for most police selection interviews.

However, there is good evidence that reliability, at least, is increased by the use of structured interviews—those in which the wording, order, and content of the interview are standardized (Rogers, 2001). It is possible for police departments to construct their own structured interviews for personnel selection purposes, using established guidelines (U.S. Office of Personnel Management, 2008), to more effectively use the advantages of structured interviewing.

Interviews are a necessary part of an evaluation, according to guidelines recommended by police psychologists (Dantzker, 2010). They are also valuable as a rapport-building introduction to the evaluation process. They increase applicants' cooperation while reducing their apprehension. Interviews are also popular because they can be flexible and economical. However, because they are subject to distortions and impression management by candidates, interviews are still more useful for orienting candidates to the evaluation than for predicting subsequent performance. Whether such interviews in the future will make more use of remote technology, using platforms such as Zoom and Microsoft Teams that were employed so much during the pandemic work conditions of 2020, remains to be seen.

Situational Tests

Situational tests incorporate tasks that are similar to those that will actually be undertaken by officers on the job. They are designed to predict performance in the training academy and in the field. At one time, this approach was a widely discussed aspect of police selection, involving tasks such as observing patrols, analyzing clues, and discussing cases (Mills et al., 1966), but does not appear to be used at present—although situational *components*, such as simulations and candidate responses, are still incorporated (IACP, 2016). The time intensiveness and cost of situational tests apparently led to the preference for more focused situational tasks such as report writing that are common aspects of police work. (For one part of the National Police Officer Selection Test (POST), refer to http://www.kacp.cc/misc/post.pdf.)

Psychological Tests

Many standardized psychological tests have good reliability and can be objectively scored and administered to large groups of participants at the same time. Consequently, they are important in police screening. Two types of tests are included in most selection batteries: tests of cognitive or intellectual ability and tests of personality traits, integrity, or emotional stability. This is consistent with the goals of identifying abnormal behavior and symptoms, and describing functioning relative to others in the general population (Corey & Zelig, 2020).

Police officers tend to score in the average to above-average range on intelligence tests (Brewster & Stoloff, 2003), and intelligence tends to correlate fairly strongly with the performance of police recruits in their training programs. However, intelligence scores are only weakly related to actual police performance in the field (Bartol, 1983; Brewster & Stoloff, 2003). This underscores a point made earlier: it is challenging to predict good job performance, but more straightforward to identify problem areas or deficits in candidates that could interfere with good performance. This is a consideration throughout our discussion of police officer selection.

The Minnesota Multiphasic Personality Inventory (MMPI; the 1989 revision of this test is called the MMPI-2, the 2008 revision is the MMPI-2-RF, and the 2020 revision the MMPI-3) is the test of personality most often used in police screening; other psychological tests often used in police selection are the California Psychological Inventory (CPI) and the Sixteen Personality Factor Questionnaire (16PF). Evidence for the validity of these tests in screening out candidates unsuitable for police work is mixed. There is research supporting the validity of the MMPI (Bartol, 1991), the MMPI-2 (Weiss et al., 2003), the MMPI-2-RF (Tarescavage et al., 2015), and the CPI (Roberts et al., 2019), although others (e.g., Hogg & Wilson, 1995) have questioned the general value of psychological testing of police recruits.

One personality test developed in 1979 specifically to identify psychologically unsuitable law enforcement candidates is the Inwald Personality Inventory (IPI; Detrick & Chibnall, 2002; Inwald, 1992; Inwald et al., 1983). It is a behaviorally based personality measure designed and validated specifically for use in high-risk occupations, such as law enforcement. Consisting of 26 scales that tap past and present behaviors presumed to have special relevance for law enforcement applicants (Lack of Assertiveness, Trouble with Law and Society, Undue Suspiciousness, and Driving Violations, for example), it can predict poor job performance better than traditional tests of personality and psychopathology such as the MMPI and its revisions (Inwald, 2008). Despite the promise and empirical support associated with the original IPI, its revision (the IPI-2) from 2012 has not been the subject of peer-reviewed studies (Corey & Zelig, 2020), and so it is no longer useful in police officer selection. Another written tool developed for the selection of entry-level police officers is the POST, noted earlier as having a job situational component. In addition to incident report writing, the POST measures arithmetic and reading comprehension. It has demonstrated adequate reliability and validity in some research (Henry & Rafilson, 1997; Rafilson & Sison, 1996). It has also been mandated as a statewide screening measure in several states, and adopted by the police chiefs' associations in some jurisdictions. It remains in use as of 2022.

The Validity of Police Screening

Although experts disagree on the usefulness of psychological screening of police, they all agree that good empirical research on this topic is difficult to conduct (Corey & Zelig, 2020; Inwald, 2008). Studying predictive validity using actual police performance in the field as the outcome is time-consuming and expensive, so most departments do not do this. Instead, they employ research that examines the relationship between screening results and performance by police recruits in police academies or training schools. This relationship is usually positive, but success or failure in the training academy is of less interest than actual performance as a police officer. One fairly inexpensive form of assessment involves gathering peer ratings from trainees as they progress through their training classes together; these ratings have been shown to correlate with job retention of police officers (Meier et al., 2016).

Another problem with studies of validity is that the police candidates who do poorly on screening evaluations are eliminated from the pool of trainees and potential employees. Although this decision is reasonable, it makes it impossible to study whether predictions of poor performance by these individuals were valid.

In addition, applicants for police work, like applicants for most jobs, are likely to try to present an unrealistically positive image of themselves. They may deny or underreport symptoms of mental illness, answer questions to convey a socially desirable impression, and respond as they believe a psychologically healthy individual generally would. If evaluators fail to detect such "fake good" test-taking strategies, they may mistakenly identify some candidates with significant behavioral health problems as well-adjusted. For these reasons, tests such as the MMPI-3 include various validity scales intended to detect test takers who are trying to "fake good" (Ben-Porath & Tellegen, 2020). Research on these scales in earlier versions of the MMPI-3 (i.e., the MMPI-2-RF) has shown that they are useful in detecting defensiveness and deception by some candidates for police positions (Ben-Porath et al., 2017).

Finally, selecting adequate criteria to measure effective police performance is difficult. Supervisor ratings are often inflated or biased by factors that are irrelevant to actual achievements or problems. Police unions may limit the accurate description of officer misconduct. In some departments, especially smaller ones, individual police officers are expected to perform so many diverse functions that it becomes unreasonable to expect specific cognitive abilities or psychological traits to be related in the same way to various aspects of performance. In addition, if we are interested in predicting which officers will act in risky or inappropriate ways, our predictions will be complicated by the fact that such behaviors are relatively rare. As a consequence, predictions about such inappropriate behavior will yield many "false positives"—erroneous predictions in which predicted events do not actually occur.

Fitness-for-Duty Evaluations

Another type of psychological assessment of police officers is the fitness-for-duty evaluation. As a result of stress, injuries, a life-threatening incident, a series of problems, or other indicators that an officer may be psychologically impaired, police administrators can order officers to undergo an evaluation of fitness to continue performing their duties (Corey & Zelig, 2020).

Such evaluations pose difficulties for everyone involved. Administrators must balance the need to protect the public from a potentially impaired officer against the legal right of the officer to privacy and fair employment. Clinicians must navigate a narrow path between a department's need to know the results of such an evaluation and the officer's expectation that the results will be kept confidential. Finally, the officers themselves face a dilemma: They can be honest and reveal problems that could disqualify them from service, or they can distort their responses to protect their jobs and consequently miss the opportunity for potentially beneficial treatment.

Two different models of fitness-for-duty evaluations have been used. In the first, a department uses the same psychologist to perform the evaluation and to provide whatever treatment is necessary for the officer. In the other, the psychologist who evaluates the officer does not provide any treatment; this avoids an ethical conflict between keeping the therapy confidential (as part of duty to the patient) and disclosing an officer's psychological functioning to supervisors (as part of duty to the department). The second approach is endorsed in the "Guidelines for Fitness for Duty Evaluations" distributed by the Police Psychological Services Section of the International Association for Chiefs of Police (IACP, 2013).

Training of Police Officers

Once police candidates have been selected, they participate in a course of police training that usually lasts several months. Many major American cities require 24 weeks of training, with 40 hours of training per week. Smaller jurisdictions have training programs averaging 14–16 weeks.

A number of departments now require that police officers complete at least some college education.

Two types of criticism of police training programs are common. One is that after rigorous selection procedures, few trainees fail the training. In a sample of 724 recruits from 15 police academies focusing on cadets who began training in 2015–2016, only about 9% either dropped out or failed mandatory academic or physical endurance exercises (Korre et al., 2019). A second criticism is that there is insufficient training in the field, as well as a lack of close supervision of trainees during the time they spend on patrol. The limited time that trainees spend with veteran training officers on patrol may give them a false sense of security and deprive them of opportunities to learn different ways of responding to citizens from various cultural backgrounds or resolving disputes other than through arrests.

In this context, it is very important to consider possible solutions. **Active Bystandership for Law Enforcement** (ABLE) is one such possible solution (described in Box 4.2). This is a project developed through Georgetown University Law Center's Innovative Policing Program. It reflects a collaboration of leaders in civil rights and law enforcement, and provides officers with strategies that are intended to reduce officer mistakes, prevent misconduct, and promote health and wellness. It aims to build a police culture in which intervening with fellow officers who engage in misconduct is encouraged, and becomes part of the department's culture by replacing silence in the face of such misconduct. It has been selected for use by over 30 police agencies, including those in Baltimore, Boston, Cleveland, Denver, and Philadelphia (https://www.law.georgetown.edu /news/police-departments-across-country-embrace-active -bystandership-to-prevent-harm/).

Training in Crisis Intervention

The police are often asked to maintain public order and defuse volatile situations involving persons who may have behavioral health challenges, or be intoxicated, angry, or motivated by politically extreme views. Because of the instability of the participants in such disputes, they pose risks to the police as well as to bystanders. In this section, we examine three types of crisis situations to which police are often called: incidents involving citizens with mental illness, family disturbances, and the taking of hostages. Psychologists have made important contributions to each of these areas by conducting research, designing interventions, and training the police in crisis intervention skills.

Interactions with Mentally Ill Citizens

For the past five decades, several influences have forced persons with mentally illness from residential mental health facilities, where they formerly lived, into a variety of noninstitutional settings, including halfway houses, community mental health centers, hospital emergency rooms, detoxification facilities, the streets, and local jails. Deinstitutionalization itself is an admirable goal; spending much of one's life in an institution can breed dependency,

---

Box 4.2

Could Bystander Training for Police Prevent Harm to Future Citizens?

One of the most powerful influences on police behavior and potential misconduct comes from other police officers. That is a fundamental tenet of ABLE (Active Bystandership for Law Enforcement), which advocates say can transform the culture of a police department. Adapted from a New Orleans Police program developed in 2015 called EPIC (Ethical Policing is Courageous), ABLE seeks to train police officers around the county, in a 20-hour training program over four days, not only that they *should* intervene when they witness fellow officers engage in misconduct (e.g., excessive force, gratuitous disrespect), but *how* to intervene. Police departments that incorporate ABLE training and philosophy into their service provide broad support for individual officers who might offer such intervention, meaning that an intervening officer is much more likely to receive support from the department *and* fellow officers. Among the cities that have adopted ABLE as part of their policing are Baltimore, Boston, Denver, Portland, OR, Seattle, Washington DC—and Minneapolis. (https://www.startribune.com/minneapolis -police-to-get-training-on-how-to-intervene-with-fellow -cops-who-are-using-excessive-forc/600.)

Critical Thought Question
How can ABLE be understood as a response to systemic racism in police departments?

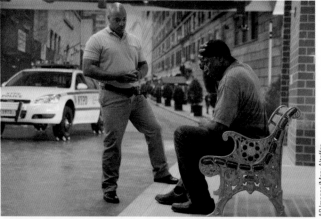

Crisis Intervention Team Training for Police.

despair, and hopelessness. People with mental illness should receive treatment in the least restrictive environment possible, allowing them to function in and contribute to their local communities. (Indeed, the contemporary focus is on the recovery of as many aspects of life as possible, rather than simply the control of symptoms and the maintenance of stability, for people with mental illness.) However, the evidence on how people with such illness have fared suggests that deinstitutionalization in the United States has not achieved its lofty goals. The problems stem from two fundamental difficulties.

First, despite important advances in medication and nonmedical interventions, severe mental illness can be difficult to treat effectively. The impairments associated with disorders such as schizophrenia and serious mood disorders can be profound, and relapses are common. For example, less than a third of non-hospitalized persons with schizophrenia are employed at any given time. Second, sufficient funding for alternative, non-institutional care has not been provided in the United States. As a result, community-based treatment of severely mentally ill persons seldom takes place under proper circumstances, despite the fact that the economic costs of severe mental disorders rival those of diseases such as cancer and heart disease and could be reduced considerably if proper care were provided.

One consequence of deinstitutionalization is that supervising people with mental illness has become a primary responsibility for the police. One review (Reuland et al., 2009) indicated that:

- The majority of law enforcement encounters with people with mental illness are for low-level charges, or for simply being a nuisance.

- The majority of such encounters are resolved by talking, rather than taking the individual into custody or to treatment.

- Possible suicide or self-harm is one of the reasons for encounters with police in an estimated 10–30% of cases.

- There is a small subset of individuals who have repeated encounters with police.

Such encounters with individuals who may have behavioral health problems are a substantial part of police responsibilities. It has been estimated that at least 20% of calls for police involve a substance use or mental health crisis (Abramson, 2021). Large-scale studies (e.g., Teplin, 1984) and broader reviews (e.g., Dvoskin et al., 2020) support the finding that individuals with mental illness are more likely to be arrested and incarcerated for reasons related to the active display of symptoms.

We will discuss some of the influences that may affect the risk of arrest for individuals with mental illness. This is important for a variety of reasons, including the minimization of fatal encounters between police officers and citizens. The *Washington Post* has maintained a database of fatal police shootings between 2015 and the present (most recently updated 3-1-22). Of the 5,105 citizens killed in the course of police encounters during this period, more than 20% (1,495) were apparently experiencing mental illness (https://www.washingtonpost.com/graphics/investigations/police-shootings-database/?itid=lk_inline_manual_3).

The Memphis Police Department started the Memphis **Crisis Intervention Team** (CIT) program after such a fatal encounter with an individual with mental illness. This approach has now become known as the "Memphis Model" for crisis intervention (CIT National Advisory Board, 2006). It was designed to increase officer and public safety while attempting to redirect those with mental illness from the judicial system to the mental health system. Along with these broad goals, the program provides law enforcement officers with the tools and skills necessary for dealing with mentally ill persons. Many police departments around the country have started their own CIT programs, some based on this "Memphis Model." A pilot program in Philadelphia made news because two officers, trained in CIT, were able to use their newly acquired skills in communicating with people with behavioral health disorders. Encountering a man who was very depressed and had climbed up on a bridge, these officers talked to him—and convinced him to come down, preventing a possible suicide. Not surprisingly, this pilot program became a full-scale attempt to train as many police officers as possible in CIT. As of 2021, more than 50% of Philadelphia officers had received this training (https://www.phila.gov/2020-11-13-our-commitment-to-making-police-and-mental-health-operational-reforms/).

There is mixed evidence on the effectiveness of CIT. Earlier reviews (Compton et al., 2008; Heilbrun et al., 2012) yielded several conclusions. First, this research provided support for the notion that CIT may be an effective way to link individuals with mental illnesses with indicated mental health treatment. Second, the training component of CIT may have a favorable impact on officers' attitudes, beliefs, and knowledge about these interactions; CIT-trained officers report feeling better prepared for their encounters with individuals with mental illnesses. Finally, CIT may result in a lower arrest rate and lower associated criminal justice costs than other diversionary approaches. Most studies show that diversion from prosecution upon first encounter with police (facilitated by CIT) is associated with greater time in the community, fewer subsequent arrests, less homelessness, greater treatment participation, and fewer community hospital days (Heilbrun et al., 2012). A more recent review (Rogers et al., 2019) concluded that CIT has beneficial officer-level outcomes such as officer satisfaction and reported less likelihood of using force, as well as the important outcome of prebooking diversion from jails to mental health facilities. This review also concluded, however, that there was limited evidence for CIT effectiveness using outcomes such as number of arrests, injury to officers or citizens, or reduced use of force.

The importance of evaluating how police interact with individuals with mental illness is underscored by the prevalence of individuals with mental illness in prisons and jails. The Bureau of Justice Statistics (2017) estimated that during 2011–2012, 26% of jail inmates met present criteria for "serious psychological distress" and over 40% reported some history of a mental health problem. This was somewhat less frequent among individuals in prison (14% reporting present serious psychological distress; nearly 40% describing some history of a mental health problem). Whether one uses the narrow definition (Steadman et al., 2009) of "serious mental illness" or the broader BJS (2017) definitions of "mental health problem" or "serious psychological distress," the proportion of those incarcerated who have this kind of difficulty is substantial.

The jailing of mentally ill persons does not reflect improper behavior by the police as much as a failure of public policy regarding the treatment and protection of people with serious mental illness. More and better training of police officers in the recognition and short-term management of mentally ill persons is necessary, but an adequate resolution to this problem requires better organization and funding of special services for those with serious mental illness (Griffin et al., 2015).

One possibility is to increase the use of **jail diversion programs** through community-based alternatives for justice-involved individuals with severe mental illness. The first contact between mentally ill individuals and the justice system is most often the police; to the extent that police are trained to use options other than arrest in such encounters, the number of justice-involved mentally ill individuals may decrease (Munetz & Griffin, 2006). Such diversion, or other community-based services, can be effective in providing needed services to individuals with severe mental illness without a commensurate increase in their risk of reoffending (Heilbrun et al., 2012).

Domestic Disturbances

When violence erupts in a family or between a couple, the police are often the first people called to the scene. What will they encounter when they arrive? Are the participants armed? Are they intoxicated or high? Do they experience behavioral health problems? How much violence has already taken place?

Responding to family disturbances is one of the most dangerous activities that police perform. The level of danger involved when intervening in a domestic dispute is not surprising, considering that strangers (not known to the victim) perpetrated only around 40% of the violent crime between 2005 and 2020—with the remaining violence perpetrated by family members, neighbors, and others known to the victim (Bureau of Justice Statistics, 2010, 2015a, 2021). During the period 2006–2015, there was an average of 1.3 million non-fatal domestic violence victimizations, with police notified of more than half—and arrests resulting in 39% of cases (Bureau of Justice Statistics, 2017). But in fewer than half the cases was a criminal complaint filed,

for reasons including privacy (32%), protecting the perpetrator (21%), and fear of reprisal (19%). The frequency and complexity of domestic violence complaints are reasons why about 90% of local police departments serving 250,000 or more residents have a full-time domestic violence unit (Bureau of Justice Statistics, 2017).

Empirical research can help improve our understanding of domestic violence. Research tells us that domestic violence is perpetrated by both men and women, and at comparable rates, although males are responsible for more serious violence and greater harm (Straus, 2011). (One way to understand this involves the presence of risk factors rather than the assumption that being male is the primary or exclusive influence on domestic violence. When risk factors are present—and we will now describe them—they influence this behavior in both men and women.) Risk factors include history of such violence (behavior, threats, escalation, violations of court orders, and related attitudes) as well as broader psychosocial adjustment (other serious criminality, relationship problems, employment and/or financial problems, substance abuse, and mental disorder) (Kropp et al., 2010). None of these influences alone is sufficient to result in domestic violence, but the presence of one or more does increase the risk of such conduct. Some of these factors might be known to responding officers when they encounter a domestic violence complaint—but in many cases, officers must make a judgment based on what they are told and what they can observe in the immediate situation.

How might we explain the behavior of individuals who are victimized by domestic violence but do not take steps to protect themselves? Such steps might include leaving the relationship, seeking a protective order, or pursuing the arrest and prosecution of a domestically violent partner. Recall some of the reasons cited for not signing a criminal complaint when police officers arrive (protecting the perpetrator, fear of reprisal), and also consider the concepts of **learned helplessness** (Walker, 1979) and **coercive control** (Dichter et al., 2018) in accounting for why some endure violence over a long period. Walker observed that women who suffer continued physical violence at the hands of their partners have a more negative self-concept than women whose relationships are free from violence. She proposed that repeated violence results in victims feeling that they won't be able to protect themselves from further assaults and that they are incapable of controlling the events in their lives. Dichter and colleagues found that women in relationships in which they experienced coercive control exerted by a partner were more likely to experience higher rates of physical, psychological, and sexual interpersonal violence—and were themselves more likely to use violence, in a way that was described as a "survival strategy."

Because of their danger and frequency, domestically violent events pose a difficult challenge for the police. Can these encounters be handled in a manner that protects potential victims, reduces repeat offenses, and limits the risk of injury to responding officers?

Much of the specialized police training during the last two decades has been associated with the Crisis Intervention Team approach. (Although work in the 1960s was termed "crisis intervention," the CIT approach of the 2000s is more formal and widespread.) CIT officers are trained to use techniques that facilitate non-violent resolutions and fewer arrests when individuals have behavioral health problems. Such problems are frequently seen in domestic disturbances.

This approach is different from policies begun by many police departments in the 1970s that called for the arrest and prosecution of those who commit domestic violence. Is arrest a better alternative than crisis intervention or counseling?

The first well-controlled evaluation of the effects of arresting domestic batterers was the Minneapolis Domestic Violence Experiment (Sherman & Berk, 1984). In this experiment, police officers' responses to domestic violence were randomly assigned to (1) arresting the suspected batterer, (2) ordering one of the parties to leave the residence, or (3) giving the couple immediate advice on reducing their violence. Judging from official police records and interviews with victims, subsequent offending was reduced by almost 50% when the suspect was arrested, a significantly better outcome than that achieved by the two nonarrest alternatives. These findings quickly changed public and expert opinion about the value of arresting domestic batterers, and soon many cities had replaced informal counseling with immediate arrest as their response to domestic violence cases.

Since the initial Minneapolis Experiment, at least five other jurisdictions—Charlotte, Colorado Springs, Miami, Omaha, and Milwaukee—have conducted studies designed to test whether arresting batterers is the best deterrent to repeated domestic violence. The results of these projects, collectively known as the Spouse Assault Replication Program, have shown that across all five sites, arresting the violent partner was associated with reduced future victimization, independent of other criminal justice sanctions or individual factors (Maxwell et al., 2002). Some other research suggests that civil protection orders may have an effect that is comparable to arrest (Broidy et al., 2016). The clear superiority of criminalizing domestic violence by promoting the arrest and prosecution of the perpetrator has been debated, however (Goodmark, 2020), leaving open the prospect of more rehabilitation-oriented alternatives that can be shown to function effectively.

What conclusion should we reach about the value of arrest as a deterrent to future intimate partner abuse? At this point, the bulk of the evidence points to the greater effectiveness of arrest and other legal mechanisms (e.g., protection orders) as a deterrent, when compared to counseling and diversion, for reducing the risk of future intimate partner violence. The impact of problem-solving courts, however, combining legal mechanisms with rehabilitation, may be greater than simply diverting an individual into rehabilitation without ongoing monitoring.

Questions about how best to limit domestic violence illustrate an interesting phenomenon often encountered with social reforms. Social problems and well-intentioned efforts to modify them tend to revolve in cycles rather than moving in a straight line toward progress and increased sophistication. A reform implemented at one time, aimed at correcting some social wrong, often fosters its own difficulties or inequities and ultimately becomes itself a problem in need of reforming at some later time.

The other important point, however, is that we cannot judge what is effective without gathering outcome data in a systematic way. Anecdotal impressions and highly publicized single cases, as much as they may resonate with the general public, do not provide a well-informed basis for decisions involving publicly funded social policies. It may also be that treatment-oriented resolutions such as those used in CIT and problem-solving courts are appropriate in some cases (e.g., seriously mentally ill individuals who have discontinued prescribed medication) but not in others (e.g., individuals with a history of battering their partner, and who inflict serious injury in the course of a violent episode).

Hostage Negotiation and Terrorism

Most experts agree that the massacre of 11 Israeli athletes taken hostage and murdered by Palestinian terrorists at the 1972 Munich Olympic Games spurred the creation of modern law enforcement techniques for resolving hostage incidents. Developed through extensive collaboration among military, law enforcement, and behavioral science experts, these hostage negotiation techniques are still being refined as more is learned about the conditions that lead to effective negotiations.

Four types of hostage situations have been described (Hatcher et al., 1998). The first type, describing more than half of hostage incidents, involves persons experiencing a mental disorder or serious personal or family problems

Police negotiators talk with hostage takers.

Jochen Tack/Image Broker/Newscom

(Feldmann, 2001). In these situations, the hostage takers often have a history of depression, schizophrenia, or other serious mental illness, or they harbor feelings of chronic powerlessness, anger, or despondency that compel a desperate act. Disturbed hostage takers pose a high risk of suicide, which they sometimes accomplish by killing their hostage(s) and then themselves. In other situations, they try to force the police to kill them; such victim-precipitated deaths are termed **suicide by cop**. This underscores the importance of incorporating mental health consultants' expertise into the effort to peacefully negotiate and resolve these hostage situations.

A second common type of hostage situation involves the *trapped offender*. Here, a person who is trapped by the police while committing a crime takes any hostage who is available and then uses the hostage to bargain for freedom. Because these incidents are unplanned and driven by panic, they tend to be very dangerous to the victims and the police, especially in their early stages.

The third type of hostage situation, involving convicted offenders, is the *takeover of prisons* by inmates who take other inmates or correctional officers as hostages. In these incidents, the passage of time may *not* increase the prospect of a non-violent resolution if the hostage takers, working as an undisciplined group with volatile leadership, have a high potential for violence.

Consider the following comment, on the relationship between psychology and hostage negotiation, by police psychologist Laurence Miller:

> Hostage negotiation is *all* about psychology, and successful crisis negotiators are among the most skilled practical psychologists I've ever met. Think about it: In the typical hostage scenario, lives are at imminent risk of violent death at the hands of a depressed, suicidal, homicidal, delusional, drug-fueled, or cold-blooded hostage-taker, often in the midst of a chaotic and uncontrolled workplace or family environment. Resolution of hostage crises may take hours or even days of incredibly focused and intense negotiation, and require the use of virtually every type of skilled communication strategy in the crisis intervention skillbox (2007, http://www.policeone.com/standoff/articles/1247470-Hostage-negotiations-Psychological-strategies-for-resolving-crises/).

This kind of hostage negotiation and skill application is most relevant to the three kinds of hostage situations just identified: an individual with a behavioral health disorder, an offender who is trapped, and a takeover of a correctional facility.

The fourth type of hostage taking, and the one that is most widely publicized, involves **terrorism**. Terrorists use violence or the threat of violence to achieve social, political, or religious aims—but in a way that is outside the traditional rules and constraints of war (Lake, 2002). Historically the term "terrorism" has focused on individuals from countries outside the United States. although there has been a recognition that **domestic violent extremists** should be included among those whose ideology and actions are outside the traditional constraints on civil conduct. This was illustrated starkly on January 6, 2021 when supporters of then-president Donald Trump stormed and briefly occupied the United States Capitol building in an apparent attempt to impede the certification of the election of Joe Biden as president.

Terrorists usually make plans in advance for the kidnapping of hostages or the taking of property, and they are typically motivated by extremist political or religious goals. One common aspect to both domestic and international terrorists is **grievance**—the perception that others have committed a wrong that must be redressed. Doing so may require their own deaths as a necessary but "honorable" sacrifice for a higher cause. For this reason, terrorists are less responsive to negotiation techniques that appeal to rational themes of self-preservation. Therefore, new ways of responding to this type of terrorism must be sought.

One terrorism specialist suggested that a country has three options in responding to international terrorism. At the lowest level of response, it may increase its internal security to prevent further attacks. A more proactive response may be to attempt to capture or eliminate the terrorists in a limited operation targeting the leaders of the terrorist organizations. Lastly, a country may implement a military retaliation with the aims of eradicating the terrorists and their organizations and deterring future attacks from other groups (Lake, 2002). Might this provide some guidance for domestic violent extremism? Using the military against U.S. citizens is generally not feasible, although National Guard troops can be used when there is a risk of violence as part of public demonstrations. Perhaps the larger point, however, is that efforts such as increasing internal security, or actively seeking to arrest and prosecute individuals who violate domestic laws, will first require that the issue of domestic violent extremism be taken seriously as a threat to the welfare of the country.

How difficult is it to identify those who might become involved in terrorism, either domestic or foreign? One review (Monahan, 2012) effectively described the challenges to assessing an individual's risk for terrorist activity in the same way that the field has assessed the risk of criminal violence for nearly 30 years: the idea of releasing and observing some "at risk" individuals to determine if they are involved in terrorist activities, a necessary part of research validation of a risk assessment measure, is obviously unacceptable from a public safety standpoint. Even retrospective validation, such as assessing individuals incarcerated for terrorist acts and comparing them with a control sample of individuals who had not committed such acts, would be enormously challenging from a practical perspective. Monahan pointed out that there are different kinds of "terrorist" activities that could be considered in a risk assessment, so specifying the target of the assessment (e.g., specific types of terrorism, specific phases in the process of becoming a terrorist, specific roles in terrorist activity) is important. He added that we know little about individual risk factors for becoming radicalized, but points to ideologies, affiliations, grievances, and "moral" emotions as promising possibilities.

Recent years have witnessed an expanded focus on what groups engage in terrorist-like activities—both foreign and domestic extremism are currently active—and on the activities in which they engage. For example, **bioterrorism**, in which biological agents such as viruses and bacteria are released or threatened, could harm far more citizens than conventional guns or bombs. In addition, there is potential for widespread apprehension about weaponizing biological agents in this fashion, particularly when there is publicity about an attack (Dougall et al., 2005). Public susceptibility to such threats may well have been enhanced by the destructive global consequences of COVID-19 beginning in 2019.

Cyberterrorism is another form of attack that has become more destructive as both perpetrators and technology have grown in sophistication. For example, ransomware attacks—in which a computer system is hacked and controlled until a ransom is paid—can take advantage of medical systems with inadequate security to interrupt the delivery of life-sustaining treatment services. The 2017 WannaCry ransomware attack, involving control of about 300,000 computers in more than 150 countries with the demand for bitcoin ransom, may provide a model of a large-scale ransomware attack with the potential to inflict damage that includes lost data, damaged equipment, chaos, and panic (Acharya & Acharya, 2017). In some respects, such large-scale cyberattacks are more harmful than a physical attack in one specific location. Effective countermeasures to such threats must also become more sophisticated, and will require enhanced collaboration among law enforcement officials, public health experts, and behavioral scientists.

Hostage Negotiation. Successful hostage negotiation requires an understanding of the dynamics of hostage incidents so that these dynamics can be applied by the negotiator to contain and ultimately end the incident with a minimum of violence (Vecchi et al., 2005). For example, in many hostage situations, a strong sense of psychological togetherness and mutual dependency develops between the hostages and their kidnappers. These feelings emerge from (1) the close, constant contact among the participants, (2) their shared feelings of fear and danger, and (3) the strong feelings of powerlessness induced by prolonged captivity. This relationship, dubbed the **Stockholm syndrome**, involves mutually positive feelings between the hostages and their kidnappers. This term derives from a 1973 event in which hostages held in a Swedish bank developed a close emotional attachment to their captors (Eckholm, 1985).

Hostages may come to sympathize with their captors and even adopt (at least temporarily) the ideological views of those who have taken them hostage. The behavior of 14-year-old Elizabeth Smart, who was kidnapped in 2002 from her family home and held for months by Brian David Mitchell, showed that she had multiple opportunities to escape during this time but did not take them. Consider how coercive control, discussed earlier as a component of domestic violence to explain why those who experience intimate partner violence do not leave the relationship, might be applied to Elizabeth Smart and others to help understand their reactions and behavior.

Hostage negotiators try to take advantage of this dynamic by becoming a part of it themselves. First attempting to become a psychological member of the hostage group who nevertheless maintains important ties to the outside world, negotiators will then try to use their outside contacts to persuade hostage-takers to bring the crisis to a peaceful end. Successful negotiators make contact with hostage takers in a nonthreatening way and then maintain communication with them for as long as necessary. Generally, the negotiator attempts to isolate the hostage takers from any "outside" communication to foster their reliance on the negotiator as the crucial link with other people. Once communication is established, the negotiator tries to reduce the hostage takers' fear and tension so that they will be more willing to agree to a reasonable solution. Negotiators structure the situation in ways that maximize predictability and calm. For example, they may offer help with any medical needs the hostage group has, thereby fostering positive feelings associated with the Stockholm syndrome. Finally, through gradual prompting and reinforcement, the negotiator tries to encourage behaviors that promote progress in negotiations (e.g., more conversation, less violence and threats as part of such conversation, and the passage of time without violence).

Many police departments have developed special crisis/hostage negotiation teams that usually include a psychologist as a consultant or adviser (Bartol & Bartol, 2006). In this capacity, the psychologist helps select officers for the team, provides on-the-scene advice during hostage incidents, profiles the hostage taker's personality, and assesses the behavior of the hostages themselves.

Do psychologist-consultants make a difference? One investigator (Butler et al., 1993) reported that using a psychologist consultant in hostage incidents was associated with fewer injuries and deaths to hostages and more peaceful surrenders by hostage takers. Investigators using police interrogation simulations considered various verbal and behavioral approaches and identified one procedure—active listening—as empirically supported (Beune et al., 2009, 2010, 2011). Consistent with this finding, psychologists have been involved in using "crisis communication" in the course of critical incidents such as hostage situations, kidnappings, suicide threats, and violence in school and workplace (Vecchi, 2009).

The Police Officer's Job

The popular conception of the job of the police officer focuses on arresting those who break the law, and enforcing the law in other ways. Actually, the major duties of the police can be divided into three general areas:

- *Enforcing the law*, which includes investigating complaints, arresting suspects, and attempting to prevent crime. Although most citizens perceive law enforcement to be the most important function of the police, it accounts for only about 10% of police activity.

- *Maintaining order*, which includes intervening in family and neighborhood disputes and keeping traffic moving, noise levels down, and disturbances to a minimum. It is estimated that 3 out of every 10 requests for police officers involve this type of activity.

- *Providing services*, such as giving assistance in medical and psychological emergencies, finding missing persons, helping stranded motorists, and escorting funerals.

Much police work is focused on the third category. Should the police spend so much time on community services? The major objections to having police provide community services are that they use police resources that could otherwise be applied to the first two areas. There have been times when there was a clear, direct attempt to move in this direction—such as the 1990s federal legislation providing funding to hire more police, which allowed police forces to implement a zero-tolerance policy leading to arrests for even minor offenses—with the results of both a reduction in crime rates and an increase in citizen complaints against the police (Green, 1999). This policy now appears to have yielded to more specialized interventions (such as when officers are trained specifically to interact more effectively with citizens with behavioral health problems) and other interventions short of arrest.

When police critics use language such as "defund the police," this should not be taken literally to mean the absence of funding for enforcing the law and maintaining order. While some critics may envision reforms in these areas, they probably mean that funding for police should not include providing an array of community-based services. There are two considerations in the debate about having police officers continue to provide an array of social services. First, it would require very substantial resources to train and employ a new cadre of community service workers. Would they be more effective? Would they be comparably available? Second, by providing these services, police officers can maintain an identity that involves helping, and potentially generating goodwill, respect, and cooperation. If police were entirely focused on criminal activity, might that *increase* the current polarization between police and some members of the community? The "us versus them" perspective can be softened when police officers and citizens interact outside the often-adversarial context of crime investigation.

A 2017 survey of about 8,000 police officers conducted by the Pew Research Center (https://www.pewresearch.org/social-trends/2017/01/11/behind-the-badge/) offers a detailed account of the perceptions of police officers regarding their interactions with the general public. Some of the findings relate directly to the present climate involving mistrust of police, and the tensions surrounding police encounters with Black citizens. The survey reported that the majority of officers considered the deaths of Black citizens during police encounters to be isolated incidents, as contrasted with the majority of the general public who, according to a separate Pew Research Center survey, regarded the problem as systemic. This varied by the race of the responding officer, however, with 57% of Black officers reporting that the problem was systemic. Almost all White officers thought that Black citizens currently have equal rights in the U.S., while most Black officers reported that continued changes were necessary to achieve such equality. A very high percentage of the general public (83%) said they understood the risks and challenges of policing, while a comparably high percentage of officers (86%) reported that the general public did not understand such risks and challenges. This survey's findings suggest that there are various topics on which police officers largely agree (e.g., the general public does not understand the risks and challenges of policing) but others on which they sharply disagree (e.g., the role of aggression). At times these disagreements are along racial lines, with the majority of White officers agreeing that there has been sufficient change to yield equal rights for Black citizens but the majority of Black officers endorsing the importance of continued focus on rights and progress.

Stress and the Police

The police officer's job is composed of multiple duties, and the stress associated with these duties may lead to personal conflicts—and sometimes to behavioral health problems including substance abuse, depression, and trauma symptoms. Much has been written about the causes and treatment of police stress (e.g., Corey & Zelig, 2020; Hille, 2010).

Certainly police work, when done well, is challenging under any circumstances. Some influences make it particularly difficult. One problem that comes with being a police officer is the "life in a fishbowl" phenomenon. Officers are constantly on public view, and they realize that their every act is being evaluated. This perception can be even more acute when police wear body cameras, and with the constant presence of smartphones that can be used to video police encounters with citizens and then post those videos immediately on social media. When police conduct is not consistent with the expectations of some citizens, there is likely to be criticism; current communications technology provides powerful tools for such critiques. In some respects this is an important advance—people perform differently when they know that they are being observed, whether in the research lab (termed the "Hawthorne Effect") or in a variety of everyday circumstances. Having convincing evidence of misconduct makes it more likely that it can be addressed fairly and appropriately. Yet the sheer volume of such criticism can also contribute to the kind of "us versus them" polarizing impact discussed in this chapter.

Some researchers have divided the stress of police work into different categories according to the sources of the stress or the type of problem involved. Project Shield, a large-scale study conducted by the National Institute of Justice, asked police officers to respond to a series of questions about the negative effects of stress in several different categories, including psychological, physical, behavioral, and organizational public health (Harpold & Feemster, 2002).

Results from the surveys showed that officers reported an increased vulnerability to alcohol abuse and heightened levels of anxiety within the first five years of employment. In addition, approximately 1% of officers in the study reported having contemplated suicide at some point. Compared to the general population, officers reported more experiences of physical and medical problems over their lifetime, including cancer, heart disease, hypertension, acute migraine headaches, reproductive problems, chronic back problems, foot problems, and insomnia. They also reported increased behavioral problems in their personal lives, such as physical abuse of their spouses and children, as a result of job-related stress. Officers reported the highest levels of organizational, or job-related, stress when faced with making split-second decisions with serious consequences, when hearing media reports of police wrongdoing, when working with administrators who did not support the officers, and when not having enough time for personal or family responsibilities.

According to questionnaire studies of police stress, the following sources of stress are common for police:

1. *Physical and psychological threats.* Included here are events related to the unique demands of police work, such as using force, being physically attacked, confronting aggressive people or grisly crime scenes, and engaging in high-speed chases. A total of 56 law enforcement officers were feloniously killed in the line of duty in 2010 (another 72 officers died in accidents while performing their duties, and 53,469 officers were assaulted in the line of duty) (FBI, 2011a). There were 51 officers feloniously killed in 2014 in the line of duty (FBI, 2015), 41 killed in 2015 (FBI, 2016), and 48 killed in 2019 (FBI, 2020). Officers also reported that specific job-related stressors in this area included responding to family disputes, exposure to abused children, and killing someone or witnessing a fellow officer killed in the line of duty (Violanti et al., 2016).

2. *Evaluation systems.* These stressors include the ineffectiveness of the judicial system, court leniency with defendants, negative press accounts of the police, the public's rejection of the police, and disrespect and mistreatment of police officers in the courts.

3. *Organizational problems and lack of support.* Examples of these stressors include bureaucracies, inadequate leadership by police administrators, weak support and confused feedback from supervisors, lack of clarity about job responsibilities, and poor job performance by fellow officers. Organizational problems may be one of the most important sources of stress—more influential even than physical danger, bloody crime scenes, and public scrutiny (Stinchcomb, 2004; Violanti et al. 2016). Officers may feel misunderstood by the public they serve and insufficiently staffed to do the job well (Pew Research Foundation, 2017). Yet police officers often find it hard to acknowledge that the stressful nature of their job is affecting them, and they may need assistance—particularly if the problems are seen as organizational, or they perceive that such a report may reflect adversely on their reputation with other officers or opportunity for advancement.

These concerns are understandable. Officers with stress-related behavioral health problems may not have these recognized as such by other officers, or may be relieved of their weapons and badges and assigned to limited-duty tasks. Fear of these consequences discourages some officers from reporting their experience of job-related stress.

Stressful working conditions also lead to **burnout**, which is "a syndrome of emotional exhaustion, depersonalization, and reduced personal accomplishment that can occur among individuals who work with people in some capacity" (Maslach & Jackson, 1984, p. 134). Emotional exhaustion reflects feelings of being emotionally overextended and "drained" by one's contact with other people. Both emotional exhaustion and depersonalization (callous or insensitive responding to people, particularly crime victims and others needing assistance) have been related to police burnout (Hawkins, 2001). Three factors—exhaustion, cynicism, and professional efficacy—were identified as part of police burnout (Storm & Rothman, 2003) in a sample of 2,396 South African police officers, applying well to officers of different races. This suggests that burnout in police officers can be more specifically described on these three dimensions.

A review of the literature on managing police burnout (Portland State University, 2014) made recommendations in different areas. These included decreasing stress in various ways, using peer support and counseling, developing reasonable "use of force" policies, increasing compatibility in officer assignments (Terpstra & Schaap, 2013), promoting better working relationships between officers and their supervisors (Hassell & Brandl, 2009; Scott, 2004), encouraging continued formal education and training, and emphasizing characteristics such as conscientiousness, stability, resilience, and coping in officer selection (Pienaar et al., 2007).

Implementing these recommendations would, one hopes, reduce the acute and chronic stress experienced by police officers to more manageable levels. That, in turn, should have a favorable impact on reducing police burnout.

Two other strategies for decreasing burnout among police are the use of team policing and counseling. Team policing involves a partial shift of decision making from a centralized authority to front-line officers and their immediate supervisors, who share the responsibility of setting policing priorities and making management decisions. Teams are often organized around neighborhoods, where they focus their efforts for extended periods of time. Within a neighborhood team, members perform several different functions so that they come to realize how important each team member is to the overall success of the group. In addition, because the team stays in the neighborhood, citizens should come to know the officers more closely and develop a better understanding of them.

In addition to team policing, many police agencies have developed their own stress management programs or referred their officers to other agencies for counseling to reduce burnout. These programs emphasize the prevention of stress through various techniques, including relaxation training, stress inoculation, detection of the early signs of stress, and effective problem solving. As useful as these types of techniques may be, the stigma associated with obtaining mental health treatment will continue to discourage some officers from participating.

But despite attempts to prevent stress and to change organizations in positive ways, some officers will experience stress-related problems that require counseling. Psychological treatment of police officers is complicated because police officers are often reluctant to become involved in therapy or counseling, for several reasons. First, they tend to believe that capable officers should be able to withstand hardships—and failure to do so shows a lack of professionalism or emotional control. Second, police fear that counseling will brand them with the stigma of mental disorder and thus diminish their peer officers' respect for them. Finally, officers are justifiably concerned that the department's need to know their psychological status related to fitness for duty will override their rights of confidentiality and lead to embarrassing disclosures of personal information.

Police departments have developed several alternatives for providing psychological counseling to their officers. Each addresses some of the obstacles that arise in police counseling programs. Peer counseling, involving the delivery of services by police officers, has the potential to overcome the stigma of being involved in treatment with a psychiatrist or psychologist. This approach offers better access to individuals who would otherwise avoid any kind of therapy or counseling. It has been used after catastrophic events such as 9/11 (Dowling et al, 2006), and has contributed to an increase in mental health referrals and a decrease in sick days, poor work performance, and job-related suicide (Levenson & Dwyer, 2003).

A second method involves providing counseling targeted at problems specific to police officers. The most noteworthy example of these focused interventions is with officers who have been involved in the use of deadly force. The emotional aftermath of shooting incidents is among the most traumatic experiences the police encounter and can lead to symptoms of posttraumatic stress disorder. Providing post-incident counseling is a common service of police psychologists and is recommended by the International Association of Chiefs of Police (2016). The goals of this counseling, which often also relies on peer support, are to reassure officers that their emotional reactions to incidents are normal, to give them a safe place to express these emotions, to help them reduce stress, and to promote a timely return to duty. Many departments also try to make counseling services available to family members of officers who have been involved in traumatic incidents.

There are several ethical considerations involved in psychological counseling for police officers, and some of the most difficult concern confidentiality. Police counseling services are usually offered either by an in-house psychologist who is a full-time employee of the police department or by an outside psychologist who consults with the department on a part-time basis. In-house professionals are more readily available and more knowledgeable about police issues. Outside consultants, because of their independence from the department, may be better able to protect the confidentiality of their clients' disclosures.

Police–Community Relations

Police work has high public visibility. Police conduct is scrutinized by the courts and evaluated by the public. Several amendments to the U.S. Constitution impose limits on law enforcement officers; such limits are part of the first ten amendments to the United States Constitution. For example, the Fourth Amendment protects citizens against unreasonable search and seizure of persons or property. Limits on police activities are frequently reevaluated on the basis of current court interpretations of these amendments. These amendments also have implications for police procedures. Protection against "cruel and unusual punishment" is provided under the Eighth Amendment, and the Fourteenth Amendment guarantees all citizens "due process."

Historically, the interrogation practices used by the police to elicit confessions from suspects, a topic we explore in a later chapter, have been a major focus of concern. The risk factors for inducing inaccurate confessions include physical custody and isolation, the presentation of false evidence, offense minimization and "unspoken promises," developmental immaturity, cognitive and intellectual disabilities, and certain kinds of personality and psychopathology (Kassin et al., 2009). A 2021 series of articles in the *Philadelphia Inquirer* detailed allegations that Philadelphia homicide detectives threatened at least 15 witnesses over the last 30 years to make "satisfactory statements" or risk having their children taken from them (https://www.inquirer.com/crime/a/

philadelphia-murder-exonerations-wrongful-convictions
-20210507.html). To the extent that such situational and
dispositional factors are present in police interrogations, or
inaccurate witness statements are provided due to this kind
of police conduct, there is a greater likelihood of false confessions—and the conviction of innocent defendants.

A second police technique that has caused widespread
concern is racial profiling—the practice of making traffic or
pedestrian stops involving a larger percentage of minority
citizens than nonminority citizens. Various terms (e.g.,
"driving while Black," "stop-and-frisk," the Terry stop) have
been used to describe the phenomenon of police being more
likely to stop African Americans in public, either while driving or on foot. This is highly problematic, creating major
concerns regarding equal protection under the law for citizens of different races and ethnic groups. According to the
Stanford Open Policing Project, an analysis of nearly 100
million records of traffic stops and searches collected since
2015 involving both state patrol and municipal police,
there is evidence of "significant racial disparities" in policing
(Pierson et al., 2020). Although some law enforcement officials have defended this procedure as a reasonable crime
control tool, the public outcry over its potential for abuse
has led several states to abandon it.

In New York City, extensive data were gathered under
Stop-and-Frisk policies. Police were required to submit a
form with basic information about who was stopped and
what was found. Between 2002 and 2015, there was a total
of 5,150,122 stops of citizens, about half of whom were
between ages 14 and 24 and about 90% of whom were Black
or Hispanic. There was no arrest or further action in close
to 90% of cases across all years (New York ACLU, 2016).
The debate about public safety (about 10% of these stops
resulted in the discovery of contraband and possible arrest)
versus individual rights (nearly 90% of these stops did not
yield anything problematic, yet youth and minorities were
clearly disproportionately subjected to Stop-and-Frisk) is
clear in this example. But even for those who are convinced
that the benefit to public safety outweighs the cost of millions of stops that yielded nothing illegal, it is easy to understand how BIPOC citizens would perceive this policy as
discriminatory—and trust the police less as a consequence.

Another major concern of some community groups is
excessive force or brutality by the police (Holmes & Smith,
2008). This is seen currently in the Black Lives Matter movement, which was influenced in its development by the perception that African American men were disproportionately
victimized by lethal force in police encounters. (We discussed
this early in this chapter, showing that minority citizens are
disproportionately the subject of force in police encounters—
but not lethal force.) A familiar example of such an encounter between police and a Black citizen involves the killing
of George Floyd in Minneapolis (described in Box 4.1).
This case differed in some important ways from other such
encounters—it was recorded on a cell phone and widely
viewed on social media, it launched a series of deadly protests

across the U.S., and it resulted in the conviction of police
officer Derek Chauvin for second-degree murder. While
such convictions of police are rare, there is growing public
pressure to investigate whether such encounters are consistent with the U.S. Supreme Court's restriction on the use
of deadly force by police (described in Box 4.3). Part of this
consideration, on a broader policy level, involves whether
such misconduct, when it does occur, is a matter of "a few
bad apples" or broader systemic influences.

How can we understand incidents in which officers
have used excessive force? The "few bad apples" explanation focuses on the personal and situational problems of
individual police officers. In this view, brutality reflects
extreme aggressiveness and toughness of a few officers. A
second explanation is more situational: police respond forcefully to violent events that might require such response. A
third explanation is that police brutality reflects a systemic

Box 4.3

The Case of Edward Garner and Limits on the Use of Deadly Force

In the 1985 case of *Tennessee v. Garner*, the U.S. Supreme
Court struck down a Tennessee law that allowed police
to shoot to kill, even when an unarmed suspect fleeing a
crime scene posed no apparent threat. In October 1974,
Edward Garner, then 15, fled when the police arrived just
after he had broken the window of an unoccupied house.
He was pursued by Officer Elton Hymon. As Garner
scaled a 6-foot fence at the back of the property, Officer
Hymon yelled, "Police—halt!" Garner didn't halt, and
Officer Hymon, knowing that he was in no shape to catch
the fleeing youth, shot and killed him with a bullet to the
back of the head.

Garner's father sued public officials and the city of
Memphis, alleging that the police had violated his son's
civil rights by the use of excessive force. The city defended
itself on the basis of a state statute giving police officers
the right to use deadly force if necessary to stop a fleeing
felon. The lower courts agreed with the city, but 11 years
later the U.S. Supreme Court struck down the statute in a
6–3 decision (*Tennessee v. Garner*, 1985).

The majority held that shooting a person, even one
suspected of a felony, violates that person's Fourth Amendment right to be free from unreasonable searches and sei-
zures. The majority opinion added, however, that deadly
force would be justified if officers had reason to believe that
the suspect posed an immediate threat to them or others.

Critical Thought Question

Should facilitating capture of a suspect be justification for
using deadly force?

bias, consistent with the ongoing presence of racism in our society. (Recall from the earlier discussion in this chapter that police officers themselves are sharply divided in their opinions on these questions.) If system-level interventions such as ABLE (described in Box 4.2) succeed in reducing the frequency of excessive force used by police officers, that provides some support for the importance of systemic influences in contributing to this problem.

Police use of excessive force is another example of a problem for which psychology seeks explanations in the interactions between persons and the situations in which they function, rather than simply in the individual's characteristics or the situational influences. From this perspective, we begin with police officers who typically are strongly committed to maintaining the conventional order and to protecting society. We repeatedly put them into potentially dangerous situations, we arm them well, we urge them to be "tough on crime," and we train and authorize them to use appropriate force. The result of mixing this type of person with these types of situations is not surprising: In some encounters, the police will use excessive force against citizens who are suspected of conduct that threatens public safety. In addition, police justifications for extreme force can be motivated by stereotypes, mistaken information, and the mutual mistrust that can develop between individuals from different cultural and ethnic backgrounds.

There have been various attempts to improve police relations with people in the community, especially in neighborhoods with large numbers of BIPOC citizens. For example, changes in the Los Angeles Police Department from what African Americans referred to as an "occupation force of hardliners" into an organization that actively courts and wins support from its African American and Latino populations is described in attorney Connie Rice's 2012 book, *Power Concedes Nothing: One Woman's Quest for Social Justice in America*. But there remains a powerful emotional component associated with the mistrust of police in many BIPOC citizens. There is also a strong emotional response from police, to the effect that they are asked to prevent crime and apprehend offenders, but are then blamed and mistrusted when they try to do that. Is there anything that would ease the historical tension between minority citizens and police, something that would promote greater legitimate trust in the police but still retain their effectiveness in preventing crime and apprehending offenders?

This is an urgent question. Psychology and other behavioral sciences can offer some steps that might help, judging from some of the earlier discussion in this chapter. First, it is clear that policing is a stressful and sometimes dangerous job, associated with the risk of suicide, death, or injury at higher rates than most other jobs. To the extent that communities can provide police officers with better training, and more effective tools for managing stress and doing their jobs, it is likely that cynicism and burnout among officers will decrease—and have less impact on their encounters with citizens.

Second, the improved documentation of police–citizen interactions using tools such as body cameras can protect both citizens from being subjected to excessive force and officers from being subjected to unwarranted complaints. Such documentation, along with associated monitoring of whether officers are consistent with applicable use of force policies, is needed for another reason: with the near-constant availability of camera-enabled smartphones, the filming and posting of parts of such encounters on social media sites are likely to increase. Having documentary evidence of the entire encounter will facilitate a fairer and more accurate consideration of complaints and investigation of events in which injury or death result.

Third, it is important to actively seek and retain a diverse police force. Having more BIPOC police officers, as well as more police who are female, gay, and otherwise underrepresented within the ranks of law enforcement, can serve the purposes of diversifying attitudes, perspectives, and behavioral propensities among officers. It can also help to enhance the credibility of a police force to have both leadership and line officers more closely resemble the characteristics of the larger population. There is ample evidence, according to the Pew survey discussed earlier in this chapter, that attitudes of officers on a number of issues differ by race.

Fourth, we must improve the communication between police and citizens. This applies to the individual encounter between a police officer and a citizen, to groups representing the public's interests, and to police leaders. Mutual respect and acknowledgment of the other's positions are a necessary precursor to sufficient trust for a good working relationship. These strategies, and others, are discussed in the next section that covers a presidential task force report on the future of U.S. policing in the twenty-first century.

Before that, we turn to one promising approach to improving this communication that has been implemented over the last four decades. This innovation in police work is **community-based policing**. In this approach, police officers develop a proactive, problem-solving approach with active collaboration from local citizens who support the police in the effort to combat crime, promote safety, and enhance the overall quality of neighborhoods.

In most versions of community policing, there are more foot patrols by officers who stay in the same neighborhoods. As a result, community-based policing seeks to humanize police and citizens in one another's eyes and to broaden the roles that police play in a community. For example, Chicago's version of community policing contained six basic features (Lurigio & Skogan, 1994):

1. *A neighborhood orientation*, in which officers develop friendly relationships with individual residents in a community, identify the "hot spots" for crime, and develop partnerships with community organizations for fighting crime.

2. *Increased geographic responsibility*, which means that officers regularly walk a given neighborhood "beat" and become highly visible, well-known experts about problems in that area.

3. *A structured response to calls for police service*, in which emergency calls are handled by a special-response

team, thereby permitting beat officers to stay available for routine calls and maintain a high-profile presence.

4. *A proactive, problem-oriented approach*, whereby more effort is devoted to crime prevention (e.g., closing down drug houses, breaking up groups of loitering youth) than to responding to discrete disturbances or criminal activities.

5. *Brokering more community resources for crime prevention*, as police enlist the help of other city agencies to identify and respond to local community problems.

6. *Analysis of crime problems*, which enables officers to focus their attention on the highest risk areas by using computer technology to keep accurate track of crime patterns.

During the first 10 years of Chicago's program, both African American and White citizens reported a decrease in crime problems and fear of crime, although Latinos did not. African Americans, in particular, perceived a decrease in social disorder and physical decay in their neighborhoods, and all groups increased their ratings of policy favorability (Chicago Community Policing Evaluation Consortium, 2004). But after the early 2000s, Chicago invested fewer resources in community policing, took a harder line on crime following an increase in homicides (that followed six consecutive years of decreases), moved officers from community-based policing to street patrol, and held fewer meetings. By 2016, the once-vibrant program had become a shadow of itself (Rhee, 2016).

There are important lessons in the rise and fall of community-based policing in Chicago. First, when properly funded and staffed, this program appeared to have a favorable impact on relations between police and the community and may have decreased both criminal activity and the fear of crime. Second, there are challenges to maintaining such a program. When there is an increase in crime, a change in

political leadership, or a crisis, there is a temptation to shift resources from a program like this into harder-line crime control. This is often a short-term solution to a long-term problem; maintaining favorable relations between police and citizens will be important over a period of decades, even if it appears to be a lower priority in a crime-driven crisis. Third, if communities succumb to the temptation to shift funding and other resources away from community policing, there will be a commensurate decrease in the program's vitality and effectiveness.

The experience with community-oriented policing in Chicago is a microcosm of the broader approach within the United States: development and rapid growth in the 1990s, continued support up to around 2008, and diminishing resources after that. For example, the Community-Oriented Policing Services, a division of the U.S. Department of Justice, received $148 million in 1994 funding, which grew rapidly to $1.42 billion in 1997. Its budget began shrinking in the mid-2000s, dropping from $495 million (2011) to $208 million (2015) (United States Department of Justice, 2016). Although funding has increased since 2017, it remains well below 2011 levels (Congressional Research Services, 2021).

Should this be considered a failed experiment, or does community policing have the potential to improve many of our current problems involving relationships between citizens and police? What is the evidence for its effectiveness? The results have been mixed. Some cities that have introduced community-policing initiatives reported large improvements in the public's attitude toward their police departments (Adams et al., 2005) and sizable reductions in rates of serious crimes. Others, such as Chicago, described substantial benefits but eventual reductions in funding that greatly limited its impact and viability.

Reforming and revitalizing community-based policing can proceed on many fronts. Technology should be used as effectively as possible. Community crime mapping can help police to identify and address problems (Hickman & Reaves, 2001). Data sharing partnerships can be facilitated by the gathering of such crime mapping and other data amenable to combination in a single database. Written agreements can help such data sharing collaborations to work more smoothly (Boba et al., 2009). The use of communications technology such as social media, websites, e-mail, and texting can ease the strain of communication associated with more traditional approaches such as 911 operators and police dispatchers. One 2016 survey found that a large majority of law enforcement agencies use social media to notify the public of safety concerns, for community outreach and citizen engagement, and for public relations and reputation management (International Association of Chiefs of Police and the Urban Institute, 2017). In our present state of communications technology, it is likely that virtually all U.S. law enforcement agencies also use texting, e-mail, and digital storage to some extent.

Stakeholders must be considered in effective partnerships between police and the community. Participants should include businesses, schools, religious institutions,

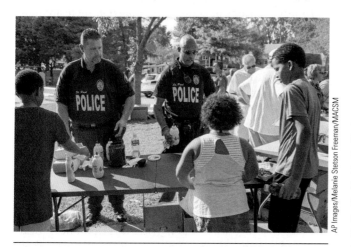

Community policing is a philosophy designed to increase the amount and quality of specific police officers' contact with citizens and to involve police more in crime prevention and community maintenance activities.

city agencies, and individual community members, particularly consumers of justice-involved services (Payne & Button, 2009). Those forming and operating these partnerships should also ensure that there is appropriate representation from underrepresented minority communities and that the program is publicized through various media and in different languages (Skogan et al., 2002).

The Future of Policing in The United States in The Twenty-First Century: The President's Task Force Report

Much research-based evidence and thinking about contemporary policing was captured in a national task force report (President's Task Force on 21st Century Policing, 2015). In December 2014, President Barack Obama signed an executive order commissioning a task force to identify best practices in policing and make recommendations on how policing practices can both promote effective crime reduction and build public trust. The final report can serve as an important guide for changes in police work over the coming decades. We describe this report in some detail, for its scholarly and practical value and because it offers a valuable perspective on the stability of the trends and evidence discussed in this chapter.

There were two overarching recommendations. First, the Task Force recommended that the president support the creation of another task force (the National Crime and Justice Task Force) to consider criminal justice reforms in the wake of the report. Second, members recommended support for programs that are community-based, addressing important issues such as poverty, education, health, and safety. In this respect, the Task Force clearly placed policing in the broader context of our communities and criminal justice system, identifying risk factors for crime and seeking to reduce them.

The report also made more specific recommendations in six topic areas: Building Trust and Legitimacy, Policy and Oversight, Technology and Social Media, Community Policing and Crime Reduction, Officer Training and Education, and Officer Safety and Wellness. We describe each of these and discuss them in the context of other material in this chapter.

Building Trust and Legitimacy

The Task Force clearly adopted a procedural justice perspective (Tyler, 1990) regarding the police: people are more likely to behave lawfully when they perceive those enforcing laws are acting on legitimate authority. Such authority is more likely to be perceived as legitimate if police act in procedurally just ways (treating people with dignity and respect, giving people "voice," being neutral and transparent in making decisions, and communicating motives that are trustworthy).

In using procedural justice as a guiding structure, the Task Force recommended that law enforcement adopt a "guardian" rather than a "warrior" mindset. Establishing transparency and accountability was perceived as very important in establishing and acting upon policies consistent with procedural justice. Promoting trust through positive, non-enforcement-based activities (similar to those described in the community policing section earlier in this chapter) was also recommended. Measuring "trust of police" by the community through regular surveys was cited, as it is difficult and often misleading to use anecdotal accounts and single cases to gauge broader trust levels. Finally, the Task Force recommended having police officers as a group reflect the diversity of race, gender, culture, language, and life experience that is part of the community that the police serve.

Policy and Oversight

Police policies should be developed and modified in collaboration with civilian representatives from the community, according to the Task Force. (Again, note the influence of community policing.) Policies on the use of force should include training on alternatives such as de-escalation (refer to the discussion of CIT earlier in this chapter). Other policies and aggregate data—in areas such as mass demonstrations, consent before searches, gender identification, and racial profiling—should be made publicly available. Routine review of such policies should be conducted, including non-punitive peer review of critical incidents. To assist law enforcement and the community to succeed in this area, the Task Force recommended technical assistance, incentive funding, interagency collaboration, and other assistance and cooperation using the U.S. Department of Justice and relevant professional organizations.

Technology and Social Media

Given the rapid and significant advances in this area, the Task Force's recommendations in this section of the report are particularly important. It is often unclear how new technology and applications can assist law enforcement in their effectiveness and efficiency without violating individual rights. Accordingly, the Task Force recommended that the Department of Justice should collaborate with law enforcement to establish standards relevant to research and development of new technologies; these would include auditory, visual, and biometric data, and "less than lethal" technologies. Such standards would also include compatibility and operation of social media for law enforcement purposes, again considered using the dual criteria of effectiveness/efficiency and respect for citizens' rights. It can be very difficult for a federal agency to develop standards that are subsequently imposed on local jurisdictions, however. Often a preferable strategy involves the development of model standards, implemented through demonstration projects and publicized widely on both a national and a local level.

Community Policing and Crime Reduction

The community policing approach is built on the assumption that positive, non-enforcement related interactions between citizens and police have favorable consequences that include the enhancement of the procedural justice components described earlier. In addition to increasing trust of the police and perception of their legitimacy, this approach is also assumed to increase the effectiveness of crime prevention and investigation through better collaboration between police and citizens. Yet the problems with community policing, described earlier using Chicago as an example, involve the temptation to divert community policing resources to equipment and crime investigation when there are changes in leadership or an increase in offending. There has been a noteworthy diminishing of the use of community policing in the last decade.

It is very interesting, therefore, to note that the Task Force has made community policing a central pillar of their recommendations. Community policing is identified as a foundational philosophy for both law enforcement and the community in the twenty-first century. This assumes that community policing can be revived, supported, and expanded. Among the recommendations in this area are the protection and promotion of dignity for citizens—particularly vulnerable children and youth—by avoiding stigmatizing them and minimizing the role of police in public schools. Youth are recognized as important in (a) contributing to community decision-making, (b) participating in research and problem-solving, and (c) developing leadership and life skills. According to Task Force recommendations, all of these should be facilitated through positive interactions between police and youth (such as the Police Athletic League).

Officer Training and Education

As the scope of law enforcement duties has expanded, so has the importance of training in areas such as mental health, cultural competence, technology, immigration, and terrorism. The Task Force recommends greater use of community experts in providing relevant training to law enforcement personnel throughout their careers. This could be facilitated by the establishment of training innovation hubs involving universities and police academies. A national center for training senior police executives would provide valuable knowledge to senior leaders. The inclusion of CIT as a mandatory aspect of training, perhaps in police academies, would help future generations of police officers move from "CIT training optional" status (where it often is currently) to including CIT skills among the mandatory competencies for police officers.

Officer Wellness and Safety

There is general recognition in the report that officer safety *and* wellness are both important. Training in tactical first aid and the use of seat belts and bulletproof vests are examples of recommendations that would enhance officer safety. Better attention to shift length, exercise, sleep, behavioral health, and medical health are all considerations that would improve the general health of police officers, which could improve performance in both routine encounters and crisis situations. The Task Force makes recommendations that rely on the collection and analysis of data, in areas such as shift length, officer injuries, and "near misses." It is very interesting to note the foundational similarity between the Task Force's assumption that empirical data and specific expertise are valuable to their mission, and the assumption in this book that psychology can contribute to the law in similar ways.

Summary

1. **What is the role of the police in our society?** Policing is necessary in any society concerned with maintaining public order, even though in a democratic society we must balance public safety with civil liberties and criminal rights. Police officers daily face the dilemma of equality versus discretion: whether to treat all suspects or lawbreakers equally or to provide an effective response that varies somewhat under different circumstances.

2. **What procedures are used to select police?** Selection of police officers is usually informed by psychological tests and an interview. Another assessment device is the use of some version of a situational test, in which

the candidate responds to real-life challenges that would face a police officer, such as intervening in a dispute between spouses or writing an incident report. Responses to these situational tasks can be valuable additions to psychological testing and interviewing, but they can also be costly and time-consuming.

3. **How has the training of police officers expanded into new areas?** Training of police officers usually involves a variety of activities, including criminal law, human relations training, self-defense, and the use of firearms. Most training programs last at least six months. Police officers are now frequently trained in crisis intervention, including handling situations involving individuals with

mental illness, resolving family disputes, and responding to hostage-taking situations.

4. **What are the respective explanations for police conduct associated with the "bad apples" and "systemic racism" positions?** Existing racism in policing is explained by some who hold that individual officers and leaders with their own biases behave in this way primarily because of such biases, whether they brought them to the job or had them strengthened by experience working as part of the police force. "Systemic racism," by contrast, holds that there are system-level influences in the selection, training, supervision, and peer interactions of police that incline them toward behaving in racially biased ways. These explanations are not mutually exclusive.

5. **Describe the different activities of the police. Is law enforcement central?** The police officer's job is multifaceted. Law enforcement (including investigation of complaints, arrest and prosecution of suspects, and efforts at crime prevention) accounts for only about 10% of police activity. Maintaining order (intervening in family and neighborhood disputes, keeping traffic moving, responding to disturbances of the peace) accounts for about 30% of police activity. Providing social services to the community is even more time-consuming. These proportions may vary if officers are involved in community policing.

6. **What stressors do the police face?** Three problems are especially significant: the high visibility of policing, job-related stress, and burnout. Job duties, perceptions of police work, system-level interventions such

as ABLE, and specific responses can be modified to reduce burnout and help officers manage chronic and acute stress. All three problems, however, can be exacerbated by public perceptions of bias and unnecessary aggressiveness.

7. **What is the relationship between the police and the communities they serve?** Some community groups and individual citizens have been critical of police behavior, focusing on unequal and disproportionate use of police force against people living in poverty and racial minorities. Efforts to improve police–community relations include team policing, crisis intervention training, reorganization of the police department that restructures the traditional chain of command, community-based policing, and greater use of communications technology. These interventions have had some success, although funding for community-based policing has decreased during the last decade.

8. **What is the future of policing in the United States in the twenty-first century?** There are six major areas identified by the President's Task Force on 21st Century Policing (2015) prioritizing recommendations for police work in the coming decades: building trust and legitimacy, policy and oversight, technology and social media, community policing and crime reduction, officer training and education, and officer wellness and safety. The Task Force used procedural justice as a guiding framework for making recommendations, and cited the importance of empirical evidence, specialized experts, and community-based policing in their implementation.

Key Terms

Active Bystandership for Law Enforcement
bioterrorism
burnout
community-based policing
coercive control
counseling

Crisis Intervention Team
Cyberterrorism
domestic violent extremists
fitness-for-duty evaluation
grievance
jail diversion programs
learned helplessness

predictive validity
President's Task Force on 21st Century Policing
procedural justice
Stockholm syndrome
structured interviews
suicide by cop

team policing
terrorism
validity scales
zero-tolerance

Chapter 5

Eyewitnesses to Crimes and Accidents

Orienting Questions

1. What psychological factors contribute to the risk of mistaken identifications in the legal system?

2. What are the defining features of estimator, system, and reflector variables in the study of eyewitness memory?

3. How do jurors evaluate the testimony of eyewitnesses, and how can psychological research help jurors understand the potential problems of eyewitness testimony?

4. Can children accurately report on their experiences of victimization? What factors affect the accuracy of their reports? Are they likely to disclose abuse?

5. Can memories for trauma be repressed, and if so, can these memories be recovered accurately?

The police investigate crimes and accumulate evidence so that suspects can be identified and arrested. At the early stages of an investigation, eyewitnesses to those crimes provide important information to police; sometimes they provide the only solid leads. Eyewitnesses also play a vital role in later stages of a prosecution. According to defense attorney David Feige, "It's hard to overstate the power of eyewitness testimony in criminal cases. In thousands of cases every year, testimony of a single eyewitness, uncorroborated by forensic or any other evidence, is used to sustain serious felony charges, including robbery and murder" (Feige, 2006).

But in their attempts to solve crimes—and especially in their reliance on eyewitnesses—police and prosecutors face a number of challenges. Although many eyewitnesses provide accurate reports, some make mistakes. The recollections of eyewitnesses can lead the police down blind alleys or cause them to arrest the wrong person. As we will show, the investigative procedures used by police sometimes compound those problems. Various studies of actual eyewitness identifications provide a startling statistic: approximately one in five eyewitnesses who feel they are capable of recognizing a perpetrator selects an innocent person during an identification procedure (Steblay, 2015). The result: wrongful convictions by judges and juries, an all-too-familiar scenario by now. By one estimate, wrongfully convicted people in the United States have spent over 25,000 years in prison for crimes they did not commit. Over $2.9 billion has been spent compensating these individuals for years behind bars, either through state government compensation programs or as the result of civil lawsuits (National Registry of Exonerations, 2021).

Beyond the enormous cost in years lost and the massive financial burden imposed by wrongful convictions, one often overlooked fact is that when an innocent person is convicted, the guilty one is still free. And while the innocent person languishes behind bars, the guilty person remains on the streets, possibly committing other offenses. One stark example of this reality comes from the case of Kirk Bloodsworth, the first person in the United States exonerated from death row by DNA evidence. Bloodsworth was convicted of raping and murdering nine-year-old Dawn Hamilton. The primary evidence against Bloodsworth was five eyewitnesses who reported seeing him in proximity to the victim. Weeks after Bloodsworth's arrest, the true perpetrator—Kimberly Shay Ruffner—committed a similar assault, one that might have been prevented, had eyewitness error not misdirected investigators toward the innocent Kirk Bloodsworth (Junkin, 2004).

It is now apparent that eyewitness errors create real problems for the justice system (and for the people mistakenly identified!). DNA procedures developed in the 1980s made it possible to take a new look at evidence left at a crime scene. Unfortunately, only a small fraction of crimes—most notably sexual assaults—have DNA-rich evidence, and even when DNA is present, it is often not tested or is destroyed. In 2009, the Supreme Court ruled that states are not required to make DNA evidence available to convicted offenders (*District Attorney's Office for Third Judicial District v. Osborne*, 2009). As a result, many wrongly convicted people have no way to prove their innocence, even if DNA evidence is available. Many others have no hope of proving their innocence because DNA evidence was never available. For example, evidence from a typical drive-by shooting will not include DNA samples.

When DNA testing *is* conducted, it sometimes reveals that the person convicted of a crime and incarcerated—sometimes for decades—was not the actual perpetrator. Further analysis of the evidence in these cases often shows that eyewitness errors are to blame. Eyewitness errors are the leading cause of wrongful convictions, particularly in sexual assaults and robberies. According to the Innocence Project, the largest and most prominent organization devoted to proving wrongful convictions, 372 people have been exonerated by DNA in the United States (as of January, 2020). Among those exonerations, mistaken identifications account for approximately 70% of wrongful convictions, more than false confessions, problems with informants, and defective or fraudulent forensic science (Innocence Project, 2022).

Beyond mistakenly identifying someone as the culprit, eyewitnesses sometimes even generate false reports about non-existent people. One famous example of this occurred in the investigation of the domestic terrorism attack in Oklahoma City in 1995. In that attack, a bomb hidden in a rental truck killed 168 people at the Alfred P. Murrah Federal Building; Timothy McVeigh was executed for this crime in 2001. In investigating the crime, the FBI encountered multiple witnesses who reported seeing two people rent the truck in question. Massive law enforcement efforts were devoted to finding this accomplice—John Doe #2. As it turns out, there is compelling evidence that McVeigh rented the truck alone and that witnesses were misremembering another man who rented a similar truck the day after McVeigh did (Memon & Wright, 1999). Indeed, empirical evidence demonstrates that people can misremember an accomplice being present, especially if someone else confidently reports remembering such an accomplice (Wright et al., 2000).

Examples of Mistaken Eyewitness Identification

Cases of wrongful convictions based on faulty eyewitness testimony abound. The ordeal of Calvin C. Johnson, Jr., is a good example. Johnson, a college graduate with a job at Delta Airlines, spent 16 years behind bars for a rape he did not commit. He is not alone. In fact, Johnson was the 61st person in the United States to be exonerated through the use of DNA testing. Such testing in Johnson's case indicated that he was not the man who raped and sodomized a College Park, Georgia, woman in 1983. Yet the victim picked Johnson out of a photographic lineup and identified him as the rapist at trial. The all-White jury convicted Johnson, who is Black, despite the fact that forensic tests excluded him as the source of a pubic hair recovered from the victim's bed. The jury also apparently chose to disregard the testimony of four alibi witnesses who claimed that Johnson was home asleep at the time. One of the jurors stated that the victim's eyewitness testimony had been the most compelling evidence in the case.

One reason why wrongful convictions happen is that when eyewitnesses make a tentative identification, police often stop investigating other leads and instead look for further evidence that implicates the chosen suspect. This is an example of **confirmation bias**, whereby people look for, interpret, and create information that verifies an existing belief. In terms of eyewitness identification, the goal of finding the truth is neglected, often unintentionally, in a rush to solve the crime. In Johnson's case, police pushed ahead with the case even after the victim picked someone else at a live lineup (conducted after the photographic lineup). She testified at trial that she had picked the wrong person at the live lineup because looking at Johnson was too much for her: "I just pushed my eyes away and picked someone else" (Boyer, 2000).

You might think that people like Calvin Johnson would have some recourse—that they could get something back for the time they lost in prison. However, according to the Innocence Project, only 38 states and the District of Columbia have provisions for compensating wrongfully convicted individuals. Furthermore, such financial compensation is generally small, and social service assistance after exoneration is rare. Calvin Johnson initially received nothing because the state of Georgia did not have a law providing compensation for people who were wrongly convicted; he ultimately received $500,000 in compensation (https://www.law.umich.edu/). Unfortunately, Calvin Johnson's experience is not unique: many exonerees leave prison with "next to nothing" (Clow et al., 2012, p. 330).

Even in states with compensation laws on the books, wrongfully convicted individuals sometimes struggle to receive that compensation. For example, Florida has a Wrongful Compensation Incarceration Act which allows $50,000 per year of wrongful incarceration (with a maximum of $2 million), but only if exonerated individuals have "clean hands," meaning no prior felony convictions. For Nathan Myers, whose murder conviction was vacated on March 28, 2019 after he spent 43 years in prison, $2 million hardly seems like enough money. Even though he had no prior felony convictions, Myers struggled to receive compensation because the Attorney General's office indicated he was not eligible because the court did not declare him "actually innocent" (they simply vacated his life sentence, Schindler, 2020). Myers was eventually able to receive the maximum compensation (https://deathpenaltyinfo.org).

Nathan Myers' uncle, Clifford Williams, was wrongfully convicted of the same murder for which Myers was convicted and also spent 43 years in prison. He was initially denied compensation because he had two prior felony convictions, but Florida's governor approved a bill in 2020 allowing $2.15 million in compensation for Williams (Turner & Sexton, 2020). Even after being released, exonerated

individuals face discrimination in critical areas, such as employment. One study demonstrated that people evaluating job applications offered exonerated individuals lower starting salaries compared with similar individuals who had no criminal justice involvement (Kukucka et al., 2020).

How Mistaken Eyewitness Identifications Occur

Mistaken identifications can happen because features of the crime make it difficult for eyewitnesses to see the perpetrator's face clearly. It may be too dark, events may move too swiftly, or the encounter may be too brief for the witness to perceive the incident accurately. All of these conditions diminish memory strength. Yet, when questioned by police, witnesses are often asked to give specific details about a criminal's height, hair color, voice, and other identifying features. When such descriptions are accurate, they make the job of law enforcement much easier. However, when such descriptions are inaccurate or inadequate, they hinder the investigation.

Mistakes can also occur during the investigation of a crime. Police often ask eyewitnesses to examine a series of photos (called a **photographic lineup** or **photospread**) or a video lineup of suspects and decide whether the perpetrator is present. At this point, eyewitnesses typically want to help the police solve the crime; they may feel pressure to identify someone, and are likely to assume that the perpetrator is in the lineup. As a result of these factors, innocent people are sometimes selected and guilty people are sometimes overlooked.

Once a mistaken identification occurs, the error can be made worse during a trial. This is because during a trial, jurors may watch an eyewitness confidently state that the defendant is the perpetrator. In DNA exoneration cases, the mistaken eyewitnesses were uniformly confident that their

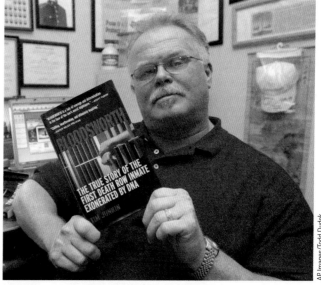

Kirk Bloodsworth, holding the book written about his case.

memories were correct, even though some had been uncertain about their initial identifications (Garrett, 2011). Not surprisingly, juries are impressed by confident eyewitnesses (Semmler et al., 2012). But by relying on confidence as an indication of accuracy, juries fail to recognize the fact that witnesses can be highly confident, even when they have identified the wrong person. We describe several ways this could happen in this chapter.

The study of eyewitness identification grew out of our understanding of the basic principles involved in perception and memory, as well as our understanding of social influence. We describe how both memory errors and social influence processes contribute to eyewitness identification errors.

Basic Information Processing

We have all had the experience of greeting someone we recognize, only to realize that we were wrong—that the person is actually a stranger. Similar mistakes can be made when crimes are observed. To process information about a crime, we must first perceive a stimulus and then retain it in our minds until there is an opportunity to make an identification, or at least until we can describe what we witnessed. But failures in this process can emerge along the way.

Perception

Although our perceptual abilities are impressive (Penrod et al., 1982), we do make errors. We tend to overestimate the height of criminals. We overestimate the duration of brief events and underestimate the duration of prolonged incidents. When watching a short film, we notice more about the actions than about the persons doing the acting. In short, we get the basic gist of events and people but we fail to notice specific details (Migueles et al., 2016). Research is increasingly considering the role of culture in these basic processes, suggesting there might be some variation in reporting tendencies as a function of cultural background. For example, one study assessed mock witness reports among people from rural Ghana, urban Ghana, and the Netherlands. Each group was shown a series of crime scene photographs in either a Ghanian setting or a Dutch setting. Both Ghanian groups reported significantly more correct central details when viewing crime scenes set in a Ghanian context compared with a Dutch context; Dutch participants' reports of central details did not differ across cultural context (Anakwah et al., 2020).

Consider a situation in which a weapon is present when a crime is committed. Eyewitnesses may devote more attention to the weapon than to the facial features or other physical aspects of the person who has the weapon. This **weapon focus effect** appears to be caused by **selective attention**: because we have limited attentional capacity and cannot process all of the stimuli available at a given time, we unconsciously select what information to attend to. The threatening aspect of a weapon draws witnesses' attention (Hope & Wright, 2007). This limits the amount of attention they can pay to other

aspects of the situation, and reduces their ability to recognize and describe the perpetrator (Fawcett et al., 2016).

The presence of a weapon can also affect the processing of auditory information. Professor Kerri Pickel and her colleagues showed a film of a man holding either a weapon (e.g., a gun, a switchblade knife) or a neutral object (e.g., a soda bottle, a ballpoint pen) and speaking to a woman in such a way that his words were either easy or difficult to understand (Pickel et al., 2003). Witnesses had difficulty understanding the man's speech in the latter condition, and the presence of a weapon further impaired their comprehension. A reasonable explanation for these results is that witnesses focus on the weapon and their attempt at language comprehension competed for limited processing time. They had a hard time doing both things at once.

Memory

Cognitive psychologists subdivide the building of a memory into three processes: encoding, storage, and retrieval. We describe how each of these stages is relevant to the memory of eyewitnesses.

Encoding. Encoding refers to the acquisition of information. Many aspects of a stimulus can affect how it is encoded. For example, stimuli that are only briefly seen or heard cannot be encoded fully, of course. The complexity of a stimulus also affects its encoding. As the complexity of an event increases (consider an earthquake, explosion, or hurricane), some aspects of the event probably will be misremembered, while others will be accurately recalled.

Contrary to what many people believe about a stressful event being "etched into memory forever," heightened arousal does not always enhance the encoding of events. The stress of being victimized causes a defensive "fight or flight" reaction that interferes with the encoding of precise details. So although mild stress or arousal may indeed increase alertness and interest in a task, extreme stress usually causes people to encode information incompletely or inaccurately (Deffenbacher et al., 2004). Performance on many tasks is best when the level of arousal is sufficient to ensure adequate attention but not so high as to disrupt accuracy.

A study of the accuracy of eyewitness memory in highly stressful military survival school interrogations provides good evidence of the effects of stress on memory (Morgan et al., 2004). Survival school interrogations are one of the greatest training challenges experienced by active-duty military personnel. (These interrogations are intended to test one's ability to withstand exploitation by the enemy, and to train people to hold up under the physical and mental stress of capture.) Over 500 military personnel participated in a series of studies as part of survival training. These soldiers, sailors, and pilots were placed in mock prisoner of war (POW) camps and deprived of food and sleep for approximately 48 hours prior to interrogation. For all participants, the interrogation lasted about 40 minutes. In the high-stress condition, participants were physically confronted by the interrogator or a guard. In the low-stress condition, there was no physical confrontation, but interrogators tried to "trick" participants into revealing sensitive information. One day after the interrogation, all personnel completed an identification procedure. Among those who saw a photospread, 76% of participants in the low-stress interrogation correctly identified their interrogator. In contrast, only 34% of participants in the high-stress interrogation condition correctly identified their interrogator.

Different expectancies about upcoming events also influence how they are encoded; in general, we have a tendency to see what we expect to see. This tendency can cause us to overlook salient, unusual stimuli, simply because we are not expecting them (Simons & Chabris, 1999). The effects are especially pronounced if the unexpected stimulus is visually similar to stimuli that are consciously being ignored, as they might be if one is concentrating on other elements of the scene.

Storage. The second step in building a memory is the storage of stimulus information. How well do we retain what we encode? Many years ago, psychologist Hermann Ebbinghaus showed that memory loss is rapid. This is relevant for eyewitness accuracy because it is likely that some time will pass between the commission of a crime and police questioning of eyewitnesses. This period of time is known as the retention interval. In one study, eyewitnesses attempted to recall details of a video one, three, or five weeks after viewing it. Eyewitnesses who recalled the video for the first time five weeks after seeing it were significantly less accurate than eyewitnesses who attempted recall after one or three weeks, supporting the notion that memory fades as the retention interval increases (Odinot & Wolters, 2006). A meta-analysis of 53 studies on this topic showed that the longer the retention interval, the more memory loss for previously seen faces (Deffenbacher et al., 2008).

A second phenomenon—both surprising and concerning—also occurs during the storage phase. Activities that eyewitnesses carry out or information they learn after they observe an event, termed post-event information, can alter their memory of the event. For example, simply talking to other witnesses can introduce new (not always accurate) details into one's memory. A study of actual eyewitnesses at an identification unit in the United Kingdom showed that 88% of cases involved multiple eyewitnesses, with approximately four co-witnesses, on average (Skagerberg & Wright, 2008). Among witnesses who saw violence against another person, 46% admitted to discussing the event with their co-witness(es). A staggering *100%* of witnesses to sexual offenses or fraud/forgery reported discussing the event with their co-witness(es).

The now-classic studies of Elizabeth Loftus (1975; 1979) showed how exposure to post-event information can affect memory. In one study, participants viewed a film of an automobile accident and were asked questions about it. The first question asked either how fast the car was going "when it ran the stop sign" or how fast it was going "when it turned right." Then all subjects were asked whether they had seen a stop sign in the film. In the first group, which had been asked about the speed of the car "when it ran the stop sign," 53% said they had seen a stop sign, whereas only 35% of the second group said they had seen the sign. The effect of the initial question was to "prompt" a memory for the sign. In a second study, Loftus included a misleading follow-up question that mentioned a nonexistent barn. When questioned one week later, 17% of the subjects reported seeing the barn in the original film. In essence, the new information conveyed as part of a question was added to the memory of the original stimulus. Not surprisingly, post-event information that matches one's beliefs is more likely to be integrated into memory (Luna & Migueles, 2008). This line of research is a good example of the interplay between the influence of other people (i.e., social influence) and basic memory processes—and how they combine to produce eyewitness errors.

Viewing photographs of suspects after witnessing a crime can also impair an eyewitness's ability to recognize the perpetrator's face in a lineup. Exposure to photographs reduces both correct identifications (identifying actual perpetrators when they are present in the lineup) and correct rejections (rejecting the choices in a lineup when the perpetrator is absent), and increases false alarms (identifying someone who is not the perpetrator) (Deffenbacher et al., 2006). The case of Larry Fuller, described in Box 5.1, provides an example of the effects of post-event exposure to photographs.

Retrieval. The third and final step in establishing memory is the retrieval of information. When eyewitnesses are asked whether they recognize the culprit from a lineup or a show-up (the presentation of a single suspect), they sometimes respond with an immediate positive identification. This suggests that there is a strong match between their memory of the culprit and the photo they have identified. Psychological scientists describe the degree of this match as ecphoric similarity (Tulving, 1981), or how much someone's memory matches the stimulus—the identified individual, in the case of an eyewitness.

At other times, the eyewitness's response is not automatic. Instead, it entails more effortful and deliberative thinking, during which various aspects of the situation (the way questions are worded, for example) can affect retrieval (Charman & Wells, 2006). Consider the question "What was the man with the mustache doing with the young boy?" Assume that the man in question had no mustache. This form of the question may influence memory of the man's appearance. Later, if asked to describe the man, eyewitnesses who lack a strong memory of the perpetrator may incorporate the detail (in this case, the mustache) embedded in the question (Leippe et al., 2006). Repeated retrieval procedures—for example, searching through a series of mug shots before viewing a lineup or seeing a suspect at various pretrial hearings—can increase an eyewitness's susceptibility to suggestion (Chan & LaPaglia, 2011) and inflate a witness's confidence (Odinot et al., 2009).

In recalling information from our memory, we can sometimes retrieve memories that are accurate but are not

Box 5.1

The Case of Larry Fuller and the Victim Who "Never Wavered"

Six o'clock on a foggy April morning in 1981, 45 minutes before sunrise in Dallas. A woman awakens to find a man with a knife atop her. The only light in the room comes from a digital alarm clock. The intruder cuts her and rapes her. Shortly afterwards, hospital personnel collect semen in a rape kit. Two days later the victim looks at photographs of possible suspects; Larry Fuller's picture is among them. Because she cannot make an identification, the investigating officer recommends that the investigation be suspended. But other detectives persist, showing the victim a second photospread several days later. Importantly, Fuller's picture is the only one in the second photospread that was also in the first. At this point, the victim positively identifies him and he is arrested. In the subsequent trial, the prosecution claimed that the victim "never wavered." Perhaps not surprisingly, Fuller is convicted and sentenced to 50 years in prison.

Larry Fuller was 32 years old at the time, raising two young children. He had served two tours of duty in Vietnam where he was shot down several times. After being honorably discharged, he pursued a degree in the arts while working several jobs. From prison he petitioned the Innocence Project to take his case but the Dallas District Attorney's Office opposed multiple requests for DNA testing. (That District Attorney has since been replaced.) A

Larry Fuller

judge finally ordered DNA testing and Larry Fuller was excluded as the perpetrator. After serving 25 years for a crime he did not commit, he became the 186th person exonerated through DNA analysis.

Critical Thought Question

Why would post-event exposure to Fuller's photograph increase the likelihood that the victim would identify him?

---

relevant to the task at hand. For example, victims sometimes pick from a lineup the person whom they have seen before but who is not the actual criminal. For example, a clerk at a convenience store who is the victim of a late-night robbery may mistakenly identify an innocent shopper who has been in the store previously. In an actual case, a Los Angeles judge who was kidnapped and attacked while jogging picked a suspect's picture from a photographic lineup. She later stated that she had forgotten that the suspect appeared before her in court for similar offenses four years earlier, and that she had sentenced him to unsupervised probation (Associated Press, 1988). This phenomenon is called **unconscious transference** (not to be confused with the psychoanalytic notion of transference in a therapeutic context). It is one reason that innocent persons are sometimes charged with a crime and eventually convicted. This phenomenon is one possible explanation for the mistaken identification of Larry Fuller (refer to Box 5.1); the witness was familiar with his face because she saw his photo in an earlier photospread, not because he was guilty of assaulting her.

The fact that eyewitnesses make mistakes should not be surprising. We all have experiences in which our own memories fail: forgetting a cousin's birthday, not recognizing someone we previously met, or failing to remember the name of a famous actress. The mistakes made by eyewitnesses are the result of the same memory processes that

operate in all of our daily lives. What makes them such an important area of study for psychological scientists is the consequence for a mistake. Forgetting your cousin's birthday is likely to result in nothing more than a guilt trip; mistakenly identifying an innocent person could send them to prison for decades, or even to death row.

How Psychologists Study Eyewitness Identification

We have already described studies of various influences on eyewitness memory. We now expand on three techniques that psychologists use to study eyewitness issues, and describe their advantages and disadvantages. Knowing how the studies are conducted can help you to understand what we can justifiably conclude from them.

Experimental methodology, in which a researcher stages a crime or shows a filmed crime to unsuspecting participant witnesses, is the primary research method. In an experiment, the researcher manipulates some variable (e.g., the presence or absence of an instruction to witnesses, prior to viewing a lineup, that the perpetrator "may or may not be in the lineup") and measures its effects (e.g., the likelihood of choosing someone from the lineup). The value of an experiment is that the researcher knows exactly what the witnesses experienced (termed **ground truth**) and can measure, fairly precisely, how the manipulated variable affected what the witnesses remember. As a result, a well-designed experiment can establish cause-and-effect relations. But any individual experiment may lack ecological validity, meaning that the study may not approximate the real-world conditions under which eyewitnesses observe crimes and police interact with eyewitnesses. Still, if a number of experiments conducted under varying conditions and with different populations tend to reach the same conclusion, we can be fairly certain that the result would apply (or generalize) to the "real world."

A second way to study eyewitness identification is via archival analysis that involves after-the-fact examination of actual cases. Archival analyses typically begin with proven wrongful convictions and examine features of the cases that could have led to the mistaken verdicts. A study of the first 200 exonerations based on DNA testing analyzed the evidence that was used in the original trials (e.g., eyewitness testimony, forensic evidence) (Garrett, 2008). These analyses helped demonstrate the overwhelming influence of mistaken eyewitness identifications on wrongful convictions. Archival analyses can also provide information about when eyewitnesses are likely to be accurate. For example, identifications tended to be accurate when witnesses had a longer time to view the perpetrator and saw them from a close distance (Horry et al., 2014). Archival analyses are most useful when there are other methods of corroborating the accuracy of the witness's identification.

Field studies combine the rigorous control of an experiment with the real-world setting of archival analyses. Field studies of eyewitness identification can examine the procedures used by the police in actual cases. For example, some field studies test different procedures for showing photos to witnesses (Wells et al., 2015). A field study may have more ecological validity than an experiment, but it also has a downside. Because we cannot be certain whether a suspect is really guilty, we cannot distinguish correct identifications of the guilty from incorrect identifications of the innocent.

The Variables That Affect Eyewitness Accuracy

Building on the research on basic information processing and using these methodologies, psychologists have identified several other variables that can influence the validity of identifications. Professor Gary Wells, a prolific researcher in the area of eyewitness identification, introduced a useful taxonomy to categorize these variables (Wells, 1978). He coined the term system variable to refer to factors that are under the control of the criminal justice system (e.g., the instructions given to eyewitnesses and the composition of the lineup). The term estimator variable refers to factors that are beyond the control of the justice system and whose impact on the reliability of the eyewitness can only be estimated (e.g., the lighting conditions at the time of the crime and whether the culprit was wearing a disguise). A third

category of variables—reflector variables—does not affect the reliability of an identification (Wells, 2020). Instead, these variables reflect accuracy because witnesses who are accurate behave differently from those who are inaccurate (these are also called postdiction variables). One example is the speed of an eyewitness's identification decision: witnesses who make decisions more quickly tend to be more accurate than witnesses who make decisions more slowly (e.g., Grabman et al., 2019).

Because system variables hold more promise for preventing errors in eyewitness identification (they are, after all, controllable), many psychologists have focused their research efforts on those variables. But research on estimator variables is important because it can help us understand situations in which eyewitnesses experience problems in perception and memory, and studies of reflector variables allow an after-the-fact assessment of eyewitness accuracy. The next sections review these kinds of variables, all relevant in different ways to our understanding of the psychology of eyewitness identification.

Assessing the Impact of Estimator Variables

We have already described two estimator variables—the witness's stress level at the time of the crime and the presence of a weapon. Other estimator variables can also be present and affect identification accuracy.

Race of the Eyewitness. Eyewitnesses are usually better at recognizing and identifying members of their own race or ethnic group than members of another race or ethnic group. The chances of a mistaken identification have been estimated to be 1.56 times greater when the witness and suspect are of different races than when they are of the same race (Meissner & Brigham, 2001). This phenomenon, termed the own-race bias, has been examined extensively in experimental studies involving a variety of racial groups, and archival analysis of DNA exoneration cases shows that it is also a significant problem in actual cases.

Understanding the reasons for the own-race bias has vexed psychologists for some time. Racial attitudes are apparently not related to this phenomenon: people with prejudicial attitudes are not more likely to experience the own-race bias than are people with unbiased attitudes (e.g., Ferguson et al., 2001). Therefore, explanations of the own-race bias have tended to involve both cognitive and social processes.

Cognitive interpretations hold that there are differences between faces of one race and faces of another race in terms of the variability in features, something called physiognomic variability. Faces of one race differ from faces of another race in terms of the type of physiognomic variability. For example, White faces have more variability in hair color; Black faces have more variability in skin tone. For eyewitnesses to make a correct identification, they must focus on the characteristics that distinguish that person from other people of the same race. Thus, witnesses who saw a White perpetrator would be better off noticing and encoding hair color rather than skin tone. In contrast, if the perpetrator was Black, witnesses who focused on skin tone rather than hair color might be better able to correctly identify the perpetrator. Because most of us have more experience with members of our own race, our natural inclination is to focus on the features that distinguish members of *our own group* from one another. We have less practice distinguishing one member of another race from other people of that race.

Additional support for the idea that people process other-race faces differently from own-race faces is provided by studies involving sophisticated eye-movement monitoring technology to assess the encoding processes people adopt when viewing own-race and other-race faces. One study showed that we fixate on more, and more distinctive, features when viewing own-race faces than when viewing other-race faces (Goldinger et al., 2009).

The influence of practice (or experience) on the own-race bias is supported by one study measuring identification accuracy and inter-racial contact among university students. This study showed that Black students from the University of Cape Town (South Africa) who reported higher levels of inter-racial contact showed less own-race bias compared with Black students from the same university who reported less inter-racial contact (Wright et al., 2003).

Social psychologists have also tried to explain the own-race bias. One reasonable hypothesis is based on social perception and **in-group/out-group differences** (Sporer, 2001). When we encounter the face of a person from another race or ethnic group (the out-group), our first job is to categorize the face as a member of that group (e.g., "That person is Asian"). Attentional resources that are directed toward categorization come at the expense of attention to facial features that would distinguish that person from other members of the out-group. But when we encounter the face of a person from our in-group, the categorization step is eliminated, so we can immediately devote attention to distinguishing that person from other members of the in-group. Because identifying people of other races involves both a cognitive and a social process, both explanations may be right.

Because the race of the victim and perpetrator are outside the control of the justice system (i.e., they are estimator variables), it might seem like there are no constructive solutions to these kinds of eyewitness errors. However, one simple solution might be to ensure that the lineup administrator assembling a photospread is the same race as the suspect (Brigham & Ready, 1985). Such a policy would ideally reduce the chances that the suspect inadvertently stands out from other photos because the person assembling the photospread has used appropriate physiognomic characteristics in selecting photos for the witness to view.

Social Media. Increasingly, some witnesses conduct their own searches on social media for images or information about culprits (e.g., Mcgorrery, 2016). For example, in one case, a victim was assaulted by a stranger who happened to be with an acquaintance of the victim. After the attack, the victim searched the acquaintance's Facebook page and "identified" the assailant from those photos. In another case, a stabbing victim was shown an Instagram photo of a potential suspect by a friend who had heard about the attack (Douglass & Smalarz, 2019). These social media "investigations" are not controlled or arranged (or endorsed) by police. Moreover, they often occur before any formal interaction with police, thereby undermining any subsequent identification procedure, even if it is conducted by police in line with all recommendations from psychological scientists. And witness accuracy has the potential to be negatively influenced by variables already discussed, such as post-event information or co-witness influence.

Controlling the Impact of System Variables

System variables are those factors over which the justice system has some control. In general, system variables tend to come into play after the crime, usually during the investigation. They are associated with how a witness is questioned and how a lineup is constructed and presented to the eyewitness. We have already described one system variable: the types of questions posed to eyewitnesses. Other system variables are also important. Research on these variables can suggest changes to procedures that investigators use with eyewitnesses.

To explain why system variables are so important, it may be helpful to draw an analogy to the steps used by researchers conducting an experiment (Wells & Luus, 1990). Like scientists, crime investigators begin with a hypothesis (that the suspect actually committed the crime); test the hypothesis (by placing the suspect in a lineup); observe and record the eyewitness's decision; and draw conclusions from the results (e.g., that the suspect is guilty).

There are certain principles that are essential to good experimental design. For example, experiments are not useful if the person recording the data is biased or careless. In similar fashion, violating the principles of good criminal investigation affects the results of the investigation. For example, if the suspect appears to be different from the other people in the lineup in some obvious way, or if the people conducting the lineup convey their suspicions to the eyewitness, then the results of that identification procedure can be erroneous. Applying the analogy of an experiment to criminal investigations enables us to evaluate the steps involved in these investigations.

Reforming Identification Procedures

One important aspect of a system variable is that because it is controllable, it can be modified. Because the police want to catch the real culprits and avoid mistakes, they have begun to incorporate procedures recommended by psychologists and other researchers for interviewing eyewitnesses and constructing and presenting lineups. Many of these changes are designed to improve the **diagnosticity** of an identification procedure or the likelihood that an identification is accurate (i.e., that the identified suspect is guilty).

Psychological scientists have published the scientific consensus on research-based recommendations for collecting and preserving eyewitness evidence (Wells et al., 1998; 2020). Many recommendations have also been endorsed by both the U.S. Department of Justice (1999) and the National Research Council (2014). In addition, several state courts have imposed requirements for eyewitness evidence by relying on social science findings (e.g., *State v. Henderson*, 2011; *State v. Lawson*, 2012). Law enforcement jurisdictions around the country have also voluntarily adopted many of the recommendations made by psychologists (Wells, 2020).

In the sections that follow, we describe some of the scientific findings on system variables that led to these policy changes. You will notice that the reforms (for example, warning an eyewitness that the suspect may or may not be in the lineup) may come with a trade-off: although they reduce the likelihood of mistaken identifications, they also reduce the likelihood of correct identifications. How people value this trade-off will depend on whether they are primarily concerned about due process rights of criminal defendants or about crime control and the conviction of guilty offenders, as well as other complicated policy issues (Clark, 2012).

Interviewing Eyewitnesses

The police often want more information from eyewitnesses than those witnesses can provide (Kebbell & Milne, 1998). So psychologists have devised ways to enhance information gathering. The **Cognitive Interview** is an interviewing protocol based on various concepts of memory retrieval and social communication (Fisher & Geiselman, 1992; Geiselman et al., 1985). Before describing the Cognitive Interview, we describe a standard police interview so you can understand why a new method was needed.

A "standard" police interview relies on a predetermined set of questions with little opportunity for follow-up, repeated interruptions, time constraints, and an expectation that the witness will be willing and able to answer all of the questions. By contrast, in a Cognitive Interview, the interviewer first engages the witness in order to develop rapport, then asks the witness to provide a narrative account of the event, and finally, probes for details with specific questions. The interviewer allows the witness to direct the subject matter and flow of the questioning, rarely interrupts, and listens actively to the witness's responses.

Perhaps the most distinctive element of a Cognitive Interview (and the reason for its name) is its reliance on a set of cues developed from research on memory retrieval. Cognitive psychologists have observed that reinstating the context in which a witness encoded an event provides retrieval cues and thereby increases accessibility of information stored in memory. With this objective in mind, the interviewer may cue a witness to mentally reconstruct the physical and emotional experiences that existed at the time of the crime. The interviewer may direct the witness to form an image of the situation, recollect sights, sounds, smells, and physical conditions (e.g., heat, cold, darkness), and recall any emotional reactions experienced at the time. When the witness has mentally reconstructed the event, the interviewer asks for a detailed narrative and then uses follow-up questions to probe for specific information. Witnesses are sometimes asked to recall events in different temporal orders (e.g., describing the event from the end to the beginning), from different perspectives, or from the point of view of different people. A Cognitive Interview allowed British police to solve a kidnapping that gripped the nation for eight days in 1992. We describe the case in Box 5.2.

A meta-analysis of 65 experiments gauged the effectiveness of the Cognitive Interview. It showed that compared with the traditional interview method, the Cognitive Interview can generate substantial increases in correct recall, though it can also produce a small increase in incorrect details (Memon et al., 2010). The Cognitive Interview is especially effective for older adults, who rely more on external cues to retrieve information from memory. Personnel from organizations including the FBI, Department of Homeland Security, National Transportation Safety Board, and some state and local police departments have been trained on Cognitive Interviewing procedures and tests in the field demonstrate the value of the Cognitive Interview in real crime situations (e.g., Ashkenazi & Fisher, 2022).

Researchers have even developed a **Self-Administered Interview** (SAI), a version of the Cognitive Interview that can be completed by witnesses themselves by answering questions—and providing drawings—in a prepared booklet (e.g., Gabbert et al., 2009; Matsuo & Miura, 2017). One benefit of the SAI is that it does not require trained interviewers to be present with the witness. Therefore, it can often be administered soon after an event because witnesses can complete the booklet independently. One obvious downside is that it requires witnesses to be literate in the language in which the booklet has been provided.

Lineup Instructions

There is ample evidence that when conducting a lineup, an investigator should instruct the witness that the offender may or may not be present (Malpass & Devine, 1981). Without this admonition, eyewitnesses may assume that their task is to pick someone, so they tend to respond by choosing the person who looks most like the perpetrator. Evaluating experimental studies on the "might or might not be present" admonition, Professor Nancy Steblay determined that this instruction reduced the rate of mistaken identifications (i.e., saying that offenders were present in the lineup when they were not) from 70% to 43% (Steblay, 2013). The rate of accurate identifications is also slightly reduced by the instruction, but that decline is much smaller than the decline in mistaken identifications.

Box 5.2

The Case of Wooden-legged Michael Sams and his Victim's Cognitive Interview

On January 22, 1992, real estate agent Stephanie Slater arranged to show property to a prospective client in Birmingham, England. But Michael Sams was no client. At the rundown house, he put a knife to Slater's throat, forced her into his car, and drove her to a remote warehouse where he held her, handcuffed, blindfolded, and gagged, for eight days. Though Sams had killed before, this time he released his victim after receiving ransom money from Slater's manager.

Now the police had a single eyewitness to the crime—the victim—and needed to find her kidnapper. Through careful questioning that included context reinstatement, Slater was able to recall that during captivity she heard nearby trains and an old telephone ring. She described the smell of the kidnapper's clothes. And she recalled the feel of walking across cobblestones. Sparse though these details were, they allowed police to piece together a physical description of her attacker and trace the place of her confinement. After releasing this information to the public they received hundreds of tips, including one that led to Michael Sams, a wooden-legged criminal who had kidnapped and murdered a sex worker the previous year. This

PA Images/Getty Images

Michael Sams

case was a landmark application of the principles of Cognitive Interviewing.

Critical Thought Question

For what reasons would Slater have been able to remember more when questioned via the Cognitive Interview than a standard police interview?

The vast majority of police officers report that they give eyewitnesses the option of not making a selection from the lineup (Wogalter et al., 2004). However, police officers can inadvertently undermine the usefulness of proper instructions if—for example—they encourage witnesses. In one experiment, when lineup administrators gave proper instructions but *also* said—"Surely, you can pick the perpetrator"—the likelihood of a false identification increased compared to a condition in which there was no such encouragement (Quinlivan et al., 2012).

How do Witnesses Decide whom to Identify?

Ideally, witnesses would only identify someone from a photospread if there is a strong match between the photo and their memory of the culprit. When the culprit is present in a set of photos, the likelihood that a witness will make a correct identification is high. However, what happens when the culprit's photo is not present? What happens if the person the police think is guilty, is actually innocent? What *should happen* is that witnesses decide not to make an identification. What *does happen* is something quite different.

Professor Gary Wells demonstrated what does happen in his "removal without replacement" study (Wells, 1993). In this study, all eyewitnesses watched a staged crime. Some were presented with a photographic lineup that included the

actual culprit and five fillers. Another group saw the same photographic lineup with one exception: The culprit's photo was removed and was not replaced with another photo. In both groups, all lineup members were presented to the witness at once. This procedure is termed **simultaneous presentation**.

If identifications of the culprit by the culprit-present group are based solely on witnesses' recognition, then the percentage of people in that group who identified him *plus* the percentage who said "not there" should be exactly the same as the percentage in the culprit-absent group who said "not there." Wells tested this idea by showing 200 eyewitnesses either a culprit-present lineup or a lineup in which the culprit was absent but was not replaced by anyone else (refer to Table 5.1). When the culprit was present in the lineup, 54% of eyewitnesses selected him, and 21% said "not there." Did 75% of eyewitnesses in the "target-absent" lineup say "not there"? Unfortunately, no. The "not there" response was given by only 32% of people in that group. The others all mistakenly identified someone else from the lineup, even though they had been warned that the offender might not be in the lineup. Why? Through a process of **relative judgment**, eyewitnesses apparently select whoever looks most like the perpetrator. The weaker one's memory, the more likely one is to use a relative judgment (Clark &

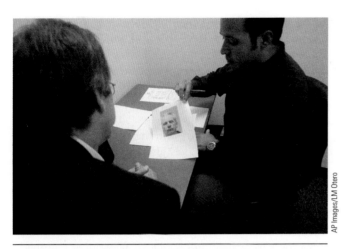

A sequential photospread identification procedure.

Davey, 2005). Importantly this shift to identifications of an innocent person happened even when the instructions were unbiased—that is, witnesses were warned that the actual culprit might not be in the photospread.

The fact that eyewitnesses tend to choose someone from a photospread—even if the culprit is not present—explains the recommendation that police adopt a **reasonable suspicion standard** for deciding to conduct an identification procedure (this is also called an evidence-based suspicion standard; Wells et al., 2015). The logic is that because witnesses tend to make choices from photospreads, and because identifications are such compelling incriminating evidence, police should have some evidence suggesting guilt before placing the "… suspect into the jeopardy of an identification procedure" (Wells, 2020, p. 1322). Such evidence might include things like self-incrimination, a unique fit to the witness's description, or physical evidence (refer to Wells et al., 2020 for additional examples). One study suggests that police officers tend to use identification procedures without any evidence against the suspect (Katzman & Kovera, 2022). If this tendency is supported in additional samples of police officers, explaining the reasonable suspicion standard will be an important area for future education efforts in law enforcement communities.

The phenomenon demonstrated in Table 5.1 motivated the recommendation that photos be presented to witnesses one at a time, in a so-called **sequential presentation**. In this presentation, the witness makes a decision about each lineup member before seeing the next one. Indeed, some field studies find that sequential procedures yielded fewer mistaken identifications of fillers (11%) than did simultaneous procedures (18%), without affecting the rate of identifying the suspect (e.g., Wells et al., 2015). But other studies find a decrease in accuracy when sequential procedures are used (e.g., Steblay et al., 2011). As a result of these empirical inconsistencies, the National Academy of Sciences (2014) wrote that the "relative superiority of competing identification procedures (i.e., simultaneous versus sequential) is unresolved" (p. 104). They recommended collaborative work among psychological scientists to continue to deepen our understanding of the relative costs and benefits of each procedure.

The Influence of Feedback

Recall our analogy between a criminal investigation and a scientific experiment. One of the cardinal rules of a good experiment is that the person conducting the experiment should not influence the results, a problem referred to as **experimenter bias**. To avoid such bias, experimenters interacting with research participants should know little about the study's hypotheses and less about the experimental condition in which any participant is placed. Nearly all clinical drug trials adhere to these rules—neither the patient taking the pills nor the doctor assessing the patient's health know whether the pills are actually a new drug or a placebo. These so-called **double-blind testing procedures**, commonplace in medicine and other scientific fields, should also be used in police investigations with eyewitnesses. Not only should the witness be blind to the identity of the suspect, but the lineup administrator should be as well.

When lineups are conducted by detectives who selected the fillers and know which person is the suspect, their knowledge can affect the eyewitness in various ways. First, it can increase the likelihood that an eyewitness will choose someone from the lineup (Phillips et al., 1999). This is

Table 5.1							
Rates of choosing lineup members when a culprit (#3) is present versus removed without replacement							
	Lineup Member						
	1	**2**	**3**	**4**	**5**	**6**	**No Choice**
Culprit present	3%	13%	54%	3%	3%	3%	21%
Culprit removed (without replacement)	6%	38%	—	12%	7%	5%	32%

Source: "What do we know about eyewitness identification?" from G. L. Wells. (1993). *American Psychologist, 48,* 553–571.

more likely to occur when the administrator has failed to provide instructions that the suspect may or may not be in the lineup, in which case the eyewitness may presume that the suspect is present and look to the administrator for cues (Greathouse & Kovera, 2009).

Furthermore, eyewitnesses who have frequent contact with the administrator—either because they are in close physical contact or because they have extensive interactions—are likely to make decisions consistent with the administrator's expectations (Haw & Fisher, 2004). Perhaps most concerning, neither the eyewitness nor the administrator is typically aware of this influence (Garrioch & Brimacombe, 2001). An obvious solution to this situation is to have the lineup administered by someone who does not know which person in the lineup is the suspect. Experimental studies now document that double-blind procedures reduce both mistaken identifications and confidence in those mistaken identifications (Charman & Quiroz, 2016).

Beyond affecting witnesses' choices, lineup administrators can affect how confident witnesses report being in their identification decision. For example, feedback from a lineup administrator about the witness's accuracy distorts eyewitnesses' certainty in that identification compared with eyewitnesses who receive no such feedback (Wells & Bradfield, 1998). Influence occurs even when witnesses are explicitly told that the lineup administrator does not know who the suspect is (Smalarz et al., 2021).

Remarkably, feedback that confirms an identification also leads eyewitnesses to report that they had a better view of, and paid more attention to, the perpetrator and that it was easier for them to identify that person. It increases their sense that they have good memory for strangers and willingness to testify about their eyewitness experience at a trial (Steblay et al., 2014). Finally, post-identification feedback also makes witnesses more persuasive to observers, even though their identifications are incorrect (Douglass et al., 2010).

Even *without* explicit confirming feedback, eyewitnesses infer from the facts of an ongoing investigation and eventual prosecution that they must have picked the culprit from the lineup. Hence, their confidence can increase. This enhanced confidence is troubling because the confidence expressed by eyewitnesses during their trial testimony is one of the most compelling reasons why jurors believe such identifications are accurate (Brewer & Burke, 2002). This is not surprising—when evaluating others' claims in multiple domains, we tend to assume that confident people are accurate. The remedy to this problem of ever-increasing certainty? A blind administrator should take a video-recorded statement of the eyewitness's confidence at the time of the identification decision, before any feedback can occur.

Eyewitness Confidence

In spite of ample evidence that post-identification feedback (and other variables) distort eyewitnesses' confidence, their confidence can be very useful in postdicting their accuracy.

The key is to ensure that confidence statements are uncontaminated by external variables, like post-identification feedback or co-witness influence. Researchers generally agree that statements of confidence made from the witness stand during a trial are uninformative because in that setting, there are many factors other than witnesses' accuracy that can boost confidence (e.g., simply seeing that the defendant has been charged with the crime). But confidence statements made immediately after a positive identification from a lineup, assuming the lineup was conducted properly, can provide useful information about accuracy (Wixted & Wells, 2017).

Whether witnesses' statements of confidence at the lineup are indicative of accuracy depends on how that identification was secured and reported. What does a properly conducted lineup look like? The suspect does not stand out from the fillers, the fillers are known to be innocent, the lineup administrator provides unbiased ("may or may not be present") instructions and avoids giving post-identification feedback, and confidence is measured immediately after an identification. Unfortunately, these conditions often don't occur in the real world (Police Executive Research Forum, 2013), despite being supported by empirical research. This can explain why eyewitnesses in hundreds of DNA exoneration cases were confident, but wrong (Smalarz & Wells, 2015). And its suggests that criminal justice personnel should review their eyewitness identification practices in order to bring them in line with "best practices." Only then can eyewitness confidence tell us something about eyewitness accuracy (Wixted & Wells, 2017).

As investigators "clean up" their identification procedures, they must be attentive to other ways that they can affect eyewitnesses' confidence statements. Research shows that a host of variables can affect witness confidence, including learning about another witness's identification decision (Charman et al., 2010) or learning whether they might be contradicted by another witness; confidence increased when there was no chance of contradiction and decreased when there was (Shaw et al., 2007). Entirely different forms of evidence can also affect eyewitness confidence. In one experiment, witnesses' confidence increased when they learned that the person they identified had confessed and their confidence decreased when they learned that all suspects denied being involved or when they learned that the person they identified denied involvement (Hasel & Kassin, 2009). Even more striking, learning that someone other than their chosen suspect confessed actually prompted some eyewitnesses in Hasel and Kassin's study to change their identification decisions to a different person.

The Eyewitness in the Courtroom

Despite limitations on the reliability of eyewitness identifications, jurors put a great deal of weight on testimony from an eyewitness. In a study showing this influence, Loftus (1974) gave subjects a description of an armed robbery that resulted in two deaths. Among mock jurors who heard a version of the case that contained only circumstantial evidence against the defendant, 18% convicted him. But when an eyewitness's identification of the defendant was presented as well, 72% of the mock jurors convicted him. This pattern is replicated in real cases where jurors acknowledge that eyewitness evidence is powerful and compelling. In one murder trial, a juror reported being heavily persuaded by the testimony of the single eyewitness, who was a friend of the murder victim: "The friend's story never changed. He didn't stutter. I thought: *If I'd seen my friend murdered, I would remember who I saw do it.*" (Kennedy, 2018). The defendant in this case was indeed convicted, only to be exonerated years later, to the dismay of the juror who belatedly realized his faith in the witness was ill-placed. This case is one of many demonstrating the power of confident eyewitnesses to convince a jury of the correctness of their testimony.

Why do jurors have difficulty inferring the accuracy of an eyewitness's memory? In particular, why do they overestimate accuracy? One reason is that, as we mentioned, jurors rely on witness confidence as an indicator of accuracy and by the time eyewitnesses get to trial, most are quite confident. Jurors themselves believe that when they are sure of something, they are likely to be correct, so why not eyewitnesses, too (Bornstein & Greene, 2017)? As a result, jurors tend to trust both overt statements of confidence such as "I'm sure that's the guy" and subtler indications of confidence such as voice pitch, intonation, and speed of making an identification.

There are other explanations for jurors' over-reliance on eyewitness testimony (refer to, e.g., Semmler et al., 2012):

- Jurors cannot verify an eyewitness's version of an event against some objective record of what occurred. Instead, they may rely on a positive stereotype about memory credibility, suggesting an insensitivity to the impact of estimator variables.

- Jurors assume that eyewitnesses' testimony is a reflection of their memory quality, and not the way they were questioned or interacted with the lineup administrator. This suggests an insensitivity to the role of system variables and social influence in shaping a witness's recollection. More broadly, it is an example of the fundamental attribution error: the tendency to assume that the causes of behavior are internal to a person rather than the result of external factors such as the role of a lineup administrator and the nature of the lineup.

Safeguards against Wrongful Convictions: Trial Remedies

The best way to prevent wrongful convictions stemming from mistaken identifications is to prevent the mistaken identifications from happening in the first place. That goal is best reached by implementing the investigative remedies described earlier (e.g., double-blind lineup administration). If a mistaken identification does occur, there are ways to address the problem at trial, none of which are very good, unfortunately. We discuss three methods below: limiting eyewitness testimony, expert testimony, and jury instructions.

Limiting Eyewitness Testimony

Suppose that an eyewitness to a convenience store robbery made a tentative identification of a suspect from a lineup, and after being presented with a second lineup in which the suspect was the only person repeated, made a more confident identification. A judge could rule that the eyewitness can testify about the initial, tentative identification, but not about the second identification. A prosecutor faced with the exclusion of powerful testimony is likely to pressure the police to use less suggestive procedures in the future (Wells & Quinlivan, 2009). However, for this remedy to be effective, judges must understand empirical evidence and apply it to the case correctly. Unfortunately, because judges are not trained on experimental or scientific procedure, their ability to correctly understand and apply science is limited (e.g., Stinson et al., 1997).

Expert Testimony

Another trial remedy is to invite an expert witness to provide information to the judge or jury about psychological science related to eyewitness identification evidence. To be most helpful, expert testimony should aid jurors in discriminating between circumstances that enhance eyewitness accuracy (e.g., double-blind lineup administration) and those that impair it (e.g., weapon focus). The data are mixed on whether this remedy is effective. Some studies find that experts can sensitize jurors to questionable viewing conditions or suggestive police procedures (e.g., Devenport et al., 2002; Laub et al., 2016). But other studies conclude that expert testimony makes jurors skeptical of eyewitness memory and less likely to convict, regardless of the quality of the witnessing conditions and identification procedures (e.g., Jones et al., 2017; Martire & Kemp, 2011). And judges are the ones who typically decide whether expert testimony is even allowed in an individual case. When it is, it is an expensive safeguard that is available in only a small fraction of the cases that come to trial each year (Wells et al., 1998). Are there other more affordable and readily available remedies?

Jury Instructions

In a case with eyewitness evidence, the defense typically requests that juries receive instructions telling them how to evaluate eyewitness evidence. The judge decides whether to grant the request. There is some evidence that jury instructions can help juries make better decisions about whether to believe eyewitness identification evidence. In one study, mock juries instructed that eyewitness identification evidence was not collected properly were less likely to convict the defendant (Lampinen et al., 2005). However, data from other studies are not so promising: In New Jersey, judges must provide instructions to juries regarding the reliability of eyewitness identification testimony (*New Jersey v. Henderson*, 2011) but empirical tests of these specific instructions suggest that they are generally unable to help jurors evaluate eyewitness identification evidence (Jones et al., 2020). As noted earlier, given the relative inefficiency of these remedies, the best approach is to try to prevent mistaken identifications from happening in the first place.

Children as Witnesses

Sometimes a child is the only witness to a crime—or its only victim. A number of questions arise in cases where children are witnesses. Can they remember the precise details of these incidents? Can suggestive interviewing techniques distort their reports? Do repeated interviews increase errors? Is it appropriate for children to testify in a courtroom? Society's desire to prosecute and punish offenders may require that children testify about their victimization, but defendants should not be convicted on the basis of inaccurate testimony. In this section we focus on the accuracy of children as witnesses, and on concerns about children testifying in court.

Children as Eyewitnesses to Crimes

Like adults, children are sometimes asked to identify strangers or to describe what they witnessed regarding crimes. In kidnappings and assaults, the child may be the only witness to a crime committed by a stranger. To test children's eyewitness capabilities, researchers create situations that closely match real-life events. In these studies, children typically interact with an unknown adult (the "target") for some period of time in a school classroom or a doctor's office. They are later questioned about what they experienced and what the target person looked like, and they may be asked to make an identification from a lineup.

Two general findings emerge from these studies. First, children ages 5 and older can make reasonably reliable identifications from lineups (Pozzulo, 2017). Second, children are generally less accurate than adults when making an identification from a lineup in which the culprit is absent. In these situations, children tend to select someone from the lineup, thereby making a false-positive error (Fitzgerald & Price, 2015). Such mistakes are troubling to the police because they thwart the ongoing investigation and implicate an innocent person.

Psychologists have attempted to devise identification procedures for children that maintain identification accuracy when the culprit is in the lineup but reduce false-positive choices when the culprit is absent. Presenting lineup members in a face-off procedure that breaks the task into a series of binary decisions, rather than showing all lineup members together, decreased guessing and the incidence of false identifications from target-absent lineups (Price & Fitzgerald, 2016).

Children as Victims of Maltreatment

The most likely reason that children become involved with the legal system is that they have been maltreated, with more than four million such cases under investigation in the United States each year (London et al., 2021). In many of these cases, the issue is not who committed the crime. Rather, the question centers around what happened to the child. Psychologists have been particularly interested in the effects—socio-emotional, neurobiological, mental health, *and* cognitive—of maltreatment. In this chapter we focus on the cognitive effects, particularly the implications for memory of child abuse, including child sexual abuse (CSA).

Most CSA cases rest solely on the words of the victim because these cases typically lack any physical evidence. (The most frequent forms of sexual abuse perpetrated on children are fondling, exhibitionism, and oral copulation.) Yet anyone who has spent time with young children knows that their descriptions of situations can sometimes mix fact and fantasy. There are concerns about whether preschoolers and even older children can be trusted to provide accurate details and to disclose experiences of abuse. There are also concerns about the accuracy of memory on the part of adolescents and adults who previously experienced maltreatment. We focus on studies that assess the effects of interviewing techniques on children's memory of events they experienced and that examine patterns of disclosure of maltreatment and the accuracy of memory for abuse.

Investigative Interviews

One feature of CSA cases is crucial to the accuracy of child witnesses: the nature of the investigative interview. Some interviewers now use a structured questioning protocol that first builds rapport between interviewer and child, and then encourages children to provide details in their own words ("Tell me everything that happened from the beginning to the end as best you can remember"). As with the Cognitive Interview described above, the protocol for children discourages the use of **suggestive questions** (questions that assume information not disclosed by the child or suggest the expected answer, such as "He touched you, didn't he?"). See Box 5.3 for an example of suggestive questions in actual forensic interviews.

Exterior of the McMartin Preschool in Manhattan Beach, California.

Box 5.3

The Case of the Suggestive Interviews

In the 1980s and 1990s, the United States was wracked by a series of horrific and sensational scandals alleging child sexual abuse in daycare settings. Two of the most prominent were the case against Kelly Michaels (Maplewood, New Jersey) and the cases against seven teachers from the McMartin preschool in Manhattan Beach, California. Michaels was convicted of sexually abusing 20 children in her care; she was sentenced to 47 years in prison. After six years in prison, her case was overturned because the jury was "permitted … to believe that the (interviewing) process was rooted in science and thus was a reliable means of determining sex abuse" (National Registry of Exonerations, 2021). Among the seven teachers initially charged at the McMartin preschool, two were tried: Peggy McMartin Buckey and her son Raymond Buckey. Peggy Buckey was acquitted at trial; charges against Raymond Buckey were eventually dropped. (For more information on these cases, refer to Nathan & Snedeker, 1995.)

Part of what gripped the nation upon learning about these cases was the graphic and disturbing nature of the allegations, as well as the young ages of the alleged victims. Some of the alleged victims were only in preschool when the abuse supposedly occurred. Children in both cases provided detailed reports of extensive physical abuse, including being repeatedly raped with Lego blocks, spoons, and forks. Some children reported that daycare workers forced them to watch animals being killed, that they were subjected to satanic ritual abuse, and that they were flown from the daycare to be subjected to abuse in far-flung locations (e.g., Zirpolo, 2005). Parents of children at the McMartin school received a terrifying letter alerting them to the potential of abuse and asking them to question their children about what they might have experienced.

The cases really gathered momentum when the children were formally interviewed as part of the criminal prosecutions. Unfortunately, the questioning tactics used on the children represented a 'how to' for collecting mistaken and false information. An extensive analysis of the actual interviews showed just how these suggestive techniques were employed (Schreiber et al., 2006).

Schreiber et al. (2006) measured the presence of five different suggestive techniques in the actual forensic interviews. For example, some children were questioned repeatedly about events, likely creating an impression in them that they were not providing the correct answer. Indeed, one former

day care student reported (as an adult) that "I remember thinking to myself, 'I'm not going to get out of here unless I tell them what they want to hear" (Zirpolo, 2005). Other children were invited to speculate on what *might have* happened. In this excerpt, the child was encouraged to use Rags Racoon (a puppet) to help her answer questions:

Interviewer: Now, I think this is another one of those tricky games. What do you *think*, Rags?

Child: Yep.

Interviewer: Yes. Do you *think* some of that yucky touching happened, Rags, when she was tied up and she couldn't get away? Do you *think* some of that touching that—Mr. Ray *might* have done some of that touching? Do you think that's *possible*? Where do you *think* he *would have* touched her? Can you use your pointer and show us where he *would have* touched her? (Schreiber et al., 2006, italics added by Schreiber et al.)

For other children, new information was introduced during questioning. Later, when that information was reported back by the child, it was interpreted as corroboration of other children's accounts. For example:

Interviewer: How about Naked Movie Star? You guys remember that game?

Child: No.

Interviewer: Everybody remembered that game. Let's see if we can figure it out.

Based on what we have already learned about the influence of co-witnesses, this technique powerfully harnesses the influence of other people's reports on one's own memory. In sum, the interviewing techniques employed in the Michaels and McMartin cases were characterized by "high levels of three suggestive techniques: reinforcement, the use of co-witness information, and introducing new information" (Schreiber et al., 2006, p. 36). Children in the McMartin case were also invited to speculate. All of the techniques employed in these cases have been tested empirically; all reduce accuracy and even promote false reporting.

Critical Thought Question

How might the suggestive questioning described in Box 5.3 affect memory reports through both social influence and effects on basic memory processes?

Investigative interviewers trained in the structured protocol questioned preschool-aged children who were suspected victims of child abuse. Five-year-olds were able to provide forensically important information in response to **open-ended questions**, and even 3-year-olds were able to share information when invited to elaborate on an earlier response (Hershkowitz et al., 2012). These findings suggest that central

details (the "gist") of victimization experiences can be remembered well when they are elicited by non-suggestive questioning.

After a child has recounted an experience in their own words and in response to open-ended questions, investigators may ask specific questions about the event. For example, if a child said that she was touched, a follow-up question might be "Where were you touched?" Although children tend to provide more detail in response to specific questions than to open-ended questions, the use of specific questions comes at a cost: Children are less accurate in answering specific questions. This difficulty is not restricted to very young children. After seeing a stranger in their classroom handing out candy the previous week, two groups of children (4- to 5-year-olds, and 7- to 8-year-olds) were asked specific, misleading questions (e.g., "He took your clothes off, didn't he?"). Older children were just as likely as younger children to assent to these suggestions (Finnila et al., 2003). And, although suggestibility typically declines with age (e.g., Paz-Alonso & Goodman, 2016), if the suggestion relates to a previously experienced and related event, adults can be more suggestible than children because adults have more experience with "scripts, stereotypes, schemas, and other forms of connected meaning" (Otgaar et al., 2018, p. 383). This knowledge can facilitate incorporations of suggestions into erroneous memory reports. Of course, most interviewers would never intentionally mislead a child, but they may have misinformation or suspicions that could unintentionally shape children's responses. Therefore, the notion of **confirmation bias**—discussed earlier in the context of eyewitness identifications—is relevant here, too.

Children are less accurate in answering specific questions than more general queries because specific questions demand precise memories of events that the child may never have encoded or may have forgotten (Poole et al., 2015). Additionally, children may answer a question that they do not fully understand in order to appear to be cooperative (Waterman et al., 2001). Finally, the more specific the question, the more likely it is that the interviewer will accidentally include information that the child has not stated (refer to Box 5.3 for a real-world example). Specific questions can easily become suggestive.

For children who experience multiple incidents of sexual abuse, the central features of the experiences may be constant, but peripheral details may change. Before prosecutors can file multiple charges, they must provide evidence that reflects the critical details of each separate incident. In other words, the child has to "particularize" their report by providing precise details about each specific allegation. Can a child do this? Studies that examine children's recall of repeated events typically expose them to a series of similar incidents with certain constant features and some details that vary across episodes. Although source monitoring (identifying the source of a memory) improves with age (Quas & Schaaf, 2002), children often recall information from one event as having occurred in another (Brubacher et al., 2011). In fact, exposure to recurring events is a double-edged sword: Repeated events enhance memory for aspects of the incident that are held constant but impair the ability to recall details that vary with each recurrence (Dickinson et al., 2005).

If they experience multiple incidents of maltreatment, children may be subjected to repeated interviews. One line of research has found negative effects of repeated interviews on children's memory and suggestibility. In these studies, experimenters describe true and false events (e.g., in one famous study, children were told that their hand had been caught in a mousetrap), imply that the children experienced all of them, and tell the children that their parents or friends said the events had occurred. After repeated questioning, approximately one-third to one-half of preschool-aged children provided additional details of the false events (e.g., Bruck et al., 2002). A separate line of research has documented beneficial effects of repeated interviews, however. These studies found that children exposed to repeated interviews were not prone to errors. In fact, their memory improved with repeated interviews (e.g., Waterhouse et al., 2016).

What accounts for these conflicting findings? One hint comes from a study that varied the number of interviews and the nature of the questions asked (Quas et al., 2007). In this study, children played alone in a laboratory setting and were questioned either once or three times about what happened while they played. The questions were either biased (implying that the child played with a man) or unbiased. Children interviewed only once by the biased interviewer were most likely to claim they played with a man, and children interviewed on multiple occasions (regardless of the type of question asked) were less likely to do so. This suggests that biased interview questions can lead to false reports in a single interview (Goodman & Quas, 2008). Stated in another way, "When and how children are interviewed is at least as important for their accuracy as is how many times they are interviewed" (Goodman & Quas, 2008, p. 386). It also suggests that forensic interviewers must question children in developmentally appropriate ways, using evidence-based techniques, and more than once if possible.

Interviewer training is most effective when reinforced over extended time periods (Brubacher et al., 2022). Increasing the impact of training might include placing interviewers in the role of *interviewees* to experience the difference in answering open-ended vs. closed-ended questions (e.g., Boud & Molloy, 2013) or using realistic avatars to simulate the experience of interviewing a child victim (e.g., Powell et al., 2022).

A robust finding in cognitive psychology, termed the **reminiscence effect,** can explain why multiple interviews might be useful. When people attempt to remember pictures or events they viewed previously, they often report (reminisce) new information on each recall attempt, suggesting that recollection may be incomplete on the first telling but unrecalled information can be produced in later interviews. The additional information reported as a function of reminiscence is most reliable when open-ended questions are used (refer to Box 5.3 for evidence of the impact of suggestive questioning techniques).

Repeated interviewing is necessary when an alleged victim is too distressed to provide useful information initially, when victims fail to disclose abuse that is subsequently documented by medical examinations or confessions, or when new evidence comes to light (La Rooy et al., 2010).

Disclosure of Child Maltreatment

Children are often reluctant to disclose abusive experiences and may even deny them when asked. One study involved interviews of approximately 4300 high school students, 45%

of whom reported previous experiences of sexual abuse. Of these, only 65% of females and 23% of males had disclosed that abuse (Priebe & Svedin, 2008). In another study of 76 undergraduate women, fewer than 10% of women formally reported abusive incidents. Only about half informally reported the abuse to individuals in their social networks. Women who were younger at the time of the abuse were less likely to report the abuse than if the abuse occurred when they were adolescents (Winters et al., 2020). These data suggest that large numbers of children fail to disclose maltreatment when they are young and, therefore, that reported cases of CSA are the tip of a large iceberg. Many abuse victims fail to disclose because they feel shame or anticipate emotional distress upon disclosure (e.g., Winters et al., 2020). Therefore, disclosure is facilitated by supportive relationships and by other people's willingness to detect and report the abuse (Jones et al., 2017). Unfortunately, data indicate that adults are not very skilled at determining when children are being truthful about reports of abuse (Domagalski et al., 2020).

Some studies have focused on what individuals remember about being maltreated. In fact, children can remember significant details of abuse experiences and, if asked directly, can describe them quite accurately. One team of developmental psychologists contacted approximately 200 adolescents and young adults who, during the 1980s, had been involved in a study of the effects of criminal prosecutions on victims of CSA (Alexander et al., 2005). Participants had been 3 to 17 years old at the time of the original data collection. All of them had been sexually abused. Upon renewing contact years later, psychologists provided a list of traumatic events (including CSA) and asked respondents to indicate which events happened to them and, among those events, which was the most traumatic. Respondents who designated CSA as their most traumatic experience were remarkably accurate in reporting details of their experiences. These data suggest that memory for emotional, even traumatic, victimization experiences can be retained quite well even decades after the events occurred.

Still, a subgroup of abuse victims either forgets the abuse or remembers it poorly. Why do some maltreated people have full access to memories of those experiences and others have none? Processes that people use to regulate their emotions—in particular, their coping strategies—may be implicated (Harris et al., 2016). People who cope with maltreatment by actively trying to suppress, inhibit, or ignore their thoughts about it may weaken or even eliminate memories of those experiences over time. As a result, they may have memory deficits for these traumatic events.

The Child Witness in the Courtroom

Though most child maltreatment cases end in admissions of guilt or plea bargains, tens of thousands of children, often preschoolers, must testify in abuse trials each year. In one study, although only 18% of all CSA cases involved children 5 years old or younger, 41% of the cases that went to trial involved children of this age (Gray, 1993). Two questions arise: What is the effect on the child of having to discuss these issues in court, and how do jurors weigh the testimony of a child witness?

Talking about victimization in a public setting may increase the trauma for many children. Sexual abuse victims can be fearful of confronting the alleged offender in criminal court (Hobbs et al., 2014). Professor Gail Goodman and her colleagues examined the short- and long-term outcomes for children who testified in CSA cases, initially interviewing a group of 218 CSA victims when their cases were referred for prosecution (Goodman et al., 1992) and reinterviewing many of them 12 years later (Quas et al., 2005). The experience of testifying was quite traumatic for some children. They had nightmares, vomited on the day of their appearance in court, and were relieved that the defendant had not tried to kill them (Goodman et al., 1992). Testifying appears to be particularly negative for older child victims (12 to 16 years old), for those whose cases ended in acquittal or lenient punishment for the offender (Quas & Goodman, 2012), and for those who testified more than once (Elmi et al., 2018).

How do jurors perceive child witnesses? Do they tend to doubt the truthfulness of children's testimony, reasoning that children often make things up and leave things out? Or do they tend to believe children in this setting? In mock jury studies, child eyewitnesses are generally viewed as less credible than adult eyewitnesses (e.g., Pozzulo & Dempsey, 2009). But something quite different happens in CSA cases. Here, younger victims are viewed as *more* credible than adolescents because they are deemed more trustworthy and honest. In fact, laypeople believe that the "ideal" witness in a child sexual abuse case would be an 8-year-old, and the least ideal would be a 12-year-old (Nunez et al., 2011). In addition, jurors can recognize the effects of suggestive questioning; mock jurors who read a transcript of a highly suggestive forensic interview tended to discount the child's testimony (Castelli et al., 2005).

Procedural Modifications When Children Are Witnesses

Judges allow various courtroom modifications to protect children from the potential stress of testifying. One innovation is the placement of a screen in front of the defendant so the child witness cannot see the defendant while testifying. This arrangement was used in the trial of John Avery Coy, who was convicted of sexually assaulting two 13-year-old girls. Coy appealed his conviction on the grounds that the screen deprived him of the opportunity to confront the girls face-to-face, a reference to the **confrontation clause** of the Sixth Amendment that guarantees defendants the right to confront their accusers. The right to confrontation is based on the assumption that the witness will find it more difficult to lie in the presence of the defendant. In a 1988 decision, the Supreme Court agreed with Coy, saying that his right to confront his accusers face-to-face was not outweighed "by the necessity of protecting the victims of sexual abuse" (*Coy v. Iowa*, 1988).

But just two years later, in the case of *Maryland v. Craig* (1990), the Court upheld a law permitting a child to give testimony in a different part of the courthouse and have the testimony transmitted to the courtroom via closed-circuit TV (CCTV). The law applied to cases where the child was likely to experience significant emotional distress by being in the presence of the defendant. *Craig* thus modified the rule of the *Coy* case (for a similar opinion, refer to *State of North Carolina v. Jackson*, 2011).

Proponents of CCTV claim that in addition to reducing the trauma experienced by a child, this technology will also provide more complete and accurate reports. Opponents claim that the use of CCTV violates the defendant's right to face-to-face confrontation of witnesses. Several studies have assessed the veracity of children who testify in and out of courtrooms and whether observers perceive differences in their credibility. A common finding is that children give more detailed statements when allowed to testify on CCTV (Goodman et al., 1998). Children also feel less nervous when allowed to testify outside of the courtroom (Landstrom & Granhag, 2010). On this basis, one might argue for its use in every case in which a child feels anxious about testifying. But things aren't quite so simple. Children who testify via CCTV or in pre-recorded videos are viewed less positively than are children who testify in open court (Antrobus et al., 2016). It seems that jurors want to see children in person in order to assess the truthfulness of their reports. Clearly, the impact of CCTV on jurors' decisions in CSA cases is complex. Perhaps it should be reserved for cases in which the prospect of testifying is so terrifying to children that they would otherwise become inept witnesses—or would not testify at all.

Judges make other accommodations when children must testify. In cases involving CSA, physical abuse, or adult domestic violence, a support person—typically a parent, guardian, or victim assistant—is almost always present with the child to decrease stress and ideally to increase accuracy and completeness. The effect may not be what the victim intended, however, as mock jurors deem child victims less accurate and trustworthy when a support person is present (McAuliff et al., 2015).

Finally, we should note that although testifying has the potential to inflict further trauma on the child, it can be a therapeutic experience for some children (Quas & Goodman, 2012). It can engender a sense of control over events, and if the defendant is convicted, provide some satisfaction to the child. Psychological science has much to offer child victims in terms of creating developmentally appropriate approaches to prosecution, ones that both maximize the potential for justice and minimize the potential for harm (e.g., Lamb, 2015).

Repressed and Recovered Memories

Retrieving memories over short time periods, as eyewitnesses must do, is a complex task. Yet it pales in comparison with retrieving memories that have been stored, and in some cases, forgotten, over lengthy intervals. Two basic processes need to be distinguished in understanding long-lost memories. The first is natural forgetting, which tends to occur when people simply do not think about events that happened years earlier. Just as you might have trouble remembering the name of your fourth-grade teacher, witnesses to crimes, accidents, and business transactions are likely to forget the details of these events, if not the entire event, after the passage of months or years. Such forgetting or misremembering is even more likely when the event is confused with prior or subsequent experiences that bear some resemblance to it. No one disputes the reality of natural forgetting.

Much more controversial is a second type of lost "memory"—the memories that are presumed to have been repressed over long time periods. In this scenario, events that are traumatizing get buried deeply in the unconscious mind through a process of emotionally motivated forgetting called **repression**. But the notion of repression is highly controversial; some suggest that evidence of repression has never been scientifically established, and that the inability to remember traumatic effects can be explained by ordinary forgetting (e.g., McNally, 2005; Engelhard et al., 2019). A similar controversy is associated with the concept of **dissociation**, in which victims of abuse or other traumas may escape the full impact of an experience by psychologically detaching themselves from it. Although some clinicians believe dissociation is one way people respond to trauma (e.g., Dalenberg et al., 2012), other psychological scientists contend that dissociation is inconsistent with what we know about how memory systems work (e.g., Otgaar et al., 2019; Lynn et al., 2014).

Repressed Memories of Child Sexual Abuse

Most reports of repressed and recovered memories involve cases in which individuals (1) report having experience sexual or physical abuse as children, often at the hands of parents or other trusted adults; (2) repressed or dissociated any memory of these horrors for many years as a form of unconscious protection; and (3) recovered their long-lost memories of the abuse when it was psychologically safe to do so.

Repressed memories are sometimes recovered after a person has participated in "memory-focused" psychotherapy that applies techniques such as hypnosis, psychopharmacology, pressures to recall, and guided imagery, all in an attempt to help clients remember past abuse. These techniques are sometimes introduced if therapists suspect clients of harboring repressed memories of abuse. In these instances, therapists might ask the clients highly suggestive questions, such as "You show many of the signs of childhood sexual abuse; can you tell me some of the things you think might have happened to you when you were a very young child?" This approach might be particularly appealing to clients who believe that they experienced childhood trauma and abuse they cannot remember (Rubin & Boals, 2010). Indeed, it may even prompt "memories" of past abuse. One survey indicates that among undergraduate students in therapy, students whose therapists suggested the possibility of repressed memory were nearly 30 times more likely to recover memories of abuse, compared with clients whose therapists did not mention repression (Patihis et al., 2022). Even though surveys indicate that some practicing clinicians vouch for the veracity of recovered memories (e.g., Magnussen & Melinder, 2012), researchers of memory tend to be skeptical, arguing that "the ongoing belief in unconscious repression can be harmful in multiple contexts" (Otgaar et al., 2021, p. 459).

Indeed, researchers and other clinicians tend to question the validity of memories that resurface years after the alleged incidents, particularly after the individual has been in therapy (Patihis et al., 2014). (These professionals are not denying the reality of CSA, of course. Not only does it occur, it is a very serious problem throughout the world, and children who were abused are at increased risk to be diagnosed with mental health disorders in adulthood.) They point out that most people who endure severe trauma do not forget the event; in fact, some of them experience intrusive recollections of it for years afterward. Skepticism is fueled by the fact that some alleged victims claim to have recalled traumas that happened when they were less than 1 year old. Nearly all research on childhood memory and amnesia shows this is not possible, for reasons related to neurological development.

The real question is whether allegations of child abuse that surfaced only after searching for them in therapy are trustworthy. In a clever study designed to compare memories of abuse recovered in therapy to memories recovered outside of therapy and memories never forgotten, Professor Elke Geraerts and her colleagues sought independent corroboration of the abuse from other people who were abused by the same perpetrator, individuals who learned of the abuse soon after it occurred, or from perpetrators themselves. They were able to corroborate 45% of the abuse memories that had never been forgotten, 37% of the memories that were recalled out of therapy, but 0% of the memories that were recalled in therapy (Geraerts et al., 2007).

Scientists now believe that there are at least two kinds of recovered memories of CSA: those that are gradually recovered in the context of suggestive therapy, and those that spring up spontaneously without prompting or attempts to reconstruct the past. Memories recovered spontaneously can be more easily corroborated, suggesting that they are more likely to be genuine and therefore the product of 'normal' forgetting and remembering (Geraerts, 2012).

So what should we make of the recollection of past abuse events that a person claims to have repressed for years? Can we be sure that alleged abuses took place? Answers to these questions are vitally important to the criminal justice system where issues related to recovered memories can be contentious. Among the issues: the admissibility of recovered memory evidence, delayed disclosure of abuse, exaggeration of CSA-related symptoms, and the impact on juries of recovered memory reports.

Clearly, it is possible that given the right circumstances, people can spontaneously recall thoughts or perhaps whole experiences they had forgotten for many years. And just as clearly, it is possible that some recovered memories, especially those that appear to have been repressed for years and then recovered through aggressive "memory work" therapy are imagined or made up.

Creating False Memories

As difficult as it might be to believe, it is relatively easy to generate false memories for events that never occurred (e.g., Zaragoza et al., 2019). One way that psychologists have been able to implant false memories is by enlisting the help of family members, who suggest to adult research participants a fabricated event. In a now-classic study, Loftus and Pickrell (1995), with help from participants' relatives, constructed a false story that the participant had been lost during a shopping trip at the age of 5, was found crying by an elderly person, and was eventually reunited with family members. After reading this story, participants wrote what they remembered about the event. Nearly 30% of participants either partially or fully remembered the made-up event, and 25% claimed in subsequent interviews that they remembered the fictitious situation.

Suggestive techniques leading to false memories can affect people in a variety of ways. They can change people's beliefs about themselves and others; inspire new, healthier habits; and affect daily behaviors. Falsely suggesting to people that they became sick, years before, after eating a particular food actually influenced their food choices. The suggestion deterred them from eating that food when it was offered (Geraerts et al., 2008).

More pertinent to the forensic context, scientists have found that people can be induced, via suggestion, to create false memories of committing serious crimes (theft, assault, and assault with a weapon) as adolescents. As researchers noted, "imagined memory elements regarding what something *could* have been like can turn into elements of what it *would* have been like, which can become elements of what it *was* like" (Shaw & Porter, 2015, p. 298). Some of the false memories were highly descriptive and multi-sensory, supporting the contention that false memories can be experienced as very similar to real (true) memories.

Psychologists have used other experimental procedures to examine the malleable nature of autobiographical memory (memory for one's past experiences). These include asking participants to imagine events that never occurred (Mazzoni & Memon, 2003) and doctoring family photographs to portray events such as hot-air balloon rides that never took place (Wade et al., 2002). Merely imagining or viewing a photo associated with a fabricated event can dramatically increase the rate of false memories. In one study, researchers provided false suggestions to adults about various school-related pranks (for example, putting Slime on a teacher's desk in elementary school). Some participants viewed group class photos from that time and others did not. The rate of false memory reports was substantially higher among participants who viewed the photographs, even though the photographs only depicted participants as they were at the age of the incident—the photographs contained no visual evidence of the alleged incident itself (Lindsay et al., 2004). This is concerning because some memory-focused therapists recommend that adults who think they have been abused should view family photo albums to cue long-forgotten memories of abuse.

Simply imagining an event from one's past can also affect the belief that it actually occurred, even when the event is completely implausible—for example, proposing marriage to a Pepsi machine (Seamon et al., 2006). This phenomenon is known as **imagination inflation** (e.g., Garry et al., 1996). In studies using memory implantation or imagination inflation techniques, scientists have measured various aspects of autobiographical memories. These include the extent to which people say they "remember" the suggested experiences, agree that those experiences occurred, embellish them, and create a coherent story to explain them. When the results of several studies and more than 400 memory reports were analyzed together in a "mega-analysis," researchers determined that 30.5% of these reports met the definition of a false memory and another 23% involved accepting the suggested event as true to some degree. Thus, more than half the participants in these studies came to believe that they experienced a suggested, fabricated event (Scoboria et al., 2017).

How can we account for this? One possibility is **source confusion**. The act of imagining may make the suggested event seem more familiar, but that familiarity is mistakenly associated with childhood memories rather than with the act of imagination itself. The creation of false memories is most likely to occur when people who are having trouble remembering are explicitly encouraged to imagine events and discouraged from thinking about whether their constructions are real.

Keep in mind that although false childhood memories can be implanted in some people, the memories that result from suggestions are not always false. Unfortunately, without corroboration, it is very hard to know whether someone is recalling an event from their past or reporting reconstructions that originated from other sources of information. This presents a challenge for courts in how to handle claims of recovered memories of childhood sexual abuse.

Recovered Memories in Court

Legal cases based on recovered "memories" have typically involved claims of personal injury against wrongdoers—for example, adult daughters suing their fathers for alleged child sexual abuse, and adults suing the Catholic Church, claiming they were abused by priests (Milchman, 2012). (The latter issue was depicted in the 2015 film, *Spotlight.*) These are civil lawsuits in which complainants must prove their case by a preponderance of evidence. Prosecutors rarely file criminal charges based on claims of recovered memories because they must prove the case beyond a reasonable doubt and doing so is difficult with only recovered memories as evidence.

These cases can be quite contentious because the alleged victim often has a close tie to the defendant and other family members may be forced to take sides, causing strain and animosity within a family. They can also be controversial because they concern events that were alleged to have happened in the distant past. For example, when Connolly and Read (2006) analyzed 2000 claims of "historic" CSA—which they defined as two years or more between the end of the offense and the trial—they found that the mean age of the complainant at the time of the alleged abuse was 12.39, but the mean age at trial was 26.09, a difference of nearly 14 years. In addition, jurors tend to be rather skeptical of recovered memory claims at trial (Bornstein & Muller, 2001), despite the fact that laypeople tend to believe traumatic memories can be repressed and then retrieved accurately in therapy (Patihis et al., 2014).

Jurisdictions have varying processes in place to deal with these issues. In some states, the statutes of limitations—the period during which a lawsuit can be pursued—have been extended for victims who claim they had forgotten the experiences or did not understand that they caused harm. Some states require corroboration of the abuse. In some jurisdictions, experts are allowed to testify about traumatic amnesia and recovered memories. So in many respects, the legal system's response to concerns about the validity of recovered memories mirrors the scientist-practitioner divide. Suffice to say, there are differences of opinion.

Summary

1. **What psychological factors contribute to the risk of mistaken identifications in the legal system?** Evidence produced by eyewitnesses often makes the difference between an unsolved crime and a conviction. In the early stages of a crime investigation, eyewitness accounts can provide important clues and permit culprits to be identified. But witnesses often make mistakes, and mistaken identifications have led to the conviction of numerous innocent people. Errors can occur at the moment the crime is committed or at any of the three phases of the memory process: encoding, storage, and retrieval. Furthermore, subsequent questioning and new experiences can alter what is remembered from the past.

2. **What are the defining features of estimator, system, and reflector variables in the study of eyewitness memory?** In describing the factors that affect the reliability of eyewitness memory, psychologists distinguish (1) estimator variables whose impact on an identification can only be estimated and not controlled, (2) system variables that are under the control of the justice system, and (3) reflector variables that correlate with the accuracy of an identification. Much research has focused on a particular set of system variables related to the way lineups are conducted.

3. **How do jurors evaluate the testimony of eyewitnesses, and how can psychological research help jurors understand the potential problems of eyewitness testimony?** Jurors are heavily influenced by the testimony of eyewitnesses, and they tend to overestimate the accuracy of such witnesses, relying to a great extent on the confidence of the eyewitness. To alert jurors to these problems, two types of remediation have been described (in addition to limiting eyewitness evidence when it was gleaned through suggestive procedures). In some cases, psychologists testify as expert witnesses about the problems inherent in eyewitness memory. Laboratory evaluations of mock juries are mixed on whether such testimony properly sensitizes jurors to factors that affect an eyewitness's reliability. The other intervention involves the judge giving a "cautionary

instruction," sensitizing jurors to aspects of the testimony of eyewitnesses they should consider. Data are mixed on its effectiveness.

4. **Can children accurately report on their experiences of victimization? What factors affect the accuracy of their reports? Are they likely to disclose abuse?** When children are questioned in a non-suggestive manner and are asked open-ended questions, the resulting report will be more accurate than when suggestive interrogation procedures are used. Children are less accurate in answering specific question than more general questions, and sometimes recall information from one event as having occurred in another. Multiple interviews can facilitate memory recall under some circumstances. Most children are able to remember details of their maltreatment and describe them accurately, though victims who suppressed their thoughts about it may have memory deficits.

5. **Can memories of trauma be repressed, and if so, can these memories be recovered accurately?** Sometimes, memories of trauma are apparently forgotten and later recovered. When spontaneously recalled, such memories tend to be accurate. But when the recollections occur in the context of therapies that use suggestive memory retrieval techniques, their accuracy is less certain. Research shows that people can "remember" events that never happened, sometimes simply by imagining them.

Key Terms

archival analysis

autobiographical memory

cognitive interview

confirmation bias

confrontation clause

diagnosticity

dissociation

double-blind testing procedures

ecological validity

encoding

estimator variable

experimental methodology

experimenter bias

ecphoric similarity

field studies

generalize

ground truth

imagination inflation

in-group/out-group differences

open-ended questions

own-race bias

photographic lineup

photospread

physiognomic variability

postdiction variables

post-event information

reasonable suspicion standard

reflector variables

relative judgment

reminiscence effect

repression

retention interval

retrieval

self-administered interview

selective attention

sequential presentation

simultaneous presentation

source confusion

storage

suggestive questions

system variable

unconscious transference

weapon focus effect

Chapter 6

Psychology of Victims of Crime and Violence

Orienting Questions

1. What is the frequency of crime victimization?
2. What types of research have psychologists conducted on victimization?
3. What factors predict the development of PTSD after being a crime victim?
4. What are the components of battered woman syndrome that make it more specific than Post Traumatic Stress Disorder?
5. How can sexual assault be prevented?
6. What are two types of sexual harassment recognized by the courts?

Perceptions of Those Who Experience Crime and/or Violence

Almost every crime has at least one victim. Even so-called victimless crimes—crimes such as prostitution and gambling—have victims, even if they do not immediately recognize it or would not describe themselves that way. The social burdens and psychological costs of these offenses—the squandering of a person's income resulting from habitual gambling losses or the physical abuse and underworld crimes that surround prostitution—are often delayed. Ultimately, however, both individuals and the larger society are victimized by these crimes.

Society has different reactions toward victims. While some feel sympathy for them, others question why they became victims—or even blame them for the events in question. One reason for this is the need to believe in a "just world." The thought of becoming victims ourselves is threatening, so we seek an explanation for why we are different from those who are victimized—and why they "deserved" (or at least share responsibility for) the own victimization (Lerner, 1980). These justifications, which rise to the level of a cognitive bias, can protect people from more threatening explanations such as randomness, callousness, and impersonal motivations. This has led to what has been called "blaming the victim" (Ryan, 1970).

When individuals are targeted for crime based on race, religion, sexual orientation, or other grounds, the impact can be exacerbated. It can be traumatic not only for the individual who is targeted, but also for others who are similar. This is the major justification for classifying such offenses as **hate crimes**, with enhanced sentences upon conviction. One such crime involved an unarmed Black man, Ahmaud Arbery, who was pursued and killed by three White individuals while he was out running (Box 6.1). This kind of crime is particularly painful as our society confronts the consequences of various kinds of prejudice that are discussed throughout this book.

Victims of Crime

Throughout this book we discuss individuals who are involved in perpetrating crime. But what about those who are victimized? In this chapter, we turn to questions about victimization experienced in different contexts—childhood, the workplace, and adult relationships. As we will see, there is a relationship between abuse and other

---

Box 6.1

The Case of Ahmaud Arbery: Victim of a Hate Crime

Ahmaud Arbery, a 25-year-old Black man, was out running in a neighborhood near Brunswick, Georgia, in February 2020 when he was spotted by three White men: Travis McMichael and his father Gregory McMichael (in one vehicle) and their neighbor Roddie Bryan (in another vehicle). The three of them chased Arbery for several minutes while Bryan recorded the events on his cell phone. Catching up to him, Travis McMichael left his truck and shot Arbery as he tried to defend himself. County police arrived but made no arrests; the video shot by Bryan was released in May, with the McMichaels and subsequently Bryan arrested later that month. They were tried in November 2021. All three were convicted of felony murder, with Travis McMichael also convicted of malice murder. Travis and Gregory McMichael were sentenced to life imprisonment with no possibility of parole, while Roddie Bryan received a life sentence but will be eligible for parole after 20 years.

These were charged as hate crimes, with the prosecution contending that Arbery was pursued because he was Black. The defense argued that the McMichaels and Bryan pursued him only because they thought he was a threat to break into neighbors' homes, but there was ample evidence that racial bias had a substantial influence on the behavior of the perpetrators. Georgia enacted hate crimes legislation—and replaced its law

UPI/Alamy Stock Photo

Ahmaud Arbery

on citizen's arrest—in the wake of the murder of Ahmaud Arbery.

Critical Thought Question

Why should an offense be considered worse because it is directed toward a member of a minority group?

adversity experienced as a child and the risk that such an individual will in turn inflict harm on others as an adult.

The primary source of information on crime victims in the United States is the Bureau of Justice Statistics' National Crime Victimization Survey, which can be found at https://bjs.ojp.gov/library/publications/criminal-victimization-2020. Each year, data are collected from a national sample of households and individuals on the frequency and consequences of criminal victimization in the form of rape and other sexual assaults, robbery, theft, assault, household burglary, and car theft. From these figures, one can calculate the rate of victimization nationwide. It is estimated that in 2020, when compared with 2019, the rate of violent victimization fell by 22% and the number of violent crimes (excluding simple assault) was 20% lower. Likewise, the number of burglary and trespassing victimizations was 23% lower. What are we to make of this, particularly in light of other information suggesting that violent crime particularly *increased* in 2020 during the COVID-19 pandemic? Consider that we are talking about information from one source (victims of crime). But respondents to this survey also said that only about 40% of violent victimizations and 33% of property crimes were reported to police—so one possibility is that crime victimization surveys such as this, when large and national in scope, provide a *better* perspective about broad patterns than do official arrest and conviction statistics.

This chapter considers four types of victims and the effects of victimization on them: people who experience adversity

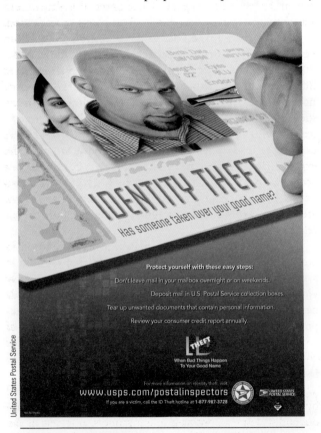

Identity theft warning.

and trauma in childhood, targets of sexual harassment, those experiencing intimate partner violence, and victims of violent crime—particularly sexual assault, the violent crime that has been studied most often. For each of these, the field of psychology has generated theory and research relevant to the laws and court decisions instituted to protect such victims. The responses of the legal system reflect conflicting views in our society about the nature of victims, especially victims of sex-related offenses. For example, how extreme does a situation need to be before we conclude that sexual harassment exists, and how distressed does the response of the victim need to be? In the case of an individual who has experienced intimate partner violence, will the legal system accept a claim of **self-defense**? Why do as many as two-thirds of sexual assault victims never report the attack to the police?

Adversity and Trauma in Childhood

There are two kinds of adverse experiences that are particularly important to consider as part of human development. The first involves experiences that are emotionally painful and overwhelming for the individual's capacity to cope effectively. Examples include the abuse of children of various kinds (e.g., sexual abuse, physical abuse, severe neglect). The second refers to the kind of chronic adversity that results from influences such as poverty, racism, and other such longstanding, less acute but more pervasive aspects of the lives of many children. Although adversity may be accompanied by the development of coping strategies, it has a cumulative impact that can affect an individual's development and adult functioning in various problematic ways.

The relationship between traumatic childhood experiences and physical and emotional health outcomes in adult life is at the core of the landmark Adverse Childhood Experiences (ACE) Study. The ACE Study involved the cooperation of over 17,000 middle-aged (average age was 57), middle-class Americans who agreed to help researchers study the following nine categories of childhood abuse and household dysfunction: recurrent physical abuse; recurrent emotional abuse; contact sexual abuse; an alcohol and/or drug abuser in the household; an incarcerated household member; a household member who is chronically depressed, mentally ill, institutionalized, or suicidal; a mother who is treated violently; one or no parents; and emotional or physical neglect. Each participant received an ACE score in the range of 0–9 reflecting the number of such experiences they reported (Felitti et al., 1998).

The study had two major findings. First, adverse childhood experiences are much more common than anticipated or recognized—even in the middle-class population that participated in the study, all of whom were receiving health care via a large health maintenance organization (HMO). (This was a large study drawn from the general population, albeit that portion that had healthcare benefits. It was not drawn from a selected clinical or criminal justice population.) It is reasonable to assume that the prevalence of ACEs is significantly higher among, for example, young Black, Indigenous, and other Persons of Color (BIPOC) males in the general population, particularly those who live with chronic stress and do not have a regular source of health care.

The study's second major finding is that adverse childhood experiences have a strong relationship to health outcomes later in life. As the ACE score increases, so does the risk of an array of social and health problems such as social, emotional and cognitive impairment; presence of health-risk behaviors; disease, disability and social problems; and early death. ACEs are strong correlated with adolescent health, teen pregnancy, smoking, substance abuse, sexual behavior, the risk of revictimization, performance in the workforce, and the stability of relationships, among other health determinants. The higher the ACE score, the greater the risk of heart disease, lung disease, liver disease, suicide, HIV and STDs, and other risks for the leading causes of death (Felitti et al., 1998).

Consequences of Early Victimization

One might wonder whether early victimization experiences increase the likelihood of adolescent and adult criminality. Cathy Spatz Widom (1989, 1992) used court records to identify a group of 908 children in a Midwestern American city who had experienced abuse (i.e., sexual abuse or physical assault leading to injury) or severe neglect (i.e., inadequate food, clothing, shelter, or medical care) between 1967 and 1971. This "abuse/neglect" group was matched to a group of 667 children who had not been exposed to abuse or neglect but who were similar in gender, age, ethnicity, and family socioeconomic status. Matching the abused and non-abused groups on these variables was important, because it enabled Widom to conclude that any differences between the groups in violent behavior in adolescence or adulthood were not due to differences in demographic characteristics.

Widom's analysis of police and court records showed that, as earlier research had suggested, abused or neglected children were significantly more likely than the comparison group to have been arrested for violent crimes as juveniles or as adults. In addition, the abused or neglected individuals were, on average, a year younger than comparison subjects at the time of their first arrest and had committed twice as many total offenses over the 15- to 20-year period studied. These differences were seen in boys and girls and in White and Black children; however, the relationship between abuse and violence was particularly strong among Black children.

Follow-up data on this sample were collected 22 to 26 years after the abuse or neglect (Maxfield & Widom, 1996). The researchers found that by age 32, almost half of the abused/neglected group (49%) had been arrested for a non-traffic offense. This percentage was considerably greater than for the matched control sample (38%). Furthermore, victims of abuse and neglect were more likely than members of the control group to have been arrested for violent crimes, even after controlling for age, race, and gender.

Widom and her colleagues next examined the impact of sexual abuse, physical abuse, and neglect in childhood on adult mental health outcomes (Horwitz et al., 2001). Findings suggested that both men and women with histories of childhood abuse and neglect displayed increased levels of mood disorders and antisocial personality characteristics when compared with matched controls. The abused and neglected women also reported more alcohol problems than both the men and the matched groups. Although this line of research has suggested a strong association between childhood experiences of abuse and neglect and elevated levels of mental health problems in adulthood, these differences decreased after controlling for other stressful life events.

Widom and colleagues (Widom et al., 2006) next conducted a follow-up study with these data focusing on potential pathways between childhood victimization and violent criminal behavior, focusing on early aggressive behavior and problematic drinking. They found different pathways for men and women. For men, child maltreatment was related to later aggression toward others as well as later problematic alcohol use. In women, early victimization was directly related to later alcohol problems, which in turn were related to later violence toward others.

Finally, Kaplow and Widom (2007) identified documented cases of children who were physically and sexually abused and neglected prior to age 12 ($N = 496$) and followed them into adulthood. Earlier onset of maltreatment predicted more symptoms of anxiety and depression in adulthood, even when controlling for gender, race, current age, and other abuse reports. Later onset of maltreatment was associated with more behavioral problems in adulthood.

A review of the scientific evidence on the relationship between trauma, adverse experience, and crime (Zelechoski, 2016) concluded that it is unclear whether trauma causes increased offense risk—but this is probably the result of not having the right kind of research to allow us to draw such a conclusion. (For obvious reasons, it would be unethical to deliberately expose children to trauma or adverse experience, and then follow up to determine whether the exposed children were more often involved in crime.) But according to Zelechoski, there is very likely a relationship between trauma exposure and juvenile offending, and we are getting closer to understanding the precise nature of that relationship.

Some of the Widom studies may *underestimate* the risks created by childhood abuse. Only offenses that resulted in arrest or trial were included in the research linking early victimization to later criminality. Members of the abused/neglected group may have committed undetected or unreported crimes. These findings highlight the importance of considering early child abuse and neglect as part of a broader constellation of life stressors rather than isolating them as independent predictors of adult outcomes.

Another major source of childhood adversity is school bullying. This has been recognized for some time as a serious and widespread problem in our schools. A review of the evidence on bullying (Arseneault, 2017) indicates that bullying is associated with distress and various behavioral health problems, which can persist until middle-life with adverse physical and economic outcomes as well.

Among those particularly targeted for bullying are children who identify as lesbian, gay, or bisexual. According to the CDC's Youth Risk Behavior Survey, LGB students continue to experience greater risk of violent victimization in school than do heterosexual youth, as measured by the results of 2015, 2017, and 2019 surveys (Johns et al., 2020). This greater risk of being bullied is also seen for transgender youth (Earnshaw et al., 2016). It is not surprising, therefore, that LGBTQIA+ students are much more likely to report feeling unsafe at school and to have been harassed. Verbal and physical victimization based on sexual identity have been related to posttraumatic stress symptoms (Dragowski et al., 2011) as well as depression, suicidal thoughts, and high levels of substance use (Espelage et al., 2008).

Technological advancements and cultural changes have provided new tools and contexts for bullying (e.g., cyberbullying). In addition to cyberbullying, psychologists have identified other subtypes of bullying: physical, verbal, social exclusion, and spreading rumors (Wang et al., 2010). Males are more likely to be victims of all types of bullying. It is not yet clear how the restrictions imposed during the COVID-19 pandemic might affect the school bullying problem, although there is evidence that broader mental health problems such as depression and anxiety among adolescents have increased substantially during the 2020–2021 period (Magson et al., 2021).

Violence, Crime, and Posttraumatic Stress Disorder

The dilemmas confronted throughout this book, especially the attempt to preserve both the rights of suspects and the rights of victims, come into sharp focus when we consider the victims of crime, particularly victims of violent crimes. Historically, society has paid less attention to crime victims than it should have. Most of the legal rights formally protected in the adversarial system are extended to defendants, not victims. Consequently, the needs and rights of those victimized by crime have often been underprioritized.

This began to change in the 1980s when victim advocacy groups, mental health professionals, police, and court officials all began to acknowledge the need to better recognize and serve crime victims. Various developments reflect these changes:

- The emergence of the interdisciplinary field of **victimology**, which concentrates on studying the process and consequences of victimization experiences and how victims (or *survivors*, which is the term preferred by many) recover

- The increasing availability of services to crime victims, including compensation and restitution programs, victim assistance programs in the courts, self-help programs, and formal mental health services

- The expanded opportunity for victims to participate in the trials of their victimizers through mechanisms such as victim impact statements

- The heightened focus on victims brought about by the establishment of professional journals (e.g., *Victimology*; *Violence and Victims*); organizations such as the National Organization for Victim Assistance; and commissions such as the American Psychological Association's Task Force on the Victims of Crime and Violence

- The growing recognition that individuals who have been wrongly convicted of crimes, though not traditional crime victims but rather, victimized by the criminal justice system, should have their cases reviewed by conviction integrity units within prosecutors' offices, and, if exonerated, provided compensation and services as they return to the community (Heilbrun et al., 2020).

For their part, psychologists have conducted research on and delivered clinical services to a diverse array of crime victims. Three areas have received special attention: the consequences of physical/sexual abuse on child victims; the role of violent victimization as a cause of psychological disorders, particularly posttraumatic stress disorder; and the psychology of sexual assault. We have discussed the consequences of child abuse earlier in this chapter; we now turn to the latter two topics.

Posttraumatic Stress Disorder

Individuals who experience a severe trauma and, weeks or months later, continue to experience intense, fear-related reactions when reminded of the trauma, may be experiencing **posttraumatic stress disorder** (PTSD). This kind of trauma must involve a threat of serious injury or death. We have seen vivid and disturbing examples of PTSD in soldiers returning from the wars in Vietnam, Iraq and Afghanistan. As well, most instances of violent crime qualify as trauma severe enough to trigger PTSD in at least some victims.

The symptoms of PTSD fall into five domains (these symptoms must last longer than one month to qualify as PTSD) after direct or indirect exposure to death, or actual or threatened serious injury or sexual violence:

1. Persistent re-experiencing of the event through intrusive thoughts, flashbacks, and repeated nightmares and dreams
2. Persistent avoidance of trauma-related thoughts, feelings, and external reminders
3. Negative alterations in thinking and mood
4. Alterations in arousal and reactivity
5. Distress or functional impairment in social or occupational areas.

The case of Joe (Box 6.2) reveals how these diagnostic criteria apply to a real-life case. Sexually abused by parents

Box 6.2

The Case of Joe: Adverse Experience, Multiple Traumas, and Posttraumatic Stress Disorder

Joe's life of adverse experience and trauma began in his childhood. He reported that both of his parents sexually abused him. He added that his father once "split my skull … because I was in his way." Joe was a ward of the state and sent to an orphanage as a young child. When he was moved to a wing housing older boys, "I was raped the first night. The rapes continued as long as I stayed at the home."

Today Joe is in his 50s. But the effects of his childhood are still with him. He experiences posttraumatic stress disorder, which includes intense anxiety, nightmares, constant fear for one's safety, and always being on guard.

Joe attempted suicide for the first time when he was 12, and his adolescence included three more attempts. He ended up leaving the orphanage and hitchhiking around, but says that he still lived in fear, could never relax, and tended to sabotage himself. He tried working so much that he became "sort of a workaholic"; he tried relationships (including a marriage) that didn't work out, and always assumed that

other people didn't want to be around him. He was on workplace disability, seeing one therapist after another (most frequent diagnosis: chronic depression), when eventually he came in contact with a psychiatrist who spent enough time with Joe and asked the right questions to diagnose Joe with PTSD. He improved a good deal, although he still experiences chronic insomnia. He works with male survivors of abuse online and with an in-person support group.

Many think of PTSD as a disorder associated with war. Joe's case demonstrates that it can be associated with adverse experience and trauma at other stages of life as well (Kopfinger, 2007).

Critical Thought Question

Does everyone exposed to life-threatening trauma develop PTSD? If not, why not?

Source: Courtesy of Sunday News, Lancaster, PA.

and older boys, Joe experienced a series of extremely traumatic and adverse events throughout his childhood and adolescence. He experienced symptoms including difficulty sleeping, avoidance of people and human relationships, hypervigilance, and nightmares. The correct diagnosis and appropriate treatment resulted in some improvement, but Joe's life was still very difficult.

How common is PTSD? According to the National Center for PTSD, about 6% of the U.S. adult population (8% of women and 4% of men) will have PTSD at some time in their lives. This is a substantial number, although most who experience a life-threatening trauma do not develop PTSD symptoms. This is not to say that they do not have reactions, of course—but these reactions often diminish over time rather than developing into full-blown symptoms. The prevalence of PTSD is higher in military veterans, with estimates of about 11–20% of military veterans who have served in Vietnam, Desert Story, Operation Iraqi Freedom, or Operation Enduring Freedom experiencing PTSD in a given year (https://www.ptsd.va.gov/understand/common/common_adults.asp). Military service appears to be one risk factor for developing PTSD, as does being a victim of crime, being physically injured, perceiving one's life to be in danger, and having no control over the events (Resnick et al., 1993).

Although traumas are unfortunate aspects of life, there is reason to believe that PTSD—in some trauma victims, at least—can be prevented. For one thing, although many persons who experience severe trauma may develop

acute stress disorder (trauma-related symptoms that last less than one month), not all go on to develop full-blown PTSD. One reason may be that those experiencing trauma, but not PTSD, tend to receive high levels of social support from family, friends, or counselors immediately following the event (Grills-Taquechel et al., 2011). Thus, providing immediate social support for trauma victims may prevent their experiences from progressing into posttraumatic stress disorder. Another consideration involves the nature of the trauma, with the experience of violence more likely to result in PTSD than accidents or illness (consider https://www.ptsd.va.gov/understand/related/acute_stress.asp#:~:text=If%20you%20have%20ASD%2C%20you,still%20develop%20PTSD%20later%20on).

Two other characteristics distinguish people who develop PTSD from those who do not. Individuals who experience PTSD often perceive the world as a dangerous place from which they must retreat, and they come to view themselves as helpless to deal with stressors. If these two misconceptions could be eliminated, full-blown cases of PTSD might be prevented in many victims. Edna Foa (well known for her use of exposure therapy in treating PTSD, involving gradually "exposing" individuals to milder forms of the trauma and thereby reducing the associated anxiety) developed a four-session prevention course designed to change these two misconceptions in women who have been assaulted, sexually or physically. The course includes education, training in relaxation, emotionally reliving the trauma through imagery-based exposure, and cognitive restructuring to help the women replace negative beliefs about their competence and adequacy. These steps apparently reduced the future experience of PTSD (Foa et al., 1995), as did evidence-based practice with individuals following a PTSD diagnosis (Foa et al., 2009).

Regardless of whether they result in PTSD, the frequency and consequences of traumatic and other adverse events may be greater than many have thought. As discussed earlier, the Adverse Childhood Experience (ACE) Study (Felitti et al., 1998) found a graded relationship between the number of categories of childhood exposure and each of the adult health risk behaviors and diseases that were studied (including alcoholism, drug abuse, depression, suicide attempts, smoking, poor health, multiple sexual partners and sexually transmitted disease, and severe obesity). Such adverse experiences have particularly been linked to increased risk of PTSD (Roberts et al., 2011) as well as anxiety disorders and lower intellectual functioning (Breslau et al., 2006).

The question of how such traumatic events affect the risk of antisocial behavior toward others, in the form of juvenile delinquency and criminal offending, is a complex one. As described earlier in the Widom research and Zelechoski summary, there is a relationship between trauma and posttraumatic symptoms in younger cohorts. In adolescents, this relationship parallels the adverse outcomes (including risk of antisocial behavior toward others) experienced by adults after trauma (Breslau et al., 2006). Adolescents may be particularly vulnerable when the trauma occurs in the family, if the individual continues to live in that family environment.

Youths at high risk of offending have often been abused or neglected (Swahn et al., 2006). Consistent with this finding, Abram and colleagues' (2004, 2007) large-scale studies of incarcerated youth found a substantially elevated risk for traumatic history and psychiatric comorbidity (multiple diagnoses) among such youth. This suggests that early victimization experiences may be related to multiple mental health diagnoses and criminal conduct among adolescents.

Findings from the National Child Traumatic Stress Network Core Data Set (Dierkhising et al., 2013) documented various forms of trauma and adverse experience among youths ($N = 658$) involved with the juvenile justice system and referred for trauma-focused treatment. These youths had experienced an average of 4.9 different types of trauma, including loss (61.2%), caregiver impairment (51.7%), domestic violence (51.6%), emotional abuse (49.4%), physical abuse or maltreatment (38.6%), and community violence (34%). These findings move from considering trauma narrowly (e.g., life-threatening experiences) to more broadly (to include other kinds of adverse experiences), a trend that led to the conclusion (Maschi et al., 2008) that youth who experience more of these traumatic events (broadly considered) are at greater risk for juvenile delinquency.

Intimate Partner Violence

Prevalence Rates

The extent of physical abuse directed toward spouses and romantic partners in the U.S. is difficult to estimate, but many observe that it is extensive. The Centers for Disease Control and Prevention (https://www.cdc.gov/violenceprevention /intimatepartnerviolence/fastfact.html) estimates the following frequencies for having experienced intimate partner violence in a lifetime: *severe physical violence* (1 in 5 women, 1 in 7 men), *sexual violence* (1 in 5 women, 1 in 12 men), and *being stulked by an intimate partner* (10% of women, 2% of men). These are national estimates that may vary by geographic region, of course. For instance, the prevalence of lifetime domestic violence estimates range from 1.9% in Washington State to 70% in Hispanic women in the Southeastern U.S. (Alhabib et al., 2010). Rates of intimate partner violence also increased over 8% in the year following the COVID-19-related lockdown (https://counciloncj.org/impact-report -covid-19-and-domestic-violence-trends/), in part because of the increased time together in the home and perhaps other risk factors, such as substance use.

Current estimates of intimate partner violence encompass gay and lesbian relationships as well as heterosexual couples, so it is not meaningful to consider only "male violence perpetrated against women" or "female violence perpetrated against men." Nonetheless, there are several important considerations here. Male aggression toward women is significantly more likely to result in serious injuries (Tanha et al., 2010). Women and Black men are more likely to be killed by an intimate partner, and a high proportion of these incidents result in suicide of the perpetrator (Velopulos et al., 2019). Finally, the problem of intimate partner violence as part of domestic abuse may be different in other countries in which women have fewer rights, and victims have fewer resources.

Risk Factors for Intimate Partner Violence

What are the main risk factors for intimate partner violence? One review points to several important risk factors in the lives of perpetrators (Rosenbaum & Gearan, 1999). Although such individuals come from all socioeconomic and ethnic backgrounds, they are more likely than non-perpetrators to be unemployed, poorly educated, and of lower socioeconomic status. They tend to have been raised in families in which they either were physically abused as children or observed an abusive relationship between their parents. Adolescents who later become perpetrators of IPV have experienced a higher rate of conduct problems and are more likely to have engaged in early substance abuse; early experiences with coercive or aggressive behavior may set the stage for similar strategies in adult relationships (Magdol et al., 1998). Different types of perpetrators have been identified: generally violent, psychopathological, and family-only (Waltz et al., 2000). These groups were distinguished by the degree of violence within the relationship and the degree of extra-relationship violence reported, as well as by personality characteristics. For instance, generally violent perpetrators displayed the highest levels of aggressive-sadistic behavior, psychopathological IPV perpetrators exhibited more passive-aggressive/dependent characteristics, and family-only perpetrators displayed violent behaviors but generally did not hold violence-supportive beliefs and attitudes.

Different specialized risk assessment measures have been developed to appraise the likelihood that an individual will commit violence toward an intimate partner, and identify intervention strategies to reduce this risk. One such measure was developed in the 1990s (the Spousal Assault Risk Assessment Guide, or SARA; Kropp et al., 1994, 1999). Subsequent specialized measures in this area include the Domestic Violence Screening Instrument (Williams & Houghton, 2004) and the Ontario Domestic Assault Risk Assessment (Hilton et al., 2004).

Considering these measures can help us understand the risk factors for domestic violence. For example, the SARA has four broad areas: *Criminal History* (past assault of family members, past assault of strangers or acquaintances, past violation of community supervision conditions), *Psychosocial Adjustment* (recent relationship problems, recent employment problems, victim/witness of family violence when young, recent substance abuse, recent suicidal or homicidal thoughts, recent psychotic symptoms, and personality disorder with anger, impulsivity, or behavioral instability), *Spousal Assault History* (past sexual assault/sexual jealousy, past use of weapons and/or credible death threats, recent escalation in frequency or severity of assault, past violation of "no-contact" orders, extreme minimization or denial of spousal assault history, attitudes that support or condone spousal assault), and *Alleged Current Offense variables* (severe and/or sexual assault, use of weapons and/or credible threats of death, and violation of "no contact" order), as well as unspecified other considerations. Using a structured professional judgment measure like the SARA allows a clinician to make a well-informed judgment about the risk of future domestic violence. Generally, the more extensive the individual's history of criminal offending and domestic violence, the poorer their psychosocial adjustment, and the more serious the current alleged violence—the greater the risk of future violence toward an intimate partner.

The Cycle of Violence

IPV perpetrators are sometimes described as displaying a cycle of violence involving a Jekyll-and-Hyde pattern of emotional and behavioral instability that makes their victims even more fearful of the violence they believe is inevitable. A perpetrator may be loving and attentive to a partner's needs early in their relationship, cultivating the partner's affection and relying on the partner to satisfy the perpetrator's dependency needs; however, when disappointments or disagreements occur in the relationship, as they invariably do, a *tension-building phase* begins, characterized by

increased criticism of the partner and perhaps even minor physical assaults.

This phase leads to a second stage in the cycle, an *acute violence episode*. By the time this more serious form of aggression occurs, the victimized partner has become too dependent on the perpetrator to break off the relationship easily. The perpetrator has succeeded in controlling their partner's behavior and curtailing their contact with friends who might have possibly helped. The partner also tends to believe that if only they can find the right way to mollify the perpetrator's anger and reassure the perpetrator of their faithfulness and obedience, things will change.

Following a violent episode, a third stage (called the *contrite phase*) occurs, in which the perpetrator apologizes for the attack, promises never to do it again, and persuades the partner that there has been a change. Often this is an empty pledge. Indeed, sometimes the humiliation that the perpetrator feels over having apologized so profusely simply fuels more intense anger and violence, and the cycle repeats itself.

How pervasive is the cycle of violence? Even when it was first proposed (Walker, 1979) it seemed to apply in only about two-thirds of the 400 women who were studied. The *cycle of violence* may be related to an underlying personality disorder that typifies a certain category of perpetrator. Donald Dutton (2000), a psychologist at the University of British Columbia, has suggested that as many as 40% of IPV perpetrators have the features of borderline personality disorder, a severe disturbance that is characterized by unstable moods and behavior. People with borderline personality disorder are drawn into intense relationships in which they are particularly unable to tolerate and modulate certain emotions. They are demandingly dependent, which causes them to feel easily slighted, which then leads to jealousy, rage, aggression, and subsequently guilt. These emotional cycles repeat themselves, providing the underlying motivation for the cycle of violence.

Battered Woman Syndrome and Its Use as a Legal Defense. Battered woman syndrome was described as a collection of symptoms and reactions by a woman to a pattern of continued physical and psychological abuse inflicted on her by her mate. Today this is more likely to be described in terms such as intimate partner violence and Post Traumatic Stress Disorder, with the recognition that not all perpetrators are male and not all victims are female. Women are disproportionately victimized by intimate partner violence, which accounts for the historical tendency to call IPV perpetrators "him" and IPV victims "her." We have not done this earlier in this section, acknowledging that IPV is seen in relationships that are gay, lesbian, and transgender. But the earlier work in this area, which we now discuss, was focused on the male perpetrator/female victim dyad, so we will use these terms in discussing that work.

Lenore Walker (2009), the psychologist who is recognized for naming battered woman syndrome, emphasized the following elements:

1. As a result of chronic exposure to repeated incidents of IPV, the woman develops a sense of *learned helplessness*, in which she comes to believe that there is nothing she can do to escape from the perpetrator or improve her life.

2. Due to *social isolation* and often *financial dependence* on the perpetrator, she increasingly feels dominated and without alternatives.

3. With growing social isolation comes *increasing fear*, with many coming to believe that the perpetrator would eventually kill them.

4. This is accompanied by *diminished self-esteem, guilt and shame, and increasing resentment* toward her partner.

5. *Increasing vigilance* and *heightened sensitivity to danger* are sometimes cited to explain killing an abusive partner even at a time when IPV was not taking place.

Only a very small minority of victims of IPV kill their perpetrators. But when they do, they sometimes receive a great deal of public scrutiny. Some rely on either insanity or self-defense as a defense; in either instance, battered woman syndrome may be incorporated into the defense. (It may not be called that. To incorporate these concepts into contemporary thinking, it is likely that an individual would be evaluated to determine whether they met criteria for Post Traumatic Stress Disorder under DSM-5, as described earlier in this chapter. In other words, it may no longer be useful to use the construct of battered woman syndrome as such, even though many of its elements remain useful.)

How have such claims worked? There are both legal hurdles and juror skepticism present (Russell & Melio, 2006), perhaps helping to explain why most defendants attempting such a defense are convicted. Historically, a claim of self-defense has applied to homicides in which, at the time of the killing, the individual reasonably believed that they were in imminent danger of death or great bodily harm from an attacker. The defense was usually invoked in cases in which a specific attack or fight put defendants in fear for their lives. However, the typical case in which IPV victims rely on a theory of self-defense to murdering their partners is different. The violence does not involve a specific episode; rather, it is ongoing. The victim's response may seem disproportionate to what a "reasonable" person believes was necessary, particularly if they killed an abuser while that individual was unarmed or sleeping.

To help jurors understand how battered woman syndrome leads to a woman's perception that she is acting in self-defense, defendants often try to introduce expert testimony about the characteristics and consequences of the syndrome. Some mock jury research has explored the effect of expert testimony in a criminal homicide case in which the defendant was an IPV victim (Schuller et al., 2004). Participants were more inclined to accept the woman's claim of self-defense when they heard from an expert testifying for the defense. In addition, compared to the no-expert control condition, those exposed to expert testimony on IPV believed that the defendant's options were far more limited (Schuller et al., 2004). Community members surveyed about a scenario in which an IPV victim had killed her abuser were more likely to convict the defendant when she waited for a longer period following the abuse, and when the abuser was sleeping (Hodell et al., 2012).

The use of battered woman syndrome in legal proceedings provides a good example of why behavioral health syndromes and diagnoses should be carefully considered for their relevance and accuracy in legal contexts. One particular critique of the battered woman syndrome notes that (a) there is no single profile of a battered woman; (b) there is no single profile of the effects of IPV; (c) the name of the syndrome itself is vague, without a clearly defined set of criteria to operationalize it; (d) battered woman syndrome (or any other syndrome or diagnosis) is not uniquely relevant to understanding IPV; (e) the relevant information needed in such cases extends beyond the psychological impact of IPV, and includes the dynamics of violence, the victim's responses, the short- and long-term outcomes of these efforts, and the context of the abuse; and (f) the term creates an image of pathology (Dutton, 2014). Even a syndrome that appears directly relevant to the facts of certain kinds of cases, therefore, should be considered with healthy skepticism to avoid overreliance on the findings in this area.

No single set of reactions or characteristics can describe all victims of IPV. Although those affected share the experience of being victimized by a violent partner, their reaction to this aggression and how they cope with it takes many different forms. This variation has implications for developing the most effective types of intervention for those who experience IPV. Rather than assuming that they need traditional services such as psychotherapy or couples counseling, it would be more effective to provide IPV victims with special advocates who can support these survivors and help them find the resources they need to improve their lives.

Sexual Assault

Historically, victims of sexual assault have often been misunderstood, harassed, and neglected. For example, if an individual does not explicitly decline a sexual act, some might mistake this for consent. Advocacy work during the last decade, particularly on college campuses, has emphasized the importance of active and affirmative agreement by both parties, who are conscious and have the capacity to consent—and the challenges associated with implementing this policy (Johnson & Hoover, 2015). There remains debate about various aspects of this crime. Is sexual assault a sexual crime or an act of violence? Does perpetration reflect a disordered mind, a flawed character, or a result of extraordinary circumstances? Does it make any difference if the perpetrator has the prominence of someone like Bill Cosby or Harvey Weinstein? One such example appears in Box 6.3.

Beginning in the 1970s, there has been a good deal of psychological research directed toward understanding

Box 6.3

The Case of Dominique Strauss-Kahn: Prominence and the Accusation of Sexual Assault

Dominique Strauss-Kahn was in New York City in his role as chief of the International Monetary Fund in May 2011 when he was accused of sexual assault by a hotel housekeeper at the Sofitel Hotel, where he was staying. According to the housekeeper, Strauss-Kahn forced her to perform oral sex and submit to anal sex after emerging naked from his suite's bathroom. Strauss-Kahn was arrested and charged with two counts of criminal sexual act in the first degree, one count of attempted rape, sexual abuse in the first degree, unlawful imprisonment, sexual abuse in the third degree and forcible touching. Prosecutors subsequently became concerned about the history of the housekeeper (she had once reported being sexually assaulted in her native Guinea, but later recanted) and her behavior following the alleged assault. Strauss-Kahn himself had a history that seemed important. The married father of four was nicknamed "The Great Seducer" and had spoken publicly about his infidelity and affinity for younger women. He was also alleged by French journalist Tristane Banon to have sexually assaulted her during an interview nine years before the New York allegations.

Because prosecutors decided that the testimony that would be provided by the alleged victim in this case would be too weak to withstand cross-examination, they eventually dropped all charges against Mr. Strauss-Kahn.

Critical Thought Question

What are the advantages and disadvantages of admitting evidence concerning the history of previous allegations of sexual assault by the alleged perpetrator? Of admitting previous allegations of sexual assault made by the alleged victim?

sexual assaults (Beech et al., 2003; Jones et al., 2004). Differing attitudes and perceptions affect responses toward both offenders and their victims. Some respondents feel more empathy toward victims of sexual assault than others do. Empathy varies by an individual's experience as a victim (or a perpetrator); women with victimization experience showed greatest empathy with female victims, while men with perpetration histories showed more empathy for a male perpetrator (Osman, 2011). The consideration of attitudes about sexual assault can clarify what different people believe about this crime, its victims, and its perpetrators.

Some early research about individuals who are unsympathetic to victims and tolerant of those who commit sexual assault identified various misleading stereotypes about sexual assault that persist. According to a study involving 598 Minnesota adults (Burt, 1980), three factors distinguish those who endorse such stereotypes about sexual assault from those who do not:

1. *Adversarial sexual beliefs.* This refers to the belief that sexual relationships are fundamentally exploitive—that participants in them are manipulative, unfaithful, and not to be trusted.
2. *Acceptance of interpersonal violence.* This involves the belief that force and coercion are legitimate behaviors in sexual relationships, approving of domination over and control of partners with violence.
3. *Sex-role stereotyping.* This involves the extent to which an individual has beliefs associated with traditional gender roles.

It is interesting to consider how well this study, which was conducted over 50 years ago, continues to describe individuals who are more supportive of the act of sexual assault. To what extent have societal attitudes changed? Those who are more tolerant of sexual assault are more likely to have traditional beliefs about gender roles, more adversarial sexual beliefs, greater needs for power and dominance, and heightened expressions of aggressiveness and anger. This appears to be true for both men and women, although participants in one study did differ by gender on rape myth acceptance (women were lower), attribution of fault to society (women were higher), and feelings of anger and fear in response to sexual assault (women were higher) (Earnshaw et al., 2011). Other reviews are consistent with the importance of rape supportive attitudes in the specific context of campus sexual assault (refer to, e.g., Suarez & Gadalla, 2010). Such attitudes include the acceptance of rape myths, adversarial sexual beliefs, and hostile attitudes towards women (Widman & Olson, 2013). It would appear, therefore, that such attitudes have been a stable risk factor for sexual offending over a period of decades.

Facts about Sexual Assault

The United States has one of the highest rates of sexual assault among the world's industrialized countries. The annual number of sexual assaults in the U.S. reported in the National Crime Victimization Survey between 2008 and 2020 has fluctuated considerably from around 300,000 (2008) to as low as about 200,000 (2011) and as high as about 650,000

(2018) (refer to https://www.statista.com/statistics/251923/usa--reported-forcible-rape-cases-by-gender/). There has not been an identifiable trend over this period. But clearly this has been, and remains, a substantial problem.

According to the National Violence Against Women Survey, almost 18 million women (and almost 3 million men) in the United States have been raped. Women who reported being sexually assaulted as minors were twice as likely to report being sexually assaulted as adults—although fewer than 20% of victims report this assault to police (Tjaden & Thoennes, 2006). This is an important reason why statistics from crime victimization surveys are likely to be more accurate than official records of complaints. Women of all ages, social classes, and ethnic groups are more likely than men to be victimized by sexual assault (National Archive of Criminal Justice Data, 2010).

Motivations and Characteristics of Those Who Commit Sexual Assault

Sexual assault involves diverse combinations of aggressive and sexual motivation and deviant lifestyles, with various typologies describing perpetrators (refer to Robertiello & Terry, 2007, for a review). Most typologies have emphasized four factors that distinguish different types of sexual assailants: (1) the amount and type of aggression the assailant used; (2) when the level of aggression was high, whether it heightened sexual arousal in a sadistic manner; (3) whether the offender showed evidence of psychopathy or antisocial personality disorder; and (4) whether the offender relied on deviant sexual fantasies to produce sexual arousal.

Acquaintance Sexual Assault

A review of the National Crime Victimization Survey from 2010–2016 (https://www.rainn.org/statistics/perpetrators-sexual-violence) indicates that most sexual assaults (nearly 80%) are committed by someone known to the victim, including "acquaintance" (39%) and current or former partner (33%). The closer the relationship between the female victim and the offender, in general, the greater the likelihood that the police were not told about the assault; assaults by strangers were much more likely to be reported (Bureau of Justice Statistics, 2002). Barriers to reporting historically (e.g., shame and not wanting friends and family to know; concerns about confidentiality; fear about not being believed) have persisted, in contexts as different as college campuses (Sable et al., 2006) and active duty military.

Consequences of Being Sexually Assaulted

Those who have been sexually assaulted may experience physical injuries, emotional pain and humiliation, and sometimes severe psychological aftereffects. Recovery from this trauma can be very slow, and victims often describe a sense that they will never be the same again. Providing psychological assistance when needed to victims of sexual assault is of utmost importance.

The consequences of being sexually assaulted have received increased attention through various highly publicized cases in which women have come forward to report their experiences. As these cases have unfolded in the public eye, sexual aggression has become a topic of increased discussion. Highly publicized reports such as the accusations of multiple women that comedian and actor Bill Cosby drugged and sexually assaulted them, or that physician Larry Nassar sexually assaulted hundreds of girls and women while treating them at Michigan State and USA Gymnastics, have helped to focus this nation's attention on matters of sexual conduct and on the plight of the victims of sexual aggression. This discussion was renewed in 2021, following Mr. Cosby's release from incarceration after his conviction was overturned by the Pennsylvania Supreme Court on a procedural question unrelated to his guilt.

One part of this discussion has been a debate about whether the names of victims of sexual assault should be made public. The tradition in this country has been to protect the identity of sexual assault victims by not using their names in media coverage. Still, in some cases, both television and online reporting break with this tradition and publish the name of the accuser. Defenders of this practice argue that not naming sexual assault victims perpetuates the stigma of having been raped, making it more difficult in the long run for victims to come forward and confront their attackers. Critics claim that publishing the victim's name invades the individual's privacy and perhaps adversely affects their future.

How Do Victims React to Being Sexually Assaulted?

Sexual assault is a form of severe trauma that can lead to the experience of Post Traumatic Stress Disorder (American Psychiatric Association, 2013). Those with PTSD have

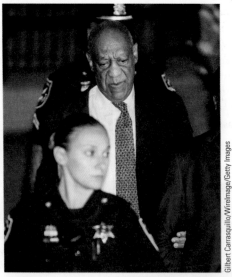

Gilbert Carrasquillo/WireImage/Getty Images

Bill Cosby

been exposed to at least one serious traumatic event (actual or threatened death, serious injury, or sexual violence), and have experienced the kind of symptoms discussed earlier in this chapter.

But not all those who are victimized by sexual assault develop PTSD. There is a range of responses in terms of severity. In some instances these responses do not combine to justify a full diagnosis of PTSD, but there are a number of commonly-experienced emotions (e.g., guilt, embarrassment, fear, distrust, sadness, vulnerability, anger, lack of control, numbness, confusion, shock) and symptoms (e.g., nightmares, flashbacks, depression, concentration problems, anxiety, disturbance in eating and sleeping, substance use) on the part of those victimized by sexual assault (National Sexual Violence Resource Center, 2010).

Contemporary thinking would probably avoid an attempt to classify such responses as specific to sexual assault (e.g., "rape trauma syndrome") for some of the same reasons that battered woman syndrome (discussed earlier) is problematic. We know that those who experience multiple traumas are more likely to have various kinds of adverse reactions.

There has been a range of adverse outcomes associated with the experience of sexual assault. The Centers for Disease Control and Prevention (refer to https://www.cdc.gov/violenceprevention/sexualviolence/fastfact.html) indicates that there can be immediate psychological reactions in the aftermath of the assault that include depression, anxiety, and suicidal thoughts. For some, these can develop into full-blown PTSD. Various health-related problems are associated as well; these include reproductive, gastrointestinal, cardiovascular, and sexual health problems—as well as "risky health behaviors" such as smoking, substance abuse, and risky sexual activity. Work-related problems such as job loss, time away from work, inability to work, and diminished performance may also result, having an adverse consequence on the individual's financial health. Whether individuals recover from this trauma, and how quickly, can depend on the support they receive, their own health and resilience, and the extent to which they can limit these other potential harms (Wolf, 2009).

Whether individuals acknowledge a previous sexual assault makes a difference. Victims who have experienced (but do not acknowledge) a previous assault were nearly twice as likely to report having experienced an attempted sexual assault during the six-month follow-up period (Littleton et al., 2009).

The long-term consequences of sexual assault are potentially serious, but can be treated. There is strong evidence for the effectiveness of certain kinds of more general interventions for trauma. One of the best-researched approaches to effective trauma treatment has been termed prolonged exposure (PE) (Foa & Kozak, 1986). In its current version, this approach includes *in vivo exposure* (real-life confrontation with feared stimuli, undertaken with low risk of harm—for example, post-assault fear of leaving home might be addressed with the goal of taking regular walks), *imaginal*

exposure (imaging the feared stimuli), and *processing* (immediately following the imaginal exposure, discussing the experience of revisiting the trauma memory—but focusing on new learning and changed beliefs). There have been numerous randomized controlled trial studies supporting the effectiveness of prolonged exposure in reducing trauma symptoms (McLean & Foa, 2011), with this effectiveness producing a "large" effect size in meta-analysis (Powers et al., 2013). An optimal treatment strategy, therefore, might involve both counseling on the sexual assault itself and prolonged exposure to treat the trauma symptoms.

Providing social support is another helpful intervention. The therapeutic power of social support may derive in part from the fact that many women tend to react to stress by seeking opportunities for attachment and caregiving—or what psychologist Shelley Taylor has termed the *tend-and-befriend* response (Taylor et al., 2000). (Men, on the other hand, are more likely to respond to stress with the well-known "fight-or-flight" strategy.) Therefore, it might be especially useful to female crime victims to have ample opportunities for social support so that their preference to be with others in times of need can be fully addressed.

Sexual Assault Trauma in Court. Psychologists, along with psychiatrists and other physicians, testify as expert witnesses in sexual assault trials, including about the nature and consequences of sexual assault (Melton et al., 2018). This testimony is best-supported when presented as an example of posttraumatic stress disorder, such as that experienced by veterans of combat, survivors of natural disasters, and victims of other violent crimes. The expert can be of special use to the prosecution in those trials in which the defendant admits that sexual intercourse took place but claims that the woman was a willing participant; evidence of sexual assault trauma can be consistent with the complainant's version of the facts. If jurors are not familiar with the reactions that sexual assault victims frequently experience, psychological experts can educate the jury. Courts around the country are divided, however, on the admissibility of such testimony, and the resulting controversy has generated considerable debate.

There is some history of presenting trauma reactions to sexual assault (and, as discussed earlier, to physical assault by an intimate partner) as "syndromes." The main argument against admitting expert testimony on a disorder as specific as rape trauma syndrome is as follows: The psychological responses of sexual assault victims are not unique to sexual assault and are not uniform, so it is impossible to say that a victim exhibiting any given set of responses has been sexually assaulted. Therefore, a psychologist should not be allowed to testify that a woman is experiencing rape trauma syndrome because to do so is tantamount to telling the judge and jury that she has been sexually assaulted, which should remain a matter for the judge or the jury to decide. Many courts also reject expert testimony on rape trauma syndrome on the basis that the reliability of the syndrome has not been established.

Source: Ad Council

It's On Us, a public service campaign, aims to reduce sexual violence against women on college campuses.

Preventing Sexual Assault

As we learn more about the frequency and consequences of sexual assault, a primary goal of concerned citizens, law enforcement officials, and social scientists has been to develop effective interventions for preventing it. Three basic strategies have been emphasized: (1) emphasizing the collective responsibility of both men and women to communicate more openly, seek affirmative consent for sexual behavior, identify high risk situations, and intervene to deter behavior that might be sexually coercive; (2) designing effective treatment for offenders so that they do not repeat their crimes, and (3) training potential victims how best to protect themselves against sexual assault. The first strategy is increasingly advocated in certain settings, such as college campuses, while the third strategy has been criticized as unfairly making women (more often victimized by sexual assault) responsible for their safety. The second strategy is generally more useful in the broader community than in a selected population such as universities, as few college students have previous convictions for sexual assault. Each will be discussed.

Emphasizing Collective Responsibility for Preventing Sexual Assault.

The first major strategy for preventing sexual assault has been implemented primarily on college campuses over the last decade. This approach has clearly

been influenced by changing views on sexual assault. There is far less tolerance for sexual misconduct generally, as we discuss in the next section. Affirmative consent is prioritized; consent is not assumed from the absence of "no." "No means no" is outdated, with "yes means yes" the appropriate standard at present. Many colleges have implemented policies requiring clear consent by both parties at each stage of a sexual encounter. Making women (who are more likely to be victimized by sexual assault on a college campuses) primarily responsible for their own safety, it has been suggested, is not only ineffective but insulting.

Yet there are some extraordinary challenges to developing policies that minimize the risk of sexual assault while respecting the privacy of those involved in sexual behavior. For example:

- Investigating sexual assault would typically fall under the jurisdiction of local police, with defendants prosecuted within the criminal justice system. But many universities have taken on the responsibility of investigating and adjudicating reports of sexual misconduct—meaning that campus police, offices of student life, and committees that may be composed of faculty members and administrators are tasked with doing what seasoned police investigators and prosecutors do in the criminal justice system. Such university officials have far less experience in these areas.

- Many college undergraduates are between the ages of 18 and 22, legally adults but often dependent on their families for financial support. Students who are accused of sexual assault may contact their families; parents, in turn, contact college leaders, who can feel pressure to support those reportedly victimized *and* be fair to those who are accused.

- Students who are experiencing less supervision, have easier access to drugs and alcohol, and are actively exploring their own sexuality may become involved in situations in which they consent to sex but later regret it, other situations in which they are uncertain (and subsequently believe they did not consent to sex), and yet others in which they clearly did not consent (e.g., they were coerced) or could not consent (e.g., they were unconscious).

Some of these are complex, while others seem straightforward. (Unconscious or extremely inebriated individuals obviously cannot give consent.) How have universities, using this "collective responsibility" strategy, attempted to minimize the risk of sexual assault while respecting the privacy of their students?

In a large study of campus sexual assault funded by the National Institute of Justice, investigators (Krebs et al., 2007) conducted the Campus Sexual Assault (CSA) Study, which gathered data on different kinds of sexual assault experienced by university students with the primary goal of informing the development of intervention strategies. Investigators surveyed over 6,800 undergraduate students (5,466 women and 1,375 men). They reported that 13.7% of undergraduate women had experienced at least one completed sexual assault since entering college, with 4.7% reporting physically forced sexual assault, 7.8% describing sexual assault when they were incapacitated after voluntarily consuming drugs and/or alcohol, and 0.6% reporting sexual assault when they were incapacitated after having been given a drug without their knowledge. Self-reported rates of sexual assault victimization and perpetration among males were very low.

There were several implications of this study for the "collective responsibility" strategy. The first involves the role of voluntarily consumed drugs or alcohol, which were implicated in most of the reported sexual assaults. Considering this, it should be the responsibility of the entire college community—men and women; students, administrators, and faculty—to strive to ensure that alcohol is used responsibly, that individuals do not drink to the point of disabling intoxication, and that there are multiple mechanisms for intervening should this occur (e.g., the person is accompanied home by friends, escorted by campus police). Second, the low rate of acknowledgment by men of committing any kind of sexual assault may indicate that many men assume that the absence of protest, even from an individual who was very intoxicated or unconscious, would translate into agreement to have sex. If this is true, then education programs focusing on the importance of affirmative consent, the influences that can preclude it, and the potential consequences for assuming consent when it has not been given should be part of student orientations, important websites, and public service messages.

The United States Congress passed the Campus Sexual Violence Elimination Act ("Campus SaVE Act") in 2013. This legislation is intended to address the needs of victims of sexual assault on university campuses by mandating certain protections for students (e.g., increased reporting of crime statistics). Under the terms of the SaVE Act, universities are required to create a plan to prevent sexual violence, to detail the procedures taken after a sexual assault is reported, and to inform reported victims of their rights and resources (Schroeder, 2014). This law remains in effect. Hopefully the combination of changing values, relevant law, and campus action under the collective responsibility strategy will substantially reduce the rate of campus sexual assault in the coming years.

Designing Effective Treatments for Perpetrators. Society is rightfully concerned about the likelihood of sexual offenders repeating their crimes. In some states, men convicted of sex crimes are required to complete a treatment program before being considered for parole. In such programs, the offender must acknowledge responsibility for his actions and participate in special interventions (Marshall et al., 2006).

The treatment of sexual offenders can involve psychological, physical, and medical procedures; in many treatment programs, different interventions are often combined. In the United States it is not uncommon for antiandrogen drugs to be prescribed to sexual offenders in order to reduce their sex drive, a procedure sometimes referred to as chemical

castration. The most common treatment involves giving male offenders a synthetic female hormone, MPA, which has the trade name of Depo-Provera. MPA decreases the level of testosterone in the body, thereby decreasing sexual arousal in most men; however, the drug has also been associated with various negative side effects, including weight gain, hair loss, feminization of the body, and gall bladder problems.

Anti-androgen treatments have problems other than negative side effects. The rate of men dropping out of such treatment prematurely is very high, and failure to complete treatment is one of the strongest predictors of recidivism for sexual offenders (Larochelle et al., 2011). In addition, the treatment does not always reduce sexual arousal and sexual offenses. In some men, arousal is not dependent on their level of testosterone, so the drugs have little effect on their sexual behavior. This is related to the fact that sexual assault is often an act of violence, not of inappropriate sexual arousal; consequently, drugs aimed at reducing sexual desire may be pointing at the wrong target. Even if the drugs inhibit sexual urges, they may not control violent behavior. Hence, they would not meaningfully control these offenders.

Another major approach to treating aggressive sexual offenders involves combining several behavior therapy techniques into an integrated program designed to increase offenders' self-control, improve their social skills, modify their sexual preferences, and teach them how to prevent relapses of their offenses. These programs are usually situated in prisons, but they have also been implemented in the community.

These integrated programs employ a wide range of treatment techniques. Sex education and training in social skills are common ingredients because of the widespread belief that those who commit sexual offenses are often socially incompetent. Aversive conditioning is sometimes used to decrease inappropriate sexual arousal and replace it with arousal to nonaggressive sexual cues. Existing programs appear to be able to produce short-term decreases in recidivism, but long-term improvements have been difficult to achieve. Consequently, relapse prevention techniques (which have proved useful in the treatment of drug addictions and cigarette smoking) are incorporated into many programs. Programs with a cognitive-behavioral orientation have shown effectiveness in reducing subsequent sexual offending against children (Beggs & Grace, 2011).

Training Potential Victims to Reduce the Risk of Sexual Assault. As we have discussed, national surveys suggest that most individuals who have been sexually assaulted were acquainted with their assailants before the assault. Research has also uncovered several risk factors associated with sexual assault, including using alcohol and drugs. Some colleges and universities have incorporated this information about risk factors into sexual assault prevention programs aimed at changing attitudes about sexuality, challenging stereotypes, promoting affirmative consent, and improving coping responses in potentially dangerous situations.

In the typical sexual assault prevention program, participants discuss factual evidence about sexual assault, describe the risks associated with heavy use of alcohol, practice resisting pressure for unwanted sexual activity, and role-play other strategies for protecting themselves. The programs try to help women change behaviors and to dispel the notion that victims cause sexual assault. They also strive to minimize the blaming of women that can occur following sexual victimization.

One study (Orchowski et al., 2008) investigated the impact of a sexual assault risk reduction program with a self-defense component for 300 college women. Using a placebo-control group, the study indicated that this program was effective in increasing levels of self-protective behaviors, self-efficacy in resisting against potential attackers, and use of assertive sexual communication over a four-month period, as well as reducing the incidence of rape among participants over the two-month follow-up. Another study of 500 college women who received a comparable sexual assault risk-reduction program also found an increase in self-protective behavior displayed by program participants during the six months following completion. In this study, however, there were no significant differences between participants and controls in rates of sexual victimization, assertive communication, or feelings of self-efficacy (Gidycz et al., 2006).

Sexual Harassment

Even though *sexual harassment* has been a significant problem in educational and work environments for many years, the term itself was coined in 1974. At that time, a group of women at Cornell University, after becoming aware that several of their female colleagues had been forced to quit because of unwanted advances from their supervisors, began to speak out against such harassment (Brownmiller & Alexander, 1992). Also in the early 1970s, the United States Equal Employment Opportunity Commission (EEOC) emerged as a major tool for redressing sexual harassment by employers.

Defining Sexual Harassment

U.S. federal law defines harassment as follows: Unwelcome sexual advances, requests for sexual favors, and other verbal or physical conduct of a sexual nature constitute sexual harassment when (1) submission to such conduct is made either explicitly or implicitly a term or condition of an individual's employment, (2) submission to or rejection of such conduct by an individual is used as the basis for employment decisions affecting such individual, or (3) such conduct has the purpose or effect of unreasonably interfering with an individual's work performance or creating an intimidating, hostile, or offensive working environment (16 Code of Federal Regulations Section 1604.11).

Some of the studies described in this section use the term *sexual harassment* to mean unwanted sexual attention. But sexual harassment also has a specific meaning under the law, as we note in the previous paragraph. Title VII of the Civil Rights Act of 1964 prohibits discrimination in the workplace because of a person's gender. It therefore provides the legal basis for banning sexual harassment, although there is continued confusion about the nature of sexual harassment. Such questions can be clearly answered with the kind of workplace harassment training described by the EEOC (2016).

In educational settings, sexual harassment is subject to Title IX of the Education Amendments of 1972 (Title IX) regarding sexual harassment. Revised guidance issued by the U.S. Department of Education (2001) reaffirms that a school should recognize and effectively respond to sexual harassment of students as a condition of receiving federal financial assistance. This is based in the legal authority indicating that sexual harassment of students can be a form of sex discrimination under Title IX. The United States Supreme Court has held (in *Gebser v. Lago Vista Independent School District*, 1998) that an educational institution in which an instructor sexually harasses a student may be liable for monetary damages, and further (in *Davis v. Monroe County Board of Education*, 1999) that such monetary damages may apply if one student sexually harasses another student. The liability set forth in the *Gebser* and *Davis* decisions is limited to private action for monetary damages.

Title IX was amended as of August 2020 to (1) narrow the definition of sexual assault, (2) limit the obligation to investigate off-campus conduct not related to school program or activity, and (3) allow the school to choose the standard of evidence used in an investigation (e.g., preponderance of the evidence versus clear and convincing). Refer to https://www.ctschoollaw.com/2020/07/new-title-ix-regulations-to-take-effect-in-august/. Effective June 2021, the U.S. Department of Education confirmed that Title IX will be applicable to protecting students from discrimination based on sexual orientation and gender identity (https://www.ed.gov/news/press-releases/us-department-education-confirms-title-ix-protects-students-discrimination-based-sexual-orientation-and-gender-identity).

There are certain differences between men and women in how sexual harassment is perceived. For instance, a meta-analysis on this topic (Rotundo et al., 2001) indicates that males and females tend to disagree about behaviors that involve workplace harassment, derogatory attitudes toward women, dating pressure, or physical sexual contact. On these topics, there were gender differences about what constitutes harassment. Sexual propositions or sexual coercion are topics upon which both men and women seem to agree as they relate to sexual harassment.

One problem with the federal definition of sexual harassment is that it leaves key terms such as *unwelcome* and *unreasonably interfering* open to varying interpretations. When men and women differ in their evaluations of potentially harassing interactions, women are more likely than men to classify a specific act as harassment (Rotundo et al., 2001). Women were more likely than men to consider online harassment "a major problem and to prioritize feeling "welcome and safe online" (as contrasted with "able to speak their minds freely online") (Duggan, 2017). Who, then, determines when an act is harassing—the alleged victim, the alleged perpetrator, or an outside, "neutral" observer?

A large-scale survey of men and women serving in the U.S. military (1,764 men; 4,540 women; Settles et al., 2014) addressed varying perceptions of perpetrator characteristics (sex and rank) and outcomes (psychological distress, role limitations, and work satisfaction). Results indicated that whether women who were sexually harassed found this conduct distressing depended upon whether it was frightening—but men who were harassed found it distressing regardless of whether it was frightening. Having a perpetrator who was male or higher status was more likely to make the behavior frightening to women. But the relationship between frightening appraisals and more psychological distress, more role limitations, and less work satisfaction was stronger for men than women. The investigators considered these results in the context of dominance, concluding that serious and more frightening harassment was distressing to both genders—but less serious harassment was more frightening and otherwise consequential to men. This is consistent with the results of an earlier meta-analysis (Blumenthal, 1998), reporting that both men and women were more likely to perceive behavior directed by someone of higher status at someone of equal or lesser rank in the workplace as harassment than if such behavior occurred between peers.

When psychologists study how individuals define sexual harassment, they usually do this by presenting participants with a set of facts and asking them whether they believe those facts indicate that sexual harassment occurred. For example, Wiener and his colleagues conducted a complex experiment that simultaneously assessed the impact of observers' gender and sexist attitudes on perceptions of allegedly harassing behavior in two workplace situations (Wiener et al., 1997). They classified participants as being either high or low in *hostile sexism* and *benevolent sexism*. Hostile sexism involves antipathy toward women, reflecting a belief that men are superior to women and should be dominant over them. Benevolent sexism is an attitude of protection toward women; it reflects a belief that as the "weaker sex," women need to be shielded from the world's harshness.

In addition to finding that females were more likely than males to believe that sexual harassment had occurred in these two situations, Wiener and colleagues (1997) examined the impact of participants' attitudes on their perceptions of sexual harassment. They predicted that those high in hostile sexism would be less inclined to conclude that sexual harassment had occurred. The results supported their prediction. Participants high in hostile sexism were less likely than those who scored low on this dimension to find that the defendant's behavior constituted sexual harassment.

The courts, following federal guidelines, have recognized two types of sexual harassment. The *quid pro quo* type involves sexual demands that are made in exchange for employment benefits; it is essentially sexual coercion. *Quid*

pro quo harassment is seen in an implicit or explicit bargain in which the harasser promises a reward or threatens punishment, depending on the victim's response (Hotelling, 1991). This would include a demand from a person having more power in a workplace or educational setting (e.g., a supervisor, a professor) for sexual favors in exchange for a tangible benefit such as a better evaluation.

The second, more common type of harassment, usually referred to as **hostile workplace harassment**, involves demeaning comments, acts of touching or attempted intimacy, or the display of provocative photographs or artwork. Under Title VII, it is illegal for employers to create or tolerate "an intimidating, hostile, or offensive working environment." In the 1986 case of *Meritor Savings Bank v. Vinson*, the U.S. Supreme Court recognized for the first time that sexual harassment creating a hostile work environment violates Title VII. Although evidence of repeated offensive behavior or behavior of a severe nature is usually required for the plaintiff to prevail, the effects of such harassment need not "seriously affect [an employee's] psychological well being" or lead the plaintiff to "suffer injury" to constitute *hostile workplace* harassment (*Harris v. Forklift Systems, Inc.*, 1993; refer to Box 6.4).

Prevalence Rates

Several cases involving sensational charges of sexual harassment have received widespread attention and focused awareness on the problem of sexual harassment.

Fox talk show host Gretchen Carlson filed suit against Roger Ailes, the head of Fox News, claiming that her June 2016 firing came after Mr. Ailes reduced her role on shows and paid her less because she refused a sexual relationship or sexual banter with him. Mr. Ailes subsequently resigned from Fox News. Harvey Weinstein, a prominent Hollywood movie producer, was convicted of sex crimes against six women and sentenced in 2021 to 23 years in prison. After years of rumors regarding his coercing female actors into unwanted sexual contact, he was openly accused by several women of sexual assault and harassment. This led to a reexamination by our society of the workplace conduct of powerful individuals, most often men, that has been called the #MeToo movement.

#MeToo has demonstrated that sexual harassment is not confined to a few.

Box 6.4

The Case of Teresa Harris: Sexual Harassment on the Job

Teresa Harris was the rentals manager at Forklift Systems in Nashville. Her boss (the company president) made various suggestive and demeaning comments to her. At first she tried to ignore him, and then she confronted him. He promised to stop, but a month later, in public, he asked whether she had slept with a client to get his account. This was the last straw; after working there two years, Harris quit. She sought relief from the EEOC and the courts, claiming that her boss's behavior had created a hostile workplace. She asked for back wages as part of the litigation.

When she did not receive satisfaction from the lower courts, she brought her appeal to the U.S. Supreme Court, which agreed to hear the case because different circuit courts had been inconsistent in their decisions in such cases. Some courts had adopted a subjective approach, focusing on the impact of the alleged harassment on the plaintiff. Others, taking a more objective approach, had asked whether a reasonable person would have found the environment abusive. Another question involved the degree of impact. Was it sufficient that the environment interfered with the complainant's work performance, or was it necessary for "psychological injury" to have occurred? Sexual harassment can produce psychological damage—but should plaintiffs be forced to prove that they were psychologically harmed to persuade a jury that the sexual harassment has occurred?

The unanimous decision of the Court, announced by Justice Sandra Day O'Connor, was in favor of Harris and held that it was not necessary for plaintiffs to prove that they had sustained psychological injuries. The Supreme Court decision listed several criteria by which to decide whether an action constitutes sexual harassment, including the frequency and severity of the behavior, whether the behavior was physically threatening or humiliating, and whether it would unreasonably interfere with an employee's work performance.

Prior to this decision there was controversy about whether to assess potentially harassing behavior from the perspective of a "reasonable man," "reasonable person," or "reasonable victim" (Gutek & O'Connor, 1995; Wiener & Gutek, 1999). Justice O'Connor's opinion suggested that if conduct was not sufficiently severe and pervasive that it created an "objectively hostile" work environment as defined by a *reasonable person*, then it was not sexual harassment. The Court's decision reflected an intermediate position; harassment was no longer defined solely by the individual doing the harassing, or the individual who was receiving it.

Critical Thought Question

If you had been Justice O'Connor trying to determine whether a workplace environment was "objectively hostile," would you have selected the perspective of "a reasonable man," "a reasonable victim," or "a reasonable person"?

How frequent is sexual harassment? Research has suggested that 38% of women and 14–15% of men experience some kind of sexual harassment and/or assault in the workplace over their lifetime. More frequent experiences with such harassment occur in "public spaces," with "online" a growing frequency (Kearl et al., 2019). Some proportion of this reported workplace harassment would be relevant to the present discussion involving harassment by supervisors. In workplace environments that are predominantly male, the rates of such harassment have been estimated to be even higher, ranging from two thirds or more of women and one third of men (Department of Defense, 2004; Department of Defense Inspector General, 2005). Outcomes of such harassment include difficulties such as anxiety, depression, and posttraumatic stress symptoms (Willness et al., 2007) that may persist beyond a year after the occurrence of the harassment (Munson et al., 2000). Finally, it may have negative consequences in the workplace: less commitment to and satisfaction with work, poorer productivity, and greater likelihood of leaving the job (Cogin & Fish, 2009; Langhout et al., 2005; Lapierre et al., 2005).

A study examining sexual harassment in academic medicine indicated that about half of female faculty experienced some form of sexual harassment, compared to very few male faculty, and these experiences were prevalent across different institutions in the sample and across all regions of the United States (Carr et al., 2000). One meta-analysis (Ilies et al., 2003) used 86,000 respondents from 55 samples to estimate that 58% of women report having experienced potentially harassing behavior, and 24% report having experienced sexual harassment at work. A subsequent meta-analysis (Sojo et al., 2016) considered the relationship between different kinds of workplace harassment (e.g., sexual coercion, organizational climate) on women's attitudes toward work and perceived job stress. Women were adversely affected by both more intense/less frequent acts such as sexual coercion, and less intense/more frequent behavior (e.g., sexist organizational climate). This impact was exacerbated when there was a power imbalance between the perpetrator and the target.

A broad survey of workplace harassment conducted by the Equal Employment Opportunity Commission in 2016 yielded various conclusions about the status of this form of harassment:

Harvey Weinstein

Workplace Harassment Remains a Persistent Problem. Almost one third of the approximately 90,000 charges received by EEOC in 2015 included an allegation of workplace harassment.

Workplace Harassment Too Often Goes Unreported. Common workplace-based responses by those who experience sex-based harassment are to avoid the harasser, deny or downplay the gravity of the situation, or attempt to ignore, forget, or endure the behavior. About 3/4 of those who experienced harassment never discussed it formally with anyone at work, citing fear of having their report disbelieved, their claim not acted upon, being blamed, or being the victim of social or professional retaliation.

There Is a Compelling Business Case for Stopping and Preventing Harassment. In 2015, the EEOC by itself recovered $164.5 million for workers alleging harassment. Those who experience workplace harassment can suffer mental, physical, and economic harm. The environment created by this behavior can also affect other workers, and decrease productivity, increase turnover, and harm reputations.

Leadership and Accountability Are Critical. Workplace culture has the most influence on whether harassment is frequent or minimal. Such leadership includes providing effective harassment prevention and a workplace environment in which harassment is not tolerated.

Training Must Change. Much training over the last three decades has been delivered with the goal of avoiding legal liability. Effective training must be part of a broader culture that does not condone harassment, should be tailored to specific work staff and environment, and include middle managers and immediate supervisors. Promising modified training approaches include "bystander intervention training" and "workplace civility training."

It's On Us. Workplace harassment may be reduced through this kind of campaign, which was originally devised to reduce sexual violence in campus settings. It incorporates the idea that students, faculty, and campus staff should all be part of the training and the campaign, distributing the responsibility far beyond those who are the immediate victims of sexual violence or harassment. This kind of campaign has yet to be implemented with respect to sexual harassment in the workplace, but shows considerable promise.

Applying Psychological Knowledge to Detecting Harassment

Psychological approaches contribute to our understanding of sexual harassment in two other ways. First, some psychologists have attempted to predict when sexual harassment will occur. Other psychologists have tried to determine the likelihood of a favorable outcome in litigation when a person who alleges sexual harassment files a complaint. We consider these issues next.

When and in what environments is sexual harassment more likely to occur? Some studies have suggested that having employees with authoritarian personality characteristics (Begany & Milburn, 2002), traditional beliefs about women's roles (Driscoll et al., 1998), or men who are higher in hostility toward women (Krings & Facchin, 2009) will increase the likelihood that workplace sexual harassment will occur. While such considerations may contribute somewhat, probably the strongest influence has been termed "organizational climate" (Pryor et al., 1995; Roofeh, 2019). This involves the extent to which organizations tolerate (or do not tolerate) various forms of "humor" and other behavior that may be overtly sexualized, thus contributing to the creation of a hostile workplace environment. It is noteworthy that this influence—situational rather than an aggregation of personality characteristics—may be considerably stronger and more influential than the individuals who work within the organization.

To determine trends in workplace harassment claims upheld by the Equal Employment Opportunity Commission, we consider data on claims filed between 2010 and 2020. During this period, the annual number of "resolutions" decreased from 8,959 (2010) to 7,278 (2020), a reflection of the number of claims presented each year to the EEOC. Findings of "no reasonable cause" (basically a denial of the merits of the claim) fluctuated between 50% and 56.4%, with no discernible pattern, while findings of "reasonable cause" dropped from 8.7% (2010) to 4.7% (2020) (https://www.eeoc.gov/statistics/charges-alleging-sex-based-harassment-charges-filed-eeoc-fy-2010-fy-2020). We may conclude that the number of claims over this period did not grow, and the percentage of findings in favor of the complainant actually decreased.

Offenders' Experience as Victims of Crime, Violence, and Trauma

When offenders are also victims, or report that they are victims, of crime, violence, or other kinds of trauma, then society's reaction becomes even more complex—and decisions made by the legal system become even more controversial. Considering the association between victimization and offending using a measure of youth lifestyles, one study found a positive association between violent and non-violent offending, and being a victim of violent and non-violent crime (Deadman & MacDonald, 2004). Consistent with this, other investigators (e.g., Abram et al., 2004) have reviewed the relationship of various kinds of trauma (perceived impending harm to self or a family member, physical assault, sexual assault, threat with a weapon, serious accident, natural disaster, exposure to violence, and exposure to dead bodies) and offending in justice-involved youth. More than half of the youth (total sample = 898 arrested and newly detained adolescents) had experienced six or more such traumatic events, and over 90% had been exposed to at least one. Findings using data from the National Child Traumatic Stress Network Core Data Set (Dierkhising et al., 2013) indicated that justice-involved youth referred for trauma-focused treatment ($N = 658$) experienced an average of about 5 different kinds of trauma, including loss and bereavement (61.2%), impaired caregiver (51.7%), domestic violence (51.6%), abuse or maltreatment (emotional: 49.4%; physical: 38.6%), and community violence (34%). Such findings led one scholar to conclude that there is clearly a relationship between trauma exposure and juvenile justice system involvement—although it may be a complex one (Zelechoski, 2016).

Consider the case of Jodi Arias and Travis Alexander. They had dated off and on for more than a year, in a distance relationship that involved travel between their homes in Arizona and California. In 2008, they planned a trip to Cancun, Mexico that overlapped with Alexander's work. They never went on the trip, scheduled for June 15. Following Alexander's disappearance, Arias was eventually charged with his death. After telling investigators that he had died in his home at the hand of two intruders who broke in, killing him and attacking her, she subsequently told police that she had killed Alexander in self-defense—and he had been abusive toward her. Arias was convicted of first-degree murder in May 2013. She was eventually sentenced to life in prison without the possibility of parole. Jurors did not seem convinced that Arias had been the victim of intimate partner violence that left her with few options to protect herself. This case is perhaps not representative of many instances in which a one partner experiences violence at the hands of another. In another respect, however, it does demonstrate very well the importance of considering a variety of explanations and following the evidence wherever it may lead. But we now know that the experience of trauma and serious adversity inclines individuals toward criminal offending. Is this an inevitable result? No. Is it something that a legal decision-maker should consider in trying to understand the motivation of a criminal offender—particularly when the consequences being considered are very serious? Probably.

Summary

1. **What is the frequency of crime victimization?** Probably the most accurate way of measuring crime involves self-reported victimization. In 2020, the rate of self-reported violent victimization fell by 22% compared to the previous year. Likewise, the number of burglary and trespassing victimizations were 23% lower. But only about 40% of violent victimizations and 33% of property crimes were reported to police.

2. **What types of research have psychologists conducted on victimization?** Four areas of victimization have received special attention from psychologists: adverse childhood experience; violent victimization and post-traumatic stress disorder, including the psychology of sexual assault; domestic violence (particularly intimate partner violence); and sexual harassment.

3. **What factors predict the development of PTSD after being a crime victim?** The extent of injury suffered in the crime and the belief that the victim has no control over their life heighten the risk of developing PTSD. Cognitive-behavioral treatments that help restore a sense of control and that help victims re-experience the trauma so that its emotional power is drained are the most effective interventions for preventing and reducing PTSD after a criminal victimization.

4. **What are the components of battered woman syndrome that make it more specific than Post Traumatic Stress Disorder?** Battered woman syndrome consists of a collection of responses that may be displayed by individuals who are repeatedly physically abused by their intimate partners. The most specific of these components are learned helplessness, social isolation, and economic dependence.

5. **How can sexual assault be prevented?** Prevention of sexual assault has been attempted in several ways. One includes promoting shared responsibility for the safety of all. A second is strengthening the capacity for

self-protection from sexual assault. The third is the use of effective treatments for convicted sexual offenders. Anti-androgen drugs, which reduce sex drive, and a combination of various behavior therapy techniques have shown some effectiveness as treatment for convicted sexual offenders.

6. **What are the two types of sexual harassment recognized by the courts?** The first type of harassment, *quid pro quo* harassment, consists of sexual demands made in conjunction with offers of benefits in exchange for compliance or threats of punishment if the respondent does not comply. The second type is harassment that creates a hostile work environment; it often involves demeaning comments, acts of touching or attempted intimacy, or the display of provocative photographs or artwork.

Key Terms

acute stress disorder

battered woman syndrome

borderline personality
   disorder

chemical castration

cycle of violence

hate crimes

hostile workplace harassment

posttraumatic stress
   disorder

quid pro quo harassment

rape trauma syndrome

self-defense

victimology

Chapter 7

Evaluating Criminal Suspects

Orienting Questions

1. What are some psychological investigative techniques used by the police?

2. What is criminal profiling?

3. Is the polygraph a valid instrument for lie detection? What are some problems associated with it?

4. What are the premises of cognitive-based methods to detect deception and how effective are those protocols?

5. What brain-based techniques are used to detect deception, and how well do they work?

6. How valid is confession evidence? What kinds of interrogation procedures can lead to false confessions?

7. What are some of the reforms proposed to prevent false confessions?

In this chapter, we discuss three additional activities that psychology can undertake to assist law enforcement: profiling criminal suspects, assessing the truthfulness of suspects, and evaluating the validity of confessions obtained through interrogations. The common thread that ties these topics together is the assumption that psychological theory and techniques can be used to improve law enforcement evaluations of criminal suspects.

These contributions occur in a logical sequence. Psychological profiling is usually performed early in a criminal investigation when the police need help focusing on certain types of people who might be the most likely suspects. Once suspects have been identified, law enforcement officials use other procedures to determine whether they should be charged. While questioning suspects, police rely on various visual and verbal cues to determine whether they are giving truthful responses. But as we will discuss, people are not especially adept at detecting deception by relying on these kinds of cues.

Suspects are sometimes given so-called lie detection (or polygraph) tests to provide more information about their guilt or innocence and, sometimes, to encourage them to confess. However, assumptions about the effectiveness of polygraph procedures conflict with some psychological findings about their accuracy. Many psychologists question the objectivity of the procedure as it is usually administered and, hence, the validity of its results.

Increasingly, law enforcement agents and industry personnel are using brain-based technologies including neuroimaging and brain-wave measurements, as well as artificial intelligence, to detect deception. Although promising, these techniques have not yet been subjected to the kind of rigorous, real-world testing that is required before they become commonplace investigatory tools. One review (Meijer & Verschuere, 2017) concluded that fMRI, a form of neuroimaging, has done a good deal to advance theory development in the detection of deception, but little to address the practical problems associated with procedures such as the polygraph.

The police interrogate suspects and encourage them to confess because confessions make it more likely that suspects will be successfully prosecuted and eventually convicted. But in the quest for conviction, confessions can be coerced. Courts have tried to clarify when a confession is truly voluntary, but psychological findings often conflict with the courts' evaluations of confessions.

Thus, a consistent theme throughout this chapter is the conflict between the legal system and psychological science regarding ways of gaining knowledge and evaluating truth. A related conflict involves the competing interests of determining the truth and resolving disputes.

Profiling of Criminal Suspects

Do offenders commit their crimes or choose their victims in distinctive ways that leave clues to their psychological makeup, much as fingerprints point to their physical identity or ballistics tests reveal the kind of gun they used? There is some evidence that psychological characteristics are linked to behavioral patterns and that these links can be detected by a psychological analysis of crime scenes. Behavioral scientists and police use criminal profiling to narrow criminal investigations to suspects who possess certain behavioral and personality features that were revealed by the way the crime was committed. (Another way to think about profiling is that it involves the attempt to "reverse engineer" a final product—the crime scene—to learn more about the individual[s] who created that final product.)

Profiling, which has also been called "criminal investigative analysis," does not identify a specific suspect. Instead, profilers offer a general psychological description of the most likely type of suspect, including personality and behavioral characteristics suggested by a thorough analysis of the crimes committed, so that police can concentrate their investigation of difficult cases in the most profitable directions. (Profiles also help investigators search for persons who fit descriptions known to characterize hijackers, drug couriers, and those who are undocumented; refer to Monahan & Walker, 2018.) The results of a careful profile may provide specific information about suspects, including psychopathology, characteristics of their family history, educational and legal history, and habits and social interests. Although profiling can be used in diverse contexts, it is considered most helpful in crimes in which the offender has demonstrated some form of repetitive behavior with unusual aspects, such as sadistic torture, ritualistic or bizarre behavior, evisceration, or staging or acting out a fantasy (Woodworth & Porter, 2000).

A successful profiler should possess several key attributes, including both an understanding of human psychology and investigative experience (Hazelwood et al., 1995). There is some controversy regarding who should be considered a successful profiler. Because of the importance of investigative experience in criminal profiling, some have suggested that mental health professionals may not be fully qualified to engage in profiling (Hazelwood & Michaud, 2001). Others maintain that clinical (forensic) psychologists possess a level of expertise that contributes to the effectiveness of criminal profiling (Copson et al., 1997; Gudjonsson & Copson, 1997). One survey (Torres et al., 2006) found that only 10% of the psychologists and psychiatrists surveyed reported any profiling experience, although 25% considered themselves knowledgeable about profiling. Fewer than 25% believed that criminal profiling was scientifically reliable or valid, but most felt it had some usefulness in criminal investigation. Certainly any professional who attempts to conduct profiling should be knowledgeable and experienced with offenders and the process of criminal investigation, which typically means that an individual must have experience as a criminal investigator. (Despite the mixed evidence on the validity of criminal profiling, a 2021 online search of "criminal profiler" yielded 11,500,000 results. Many appear to be from training programs purporting to help individuals obtain jobs in this area. Others are appropriately cautious, noting that there are relatively few such full-time positions, typically held by individuals with substantial experience in criminal investigation as a law enforcement agent.)

Many famous fictional detectives have been portrayed as excellent profilers because they could interpret the meaning of a small detail or find a common theme among seemingly unrelated features of a crime. Lincoln Rhyme, the "criminalist" in Jeffrey Deaver's novels, focuses on learning everything humanly possible from painstaking scrutiny of the crime scene, and using that information to support (or disconfirm) possibilities about potential perpetrators. Profiling even infiltrated popular culture through TV programs such as *Law and Order* and its offspring (*Criminal Intent, UK,* and *Special Victims Unit*), as well as *Criminal Minds, FBI, and FBI: Most Wanted.*

One of the earliest cases of criminal profiling involved the 1957 arrest of George Metesky, otherwise known as the Mad Bomber of New York City. Over an eight-year period, police had tried to solve a series of more than 30 bombings in the New York area. They finally consulted Dr. James Brussel, a Greenwich Village psychiatrist, who, after examining pictures of the bomb scenes and analyzing letters that the bomber had sent, advised the police to look for a heavyset, middle-aged, Eastern European, Catholic man who was single and lived with a sibling or aunt in Connecticut. Brussel also concluded that the man was very neat and that, when found, he would be wearing a buttoned double-breasted suit. When the police finally arrested Metesky, this composite turned out to be largely accurate.

Not all early profiles were so useful, however. For example, the committee of experts charged with the task of profiling the Boston Strangler predicted that the killer was not one man but two, each of whom lived alone and worked as a schoolteacher. They also suggested that one of the men would be gay. When Albert DeSalvo ultimately confessed to these killings, police discovered that he was a heterosexual construction worker who lived with his wife and two sons (Porter, 1983).

Two important aspects to this kind of reconstructive activity have involved *crime scene analysis* (detecting physical evidence that would provide important investigatory and prosecution support) and *inferences about offender characteristics* (patterns of perpetrator thinking, feeling, and behavior deduced from evidence left at the crime scene). Disciplines such as biology and biochemistry have provided tools for advances in the former area, while psychology, psychiatry, and criminology have provided important contributions in the latter (refer to Turvey, 2012, for an extensive discussion).

A major source of research and development on criminal profiling has been the FBI's Behavioral Science Unit (the BSU), which worked on criminal profiles between the 1970s and 2014, when it was disbanded. The BSU was one of the instructional components of the FBI's Training and Development Division, located at the FBI Academy in Quantico, Virginia. It provided training, conducted research, and offered consultation in the behavioral and social sciences. The BSU also coordinated with other FBI units, such as

the National Center for the Analysis of Violent Crime (NCAVC), which continues to provide operational assistance to FBI field offices and law enforcement agencies. The NCAVC now has separate units that focus on (1) counterterrorism, arson, and bombings; (2) threats, cyber crime, and public corruption; (3) crimes against children; (4) crimes against adults; and (5) research, strategy, and instruction. Its mission is to provide behaviorally based support to a range of law enforcement agencies, including the FBI, other U.S. security agencies, and law enforcement agencies ranging from international to federal, state, and local. This is offered particularly in the context of investigation of unusual or repetitive violent crimes (refer to https://www.fbi.gov/services/cirg and go to "CIRG" under "Services").

Historically, much of the BSU's focus was on violent offenders, especially those who commit bizarre or repeated crimes (Jeffers, 1991). Particular attention was given to those who committed serious sexual offenses (Ressler et al., 1988), arson (Rider, 1980), sexual homicide (Hazelwood & Douglas, 1980), or mass or serial homicide (Porter, 1983). Interest in these topics continues, particularly in serial and mass homicide (Fox & Levin, 2005; Hickey, 2009; Morton & Hilts, 2008; Mullen, 2004). There is also continued interest in the topic of crime scene analysis and offender profiling (Ainsworth, 2001; Owen, 2004; Petherick, 2005). The focus of such work is on describing those who have committed a specific type of offense to learn how they select and approach their victims, how they react to their crimes, what demographic or family characteristics they share, and what personality features they have. For example, as part of its study of mass and serial murder, the FBI conducted detailed interviews with some of the United States' most notorious homicide offenders—among them Charles Manson, Richard Speck, and David Berkowitz—to determine the similarities among them.

Following September 11, 2001, the FBI placed a higher priority on counterterrorism (FBI Academy, 2002). Profiling terrorist suspects in the United States has proved challenging, and no reliable profile has been developed. There are various reasons for this, described succinctly in a review on the topic (Monahan, 2012). The author observes that individual risk factors for criminal behavior (e.g., age, gender, marital status, social class, past crime, major mental illness, and personality) do not serve as risk factors for terrorism. Indeed, while there are some advantages to considering "terrorism" broadly, Monahan describes the strategy of being more specific about types of terrorism, such as suicidal, homegrown, inside, jihadist/Salafist, and so on, as also potentially useful. Finally, he offers four categories of "promising" risk factors in this area: ideology, affiliation, trauma/loss, and disgust. Even focusing on these more promising strategies, however, would not allow the prospective validation of a risk assessment tool for terrorism. (Imagine "validating" such a tool by administering it to many individuals and releasing some of them to observe how often they became involved in subsequent terrorist activity.) In addition, applying such risk factors in the United States would risk violating Americans' civil liberties and producing many "false positives" (those who are predicted to present a threat but who actually do not).

Nonetheless, it is domestic terrorism—sometimes called "domestic violent extremism" (DVE)—that in 2021 posed a far greater threat to the security of U.S. citizens than did the radical Islamic terrorism associated with September 11 and discussed by Monahan in the previous paragraph. The Office of the Director of National Intelligence made the following points regarding domestic violent extremism in a 2021 summary:

- Existing biases against minority populations and government actions will continue to influence DVE radicalization and violence. These will be supplemented by newer influences, such as perceived election fraud, the U.S. Capitol insurrection, and the COVID-19 pandemic.

- Individuals or small DVE cells are more likely than organizations to perpetrate attacks in the U.S. It is harder to detect these individuals and small groups because their radicalization is often via consumption of online material.

- The most serious DVE threats are from racially motivated violent extremists (RMVEs) and militia violent extremists (MVEs). RMVEs are more likely to engage in mass-casualty attacks against civilians; MVEs are more likely to select law enforcement and government personnel and facilities as targets.

- White supremacist RMVEs pose the greatest threat across nations because there are similar beliefs held by others in various countries, and these individuals communicate with and influence each other.

- Domestic violent extremists use social media, smaller websites, and encrypted chat applications for recruiting, planning, and mobilization to violence.

- DVE threats could be increased by influences such as increased support (domestic or international), high-profile attacks, and growing perceptions of government overreach.

- DVE lone offenders present particular problems because of their independent radicalization, firearm access, and ability to act without easy detection (https://www.dhs.gov/sites/default/files/publications/21_0301_odni_unclass-summary-of-dve-assessment-17_march-final_508.pdf).

Contemporary law enforcement must consider various influences on violent offending, therefore. We continue with a description of necessary approaches to mass and serial homicide motivated by personal factors, but add that domestic violent extremism committed for ideological reasons is likely to play a prominent part in the criminal and national security landscape in the United States as long as the country is as polarized as it now seems to be. In addition, religious and ideological influence may sometimes be a part of the motivation of lone actors, as we discuss in the next section.

Classifying Homicide Offenders: Mass and Serial Murderers

Two types of multiple homicides have been identified: mass murder and serial murder. These types share some similarities but are marked by several differences (Meloy & Felthous, 2004). The most frequent definition of **mass murder** involves killing four or more victims in one location during a period of time that lasts anywhere from a few minutes to several hours. **Serial murder** involves the killing of at least two individuals by the same person, in events separated by a "cooling off" period of at least several hours.

In 2019, there were 34 events in the United States that involved the death of at least four people—but 417 events in which at least four people were injured. The number of events with at least four fatalities was lower in 2020 (21) but the total number of events was higher (611) (http://www.shootingtracker.com/). These numbers illustrate some of the challenges in using data to better understand mass killings. Are we considering only perpetrators who actually kill at least four people, or also those who try? (The latter event is much more common than the former.) Is the number of highly lethal events increasing? It was estimated that about two mass murders were committed every month in the United States in the 1990s (Fox & Levin, 1998.) This is not very different from the numbers in 2019 and 2020. Do the small number of events detract from the tragedy of multiple deaths associated with mass killings? (This question involves both numbers and moral values.) Learning more about mass and serial killing seems both challenging and important to us, even considering their rarity. So what do we know?

Based on research to date, behavioral scientists have been able to classify individuals who commit mass homicide, and add to the portrait of contemporary homicide offenders. Historically, most homicides have been committed by killers who were well acquainted with their victims, had a personal but rational motive, killed once, and were then arrested. In recent decades, however, increased attention has been paid to patterns of homicide involving killers who attack multiple victims, sometimes with irrational or bizarre motives, and who are less likely to be apprehended than in former days because their victims are strangers. There is also a question of whether a given attack might have been motivated by religious ideology. For example, Omar Mateen, a 29-year-old security guard, killed 49 people and wounded 53 others in June 2016 at Pulse, a gay nightclub in Orlando, in the deadliest mass killing of LGBT individuals in U.S. history. Before this crime was carried out, Mateen attributed his actions to his allegiance to the Islamic State of Iraq and the Levant (ISIL)—although there was no credible evidence that he was involved with this group. Mateen was killed by police after negotiations over three hours did not convince him to surrender.

The criminal trails of those who commit mass homicide may center on one locale and period of time, or cross through different locations and stretch over a longer period of time. This does not mean, of course, that the patterns of homicide offending have necessarily changed. It is quite likely that changes in communication technology have changed the *awareness* of homicide offending with multiple victims. (Refer to http://www.shootingtracker.com/ for figures on mass killings between 2013 and 2020.) It has also been difficult to get scientifically sound information about mass homicide. According to a 2020 review by the National Institute of Justice, there are two systematic deficiencies associated with 44 identified studies (1997–2016) in this area: (1) the absence of a uniform definition of mass shootings and related concepts, and (2) the absence of consistent databases that gather, sort, and communicate information on attempted and completed events (https://nij .ojp.gov/topics/articles/advancing-mass-shooting-research -inform-practice). Definitions range from "two victims" (5% of studies) or "three victims" (9% of studies") to "four or more victims" (48% of studies) or "multiple victims" (38%). Data were drawn from publicly accessible databases (65%), official records (33%), and interviews with perpetrators (2%). Until research in this area uses more uniform definitions and reliable sources of data, we are left with questions about whether these findings *in aggregate* are meaningful.

Because mass homicides and serial killings are relatively rare, it is virtually impossible to formulate statistical models that predict them accurately. The particular problem with trying to predict such rare events is the "false positive" error rate: even approaches that have a good overall accuracy rate result in more errors in the false positive direction (those who are predicted to be violent, but actually are not) than the false negative direction (those who are predicted not to be violent, but actually are). As an alternative to prediction, some research has focused on identifying characteristics of these homicide offenders and examining patterns among individuals. One study comparing 30 adult versus 34 adolescent mass murderers found striking similarities between the two groups (Meloy et al., 2004). Three-quarters of the entire sample were White (75%); the majority of both the adolescents (70%) and the adults (94%) were described as "loners"; almost half of the adolescent sample (48%) and almost two-thirds of the adult sample (63%) demonstrated a preoccupation with weapons and violence; and about 43% of both groups had a violent history.

The majority of mass homicide offenders do not attack strangers at random; in almost 80% of studied mass homicides, the assailant was related to or well acquainted with the victims, and in many cases, the attack was a carefully planned assault rather than an impulsive rampage. For every Seung-Hui Cho, who killed 32 people and wounded 25 others in a mass shooting at Virginia Tech in 2007, there are many more people like Bruce Pardo, who, dressed as Santa Claus, opened fire at a Christmas party at the home of his former in-laws and killed nine people before killing himself. Most mass murders are solved by law enforcement; the typical assailant is killed at the location of the crime, commits suicide, or surrenders to police. **Spree killers** are a special form of mass murderers: attackers who kill victims at two or more

Crime scene investigator testifies during a murder trial.

different locations with no "cooling-off" interval between the murders. The killing constitutes a single event, but it can either last only a short time or go on for a day or more.

Serial homicide offenders kill four or more victims, each on a separate occasion. Unlike mass murder offenders, serial murderers usually select a certain type of victim who plays a part in the killer's fantasies. There are cooling-off periods between serial murders, which are usually better planned than mass or spree killings. Some serial killers (such as Angel Maturino Resendiz, called the Railway Killer because the murders he was charged with took place by railroad tracks) travel frequently and murder in several locations. Dr. Michael Swango, trained as a physician, is suspected by the FBI of killing up to 60 individuals, typically by poisoning them, between 1981 and 1997. He moved around a great deal, and was suspected of killings in Illinois, New York, Ohio, and South Dakota—as well as Zimbabwe. Others (such as Gary Ridgway, the so-called Green River Killer, who confessed to killing 48 women, mostly prostitutes, and dumping their bodies along the Green River in Washington) are geographically stable and kill within the same area. Ted Kaczynski, the so-called Unabomber, who apparently remained in one place but chose victims who lived in different parts of the country to receive his carefully constructed mail bombs, reflected an unusual combination of serial killer characteristics.

When they are clever in the way they plan their killings, capable of presenting themselves as normal members of the community, kill for idiosyncratic reasons, and wait months between killings, serial murderers are hard to catch. It took 30 years for Wichita police to figure out that Dennis Rader, a Boy Scout leader and president of Christ Lutheran Church, was a brutal serial killer who used the moniker "BTK"—an acronym for "bind, torture, kill." He confessed to 10 counts of first-degree murder in 2005.

Social scientists have gained some knowledge about these criminals, who may number as many as 100 in the United States. One study compiled a list of characteristics from 157 serial offenders and found that most were White males in

Dennis Rader, the "BTK Killer"

their early 30s (Kraemer et al., 2004). More than half were employed at the time of the offense, and approximately one-third were married. The average offender had an 11th-grade education. Victims of these offenders were most often White females in their early to mid-30s who were strangers to their killers. More than half of the killings were sexually motivated. These characteristics differ from those of single-homicide offenders, who often know their victims and kill for emotional reasons such as anger or sexual jealousy (Kraemer et al., 2004).

In another study that compared multiple homicide offenders (MHOs, N = 160) with single homicide offenders (SHOs, N = 494), investigators (DeLisi & Scherer, 2006) reported that almost 30% of MHOs were habitual offenders before their final homicide. Some distinguishing features between these two groups were prior rape convictions, misdemeanor convictions, more extensive prison histories, and current involvement in rape and burglary—all were observed more often in the MHO group. This notwithstanding, nearly 40% of MHOs had never been arrested prior to their current justice involvement.

Serial killers tend to select vulnerable victims of some specific type who gratify their need to control people. Consistent with the motive of wanting to dominate people, they prefer to kill with "hands-on" methods such as strangulation and stabbing, rather than with guns, which are the preferred weapons of mass homicide offenders. Serial offenders are often preoccupied with sexualized or sadistic fantasies involving capture and control of their victims. Many serial killers use pornography and violent sexual fantasies intensively as "rehearsals" for and "replays" of their crimes, and they often keep souvenirs (sometimes in the form of body parts from victims) as trophies of their attacks. Despite the apparent "craziness" of their behavior—this adjective can mean "we don't understand why" offenders do this—serial killers are not typically seriously mentally ill. Many, however, have personality disorders and lack the ability to experience empathy and remorse. In fact, serial killers often revel in the publicity that their crimes receive. Fox and Levin (2005) have provided examples of different motivations for serial and mass murder (including power, revenge, loyalty, profit, and terror), along with brief vignettes illustrating these motivations (refer to Table 7.1).

Similar examples of possible motivations for homicide, as well as additional information (e.g., signature aspects of violent crime, staging and undoing at crime scenes, and recommendations for interrogation) are contained in the *Crime Classification Manual* (Douglas et al., 2006). As you might suspect, the classification with respect to offender motivation can be complex. For example, was the Virginia Tech shooter Seung-Hui Cho motivated by power? What about revenge? Some evidence suggests that both may have influenced him. This example vividly illustrates the point that many influences and motivations may come together in the rare and tragic context of multiple homicide.

Steps Involved in Criminal Profiling

Douglas et al. (1986) divided the FBI's profiling strategy into five stages, with a final, sixth stage being the arrest of the correct suspect. The six stages, as they evolve in a murder investigation, seem to apply reasonably even decades later. They are as follows:

1. *Profiling inputs.* The first stage involves collecting all information available about the crime, including physical evidence, photographs of the crime scene, autopsy reports and pictures, complete background information on the victim, and police reports. The profiler does not want to be told about possible suspects at this stage, because such data might prejudice or prematurely direct the profile.

2. *Decision process models.* In this stage the profiler organizes the input into meaningful questions and patterns along several dimensions of criminal activity. What type of homicide has been committed? What is the primary impetus for the crime—sexual, financial, personal, or emotional disturbance? What level of risk did the victim experience, and what level of risk did the murderer take in killing the victim? What was the sequence of acts before and after the killing, and how long did these acts take to commit? Where was the crime committed? Was the body moved, or was it found where the murder was committed?

3. *Crime assessment.* On the basis of the findings in the previous phase, the profiler attempts to reconstruct the behavior of the offender and the victim. Was the murder *organized* (suggesting an intelligent offender who carefully selects victims against whom to act out a well-rehearsed fantasy) or *disorganized* (indicating an impulsive, less socially competent, possibly even psychotic offender)? Was the crime staged to mislead the police? Can details such as cause of death, location of wounds, and position of the body reveal anything

Table 7.1 Generic examples of motivations for multiple murder

Motivations for Multiple Murder	Type of Multiple Murder	
	Serial Murder	Mass Murder
Power	Inspired by sadistic fantasies, a man tortures and kills a series of strangers to satisfy his need for control and dominance.	A pseudo-commando, dressed in battle fatigues and armed with a semiautomatic weapon, turns a shopping mall into a "war zone."
Revenge	Grossly mistreated as a child, a man avenges his past by slaying women who remind him of his mother.	After being fired from his job, a gunman returns to the work site and opens fire on his former boss and coworker.
Loyalty	A team of killers turns murder into a ritual for proving their dedication and commitment to one another.	A depressed husband/father kills his family and himself to spare them from a miserable existence and bring them a better life in the hereafter.
Profit	A woman poisons to death a series of husbands to collect on their life insurance policies.	A band of armed robbers executes the employees of a store to eliminate all witnesses to their crime.
Terror	A profoundly paranoid man commits a series of bombings to warn the world of impending doom.	A group of antigovernment extremists blows up a train to send a political message.

Source: From Fox & Levin, 2005, p. 20.

about the killer's motivation? Criminal profilers are often guided by the following hypotheses:

- Brutal facial injuries point to killers who knew their victims.
- Murders committed with whatever weapon happens to be available are more impulsive than murders committed with a gun and may reveal a killer who lives fairly near the victim.
- Murders committed early in the morning seldom involve alcohol or drugs.

4. *Criminal profile.* In this stage, profilers formulate an initial description of the most likely suspects. This profile includes the perpetrator's race, sex, age, marital status, living arrangements, and employment history; psychological characteristics, beliefs, and values; probable reactions to the police; and past criminal record, including the possibility of similar offenses in the past. This stage also contains a feedback loop whereby profilers check their predictions against stage-2 information to make sure that the profile fits the original data.

5. *Investigation.* A written report is given to investigators, who concentrate on suspects matching the profile. If new evidence is discovered in this investigation, a second feedback process is initiated, and the profile can be revised.

6. *Apprehension.* The intended result of these procedures—the arrest of a suspect—allows profilers to evaluate the validity of their predictions. The key element

in this validation is a thorough interview of the suspect to assess the influences of background and psychological variables.

The Validity of Criminal Profiling

What is the evidence for the validity of psychological profiling of offenders? Are profilers more accurate than other groups in their descriptions of suspects, or is this activity little more than a reading of forensic tea leaves? Do profilers use a different process in evaluating information than other investigators?

In a review of criminal profiling, Homant and Kennedy (1998) concluded that different kinds of crime scenes can be classified with reasonable reliability and that differences in these crimes do correlate with certain offender characteristics, such as offenders' prior relationships and interactions with victims (Salfati & Canter, 1999); organized versus disorganized approaches; and serial versus single offenders (e.g., Kraemer et al., 2004). At the same time, this research suggests several reasons for caution: (1) Inaccurate profiles are quite common, (2) many of the studies have been conducted using FBI data describing a fairly small number of offenders, and (3) the concepts and approaches actually used by profilers have often not been objectively and systematically defined. A majority of the psychologists and psychiatrists responding to one survey (Torres et al., 2006) did not view criminal profiling as scientifically reliable or valid—but nonetheless endorsed it as a potentially useful tool in criminal investigation.

One important early study (Pinizzotto & Finkel, 1990) investigated the effectiveness of criminal profiling as practiced by real-life experts. In this investigation, four different groups of participants evaluated two criminal cases—a homicide and a sex offense—that had already been solved but were completely unknown to the subjects. The first group consisted of four experienced criminal profilers who had a total of 42 years of profiling experience and six police detectives who had recently been trained by the FBI to be profilers. The second group consisted of six police detectives with 57 years of total experience in criminal investigations but with no profiling experience or training. The third group was composed of six clinical psychologists who had no profiling or criminal investigation experience. The final group consisted of six undergraduates drawn from psychology classes.

All participants were given, for each case, an array of materials that profilers typically use, including crime scene photographs, crime scene descriptions by uniformed officers, autopsy and toxicology reports (in the murder case), and descriptions of the victims. Three tests of profiling quality were used: All subjects prepared a profile of a suspect in each case, answered 15 questions about the identity (e.g., gender, age, employment) of the suspects, and were asked to rank order a written "lineup" of five suspects, from most to least likely to have committed each of the crimes.

The results indicated that, compared with the other three groups, the profiler group wrote longer profiles that contained more specific predictions about suspects, included more accurate predictions, and were rated as more helpful by other police detectives. Profilers were more accurate than the other groups in answering specific questions about the sex offense suspect, though the groups did not differ in their accuracy about the homicide suspect. Similar results were found with the "lineup" identification: Profilers were the most accurate for the sex offense, whereas there were no differences for the homicide case.

This study suggests that profilers can produce more useful and valid criminal profiles, even when compared to experienced crime investigators. This advantage may be limited, however, to certain kinds of cases or to the types of information made available to investigators.

Another study (Canter et al., 2004) tested the "organized/ disorganized" dichotomy by using specialized statistics to analyze aspects of serial killing derived from murders committed by 100 U.S. serial killers. There was no distinct subset of offense characteristics associated with organized versus disorganized killings. Researchers did find a subset of organized features (e.g., evidence of planning, bringing a weapon, use of a vehicle) that were characteristic of most serial killings, but disorganized features such as impulsivity, failure to use precautions that would limit evidence left at the scene, and related behaviors were far more unusual. The investigators suggested that these results cast doubt on whether killings can be reliably and validly classified using this dichotomy.

Based on the absence of empirical scientific data supporting the process of profiling, some (e.g., Note, 2008; Risinger & Loop, 2002) have argued that profiling lacks the requisite

scientific support to allow experts to testify to the findings in the course of litigation. On this point, one investigator (Kocsis, 2003) concluded that there is some support for the view that professional profilers can produce a more accurate description of an unknown offender than can other groups. This conclusion was strongly criticized by other investigators, however. One review criticized the methodology used by Kocsis, suggesting that greater scientific rigor would yield less support for profiling accuracy (Bennell et al., 2006, but refer to Kocsis, 2006, for a response). Subsequent meta-analysis (Snook et al., 2007) indicated that experienced profilers performed comparably to other groups in many respects and somewhat better in a few other domains. This led to the question of whether perceptions of the validity of profiling are based upon illusory belief, influenced by anecdotes and repeated messages that it does work (Snook et al., 2008).

Where does that leave us on the question of offender profiling validity? Some (Kocsis & Palermo, 2015) argue that because profilers are often "trait-based" (seeking to identify stable aspects of offenders' functioning), they are not as accurate as they could be if they also incorporated situational influences—but still conclude that there is scientific support for profiling validity. Others (e.g., Chifflet, 2015) describe profiling as supported by uncertain theories and limited data.

A noteworthy different approach to profiling—using statistically derived algorithms describing behavioral profiles of burglary offenders—showed that burglary arrest rates for agencies receiving the statistical profile were significantly higher than agencies that relied on human judgments alone (Fox & Farrington, 2015). This approach may offer an interesting and potentially valuable alternative to the use of human profilers.

Given the mixed reviews on the question of profiling validity, there does not appear to be an adequate scientific foundation for expert testimony in this area. Whether courts admit profiling evidence will probably continue to depend on the particular judge. But profiling that is used as an investigatory tool—an approach to "reverse engineering" a homicide yielding leads to be investigated but not conclusions—appears more promising. It is used in some form in different countries (Woodworth & Porter, 2000).

Becoming an FBI Profiler

Despite the mixed evidence about the scientific validity of profiling, it is used with some frequency and perceived as a helpful investigatory tool by many. One of the questions frequently asked by those considering a career in law enforcement is "How do I become an FBI profiler?" Of course, the FBI is not the only law enforcement agency that uses profiling— it may be used as well in other agencies at the federal, state, and community levels. But our discussion here considers the FBI as an example of an agency that has been prominently associated with this profiling, and has incorporated the contributions of psychology in a significant way.

The question about "becoming a profiler" may be answered in different ways. Consider the advice offered by Mary Ellen O'Toole, PhD, a retired FBI agent and criminal profiler, to those with interest in FBI profiling:

- Consult the website (www.fbi.gov) and review the current information on job requirements for becoming an FBI agent. FBI profilers are all agents. If you are interested, you can get further details from your local FBI office (applicant coordination).

- To become an agent, you would need, at minimum, a four-year college degree (any major). You would spend about 4 months in rigorous training at the FBI Academy if accepted; such training includes psychology, interviewing, and legal issues as well as physical fitness and firearms use.

- Following graduation from the Academy, you would be placed in a specific FBI field office, so you must be willing to relocate. You would work on a variety of investigations as part of this assignment.

- Field experience as an FBI agent is important before applying to the Behavioral Analysis Unit or other FBI unit that provides profiling services. Most FBI profilers have 7–15 years of investigative experience before being accepted into such a unit.

- Work as an FBI profiler includes analysis, interviewing, writing, public speaking, and assessing individual and group behavior. Coursework in psychology, sociology, philosophy, journalism, and public speaking might be particularly helpful (http://maryellenotoole.com/meo/becominganfbiprofiler/).

One particularly important aspect of this advice is the emphasis on criminal profiling as only one aspect of law enforcement, improved by competence and experience in other aspects of criminal investigation.

Detecting Deception

In the short-lived television crime drama *Lie to Me*, actor Brendan Hines assisted law enforcement by investigating criminals and trying to ascertain their truthfulness. The twist was that he felt a moral imperative to tell the truth himself, to "shoot out the truth" without censoring himself. Unfortunately, such "radical honesty" is far more likely to appear on television than in reality.

People tell lies fairly often—on average, between once and twice a day, according to self-report studies (Hartwig, 2011). They do so for a variety of reasons: so that others will perceive them favorably, to avoid tension and conflict in social situations, and to minimize hurt feelings (Vrij et al., 2010). People also lie to conceal their wrongdoings, and successfully detecting these individuals can have profound societal benefits. Consider the work of a customs official who intercepts a cache of weapons, a detective who doubts the veracity of

someone suspected of child molestation, or an airport security officer who suspects that a passenger about to board a plane harbors ill intent. Consider the fact that each of the 19 terrorists who launched the September 11 attacks lied to authorities on at least three occasions, and that none of their lies was ever detected (Honts & Kircher, 2011).

Throughout history, many societies have assumed that criminals can be detected by the physical manifestations of their denials. Ever since King Solomon tried to discover which of two women who claimed to be the mother of an infant was lying by watching their emotions when he threatened to cut the baby in half and divide it between them, people have believed that the body will reveal when the mind is lying. People judge others' truthfulness by observing their behavior, often without conscious awareness of doing so. In late-night conversations, parents gauge the veracity of their teenagers' stories about where they had been and with whom. During job interviews, employers make quick judgments of the candor and honesty of prospective employees.

Detecting Deception via Observation

Police officers and other law enforcement officials know that deception is common, and their ability to detect lying has profound implications for the people who pass through the criminal justice system. Being deemed "truthful" can absolve guilty people of suspicion, allowing them to remain on the streets to commit more crimes. Being deemed "deceptive" can launch someone—perhaps an innocent person—into a criminal prosecution and toward eventual conviction and imprisonment. How well law enforcement officials can assess deception during investigative interviews is vitally important to the fair and effective operation of the justice system. Fortunately, psychologists have provided tools to help them. In this section, we describe what psychologists have learned about people's ability to detect deception unaided, using only their eyes and ears and relying only on verbal and behavioral cues. This technique—simple observation—is actually the most common form of deception detection (Vrij et al., 2010).

It is difficult to be certain when people are fibbing and when they are telling the truth (at least as they believe it). It is also difficult to assess how people distinguish honesty from dishonesty in others. For this reason, psychological scientists have developed research protocols that mimic real-world lying and truth-telling.

In these studies, researchers instruct some participants to lie and others to tell the truth about a particular experience or intention—a film they saw or intend to see, the contents of their pockets, or what they plan to do that evening. Some studies have involved more forensically relevant situations such as asking participants to provide a true or false statement about their whereabouts during a certain timeframe on a particular day (e.g., Evans et al., 2017). These stories—lies and truths alike—are videotaped and shown to observers who then judge the truthfulness of those statements. Scientists measure the ability to detect deception—that is, to realize that a truthful person is telling the truth and that a liar is lying—as the percentage of correct judgments. In a simple two-alternative forced choice, the chance level of an accurate decision is 50%.

How accurately can people detect deception? In a meta-analysis that evaluated the decisions of nearly 25,000 observers in hundreds of studies, Bond and DePaulo (2006) determined that people are correct only 54% of the time, hardly better than chance. The analysis revealed several other interesting clues to how people judge deception. For example, it uncovered a **truth bias**, meaning that people were biased toward judging statements as being truthful. People tend to take most assertions at face value, assuming that they are true unless their authenticity is called into question for some reason. (Think about asking someone what time it is.) As a result, subjects in the meta-analysis correctly classified 61% of truthful statements as nondeceptive but only 47% of lies as deceptive.

Many of the people involved in these deception studies were college students who had no expertise or specialized training (and perhaps little desire) to do the tasks well. In addition, there were few consequences for failing to convince observers of their honesty. Are people more accurate at detecting lies under more realistic circumstances, for example, in conditions that involve high emotions and strong motivations to be believed? This question was addressed in a meta-analysis of 144 samples involving more than 9,000 individuals telling lies or truth, some of whom provided statements during criminal investigations or legal proceedings (Hartwig & Bond, 2014). The meta-analysis revealed that deception was equally detectable regardless of circumstances, meaning that the heightened motivations and emotions elicited in more realistic settings did little to help observers distinguish lies from truthful statements. It also revealed an accuracy rate for detecting lies of 67%, an improvement over the 54% noted in the Bond and DePaulo (2006) meta-analysis. Researchers attributed improved accuracy to the fact that studies done after 2006 incorporated multiple behavioral cues to deception, rather than single cues. Even so, an accuracy rate of 67% means that one of every three judgments was incorrect.

Might people who have more experience judging deception be better at it? When playwright Tennessee Williams wrote that "mendacity is the system we live in," he may have been referring to people whose occupations expose them to multiple lies on a daily basis: police officers, judges, customs officials, border patrol officers, and the like. A classic study supports the idea that it helps to have experience with people who both lie and tell the truth. Ekman and O'Sullivan (1991) found that U.S. Secret Service agents (who frequently interview individuals who may present a threat to the president or vice-president and their families) were the only participants—among others from the CIA, FBI, National Security Agency, Drug Enforcement Agency, and California police and judges—who could detect deception at greater than chance levels. But a study by Bond and DePaulo (2008) found only very small individual differences in detecting deception.

These studies raise the question whether people can be trained to become better lie catchers. To some extent, yes, although trained observers are only *somewhat* better than untrained observers at distinguishing between truths and lies (Hauch et al., 2016). And while training generally improves people's ability to tell that someone is lying, it has less effect on the ability to tell that someone is truthful. Still, training may be useful to police and parole officers who tend to be biased toward judging statements as lies, even when they are true, a phenomenon known as **lie bias** or investigator bias (Meissner & Kassin, 2002).

Yet another factor that complicates judgments about deception is that people often lack precise memories about where and with whom they were, and what, exactly, they were doing at some point in the past. So when asked if they have a credible alibi, their responses may be at odds with documented events. A clever study used a smartphone app to record people's locations via GPS over the course of a month and tested participants' memories of those situations (Laliberete et al., 2021). Results showed that people confused days of the week and hours of the day and that their memories blended with details from similar experiences, suggesting that suspects may be perceived as liars even when they attempt to tell the truth.

Others Methods of Detecting Deception

Arousal-based methods of detecting deception. Over the years, people suspected of wrongdoing have faced various tests of their veracity. The ancient Hindus forced suspects to chew rice and spit it out on a leaf from a sacred tree. If the rice was dry, the suspect was deemed guilty. Arabian Bedouins required conflicting witnesses to lick a hot iron; the one whose tongue was burned was thought to be lying (Kleinmuntz & Szucko, 1984). These procedures reflect activity of the sympathetic nervous system (under emotional stress, salivation usually decreases) and thus are crude measures of emotion.

In modern times, police investigators have developed interview protocols to help them garner insights into a person's truthfulness. These tools, which analyze both verbal and nonverbal behavior, are based on the premise that liars will be more nervous than truth-tellers and exhibit more nervous behaviors. One of the early methods to detect nonverbal behavior was the Behavior Analysis Interview (BAI; Inbau et al., 2013), an accusatory style of questioning still in use today (Vrij, 2019). The BAI consists of a set of predetermined questions—both nonthreatening and behavior-provoking—designed to assess whether a suspect is likely to be guilty. Among other things, suspects are asked whether they committed the crime themselves and whether they know who committed the crime. Police investigators assume that guilty suspects are more likely than innocent people to display nervous behaviors such as crossing their legs, shifting their position, avoiding eye contact, and performing grooming behaviors. These suspects are then subjected to the Reid method of interrogation, which we describe later in the chapter.

Studies of the effectiveness of the BAI and similar, accusatory techniques to detect deceit yield rather disappointing results, however. When compared with a nonaccusatory, information-gathering interview method, which we also describe later in the chapter, they result in less information and fewer useful cues to deception (Brimbal et al., 2021; Meissner et al., 2014).

For many years, a standard way to assess truthfulness was to measure signs of physiological arousal in combination with a specific questioning strategy. The **polygraph** (sometimes referred to as the *lie detector*) is a computer-based machine that measures blood pressure, electrodermal activity, and respiratory changes during questioning. Its use is also based on the premise that liars will exhibit a particular constellation of emotional responses that distinguish them from truth-tellers.

The **Control Question Test** (CQT, sometimes referred to as the *Comparison Question Test*) has become the most popular approach to polygraphic examinations (Meijer & Verschuere, 2010). The polygrapher focuses on responses to two kinds of questions. *Relevant questions* inquire about the crime under investigation (e.g., "Did you steal the law school's video monitor?"). *Comparison questions* are not directly concerned with the crime but are designed to induce an emotional reaction because they cover common misdeeds that nearly all of us have committed (e.g., "Prior to the age of 21, did you ever do anything that was dishonest or illegal?"). Most polygraphers consider a denial to be a "known lie." But subjects *will* deny, thereby providing a characteristic physiological response to a lie. Polygraphers expect that guilty subjects will be more aroused by the relevant questions (to which they must respond with a lie in order to maintain their innocence) whereas innocent subjects will be more aroused by the comparison questions (because they will worry that admitting to a past misdeed might make them look more like a criminal). Therefore, this procedure works best when innocent subjects lie or show greater emotional arousal in response to the comparison questions, and guilty subjects lie and become more emotionally aroused in response to the relevant questions.

The level of accuracy has been of great concern in debates about the validity of the polygraph. Examiners are accurate when they expose liars and believe truthful suspects. They err when they believe that an individual who lies is truthful (a *false negative*) or that a truthful subject is lying (a *false positive*). How accurate are judgments based on CQT results? In 2003, a panel of scientists reviewed studies on the CQT and concluded that it could discriminate lying from truth-telling at rates above chance, but far below perfection (National Research Council, 2003). This conclusion holds true even when newer studies are considered (Iacono & Ben-Shakhar, 2019), although a 2021 meta-analysis based on 42 field studies was somewhat more optimistic (Honts et al., 2021). It concluded that the CQT, though an imperfect tool, is accurate enough to provide useful information to decision makers and to move them well beyond the 54% accuracy level reported in 2006 by Bond and DePaulo.

An alternative to the CQT is the **Concealed Information Test** (CIT). Both the procedure and the purposes of this method are fundamentally different from the control question approach. The goal is to detect the presence of concealed information in the suspect's mind, not to detect lying. The procedure relies on the accumulation of facts that are known only by the police, the criminal, and any surviving victims. The polygrapher creates a series of multiple-choice questions and presents them to the suspect. For example, the polygrapher may ask, "In what room was the victim's body found? What strange garment was the victim wearing? What was the victim clutching in his hand?" Each alternative would appear equally plausible to an innocent person. But the true criminal will, in theory, be revealed by heightened physiological reactions that accompany recognition of concealed information.

The CIT has several limitations. It can be used only when the details of the crime have been kept from the public. Even then, it is conceivable that the suspect is not the perpetrator but, rather, was told about the crime by the true criminal and therefore possesses concealed knowledge. It is possible that some guilty subjects are so distraught or pay so little attention to the details of their crimes that they actually lack the required information on which this method relies. Finally, guilty suspects can use **countermeasures** to avoid detection—a feature the CIT shares with the CQT. Because of the variable and questionable reliability of polygraph tests, their results are generally not admissible as evidence in court, although they are used in the investigatory stage of a case.

Arousal-based theories of deception detection all stem from the idea that because deceivers fear being caught in a lie, they will exhibit predictable behaviors that signal their stress and possibly, their guilt. Without much evidence, people have come to associate deception with lack of eye contact, fidgety movements, and certain grooming behaviors (e.g., Strömwall & Granhag, 2003). But in fact, those who lie and those who tell the truth use many of the same nonverbal strategies to attempt to appear honest: looking interviewers directly in the eye and suppressing fidgety behaviors (Hartwig et al., 2010). Observers also tend to interpret suspects' anger as a sign of their guilt. But people tend to be angrier when they are *falsely* accused than *accurately* accused (DeCelles et al., 2021), so paradoxically, anger may be a better indicator of innocence than of guilt. More generally, both laypeople and professionals in important decision-making roles err in their judgments of truth and deception.

Finally, it is important to acknowledge the influence of cultural norms on verbal and nonverbal behaviors. Whereas it is expected for European Americans to look into the eyes of their conversational partners, Japanese consider direct eye contact to be rude, and African Americans avert their gaze more often than European Americans (Johnson, 2006). Chinese speakers tend to use higher pitched voices when lying than when telling the truth; just the opposite is true among Hispanics (Matsumoto & Hwang, 2015). But most importantly, people who are telling the truth can experience the same emotions as liars, particularly when they are worried that they won't be believed. As Aldert Vrij, a psychologist at the University of Portsmouth, reminds us, there is nothing as obvious as Pinocchio's growing nose to alert us to a lie.

Cognitive methods of detecting deception. Given the difficulty of using behavioral cues to detect deception, a new paradigm for detecting deception has emerged in recent years. Cognitive methods of deception detection are based on the assumptions that lying is more mentally taxing than telling the truth, and that truth-tellers and liars use different strategies in responding to questions. These premises have led to the development of new questioning methods to detect deceit.

There are many reasons that lying is mentally taxing. Liars must first formulate their fabrications and then remember what they said earlier and to whom. They need to avoid providing any new information to interviewers. Because they know they are being deceitful, they may have to pay more careful attention to their own demeanor and to reactions from the interviewer to determine if they are getting away with their lies. Finally, they have to suppress the truth. All of these activities require mental effort which, when compounded by the need to answer interviewers' questions, can confound and confuse deceitful subjects. One group of researchers summed it up simply: "lying takes time" (Suchotzki et al., 2017).

Exploiting this reality, researchers have developed interview protocols that elicit and increase **cognitive load** more in liars, who are already preoccupied, than in truth-tellers. Among the techniques that effectively increase cognitive load is asking subjects to recall a series of events in reverse chronological order, and requiring them to perform a secondary task during the interview, such as determining whether a figure that reappears on a computer screen is similar to a target figure shown earlier. These interventions cause liars to show more **diagnostic cues** to deception. In other words, by making subjects think harder in an interview, investigators are better able to distinguish lying from truth-telling (Vrij et al., 2008).

Another cognitive approach to detecting deception exploits the fact the liars prepare themselves for anticipated questions by rehearsing—indeed, *over*-rehearsing—their responses. But rehearsal works only when liars correctly anticipate the questions they will be asked. Although they may anticipate certain predictable questions (e.g., "What did you do in the restaurant?"), they typically do not anticipate spatial questions (e.g., "In relation to the front door and where you sat in the restaurant, where were the closest diners?"), temporal questions (e.g., "Who finished their food first, you or your friend?"), or requests to draw the scene. In one study, when observers viewed responses to anticipated questions, they could not distinguish truth-tellers from liars above chance level. But when they viewed responses to unanticipated questions, they correctly classified 80% of the truth-tellers and liars (Vrij et al., 2009). These findings suggest that asking unanticipated questions can be a surprisingly effective way to detect lying.

Yet another cognitive method for detecting deceit relies on the premise that those who lie and those who tell the truth use different verbal strategies in investigative interviews. Those who lie tend to keep it simple and truth-tellers are apt to "tell it all," particularly when asked to include details that can be verified (Verschuere et al., 2021). Whereas truth-tellers are generally forthcoming, those who lie tend to avoid certain topics and deny certain behaviors. This distinction allows investigators to be strategic about revealing evidence they possess about the suspect's actions. For example, withholding evidence until late in the interview leaves room for deceitful suspects to blatantly lie, denying any involvement in the crime. But when the interviewer eventually reveals incontrovertible evidence—a surveillance video, for example—suspects must scramble to explain away the lie, often by telling another lie. This strategic use of evidence also increases investigators' abilities to distinguish lying from truth-telling (Oleszkiewicz & Watson, 2021).

How well do these cognitive methods of deception detection stack up against standard methods of questioning? According to one meta-analysis, cognitive lie detection approaches are effective, increasing accuracy rates from 56% using standard questioning procedures to 71% (Vrij et al., 2015). Should we be concerned that even these newer techniques yield correct classifications just 71% of the time? Absolutely; before lie detection procedures can be applied with confidence by police, border control agents, or others who assess people's truthfulness, they should be more accurate even than this. Might other methods work better?

Brain-based lie detection. Rather than relying on measures of physiological arousal as the polygraph does, or verbal responses as cognitive approaches do, recent developments in deception detection monitor changes in the brain's activity in response to stimuli. Two of the prominent brain-based methods of lie detection are neuroimaging and brain-wave analysis.

Neuroimaging in Deception Detection. Neuroimaging techniques such as **functional magnetic resonance imaging** (fMRI) use scanners fitted with powerful electromagnets to measure blood flow and oxygen utilization in selected parts of the brain. Increases in oxygen consumption and blood flow in a particular part of the brain indicate that that region of the brain is involved when a subject undertakes a certain task. The primary function of fMRI is to diagnose neurological disorders. But because it is highly sensitive to cognitive processes involved in memory (Binder et al., 2009) and motivation (Hare et al., 2008), it holds promise as a way to monitor deception.

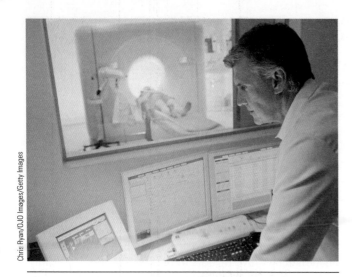

fMRI monitors changes in brain activity to detect deception.

Early studies using fMRI to detect deception typically asked simple questions about one's past experiences or knowledge (e.g., "Who was your best friend in primary school?" "Does a bicycle have six wheels?"). Participants pressed buttons to answer "yes" or "no." Some were told to conceal information by lying in response to specific questions, whereas others were told to respond truthfully. Scientists then compared brain activity in response to truthful answers and lies.

At this point, you may wonder whether lying about the name of a best friend is comparable, in any way, to lying about criminal activity. In doing so, you are asking whether these studies have **external validity**. Many neuroscientists—particularly those who are skeptical that neuroimaging can identify deception—have wondered the same thing.

So scientists have now begun to use more realistic methods to simulate the processes of truth-telling and lying. For example, one team of researchers asked some research participants to fire a starter pistol with blank bullets in the testing room of a neuroimaging center. Prior to fMRI questioning, half of each group was instructed to tell the truth and the other half was instructed to lie when asked, "Did you shoot that gun?" (Mohamed et al., 2006). Results showed that different patterns of brain activation were associated with truth-telling and lying. Several brain regions in the frontal, parietal, and anterior cingulate cortex responded more strongly during lies, a result that is consistent across studies (Farah et al., 2014). These brain areas are associated with planning and other high-level executive functions, underscoring the fact that telling lies requires more cognitive effort than telling the truth because liars must keep two versions of the story in working memory.

Although fMRI holds some promise as a method of detecting deception, a number of issues have not yet been resolved. It is not clear whether fMRI technology can handle situations in which a subject's response cannot be neatly categorized as the truth or a lie. This occurs when a response

is partly true and partly false, and when people consider the possibility of lying but ultimately decide to tell the truth (Appelbaum, 2007). Also, questions remain about the use of fMRI for detecting deception in those with medical and psychiatric conditions, youth, and the elderly. Consider also that a relatively high proportion of criminals meet the diagnostic criteria for psychopathy, which is associated with frequent deception and atypical fMRI responses (Anderson & Kiehl, 2012). Finally, there is only limited evidence of the accuracy of fMRI in lie detection, and it is not particularly encouraging: accuracy levels range from 76% to 90% but drop precipitously when countermeasures are employed (Langleben & Moriarty, 2013). Despite these lingering concerns, fMRI techniques are being marketed commercially and occasionally used in court. Joel Huizenga, who founded a company called No Lie MRI, asserts confidently, "Once you jump behind the skull, there's no hiding." Not all neuroscientists agree, but fMRI test results were used in the case we describe in Box 7.1.

Brain-Wave Analysis in Deception Detection. Imagine that a suspect denies being at the scene of a crime. Further imagine that they are confronted with pictures or verbal descriptions of the scene. Relatively new technology that measures brain-wave patterns that occur in response to familiar and unfamiliar images may eventually help investigators determine whether people are being deceptive when they claim, "I wasn't there." This technique, termed **brain fingerprinting**, was the "brainchild" of Lawrence Farwell. It uses an electroencephalogram (EEG) to record electrical activity on the surface of the scalp, reflecting spontaneous activity from the underlying cerebral cortex.

The premise of brain fingerprinting is that the brain houses information about experienced events and emits electrical signals in response to stimuli. A unique brain-wave pattern—the P300 wave—is elicited by a stimulus that is meaningful to the subject. It derives its name from its positive polarity and its occurrence approximately 300–900 milliseconds after the onset of a stimulus. Brain fingerprinting evaluates neural activity to assess how a suspect responds to crime scene details known only to the perpetrator. For example, after showing a suspect a series of common images while measuring P300 waves, investigators might show critical images of the crime scene and compare activation patterns. A guilty person, but not an innocent subject, would react differently to the critical details because they are meaningful. (You can probably recognize that this protocol borrows heavily from the Concealed Information Test used with the polygraph.)

Researchers estimate the accuracy of brain fingerprinting by asking some participants to lie and others to tell the truth about a witnessed mock crime or autobiographical event when answering questions. They measure detection rates based on the resulting patterns of brain waves. Estimates range from 85% to 95% accuracy in distinguishing liars from truth-tellers under optimized laboratory conditions (Rosenfeld et al., 2004). Meta-analysis showed that the P300 component of the brain wave measured in conjunction

Box 7.1

The Case of Contested Poisoning: Munchausen's Syndrome by Proxy or Not? Can fMRI Tell the Difference?

Munchausen syndrome by proxy is a mental health disorder in which parents, guardians, or other caregivers deliberately inflict pain and injury on vulnerable children in order to attract attention to themselves. Perpetrators are overwhelmingly female, and often are mothers of the victims. The disease is difficult to diagnose because many of the child's symptoms could result from organic causes or undiagnosed illnesses. The question posed by a case in England was whether a child's poisoning had been carried out by the victim's mother. She was convicted of the charge and served four years in prison.

In a groundbreaking experiment, Professor Sean Spence, a pioneer of fMRI technology to detect deception, examined the woman's brain activity as she alternately repeated her protestations of innocence and her accusers' account of the poisoning (Spence et al., 2008). The tests, repeated four times, showed that her prefrontal and anterior cingulate cortices were activated when she endorsed statements that she believed to be false, namely her accusers' versions of the event. In short, the data suggested that she lied when she agreed with her accusers' statements. According to Professor Spence, "[A]t the present moment, this research doesn't prove that this woman is innocent. Instead, what it clearly demonstrates is that her brain responds as if she were innocent … If proved to be accurate, and these findings replicated, this technology could be used alongside other factors to address questions of guilt versus innocence."

Critical Thought Question

A question arises whenever new technology is introduced into legal proceedings: At what point is the technology sophisticated enough to merit its use in investigations and trials? In your opinion, should the answer be different depending on whether the new technology is used for investigative purposes (e.g., to assess suspects' truthfulness), or offered as evidence during a trial (e.g., to show that a witness had lied)?

with the Concealed Information Test reliably detects concealed information under laboratory conditions, though the technique is less accurate with realistic mock crime scenarios (Meijer et al., 2014). The technique's originator, Lawrence Farwell, has patented, developed, and promoted a commercial version of the tool that he claims is 100% accurate (Farwell, 2012). But this is hardly "settled science" and others, citing lack of methodological rigor in Falwell's work, dispute his claims (e.g., Meijer et al., 2013).

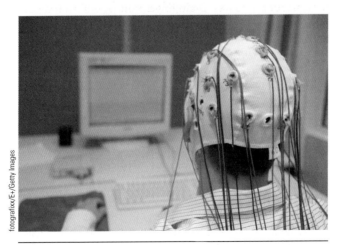

Brain fingerprinting, one method of detecting deception, uses electroencephalogram (EEG)—like the one shown here—to record electrical activity on the surface of the scalp, reflecting spontaneous activity from the underlying cerebral cortex.

Brain-Based Lie Detection in Court. Brain-based technologies could be used in various ways in legal contexts. Defendants and witnesses could try to introduce the results of these tests to bolster their credibility. In one U.S. case, defendant Terry Harrington's murder conviction was reversed after Lawrence Farwell used brain fingerprinting to conclude that the record of the crime stored in Harrington's brain did not match the crime scene, but did match the alibi. When confronted with this information, a key prosecution witness recanted his testimony and admitted that he accused Harrington to avoid being prosecuted (*Harrington v. Iowa*, 2003).

Many people would agree that defendants and witnesses should be able to offer neuroscience evidence to support their version of the facts, so long as that evidence is based on valid and reliable scientific testing procedures. But many observers believe that the processes underlying these methods of deception detection are not sufficiently developed and understood to be routinely used in courts of law (e.g., Meijer et al., 2016). And when one ponders another use of this type of evidence—demanding that defendants and witnesses be screened for deception—even more people will balk.

A host of legal issues arise when brain-based techniques are conducted against the wishes of the subject being scanned. What happens if people refuse to undergo an fMRI or brain-wave test? Can their credibility be questioned? Some have pondered whether these practices constitute a "search" of the brain that should be governed by the Fourth Amendment's prohibition against unreasonable search and seizure (Farah et al., 2014). A related question is whether brain-based tests conducted without the consent of the subject violate the protection against self-incrimination guaranteed by the Fifth Amendment. Alternatively, perhaps brain fingerprinting is just another form of physical evidence, similar to DNA or fingerprint evidence.

Although probing a person's brain to detect a lie may seem highly intrusive, the government's interests in crime control and public protection may offset these concerns. How far the law can extend into the realm of exposing (and protecting) private thoughts is unclear. Many commentators urge judges to resist the temptation to admit this evidence until more conclusive data are available (Aronson, 2010) and a team of legal scholars has proposed legislation that would prohibit the use of brain-based lie detection techniques until regulatory systems can be put in place to evaluate and monitor their safety and effectiveness (Greely & Illes, 2007). Perhaps the only certainty is that the controversy over brain-based lie detection systems will continue for some time.

Novel technologies to detect deception. New frontiers in deception detection are now emerging, even as controversy swirls around brain-based techniques. Researchers are now using **artificial intelligence** (AI) to attempt to recognize deception. This technology functions by scouring reams of data to spot complex patterns of behaviors that could, in theory, signal lying better than an elevated pulse, blood pressure, or a suspect's own words.

Silent Talker was one of the first such technologies developed (Bittle, 2020). Its software analyzes video, monitoring approximately 40 physical "channels" on a person's body such as facial expressions, eyeblinks, the angle of one's head, and postural changes many times per second. It then evaluates these complex patterns in light of previously learned data—a feature typical of machine-learning systems—from liars and truth-tellers.

Can artificial intelligence move us closer to the truth in detecting deception? Despite promises from developers of Silent Talker that it would make the polygraph obsolete, studies show that it has never achieved more than 80% accuracy in guessing whether someone was lying or telling the truth, and that other AI software generates a high number of false positives (Bittle, 2020). So observers suspect that, like the polygraph, results of AI lie detection would likely be barred from courtrooms. Still, entrepreneurs have started private companies to market AI-based technologies to use at border crossings and in police departments, and to screen job and loan applicants.

Interrogating Suspects

When investigators have a hunch that a person is acting deceptively—due to a "failed" polygraph, neuroscientific test results, artificial intelligence, or simply through observation and interview—they may target that person for more formal interrogation, with the hope of extracting a confession. Throughout history, confessions have been accorded enormous importance. Many religions maintain that confession is the first step toward redemption and have evolved special rituals to encourage it. Interrogations and confessions also play a role in military and intelligence matters. People detained as terrorist threats in military jails in Afghanistan, Iraq, Guantanamo Bay, and elsewhere have been interrogated by harsh methods. These include both physical and psychological torture practices deemed illegal and condemned by the American Psychological Association. But tactics used in military and intelligence-gathering interrogations have been applied in criminal interrogations as well (Evans et al., 2010).

Confessions play a prominent role in the criminal justice system; many consider them to be the most powerful weapon at the state's disposal (Kassin & Gudjonsson, 2004). When the police capture suspects, one of their first acts is to interrogate and in the process, encourage them to confess. A confession will, of course, permit a district attorney or grand jury to bring charges. Even if the suspect later denies the confession and pleads not guilty, the confession can be introduced into evidence at the trial.

Although disputed "confessions" by defendants occur surprisingly often and observers have documented many false confessions (refer to, e.g., Center for Wrongful Convictions), the number of false confessions is actually a matter of contention. Prosecutors observe that defendants can easily recant confessions by alleging that police coerced them, but defense attorneys say that false confessions happen more often than prosecutors acknowledge.

Historical Background and Current Legal Standing

Until the mid-twentieth century, many "confessions" came only after intense questioning by the police—questioning that involved promises, threats, harassment, and even brutality. Until 1966, the traditional test for admissibility of a confession in court was voluntariness. A voluntary confession is given without overt inducements, threats, promises, or physical harm. The trustworthiness of a confession was believed to be lost when it was obtained through one or more of those means (*Hopt v. Utah*, 1884).

But assessing the voluntariness of confessions proved difficult for many reasons. The task was highly subjective, and it resulted in countless "swearing contests" between police and suspects about what went on behind the closed door of interrogation rooms. Therefore, in *Miranda v. Arizona* (1966), the Supreme Court held that a confession resulting from in-custody interrogation was admissible in court only if, in addition to being voluntary, it was obtained after the police had given the so-called *Miranda* warnings, intended to ensure the suspect's protection from self-incrimination (described in Box 7.2). One year later, the Supreme Court extended those rights to juveniles (*In re Gault*, 1967). The

Box 7.2

The Case of Ernesto Miranda and the Right to Remain Silent: Changing Forever the Nature of Police Work

One of the best-known U.S. Supreme Court cases decided during the last century, *Miranda v. Arizona* (1966), dealt with the problem of coerced confessions. Late on a Saturday in May of 1963, an 18-year-old woman left her job in downtown Phoenix. As she was walking home, a man grabbed her and dragged her to his car, tied her hands and laid her down in the back seat, then drove to the desert and raped her. As he waited for her to get dressed, he demanded money. She gave him the four $1 bills in her purse.

A week after the rape, the victim's brother-in-law spotted a car like the one she had described. He remembered enough of the license plate for the police to trace the car to Ernesto Miranda. When police located the car, they saw a rope strung along the front seat, just as the victim had described. They put together a lineup, selecting three Mexican Americans to stand with Miranda. But he was the only person with eyeglasses and tattoos—features the victim remembered about her assailant. Still, she couldn't identify anyone.

Frustrated, the police then took Miranda to an interrogation room for what they thought was routine questioning. But the exchanges that occurred in that tiny chamber changed forever the way police interact with citizens. Miranda asked about the lineup: "How did I do?" "You flunked," a police officer replied, and began to question Miranda. No attorneys, witnesses, or tape recorders were present. The police later reported that Miranda voluntarily confessed. Miranda described the interrogation differently:

> Once they get you in a little room and they start badgering you one way or the other, "You better tell us … or we're going to throw the book at you.… And I haven't had any sleep since the day before. I'm tired. I just got off my work, and they have me and they are interrogating me. They mention first one crime, then another one; they are certain I am the person.… Knowing

Ernesto Miranda

what a penitentiary is like, a person has to be frightened, scared. And not knowing if he'll be able to get back up and go home. (Quoted in Baker, 1983, p. 13)

Whichever story one believes, Ernesto Miranda emerged from the questioning a confessed rapist. In June of 1963, he was convicted of rape and kidnapping, and was sentenced to 20 to 30 years for each charge. He appealed his conviction to the U.S. Supreme Court, and the Court—by a 5–4 vote—concluded that his right against self-incrimination had been violated. Henceforth, they stated, the police must warn suspects of certain rights before starting a custodial interrogation. If these procedures are not followed, any damaging admissions made by suspects cannot be used by the prosecution in a trial.

Ironically, on the night of January 31, 1976, Miranda was playing poker in a flophouse section of Phoenix. A drunken fight broke out and Miranda was stabbed. He was dead on arrival at the hospital. Miranda's killer fled, but his accomplice was caught. Before taking him to police headquarters, a police officer read to him from a card:

> You have the right to remain silent. Anything you say can be used against you in a court of law. You have the right to the presence of an attorney to assist you prior to questioning and to be with you during questioning, if you so desire. If you cannot afford an attorney, you have the right to have an attorney appointed for you prior to questioning. Do you understand these rights? Will you voluntarily answer my questions?

Critical Thought Questions

What problems are the *Miranda* warnings intended to solve? What aspects of Miranda's case might have led Supreme Court justices to decide that his confession was not given freely?

Miranda warnings are intended to protect suspects from conditions that might give rise to unfounded confessions.

The *Miranda* case did not solve all problems associated with the validity of confessions. Although the warnings add a new element to interrogations, intense and secretive interrogations continue to this day, with the interrogator intent upon persuading the suspect to confess. Furthermore, most suspects waive their *Miranda* rights, and after a suspect voluntarily enters the interrogation room, investigators can use any number of tactics to obtain a confession.

Why do suspects waive their rights? A primary reason is because they do not understand them. Psychologists have documented problematic vocabulary and terminology of some *Miranda* warnings (Rogers et al., 2011), widely held misperceptions about the warnings (Rogers et al., 2020), and juveniles' difficulties understanding them (Rogers et al., 2016). The stress that comes from being accused of wrongdoing undermines comprehension of *Miranda* warnings, even in well-adjusted, intelligent adults (Scherr & Madon, 2012). As we will show, some young and mentally impaired suspects waive their rights because they are vulnerable to the tactics of a skillful interrogator (Zelle et al., 2015).

Whittling Away at *Miranda*

Miranda v. Arizona (1966) was one of the most controversial decisions of the past century. The chief justice at the time, Earl Warren, was castigated in congressional committees and on the floor of Congress (Warren, 1977), and "Impeach Earl Warren" billboards were widely seen. Although the decision has survived for nearly 60 years, it remains controversial to this day. It survived a major challenge in 2000 when the Supreme Court reaffirmed that *Miranda* was a constitutional ruling and that the warnings are part of the national culture (*Dickerson v. United States*, 2000). The *Dickerson* case is a good example of *stare decisis*—the court's preference for maintaining stability in the law through "abiding by settled principle" whenever possible. Given *Miranda's* long-standing acceptance in the United States, the Court opted against changing the law of confessions.

The U.S. Supreme Court has weakened the *Miranda* requirements through a series of other decisions, however. Here are some of the changes:

1. *Confessions that violate* Miranda *may still be used at a trial.* Suppose a person confesses when arrested, and the confession is taken in violation of the *Miranda* warnings. If the defendant claims to be innocent at trial, the prosecutor may use the confession to show that the defendant should not be believed (*Harris v. New York*, 1971).

2. Miranda *does not apply unless the suspect is in the custody of the police.* The Supreme Court has interpreted *custody* in various ways. For example, the Court held that roadside questioning of a motorist stopped for drunk driving is not "custody," even though the motorist is not free to go (*Berkemer v. McCarty*, 1984). Warnings are not required in this circumstance. "Stop-and-frisk" questioning is also usually viewed as noncustodial because such questioning merely accompanies temporary detentions in public places.

3. Miranda *does not apply unless the defendant is being interrogated.* A volunteered confession is always admissible. Suppose the police arrest a robbery suspect and decide, for whatever reason, not to question him. On the way to the station, the accused person volunteers that he wouldn't have been caught if he'd kept his mask on. This confession is admissible because it was not in response to police questioning (*Rhode Island v. Innis*, 1980).

The Validity of Confession Evidence

In a perfect world, guilty people would always confess, and innocent people would never do so. Unfortunately, this is far from reality. Scientists know that two kinds of erroneous outcomes are possible: **false denials** (when guilty suspects proclaim their innocence and deny involvement in actual crimes) and **false confessions** (when innocent suspects confess to alleged crimes). False denials occur when crime perpetrators lie by saying "I didn't do it," and false confessions occur when innocent suspects say "I did it" and provide factually untrue descriptions of how and why the crime occurred.

Relatively few studies have looked at how guilty suspects tend to lie to authorities, although one study involved questioning prison inmates about the strategies they used to tell lies during interrogations (Stromwall & Willen, 2011). It documented both verbal and nonverbal techniques of deception, including providing statements that are close to the truth (but not the *whole* truth), and not giving away any information. These strategies reveal a sophisticated understanding of how to manage impressions and information during an interrogation.

Although false denials occur more often than false confessions, the latter have captured the attention of psychological scientists, lawyers, judges, and the public. Indeed, we focus a great deal of attention on the reasons for false confessions later in this chapter. But it is important to bear in mind that false denials are also critical errors for the criminal justice system and the public. Because they are more frequent than false confessions and can result in the release of guilty and potentially dangerous offenders back into the community, their costs should not be underestimated. As we discuss some of the reasons, including coercive questioning, for why false confessions occur, keep in mind that these coercive influences promote confessions by the guilty—important in the investigation and conviction of criminal offending.

One might ask why so much attention has been devoted to uncovering false confessions and relatively little to understanding false denials. There are various answers to that question. It may reflect widespread philosophical agreement that it is "better for ten guilty persons to go free than one innocent person to be convicted," and it may reflect the interests of many psychology and law scholars in illuminating ways that the criminal justice system ensnares innocent people (Cutler, 2011; Garrett, 2011). But it is worth remembering that if society wants the police to refrain from using tactics that yield false confessions, there will be a corresponding reduction in the number of true confessions that lead to the convictions of guilty suspects. Consider, for a moment, the possibility that among those fewer convictions are people who are guilty of multiple counts of sexually abusing children over a period of many years. False denials, like false confessions, come at a cost to society.

Why Would Innocent Suspects Falsely Confess? Why would truly innocent people falsely confess to a crime that they did not commit? How often does this really happen? Any attempt to quantify the problem is almost certainly an underestimation because false confessions often are not revealed, and thus go unacknowledged by police and prosecutors and unreported by the media. But researchers who interviewed people incarcerated in German prisons provided some answers (Gubi-Kelm et al., 2020). Via interviews, they learned that 32% of respondents reported having falsely confessed. These inmates did so because 1) they feared negative consequences had they not confessed; 2) they were presented with false evidence against them; and 3) they believed that the truth of their innocence would eventually emerge. We explore each of these themes in this chapter.

In 2021, the Innocence Project reported that approximately 27% of cases in which DNA evidence led to exonerations involved false confession evidence. Interrogation-induced false confessions tend to occur in more serious cases like homicides and other high-stakes felonies when the police are under pressure to solve the crime, and thus use more psychologically coercive tactics to wear the suspect down (Gross et al., 2005). Lacking a victim or an eyewitness to describe the crime, the police may need a confession to secure a conviction.

Another important question is "under what circumstances would someone confess falsely?" Scientists understand some of the circumstances that give rise to false confessions. But before we describe them, we ask how one can know for certain that a confession is false. Do we simply take suspects or defendants at their word when alleging that an admission of guilt was wrong? Alternatively, do we need some kind of evidence that proves, unequivocally, that they could not have committed the crime to which they confessed?

Proving That a Confession Is False. There are four reasons one can be certain that a disputed confession is false (Drizin & Leo, 2004). First, a suspect could confess to a crime that never happened. For example, three intellectually disabled defendants were convicted by an Alabama jury of killing Victoria Banks's newborn child. One was Banks' husband Medell who gave a police-induced confession after making the short-sighted decision that a guilty plea was preferable to almost-certain conviction and a death sentence. Only after the three had served time in prison was it determined that Ms. Banks was incapable of giving birth to a child because she had had a tubal ligation operation that prevented her from getting pregnant (Herbert, 2002).

Confessions can be proved to be false in situations where it was physically impossible for a suspect to commit the crime, as, for example, when jail records show that the defendant was incarcerated at the time the crime was committed. Three men suspected of committing crimes in Chicago were actually in jail when those crimes were committed (Drizin & Leo, 2004).

A third way in which a disputed confession can be proved false is that the actual perpetrator is identified and guilt is objectively established. This happened in the case of Christopher Ochoa, a high school honor student, who confessed to robbing, raping, and murdering a woman in an Austin, Texas, Pizza Hut in 1988. Ochoa, who served 12 years in prison, claims that he confessed in order to avoid the possibility of a death sentence. He was released and exonerated only after the real perpetrator confessed to killing the

woman and led authorities to the weapon and the bag in which he had placed the money (Drizin & Leo, 2004).

Finally, a confession is false when there is scientific evidence—most commonly DNA—that definitively establishes the defendant's innocence. For example, Angel Gonzalez, a Mexican national with very limited ability to speak English, was misled by police into confessing to sexually assaulting a woman in Waukegan, Illinois in 1994. Gonzalez was convicted and served 20 years before being exonerated in 2015 after DNA testing proved his innocence.

Few cases involving disputed confessions come with independent evidence that the suspect is innocent, however (Leo, 2008). Rarely will the actual perpetrator come forward to claim responsibility and remove the blame from an innocent confessor, and in most cases there is no DNA evidence to compare to the confessor's DNA. As a result, few confessors can prove definitively that their confessions were false. And even when DNA evidence exonerates a false confessor, prosecutors sometimes refuse to concede innocence and juries sometimes convict. For example, in 1991, Jeffrey Deskovic was convicted of raping and murdering a high school classmate despite DNA testing that excluded him as a perpetrator. Why? Probably because in the course of a manipulative and grueling interrogation, the 16-year-old confessed. Since then, several other cases have come to light in which confessors were convicted despite unequivocal DNA evidence of their innocence (Drizin & Riley, 2014). In cases like these, prosecutors explain away inconsistencies between the confession and the DNA evidence by suggesting, for example, that the victim had prior consensual sex with another man (the so-called "unindicted co-ejaculator") (Appleby & Kassin, 2016; McMurtrie, 2015).

Let's return to the question of why people would confess to a crime they did not commit. One reason is to protect someone else. Another is to escape the pressures of a harsh interrogation. Yet another reason is that various tactics of psychological coercion induce suspects to confess, particularly when those suspects are young or have mental limitations. Brendan Dassey, who confessed to raping and murdering a woman with his uncle, Steven Avery, in the Netflix series, *Making a Murderer*, was both young and cognitively impaired. Before confessing, he endured hours of questioning without his lawyer present. Although a judge threw out his conviction because investigators had falsely promised Dassey that he would not be prosecuted, that ruling was overturned by an appellate court. In Box 7.3 we provide another example of the compounding effects of interrogators' coercive tactics and suspects' vulnerable state at the time of questioning.

Inside the Interrogation Room: Common Interrogation Techniques

Based on his observations of more than 100 police interrogations and his review of recorded interrogations in several hundred other cases, Professor Richard Leo noted a

Box 7.3

The Case of Henry McCollum and Leon Brown: Young, Intellectually Disabled Half-Brothers Who Falsely Confessed

Red Springs, North Carolina; September, 1983. Eleven-year-old Sabrina Buie had been raped and suffocated by underwear stuffed down her throat. Nineteen-year-old Henry Lee McCollum and his 15-year-old half-brother Leon Brown were picked up after police received a tip from a local teenager, despite the absence of physical evidence tying them to the crime. Their interrogations went on for five hours with no lawyers present and with their mother weeping in the hallway, unable to join them. McCollum cracked first. He concocted a story about how he and three others attacked and killed the girl, and then asked, "Can I go home now?" (Years later, McCollum recounted that he had never before been under such pressure, with detectives "hollering at me and threatening me.") Armed with a confession from his half-brother, police worked on Brown next, threatening him with execution if he failed to cooperate. He also confessed and signed a statement prepared by police. Even though both men claimed their confessions were coerced, they were convicted, sentenced to death, and languished in prison for 30 years. But after decades of legal battles, their fortunes turned in 2014 when DNA evidence from a cigarette butt found near the victim's body implicated another man who lived only a block away. McCollum and Brown were freed later that year. But like other

Henry McCollum and Leon Brown

prosecutors who attempt to explain away contradictory DNA evidence by invoking the theory of an "unindicted co-ejaculator," the original prosecutor, Joe Freeman Britt, continues to believe in their guilt.

Critical Thought Question

What police tactics may have led to McCollum and Brown's false confessions? How do you suspect those tactics influenced them?

---

fundamental contradiction concerning the nature of interrogations: "On the one hand, police need incriminating statements and admissions to solve many crimes, especially serious ones; on the other hand, there is almost never a good reason for suspects to provide them. Police are under tremendous organizational and social pressure to obtain admissions and confessions. But it is rarely in a suspect's rational self-interest to say something that will likely lead to his prosecution and conviction" (Leo, 2008, pp. 5–6).

Because physical intimidation and "third-degree" tactics are virtually nonexistent today, interrogators now use psychologically oriented coercion to overcome the anticipated resistance of suspects and to yield legally admissible confessions (Kassin et al., 2010). Most of these techniques are detailed in interrogation training manuals; the most popular are *Criminal Interrogation and Confessions*, commonly referred to as the Reid technique (Inbau et al., 2013), and *The Investigator Anthology* (Jayne & Buckley, 2017). For example, the Reid technique consists of nine steps that interrogators are instructed to use in order to obtain confessions. To understand why someone would falsely confess, one must be aware of the techniques of social influence recommended by these manuals and put into practice in interrogation rooms.

One can divide an interrogation into the pre-interrogation "softening up" stage and the interrogation itself. Throughout the encounter, police use well-crafted, deliberate strategies to secure incriminating evidence from suspects.

Pre-Interrogation—"Softening Up" the Suspect. Would you prefer to be "interviewed" or "interrogated"? (Probably the former.) When the police arrange to question a suspect, they may "invite" that person to the station house because they "just want to ask a few questions" to "clear up a little matter." They may explicitly tell suspects that they do not consider them a suspect. This all sounds innocuous enough. But the police have actually misrepresented the nature and purpose of the "discussion" to disarm the suspect and reduce resistance (Leo, 2008).

When suspects arrive at the police station for questioning, they are typically shuffled off to a small, soundproof room with armless, straight-backed chairs, thereby removing sensory stimulation and distractions. By physically and socially isolating suspects, the police begin to subtly exert pressure on them to talk. The interrogator may then try to soften up the suspect by using flattery, ingratiation, and rapport building—asking benign questions and engaging in pleasant small talk. According to one detective, "I don't care whether it is rape, robbery or homicide … the first thing you need to do is build rapport with that person … I think from that point on you can get anybody to talk about anything." (Leo, 2008, p. 123) All the while, detectives are concealing the fact that they have already determined that the suspect is guilty of a crime and are intent on extracting incriminating evidence.

Although the police are required by law to give the *Miranda* warnings prior to questioning, there are various ways they can circumvent these warnings, such as trivializing the warning as a minor administrative detail rather than a statement of one's constitutional rights (Woody & Forrest, 2020). Leo observed a detective who stated, "Don't let this ruffle your feathers or anything like that, it's just a formality that we have to go through, okay. As I said this is a *Miranda* warning and what it says is …." The intent here is to get suspects to waive their rights and begin to talk, thereby increasing the police's chances of hearing incriminating information. Recall that the warnings are required only when the suspect is being interrogated while in custody. By telling suspects that they are not under arrest and are free to go, there is no need to warn them that their statements may be used against them. On other occasions, police can persuade the suspect to talk in order to tell "his (or her) side of the story." Almost all suspects waive their *Miranda* rights and talk to interrogators (Leo, 2008).

The Interrogation Itself. During the heart of the questioning, interrogators use a set of carefully orchestrated procedures with the goal to eventually overwhelm even the most reluctant suspects and get them to provide incriminating statements. These procedures can be reduced to a few basic strategies. One strategy is the use of **negative incentives** to break down a suspect's defenses, lower resistance, and instill feelings of fear, despair, and powerlessness. Negative incentives like accusations, attacks on denials, and evidence fabrications convey to the suspect that there is no choice but to confess. The police also use **positive inducements** to motivate suspects to recognize

that an admission is in their best interest. All interrogators try, implicitly or explicitly, to send the message that suspects will receive some benefit in exchange for an admission of wrongdoing.

After suspects have either implicitly or explicitly agreed to talk, the interrogation can become accusatorial, with the interrogator confronting the suspect with a statement indicating absolute belief in guilt. Accusations are one of the most basic tactics in interrogations; police use them routinely. One subtle effect of this accusation is shifting the burden of proof from the state to the suspect. In what may be one of the most "ingenious psychological aspects of American interrogation" (Leo, 2008, p. 135) suspects must now work to convince the police of their innocence.

During questioning, interrogators also challenge denials that suspects make by simply cutting them off, expressing disbelief in their version of events and disparaging them (Kaplan & Cutler, 2022). They also deliberately introduce information about important details of the crime. In an experimental setting, mock interrogators provided crime information and those same details showed up later in both true and false confessions (Alceste et al., 2020). The effect of these ploys is to undermine suspects' confidence in their memories, which may cause inconsistencies in later retellings of the truth, and eventually, false confessions consistent with interrogators' version of the facts.

The most powerful, and arguably the most controversial, tool in the interrogator's arsenal is the opportunity to present **fabricated evidence**. Even if interrogators have no evidence of suspects' wrongdoing, they can make them believe that they do. They can point to "signs" of nonverbal behavior that indicate guilt, tell suspects that other people including eyewitnesses and accomplices have implicated them, and make up stories about the existence of fraudulent fingerprint and DNA evidence and surveillance videos that capture their images. (Interrogators are actually advised to carry file folders into the interrogation room to suggest the presence of such "evidence.") On occasion, suspects may take a polygraph examination, presented as an opportunity to prove innocence, when all along investigators plan to confront them with evidence of a failed test and urge them to confess. Fabricated evidence ploys are implicated in many cases of false confessions (Woody & Forrest, 2020).

Finally, police use positive inducements to persuade suspects that they will benefit from complying with authorities and confessing. This can take the form of providing scenarios to explain or justify suspects' actions (e.g., suggesting that they were probably acting in self-defense or in the "heat of the moment"), or of promising some sort of a deal for confessing. Sometimes detectives simply imply that suspects can go home if they accept interrogators' demands. In one of the most famous cases involving false confessions—the Central Park jogger case, in which five young men confessed to brutally raping and beating a female jogger—each suspect

A suspect being interrogated

Maxim Vasiliev/Shutterstock.com

confessed in a way that minimized his own involvement, and each thought that after confessing he could go home (Kassin, 2005).

A 2007 survey of more than 600 police investigators showed that they commonly practiced many of these ploys, including physically isolating suspects, establishing rapport, finding contradictions in their accounts, confronting them with evidence of their guilt, and appealing to their self-interest (Kassin et al., 2007). In fact, 92% of interrogators reported lying to suspects at least some of the time! Furthermore, the tactics are typically used in a prescribed order for maximum persuasive impact. For example, accusations of guilt and attempts to shame the suspect often precede justifications and rationalizations for the crime (Kaplan & Cutler, 2022).

But one study hints that interrogation tactics may have changed somewhat over the intervening years, at least in one jurisdiction. By analyzing 29 recorded interrogations provided by the Robbery-Homicide Division of the Los Angeles Police Department, Kelly et al. (2016) found that rapport-building was the favored tactic at the beginning of the interrogation, and that provoking emotions by offering rationalizations or appealing to one's conscience tended to increase as the interrogation progressed. Confrontational tactics such as accusations of guilt and implied threats for noncompliance were used relatively infrequently. Moreover, interrogations that ended in a confession contained fewer confrontations than those that ended in denial, suggesting that suspects are less likely to cooperate with detectives when questioned in an accusatory or threatening manner. Whether these findings hold up in a larger sample and these practices take place in other departments are questions for future research.

An Empirical Look at Interrogation Tactics. Psychological scientists have examined some of these interrogation tactics and now understand why innocent people waive their *Miranda* rights; how interrogators' presumption of guilt affects the nature of the questioning which, in turn, affects the suspect's responses; and how false evidence ploys elicit confessions.

In the first study to examine whether innocent people are likely to waive their rights and submit to questioning, Kassin and Norwick (2004) instructed participants either to steal $100 from a drawer (guilty condition) or to open the drawer but not take any money (innocent condition). When questioned by a "detective" who sought a waiver of their *Miranda* rights, innocent participants were considerably more likely to grant the waiver than those who were guilty, by a margin of 81% to 36%. When asked to explain why, 72% of innocent people said that they waived their rights precisely because they were innocent. A typical comment: "I did not have anything to hide." Innocents may waive their rights and answer questions because they assume, naively, that their innocence will set them free. But ironically, "innocence may put innocents at risk" (Kassin, 2012, p. 433).

Recall that many interrogations begin with the detective issuing a statement of belief in the suspect's guilt. This presumption of guilt can influence the way a detective conducts the questioning, causing the suspect to become defensive or confused, and increasing the chances of a false confession. This phenomenon—referred to as a self-fulfilling prophecy or **behavioral confirmation** (Meissner & Kassin, 2004)—has been demonstrated in a wide range of settings (McNatt, 2000; Rosenthal & Jacobson, 1968). After people form a particular belief (e.g., in the guilt of a suspect), they unwittingly seek out information that verifies that belief, disregard conflicting data, and behave in a manner that conforms to the belief. In turn, the target person (here, the suspect) behaves in ways that support the initial belief.

Psychologists have examined the effects of an implicit assumption of guilt on the behavior of interrogators and suspects, and on judgments of the interrogation by neutral observers. In one study, some participant-interviewers were led to believe suspects were guilty of cheating on a test while others believed they were innocent. Researchers examined the kinds of questions interviewers asked suspects. As expected, expectations of guilt resulted in more guilt-presumptive questions, indicating that confirmation bias led interviewers to seek information confirming their expectations. Later, independent observers listened to audiotaped interviews of "suspects" who had been questioned with either guilt-presumptive or neutral questions and rated their behavior. Importantly, observers did not hear the questions asked, only the suspects' responses, and none of the responses contained a confession. Still, observers rated the suspects questioned in a guilt-presumptive manner as more nervous and defensive than suspects questioned in a neutral manner, and judged the former to be guiltier than the latter (Hill et al., 2008).

The presumption of guilt apparently ushers in a process of behavioral confirmation by which the expectations of interrogators affect their questioning style, suspects' behavior, and, ultimately, judgments of the guilt of the suspect. These findings may actually *underestimate* the risks of behavioral confirmation in actual interrogations, where questioning can go on for hours rather than minutes and interrogators have years of experience in questioning suspects, as well as confidence in their ability to get a confession (Meissner & Kassin, 2004).

Finally, we consider the role of **evidence ploys** in eliciting confessions. As we mentioned, it is legal for interrogators to lie to suspects about the existence of evidence linking them to the crime, and most do. Researchers have now investigated how these ruses lead people to believe they committed acts they did not actually commit. In one study (Nash & Wade, 2009) participants were falsely accused of cheating on a computerized gambling task. Some were shown a doctored video that portrayed them doing so, and others were only told that their cheating was documented on video. Participants who saw the fake video were more likely to provide confabulated details and confess without resistance. Feeding false information to suspects can apparently cause them to doubt their memories and rely instead on external sources to infer what happened.

So far, we have considered the effects of interrogation tactics on adults accused of committing crimes. But the psychological processes we've discussed—innocent suspects' naiveté, short-sighted decision making in light of guilt-presumptive questioning, and the impact of manipulative police techniques—have arguably even more profound effects on juveniles.

One particularly troubling picture of juvenile interrogations came from observations of 57 recorded interviews (Cleary, 2014). An account of those interrogations noted, "Even when police interrogators left the room, cameras kept recording the teenage suspects. Some paced. Several curled up and slept. One sobbed loudly, hitting his head against the wall, berating himself…What none did, however, was exercise his constitutional rights. It was not clear whether the youths even understood them. Therefore, none had a lawyer at his side. None left, though all were free to do so, and none remained silent. Some 37% made full confessions, and 31% made incriminating statements" (Hoffman, 2014).

False Confessions

As we've shown, detectives draw out confessions from innocent people as well as from the guilty. Yet not all false confessions are alike; they occur for different reasons and can be explained by different situational and dispositional factors. Kassin and Wrightsman (1985) devised a taxonomy of false confessions. Although it has been refined over the years (Kassin & Gudjonsson, 2004), it still serves as a good framework for understanding why false confessions happen.

Some innocent people confess to criminal acts with little prodding. When Charles Lindbergh's baby was kidnapped in 1932, more than 200 people came forward and claimed responsibility. After the murder of child beauty-pageant contestant JonBenét Ramsey had gone unresolved for several years, prosecutors were eager to consider the confession of Mark Karr. But Karr's DNA did not match the sample found on the victim and he was never charged. These **voluntary false confessions** arise because people seek notoriety, desire to cleanse themselves of guilty feelings from previous wrongdoings, want to protect the real criminal, have difficulty distinguishing fact from fiction (McCann, 1998), or, as in one reported case, want to impress a girlfriend (Radelet et al., 1992).

Sometimes suspects confess in order to escape or avoid ongoing aversive interrogations or to gain some sort of promised reward. Legal history is full of examples, including the false confessions in the Central Park jogger case in which defendants said they confessed because they wanted to go home. These confessions are termed **compliant false confessions** because the suspect is induced to comply with the interrogator's demands to make an incriminating statement. They occur when suspects know that they are innocent but publicly acquiesce to the demand for a confession because the short-term benefit of confessing—such as being left alone or allowed to leave—outweighs the long-term costs—such as being charged with or convicted of a crime (Madon et al., 2011).

Some suspects confess because they actually come to believe that they have committed the crime. These so-called **internalized false confessions** can be directly related to the highly suggestive and manipulative techniques that interrogators sometimes use during questioning. An internalized false confession can result when, after hours of being questioned, badgered, and told stories about what "must have happened," suspects begin to develop a profound distrust of their own memory. Being vulnerable, they are easily influenced by external suggestions and come to believe that they "must have done it."

An example is the case of 14-year-old Michael Crowe, who falsely confessed to the 1998 murder of his sister in Escondido, California. Despite his initial vehement denials, Michael apparently came to believe, over the course of three grueling interrogations, that he had actually stabbed her: "I'm not sure how I did it. All I know is I did it" (Drizin & Colgan, 2004, p. 141). During the interrogations, detectives told Michael at least four lies: that his hair was found on his sister's body, that her blood was in his bedroom, that all of the doors to the house had been locked, and that he failed a lie detector test. With no memory of the killing but persuaded by these details, Michael was apparently convinced that he had dissociative identity disorder and that the killing was accomplished by the "bad Michael" while the "good Michael" blocked out the crime (Drizin & Colgan, 2004). But in fact, he was innocent.

Inside the Courtroom: How Confession Evidence Is Evaluated

The first sources of error involving confession evidence stem from what happens in the pre-interrogation interview and the interrogation itself. A compounding error occurs when prosecutors, defense attorneys, judges, and especially juries fail to understand why the suspect might have confessed and uncritically accept a false confession as valid. The false confession sets in motion a chain of events with adverse consequences for the suspect because attorneys, juries, and judges make decisions—about plea-bargaining, convicting, and sentencing—assuming that what the suspect said was true.

Many prosecutors assume that only guilty suspects confess. So when they secure a confession, they tend to treat suspects harshly, charging them with the highest number and types of offenses possible, requesting higher bail, and dismissing exculpatory evidence. Prosecutors offer fewer plea bargain discounts to confessors than non-confessors (Redlich et al., 2016). The confession becomes, in essence, the crux of the prosecution's case. Even defense attorneys assume that people who confess are guilty and urge them to accept plea bargains rather than risk their chances in a trial with confession evidence (Alschuler, 2016).

Judges are also likely to treat confessors harshly. In cases of disputed confessions, they almost always decide that confessions are voluntary and thus admissible as evidence in a trial (Givelber, 2001). In some cases, defendants who confessed will nevertheless enter a plea of not guilty and go to trial. If the jury convicts, judges' sentences are likely to be harsh because they tend to punish offenders who claim innocence, waste resources in a trial, and fail to show remorse or apologize (Leo, 2008).

Confessions are an especially potent form of evidence to jurors, even more influential than eyewitness and character testimony (Kassin & Neumann, 1997). Juries are quite likely to convict defendants who confessed, even when confessions are false. Archival analyses of actual cases in which false confessors pled not guilty and proceeded to trial show that conviction rates ranged from 73% (Leo & Ofshe, 1998) to 81% (Drizin & Leo, 2004).

For several reasons, jurors tend to accept confession evidence as valid. They assume that suspects would not act against their own self-interests and confess to something they had not done (Kassin et al., 2010) and that interrogators are adept at identifying liars (Costanzo et al., 2010). They are persuaded by secondary confessions in which suspects confess to another person who provides information to the police, even when those informants are motivated to lie (Key et al., 2018). Jurors are impressed by contextual details in confessions, particularly if the details include nonpublic information, but they fail to account for the fact that police could have scripted the confession in a manner consistent with their theory of the case. But jurors' awareness may be changing in subtle ways. Woestehoff and Meissner (2016) showed that jurors can be made aware that situational pressures, rather than guilt, may have motivated defendants to confess.

In general though, when people, including jurors, explain the causes of others' behavior, they often commit the **fundamental attribution error**: They do not give sufficient weight to the external situation as a determinant of behavior; instead, they believe the behavior is caused by stable, internal factors unique to the actor. In many instances, jurors take a confession at face value, fail to adjust or correct for situational forces on behavior, and assume that if suspects confess, they must be guilty (Wrightsman & Kassin, 1993). So a jury trial will not provide much of a safeguard for defendants who falsely confess and then claim their confessions were coerced (Bornstein & Greene, 2017).

Psychologists sometimes participate in cases of disputed confessions, functioning as consultants to defense attorneys or testifying as expert witnesses in pretrial hearings and during trials. The objective is to educate jurors and judges about the nature of police interrogations and the dispositional and situational factors that lead to false confessions. Though it is unclear whether expert testimony generates general juror skepticism or sensitivity to the coercive nature of interrogations (Woody & Forrest, 2020), one study showed that it can successfully alert jurors to whether the confession is consistent with other trial evidence (Henderson & Levett, 2016).

Putting It Together: A "Cumulative Disadvantage Framework" for Understanding How Innocence Can Lead to Confession

As we have shown, many innocent people waive their rights and police presume their guilt, and these events set off a cascade of additional processes that can prompt confessions and, in some cases, result in convictions. These seemingly distinct events are actually not isolated phenomena, but rather, accumulated disadvantages that can link together to transform an innocent person into a convicted felon (Scherr et al., 2020).

How does that happen? Consider how errors in the early stages of an investigation can taint the procedures that follow and collectively lead to wrongful convictions: Police sometimes question innocent people and, misperceiving their nonverbal behavior, deem them to be deceptive. These suspects, believing they have nothing to hide, waive their *Miranda* rights to silence and an attorney and submit to an interrogation. They are then questioned by detectives who almost certainly use manipulative interrogation techniques to pressure them to confess. A confession then biases the course of the investigation in a manner consistent with guilt: informed of a confession, eyewitnesses change their identifications, alibi witnesses retract their support, and forensic scientists alter the nature of their analyses (Scherr et al., 2020). By this point, a conviction or guilty plea is almost inevitable. Consider also how these errors are compounded when suspects are especially vulnerable. Are there ways to "contain the momentum that builds in these cases" (Scherr et al., p. 18)? We turn to that question next.

Reforming the System to Prevent False Confessions and Wrongful Convictions

One way to assess whether a suspect's confession resulted from a coercive interrogation would be to record the interrogation. A recording can provide a complete, objective, and reviewable record of how the suspect was questioned and deter the use of manipulative tactics by investigators *and* frivolous claims of coercion by defendants (Kassin et al., 2014). It can preserve an objective record of the entire session—an important benefit because police reports of interrogations frequently understate the use of confrontation, negative incentives, positive inducements, and false evidence ploys (Kassin et al., 2017). Moreover, video-recording neither inhibits suspects who wish to speak nor alters case outcomes (Kassin et al., 2019). Approximately half the states and the federal government require video-recording and hundreds of other jurisdictions voluntarily record interrogations. Law enforcement agencies that do so are highly supportive of the practice (Sullivan, 2008).

A more radical reform would reconceptualize the fundamental nature of police interrogations. At present, American interrogation practices are confrontational and accusatorial, and police claim that deceptive techniques are necessary to get reluctant suspects to confess. But we now have a robust body of empirical research documenting the detrimental effects of such trickery and deception. In contrast to these practices, police interviews in the United Kingdom are not coercive or overtly confrontational, and interviewers are not allowed to lie to suspects or present false evidence. The goal is to obtain useful information about a crime, rather than to extract a confession (Gudjonsson & Pearse, 2011). Data suggest that the nonconfrontational, U.K.-type interviews produce fewer false confessions and more true confessions than accusatory interrogations (Meissner et al., 2014), probably because they encourage suspects to say more (Evans et al., 2013), which leads to more accurate credibility judgments (Vrij et al., 2015). One prominent observer of the Supreme Court, the scholar for whom this textbook is named, advocated that judges take a stand against deception in police interrogations (Wrightsman, 2010). Having read this chapter, you might ask yourself whether other officials involved in ascertaining the truth about alleged criminal activity should do the same.

Summary

1. **What are some psychological investigative techniques used by the police?** The police use a variety of techniques to increase the likelihood that suspects will be prosecuted and convicted. Among these are criminal profiling; unaided judgments of deception; the polygraph; brain-based techniques for gauging deception; artificial intelligence, and procedures to induce confessions.

2. **What is criminal profiling?** Criminal profiling is an attempt to use what is known about how a crime was committed to infer what type of person might have committed it. Evidence about profiling suggests that it may have some utility as a means of narrowing police investigations to the most likely suspects.

3. **Is the polygraph a valid instrument for lie detection? What are some problems associated with it?** No measure of physiological reactions can precisely distinguish between guilt and other negative emotions, such as fear, anger, or embarrassment. Although some studies show high rates of accuracy in distinguishing between subjects who are lying and those who are not, many scientists are skeptical of those claims.

4. **What are the premises of cognitive-based methods to detect deception and how effective are those protocols?** Cognitive methods of deception detection are based on the facts that lying is mentally taxing, and that truth-tellers and those who lie reveal information in different ways. Researchers have developed interviewing protocols that increase cognitive load on already-taxed liars and that reveal evidence strategically, forcing deceptive suspects to be caught in their lies.

5. **What brain-based techniques are used to detect deception, and how well do they work?** Two techniques, neuroimaging using fMRI and brain fingerprinting using electroencephalograms, record brain activity while people are either lying or telling the truth. Studies show that different patterns of brain activation are associated with truth-telling and lying. Advocates of these procedures promote their effectiveness in detecting deception, but a number of complicating issues have not been resolved.

6. **How valid is confession evidence? What kinds of interrogation procedures can lead to false confessions?** Two kinds of errors arise in the context of confessions: guilty suspects falsely proclaiming their innocence, and innocent suspects falsely confessing. Among the interrogation techniques that can lead to false confessions are prolonged social isolation, confronting suspects and expressing a belief in their guilt, exaggerating or fabricating evidence against the suspect, and offering psychological and moral justification for the offense.

7. **What are some of the reforms proposed to prevent false confessions?** Critics of police interrogations suggest that these interrogations should be recorded in order to improve the quality of questioning, deter police misconduct, and preserve a record that can be evaluated at a later time. A more radical approach would replace the accusatorial style of interrogations with nonconfrontational interviews such as are now being conducted in the United Kingdom.

Key Terms

artificial intelligence

behavioral confirmation

brain fingerprinting

cognitive load

compliant false confessions

Concealed Information Test

Control Question Test

countermeasures

criminal profiling

diagnostic cues

evidence ploys

external validity

fabricated evidence

false confession

false denial

functional magnetic
    resonance imaging

fundamental attribution error

internalized false confessions

lie bias

mass murderer

negative incentives

polygraph

positive inducements

serial killers

spree killers

serial murder

truth bias

voluntary false confessions

Chapter 8

Traditional Steps in Criminal Prosecution and Civil Litigation: Arrest, Bail, Plea Bargains, Settlements, and Trials

Orienting Questions

1. What are the major legal proceedings between arrest and trial in the criminal justice system?
2. What is bail, and what factors influence the amount of bail set?
3. Why do defendants and prosecutors agree to plea bargain?
4. What are settlement negotiations, and why are most civil lawsuits resolved through settlement rather than trial?
5. What is the purpose of a trial?
6. What are the steps involved in a trial?
7. How has the introduction of emerging technologies changed the way that trials are conducted?

Between the time that the police make an arrest and a case is resolved at sentencing, traditional legal proceedings involve several steps with psychological implications. One feature of these proceedings has obvious psychological overtones: a trial. The trial is the penultimate act in our adversarial system of justice. (For criminal defendants found to be guilty, sentencing and punishment come afterwards and for civil litigants, further wrangling sometimes ensues.) Trials are public battles waged by two opponents (prosecution versus defense in a criminal trial, plaintiff versus defendant in a civil trial), each vying for a favorable outcome. They can be fiercely contested; prosecutors desire convictions, criminal defendants seek their freedom through acquittals, civil plaintiffs want compensation for wrongs they have suffered, and civil defendants hope to be absolved of wrongdoing and not required to pay damages. Psychological issues abound.

Although the trial may be the most visible and dramatic ritual in our system, many other factors play larger—often decisive—roles in determining case outcomes. For example, in the weeks and months following arrest, many criminal cases are simply dismissed for lack of evidence or other difficulties that prosecutors perceive in the case. For example, of the nearly 80,000 federal criminal cases charged in 2018, 8% were simply dismissed (Gramlich, 2019).

For the overwhelming majority of people charged with crimes who do not have their charges dropped, **plea bargains**, not trials, resolve their cases. Fully 90% of 2018 federal criminal cases ended this way (Gramlich, 2019). Plea bargaining, described in more detail in this chapter, is a process in which a defendant agrees to plead guilty in exchange for some concession from the prosecutor. Such concessions typically involve a reduction in the type of charge, the number of charges, or the recommended sentence. By pleading guilty, defendants give up their right to a trial, allowing attorneys and judges to move on to other cases. The vast majority of civil cases are also resolved without a formal trial in a process termed *settlement negotiation*, also described in more detail in this chapter.

If most cases are settled without a trial, why is our society (including psychologists who work in the legal arena) so fascinated by trials and trial procedures? Without a doubt, there are theatrical aspects to many trials, especially those featured in news media, films, and novels. Trials grab our attention because they vividly portray the raw emotions of sad, distraught, and angry people. Interest in trials is also related to their very public nature; most trials are conducted in open court for all to observe. Some are televised or even available for online viewing.

In contrast, negotiations about plea bargains and settlements are off the record and largely hidden from public view. Prosecutors offer concessions to defense attorneys over the phone or in courthouse hallways. Defense attorneys convey these offers to their clients in offices, jails, or via remote calls. Settlement negotiations in civil cases are also conducted in private. In fact, the eventual settlements in civil cases are often never made public.

In addition to plea bargains and settlements, this chapter examines other pretrial proceedings in criminal cases including pretrial motions and bail setting, and outlines the basic steps involved in a trial. All of these procedures raise important psychological questions that have been addressed through experimentation, observation, or empirical analysis. We preface those issues by describing the customary sequence of activities that occur after an arrest has been made in a criminal case.

What Happens After an Arrest?

If the police believe that a suspect committed a crime, they will probably arrest the suspect. However, being arrested for a crime and being charged with a crime are two different events, and a person may be arrested without being charged. For example, the police may arrest people who are intoxicated to detain them and allow them to sober up in a safe and controlled environment, but formal charges might never be filed. Charging implies a formal decision to continue with the prosecution, and that decision is made by the prosecuting attorney rather than the police. A few studies have focused on psychological factors associated with prosecutors' decisions to pursue criminal charges. For example, by reviewing files in 400 child maltreatment cases in North Carolina, Eldred and colleagues determined that only 40% of individuals arrested for child maltreatment were charged, and that the presence of a concurrent non-child maltreatment charge was associated with that decision (Eldred et al., 2016).

The Initial Appearance

Following arrest, the **initial appearance** is a crucial step in the criminal process. The Fourth Amendment to the United States Constitution requires that any person arrested be brought before a judge within 48 hours of arrest. This is one of the most important protections of the Bill of Rights. In many countries the police arrest people (or "detain" them, a euphemism for arrest) and hold them without charge for extended periods—or indefinitely. In the United States, however, anyone who is arrested must be taken without delay before a judge, an essential protection against abuse of power by the police. The primary purpose of the initial appearance is for the judge to review the evidence summarized by the prosecutor and determine whether there is reason to believe that the suspect committed the crimes charged. In addition, the judge will inform defendants of the charges against them, inform them of their constitutional rights, review the issue of bail, and appoint attorneys for those that cannot afford to hire their own.

The Preliminary Hearing

The next step is the **preliminary hearing**. One of its purposes is to filter out cases in which the prosecution has insufficient evidence. At a preliminary hearing, the prosecution must offer some evidence on every element of the crime charged and the judge must decide whether the evidence is sufficient to pursue the case further. No jury is present and defendants rarely testify or offer any evidence of their own. The judge will sometimes send the case to a grand jury (described next) or reduce the charges, either because the judge believes the evidence does not support the level of crime charged by the prosecutor or because of a plea bargain between the prosecutor and the defense attorney.

The Grand Jury

Consisting of citizens drawn from the community, the **grand jury** meets in private with the prosecutor to investigate criminal activity and return **indictments** (complaints prepared and signed by the prosecutor describing the crime charged). In about one-third of the states, a criminal defendant cannot be prosecuted unless a grand jury has found grounds to do so. The remaining states permit the prosecutor to proceed either by grand jury indictment or by a preliminary hearing.

If the grand jury decides there is sufficient evidence to justify the defendant being tried, it issues an indictment. For example, six Baltimore police officers were indicted by a grand jury in relation to the death, in April 2015, of Freddie Gray, a young Black man who died while in police custody. None of the officers was convicted.

Arraignment

A grand jury gives its indictments to a judge, who summons those indicted to court for arraignment. At the **arraignment**, the judge makes sure that the defendant has an attorney and appoints one if necessary. The indictment is then read to the defendant, and the defendant is asked to plead guilty or not guilty. It is customary for defendants to plead not guilty at this time, even those who ultimately plead guilty. The reasons for a not-guilty plea at this stage involve providing opportunities for both plea bargaining and discovery (described next), so that the defendant's attorney can review some of the evidence against the defendant.

Courtroom trial in session.

Discovery and Pretrial Motions

In criminal cases, defendants and their attorneys want to be aware of the evidence the prosecution will use to try to prove its case. In civil trials, each side is entitled to **discovery**—that is, each side has a right to depose (or question) the witnesses on the opposing side, and to review and copy documents that the other side might use at trial.

Just how much the prosecution must reveal to the defense varies widely. Some states require prosecutors to turn over to the defense all reports, statements by witnesses, and physical evidence. Most states require only that the prosecutor share certain evidence (e.g., laboratory reports) and evidence that is **exculpatory** (i.e., that tends to show the defendant is not guilty or suggests that prosecution witnesses are not credible). In part because prosecutors failed to share exculpatory evidence, a Colorado man spent eight and a half years in prison for a crime he didn't commit. We describe his case in Box 8.1.

Discovery is a two-way street. In general, states require the defense to turn over the same types of materials that the prosecution must turn over. If the prosecution is required to reveal laboratory reports, the defense will likewise be required to share such reports. In many states, the defense is required to notify the prosecution if it intends to rely on certain defenses, notably insanity and alibi defenses. The reason for requiring such pretrial notice is to give the state an opportunity to investigate the claim and avoid being surprised at trial.

During the discovery phase of the case, both sides file pretrial motions seeking favorable rulings on the admissibility of evidence. Motions commonly filed by the defense are the following:

1. *Motion for separate trials.* When two or more defendants are jointly indicted, one of them often requests a separate trial, claiming that to be tried together would be prejudicial. Research findings support this idea: in a mock jury study, defendants who were tried together were more likely to be convicted than those tried alone (Wilford et al., 2018). In 1996, Terry Nichols requested a trial separate from co-defendant Timothy McVeigh on charges related to the bombing of the federal building in Oklahoma City that killed 168 people. Being granted a separate trial served Nichols well because he was convicted of conspiracy and sentenced to life imprisonment whereas McVeigh was convicted of murder, sentenced to death, and executed in 2001.

2. *Motion to sever counts.* Suppose the indictment charges the defendant with robbing a convenience store on April 13 and burglarizing a house on April 15. The defendant may request separate trials on these offenses. A defendant may argue that it is prejudicial for the same jury to hear evidence about separate crimes because the jury will be tempted to combine the evidence introduced on the separate crimes to find the defendant

Box 8.1

The Case of Tim Masters and Prosecutors' Failure to Disclose Evidence

Helen H. Richardson/Denver Post/Getty Images

Tim Masters

In late January, 2008, Tim Masters became perhaps the first person in Colorado to walk up to a counter at the Department of Motor Vehicles and, without first taking a number and waiting in line, get a drivers' license. The crowds of people waiting their turns were happy to give Masters a break; after all, he had been released from prison just a few days before when his murder conviction and life sentence were wiped out by DNA evidence that pointed to another suspect. The DNA testing was the final chapter in a long saga of misplaced hunches, shoddy procedures, and prosecutors' failure to disclose crucial evidence.

In 1987, Masters—then only 15 years old—lived with his father in a trailer outside of Fort Collins, Colorado.

A woman's body was found in a field about 100 feet from his home; she had been stabbed and sexually mutilated. Detectives interrogated Masters, who admitted to walking past the body on his way to catch a school bus and failing to report it. They also searched his home, confiscating violent pictures he had drawn in his school notebooks. Over the next several years, prosecutors built a circumstantial case against Masters based on "psychological analysis" of his drawings, the fact that the murder coincided with the anniversary of his mother's death, and their suspicions. Masters was convicted of murder and sentenced to life imprisonment in 1999.

But several years later, a new team of investigators and attorneys began to glean clues that prosecutors knew more than they revealed in 1987. They learned that police had an alternate suspect back then, something not revealed to the defense. They learned that counter to the judge's orders, prosecutors had taken evidence from the case for their own examination. They alleged that prosecutors deliberately "stonewalled, delayed, and obstructed" in order to preserve the conviction. Eventually, DNA tests excluded Masters as a suspect. His conviction was set aside, he was released from prison, and he finally got the chance to drive.

Critical Thought Questions

What had the prosecutor in this case failed to do, and why was that mistake costly to Masters, and eventually, to the police department, prosecutor's office, and the community?

---

guilty of each crime. There is good reason for defendants to be concerned because psychological research studies have shown that mock jurors are more likely to convict a defendant on any charge (e.g., robbery) when it is combined with another (e.g., burglary) than when it is tried alone (e.g., Greene & Loftus, 1985). A review of nearly 20,000 federal criminal trials over a five-year period reached a similar conclusion (Leipold & Abbasi, 2006).

3. *Motion for change of venue.* The defendant may request a **change of venue** (moving the proceedings to a different location) on the ground that community opinion, usually the product of prejudicial pretrial publicity, makes it impossible to seat a fair-minded jury. Psychologists are sometimes involved in analyzing the extent and impact of the publicity on prospective jurors.

4. *Motions* in limine. Perhaps the most common pretrial motions are those that seek advance rulings on evidentiary issues that will arise at trial. A **motion in** *limine* is simply a request for a pretrial ruling. Suppose, for

example, that the defendant was previously convicted of burglary. The judge must decide whether to allow the prosecution to introduce that conviction into evidence in order to discredit the defendant if he chooses to testify. The defendant obviously wants a pretrial ruling on this issue in order to plan the questioning of the jurors and to decide whether to testify. Similarly, the prosecutor may want a pretrial ruling on the admissibility of a certain piece of evidence in order to plan the opening statement.

The Decision to Set Bail

Judges must decide whether to keep criminal defendants in custody during the time between arrest and plea bargaining or trial, or whether to release them into the community with a promise to reappear for subsequent hearings. Judges have many options. In capital cases (those rare cases in which the prosecutor is seeking a death sentence) and cases in which the defendant poses a serious risk of fleeing or committing

Box 8.2

The Case of Sandra Bland, Denied Bail After a Traffic Stop

A memorial at the site of
Sandra Bland's arrest

On July 10, 2015, en route to a new job at Prairie View A&M University, Sandra Bland was pulled over by a Texas state trooper for failing to signal a lane change. During the angry exchange that followed, the officer pulled out a stun gun, yelled "I'm going to light you up!" and ordered her out of the car. Following her arrest for allegedly assaulting the officer, the judge set bail at $5,000, requiring Bland to come up with $500 in order to be released. Because she didn't have the money, she was jailed. Three days later, Bland committed suicide by hanging herself in her cell. After a video of the traffic stop came to light, the state trooper was indicted on a charge of perjury for falsely claiming that he ordered Bland out of her car to investigate more safely, and the case led to the 2017 Sandra Bland Act which requires all police officers in Texas to undergo de-escalation training.

Critical Thought Question

How might this case have been different if, rather than being Black and poor, Bland had been White and from a privileged background?

---

other crimes, they can deny bail altogether. For example, Stewart Rhodes, leader of the Oath Keepers militia, was denied bail after being charged with seditious conspiracy for his role in the attack on the U.S. Capitol on January 6, 2021. The judge deemed Rhodes a flight risk because of the elaborate escape tunnels in his backyard. Approximately half of all murder defendants are denied bail, compared with less than 10% of defendants charged with other crimes (Reaves, 2013).

Short of denying bail, judges can require that money (or a bail bondsman's pledge) be deposited with the court or that a third person agrees to be responsible for the defendant's

future appearances and to forfeit money if the defendant does not appear. When bail is higher than defendants can afford, they have no choice but to remain in jail. In fact, nearly three-quarters of people awaiting trial in New York City jails in 2016 were detained because they could not pay bail, yet fewer than 8% of them had committed a serious crime (Bellafante, 2017). Unfortunately, this burden falls most heavily on low-income people and people of color who constitute a disproportionate share of the detained population. The case of Sandra Bland, described in Box 8.2, is one example.

States enacted various bail reforms in the late 2010s, and a bill to reform the federal system has been introduced in Congress. The state-level reforms, intended to decrease jail and prison populations, typically reduce or eliminate cash bail for low-level offenses. Lawmakers in New York passed one of the most sweeping reform bills, abolishing bail for many misdemeanors and non-violent crimes and requiring judges to consider a defendant's financial resources when setting bail. But a 2020 spike in crime rates in New York City fueled a backlash and many of those provisions were rolled back.

In addition to ensuring the defendant's return to court, bail has a secondary purpose: protecting public safety. In fact, bail evolved in the American legal system as an attempt to resolve the basic conflict between an individual's right to liberty on the one hand, and societal rights to be protected from criminal behavior on the other. The Eighth Amendment to the U.S. Constitution says that excessive bail shall not be required, but the Supreme Court has ruled that this provision does not guarantee a right to bail; it simply requires that bail, if any, should not be excessive (*United States v. Salerno*, 1987). Although various laws govern the bail decision, they are typically vague and loosely defined, allowing judges considerable leeway in the factors they consider and the way they make the decision about bail.

What Considerations Affect the Decision to Set Bail?

Psychologists and other social scientists have examined how judges make bail-setting decisions (e.g., Beattey et al., 2014). In particular, they have evaluated the factors that judges consider and the cognitive processes by which judges weigh and combine these factors.

Bail decisions are influenced by both legal and extralegal factors. **Legal factors** are related to the offense or the offender's legal history. Research has shown that bail is likely to be denied or set very high when the offense was serious and when the offender has prior convictions (Williams, 2016). Even *perceptions* of crime seriousness matter: In one study, judges imposed higher bail on those charged with sexual offenses than on those charged with non-sexual offenses at the same statutory offense level (Beatty et al., 2014). Since there is not strong, consistent evidence that defendants charged with sexual offenses are at higher risk to reoffend (Beattey et al., 2014), they may be particularly disadvantaged in the bail-setting context. This suggests that judges may be considering even the legally relevant factor of crime serious-ness in an unsystematic, stereotype-influenced way.

Because laws relevant to bail decisions are ill defined and there is little public scrutiny of this step in the criminal process, extralegal factors such as offenders' race and gender can affect judges' decisions as well (Kutateladze & Andiloro, 2014; Rachlinski & Wistrich, 2017). For exam-ple, in cases prosecuted by the New York County District Attorney in 2010–2011, judges detained a higher percentage of Black felony defendants (61%) than Latinos (56%), Whites (43%), or Asians (28%). Even after controlling for charge seriousness and prior record, Blacks were 10% more likely to be detained than Whites. These results can be explained by a focal concerns perspective, which proposes that judges' desire to protect the community is an import-ant factor in their decisions. So even if race *per se* did not influence bail-setting (in fact, it does), factors correlated with race, such as a defendant's perceived probability of re-arrest, may guide decisions (see, e.g., McIntyre & Baradaran, 2013). In other words, racial and gender disparities emerge because judges regard Black defendants as more likely to be re-arrested than Whites, and female defendants as less likely to be re-arrested than males.

Psychologists have assessed the cognitive processes that judges use in determining whether bail should be allowed. In some studies, judges respond to simulated cases presented as vignettes. In other studies, researchers observe judges dealing with real cases in the courtroom (Dhami, 2003; Dhami & Ayton, 2001). In both settings, judges tend to use a mental shortcut called the matching heuristic: They search through a subset of available case information and make a decision on the basis of only a small number of fac-tors (for example, offense severity and prior record), often ignoring other seemingly relevant information. This is not especially surprising; judges' large caseloads force them to make fast decisions, and people often use shortcut reasoning strategies when forced to think quickly (Kahneman, 2011).

The opinions of police and prosecutors can also sway judges' decisions about bail. Dhami (2011) analyzed bail-setting decisions in two London courts and found that prosecutors' requests and the position of the police strongly influenced judges' choices. Problematically, neither of these recommendations was related to an offender's risk of com-mitting further crimes while out of jail. Finally, although judges were highly confident that they had made the appro-priate decisions, there was significant disagreement among judges who responded to the same simulated fact patterns, raising troubling questions of fairness and equality.

Does Pretrial Detention Affect Trial Outcome?

What if the defendant cannot provide bail and remains in jail until the time of trial? Does pretrial detention affect the outcome? Apparently so. Defendants who are detained in jail are more likely to plead guilty or be convicted and to receive longer sentences than those who can afford bail, even when the seriousness of their offenses and the evidence against them are the same (Phillips, 2012). Pretrial deten-tion also decreases employment opportunities and receipt of government benefits, while having no net effect on future crime (Dobbie et al., 2018).

Some data suggest that prosecutors use pretrial detention as a "resource" to encourage (or coerce) guilty pleas. Pretrial detention is likely to cost defendants their jobs, making it harder for them to pay attorneys, so the threat of it may make them more likely to plead guilty. Among defendants who do go to trial, an accused person who is free on bail finds it easier to locate witnesses and prepare a defense. Jailed defendants cannot go to their attorneys' offices for meetings, have less time working with the attorney to pre-pare for trial, and have less access to records and witnesses. Detention also corrodes family and community ties.

Can High-Risk Defendants Be Identified?

Since 1970, judges have had the authority to preventively detain people who pose a risk of flight or danger, including violent offenders, individuals with severe mental illness, and those suspected of terrorism. Civil libertarians oppose the preventive detention of individuals believed to be at high risk of re-offending because it conflicts with the fundamen-tal assumption that a defendant is innocent until proven guilty (Cole, 2014; Margulies, 2011).

Preventive detention of so-called "high risk offenders" assumes that valid assessments of risk and accurate predic-tions of future dangerous conduct can be made. Kraemer and colleagues defined the assessment of risk as the "process of using risk factors to estimate the likelihood (i.e., proba-bility) of an outcome occurring in a population" (Kraemer et al., 1997, p. 337). Mental health professionals now have the capacity to assess violence risk in some situations, partic-ularly when using specialized tools (Desmarais & Zottola, 2020). How valid are these predictions?

A meta-analysis combined data from 11 studies that used 6 risk assessment instruments and concluded that the tests showed good to excellent predictive validity with few differences in validity for men and women (Desmarais et al., 2021). Predictive validity was generally comparable across racial and ethnic groups, although when differences emerged, predictions were less accurate for defendants of color than White defendants.

A related question is whether the general public supports the use of risk assessment algorithms in pretrial decisions. Californians queried about this approach voiced mixed sup-port and concerns—partly borne out by the meta-analysis—that it would augment racial and socioeconomic disparities in criminal case processing (Scurich & Krauss, 2020).

The preventive detention of those suspected of terrorism is an altogether different matter, though no less contentious. (Recall the outcry over former President Trump's 2017 order banning citizens from seven predominantly Muslin countries from entering the U.S. until a stricter vetting system could be developed to ensure they did not pose a national security risk.) Many citizens approve of preventive detention of suspected terrorists, believing that society's need to be protected from possible future harm outweighs individual rights. But though some risk factors have been identified (e.g., ideologies, affiliations, grievances, identities), there is still uncertainty about how lone-actor terrorists differ from groups and about how to put these findings into action (Monahan, 2017).

Plea Bargaining in Criminal Cases

More than 90% of criminal cases end prior to trial when the defendant pleads guilty to some charge, usually in exchange for a concession by the prosecutor. Plea bargaining is so pervasive that in *Missouri v. Frye* (2012), Supreme Court Justice Anthony Kennedy wrote "…horse trading [between prosecutor and defense counsel] determines who goes to jail and for how long. That is what plea bargaining is. It is not some adjunct to the criminal justice system; it *is* the criminal justice system" (quoting Scott & Stuntz, 1992, p. 1912).

Previous editions of *Psychology and the Legal System* had relatively little to say about the psychology inherent in plea bargaining because it has been difficult to study. Plea bargaining occurs in non-public settings, often in courthouse hallways and over the phone. So examining the negotiating that takes place—what offers a prosecutor might make and how a defendant might respond—has been hard to gauge. But new research using archival analyses of settled cases, lab-based experimental studies, field research, and interviews with the parties involved, can now shed light on this crucial process in resolving cases (see, for example, the 2018 special issue of the journal *Psychology, Public Policy and Law* devoted to this topic). In addition, researchers have advanced an agenda for additional psycholegal research on plea decisions, including questions concerning judicial involvement in plea deals, baseless pleas, and the waiver of rights that accompany guilty pleas (Zottoli et al., 2019). We hope that, given the scope of plea bargaining in the criminal justice system, future editions of this book will have even more to say about this important topic.

Plea bargaining has been practiced in the United States since the middle of the nineteenth century, and lately it has threatened to put the trial system out of business. Of nearly 50,000 felonies adjudicated in the 75 largest counties in the U.S. during 2009 (the most recent year for which data were collected), 96% were resolved via guilty pleas (Reaves, 2013). By one estimate, plea bargains resolve cases every 2 seconds during a typical work day in the United States (Colquitt, 2001). Interestingly, murder defendants were less likely to plead guilty than defendants charged with other violent felonies. Guilty pleas were offered by 97% of robbery suspects but by only 73% of murder suspects. The harsh sentences imposed on most convicted murderers—often life in prison without parole—make it worthwhile for murder defendants to go to trial and hope for sympathetic judges or juries.

Both mundane and serious cases are resolved by plea bargains. In a routine case that would never have been publicized if the defendant had not been a judge, Roger Hurley, a judge from Darke County, Ohio, pled guilty in a domestic violence case. He was accused of grabbing his estranged wife by the neck during an argument and threatening her with a bread knife. According to Hurley, he accepted a plea bargain in order to get on with his life and end the hurt and friction that this incident caused his family. In a more notorious case, James Earl Ray, the assassin of Martin Luther King, Jr., died in prison while serving a life sentence as a result of a plea bargain. That plea deal was not well received: many thought Ray had not acted alone, and the plea agreement meant that the facts would never be aired in a public forum. After Ray's death in 1998, the King family released a statement expressing regret that Ray had never had his day in court and the American people would never learn the truth about Dr. King's death.

The defendant's part of the plea bargain requires an admission of guilt and willingness to waive many rights. The admission relieves the prosecutor of any obligation to prove that the defendant committed the crimes charged. The prosecutor's part of the bargain may involve an agreement to reduce the number of charges or allow the defendant to plead guilty to a charge less serious than the evidence supports. For example, manslaughter is a lesser charge than murder, and many murder prosecutions are resolved when a defendant pleads guilty to manslaughter.

In a common procedure known as **charge bargaining**, the prosecutor drops some charges in exchange for a guilty plea. But charge bargaining may lead prosecutors to charge the defendant with more crimes or with a more serious crime than could be proven at trial, as a strategy for enticing defendants to plead guilty. Indeed, until 2013, unless defendants were willing to enter a plea bargain at the first opportunity, federal prosecutors were required to charge defendants with the most serious crimes that could be proved (Rakoff, 2014). Laboratory research using role-playing procedures indicates that "overcharging" is effective: Research participants were more likely to accept a plea bargain when more charges were filed against them (Gregory et al., 1978). The defendants who engage in this type of bargaining may win only hollow victories. Cases in which prosecutors offer to drop charges are likely to be ones for which judges would have imposed concurrent sentences for the multiple convictions anyway.

Plea bargaining may also take the form of **sentence bargaining**, in which prosecutors recommend reduced or less restrictive sentences in return for guilty pleas. In role-playing research, adults (but not juveniles) were less likely to accept a plea bargain when the offer included jail time than when it did not (Redlich & Shteynberg, 2016), suggesting that sentencing bargaining can be an effective tool, at least for adult defendants. As you can see, prosecutors have a great deal of control over the terms of a plea deal.

Some court observers suspect that tougher sentencing laws of the past few decades have allowed prosecutors to gain even greater leverage over criminal defendants, threatening them with mandatory or harsh sentences. So no matter how convinced defendants are of their innocence, they take a risk by turning down plea bargains and facing the possibility of additional charges or mandatory sentences (Oppel, 2011). In essence, they choose a certain more lenient option over a potential more serious one (Helm & Reyna, 2017). We describe one such case in Box 8.3.

Sentencing that follows a guilty plea is ultimately the judge's decision, and judges vary in their willingness to follow prosecutors' recommendations. But after ensuring that defendants understand the rights they are waiving and the consequences of a guilty plea, many simply rubber-stamp prosecutorial sentencing recommendations and accept the defendant's plea. In general then, defendants can expect that judges will follow the sentences that have been recommended by a prosecutor, and prosecutors can earn the trust of judges by recommending sentences that are reasonable and fair.

The Decision to Plead Guilty

Defendants plead guilty for a variety of reasons: because the evidence of guilt is strong and therefore, the likelihood of conviction is high; because, if convicted, they would face lengthy sentences; and because their attorney has recommended doing so (Redlich et al., 2017). These considerations are consistent with the notion of "bargaining in the shadow of trial," in which a decision to plead guilty or go to trial is rational and based on expectations of what is likely to happen at trial: as the likelihood of conviction increases, so too does the likelihood of a guilty plea.

But the "shadow of trial" theory has not held up well over time. A 2021 study challenged the theory by finding that, like home sellers in a hot real estate market, defendants require progressively better deals as the likelihood of conviction goes up (Bartlett & Zottoli, 2021). This challenge to the "shadow of trial" theory certainly complicates predictions of plea decision making. In fact, a number of other psychological factors also affect plea-bargaining behavior. In large part, they illustrate the role of biases and heuristics in decisions to plead guilty (Redlich et al., 2017).

One such factor is **framing effects**. Psychologists who study decision making have learned that the way decision alternatives are presented (or framed)—as either *gains* or *losses*—can have a significant impact on a person's choice. Individuals are more willing to take chances when the decision alternatives are presented in terms of gains rather than losses. Imagine that two defendants have been charged with the same crime, each has a 50% chance of being convicted at trial, and, if convicted, each is likely to be sentenced to 20 years in prison. The prosecutor has offered both defendants a deal that would result in only 10 years imprisonment in exchange for a guilty plea. Now imagine that Defendant A's options are framed as a *gain* and Defendant B's options are framed as a *loss*. Defendant A is told that if he or she went to trial, there would be a 50% chance of being acquitted and *gaining 10 years* outside of prison compared to the plea-bargain offer. Defendant B is told that if he or she went to trial, there would be a 50% chance of being convicted and *losing an additional 10 years* of life in prison compared to the plea-bargain offer. Although the two situations are identical except for the decision frame, Defendant A is more likely to take a chance at trial and Defendant B is more likely to take the plea bargain to avoid a loss.

The desire to optimize gains and avoid losses also explains the plea decisions of defendants who are detained pending trial. By tracking the outcomes of 1,800 criminal cases, Kellough and Wortley (2002) found that defendants denied bail were 2.5 times more likely to plead guilty than those not detained. Why? Because jailed defendants view their eventual freedom as a gain, whereas released defendants view

Box 8.3

The Case of Shane Guthrie and the Power of the Prosecution in Plea Bargaining

Shane Guthrie, age 24, was arrested in Gainesville, Florida in 2010 and charged with aggravated battery on a pregnant woman and false imprisonment. The charges stemmed from Guthrie allegedly beating his girlfriend and threatening her with a knife. The prosecutor initially offered Guthrie a plea deal of two years in prison and probation. Believing in his innocence, Guthrie rejected that offer, as well as a subsequent offer of five years in prison, despite apparently being warned that higher charges would be filed if he refused to accept the offer. But Guthrie's attorney maintained that there was no evidence the girlfriend was pregnant, that she started the fight by hitting Guthrie in the forehead with a pipe and changed her story several times, and that she had been arrested in 2009 for attacking Guthrie and telling police that he struck her.

The prosecutor's response to Guthrie's unwillingness to plead guilty? A year later, he filed more serious charges, including first-degree felony kidnapping, which would have meant life imprisonment if Guthrie, who had already spent time in prison, was convicted. "So what he could have resolved for a two-year term could keep him locked up for 50 years or more" (Oppel, 2011). This case illustrates the power that a prosecutor, who determines what charges to file, has over a defendant's destiny.

Critical Thought Question

How do the prosecutor's actions in this case differ from the more typical ways that prosecutors handle plea bargains?

any conviction and sentence as a loss. More recently, Edkins and Dervan (2018) showed that this effect was stronger for innocent defendants than for the guilty.

The choice to plead guilty to reduced charges also implicates an **anchoring** effect whereby the initial charge serves as a reference point against which other offers are compared. If the initial charge is excessive (which is often the case), then anything less will be perceived by a defendant as a good deal, even if it is still more serious than what the evidence could prove at trial (Haby & Brank, 2013).

Other psychological factors affect and sometimes distort offenders' and attorneys' decisions concerning plea bargains. In general, people—especially young people—tend to be too optimistic about their chances of securing favorable outcomes and are therefore overconfident. The **overconfidence bias** suggests that because defendants and their attorneys believe (incorrectly) that they have a chance to win at trial, they might reject reasonable offers from prosecutors. Some defendants may continue to rely on a strategy that they have long used: do not admit culpability, whatever the circumstances.

For other defendants, any admission of culpability is difficult for different reasons. They have trouble acknowledging guilt to their attorneys; some cannot even admit it to themselves (Bibas, 2004). Thinking about one's immoral or illegal actions is painful and depressing, and denial mechanisms allow people to avoid dealing with those thoughts. But denial results in minimizing the harm caused to others and an unwillingness to accept responsibility for wrongdoing. Defendants in denial are unlikely to take a plea bargain even when it is advantageous for them to do so.

Finally, plea decisions are influenced by the recommendations of authority figures—in particular by defense attorneys who, by virtue of their training and experience, are assumed to make better trial predictions and to have their client's interests at heart. As we describe in the next section, their recommendations are especially likely to hold sway with younger and less educated defendants (Redlich et al., 2017).

Plea decisions by juvenile offenders. Adolescents are just as likely as adults to accept plea deals (Kaban & Quinlan, 2004), so nearly all juvenile court convictions happen via plea bargaining. There is reason to be concerned about this state of affairs. Juveniles tend to be more suggestible, impulsive, and risk-taking than adults, which positions them to make less rational decisions in legal settings. In particular, they are likely to consider the short-term, rather than long-term, consequences of a guilty plea (Daftary-Kapur & Zottoli, 2014). Defense attorneys questioned about why their juvenile clients pled guilty cited the desire to go home and not be incarcerated, to avoid a trial in which witnesses would testify against them, and to get the process over with as quickly as possible (Fountain & Woolard, 2018). Obviously, this focus on immediate needs means that juveniles pay little heed to the long-term consequences

of their decision. Innocent adolescents are especially at risk, assuming—like adults—that that they will be able to withdraw a guilty plea and claim innocence (Helm et al., 2018).

Another reason for concern is that juveniles typically lack the comprehension skills necessary to understand the terminology used in plea materials and to intelligently weigh the trade-offs inherent in the process. When juveniles awaiting adjudication were asked to define words used in the plea form (e.g., disposition, assurance, restitution), they were correct only 14% of the time (Kaban & Quinlan, 2004). Because the plea bargain process happens quickly (averaging only 38 minutes, according to defense attorneys), there is little time available for defense counsel to educate or advise their clients or to encourage them to consider collateral and long-term consequences of their choice.

Attorneys' Roles in Plea Bargaining

The role of prosecutors. Defendants plead guilty in order to obtain less severe punishment than they would receive if they went to trial and were convicted. But why do prosecutors plea bargain? What advantages do they seek, given that they hold the more powerful position in this bargaining situation? Prosecutors are motivated to plea bargain for one or more of the following reasons: (1) to dispose of cases in which the evidence against the defendant is weak or the defense attorney is a formidable foe; (2) to ensure a "win" when their office keeps a record of the "wins" (convictions) and "losses" (acquittals) of each prosecuting attorney in the office; (3) to obtain the testimony of one defendant against a more culpable or infamous codefendant; and most importantly, (4) to expedite the flow of cases for an overworked staff and a clogged court docket.

Prosecutors have considerable authority in plea negotiations. They have discretion about the charges that are filed, the disclosure of evidence that supports those charges, the terms of the initial offering, and any subsequent modifications of that offer. One might assume that, given these powers, prosecutors' discretion is somehow constrained by various statutes and rules. But there is little clarity in the law even about whether prosecutors are required to share exculpatory evidence—that which supports an acquittal—with the defense during plea bargaining (Zottoli et al., 2019).

Prosecutors can also frighten defendants with the possibility of additional charges, severe punishment, and reprisals for failure to accept an offer. In fact, from interviewing convicted offenders about their reasons for accepting a plea bargain, Bordens and Bassett (1985) learned that pressure from the prosecutor was one of the most commonly cited reasons. A classic legal case that illustrates the threat of a "trial penalty" is *Bordenkircher v. Hayes* (1978) (Redlich et al., 2017). The prosecutor offered the small-time criminal defendant, Hayes, a deal that would sentence him to 5 years for passing a forged check for $88.93. Along with the offer came the threat that if Hayes opted to go to trial, the prosecutor would try him under Kentucky's habitual offender statute (for which Hayes was eligible because of two prior convictions). A trial conviction would result in a mandatory life sentence. Hayes famously rejected the deal, went to trial, and was convicted. On appeal, the U.S. Supreme Court upheld the conviction and sentence, reasoning that Hayes made his choice freely and voluntarily and that the prosecutor was exercising discretion as allowed by law.

The role of defense counsel. Although prosecutors have most of the power in plea-bargaining, defendants have the final say in any decision. Before accepting a guilty plea, judges ask defendants if they made the decision freely and of their own accord. Defense attorneys can have an impact in this decision by informing defendants about the evidence against them and predicting how that will affect their chances of being convicted. They gauge whether to recommend a plea offer based on legal variables such as the strength of the evidence against the defendant and the severity of the punishment (Brank & Scott, 2012). When the evidence points toward conviction and the defendant is facing a lengthy prison sentence, defense attorneys will typically recommend that defendants accept plea offers. Unfortunately, most criminal defendants are represented by court-appointed attorneys, often overworked public defenders who, like prosecutors, lack the time and resources to investigate cases thoroughly and bring them to trial. This has led to a situation in which under-resourced defense counsel can do little more for their clients than "meet 'em and greet 'em and plead 'em" (Rhode, 2001, p. 1793.)

Defense attorneys' recommendations interact with defendants' wishes in complex ways to yield a decision. At least in some circumstances, attorneys take their clients' preferences into account. Kramer et al. (2007) had attorneys read vignettes that varied the strength of the evidence against a hypothetical defendant, the potential sentence if convicted, and the defendant's wishes. When the probability of conviction was high and the likely prison sentence was long, attorneys strongly recommended the plea offer, regardless of the defendant's desires. But when the probability of conviction was low and the prison sentence was short, attorneys were willing to consider the defendant's wish to proceed to trial.

Unfortunately, zealous representation by defense attorneys in plea negotiations may not apply to all defendants equally. When she asked defense attorneys from across the country to respond to scenarios that varied the race of the defendant, Edkins (2011) found that the plea deals that attorneys felt they could secure for White clients contained shorter sentences than those they felt they could obtain for Black clients, even though they were slightly more likely to think that the White clients were guilty. Defense attorneys' own biases, and possibly, their knowledge of judges' biases, may come into play when they advocate for their clients. But broadly speaking, plea bargaining serves the need of defense attorneys to appear to gain something for their clients.

In most plea deals, both the prosecutor and defense attorney believe they are making the "punishment fit the crime" by individualizing the law to fit the circumstances of the case, and both are comfortable with a system in which cases are resolved without clear winners or clear losers. Experienced prosecutors and defense attorneys teach plea bargaining to the rookies in their offices, and lawyers from both sides engage in a ritual of give and take, with changing facts and personalities but with the same posturing and rationalizations. In fact, plea bargaining procedures are so well known that in some cases no formal bargaining even takes place. Rather, everyone involved—prosecutor, defense attorney, defendant, and judge—knows the prevailing "rate" for a given crime, and if the defendant pleads guilty to that crime, the rate is the price that will be paid.

Evaluations of Plea Bargaining

The U.S. Supreme Court has called plea bargaining "an essential component of the administration of justice" (*Santobello v. New York*, 1971), and has also ruled that defendants have a constitutional right to effective representation in plea negotiations, including competent advice and information about prosecutors' offers (*Lafler v. Cooper*, 2012). Still, plea bargaining remains a controversial and largely unregulated procedure (Turner, 2021). It has been defended as a necessary and useful part of the criminal justice system (American Bar Association, 1993), and condemned as a practice that should be abolished from our courts (Lynch, 2003). Advocates justify the procedure by pointing out that guilty pleas lessen the backlog of cases that would otherwise engulf the courts, facilitate the prosecution of other offenders, and reduce the involvement of criminal justice participants, including (in addition to judges and attorneys) police officers who don't have to spend hours in court, and victims who are spared the trauma of a trial.

Critics urge the abolition, or at least a revision, of plea-bargaining practices. They claim that (1) improper sentences—sometimes too harsh but more often too lenient—are likely; (2) plea bargaining encourages defendants to surrender their constitutional rights; (3) prosecutors exert too much power in negotiating guilty pleas; and (4) innocent defendants might feel pressure to plead guilty because they fear the more severe consequences of being convicted by a jury.

Data on these contentions are limited, but the available evidence suggests that plea bargaining works approximately as advertised. Defendants who are convicted at trial do indeed suffer more severe sanctions than those who accept plea bargains. In 2006, 89% of felons convicted during a trial were sentenced to jail or prison, compared with only 76% of those who committed the same crime and accepted plea bargains. In addition, judges imposed longer sentences on offenders who went to trial (an average sentence of 8 years and 4 months) than on those who pled guilty (an average sentence of 3 years and 11 months) (Rosenmerkel et al., 2009).

There are some "dark sides" to plea bargaining, however. The large-scale study of all cases disposed of by the New

Box 8.4

The Case of Brian Banks and Football Aspirations Derailed by a False Guilty Plea

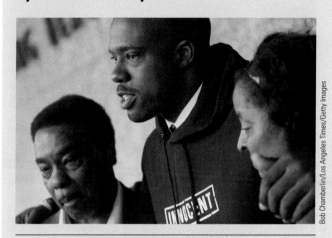

Brian Banks, center, with mother and father.

Most exonerees—people convicted of crimes and later proven innocent—have no reasonable expectation of playing in the National Football League (NFL). But Brian Banks did. His performance as a star linebacker in high school attracted the attention of college coaches and recruiters and he dreamed of playing in the big leagues. In fact, in 2002, he verbally committed to play for the University of Southern California. But that all unraveled when a high school acquaintance, Wanetta Gibson, accused Banks of rape and kidnapping after first claiming that the two had consensual sex on the school campus. (Years later, Gibson admitted she lied, but not before

receiving $1.5 million from the Long Beach Unified School District for lax security on the school grounds, an award that was later rescinded.)

Banks faced an excruciating choice: either fight the charges and face a sentence of 41 years to life, or agree to a plea bargain that would land him in prison for just 5 years. He opted for the latter, though it meant curtailing his football aspirations and lifetime registration as a sex offender. In 2012, following Gibson's recantation, Banks' conviction was overturned, but by then he had served five years in prison and another five on probation as a registered sex offender. He did have a short stint in the NFL in 2013.

Federal judge Jed Rakoff, who served as both prosecutor and defender prior to assuming the bench, provides a succinct explanation for why false plea bargains occur: "The typical person accused of crime combines a troubled past with limited resources: he thus recognizes that, even if he is innocent, his chances of mounting an effective defense at trial may be modest at best. If his lawyer can obtain a plea bargain that will reduce his likely time in prison, he may find it 'rational' to take the plea" (Rakoff, 2014). Banks' trial attorney practically told him as much: that as a big Black teenager, no jury would believe anything he said.

Critical Thought Question

In addition to concerns about whether a jury would believe him, what other factors were working against Banks in the plea-bargaining context?

York County District Attorney's Office in 2010–2011 revealed various racial disparities: Blacks were less likely than Whites to receive reduced charge offers, and more likely to receive offers that included incarceration rather than community service, probation or fines (Kutateladze & Andiloro, 2014). Prosecutors in misdemeanor marijuana cases were also more likely to offer deals that involved incarceration to Black defendants than to White defendants (Kutateladze et al., 2016). Given these differences, it is not surprising that Black defendants are less likely than White defendants to accept plea deals (Metcalfe & Ciricos, 2018).

Plea bargaining may also work against the long-range goal of achieving justice. First, it may prevent families of victims from seeing the defendants "get justice" or hearing them acknowledge full responsibility for their offenses, as exemplified by the King family's reaction to James Earl Ray's plea agreement.

Second, plea-bargaining removes the opportunity for juries—ostensibly comprised of defendants' peers—to decide whether people should be punished and incarcerated for their

actions. It also diminishes the chance for laypeople to act as a check on prosecutors, legislators, and judges. One commentator has suggested that allowing juries to hear information about any plea offer would remove the incentive that pushes criminal defendants to give up jury trials (Thomas, 2017).

Finally, the pressures to enter into a plea agreement can lead some defendants to plead guilty to crimes they never committed, though certainly, innocent defendants are more likely than guilty defendants to reject a plea deal. Extensive interviews of defendants who pleaded guilty to felonies in New York City revealed that 27% of the youth and 19% of the adults claimed they were completely innocent of the charges (Zottoli et al., 2016). One estimate is that approximately 10% of legally acknowledged exonerations involve guilty pleas by innocent defendants (Rakoff, 2014). We provide an example in Box 8.4.

What would lead an innocent person to plead guilty falsely? In one experimental study that asked participants to imagine they were either innocent or guilty of a cheating violation, the innocent were as likely as the guilty to accept plea deals when the likelihood of conviction was high (Tor et al., 2010). Because expected trial outcomes are probabilistic and known only after-the-fact, the anticipation of being convicted can apparently push some innocent defendants to accept a guilty plea. Additionally, judges rarely inquire about the evidence supportive of guilt, but rather, assume that defendants' willingness to plead guilty is indicative of factual guilt.

It is troubling that cases are not always resolved in line with the gravity of the offense (or with the truth, for that matter). When these "errors" are in the direction of sentencing leniency, they often are attributed to a perceived overload in the prosecutor's office or the courts. A defendant should not be able to plead to a greatly reduced charge simply because the criminal justice system lacks the resources to handle the case. However, the answer to problems of unwarranted leniency is not the abolition of plea bargaining; rather, adequate funding must be provided for indigent defense, the court system, and the correctional system, so that when severe penalties are necessary, severe penalties can be given. In the long run, if plea bargaining serves primarily as a method for managing the underfunded budgets of our courts and correctional systems, it will cease to be a bargain in the larger sense and will become, instead, too great a price for our society to pay.

Settlements in Civil Cases

Just as most criminal cases are resolved through plea-bargaining procedures prior to trial, the vast majority of civil disputes are also resolved (or settled) without a trial, typically in private negotiations between attorneys representing the disputing parties. This process is known as **settlement negotiation**. (Attorneys also negotiate with insurers, regulators, and sometimes even their own clients in an attempt to settle a dispute.) Most divorces, landlord–tenant disputes, claims of employment discrimination, and accident cases are resolved without a trial.

Large class-action lawsuits that may involve hundreds or thousands of plaintiffs are also typically resolved in settlement negotiations. In 2012, attorneys representing the oil giant BP and more than 100,000 Gulf Coast residents and businesses affected by the 2010 Deepwater Horizon oil spill reached a settlement that eliminated the threat of a trial. One commentator suggested that as lawsuits go, "this was going to be the Super Bowl wrapped up in the World Series—only with much, much more money at stake" (Walsh, 2012).

Lawyers spend considerable time negotiating settlements because they would almost always prefer the certainty of a negotiated compromise to the uncertainty of a jury trial. Because their caseload (or docket) is so large, judges would always prefer that the participants in a civil dispute resolve their differences themselves, without using the considerable resources necessary for a trial.

Disputing parties obviously have different objectives in settlement negotiations. Hence, the attorneys representing

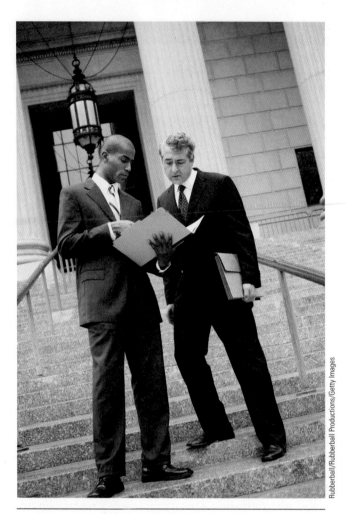

Attorneys often informally negotiate settlements in civil cases.

these parties will have very different roles to play in the negotiation. In a personal injury case, a common type of civil dispute, plaintiffs' lawyers will try to extract every dollar that a defendant will pay, whereas defendants' lawyers will try to avoid paying all but the minimal cost necessary to settle the case. In the Deepwater Horizon case, plaintiffs' attorneys were motivated to avoid years of uncertain litigation and the possibility of obtaining less money for their clients than they would receive in the settlement. Defense attorneys representing BP opted to settle in order to avoid having the company's mistakes paraded in open court, particularly in light of ongoing litigation with federal, state, and local governments.

Some lawyers have become highly skilled at negotiating settlements. Consider, for example, the case of Valerie Lakey, who, at age 5, was disemboweled by the suction power of a pool drain pump produced by Sta-Rite Industries. Valerie sat on an open pool drain after other children removed the protective cover that a swim club had failed to install properly. Despite 12 prior suits with similar claims, Sta-Rite continued to make and sell drain covers lacking installation warnings. After lengthy negotiations,

Sta-Rite eventually settled and the Lakey family received $25 million—at the time, the largest personal injury award in North Carolina history. (Importantly though, most personal injury awards are far smaller; typically in the range of $10,000 to $50,000.)

What makes some lawyers skilled at negotiating and winning large damage awards? Do they have a knack for deciding whether a case is worth pursuing and an ability to assess accurately what it might be worth? Do they have a particular interpersonal style that facilitates compromise? Are they particularly skilled negotiators? Psychologists, economists, and game theorists (scientists who study behavior in strategic situations) have conducted studies of actual and simulated settlement negotiations to determine what factors predict settlement amounts.

Factors That Determine Settlement Amounts

The legal merits of the case matter most, of course. In an automobile accident case in which there is strong evidence of the defendant's reckless driving and in which there are obvious and severe injuries, a plaintiff will recover more money than will a plaintiff whose case is weak on liability or damages.

But other factors matter as well. Negotiation theory suggests that outcomes are also influenced by the negotiators' reservation price, or bottom line (Korobkin & Doherty, 2009). The defendant's reservation price is the *maximum* amount of money that he or she would be willing to pay to reach an agreement, whereas the plaintiff's reservation price is the *minimum* amount of money that he or she would accept to settle the claim. Let's assume that multiple plaintiffs were injured when a piece of machinery malfunctioned, injuring them and resulting in medical and other costs of approximately $100,000. The defendant manufacturer may set a reservation price of $75,000, authorizing the defense attorney to negotiate a settlement that does not exceed that amount, while the plaintiffs may set a reservation price of $25,000, meaning that they will accept nothing less. Though the parties are not initially aware of one another's reservation prices, they have a $50,000 "bargaining zone" in which to negotiate a compromise. If they fail to reach a compromise, negotiators walk away from the bargaining table and the case goes to trial. Various psychological factors influence reservation points, including perceptions of the likely outcome if the case goes to trial and negotiators' goals and views on the merits of the case.

In considering the merits of their case, plaintiffs, defendants, and attorneys alike are influenced by psychological biases, often referred to as heuristics, which affect their ability to gauge when it is in their best interest to settle the case prior to trial (Knutson et al., 2015). Because of these reasoning errors, both plaintiffs and defendants lose more by going to trial than by settling. In one study, 61% of plaintiffs who passed up a settlement offer and proceeded to trial were awarded less than had been offered, and 24% of defendants were forced to pay more than they had offered—specifically, an average $1,140,000 more in damages (Kiser et al., 2008).

One such heuristic, the self-serving bias (sometimes referred to as the myside bias), occurs when people interpret information or make decisions in ways that are consistent with their own interests, rather than in an objective fashion. When evaluating their cases, people often have difficulty seeing the merits of the other side, believing that the evidence favors their position, and that the fairest resolution is one that rewards them. For example, law students who were randomly assigned to represent one side or another in an appellate court case judged the evidence and moral value of their arguments as strongly supporting their arbitrarily assigned roles (Eigen & Listoken, 2012). Self-serving biases also lead to impasse because people who are unable to consider the perspective of their negotiation opponents are less likely to reach a deal than those who can take their adversaries' perspective into account (Simon et al., 2020).

A heuristic that we mentioned in the context of plea bargaining—anchoring—occurs when negotiators are strongly influenced ("anchored") by an initial starting value and when, in subsequent discussion, they do not sufficiently adjust their judgments away from this starting point. This bias is quite pervasive, and even wildly extreme anchors can influence judgments. For example, people provided higher estimates of the average temperature in San Francisco when first asked whether it was higher or lower than 58 degrees, a number that may have induced people to consider the (unlikely) possibility that San Francisco temperatures are high (cited by Guthrie et al., 2001). In the context of settlement negotiations, the first offer can serve to anchor the final negotiated compromise: the higher the offer, the higher the ultimate settlement (Korobkin & Doherty, 2009).

Many legal disputes involve intense emotions that can also influence the likelihood of resolution. Imagine, for example, the despair and anguish that Rachel Barton Pine must have experienced after being dragged 200 feet underneath a Chicago commuter train in 1995. The then–21-year-old classical violin prodigy had her left leg severed above the knee, lost part of her right foot, and badly injured her right knee as terrified passengers tried to alert the engineer to halt the train. Barton sued the train company for $30 million. After several years of negotiations and 25 operations, she received nearly that amount and gave a sizeable portion to charity.

Emotions on the part of plaintiffs, defendants, and their attorneys all play a role in negotiation. The emotion most closely associated with disputes may be anger; parties involved in settlement discussions often feel resentment, antagonism, and sometimes, outright fury. Presumably, those expressions would harm the chances for concessions and compromise, and psychological data suggest that they do. Higher levels of anger on the part of negotiators are related to angry responses from the other party (Friedman et al., 2004), a greater likelihood of deception (Yip & Schweitzer, 2016), and a greater frequency of impasse (Hillebrandt & Barclay, 2017). Angry disputants have difficulty resolving their competing claims.

If anger tends to inhibit dispute resolution, do positive emotions tend to enhance it? The answer is yes; positive emotions such as happiness foster cooperation and concession making (Kopelman et al., 2006), stimulate creative problem solving (deVries et al., 2012), increase the likelihood that parties will disclose personal information (Forgas, 2011), and positively influence negotiators' expectations (Carnevale, 2008). Experiencing positive emotions improves one's chances for successful settlement negotiations.

What Is the Purpose of a Trial?

Sometimes settlement negotiations fail and plea bargains prove to be elusive. In those situations, disputants have no choice but to have their case resolved in a trial, a topic to which we devote the remainder of this chapter. Every trial, civil or criminal, presents two contrasting versions of the truth. Both sides try to present the "facts" in question so as to convince the judge or the jury that their claims are true. The judge or jury must render judgments on the probable truth or falsity of each side's statements and evidence.

The jury system evolved from an ancient ritual during which a defendant stood before a priest, surrounded by friends who swore that the defendant had not committed the crime. But the victim also brought friends who swore to just the opposite (Kadri, 2005). Because this arrangement was not especially satisfactory to anyone, the English monarchy began to have defendants appear in front of a panel of citizens whose task was to assess the innocence or guilt of the defendant.

If one is asked about the purpose of a modern trial, the first response might be "to determine the truth, of course." But in fact, trials also serve other purposes: They provide a sense of stability and a way to resolve conflicts so that the disputants can receive satisfaction. Many years ago, Miller and Boster (1977) identified three images of the trial that reflect these contrasting conceptions and that still hold true today.

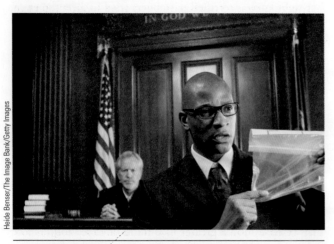

After a witness testifies during a trial, the witness is then crossexamined by the opposing attorney, followed by redirect questioning by the original attorney, if needed.

The Trial as a Search for the Truth

Many people believe that a trial is a rule-governed event involving the parties' collective search for the truth. This view assumes that what really happened can be clearly ascertained and that witnesses are capable of knowing, remembering, and describing events completely and accurately. Although this image of the trial recognizes that the opposing attorneys present only those facts that buttress their positions, it assumes that the truth will emerge from the confrontation of conflicting facts. It also assumes that judges or jurors, in weighing these facts, can "lay aside their prejudices and preconceived views regarding the case and replace such biases with a dispassionate analysis of the arguments and evidence" (Miller & Boster, 1977, p. 25).

But this image of the trial as a rational, rule-governed event has been challenged on several grounds. Eyewitnesses are not always thorough and accurate reporters, as the legal system would like to believe. Interrogations can sometimes result in false confessions, and jurors are not particularly good at distinguishing false confessions from true confessions. Jurors may have difficulty setting aside their own experiences and prejudices. Although this image of the trial remains as an inspiring ideal, other images need to be considered as well.

The Trial as a Test of Credibility

A second conception—that the trial is a test of credibility—acknowledges that facts and evidence are always incomplete and biased. Hence the decision makers, whether judge or jury, must not only weigh the information and evidence but also evaluate the truthfulness of the opposing sources of evidence (Miller & Boster, 1977). They must focus on the way evidence is presented, the qualifications of witnesses, and the inconsistencies between witnesses. Competence and trustworthiness of witnesses take on added importance in this image.

The image of the trial as a test of credibility also has problems. Both judges and jurors can make unwarranted inferences about witnesses and attorneys on the basis of race, gender, mannerisms, or style of speech. Judges' and jurors' judgments of credibility may be based more on stereotypes, folklore, or "commonsense intuition" than on the facts.

The Trial as a Conflict-Resolving Ritual

The first two images share the belief that the primary function of a trial is to produce the most nearly valid judgment about the guilt of a criminal defendant or the responsibility of a civil defendant. The third image shifts the function of the trial from determining the truth to providing a mechanism to resolve controversies. Miller and Boster (1977) express it this way: "At the risk of oversimplification we suggest that it removes primary attention from the concept of doing justice and transfers it to the psychological realm of *creating a sense that justice is being done*" (p. 34). Truth remains a goal, but participants in the trial process also need both the opportunity to have their "day in court" and the reassurance that, whatever the outcome, "justice was done." In other words, they need closure that only a trial can provide.

A criminal trial conducted in federal court in Georgia in 2022 exemplified this desire for doing justice. A few months prior, three White men had been convicted of murder and sentenced to life in prison for their role in the shooting death of 25-year-old Ahmaud Arbery, a Black man who was jogging through their neighborhood. Even after this conviction, there was interest in determining whether the killing was racially motivated and whether the defendants violated Arbery's civil rights—issues addressed in a federal hate crimes statute. Arbery's family objected to a plea bargain arranged by federal prosecutors (his mother told the judge "They killed my son because he's a Black man. I'm asking on behalf of his family, on behalf of his memory, and on behalf of fairness that you do not grant this plea"). As a result, a trial ensued and defendants were convicted of violating Arbery's civil rights.

The stabilizing function of a trial is worthless, of course, if the public doubts that justice was done in the process. That sense of closure is sometimes missing after a trial; the widespread dissatisfaction in some segments of our society with the outcome of O. J. Simpson's murder trial (Brigham & Wasserman, 1999) ensured continued media interest and public fascination with his actions and statements. (In 2016 alone, the public had two opportunities to relive the details: the TV series *The People v. O.J. Simpson: American Crime Story*, and *O.J.: Made in America*.) The belief that "he got away with murder" even led to proposals to reform and restrict the jury system. Other segments of society were equally dissatisfied with the verdict in Simpson's civil trial, in which he was found liable for the deaths of his ex-wife and her friend. Perhaps together, the verdicts in the two trials converged on a reasonable outcome—while Simpson may have been the killer, this couldn't be proven beyond a reasonable doubt, the level of certainty required for a criminal conviction.

These three contrasting images remind us that truth in the legal system is elusive, and that truth seekers are subject to human error, even though the system seems to assume that they approach infallibility. The failure to achieve perfection in our decision making will become evident as we review the steps in the trial process.

Steps in the Trial Process

In the next section, we sketch out the usual steps in a trial in brief detail. Though some of these procedures are conducted out of the public eye, they all involve—either implicitly or explicitly—issues of interest to psychologists.

Preliminary Actions

Discovery is the pretrial process by which each side tries to gain vital information about the case that will be presented by the other side. This information includes statements by witnesses, police records, documents, material possessions, experts' opinions, and anything else relevant to the case.

The U.S. Constitution provides criminal defendants with the right to have the charges against them judged by a jury of their peers, though a defendant can decide instead to have the case decided by a judge. If the trial is before a jury, the selection of jurors involves a fairly complicated process that we describe in Chapter 12.

The Trial

All trials—whether related to criminal law or to civil law—include similar procedural steps. At the beginning of the trial itself, lawyers for each side are permitted to make **opening statements**. These are not part of the evidence, but they serve as overviews of the evidence to be presented. The prosecution or plaintiff usually goes first, because this side bears the burden of proving the allegations. Attorneys for the defendant, in either a criminal or civil trial, can choose to present their opening statement immediately after the other side's opening statement or to wait until it is their turn to present evidence.

Some psychologists have wondered whether the timing of the opening statement matters. In other words, would it be preferable for the defense attorney (and more beneficial to the defendant) if the defense's opening statement immediately followed the prosecutor's opening statement or would it be better for the defense to wait until all of the prosecution witnesses have testified? Their study, using a mock jury simulation, varied the timing of the defense opening statement in an auto theft case (Wells et al., 1985). The results were striking: When the defense opening statement was given earlier rather than later, verdicts were more favorable to the defense, and the perceived effectiveness of the defense attorney was enhanced. Defense attorneys who take their first opportunity to make an opening statement can apparently counter the story told by the prosecutor, or at least urge jurors to consider an alternative interpretation of the evidence.

After opening statements, the prosecution or plaintiff calls its witnesses. Each witness testifies under oath, with the threat of a charge of **perjury** if the witness fails to be truthful. That witness is then cross-examined by the opposing attorney, after which the original attorney has a chance for **redirect questioning**. Redirect questioning is likely if the original attorneys believe the opposition has "impeached" their witness; **impeachment** in this context refers to a cross-examination that has effectively called into question the credibility (or reliability) of the witness.

The purpose of redirect examination is to "rehabilitate" witnesses, or to salvage their original testimony. The defense, however, has one more chance to question the witness, a process called **recross** (short for "re-cross-examination"). After the prosecution or plaintiff's attorneys have presented all their witnesses, it is the defense's turn.

The same procedure of direct examination, cross-examination, redirect, and recross is used. After both sides have presented their witnesses, one or both may decide to introduce additional evidence and witnesses and so ask the judge for permission to present **rebuttal evidence**, which attempts to counteract or disprove evidence given by an earlier witness.

Once all the evidence has been presented, each side is permitted to make a **closing argument**, also called a summation. Although jurisdictions vary, typically the prosecution or plaintiff gets the first summation, followed by the defense, after which the prosecution or plaintiff responds and has the final word.

The final step in the jury trial is for the judge to give instructions to the jury. (In some states, instructions precede the closing arguments.) The judge informs the jury of the relevant law. For example, a definition of the crime is given, as well as a statement of what elements must be present for it to have occurred—that is, whether the defendant had the motive and the opportunity to commit the crime. The judge also instructs jurors about the standard they should use to weigh the evidence.

With criminal charges, the jurors must be convinced beyond a reasonable doubt that the defendant is guilty before they vote to convict. Although the concept of "reasonable doubt" is difficult to interpret, generally it means that jurors should be strongly convinced (but not necessarily convinced beyond *all* doubt). Each of us interprets such an instruction differently, and this instruction is often a source of confusion and frustration among jurors.

In a civil trial, in which one party brings a claim against another, a different standard is used. A **preponderance of evidence** is all that is necessary for a finding in favor of one side. Preponderance is often interpreted as meaning at least 51% of the evidence, though it is difficult (and potentially misleading) to quantify a concept that is expressed verbally.

The jury is sometimes given instructions on how to deliberate, but these are usually sparse. Jurors are excused to the deliberation room, and no one—not even the bailiff or the judge—can be present during or eavesdrop on their deliberations. When the jury has reached its verdict, its foreperson informs the bailiff, who informs the judge, who in turn reconvenes the attorneys and defendants (and plaintiffs in a civil trial) for announcement of the verdict. Chapter 13 focuses on how jurors and juries make their decisions.

Now that we have detailed the steps involved in trials, we consider the advantages accorded by these procedures to the prosecution and the defense in criminal trials. You will notice that opposing sides have roughly offsetting advantages. For example, the prosecution gets the first and last chance to address the judge or jury. In other words, it has the advantages of both *primacy* and *recency* in its attempts at jury persuasion, and research shows that information presented first (primacy) and last (recency) has more persuasive influence than information presented in the middle of a discussion. Of course, the prosecution also has the burden of proving its case.

The defense, on the other hand, is not given the opportunity to speak first or to speak last. But it has the advantage of not needing to prove anything to the judge or jury. In fact, the defense does not have to call any witnesses at all. If the prosecution is unable to meet its obligation to convince the judge or jury of the defendant's guilt, then the defendant prevails. Defendants are entitled to all exculpatory evidence (evidence that would tend to absolve the defendant) and those found not guilty can never be tried again for that specific crime.

Sentencing

If the defendant in a criminal trial is deemed guilty, a punishment must be decided. In the vast majority of jurisdictions, the trial judge decides punishment in a sentencing hearing conducted some weeks after the trial. In a handful of states, sentencing is determined by a jury. In these jurisdictions, the jury reconvenes after the verdict is rendered, and attorneys present evidence relevant to the sentencing decision. The jury then deliberates until it agrees on a recommended punishment. In cases involving the death penalty, jurors, rather than judges, decide the sentence (*Ring v. Arizona*, 2002). We cover judges' and capital juries' sentencing decisions in Chapter 14.

The Appellate Process

Involvement of guilty defendants in the legal system does not end when they are sentenced to a prison term or to probation. To protect their rights, defendants who claim they have been convicted unjustly can appeal to a higher level of court. (Defendants who plead guilty are often required to waive their appellate rights as a condition of the plea agreement.) Appeals are also possible in virtually every civil suit.

As in earlier steps in the legal process, a conflict of values occurs as appeals are pursued. One goal is equality before the law—that is, to administer justice consistently and fairly. But appellate courts also try to be sensitive to differences in cases which, at first glance, appear to be similar. Appellate courts recognize that judges and juries can make errors. The appellate process can correct mistakes that impair the fairness of trials; it also helps promote a level of consistency in trial procedures.

When a decision is appealed to a higher court, the appellate judges read the transcript of the trial proceedings, the motions and accompanying documents filed by the attorneys, and written arguments, called briefs, from both sides about the issues on appeal. They then decide whether to overturn the original trial decision or to let it stand. Appellate judges rarely reverse a verdict on the basis of the facts of the case or the apparent legitimacy of that verdict. When they do reverse a verdict, it is usually because they believe that the trial judge made a procedural error, such as allowing controversial evidence to be presented or failing to allow the jury to consider some evidence that should have been included.

If a verdict in a criminal trial is overturned or reversed, the appeals court will either order a retrial or order that the charges be thrown out. In reviewing the decision in a civil case, an appellate court can let the decision stand, reverse it (rule in favor of the side that lost rather than the side that won), or make some other changes in the decision and return the case to a lower court for reconsideration. One possible conclusion in either civil or criminal appeals is that certain evidence should not have been admitted or that certain instructions should not have been given; hence, a new trial may be ordered.

There is relatively little psychological research on the appellate court decision-making process. Exceptions include an evaluation of small group dynamics in appellate court decisions (Miller & Curry, 2017) and two books on the psychology of judicial decision making that touch on issues arising in appellate courts (Klein & Mitchell, 2010; Wrightsman, 1999).

Courtroom of the Future

With only minor variations, courtroom trials and appeals have followed these procedures for much of our nation's history. The trials of John Scopes (tried in 1925 for teaching the theory of evolution in a Tennessee public school science class), Julius and Ethel Rosenberg (tried in 1951 on espionage charges), and defendants facing charges across the United States today all follow essentially the same format. But recently, the introduction of emerging technologies into the legal system has begun to change the look of trials. Today, juries and judges expect attorneys to use more than yellow legal pads and grainy videos. Many jurors, especially younger jurors and those who are more tech-savvy, now expect to see and hear multimedia approaches (Griffin, 2008), and some judges want all documents presented during a trial to be displayed electronically. People are already considering how, in 2030, a well-designed courtroom could enhance the delivery of forensic science evidence (Horan & Maine, 2014). In this hypothetical scenario, mathematical models are used to prepare visual crime scene animations; witnesses use high-quality holograms and 3D holographic displays; internationally acclaimed experts testify from remote locations over holographic link-ups; all evidence is retrieved instantaneously without interrupting the flow of proceedings; and each juror has a tablet with a video transcript in time- and word-searchable form and custom-designed questions to work through during deliberation.

Even today, technologies being used in courts extend far beyond surveillance videos, which would have been novel only a few years ago. One noteworthy development is the proliferation of smartphone videos, particularly clips of encounters between citizens and police, which have dominated the news recently. Scores of websites dedicated to "cop-watching" now exist and various groups monitor high-crime areas for examples of hostile police–citizen interactions (Hoffberger, 2013). Federal courts have affirmed the right to film police in action, and police departments have responded by investing in wearable cameras ("body-cams"), which film their actions automatically. In Box 8.5, we describe a case that turned heavily on a smartphone video.

Box 8.5

The Case of Antonio Buehler and the Power of Visual Technology

Antonio Buehler, a Stanford and West Point graduate and Afghan war veteran, was arrested outside a 7–11 in Austin, Texas in the early hours of New Years Day, 2012 after an altercation with police. While stopped for gas, Buehler witnessed a drunk driving investigation in which police were pulling a woman from her car as she urged bystanders to "film this!" (Bock & Schneider, 2017). Buehler took some still shots while calling out to police that their tactics were overly aggressive. An officer then confronted him and arrested him for public intoxication, assault related to allegedly spitting on an officer, and refusing to obey a lawful order. The first two charges were dropped and Buehler opted to go trial on the last charge, claiming that the reason he was charged was because he filmed police activity.

At trial, jurors saw four videos: two dash-cam videos from the arresting officer's car, a clip from a surveillance camera at the convenience store, and a smartphone video shot by a bystander across the street that showed the entire scene. Crucially for Buehler, the bystander's video showed him being thrown to the ground while shouting "Why are you doing this?" This evidence bolstered Buehler's testimony that he thought the officer was the aggressor in the incident and seemed to contradict the officers' recollection that Buehler was verbally abusive and spat on him. In fact, dash-cam clips revealed that the arresting officer was loud and agitated throughout the incident. Much of the prosecution's case was an attempt to downplay the video evidence and explain to the jury why it is important for officers to control situations and defend themselves. But Buehler was acquitted, perhaps because jurors could witness the officer's demeanor for themselves from the vantage point of the bystander's smartphone. Those images may have revealed more than words could ever say.

Critical Thought Question

In what ways might visual technologies such as smart phones and dashboard and body cameras transform the bail-setting, plea-bargaining, and trial stages of a case?

Technology has provided other tools for attorneys and judges to employ during pretrial hearings and trials, and the coronavirus pandemic accelerated their use. These include:

- videoconferencing that permits live, two-way video and audio communication between courtrooms and remote sites—useful when witnesses and defendants are medically incapacitated or incarcerated, and, during the pandemic, to allow arraignments, guilty pleas, and even entire trials to be conducted online.

- electronic and digital evidence, such as digital recordings, documents, and photographs, that allows judges and jurors to easily observe the evidence themselves, rather than hear others' descriptions of it.

- computer animations and simulations that feature computer-generated depictions of complex physical events like accidents and crimes, often accompanied by voice-overs from participants in the event.

- virtual reality (VR) technologies that allow observers to experience a re-creation of an event as if they were present when it occurred. Virtual reality environments allow judges and jurors to immerse themselves in an artificially created world such as a crime scene, operating room, factory, or accident site to gauge for themselves what could be seen from different points of view and what likely happened given the circumstances (see Box 8.6).

Each of these high-tech methods raises interesting and complex questions that psychologists have begun to address. What effect does remote viewing have on a judge or juror's ability to determine whether a witness is credible and sincere? How does a witness's mask-wearing, as occurred during the pandemic, affect these assessments? Are nuances of body language and verbal expression adequately captured in videoconferencing, or are they missed? Does the person testifying at a remote site—a setting that lacks the trappings and formality of a courtroom—feel less obligated to show respect and tell the truth? Are jurors less focused and disciplined in online trials and especially when the quality of their audio or video is low? (In one of the nation's first online trials—conducted in 2020 over a speeding ticket in Texas—the jury appeared to treat the proceedings rather informally, with one juror's kitten pawing at a window curtain behind her and another displaying a photo of a Texas longhorn as his backdrop.)

Answers to these questions are beginning to emerge and they suggest that, among other things, defendants may be disadvantaged by videoconferencing. It results in less favorable outcomes for defendants in bail hearings, perhaps because it tends to be brief (Diamond et al., 2010; describing videoconferencing as a "cattle call" approach to justice, p. 885). Defense attorneys report that remote conferencing reduces their ability to develop meaningful relationships and mutual trust with their clients (Daftary-Kapur et al., 2021).

Box 8.6

The Case of U.S. Army Staff Sergeant Terrence Dillon in Virtual Reality

To treat his high cholesterol levels, U.S. Army Staff Sergeant Terrence Dillon underwent a surgical procedure in February 2002, in which doctors implanted a "new life stent." The stent was designed to cleanse blood of cholesterol and to dissolve cholesterol-forming plaque blocking the arteries. But for Dillon, the stent worked too well, loosening large amounts of plaque that clogged his circulatory system and causing a stroke. Dillon died in March, 2002. Shortly thereafter, the stent's manufacturer, NewLife MedTech, was criminally indicted for manslaughter (Horrigan, 2002).

In truth, none of this actually happened. But these facts served as the basis for a simulated trial, one feature of a legal technology program dubbed "Courtroom 21 Project" by the National Center for State Courts. The project provides technology information to lawyers and judges.

During the "trial," the defense argued that NewLife MedTech was not at fault and that blame lay with the surgeon who allegedly placed the stent in the wrong part of the artery. To bolster that argument, the defense offered the testimony of a nurse who donned a virtual reality headset and specialized goggles, giving him a three-dimensional view of the operating room and allowing him to describe the stent's placement. The prosecution countered by arguing that because the nurse's view of the surgery was obstructed, he was unable to see where the stent had been implanted. Because virtual environment technology allowed jurors themselves to watch a reenactment of the surgery on laptops, they could decide for themselves what the nurse was able to observe. Images were also projected to wide-screen monitors in the courtroom, allowing the judge, lawyers, trial-watchers, and even observers outside the courtroom to view the virtual operation and reach their own conclusions. Whether NewLife MedTech was convicted is largely irrelevant; the noteworthy fact is that the "trial" introduced many people to the courtroom of the future.

Critical Thought Question

Why might evidence presented via virtual environment technology be more persuasive to decision makers than evidence presented verbally or even visually?

In a study that involved virtual court proceedings, people who heard witness testimony in low-quality audio, relative to those with high-quality audio, had poorer memory for important facts and attributed less weight to this testimony in their guilt judgments (Bild et al., 2021). Remote video technologies also result in more deportations in immigration cases than in-person hearings because detained persons on video are less engaged in the adversarial process (Eagly, 2015).

There may also be advantages to virtual court proceedings, however. Prospective jurors questioned in the familiar environment of their homes, where the formality and social pressures of a courtroom are less salient, seem to respond more honestly during voir dire (Gates et al., 2021). Similarly, attorneys can glean different—and perhaps better—information to assess prospective jurors' ability to be impartial by seeing them in their home settings (Gordon, 2022).

Yet, other questions remain. Do computer animations, simulations, and virtual reality reenactments make difficult or technical concepts easier to visualize and, hence, to understand? Might they also serve to cement one version of a contested event in observers' minds, making it harder to construe alternative explanations? In other words, might observers assume that animations, simulations, and virtual realities represent true and uncontroversial facts, rather than just one party's theory of the case?

Lawyers and judges should be especially interested in the answers to these questions because according to the Federal Rules of Evidence (2009), evidence may not be introduced into a trial if its **probative value** (relevance to legal proof) is outweighed by any prejudicial effects on the opposing party or if it misleads or confuses the jury. Thus, it is imperative that judges have good information about the effects of high-tech evidence presentations on legal judgments.

Empirical research can now provide some relevant information. One study examined the effects of visual presentations on jurors' verdicts in a case involving statistical evidence (Park & Feigenson, 2013). In a simulated trial in which Black employees had sued their employer, a railroad company, for racial discrimination, mock jurors saw different versions of the plaintiffs' and defendant's opening statements. Researchers varied whether attorneys' spoken statements were accompanied by visual presentations that illustrated the statistical evidence.

The results of these variations on liability determinations were most pronounced when one party used a visual presentation and the other party did not. When the plaintiffs included a visual presentation and the defendant did not, jurors deemed the defendant most responsible. Apparently, even a relatively simple visual presentation by the plaintiffs helped participants understand the statistical evidence that supported their racial discrimination claim. But that pattern was reversed when only the defendant included a visual presentation. Here, jurors deemed the defendant least responsible. Presumably, more extensive or dramatic visual displays would have an even greater impact.

Why do visual displays persuade people in ways that words cannot? Basic psychological theorizing about the **vividness effect** suggests that information has a greater impact on judgments and decisions when it is vivid and attention grabbing than when it is pallid and bland. In the racial discrimination study we just described, recall of each party's evidence improved when that party presented visual displays, suggesting that information presented in a highly imaginable way is more memorable than simple verbal descriptions of the same material. By itself, vivid information is not necessarily prejudicial in a courtroom, but it rises to that level when the likelihood of prejudice exceeds the objective probative value of the evidence (Young, 2014).

Virtual reality environments have piqued psychologists' interests in the notion of **presence**, or the degree to which a user or observer has the impression of actually "being in another world" and present in the virtual environment. Because complete immersion of the senses—a sense of presence—is persuasive in ways that two-dimensional computer animations are not (Young, 2014), virtual environments also raise questions about whether observers will give this evidence more weight than it deserves; in short, whether its prejudicial effects outweigh its probative value.

Another concern about the use of virtual environments in court is that people who witness them may be so swept up in the experience and persuaded by the lifelike nature of these scenes that they have difficulty imagining or visualizing a different point of view. This notion, termed **experiential inflammatory bias**, suggests that virtual environment demonstrations may be prejudicial to the side that did not introduce them, and that both sides should have the opportunity to manipulate and alter any virtual environment introduced into evidence (Bailenson et al., 2006).

A 2021 study that investigated the use of VR technology in a simulated jury trial (Reichherzer et al., 2021) suggested an upside to this technology. Researchers varied whether the crime scene in a hit-and-run homicide case was depicted via VR or still images and found that VR led to more consistent decisions; that is, participants who viewed VR were more likely to agree on a verdict, perhaps because they were more likely than jurors who saw still images to interpret the evidence in a uniform manner.

Although virtual environment technology is not yet routinely used in actual trials, that day may arrive soon. Indeed, proponents believe that the technology is already mature enough to warrant its use in court: "If a picture is worth a thousand words, then a … virtual reality simulation should be worth at least ten thousand" (Bailenson et al., 2006, p. 265). The day has already arrived for body- and dash-cam recordings, animations, simulations, remote videoconferencing, and other forms of digitally presented evidence. To what extent do they alter the way that trials are conducted? Psychologists, judges, and lawyers will grapple with this question for some time to come.

Summary

1. **What are the major legal proceedings between arrest and trial in the criminal justice system?** (1) An initial appearance, at which defendants are informed of the charges, of their constitutional rights, and of future proceedings; (2) a preliminary hearing, in which the judge determines whether there is enough evidence to hold the defendant for processing by the grand jury; (3) action by the grand jury, which decides whether sufficient evidence exists for the defendant to be tried; (4) an arraignment, involving a formal statement of charges and an initial plea by the defendant to these charges; (5) a process of discovery, requiring that the prosecutor reveal to the defense certain evidence; and (6) pretrial motions, which are attempts by both sides to win favorable ground rules for the subsequent trial.

2. **What is bail, and what factors influence the amount of bail set?** Bail is the provision, by a defendant, of money or other assets that are forfeited if the defendant fails to appear at trial. In determining whether to release a defendant prior to trial, the judge should consider the risk that the defendant will not show up for his or her trial. Judges also consider the seriousness of the offense and the defendant's prior record as well as the defendant's race and gender.

3. **Why do defendants and prosecutors agree to plea bargain?** Plea bargaining is an excellent example of the dilemma between truth and conflict resolution as goals of our legal system. The vast majority of criminal cases conclude between arrest and trial with the defendant pleading guilty to some (often reduced) charges. Plea bargaining benefits both defendants and prosecutors. Defendants who plead guilty often receive reductions in the charges or in their sentences; prosecutors secure a "conviction" without expending their time at trial.

4. **What are settlement negotiations, and why are most civil lawsuits resolved through settlement rather than trial?** Settlement negotiations are private discussions held between the attorneys representing disputing parties in a civil lawsuit. The objective of the negotiations is to resolve the dispute in a manner agreeable to both sides. Settlement negotiations are often preferable to trials because (1) a negotiated compromise is more appealing to most litigants than the uncertainty of a jury trial, and (2) judges have large caseloads (or dockets) and therefore prefer that participants in civil disputes resolve their differences themselves without using the considerable resources necessary to a trial.

5. **What is the purpose of a trial?** Every trial presents two contrasting views of the truth. Although at first glance, the purpose of a trial seems to be to determine truth, conflict resolution may be an equally valid purpose. This debate is exemplified by three contrasting images of a trial: (1) as a search for the truth, (2) as a test of credibility, and (3) as a conflict-resolving ritual.

6. **What are the steps involved in a trial?** Pretrial procedures include discovery, or the process of obtaining information about the case held by the other side. Once the jury is selected, the following sequence of steps unfolds in the trial itself:

   a. Opening statements by attorneys for the two sides (prosecution or plaintiff goes first)

   b. Direct examination, cross-examination, and redirect and recross of witnesses, with prosecution witnesses first, then defense witnesses

   c. Presentation of rebuttal witnesses and evidence

   d. Closing statements, or summations, by the two sides, usually in the order of prosecution, then defense, then prosecution again

   e. Judge's instructions to the jury (in some jurisdictions, these come before the closing statements)

   f. Jury deliberations and announcement of a verdict

   g. If the verdict is guilty, determination of the punishment and sometimes, appellate proceedings.

7. **How has the introduction of emerging technologies changed the way that trials are conducted?** Over time and especially during the coronavirus pandemic, the emergence of more sophisticated technologies into the legal system has begun to change the look of courtroom trials and appeals. As judges, lawyers, and jurors have become more tech-savvy, documentation and presentation methods of the past are being replaced by newer technologies such as computer animations and simulations, videoconferencing, virtual reality, electronic and digital presentations of evidence, and even online trials. These high-tech methods have raised a number of interesting and complex psychological questions regarding the influence and effectiveness of technology in the courtroom.

Key Terms

anchoring

arraignment

change of venue

charge bargaining

closing argument

discovery

exculpatory

experiential inflammatory
    bias

extralegal factors

focal concerns perspective

framing effects

grand jury

heuristics

impeachment

indictments

initial appearance

legal factors

matching heuristic

motion in *limine*

opening statements

overconfidence bias

perjury

plea bargains

preliminary hearing

preponderance of evidence

presence

preventive detention

probative value

rebuttal evidence

recross

redirect questioning

reservation price

self-serving bias

sentence bargaining

settlement negotiation

vividness effect

Chapter 9

Alternatives to Traditional Criminal Prosecution and Civil Litigation

Orienting Questions

1. What is alternative dispute resolution (ADR)? What are some types of ADR?

2. What is the Sequential Intercept Model?

3. What are the major stages (or intercepts) for community-based alternatives to standard prosecution?

4. What are the similarities and differences between community court and other kinds of problem-solving courts?

The previous chapter described the components of our legal system that have been in place for centuries. Valuing precedent as it does, the law is slow to change, but the last three decades have witnessed various innovations that are important and useful. These will be discussed in the present chapter. The first major area—alternative dispute resolution—has been applied in both criminal and civil contexts. The second major area of discussion is community alternatives to standard criminal prosecution. Our discussion of this area is framed within the Sequential Intercept Model, which identifies different points at which certain groups of individuals can be diverted from standard prosecution into an approach that is more rehabilitation oriented. The discussion will include relevant research findings, which are very important in considering the effectiveness of interventions at these different stages.

Alternative Dispute Resolution

In contemporary times, you might easily get the impression that most lawsuits are resolved by a jury trial. In fact, most cases are resolved through negotiation or by alternative dispute resolution (ADR), and relatively few cases are settled in trials. This trend toward fewer jury trials, both civil and criminal, has been described as the "disappearing jury trial" (Diamond & Salerno, 2020). This decrease in jury trials may be considered in the larger context of a diminishing number of trials of any kind: bench (judge only) or jury. In 1962, 11.5% of federal civil cases were decided in a trial, compared with 6.1% in 1982, 1.8% in 2002, and only 1.2% in 2009 (Qualters, 2010). In 2016, the figure dropped to 0.7%. On the criminal side, trials also decreased, though not as sharply. In 1962, 15.4% of criminal cases went to trial; in 2002 only 4.7% involved a trial (Galanter, 2004). These trends continued into the second decade of the twenty-first century (Galanter & Frozena, 2014), with another review citing a decrease of more than 60% in federal civil jury trials between 1990 (n = 4,765) and 2016 (n = 1,758) and a comparable decrease of 63% in federal criminal jury trials between 1990 (n = 5,061) and 2016 (n = 1,889) (Smith & MacQueen, 2017).

These declines have been attributed to different influences. These include the perceived cost of litigation—the "transaction costs," in economists' language. Lawyers' fees to prepare for and try a case, as well as the fees paid to expert witnesses, often make a trial economically unfeasible. In addition, federal courts pressure litigants to settle or to plead guilty. The federal sentencing guidelines give criminal defendants an incentive to plead guilty because judges can decrease the length of a sentence considering "acceptance of responsibility" (which normally requires a guilty plea) (Galanter, 2004). The increased reliance on summary judgments, the perceived impact of tort reforms, and more stringent requirements for claims for relief have all been cited in civil contexts (Diamond & Shapiro, 2020). Finally, federal trials have decreased because it has been some time since Congress passed sweeping legislation that creates liability for certain actions and that brings lawsuits into the courts to determine the boundaries around that liability. Legislation such as the Americans with Disabilities Act of 1990 is an example (Qualters, 2010).

In civil cases, federal judges are required to attempt to resolve disputes through ADR, and in both state and federal courts, judges can require litigants to try to settle their cases without going to trial. Increasingly, American courts assume that cases will be settled rather than tried, to the point where a trial is viewed "as a failure of the system" (Sanborn, 2002, p. 25). Edmund Ludwig, a federal judge with over 30 years of experience, describes it this way:

> Litigation represents a breakdown in communication, which consists in the civil area of the inability of the parties to work out a problem for themselves and in the criminal area, of ineffectively inculcating society's rules and the consequences for violating them. Trials are the method we have ultimately used to deal with those breakdowns. However, the goal of our system is not to try cases. Rather, it is to achieve a fair, just, economical, and expeditious result by trial or otherwise (Ludwig, 2002, p. 217).

Many cases are settled by **negotiation**, without the assistance of a third party. Negotiation might be formal, as when management and union representatives negotiate a labor contract, or informal, as when attorneys have a series of discussions to settle a personal injury claim. Another informal mechanism involves collaborative divorce, in which lawyers and psychologists work with a divorcing couple to finalize all issues without going to court. Typically, there is a heightened sense of trust, openness, and disclosure in collaborative divorce (Degoldi, 2008). We describe one example in Box 9.1.

As in trials, procedural justice considerations are important in successful negotiations. People care about both the outcome of negotiations and the fairness of the process. In a study in which law students role-played attorneys in a simulated negotiation about a contract dispute, participants thought negotiations were fair when they believed that they had been listened to and treated with courtesy—and when they perceived the other party as trustworthy (Hollander-Blumoff & Tyler, 2008).

Arbitration

One form of ADR, binding **arbitration**, bears the closest resemblance to a trial. When the parties agree to binding arbitration, they agree to accept the decision of an arbitrator. Salary arbitration in major league baseball is a good example. The contract between the owners and the players' union provides that players' salary disputes be settled by binding arbitration, and that the arbitrator must accept either the owner's offer or the union's offer but cannot split the difference. The parties have an incentive to make an offer as close as possible to the player's "value" (their estimate of the arbitrator's valuation of the player's worth). Although many cases require binding arbitration, other cases are resolved by

Box 9.1

The Case of Sarah Smith, David Boyle, and Their Swift Collaborative Divorce

Whereas a full-scale divorce litigated in a courtroom can cost more than $75,000 and a negotiated divorce involving adversarial lawyers can total more than $25,000, Sarah Smith and David Boyle spent roughly $5,000 for their collaborative divorce. Smith and Boyle, who live in neighboring suburbs of Boston, were mainly concerned about the welfare of their children, ages 5 and 9 at the time. Together with their lawyers, Smith and Boyle worked out an arrangement by which the children spend time with each of them.

Lawyers are increasingly likely to embrace collaborative divorce. As of 2007, more than 20,000 had received training in collaborative law, which requires them to pledge to work together with their clients and other professionals to devise outcomes that are beneficial to all parties.

Children of a divorcing couple reap a secondary benefit from collaborative divorce. Psychologists have shown that an important factor in emotional well-being in children is the nature of the parents' post-divorce relationship (Baxter et al., 2011). The extent of court involvement during the divorce (little, moderate or high levels of litigation) is associated with children's coping ability: the higher the level of court involvement, the less successful the coping ability (Bing et al., 2009).

Critical Thought Question

What factors explain the increasing popularity of collaborative divorce as compared to traditional, adversarial methods of divorcing?

---

nonbinding arbitration. If one of the parties is dissatisfied with the arbitrator's decision, that person may ask that the case be tried before a judge or jury.

Arbitration, whether binding or nonbinding, uses trial-like procedures. The parties present evidence and argue the case, and the arbitrator makes a decision. Initially promoted as a way to avoid the contentiousness and expense of a trial, arbitration was subsequently criticized for being overly formal and time consuming (Stipanowich, 2010). Other methods for resolving disputes, such as mediation (which we discuss later), are more streamlined.

Summary Jury Trial

The **summary jury trial** is an interesting variation on arbitration. The concept was created by Federal District Court Judge Thomas Lambros in the early 1980s following his difficulty resolving two personal injury cases using other forms of ADR. The parties in these cases refused to settle, each assuming a more favorable verdict would result from a jury trial. Judge Lambros reasoned that chances for settlement would increase if the parties had a sense of what a jury would do. He instituted an abbreviated and expedited form of a jury trial that he suspected would be especially helpful in resolving relatively simple, lower-value cases.

A summary jury trial is much like a conventional jury trial, though shorter. A jury is empanelled, and the lawyers tell the jurors what the witnesses would say if they were present. The lawyers argue the case and try to answer the jurors' questions about the facts. The judge tells the jury what the law is and tries to answer jurors' questions about the law. The jurors then deliberate and decide the case. In the original conception of a summary jury trial, the "verdict" did not bind the parties, it was merely advisory. Subsequently, verdicts became binding and enforceable. Regardless of

these variations, the intent is the same: the process educates the lawyers and clients on how a conventional jury might view the facts and the law. Once educated, the lawyers and their clients are more amenable to settling the case (National Center for State Courts, 2012).

The *American Bar Journal* has reported favorable comments from lawyers and judges who had used this form of ADR (McDonough, 2004). Commenting on the summary jury trial, federal judge William Bertelsman said,

> I believe that substantial amounts of time can be saved by using summary jury trial in a few select cases. Also … the summary jury trial gives the parties a taste of the courtroom and satisfies their psychological need for a confrontation with each other. Any judge or attorney can tell you that emotional issues play a large part in some cases. When emotions are high, whether between attorneys or parties, cases may not settle even when a cost-benefit analysis says they should. A summary jury trial can provide a therapeutic release of this emotion at the expenditure of three days of the court's time instead of three weeks (McKay v. Ashland Oil Inc., 1988, p. 49).

In the period leading up to 2000, little was being written about summary jury trials and there was apparently diminishing interest in using them. Since 2000, however, there seems to be renewed interest in this form of dispute resolution, influenced particularly by growing constraints on time and costs of trials (Murphy et al., 2021).

Mediation

Mediation, another form of ADR, involves a neutral person (the mediator) who works with the litigants and their lawyers to achieve a settlement of the controversy. The mediator does not have authority, as an arbitrator does, to decide the controversy. Rather, the mediator acts as a facilitator. Mediation often involves *shuttle diplomacy*, a term that could describe former Secretary of State John Kerry. Much as Kerry would "shuttle" between the two sides in international diplomacy, the mediator goes back and forth between the parties, meeting first with one side, then with the other, trying to broker an agreement between the two.

One thinks of lawyers as eager to do battle—to slay their opponents with rhetorical swords. Increasingly, though, disputants prefer procedures in which a neutral third party helps them to craft a resolution of their own. In short, many prefer mediation (Shestowsky, 2014). Why? People are **risk averse**; they work to avoid taking risks. They prefer that controversies be settled *by them* rather than decided *for them*. A mediator can assist in facilitating a resolution, and people prefer the certainty of a settlement over the uncertainty of arbitration or trial.

Mediation also has a role in divorce proceedings. An alternative to collaborative divorce (in which both parties employ their own lawyers, who agree to cooperate), a mediated divorce involves a third party who helps the couple to dissolve their marriage. Psychologists have assessed whether a mediated divorce leads to more desirable outcomes than litigation. One remarkable study assessed parent–child contact and co-parenting in families whose custody disputes had been resolved 12 years earlier by either mediation or litigation (Emery et al., 2001). Families who mediated custody showed more cooperation and flexibility than families who litigated. Nonresidential parents who mediated had more contact with their children and were more intimately involved in parenting, and fathers who mediated were much more satisfied with their custody arrangements. Compared to litigated divorces, mediation apparently encourages parents to comply with divorce agreements, remained involved in their children's lives, and renegotiate relationships in a more adaptive way.

Building on the findings from this study, other investigators (Ballard et al., 2013) conducted a randomized

controlled trial involving "mediation as usual" in one condition and two variations of mediation: "child focused" (parents were presented with general information about children and divorce) and "child inclusive" (children were interviewed and parents provided with feedback about their specific case). All three conditions resulted on comparable rates of agreement, but both the child-focused and child-inclusive conditions had significantly better outcomes as measured by parents reporting learning something useful, and mediators preferring that version as compared with mediation as usual.

Beliefs about Alternative Dispute Resolution

What form of ADR do people tend to favor? The answer to this question is important because ADR procedures will be accepted and used when they are respected and considered legitimate. One study investigated the preferences for different dispute resolution features among people involved in actual disputes. They indicated their preferences for a certain process and set of rules. The most consistent finding was that participants favored options that offered them control (e.g., a neutral third-party helping disputants to arrive at *their own* resolutions, and processes that allow disputants to control *their own* presentation of evidence) (Shestowsky, 2014).

Should courts force litigants to try ADR before setting a case for trial? The reports from courts that require ADR are mixed. Some attorneys like the process, believing that both the process and the outcomes are fair (Wissler & Dauber, 2007). But other attorneys doubt that arbitration saves time or money—and express concerns about whether arbitrators have adequate knowledge of the issues (Wissler & Dauber, 2007). Another consideration is that litigants have a Constitutional right to trial by judge or jury. Judges are tasked with protecting this right, and mandating ADR undermines it. There has been renewed debate about the prospect of making ADR mandatory in the United States given the change in that direction occurring elsewhere (e.g., the United Kingdom; review https://www.lexisnexis.com /uk/lexispsl/personalinjury/document/393747/55KB-BXG1 -F18B-704H-00000-00/ADR_and_dispute_resolution _clauses_overview). For the present, ADR in the United States remains a useful tool, but whether it is mandatory varies by jurisdiction.

Community Alternatives to Standard Prosecution

We now move from ADR, which is practiced in both civil and criminal law, to community alternatives to standard prosecution (criminal law only). Have you ever wondered whether there was a more effective way (different from conviction and incarceration) for our society to respond to certain kinds of offenders? Consider those found guilty of drug offenses. Drug misuse was once considered an indication of poor motivation and weak character; now it is treated as a disease. So what about the individual who continues

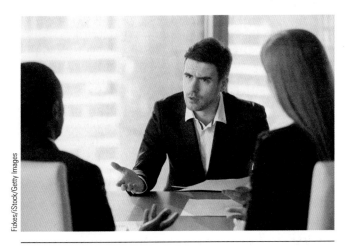

Mediators work with litigants to settle legal cases.

Fizkes/iStock/Getty Images

to break the law by stealing in order to buy substances that are illegal, and then behaving under their influence? If such individuals were successfully treated for drug misuse and monitored to ensure that they did not continue to behave illegally, that would seem preferable to incarceration. This is the kind of individual who is well-suited for a drug court—a specialized kind of **problem-solving court**, developed to rehabilitate and monitor individuals in the community rather than incarcerate them. Problem-solving courts are discussed in this section.

There has been increasing attention over the last two decades to community-based alternatives to conviction and imprisonment for certain individuals. Such community-based alternatives have developed because they are more humane, less expensive, and make our society safer (or at least do not increase the risk of crime). Often these individuals are members of a certain subgroup whose experience or behavioral health symptoms might account for a number of minor offenses committed by members of this group. For example, individuals with severe mental illness—schizophrenia, bipolar disorder, major depressive disorder, and other psychotic disorders—might be arrested for domestic disturbances, encounters with police, or problematic interactions with other citizens when the symptoms of such disorders are active. Individuals with serious drug problems may become involved in offenses such as theft, prostitution, and public intoxication for reasons related directly to the need to buy drugs and the consequences of taking them. Military veterans could be charged with traffic violations, drug or weapon possession, or problematic interactions with police, influenced in part by posttraumatic stress disorder or traumatic brain injury. Each of these examples recognizes that some criminal behavior involves acting upon symptoms that could be contained with targeted treatment and rehabilitation.

This is the basic philosophy underlying the development of community alternatives to standard criminal arrest, prosecution, and incarceration. Three major justifications have been offered for the development and expansion of such community alternatives. The first is humanitarian. In the words of the U.S. Supreme Court, the Eighth Amendment (which states that "cruel and unusual punishments" may not be inflicted) must draw its meaning from the "evolving standards of decency" that characterize a "maturing society" (*Trop v. Dulles*, 1958). But *Trop v. Dulles* was a death penalty case. What about criminal offenses that are much less serious? When behavioral health disorders are associated with minor offending, this could be handled through standard criminal justice processing—but might also be addressed in a more humane and rehabilitative fashion through alternative approaches. Some offenders with severe mental illness are similar to justice-involved individuals without severe mental illness in most of their rehabilitation needs (Skeem & Eno Louden, 2006). But those whose crimes involve behavior that simply reflects their symptoms (e.g., an acutely psychotic individual who is confused and frightened, responds badly to an encounter with police, and is charged

with resisting arrest) may be very good candidates for lower-intensity, briefer, community-based interventions—particularly when those individuals present a low risk for criminal offending, and this risk is reduced even further by treating the disorder.

The second justification for community-based alternatives to standard prosecution is cost. It is much less expensive to monitor and treat an offender in the community than it is to incarcerate that individual. State-level spending on prison incarceration ranges from around $60 million to over $8 billion annually, a very substantial part of any state budget, with most states averaging about $25,000–$30,000 per incarcerated individual, according to 2021 information from the Vera Institute (https://interrogatingjustice .org/prisons/annual-prison-costs-budgets/). Individuals who are provided with treatment and monitoring services in the community but do not need housing or board—and may be able to continue working—cost much less to rehabilitate.

The third justification involves the kind of specialized treatment services that can be provided in the community, as contrasted with services that can be delivered in a prison or jail. Correctional facilities house inmates who, as a group, have wide-ranging rehabilitation needs. More inmates need job training, housing assistance, or substance misuse rehabilitation, for example, than require the combination of medication, psychosocial skills intervention, co-occurring disorder treatment, and recovery focus that is optimal in working with inmates with severe mental illness. In addition, correctional facilities must highly prioritize security and rule compliance, which reduces the resources available for treatment and rehabilitation. When populations are more homogeneous (e.g., as in mental health or drug treatment settings), and security concerns are fewer, then specialized and intensive treatment is more feasible.

Some of these trends have been affected by the COVID-19 pandemic, particularly between 2020 and 2021. In a series of panels including representatives from law enforcement, courts, corrections, the community, and victim services, participants in the Priority Criminal Justice Needs Initiative (managed by the Rand Corporation in partnership with the National Institute of Justice) identified two major changes that are promising. These were termed a "lighter touch" justice system and a shift to virtual models (Jackson et al., 2021). The former refers to a greater rehabilitative and less punitive focus, while the latter anticipates less reliance on in-person conduct of proceedings and decision-making. While it remains to be determined whether both will continue after the pandemic has receded, we expect they will—as both are consistent with pre-COVID trends.

Community-Based Alternatives and the Sequential Intercept Model

One of the useful models describing community-based alternatives is the **Sequential Intercept Model** (SIM) (Munetz & Griffin, 2006). It identifies five stages of the overall criminal justice process at which standard prosecution and incarceration could be interrupted and a community treatment alternative substituted. These stages are: (1) law enforcement and emergency services; (2) post-arrest: initial detention/initial hearing and pre-trial services; (3) post-initial hearings: jail/prison, courts, forensic evaluations, and commitments; (4) re-entry from jails, prisons, and forensic hospitalization; and (5) community corrections (including parole) and community support. A review of the evidence for intervention effectiveness at each of these intercepts has been published (Heilbrun et al., 2012), as has a book describing its applications (Griffin et al., 2015). A sixth intercept—Intercept 0, Community Services—has also been described (e.g., https://www.samhsa.gov/criminal-juvenile-justice/sim-overview). Since this section focuses on community-based alternatives prior to incarceration, we will consider only the first four intercepts (0–3) in this discussion.

Community Services (Intercept 0). This addition to the SIM emphasizes the quality and impact of community-based services that are delivered without contact with any aspect of the justice system. For example, an individual with severe mental illness living at home with their aging parent and inclined to become angry and argumentative when no longer taking prescribed medication is at risk for contact with first responders (as discussed in the next Intercept). But suppose the community mental health center providing that individual with outpatient treatment, including psychotropic medication, began a skills-based group focusing on improving communication with prescribing physicians and attempting to improve the consistency of taking prescribed medication—with improved problem-solving associated with medication side-effects rather than simply stopping the medication? This intercept focuses generally on diverting individuals into local crisis care and other relevant behavioral health services *without* involving 911, police, or other first responders. It is an informal way of linking those in need to services without resorting to possible arrest or criminal charges. Because it does not require interactions between justice personnel, mental health personnel, and individuals in need of services, this intercept is fundamentally different from the other five. Its presence underscores the important point that appropriate and indicated behavioral health services can promote recovery and lessen the likelihood of a crisis that will lead to any possible justice system involvement—which is described in the remaining intercepts.

Law Enforcement and Emergency Services (Intercept 1). Encounters between police or other "first responders" and individuals with behavioral health disorders is the first step in a process that can result in arrest, criminal charges, conviction, and incarceration. Annual police encounters with citizens with mental health problems have been estimated through a review of 21 studies and nearly 330,000 individuals, finding that (1) one in four people with mental disorders have been arrested; (2) one in ten individuals with mental disorders have experienced police encounters;

and (3) one in one hundred police dispatches and encounters involve people with mental disorders (Livingston, 2016). These findings supplement the estimate that there are more than 300 such police encounters per 100,000 population across jurisdictions, with this rate increasing annually (Durbin et al., 2010). In some such encounters, arrest is unnecessary. What if police officers received specialized training in recognizing behavioral health symptoms and interacting with such individuals in a way that did not result in the escalation of conflict—but instead yielded the opportunity for needed treatment? This is the goal of **specialized police responding**. In particular, the approach known as **Crisis Intervention Team** (CIT) (Compton et al., 2008) provides police and other first responders (e.g., fire fighters, emergency medical personnel) with enhanced knowledge and skills for use when they encounter individuals who may be experiencing a behavioral health crisis. (Discussed also in Chapter 4.) CIT is intended to increase the number of treatment-oriented dispositions and decrease the number of minor arrests in such cases, and to reduce the number of incidents in which the individuals or the police officers are harmed. For instance, an individual with bipolar disorder, off medication and experiencing a manic episode, might be taken by CIT-trained police to the local psychiatric emergency room rather than arrested for disturbing the peace and battery on an officer. We share a representative story in Box 9.2, provided by a CIT-trained officer in Florida, describing the difference that such CIT training can make in correctional facilities as well as in the community.

What is the evidence that CIT is effective in diverting such individuals, resulting in more treatment dispositions and fewer arrests? Research on this topic has been summarized (Heilbrun et al., 2012) on several points related to CIT: characteristics and knowledge of CIT-trained officers; characteristics of diverted individuals; and outcomes such as the number of diverted individuals, services delivered to

Police Crisis Intervention Teams are specially trained to help people in the midst of emotional crisis or psychiatric distress. These officers are part of a mobile CIT run jointly by a hospital and local police department.

Box 9.2

CIT for Police, First Responders and Correctional Officers

Please allow me to share this story with you. It is a little long, so be patient. The other day a 65-year-old transient female was arrested on two out-of-county misdemeanor warrants. It seems the woman was involved in a fight earlier in the day, which resulted in numerous cuts, bruises, and abrasions. Upon her arrest, she was initially transported to (a local medical facility) for medical clearance prior to being transported to the county jail. Unable to accurately detail the events leading to her arrest, she was subsequently treated and cleared from the hospital, then sent to directly to the county jail.

Upon arrival, the woman, who is elderly and petite in stature, now bruised and battered and obviously in some form of physical distress, is placed in a female dorm along with other offenders of various classifications. It always amazes me ... that most female offenders will come to the aid of the elderly and help them along with their personal needs. They help them shower, tend to personal needs, and even assist in changing their sheets and clothing. There seems to be an inmate code with the elderly and disabled. Well, as fate would have it, the woman begins to require additional needs which cannot be met in a county jail and this concern is finally brought to the attention of the supervisor by an attentive block officer.

Now here is where it starts to come together. The supervisor in this matter is CIT-trained and just knows in the pit of his stomach that something is wrong and just doesn't make sense. He immediately realizes that the woman needs supplementary care, medical attention, and proactive intervention. He instructs the officers to bring the female to booking, where she can be isolated from the general population. He then notifies the on-duty medic and initiates a 15-minute watch on her so she can be observed on a more regular basis. He instructs the female officers, with the assistance of some female inmates, to change her linen and clothing, which is soiled—and make her comfortable until the medic arrives. The woman appears to be resting comfortably on her bunk, but shortly after the supervisor notices she is extending her arm above her body as if to motion for assistance. The supervisor approaches the cell and realizes something is not right; he gets that gut feeling again. Her breath appears labored and she just had a look on her face that she was in need of some assistance, but was unable to ask. He summoned a female officer for additional aid and again notified the

on-duty medic. Weak, frail, and pathetic, she is unable to properly communicate her concerns.

While ... the medical responders (are treating her, they learn) that the woman is asthmatic, experiences emphysema, requires immediate oxygen, and was in pulmonary distress. The woman was immediately sent to the hospital. After returning, one of the female deputies assigned to the woman ... noticed that when she was assisting the woman with her change of clothing...(there) appeared to be some bruising on and about the woman's groin area. The Deputy then stated that "I think this woman was a victim of a sexual assault" and went on to say, "I wonder if they (hospital) did a rape kit on her?" After piecing various facts together, the supervisor, a trained CIT member, knew something was wrong. Shortly after, while officers were discussing what had happened, the classification officer mentioned that he had received a phone call from a victim in another matter, who stated something to the effect that the guy that assaulted her also tried to rape an elderly female the same night.

Now here is where it all finally comes together. The supervisor, aware of what might have happened to this woman, immediately contacted the Victim Services Advocate and the CID Detectives Bureau. After explaining the circumstances surrounding this matter, the detectives interviewed the woman in the safety of her hospital room. The victim's advocate immediately (pointed out that the perpetrator in this case) might very well be incarcerated in the very same jail on unrelated charges. Subsequently, the county which issued the charges against the woman rescinded the warrants and she was released and transferred to another hospital for treatment. The woman ultimately had a stroke while in the hospital and is currently being treated for her injuries and current medical condition. Without the intervention of a trained Crisis Intervention Team member, perhaps this end result would have been much different. Doctors stated that the woman was operating with only 1% lung capacity, and if (she had) gone untreated would not have made it through the night. The woman is alive today ... due to the actions of a CIT-trained individual.

Critical Thought Question

How might CIT training, which is increasingly provided to correctional officers as well as police and first responders, have made a difference in this case?

them, and number of arrests following police encounters. CIT-trained police officers reported better preparation for handling interactions with those experiencing a behavioral health crisis (Borum et al., 1998), were more likely to help

individuals obtain mental health services (Compton et al., 2008), and were less likely to use physical force (Compton et al., 2008; Skeem & Bibeau, 2008). Jail days were fewer for such individuals, and costs were shifted from criminal justice to treatment sources; diverted participants were also more likely to utilize mental health treatment (comply with medication, use hospital stay and emergency room visits, participate in counseling) and less likely to receive residential treatment for substance misuse (Steadman & Naples, 2005). Following such diversions, those who were diverted did not differ from others in their number of arrests over the next year (Teller et al., 2006; Watson et al., 2010). A review of the evidence in this area (Rogers et al., 2019) concluded that CIT has favorable officer-level outcomes (e.g., officer satisfaction, self-perceived decreased use of force), and also likely is related to prebooking diversion from jails to mental health facilities. The authors added, however, that there was little evidence that CIT had benefits on outcomes such as reduced arrests, officer or citizen injuries, or use of force.

Post-Arrest: Initial Detention/Initial Hearing and Pre-trial Services (Intercept 2).
Assume an individual has been arrested upon first encounter with police or another first responder. The second intercept identifies the point at which that person is brought to "first appearance" before a judge. This occurs before the individual enters a plea. In some jurisdictions, there is a specialized team that works as part of the court system, identifying defendants who would be appropriate for behavioral health diversion. While some specialized problem-solving courts (e.g., drug court, mental health court, veterans' court, community court) function at this stage, it is more typical to have them take referrals at Intercept 3. Accordingly, Intercept 2 diversion is more likely to send individuals directly to treatment, or assign them to specialized probation.

A number of studies on Intercept 2 have used effectiveness criteria like those employed in studies on Intercept 1. Addressing outcomes for individuals who receive diversion following arrest, investigators have examined services use, mental health, substance use, offending, and quality of life (Broner et al., 2004, 2005). They have also employed criteria such as whether the individual had housing (National GAINS Center, 2002).

Almost all the existing research identifies differences between diverted and non-diverted individuals at this stage. It is not necessarily accurate to conclude that such differences are *attributable* to the diversion; that would require the use of experimental designs (using random assignment to condition) that are virtually impossible to implement in a criminal justice context. (Judges and clinical administrators are understandably reluctant to allow random assignment of defendants to conditions, because an unfortunate outcome such as a serious offense committed by an individual in a no-treatment control group is hard to justify after the tragic event.) However, correlational designs, particularly when accompanied by a comparison group, can provide useful information on the strength (although not the causal direction) of the relationship between the diversion variable and the different outcomes. For example, the studies described later in this paragraph using a comparison group typically obtain their groups from (1) individuals who have been diverted, or (2) those in a standard condition such as probation, and consider how these two groups fare on certain relevant outcomes. This is sometimes called a quasi-experimental design, because it does not have the genuine experimental attribute (random assignment to group) that allows the researcher to control all variables except the one of interest—diversion status—and hence draw conclusions about whether diversion causes differences in outcomes.

For this intercept, several investigators reported that diverted individuals had more time in the community (Broner et al., 2005; Hoff et al., 1999; Lamberti et al., 2001; Steadman & Naples, 2005), fewer hospital days in the community (Lamberti et al., 2001), fewer arrests (National GAINS Center, 2002; Shafer et al., 2004), and less homelessness (National GAINS Center, 2002). A national survey of criminal justice diversion programs is available (Center for Health and Justice at TASC, 2013), along with data supporting such initiatives at Intercepts 1, 2, and 3.

Using a naturally occurring experiment in Harris County, Texas, investigators (Mueller-Smith & Schnepel, 2021) found evidence that two different forms of diversion for first-time felony defendants cut reoffending rates in half and increased quarterly employment rates substantially over a 10-year outcome period. The investigators cited evidence strongly suggesting that stigma associated with a felony conviction played an important part in these results, as they could rule out alternatives such as change in incarceration, other adjustments in policy or practice, and differences in criminal processing.

Post-Initial Hearings: Jail/Prison, Courts, Forensic Evaluations and Commitments (Intercept 3).
The third intercept in the Sequential Intercept Model is the most widely recognized of the five. This is the stage at which problem-solving courts (also called specialty courts) such as drug courts, mental health courts, homeless courts, domestic violence courts, and community courts have been developed. There have also been courts developed for other groups, such as veterans and prostitutes, but these problem-solving courts are sufficiently new that there has not been much research investigating how well they work. Specialized problem-solving courts are also discussed later in this book in Chapter 15.

Collecting data across the intercepts of the SIM is important, both in general (to demonstrate the nature and impact of interventions broadly) and in specific cases (often to demonstrate the impact of a change from before an intervention to after). The various data elements that can be used to guide meaningful scientific research *and* specific cases are described in a manual published by the Substance Misuse and Mental Health Services Administration (SAMHSA) (https://store.samhsa.gov/sites/default/files/d7/priv/pep19 -sim-data.pdf). This describes either collecting data on one (or more) intercepts, or tracking individuals' progress through more than one intercept. It includes recommendations to obtain baseline data, perform analyses, continue with ongoing data collection, and track people with mental illness and substance use disorders.

Problem-Solving Courts

Certain offenders are summoned back to court and returned to prison repeatedly. For them, the criminal justice system has become all-too-familiar home (Wiener et al., 2010). Fed up with this model of "revolving-door" justice, states and communities have created problem-solving courts using treatment-oriented principles to address certain specific causes of antisocial behavior (Casey & Rottman, 2005).

The premise of specialty courts is that the legal system should help troubled individuals cope with the chronic problems that brought them into contact with the criminal justice system in the first place. This collaborative, non-adversarial nature of specialty courts, in which judges work side by side with mental health professionals, community agencies, and offenders themselves, focuses more on meeting the ongoing needs of participants than on punishing them.

This approach, in which the law is used as a vehicle to improve people's lives, is called **therapeutic jurisprudence**. Examples include courts specialized to deal with problems involving drugs, mental health, homelessness, and domestic violence, as well as veterans' issues, and courts that treat more than one of these problems (Winick et al., 2010). Regardless of the problem, all specialty courts involve a few common elements, including immediate interventions such as drug or alcohol counseling, frequent court appearances in a non-adversarial context, an interdisciplinary team approach, and a set of clearly defined objectives (DeMatteo et al., 2019).

Working together with mental health providers, attorneys, and probation officers, judges in these courts become social workers and cheerleaders as much as jurists. Rather than impose punishment, they offer opportunities for people to deal with their addictions, anger, and disputes (Hartley, 2008). Those who comply with the judges' orders may have their sentences reduced or dismissed.

Although some aspects of these courts are traditional—for instance, judges wear robes—many characteristics of specialty courts are unconventional. For example, the people who appear in court are often called clients rather than defendants. These "clients" are able to speak directly to the judge, rather than communicating through their attorneys. Judges often have a great deal of information about clients, and may interact with them over a number of years. On occasion, a friendly relationship develops, as described in Box 9.3.

By the end of 2020, the National Drug Court Resource Center (2020) provided the following totals for adult problem-solving courts in the United States: drug (1,753), veterans (476), mental health (469), family treatment (317), DUI (273), hybrid drug/DUI (271), co-occurring disorder (74), reentry (64), opioid (16), and other (16).

Drug Courts. The most common kind of specialty court is drug court, created to deal with offenders whose crimes are related to addiction. Drug courts developed in response to an increase in antidrug law enforcement efforts and stiffer sanctions for drug offenders during the 1980s and 1990s. Drug courts were developed to address the misuse of alcohol and other drugs and criminal activity related to their misuse. Drug courts divert cases from the traditional criminal justice system and link offenders with a drug addiction with treatment programs and extensive supervision. In exchange for successful completion of the program, the court may dismiss the original charge, reduce or set aside a sentence, assign some lesser penalty, or make a combination of these adjustments. The ultimate goal, in addition to improving the lives of individuals with a drug addiction, is to reduce the number of drug offenders in prisons.

How successful are drug courts in reducing drug-related criminal activity? The findings are encouraging, though some drug courts work better than others. A **meta-analysis**—a

Box 9.3

The Case of a "Client" of Justice Matthew D'Emic

An immigrant from Barbados in his early 20s arrived in the New York courtroom of Justice Matthew D'Emic facing a serious charge of arson after starting a fire that damaged a small public housing complex (Eaton & Kaufman, 2005). The man was delusional, believing that he was the son of God; he had been hospitalized nine times in five years. In a traditional courtroom, the case would have been disposed of by a guilty plea or verdict, and the defendant would have been sent to prison. But in the mental health court over which Justice D'Emic presided, something very different happened. The judge decided that the young man could safely return to live with his mother, provided that he continued to take his medications. Later, when the man complained of stomach cramps and began to miss appointments, the judge suggested that he change his medicine. The judge insisted that the man sign up for job training, allowing him to "graduate" from court with only a misdemeanor on his record. Most remarkably, Justice D'Emic gave the client his cell phone number and urged him to call if he got into a jam. The man said he used it just once, to ask the judge for advice about a woman he was considering marrying.

Critical Thought Question

What are the pros and cons of resolving this dispute in a mental health court, rather than through the workings of the traditional criminal justice system?

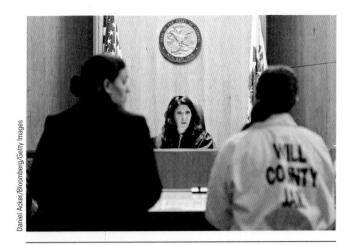

Drug courts, like this one in Illinois, only address crimes related to drug and alcohol abuse.

statistical technique that combines the results of individual studies with similar research hypotheses—of 60 studies that compared a treatment condition to a control condition, and that included at least one measure of criminal behavior as an outcome measure, concluded that drug courts have a statistically significant effect on recidivism. Offenders assigned to drug court had a 45.5% recidivism rate, while the comparison group had a 54.5% recidivism rate (Shaffer, 2011). The most successful programs were those that excluded violent offenders, worked with and treated offenders who had not yet entered a plea, and employed well-qualified and competent staff who ensured that the program was delivered as designed and who interacted positively with participants. This moderate effectiveness of drug courts in reducing criminal recidivism is also supported by other meta-analyses (see, e.g., Marlowe et al., 2016; Mitchell et al., 2012). A large multisite study with nearly 3,000 participants in drug court identified being employed and older age as two factors reducing the risk of subsequent criminal offending (Wilson et al., 2018).

According to Seattle Judge J. Wesley Saint Clair, "Drug courts work, and not because they're fuzzy—let me tell you, I can be a hard man to deal with." One offender to appear in Judge Saint Clair's courtroom was 36-year-old Jenifer Paris, who, after 22 years of heroin and cocaine use and stretches of prostitution and homelessness, was now clean. "You guys are the first people to believe in me … I'm full of gratitude for the opportunity and for you not kicking me out," she said, tearfully. Replied Judge Saint Clair with a hint of a smile, "We're not done yet" (Eckholm, 2008).

Problem-solving courts have particular appeal within communities, as judges often interact with treatment providers and advocacy groups in a way that does not typically occur in traditional courts. Judges like Wesley Saint Clair often play a much more active role, setting aside judicial restraint and impartiality in favor of more direct involvement in the interventions and responses of problem-solving court participants.

Mental Health Courts. The number of individuals hospitalized long term for mental illness has dropped significantly in the past four decades. But **deinstitutionalization**, the long-term trend of closing mental hospitals and transferring care to community-based mental health treatment facilities, has left many mentally ill individuals without services or medication. As a result, the mentally ill have experienced higher rates of homelessness, unemployment, alcohol and drug use, and physical and sexual misuse. They also experience high rates of incarceration: 17% of men and 34% of women in jails suffer from a serious mental illness or post-traumatic stress disorder (Steadman et al., 2009). Unfortunately, most local jails lack treatment resources and are highly stressful environments, especially for people experiencing severe mental illnesses.

According to the **criminalization hypothesis**, a subgroup of mentally ill offenders are arrested for offenses *caused* by their untreated symptoms of mental illness. Mental health courts were developed for offenders dealing with serious mental illness and seek to "decriminalize" this population. By 2020, there were 469 mental health courts in the United States (National Drug Court Resource Center, 2020).

As with the drug court model, the first decision in a mental health court is whether to divert the offender from the regular criminal courts to treatment programs associated with the mental health court. This decision, which usually requires the consent of both the offender and the victim, is made after an evaluation of the offender and by considering the nature of the offense. If the offender is diverted, the mental health team prepares a treatment plan for mental health care and reintegration into society. Close monitoring is essential. Defendants are often assigned to a probation officer who is trained in mental health and who carries a greatly reduced caseload to provide a more intensive level of supervision and expertise. The charges are typically dismissed if the offender follows the treatment plan (DeMatteo et al., 2019).

Evaluations of mental health courts suggest that they have been effective in reducing recidivism (Honegger, 2015). A meta-analysis found a medium effect size for the relationship between mental health court participation and reduced future offending (Sarteschi et al., 2011). This research suggests some favorable impact of mental health courts, although it is limited by considerations such as sampling (White males are overrepresented) and the quasi-experimental designs of most of the studies, limiting the ability to draw conclusions about causality.

Whether mental health courts provide therapeutic value to participants is less clear (Honegger, 2015). For instance, the Sarteschi et al. (2011) meta-analysis could not calculate an effect size for the behavioral health outcomes for participants in mental health court because the eight studies were insufficiently similar. Research on linkage to services for mental health court participants has shown varying outcomes, from no differences in hospitalization rates between mental health court participants and non-diverted offenders

(Luskin, 2013) and no difference in emergency room visits or contact with crisis services (Keator et al., 2013) to greater provision of inpatient and detoxification services to mental health court participants (Keator et al., 2013). Although findings are limited, it appears that mental health courts are also cost effective, reducing the need for services such as psychiatric emergency room visits and other crisis interventions.

There are two broad concerns associated with mental health courts, however. First, participants may feel coerced into participating. In one study involving over 200 participants, investigators found that although most said they had agreed to participate, the majority were unaware that the program was voluntary and did not understand many of the nuances of the program. This led the researchers to question whether diversion to mental health courts is truly voluntary (Redlich et al., 2010).

The second concern involves the selection of participants. Specialty courts, including mental health courts, admit only a fraction of the people who are eligible, and admission decisions typically involve multiple perspectives and parties (e.g., clients, treatment providers, judges, prosecutors, defense attorneys, and victims) (Wolff, et al., 2011). Research suggests that gender and racial bias may influence the way that potential clients are identified, recruited, and eventually selected to participate. Specifically, White males are overrepresented in mental health courts. According to one meta-analysis (Sarteschi et al., 2011), the majority of participants in mental health courts are White males in their mid-30s, whereas Black males continue to be incarcerated at higher rates than either White or Hispanic males, although this gap is narrowing (Pew Research Center, 2020). Mental health service availability is often marked by disparities disadvantaging minority groups (McKnight-Eily et al., 2021).

A related concern is the possibility that the selection process, rather than the interventions provided, accounts for the modest positive outcomes associated with participating in mental health courts. This could happen if only those potential clients who accept their mental health disorder and are amenable to treatment are invited to participate. After evaluating the selection procedures in six demographically diverse mental health courts, Wolff et al. (2011) concluded that client selection might explain findings on the effectiveness of mental health courts.

Homeless Courts. People living on the streets are frequently cited for public nuisance offenses such as public intoxication and loitering; they often fail to appear when summoned to court. Consequently, they are unable to access vital services such as housing, employment opportunities, and public assistance.

Homeless courts were started in southern California in the late 1980s. They are designed to assist individuals by addressing the underlying problems that resulted in their homelessness, and reintegrate them into society. Homeless "court" is typically held in shelters or agencies that serve this population. Rather than being fined or taken into custody, participants are given alternative sentences—including assignment to programs and activities such as employment training, counseling, Alcoholics Anonymous meetings, and volunteer work.

New York City has created a variant on this approach termed community courts (discussed in more detail later in this section) in Times Square and the Red Hook area of Brooklyn (Post, 2004a). Meeting in a refurbished Catholic school, the judges, prosecutors, and defenders in the Red Hook community court regard their goal as improving the quality of life for citizens. They know the people of the community. They also make it a point to know the offenders and to make sure the offenders know them. "The clerk of court has been known to stop her car at street corners and tell defendants the judge has issued a warrant for them and they'd best get over to court" (Carter, 2004, p. 39). The result is a reduction in low-level crime, and decreased recidivism by those under the jurisdiction of this problem-solving court. Some community courts also aim to reduce homelessness by dealing with landlord-tenant problems, and addressing some of the underlying causes of homelessness—mental illness, poor job skills, and language barriers.

Domestic Violence Courts. Historically, legal responses to domestic violence cases have been fragmented, with different court divisions issuing restraining orders, prosecuting perpetrators, and protecting children. Victims have been considered merely "witnesses" and the needs of children have been largely ignored (Casey & Rottman, 2005). As this kind of problem-solving court has matured, however, there have been coordinated efforts to hold perpetrators accountable, enhance victim and child safety, and promote informed judicial decision making. Domestic violence court personnel work with community-based agencies to strengthen the entire community's response to domestic violence (Sack, 2002). Estimates of the number of domestic violence courts in the United States range from 160 (Keilitz, 2004) to 208 (Labriola et al., 2010), to more than 300 (Casey & Rottman, 2005). This discrepancy probably depends on whether the court has at least one specialized unit, process, or service for domestic violence cases—or handles these cases as part of a broader problem-solving court.

Like other specialty courts, domestic violence courts involve judges and staff specially trained in the relevant domain, coordination among community resources, and close monitoring of the perpetrator both before and after case disposition. But domestic violence courts differ from other specialty courts in important respects. They start from the premise that offenders' behavior is learned rather than rooted in a treatable addiction or illness. Therefore, court proceedings are primarily adversarial rather than therapeutic. They often involve both victim and offender attempting to reach agreement on protection orders. The needs of children are considered, and co-occurring child misuse and neglect are addressed.

Although few studies have evaluated the effectiveness of domestic violence courts, including their ability to reduce recidivism (Wiener et al., 2010), victims, perpetrators, advocates, and judges have generally reacted positively. Both victims and perpetrators express satisfaction with the court processes and outcomes. Compared with traditional courts, domestic violence courts process cases faster and have higher rates of guilty pleas (reflecting their greater emphasis on rehabilitation as opposed to an adversarial process). In addition, perpetrators are more likely to comply with court-ordered conditions (Casey & Rottman, 2005).

Community Courts. In contrast to drug courts and mental health courts, each of which is characterized by jurisdiction over a very specific group, a community court is neighborhood-focused and designed to address local problems such as vandalism, prostitution, shoplifting, vagrancy, and the like. Community courts use problem solving and strive to create relationships with outside stakeholders such as residents, merchants, churches, and schools (Center for Court Innovation, 2012).

Community court participants generally like how they are treated in this kind of court. Participants regard them as fairer than traditional courts (Frazer, 2006), and give them high marks in achieving goals such as working productively, assigning useful community service, and treating participants equally (Justice Education Center, 2002). Perhaps one reason for such favorable ratings has been the use of alternative sanctions by community courts; they are less likely to incarcerate individuals as part of disposition of charges (Hakuta et al., 2008). Although such courts are slightly more expensive when measured by cost per case, they are also associated with higher levels of compliance with sanctions and greater reduction of outcomes such as prostitution, illegal vending, and other problems particular to community courts (Kralstein, 2005). We provide one example of a community court in Box 9.4.

Box 9.4

Seattle Community Court: Creative Solutions for High-Impact, Low-Level Crime

When a minor crime is committed over and over, is it still too small for concern? Judge Fred Bonner, presiding over the Seattle Community Court, said that people in survival mode commit acts of theft to survive, and these small crimes often indicate larger societal problems that are significant. Many of the low-level crimes, such as theft and prostitution, committed in Seattle were by individuals who were homeless or mentally ill. "Criminal trespass, theft, prostitution, alcohol and drug-related crime—those were the main kinds of crimes we were dealing with," said Assistant City Attorney Tuere Sala. "They are what we call quality-of-life crimes— and they are usually crimes that are committed more out of a need to survive than an intention to injure others."

Although the intention of such offenses may not be to injure any one individual, the cumulative effect of this kind of offending on a community can be very substantial. "Even if you think it's a faceless crime," said defense attorney Nancy Waldman, "somebody is violated. If a business feels that way, they're more inclined to move their business away from any given district. It has an effect on the whole city." Seattle City Attorney Peter S. Holmes said, "This is a non-partisan issue: Everyone wants to reduce crime and save money, and that's ultimately what community court is about."

In the search for an appropriate response to Seattle's low-level crime, the Seattle Community Court opened in 2005 to serve the downtown district. "We took those individuals who had no place to go, who had spent many days in jail over the years," said Judge Bonner, "and we designed our program to address those needs." Like most community courts across the United States, by combining punishment with help, the Seattle Court seeks to address the social needs associated with crime, repair the harm done, and help transform offenders into productive members of the community. The Seattle Community Court handles only defendants who have committed low-level misdemeanors and do not present a public safety risk. Rather than paying a fine or spending time in jail, all defendants who agree to participate in community court are assessed for social service needs and then must contact each social service link, such as community service opportunities identified during assessment. It is common practice in community courts to use alternatives to detention, such as community service, as a sanction. Participants in the Seattle Court have completed over 50,000 hours of community service, but Judge Bonner stresses the importance of developing such programs to also educate people about the effects that quality-of-life crime has on the community.

Seattle continues to develop its programs and services to address the needs of offenders as those needs change. "We've just developed a theft awareness class and life-skills training, which would constitute community service," said Judge Bonner, who added that Seattle Community Court also launched three stand-alone sites that provide young prostitutes with housing and classes on avoiding sexually transmitted diseases. They can earn community service hours at these sites, as well as receive literacy training and counseling. Seattle Community Court also has new protocols that allow for community service alternatives for individuals with disabilities. The court already partners with 25 community service organizations, and coordinators from the Seattle Community Court have recently started to expand options for individuals not physically able to perform traditional community service. For example, individuals who are unable to pick up trash could be required to answer phones or do filing. "Offenders find that they feel proud of putting in a full day's work," said Karen Murray, of the Associated Counsel for the Accused. "Then we can link them to employment services. Landlords and employers can see people's capacity to change." Seattle Community Court is also evolving to address the different needs that veteran offenders have. "We have a marvelous caseworker from the veterans' hospital coming to our court, and we're trying to do a docket right now just for veterans," said Murray. "They never had criminal histories before and suddenly they're coming back and they're acting out. Do we actually expect people to get off the plane and come back into society as though nothing happened? That's another role for community court in our time."

Another defining element of our time is the strained economic climate experienced throughout the country, and community courts are not immune to this struggle. "We have been suffering some serious budget issues here," said Judge Bonner, "but one of the things that the city council has said is, 'We don't want to reduce or cut community court.' It has been recognized that not only does it save the city money, it also saves lives."

In 2009, the Justice Management Institute issued an independent evaluation of Seattle Community Court. The report stated that individuals involved in the community court committed 66% fewer offenses within 18 months of community court intervention, while those in the control group (undergoing traditional prosecution, and receiving probation if convicted) showed an increase of 50%, suggesting that the court is significantly more effective at reducing the frequency of recidivism than the traditional court process. "The study adds to the value of understanding these kinds of interventions; even though they seem at the surface to be cost-intensive, that may actually not be the case," said Elaine Nugent-Borakove, president of the Justice Management Institute and primary researcher on the evaluation.

Furthermore, the Seattle Mayor's Office of Policy and Management estimates that through reduced recidivism and jail use the community court saved the city $1,513,209 during the court's first three years of operation. "We're still studying why crime is down nearly double digits percentage-wise in Seattle over the past 16 months," said City Attorney Holmes, "but I have to think that community court is a factor." Holmes also discussed how community court may have helped alleviate the strain on funds. "When I was on the campaign trail in 2009, it was seen as inevitable that Seattle was going to break ground on a new jail with a price tag of 400 million dollars within the next five years. We have to give some credit to the community court diverting people from incarceration for the fact that Seattle is no longer seriously on the track to build a new jail."

For some who work in the court, the problem-solving approach is new. Craig Sims, chief of the Criminal Division, said, "When I came here in January 2010, I didn't know much about community court. I've been a prosecutor since the late nineties, working in the traditional mode of prosecution: Someone does something wrong, they go to court, they get prosecuted, they go to jail, and we move on to the next one. It was quite refreshing for me to collaborate with the court and the defense to figure out a different way to resolve lower-level crimes." "We're all partners in this," added Holmes, and the Seattle community can see the tangible benefits of this partnership. "We've had some wonderful public events," said Holmes. "Rather than spending time in jail, low-level offenders were out beautifying the community and giving back. Community murals have had unveiling events, heavily attended by local community groups and local media, and the community is able to feel less cynical about the criminal justice system."

"I like the fact that it's an opportunity court," said Sala. "You have an opportunity to make a difference, to change something. As a prosecutor, I would rather see that than the same offenders constantly coming back."

Critical Thought Question

How is community court similar to other kinds of problem-solving courts, such as drug court, mental health court, and veterans' court? How is it different?

Veterans' Courts. In 2008, the most recent version of specialty court—veterans' courts—was launched to address the complicated psychological and legal problems of members of the U.S. military who have returned from war. There are now nearly 500 such courts across the country (National Drug Court Resource Center, 2020).

More than 2 million Americans have served in the wars in Iraq and Afghanistan, making these the largest deployments since the Vietnam War. Approximately one-third of them experience posttraumatic stress disorder (PTSD), traumatic

brain injury, depression, or other mental illness, and one-fifth are addicted to drugs or alcohol (Marvasti, 2010). Sadly, only about half of the veterans with PTSD or depression have sought help, and of those, only about half received satisfactory care (Tanielian & Jayco, 2008). Given their training in the military to react immediately to any perceived threat, it is not surprising that thousands of returning veterans have reacted strongly and aggressively in certain situations. This training and experience may have contributed to subsequent arrests for criminal offenses, some of them very serious.

Veterans' courts, like this one, aim to address crimes perpetrated by members of the U.S. Military returning from war.

In a typical veterans' court, a district attorney may opt to defer prosecution or offer a plea bargain to a reduced charge if it appears that the offense was related to the veteran's disability and the veteran agrees to seek treatment. Veterans who plead guilty to a nonviolent felony or misdemeanor are teamed with volunteer veteran mentors who ensure that the offender adheres to a strict regimen of counseling, personalized rehabilitation programs, and court appearances. Judges may issue alternative sentences that require offenders to seek psychological treatment. By completing the required program, an individual may avoid going to prison. Whether these provisions should be made available to veterans charged with felonies is a matter of ongoing debate.

There are few studies of their effectiveness at present. The limited data that exist suggest that offenders who are diverted to veterans' court are less likely to reoffend than those whose cases go through the traditional criminal justice system (Mador, 2010). One study (Knudsen & Wingenfeld, 2016) included 86 veterans in an Ohio jail diversion and trauma recovery treatment court who were interviewed at baseline, then 6 and 12 months later to determine if the program led to improvements in jail recidivism, psychiatric symptoms, quality of life, and recovery. Results suggested that participants experienced significant improvement in various outcomes relative to baseline (PTSD, depression, substance misuse, overall functioning, emotional well-being, relationships with others, recovery status, social connectedness, family functioning, and sleep). However, without a control or comparison group, we do not know whether this improvement was significantly better than other approaches to processing participants in the criminal justice system.

There is some other relevant research, although it is limited. In a study of 59 participants in 14 veterans' courts, investigators found a criminal recidivism rate of less than 2% (Holbrook & Anderson, 2011). In an uncontrolled pre-post study of the Rochester Veterans Treatment Court in New York, researchers (Commaroto et al., 2011) described a 59% reduction in arrests for participants after joining the program. Using symptomatic outcomes, other investigators (Slattery et al., 2013) considered symptoms of PTSD and substance misuse and observed reductions in both at 6- and 12-month outcomes. Finally, a study of a veterans' court in San Antonio (Frantzen, 2015) cited lower rearrest rates for participating veterans than for other veterans who declined to enter the program. While modestly encouraging, these studies also reflect some of the methodological difficulties with the existing research—particularly the absence of a comparison group, or the absence of random assignment to group when there is such a comparison group.

Finally, a study using a VA database of about 1,200 individuals (Johnson et al., 2017) identified variables associated with eventual incarceration for veterans' court participants. Variables positively associated with incarceration included a longer period of participation in treatment court, and receiving mental health services. Variables associated with a *lower* rate of incarceration included stable housing and participation in substance misuse services. This might suggest that individuals who are treated for substance misuse and require shorter periods of intervention (and who also have stable housing) are less likely to commit violations that result in their incarceration.

Criticisms of Problem-Solving Courts. Despite the apparent successes of problem-solving courts, they have also been criticized. One concern is that regardless of the type of specialty court, they are presided over by middle-class judges who inevitably reflect their own values and who may become inappropriately paternalistic in what they require of people (Eaton & Kaufman, 2005). Some have argued that problem-solving courts lack legitimacy because threatening punishment to coerce rehabilitation is unfair and because guilt or innocence is not determined by a trial (Casey, 2004). Both prosecutors and public defenders have expressed concern over the "social worker" roles inherent in drug court philosophy; prosecutors feel pressured to favor rehabilitation of the offender over protection of society, and defenders feel pressure to encourage their clients to plead guilty and to inform the court of clients' failure to comply with the terms of probation (Feinblatt & Berman, 2001). Finally, social scientists worry about the lack of rigorous, empirical studies that assess *how* specialty courts influence (or fail to influence) offenders' conduct and what impact they have on the underlying social and psychological problems of offenders (Wiener et al., 2010).

Despite these criticisms, problem-solving courts have shown remarkable growth and the ability to address some of the influences on criminal offending that respond to interventions. Consequently, they have the potential to reduce recidivism rates and to improve the lives of participants and their families. Problem-solving courts will probably continue to develop and evolve, focusing on the reasons why people are in court in the first place.

Research on Intercept 3 of the Sequential Intercept Model is the most mature and consistent of the evidence described thus far. Specialty courts of different kinds have been studied, with the general focus on the characteristics of participants, the perceptions of favorability on the part of such participants, and outcomes such as cost, the nature of appropriate services delivered, and change in justice-relevant outcomes such as rearrest and subsequent incarceration. The evidence on the delivery of appropriate services, the perception of favorability on the part of participants, and the reduction in subsequent arrests and incarcerations seems largely favorable for drug courts, community courts, and mental health courts.

The Sequential Intercept Model describes two other points at which specialized interventions can occur for offenders in the community: during the transition from incarceration back to the community (the reentry process) and while on parole following release from incarceration. These are both discussed later in this book, in Chapter 15.

The Future of Community-Based Alternatives to Prosecution

The alternatives to traditional prosecution described in this chapter have grown substantially during the last two decades. One explanation for this is their potential appeal to lawmakers across the political spectrum. For conservative legislators who focus on public safety and cost, there is growing evidence that alternative approaches such as specialized police responding and problem-solving courts reduce the risk of criminal offending and hold down criminal justice costs (although they may shift costs to systems that deliver rehabilitation services). For progressive legislators who might be inclined to emphasize rehabilitation, there is more specific treatment and rehabilitation associated with such alternative approaches. But such approaches have also grown because the original areas of rehabilitation need (e.g., substance misuse, mental health) have been expanded to include other areas as well.

Will this trend continue? Will similar problem-solving courts be established? The expansion of the current number of courts? If so, we hope that research is used both in the development and the maintenance of these new courts, so our society has evidence that they work as intended. But it seems unlikely that the community alternatives approach will ever replace our traditional system of prosecution and incarceration, particularly for serious crime. Our society also values the importance of punishing criminal offending through incarceration.

Summary

1. **What is alternative dispute resolution (ADR)? What are some types of ADR?** Alternative dispute resolution (ADR) is an umbrella term for alternatives to the court and jury as a means of resolving legal disputes. The most common forms are arbitration, in which a third party decides the controversy after hearing from both sides, and mediation, in which a third party tries to facilitate agreement between the disputants. The summary jury trial is another ADR mechanism.

2. **What is the Sequential Intercept Model?** The Sequential Intercept Model is a model identifying the most relevant points of interception from the standard process of arrest, prosecution, conviction, and incarceration of criminal offenders.

3. **What are the major stages (or intercepts) for community-based alternatives to standard prosecution?** The intercepts that are most relevant to community-based alternatives, diverting offenders from jail or prison into a rehabilitative community disposition, are (0) informal way of linking those in need to services without resorting to possible arrest or criminal charges; (1) specialized law enforcement and emergency services responding; (2) post-arrest initial detention/hearing; and (3) jail/prison, courts, forensic evaluations, and commitments.

4. **What are the similarities and differences between community court and other kinds of problem-solving courts?** The underlying philosophy of all problem-solving courts reflects the view that identifying and rehabilitating a subset of criminal offenders can be accomplished less expensively, less restrictively, more effectively, and more safely in the more rehabilitation-oriented problem-solving court than with the traditional criminal process. Most problem-solving courts accept a specific subgroup of offenders, based on their symptoms (e.g., mental health court, drug court) or experience (e.g., veterans' court), with the assumption that those in such groups have a specific constellation of rehabilitation needs which, if addressed, would make them less likely to reoffend. By contrast, community court is more heterogeneous, and may include a variety of groups of offenders in need of rehabilitation for reasons that relate strongly to their risk for future offending.

Key Terms

arbitration

criminalization hypothesis

Crisis Intervention Team

deinstitutionalization

mediation

meta-analysis

negotiation

problem-solving court

risk averse

Sequential Intercept Model

specialized police
  responding

summary jury trial

therapeutic jurisprudence

Chapter 10

Forensic Assessment in Juvenile and Criminal Cases

Orienting Questions

1. What is the scope of forensic psychology?
2. What is meant by competence in the criminal justice process?
3. How do clinicians assess competence?
4. What are the consequences of being found incompetent to proceed in the criminal justice process?
5. What is the legal definition of insanity?
6. How frequently is the insanity defense used, and how successful is it?
7. What are the major criticisms of the insanity defense, and what attempts have been made to reform it?
8. What are the important criteria in deciding on juvenile transfer?

The Scope of Forensic Psychology

Forensic psychologists use knowledge and techniques from psychology, psychiatry, and other disciplines to answer questions about individuals involved in legal proceedings. Forensic psychological assessments—evaluations that appraise a person's capacities or culpability at a given time—are performed mostly by clinical psychologists or clinical neuropsychologists, and the field of forensic psychology has prospered and matured considerably in the last 40 years (Melton et al., 2018). For example:

- Forensic psychology is recognized as a specialty by the American Board of Professional Psychology and by the American Psychological Association.

- A second edition of specialty guidelines for the practice of forensic psychology has been published (American Psychological Association, 2013), updating the original version (Committee on Ethical Guidelines for Forensic Psychologists, 1991). The revision of these 2013 guidelines into a third edition is underway.

- Forensic psychology predoctoral training concentrations and postdoctoral fellowships are available, providing formal training in the field.

- The research and clinical literatures on forensic practice have increased dramatically.

It appears likely that growth in this field will continue. There are several reasons for this. First, mental health experts have expertise in a variety of areas relevant to litigation. As scientists learn more about human behavior, attorneys will find new ways to use this information in various legal proceedings. In this and the following chapters, we focus on several topics that mental health professionals are called on to assess for individuals involved in court proceedings.

Second, forensic psychology is flourishing because the law permits, and even encourages, the use of expert testimony in a host of areas, including psychology, anthropology, criminology, engineering, toxicology, genetics, and medicine (National Research Council, 2009). Expert testimony is used in all these areas, but psychological topics have received particular attention.

Finally, expert testimony by forensic psychologists thrives because it can be very lucrative. With hourly rates between $200 and $800, forensic experts can earn thousands of dollars per case. If one party in a lawsuit or criminal trial hires an expert, the other side may respond with its own expert. Consequently, the use of psychological experts promotes the further use of such experts, and it has become a significant source of income for many professionals.

In general, a qualified expert can testify about a topic if such testimony is relevant to an issue in dispute and if the usefulness of the testimony outweighs whatever prejudicial impact it might have. If these two conditions are satisfied—as they must be for any kind of testimony to be admitted—an expert will be permitted to give opinion testimony if the judge believes that "scientific, technical, or other specialized knowledge will assist the trier of fact to understand the evidence or to determine a fact in issue" (Federal Rule of Evidence 702). The U.S. Supreme Court ruled in the 1993 case of *Daubert v. Merrell Dow* that federal judges could decide whether expert testimony has a sufficiently relevant and reliable scientific foundation to be admitted into evidence. For opinions offered by behavioral scientists and mental health experts, the *Daubert* standard requires that admissible expert testimony be grounded in scientifically based methods and theory (Melton et al., 2018). In addition, the U.S. Supreme Court has held (in *Kumho Tire Co., Ltd v. Carmichael*, 1999) that this requirement also applies to expert opinions that are provided by those with technical or professional skills, such as clinicians.

Expert testimony plays a crucial role in the insanity defense, one of the most difficult and controversial legal questions faced by courts and forensic evaluators. Our discussion of the insanity defense begins in Box 10.1, describing the case of Andrea Yates.

The question of whether Andrea Yates—or any criminal defendant—was insane at the time of a criminal offense is one of the most challenging questions that forensic psychologists and psychiatrists are asked to help courts decide. The question has generated a good deal of research by social scientists, although less in the 21st century. In this chapter, we discuss the construct of insanity—its definition, assessment by mental health professionals, and implications when used as a legal defense. Prior to that, we describe competence to stand trial, which is sometimes confused with insanity. We cover trial competence and insanity together in this chapter because these issues both occur in the criminal context, are raised together in some cases, and are close to one another within the sequence of criminal adjudication. We also discuss two other important issues that involve assessment by forensic psychologists: capital sentencing evaluations, and the transfer of juveniles from juvenile to criminal (adult) court. In Chapter 11, we explore several other forensic questions that clinicians assess, including questions that arise in civil litigation, divorce and child custody disputes, commitment hearings, and other types of legal proceedings.

Competence

The Andrea Yates case also highlights the importance of evaluating a defendant's competence to stand trial. Did Yates understand the nature of her charges—murder involving drowning her children—and the possible consequences of those charges? This question is particularly salient considering an interview with Yates's mother, who recalled that Andrea Yates (while in prison for these murders) asked her mother who would be watching them (Gibson, 2005). Questions were also raised about whether Yates was taking her antipsychotic medication at the time of the murders as well as during her trial.

Box 10.1

The Case of Andrea Yates: Tragedy and Insanity

Reuters/Alamy Stock Photo

Andrea Yates with her family

On the morning of June 20, 2001, Andrea Yates, a 37-year-old wife and mother of five, said goodbye to her husband as he left for work. Before her mother-in-law arrived to help care for the children, who ranged in age from six months to seven years old, Yates filled the bathtub of her Texas home with water. Beginning with her middle son, Paul, she drowned each of her children in turn. She laid the four youngest children on the bed, covering them with a sheet. Her oldest boy was left floating lifelessly in the bathtub. She then called the police and her husband to tell them what she had done.

Prior to the killing of her children, Yates had a long history of severe mental illness. She reportedly experienced numerous psychotic episodes and had been diagnosed with schizophrenia and postpartum depression. These episodes resulted in several hospitalizations, including one just a month prior to the killings, and required psychotropic

medications to help stabilize her ("The Andrea Yates Case," 2005).

Yates pled not guilty by reason of insanity to drowning three of her children; she was not charged in the other two deaths. (Prosecutors may have been preserving their options in case she was acquitted of drowning her first three children; they might have subsequently charged her with the other two homicides.) Her insanity plea was based on her claim that she had no choice but to kill them while they were still innocents, to prevent them from burning in hell (Wordsworth, 2005). No one disputed that Yates systematically killed each of her children, but the question remained: Was she so disturbed by the symptoms of her severe mental illness that she could not be held criminally responsible for the murders?

At the conclusion of her trial, Yates was found guilty and sentenced to life in prison. After she had served three years of her sentence, however, the court declared a mistrial and Yates's conviction was overturned. During the trial, one of the psychiatric experts testified that the television show "Law and Order" had aired an episode in which a defendant had been acquitted by reason of insanity after drowning her children in the bathtub. Although the expert himself did not link this observation to Ms. Yates's thinking or motivation, the prosecutor did so in closing arguments. In fact, there had never been an episode of "Law and Order" with this specific story line. Yates was subsequently found not guilty by reason of insanity in a retrial, and is now hospitalized in the Texas state forensic hospital system.

Critical Thought Question

Why would it make a difference in the jury's consideration of the insanity defense for Andrea Yates if "Law and Order" had shown an episode in which an individual had drowned her children in a bathtub—and Ms. Yates had viewed this episode?

What do we mean by competence to stand trial? How do clinicians assess this kind of legal competence? What legal standards should be applied? The question of a defendant's **competence** is the clinical-legal issue most frequently assessed in the criminal justice system. **Competence to stand trial** refers to a defendant's capacity to function meaningfully and knowingly in a legal proceeding. Defendants may be adjudicated (i.e., formally determined by a judge) to be incompetent if they are seriously deficient in one or more abilities, such as understanding the legal proceedings, communicating with their attorneys, appreciating their role in

the proceedings, or making legally relevant decisions. Concerns about a defendant's competence are tied to one fundamental principle: Criminal proceedings should not continue against someone who cannot understand their nature and purpose, or who cannot assist in defending against prosecution on these charges.

Competence is an important doctrine in our legal system, and the law requires defendants to be competent for several reasons (Melton et al., 2018). First, defendants must be able to understand the charges against them so that they can participate in the criminal justice system in a meaningful way, making it more likely that legal proceedings will arrive at accurate and just results. Second, punishment of convicted defendants is morally acceptable only if they understand the reasons why they are being punished. Finally, the perceived fairness and integrity of our adversarial system of justice requires participation by defendants who have the capacity to defend themselves against the charges of the state.

The accepted national standard for competence to stand trial in the United States is a "sufficient present ability to consult with [one's] attorney with a reasonable degree of rational understanding, and ... a rational, as well as factual, understanding of the proceedings against [one]" (*Dusky v. United States*, 1960). With minor differences across jurisdictions, this is the standard for competence to stand trial in all U.S. courts. It establishes the basic criteria for competence as the capacities for factual and rational understanding of the court proceedings and for consulting with one's attorney in a rational way. These criteria refer to *present* abilities rather than to the mental state of the defendant at the time of the alleged offense, which, as we will discuss later, is the focus of evaluations of a defendant's sanity.

The *Dusky* standard does not specify how the evaluator assessing competence should judge the *sufficiency* of rational understanding, ability to consult, or factual understanding. That is ultimately the role of the judge. However, to allow evaluators to provide courts with more detailed information in these areas, various courts and mental health groups have expanded on *Dusky* by listing more specific criteria related to competence. For example, evaluators may consider different relevant psycholegal abilities (Zapf & Roesch, 2009):

- Understanding
  - The roles of key participants within the legal process
  - The current charges faced by the defendant
  - The elements of an offense
  - The consequences of conviction
  - The rights waived in making a guilty plea
- Appreciation
  - The likelihood that one will be found guilty
  - The consequences for the defendant of being convicted
  - The available legal defenses and their likely outcomes
  - Whether or not to testify
  - The ability to make rational decisions regarding the specific case
- Reasoning
  - Distinguishing more relevant from less relevant information
  - Seeking relevant information
  - Weighing and evaluating various legal options and their consequences
  - Making comparisons
  - Providing reality-based justifications for making particular case-specific decisions or conclusions
- Assisting in one's defense
  - Consulting with one's lawyer
  - Relating to the lawyer
  - Planning legal strategy
  - Engaging in one's defense
  - Challenging witnesses
  - Testifying relevantly
  - Managing one's courtroom behavior
- Decision-making abilities relevant to decisions likely to arise during the proceedings.

The issue of competence also arises when defendants plead guilty. By pleading guilty, defendants waive several Constitutional rights: the right to a jury trial, the right to confront their accusers, the right to call favorable witnesses, and the right to remain silent. The U.S. Supreme Court has held that waiving such important rights must be done knowingly, intelligently, and voluntarily (*Johnson v. Zerbst*, 1938), and trial judges are required to question defendants about their pleas to establish clearly that they understand that they are waiving their Constitutional rights by pleading guilty. A knowing, intelligent, and voluntary guilty plea also includes understanding the charges and the possible penalties that can be imposed, and requires the judge to examine any plea bargain to ensure that it is "voluntary" (i.e., that it represents a considered choice between constitutionally permissible alternatives). For example, prosecutors can offer lighter sentences to a defendant in exchange for a guilty plea, but they cannot offer the defendant money to encourage a guilty plea.

Logically, **competence to plead guilty** would require that defendants understand the alternatives they face and can make a reasoned choice among them. In some respects, this standard is more demanding than that for competence to stand trial. Defendants standing trial must be aware of the nature of the proceedings and able to cooperate with counsel in presenting the defense, paying attention to the proceedings and controlling their behavior over the course of a trial. This creates a strong demand for *attention, concentration*, and *behavioral control*. Defendants pleading guilty, on the other hand, must understand the possible consequences of pleading guilty instead of going to trial and must be able to make a rational choice between the alternatives. This underscores the importance of the defendant's *cognitive awareness* and *reasoning*.

Adjudicative Competence

Despite this, the U.S. Supreme Court ruled that the standard for competence to stand trial would be applied in federal courts to other competence questions that arise in the criminal justice process (*Godinez v. Moran*, 1993). In so doing, it rejected the idea that competence to plead guilty involves a different standard than competence to stand trial. Consequently, the terms *competence to plead guilty* and *competence to stand trial* have become somewhat confusing. Some scholars have suggested that **adjudicative competence** is a clearer description of the various capacities that criminal defendants need in different legal contexts (Bonnie, 1993; Hoge et al., 1997). The term competence to stand trial is still used frequently, although it acquired a broader meaning after the *Godinez* decision. We discuss adjudicative competence with the understanding that it is synonymous with competence to stand trial, post-*Godinez*. We begin this discussion with the case of Jared Loughner, described in Box 10.2.

Box 10.2

The Case of Jared Loughner: Assessing Competence

Jared Loughner, following his arrest

Jared Loughner was arrested after being wrestled to the ground in a grocery store parking lot in Tucson, Arizona on January 8, 2011, after he walked up to United States Congresswoman Gabrielle Giffords, an Arizona Democrat, and shot her. Following that, Mr. Loughner turned his gun on others in the crowd. Those dying in the shooting included John Roll, a federal judge in Tucson; 9-year-old Christina-Taylor Green; and four other bystanders. Twelve other individuals in addition to the congresswoman were injured.

Mr. Loughner was a troubled young man with a history of classroom outbursts at Pima Community College, which had expelled him, and bizarre postings on the Internet. Before he could be tried for these offenses, however, the issue of Mr. Loughner's competence to stand trial was raised. Among the questions that the mental health experts were asked to address, and the court ultimately had to decide, were whether Mr. Loughner indeed had a mental illness—and, if so, how the symptoms of that illness affected his capacities to understand his legal circumstances, assist counsel in his own defense, and make rational decisions in the process.

Judge Larry A. Burns of the U.S. District Court considered the findings of two mental health experts in the case: Christina Pietz, Ph.D., a psychologist appointed at the request of the prosecution, and Matthew Carroll, M.D., a psychiatrist appointed by the judge. Dr. Pietz reported that Mr. Loughner's thoughts were random and disorganized, that he experienced delusions, and that he responded to questions in an irrelevant fashion. Dr. Carroll also described delusions as well as bizarre thoughts and hallucinations. Both experts concluded that Mr. Loughner experienced schizophrenia, a form of severe mental illness. They described these symptoms as seriously impairing Mr. Loughner's ability to understand his legal circumstances and assist counsel in his own defense. The judge adjudicated him incompetent to stand trial and committed him to the Federal Medical Center in Springfield, Missouri for treatment to improve his symptoms and restore these capacities. Following treatment, he was adjudicated competent to stand trial in August 2012 and pled guilty to criminal charges, resulting in a sentence of life plus 140 years in federal prison.

Because of the horrific and widely publicized nature of these alleged offenses, there was (and will continue to be) a great deal of scrutiny of Mr. Loughner's case. The prosecution in such cases experiences pressure to consider the death penalty, and to bring the defendant to trial and convict. The defense may struggle in working with a severely mentally ill defendant, even an individual whose symptoms are in remission, because the defendant may continue to show irrational thinking and behavior that is not consistent with defense attorneys' strategic recommendations. A judge must balance the arguments of both prosecution and defense in a highly charged, widely scrutinized atmosphere. Such cases test the limits of our legal system in the pursuit of justice under very trying circumstances.

Critical Thought Question

Why does the highly publicized nature of an alleged offense like Jared Loughner's affect the proceedings on a question like competence to stand trial?

Would Jared Loughner have been a good candidate for an insanity defense? Explain.

Raising the Issue of Competence

The question of a defendant's competence can be raised at any point in the criminal process, and it can be raised by the prosecutor, the defense attorney, or the presiding judge. Once the question of incompetence is raised, the judge will order an evaluation of the defendant if a "bona fide doubt" exists that the defendant is competent. Judges consider the circumstances of each case and the behavior of each defendant when making this determination. However, if the question of competence is raised, an examination will usually be conducted. Because it is relatively easy to obtain such evaluations, attorneys often seek them for reasons other than a determination of competence. Competence evaluations are used for several tactical reasons: to obtain information about a possible insanity defense, to guarantee the temporary incarceration of a potentially dangerous person without going through the cumbersome procedures of involuntary civil commitment, to deny bail, and to delay the trial as one side tries to gain an advantage over the other (Winick, 1996). Defense attorneys have questions about their clients' competence in up to 10–15% of felony cases (approximately twice the rate for defendants charged with misdemeanors); it is estimated that formal evaluations occur in about half of these cases (Danzer et al., 2019). (There could be different reasons why a defense attorney might not formally raise the issue of a defendant's competence to stand trial. These include preferring an alternative disposition such as diversion, the perception that a client had challenges but was able to sufficiently understand and assist to dispose of charges, a client's expressed preference to avoid a mental health evaluation, and others.) Estimating the number of evaluations of competence to stand trial performed across the U.S. each year is difficult, with contemporary estimates ranging from 60,000 to 94,000 (Morris et al., 2021).

Evaluating Competence

After a judge orders a competence examination, arrangements are made for the defendant to be evaluated by one or more mental health professionals. Although these evaluations were historically conducted in a special hospital or inpatient forensic facility, the majority began to be conducted in the community on an outpatient (nonhospitalized) basis in the 1980s (Grisso et al., 1994), with this trend accelerating given that the period 2010–2020 has witnessed a shortage of beds accompanied by a substantial waiting list for hospital admission for those already adjudicated incompetent to stand trial (IST) in several states (Callahan & Pinals, 2020). The transition from inpatient to outpatient pre-adjudication evaluation remains in place because inpatient evaluations are more costly and time-consuming, and community-based evaluations are appropriate for most evaluative purposes (Melton et al., 2018).

Physicians, psychiatrists, psychologists, and social workers are authorized by most states to conduct competence examinations, but psychologists and psychiatrists are the professional group responsible for the largest number of reports. Some data suggest that it is forensic specialization (training and experience) rather than discipline (psychology or psychiatry) that is most strongly associated with report quality (Lander & Heilbrun, 2009; Sanschagrin et al., 2006).

Under the *Dusky* standard, the presence of mental illness or intellectual disability does not guarantee that a defendant will be found incompetent to stand trial. The crucial question is whether the disorder impairs a defendant's ability to participate knowingly and meaningfully in the proceedings and to work with the defense attorney. An individual who is experiencing active symptoms of severe mental illness might be competent to stand trial in a relatively straightforward case but incompetent to participate in a complex trial that would demand more skill and understanding. Consider the case of Theodore Kaczynski, also known as the Unabomber, who was charged in federal court with murder as part of mailing explosive devices to individuals he thought were harming society through the application of technology. He was evaluated by a forensic psychiatrist, who concluded that he experienced a severe mental illness (what was then termed "paranoid schizophrenia"). But Mr. Kaczynski did not wish to pursue any defense or present any evidence that would imply that he had a mental illness. Eventually he was offered a plea bargain involving a sentence of life without parole, and he accepted the offer. Before he did, however, both the defense and the prosecution had to agree to consider him competent to stand trial (Reisner et al., 2013). In this case, even though there was strong evidence that the defendant experienced a severe mental illness, there was agreement that he could understand the charges against him and the operation of the legal system, and could assist in his own defense.

Trial competence evaluations focus on the defendant's present ability to function adequately in the legal process. This focus has been sharpened by the development of several structured tests or instruments specifically aimed at assessing the capacities relevant to competence to stand trial. Psychological testing remains a common ingredient in competence evaluations, and although clinicians have begun to use one or more of these specially designed competence assessment instruments in their practice, their use is not as widespread as it should be (Lander & Heilbrun, 2009; Rogers & Johansson-Love, 2009)—although it does appear to be increasing (McLaughlin & Kan, 2014; Neal & Grisso, 2014). There have been various such instruments developed for this purpose. The most current and best supported empirically are described in the following paragraphs.

Interdisciplinary Fitness Interview (IFI). The IFI and its revision, the IFI-R (Golding, 1993), are versions of a semi-structured interview that evaluates a defendant's abilities in five specific legal areas. It also assesses 11 categories of psychopathological symptoms. Evaluators rate the weight they attached to each item in reaching their decision about competence. These weights vary depending on the nature of the defendant's case; for example, hallucinations might impair a defendant's ability to participate in some trials, but they would have limited impact in others and would therefore be given less weight. Golding et al. (1984) found that interviewers using the IFI agreed on final judgments of competence in 75 of 77 cases evaluated. These judgments agreed 76% of the time with independent decisions about competence made later at a state hospital.

Fitness Interview Test—Revised. The Fitness Interview Test—Revised (FIT-R) is a structured interview for assessing a person's competence to stand trial. Like the IFI-R, it uses a structured professional judgment approach to assessing competence capacities. Using this approach, various areas are considered but not "scored," and there is not a total score that is related to a category or level of impairment. It was originally designed for use in Canada, but has been updated for use in the United States and Great Britain as well. It includes 16 items in three broad domains (Factual Knowledge of Criminal Procedure, Appreciation of Personal Involvement in and Importance of the Proceedings, and Ability to Participate in Defense). Research on the FIT-R (Roesch et al., 2006; Zapf et al., 2001) suggests that it is a promising screening tool.

The MacArthur Measures of Competence. Growing out of the concept of adjudicative competence, which describes several interrelated components that need to be considered in the evaluation of competence, the *MacArthur Structured Assessment of the Competence of Criminal Defendants* (MacSAC-CD; Hoge et al., 1997) is a highly regarded research instrument. Most of the 82 items in the MacSAC-CD rely on a hypothetical vignette about which the defendant is asked questions that tap foundational and decisional abilities. Defendants are asked the questions in a sequence. Open-ended questions come first. If there is a wrong answer, correct information is provided to the defendant. Defendants are then asked additional open-ended questions to determine whether they now have the necessary understanding based on this disclosure; a series of true–false questions concludes each area of assessment. This format has several advantages. It offers a more standardized evaluation across different defendants, and it makes it possible to assess separately defendants' preexisting abilities as well as their capacity to learn and apply new information.

One major disadvantage of the MacSAC-CD is that it was developed as a research instrument and takes about two hours to complete, too long to be used routinely in practice. To overcome this limitation, a 22-item clinical version of this measure, called the *MacArthur Competence Assessment Tool—Criminal Adjudication* (MacCAT-CA) was developed (Poythress et al., 1999). This instrument begins with a hypothetical vignette about a crime, upon which the first 16 items are based. These items assess the defendant's general understanding of the legal system and adjudicative process and their reasoning abilities in legal situations. The remaining six items are specific to the defendant's own legal situation. The reliability and construct validation of the MacCAT-CA has been supported by different studies (Otto et al., 1998; Poythress et al., 2002).

The Evaluation of Competence to Stand Trial–Revised. The *Evaluation of Competence to Stand Trial–Revised* (ECST-R) (Rogers et al., 2004) is a semi-structured interview that was developed using the *Dusky* criteria. Its three factors (factual understanding of proceedings, rational understanding of proceedings, and consultation with counsel) have been empirically tested using a statistical technique known as confirmatory factor analysis. It focuses on information that is specific to the case of the individual being evaluated (unlike the MacCAT-CA, which uses a general vignette involving two individuals who fight in a bar). It also addresses the question of whether the evaluee is trying to exaggerate or fake deficits that might make that person appear incompetent to stand trial. Both the case specificity and the built-in measure of possible exaggeration are useful features of the ECST-R, which appears well supported by the relevant research (Norton & Ryba, 2010; Rogers et al., 2001, 2004).

Competence Assessment for Standing Trial for Defendants with Mental Retardation. One specialized measure, the *Competence Assessment for Standing Trial for Defendants with Mental Retardation* (CAST-MR; Everington & Luckasson, 1992), was developed specifically for assessing defendants with mild to moderate intellectual disability (previously called mental retardation). Two validation studies have been conducted; although the number of participants has been small, the results have been somewhat encouraging (Grisso, 2003). In addition, the CAST-MR is the only specialized tool developed specifically for assessing trial competence with individuals with developmental disabilities.

One important issue being studied by researchers is the extent to which defendants can successfully fake incompetence on these tests. Some research suggests that although offenders can simulate incompetence, they often take such simulations to extremes, scoring much more poorly on specialized measures of competence capacities than those who are genuinely incompetent to stand trial (Gothard et al., 1995; Gottfried et al., 2015). Therefore, very poor performance should underscore the possibility that defendants might be exaggerating their deficiencies. As noted earlier, one specialized tool (the ECST-R) has a built-in measure to help the evaluator determine whether the defendant is exaggerating deficits. Research indicates that the ECST-R is sensitive to the exaggeration of both symptoms of mental illness and intellectual deficits (Vitacco et al., 2009).

This issue has gained a great deal of attention because malingering (faking or grossly exaggerating) mental illness in competence evaluations has been estimated in nearly one third (31%) of defendants who have been adjudicated incompetent for trial (Nesbit-Bartsch et al., 2021). Therefore, screening tools have been developed to offer a more scientific method of detecting malingering in patients being evaluated for their competence to stand trial. One of these instruments is the Miller Forensic Assessment of Symptoms Test (M-FAST; Miller, 2001). The M-FAST is a brief, 25-item structured interview that can accurately identify individuals who are attempting to feign mental disorders (see Miller, 2004). Empirical evidence thus far supports the use of the M-FAST in detecting malingering (Detullio et al., 2019), but it is a screening instrument and should be used in conjunction with a wider array of assessments to determine whether the defendant is genuinely malingering.

Consider the case of former pro wrestler Jimmy "Superfly" Snuka. Mr. Snuka was charged with the beating death of his girlfriend more than three decades after the crime, when a newspaper story in 2013 raised new questions about his culpability. When he appeared before a Pennsylvania judge in Lehigh County for a competence to stand trial hearing in 2016, his lawyer argued that he experienced dementia after many years of head injuries in the ring. The prosecution, by contrast, suggested that Snuka (who was 73-years-old at the time of the hearing) experienced only problems associated with normal aging, and was faking his symptoms of confusion when asked simple questions such as his age or the current year. The judge was not convinced that he was faking, however, describing him as "vacant" and not "smart enough" to malinger—and formally adjudicated him incompetent to stand trial (http://www.foxnews.com/entertainment/2016/06/02/judge-declares-jimmy-superfly-snuka-incompetent-to-stand-trial-in-death.html). This is the kind of case in which a formal evaluation of symptoms of cognitive impairment would be helpful. Were Mr. Snuka's symptoms genuine? Did he more closely resemble defendants with real symptoms of dementia—or those who fake such symptoms? But in addition to an assessment of malingering, it would also be useful for the evaluator to obtain other sources of information. Had Mr. Snuka ever received medical treatment for dementia? Would collateral observers who saw him frequently (e.g., friends, caretakers, relatives) describe him as displaying such symptoms? Clearly there are multiple sources of information that could be useful in answering this question.

Following the collection of assessment data, evaluators communicate their findings to the judge. Often, they submit a written report that summarizes the evidence on competence to stand trial, as well as the likelihood that appropriate treatment will sufficiently improve competence-relevant deficits. In controversial or strongly contested cases, it is more likely that there will be a formal competence hearing where the evaluating experts testify and are questioned by attorneys from both sides.

In formal competence hearings, who bears the burden of proof? Must prosecutors prove that defendants are competent, or are defendants required to prove their incompetence? In the 1992 case of *Medina v. California*, the U.S. Supreme Court held that a state can require criminal defendants to shoulder the burden of proving that they are incompetent. But how stringent should that burden be? Most states established the criterion to be a "preponderance of the evidence," meaning that the defendant had to show that it was more likely than not that they were incompetent. But four states—Oklahoma, Pennsylvania, Connecticut, and Rhode Island—required a higher standard of proof: evidence that was "clear and convincing." In 1996, the U.S. Supreme Court addressed the standard of proof question, holding that this higher standard was too stringent (*Cooper v. Oklahoma*, 1996)—so the current standard is "preponderance of the evidence."

Results of Competence Evaluations

About 70% of the defendants referred for evaluation are ultimately found competent to stand trial (Melton et al., 2018); when very rigorous examinations are conducted, the rate of defendants found competent approaches 90%. Judges seldom disagree with clinicians' recommendations regarding competence, and opposing attorneys often will **stipulate** (agree without further examination) to clinicians' findings (Melton et al., 2018).

Should evaluators directly answer the "ultimate legal question"—whether the defendant is competent to stand trial—or provide information about clinical condition and functional-legal capacities, leaving matters of sufficiency, values, and community sentiment to the judge? One study asked judges, prosecutors, and defense attorneys to rank in order of importance eight items typically offered by expert witnesses in competence evaluations (e.g., clinical diagnosis of the defendant, weighing different motives and explanations, providing an ultimate opinion on the legal issue) (Redding et al., 2001). Judges and prosecutors agreed that the expert's ultimate opinion on the legal issue was one of the three most important pieces of information the expert could provide.

Another study asked juvenile and criminal court judges (*N* = 166) about information they considered valuable in competence evaluations. Results showed that judges (1) consider clinicians' ultimate opinion to be an essential component of reports, (2) regard forensic and psychological testing as valuable, (3) seek similar but not identical characteristics in juvenile and adult competence evaluations, and (4) consider opinions about maturity to be an important component of competence evaluations in juvenile court (Viljoen et al., 2008). Depending upon how such "ultimate opinions" are used, this may suggest that mental health professionals exert great—perhaps excessive—influence on this legal decision. Is that a problem?

Even though this research evidence suggests that many judges want to hear evaluators' ultimate legal conclusions, there are reasons to avoid offering them. Whether a defendant shows certain symptoms or has a certain understanding of the proceedings are matters well within the expertise of psychologists and psychiatrists. Whether this information translates directly into a conclusion about the defendant's competence to stand trial is a different question. Many in the field have debated this question, and after 40 years it is not resolved (see, e.g., Heilbrun, 2001; Melton et al., 2018; Rogers & Ewing, 2003; Tillbrook et al., 2003).

What are the characteristics of those judged to be incompetent? In his study of more than 500 defendants found incompetent to stand trial, Steadman (1979) described them as often "marginal" men who were poorly educated, and had limited job skills with long histories of involvement in both the legal and the mental health systems. Problems of substance abuse were common. Minorities were overrepresented. Others report relatively high percentages of serious mental illness, lower intelligence, and more problems with certain aspects of memory among incompetent defendants (Cooper & Zapf, 2003), as well as co-occurring substance use disorder, unemployment, and homelessness (Schreiber et al., 2015). Among defendants who are both charged with violent crimes and have been adjudicated incompetent to stand trial, there is frequent co-occurring (mental health and substance use) disorder, homelessness, unemployment, and lengthy history of prior hospitalizations for mental health treatment as well as prior arrests (Schreiber et al., 2015). A 2019 review underscored the presence of three primary classes of clinical deficits among those who are incompetent to stand trial: symptoms of severe mental illness, intellectual disability, and cognitive deficits (Heilbrun et al., 2019).

If a defendant referred for a competence evaluation is adjudicated competent to stand trial, the legal process resumes, and the defendant again faces the possibility of trial or disposition of charges through plea bargaining. If the defendant is found IST, however, the picture becomes more complicated. For crimes that are not serious, the charges are occasionally dropped, sometimes in exchange for requiring the defendant to receive treatment. In other cases, however, the defendant is hospitalized to be treated for restoration of competence, which, if successful, will result in the defendant proceeding with disposition of charges.

Prior to the 1970s, defendants found incompetent were often confined in state psychiatric hospitals for excessive periods of time. (Sometimes such confinements were even longer than their sentences would have been had they stood trial and been convicted.) This was the subject of a 1972 U.S. Supreme Court case (*Jackson v. Indiana*). The decision held that defendants who had been committed because they were incompetent to stand trial could not be held "more than a reasonable period of time necessary to determine whether there is a substantial probability that [they] will attain that capacity in the foreseeable future." Consequently, the length of time an incompetent defendant can be confined is now limited, and many states have passed statutes that "limit" such hospitalization to a period not to exceed the maximum sentence that could have been imposed if the defendant were convicted of charges (see Heilbrun et al., 2021).

How successful are efforts to restore defendants' competence? One study evaluated an experimental group treatment administered to a sample of incompetent defendants sent to one of three Philadelphia facilities (Siegel & Elwork, 1990). In addition to receiving psychiatric medication, defendants assigned to these treatment groups watched videotapes and received instructions on courtroom procedures. They also discussed different ways of resolving problems that a defendant might face during a trial. A matched control group received treatment for their general psychiatric needs, but no specific treatment relevant to incompetence. Following their treatment, defendants participating in the competence restoration group showed significant increases in their assessment scores compared to the controls. In addition, hospital staff judged 43% of the experimental subjects competent to stand trial after treatment compared to 15% of the control subjects. Other research, however, indicates that providing general legal information is about as effective as highly specialized programs focusing on individual deficits (Bertman et al., 2003). In general, most defendants have their adjudicative competence restored, usually with about six months of treatment (Heilbrun et al., 2019; Zapf & Roesch, 2011), and the most important intervention for most defendants is the administration of appropriate psychotropic medication (Zapf & Roesch, 2009).

The real dilemma for IST defendants occurs when treatment is not successful in restoring competence and holds little promise of success in the future. Theoretically, the previously described *Jackson* ruling bars the indefinite confinement of an individual adjudicated incompetent to stand trial. Once such a defendant has been hospitalized for this period, however, they can be found "unrestorably incompetent." Research indicates that the major influences associated with unrestorable incompetence are intellectual disability, dementia, lower global functioning, psychotic disorder accompanied by lengthy hospitalization, and poorer response to interventions such as psychotropic medication and psychoeducational rehabilitation (Heilbrun et al., 2021).

Typically, unrestorably incompetent defendants are committed to a hospital through involuntary civil commitment proceedings. Standards for this type of commitment are often narrower than for IST commitment, however. Under civil commitment statutes, the state must show that the person is mentally ill and either imminently dangerous to self or others or so gravely disabled as to be unable to care for themselves.

Should an incompetent defendant not meet the criteria for involuntary hospitalization, what happens? Despite the ruling in the *Jackson* case, some states simply continue to confine incompetent defendants for indefinite periods. Although this "solution" might appease the public, it also jeopardizes defendants' due process rights and results in lengthy periods of confinement without a conviction. Several alternative procedures have been proposed to resolve this problem, including abolishing the IST concept altogether (Burt & Morris, 1972), allowing defendants to seek trial continuances without going through an elaborate evaluation, or waiving their right to be competent under certain circumstances (Winick, 1996). To date, however, there has been no effectively implemented alternative to the Constitutional requirement that a defendant be competent to stand trial in order to proceed.

One recent proposal involves what researchers termed the "Demonstration Model," which identifies individuals who do not appear restored to competence after about six months of hospital milieu, medication, and other standard interventions. Targeting these individuals for more individualized and intensive interventions over another year or so, this proposal (Heilbrun et al., in press) identifies two possible outcomes: (1) the individual responds favorably to the more individualized and intensive interventions, or (2) the individual does not, leaving hospital staff with no reasonably remaining interventions to try. When this process is carefully documented, it can lead to a well-informed opinion that the individual either has been restored—or is, under *Jackson v. Indiana*, unlikely to be restored within the foreseeable future—either of which is useful for the judge who must decide about potential unrestorability.

Competent with Medication, Incompetent Without

For most defendants found IST, psychotropic medication has been the treatment of choice, as it is considered the best intervention for restoring defendants to competence in a reasonable period. Can incompetent defendants refuse this treatment? If medicated, will defendants be found competent to stand trial even though the medication, because of its temporary impact, might undercut a defense such as insanity? The U.S. Supreme Court case *Sell v. U.S.* (2003) concerns questions of competence and forced medication (Box 10.3).

Other Legal Competencies

Because questions about competence can be raised at any point in the criminal process, several other competences are also relevant. Competence for any legal function involves (1) determining what functional abilities are necessary, (2) assessing the context where these abilities must be demonstrated, (3) evaluating the implication of any deficiencies in

Box 10.3

The Case of Charles Sell: Involuntary Medication to Restore Competence?

Charles Sell, once a practicing dentist, had an extensive history of severe mental illness and was hospitalized several times. He was accused of fraud after he allegedly submitted fictitious insurance claims for payment. His competence to stand trial was evaluated, and he was found competent and released on bail. Subsequently, a grand jury indicted Sell on 13 additional counts of fraud and, later, attempted murder. During his bail revocation hearing, Sell's mental illness was markedly worse, and his behavior was "totally out of control," including "spitting in the judge's face" (*Sell v. United States*, 2003, p. 2). His competence was again evaluated, at which time he was adjudicated incompetent to stand trial. He was hospitalized for treatment to help restore his competence. Hospital staff recommended antipsychotic medication, which Sell declined to take. The hospital administered these medications to him involuntarily. Sell challenged this in court, arguing that involuntary medication violates the Fifth Amendment right to "liberty to reject medical treatment" (p. 10). The lower court found that Sell was a danger to himself and others, that medication was the only way to render him less dangerous, that the benefits to Sell outweighed the risks, and that the drugs were substantially likely to return Sell to competence. The court further held that medication was the only viable hope of rendering Sell competent to stand trial and was necessary to serve the Government's interest in obtaining an adjudication on the

issue of his guilt. Sell appealed and this case was granted *certiorari* by the United States Supreme Court.

At the heart of this case is the question of whether involuntary medication to restore a defendant's competence to stand trial, with the associated possibility of conviction and incarceration, is a violation of that defendant's rights. Of course, if a defendant cannot be restored to competence without medication, they may remain hospitalized, and thus also deprived of their liberty, for a lengthy period. In the *Sell* decision, the Court weighed these considerations and outlined the conditions under which the government may forcibly administer psychotropic medication to render a mentally ill defendant competent to stand trial. The treatment must be (1) medically appropriate, (2) substantially unlikely to have side effects that may undermine the trial's fairness, and (3) necessary to significantly further important government trial-related interests.

Critical Thought Question

Assume that a defendant is hospitalized as incompetent to stand trial with a severe mental illness, and assume further that he is actively psychotic and declines to take prescribed medication while in the hospital. Finally, assume that he does not present a threat of harm toward others or himself. Under those circumstances, what are the advantages and disadvantages of forcing him to take psychotropic medication?

the required abilities, and (4) deciding whether the deficiencies warrant a conclusion that the defendant is incompetent (Grisso, 2003). Mental health professionals are sometimes asked to evaluate each of the following competencies (see also Melton et al., 2018).

Capacity to Waive *Miranda* Rights. The waiver of *Miranda* rights is required for defendants in police custody to make a legally-admissible confession—and the waiver of these *Miranda* rights (Fifth Amendment right to avoid self-incrimination and Sixth Amendment right to counsel and trial) must be made in a knowing, intelligent, and voluntary fashion. It is difficult to assess these abilities because, in most cases, the waiver and confession have occurred months before the professional's evaluation, requiring a reconstruction of the defendant's mental and emotional state at the time.

One aspect of a defendant's rights guaranteed by *Miranda* involves the Sixth Amendment right to be represented by counsel when in police custody. The same standard to waive this right—knowing, intelligent, and voluntary—is applied to the questions of waiving counsel and making a confession.

A slightly different twist on the right to be represented by counsel involves the question of whether defendants can decide that they do not want a lawyer to represent them at trial. The U.S. Supreme Court has held that defendants have a Constitutional right to waive counsel and represent themselves at trial, if they make this decision competently (*Faretta v. California*, 1975). In addition, the presiding judge must be convinced that the waiver of counsel is both voluntary and intelligent. Defendants do not have to convince the court that they possess a high level of legal knowledge, although some legal knowledge is probably important.

Questions concerning competence to waive the right to counsel arose in the case of Andrew Kowalczyk, a 33-year-old man charged with possession of child pornography involving images allegedly found on his laptop computer (*United States v. Kowalczyk*, 2015; Thiele & Martinez, 2016). Over a period of nearly 7 years, a total of 9 different defense attorneys were appointed and subsequently withdrew as defense counsel. One psychological evaluation found that Mr. Kowalczyk experienced paranoid schizophrenia that made him irrationally suspicious of his various attorneys; he filed lawsuits against several of them. Another evaluation, conducted at the Federal Medical Center in Springfield (where he had been sent after being adjudicated incompetent to stand trial), concluded that Mr. Kowalczyk was malingering. Mr. Kowalczyk stated that he did not want to represent himself—but his extreme dissatisfaction with every lawyer appointed to represent him created a major problem for the judge. Eventually the court appointed "amicus counsel" who advised Mr. Kowalczyk in the proceedings, after the judge informed the defendant that if he could not work with the last attorney appointed for him, he was effectively asserting a waiver of his right to be represented by a lawyer. This is interesting because Mr. Kowalczyk had a right to have an attorney provided (*Gideon v. Wainwright*, 1963) and a right to represent himself (*Faretta v. California*, 1975), but had to satisfy the court that he was both competent to stand trial *and* could perform the additional tasks necessary to represent himself (*Indiana v. Edwards*, 2008). Did the court successfully navigate this maze in Mr. Kowalczyk's case?

Competence to Refuse the Insanity Defense. In cases in which it is likely that the defendant was insane at the time of the offense, can the defendant refuse to plead insanity? If there is evidence that a defendant was not mentally responsible for criminal acts, do courts have a duty to require that the defendant plead insanity when the defendant does not want to do so? Courts have been divided on this question. In some cases, they have suggested that society's stake in punishing only mentally responsible persons requires the imposition of an insanity plea even on unwilling defendants (*Whalen v. United States*, 1965). Other decisions (*Frendak v. United States*, 1979) use the framework of competence to answer this question—if the defendant understands the alternative pleas available and the consequences of those pleas, the defendant should be permitted to reject an insanity plea. This latter approach is followed in most courts.

This question was at the heart of the prosecution of Theodore Kaczynski, a reclusive mathematician who was dubbed the "Unabomber" for sending a series of mail bombs to universities and airlines between 1978 and 1995. Although the consensus of several experts was that Kaczynski experienced paranoid schizophrenia, he adamantly refused to let his attorneys use an insanity defense, arguing that he did not want to be stigmatized, in his words, as "a sickie." Was Kaczynski competent to make this decision, or was Judge Garland E. Burrell, Jr. correct in ruling that Kaczynski's lawyers could control his defense, even over the defendant's persistent objections? It is doubtful that an insanity defense would have been successful—Kaczynski's own diary showed that he understood and intended to commit his crimes—but we will never know. Ultimately, to avoid the possibility of the death penalty, Kaczynski pled guilty to murder and was sentenced to life in prison.

Competence to Be Sentenced. For legal and humanitarian reasons, convicted defendants are not to be sentenced unless they are competent. In general, the standard for this competence is that defendants can understand the punishment and the reasons why it is being imposed, and can meaningfully execute their right to address the court at sentencing. Competence to be sentenced is often a more straightforward question for the clinician to evaluate than adjudicative competence, which involves issues of whether the accused can interact effectively with counsel and appreciate alternative courses of action.

Competence to Be Executed. A particularly controversial aspect of this area is determining whether a defendant is competent to be executed. The U.S. Supreme Court decided,

Adolescent in Juvenile Court

in *Ford v. Wainwright* (1986), that the Eighth Amendment ban against cruel and unusual punishments prohibits the execution of defendants while they are incompetent. In a subsequent decision (*Panetti v. Quarterman*, 2007), the Supreme Court clarified that competence for execution includes a factual awareness of the impending execution and the reason for it—but also a rational understanding of why the convicted individual is to be executed. (Scott Panetti was aware that he was to be executed, but delusionally believed that the reason was to stop him from preaching.) Mental health professionals are sometimes asked to evaluate inmates waiting to be executed to determine whether they are competent to be executed. The practical problems and ethical dilemmas involved in these evaluations are enormous (Heilbrun, 1987; Mossman, 1987) and have led some psychologists to recommend that clinicians refrain from performing such evaluations. When they are conducted, consequently, it is preferable to use relevant guidelines and a structured approach (see, e.g., Zapf et al., 2003).

Juvenile Competence to Stand Trial

In a series of decisions about justice-involved adolescents, the U.S. Supreme Court has held that developmental immaturity distinguishes adolescents in some important ways from adult defendants (*Roper v. Simmons*, 2005; *Graham v. Florida*, 2010; *JDB v. North Carolina*, 2011; *Miller v. Alabama*, 2012; *Montgomery v. Louisiana*, 2016). This complicates the question of juvenile competence for trial, because adolescents may experience severe mental illness or intellectual disability (the two major reasons why adult defendants may be incompetent to stand trial)—but developmental immaturity is a third important influence.

Are juveniles competent to stand trial? Does it make a difference whether they are being processed in juvenile court or tried as adults? Do adolescents differ from adults in their abilities to participate in trials, and if so, what are these differences? These were questions posed by researchers

(Grisso et al., 2003) when they studied a group of 927 adolescents in juvenile detention facilities and community settings. Participants were administered a specialized measure of competence for adults (the MacCAT-CA) as well as the MacArthur Judgment Evaluation (MacJen), which was designed to examine immaturity of judgment. Their research goal was to provide data on *competence to proceed* (comprehension of the purpose and nature of the trial process, ability to provide relevant information to counsel and to process information, and ability to apply information to oneself without distortion or irrationality) and *decisional competence* (ability to make important decisions about waiver of constitutional rights and maturity of judgment).

Results indicated that participants who were age 15 and younger were significantly impaired in ways that compromised their abilities to function as competent defendants in a criminal (adult) proceeding. More specifically, one-third of 11–13-year-olds and one-fifth of 14–15-year-olds were as impaired in their functional legal capacities as mentally ill adults who were incompetent to stand trial. Below-average intelligence was also associated with deficits in these functional legal capacities. Since a large proportion of adolescents in the juvenile justice system have below-average IQ, the risk for incompetence is further increased when adolescents in this system are transferred into criminal court (Grisso et al., 2003).

These findings have fewer implications for adolescents when they are in juvenile court, however. Since the expectations for competence in juvenile court are different— adolescents are being tried in a setting that is designed for juveniles—it is more likely that an adolescent with limited functional legal capacities would be adjudicated competent in juvenile court than if they were tried in adult criminal court. But it is still important for lawmakers to consider the evidence on adolescent maturity and other functioning related to competence to stand trial. Policy researchers have developed a guide to help them with this task (see Larson & Grisso, 2011). Some states (e.g., Virginia, California) have established specialized rehabilitation placements with the goal of assisting juveniles who are adjudicated incompetent to stand trial in regaining competence (Jackson, 2018).

The Insanity Defense

Any society that respects the rights of individuals recognizes the possibility that some of its citizens cannot comprehend the consequences or the wrongfulness of their actions. Our legal system allows defendants who claim that they lack these abilities to invoke the insanity defense. Yet the evaluation of insanity defense claims is challenging. For example, it may be very difficult to accurately gauge a defendant's mental state at the time of the offense, as must be done when a defendant uses insanity as a defense. The jury or judge must answer the question "What was he experiencing when he fired the gun?" This is more complex in many cases than determining whether he fired the gun, and had the requisite intent. How can we determine whether a defendant is legally insane? Can we know what a person's state of mind was when they committed an antisocial act? This becomes even more difficult when the fact finders—juries and judges—must determine not whether the person is currently insane, but rather whether they were insane at the time of the crime, possibly months or years earlier.

This problem is further complicated by the reality that there are far fewer specialized tools specifically designed to assess insanity than there are to assess competence. One brief screening instrument—the Mental Status Examination at the Time of the Offense (Slobogin, et al., 1984)—has been developed, but research on its reliability and validity is limited to one study. More research has been conducted on the Rogers Criminal Responsibility Scales (RCRAS; Rogers, 1986), a set of 25 scales that organize the many factors and points of decision that clinicians need to consider when assessing criminal responsibility. Although the RCRAS has clear limitations, it is the only formal instrument with some demonstrated reliability and validity for guiding clinicians' decision-making process in insanity evaluations (Melton et al., 2018).

Another reason why insanity questions are so difficult involves the conflict between law and behavioral sciences as alternative pathways to knowledge. Insanity is a legal concept, not a medical or psychological one. In many states, a defendant could be hallucinating, delusional, and diagnosed with schizophrenia, but if the individual knew the difference between right and wrong, they would be legally sane. Thus, psychiatrists and clinical psychologists are called upon as forensic experts to provide information regarding a decision that is ultimately outside the traditional diagnose-and-treat framework of these professions. (Of course, the same could be said about *any* legal question that is the focus of a forensic mental health evaluation—but evaluations with clear clinical-legal criteria and that are focused on present mental state and capacities are more straightforward.) The therapeutic goals of psychiatry and clinical psychology (diagnoses and assessments that are probabilistic and complex) do not fit well with the legal system's demand for a straightforward "yes-or-no" answer (Heilbrun, 2001). Furthermore, although mental health experts can offer diagnoses, any one diagnosis is less important than the specific symptoms and their impact on the functional legal demands associated with the insanity standard (whether the defendant "knew" the behavior was wrong; in some states, additionally, whether the defendant could conform their conduct to the requirements of the law). In addition, insanity is not a conclusion that should be applied to behavior simply because it is something we don't understand, doesn't appear rational, or may be a radicalized expression of religious or political views (see Box 10.4).

Rationale for the Insanity Defense

Insanity refers to the defendant's mental state at the time the offense was committed (as contrasted with *competence*

to stand trial, which refers exclusively to the defendant's relevant legal capacities at the time of the trial or plea bargain). Why do we have laws about insanity? Wouldn't it be simpler to do away with insanity in the legal system? Allowing a criminal defendant to plead not guilty by reason of insanity reflects a fundamental belief that a civilized society should not punish people who do not know what they are doing or are incapable of controlling their conduct. Thus, the state must occasionally tell the victim's friends and family that even though it abhors the defendant's acts, some offenders do not deserve punishment. Before it can do that, however, a judgment must be made about whether such persons were responsible for their actions.

What is the legal standard for insanity? There is no single answer. The following sections describe several definitions currently in use. The legal standards that define criminal responsibility vary from state to state, but in all states, the defendant is initially presumed to be responsible for their alleged offense. Therefore, if pleading insanity, defendants must present some evidence that would rebut the initial presumption of criminal responsibility in their case. A related legal issue is the assessment of *mens rea*, or the mental state of knowing the nature and quality of a forbidden act. To be a criminal offense, an act not only must be illegal but also must be accompanied by the necessary *mens rea*, or guilty mind.

Varying Insanity Defense Rules

The M'Naghten Rule: An Early Attempt to Define Insanity. In 1843, an Englishman named Daniel M'Naghten shot and killed the private secretary of the British prime minister. Plagued by paranoid delusions, M'Naghten believed that the Prime Minister, Sir Robert Peel, was part of a conspiracy hatched by the Tory party against him. M'Naghten initially sought to escape his imagined tormentors by traveling through Europe. When that didn't work, he stalked the Prime Minister and, after waiting in front of the official residence at No. 10 Downing Street, shot the man he mistakenly thought was Peel.

M'Naghten was charged with murder, and his defense was to plead not guilty by reason of insanity. Nine medical experts, including the American psychiatrist Isaac Ray, testified for two days about his mental state, and all agreed that he was insane. On instructions from the lord chief justice, the jury rendered a verdict of not guilty by reason of insanity without even leaving the jury box to deliberate. M'Naghten was committed to the Broadmoor Asylum for the Insane, where he remained for the rest of his life.

The public was infuriated, as was Queen Victoria, who had been the target of several attempts on her life. She demanded a tougher test of insanity. Subsequent debate in the House of Lords led to such a "tougher" standard: the M'Naghten rule, which was announced in 1843, long before psychiatry became a household word. The M'Naghten rule, which became the standard for defining insanity in Great

Box 10.4

Is The Insanity Defense Relevant to Possible Terrorist Acts? The 2016 Ohio State Attack

On November 28, 2016, a young man who was a student at Ohio State University drove a car on campus and deliberately rammed students, and then jumped out and stabbed a number of them with a knife. The man was identified as Abdul Razak Ali Artan; he was a Somali refugee who was a legal permanent resident of the United States. He was quickly shot and killed by a nearby campus police officer. Ironically, Artan had been selected earlier that year, at random, for an interview for the campus paper, with the interview appearing in August. In the interview, Artan talked about his Muslim faith, and why it was important for him to have a quiet place to pray. He added that Ohio State seemed "huge" to him, and that he was "kind of scared" as a Muslim, considering how the media portrayed those of his faith. Early investigations following the attack could not definitively conclude that this was an act of terrorism—that kind of conclusion should be reached only after an intensive and detailed review—but authorities could not rule out terrorist motivation, despite the absence of an immediate indication that Abdul Artan was acting with such motivations.

Is the insanity defense ever relevant to such acts? For the answer to this question to be "yes" (or even possibly), several considerations would be relevant. First, unless a criminal court were to interpret radical Jihadist ideology as a "mental disease or defect" (without the defendant showing signs of having a severe mental illness or intellectual disability), then there would be no "threshold issue" on which to base the claim of insanity. Assuming, however, that a defendant could make a convincing argument about having both symptoms of a severe mental illness *and* radical Jihadist beliefs, then the next question would be whether this combination kept the individual from understanding the nature, quality, or wrongfulness of terrorist acts—or conforming his conduct to the requirements of the law.

Perhaps we should not be surprised that terrorist acts and the insanity defense are rarely mentioned together. Our best evidence is that the strongest influences on the development of radical Jihadist ideology are cultural, religious, and political—not the result of mental illness. Even for individuals who might have a recognizable mental disorder and become radicalized, it would seem far more likely that they would remain committed to their radical beliefs than agree to a defense that excuses criminal conduct based on mental illness or intellectual disability.

Britain and the United States, "excuses" criminal conduct if defendants, as a result of "disease of the mind," (1) did not know what they were doing (e.g., believed they were shooting an animal rather than a human), or (2) did not know that what they were doing was wrong (e.g., believed killing unarmed strangers was "right").

The M'Naghten rule (or a close variation) is used in 26 states and the federal jurisdiction (https://criminallaw.uslegal.com/defense-of-insanity/the-insanity-defense-among-the-states/), so it is the most frequently employed legal standard for insanity in the United States. It has often been criticized on the basis that the cognitive focus ("knowing wrongfulness") is too limiting, and does not allow consideration of motivational and other influences affecting the control of behavior. There have been different legal tests of insanity since the M'Naghten rule was first established. These are described in the sections that follow.

The Brawner Rule, Stemming from the Model Penal Code. A committee of legal scholars in the American Law Institute developed the Model Penal Code, intended to standardize penal laws in the U.S. Included in the Model Penal Code is the Brawner rule, which states that a defendant is not responsible for criminal conduct if the defendant "at the time of such conduct as a result of mental disease or defect, [lacks] substantial capacity either to appreciate the criminality [wrongfulness] of his conduct or to conform his conduct to the requirements of the law." This standard, or a variation, allows judges and juries to consider whether mentally ill defendants have the capacity to understand the nature of their acts or to behave in a lawful way. As of 2022, it was used in 20 states (https://criminallaw.uslegal.com/defense-of-insanity/the-insanity-defense-among-the-states/). Federal courts have also adopted the Brawner rule in drastically altered form (which we describe later).

The Brawner rule differs from the M'Naghten rule in three substantial respects. First, by using the term *appreciate*, it incorporates the emotional as well as the cognitive influences on criminal behavior. Second, it does not require that offenders exhibit a total lack of appreciation for the nature of their conduct, but only a lack of "substantial capacity." Finally, it includes both a cognitive element and a volitional element—appreciation of wrongfulness *and* capacity to conform conduct to the requirements of the law—making defendants' inability to control their actions a sufficient criterion by itself for insanity.

The Insanity Defense Reform Act. In the wake of the trial of John Hinckley, Jr., who attempted to assassinate President Ronald Reagan, the U.S. Congress enacted the Insanity Defense Reform Act (IDRA) in 1984. The law modified the existing insanity defense (eliminating the "volitional" prong and retaining the "cognitive" prong), with the expectation that fewer defendants would be able to use it successfully. This law did not abolish the insanity defense, but changed it substantially. In addition to eliminating the volitional prong, it also changed the insanity defense process as follows:

1. It prohibited experts from giving ultimate opinions about insanity (i.e., whether the defendant was insane at the time of the crime). Although this prohibition may have little effect on jurors, reformers believed it would prevent expert witnesses from having excessive influence over the jury's decision.

2. It placed the burden to prove insanity on the defendant, replacing the previous requirement that the prosecution must prove a defendant's sanity.

Empirical Research Relevant to Varying Insanity Defense Rules. What little research has been conducted on the Insanity Defense Reform Act suggests that it does not accomplish either what its proponents envisioned or what its critics feared. At least in mock jury studies, verdicts do not significantly differ regardless of whether the jurors have heard IDRA instructions, Brawner instructions, or no instructions (Finkel, 1989). In addition, states with the broadest test of insanity (Brawner) do not show higher rates of insanity acquittals than states with the narrowest test (M'Naghten) (Melton et al., 2018).

In theory, varying rules for insanity should influence jurors' understanding of the defense, but psychologists have questioned whether the typical juror can comprehend the legal language of these definitions and then apply them as intended by the courts. Elwork et al. (1981) found jurors correct on only 51% of their responses to questions regarding their comprehension of instructions regarding the M'Naghten rule. Ogloff (1991) obtained similar results: Regardless of what insanity rule was used, college students showed very low rates of recall and comprehension of crucial components in various insanity definitions. It may be that jurors (or mock jurors) do not understand the differences between these different tests very well, consistent with the broader conclusion that jurors do not understand the nuances of a variety of legal instructions that are provided to them (Lieberman, 2009). When mock jurors receive simplified instructions, this improves their knowledge—but individual juror factors such as myth endorsement and attitudes, as well as perceptions of the defendant, had more influence on their verdicts (Tsao, 2014).

The limited empirical evidence indicates that different standards of insanity also make little difference in verdicts. Although instructions have some effect on jury decision making in insanity cases, they tell only part of the story—and perhaps a minor part at that (Finkel & Slobogin, 1995; Helm et al., 2016).

A much greater influence may be exerted by preexisting attitudes toward the insanity defense (Eno Louden & Skeem, 2007). This decision process is an example of how jurors are prone to interpret "facts" in the context of a personal story or narrative that "makes the most sense" to each of them subjectively. Differences among jurors in the individual narratives they weave about the same set of trial "facts" may be related, in turn, to the different attitudes they hold about the morality of the insanity defense and the punishment of mentally ill offenders (Roberts & Golding, 1991). For instance, one study found that jurors conceptualized the prototypical insanity defendant in one of three ways: (1) severely mentally disordered (SMD), characterized by extreme, chronic, uncontrollable mental illness and/or intellectual disability that impair the defendant's ability to function in society; (2) morally insane (MI), typified by symptoms of psychosis and psychopathy, a categorization used to represent a malevolent, detached, and unpredictably violent offender; or (3) mental-state-centered (MSC), describing a defendant who experienced varied, but clearly supported, impairments in his mental state at the time of his offense (Skeem & Golding, 2001). Jurors who held SMD- or MI-like prototypes made up the vast majority of the sample (79%), and they tended to believe that the insanity defense was frequently raised, was easily abused, and jeopardized public safety. By contrast, those jurors who held MSC-like prototypes (21%) were less likely to perceive the insanity defense as unjust and tended to believe that the Constitutional rights ascribed to defendants were necessary components of the legal process.

Some data suggest that the race of mock jurors may affect a decision regarding whether a defendant is Not Guilty by Reason of Insanity. Jurors who are Black, Indigenous, or other People of Color (BIPOC) were less likely to support an insanity defense than were jurors who were White (Bolin, 2020).

Famous Trials and the Use of the Insanity Plea

Before reporting on the actual frequency and effectiveness of attempts to use the plea, we will review the results of several highly publicized trials that have molded public opinion about insanity pleas.

Trials in Which the Insanity Plea Failed. Among murder defendants who have pleaded insanity as a defense are Jack Ruby, whom millions of television viewers saw kill Lee Harvey Oswald, President John F. Kennedy's alleged assassin; Sirhan Sirhan, charged with the assassination of Robert F. Kennedy; John du Pont, a wealthy heir to a family fortune who killed an Olympic champion wrestler living and working on his estate; Andrea Yates, charged with drowning her children in the bathtub; Lee Boyd Malvo, an adolescent who traveled with an older defendant (John Muhammad) and participated in the killing of a number of individuals in Maryland and Virginia from a car with a sniper hole cut in the trunk: and Eddie Ray Routh, an Iraq war veteran charged with killing Chris Kyle, a former Navy SEAL who was the model for the movie "American Sniper." All these defendants were convicted of murder despite their pleas of insanity, although Ms. Yates was found not guilty by reason of insanity in a second trial granted after her appeal of her conviction in the first.

In another unsuccessful insanity defense asserted by a widely-recognized defendant, Jeffrey Dahmer, jurors rejected a plea of insanity as a defense against murder charges. Dahmer admitted killing and dismembering 15 young men in Milwaukee over about a 10-year period, but his attorney, Gerald Boyle, argued that Dahmer was insane at the time—a sick man, not an evil one. Prosecutor Michael McCann disagreed, arguing that Dahmer knew that what he was doing was wrong. After listening to two weeks of evidence, including taped interviews in which Dahmer explained how he had dismembered his victims and expert testimony about Dahmer's mental condition, the jury voted, by a 10–2 margin, that Jeffrey Dahmer was sane. He was subsequently sentenced to life in prison for his crimes, and was killed in prison by a fellow inmate.

Wisconsin defines insanity using the Brawner rule; consequently, to have found Dahmer insane, the jury would have had to conclude that he experienced a mental disorder or defect that made him unable either to appreciate the wrongfulness of his behavior or to control his conduct as required by the law. The jury rejected both conclusions, perhaps because of evidence that Dahmer was careful to kill his victims in a manner that minimized his chances of being caught. This cautiousness suggested that he appreciated the wrongfulness of his behavior *and* could control it when it was opportune to do so.

This is not to say that all those who assert the insanity defense—unsuccessfully or even successfully—are widely recognized and charged with heinous killings. The defense of insanity may be attempted as part of a defense to any criminal charge. For reasons discussed in more detail later in this chapter, it is not necessarily a good defense strategy even for defendants with severe mental illness. The defense is rarely successful; even when it is, the consequence is typically secure hospitalization until the individual is no longer considered dangerous. But for defendants with homicide charges, facing a very long sentence if convicted, the prospect of such an open-ended hospital commitment may be less daunting. We now turn to a more detailed consideration of cases in which the insanity defense has been successful.

Trials in Which the Insanity Plea "Succeeded." The case of John W. Hinckley, Jr. has had the greatest influence of any of those discussed in this chapter, triggering much of the court reform and legislative revision regarding the insanity plea since 1982. It is summarized in Box 10.5.

Even though the Hinckley case is one in which the insanity defense was successful in the narrow sense of the word, that outcome was largely a result of a decision by the presiding judge regarding the burden of proof. Judge Barrington Parker instructed the jury in accordance with federal law at the time, which required the prosecution to prove the defendant sane beyond a reasonable doubt. After listening to two months of testimony, the Hinckley jury deliberated for four days before finding the defendant not guilty by reason of insanity. Afterward, several jurors said that, given the instruction that it was up to the government prosecutors to prove Hinckley sane, the evidence was too conflicting for them to agree. They thought that Hinckley's meandering travels raised a question about his sanity, and both sides' expert psychiatric witnesses had testified that he experienced some form of mental disorder.

Research on the Insanity Defense

Much of the research on this topic was conducted prior to 2000 and in a few instances before 1990. For whatever reasons, the insanity defense as a research topic is not pursued currently with the same frequency and depth as it was three decades ago—and even then, there were not many such studies.

When the Insanity Defense Is Used. The insanity defense is most often used in cases in which the defendant is charged with a violent felony. In the largest study to date, data on defendants found not guilty by reason of insanity (NGRI) from four states ($N = 1,099$) were obtained (Steadman et al., 1993). These investigators found that 22.5% of the insanity acquittees had been charged with murder and that a total of 64% had been charged with crimes against persons (murder, rape, robbery, or aggravated assault).

Available research consistently suggests that the majority of defendants found NGRI have been diagnosed with some form of psychosis, suggesting severe and probably chronic mental impairments (Melton et al., 2018). Steadman and colleagues (1993) reported that 67.4% of the insanity acquittees described in their study were diagnosed with a schizophrenic disorder and that another 14.9% were diagnosed with another major mental illness. Co-occurring disorders, particularly major mental illness and substance abuse, are also common in those acquitted by reason of insanity.

How often do criminal defendants being assessed for insanity try to fake a mental disorder? It has been estimated using empirical research (Rogers & Sewell, 1999) that about one of four or five defendants being assessed for insanity engages in at least moderate malingering of mental disorders. This figure suggests that exaggeration or fabrication of self-reported symptoms is not rampant—but is frequent enough to merit attention. Psychologists have developed various assessment methods to detect persons who are trying to fake a mental disorder. These methods include special structured interviews, individual psychological tests, and specialized measures (Rogers & Bender, 2018). These techniques have shown promising results in distinguishing between subjects who were trying to simulate mental illness (to win monetary incentives for being the "best" fakers) and those who were reporting symptoms truthfully.

Box 10.5

The Case of John W. Hinckley, Jr. and the Attempted Assassination of President Reagan

John W. Hinckley, Jr.

Bettmann/Getty Images

Television replays show John Hinckley's March 30, 1981, attempt to kill President Ronald Reagan. When Hinckley came to trial 15 months later, his lawyers didn't dispute the evidence that he had planned the attack, bought special bullets, tracked the president, and fired from a shooter's crouch. But he couldn't help it, they claimed; he was only responding to the driving forces of a diseased mind. Dr. William Carpenter, one of the defense psychiatrists, testified that Hinckley did not "appreciate" what he was doing; he had lost the ability to control himself.

The defense in John Hinckley's trial made several other claims:

1. Hinckley's actions reflected his pathological obsession with the movie *Taxi Driver*, in which Jodie Foster starred as a 12-year-old prostitute. The title character, Travis Bickle, is a loner who is rejected by the character played by Cybill Shepherd and subsequently befriends Foster's character; he stalks a political candidate but eventually engages in a bloody shootout to rescue the Foster character. It was reported that Hinckley had seen the movie 15 times and that he so identified with the hero that he had been driven to reenact the fictional events in his own life (Winslade & Ross, 1983).

2. Although there appeared to be planning on Hinckley's part, it was the movie script that provided the greatest influence on his planning. The defense argued, "A mind that is so influenced by the outside world is a mind out of control and beyond responsibility" (Winslade & Ross, 1983, p. 188).

3. The defense tried to introduce the results of a CAT scan—an image of Hinckley's brain using computerized axial tomography—to support its contention that he had schizophrenia. The admissibility of this evidence created a controversy at the trial. The prosecution objected, claiming that all the apparent scientific rigor of this procedure—the physical evidence, the numerical responses—would cause the jury to place undue importance on it. The prosecution also contended that there were no grounds for concluding that the presence of abnormal brain tissue necessarily denoted schizophrenia. Initially, the judge rejected the request to admit this testimony, but he later reversed the decision on the basis that it might be relevant.

Critical Thought Question

The Hinckley defense argued that he was so influenced by the movie "Taxi Driver" that he was not in control of his actions and therefore (under the prevailing federal insanity standard at that time) not guilty by reason of insanity. If you had been a member of the jury, how much weight would you have placed on evidence that he had seen the movie many times and seemed to be reenacting parts of it in his own life?

In their large study, Steadman et al. (1993) observed that the decision to acquit by reason of insanity was most strongly influenced by clinical factors. They compared those who successfully employed the insanity defense with others who entered this plea but were nevertheless found guilty, and reported that 82% of the former group but only 38% of the latter group had been diagnosed with a major mental illness.

Based on relevant research, we have learned more about defendants who are found not guilty by reason of insanity (NGRI). For instance:

1. Individuals hospitalized following acquittal by reason of insanity stay longer if they have been acquitted of more serious offenses, particularly homicide (Dirks-Linhorst & Kondrat, 2012; Steadman et al., 1993).

2. Longer duration of hospitalization is not associated with better outcomes following release; rearrest is more strongly associated with demographic and criminal history variables (Miraglia & Hall, 2011).

3. Most defendants found NGRI have a prior history of psychiatric hospitalizations and have been diagnosed with serious forms of mental illness, usually psychoses (Dirks-Linhorst & Kondrat, 2012; Steadman et al., 1993).

4. Most NGRI defendants have previously been found incompetent to stand trial (Boehnert, 1989).
5. Although most studies have concentrated on males, some research (e.g., Heilbrun et al., 1988) indicates that female defendants found NGRI have similar socioeconomic, psychiatric, and criminal backgrounds to their male NGRI counterparts. Other studies have indicated that women are more likely to be older and married, less likely to abuse substances, have less criminal history and prior violence, and are more likely to be acquitted of murder (see Veysey, 2015).

Public Perceptions of the Insanity Defense

The American public has repeatedly expressed its dissatisfaction with the insanity defense. Several surveys have concluded that most U.S. citizens view the insanity defense as a legal loophole through which many guilty people escape conviction (Skeem & Golding, 2001). After John Hinckley was found not guilty by reason of insanity, a public opinion poll conducted by ABC News showed that 67% of Americans believed that justice had not been done in the case; 90% thought Hinckley should be confined for life, but 78% believed he would eventually be released back into society.

The public's disapproval of the insanity defense appears to be stimulated by trials such as Hinckley's that receive massive publicity. Melton et al. (2018) reported the following three beliefs to be prevalent among the public: (1) Many criminal defendants use the insanity defense, (2) those defendants found NGRI are released back into society shortly after their NGRI acquittals, and (3) persons found insane are extremely dangerous.

How accurate are these views? Are they myths or realities? Given the interest and debate surrounding the insanity defense, it is surprising that so few empirical studies have been conducted to investigate its actual outcomes. But there are some data concerning each of these questions.

How Often Is the Plea Used, and How Often Is It Successful?

The plea is used much less often than many assume. A survey of the use of the insanity defense in eight states between 1976 and 1985 found that although the public estimated that the insanity defense was used in 37% of the cases, the actual rate was only 0.9% (Silver et al., 1994); other research (e.g., Hans, 1986) also shows that the general public greatly overestimates the frequency with which the insanity defense is used. Data from the states of California, Georgia, Montana, and New York (Steadman et al., 1993) described as part of the largest multi-state study of individuals acquitted by reason of insanity indicate that defendants in those states, over a 10-year period, entered an insanity plea in 0.9% of felony cases and were successfully acquitted as NGRI in 22.7% of the cases in which this plea was entered.

Studies such as these are particularly valuable because few individual states keep complete records on the use of the insanity plea and its relative success. The findings reported in these studies suggest that of the nine insanity pleas raised in every 1,000 criminal felony cases, about two will be successful.

To gather data on the question of how many people are acquitted by reason of insanity each year, Cirincione and Jacobs (1999) contacted officials in all 50 states and asked for the number of insanity acquittals statewide between the years 1970 and 1995. After persistent attempts to collect these data from a variety of sources, they received at least partial data from 36 states. Few states could provide information for the entire 25-year period, but the results shown in Table 10.1 were obtained.

What Happens to Defendants Who Are Found NGRI?

Many mistakenly assume that defendants who are adjudicated NGRI go free. Steadman and Braff (1983) found that defendants acquitted by reason of insanity in New York had an average hospital stay of three years in a secure hospital. Researchers also found a clear trend for longer detentions of defendants who had committed more serious offenses: the average length of involuntary hospitalization was greater for those who had been charged with violent offenses (34.1 months) than for individuals with other categories of offenses (Steadman et al., 1993). The average length of confinement for all NGRI individuals was 28.7 months. But this figure undoubtedly underestimates the "true" average period of confinement. Why? These data describe only individuals who were hospitalized and released—they cannot tell us about individuals who were hospitalized but not released. This points to one of the important differences between a criminal sentence, which often is determinate (of fixed length), and the hospital commitment following acquittal by reason of insanity, which is indeterminate (depending on the individual no longer meeting criteria for hospitalization).

A subsequent study of insanity acquittals in Missouri (Dirks-Linhorst & Kondrat, 2012) provides additional data that can help answer the question of length of hospital stay. Reviewing 27 years of insanity acquittals in the state involving 1,130 individuals, it reported an average duration to conditional release of 45.9 months, and average duration to unconditional release of 92.0 months, and an average of 135.2 months for individuals who had never been released. In other words, those who had not been released had been in the hospital for an average of over 11 years—and that group contained individuals who had been in the hospital for a relatively short time, reflecting the presence of some who had been hospitalized for a very long duration.

Researchers have been particularly interested in learning whether defendants found not guilty by reason of insanity are confined for shorter periods than defendants who are found guilty of similar crimes. A survey of the use of the insanity defense across several states, covering nearly one million felony indictments between 1976 and 1985, sought answers to that question (Silver, 1995). Considering more than 8,000 defendants who pleaded insanity during this period, the investigator found that compared to convicted defendants, insanity acquittees spent less time in confinement in four states and more time in confinement in three states. It is possible to spend *longer* confined as NGRI than following a conviction because the NGRI commitment bases confinement on the question of whether a released individual would be dangerous to others in the community—a broad standard that (it has been suggested) might violate the equal protection doctrine (Wendzel, 2020).

Some states use a procedure known as *conditional release*, in which persons found NGRI are released to the community (following a period of hospital confinement) and are monitored and supervised by mental health personnel. Conditional release is the mental health system's counterpart to parole; it functions like a form of outpatient commitment. One four-state follow-up of 529 persons found NGRI reported that about 60% of these individuals were conditionally released within five years of their confinement (Callahan & Silver, 1998). Of those released, the median period of hospital confinement was 3.6 years for violent offenders and 1.3 years for those charged with less serious offenses. One review noted that those released on conditional release had revocation rates ranging from 35 to 50% (McDermott et al., 2008).

How Risky Are Defendants Found NGRI? Because most defendants who are found NGRI are quickly committed to a secure hospital following their acquittal, it is difficult to assess the risk they pose to public safety at that time. In addition, they are likely to receive treatment in the hospital to which they are committed, further complicating the question of their risk of reoffending without this treatment. The limited evidence available on this question suggests either no difference in recidivism rates between defendants found NGRI and non-NGRI felons or slightly lower recidivism rates among the NGRI group (Melton et al., 2018). For instance, in a year-long study examining rehospitalization and criminal recidivism in 43 NGRI acquittees, nearly half (47%) were rehospitalized, a minority of the patients (19%) were rearrested or had committed a new crime, and about a fourth of the patients (24%) were reintegrated into the community without difficulty (Kravitz & Kelly, 1999). Revocations in conditional release noted in the last paragraph (McDermott et al., 2008) could be for a variety of reasons beyond harming others or further offending—including a failure to comply with conditions related to substance use, treatment compliance, and other specified aspects of the plan. Individuals acquitted by reason of insanity may continue to have legal and/or behavioral health problems. But their overall rate of criminal recidivism does not exceed that for individuals who have been convicted, incarcerated, and subsequently returned to the community.

Current Criticisms of the Insanity Defense

Even if the insanity defense is not successful as often as presumed, legitimate concerns remain about its continued use. We will now evaluate several of these.

It Sends Undeserving Individuals to Hospitals and Then Frees Them. Those without mental illness but charged with a serious offense can try to capitalize on the insanity defense to avoid prison incarceration and eventually be released from the hospital. How often this happens is unknown. Some research described in the previous section indicates that persons found NGRI may be confined for long periods and are never required to be released, as the commitment is indeterminate. Other research finds that those acquitted by reason of insanity *when they are subsequently released* are confined for a shorter average time than those convicted of comparable offenses (Steadman et al., 1993). After confinement, those who have been acquitted by reason of insanity also may undergo an additional period of conditional release.

One major problem with such insanity acquittals is that they can be highly publicized, contributing to the public's perception that they "happen all the time," and that the insanity defense is therefore a constant threat to justice. But insanity acquittals are relatively rare, actually. Furthermore, if in the interest of protecting society all defendants found NGRI were kept hospitalized until they no longer showed symptoms of mental illness, then society would have to be willing to violate the rights of many mentally ill persons to protect against harm inflicted by a few.

It Is a Defense for the Privileged. Of all the criticisms leveled at the insanity defense, this one is perhaps the most clearly contradicted by the data. Earlier studies did not find socioeconomic or racial bias in the use or the success of the insanity defense (Boehnert, 1989; Howard & Clark, 1985; Nicholson et al., 1991; Pasewark & Pantle, 1981; Steadman et al., 1993) although subsequent research has identified BIPOC status as associated with greater reluctance to find a defendant insane (Bolin, 2019). In addition, the U.S. Supreme Court held in *Ake v. Oklahoma* (1985) that indigent defendants who plead insanity as part of capital (death penalty) cases are entitled to psychiatric assistance at state expense in pursuing this defense. Many states and communities have extended this ruling by providing public funding for indigent defendants asserting an insanity defense.

Although defendants who can afford to hire their own experts might be more likely to benefit from raising the issue of insanity, this is not a problem unique to the insanity defense. Defendants who can afford ballistics experts, chemists, and their own private detectives also have an advantage over poor defendants, but no one suggests that a defense based on ballistics evidence, blood analyses, or mistaken identity should be prohibited because of the expense.

It Relies Too Much on Mental Health Experts. Several issues are pertinent here. One criticism is that testifying about insanity requires psychiatrists and clinical psychologists to give opinions about things they are not competent or trained to do—for example, to express "reasonable certainty" rather than probability about a person's mental condition, and to claim greater knowledge about the relationship between psychological knowledge and legal questions than is justified.

Within the field of psychology, there is debate on these matters. The debate centers on two related questions: (1) Can clinicians reliably and validly assess mental illness, intellectual disability, neuropsychological disorders, trauma symptoms, and disorders occurring in childhood and adolescence? (2) Will this assessment permit the formulation of accurate opinions about a defendant's criminal responsibility for acts committed in the past? Researchers have found some support for the reliability and validity of psychologists' evaluations of criminal responsibility. Results from several studies revealed strong agreement (88% to 93%) between evaluators' recommendations and courts' decisions about defendants' criminal responsibility (see Viljoen et al., 2003), which is important because courts' decisions are one kind of "outcome validation measure" in this kind of research.

Additionally, critics are concerned over the intrusion of psychology and psychiatry into the decision-making process. They want to reserve the decision for the judge or jury, the fact finder in the trial. This criticism is an example of the general concern over the use and willingness of experts to answer legal questions for which they possess limited scientific evidence and mental health data. One remedy proposed to solve this problem is to prevent experts from giving what is often called **ultimate opinion testimony**; that is, they could describe a defendant's mental condition and the effects it could have had on their thinking and behavioral control, but they could not state conclusions about whether the defendant was sane or insane. As we've noted, the federal courts, as part of certain reforms of the insanity defense (the Insanity Defense Reform Act) prohibit mental health experts from offering ultimate opinion testimony about a defendant's insanity. But does this prohibition solve any problems, or is it merely a "cosmetic fix" (Rogers & Ewing, 1989) that has few effects?

In a study of whether prohibiting ultimate opinion testimony affects jury decisions (Fulero & Finkel, 1991), subjects were randomly assigned to read one of 10 different versions of a trial, all of which involved a defendant charged with murdering his boss and pleading insanity as a defense. For our purposes, the comparisons among three different versions of the trial are of greatest interest. Some subjects read transcripts in which the mental health experts for both sides gave only *diagnostic testimony* (that the defendant experienced a mental disorder at the time of the offense); a second group read a version in which the experts gave a diagnosis and then also offered differing *penultimate opinions* about the effects this disorder had on the defendant's understanding of the wrongfulness of his act; a final group read a transcript in which the experts offered differing diagnoses, penultimate opinions, and *ultimate opinion testimony* about whether the defendant was sane or insane at the time of the killing. Did ultimate opinion testimony affect the subjects' verdicts? Not in this study; subjects' verdicts were not significantly different regardless of the type of testimony they read. The lack of difference could be interpreted as evidence that the prohibition of ultimate opinion testimony is unnecessary, or it could indicate that the ban streamlines the trial process without sacrificing any essential information.

Finally, there is the criticism that the process of assessing sanity in criminal defendants harms the reputation of the mental health professions. When the jury sees a parade of mental health experts representing one side and then the other, their confidence in the behavioral sciences is jeopardized; this is also true for the general public, when they read about this process involving a number of different experts (Slater & Hans, 1984). This negative public perception may detract from generally favorable perceptions of the treatment activities of psychiatry and psychology (Angermeyer et al., 2017). Further, some experts, influenced by implicit bias, offer explanations favoring the retaining side that are not well-supported by the evidence, so their profession loses its credibility with jurors and the public. (This has been called the "allegiance effect" and pertains to the tendency for experts to favor the side that retained them. Refer to Murrie et al., 2013.) However, in some cases involving claims of insanity, the experts retained by each side basically agree on the question of insanity. These cases receive less publicity because they often end in a plea agreement, and are hard for researchers to access because they may not have resulted in an insanity plea.

Revisions and Reforms of the Insanity Defense

Several reforms in the rules and procedures for implementing the insanity defense have been introduced. Proposals have ranged from abolition of the insanity defense (as has already been done in four states), to provision of a "guilty but mentally ill" verdict, to reform of insanity statutes, to maintenance of the present procedures. We review three reforms in this section.

The Guilty but Mentally Ill (GBMI) Verdict. As of 2021, six states (Alaska, Arizona, Georgia, Idaho, Montana, and Utah) allow juries to reach a verdict of guilty but mentally ill (GBMI) in cases in which a defendant pleads insanity. GBMI rules differ from state to state, but generally they give a jury the following verdict alternatives for a defendant who is pleading insanity: (1) guilty of the crime, (2) not guilty of the crime, (3) NGRI, or (4) GBMI. Typically, a judge will sentence a defendant found GBMI as they would another defendant found guilty of the same offense. In some jurisdictions, the GBMI-convicted individual starts their term in a hospital and then is transferred to prison after treatment is completed. In others, the individual simply receives treatment (if needed) while serving a prison sentence.

Proponents of GBMI verdicts hoped that this compromise verdict would decrease the number of defendants found NGRI. However, actual GBMI statutes have not produced decreases in NGRI verdicts in South Carolina or Michigan (two states that have since abolished the GBMI option). One possible explanation for the lack of change in NGRI verdicts in states with GBMI statutes is that jurors do not understand the differences between the verdicts. One study examined jurors' knowledge about the two verdicts and found that only 4% of potential jurors correctly identified meanings and outcomes of both NGRI and GBMI verdicts (Sloat & Frierson, 2005).

Skepticism about the GBMI has been raised by various scholars (Borum & Fulero, 1999; Melton et al., 2018), for different reasons. First, if regular insanity instructions are confusing to jurors, then imagine how the GBMI option adds to the confusion by introducing the difficult distinction for juries to make between mental illness that results in insanity and mental illness that does not.

Also, the claim that the GBMI option will make it more likely that mentally ill offenders will receive treatment is largely a false promise. In Michigan, a group of 30 Guilty but Mentally Ill women received no discernably different treatment in prison than did a group of convicted women matched for symptoms of mental illness (Naidoo et al., 2018). One review of the GBMI verdict observed a "typical absence of treatment" for GBMI defendants (Palmer & Hazelrigg, 2000). State-level prison systems classify individuals who are sent to prison and, according to that classification, make decisions involving security, rehabilitation—and mental health treatment. It has not seemed to matter whether an individual arrives with a designation of Guilty but Mentally Ill.

The Defense of Diminished Capacity. Several states allow a defense of diminished capacity, which is a legal doctrine that applies to defendants who lack the ability to commit a crime purposely and knowingly. Like the insanity defense, diminished capacity often involves evidence that the defendant experiences a mental disorder. It differs from insanity in that it focuses on whether defendants had the state of mind to act with the purpose and the intent to commit a crime—that is, to consider the consequences of their contemplated actions—not on whether they knew the crime was wrong or whether they could control their behavior. Suppose M'Naghten knew that murder was wrong but, because of his mental condition, wasn't thinking clearly enough to form the intent to kill Peel's secretary. Under these conditions, he would not be insane, but he would lack the *mens rea* (the necessary specific intent) for first-degree murder, so he could have been convicted of second-degree murder or manslaughter.

The rationale for this defense is straightforward: Offenders should be convicted of the crime that matches their mental state, and expert testimony should be offered on the issue of their mental state. The majority of states permit expert testimony about a defendant's *mens rea*, thereby allowing clinicians to present testimony that could be used in support of a diminished-capacity defense (Melton et al., 2018). As long as proof of a defendant's *mens rea* is required, defendants are likely to put forward expert evidence about it, especially in those states that have abolished the insanity defense. Even when the diminished capacity defense "works," it still usually leads to a prison sentence.

Elimination of the Insanity Defense. Winslade and Ross (1983) reviewed seven trials (mostly for murder) in which the insanity defense was used and psychiatric testimony was introduced to justify it. Using an analysis of the outcomes of these trials, they recommended that the insanity defense be eliminated. This has occurred in four U.S. jurisdictions—the states of Idaho, Kansas, Montana, and Utah have abolished their respective insanity defenses—and the question of whether such abolition is unconstitutional has been addressed by the U.S. Supreme Court in *Kahler v. Kansas* (2020). The Court concluded that states could abolish the insanity defense without violating the Constitution.

A careful analysis suggests, however, that other states are unlikely to eliminate their own versions of the insanity defense (Appelbaum, 2020). This was also discussed by Morse and Bonnie (2013), who argued that it is morally justified to have an insanity defense available to those who genuinely meet the standard.

Like Appelbaum, Morse and Bonnie, we have concluded that the NGRI plea should be maintained as an option. We have further concluded that modifications of the system should be restricted to clarifying the standard and process, and defendants for whom the defense was successful should be evaluated. For example, the Insanity Defense Reform Act changed the law that required the prosecution to prove that John Hinckley was not insane. If a crime like Hinckley's were committed today in a federal jurisdiction or in the vast majority of states, the defendant, not the prosecution, would bear the responsibility of proving the plea; otherwise, the defendant would be found guilty. States should carefully monitor people committed after NGRI verdicts to ensure that they are not released while still mentally ill and dangerous. Indications are that this precaution is being taken.

Capital Sentencing Evaluations

Although mental health professionals are involved in many aspects of the legal process, none has more implication for a defendant's life than capital sentencing evaluations, which have been described as literally "a life or death matter" (*Satterwhite v. Texas*, 1988, p. 1802). The U.S. Supreme Court, in *Eddings v. Oklahoma* (1982), held that a trial court must consider any potentially mitigating information—evidence that argues *against* a death sentence. Mitigating factors are defined as "… any aspect of a defendant's character or record, or any of the circumstances of the offense that the defendant proffered as a basis for a sentence less than death" (*Lockett v. Ohio*, 1978, p. 604). This leaves the forensic clinician with a very broad focus for the evaluation.

Evaluators must consider information about a defendant's physical, cognitive, social, and developmental history. Understanding, judgment, impulsivity, and values are influenced by developmental, cognitive, neuropsychological, cultural, community, situational, and other life influences, and it is important to consider these dimensions as part of a capital sentencing evaluation.

Some jurisdictions also consider the question of a defendant's future risk to society, and forensic clinicians often evaluate and testify about these risks. Texas requires that the jury consider future risk in weighing a sentence of death (Cunningham, 2010). Oregon and Virginia also specify future dangerousness as a consideration in capital sentencing. Two other states (Oklahoma and Wyoming) list future dangerousness as a potential aggravating factor when present, and four additional states (Colorado, Maryland, New Mexico, and Washington) note its absence as a potential mitigating factor. The U.S. Supreme Court has also held that the *absence* of dangerousness in prison can be considered a mitigating factor in all capital cases (*Skipper v. South Carolina*, 1986).

In addition to considering factors encompassing mitigation and future violence risk, clinical evaluations must also address the question of eligibility for capital sentencing if the defendant may be intellectually disabled, which would exempt the defendant from the death penalty, consistent with the Supreme Court decision in *Atkins v. Virginia* (2002). It is also useful to consider the quality of such evaluations, given the enormous importance of the sentencing decision (DeMatteo et al., 2011). There has been a robust debate about the use of the Psychopathy Checklist-Revised in capital sentencing, insofar as it is used to appraise the risk of future harm to others in prison (DeMatteo et al., 2020a, 2020b; Olver et al., 2020). Much of the debate centers around how accurately the PCL-R predicts serious institutional violence—and how good it should be for such use, given that "death is different."

Juvenile Transfer

During the 1980s and 1990s, there was substantial reform in the juvenile and criminal justice systems in the United States to allow more frequent prosecution of juveniles in criminal (adult) court. Such reform was motivated largely by the perception that juvenile crime had increased—and become more serious. A "get tough" approach was adopted in the attempt to decrease the rate of juvenile offending. One aspect of this "do the crime, do the time" philosophy involved expansion of ways in which adolescent (under 18 years old) offenders could be **transferred** (also called certified or waived) into criminal court.

States vary in their specification of the age at which an adolescent is eligible for prosecution in the criminal system. Some states do not have any age limit; others have passed legislation decreasing the age of eligibility. Most still use the age of 14 or 15, however.

There are several justifications for transferring an adolescent into the criminal system: (1) a charge of homicide; (2) a charge of other specific violent felonies (e.g., sexual assault, armed robbery, aggravated battery); or (3) a history of prior juvenile offending, suggesting a failure to respond to interventions provided by the juvenile system. In addition, some states have a policy involving "once an adult, always an adult," under which any adolescent convicted (or even tried) in criminal court will be charged in criminal court for future offenses, regardless of their nature or that individual's age.

Different criteria are described in state laws on juvenile transfer. Two of the most important are public safety and **treatment needs and amenability**. Another criterion often used is **sophistication-maturity**. Those evaluating a juvenile for a possible transfer must focus on the risk of future offending, the interventions needed to reduce this risk, and the likelihood that the youth will respond favorably to such interventions. The extent to which juveniles are mature—cognitively and psychosocially—and the degree to which they are "adult-like" in their criminal thinking and behavior can both affect their response to interventions. The risk/need/responsivity (RNR) model (Andrews & Bonta, 1990) is useful in this respect, as it prompts the evaluator to consider risk of reoffending and risk-relevant deficits (e.g., substance abuse, family problems, education/employment problems) carefully. This consideration can be facilitated by using an empirically supported specialized tool, such as the Structured Assessment of Violence Risk in Youth (SAVRY; Borum, Bartels, & Forth, 2005), the Youth Level of Service/Case Management Inventory (YLS/CMI; Hoge & Andrews, 2002), or the Risk-Sophistication-Treatment Inventory (Salekin, 2004).

Assessing a youth being considered for transfer is a forensic evaluation. It involves a legal question that will be answered by the judge, just as competence and insanity do. With juveniles, this means that evaluators must pay particular attention to school and family functioning, often by obtaining school records and conducting interviews of family members. Evaluators should also obtain information in other important areas. Peers, for example, can have an important influence on an adolescent's behavior. Was the offense committed alone, or was the youth with peers who may have encouraged one another to offend—or at least refused to back down? Substance abuse is another very important risk factor for offending; both using drugs and selling drugs are areas that should be targeted for intervention. Determining whether interventions addressing such risk factors will be effective with a particular individual is difficult. Whether intervention will help a particular youth to desist from offending may be judged partly from the individual's expressed motivation, capacity to admire and respect authority figures, and responses to previous interventions (Grisso, 1998).

Juveniles can be transferred to criminal (adult) court in several different ways. The state legislature in a jurisdiction can determine that certain offenses allegedly committed by an adolescent must be filed directly in adult court (Griffin, 2003). For example, a state legislature may pass a law dictating that certain serious felony charges (e.g., armed robbery, sexual battery) be prosecuted in criminal court if the defendant is over a certain age. This approach to transfer has been called **statutory exclusion**. As of 2018, 28 states had statutory exclusion for certain offenses (OJJDP, 2018).

A second approach to transferring juveniles to criminal court has been termed **judicial discretion**. When this procedure is used, the juvenile court judge decides whether the youth should be transferred to criminal court. Some 46 states provide for this type of transfer (OJJDP, 2018). In making such a decision, the judge typically considers statutorily specified influences such as the youth's risk to public safety, amenability to treatment, and maturity (Brannen et. al., 2006; Heilbrun et al., 2017). Such factors can be evaluated by mental health professionals, and the results described in the report and in expert testimony, to help inform the judge in making this decision.

A third approach to juvenile transfer is called **prosecutorial discretion**. Prosecutorial discretion requires prosecutors to decide whether cases are filed initially in juvenile or adult court. As of 2018, 13 states had the option of prosecutorial discretion for certain offenses (OJJDP, 2018).

Is putting juveniles in the adult system effective in reducing reoffending? Common sense might suggest that adolescents would be less likely to offend if they knew that offending could result in more severe punishment. But research has not supported this. Research on general deterrent effects has reflected no decline in juvenile crime after these transfer laws came into effect. One study found no differences in the juvenile homicide/manslaughter rates in the states with prosecutorial discretion policies in the first five years after transfer laws were enacted (Steiner & Wright, 2006). Housing juveniles with adult criminals may also promote criminal attitudes and motivations (Forst et al., 1989). Juveniles detained in New York's adult system were 89% more likely to be rearrested for a violent offense and 44% more likely to be rearrested for a property offense than juveniles in the New York metropolitan area who were detained within New Jersey's juvenile court system (Fagan, 1996). Higher rates of recidivism have also been observed in other studies with youth detained in the adult correctional system (Bishop et al., 1996; Fagan et al., 2004; Mason & Chang, 2001; Myers, 2001, 2003; Steiner et al., 2006). Research also suggests that juveniles in adult facilities were more likely to be sexually and physically assaulted than were youth in the juvenile facilities (Beyer, 1997).

Juvenile transfer may also occur in the other direction (when juveniles placed in adult court are returned to juvenile court). This procedure has been called **reverse transfer**. Many states provide this option, allowing the criminal court judge to review the case and determine whether the youth should remain in adult court. Some 23 states have reverse transfer procedures that allow juveniles in adult court to petition for transfer back to juvenile court (King, 2017).

Summary

1. **What is the scope of forensic psychology?** Forensic psychology is a specialty that involves the application of knowledge and techniques from the behavioral sciences to answer questions about individuals involved in legal proceedings. The legal questions that psychological and psychiatric experts are asked to help address through evaluation and testimony are better informed by scientific research and applicable specialized forensic assessment measures.

2. **What is meant by competence in the criminal justice process?** Adjudicative competence entails having a sufficient present ability to consult with one's attorney with a reasonable degree of rational understanding and having a rational, as well as factual, understanding of the proceedings. This same standard is applied to the questions of whether a defendant is competent to plead guilty and whether a defendant is competent to stand trial, so the phrase "competence to stand trial" is often used to refer to the entire process of disposition of charges, not merely the trial.

3. **How do clinicians assess competence?** When mental health professionals assess a defendant's competence, they can use one of several specialized instruments designed specifically for evaluating how well a defendant understands the charges and potential proceedings. These specific tests and structured interviews have made competence assessments more reliable, valid, and useful. Competence evaluations are sometimes complicated by such factors as malingering, amnesia, and the problem of whether incompetent defendants can be treated against their will. Other competence issues (e.g., competence to refuse the insanity defense and competence to be sentenced) can arise at different points in the criminal process.

4. **What are the consequences of being found incompetent to proceed in the criminal justice process?** When defendants are found incompetent to stand trial, they can be committed for a period of treatment designed to restore their competence. If they are subsequently adjudicated as competent to stand trial following experts' recommendations and a judge's decision, they will stand trial

or dispose of their charges through the plea-bargaining process. If treatment is not successful in restoring competence and the defendant is adjudicated as unrestorably incompetent, the state will usually attempt to civilly commit the person to a state psychiatric hospital. The use of the Demonstration Model (involving more intensive and individualized treatment, accompanied by careful documentation) has been proposed to help guide the consideration of whether incompetent defendants are unrestorable. This involves an alternative to hospitalization or other treatment that is too brief or too long.

5. **What is the legal definition of insanity?** Two major definitions of insanity are used currently in the United States. The M'Naghten rule defines insanity as not knowing the nature, quality, or wrongfulness of behavior because of mental disease or defect. The Brawner rule states that a person is not responsible for a criminal act if, as a result of mental disease or defect, the person lacked "substantial capacity either to appreciate the criminality of his conduct or to conform his conduct to the requirements of the law." The federal system now requires the defense to show that, as a result of a severe mental disease or defect, the defendant was unable to appreciate the nature and quality or the wrongfulness of their acts. Four states have outlawed insanity as a defense, although these states still allow the defendant to introduce evidence about their mental condition that is relevant to determining *mens rea*. Some highly publicized trials have led to "successful" use of the insanity defense. But many others who used this defense were found guilty.

6. **How frequently is the insanity defense used, and how successful is it?** The insanity plea is used much less frequently than many assume; it is attempted in fewer than 1% of cases, and it succeeds in only about 23% of these cases. When it does succeed, there is no guarantee that the defendant will be released from the hospital any sooner than they would have been paroled from prison.

7. **What are the major criticisms of the insanity defense, and what attempts have been made to reform it?** Some examples of early release of defendants found NGRI have led to justified criticism of the procedure. Other criticisms are that insanity cannot be reliably and validly assessed and that the insanity defense relies too much on mental health expert testimony. Reforms include the Insanity Defense Reform Act and the adoption in several states of a "guilty but mentally ill" verdict. Some states also allow the diminished capacity plea, a partial defense based on mental condition.

8. **What are the important criteria in deciding on juvenile transfer?** One important consideration is public safety—the risk that a youth would commit further offenses following rehabilitation in the juvenile system. A second related consideration is the youth's needs and likely response to interventions reducing the risk of future offending, often called "treatment needs and amenability." Many jurisdictions also cite a youth's "sophistication-maturity," involving the extent to which the developmental level and the approach to offending resemble those of adults.

Key Terms

adjudicative competence

Brawner rule

competence

competence to plead guilty

competence to stand trial

diminished capacity

insanity

judicial discretion

M'Naghten rule

mens rea

Miranda rights

prosecutorial discretion

reverse transfer

sophistication-maturity

statutory exclusion

stipulate

transferred

treatment needs and amenability

ultimate opinion testimony

Chapter 11

Forensic Assessment in Civil Cases

Orienting Questions

1. What problems are associated with expert testimony, and what reforms have been proposed?

2. Under what conditions can a plaintiff be compensated for psychological damages?

3. What is workers' compensation, and how do mental health professionals participate in such cases?

4. What capacities are involved in civil competence?

5. What criteria are used for decisions about disputes involving child custody or parental fitness?

6. What steps are taken in civil commitment? How well can clinicians assess the risk of dangerousness or violent behavior, a key criterion for civil commitment?

Whether a defendant is competent to stand trial (often called *adjudicative competence*, because it refers to a defendant's capacities to dispose of charges either through a trial or via plea bargaining) and whether a defendant was insane at the time of an alleged criminal offense are two of the best-known legal questions that mental health professionals help courts decide. However, they are certainly not the only questions. Throughout earlier chapters, we examined other questions arising in the legal system that psychologists are often asked to consider. Is a given individual a good candidate to become a police officer? Will a person who is experiencing from mental illness be violent in the future? How accurate is one's memory for, and testimony about, highly traumatic events likely to be? These questions—like those of competence and insanity—are often asked of forensic psychologists and psychiatrists, and they are usually answered through a combination of research knowledge and the results of individual assessments performed by forensic clinicians.

Different kinds of litigation are making use of scientific knowledge and expert opinion. Psychology and psychiatry are two fields in which the use of experts has proliferated. Melton et al. (2018) offer a comprehensive listing and description of the legal questions that are most often addressed in civil, juvenile/family, and criminal cases. In addition to the legal questions discussed in previous chapters, mental health experts are involved in hearings or trials in the areas of civil commitment; psychological damages in civil cases; psychological autopsies (i.e., after-death appraisal of the extent to which psychological problems may have influenced the causes of death, particularly in cases that may have involved self-inflicted harm); negligence and product liability; trademark litigation; discrimination; guardianship and conservatorship (a guardianship-like arrangement for an individual's financial assets); child custody; adoption; termination of parental rights; professional malpractice; and other social issues such as sexual harassment in the workplace. In certain jurisdictions, therefore, judges must decide whether the expert testimony that an attorney seeks to introduce meets the criteria that the U.S. Supreme Court has established in the federal courts as the standard for admitting scientific evidence and expert testimony.

In this chapter, we provide information about expert testimony in civil cases, and describe six areas of forensic assessment in which psychologists and psychiatrists are involved: (1) psychological damages to civil plaintiffs, (2) workers' compensation claims, (3) the assessment of civil competencies and capacities, (4) psychological autopsy, (5) child custody and parental fitness, and (6) civil commitment and risk assessment. Although these areas do not receive the publicity commanded by adjudicative competence or insanity at the time of the offense, they illustrate several ways in which psychological expertise can be applied to important legal questions. For each of the six areas, we:

- discuss the basic psycholegal questions that experts are expected to address,

- describe the techniques typically used by forensic clinicians to evaluate these questions, and

- summarize the empirical evidence and legal status associated with the forensic activity.

Experts in the Adversarial System

In general, a qualified expert can testify about a topic if such testimony is relevant to an issue in dispute and if the usefulness of the testimony outweighs whatever prejudicial impact it might have. If these two conditions are met, an expert will be permitted to testify if the judge decides that the testimony is based on sufficiently relevant and reliable scientific evidence. In other words, under criteria established by the U.S. Supreme Court in *Daubert v. Merrell Dow Pharmaceuticals* (1993) and *Kumho Tire Co. v. Carmichael* (1999), the judge serves as a "gatekeeper" who must determine whether the theory, methodology, and analysis that are the basis of the expert's opinion measure up to scientific standards. If they meet this standard, the judge will probably admit relevant expert testimony; if they do not, the judge should not allow the testimony. The *Daubert* and *Kumho* decisions apply to all cases in federal court. In state court, the prevailing standard may also be *Daubert*—or it may stem from an earlier decision (*Frye v. United States*, 1923) holding that expert testimony must be based on techniques and process that are "generally accepted" in the field to which they belong. States have the discretion to decide which standard they will use by passing state legislation.

Judges generally do not perform the gatekeeper function well (Gatowski et al., 2001). Many judges lack the scientific training that *Daubert/Kumho* appears to require. Even for those with substantial scientific training, the range of expert topics about which judges need information is staggering. As a result, many critics, including experts and judges themselves, believe that the difficulty of distinguishing valid from invalid scientific evidence will result in jurors too often being exposed to "expert" testimony that is based on little more than "junk science" (Grove & Barden, 1999; consider Box 11.1). The presence of such junk science is a substantial problem when it forms the basis for expert testimony. Review https://www.nj.com/opinion/2020/05/netflix-series-reveal-injustice-and-junk-science-are-plaguing-our-nations-courts.html for examples—and https://www.usnews.com/news/best-states/california/articles/2022-01-26/california-senate-aims-to-limit-junk-science-in-courtrooms for legislative attempts to reduce it.

There are clear advantages to having mental health professionals provide expert testimony. Mental health professionals have specialized knowledge and training that can provide the court with valuable information in a variety of cases. For example, some psychologists are trained to administer tests to determine neuropsychological problems and symptom genuineness in workers' compensation cases, or are experienced in conducting interviews and obtaining other information from multiple sources to assess parental fitness.

However, judges, lawyers, and mental health professionals themselves have expressed great concern about the reliability, validity, propriety, and usefulness of expert testimony and the forensic assessment on which it is based. Former federal appellate judge David Bazelon (1974) once complained that "psychiatry … is the ultimate wizardry … in no case is it more difficult to elicit productive and reliable testimony than in cases that call on the knowledge and practice of psychiatry." Critiques of psychologists' and psychiatrists' expert testimony have continued over the decades (see, e.g., Faust, 2012; Grisso, 2003; Melton et al., 2018; Tillbrook et al., 2003).

What are the main problems with testimony by psychological or psychiatric experts? Grisso (2003) discussed

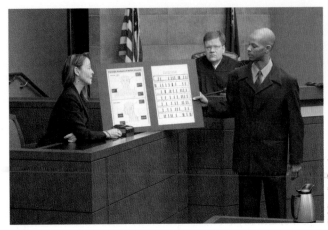

An expert witness in direct examination.

Box 11.1

The Case of Columbine Shooter Eric Harris, Antidepressant Medication, and Violence: Expert Opinion or Junk Science?

In 2002, Mark Taylor, a survivor of the Columbine High School shooting, sued the pharmaceutical company that manufactures Luvox, the antidepressant drug that one of the shooters, Eric Harris, was taking at the time of the shooting. Is there scientific evidence that this drug caused Eric Harris to be violent? Peter Breggin, M.D., one of the experts involved in the litigation, thought so. Was his testimony impartial and based on good science? Or was it an example of expert bias, poor science, or both?

Breggin opined in a preliminary report filed with the U.S. District Court in Denver that Luvox triggered Harris's rampage. "Absent persistent exposure to Luvox, Eric Harris would probably not have committed violence and suicide," noted Breggin.

Breggin, a psychiatrist who was then based in Washington, D.C., described himself as a medical expert with 30 years of experience in product liability lawsuits involving psychiatric drugs. However, some of this history reflects the skepticism of legal fact finders about his impartiality. A Wisconsin judge in 1997 observed, "Dr. Breggin's observations are totally without credibility. I can almost declare him [to be a] fraud or at least approaching that. I cannot place any credence or credibility in what he has to recommend in this case." On the question of whether his opinion reflects good science, another court held in 1995 that "Dr. Breggin's opinions do not rise to the level of an opinion based on 'good science.' The motion to exclude his testimony as an expert witness should be granted." The question of Breggin's impartiality may be one reason that Taylor eventually dropped his lawsuit in exchange for a contribution from the pharmaceutical company to the American Cancer Society.

Eric Harris and Dylan Klebold, Columbine High shooters, shown via school surveillance video.

Critical Thought Questions

1. What are some of the characteristics you would expect from an expert whose testimony is grounded in science?

2. How might "litigation bias" influence an expert who was conducting the scientific research, as opposed to citing the research of others?

3. How might one court's critical language about an expert influence that expert's work on similar litigation matters in the future?

criticisms of forensic mental health assessment that he calls "the five I's": ignorance, irrelevance, intrusion, insufficiency, and incredibility. These refer to not knowing (or not using) the proper legal standard; providing evidence that goes beyond what is relevant to the proceeding; offering conclusions that impinge upon the court's domain; providing limited supporting evidence for one's conclusions; and offering conclusions that are not justified by the evidence one does provide. These criticisms are similar in some respects to those described by others (e.g., Smith, 1989) over three decades ago. Although Smith was talking about expert testimony and Grisso was referring to forensic assessment more broadly, their overlap underscores an important point: good expert testimony is based on a good evaluation.

Various reforms of expert testimony have been proposed. Most of these suggestions are aimed at reducing the undue influence or excessive partisanship that can adversely affect expert testimony. Of course, reforming expert testimony without also applying such reforms to expert reports would substantially limit the impact of such reform—as most adjudications of not guilty by reason of insanity, like other adjudications, result from plea negotiations rather than trials (Melton et al., 2018).

One reform involves prohibiting testifying experts from directly answering the ultimate legal question (e.g., guilt or innocence; liability or no liability). Since 1984, as part of the Insanity Defense Reform Act, the federal courts have not permitted expert testimony that directly answers the ultimate legal question of insanity when a plea of not guilty by reason of insanity has been entered. However, there is little evidence that such limitation of expert testimony has much impact on the use or success of the insanity defense (Borum & Fulero, 1999)—it applies only to testimony in federal cases—and it also would not affect the other kinds of cases we discuss in this chapter.

Increasing the impartiality of experts would be a useful reform. Most authors and sources of authority suggest that partisanship in expert witnesses should be reduced or eliminated entirely. But a few do not. For instance, in his book entitled *Behind the Scenes with an Expert Witness*, Tanay (2010) describes his own experience as a psychiatric expert—particularly on the legal question of insanity—and argues that the expert should be a strong advocate so that unjust jury verdicts are less likely. Reviewing this book, prominent psychologist Stan Brodsky (who has done a great deal of research and scholarship on the topic of expert testimony) discusses the personal and idiosyncratic approach taken by Dr. Tanay to expert testimony. Such an approach, says Brodsky, makes for interesting reading—but it also involves more advocacy (and less impartiality) than is appropriate for the forensic expert.

Other suggestions have involved reducing the overly adversarial nature of expert testimony by limiting the number of experts on a given topic, requiring that the experts be chosen from an approved panel of individuals reputed to be impartial and highly competent, and allowing testimony only from experts who have been appointed by a judge rather than hired by one of the opposing attorneys. Although these changes would appear to reduce the "hired gun" problem, it is not clear which experts would belong on an approved list, or whether being appointed by a judge ensures an expert's impartiality. Furthermore, some research suggests that jurors might already be inclined to discount the testimony of experts whom they perceive to be "hired guns" because of the high fees such experts are paid and their history of testifying frequently (Cooper & Neuhaus, 2000).

It may be that there are a few forensic psychologists and forensic psychiatrists who are motivated primarily by money and can be consistently relied upon to render opinions that are favorable to the attorney who retains them. In our view, however, this is a small number—and these individuals develop a certain reputation in forensic mental health and legal circles. The more common problem that may influence many experts is what has been called "allegiance bias" or "retention bias." The question of whether experts can remain impartial and accurate without regard to which side has retained them has been addressed through research. In a comprehensive review of relevant studies, Murrie and Boccaccini (2015) summarized the factors that can diminish impartiality and concluded that working at the request of one side in an adversarial proceeding can cause experts' opinions to "drift" toward the retaining party, even in scoring "objective" testing. They suggest that this process is part of a larger influence on human decision-making, in which "cognitive biases" have an important influence on how human beings make decisions.

There are other kinds of bias that apply to human decision-making more broadly. The work of Daniel Kahneman and Amos Tversky (see, e.g., Kahneman, 2011; Lewis, 2017) identified a number of factors that affect how people make decisions under conditions of uncertainty, when there are no clear and objectively "right" answers. These influences can impair the impartiality and accuracy of evaluations and testimony presented by forensic clinicians, particularly in the context of an adversarial system. As they apply to forensic assessment and testimony six biases are particularly relevant:

- Representativeness—overemphasizing evidence that resembles a typical representation of a prototype (e.g., making attributions about an individual's motivation because that individual resembles a "drug addict" in many ways);

- Base rate neglect—judging the likelihood of an outcome without considering information about the actual probability of this outcome, as conveyed by base rates (e.g., predicting a serious act of violence by someone who shows predictors consistent with a group that rarely behaves this way);

- Availability—overemphasizing the probability of occurrence when similar instances are easy to recall (e.g., from a recent, highly publicized case);

- Confirmation bias—selectively gathering and interpreting evidence that confirms a hypothesis while ignoring evidence that might disconfirm it (e.g., as a result of using early impressions in an evaluation to shape the gathering of additional evidence);

- WYSIATI (what you see is all there is)—organizing activated information to derive the most coherent "story" while leaving out non-activated information (e.g., by focusing on information that has been "activated," perhaps via confirmation bias, and consequently constructing an account that is excessively consistent because it excludes contradictory information); and

- Anchoring—information encountered first is the most influential.

Acknowledging the presence of such biases among forensic mental health professionals, and developing "debiasing" strategies, thus seem to have broad potential for improving both forensic mental health evaluation and the expert testimony that may result. One such debiasing strategy is to conduct forensic evaluations that are guided by foundational principles, and basing expert testimony on the results of such evaluations (Heilbrun et al., 2009). Another is to conduct training, and periodically review one's professional performance, by reviewing whether the biases described in the last paragraph are affecting performance.

A detailed empirical consideration of debiasing strategies for forensic assessment (Neal & Brodsky, 2016) identified four categories of debiasing strategy: (1) *effective*—identified by empirical research and supported by clinicians; (2) *ineffective*—contraindicated by research but supported by clinicians; (3) *overlooked* (research-identified effective strategies not cited by clinicians); and (4) *newly identified by clinicians and promising*. Effective strategies include training about human decision-making, taking time to think about evaluation information, consulting with colleagues, using structured evaluation methods, examining patterns of decision-making (e.g., agreement with the retaining party), and critically examining conclusions by first generating alternative hypotheses. Ineffective strategies, by contrast, include introspection and failing to account for the bias blind spot (the assumption that one is not subject to the same biases that others are). In the "overlooked" category, Neal and Brodsky cite exposure control (limiting information that is influential but largely irrelevant) and blinding (not including information in the report about the retaining side). Newly identified strategies, while not yet evaluated for their effectiveness, include taking careful notes, and strengthening pride in one's professional identity. To this nuanced description we might add "carefully avoiding any comment about specific cases that are active."

Several scholars have suggested that courts not permit clinical opinion testimony unless it can be shown that it satisfies standards of scientific reliability. The standard required by the *Daubert/Kumho* decisions has made this recommendation more feasible (Imwinkelried, 1994). Such a requirement might reduce the frequency of testimony by forensic psychologists and psychiatrists, but unless lawyers and judges are educated more thoroughly about scientific methodology, it is unlikely that many of them will be able to correctly apply the concepts described in *Daubert* (e.g., falsifiability, error rate) toward making informed distinctions between "good" and "bad" science (Melton et al., 2018).

Psychological Damages to Civil Plaintiffs

When one party—a person, business, or other entity—is injured by the actions of a second party, the injured party can sue the second party to recover monetary damages as compensation for the injury. This action is covered by an area of civil law known as torts. A **tort** is a wrongful act that causes harm. The criminal law also exacts compensation for wrongful acts, but on behalf of society as a whole; by punishing an offender, the criminal law attempts to maintain society's overall sense of justice. Tort law, on the other hand, provides a mechanism to more specifically remedy the harms that individuals or other entities have suffered from wrongful acts by another party.

As illustrated by the January 6, 2021 insurrection at the U.S. Capitol, both criminal punishment and civil remedies can be sought for the same act. Consider the possibility that a Metropolitan Police Officer could file suit against someone alleged to have conspired in planning the events of that day, with the officer seeking compensatory and punitive damages for physical and emotional injuries. This action would be independent of any criminal prosecution of that individual. This was also seen historically in the O.J. Simpson case. Simpson was prosecuted for the murder of Nicole Brown Simpson under criminal law (and acquitted); he was also sued for monetary damages by the surviving relatives of Nicole Brown Simpson and Ronald Goldman (and found liable under this civil litigation).

Many kinds of behavior can constitute a tort. Slander and libel are torts, as are cases of professional malpractice, invasion of privacy, the manufacture of defective products that result in a personal injury, and intentional or negligent behavior producing harm to another person.

Four elements are involved in proving a tort in a court of law and all involve behavioral issues. First, torts occur in situations in which one entity owes a **duty**, or has an obligation, to another. For instance, a physician has a duty to treat patients in accordance with accepted professional standards, and individuals have a duty not to harm others physically or psychologically. Second, a tort typically requires proving that one party breached or violated a duty that was owed to other parties. The **breached duty** can be due to negligence or intentional wrongdoing. **Negligence** is behavior that falls below a standard for protecting others from unreasonable risks; it is often measured by asking whether a "reasonable person" would have acted as the civil defendant acted in similar circumstances. **Intentional behavior** is conduct in which a person meant the outcome of a given act to occur. Third, the violation of the duty must have been the proximate cause of the harm suffered by a plaintiff. A **proximate cause** is one that constitutes an obvious or substantial reason why a given harm occurred. It is sometimes equated with producing an outcome that is "foreseeable." So if a given event would be expected to cause a given outcome, it is a proximate cause. Fourth, a **harm**, or loss, must occur, and the harm has to involve a legally protected right or interest for which the person can seek to recover damages that have been suffered. If it can be established that (1) there was a duty, (2) that was breached, (3) which proximately caused the (4) resulting harm, then a tort can be proven in a civil lawsuit.

The damages suffered from a tort can involve destruction of personal property, monetary loss, physical injuries, and/ or emotional distress (sometimes called "pain and suffering"). Historically, the law has always sought to compensate victims who are physically hurt or sustain property losses, but it was reluctant to allow compensation for emotional distress, largely out of concern that such damages are too easy to fake and too difficult to measure. In cases in which recovery for emotional damages has been allowed, the courts have historically required that a physical injury has accompanied the psychological harm or that a plaintiff who was not physically injured was at least in a "zone of danger." (For example, even if the plaintiff was not injured by the attack of an escaped wild animal, the plaintiff was standing next to their children when the animal attacked them.)

One case that received extensive international coverage illustrates this historical approach to emotional damages. On the afternoon of March 22, 1990, the *Aleutian Enterprise*, a large fishing boat, capsized in the Bering Sea. Within 10 minutes, the boat sank, killing nine crew members. Twenty-two sailors survived the disaster; of these men, two returned to work in a short time, but the other twenty filed a lawsuit against the company that owned the ship. Of the 20 plaintiffs, 19 consulted a psychologist or psychiatrist, and every one of these 19 individuals was subsequently diagnosed with posttraumatic stress disorder (PTSD) by his evaluating mental health professional (Rosen, 1995). (The defendant company hired its own psychologist, who evaluated the plaintiffs and diagnosed PTSD in only five of them and some other post-incident disorder in three others.) The surviving sailors were entitled to recover for their psychological injuries because they had been in the "zone of danger."

Subsequently, the courts have progressed to a view in which psychological symptoms and mental distress are more likely to be compensated regardless of whether the plaintiff suffered physical injuries. Two types of "purely" psychological injuries are now claimed in civil lawsuits: those arising from "negligent" behavior and those arising from "extreme and outrageous" conduct that is intended to cause distress. In the former type of case, plaintiffs are often allowed to sue for psychological damages if they are bystanders to an incident in which a loved one is injured (e.g., a parent sees their child crushed to death when a defective roller coaster—on which the child was riding—derails).

In the case of intentional torts causing psychological distress, a plaintiff must prove that a defendant intentionally or recklessly acted in an extreme and outrageous fashion (sometimes defined as "beyond all bounds of decency") to cause emotional distress. In addition, the plaintiff must prove that the distress is severe. What kinds of behavior might qualify? Consider the conduct of a debt collector who was trying to locate a debtor when he posed as a hospital employee—and told the debtor's mother that her grandchildren had been seriously injured in a wreck and that he needed to find the debtor to inform him of this fact (*Ford Motor Credit Co. v. Sheehan*, 1979). Under the court's decision in this case, the conduct was "extreme and outrageous."

An increasing number of subsequent cases have dealt with psychological injuries resulting from the tort of sexual harassment, usually in the workplace. A plaintiff who claims to have been sexually harassed at work can sue the workers responsible for the harassment and can also sue the company itself, if the plaintiff can show that the company knew (or should have known) about the harassment and failed to stop it. These cases can be filed either in state court or in federal court, where Title VII of the federal Civil Rights Act of 1991 applies to companies with at least 15 employees. Plaintiffs can seek both **compensatory damages** (payment for injuries suffered) and **punitive damages** (punishment of the company for its failure to respond properly to the misconduct).

Of course, the tort of harassment is not always based on sexual misconduct. It may incorporate other characteristics—including racial/ethnic group or religious beliefs, as we see in the case of antiterrorism officer "John Doe," described in Box 11.2.

Assessment of Psychological Damages

When a mental health professional assesses a plaintiff, the clinician will typically conduct an evaluation that, like most forensic mental health assessments, includes a social history, a clinical interview, and possibly psychological tests and specialized forensic measures (Melton et al., 2018). One major difference, however, between standard clinical evaluations and forensic assessments is the much greater use of third-party interviews and review of available records in forensic examinations. This practice is based on two basic considerations (Heilbrun, 2001; Melton et al., 2018). First, forensic experts must be confident that their opinions are based on accurate information, and self-reported information in the context of litigation is not necessarily accurate. Second, forensic experts are often asked to evaluate an individual's psychological condition at some specific time or circumstance in the past. Therefore, clinicians must use independent sources of information, when possible, to verify their descriptions and judgments about such matters.

Box 11.2

The Case of Antiterrorism Officer "John Doe": Racial/Ethnic and Religious Discrimination in the Workplace

Discrimination in the workplace can occur for different reasons. Consider the case of "John Doe," an undercover police officer in the New York City Police Department (NYPD). Egyptian-born and Muslim, he was subjected to treatment that may have been discriminatory for ethnic and religious reasons. The NPYD has contained an undercover unit of investigators, most of whom are of Middle Eastern or Asian backgrounds, who use their language and cultural skills to investigate potential terrorist threats against New York City. But one Egyptian-born analyst in the unit filed a suit charging that he was subjected to hundreds of anti-Muslim and anti-Arab e-mail messages sent out by a city contractor over the course of three years. In an interview, "Mr. Doe" (who was not named because he was still in the unit) said he complained repeatedly to supervisors but that no one took action.

The lawsuit cites e-mail briefing messages sent out several times a day to members of the unit by Bruce Tefft, a former Central Intelligence Agency (CIA) official who has identified himself in the past as the Police Department's counterterrorism adviser. (The suit was filed against both the NYPD and Tefft.) The e-mail messages were sent to everyone in the division, according to the suit, which also alleges that the briefing messages were preceded by anti-Muslim and anti-Arab statements like, "Burning the hate-filled Koran should be viewed as a public service at the least" and "This is not a war against terrorism … it is against Islam and we are not winning." In one, he asked, "Has the U.S. threatened to vaporize Mecca?" and responded, "Excellent idea, if true." The lawsuit alleged that e-mails "ridiculed and disparaged the Muslim religion and Arab people, and stated that Muslim- and Arab-Americans were untrustworthy and could

not reliably serve in law enforcement positions or handle sensitive data."

According to a NYPD spokesman, the police commissioner was not aware of the "offensive commentary" until the complaint was made. "As soon as the Police Department became aware of a complaint about the content of e-mail sent by an individual not employed by the Police Department, we took immediate action to block his e-mails, followed by a cease and desist letter to the individual and his employer, a consulting firm," he wrote.

Reportedly the department's contract with this advisor ended in 2003, but Tefft continued to send the e-mail messages on his own, circumventing attempts by the department to block them. Mr. Doe's lawyer commented, "It's incredible in this day and age that hundreds of racist e-mails could be sent to hundreds of NYPD officials over three years, and not one person did a thing to stop it."

This unit was profiled on "60 Minutes" and in the *Wall Street Journal* and the New York *Daily News*. Mr. Doe said, "The NYPD was happy to introduce us to the press—'Here these guys are, the best of the best, they are doing a great job.' But then they failed to protect us under this smear, this constantly daily attack against my religion and against good Muslim Arab-Americans, and I will say good because the majority are good."

Critical Thought Question

Can you apply a tort law framework in analyzing this lawsuit? What are the questions that a court will need to answer in deciding whether the lawsuit should be decided in favor of the plaintiff (the officer who filed the suit)?

Using data from these sources, the clinician arrives at an opinion about the psychological condition of the person in question. With the exception of greater reliance on third-party interviews and records, this part of the evaluation resembles a standard clinical evaluation of individuals assessed for diagnostic and treatment purposes. The more difficult question the clinician must answer in litigation, however, is whether the psychological problems were caused by the tort, were aggravated by the tort, or existed before the tort. In fact, given that some research suggests that psychological problems make people more prone to accidents, the clinician needs to consider whether certain psychological conditions might have contributed to the plaintiff being injured in the first place.

There is no established procedure for answering these questions, although most clinicians try to locate records

and other sources of information that help them describe the development of any disorder that is diagnosed. In some situations, a plaintiff might allege that they were targeted for harassment precisely because the defendants knew of some prior difficulty that made the plaintiff vulnerable to such harassment. In such cases, the clinician must consider this additional information before reaching a conclusion about the significance of the prior psychological problem.

Another complication may affect the evaluations of individuals who claim to have suffered psychological harm: Plaintiffs may be motivated to exaggerate their symptoms in order to improve their chances of winning large awards. Sometimes such symptom exaggeration or fabrication (called **malingering**) involves outright lying. In other cases, a genuine behavioral health disturbance is present, but the plaintiff exaggerates its seriousness.

A meta-analysis found that the possibility of receiving compensation for an injury was associated with more frequent reports of pain (Rohling et al., 1995). Similar findings were observed in a second meta-analysis, focusing particularly on mild traumatic brain injury (Belanger et al., 2005). Of course, such findings do not necessarily show that litigation involvement causes exaggeration. It might work in the other direction as well—individuals with more intransigent pain might be more likely to litigate their claims. Or a third influence might affect both; for instance, lifestyle might influence both recovery from injury and propensity toward litigation. But it is certainly possible that litigation involvement increases both the experience of pain and the report of such pain resulting from injury (Greene, 2008).

In a review of the ethics of attorneys "coaching" their clients on how to "beat" psychological tests in civil litigation cases, Victor and Abeles (2004) argued that these techniques are well within the ethical boundaries of legal practice and that attorneys often view such coaching as an important part of advocating for their clients. Indeed, it was estimated that more than half of attorneys practicing in specialty areas of law in which it is common to seek psychological testing (family, juvenile, personal injury, criminal, disability, workers' compensation) provide coaching to their clients about the psychological testing they will take (Spengler et al., 2020). Of course, it has also been strongly argued (Victor & Abeles, 2004) that such coaching results promote inaccuracy in psychological evaluations for the courts, and that evaluators should take steps to prevent it. If it is not prevented, such coaching could create ethical problems for the evaluating psychologist—but such ethical problems are not the same for attorneys seeking to have their clients evaluated. It might be that a "coached" client, if advised by an attorney to respond to psychological evaluation in a certain way to achieve a certain impression, might be charged with perjury if they knowingly provided false testimony in a hearing or trial—and attorneys cannot ethically advise their clients to commit perjury.

These coaching strategies may be effective. Some evidence shows that the *F* scale on the MMPI-2 (one of the instrument's validity scales designed to detect possible malingering) was not as effective at identifying coached malingerers as at identifying non-coached malingerers (Storm & Graham, 2000). Of course, forensic evaluators who suspect that coaching has occurred are likely to compensate by gathering additional information from sources other than self-report.

Spurred by results like these and by estimates from experienced clinicians that malingering and self-serving presentations are not at all uncommon in forensic evaluations (Rogers & Bender, 2008), some have recommended that clinicians consistently consider response style in forensic evaluations. This refers to whether evaluees are responding as accurately as they can ("reliable"), exaggerating or fabricating symptoms ("malingering"), denying or minimizing symptoms ("defensive"), or failing to engage in the evaluation and respond meaningfully to questions ("uncooperative"). When response style appears anything other than reliable, then evaluators should take extra steps to evaluate it, such as additional collateral interviews and record review, and administer specialized measures of response style (Heilbrun, 2001).

Workers' Compensation

When a worker is injured in the course of their job, the law provides for the worker to be compensated through a streamlined system that avoids the necessity of proving a tort. This system is known as *workers' compensation law*. All 50 states and the federal government have some type of workers' compensation system in place. Prior to workers' compensation, a person who was injured at work had to prove that the employer was responsible for a tort in order to receive compensation. This was difficult because employers had several possible defenses to the worker's claim. They often blamed the employee's negligence or the negligence of another worker for the injury. In other cases, employers said that a worker's injuries were simply the unavoidable risks of particular jobs and that the worker was well aware of these risks at the time of employment. As a result, until early in the twentieth century, many seriously injured workers and their families were denied any compensation for their work-related injuries.

Workers' compensation systems were developed around the beginning of the twentieth century to provide an alternative to the tort system. In workers' compensation systems, employers contribute to a large fund that insures workers who are injured at work, and employers also waive their right to blame the worker or some other individual for the injury. For their part, workers give up their right to pursue a tort case against their employers, and if they are compensated, the size of the award they receive is determined by (1) the type and duration of the injury and (2) their salary at the time of the injury. Workers can seek compensation for:

- physical and psychological injuries suffered at work;
- the cost of whatever treatment is given;
- lost wages; and/or
- the loss of future earning capacity.

Determining how much impairment in future earning capacity a given mental disorder or psychological condition might produce is very difficult. Physicians can assess the degree of impairment from a ruptured disc or a paralyzed arm, but how can we measure the degree or permanence of a mental disability? To bring some uniformity to these assessments, many states require evaluators to use the American Medical Association's *Guides to the Evaluation of Permanent Impairment* (AMA, 2007). The *Guide* provides five categories of impairment, ranging from "no impairment" to "extreme impairment," that clinicians can use to organize their descriptions of a claimant. In general, however, ratings of psychological impairments are hard to quantify reliably.

Both employers and employees should benefit from a process in which workers' claims can be resolved fairly quickly, which is a major goal of the workers' compensation system. Formal trials are not held, and juries do not resolve these cases; they are heard and decided by a hearing officer or commissioner. (These decisions can be appealed.) In theory, workers' compensation cases should be handled expeditiously, but they often drag on for years as both sides go through a process of hiring one or more experts to examine the worker and give opinions about the injuries and any disability suffered.

How do mental health professionals become involved in workers' compensation claims? Because psychological injuries or mental disorders arising from employment can be compensated, clinicians are often asked to evaluate workers and render opinions about the existence, cause, and implications of any mental disorders (Piechowski, 2011).

Claims for mental disability usually arise in one of the two ways, though there is a third (less likely) basis for a claim as well. First, a physical injury can lead to a mental disorder and psychological disability. A common pattern in these *physical–mental* cases is for a worker to sustain a serious physical injury (e.g., a broken back or severe burns) that leaves the worker suffering chronic pain. As the pain and the disability associated with it continue, the worker also experiences associated psychological problems, usually depression and anxiety. These problems can worsen until they become full-fledged mental disorders, resulting in further impairments of the worker's overall functioning.

The second work-related pathway to mental disability is for an individual either to suffer a traumatic incident at work or to undergo a long period of continuing stress that leads to substantial psychological difficulties. A night clerk at a convenience store who is the victim of an armed robbery and subsequently develops posttraumatic stress disorder is an example of such *mental–mental* cases. Other examples include clerical workers who are overworked and pressured by a boss, and essential workers who feared exposure to COVID-19 during the pandemic, and who experience an anxiety disorder.

In a third kind of case, known as *mental–physical*, work-related stress leads to the onset of a physical condition such as high blood pressure. Many states have placed restrictions on these types of claims, and psychologists are seldom asked to evaluate them.

The number of psychological claims in workers' compensation litigation has increased dramatically in the last 30 years, and much of the increase can be attributed to a surge in mental–mental cases (Melton et al., 2018). At least three explanations have been proposed to account for this increase in psychological claims. First, because more women have entered the workforce, and because women are more often diagnosed with anxiety and depressive disorders than men, the rise in psychological claims might be due to the increased percentage of female workers. Of course, this explanation does not take into account that a higher percentage of women in the workforce may be associated with a more gender-related misconduct toward female workers, which might account for a justifiably larger number of complaints. A second possibility is that a shift in the job market from manufacturing and industrial jobs to service-oriented jobs has produced corresponding increases in job-related interpersonal stressors and decreases in physical injuries. A third possibility is that claims of psychological impairments are motivated primarily by financial incentives, generating a range of cases in which genuine impairments are mixed in with exaggerated or false claims of disability.

Assessment in Workers' Compensation Claims

Some empirical studies have been conducted on the assessment of psychological damages in workers' compensation cases. They usually focus on one of the following questions:

- How do workers' compensation claimants score on standard psychological tests such as the MMPI-2-RF and the MMPI-3?

- Are certain injuries or stressors associated with a particular pattern of psychological test scores?

- Can psychological tests distinguish claimants who are experiencing a genuine disorder from those who are faking or exaggerating their problems?

- What factors threaten the impartiality of forensic evaluations in workers' compensation cases?

In a study relevant to the first bullet point, investigators analyzed archival MMPI-2s produced by 192 women and 14 men involved in litigation related to alleged workplace sexual harassment and discrimination. Among the women, 28% produced a profile that was within normal limits. The remaining profiles fell into four distinctive clusters representing different approaches to the test items (Long et al., 2004). This is relevant because the MMPI-2-RF is effective

When injured at work, the worker's compensation law helps employees seek compensation from the employer.

in identifying over- and under-reporting—and it is also better about describing the sources of evidence supporting the descriptions in different profiles (Chmielewski et al., 2017; Ingram & Ternes, 2016).

Regarding the association between injuries and test scores, the research does not suggest that particular injuries or claims are reliably linked with different patterns of test scores (Melton et al., 2018). One reason for the lack of distinguishing patterns might be that regardless of the injury or the stressor, most people manifest psychological distress through a mixture of physical complaints and negative emotions such as anxiety, depression, and feelings of isolation.

We now turn to the question of whether psychological tests can distinguish between claimants with genuine disorders and those who are exaggerating. The MMPI-2-RF and the MMPI-3 contain sets of items that are sometimes used to assess the test-taking attitudes of a respondent. These validity scales can be examined to determine whether respondents might have tried to fool the examiner by exaggerating or denying psychological problems. Other tests such as the Validity Indicator Profile (Frederick, 1997, 2000; Frederick & Crosby, 2000), the b Test (Boone et al., 2002), and the Test of Memory Malingering (Tombaugh, 1997) have been developed to detect malingering on cognitive and neuropsychological measures.

The typical case of a person trying to exaggerate or fake mental disorder involves the individual answering many items in the "bad" direction, thereby attempting to look as disturbed as possible. However, the strategy might be more complicated in the case of a person who is faking or exaggerating a disorder in a workers' compensation case. These individuals usually want to appear honest, virtuous, and free of any psychological problems that might have existed prior to the injury, while at the same time endorsing many symptoms and complaints consistent with being harmed by a work-related incident. In other words, their motivation involves a combination of faking good and faking bad.

The impartiality of psychological evaluations performed in workers' compensation cases can be threatened by several factors (Melton et al., 2018). Chief among these problems is that attorneys often retain the same expert to conduct evaluations of different cases. An expert who is repeatedly hired by the same attorney, whether a plaintiff's or defense attorney, may risk opining what the attorney wants rather than rendering impartial opinions about each case.

One study investigated experts' impartiality by examining whether psychological assessments of workers' compensation claimants were related to the side that had retained the expert. Hasemann (1997) collected and compared 385 reports that had been prepared by various mental health professionals. Of these reports, 194 had been conducted by defense-hired experts, 182 were completed by plaintiff-hired experts, and 9 evaluations could not be classified. Did plaintiff and defense experts differ in their opinions in these cases? Several results indicate that they did and that they might have been unduly influenced by the adversarial system.

Consider these three results:

- Plaintiff experts gave impairment ratings to claimants that were nearly four times larger than the impairment ratings assigned by defense experts.
- Defense experts concluded that MMPIs completed by claimants were invalid or malingered in 72% of their evaluations, whereas plaintiff experts reached this conclusion in 31% of their evaluations.
- Of the 19 experts who had conducted three or more evaluations, 17 tended to do so almost exclusively for one side. Ten experts conducted a total of 107 plaintiff evaluations and only 8 defense evaluations. Seven experts completed 147 assessments for the defense and only 36 for the plaintiffs.

Comparing the numbers of evaluations conducted for plaintiffs with the number conducted for defendants can be misleading, however, because these numbers depend on the number of referrals from each side. A better measure of evaluator impartiality involves the proportion of "useful" opinions (i.e., opinions helpful to the referring attorney) relative to the overall number of referrals. For example, an evaluator who has conducted 90 evaluations for the defense and 10 for plaintiffs might appear less impartial than the evaluator who has done 50 for the defense and another 50 for plaintiffs. However, looking more closely at the "usefulness" proportion might reveal that the first evaluator has reached a conclusion favorable to the referring attorney in 50% of the defense cases and 45% of the plaintiff cases, whereas the second evaluator has favored the referring attorney in 98% and 100% of defense and plaintiff cases, respectively. Which evaluator appears less impartial?

Other influences can affect the apparent impartiality of forensic evaluations. Even if experts are reasonably impartial, attorneys may selectively introduce expert opinions depending on whether those opinions support their side. To evaluate this possibility, investigators would need to review evaluations requested by attorneys but not subsequently presented as evidence. This is comparable to the "file drawer problem" encountered by investigators performing meta-analysis: Because research reporting non-significant differences is often not accepted for publication, such results tend to languish, unpublished, in a file drawer, which limits the accuracy of the investigator's ability to determine an overall "effect" of a research phenomenon based on all the evidence. (Perhaps this should be renamed the "hard drive problem.") Even if forensic evaluators can be reasonably impartial, they still conduct such evaluations in the context of an adversarial system, and decisions about whether to introduce such reports as evidence are often made by attorneys who are advocates for their clients.

It is these kinds of concerns that prompted the development of a series of "best practice" books in forensic mental health assessment. Several of these books address questions relevant to this chapter. One (Piechowski, 2011) focuses on evaluation for workplace disability. The second (Goodman-Delahunty & Foote, 2011) addresses the topic of workplace discrimination and harassment. A third (Kane & Dvoskin, 2011) describes the process of conducting evaluations for personal injury claims more broadly. These books discuss the steps that potential evaluators can take to conduct thorough, accurate, and balanced evaluations on this topic. They do not, of course, ensure that evaluations will be conducted as recommended. But they do identify best practices, as well as steps to avoid, so evaluators who wish to use the strongest approaches developed in the field have clear guidance in doing so.

Civil Competencies

The concept of legal competence extends to many kinds of decisions that individuals are called on to make throughout their lives. When we discussed competence to stand trial, we focused on the knowledge that criminal defendants must have and the decisions they are required to make. However, the question of mental competence is raised in several non-criminal contexts as well; we refer to these other situations with the general term **civil competencies**.

The question of civil competence focuses on whether an individual has the capacity to understand information that is relevant to decision-making in a given situation and then make an informed choice about what to do in that situation. Here are some questions that address issues of civil competence:

- Is a person competent to manage their financial affairs?

- Can an individual make competent decisions about their medical or psychiatric treatment?

- Is a person competent to execute a will and decide how to distribute property to heirs or other beneficiaries?

- Can a person make advance decisions about the kind of medical treatment they want or do not want to receive if terminally ill or seriously injured?

Scholars who have studied this issue usually point to four abilities that contribute to competent decision-making (Appelbaum & Grisso, 1995; Grisso, 2003). A competent individual is expected to be able to (1) understand basic information that is relevant to making a decision; (2) apply that information to a specific situation in order to anticipate the consequences of various choices; (3) use rational thinking to evaluate the pros and cons of various strategies and decisions; and (4) communicate a personal decision or choice about the matter under consideration.

The specific abilities associated with each of these general criteria depend on the decision that a person must make. Deciding whether to have risky surgery demands different information and thinking processes than deciding whether to leave property to children or to a charitable organization.

Decisions about medical treatment that one might receive in the future, including the desire to have life-sustaining medical treatments discontinued, involve a special level of planning that has been encouraged by a 1990 federal statute known as the Patient Self-Determination Act. Planning about future medical treatments is formalized through what are known as **advance medical directives**, in which patients indicate what kinds of treatment they want should they later become incapacitated and incompetent to make treatment decisions.

One of the most important of these advance directives is the "living will," in which a patient essentially asserts that they prefer to die rather than to be kept alive on a ventilator or feeding tubes. The ethical and practical issues involved in determining patients' competence to issue advance medical directives are substantial, but the trend, revealed in U.S. Supreme Court decisions such as *Cruzan v. Director, Missouri Department of Health* (1990), is to recognize that patients have great autonomy in accepting or rejecting a variety of treatments and health care provisions (Hanson & Doukas, 2009).

Advance medical directives seem like a simple and direct way to communicate end-of-life decisions. One Canadian study (Bravo et al., 2003) estimated the prevalence of advance directives for health care at around 42% of respondents. Those having such directives were older, more likely to be female, and had more often known someone with cognitive impairment.

But for living wills to be effective, individuals must be able to generate preferences that are stable over time and across changes in health. Unfortunately, individuals' predictions about what kind of care they might want in the future vary from one occasion to the next and are affected by the status of their present health. In studies that examined the stability of advance directives, participants were asked to record their preferences for various life-sustaining treatments (e.g., cardiopulmonary resuscitation [CPR]) in different medical scenarios, such as coma. After an interval ranging from one month to two years, these individuals recorded their preferences again. The average stability of preferences across all judgments was 71%, suggesting that over time periods as short as two years, there were substantial changes in stated treatment preferences (Ditto et al., 2003). Of course, a person could change their preferences for good reason—perhaps as a result of intervening life experiences such as a health crisis, or a relative's need for life-sustaining treatment. However, most people were unaware that their preferences change; they mistakenly believed that the preferences they express at the second interview were identical to those they provided at the first interview (Gready et al., 2000).

Preferences are also dependent on the context in which they are made. For example, when patients recently discharged from hospitals were asked about their desire for life-sustaining treatment, they showed a characteristic "hospital dip"; they reported less desire for interventions than they did prior to hospitalization—and less than they did several months after their discharge (Ditto et al., 2006). Apparently people do not have stable preferences for future medical care.

Assessing Competence to Make Treatment Decisions

The question of competence to consent to treatment usually arises when a patient refuses treatment that seems to be medically and psychologically justified. Under these circumstances, the first step might be to break down the explanation of the treatment decisions facing the patient into smaller bits of information. (Research results have shown that patients can better understand treatment information when it is presented to them one element at a time.) Using this kind of presentation might facilitate a patient's appreciation of whether a recommended treatment would be in their best interest. If there were still an impasse between the patient and treating professionals after such a presentation, it would be important to administer a clinical assessment instrument to determine whether a given patient lacks the necessary ability to reach a competent decision. Such an instrument—the MacArthur Competence Assessment Tool for Treatment Decisions (MacCAT-T)—is commercially available (Grisso & Appelbaum, 1998a, 1998b).

The research for the MacCAT-T, conducted as part of a larger MacArthur Research Network on Mental Health and Law study on competencies, coercion, and risk assessment, focused on the capacities of individuals with severe mental disorders to make decisions and give informed consent about their own psychiatric treatment. Can persons with serious mental disorders make competent treatment decisions for themselves? Do their decision-making abilities differ from those of persons who do not experience mental disorders?

Researchers in the MacArthur Treatment Competence Study developed a series of structured interview measures to assess the four basic abilities—understanding information, applying information, thinking rationally, and expressing a choice—involved in legal competence (Grisso et al., 1995). For example, here is an item that taps a person's ability to apply information to the question of whether they have a condition that could be effectively treated:

> "Most people who have symptoms of a mental or emotional disorder like your doctor believes you have can be helped by treatment. The most common treatment is medication. Other treatments sometimes used for such disorders are having someone to talk to about problems, and participating in group therapy with other people with similar symptoms." "… [D]o you believe that you have the kind of condition for which some types of treatment might be helpful?" "All right, you believe that … (paraphrase of the patient's expressed opinion). Can you explain that to me? What makes you believe that … (again paraphrase as above)?" For a patient who believes that treatment will not work because they are "just too sick," the interviewer would ask: "Imagine that a doctor tells you that there is a treatment that has been shown in research to help 90%

of people with problems just as serious as yours. Do you think this treatment might be of more benefit to you than getting no treatment at all?" (Grisso et al., 1995, p. 133)

Standardized interviews, using items of this type, were conducted with three groups of patients—those with schizophrenia, those with major depression, and those with heart disease—and with groups of people from the community who were *not* ill but were demographically matched to the patient groups (Grisso & Appelbaum, 1995). Only a minority of the persons in all the groups showed significant impairments in competent decision-making about various treatment options. However, the patients with schizophrenia and major depression tended to have a poorer understanding of treatment information and used less adequate reasoning in thinking about the consequences of treatment than did the heart patients or the members of the community sample. These impairments were more pronounced and consistent across different competence abilities for patients with schizophrenia than for patients with depression, and the more serious the symptoms of mental disorder (especially those involving disturbed thinking), the poorer the understanding.

These results obviously have implications for social policies involving persons with mental disorders. Contrary to popular impressions, the majority of patients experiencing from severe disorders such as schizophrenia and major depression appear to be capable of competent decision-making about their treatment. On the other hand, a significant number of patients—particularly those with schizophrenia—show impairments in their decision-making abilities.

Assessing Competence to Execute a Will

Clinicians may also be asked to evaluate whether a person (called a "testator") was competent to execute a will; such competence is a requirement for the provisions of the will to be valid. Typically, challenges to this capacity are raised when there is reason to think that the testator lacked the necessary mental capacity to execute a valid will (Melton et al., 2018).

We find one example of the influences on **testamentary capacity** in an article (Alton, 2017) that considers Stevenson's classic "The Strange Case of Dr. Jekyll and Mr. Hyde" (1886) from the perspective of what is needed to make a will. Alton suggests that the *general soundness of mind*, the question of whether there are *particular symptoms that might interfere with it* (e.g., delusions, cognitive impairment), and the *presence of undue influence and duress* are as relevant today as they were in England during Queen Victoria's reign, when the fictional Dr. Jekyll was making his will. (This nineteenth century novella is also a superb consideration of the coexistence of good and evil within an individual—and is well worth reading or rereading for that reason also.)

According to one study, situations that may raise concern about capacity to execute a will include the following: There is a radical change from a previous will (seen in 72% of cases); undue influence is alleged (56% of cases); the testator has no biological children (52% of cases); the testator executed the will less than a year prior to death (48% of cases); and the testator experienced comorbid conditions such as dementia (40% of cases), alcohol abuse (28% of cases), or other neurological/psychiatric conditions (28% of cases) (Shulman et al., 2004).

The legal standard for testators' competence to execute a will is derived from *Banks v. Goodfellow* (1870), in which the court held as follows:

1. Testators must know at the time of making their wills that they are making their wills.

2. They must know the nature and extent of their property.

3. They must know the "natural objects of [their] bounty" (those who would inherit their property).

4. They must know the manner in which the wills they are making distribute their property.

This type of competence has a lower threshold than other competencies because it requires only that persons making a will have a general understanding of the nature and extent of their property and of the effect of their will on members of their family or others who may naturally claim to benefit from the property cited in the will (Melton et al., 2018). A person cannot be deemed incompetent to execute a will simply because they have a mental illness, unless there is clear evidence that the mental illness specifically interfered with the individual's ability to meet the standard applicable when the will was written.

Assessment of this competence focuses on the individual's functional abilities at the time their will was written. Melton and colleagues (2018) outline some strategies used by mental health professionals in assessing competence to execute a will. First, they recommend structuring the evaluation to conform to the associated legal elements. They suggest using the sources available (e.g., the testator, family, friends, records) to first determine the purpose of the will and why it was written at that time. Second, they recommend gathering information about the testator's property holdings, which may include asking questions about occupation and salary, tangible property, and intangibles (e.g., bank accounts, investments). Third, the clinician should determine the testator's preferences and their values to better understand the family dynamics (e.g., with whom does the testator have a good relationship, with whom do they not get along). This information can shed light on the testator's rationale for bequeathing their belongings to specific individuals. Finally, Melton and colleagues recommend that clinicians assess the general consequences of the dispositions outlined in the will.

One of the obvious difficulties in these types of evaluations is that the testator, the subject of the evaluation, is often deceased at the time the question of competence to execute the will arises. Thus, the sources of information will be different. If the testator is alive, they will be a primary informational source—but if they are deceased, the evaluator must gather information from family, friends, acquaintances, medical records, and other available sources without the testator's specific input.

Psychological Autopsies

Like most clinical assessments, the typical forensic assessment involves a clinician interviewing, observing, and testing a client to reach an understanding of the case. However, in a few unusual circumstances, clinicians may be called on to give an opinion about a deceased person's state of mind as it existed at a specific time before death. Obviously, in these cases, the clinician must conduct an evaluation without any participation by the individual whose prior condition is in question. These evaluations are termed **psychological autopsies** (Ogloff & Otto, 1993).

Psychological autopsies originated in the 1950s when a group of social scientists in the Los Angeles area began assisting the coroner's office in determining whether suicide, murder, or accident was the most likely mode of death in some equivocal cases. Their use has spread over the years, and now they are encountered most often in cases such as determining the cause of death in situations where an insurance company could deny death benefits if the policy holder committed suicide; assessing claims in workers' compensation cases that stressful working conditions or work trauma contributed to a worker's death or suicide; evaluating a deceased individual's mental capacity to execute or modify a will; and assessing the validity of an argument occasionally made by criminal defendants that a victim's mode of death was suicide rather than homicide.

Although there is no standard format for psychological autopsies, most of them rely on information from two sources: interviews with third parties who knew the decedent and prior records. General guidelines for what should be included in psychological autopsies have been published (La Fon, 2008), and the "next generation" of psychological autopsy studies described (Conner et al., 2012). Some investigators concentrate on more recent data, generated close in time to the person's death. What was the person's mood? How was the person doing at work? Were there any pronounced changes in the person's behavior? Others—especially those who take a developmental perspective on behavior—look for clues early in the person's life. As a child, how did the person interact with their parents and siblings? What was the individual's approach to school? Peers? Hobbies and other activities?

As with any assessment technique, the first question to be considered is the reliability of the psychological autopsy. There are several reasons to suspect that the reliability of psychological autopsies is low. If the person in question is not available to be interviewed or tested, then obviously, the decedent's "true" state of mind is unknown. If it *were* known, the autopsy would be unnecessary. Also, the persons who are interviewed might not remember the past accurately, or they might have reasons to distort their answers.

A review of research on psychological autopsy studies (Foster, 2011) revealed specific life events (particularly interpersonal conflict) as risk factors for suicide, with some evidence that the greater the conflict, the higher the risk. However, limitations of psychological autopsy studies suggest the need for complementary research into life events prior to serious suicide attempts. One study addressed the question of reliability of psychological autopsy indirectly, using information from the investigation of the U.S.S. *Iowa* explosion (see Box 11.3).

How has testimony about psychological autopsies fared in court? In cases involving workers' compensation claims and questions of whether insurance benefits should be paid, the courts have usually admitted psychological autopsy testimony; in criminal cases or in cases involving the question of whether a person had the mental capacity to execute a will, the courts have been more reluctant to permit the testimony (Ogloff & Otto, 1993). In particular, the application of the *Daubert* standard for admission of expert evidence may limit the admissibility of psychological autopsy results. Consider the case of *Bevan v. Valencia* (2018), a wrongful death lawsuit stemming from Desiree Gonzales' admission to a hospital following a heroin

overdose. After she was given medical approval for hospital discharge, she was taken to the Santa Fe Youth Development Program—where there was no nurse on duty. She stopped breathing and was returned to the hospital, where it was determined that she had died of the lingering effects of the heroin overdose. The plaintiff succeeded in excluding expert testimony from a forensic psychiatrist who would have offered conclusions obtained from using a psychological autopsy (see https://www.expertinstitute.com/resources/case-studies /psychological-autopsy-method-fails-to-meet-daubert-reliability -requirements-according-to-new-mexico-district-court/). The plaintiff argued that psychological autopsy results should not be admitted under *Daubert* because they were not based on scientific principles and methods.

Judges are more hesitant to allow expert testimony based on psychological autopsies in criminal cases than in civil ones, perhaps because the risks of prejudicial testimony are greater when one's liberties can be taken away. One reason for the courts' hesitancy in permitting psychological autopsy testimony in cases involving the validity of wills might be that, in such cases, the state of mind of the deceased is the critical question for the jury. Allowing expert testimony on this matter might therefore be viewed as invading the province of the jury, a perception that judges usually want to avoid.

Box 11.3

The Case of the U.S.S. *Iowa*: Gauging Reliability of the Psychological Autopsy

On April 19, 1989, 47 U.S. Navy sailors were killed when an explosion ripped through turret 2 of the U.S.S. *Iowa*. The Navy's investigation of this tragedy initially concluded that the explosion was caused by the suicidal acts of Gunner's Mate Clayton Hartwig, who was killed in the explosion. The major foundation for this conclusion was a psychological autopsy conducted by FBI agents working at the National Center for the Analysis of Violent Crime. The Navy's conclusions were later evaluated by a congressional committee, which commissioned its own panel of 14 psychological and psychiatric experts to review the FBI's analysis. Partly on the basis of this panel's input, the congressional committee rejected the FBI analysis as invalid. Ultimately, the U.S. Navy also concluded that the cause of the explosion could not be determined.

Forensic psychologist Randy Otto and his colleagues asked 24 psychologists and psychiatrists to rate the reports of the 14 experts who reviewed the FBI analysis of the U.S.S. *Iowa* explosion (Otto et al., 1993). Three raters judged each of the 14 reports, and although they failed to show precise agreement in how they thought the reports should be interpreted, they did achieve a moderate amount of broad agreement in their ratings. Note, however, that this agreement pertains only to how the raters interpreted the 14

The U.S.S. *Iowa*, damaged in an explosion

panelists' reports, not to the contents or opinions in the reports themselves.

Critical Thought Question

What are the major challenges in conducting a psychological autopsy—and what kind of forensic mental health assessments in particular include such challenges?

Child Custody and Parental Fitness

The "Best Interests of the Child" in Custody Disputes

An important area in forensic psychology involves the evaluation of families for the purpose of recommending custodial arrangements that are in the best interests of children whose parents are divorcing or separating. The increase in the number of these cases is attributable to two facts. First, about 50% of marriages in the United States now end in divorce, with the rates even higher for second marriages (60%) and third marriages (over 70%) (see https://worldpopulationreview.com/state-rankings/divorce-rate-by-state). As of 2019, 23% of households with children in the United States were single-parent families. The issue of custody is a practical concern for millions of families. Second, from the end of the nineteenth century to about the middle of the twentieth century, the prevailing assumption was that awarding custody of young children (sometimes called children of "tender years") to their mothers was usually in their best interests. This preference for maternal custody has diminished at the beginning of the twenty-first century; now many courts want to know about the parenting abilities of each parent before deciding about custody (Fuhrman & Zibbell, 2012).

Currently, the prevailing standard for custody decisions is the **future best interests of the child**. Although the child's "best interests" must be assessed on a case-by-case basis, the Uniform Marriage and Divorce Act indicates that courts should consider the following criteria: (1) the wishes of the child; (2) the wishes of the child's parents; (3) the relationships between the child and the parents, siblings, and significant others who interact with the child; (4) the child's adjustment at home and school and in the community; and (5) the physical and mental health of the parties involved.

Child custody evaluations usually arise in situations in which divorcing parents disagree about which of them can better meet the needs of their children and should therefore have custody. Most states permit two kinds of custodial arrangements—sole and joint custody, each with two aspects (physical and legal). *Physical custody* refers to the living arrangement, whereas *legal custody* concerns the responsibility for decision-making. In **sole custody**, the child will live only with one parent (although the other parent may be granted visitation rights), and/or all legal decision-making authority for that child will rest with one parent. In **joint custody**, both parents can retain parental rights concerning decisions about the child's general welfare, education, health care, and other matters (this is called joint legal custody), and the child can alternate living in the home of the mother and in the home of the father according to the schedule provided in the custody decision (this is called joint physical custody). Joint custody does not necessarily mean that the child spends equal time with each parent, however. Usually, one parent is designated the residential parent, and the child spends more time living at the home of that parent.

The "best interests of the child" are the focus of the judge's decision-making in custody cases.

The three main differences between sole custody and joint custody are as follows:

1. Joint custody distributes the frequency of interaction more evenly between the children and each parent.

2. Joint custody requires more interactions between the divorced parents and generates more demands for cooperation concerning the children.

3. Joint custody results in more alterations in caregiving arrangements, along with more separations and reunions between children and parents (Fuhrman & Zibbell, 2012).

An interesting and methodologically sophisticated Spanish study sought to identify predictors of custodial decisions in 1,884 cases (Munoz Soro & Serrano-Cinca, 2021). Results indicated that couples who have a good relationship are more likely to request joint custody—and the least likely to prevail before the court are men who apply for joint custody, have a poor relationship with their former spouses, and have child circumstances unfavorable to joint custody. This is the kind of research that could be replicated in the United States—and would provide valuable larger-scale data about the process of awarding child custody.

Psychologists have examined the effects of sole custody and joint custody on children and parents. Although the findings are not clear-cut, there appear to be several advantages to joint custody arrangements. Using meta-analysis, Bauserman (2002) concluded that children in joint custody fared better than children in sole custody on various measures related to adjustment and interpersonal relations: general adjustment, family relationships, self-esteem, emotional and behavioral adjustment, and divorce-specific adjustment. There was less conflict between parents in joint-custody (rather than sole custody) situations, but this factor did not account for the better adjustment of children in joint-custody arrangements.

Some research has also addressed the impact of having one or both parents who are gay or lesbian on the subsequent adjustment of children in custody following a divorce or other ending of the parental relationship. A review of the legal and empirical literature in this area (Haney-Caron & Heilbrun, 2014) summarized empirical findings on parenting ability, impact on children's sexual orientations, social stigma confronting children, and children's general adjustment. This review provided no evidence that lesbian and gay parents differ from heterosexual parents in these domains. The authors recommended that research-informed policy should promote equitable decisions under the law regarding gay and lesbian parents in the area of child custody—particularly since some judges have expressed concerns about adverse impact on children unless custody is awarded to the parent who is not gay or lesbian.

Other evidence on the effects of divorce on children comes from long-term longitudinal studies (Hetherington & Kelly, 2002; Wallerstein & Kelly, 1980), retrospective perceptions of parents' separation or divorce (Braver et al., 2003; Marquardt, 2006), reviews (American Academy of Child and Adolescent Psychiatry, 2017; Anderson, 2014; Brand et al., 2019), and meta-analyses (Amato, 2001; Bauserman, 2002). Based on this evidence, it appears that the most significant effects of divorce on children occur in the first year or two. Temporary behavioral changes are frequent (Hetherington et al., 1982; Wallerstein & Blakeslee, 2003), including problems in emotional regulation, disturbed sleep patterns, behavioral or academic problems, grief reactions, and loyalty conflicts. Most parents and children return to behavior that is more typical for them after this one- to two-year period (Laumann-Billings & Emery, 2000; Marquardt, 2006).

Both the well-being of the primary parent and the level of parental conflict are major factors influencing outcomes (Hetherington & Kelly, 2002). Children from families in which the parents had a great deal of conflict seem to do better following divorce than do children from low-conflict families (Amato, 2001). Importantly, around 75% of children whose parents divorce will not experience significant developmental challenges or long-term negative effects of the divorce (Kelly & Emery, 2003).

Other research (Nielsen, 2017) has updated our knowledge about the impact of parental conflict on child custody outcomes. Nielsen reported that parents with joint physical custody do not differ in their cooperativeness or conflict from parents with sole physical custody. Indeed, the quality of the relationship between parents and children is more strongly associated with outcomes than is conflict, except when such conflict is extreme. Accordingly, we should be particularly attentive to helping parents strengthen their relationships with their children as part of divorce and custody actions.

What makes it more or less likely that divorce will adversely affect the children involved? Risk and protective influences have been summarized (Fuhrmann & Zibbell, 2012) as follows:

Risk factors:

- stress of the initial separation

- diminished parenting

- loss of significant relationships (including extended family, e.g., grandparents), and friends

- multiple moves (including change of schools and loss of friends)

- financial problems (the stress of which can affect parenting style or quality)

- either parent becoming involved with a new partner

Protective factors:

- A capable and well-adjusted custodial parent

- The noncustodial parent having regular and consistent contact and (particularly important) taking an active interest in the activities and school performance of the child

- A good relationship between parent and child

- Extended family support for the custodial parent

Consider these risk factors and how they might be influenced in an unusual custodial arrangement in which the divorcing parents actually remained in the same household (consider Box 11.4).

Assessment in Custody Disputes

Many mental health professionals regard child custody cases to be the most ethically and clinically difficult forensic evaluations they perform. There are four main reasons for this. First, the emotional stakes are extremely high, and both parents are often willing to spare no expense or tactic in the battle over which of them will win custody. The children involved are usually forced to live—for months, if not years—in an emotional limbo in which they do not know in whose home they will be residing, where they will be going to school, or how often they will see each parent.

Second, a thorough custody evaluation requires that the clinician evaluate the children, both parents, and others who have interacted with the child, such as relatives, teachers, and family health care providers. Often, not all the parties agree to be evaluated or do so only under coercion, resulting in a lengthy and sometimes tense process. Such tension can be increased if the evaluation is requested by the attorney for one of the two divorcing spouses, which may lead the other spouse to perceive the evaluator as unfairly biased in favor of the spouse who retained this evaluator. An alternative arrangement—having the court order the evaluation and designate a neutral expert, with both parties agreeing to this appointment—can help to reduce this perception of bias.

Box 11.4

A Kinder, Gentler Divorce Where Nobody Moves Out

When a couple divorces, all kinds of disruption can occur in the lives of the divorcing parties and their children. In recent times, there have been "out of the box" attempts to limit the consequences of moving (cost, distance, time, limited visitation) by having everyone remain in the same home. Consider the story (Jacobs, 2022) that appeared in the *New York Times* about the author, her ex-husband, their son, and her ex-husband's new partner.

…my ex-husband's girlfriend stepped out of the bathroom wrapped in a towel, beads of water dripping from her brown hair, she ran into me, the ex-wife, dashing from the bedroom they often share, with my ex-husband's dirty clothes in my arms.

"Hi, I was just getting his clothes" I said before scurrying back downstairs, where I was doing our laundry.

He and I live on separate floors of a two-family house in Brooklyn. Our 8-year-old son can run upstairs to beg his father to let him play Minecraft and run downstairs to have the Cheerios he likes with me. I dip into my ex's apartment when a recipe calls for chia seeds, and he knocks on my door when I need help resetting the clock that is too high up for me to reach.

We have been like this for more than two years.

Technically, we are still married, although we have filed for divorce. Some of the neighbors still seem to think we are together. The kindly pharmacist always asks for updates and sends his regards. But we aren't a couple: We no longer share a bed, no longer smooch, no longer take turns making the salad, no longer give each other halfhearted back rubs, no longer dream of trips to Italy, no longer put our arms around each other in public, no longer fight about the shades being crooked, no longer outsource our intimacy to Netflix, no longer write checks to a couples' counselor, no longer hope to fix it.

How would this work? For many couples and their children, it would not. The animosity associated with some relationships ending in divorce wouldn't allow it. But just as mediation has become a preferred alternative to custodial litigation for couples who can do it, so too is the kind of creativity seen in this arrangement. Definitely not for everyone—but for those who can live with the disadvantages, it might be far less disruptive to their lives in many ways.

Critical Thought Question

In this story, what are some of the characteristics of this couple that might make them good candidates for custody mediation?

Third, to render a valuable expert opinion, a clinician must be quite knowledgeable—about the children and parents under evaluation, but also about child development, bonding and attachment, family systems, the effects of divorce on children, adult and childhood mental disorders, and several different kinds of testing. Evaluators should also be knowledgeable about scientific evidence regarding the impact of any specific aspects of a particular evaluation, such as parents' sexual orientation and behavioral health (Haney-Caron & Heilbrun, 2014).

Finally, child custody evaluations are often highly adversarial, with each parent trying to expose all the faults of the other and each side vigorously challenging any procedures or opinion by an expert with which it disagrees. Clinicians who conduct custody evaluations must be prepared for challenges to their evaluation methods, scholarly competence, and professional ethics. Even evaluators who operate under court appointment may have their findings challenged in some cases.

There are three different approaches to appointing evaluators: (1) a judge can appoint one clinician to conduct a custody evaluation that is available to all the parties, (2) each side can retain its own expert to conduct independent evaluations, or (3) the litigants can agree to share the expenses of hiring an expert to conduct one evaluation (Fuhrmann & Zibbell, 2012). It is likely that evaluators prefer either the first or third option, as there is less adversarial pressure associated with these. In addition, consider the various forms of bias that might affect evaluations performed in the context of highly contentious proceedings involving parties who are litigating for the opportunity to spend more time with their children.

Specific guidelines for conducting custody evaluations have been developed by the American Psychological Association (2010) and the Association of Family and Conciliation Courts (AFCC, 2006a, 2016), Although the methods used in custody evaluations vary depending on the specific issues in each case, most evaluations include the following components: (1) clinical, social history, and mental status interviews of the parents and the children; (2) standardized testing of the parents and the children; (3) observation of interactions between each parent and the children, especially when the children are minors; (4) assessments or interviews with other people who have had opportunities to observe the family (adult children of the parents, grandparents, neighbors, the family physician, schoolteachers, and other observers); and (5) documents or records that might be relevant to the case (medical records of children and parents, report cards, and arrest records).

In any forensic psychological evaluation, it is useful to include a specialized tool that has been developed to measure capacities associated with the legal decision. In child custody evaluations, these include parenting skills and capacities (for the parents) and needs (for the children). Although specialized approaches are available for child custody evaluations, these tests are of questionable validity (see Melton et al., 2018; Otto & Edens, 2003), so it remains for the field to develop a specialized measure that is consistent with the principles of scientific test development.

Custody evaluations are time-consuming. It has been estimated from national surveys of mental health professionals that evaluators spend an average of about 30 hours (Ackerman & Ackerman, 1997) or more (Brey, 2009) on each evaluation. Much of this time was devoted to interviewing and observing the parties in various combinations. In fact, more than two-thirds of the respondents indicated that they conducted individual interviews with each parent and each child, observed each parent interacting (separately) with each child, and conducted formal psychological testing of the parents and the children.

There have been a number of problems associated with child custody evaluations in terms of scientific support and relevance of measures. These include inadequate scientific support and limited relevance for "best interests of the child," the foundation of the custody decision (Emery et al., 2005). Nonetheless, there have clearly been noteworthy developments over the last four decades in the evaluation of child custody. These include more clearly established procedures influenced by the APA Ethics Code and specialized guidelines, and better understanding by evaluators of legal issues such as the basis for evaluation and the admissibility of expert evidence (Ackerman et al., 2021).

Because divorce is a common experience of childhood and because protracted custody battles tend to leave a trail of emotionally battered family members in their wake, increasing attention is being given to helping parents and children cope with these transitions or to finding alternatives to custody fights (Silver & Silver, 2009). Many judges require divorcing couples to attempt to settle issues of custody, visitation, and support through mediation, a form of alternative dispute resolution that minimizes the adversarial quality of the typical custody dispute. If mediation fails, the couple can return to court and have the judge decide the issues. The benefits of custody mediation are that resolutions are reached more quickly, and with better compliance among the participants, than with adversarial procedures.

The Association of Family and Conciliation Courts (2000a) has developed model standards for the practice of family and divorce mediation, indicating that a mediator shall (among other things):

- Recognize that mediation is based on the principle of self-determination by the participants.

- Conduct the mediation process in an impartial manner; disclose all actual and potential grounds of bias and conflicts of interest reasonably known to the mediator; and structure the mediation process so that participants make decisions based on sufficient information and knowledge.

- Assist participants in determining how to promote the best interests of children.

- Recognize a family situation involving child abuse or neglect or domestic violence and take appropriate steps to shape the mediation process accordingly.

- Suspend or terminate the mediation process when the mediator reasonably believes that a participant is unable to effectively participate or for other compelling reasons.

Research generally supports the favorable adjustment of those who go through mediation. Earlier research reviews (Hahn & Kleist, 2000; Kelly, 1996) indicated that families that go through mediation to determine custody have better adjustment than those going through the more traditional child custody litigation process. A subsequent meta-analysis (Shaw, 2010) showed that mediation is a beneficial alternative to litigation for couples who are divorcing. Outcomes considered in this meta-analysis include satisfaction with process and outcome, emotional satisfaction, spousal relationship, and understanding children's needs. Some of the reasons for the more favorable outcomes associated with mediation, as compared with custody litigation, may include the "active ingredients" of mediation: (1) parental cooperation extending beyond the initial separation; (2) addressing underlying emotions; (3) helping parents set up a good working relationship; and (4) avoiding divisive negotiations around the time of the custody decision (Emery et al., 2005).

Assessing Fitness to Be a Parent

Evaluations of parental fitness involve different questions than those involved in the typical custody dispute (Condie, 2003). In every state in the United States, the agency responsible for the protection of children will intervene if it receives a credible report that a child is being abused or neglected. After an investigation, the agency might file a petition asking a court to remove the child from the home and arrange placement with a relative or in foster care. In such cases, the issue before the court is whether the child should be left with the parents or removed from the home because of parental unfitness.

The question for the evaluator is what arrangement protects the child's well-being, while properly respecting the rights of the parents. Although parental rights are important, the state must protect children from parents who cannot or will not provide adequate food, shelter, and supervision. The state must also protect children from parents who abuse them, physically or psychologically. A clinician might recommend that the child be placed temporarily in foster care and that the parents receive training in parenting skills as a condition of having the child returned to them. In extreme cases—those in which parents abandon a child or are clearly incapable of caring for a child—the state might seek to terminate parental rights. This is done most often when relatives or others wish to adopt the child (Kuehnle & Kirkpatrick, 2104).

Civil Commitment and Risk Assessment

All 50 states and the District of Columbia have **civil commitment** laws that authorize the custody and restraint of persons who, as a result of mental illness, are a danger to themselves or others or who are so gravely disabled that they cannot care for themselves. This restraint is usually accomplished by compulsory commitment to a mental health facility. The courts also provide safeguards and rules for how these involuntary commitments are to be accomplished.

Many of these procedures were instituted in the 1970s, in response to a concern that in the 1950s and 1960s it was too easy to commit people to state psychiatric facilities. At that time, people who were mentally ill could be involuntarily committed whenever the state believed they needed treatment. Beginning around 1970, commitment proceedings began to be reformed, resulting in more legal rights for those with mental illness to resist compulsory commitment. A key case in this reform movement was *O'Connor v. Donaldson* (1975), in which the U.S. Supreme Court held that mental illness and a need for treatment were insufficient justifications for involuntarily committing mentally ill persons who were not dangerous.

Similar limits on involuntary hospitalizations were upheld by the Supreme Court in the 1990s (e.g., *Foucha v. Louisiana*, 1992). The standard for commitment changed from mental illness combined with a need for treatment, to mental illness that is associated with dangerousness or a grave lack of ability to care for oneself. This narrowing of the commitment standard, along with other societal influences during the last 40 years (e.g., the community mental health movement, deinstitutionalization), has resulted in fewer public hospital beds for mental health treatment, and shorter hospital stays.

Although the legislative changes of the 1970s were intended to protect the rights of individuals with mental illness, an exclusive concern with rights can sometimes leave patients without adequate care, housing, or the effective psychiatric treatment that can be provided in some hospitals (Wexler, 1992). Resources in the community devoted to treatment and recovery for individuals with mental illness—focusing on such necessities as housing and employment as well as mental health care and case management—could have replaced the need for extended hospital care in most cases. Unfortunately, however, community-based resources for individuals with mental illness have not been increased substantially following the downsizing of public psychiatric hospitals, starting in the 1970s and continuing to the present. As a consequence, some individuals have not had access to adequate treatment in either hospitals or the community during these decades (Leifman & Coffey, 2015).

Four Types of Commitment Procedures

The law permits four types of civil commitment: (1) emergency detention, (2) voluntary inpatient commitment, (3) involuntary inpatient commitment, and (4) outpatient commitment. Emergency detention is the means by which most individuals are initially admitted to hospitals. A police officer, a mental health professional, or sometimes a private citizen can initiate involuntary detention of another person. Usually, the cause is actual or anticipated harmful behavior by the patient either against self (e.g., attempted suicide) or against others. An examination is performed by a physician or a qualified mental health professional. Patients committed on an emergency basis can be detained for only a specified length of time—usually two or three days—before a review takes place. At that time a preliminary hearing must be held before the patient can be confined any longer.

A person may agree to enter a psychiatric hospital, although they still must meet the criteria for hospitalization (typically some version of "mentally ill and in need of treatment"). But even those who are being hospitalized "voluntarily" may feel pressure from family, mental health personnel, or the legal system to enter the hospital. Individuals who have been provided with more information and given the chance to express their views report feeling less coercion, regardless of whether they are voluntarily or involuntarily hospitalized (Dennis & Monahan, 1996). While voluntarily hospitalized, the patient may find that the hospital has instigated commitment proceedings to challenge or delay release.

The third type of commitment—involuntary inpatient commitment—requires a court order. The criteria for obtaining an involuntary civil commitment vary from state to state; in general, however, the person must be mentally ill and must also be dangerous to self and others, or so gravely disabled as to be unable to provide for their own basic needs. Although the criterion of "dangerousness" is the most often discussed standard and therefore is deemed the most important for involuntary hospitalization, grave disability is the standard that determines most commitments (Melton et al., 2018).

To obtain an involuntary commitment, the concerned persons must petition the court for a professional examination of the individual in question. A formal court hearing usually follows the examination. In most states, the hearing is mandatory, and persons whose commitment is sought can call witnesses and have their lawyer cross-examine witnesses who testify against them.

A fourth type of commitment procedure, known as outpatient commitment, allows a patient to be mandated to receive treatment in an outpatient setting, such as a community mental health center, rather than in a hospital—and it appears to reduce the potential for minor harmful acts toward others. (Its potential for reducing major violence, including mass shootings, is unknown because such events are relatively rare. Consider Swartz et al., 2017). Those released from involuntary hospitalization into outpatient commitment were more likely (relative to a group released without any kind of commitment) to use outpatient and residential mental health services and psychotropic medication (Pollack et al., 2005). However, outpatient commitment should not simply be used as a mechanism for ensuring compliance with treatment if the individual does not meet the commitment criteria (which typically have a public safety component).

Dangerousness and Risk Assessment

Dangerousness is one of the central constructs of mental health law. Whether a person is now or could in the future be dangerous is an issue that underlies many decisions in our system of justice, including questions of civil commitment. Although the law often uses the terms *dangerous* and *dangerousness*, these terms are difficult to define. They actually merge three distinct constructs: (1) risk factors (variables associated with the probability that violence or aggression will occur), (2) harm (the nature and severity of predicted and actual aggression), and (3) risk level (the probability that harm will occur) (National Research Council, 1989). In some combination, these factors provide a major justification for involuntarily committing those with mental illness to hospitals.

The construct of dangerousness to others recurs throughout the law. Dangerousness is the basis for requiring therapists to protect third parties from possible acts of violence against them by the patients of these therapists. It is also a reason for denying bail to certain defendants and the justification for hospitalizing defendants after they have been found not guilty by reason of insanity. Some states also use future dangerousness as one factor a jury can consider when deciding whether to sentence a convicted murderer to life in prison or death by execution.

Difficulties in Assessing Dangerousness

Because dangerousness is hard to define, we prefer to use the term *violence risk* and will do so throughout the remainder of this chapter. Can mental health experts accurately assess a person's present violence risk and then predict whether that person will be violent in the future? Is mental illness a sign that a person is likely to be violent? Do certain types of mental illness make a person more prone to violent behavior? These questions have been examined extensively by researchers for more than three decades, and they are at the heart of many real-life cases. For example, should the mental health professionals who treated Jeffrey Dahmer, who killed a number of young men and had sex with the bodies, have predicted that he was at risk for this kind of brutal conduct?

Clinicians who attempt to answer these questions perform **risk assessments**; using the best available data and research, they try to predict which persons are and which are not likely to behave violently in certain circumstances, give some estimate of the risk for violence, and offer suggestions on how to reduce the risk (Douglas & Otto, 2021; Heilbrun, 2009).

Many factors make such predictions difficult. For example, the base rate of violence in some groups is low, so clinicians are being asked to predict a phenomenon that rarely occurs. The clinical assessments of persons assessed for violence risk are often conducted in hospitals or prisons, whereas the environment where violence is being predicted is the community. The predictions have often been for long-term risk, which is harder to predict than violence risk over a shorter time frame.

The original consensus of researchers was that clinicians could not accurately predict future violence. Leading scholars such as John Monahan (1984) summarized the research this way: "In one study after another, the same conclusion emerges: For every correct prediction of violence, there are numerous incorrect predictions" (Pfohl, 1984). Another early summary of the research on clinicians' ability to predict violence was that their predictions were wrong in two of every three cases in which a "yes" prediction of future violence was made.

Subsequent research changed the early pessimism about clinicians' ability to predict violence, however. Researchers have learned that these predictions can sometimes reach moderate to good levels of accuracy under certain conditions (Douglas & Otto, 2021). Specifically, clinicians who consider factors that are empirically related to future violence can predict such violence considerably better than they could before 1990 (Heilbrun, 2009). When clinicians have information about a range of historical, personal, and environmental variables related to violence, when they limit their predictions to specific kinds of violent behavior, and when they concentrate on appraising risks in certain settings rather than in all situations, they can assess violence risk with a fair degree of accuracy. Although they still make a large number of errors, they do significantly better than chance.

One of the most important advances in the area of risk assessment has involved the development and use of specialized risk assessment tools (Heilbrun, 2009). A number of specialized tools are now available (Douglas & Otto, 2021), some of which are actuarial. An actuarial tool (such as the Violence Risk Appraisal Guide-Revised; Harris et al., 2013) uses specified risk factors that are rated and scored, with scores being combined into a final score that is then applied to the prediction in a way that is specified by a formula (which in turn has been developed through empirical research). Other tools (such as the HCR-20[V3], which measures historical, clinical, and risk management variables [Douglas et al., 2013]) employ "structured professional judgment." They do not combine scores on included variables to yield a total score. Rather, the evaluator is asked to make a judgment about risk in light of the status of these risk factors. Evidence indicates that good actuarial and structured professional judgment approaches to risk assessment are comparably accurate in predictions of violence (Heilbrun et al., 2021).

Summary

1. **What problems are associated with expert testimony, and what reforms have been proposed?** The main objections to expert testimony are that it is too adversarial and insufficiently impartial, introduces irrelevant information, and is often founded on an inadequate scientific base that may also be influenced by cognitive biases that affect human decision-making more generally. Proposed reforms have focused on using greater structure by linking testimony to evaluation reports that are consistent with foundational principles. Following such principles reduces the potential influence of factors such as retention bias and more general cognitive bias, provides judges with more information about the scientific foundation of expert testimony, and limits the scope of expert testimony to the highly relevant aspects of the evaluation. Limiting such testimony's scope and having judges consider the scientific foundation more carefully are proposals that have been implemented.

2. **Under what conditions can a plaintiff be compensated for psychological damages?** Plaintiffs can seek damages in civil trials if they allege that they have been victimized by a tort, which is a wrongful act that must be proved to have caused them harm. Although the law has historically been skeptical of claims for psychological harm and emotional distress unless they are accompanied by physical injuries, the subsequent trend has been to allow plaintiffs to be compensated for emotional damages (without any physical injuries) resulting from intentionally outrageous or negligent conduct.

3. **What is workers' compensation, and how do mental health professionals participate in such cases?** Workers' compensation is a no-fault system now used by all states and in the federal system to provide a streamlined alternative for determining the compensation of workers who are injured in the course of their jobs. Formal trials are not held nor juries used in workers' compensation cases. Psychologists may testify in workers' compensation hearings about the extent, cause, and likely prognosis for psychological problems that have developed following a physical injury and/or work-related stress.

4. **What capacities are involved in civil competence?** Questions of civil competence focus on whether an individual has the mental capacity to understand information that is relevant to decision-making in a given situation and then make an informed choice about what to do. The issue of civil competence is raised when it is not clear that an individual is capable of meeting the demands of a given task specified under civil law. Examples of such tasks include giving informed consent to current or future medical treatments, and executing a will.

5. **What criteria are used for decisions about disputes involving child custody or parental fitness?** The best interest of the child is the main criterion applied to disputes about which parent should have custody of a child following divorce. Evaluations of parental fitness address a different question: Should a parent's custody of a child be limited or terminated because of indications of parental unfitness? Many mental health professionals regard custody and parental fitness assessments as the most difficult evaluations they perform. For this reason, and in an attempt to reduce the stress of custody battles, custody mediation has been developed as a less adversarial means of resolving these disputes, and has been shown to be associated with more favorable subsequent adjustment of parents and children than is custody litigation.

6. **What steps are taken in civil commitment, and how well can clinicians assess dangerousness or the risk of violent behavior, a key criterion for civil commitment?** People who are considered gravely disabled or dangerous to themselves or others may be committed to a state psychiatric hospital against their will, but they have the right to a hearing shortly thereafter to determine whether they should be retained. After (or instead of) being hospitalized, some patients may be placed on outpatient commitment. Long-term predictions of violent behavior are more difficult to make with accuracy, but there is a reliable association among historical, personal, and environmental factors and dangerous behavior that provides a basis for reasonably accurate short-term assessments of risk. The use of structured risk assessment, whether through the use of a specialized actuarial risk assessment measure or a tool using structured professional judgment, can increase predictive accuracy beyond what is possible with unstructured judgment.

Key Terms

advance medical
  directives

breached duty

civil commitment

civil competencies

compensatory damages

dangerousness

duty

future best interests of
  the child

harm

intentional behavior

joint custody

malingering

negligence

proximate cause

psychological
  autopsies

punitive damages

risk assessments

sole custody

testamentary
  capacity

tort

Chapter 12

Preparing for Trials

Who Should Decide: Jury or Judge?

How Judges and Juries Compare

Determinants of Discrepancies

Newer Data on Judge-Jury Differences

Jury Selection Begins in the Community: Forming a Panel, or *Venire*

Judicial and Legislative Reforms

Jury Selection Continues in the Courtroom: The *Voir Dire* Process

Challenges for Cause and Peremptory Challenges

Box 12.1: The Case of Timothy Foster and Racial Bias in Jury Selection

Box 12.2: The Case of *J. E. B. v. Alabama ex rel. T. B.*: Whose Child Is This and Who Gets to Decide?

Pre- and Midtrial Publicity

Conflicting Rights

Assessing the Effects of Pretrial Publicity

Box 12.3: The Case of the Parkland School Shooter Amidst Massive Publicity and Another School Shooting

Assessing the Effects of Midtrial Publicity

Remedying Exposure to Publicity and Other Extraneous Information

Summary

Key Terms

Orienting Questions

1. How do juries' verdicts differ from those of judges?

2. What does the legal system seek in trial juries?

3. What stands in the way of jury representativeness?

4. What procedures are used in *voir dire*?

5. What personality and attitudinal characteristics of jurors, if any, are related to their verdicts? How effective are lawyers at responding to these characteristics?

6. What role do trial consultants play in a trial?

7. In what ways do pretrial publicity and midtrial information pose a danger to fair trials? How can these dangers be reduced?

The majority of legal disputes are resolved before they reach a courthouse. They are diverted from the criminal justice system, plea bargained, or settled through alternative dispute resolution mechanisms such as mediation and negotiation. Still, many civil and criminal cases are resolved through courthouse trials, and each year about 15% of adults in the United States are summoned to those courthouses to serve as jurors (Nekritz, 2022). So the trial is a foundational aspect of our legal system and Constitution. But before a trial commences, various issues must be resolved. We address three of these issues in this chapter: (1) whether the case should be decided by a jury or a judge; (2) if the choice is a jury, how a representative group of fair-minded citizens can be chosen to serve as jurors; and (3) what happens when those citizens are exposed to information about the case prior to setting foot in a courtroom or go online during a trial to search for case-related facts. Each of these topics has been examined by psychological research.

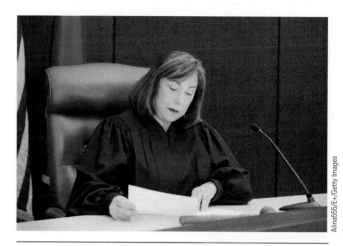

In bench trials, a judge determines the verdict.

Who Should Decide: Jury or Judge?

Before a trial begins, one choice looms large for all criminal defendants and most civil plaintiffs: Should the case be resolved by a judge or a jury? If the opposing party consents, defendants and plaintiffs can opt to have the verdict decided by a judge, in a proceeding called a **bench trial**. Several of the defendants involved in the January 6, 2021 U.S. Capitol riot have requested bench trials, believing that a single judge would be more lenient than a group of 12 Washington, DC residents. It is tempting to say that they gambled correctly, because the sole acquittals in a handful of prosecutions that have gone to trial so far have come from two bench trials. But might they have been equally (or even more) likely to be acquitted by a jury? Later, in this section, we present data on the rates of conviction by juries and judges that will help answer this question.

The preference for a bench trial or a jury trial obviously involves thoughts of who will issue the most favorable ruling (Bornstein & Greene, 2017). But it may be influenced by race and ethnicity as well. When researchers asked approximately 1,500 Texas residents whether they would favor a bench trial or a jury trial, Black and Latino respondents showed less support for a jury trial than Whites, reflecting, perhaps, the belief that the majority group's views, including any prejudices and biases, might predominate during deliberations. For these citizens, judges appear to be the less risky choice (Rose et al., 2008).

How Judges and Juries Compare

In general, does it matter who decides? Do juries and judges generally agree with each other? When they disagree, can we say who made the better decision? Of course, jury verdicts are not systematically compared against some "correct," back-of-the-book answer—even if there were such a thing (which there is not!). Fortunately, we have some data that

illustrate how frequently judges and jurors agree and why they might disagree.

The groundbreaking data were collected between 1954 and 1961 by Harry Kalven and Hans Zeisel (1966), professors at the University of Chicago, who carried out an extensive survey of the outcomes of jury trials. They asked every district court judge in the United States to provide information about recent jury trials over which they had presided and collected data from approximately 3,500 trials. In each, judges gave their assessments of the case while jurors were deliberating. Because of the large sample size and the careful way the study was conducted, we have faith in its findings despite its age. Later in this chapter, we describe research conducted more recently that borrows from the methodology used in this early, classic study.

Two questions addressed by Kalven and Zeisel are relevant to our discussion: (1) What was the jury's verdict? and (2) Did the judge agree? In criminal trials, the judges reported that their verdict would have been the same as the jury's actual verdict in 75% of the cases. (Table 12.1 presents detailed results.) Similar consistency was found for civil trials: judges reported that their verdict would have favored the side favored by the jury in 78% of cases. (Table 12.2 presents results.) These levels of agreement suggest that jurors are not deviating to a great extent from their mandate to follow the law and use only the judge's instructions plus the actual evidence to reach their verdict.

In most criminal cases in which the judge and jury disagreed, the jury was more lenient than the judge. The judge would have convicted the defendant in 83.3% of these cases, whereas the jury convicted in only 64.2% of them. For every trial in which the jury convicted and the judge would have acquitted, there were almost eight trials in which the reverse was true.

Other interesting results emerged from civil cases. Many commentators believe that civil juries are swayed by sympathetic plaintiffs, particularly in cases involving defective products or negligent doctors (Bornstein & Greene, 2017).

Table 12.1

Agreement of judges' and juries' verdicts based on 3576 criminal trials (in percentage of all trials). Jury verdicts shown in columns, and judge verdicts shown in rows

Judge Verdict	Jury Verdict		
	Acquit	Convict	Hung
Acquit	**13.4**	2.2	1.1
Convict	16.9	**62.0**	4.4

Source: Adapted from Kalven and Zeisel (1966, p. 56). Figures in bold show cases in which judge and jury agreed on the verdict.

Table 12.2

Agreement of judges' and juries' decisions in civil trials (as percentage of all trials). Jury verdicts shown in columns, and judge verdicts shown in rows

Judge Verdict	Jury Verdict	
	Plaintiff	Defendant
Plaintiff	**47**	10
Defendant	12	**31**

Source: Adapted from Kalven and Zeisel (1966, p. 63). Figures in bold show cases in which judge and jury agreed on the verdict.

But the data show otherwise: juries decided in favor of plaintiffs in only 59% of cases; judge did so in 57%.

Juries do occasionally make high awards to injured plaintiffs, sometimes higher than what judges would award (Hersch & Viscusi, 2004). What's more, media tend to report these uncharacteristically large damage awards (Kritzer & Drechsel, 2012). But in controlled studies, most juries make decisions—verdicts and awards—quite like those made by judges and experienced lawyers. In fact, some would argue that because the jury can apply its sense of community standards to a case, their award of damages in a civil case might actually be more fitting than a judge's award: "The appreciation of pain and suffering, and the likely impact on an individual's life and his or her ability to earn a living, are not matters which judges are any more qualified to assess than is a member of the public applying his or her life experience" (Watson, 1996, p. 457).

Determinants of Discrepancies

In cases where jurors and judges disagree, what accounts for the discrepancies? Are jurors less competent than judges and less able to apply the law in predictable ways? Or are there other, subtler factors at work? Kalven and Zeisel attempted to answer these questions by delving more deeply into the judges' reactions to the cases and comparing them to the juries' verdicts.

A few of the jury–judge discrepancies resulted from facts that one party knew but the other did not. For example, in several cases, the judge was aware of the defendant's prior arrest record (a matter not introduced into evidence or known to jurors) and would have found the defendant guilty, but the jury acquitted. The opposite can also occur. Especially in a small community, a member of the jury might share with fellow jurors some information about a witness or a defendant that was not part of the evidence and was not known by the judge at the time.

A second, smaller source of judge—jury discrepancies was the relative effectiveness of the two attorneys. In some trials, the jury was apparently swayed by the superiority of one lawyer over the other and produced a verdict that was, at least in the judge's opinion, contrary to the weight of the evidence.

Perhaps the most important explanation of judge–jury differences, accounting for roughly half of the disagreements, involves what Kalven and Zeisel called **jury sentiments**. They used this term to cover situations in which, *in the judge's view*, the jury's verdict was detrimentally affected by factors beyond the evidence and the law. (There is an implicit assumption here that the judge's decision was free of sentiments—a dubious claim, given that judges are all too human and subject to the same influences as most jurors.)

Jurors' sentiments play a role in decision making when jurors believe, for example, that the "crime" is just too trivial for any punishment or at least for the expected punishment, and find defendants not guilty to ensure that they will not be punished. In other instances, jurors believe that the defendant has already been sufficiently sanctioned, and therefore punishment by the legal system is unnecessary.

Jurors sometime acquit (when judges would have convicted) because they believe that a law is unfair. In trials for the sale of beer and liquor to minors who were in the military, juries have concluded that there was minimal social harm. Apparently they felt that if a young person can be forced to die for his country, "he can buy and consume a bottle of beer" (Kalven & Zeisel, 1966, p. 273). Jury sentiments have surfaced in many cases involving "unpopular" crimes—for example, small misdemeanors such as traffic offenses and arguably victimless crimes such as prostitution. "Why waste our time over such minor affairs?" jurors might have been thinking.

So jury–judge discrepancies should probably not be attributed to a lack of competence on the part of juries. Such disagreements might more appropriately be attributed to the jury's interest in fairness, or its consideration of a range of factors that are broader than those considered by an individual judge (Shuman & Champagne, 1997).

The study by Kalven and Zeisel was a massive undertaking and in the intervening decades, the methodological limitations of the study, including an unrepresentative sample and overreliance on judges' impressions, have become apparent (Hans & Vidmar, 1991). What do newer studies have to say on this topic?

Newer Data on Judge-Jury Differences

Updating Criminal Case Comparisons. A replication of this study was long overdue when researchers at the National Center for State Courts collected data from jurors, judges, and attorneys in more than 350 trials in four jurisdictions: Los Angeles, Phoenix, the Bronx (in New York City), and the District of Columbia (Eisenberg et al., 2005). They examined some of the same issues that Kalven and Zeisel had explored, including how often judges and juries agreed on verdicts in criminal trials.

As before, judges stated, prior to hearing the juries' verdicts, whether they would opt to acquit or convict and what they thought about the evidence. One obvious advantage of this study over its predecessor is that all groups (judges, attorneys, and jurors alike) gave their views of the evidence, thus addressing an important concern about Kalven and Zeisel's work—that all the information about a trial came from the judge.

The most striking finding was how closely the new results mirrored those of the earlier study. The rate of jury–judge agreement was 70% (compared to Kalven and Zeisel's 75%). When there was disagreement, it also mirrored the earlier asymmetry: Juries were more lenient. They were more likely to acquit when judges opted to convict than they were to convict when judges would have acquitted. The data are presented in Table 12.3.

Further scrutiny of the information collected by the National Center for State Courts revealed the circumstances in which jurors were more likely than judges to return "not guilty" verdicts (Givelber & Farrell, 2008). Jurors were more impressed than judges by the presence of a third-party defense witness (someone other than the defendant). Thus, when the defendant *and* another defense witness testified,

Table 12.3

Agreement of judges' and juries' verdicts based on 350 trials (National Center for State Court data, in percentage of all trials). Jury verdicts shown in columns, judge verdicts shown in rows

Judge Verdict	Jury Verdict		
	Acquit	Convict	Hung
Acquit	**11.6**	5.0	1.9
Convict	16.0	**58.5**	6.9

Source: Adapted from Eisenberg et al. (2005). Figures in bold show cases in which judge and jury agreed on the verdict.

jurors were 50% more likely than judges to acquit. Jurors were also impressed by the absence of a prior criminal record: When the defendant and another defense witness both testified *and* when the defendant had no prior record, jurors were 90% more likely to acquit!

Juries are also more lenient than judges in death penalty cases. Although the Supreme Court has ruled that only juries may impose a death sentence (*Ring v. Arizona*, 2002), this was not always so. Therefore, it is possible to compare sentencing outcomes from the era when judges made decisions and the period when juries did. Hans and her colleagues (2015) conducted a historical analysis of all 146 capital trial outcomes in Delaware from 1997 to 2007 and found that judges were significantly more likely than juries to impose a death sentence.

A reasonable explanation for these differences is that jurors and judges assume their roles differently. While jury duty is a unique experience for most jurors, judges have probably heard it all (or most of it) before. So jurors may take more seriously their instruction to acquit (or sentence to life in prison rather than death) unless the prosecution can prove the case beyond a reasonable doubt, may feel sympathy for someone in the defendant's situation, and may possess a commonsense understanding of what motivates people to act impulsively.

Updating Civil Case Comparisons. There are also newer findings on how judges compare to juries in civil cases. One of the largest studies examined plaintiff win rates (the proportion of cases in which the verdict favored the plaintiff) in federal cases tried before either juries or judges from 1979 to 1989 (Clermont & Eisenberg, 1992). For many types of cases, including contracts, property damage, civil rights, and labor disputes, plaintiffs' win rates were equivalent regardless of who decided.

But differences emerged in two types of cases—product liability and medical malpractice—where plaintiffs had more success with judges (48% win rate) than with juries (28% win rate). Researchers attributed these differences to selection effects by which the selection of cases tried by juries differed in important ways from those tried by judges. Because defense lawyers expected juries to be biased in favor of plaintiffs, they tended to settle cases in which the plaintiff had a strong case. That meant that on average, juries were left to decide relatively weaker cases for the plaintiff and appeared to make different decisions than judges. The selection effect makes it rather difficult to compare judge verdicts and jury verdicts in different cases because features of the cases themselves, rather than the decision makers, could explain any discrepancies (Bornstein & Greene, 2017).

A related question is whether jury awards for punitive damages are different from awards assessed by judges, and whether the two groups differ on the reasons for those awards. Punitive damage awards are used to punish and deter corporations that have engaged in serious wrongdoing. A study of jury–judge agreement on punitive damages, conducted by Theodore Eisenberg and his colleagues (Eisenberg et al., 2002), analyzed data from more than 9,000 trials that ended in 1996. Their primary finding was that judges and juries did not differ substantially in these cases, awarding punitive damages at about the same rate (i.e., in only 4–5% of cases).

These results call into question the notion that juries are unable to set reasonable limits on punitive damages. In fact, jurors also do about as well as judges in attending to the relevant evidence in these cases and setting aside any sympathy for the plaintiff. They tend to focus on the factors that *should* matter to the determination of punitive damages, such as the actions of the defendant, rather than factors that *should not*, such as the extent of harm to the plaintiff (Robbennolt, 2002).

Returning to the question we posed earlier—whether jurors perform as well as judges when deciding damage awards—we find little evidence that jurors' reasoning is much different from that of judges. A few studies suggest that jurors render erratic and unpredictable awards, in part because their decision-making processes are influenced by various cognitive biases (Sunstein et al., 2002). But judges are also human, and apparently affected by the same cognitive illusions as juries (Wistrich et al., 2015). More generally, it is satisfying to know that Kalven and Zeisel's landmark study has withstood the test of time, even as the makeup of juries has changed in the intervening years.

When a lawsuit reaches the trial stage and the parties opt to have a jury, rather than judge, be the arbiter, specific procedures for selecting that jury come into play. We describe those procedures next, focusing on the psychological considerations and consequences of jury selection that begin not in the courtroom, but in the community.

Jury Selection Begins in the Community: Forming a Panel, or *Venire*

Jury selection begins before potential jurors arrive at the courthouse, as officials assemble a panel, or *venire*, of prospective jurors. Each state, as well as the federal government, has its own procedures for determining how the panel of prospective jurors will be chosen. But the general rule is the same: jury selection must neither systematically eliminate nor underrepresent any subgroups of the population.

To encourage representativeness, U.S. Supreme Court cases going back to 1880 (*Strauder v. West Virginia*) have forbidden systematic or intentional exclusion of religious, racial, and other cognizable groups (members of which, because of certain shared characteristics, might also hold unique perspectives on selected issues) from jury panels. But as recently as 55 years ago, the composition of most *venires* was homogeneous, with middle-aged, well-educated White men generally overrepresented (Beiser, 1973; Kairys, 1972). And even today, despite various reforms intended to broaden diversity on jury panels, persons of color and indigent people continue to be underrepresented. In this chapter, we examine the reasons for, and the implications of, that reality.

Judicial and Legislative Reforms

In a series of decisions and legislation, the U.S. Supreme Court and the Congress established the requirement that the pool from which a jury is selected must be a representative cross-section of the community. (Note that criminal defendants are not entitled to a *jury* of peers that look and think like them, but rather, a *jury pool* of peers that represent the community from which it is drawn.) Relevant court decisions and lawmaking were driven by two policy concerns, each of which includes psychological assumptions (Vidmar & Hans, 2007).

First, the government believed that if the pools from which juries were drawn represented a broad cross-section of the community, the resulting juries would be more heterogeneous. That is, they would be composed of people who were more diverse with respect to age, gender, race, ethnic background, occupation, and education. The courts assumed that this diversity would produce various benefits—for example, that members of underrepresented groups might discourage majority group members from expressing prejudice. This assumption seems logical; casting a wider net will yield members of smaller religious and ethnic groups whose presence might reduce overt prejudicial remarks.

Another assumed benefit was that heterogeneous juries would be better fact finders and problem solvers. Extensive research on the dynamics of groups shows that, other things being equal, groups composed of people with differing abilities, personalities, and experiences are better problem solvers than groups made up of people who share the same background and perspectives (Crisp & Turner, 2011). Heterogeneous groups are more likely than homogeneous groups to evaluate facts from different points of view and to have richer discussions.

Does this also happen in juries? Apparently so. Samuel Sommers (2006) used actual jury pool members to examine the effects of racial heterogeneity on jury deliberations in a rape trial. Jurors took part in simulated (mock) trials in which the racial mix of the jury was varied. Sommers found that mixed-race groups had several advantages over juries composed of only White jurors. First, the mixed-race groups had longer, more thorough deliberations and were more likely to discuss racially charged topics such as racial profiling. Second, White jurors on racially mixed juries mentioned more factual information and were more aware of racial concerns than were their counterparts on all-White juries.

Other studies have shown that diversity can lead to more thorough evaluation of trial evidence and enhanced contributions to deliberations. White jurors who expected to discuss a race-relevant topic in diverse groups showed better comprehension of relevant background information than did White jurors in all-White juries (Sommers et al., 2008), and low-status jurors in diverse groups made more high-quality contributions to deliberations than those in nondiverse groups (Bergold & Kovera, 2021). Even though deliberating in a racially diverse group can require significant cognitive work (Peter-Hagene, 2019) and Black, Indigenous, and people of color (BIPOC) individuals may perceive themselves to be token members of these groups (Richeson & Sommers, 2016), the data certainly suggest that representative and diverse *venires* result in juries who undertake better, more thorough and accurate fact-finding and discussion.

The second policy reason for the U.S. Supreme Court's and Congress's decisions on representativeness is related to the *appearance* of legitimacy, rather than to the jury's actual fact-finding and problem-solving skills (Vidmar & Hans, 2007). Juries should reflect the standards of the community. When certain components of the community are systematically excluded from jury service, the community is likely to reject both the legal process and its outcomes as invalid.

The racial composition of a jury does affect public perceptions of the fairness and legitimacy of a trial and of the resulting verdict. Participants in one survey study read a description of a shoplifting trial in which the racial makeup of the jury and the verdict were varied (Ellis & Diamond, 2003). Half of the respondents read that there were 12 Whites on the jury (racially homogeneous), and half read that there were 8 Whites and 4 Blacks (racially heterogeneous). In half of the descriptions, the jury's verdict was guilty and in the other half, not guilty. The researchers measured observers' perceptions of the fairness and legitimacy of the trial procedures. As presented in Figure 12.1, when the verdict was not guilty, racial composition of the

jury had no effect on fairness ratings. But when the verdict was guilty, the racial composition of the jury *was* important. Observers considered a trial with a homogeneous jury less fair than a trial with a heterogeneous jury. Different elements of the community must perceive that they are well represented among those entrusted with doing justice—that they have a voice in the process of resolving disputes (Hans, 1992).

The historic 1992 riots in Los Angeles that erupted after four White police officers were acquitted of assault in the beating of Black motorist Rodney King illustrate this problem dramatically. The jury eventually selected for the trial contained no Black jurors. After the jury found the police officers not guilty, the Black community rejected the verdict as invalid and angrily challenged the legitimacy of the entire criminal justice system. Shaken by the surprising verdicts and shocked by the ensuing riots, many Americans, regardless of their race, questioned the fairness of the jury's decision, in part because of the absence of Black citizens from its membership. Yet, as we explain later, persons of color continue to be systematically underrepresented on criminal juries.

Representativeness of jury pools that involves both demographic and attitudinal diversity is a worthwhile goal. So how should courts go about forming the *venire* in order to reach this goal? For many years, voter registration lists were the primary source for assembling a jury pool. However, such lists underrepresent certain segments of the community because smaller percentages of those who are young, low-income, unemployed, and persons of color register to vote. Other sources such as lists of licensed drivers, persons receiving public assistance, and unemployed people now supplement voter lists as a source of prospective jurors (Mize et al., 2007).

From those persons who are eligible for jury service, members of the *venire* are randomly selected and summoned to appear at the courthouse for jury service. Unfortunately, many people never receive the summons and other simply opt to ignore it. Because they move more, persons of color are harder to reach by mail, the primary method of contacting prospective jurors. Also, a study in Washington state revealed that nearly half of all qualified jurors, and three-quarters of Latino and Asian-American prospective jurors, ignored the jury summons, even though doing so constitutes a violation of law (Bloeser et al., 2012). Cultural barriers contribute to low compliance rates, as do worries about language proficiency, doubts about one's ability to serve, and concerns about disrespectful treatment by court personnel (Rose et al., 2012).

Several structural factors—underrepresentation of some groups in jury pool source lists, difficulty contacting certain prospective jurors, and cultural hurdles—threaten the representativeness requirement for jury pools. As a result, persons of color are typically underrepresented on criminal juries. By analyzing the racial mix of federal juries in 764 U.S. counties, Rose and her colleagues (2018) observed that

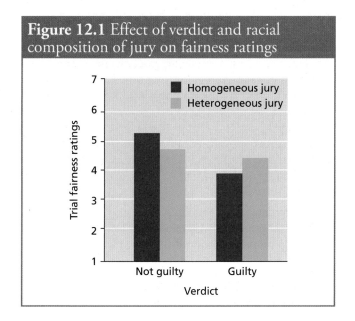

Figure 12.1 Effect of verdict and racial composition of jury on fairness ratings

roughly 40% of Black citizens and 31% of Latino citizens were not part of the jury pools in their respective communities. It is unsurprising then, that in most locations in the U.S., including those that are racially diverse, juries are primarily White (Wilkenfeld, 2004). A study of the racial composition of juries from one jurisdiction in the southeastern U.S. shows the stark result of this disparity: although Whites constituted roughly half of the adult population in 2013 and 2014, they constituted nearly two-thirds of those called for jury selection, which meant that a sizeable majority of criminal defendants were tried by juries in which non-Whites were absent or vastly outnumbered (Gau, 2016).

Another concern is that people will often go to great length to avoid serving on a jury, and some have concocted creative ways to escape jury service. As Liz Lemon on "30 Rock," Tina Fey once dressed up as Princess Leia, complete with toga and ear buns, to avoid jury service. Vincent Homenick, the chief jury clerk of the courthouse in Manhattan, once received a summons that someone had returned with the word "deceased" written on it, along with a plastic bag supposedly containing the ashes of the prospective juror (Green, 2004)! As Phoenix lawyer Patricia Lee Refo, past-president of the American Bar Association, put it aptly: "Everyone likes jury duty—just not this week."

Prospective jurors sometimes avoid jury service by claiming personal hardship. Some judges are sympathetic to claims of ill health, business necessity, caregiving responsibilities, vacation plans, and the like. But many other judges are unwilling to dismiss individual jurors because of perceived "hardships." During the jury selection for the O. J. Simpson civil trial, Judge Hiroshi Fujisaki responded to one prospective juror who had requested dismissal because she experienced symptoms of claustrophobia, "How big is your living room? Is it as big as this courtroom?" She remained in the pool.

When prospective jurors are excused for reasons of hardship, the result is a further winnowing down of the pool. Thus, even before the formal jury selection begins in a courtroom—that is, before jurors are questioned by attorneys and the judge—a sizeable portion of the community is left out of the jury system. Courts have struggled with how to get more citizens to the courthouse. Can the problem be remedied?

Suggestions abound. They include expanding summons lists, increasing juror pay, providing childcare, mandating that employers cover some portion of their employees' jury service, educating citizens about what jury duty entails, updating address lists, providing multiple reminders, and toughening penalties for non-responses. Other remedies, such as allowing noncitizens who are legal permanent residents and convicted felons to serve, aim to further broaden the pool. Providing interpreters for non-English speaking citizens would make courtrooms more welcoming. Even big data technologies, with vast public and quasi-public information about most Americans, could, within limits, be enlisted to democratize jury selection practices (Ferguson, 2016).

Jury Selection Continues in the Courtroom: The *Voir Dire* Process

Once the panel of prospective jurors has been assembled and summoned to the courthouse, selection issues change. The focus shifts from concerns about the representativeness of prospective jurors to questions about a given juror's ability and willingness to be fair and impartial.

As part of the constitutional right to be tried by an "impartial" jury, a defendant is afforded the opportunity to screen prospective jurors to determine whether any of them are prejudiced. The forum in which the judge and/or the attorneys question prospective jurors is called *voir dire*, a French term that literally means "to speak the truth." *Voir dire* is conducted in a variety of ways, depending on a jurisdiction's rules and a judge's preferences, though guidelines are typically more rigid in federal courts. In state courts, who asks the questions, what questions are asked and how they are phrased, how long the questioning goes on, and whether the questions are posed to individual jurors or to a group are generally matters left to judges' discretion.

The most limited form of *voir dire* involves a small number of questions asked in yes-or-no format by the judge and features group rather than individual questioning of prospective jurors. An example: "Do any of you have an opinion at this time as to the defendant's guilt or innocence?" Yes-or-no questions are effective in controlling the answers of respondents and reducing the time spent in *voir dire*, but they offer little insight into jurors' beliefs and attitudes. Additionally, this form of questioning requires jurors to self-identify any biases and report them to the judge. But **implicit biases**—beliefs borne of experiences and attitudes that predispose us to think in a certain way and of which we are unaware—make it difficult for jurors to accurately know their own predilections. And yet, those biases can affect how jurors remember the facts, evaluate and interpret the evidence, form impressions of witnesses, and reach verdicts (Roberts; 2019; Yokum et al., 2019).

Limited *voir dire* has limited effectiveness in identifying biased jurors. A compelling demonstration came from a project initiated by District of Columbia Superior Court Judge Gregory Mize (1999). Prior to this study, Judge Mize, like many judges, conducted limited *voir dire* during which he asked questions in open court to a group of prospective jurors. He and the attorneys would then pose follow-up questions to those who responded affirmatively to the initial question. Judge Mize revised his procedures for the study by interviewing *all* prospective jurors, regardless of whether they had responded affirmatively to the first question. In doing so, he determined that a number of jurors who were silent in response to a preliminary question actually had a great deal to say when prompted individually. Among the responses:

- "I was frightened to raise my hand. I have taken high blood pressure medications for twenty years. I am afraid I'll do what others tell me to do in the jury room."

- "My grandson was killed with a gun so the topic of guns makes my blood pressure go up."
- And remarkably, this one: "I'm the defendant's fiancée."

A 2021 study also documented the reduced utility of limited *voir dire.* It found that mock jurors' responses to generic *voir dire* questioning (e.g., "Do you know of any reason you may be prejudiced for or against the plaintiffs of defendants because of the nature of the case?") were unrelated to their case judgments (Salerno et al., 2021), suggesting that limited *voir dire* was woefully ineffective at uncovering juror bias. Why? Obviously, some jurors will fail to disclose important information because of privacy concerns, embarrassment, or a failure to recognize implicit biases. But another important psychological dynamic, the **social desirability effect**, is also a factor at this stage. Most people want to present themselves in a positive, socially desirable way. This desire to appear favorably, especially in the presence of a high-status person such as a judge, shapes how people answer questions and influences what they disclose about themselves.

At the other extreme is extended (or expanded) *voir dire,* in which both the judge and attorneys ask open-ended questions that require elaboration, cover a wide range of topics, and probe jurors individually. If the goal is to expose biases, extended *voir dire* has several advantages. Open-ended questions (e.g., "What experiences have you had in your life that caused you to believe that a person was being discriminated against because of the color of their skin?") encourage jurors to talk more about their feelings and experiences, and the answers to these questions *are* helpful in predicting jurors' case judgments (Salerno et al., 2021). But extended *voir dire* can take a long time, so most courts tend not to favor it. Typical *voir dire* procedures in state courts involve a compromise between the limited and extended versions; both the attorneys and the judge pose questions to a group of

prospective jurors, and then they ask brief follow-up questions of selected individuals.

Challenges for Cause and Peremptory Challenges

Technically, attorneys do not select a jury; rather, the judge gives them the opportunity to challenge, and effectively dismiss, a number of potential jurors from the jury. There are two mechanisms—challenges for cause and peremptory challenges—by which panelists are excluded from serving on a jury. We explain both in detail shortly. Here, we simply point out that after all the challenges have been made and ruled on, and some prospective jurors have been dismissed, the people who remain are sworn into service as the jury. In theory, because attorneys strive to exclude those jurors who seem unfavorable to their client, the challenges made by each side should tend to balance out and both extremes should be eliminated, leaving a jury composed of people who are less biased and more open minded.

In any trial, attorneys can claim that particular jurors should be excluded because they are inflexibly biased or prejudiced or because they have a relationship to the parties or the issues that creates an appearance of bias. These exclusions are known as **challenges for cause**. For example, a relative or business associate of a defendant would be challenged, or excused, for cause. Additionally, the judge may excuse a panelist for cause if the prospective juror is unfit to serve. In criminal cases, judges often inquire about whether prospective jurors have been crime victims and may excuse those who say that their own victimization experiences would affect their ability to be fair jurors. There is good reason to ask, because mock jurors who had been victims of the crime for which the defendant was being tried were more likely than nonvictims to convict (Culhane et al., 2004). In cases where the prosecution seeks the death penalty, prospective jurors whose strong opposition to the death penalty might make it difficult for them to be impartial are also dismissed for cause—a controversial practice we explore further in Chapter 14.

After one of the attorneys or a prospective juror has raised a concern about the ability to be fair and impartial, the judge will typically ask the juror whether they can be impartial. Then, using the juror's assessment of those abilities and observing the juror's demeanor, the judge decides whether to dismiss that person for cause. But judges may have difficulty determining which jurors are truly impartial (Crocker & Kovera, 2010). In making that decision, judges are often overly reliant on the juror's assertion of impartiality. Unfortunately though, jurors are not particularly insightful about their ability to be fair, and their confidence is not a reliable gauge of their open-mindedness (Rose & Diamond, 2008). So jurors who can be fair are sometimes dismissed, and those who cannot are sometimes seated on the jury.

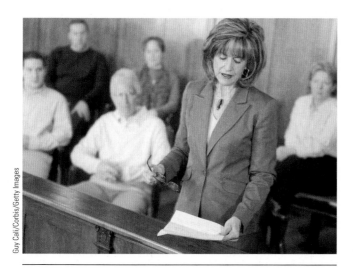

During jury selection, jurors are questioned by both the judge and attorneys.

In theory, each side has an unlimited number of challenges for cause. In reality, few prospective jurors are excused for reasons of bias. In a survey of New Mexico courts over a three-year period, only about 1 of every 20 jurors was dismissed for cause (Hans & Vidmar, 1986).

As jury selection proceeds, each side may also exclude a designated number of prospective jurors "without a reason stated, without inquiry, and without being subject to the court's control" (*Swain v. Alabama*, 1965). This procedure is known as a **peremptory challenge**. Most states and the federal courts allow six or more peremptory challenges per side, and some allow more than that in serious felony cases.

Peremptory challenges have multiple purposes. First, they allow attorneys to dismiss potential jurors whom they believe will be unsympathetic to their client, for whatever reason. The peremptory challenge has a second, largely symbolic function: When the parties in a lawsuit play a role in selecting the people who decide the outcome, they may be more satisfied with that outcome (Saks, 1997). The third function of peremptory challenges is to allow the attorney to begin to indoctrinate prospective jurors and influence those who ultimately will make up the jury. Attorney folklore in Texas is that an entire case can be tried during *voir dire* (Drummond, 2017). Consider the question "Do you agree with the rule of law that requires acquittal in the event there is reasonable doubt?" The real purpose of this question is to alert prospective jurors that reasonable doubt could exist in the case, and to make jurors aware of the rule so that they will look for reasonable doubt and then vote to acquit.

Since peremptory challenges came into effect after the Civil War when Black people were first included in jury selection, there has been concern that they were being used in a discriminatory manner. Concerns linger to this day, as exemplified by the six times that Curtis Flowers, who is Black, was convicted by all-White or nearly all-White juries from which 41 of 42 eligible Black jurors had been dismissed. (The case was featured on the popular podcast, *In the Dark*.) Many of those convictions were overturned due to prosecutorial misconduct and the U.S. Supreme Court opinion in the case was explicit: "The State's relentless, determined effort to rid the jury of black individuals strongly suggests that the State wanted to try Flowers before a jury with as few black jurors as possible, and ideally, before an all-white jury" (*Flowers v. Mississippi*, 2019, p. 2246). After the sixth verdict reversal in 23 years, the State of Mississippi dropped charges against Flowers and he was released in 2020. In the *Flowers* case and others like it, the U.S. Supreme Court has imposed more and more limits on the exercise of peremptory challenges and the overall status of this jury selection tool is in considerable flux. (They were abolished in Canada in 2019 and in 2022, Arizona became the first U.S. state to do so.)

Although opinions about the importance of peremptory challenges remain divided—some experts favor their elimination altogether and others consider them crucial for fair trials—we now have useful data on the use of peremptory challenges in real cases. Among the questions researchers asked: Do peremptory challenges disproportionately remove BIPOC individuals or other specific groups from juries? Do the prosecution and defense systematically dismiss different types of jurors? In one study researchers tracked the fate of more than 2,500 *venire* members in 89 criminal trials in Mississippi (DeCamp & DeCamp, 2020). Jurors' race clearly factored into the exercise of peremptory challenges: prosecutors dismissed 46% of Black venirepersons, and defense attorneys struck 10% of White venirepersons, making Black individuals 4.5 times as likely to be challenged. Other studies have also documented systematic racial discrepancies (e.g., Gau, 2016) which are especially pronounced in death penalty cases (Baldus et al., 2001; Grosso & O'Brien, 2011–2012).

Peremptory Challenges: No Exclusion on Account of Race or Gender. The Supreme Court has ruled that peremptory challenges may not be based *solely* on a juror's race or gender. The decision regarding race was triggered by the case of James Batson, a Black man convicted of second-degree burglary by an all-White jury. During *voir dire*, the prosecutor used four of six peremptory challenges to dismiss all the Black persons from the *venire*. In *Batson v. Kentucky*, decided in 1986, the Court held that James Batson was denied his Fourteenth Amendment right to equal protection by the prosecution's dismissal of Black members of the panel. The Court clarified that decision in *Powers v. Ohio* (1991) when it ruled that basing peremptory challenges on race harms not just *defendants*, but wrongly excluded *jurors* as well. And the following year, the Court held defense counsel to the same standard as prosecutors, effectively prohibiting race-based challenges for both sides (*Georgia v. McCollum*, 1992).

These decisions address the concern that attorneys will make unwarranted assumptions about certain jurors (assuming, for example, that Black jurors will acquit non-White defendants) and then use peremptory challenges in a discriminatory way in order to keep them from serving on juries (Hunt, 2015). They also reflect the Supreme Court's stance that systematic efforts by attorneys to exclude members of cognizable groups violate the constitutional rights of members of those groups. Simply stated, all citizens—regardless of race, religion, or creed—have the right to serve on juries.

In the *Batson* case, the Supreme Court developed a procedure for determining whether a peremptory challenge was race-based. Defense attorneys who believe that the prosecution's peremptory challenge was motivated by racial factors can initiate a so-called "*Batson* challenge," and the judge then asks the prosecutor for an explanation. The prosecutor typically advances a race-neutral explanation for the challenge—for example, that the prospective juror has a brother in prison or has filed a lawsuit against the police. The judge then determines whether the explanation is genuine, taking into account the other jurors who were not challenged by the attorney. For example, if a prosecutor stated that she dismissed a Black juror because he had been robbed, the judge would want to know why she had not dismissed a White juror who also had been robbed.

It might appear that creative prosecutors would be tempted to lie by citing "race-neutral" reasons for excluding BIPOC individuals from the jury. In fact, this is not hard to do because their reasons do not have to be particularly compelling (*Purkett v. Elem,* 1995), and because people are quite adept at generating benign explanations to justify their biased judgments.

The ease of generating neutral-sounding explanations was shown in a study in which college students, law students, and practicing attorneys assumed the role of a prosecutor trying a Black defendant (Sommers & Norton, 2007). They were given profiles of two prospective jurors, one Black and the other White, and had to use one remaining peremptory challenge. When the first juror was Black, he was challenged 77% of the time but when the first juror was White, he was challenged only 53% of the time. More to the point, participants rarely cited race as a factor in their decision. It was relatively easy for them to generate an ostensibly neutral explanation, such as the prospective juror's skepticism of statistics, to justify their choice. This is an example of **casuistry**, defined as fallacious reasoning in order to justify questionable behavior.

Psychological research on **social judgments** can explain why we are adept at generating false but plausible explanations of unseemly behavior. People hesitate to admit (even to themselves) that social category information such as race influences their decisions, often because they want to appear to be unprejudiced and to avoid the social consequences of showing racial bias (Axt et al., 2016). Furthermore, because of implicit biases, people make judgments influenced by racial factors without any awareness that those features affect their beliefs. These findings suggest that attorneys are unlikely to acknowledge that they considered the race of prospective jurors in their challenges, even when race was indeed a factor.

Recall that the judge, after hearing the prosecutor's explanation, must ultimately decide whether the attorney dismissed a prospective juror because of race. Easily concocted, plausible, and (above all) race-neutral justifications leave judges with little reason to reject them, and archival analyses of actual *voir dire* proceedings show that judges are unlikely to find that peremptory challenges violate the *Batson* rule (Melilli, 1996). But one high-profile case proved the exception to the rule—probably because it involved flagrant attention to prospective jurors' race. We describe it in Box 12.1.

Box 12.1

The Case of Timothy Foster and Racial Bias in Jury Selection

Thomas Foster

During jury selection in the 1987 murder trial of Timothy Foster, a Black man charged with killing an elderly White woman in Georgia, prosecutors struck all four Black prospective jurors and an all-White jury convicted Foster and sentenced him to death. But in notes that surfaced decades later, prosecutors left tell-tale signs of their intentions to remove Black jurors from the panel, and in 2016, the U.S. Supreme Court deemed those peremptory strikes unconstitutional (*Foster v. Chatman,* 2016).

The notes included highlighting on names of all Black prospective jurors and circles drawn around the word "black" where jurors indicted their race on questionnaires. These prospective jurors were rank-ordered in the event that

prosecutors had to pick one. Yet when questioned about their strikes, the prosecutors vehemently denied that race was a factor and even demanded an apology for the accusation. They said that the stricken jurors seemed disrespectful, nervous, or hostile. In fact, the chief prosecutor offered 11 reasons for striking 34-year-old Marilyn Garrett, including the fact that she was too young and was divorced. But the Supreme Court found these reasons "pretextual," noting that the state declined to strike eight prospective White jurors who were under the age of 36, including one who was only 21, and three of the four prospective White jurors who were also divorced (Liptak, 2016). It concluded that the strikes of Black jurors were motivated "in substantial part by discriminatory intent." So the *Foster* case has turned out to be an exception to the largely "toothless and symbolic" Batson framework (Liptak, 2015). Rarely will evidence of discrimination be so well documented or so blatant (O'Brien & Grosso, 2019).

Critical Thought Question

In examining attorneys' peremptory challenges during the *voir dire* in Foster's trial, appellate justices read the trial transcript that provided a verbatim account of everything that was said in the courtroom. But it took the discovery of handwritten notes and highlighting to bring the discriminatory nature of those choices to light. Why would it have been difficult for justices to find evidence of racial bias in attorneys' explanations of which jurors they excused?

Generally then, the procedures created in the *Batson* case for removing racial considerations from jury selection have not been effective, and discrimination persists despite U.S. Supreme Court attempts to eliminate it. In response, state supreme courts in Washington, Connecticut, and California have begun to question the *status quo* and now provide lists of reasons previously deemed "race-neutral" but which are essentially stand-ins for race, such as receiving public benefits or expressing a distrust of law enforcement. Judges in those states should assume that excluding jurors for those reasons is essentially "racism by another name" (Schwartzapfel, 2020).

As another remedy, some observers advocate for "race-related *voir dire*" to moderate the impact of racial attitudes. By talking about race explicitly during *voir dire*, judges could issue strongly worded messages intended to reduce the influence of bias, and attorneys and jurors alike may gain insight into their own implicit prejudices. Brayer (2015) claims that if such discussion is conducted in "an unhurried, relaxed, and non-judgmental environment," the impact of racial attitudes can be reduced (p. 3). Accordingly, the two most important factors in overcoming implicit racial biases may be race-relevant *voir dire* and the presence of Black people in the jury pool—the latter suggestion consistent with psychological research on the effects of racial heterogeneity on deliberations (Sommers, 2008).

In 1994, the U.S. Supreme Court extended the logic of *Batson* to peremptory challenges based on another cognizable characteristic—gender. No longer could attorneys base their peremptory challenges solely on jurors' gender. The leading case of *J. E. B. v. Alabama ex rel. T. B.* (1994) is described in Box 12.2.

How many different cognizable groups are there, and could limitations on peremptory challenges eventually be extended to cover all of them? In Houston, Texas, the attorney for accused murderer Jeffrey Leibengood asked to include only people less than five feet tall in the jury pool because his client's height was four feet six inches. The attorney told the judge, "We say a short person is subject to discrimination, and we hope to have two or three short people end up on the jury. *Batson* should be extended to include the little people" (quoted by Taylor, 1992, p. 43). The judge disagreed.

On a more serious note, courts are divided on the use of peremptory strikes based on prospective jurors' gender identity or expression. In many states, attorneys are free to base peremptory strikes on prospective jurors' gender identity or expression which, some argue, exposes transgender and gender-nonconforming jurors to sex discrimination (Maddera, 2016). By and large, attorneys' discretion in jury selection remains relatively unfettered, except that they cannot challenge jurors because of their race or gender.

Lawyers' Theories: Stereotypes in Search of Success. We now turn from the legal system's framework for jury selection and ask a more fundamental, and psychological, question: How do lawyers go about selecting or excluding jurors, and do their strategies work?

In everyday life, our impressions about others are governed largely by what psychologists have termed implicit personality theories. An **implicit personality theory** is a person's organized network of preconceptions about how certain attributes are related to one another and to behavior. Trial lawyers often apply their implicit personality theories

---

Box 12.2

The Case of *J. E. B. v. Alabama ex rel. T. B.*: Whose Child Is This and Who Gets to Decide?

The facts of this case are relatively simple: Teresia Bible gave birth to a child in May 1989; she named the child Phillip Rhett Bowman Bible, claimed that James E. Bowman, Sr. was the father, and filed a paternity suit against him to obtain child support. Even though a blood test showed that there was a 99.92% probability that he was the father, Mr. Bowman refused to acknowledge paternity, so a trial was held.

The jury pool was composed of 24 women and 12 men. After three jurors were dismissed for cause, the plaintiff's attorney used 9 of her 10 peremptory challenges to remove men, the defendant's attorney used 10 of his 11 challenges to remove women, and the resulting jury was composed of 12 women. (Note that in this case, it was men who were systematically excluded from the jury.) The jury concluded

that Mr. Bowman was the child's father and ordered him to pay child support of $415.71 per month.

Bowman appealed and the U.S. Supreme Court eventually ruled that peremptory challenges that were used to eliminate one gender were, like those used to exclude a race, unacceptable. The Court's decision acknowledged that peremptory strikes against women harken back to stereotypes about their competence and predispositions, traced from a long history of sex discrimination in the United States (Babcock, 1993).

Critical Thought Question

Given what you know about how attorneys support their exclusions in "Batson challenges," how might creative attorneys justify excluding jurors of a particular gender?

to jury selection. Years ago, one observer advised prosecutors to "never accept a juror whose occupation begins with a P. This includes pimps, prostitutes, preachers, plumbers, procurers, psychologists, physicians, psychiatrists, printers, painters, philosophers, professors, phonies, parachutists, pipe-smokers, or part-time anythings" (Bryan, 1971, p. 28). Another attorney vowed always to use a peremptory strike against any prospect who wore a hat indoors.

Implicit personality theories lead to stereotypes when a person believes that all members of a distinguishable group (e.g., a religious, racial, age, or occupational group) have the same attributes. They also produce assumptions that two personal characteristics are associated—for example, that slow-talking jurors are less intelligent than fast talkers—when they actually may not be.

We tend to link characteristics together to form our own implicit personality theories. Sometimes these judgments are rationally based; we may have had sufficient experience to draw a valid conclusion about the linkage. Other theories, however, such as the examples just presented, are only intuitive or are based on limited experiences and purely coincidental associations. Furthermore, these theories ignore within-group variability. But the emergence of implicit personality theories is almost inevitable when people form impressions of others and make interpersonal decisions. After all, human behavior is very complex and one must simplify it in some way. When attorneys have only limited information on which to judge a prospective juror, it is likely that implicit personality theories will influence their thoughts.

The jury selection decisions in the trial of *J. E. B. v. T. B.* reflect the use of implicit personality theories and stereotypes. Ms. Bible's attorney dismissed male jurors, assuming they would be sympathetic to the man alleged to be the baby's father, whereas Mr. Bowman's attorney dismissed female jurors because of similar beliefs that women would be biased in favor of another woman. But the courts prohibit the use of such stereotypes. In his majority opinion in the *J. E. B.* case, Justice Harry Blackmun wrote, "Virtually no support [exists] for the conclusion that gender alone is an accurate predictor of [jurors'] attitudes," and if gender does not predict a juror's predisposition, then there is no legitimacy to dismissing jurors on this basis only (quoted by Greenhouse, 1994, p. A10).

Lawyers must choose which prospective jurors to challenge with their quota of peremptory challenges. Hence, their own implicit personality theories and stereotypes come into play. Richard "Racehorse" Haynes, a highly successful lawyer, once defended two White Houston police officers charged with beating a Black prisoner to death. Like all lawyers, Haynes had his ideas about the kind of juror who would be sympathetic to his police officer clients, but his candor was a surprise. After the trial was over, Haynes was quoted as saying, "I knew we had the case won when we seated the last bigot on the jury" (Phillips, 1979, p. 77).

Even if they are allowed to question prospective jurors individually, lawyers cannot be certain they are being told the truth. By necessity then, they fall back on their own impressions. What attributes do lawyers find important? Textbooks and journal articles on trial advocacy provide a wealth of folklore about jurors' characteristics and their relation to beliefs and attitudes. Not surprisingly, characteristics that are visible or easily determined—age, gender, race, occupation, country of origin—receive special attention, and attorneys are naively "advised" about how jurors with certain attributes tend to think.

In addition to applying their own theories of personality to juror selection, some attorneys use their understanding of group structure. For example, they play hunches about which jurors will be the most dominant during the deliberations. Who will be selected as foreperson if, as in most jurisdictions, that choice is left up to the jury? Understanding group dynamics is more complicated than relying on simple stereotypes about individual jurors, so lawyers who try to forecast group behavior also make assumptions. Some lawyers maintain a simple "one-juror verdict" theory—that is, they believe that the final group decision is usually determined by the opinions of one strong-willed, verbal, and influential juror. Lawyers who adhere to this maxim look for one juror who is likely to be both sympathetic and influential and then, during the trial, concentrate their influence attempts on that individual. In pursuing this search for a "key juror," the typical attorney follows one basic rule of thumb: "In general, an individual's status and power within the jury group will mirror his status and power in the external world" (Christie, 1976, p. 270).

Another common attorney strategy is based on the assumption that jurors who are demographically or socially similar to a litigant will be predisposed to favor that litigant, a belief known as the similarity–leniency hypothesis. Does this rule of thumb hold true? Are jurors more likely to favor litigants with whom they share certain characteristics? One could make the opposite prediction in some cases—that sharing similar qualities with another might make a juror more skeptical of that person's excuses or justifications for behavior that the juror dislikes. Here, the so-called black sheep effect may apply: Although people generally favor individuals who are part of their in-group, they may sometimes strongly sanction those fellow members who reflect negatively on and embarrass the in-group.

Although the strength of evidence against a defendant is the most powerful predictor of jurors' sentiments in criminal cases (Devine et al., 2016), similarity between jurors and defendants may also have an influence. But the nature of that influence depends on whether the defendant has a prior record. When that person has committed previous wrongdoings, jurors render harsher judgments against members of their in-group than members of an out-group. This supports the black sheep effect: people distance themselves from others like them who are deviant in some way. But for defendants without prior wrongdoings, the similarity–leniency hypothesis seems more apt: jurors tend to view law-abiding members of their in-group more positively than members of an out-group (Gollwitzer & Keller, 2010).

Do Jurors' Demographic Characteristics Predict their Verdicts? To exercise peremptory challenges effectively, trial attorneys must make informed guesses about which prospective jurors will be favorable to their side. In doing so, they often rely on demographic features of jurors because many of these characteristics (e.g., age, race, gender, socioeconomic status [SES]) are easily observable (Kovera et al., 2002). Indeed, many attorneys actively select (or, rather, deselect) jurors on the basis of demographic information. But though demographic characteristics of jurors and juries are *sometimes* related to their verdicts, the correlations are weak and inconsistent from one type of trial to another (Devine & Caughlin, 2014). The relationships that emerge are usually small and offer no guarantee of success to the attorney who deals with only a few individuals and one trial at a time.

For example, in trials that involve issues such as sexual assault, domestic violence, and sexual harassment, women are somewhat more likely than men to convict (e.g., Golding et al., 2007), but gender differences are not apparent in other kinds of cases (Devine & Caughlin, 2014). The most consistent gender difference involves social influence rather than content; men are generally perceived by other jurors as more influential during deliberations than women (Marcus et al., 2000).

From the few studies that examined the relationship between jurors' SES and verdicts, the general consensus is that wealthy jurors are somewhat more likely than less wealthy jurors to assume that criminal defendants are guilty, particularly in trials involving theft, burglary, and fraud. As with gender though, the most powerful effect of SES occurs at the deliberation table, where jurors of higher SES are regarded as more influential because of what others believe about their competence (York & Cornwell, 2006).

Using jurors' race to predict verdicts is also complicated because, as we described, the racial mix of the jury influences an individual juror's decision. We can tentatively predict that Black jurors will be more lenient than White jurors in the typical criminal case (Devine et al., 2016), but only if the defendant is also Black (Sommers & Ellsworth, 2000). The mix of races and genders on juries—i.e., jury demographic diversity—may also be important, as individual jurors on juries with more race-gender subgroups (e.g., Latinas, Asian-American males) are less likely to convict (Devine et al.).

In general then, with regard to jurors' demographic features, there is little evidence that these characteristics can consistently predict verdicts in criminal cases (Devine et al., 2016) or damage awards in civil cases (Vinson et al., 2008). This is probably good news because verdicts should be based on the evidence presented during the trial and not on the personal features of the decision-makers.

Jurors' Personality and Attitudinal Characteristics as Predictors of Verdicts. Given that demographic variables have only a weak and inconsistent relationship to verdicts, one might wonder whether jurors' personality and attitudinal characteristics are better predictors. Personality characteristics are relatively stable patterns of behavior that describe "how people act in general" (Funder, 2004, p. 109). Attitudinal characteristics are evaluative reactions toward someone or something that are exhibited in feelings, beliefs, and intended actions (Olson & Zanna, 1993).

Enduring aspects of one's personality and attitudes do influence courtroom decisions, though usually only to a modest degree. Using simulated and real juries, research has indicated that certain personality attributes of mock jurors such as Authoritarianism and the Need for Cognition may be related to jurors' verdicts.

The personality characteristic **Authoritarianism** is modestly correlated with verdicts in criminal cases. People with an authoritarian personality tend to adhere to traditional values, identify with and submit to powerful figures, place less emphasis on civil liberties, and tend to be punitive toward those who violate established norms. Thus, authoritarian jurors are more likely to vote for conviction in criminal cases (Devine & Caughlin, 2014).

Authoritarian beliefs may be more powerful determinants of decisions in death penalty trials than in noncapital trials. In one study, prospective jurors reporting for jury duty in Florida read a condensed version of a capital case and recommended an appropriate sentence (life without parole or death). They also rated the extent to which various aggravating factors (those aspects of a crime that support a death sentence) and mitigating factors (aspects that support a life sentence) were present in the evidence (Butler & Moran, 2007). Jurors who scored high on a measure of Authoritarianism endorsed more aggravating factors and fewer mitigating factors and were more likely to select a death sentence than their counterparts lower in Authoritarianism.

Interestingly, when highly authoritarian jurors encounter a defendant who symbolizes authority, their usual tendency to punish the defendant is reversed (Nietzel & Dillehay, 1986). In fact, about the only time that authoritarian mock jurors are not more conviction-prone than nonauthoritarians is in trials in which the defendant is a police officer. In such cases, the more authoritarian jurors tend to identify with the powerful and punitive image of the officer.

Another personality variable—the **Need for Cognition**—may influence how jurors evaluate evidence in a trial. The Need for Cognition refers to a person's inclination to engage in and enjoy effortful cognitive work (Cacioppo et al., 1996) and explains why some people are motivated to think hard and analyze arguments thoroughly, and others are disinclined to do so. In a courtroom, the Need for Cognition can distinguish those jurors who scrutinize the evidence carefully and examine its weaknesses from jurors who accept trial testimony at face value and have little desire to pore over the evidence (DeWitt et al., 1997). Jurors with low Need for Cognition may pay more attention to witnesses' credentials than to the essence of their testimony.

The Need for Cognition influences how jurors process evidence presented by an expert witness. This evidence is often complicated, technical, or scientific, and may require effortful thinking on the part of jurors. When mock jurors read a summary of a sexual harassment trial in which an expert witness presented research that varied in terms of scientific rigor and quality, jurors high in Need for Cognition were attentive to the validity of the research. They evaluated the expert evidence more favorably when the research was valid and tended to support the side that presented that evidence. Jurors low in Need for Cognition were not attentive to flaws in the expert evidence and were less likely to support the side that presented the valid study (McAuliff & Kovera, 2008).

We can safely say that personality and attitudinal variables are better predictors of verdict decisions in criminal cases than are demographic factors (Lieberman & Olson, 2016), though the relationships between personality and attitudinal factors on the one hand, and verdicts on the other hand, are still only modest. The relationships seem less strong in civil cases and, in both contexts, probably depend upon the type of case (Vinson et al., 2008). In any event, behaviors are better predicted by attitudes specific to those behaviors than by general attitudes (Ajzen & Fishbein, 1977). For example, beliefs about mental health and illness in a case involving the insanity defense and attitudes toward the death penalty in a capital murder case will provide better information about how a prospective juror might reason than general beliefs about the law and legal system (Kovera & Austin, 2016).

Attorney Effectiveness in *Voir Dire*. Attorneys take pride in their skill in selecting a favorable jury. For example, a president of the Association of Trial Lawyers in America wrote, "Trial attorneys are acutely attuned to the nuances of human behavior, which enables them to detect the minutest traces of bias or inability to reach an appropriate decision" (Begam, 1977, p. 3). But psychologists and other observers of jury trials are less sanguine. They have noted that because attorneys rarely get extensive training or feedback on the wisdom of past choices, they may overvalue the role of obvious, identifiable demographic variables and undervalue the importance of specific attitudes when making peremptory challenges. As psychologist Reid Hastie has suggested, "[a]n attorney's ability to predict appears limited by a very low ceiling of precision" (1991, p. 712).

There is good reason for social scientists to be skeptical of how much lawyers can accomplish in *voir dire*. In one study, when asked to rate jurors after watching video of a previous *voir dire*, attorneys were no better than chance at detecting those who were biased against them (Kerr et al., 1991). In another study, attorneys tended to ask general questions about prospective jurors' backgrounds rather than specific questions related to the facts of the case that would have been more useful (Kovera et al., 2014). In short, as jury scholar Dennis Devine opined, "attorneys cannot read jurors like open books" (Devine, 2012).

Why are attorneys' judgments hampered in this way? One reason is that, like all of us, they are affected by their assumptions and expectations about other people. Kennard and colleagues demonstrated the powerful pull of expectations by recruiting practicing prosecutors and defense attorneys to conduct mock *voir dire* of community members (Kennard et al., 2014). They manipulated attorneys' expectations of the pro-prosecution and pro-defense attitudes of 12 community members (venirepersons) in a random fashion, meaning that the information researchers provided to attorneys was often at odds with what a community member *actually* thought. The attorneys then conducted a mock *voir dire* and indicated which six prospective jurors they would most want on the jury. Attorneys' expectations about a venireperson's verdict leanings persisted even after they had the chance to ask questions of these individuals and regardless of a person's actual inclinations. In other words, prosecutors struck more people whom they assumed to have pro-defense leanings and defense attorneys struck more people whom they assumed were pro-prosecution.

Interestingly, when venirepersons then reviewed evidence in a capital murder case and reached a verdict, those who were expected to be pro-prosecution rendered more guilty verdicts than those expected to favor the defense. This result is an example of **behavioral confirmation processes** that occur when someone's (e.g., an attorney's) perception of another person (e.g., a prospective juror) causes that person to behave in a manner consistent with the perceiver's expectation (Stukas & Snyder, 2002).

This relatively poor performance by attorneys during jury selection has been analogized to biased hypothesis testing in scientific endeavors (Kovera & Austin, 2016). In order to make effective choices—that is, in order to select jurors who will be favorably inclined toward one's position—attorneys must generate hypotheses about the relationship among jurors' traits, attitudes, and preferences, gather information during *voir dire* to test their hypotheses, and then make inferences about how those predilections will play out in their case. Each of these tasks—generating hypotheses, gathering information, and making inferences—is made more difficult by the cursory nature of jury selection in terms of time allotted and the depth of questioning. So, it is not surprising that attorneys make inaccurate decisions about a venireperson's leanings.

Scientific Jury Selection: Does It Work Any Better?
For years, trial lawyers have been "picking" jurors on the basis of their own theories about how people behave. But some attorneys—convinced of the importance of jury selection yet skeptical of their ability to do it well or limited in the time they can devote to it—hire social scientists as jury selection consultants. These consultants use empirically based procedures, such as focus groups, shadow juries, systematic ratings of prospective jurors, and surveys of the community, to identify desirable and undesirable jurors

(Lieberman, 2011). This collection of techniques is known as **scientific jury selection**. These techniques were first used to aid defendants in several highly publicized "political" trials of the Vietnam War era and are now practiced in high profile criminal and civil trials (Posey, 2016). The prime-time TV series *Bull*, loosely based on the experiences of Texas trial consultant Phil "Dr. Phil" McGraw, depicts aspects of scientific jury selection, though real-life consultants claim that it contains a fair amount of... bull (Tedder-King & Marinakis, 2016).

Scientific jury selection raises a number of complex issues and generates significant controversy. Some critics claim that it subverts the criminal justice system because it favors the wealthy and well-heeled over individuals of modest means (Strier, 1999) and creates a perception among the public that the system is rigged (Brown, 2003). Others claim that it is ineffective (Kressel & Kressel, 2002; Saks, 1997). Not surprisingly, consultants (and some attorneys) dispute these claims, pointing out that public defenders have benefitted from their services and touting the value of professional training and experience: "We've collected a lot of research and we can spot things a lawyer wouldn't normally be paying attention to.... Most attorneys do just one or two trials a year, if they're lucky. But a good consultant has studied hundreds of juries and knows which behaviors and characteristics to look out for" (quote by consultant Dan Wolfe, cited by McCann, 2004). Moreover, because the American system of justice is fundamentally adversarial, litigants are expected to present their version of the case as zealously as possible and should be able to use any legal means to convince the jury to reach a favorable decision.

How effective *are* trial consultants at selecting juries? When attorneys in criminal trials first began to rely on empirically grounded scientific jury selection, they were often successful. Although the procedure seemed to work, the success rate may have been inflated by the following factors: (1) Many of the more widely discussed cases involved weak or controversial evidence against defendants. (2) Attorneys who made the extra effort to enlist jury consultation resources may also have been more diligent and thorough in other areas of their case preparation.

To assess the impact of trial consultants, ideally one would conduct an experiment in which two, identically composed juries would decide two identically tried cases, one that involved the services of a consultant and another that did not. By holding constant all aspects of the trial, including the nature of the evidence and the identities of the participants, and by varying only the involvement of a trial consultant, one might be able to reach some conclusion about that person's impact. Unfortunately, it is impossible to conduct such an experiment, so we may never know with any precision or certainty whether and to what extent trial consultants are changing the outcomes of trials.

In addition, the effectiveness of scientific jury selection depends on a number of variables over which the consultant has no control. These include how many peremptory challenges are allowed; the extent to which questions delve into matters beyond superficial demographic details of prospective panel members; whether attorneys act on the guidance of the consultant; and, perhaps most importantly, the extent to which jurors' attitudes and beliefs will determine the outcome of the case (Greene, 2002). The more freedom and flexibility inherent in the jury selection procedures and the more the case hinges on jurors' belief systems, the more room exists for consultants to ply their trade and the greater the chances they can succeed.

Recognizing that jurors' demographic and personality characteristics do not correlate strongly with verdicts in general, many trial consultants have shifted their focus from advising lawyers about jury selection to providing services in realms other than jury selection (Posey, 2016). These include developing case themes and testing those themes in pretrial focus groups, preparing witnesses to testify in court, monitoring the effectiveness of evidence presentation during the trial, and interviewing jurors after the trial has ended. Consultants also assist attorneys during mediations.

Pre- and Midtrial Publicity

Legal cases have always attracted public attention, and the judicial system has struggled for years with the fallout of publicity that occurs prior to and during a trial. With the advent of 24-hour news networks, thousands of cable and satellite channels, online news sources, and social media, trial-related information is more available to the public, and more easily accessed and shared by jurors, than ever before. As a result, there are growing concerns about the impact of this communication on prospective jurors prior to serving, and on impaneled jurors post-jury selection. The criminal and civil justice systems are both affected: The number of criminal defendants claiming their cases have been jeopardized by pretrial publicity has more than doubled since the 1990s (Daftary-Kapur et al., 2010), and in the civil realm, publicity surrounding product liability and medical malpractice claims, along with the reporting of unusually large damage awards, is commonplace (Kritzer & Dreschel, 2012).

In this section, we address two distinct ways that information gleaned from outside of the courtroom can threaten jurors' fact-finding abilities and impartiality. The first concerns exposure to publicity prior to trial: that jurors bring this information with them into the courthouse, that such knowledge is not detected during *voir dire*, that it influences their interpretation and evaluation of the evidence, and that it can be shared with other panelists during deliberation. The effects of pretrial publicity (PTP) have been extensively researched over the past 50 years (e.g., Hoetger et al., 2022; Steblay et al., 1999).

But because "we now live in the Internet age of 140 characters or less and jurors are used to constant and immediate access to information in small sound bites" (Daftary-Kapur &

Penrod, 2019, p. 157), a second threat to jury fairness has emerged: the prospect that jurors will use social media, blogs, and news websites to conduct independent research during the trial and post about their experiences while the trial is ongoing. Legal commentators and researchers have begun to raise concerns related to such *midtrial publicity* (MTP): how this information, picked up from and shared via social media and the Internet, might affect jurors' understanding of evidence presented in the courtroom, and how courts can manage such two-way communications (Daftary-Kapur & Penrod; Hoffmeister & Watts, 2018). Although this issue is not typically addressed *before* the trial begins—as are the other topics covered in this chapter—we discuss it here because MTP has much in common with PTP.

Conflicting Rights

Pretrial and midtrial publicity expose tensions between cherished rights protected by the U.S. Constitution: freedom of speech and of the press as guaranteed by the First Amendment on the one hand, and the right to trial by jury as guaranteed by the Sixth Amendment in criminal cases and the Seventh Amendment in civil cases, on the other. The language of the Sixth Amendment is explicit about impartiality, noting that all criminal defendants have "the right to a speedy and public trial, by an impartial jury of the State and district wherein the crime [was] committed." Although the Seventh Amendment does not mention impartiality explicitly, courts have considered it an implicit guarantee.

In most instances, the liberties ensured by these constitutional protections are compatible and even complementary. The press informs the public about criminal investigations, alleged civil wrongs, and trials, and the public learns the outcomes of these actions and gains increased appreciation for both the justness and the foibles of our system of justice.

On occasion, however, the First Amendment clashes with the Sixth and Seventh. The press publishes information that, when disseminated among the public, threatens the right to a trial by impartial jurors. This can occur in cases in which defendants and/or victims, because of their fame or infamous acts, have gained national reputations. More commonly, it happens when local news media, online postings, and press releases disseminate information about a crime or the parties involved that is inflammatory, biased, emotion-laden, or factually erroneous. Examples of this information include details about a person's prior criminal record, a confession made by the accused, unfavorable statements regarding someone's character, and criticisms of the merits of pending cases. Impaneled jurors' online activities—examining case files, downloading medical information, viewing crime scenes on Google Earth, seeking guidance on legal terminology, tweeting about their deliberations, and the like—have been so pervasive as to cause mistrials and overturned verdicts. According to Reuters, "as jurors go online, U.S. trials go off track" (Grow, 2010).

The Supreme Court has considered several cases involving claims that the right to an impartial jury was compromised by jurors' exposure to extraneous information. In one case, Jon Yount's confession that he had killed a high school student was published in two local papers in 1966. Prior to trial, Yount cited continuing publicity about the case and the fact that 77% of prospective jurors admitted they had an opinion about his guilt. Yount appealed his conviction, claiming that the publicity had made a fair trial impossible. The Supreme Court ruled against him, reasoning that a "presumption of correctness" should be given to the trial judge's opinion because, being present at the trial, the judge was in a better position to evaluate the demeanor, credibility, and, ultimately, the competence of prospective jurors (*Patton v. Yount*, 1984).

But in *Rideau v. Louisiana* (1963), the Court decided that dissemination of news that strongly pointed to the defendant's guilt violated his rights. On three occasions, a local TV station broadcast a 20-minute clip of Wilbert Rideau, surrounded by law enforcement officials, confessing to charges of robbery, kidnapping, and murder. Rideau was convicted and sentenced to death by a jury, of which at least three members had seen the televised confession. The Supreme Court reversed the verdict, Rideau was granted a new trial, and he was eventually convicted of manslaughter. (In the 43 years he spent in prison, Rideau transformed from an eighth-grade dropout who could neither read nor write to a national advocate for prison reform, a filmmaker, and an award-winning editor of Angola State Prison's *Angolite* magazine. Perhaps most important, he acknowledged responsibility for his crime and apologized for the harm he caused [Green, 2005].)

The Supreme Court has also chimed in on whether jurors' online activities constitute an outside influence that necessitates a new trial. In *Dietz v. Bouldin* (2016), the Court affirmed that a judge has authority to re-impanel an already-discharged jury but, in a nod to the pervasive impact of the Internet, noted that this authority must be exercised with caution because jurors might instinctively check their phones or communicate about the case while discharged. According to Justice Sonia Sotomayor, "Immediately after discharge, a juror could text something about the case to a spouse, research an aspect of the evidence on Google, or read reactions to a verdict on Twitter. Prejudice can come through a whisper or a byte."

If asked whether they have been unduly influenced by information gleaned from or shared with outside sources, most jurors will say no. Yet it is difficult to know how much trust to place in their claims of impartiality. The problem is not that jurors lie about their beliefs, although some probably do. The issue is that people might not be aware of or admit the full measure of their knowledge and beliefs in public. Prospective and impaneled jurors alike would have to acknowledge that they received or shared biasing information, know that they integrated those details with evidence presented in court, and be able to reverse or control the biasing effects of this information—all very difficult cognitive tasks (Bornstein & Greene, 2017).

Even if fully aware of their biases, jurors might not be willing to disclose them in an open courtroom before a judge who encourages them to be fair and open-minded. They might experience evaluation apprehension, whereby they provide the answers that they perceive the judge wants to hear, regardless of whether their responses are truthful.

Assessing the Effects of Pretrial Publicity

We now turn to what psychologists and other researchers have learned about the impact on prospective jurors of exposure to pretrial information. Later in the chapter, we discuss the scant research that addresses jurors' online activities during the trial. Interestingly, the remedies to both issues converge on a number of methods, including enhanced jury instructions, which research has also examined and which we describe.

Both experimental and field studies have measured the effects on jurors of various kinds of pretrial publicity presented via different media. In experimental studies, participants are first exposed (or not exposed, in the control group) to some form of publicity and then are asked to assume the role of jurors in a simulated criminal trial. In field studies, community-respondents are surveyed to assess the effects of naturally occurring publicity about an actual criminal case. Taken together, these studies point to the conclusion that jurors exposed to pretrial publicity are more likely than those not so exposed to favor the prosecution and prejudge the defendant as guilty.

Experimental Studies of the Effects of Pretrial Publicity. Using experimental procedures, researchers manipulate the presence and type of pretrial publicity and measure its impact on perceptions of witnesses and the defendant, evaluations of evidence, and the final verdict. Because all aspects of the trial except the publicity are held constant, scientists can assess whether variations in publicity cause differences in responses.

Many experimental studies have examined the effects of negative or anti-defendant information on verdicts. These studies generally show that negative pretrial information has a modest effect on both individual and group verdict preferences: jurors and juries exposed to such publicity are more likely than those not exposed to convict (Hoetger et al., 2022). This effect is stronger for nonviolent crimes than violent crimes, perhaps because people have preconceived notions about how violent crime unfolds. For less serious crimes, there is room for extraneous information to fill in details. Some studies have explored the effects of positive or pro-defendant pretrial publicity. (Consider the case of Brock Turner, a Stanford University student convicted of sexual assault in 2016. Some of the pretrial reporting focused on the records Turner set as a standout collegiate swimmer.) This form of PTP also has an impact on individual jurors' verdicts but in the opposite direction: namely, decreasing guilty verdicts (Hoetger et al.)

Still other studies have attempted to explain why these effects occur. Three explanations seem reasonable. First, pretrial publicity may bias jurors' interpretations of the evidence to which they are exposed at trial. If pretrial publicity about the defendant is negative, jurors evaluate trial testimony—even ambiguous testimony—in a manner adverse to the defendant yet consistent with the publicity (Ruva & Guenther, 2015). In short, the publicity affects jurors' ability to determine the true probative value of the evidence. Second, jurors exposed to publicity come to believe, wrongly, that the pretrial information was actually presented as part of the evidence at trial. This is a source monitoring error: Jurors are mistaken about the source of their information (Ruva et al., 2007). Finally, jurors exposed to PTP can share that information during deliberations with jurors not previously exposed, thereby extending the bias to the group (Ruva & Guenther, 2017).

Up to this point, we have considered the effects of specific pretrial publicity, showing that case-specific information made available prior to trial can affect the sentiments of jurors in that trial. But jurors can also be influenced by generic prejudice—that is, prejudice arising from media coverage of issues not specifically related to a particular case but thematically relevant to the issues at hand. In Box 12.3 we consider how publicity about one school shooting could influence the sentiments of prospective jurors in a trial involving a wholly separate school shooting. The late Judge Abner Mikva of the Court of Appeals for the District of Columbia suggested that generic prejudice may be more problematic than specific pretrial publicity:

> Pretrial publicity is not the big difficulty. It is generic prejudice. I do not think you can get a fair child abuse trial before a jury anywhere in the country… I do not care how sophisticated or how smart jurors are, when they hear that a child has been abused, a piece of their mind closes up, and this goes for the judge, the juror, and all of us (cited by Doppelt, 1991, p. 821).

Psychological research seems to support Judge Mikva's assertion. For example, Wiener et al. (2006) found evidence of generic prejudice among mock jurors, and the effects of prejudice were greater in cases of sexual assault than homicide. Kovera (2002) showed that media exposure and preexisting attitudes interact: exposure to a story about a rape case influenced participants' appraisals of the witnesses and verdicts in a different rape case, and preexisting attitudes also affected the impact of the media on mock jurors' judgments.

Generic prejudice probably works by transferring preexisting beliefs and stereotypes about categories of people to a particular defendant in a trial setting (Vidmar, 2002). As a result, the facts of the case and the personal characteristics

The Case of the Parkland School Shooter Amidst Massive Publicity and Another School Shooting

On Valentine's Day 2018, Nikolas Cruz killed 17 people and wounded 17 more at Marjory Stoneman Douglas High School in Parkland, Florida. He pleaded guilty to all charges in 2021. The sole remaining issue was punishment: prosecutors sought the death penalty and selection of a jury for the expected four-month long sentencing trial began in April, 2022. Even before questioning began, Cruz's attorneys raised concerns about pretrial publicity:

> "This case has received extensive media coverage, frustrating the power of this court to provide a fair trial before an impartial jury in Broward County or anywhere else. Neither the passage of time nor a change in venue will make the digital publicity covering this case less accessible or contemporary to potential jurors."

Jury selection proceeded and then, a month later, coincided with the Uvalde, Texas school shooting that left 21 dead and another 17 injured. The two attacks had eerily similar facts: the lone gunman was a young man who targeted a school in his hometown, armed with a military-style AR-15 rifle and hundreds of rounds of ammunition. Citing publicity from the Uvalde shooting, as well as other mass shootings around the same time, Cruz's defense team asked for a continuance—a delay in jury selection. Given one prospective juror's remark ("If imposing the death

Students marching in support of policies to reduce gun violence after the Parkland shooting.

penalty on him would prevent some other wannabe mass murderer from doing it, that would have some weight with me for saying yes to the death penalty"), they had reason to worry about impartiality. The judge denied their request.

Critical Thought Question

How might news about the Uvalde school shooting affect prospective jurors being questioned at the sentencing trial in the Parkland school shooting case?

of the defendant may be given less weight than warranted. Racial and ethnic stereotypes, along with stereotypes related to gender identity, are probably the most common forms of generic prejudice but cases that share similar features (e.g., workplace shootings, tainted products) can also result in generic prejudice in the courtroom.

Field Studies of the Effects of Naturally Occurring Publicity. Critics have long suggested that studies of pretrial publicity lack usefulness because they do not measure the public's reactions to naturally occurring publicity. (As we pointed out, experimental studies typically "expose" participants to news reports in the context of a research study.) But serious crimes attract extensive news coverage, typically from the prosecutor's view of the case, so it is imperative to also assess the real-world impact of such information. Field studies, a research technique favored by trial consultants, can determine the saturation of a news story in a community by polling people about their knowledge of an actual crime. In these studies, participants are typically asked what they know about the crime in question, what they believe

about a criminal defendant's culpability, and whether they can be impartial in light of their knowledge. (As we noted, responses may be of questionable validity because of jurors' inability to detect their own biases.) In some instances, polling occurs in the community where publicity is assumed to be widespread, as well as in jurisdictions farther from the crime, allowing for comparisons among respondents in two or more locales.

Whether surveying opinions about notorious crimes (Studebaker et al., 2002) or cases of only local interest (Vidmar, 2002), these studies consistently find that persons exposed to pretrial publicity possess more knowledge about the events in question, are more likely to have prejudged the case, and are more knowledgeable of incriminating facts that would be inadmissible at the trial. On rare occasions, when a field study demonstrates that the volume of publicity has been overwhelming and when a crime has touched the lives of large numbers of local residents, a judge will have no option but to move the trial. That happened in the 1997 trial of Timothy McVeigh, charged with the Oklahoma City bombing that killed 163 people.

In light of extensive and detailed publicity about the case in Oklahoma, the trial was moved to Denver where McVeigh was convicted and sentenced to death.

As with experimental studies, field studies have revealed both specific prejudice, which stems from media coverage of a particular case (as in the Oklahoma City bombing), and more generic prejudice, which derives from media reports of social and cultural issues (as in cases involving police shootings and school shootings). Moran and Cutler (1991) showed that media descriptions of drug crimes influenced attitudes toward particular defendants charged with drug distribution. Generic prejudices can also be engendered by publicity about large jury damage awards (Kritzer & Drechsel, 2012), which then negatively inclines prospective jurors to civil plaintiffs (Greene et al., 1991). And although publicity about lawsuits involving consumer safety issues such as contaminated food or dangerous products can be valuable in informing the public to avoid those items (Kritzer & Drechsel), such publicity can also prejudice parties in ongoing litigation.

Field studies have several strengths. For example, they use large and representative samples of prospective jurors, and they rely on naturally occurring publicity about actual cases. They also have a weakness: the data are correlational in nature and cannot indicate the direction of any relationship between exposure to publicity and prejudice. For example, does exposure to publicity lead to prejudicial sentiments about a defendant, or, alternatively, do people with an antidefendant bias voluntarily expose themselves to such publicity? Reasoning from Kovera's (2002) study on the interactive effects of the media and preexisting attitudes in a rape case, we suspect that both alternatives are possible.

Some scholars (e.g., Carroll et al., 1986) have suggested another weakness in field surveys. They argue that courts should not conclude that pretrial publicity biases jurors just because it affects their attitudes; to be truly prejudicial, it must also affect their verdicts. According to this logic, we need to know whether the effects of pretrial publicity persist through the presentation of trial evidence. Some research suggests that antidefendant biases held at the beginning of the trial linger through the presentation of evidence and may influence the way that the evidence is interpreted (Ruva & Guenther, 2015; 2017).

A Novel Method to Assess Effects of Pretrial Publicity. Another way to gauge the likely impact of media coverage is to delve into details of the coverage itself. This is what Bakhshay and Haney (2018) did for 20 capital cases in California in which defendants had sought a change of venue. Noting that the life and death sentencing decision is highly subjective and less factually based than guilt determinations, and that these cases typically receive extensive and sensationalized media coverage, the researchers raised concerns about the biasing effects of PTP. Using more than 1,300 historic records (e.g., news articles) and a detailed coding scheme, they determined that 75% of all articles contained negative PTP, including half that featured sensationalistic details of the crimes, a third that made explicit negative character statements about the defendant, and a third that mentioned the community's outrage over the crime. Many of these details would have been excluded from the trial. Bakhshay and Haney also found that news coverage relied heavily on information provided by law enforcement and prosecutors: these sources were cited six times more often than defense sources. Nonetheless, change of venue was granted in only 6 of the 20 cases. The study provides a novel perspective and important data on the potential impact of PTP in capital punishment trials.

Assessing the Effects of Midtrial Publicity

As we have said, the impartiality of jurors is a key requisite for fair trials. Impartial jurors are those who say they can consider the evidence presented during the trial, apply the relevant laws, and reach a verdict unfettered by extraneous information. For most of the twentieth century, this ideal was within the realm of possibility. But with a rapidly expanding universe of Internet-based technologies and social media platforms such as Facebook, Twitter, WhatsApp, Instagram, and TikTok, that scenario now seems naïve. According to staff at the National Center for State Courts, "reliance on new media has become so ingrained that it would require conscious effort for many jurors to refrain from [using media] for the duration of the trial" (Hannaford-Agor et al., 2021, p. 5).

The "typical" incident of jurors' online access occurs in a criminal trial involving serious charges against a defendant. During the trial, a juror (or jurors) goes online to search for trial-relevant facts or clarification of legal terms and concepts, or to communicate with others via social media. That person (or persons) subsequently shares the online information with other jurors during deliberation. Such misconduct comes to light when those jurors report the behavior to the judge who then questions the panel to determine whether it was prejudicial to the parties.

There are significant reasons to be concerned about whether jurors access information midtrial, and how they make use of that information as the trial progresses. After the jury has been impaneled and the evidence has begun to emerge, jurors become involved with and invested in the case, so any online information to which they are exposed at this point could become increasingly salient and relevant to their decisions. Information consistent with the point-of-view jurors are developing at this stage of the trial has the potential for even greater influence (Daftary-Kapur & Penrod, 2019). Yet none of this information has been vetted by a judge or introduced in any formal way during the trial. Much of it could be prejudicial and inadmissible in court.

No one knows for sure how often jurors go online to access or share information during the course of a trial. Most of the evidence of juror exposure to midtrial information is anecdotal. It relies on analysis of cases where verdicts were challenged because of claimed juror misconduct and on survey responses of judges, attorneys, and jurors. A 2010 analysis of appellate cases involving claims of juror misconduct revealed wrongdoing in half the cases (Grow, 2010), but a 2021 study identified only a small number of such cases (Hannaford-Agor et al., 2021). When state trial judges and attorneys (n = 451 respondents) were queried, only one-quarter reported any personal experiences with juror misconduct involving online activity (Hannaford-Agor et al., 2021).

It is likely that the small number of verdicts overturned because of jurors' online activities is a function of appellate courts' deference to the trial court's discretion and the lack of consensus about how to assess prejudice in these cases. Jurors' own responses in one study reveal reasons for ongoing concern though. When questioned directly, nearly one-third said they would like to go online during the trial, and 15% admitted that they would not be able to refrain from doing so even if instructed (Hannaford-Agor et al., 2012). The upshot? We suspect that during trials, jurors are engaging in a healthy amount of poking around online that is simply never brought to light.

Remedying Exposure to Publicity and Other Extraneous Information

Given that pretrial and midtrial publicity both adversely affect jurors' impartiality, what procedures should be used to enhance the likelihood of a fair trial? Four alternatives are available; all have been applied to counter the effects of inflammatory PTP and some could be useful to head off prejudice related to midtrial exposure.

Improved jury instructions. A fairly straightforward remedy for any biasing effects of pretrial publicity is an instruction from the judge telling jurors to ignore what they learned about the case prior to trial and admonishing them to base their decision on the evidence presented in the courtroom. But cautionary instructions may not be sufficient to reduce the biasing effects of exposure to pretrial publicity (Ruva & Guenther, 2015). An instruction probably falls short as a safeguard because of the way that people remember and use information to form impressions and make judgments. Unless they have some reason to discount or ignore pretrial publicity when it is first encountered, most people will use it to help them interpret subsequent information and to make various pieces of information "fit" together in a coherent theme. For example, once the idea of a guilty perpetrator is established, it can become an organizing principle for the processing of additional information about that person. For these reasons, safeguards that attempt to remove an existing bias may never work as well as trying to find jurors who never had a bias to start with.

Whether an admonition telling jurors to steer clear of information gleaned online could be effective is an open question. A model instruction to that effect has been developed by the Federal Judicial Center. A portion reads,

> "I know that many of you use cell phones…the Internet and other tools of technology. You must not…use these tools to communicate electronically with anyone about the case…You may not communicate with anyone about the case on your cell phone, through e-mail…text messaging, or on Twitter, through any blog or website…I expect you will inform me as soon as you become aware of another juror's violation of these instructions."

Commentators encourage judges to use updated instructions along these lines and to give them at the beginning of jury service, at various times throughout the trial, and prior to deliberations. Robinson (2011) believes that when used in this way and combined with other tactics to deter juror misconduct, such instructions can be effective. In fact, a scale has now been developed to identify those individuals who will follow these instructions and those who are prone to break the rules (Knutson et al., 2015).

Expanded *voir dire*. If a goal of jury selection is to identify prospective jurors who have strong pre-existing biases regarding issues in a trial, then in-depth questioning may be necessary. In fact, a common method for handling pretrial prejudice involves conducting a thorough *voir dire* of potential jurors in order to identify and dismiss those with particularly strong prejudices. Extended questioning could also help to detect jurors who would be unlikely to refrain from online activities during the trial. But expanded *voir dire* requires that jurors recognize and acknowledge their own biases and predilections and be willing to disclose those in a public courtroom. As we have noted, jurors are inclined to provide socially acceptable responses to probing questions regardless of their true sentiments. Paradoxically, some research has found that the impact of pretrial publicity actually increased, rather than decreased, when jurors were questioned about their exposure prior to trial (Freedman et al., 1998).

Continuance. To reduce the impact of pretrial publicity, a trial can be postponed until a later date, with the expectation that the passage of time will lessen the effects of the prejudicial material. (We described the defense's request, and the judge's denial, of a continuance in the Parkland school shooting case.) But although a continuance may decrease jurors' reliance on factual pretrial publicity, it does not dampen jurors' recall or use of emotionally biasing information (Kramer et al., 1990). Furthermore, the prejudicial effects of pretrial publicity can linger for at least eight weeks post-exposure (Daftary-Kapur et al., 2014), and judges may hesitate to delay a trial for such a lengthy period. Obviously, a continuance will not prevent any midtrial online activity by jurors. In fact, any juror with a hazy memory of case-related details may, with the passage of time, become more, rather than less, likely to "just Google it."

Change of venue. The most extreme remedy for pretrial prejudice, a change of venue, is typically requested by criminal defense attorneys in cases that have generated a great deal of biasing publicity. Changing venue means that the trial is held in a different geographic location and that jurors for the trial are drawn from this new location. But venue changes are expensive, inconvenient, and time-consuming, so judges are reluctant to grant them, though some evidence suggests that they are more easily persuaded when defense attorneys provide media analyses documenting the extent of news coverage (Spano et al., 2011).

Venue changes can result in significant variations in characteristics of the communities, and hence, the jurors involved, as illustrated by the case of William Lozano, a Latino police officer who was convicted of killing a Black motorist in Miami. After the conviction was reversed because of pretrial publicity and a retrial granted, the judge moved the case to Tallahassee, which has a much smaller Latino population. But a Florida appellate court reasoned that in cases in which race may be a factor and changes of venue are appropriate, trials should be moved to locations where the demographic characteristics are similar to those of the original location (*State v. Lozano*, 1993). In the end, Lozano was retried in Orlando, where the Latino population is sizeable.

In some instances, judges import jurors from a nearby jurisdiction under the assumption that they are less likely to be influenced by local publicity. The judge in Bill Cosby's 2017 sexual assault trial undertook this plan and brought in jurors from outside of suburban Philadelphia, where the trial was held. This solution reduces inconveniences for the judge, other court personnel, and attorneys, but obviously increases hardships on jurors. As with a continuance, a change of venue would not be an effective way to limit midtrial online activity.

On occasion, psychologists have been enlisted to support a lawyer's motion for one or more of these protections against pretrial prejudices. When publicity is pervasive, a professionally conducted public opinion survey is the technique of choice for evaluating the degree of prejudice in a community. Public opinion surveys gauge how many people have read or heard about a case, whether they have formed opinions, and how their opinions might influence perceptions of the case.

Public opinion surveys can yield valuable information but require more resources than the typical client can afford. And yet, a change of venue is probably the most effective procedure available for improving the chances for a fair trial in a highly publicized case. Even if the venue is not changed, survey results can be used in jury selection. Because of these multiple purposes, public opinion surveys are a popular tool among trial consultants.

Finally, we describe a solution to pretrial publicity and online access that focuses a wider lens on jurors' experiences. As we describe in Chapter 13, jurors are active "thought processors" when seated in a courtroom. They evaluate the evidence in light of their own experiences and frames of reference, ask questions of themselves, and construct narratives to tie facts together. Why not allow them, as some judges now do, to question witnesses, view crime scenes, and engage in pre-verdict discussions with other jurors? These measures could help jurors better understand and use the evidence presented to that point, reduce the biasing influence of pretrial publicity, and decrease the likelihood they will go online in search of missing details about the case.

Summary

1. **How do juries' verdicts differ from those of judges?**
The question of whether juries' and judges' verdicts differ significantly was answered in a massive empirical study by Harry Kalven and Hans Zeisel. In actual trials, 75% of the time the jury came to the same verdict that the judge would have reached. In the vast majority of cases in which judge and jury disagreed, the jury was more lenient than the judge. The major source of discrepancies was what Kalven and Zeisel called "jury sentiments," or factors beyond the evidence and the law. Replications of this classic study in the 2000s showed remarkably similar results: In criminal cases, the judge and jury agreed on a verdict in 70% of trials, and when there was disagreement, jurors were more likely than judges to acquit.

2. **What does the legal system seek in trial juries?**
The legal system seeks representative and unbiased juries. Both are hard to achieve. The jury selection process can, in some instances, create an unrepresentative jury.

3. **What stands in the way of jury representativeness?**
The lists from which jurors' names were selected—originally only voter registration lists—underrepresent certain segments of society such as youth, older adults, and people of color. Many people fail to respond to their jury summons. Others seek dismissal by claiming personal hardship. To make jury pools more representative, jurisdictions have broadened the sources of names of prospective jurors and expanded outreach efforts.

4. **What procedures are used in voir dire?** The goal of *voir dire* is to assemble an unbiased jury. Prospective jurors who have biases or conflicts of interest can be challenged for cause and discharged. Using peremptory challenges, each side may also dismiss a certain number of prospective jurors without giving any reason, although jurors may not be dismissed because of their race or gender. Questioning of the prospective jurors is done at the discretion of the judge. In most trials, there is some combination of questions from the judge and the attorneys. When questioning jurors, most attorneys also try to sway them to their viewpoint through various ingratiation and indoctrination techniques.

5. **What personality and attitudinal characteristics of jurors, if any, are related to their verdicts? How effective are lawyers at responding to these characteristics?** Two personality and attitude-related characteristics of jurors—Authoritarianism and Need for Cognition—are related to their verdicts. Attorneys tend not to focus on jurors' personality characteristics during jury selection, probably because they are difficult to identify. In choosing jurors, lawyers base decisions on their implicit personality theories and stereotypes.

6. **What role do trial consultants play in a trial?** Initially, practitioners of scientific jury selection tried to determine which demographic characteristics of jurors were related to sympathy for one side or the other in trials. Consultants have now broadened their work to include pretrial assessments of reactions to the evidence and the development of themes that organize the evidence for jurors likely to be swayed by this approach. There is some evidence that science-oriented consultation may be useful in cases in which jurors' attitudes about the evidence are especially important.

7. **In what ways do pretrial publicity and midtrial information pose a danger to fair trials? How can these dangers be reduced?** Free speech and the right to a fair trial are usually complementary, but some trials generate so much publicity that the parties' right to an impartial jury is jeopardized. In addition, publicity about other cases or about social or cultural issues can create generic prejudice that can influence jurors' reasoning in a particular case. In addition, jurors' online activities during trial can introduce extraneous or inadmissible information into the proceedings. Psychologists have studied these effects and have also evaluated various mechanisms for reducing them. Improving and updating jury instructions is a relatively easy remedy, though of questionable effectiveness. Changing venue may be the most effective solution for extensive pretrial publicity because it does not require jurors to disregard information to which they have been exposed. But it does not address midtrial Internet access. Allowing jurors to ask questions during trials could be helpful with that.

Key Terms

Authoritarianism

behavioral confirmation
  processes

bench trial

black sheep effect

casuistry

challenges for cause

change of venue

cognizable groups

evaluation apprehension

generic prejudice

implicit biases

implicit personality theory

jury sentiments

Need for Cognition

peremptory challenges

scientific jury selection

selection effects

similarity–leniency
  hypothesis

social desirability effect

social judgments

source monitoring

specific pretrial publicity

venire

voir dire

Chapter 13

Jurors and Juries

Orienting Questions

1. How have psychologists described jurors' thought processes?
2. Describe the issue of jury competence.
3. What evidence is most important to jurors when deciding guilt in criminal trials? When deciding liability and damages in civil trials?
4. How can jurors be helped to understand their instructions?
5. What is the impact of extralegal information on jurors?
6. Can jurors disregard inadmissible evidence?
7. What is meant by the statement "Bias is inevitable in jurors"?
8. What reforms of the jury system do psychologists suggest?

One out of three Americans will serve as a juror at some point in their lives. Other than voting, there is no more direct way that citizens can be involved in their government. Juries are a vital institution of a democratic society. A trial by jury is the only right to appear in both the main body of the U.S. Constitution (Article 3) and the Bill of Rights (Sixth Amendment for criminal cases and Seventh Amendment for civil cases). The U.S. Supreme Court underscored the importance of the jury by stating that "[t]he guarantees of jury trial in the state and federal constitutions reflect a profound judgment about the way in which the law should be enforced and justice administered" (*Duncan v. Louisiana*, 1968, p. 149). In 2004, the Supreme Court acknowledged the preeminent role of juries in the United States' legal system when it announced that nearly any contested fact that increases the penalty for a crime must be determined by a jury (*Blakely v. Washington*, 2004).

Trial by jury is an institution that routinely draws ordinary citizens into the apparatus of the justice system. In fact, jury trials occur all over the world, from Venezuela to Japan and from Ireland to Ghana (Hans et al., 2017). But as many countries have instituted trial by jury to increase the legitimacy of their legal systems, jury trials in the U.S. have become less frequent. In federal courts, the percentage of civil cases going to trial has declined from roughly 12% in 1962 to approximately 1% in 2017. A similar pattern emerges in criminal cases, where jury trials accounted for about 20% of case resolutions until the early 1980s but dropped to 2% by 2017 (Smith & MacQueen, 2017). State court data are harder to come by but tend to produce similar trends.

What accounts for these declines? According to Yale Law Professor John Langbein (2012), litigants "no longer go to trial because they no longer need to" (p. 569). In civil cases, pretrial rules that allow disclosure of the strengths and weaknesses of each side's case facilitate settlements because the parties have similar expectations about who will prevail and what the damages are likely to be. The availability of alternative dispute resolution, primarily mediation and arbitration, allow the parties to control the outcome and avoid a public trial. The rising costs of litigation also play a role. In criminal cases, the desire to eliminate risk through plea bargaining motivates many defendants to "cop a plea" (Smith & MacQueen, 2017). The demise of the jury trial comes with significant costs, however, reducing direct participation in the justice system at the very time that trust in governmental institutions is eroding and systemic inequities are increasing (Wilford & Bornstein, 2021).

Despite the declining numbers, it is important to remember that the right to a jury trial—enshrined in the Constitution—will remain and will continue to provide transparency and due process protections for any litigants who wish to exercise it. Furthermore, given the vast scope of the U.S. civil and criminal justice systems, even the small percentage of cases that juries decide still translate into thousands of trials every year. So notwithstanding current trends, attention to what happens in jury trials is useful for advancing our understanding of basic psychological processes inherent in legal reasoning and decision making, and for improving the justice system.

The American legal system relies on laypeople to serve as jurors in both criminal and civil trials, and in both federal and state courts. Although laws and procedures differ somewhat in the state and federal systems, the task for jurors is essentially the same: listen attentively to the evidence, decide what "facts" are true, and consider those facts in light of the relevant laws as explained by the judge to reach a verdict. Jurors in criminal trials have a different objective than those in civil trials, however. In criminal trials, the question is whether the government, by way of the prosecutor, has proven that the defendant is guilty of the crime charged. In civil trials, juries typically make two decisions: first, whether the defendant (or, in some instances, the plaintiff) is **liable**, meaning responsible for the alleged harm, and second, whether the injured parties (typically the plaintiffs) should receive any money to compensate their losses, and if so, how much. These monies are called **damages**. For example, if a pedestrian is injured by a fast-moving bicyclist, jurors can be called on to decide whether the bicyclist was at fault and how much money the pedestrian should receive.

The jury system casts its shadow well beyond the steps of the courthouse because predictions about jury verdicts influence decisions to settle civil lawsuits and to accept plea bargains in criminal cases. Thus, the jury trial is an important and influential tradition and the outcomes of those trials ripple throughout the criminal and civil justice systems. Moreover, no other institution of government places power so directly in the hands of the people and allows average citizens the opportunity to judge the actions of their peers (Abramson, 1994).

Antecedents of the contemporary jury system may be seen in citizen juries used by the ancient Greeks and Romans and formalized in English laws more than 800 years ago. Despite this long history, the jury system has often been criticized. One commentator described the jury as, at best, 12 people of average ignorance. Another critic, Judge Jerome Frank, who served on the federal appeals court, complained that juries apply law they don't understand to facts they can't get straight. Even Mark Twain took a swing at the jury system. In *Roughing It*, he called the jury "the most ingenious and infallible agency for defeating justice that wisdom could contrive." Without a doubt, not all jury verdicts are correct—as evidenced by cases in which criminal defendants were wrongly convicted and later exonerated. (According to the National Registry of Exonerations, there have been more than 3,150 exonerations since 1989; https://www.law.umich.edu/special/exoneration/Pages/about.aspx).

But the jury system also has its defenders. Contemporary authors (e.g., Bornstein & Greene, 2017) point out that claims about juries are often based on anecdotes that are unrepresentative or fabricated and on studies that lack scientific validity. Most of us never hear about the hundreds of thousands of juries that each year toil out of the spotlight and, after careful deliberation, reach reasonable verdicts. In fact, the bulk of scientific evidence shows that juries generally do a commendable job (Bornstein & Greene, 2011).

Proponents further argue that trial by jury epitomizes what is special about the justice system in that it ensures public participation in the process. Verdicts reached by representative juries can and often do increase the legitimacy of the process in the eyes of the public, particularly in controversial trials. Juries can serve as a check on the arbitrary or idiosyncratic nature of a judge. Because juries do not give a reason for their verdicts (as judges are required to do), they retain a flexibility that is denied to judges. Finally, participating on a jury can both educate jurors and enhance their regard for the justice system. Alexis de Tocqueville (1900), a 19th-century French statesman, wrote, "I do not know whether the jury is useful to those who are in litigation, but I am certain it is highly beneficial to those who decide the litigation; and I look upon it as one of the most efficacious means for the education of the people which society can employ" (p. 290). Tocqueville was right: engaging in meaningful deliberations reinforces jurors' confidence in fellow citizens and public institutions and enhances civil involvement and participation (Gastil et al., 2010). It would be a shame if these many benefits were jeopardized by the dwindling rates of jury trials.

How Do Jurors Think?

Jurors are expected to evaluate and weigh the evidence presented by both sides in a trial in order to determine the "facts"—that is, what actually happened sometime in the past. The evidence can come from laypeople who witnessed or have first-hand knowledge of the events and people involved. Evidence can also come from experts who, given their training or experiences, can offer professional opinions relevant to the issues in dispute. Jurors then consider that evidence in light of the relevant law, as explained by the judge, and in terms of the standard of proof. In civil trials, they must ask themselves whether plaintiffs' attorneys have proven their claims "by a preponderance of evidence" and in criminal trials, whether prosecutors have proven their cases "beyond a reasonable doubt." As we've noted, civil juries decide whether plaintiffs have proven that defendants are liable for the harms they suffered and if so, what damages should be paid, and criminal juries decide whether prosecutors have proven that defendants are guilty. (Except in cases where prosecutors seek the death penalty, juries have no role in sentencing. That decision rests with the judge.) How do jurors undertake these tasks? One hint comes from a notorious criminal trial where prosecutors apparently failed to meet their high burden of proof. We describe that surprise verdict in Box 13.1.

Box 13.1

The Case of Ammon and Ryan Bundy and Prosecutors' Failure to Convince Jurors of their Guilt

Armed antigovernment protestors, at times 25 strong and led by brothers Ammon and Ryan Bundy, occupied a federal wildlife sanctuary in a remote corner of Oregon for six weeks in early 2016. The Bundys and their father had been engaged in a decades-long dispute with federal authorities over ownership of public lands in the West. The Oregon standoff had a "Wild West quality" with armed men in cowboy hats demanding that the federal government release the 188,000-acre property to local residents. Prosecutors eventually charged seven defendants, including the Bundys, with conspiracy to impede federal employees from exercising their duties and various weapons charges. But what many expected to be a slam-dunk case for the prosecution instead ended in acquittals of all seven defendants. Why? According to an email from one of the jurors to a Portland (OR) newspaper, prosecutors had failed to prove that the defendants *intended* to keep federal employees from doing their jobs, a key element of the conspiracy charge. The juror wrote, "It should be known that all 12 jurors felt that this verdict was a statement regarding the various failures of the prosecution to prove 'conspiracy'... and not any form of affirmation of the defense's various beliefs, actions, or aspirations" (Bernstein, 2016).

Ammon and Ryan Bundy, activists who led an anti-government protest in Oregon in 2016.

Jim Urquhart/Reuters

Critical Thought Question

What does this verdict suggest about how juries think when they attempt to apply the law to the relevant facts?

Returning to the issue of how jurors think, we can ask whether they are capable of making fair and intelligent decisions, or whether criticisms of juries are justified. And if the criticisms are fair, can the legal system do anything to improve the functioning of juries?

Psychologists are in a good position to answer these questions because their studies of juror and jury decision making have become so plentiful that they occupy a central place in psychology-law research. Over the past five decades, researchers have subjected the jury to careful scientific scrutiny by applying theories and principles of social psychology (e.g., persuasion, stereotyping, attribution, social influence, conformity, and small-group behavior) and cognitive psychology (e.g., memory, reasoning, judgment, and decision making). From their findings, psychologists have been able to obtain a fairly clear picture of how the jury system works.

Next, we describe three influential theories that characterize aspects of jurors' thought processes. The theories are complementary in the sense that none of them captures entirely how jurors manage their fact-finding and decision-making tasks. But neither are they contradictory, and together, they provide an effective framework for understanding the workings of jurors' minds while they listen to evidence and begin to formulate judgments. Later in the chapter we consider how the pre-deliberation preferences of individual jurors are integrated into the collective experience of deliberating as a jury.

Thinking Rationally or Intuitively. Jurors are routinely subjected to conflicting sets of facts and off-setting arguments about how those facts fit together. How do they perform in this "unruly decision-making environment" (Simon, 2018, p. 423)? Cognitive psychologists rely on **dual-process models** of information processing to capture how individual jurors think as they attend to and evaluate clashing evidence presented during a trial. Several dual-process models exist (including one espoused by Nobel Prize-winning psychologist Daniel Kahneman in his 2011 book, *Thinking, Fast and Slow*), but they all propose two ways in which people process information—either by rationally and deliberately evaluating the content of the information, or by reacting to it quickly and intuitively, without careful analysis. The former requires motivation, effort, and ability; the latter does not.

One dual-process model, termed cognitive–experiential self theory, is especially relevant to decisions that jurors make (Krauss et al., 2012). This theory suggests that when people rely on analysis and logical arguments, they are using a rationally based cognitive system that is active, deliberate, and effortful. On the other hand, when people rely on emotion, intuition, or stereotypical thinking from past events, they are using an experientially based system that is unconscious and effortless. The experiential mode is the default mode of processing, and jurors will shift to rational processing only if the importance of careful analysis is stressed to them. When they *do* think rationally about the evidence, they are alerted to possible reliability issues with the evidence (Rassin, 2016) and their verdicts reflect more accurately the strength of arguments presented by expert witnesses (Salerno et al., 2017). But they will revert to experiential processing when they are emotionally aroused (Feigenson, 2016) or required to decipher complicated evidence (Levett & Kovera, 2008).

Reasoning Coherently. Another description of jurors' thoughts has been termed **coherence-based reasoning**. According to the theory, a hard case morphs into an easier one through a series of coherence shifts in jurors' minds that move them ever closer toward a decision, and eventually, to a strong and confident verdict (Simon, 2004). At the beginning of a criminal trial, jurors' mental representation of the facts is naturally incoherent because there seems to be equivocal support for both the prosecution and defense. But over time, pieces of evidence that tend to support a particular decision are linked together, endorsed, and remembered, while rival evidence—that which supports a different decision—is rejected. As the evidence accumulates in this way, the task gradually become more coherent and a decision emerges, along with confidence that it is the correct one.

Support for this theory comes from a study in which participants were first presented with a vignette that concerned an eyewitness identification and were asked questions about the likelihood that the identification was correct (Simon et al., 2004). Participants then assumed the role of jurors in a theft case with facts similar to those in the vignette, including an eyewitness identification of the defendant. After hearing attorneys' arguments on both sides, they rendered verdicts and were asked the same questions they had answered about the vignette. Researchers evaluated separately responses from mock jurors who convicted and those who acquitted the alleged thief, and compared them with responses to the vignette. They found large differences in how much participants agreed with various pieces of evidence post-verdict (for example, those who acquitted agreed more strongly with the exculpating evidence than those who convicted) yet ratings of those same pieces of evidence following the vignette were essentially identical in the two groups. By the time mock jurors rendered verdicts, evidence that once seemed ambiguous and incoherent had developed into strong support of their preferred verdicts.

Telling Stories. In many ways, the juror's task is like that of a mystery reader. The joy of reading a mystery comes from savoring each clue, combining it with prior clues, and evaluating its significance in the overall puzzle of who committed the crime. Another core cognitive process that jurors often undertake is constructing a story or narrative summary of the events in dispute.

One influential model of individual jurors' decision making is the **story model**, developed decades ago by psychologists Reid Hastie and Nancy Pennington (e.g., Pennington & Hastie, 1993) and still widely accepted today (Levett & Devine, 2017; Vorms & Lagnado, 2022). According to the story model, as jurors listen to the evidence, they form a **schema**, or mental structure that aids in the processing and interpreting of information. Just like mystery readers who remember clues that fit their hypothesis and forget clues that do not, jurors construct their own private stories about the evidence so that it makes sense to them. In the process, they pay inordinate attention to certain pieces of evidence while ignoring others. Good lawyers know this. In fact, really great lawyers know that an important task is to convince the jury that their story, and not their opponent's story, is the right one. Famed criminal defense attorney "Racehouse" Haynes once said, "The lawyer with the best story wins."

According to the model, jurors actively construct stories by considering three sources of information: the evidence presented during the trial, their personal experience in similar situations, and their broad knowledge of the elements of a story. After jurors learn about the verdict options in the case, they map their story onto the verdict options and determine which verdict fits best with their constructed story.

In an early study, Pennington and Hastie (1986) interviewed mock jurors who had seen a filmed reenactment of a murder trial and talked out loud while making a verdict decision. The evidence summaries constructed by jurors had a definite narrative story structure, and, importantly, jurors who reached different verdicts had constructed different stories. In a later study, Pennington and Hastie (1988) found that the order in which evidence is presented influences jurors' judgments. Stories were easy to construct when the evidence was presented in a temporal order that matched the original events (chronological order), but harder to construct when the evidence was presented in non-chronological order. This variable also affected verdicts: convictions were more likely when the prosecution's evidence was presented in chronological order than when it was not.

Is the story model a complete and accurate description of how jurors decide the verdict in a trial? No. For starters, like the other theories described here, it focuses only on *jurors* and does not address the complex nuances that come into focus when jurors deliberate as a jury. Furthermore, as Professor Dan Simon points out, a good story is not necessarily an accurate one: "[An] appreciation for the truth could be overwhelmed by the narrative features of a particular case or by the storytelling acumen of the witnesses and attorneys who deliver it" (2018, p. 424). But as a general framework for understanding the strategies jurors use to process trial information prior to deliberating, it is highly useful.

Are Jurors Competent?

In this section, we focus on another broad question about jurors: are they competent to execute their duties properly? Some commentators have suggested that jurors in criminal cases make more mistakes than the public should tolerate, in part because they are faced with tough cases—cases in which the evidence is neither flimsy enough to warrant dismissal nor compelling enough to induce a guilty plea (Arkes & Mellers, 2002). Reexamining the data on jury–judge comparisons first presented by Harry Kalven and

Hans Zeisel (1966; described in Chapter 12), Professor Bruce Spencer estimates that jury verdicts are incorrect in at least one out of every eight cases (Spencer, 2007). He asks, "Can we be satisfied knowing that innocent people go to jail for many years for wrongful convictions?" (Science Daily, 2007).

Psychologists have examined the impact of specific kinds of evidence and other factors on the accuracy of jurors' verdicts. Some of their studies focused on whether jurors can listen attentively to expert testimony and use it appropriately, i.e., without giving it undue weight. Some studies assessed whether jurors' determinations of damages are predictable and reasonable. Other studies have asked whether, as the legal system assumes, jurors understand and correctly apply the judge's instructions on the law and have the necessary reasoning skills to understand protracted and complex cases. Researchers have also examined the assumption that in reaching their verdicts, jurors rely only on the evidence and disregard information that is not evidence (e.g., preexisting beliefs; irrelevant facts about the defendant, victim, plaintiff, or witnesses; and any information that the judge asks them to disregard).

To address these issues, psychologists have used a variety of research methods, including questioning jurors after trials, analyzing archival records of past verdicts, and conducting field studies and jury simulation studies. In simulation studies, the researcher introduces and experimentally manipulates some piece of information (e.g., the defendant's race or gender, the presence of an alibi witness) and measures the extent to which that information, as well as the actual evidence, influences jurors' reasoning and verdicts. Although simulation studies sometimes cast this information in a more prominent light than would be likely in real trials (e.g., a defendant's physical appearance might seem salient in an abbreviated and simulated trial but would lose its impact in a lengthy proceeding), they are nonetheless useful techniques for exploring how jurors reason and make decisions. They involve random assignment of research participants to conditions (the "gold standard" in experimental methodology) and allow researchers to control what the participants experience. As a result, researchers have learned what effects their manipulations have on resulting jury performance. And importantly, they have learned that mock juries do not differ in appreciable ways from real juries (Bornstein, 2017).

Jurors Rely on Relevant Evidence, Seen through the Lens of their Emotions

On the basis of these studies, psychologists have learned something very important: jurors in both criminal and civil cases pay considerable attention to the strength of the evidence. In fact, **evidentiary strength** is the most important determinant of jurors' verdicts (Devine et al., 2016). Differences in strength of the evidence can have profound effects on jury verdicts: Some studies have found a 70% increase in conviction rates as the evidence against the accused increases (Devine et al., 2001).

Professor Stephen Garvey and his colleagues (2004) analyzed the verdicts of 3,000 jurors in felony trials in four metropolitan areas to find out what explained jurors' first votes. They measured the strength of the evidence by asking the judge who presided in the case to estimate it. They then determined that the judge's assessment of the strength of the evidence was powerfully associated with the jurors' first votes: The stronger the evidence against the defendant, the more likely the juror was to convict.

Jurors' judgments in civil trials also tend to reflect the strength of the evidence, particularly regarding the severity of the plaintiff's injury. More seriously injured plaintiffs engender more sympathy and receive greater compensation than less seriously injured plaintiffs (Bright & Goodman-Delahunty, 2011; Greene & Bornstein, 2003). Jurors are also sensitive to evidence strength in statistical evidence (Bali et al., 2021).

These findings are important because they speak to the question of whether jurors are competent to execute their duties as the law intends. One would hope that jurors in criminal trials would convict when the strength of the evidence against a defendant was strong and acquit when it was weak. Apparently, they do just that. And one would hope that jurors would assess damage awards by taking into account the extent of the plaintiff's losses. They do that, too. So there is reason for optimism about jurors' abilities to manage their assigned tasks.

Although the legal system expects jurors to evaluate guilt, liability, and losses objectively, jurors' emotional reactions also influence assessment of the facts and evidence. In fact, the notion of a purely rational juror is inconsistent with decades of studies showing that jurors' emotional experiences affect their ability to render objective decisions (Holloway & Wiener, 2019). Of particular concern are emotions that are integral to the case itself—that is, emotions that arise out of the contentious, graphic, or violent nature of the evidence. Emotionally disturbing evidence is extremely common in trials that involve homicides and accidental injuries and can be presented in high-resolution photographs, video, and realistic reenactments of violence and accidents. Determining whether this evidence is informative on the one hand, or prejudicial on the other, is extremely complicated and case-specific (Salerno, 2021). Regardless, emotionally arousing evidence raises concerns about jurors' objectivity.

The experience of one particular emotion—anger—has an especially powerful effect on judgments of culpability and responsibility. As you might expect, as anger increases, the motivation to be fair-minded and objective decreases. Jurors then become more likely to convict (Bright & Goodman-Delahunty, 2006) and more punitive (Georges et al. 2013; Nunez et al., 2017). Understandably, jurors also have strong emotional reactions to seeing gruesome photographs of victims of severe injuries. In those cases, convictions increase as jurors' sense of disgust increases (Salerno & Phalen, 2019).

When emotionally arousing evidence is informative—as, for example, when jurors' empathetic fear helps them know whether to believe a defendant who claims self-defense—we would expect it to influence jurors' judgments. But evidence can also affect jurors' judgments because it simply inflames their emotions and biases their decision-making capabilities. Evidence that evokes strong emotions can lead jurors to support a conviction if only to satisfy their need to know that someone is blamed and punished for the harm caused.

Understanding Expert Testimony

Another aspect of competent decision making is appropriate attention to witness testimony, which can be problematic if the testimony entails complicated or technical information. As society has become increasingly specialized and knowledge has accumulated rapidly, the legal system has come to rely on expert witnesses to inform jurors about these advances. Experts typically testify about scientific, technical, or other specialized topics with which most jurors are not familiar. In accident cases, they may describe the nature and causes of various claimed injuries. In commercial cases, they may detail complex financial transactions and contractual arrangements. In criminal cases, they may describe procedures used to gather and test forensic evidence such as blood, fingerprints, DNA, and ballistics.

In general terms, expert testimony exerts a small, reliable effect on jurors' decisions, particularly when the testimony is not overly technical and can be understood by jurors (Vidmar, 2005). In these sorts of trials, when prosecutors introduce expert testimony, convictions are more likely, and when the defense introduces expert testimony, convictions are less likely. In Box 13.2 we describe a case in which expert testimony appeared to exert appropriate influence.

One concerning issue is whether, because many jurors lack rigorous analytical skills, they resort to unsystematic or effortless (i.e., experiential) processing of expert testimony and attend to peripheral or superficial aspects of experts' testimony (their credentials, appearance, personality, or presentation style), rather than the content of the testimony. But analysis of 50 real jury deliberations in civil trials, recorded as part of the Arizona Jury Project, and results of other studies find that, in most cases, characteristics of the messenger (i.e., the expert) have minimal influence. In fact, jurors are affected by peripheral details only when they do not fully understand the content of the expert's testimony (Bornstein & Greene, 2017). Even then, jurors can rely on other members of the jury with more sophisticated knowledge or experience (Greene, 2009). So there is little reason to believe that jurors focus excessively on superficial aspects of expert testimony.

Still, one kind of expertise—complicated scientific and technical expertise involving quantitative, statistical and probabilistic information—certainly challenges jurors. As a result, they tend to underutilize expert testimony that involves scientific information such as DNA or other forensic science evidence (Koehler et al., 2016). Jurors also

Box 13.2

The Case of Dharun Ravi: Expert Testimony from an I.T. Specialist

In a case that galvanized concerns about suicide by gay teens, Rutgers University student Dharun Ravi used a webcam to remotely spy on his roommate kissing another man and sent Twitter and text messages to other dormitory residents, encouraging them to watch when the roommate, Tyler Clementi, invited the man back two nights later. After discovering Ravi's actions, Clementi committed suicide by jumping off the George Washington Bridge, a mere three weeks into his freshman year. Ravi then deleted his text messages.

Former Rutgers University student, Dharun Ravi, was convicted of using a webcam to spy on his roommate.

The controversy that swirled around this case for more than a year focused on whether this was a hate crime or simple boorish and childish behavior on Ravi's part. Eventually he was charged with 15 crimes.

One of the witnesses who testified for the prosecution at Ravi's 2012 trial was Douglas Rager, a former Rutgers University police detective and information technology expert. He established the trail of electronic evidence, including Twitter feeds, cell phone records, dining card swipes, and dormitory surveillance cameras, and provided a "net flow" analysis that described how the computers in the dormitory were connected. His testimony must have been useful to jurors, as they convicted Ravi on all 15 counts, including invasion of privacy, bias intimidation, lying to investigators, and tampering with evidence. Adding further controversy to an already contentious case, the judge sentenced Ravi to a mere 30 days in jail. Said Judge Glenn Berman, "I do not believe he hated Tyler Clementi. I do believe he acted out of colossal insensitivity."

Critical Thought Question

Given what you've learned about the ways that jurors use expert testimony, what do you suspect they focused on when discussing Detective Rager's testimony during deliberations?

---

tend to discount testimony when presented by opposing experts, a common practice in civil cases under adversarial proceedings (Scurich et al., 2015). In these situations, cross-examination that casts doubt on the qualifications or biases of opposing experts engenders skepticism of expert testimony more broadly. Underutilizing complex information, especially when presented by a battle of experts, means that jurors will have difficulty distinguishing between reliable scientific evidence and "junk science."

Jurors also tend to be inattentive to the nuances of scientific methodology. In one study, mock jurors' guilt ratings were largely unaffected by the validity of the scientific tests about which an expert testified. So whether a fingerprint matching method had been scientifically validated was irrelevant to their judgments (Koehler et al., 2016). Jurors even have difficulty evaluating the validity of scientific research when sensitized to the flaws of the methodology by an opposing expert (Chorn & Kovera, 2019). In these circumstances, they *do* tend to place undue weight on the experts' experience and qualifications (Koehler et al., 2016).

How can jurors be made more attentive to the quality of scientific evidence? Hans and Saks (2018) recommend that because trials are, after all, educational forums, the proceedings should be tweaked to better educate jurors on

these difficult subjects. They suggest that judges first educate *themselves* about scientific and technical evidence in order to better structure jurors' decisions. They also suggest pretrial training for jurors through relevant tutorials, requiring opposing parties to agree on the scientific and technical evidence not in dispute, and allowing jurors to actively participate in the proceedings. We explore some of these recommendations later in the chapter.

Determining Damages

In civil cases, if a jury decides that a defendant is liable for injuries and harm to a plaintiff, another important task awaits. Jurors must also award damages to the injured plaintiff, which requires translating perceptions of an injury into dollars and cents. This determination is difficult because the task itself is inherently subjective, especially when it concerns issues like pain and suffering which lack agreed-upon metrics. Furthermore, jurors get little guidance on how to make these calculations. It's not surprising, then, that juries are frequently criticized for the unpredictable nature of their damage awards, though professionals and even judges are also prone to erroneous decisions in this realm (Greene et al., 2016; Guthrie et al., 2007). The main concern is that awards are variable and unpredictable. And although jury awards correlate positively with the degree of injury, meaning that more seriously injured plaintiffs receive higher awards (Saks et al., 1997), similar injuries do not always result in similar awards (Diamond & Rose, 2018). So inequities, and hence, criticism, linger.

To understand how jurors assess damages and whether awards could become less variable, Professors Valerie Hans and Valerie Reyna have devised a model that distinguishes between gist and verbatim judgments relevant to damages. After jurors decide that damages are warranted, they make an ordinal gist judgment, for example, that the plaintiff deserves an award that is low, medium, or high. Presumably, they have little difficulty with this task because most people are accustomed to making these categorical decisions. But their next task—assigning a specific number to that judgment—will be more difficult, particularly for jurors with low numeracy, or number sense, skills. Hans and Reyna have termed this part of the damages calculation the "verbatim judgment" (Hans & Reyna, 2011).

How well do people make gist judgments and how well do those gist judgments correspond to their verbatim judgments? Participants in one study reviewed details of a case in which plaintiffs were seeking damages for pain and suffering stemming from concussion injuries of varying severity (Hans et al., 2022). Mock jurors had little difficulty differentiating low from high severity injuries (i.e., making gist judgments), and they gave higher awards for more severe injuries. These researchers have also found that allowing attorneys to provide anchor numbers and hints about the relative magnitude of numbers reduces variability in awards and increases jurors' confidence in their decisions (Hans et al., 2022).

Understanding Jury Instructions

Jury instructions, provided by the judge near the end of a trial, play a crucial role in every case. They explain the laws that apply to the case and direct jurors to reach a verdict in accordance with those laws. Ironically, jurors are often treated like children during the evidence phase of the trial—expected to sit still and pay attention, and infrequently allowed to ask questions—but are treated like accomplished law students during the reading of the judge's instructions, when they are expected to understand the complicated legal terminology of the instructions. An appellate court acknowledged as much in granting a plaintiff a new trial in 2012. One judge called the jury instructions "a dreadful muddle" (Qualters, 2012).

Psychologists assess comprehension by providing instructions to jurors, typically in the context of a mock trial, and then testing them using multiple-choice or paraphrase tests and by asking them to apply the instructions to a hypothetical scenario (Baguley et al., 2020). Useful information as also come from analyses of the jury deliberations in civil trials that constituted the Arizona Jury Project (Diamond et al., 2012).

According to the Arizona study, discussion about instructions constituted 17% of the comments made during deliberations. Importantly, jurors were reasonably accurate in how they discussed the instructions: only 19% of their comments were incorrect. Nonetheless, they averaged 52 errors per case. One source of confusion was the legal language itself. In general, jury instructions repeat statutory language and therefore contain legal terms that are unfamiliar to laypeople. (For example, in most civil cases, jurors are informed that the burden of proof is on plaintiffs to establish their case by a *preponderance* of the evidence; the word *preponderance* appears 0.26 times per million words in the English language!).

Numerous research studies have focused on improving comprehension by modifying the language of the instructions—in other words, by reducing linguistic complexity. These studies borrow principles from the field of **psycholinguistics** (the study of how people understand and use language), including minimizing or eliminating abstract terms, negatively modified sentences, and passive voice, and reorganizing the instructions in a more logical manner. These simplified instructions are easier for jurors to understand and use (Lieberman, 2009).

Many states have revised portions of their jury instructions. California was the first state to finalize "plain-English" instructions for both civil and criminal trials (Post, 2004b). Consider these changes to the California civil jury instruction on standard of proof:

Old: "Preponderance of the evidence means evidence that has more convincing force than that opposed to it. If the evidence is so evenly balanced that you are unable to say that the evidence on either side of an issue preponderates, your finding on that issue must be against the party who had the burden of proving it."

New: "When I tell you that a party must prove something, I mean that the party must persuade you, by the evidence presented in court, that what he or she is trying to prove is more likely to be true than not true."

Not surprisingly, simplified instructions enhance jurors' comprehension of the law and result in far fewer questions to the judge about what the jury instructions mean (Post, 2004b).

But confusion about language was not the primary source of comprehension errors in the Arizona deliberations: only approximately 30% of the errors involved language misunderstanding and these were often corrected by other jurors. The more common errors stemmed from the piecemeal construction of jury instructions and the fact that they failed to address crucial topics. According to Diamond and her colleagues, the instructions are put together "like a patchwork quilt with pieces from the defense, pieces from the plaintiff, and pieces from the judge" (Diamond et al., 2012, p. 1598). This means that jurors must fit the pieces together without much advice or guidance from the judge. On the other hand, instructions about seemingly important topics like insurance and attorneys' fees are typically omitted altogether from judges' directives. As a result, jurors use their own knowledge and assumptions about these topics, which can result in unwarranted disparity in their decisions.

Another way that instruction comprehension can be improved is by providing instructions at the beginning of the trial, rather than waiting until the end. Instructions are typically given after the evidence has been presented, just before the jury retires to deliberate. Instructing the jury in this way reflects a belief in the **recency effect**: that the judge's instructions will have a more powerful impact on a jury's decision when they are given at the end of the trial. Having just heard the judge's instructions, jurors will be more likely to use them.

Logical as it might seem, this idea has been questioned by a number of authorities who worry that instructions at the end of the trial come after jurors have already made up their minds. Judge E. Barrett Prettyman's (1960) position reflects this concern:

It makes no sense to have a juror listen to days of testimony only then to be told that he and his conferees are the sole judges of the facts, that the accused is presumed to be innocent, that the government must prove guilt beyond a reasonable doubt, etc. What manner of mind can go back over a stream of conflicting statements of alleged facts, recall the intonations, the demeanor, or even the existence of the witnesses, and retrospectively fit all these recollections into a pattern of evaluations and judgments given him for the first time after the events; the human mind cannot do so (p. 1066).

The obvious alternative is to give the instructions earlier in a trial. This idea reflects schema theory—that jurors should be instructed *before* the presentation of testimony because this gives them a mental framework to appreciate the relevance of testimony as it unfolds. This line of reasoning is consistent with research in cognitive psychology showing that people learn more effectively when they know in advance what the specific task is, and that schematic frameworks facilitate comprehension and recall (Bartlett, 1932; Neisser, 1976).

The delivery of jury instructions at the beginning of the trial rests on the notion of a **primacy effect**—that instructions will have their most beneficial effect when presented first, because jurors will know the rules of the trial and the requirements of the law before the trial commences. ForsterLee and Horowitz (2003) reported that mock jurors who received instructions at the beginning of the trial recalled and used more of the evidence than did jurors who were instructed after the evidence. Jurors who receive pretrial instructions also focus better during the trial (Judicial Council of California, 2004).

We would argue that judicial pre-instructions are vastly underutilized. General instructions about the law (e.g., burden of proof, assessment of the credibility of witnesses) can be given at both the beginning and the end of trials. Interim instructions can be given as needed to explain issues that come up during the trial, and instructions that depend on the specific evidence in a trial can be given at the end (Ellsworth & Reifman, 2000).

Finally, we consider a novel approach used on occasion in Australia and New Zealand to improve understanding and application of jury instructions. This approach embeds legal concepts in a series of factual questions that the jury must answer to reach a verdict. Under this method, known as the "fact-based approach," jurors do not have to recall or apply abstract legal principles to their case. Rather, they answer a series of written questions ordered logically to mirror the jury instructions. Here is an example: "Are you satisfied beyond a reasonable doubt that Mr. X consciously and voluntarily shot Mr. Y? If the answer is 'no', you should find the accused not guilty. If 'yes', you should move to question (2)." The fact-based approach has been found to improve jurors' ability to resolve factual questions in accordance with the law (Spivak et al., 2020).

Willingness to Apply Jury Instructions

Must jurors follow the letter of the law if doing so violates their sense of justice and results in an unfair verdict? This question concerns **jury nullification**, the implicit power to acquit defendants despite evidence and judicial instructions to the contrary. Throughout history, juries have, on occasion, ignored the law rather than enforced it, particularly when they believed the law was unjust or was applied in a racially discriminatory way. In the mid-1800s, juries acquitted abolitionists of helping slaves escape from the South even though the abolitionists' actions violated the fugitive slave law. There have also been cases of nullification where White southern juries refused to convict members of the Ku Klux Klan and others who terrorized Black citizens during the early years of the civil rights movement. One case concerns Byron de la Beckwith and the murder of civil rights leader Medgar Evers (refer to Box 13.3).

The controversy about jury nullification resurfaced in the turbulent Vietnam War period when the government began to prosecute antiwar activists, usually on charges of conspiracy, and juries often acquitted. Similarly, juries in the District of Columbia, where consensual gay sex was a crime at the time, sometimes acquitted defendants of sodomy, believing that the law was an overreach. In the 1990s, some Black jurors in the District of Columbia favored acquitting defendants of nonviolent drug crimes, reasoning that they didn't want to send yet another Black man to jail (Butler, 2016). In each of these examples, jurors' moral attitudes conflicted with the letter of the law. Jury nullification acknowledges that while the public trusts jurors to

Box 13.3

The Case of Byron De La Beckwith: Jury Nullification and Race

Eager to see his children after a long day at work, civil rights leader Medgar Evers stepped out of his car in Jackson, Mississippi, on a hot June night in 1963 and was gunned down from behind by an assassin. The shooting ignited a firestorm of protest that ended in several more deaths and galvanized the civil rights movement.

The case against Byron de la Beckwith was strong but circumstantial. His rifle with his fingerprint was found at the scene, and a car similar to his was seen in the vicinity of Evers's home. But no one saw Beckwith pull the trigger, and his claim that he was 90 miles away at the time of the shooting was substantiated by two former police officers.

Beckwith was tried twice in 1964; both times the all-White, all-male jury deadlocked and failed to reach a verdict. This was an era of volatile race relations in which Black people were excluded from jury service and in which attorneys for Ku Klux Klan members charged with killing civil rights leaders openly appealed to White jurors for racial solidarity. Beckwith's segregationist views were a common bond

Byron De La Beckwith was convicted in the slaying of civil rights leader Medgar Evers.

between himself and the juries that opted to acquit him.

But things were different when Beckwith was retried in 1994. Despite the obstacles presented by stale evidence, dead witnesses, and constitutional questions, prosecutors put Beckwith on trial for the third time. This time, Beckwith's racist ideology was a liability. Despite pleas from defense attorneys that jurors not focus on Beckwith's sensational beliefs, a jury of eight Black people and four White people convicted him of murder in 1994. He was immediately sentenced to life in prison. Darrell Evers, the slain civil rights leader's son, who was nine years old at the time of the shooting, said he attended the trial to confront Beckwith: "He never saw my father's face. All he saw was his back. I wanted him to see the face, to see the ghost of my father come back to haunt him."

Critical Thought Question

Contrast jury nullification in trials that occurred in the mid-1800s, in the early years of the civil rights movement, and in Beckwith's retrial in 1994. What do these examples have in common? How are they different?

resolve the facts and apply the law in a given case, they also expect them to represent the conscience of the community (Abramson, 1994).

So should jurors be explicitly informed of their power to nullify the law? Courts have historically said no on this issue, reasoning that such information would allow personal attitudes and emotions to influence verdicts (*U.S. v. Dougherty, 1972*). Is that a correct assumption? How would juries behave if they were told that they have the option to disregard the law? Would there be "chaos in the courtroom" as opponents of nullification suggest?

Fortunately, we have some empirical evidence on this question. In a mock jury study, Peter-Hagene and Bottoms (2017) tested the impact of nullification instructions and jurors' attitudes on judgments in a morally ambiguous case involving physician-assisted suicide. When informed of their ability to nullify, jurors with pro-euthanasia attitudes were indeed more likely to acquit than jurors with anti-euthanasia attitudes. Nullification instructions also exacerbated the impact of jurors' emotions toward the defendant on their verdicts.

In the end, whether juries should be allowed or even encouraged to defy the law depends on how one views their role in the justice system (Peter-Hagene & Bottoms, 2017). If their obligation is merely to match case facts with the relevant law to determine whether the law was violated, nullification has no role. But if their role is to reflect public notions of justice and morality, particularly when harsh laws have been applied disproportionately, then, in exceptional cases, juries could be informed that they have the ability to disregard the law. Which position do you favor?

Deciding Complex Cases

Judge John V. Singleton looked up as his law clerk leaned against his office door as though to brace it closed. "You won't believe this," she said breathlessly, "but there are 225 lawyers out there in the courtroom!" (Singleton & Kass, 1986, p. 11). Judge Singleton believed it. He was about to preside over the first pretrial conference in *In re Corrugated Container Antitrust Litigation* (1980), at that time one of the largest and most complicated cases ever tried by a jury.

A more recent example is the case between Apple and Samsung over technology patents. In a 2012 trial (there have been several trials, held all across the globe), jurors received a 109-page set of instructions and a 20-page verdict form with approximately 700 very detailed questions. Among the questions were per-device dollar amounts that Apple and Samsung might owe each other for violating various intellectual property rights. Apple won that round, as jurors determined that Samsung infringed on its patents for mobile devices and awarded Apple nearly $400 million in damages. But the Supreme Court set aside that decision in 2016.

The case in Judge Singleton's court actually entailed three trials: a 15-week criminal trial that involved four corporations, 27 corporate officers, scores of witnesses, and hundreds of documents; a four-month-long trial with 113 witnesses and 5,000 exhibits; and a third trial involving plaintiffs who had opted out of the original lawsuit. Discovery and trials took five years. In the midst of this organizational nightmare, Judge Singleton worried about the "unsuspecting souls out there in the Southern District of Texas whose destiny was to weigh the facts under the complex antitrust law" (Singleton & Kass, 1986, p. 11).

The loudest and most vehement concerns about juror competence center on their abilities to decide complex cases. In product liability and medical malpractice cases, for example, there are difficult questions related to causation (i.e., who or what actually caused the claimed injuries), and in business cases there are intricate financial transactions that must be dissected and evaluated. These cases can require jurors to render decisions on causation, liability, and damages for multiple plaintiffs, multiple defendants, or both. In criminal cases, the use of forensic evidence contributes to case complexity.

Some have argued against the use of juries in complex cases. Among their concerns is that (1) the evidence is too difficult for a layperson to understand; (2) the general information load on juries is excessive because of the large number of witnesses, particularly expert witnesses, who testify in these cases; and (3) because *voir dire* procedures can result in the exclusion of jurors with understanding of or interest in the case, less-capable jurors are left to decide.

Data about jurors in complex trials support some, but not all, of these concerns. (Because the studies themselves are sprawling and complicated, examining multiple trials with dozens of jurors, relatively few such studies exist.) From interviewing jurors in complex cases, Sanders (1993) documented a substantial range in their abilities to understand and summarize the evidence. Some jurors are willing and able to attend to the complicated nature of the testimony and the sometimes-arcane questions of law that they raise; others are overwhelmed by the task. Lempert (1993) systematically examined jury issues in 12 complex trials. He concluded that in two of the 12 cases, the expert testimony was so complicated and esoteric that only professionals in the field could have understood it. But Lempert found little

evidence that jurors were befuddled—and concluded that their verdicts were largely defensible.

Jurors *can be* confounded by the presence of multiple parties and claims, however. When Reiber and Weinberg (2010) presented hypothetical cases of varying complexity to individuals summoned for jury duty, they found that comprehension worsened as the number of parties and claims increased. Mock jurors had difficulty deciding a breach of contract case that involved a claim, an affirmative defense, a permissive counterclaim, and a third-party claim (no surprises there!). They managed capably to decide an automobile negligence case that involved a single plaintiff and single defendant.

These findings point to the need for attention to how a complex case is presented to the jury. A judge has wide discretion to set the tone and pacing of the trial, to implement procedures to assist the jury, and, ultimately, to ensure equal justice under law. Jury aids such as written summary statements of expert testimony and interim summaries can enhance the quality of jurors' decision making, as can other reforms discussed later in the chapter.

One would not expect a college student to pass a course without taking notes, asking questions to seek clarification, or discussing an interesting concept with a professor or fellow student. Yet all too often, jurors are handicapped by trial procedures that discourage or even forbid these simple steps toward better understanding. We suspect that jurors would have an easier time—and their verdicts would be more reasoned—if judges structured jurors' tasks to be more conducive to their learning (e.g., giving well-organized pre-instructions and simplifying the language of the instructions). Fortunately, as we point out later in the chapter, many judges now do so.

Effects of Extralegal Information

A basic assumption of trial by jury is that verdicts will be based on the evidence produced in the courtroom. Regarding jurors and juries, there is good news and bad news. As we've demonstrated, jurors do a reasonably good job in their role as legal decision makers: they put appropriate weight on the most important evidence presented during a trial, namely, the strength of the relevant evidence. They understand and utilize most expert testimony properly, and according to analyses of their deliberations, they understand most of their instructions. But research shows that jurors are also affected by irrelevant information such as the defendant's background or appearance, what they read in a newspaper or online, and other sources of extraneous details, all of which constitute extralegal information. For example, certain physical traits of defendants (tattoos and untrustworthy faces) make them appear more criminal looking, which increases the likelihood of conviction (Sorby & Kehn, 2021). In this section, we consider the myriad ways that jurors' decisions are affected by legally irrelevant information.

Jurors' decisions in criminal trials are influenced by a complicated interaction of defendants' race, jurors' race, and the type of crime charged. There is a general tendency, albeit weak, for jurors to be harsher toward defendants of different races than their own (Devine & Caughlin, 2014). In one study, Black jurors rated White defendants as more aggressive, violent, and guilty than Black defendants, and White jurors were harsher on Black defendants than on White defendants, but only when the crime was *not* racially charged (Sommers & Ellsworth, 2000). When the crime *was* racially charged, the defendant's race did not influence White jurors' verdicts. These race-based results can be understood in the context of **aversive racism**, a social-psychological concept that proposes that many White jurors are motivated to avoid showing racial bias (Estrada-Reynolds et al., 2022). When cued about racial considerations (e.g., when the crime is racially charged or when jurors are instructed to avoid prejudice), they tend to render color-blind decisions. But without those explicit reminders to be objective, subtle racial biases influence their decisions.

What accounts for the fact that although evidence strength is, in many cases, the primary influence on jurors' decisions, extralegal evidence exerts an impact in other cases? One possibility is that jurors use extralegal information when doing so leads them to a preferred result (e.g., convicting a defendant whose appearance, race, and crime type comport with their stereotype of a guilty offender). Another is that the impact occurs unconsciously when jurors become confused about whether the information was presented as evidence in the trial or gleaned through other means (Simon, 2012).

One can understand jurors' attention to extralegal information by applying the cognitive–experiential self theory we introduced earlier. When jurors deliberately focus on the arguments or evidence provided during a trial, they are relying on a rationally based system of information processing. That is likely to occur when the evidence is unambiguous and comprehensible. But when the evidence is contradictory or confusing, jurors may rely on an experientially based system. In these circumstances, extralegal information can assert its influence.

Support for these ideas comes from post-trial questions asked of jurors, judges, and attorneys in 179 criminal cases. Professor Dennis Devine and his colleagues determined that extralegal factors such as demographics of the foreperson and exposure to pretrial publicity were related to jury verdicts only when the prosecution's evidence was weak (Devine et al., 2009). In the face of ambiguity, jurors were more likely to use experiential processing, and extralegal information had an impact. But when the evidence was unambiguous—clearly favoring one side—they were likely to rely on the logic of the arguments and think rationally. As a result, extralegal evidence had less effect. Consistent with these findings, people who tend to process information experientially are more likely than rational processors to acknowledge that extralegal factors would affect their verdicts (Gunnell & Ceci, 2010).

Impact of Extralegal Information in Criminal Trials

The Influence of Prior-Record Evidence. In 2009, church custodian Jose Feliciano was a fugitive on charges related to assault on a 7-year-old girl in 1999. When the parish priest, Edward Hinds, learned of these charges, he threatened to fire Feliciano. This led Feliciano to stab Hinds multiple times, according to Chatham, New Jersey prosecutors. Feliciano was charged with murder, and prosecutors moved to introduce the 1999 charges to demonstrate that he was motivated to kill Hinds.

Once jurors hear evidence about a defendant's prior criminal record or prior criminal charges, they may find it difficult to suspend judgment about that defendant and decide his or her fate solely on the basis of evidence introduced at trial. Therefore, the prosecution is often not permitted to introduce evidence of a defendant's criminal record, for fear that jurors will be prejudiced by it and judge the current offense in light of those past misdeeds. However, if defendants opt to testify, then prosecutors may be able to question them about certain types of prior criminal involvement to impeach their credibility as witnesses. In that circumstance, the judge may issue a **limiting instruction** to the effect that evidence of a defendant's prior record can be used for limited purposes only: to gauge the defendant's credibility but not to prove the defendant's propensity to commit the charged offense. Defense attorneys and even some judges are decidedly suspicious of jurors' ability to follow this rule, as well they should be; limiting instructions are rarely effective. Thus, defendants with prior criminal records have three bad choices: take a plea bargain regardless of actual guilt, go to trial but do not testify, or testify and risk the possibility that jurors will learn about a prior record and be more likely to convict (Rickert, 2010).

Some of these possibilities have been assessed empirically by researchers who studied more than 300 criminal trials in four jurisdictions across the country: Los Angeles, Phoenix, the Bronx (New York City), and the District of Columbia (Eisenberg & Hans, 2009). They determined that the existence of a prior record affected a defendant's decision to testify: 60% of those without criminal records testified on their own behalf, compared to only 45% with criminal records. In about half of the cases in which defendants with prior records opted to testify, the jury learned about that prior record. This rarely occurred when defendants did not testify. Finally and most importantly, juries apparently relied on their knowledge of the prior record to convict defendants when other evidence in the case against them was weak. This suggests that a prior record can lead to a conviction even when the evidence in a case normally would not support this verdict.

Why does evidence of a prior record increase the likelihood of conviction? For some jurors, the prior record, in combination with allegations related to the new charge, may indicate a pattern of criminality; together they point to an individual who is prone to act in an illegal or felonious manner. Other jurors, upon hearing evidence of a prior conviction, may need less evidence to be convinced of the defendant's guilt beyond a reasonable doubt on the new charge. Prior-record evidence may lead a juror to think that because the defendant already has a criminal record, an erroneous conviction would not be serious. This juror might therefore be satisfied with a slightly less compelling demonstration of guilt.

The Impact of Character and Propensity Evidence.

Evidence about a defendant's character—for example, that he or she is a kind and gentle person—is generally not admissible on the issue of whether the defendant committed a crime. There are exceptions, however. Character evidence can be used to provide evidence on guilt when it is relevant to the defendant, the alleged victim, or a witness.

Character evidence can be either glowing or damning, of course. In the former category was testimony elicited by the defense team of Kim Potter, a Minnesota police officer who claimed, prior to shooting and killing Daunte Wright in 2021, that she thought she was reaching for her taser, rather than her service revolver. During her trial, colleagues described Potter as a fine officer, extremely peaceful, and always willing to help out. (Potter was convicted of manslaughter.) In contrast, negative character evidence came to light during the trial of Timothy Hale-Cusanelli, an alleged White supremacist who was charged with multiple crimes stemming from the January 6 Capitol riot. Prosecutors provided evidence of Hale-Cusanelli's sexist, racist, anti-immigrant, and anti-Semitic views and allegations that he was a Nazi sympathizer. (He was convicted of all charges.)

When admitted in trials, varying kinds of character evidence affects jurors differently. Professor Jennifer Hunt and colleagues have demonstrated that although positive character evidence has little impact on jurors' judgments, evidence about negative character traits increases the likelihood of conviction (Hunt & Budensheim, 2004; Maeder & Hunt, 2011). This is consistent with social-psychological findings that judgments are more influenced by negative information than by positive information.

Evidence of other crimes or wrongdoing—so-called **propensity evidence**—is also typically inadmissible because of its potential for prejudice. Thus, prosecutors may not suggest that because defendants had the propensity to act in a criminal manner, they are guilty of the crime charged. But if defendants opt to testify, prosecutors may question them about any prior bad acts and that information has the potential to inflame jurors' sentiments. This is another reason that few defendants testify in their own defense. In Box 13.4 we describe a case in which the issue of propensity evidence featured prominently.

One wonders whether the addition of evidence regarding "prior bad acts" swayed jurors' minds in the second Cosby trial. What effect might propensity evidence of this sort have on jurors' judgments? In a study of mock jurors'

Box 13.4

The Case of Bill Cosby and Propensity to Commit Sexual Assault

Perhaps you wondered why, in the case of famed comedian Bill Cosby who faced numerous allegations of predatory sexual assault, his 2017 trial involved only one incident with one woman, Andrea Constand. Before the trial began, prosecutors and Cosby's defense attorneys sparred over whether the testimony of other women should also be allowed. Prosecutors argued that Cosby showed a pattern of behavior that included befriending and isolating young women and then drugging and molesting them. (For several reasons, prosecutors may have worried that on its own, the case involving Constand was weak: the alleged incident had occurred 12 years prior to trial and Constand, who had other unpleasant experiences with Cosby, waited a full year to report the alleged crime.) Defense attorneys argued that Cosby should be judged *only* on the basis of particular allegations involving Constand.

Cosby's first trial, with just one accuser (Constand) ended in a hung jury. But the issue of "prior bad acts" evidence came up again before his 2018 retrial. This time, the judge allowed five other witnesses to describe their own accusations of sexual abuse by Cosby years before. Their testimony was graphic, detailed, and most importantly, consistent with Constand's account. And this time, Cosby was convicted and sentenced to three to 10 years in prison. The story does not end there, however. In 2021, the conviction was overturned by an appellate court on an unrelated issue and Cosby was released from prison. Through her lawyers, Constand expressed disappointment and concern that the reversal might discourage others from seeking justice for sexual assault via the criminal justice system.

Critical Thought Question

Why is propensity evidence generally *not* admissible in most cases?

responses to uncharged acts of sexual misconduct by a male soccer coach, the inclusion of evidence of uncharged acts made jurors more likely to infer criminal intent and to believe that the accused committed the acts for which he was charged (Goodman-Delahunty & Martschuk, 2020). The prosecutors in Cosby's retrial were probably wise to request the inclusion of evidence from other accusers, and Cosby's defenders were equally wise to try to keep that evidence out.

Impact of Extralegal Information in Civil Trials

Although the bulk of psychological research on jury behavior has focused on the criminal realm, many studies have assessed the workings of civil juries. As a result, we can ask whether jurors are competent to decide civil cases fairly and rationally. Do they determine liability and assess damages in a rational way, relying on the legally appropriate sources of information? Or are they swayed by emotion and prejudice or overly attentive to extralegal factors?

The Impact of Injury Severity on Liability Judgments.

An important decision that jurors must make in civil cases concerns the parties' respective responsibility for the harm that was suffered. When psychologists study juries' liability judgments, they are really asking how people assign responsibility for an injury. When a baby is stillborn, do jurors perceive the doctor to be at fault for not performing a caesarean section? Would the child have died anyway? When a smoker contracts lung cancer, do jurors blame the cigarette manufacturer for elevating the nicotine level in its product, or the smoker who knowingly ingested a dangerous product over the course of many years? Or do they blame both?

Jurors should decide liability based on the defendant's conduct. Were that person's actions reckless? Were they negligent? Were they malicious and evil? For the most part, jurors' liability decisions align with evidence regarding the defendant's conduct: defendants whose actions were clearly negligent or malicious are likely to be found liable. But jurors also consider the severity of an injury or accident, sometimes referred to as outcome severity, when judging a defendant's liability. Although outcome severity is legally relevant to decisions about the damage award, it is largely irrelevant to a judgment concerning liability or legal responsibility. The defendant should not be saddled with a liability judgment simply because the plaintiff was seriously injured. But in their simulation of an automobile negligence case, one of the authors and her colleagues found that the defendant was perceived to be more negligent when the plaintiff suffered more serious injuries (Greene et al., 2001). These results are consistent with a meta-analysis (Robbennolt, 2000) showing that people attribute more responsibility to a wrongdoer when the outcome of an incident is severe than when it is minor. Even with accidental injuries, harm severity affects people's notions of blame and punishment (Schwartz et al., 2022).

Why would people assign more responsibility to individuals as the consequences of their conduct become more serious? One reason is defensive attribution (Fiske & Taylor, 1991), an explanation of behavior that defends us from feelings of vulnerability. As the consequences of one's actions become more severe and more unpleasant, we are likely to blame a person for their occurrence, because doing so makes the incident somehow more controllable and avoidable.

As in criminal cases, jurors' emotional state during a trial can affect their judgments in civil cases. For example, jurors who are angered by evidence of wrongdoing and harm to others feel more sympathy for a plaintiff (Feigenson et al., 2001) and less sympathy for a defendant (Bornstein, 1994). These experienced emotions are likely to interact with jurors' preexisting emotional states, implying that the legal assumption of strict objectivity in how jurors evaluate evidence is probably inaccurate (Wiener et al., 2006). A second implication is that both plaintiffs' and defendants' attorneys should try to induce empathy for their clients, hoping that in a state of heightened emotion, jurors will recognize the unjustness of their plights (Phalen et al., 2021).

Irrelevant Considerations Related to Damages Assessments.

Pity the poor man. Michael Brennan, a St. Paul, Minnesota bank president, was simply responding to nature's call when he was sprayed with more than 200 gallons of raw sewage as he sat on the toilet in the bank's executive washroom. The geyser of water came "blasting up out of the toilet with such force that it stood him right up," leaving Brennan "immersed in human excrement." He sued a construction company working in the bank at the time, but the jury awarded Brennan nothing. Why, then, did a jury award $300,000 to a workman who slipped from a ladder and fell into a pile of manure (a story aired on CBS's "60 Minutes")?

One of the most perplexing issues related to juries is how they assess damages (Bornstein & Greene, 2017). This complex decision seems especially subjective and unpredictable because people value money and injuries differently and because jurors are given scant guidance on how to award damages (Greene & Bornstein, 2000). The awards for punitive damages—intended to punish the defendant and deter future malicious conduct—are of special concern because the jury receives little instruction about how those awards should be determined. Consider the staggering $145 billion punitive damage award against the tobacco industry in a case brought by many state attorneys general in 2000. Even the judge in the case was amazed. "A lot of zeros," he observed dryly, after reading the verdict.

Social scientists have conducted research on this issue and have learned that few people get rich by suing for damages. The median award in 2020 for injuries suffered in a vehicle accident was $50,000 (https://www.iii.org/graph-archive/96044). Although the media are eager to tell us about multimillion-dollar damage awards, these colossal awards are very unusual. Also, the monies requested by the plaintiff—when grounded in quantitative evidence presented during the trial—serve as "anchor points" for jurors' damage awards. But when the requests are unsupported by the evidence, they are viewed as outrageous and are disregarded (Diamond et al., 2011).

What factors do jurors consider in their decisions about damages? Data from interviews with actual jurors, simulation studies, and videotapes of actual jury deliberations show that, as in criminal cases, jurors put most weight on the evidence they hear in court. But discussions about insurance coverage and attorney's fees—issues that are theoretically irrelevant to decisions about the amount of damages—are also quite common in jury rooms. Reviewing the deliberations of juries in the landmark Arizona Jury Project, Diamond and Vidmar (2001) found that conversations about insurance occurred in 85% of these cases and the topic of attorneys' fees came up in 83% of discussions. Other research has found that although jurors discuss these issues, the resulting awards are not directly influenced (Greene et al., 2008).

Disregarding Inadmissible Evidence

Most of the time, false or irrelevant information is prevented from being introduced during a trial. But on occasion, it slips in and anyone who has watched crime shows depicting courtroom drama is familiar with the attorney's statement, "I object!" If the judge sustains an objection, the opposing attorney's objectionable question or the witness's objectionable response will not be recorded, and the judge will instruct, or admonish, the jury to disregard the material. Are jurors able to do so?

Inadmissible evidence is evidence that is presented in court but is unrelated to the substance of the case. Studies show that jurors are influenced by inadmissible evidence (Pantazi et al., 2020) and that a judge's admonition to disregard the evidence is relatively ineffective (Steblay et al., 2006). On occasion, instructions to ignore inadmissible evidence actually backfire and result in jurors being *more* likely to use the inadmissible evidence than if they had not been told to ignore it (Lieberman & Arndt, 2000).

One explanation of this phenomenon involves **reactance theory** (Brehm & Brehm, 1981) which suggests that instructions to disregard evidence may threaten jurors' freedom to consider all available evidence. When this happens, jurors may respond by acting in ways that restore their sense of decision-making freedom. Interestingly, simply providing jurors with a reason for the inadmissibility ruling makes them more likely to comply with it.

A complementary explanation of why jurors rely on inadmissible evidence when cautioned not to focuses on their motivations: jurors are influenced by evidence when they believe it is relevant to their decision or that using it will render a just verdict. In other words, they *want to* use the evidence and their desire to reach an "appropriate" verdict overrides their willingness to follow proper procedures (Dietvorst & Simonsohn, 2019). In one study, mock jurors told to disregard certain evidence because of a legal technicality still allowed that evidence to influence their verdicts when they thought that it enhanced the accuracy of their decisions (Sommers & Kassin, 2001). In another, many jurors deemed it more important to arrive at a decision that protects society than to adhere to legal procedures (Politis et al., 2021)

Jurors' overreliance on evidence they are admonished not to use may also reflect a cognitive process described in **thought suppression** studies. In a now-classic study, Professor Daniel Wegner found that asking people "not to think of a white bear" increased the tendency to do just that. In fact, the harder people try to suppress a thought, the less likely they are to succeed (Wegner, 1994). Jurors may think more about inadmissible evidence as a direct consequence of their attempts to follow the judge's request to suppress thoughts of it (Clavet, 1996). An appellate court was aware of that possibility: "(the judge) could reasonably have believed that an instruction to the jurors to disregard what they had just heard…would have been just about as effective as a directive not to think about a pink elephant" (*Sowell v. Walker,* 2000, pg. 448).

Jurors' decision could also be influenced by many other irrelevant factors including pretrial and midtrial publicity, the personal style and credibility of attorneys, the order of presentation of evidence, and the gender, race, age, physical appearance, and attractiveness of the litigants and other witnesses (Devine et al., 2009). Sometimes the extraneous information comes from jurors themselves, rather than from the trial. For example, explicit reference to a defendant's ethnicity during deliberations in a sexual assault trial in Colorado (i.e., "Mexican men are physically controlling of women because they have a sense of entitlement and think they can do whatever they want with women") resulted in a U.S. Supreme Court ruling that racial or ethnic bias in the deliberation room will not be tolerated. The decision creates an exception to the rule that jury deliberations must be kept secret (*Pena-Rodriguez v. Colorado,* 2017).

As we have demonstrated, jurors have difficulty performing the mental gymnastics required to use evidence for a limited purpose or to ignore it altogether. But strongly worded explanations about the importance of *not* considering the evidence have some effectiveness in getting jurors to ignore inadmissible evidence (Dietvorst & Simonsohn, 2019).

Are Jurors Biased?

The Assumption of a Blank Slate

Courts assume that jurors can put aside any preconceptions about the guilt of a criminal defendant or the merits of civil plaintiffs when forming their judgments. But is that a reasonable assumption? Do jurors enter a trial as "blank slates," free of overwhelming biases? (In criminal cases, the "blank slates" should be tinted at the outset by a presumption that the defendant is innocent of the charges.) This concern has practical importance because if jurors cannot set aside their biases, they should be excused for cause.

The judge and the attorneys inquire about a prospective juror's biases during the jury selection process. A frequent question during *voir dire* takes the following form: "Do you believe that you, as a juror, can set aside any negative feelings you might have toward the defendant because he is (wealthy or a police officer or a used-car salesman—whatever the

Box 13.5

The Case of Dzokhar Tsarnaev and the Search for Unbiased Jurors

Courtroom sketch of Boston Marathon bomber, Dzhokhar Tsarnaev in federal court in Boston.

In 2015, the lone surviving Boston marathon bomber, Dzokhar Tsarnaev, was convicted on multiple counts of conspiracy and use of a weapon of mass destruction and sentenced to death. His appeal on the grounds that jury selection had improperly examined potential bias resulting from panelists' exposure to media coverage played out over several years. Prior to trial, the judge had denied Tsarnaev's multiple requests for a change of venue, leading his defense team to argue vehemently that a thorough *voir dire* was necessary to ensure a fair trial. In fact, an appellate court faulted the judge for asking jurors "only whether they had read anything that might influence their opinion" and not inquiring about "what, if anything, they had learned."

Tsarnaev's appeal raises the thorny question of how much control judges should exercise over the *voir dire* process when a case garners such widespread media coverage that finding a full panel of unbiased jurors would be difficult. Should trial judges have flexibility and autonomy? Or should they be *required* to examine jurors at some length about sources of potential bias? In a 6–3 decision, the Supreme Court opined that the jury selection process in Tsarnaev's case had been reasonable and that he had received a fair trial (*U.S. v. Tsarnaev*, 2022).

Critical Thought Question

Why, in the digital age, will it become increasingly difficult to find objective, unbiased jurors?

group membership is that possibly elicits prejudice) and make a judgment based on the law and the facts of this case?" If prospective jurors say yes, the judge usually believes them, and they are allowed to serve as jurors.

A concern about jurors' biases was a central feature of a well-known case decided by the U.S. Supreme Court in 2021. We describe it in Box 13.5.

The courts assume that individual jurors can divest themselves of any improper "leaning" toward one side or the other, and that through jury selection procedures the ideal of open-minded jurors can be achieved. Courts also assume that attorneys can identify and dismiss prospective jurors whose preconceptions would affect their verdicts, so the trial can begin with a fair and unbiased panel. For various reasons, this optimism may be misguided. First, attorneys are motivated to select jurors who are favorable to their own side, rather than those who are neutral and thus unpredictable. Second, it is impossible for anyone to be entirely free of influence by past experiences and resulting prejudices.

Inevitability of Juror Bias

In a society that respects all persons, some biases (e.g., age, race, or gender bias) are clearly prejudicial and should be shunned. But many biases—including those based on expectations and experiences—may actually be inevitable. As we use the term here, **juror bias** is a juror's predisposition to interpret and understand information based on past experience. When people are exposed to new events, they respond by relying on past experiences. When they view a traffic accident, for instance, they may make judgments that one car ran a red light or that another car was in the wrong lane. They may assume that an accident involving teenaged drivers was caused by excessive speed or texting while driving.

Bias in responses to the actions of others is inevitable because people must make assumptions about the causes of behavior. Why was Emily so abrupt when she spoke to me this morning? Why did Juan decide to buy a new car? Why did the defendant refuse to take a breathalyzer test? Individuals also make decisions on the basis of their assumptions. College admission officers decide who will be admitted on the basis of applicants' credentials and academic promise. Judges decide who should be paroled based on the belief that the parolee will not commit additional crimes. Criminal defense lawyers make recommendations to their clients on how to plead on the basis of expectations about the reactions of prosecuting attorneys, judges, and jurors. Expectations about the outcomes of one's choices rest partly on one's biases.

Because bias is inevitable, most jurors come to this task with either a pro-prosecution bias or a pro-defense bias. Jurors with a pro-prosecution bias view conflicting evidence in the case through the filter of their experiences and beliefs, which make them more likely to think that the defendant committed the crime. Persons with pro-defense biases filter the same evidence in light of *their* experiences and reactions, which make them more sympathetic to the defense.

To determine how bias affects verdicts, Lecci and Myers (2009) asked jury-eligible adults to complete the Pretrial Juror Attitudes Questionnaire (PJAQ), which includes statements such as "Criminals should be caught and convicted by any means necessary" and "Defense lawyers are too willing to defend individuals they know are guilty." Later, mock jurors watched a videotaped armed robbery trial, gave individual verdicts, deliberated as a jury, and gave post-deliberation individual verdicts. Jurors who voted guilty prior to deliberating were compared with those voting not guilty to determine whether their personal biases differed. Indeed they did: jurors who convicted were more likely to endorse pro-prosecution sentiments on the PJAQ than jurors who acquitted. Biases revealed by the PJAQ predicted post-deliberation verdicts as well, suggesting that the deliberation process did little to correct for individuals' bias. It appears that even when jurors all hear the same evidence during the trial, their personal beliefs and values can affect their verdicts.

Personal predispositions may also affect the way evidence is evaluated. Professor Jane Goodman-Delahunty and colleagues found that mock jurors' beliefs about the death penalty influenced their perceptions of evidence (Goodman-Delahunty et al., 1998). Participants watched the actual murder of a convenience store clerk that was captured on video. When asked about the defendant's motive and intentions, mock jurors who favored the death penalty were more likely than those who opposed it to "read" criminal intent into the actions of the defendant. For example, they were more likely to infer that the defendant intended to murder the victim and that his specific actions indicated premeditation. These findings remind us of the common situation in which two people experience the same event—a movie or a play, for example—and interpret the actions in very different ways, partly because of the "mindset" with which they watched or experienced that event. These beliefs, or schemas, can influence the way jurors make sense of the evidence in a trial.

Psychologists have learned something interesting about how those schemas affect jurors' verdicts. When jurors are exposed to a new piece of evidence, they evaluate the evidence in a way that is consistent with their current verdict preferences rather than in an objective fashion. Assume that two jurors hear the same evidence that favors the prosecution. Also assume that, at that point in the trial, Juror A favors the prosecution and Juror B favors the defense. According to the notion of **predecisional distortion**, these jurors will distort their evaluation of the evidence in a direction that supports their verdict choice. Thus, Juror A would

Juror decisions are influenced by relevant and irrelevant factors, including the evidence, prior experience, and the attorneys' person style and presentation.

evaluate this evidence as favoring the prosecution, whereas Juror B might evaluate it as favoring neither party, distorting the interpretation of the evidence away from its objective value (i.e., in favor of the prosecution) and in the direction of the side favored (Blanchard et al., 2014).

Do jurors' biases predispose them to favor one side over another in a civil case? It seems natural for people to have feelings of compassion for injured persons and for these feelings to translate into favorable verdicts and lavish damage awards for plaintiffs. When jurors awarded $10 million in compensatory damages and $5 million in punitive damages to Johnny Depp in his 2022 defamation case against Amber Heard, did sympathy influence their thinking?

Surprisingly, perhaps, a variety of studies using different methodologies suggest that sympathy plays only a minor role in civil jurors' judgments. In a far-reaching study of claims by individuals against corporate defendants, Professor Valerie Hans (1996) interviewed jurors and ran experimental studies that manipulated variables related to this **sympathy hypothesis**. All the data pointed to the same conclusion: that the general public is "quite suspicious of, and sometimes downright hostile to, civil plaintiffs" (p. 244). A survey conducted by the consulting firm DecisionQuest yielded similar results: 84% of the 1012 people polled agreed with the statement, "When people are injured, they often try to blame others for their carelessness." According to the same survey, potential jurors do not think highly of civil defendants, either. For example, more than 75% of respondents believe that corporate executives often try to cover up evidence of wrongdoing by their companies, and more respondents say that product warnings are intended to protect manufacturers than say they are intended to keep consumers safe.

How Juries Deliberate

To this point in the chapter, we have focused on individual jurors' reasoning process. But verdicts are not issued by twelve individuals in criminal cases or by some variable number of individuals in civil cases, depending on where the trial takes place. Rather, they come from a group, a jury. So how do individual preferences, biases, and reactions to the evidence combine to result in an agreed-upon consensus? (A unanimous verdict is required in all criminal trials in the U.S., and at least a majority verdict is required in civil trials.) In the process of reaching agreement, how and why will some jurors change their minds to coalesce around the group's decision?

Deliberations are important to the final resolution of a trial. Jurors do not simply pool their individual pre-deliberation verdict preferences, engage in a bit of horse-trading, and call it a day. Many jurors—in one study, 20% of those questioned after their trials—have no strong leanings one way or another at the start of deliberations (Hannaford-Agor et al., 2002). So discussion is imperative. Even on the question of damages, when it might seem logical for jurors to average their individual judgments, their joint analysis of the evidence and of their verdict options is crucial. Indeed, what happens over the course of the group discussion has a significant impact on the final verdict (Diamond & Rose, 2018).

The deliberation process can also improve the quality of jury decisions. Jurors can correct each other's mistaken interpretations of the jury instructions during group discussion, and, though findings are mixed, some mock jury studies have shown modest improvement in comprehension with deliberations (e.g., Diamond et al., 2012; Greene & Johns, 2001). Deliberations can also improve understanding of scientific expert testimony in people with limited backgrounds in science or mathematics (Hans et al., 2011).

Can deliberations have the additional benefit of reducing jurors' reliance on inadmissible evidence? There is reason to suspect that they can. Psychologists have studied this issue by comparing the decisions of mock jurors who deliberate and those who do not, and by comparing a single group of mock jurors prior to and after deliberating. The conclusion they draw from these studies is that deliberation can serve to decrease reliance on irrelevant information. For example, London and Nunez (2000) assessed the impact of inadmissible evidence on jurors before and after deliberation. The defendant in their mock trial was charged with taking nude photographs of a child. This evidence was deemed admissible in one condition, inadmissible in another, and was not presented in a control condition. Prior to deliberations, jurors who were told that the photos were inadmissible were as likely to convict as jurors who were told the photos could be considered, demonstrating the powerful biasing effect of inadmissible evidence. But after deliberating, the conviction rate in the inadmissible evidence condition dropped significantly and was comparable to the control condition. Group discussion reduced the influence of inadmissible evidence, probably because jurors reminded each other of the mandate not to consider that evidence.

Deliberating juries do not *always* make better decisions than individual jurors, however. One example: jurors exposed to pretrial publicity are apparently inclined to discuss it during deliberations, even when admonished not to (Ruva et al., 2022) and their inaccuracies can go uncorrected. Closely related, jurors make mistakes about the source of their memories, so mock jurors exposed to misinformation while deliberating erroneously recall that it came from the trial. Discussing the misinformation leads to the spreading of that false information. When such misinformation favors the prosecution, convictions become more likely (Thorley et al., 2020).

What do jurors actually talk about when they deliberate? Answers to that question come from recordings of mock juror deliberations and from the civil juries that constituted the Arizona Jury Project (Diamond & Vidmar, 2001; Diamond et al., 2012). Observers identified three stages of jury deliberations: orientation, when jurors discuss general procedures, elect a foreperson, and begin discussion; open conflict in which jurors actively try to persuade others to see things their way; and reconciliation or resolution, when jurors strive to guarantee that the chosen verdict is acceptable to everyone. On occasion, juries have opted to "sleep on it," that is, to reach a verdict one day, but not announce it until the next day, giving members some time to decide if they are comfortable with the choice.

The open conflict portion of the deliberation is obviously the most contentious. During this period, jury members use various forms of persuasive influence. Social psychologists have learned that persuasion occurs through informational and normative social influence. **Informational social influence** occurs when some compelling information, data, or interpretation convinces jurors that their personal perspectives were incorrect or incomplete, and that it makes sense for them to change their minds. In doing so, they might state publicly, and believe privately, that they reached the correct decision. By contrast, **normative social influence** occurs when jurors simply go along with the group's decision in order to be conciliatory. So whereas jurors might state publicly that they agree with a certain verdict, privately they think otherwise (Kaplan & Miller, 1987). Which type of influence predominates during deliberation is determined by the question being debated. If the verdict choices require careful and deliberative analysis—determining the precise amount of money to award in compensatory damages, for example—informational social influence is more likely to occur. But if the choices are more subjective, then normative influences prevail.

Approximately 40 years ago, jury scholars described the open conflict portion of deliberations as either verdict-driven or evidence-driven (Hastie et al., 1983). A **verdict-driven deliberation** is one in which jurors would take a straw poll very early in their discussion to reveal the general sentiment of the group and to establish the factions that see things in different ways. From here on, those deliberations would involve each faction attempting to gain support from members of other factions by arguing that their interpretation of the evidence is the appropriate one. By contrast, an **evidence-driven deliberation** is one in which jurors do not take an early vote. Instead, they review crucial pieces of evidence in order to reach an agreed-upon consensus about how to interpret that evidence. Only then do they try to match their interpretation to various verdict options.

From research conducted since that distinction was made, psychologists have learned that juries infrequently take a vote immediately after settling into the deliberation room. Even if a juror suggests doing so, other jurors are likely to derail the process by raising questions about how others interpreted the evidence, and the discussion quickly becomes evidence-driven (Diamond & Rose, 2018). The longer the trial, the longer the deliberation continues before a first vote is taken (Diamond et al., 2003). As you might suspect, evidence-driven deliberations last longer, but are ultimately more satisfying for jurors (Hastie et al., 1983).

Psychologists have tried to integrate models of juror and jury decision making. For example, Professor Dennis Devine (2012) suggests that individual jurors create narrative explanations of the evidence that they bring to the deliberating table. Then, by means of a process termed "story sampling," they exert informational influence by sampling from their memory and sharing their perspectives. Voting factions exert normative and informational influence in proportion to their size and the cohesiveness of their arguments. After various iterations of this process, if all goes well, a large majority faction will emerge and eventually, the jury will agree on a compelling story that is consistent with the evidence.

Jury Reform

Jury trials are conducted under strict rules developed over the years by statutes, case law, and tradition. These imperatives stem from the belief that justice is best served by an adversarial system in which the evidence is vetted through a neutral judge and limited by rules of the court. Under these rules, jurors were prohibited from investigating the facts themselves and asking questions during the trial, and they were warned not to discuss the evidence until deliberations begin.

This model treats jurors as passive recipients of information who, like digital recorders, take in a one-way stream of communication. Jurors were expected to process all incoming information impassively, without interpretation, until finally instructed by the judge to decide something. As we pointed out earlier, this conception of juror-as-blank-slate is largely wrong; jurors actively evaluate the evidence through the lens of their personal experiences and frames of reference, pose questions to themselves, and construct narratives or stories to help them understand the evidence and make a judgment about it.

Acknowledging that most jurors are active "thought processors," psychologists and other social scientists started suggesting reforms to the jury system in the 1970s. By the 1990s, judges were also beginning to question the traditional view of jurors as passive blank slates. Against this backdrop, creative court personnel and forward-thinking judges made changes in trial procedures that take advantage of jurors' natural inclinations and encourage them to be more involved in the trial. Many of these reforms have now been implemented in courts across the country.

Some reforms are uncontroversial and benign: providing notebooks that list the witnesses and summarize their testimony in long or complex cases; giving pre-instructions or interim instructions during the course of a lengthy trial; allowing jurors to take notes; designating alternate jurors only after the presentation of evidence is completed; providing a written copy of the judge's instructions to each juror; and allowing jurors to examine the demonstrative evidence during their deliberations. Some proposed reforms are downright radical. This includes the possibility of having opposing experts testify together in a process called a hot tub (though it does not involve a physical hot tub!), explaining to the judge or jury what they agree about and why they disagree (Greene & Gordon, 2016). Such a system could, in theory, reduce the adversarial nature of expert testimony and enable jurors to make better comparisons between opposing viewpoints. In practice, there is limited evidence of its effectiveness (Krauss et al., 2018).

Two reforms are moderately controversial: allowing jurors to pose questions to witnesses (questions are screened by the judge, who decides whether they are appropriate) and to discuss the evidence in the midst of trial. These reforms have also been implemented in many jurisdictions, and research studies have charted their effectiveness. Through such studies, psychologists have learned the pros and cons of implementing them during trials.

Jurors questioned about the opportunity to submit written questions have been strongly supportive: 83% of those surveyed by the Seventh Circuit American Jury Project reported that asking questions of witnesses enhanced their understanding of the facts (Seventh Circuit American Jury Project, 2008). Examining the questions jurors asked and how jurors discussed the answers, Arizona Jury Project researchers found that questions helped to clarify conflicting evidence and produced a plausible description of the events in dispute (Diamond et al., 2006). By analyzing the questions jurors asked of alleged victims of child sexual abuse, St. George and colleagues (2020) learned that questions often explored misunderstood abuse dynamics and the child's disclosure processes, such as whether it is credible to maintain contact with the alleged perpetrator and to delay disclosure.

We believe there are no serious drawbacks to allowing jurors to ask questions of witnesses. Doing so can clarify their understanding of the evidence, enhance involvement in the trial, and create an environment more conducive to learning. We also believe they should be allowed to ask questions about their instructions, rather than listen passively as the judge reads the instructions aloud, as is common practice now. Wouldn't it make sense for them to have the chance to inquire about any confusions or lack of clarity in the law itself?

The more radical reform permits jurors to discuss the evidence during the trial, rather than having to wait until formal deliberations begin. The rules are simple: All jurors must be present in the deliberation room during these discussions, and jurors must keep an open mind and avoid debating verdict options. Psychologists have described a number of potential advantages of such mid-trial discussions based on fundamental principles of cognitive and social psychology. In theory, juror discussions about the evidence can

- Improve comprehension by permitting jurors to sift through and organize the evidence into a coherent framework over the course of the trial.

- Improve recollection of the evidence and testimony by emphasizing and clarifying points made during trial.

- Promote greater cohesion among jurors, thereby reducing the time needed for deliberations (Bregant, 2009).

But there are also several potential drawbacks, and these, too, are based on well-established psychological principles. They include the possibility that jury discussions may

- Facilitate the formation or expression of premature judgments about the evidence.

- Diminish the quality of the deliberations as jurors become more familiar with each other's views.

- Produce more interpersonal conflicts prior to formal deliberations (Bregant, 2009).

The first empirical test of this reform was a field experiment in which researchers randomly assigned approximately 100 civil jury trials to an experimental "trial discussion" condition and an equal number to a control "no discussion" condition (Hannaford et al., 2000). After assessing jurors' impressions of this experience, researchers painted a fairly rosy picture: Jurors said that trial evidence was remembered very accurately during predeliberation discussions, that discussions helped them understand the evidence, and that all jurors' points of view were considered during those discussions. The perceived drawbacks were mostly logistical: Jurors said it was hard to get all members together at the same time. (After all, these short breaks represent the only time in the course of several hours for jurors to use the rest rooms or smoke a cigarette. Some people's desire for these comforts apparently outweighed their interest in talking about the evidence!)

But other research, using experimental jury simulation methodology, has called into question some of the benefits revealed by that early field study. Kerr and Jung (2018) manipulated the opportunity for jurors to engage in predeliberation discussions in an age discrimination trial and found that when discussion was allowed, evidence that came *after* the discussion had a greater impact on the verdict than evidence that came before. This is a type of recency effect and suggests that implementing predeliberation discussions

may bias juries in favor of the side that presents the bulk of its evidence last. Based on this finding and the lack of evidence for any of purported benefits of predeliberation discussion, Kerr and Jung support the long-standing tradition of prohibiting it. And, though they acknowledge that making jury service more palatable is a worthy goal, they point to other trial practices that jurors dislike (e.g., being denied information about a criminal defendant's prior record or a judge's sentencing options) but that level the playing field for litigants. So, at present, the jury seems to be out on the value of predeliberation jury discussions.

The Jury: Should It Be Venerated or Vilified? Revered or Reviled?

The jury system brings together individuals with diverse backgrounds, experiences, and biases who pool their perceptions of the evidence to reach a verdict (Diamond, 2006). In this way, the jury is a remarkable institution and, in important respects, a unique one. Having average citizens determine trial outcomes for rich and powerful figures such as Elizabeth Holmes, the former CEO of a Silicon Valley biotech firm, and for celebrities accused of sexual harassment in the 2020s underscores the United States' commitment to egalitarian values. It is no exaggeration to say that jury trials, even as they become less frequent, are still sanctified as one of the fundamental democratic institutions. Political scientist Jeffrey Abramson (1994), author of *We, the Jury*, put it eloquently:

> [T]here are all the jurors we never read about, who toil out of the limelight every day, crossing all kinds of racial and ethnic lines to defend a shared sense of justice. These examples convince me that the jury, far from being obsolete, is more crucial than ever in a multiethnic society struggling to articulate a justice common to [all] citizens. Though the jury system is a grand phenomenon—putting justice in the hands of the people—we still have lessons to learn about how to design an institution that gathers persons from different walks of life to discuss and decide upon one justice for all (p. 5).

Although there remains much to learn, psychologists now know a good deal about how juries function. They know that juries don't always get it right; on occasion, jurors are overwhelmed by the sheer volume of evidence, misunderstand their instructions, and use evidence in inappropriate ways. They know that jurors' biases and prejudices can rise to the surface and color their judgments. But by and large, psychologists find little support for the extreme claims that charge juries with poor and irresponsible performance. On the contrary, it seems that the institution of the jury is worth defending and worth improving.

Summary

1. **How have psychologists described jurors' thought processes?** Research studies have shown that if the importance of careful analysis is emphasized, jurors will reason rationally and their verdicts will reflect the strength of the evidence. But they will revert to intuitive reasoning if they are emotionally aroused. Other research describes jurors' mental representations of the evidence as becoming more coherent as jurors filter through evidence and begin to align themselves with one side in the case. Still other research points to the persuasive impact of a structured story on jurors' judgments.

2. **Describe the issue of jury competence.** Some commentators have wondered whether jurors and juries are overly attentive to extralegal information that, in theory, is irrelevant to the guilt decision in criminal cases and to the liability judgment in civil cases. Others have asked whether jurors will not understand expert testimony and dismiss it outright. Whether jurors and juries are able to understand and apply their instructions is another question. Finally, some have asked whether jurors can decide the complicated issues that arise in so-called complex cases.

3. **What evidence is most important to jurors when deciding guilt in criminal trials? When deciding liability and damages in civil trials?** In accord with legal expectations, jurors put most weight on the strength of the evidence against a defendant in a criminal trial; convicting when they are convinced beyond a reasonable doubt that the defendant is guilty. When determining liability in a civil trial, jurors focus on the defendant's conduct, although the severity of the plaintiff's losses matter, too. When assessing damage awards, they put most weight on the severity of the plaintiff's injuries.

4. **How can jurors be helped to understand their instructions?** Jurors can be instructed before the trial begins about the relevant elements of the law that they will apply to the facts they hear. Judges can provide written copies of the instructions for all jurors. Unfortunately, judges rarely provide much guidance when jurors raise questions about their instructions.

5. **What is the impact of extralegal information on jurors?** Research studies suggest that occasionally jurors are influenced by evidence of a defendant's prior record or character and propensity to commit crimes. In civil cases, evidence related to an accident victim's injury may influence the judgment of a defendant's liability.

6. **Can jurors disregard inadmissible evidence?** When a question posed or an answer offered during a trial is ruled inadmissible by the judge, jurors are instructed to disregard it. Psychological evidence indicates that it is difficult for jurors to disregard this testimony; in fact, the stronger the judge's admonition, the less effective it may be. Deliberations tend to reduce reliance on inadmissible evidence.

7. **What is meant by the statement "Bias is inevitable in jurors"?** *Bias*, as used here, refers to the human predisposition to make interpretations on the basis of beliefs and past experiences. Bias is inevitable because it is inescapable human nature to make assumptions about human behavior.

8. **What reforms of the jury system do psychologists suggest?** The information-processing demands placed on jurors should be simplified. More clearly worded instructions, in written as well as oral form, delivered at the beginning and at the end of the trial would be helpful. Preinstructions and simplifying complex language may be especially helpful. During the trial, jurors should be able to pose questions that the judge would then ask of the witnesses. Finally, mid-trial discussion of the evidence could, theoretically, help jurors organize the evidence and improve their memory of the testimony, though one study showed that it biases jurors against the side whose evidence they have already heard.

Key Terms

aversive racism
coherence-based reasoning
damages
defensive attribution
dual-process models
evidence-driven deliberation
evidentiary strength

extralegal information
inadmissible evidence
informational social influence
juror bias
jury nullification
liable

limiting instruction
normative social influence
outcome severity
predecisional distortion
primacy effect
propensity evidence
psycholinguistics

reactance theory
recency effect
schema
story model
sympathy hypothesis
thought suppression
verdict-driven deliberation

Chapter 14

Punishment and Sentencing

Orienting Questions

1. What are the purposes of punishment?
2. How are the values of discretion and fairness reflected in sentencing decisions?
3. What factors influence sentencing decisions?
4. What special factors are considered in the sentencing of juveniles? Of those who commit sexual offenses?
5. How is the death penalty decided by juries?
6. In what ways has the Supreme Court recently limited the use of capital punishment, and what role have psychologists played in these decisions?

A sentencing decision comes near the end of a criminal prosecution, after a defendant pleads guilty or is convicted by a jury. It is typically made by a judge or magistrate, encapsulates legal, pragmatic, and policy considerations, and involves predictions of future criminal conduct (Ruback, 2015). Options include probation, restitution, compensation, fines, community service, imprisonment, and even death. The purposes of the sentence—punishment, deterrence, incapacitation, or rehabilitation, for example—depend on the nature of the crime, the characteristics and experiences of the offender, the temperament of the judge, and, in some cases, public sentiment. As you might suspect, judges have considerable latitude or discretion in the sentences they impose in this system, and disparities in sentence type (probation vs. incarceration), length, and location can result. **Sentencing disparities** occur whenever offenders who committed similar crimes receive different sentences. Various efforts to reduce disparity, including maximum and minimum sentences, sentencing guidelines, and even revisions in sentencing guidelines, have been instituted, with somewhat mixed success.

Great numbers of offenders in the United States are sentenced to prison. One of the most unusual is Sylvester Jiles, who, in 2010, was sentenced to 15 years for attempting to break into the Brevard County (FL) jail one week after he had been released from that very jail! Jiles begged jail officials to take him back into custody because he feared retaliation from his victim's family (https://www.nbcnews.com/id/wbna36000255).

Unusual cases like this aside, the United States leads the world in total number of people incarcerated (more than 2 million in 2021) and has one of the highest rates of incarceration (810 per 100,000 people in 2019) (Minton, Beatty, & Zeng, 2021). Even though this rate has been declining for several years, the U.S., which has less than 5% of the global population, houses roughly one-quarter of the world's prison population, and that number is still five times greater than it was in 1975 (https://www.prisonpolicy.org/blog/2020/10/30/prisoners_in_2019/). This stark situation is a result of what Professor Craig Haney, a psychologist and a lawyer, called America's "rage to punish" (Haney, 2006, p. 4). According to Haney, "hundreds of thousands of people have been locked up in American jails and prisons who would not have been incarcerated (for the same misdeeds) in any other modern Western society" or "if they had committed their crimes at almost any other time in American history" (Haney, 2006, p. 11). Reasons for Americans' focus on punishment—relative to other countries—are described below.

High rates of incarceration are troubling for many reasons. Incarceration removes offenders from their families, leaving spouses, partners, and children economically and psychologically vulnerable. Incarceration instills fears, anxieties, and uncertainties in offenders and intensifies psychiatric disorders, diminishes their ties to their communities, reduces their chances for future employment, makes their reintegration into society difficult, and simultaneously contributes to prison overcrowding.

COVID-19 had a significant impact on incarceration rates and jail populations. Because the virus was highly transmissible in its early stages and social distancing is nearly impossible in correctional facilities, the only way to control its spread, according to health experts, was to reduce the size of incarcerated populations. Jail numbers dropped precipitously at the beginning of the pandemic: by 18% during March 2020, and another 11% during April 2020 (Minton, Zeng, & Maruschak, 2021). Still, an unfortunate effect of COVID-19 on inmate populations was a rise in the death rate. In prisons run by the Federal Bureau of Prisons, for example, that rate was 50% higher in 2020 than in 2015. According to an inmate in the Lompoc, California federal prison complex where 70% of inmates tested positive by May 2020, "At nighttime…all you heard was just coughing all night, all night" (https://www.npr.org/2022/03/07/1083983516/as-covid-spread-in-federal-prisons-many-at-risk-inmates-tried-and-failed-to-get-out).

One method to reduce prison populations, "compassionate release," allows for the release of older and dying inmates prior to the completion of their terms. This generally requires the sentencing judge to determine that an inmate has "extraordinary and compelling reasons" to be released. Prior to the pandemic, it was rarely used (Wylie et al., 2017). But eligibility criteria were expanded in the First Step Act of 2018 and the number of offenders granted compassionate release increased in response to the pandemic (U.S. Sentencing Commission, 2022). Still, the number was relatively small (e.g., 1,805 federal offenders in 2020).

Even with this high rate of incarceration, imprisoned persons represent less than a quarter of the population under correctional supervision in the U.S. (Minton, Beatty, & Zeng, 2021). At the end of 2019, there were more than 6 million adults—approximately 1 of every 40 people—under some form of supervision by correctional systems (i.e., incarceration, probation, or parole). As high as that number is, it represents a decline from 2009 when 1 in 32 people were supervised by U.S. correctional systems.

Another notable feature of criminal sentencing practices are disparities by race. Although they constitute only 13% of the U.S. population, Black inmates account for 30% of those imprisoned (Bronson & Carson, 2019). A similar, though less extreme, picture emerges of Latino inmates, who constitute 18% of the population but represent 22% of those incarcerated (Bronson & Clark, 2019). In twelve states, more than half of the prison population is Black; in Maryland, that figure is 72%. And in Oklahoma, which has the highest overall Black incarceration rate, 1 of every 15 Black men is imprisoned (Nellis, 2016). Structural disadvantages in communities of color, along with biased decision making by police, prosecutors, juries, and judges regarding arrests, charged crimes, plea deals, convictions, and sentencing, all play a role. Racially biased disciplinary practices in schools can set the stage for criminal justice system involvement, and eventually, incarceration (Kovera, 2019). This is called the school-to-prison pipeline.

How should a society respond to individual criminals? With an inmate population over 2 million, does it make sense to continue locking up more offenders every year? Incarceration comes at a price; every dollar spent on corrections means one less dollar for public schools, health care, parks, and higher education.

A controversial method to scale back prison populations uses risk assessment measures (described in Chapter 3) to apportion sentences. So-called evidence-based sentencing aims to reduce incarceration rates by sentencing offenders based on risk factors for recidivism such as criminal history, education, substance abuse, and employment history. Those assessed to be at low risk are given shorter terms than those assessed at higher risk. Critics claim that this process unfairly targets racial minorities, though a study comparing risk scores for Blacks and Whites found that regardless of offenders' race, evidence-based sentencing can effectively predict recidivism risk (Skeem & Lowenkamp, 2016). But what about the majority of cases in which sentences are negotiated during plea bargaining with no formal assessment of risk? Although both prosecutors and defense attorneys are at least somewhat attentive to considerations of risk, defense attorneys are more averse to relying on them, perhaps because they believe that risk assessments contribute to racial and ethnic disparities in the criminal justice system (Monahan et al., 2020). The public also has very mixed feeling about this approach (Scurich & Monahan, 2016).

Philosophical questions about the costs and benefits of punishment and incarceration, as well as the methods for meting out punishment, have been debated for many years and public sentiment about those issues has swung back and forth. Americans generally hold more punitive attitudes than citizens of other countries, in part because they experience more violent crime (Schwaeble & Sundt, 2020). Legislators, judges, and prosecutors are responsive to such sentiments. So when public opinion became punitive as crime rates rose in the 1980s and 1990s, sentencing options and patterns became harsher. Prison sentences increased in length, as did the kinds of behaviors punishable by incarceration. Then, when crime moderated toward the end of the 2000s and fiscal constraints forced policymakers to confront the high cost of imprisonment, sentencing policies became more lenient. Americans became increasingly supportive of alternatives to harsh punishments that focused on prevention and treatment, rather than "tough on crime" rhetoric, particularly for nonviolent and juvenile offenders. During this time, problem-solving courts were developed to address the underlying reasons for criminality (e.g., drug addiction, homelessness, trauma), and diversion to community-based services such as probation and parole was common. (We discuss both of these developments in Chapter 9.) But since 2019, the crime rate, particularly violent crime in large U.S. cities, has been on the uptick. So we may again experience a pendulum swing in sentencing policies in response to this new social reality.

In this chapter and against this backdrop, we address the topics of punishment and sentencing by describing their multiple goals and purposes, some of which aim to exact retribution from an offender and others that favor practical ends such as deterrence, incapacitation, and rehabilitation. In nearly all U.S. jurisdictions, the sentencing decision is made by a judge, and we describe the factors that judges consider in those decisions. We also detail specific issues that arise in judges' sentencing of juvenile and sex offenders. Finally, we examine the one domain in which juries make sentencing decisions: the death penalty. The ultimate punishment of death encompasses various psychological issues.

The Purposes of Punishment

The crime control model of criminal justice has heavily influenced police, prosecutors, and many judges over the past half century. It interprets the primary aim of law enforcement as the apprehension and punishment of criminals so they will not repeat their offenses and others will be deterred from similar acts. But as resources have dwindled, policymakers have become increasingly interested in punishments that serve some beneficial function, particularly because the majority of incarcerated individuals will reenter society after spending time behind bars.

These differing viewpoints illustrate the multiple purposes of punishment. Psychologists have identified at least seven different goals of punishment (e.g., Ruback, 2015).

1. *General deterrence.* The punishment of an offender—and the subsequent publicity that comes with it—are assumed to discourage other potential lawbreakers. Some advocates of the death penalty, for example, believe that fear of death may be our strongest motivation; hence, they believe that the death penalty serves as a general deterrent to murder.

2. *Individual deterrence.* Punishment of the offender is presumed to keep that person from committing other crimes in the future. Some theories assume that many criminals lack adequate internal inhibitors; hence, punitive sanctions must be used to teach them that their behavior will be controlled—if not by them, then by society.

3. *Incapacitation.* If convicted offenders are sent to prison, society can feel safe from those individuals while they are confined. One influential position (Wilson, 1975) sees a major function of incapacitation as simply to age the criminal—an understandable goal, given that the rate of offending declines with age.

4. *Retribution.* Society believes that offenders should not benefit from their crimes; rather, they should receive their "just deserts," or "that which is justly deserved." The moral cornerstone of punishment is that it should be administered to people who deserve it as a consequence of their misdeeds.

5. *Moral outrage*. Punishment can give society a means of catharsis and relief from the feelings of frustration, hurt, loss, and anger that result from being victims of crime; it promotes a sense of satisfaction that offenders have paid for what they have done to others.

6. *Rehabilitation*. One goal in sentencing has always been to help offenders recognize the error of their ways and develop new skills, values, and lifestyles so that they can become law abiding. This has been a primary consideration in punishing juveniles.

7. *Restitution*. Wrongdoers should compensate victims for their damages and losses. Typical statutes require that defendants pay for victims' out-of-pocket expenses, property damage, and other monetary losses. Restitution is often a condition of probation.

Utilitarian Approaches

Most of these goals are **utilitarian**: They are intended to accomplish a useful outcome, such as compensating the victim, deterring crime, or incapacitating or rehabilitating the defendant. Utilitarian goals have a practical objective; they are designed to right the wrongs of past misconduct and reduce the likelihood of future criminal behavior.

Rehabilitation as a utilitarian goal has been in and out of favor throughout history. The basic notion of rehabilitation is that offenders who receive treatment for the underlying causes of criminality will be less likely to reoffend. Observers of trends in mass incarceration point to a shift from rehabilitative to punitive policies occurring in the 1970s (Phelps, 2011). When rehabilitation *was* the dominant goal (e.g., pre-1970s), criminal sentences were expected to accomplish something other than incarceration and punishment.

Though the original purpose of prisons was to rehabilitate (many prisons are still called *correctional* institutions), high recidivism rates indicate that prisons have not been very effective at rehabilitating offenders. The extreme version of this view, dubbed the "nothing works" position, is attributed to Robert Martinson. He concluded, after reviewing a large number of outcome studies, that most attempts at offender rehabilitation fail (Martinson, 1974). Martinson's advocacy of another utilitarian approach—deterrence—led to a "get-tough" attitude toward offenders, and to increasingly punitive measures such as the three-strikes laws (laws stating that after a third criminal conviction, offenders go to prison for a very long time), and zero-tolerance policies enacted in the 1980s and 1990s.

But after more than 40 years of this "get-tough" approach with no reduction in recidivism, the pendulum began to swing back slowly in the direction of rehabilitative policies. Psychologists now know that rehabilitation can be effective when it is tailored to one's age, race, criminal history, religion, and other personal attributes (Andrews & Bonta, 2010). Unfortunately, many institutions continue to offer only one-size-fits-all interventions, and some provide none at all. How rehabilitation efforts will fare amidst the recent crimewave is, of course, an open question.

Retributive Approaches

Two of the punishment goals we described are **retributive**: they involve looking back at the offense and determining what the criminal "deserves" as a consequence of committing it. These goals are retribution (sometimes called "just deserts") and moral outrage, a close cousin of retribution (Kaplan, 1996). The notion of retribution implies that an offender deserves to be punished and that the punishment should be proportionate to the severity of the wrongdoing. But in deciding how much punishment is the right amount, the offender's blameworthiness, or **culpability**, must be assessed. This is no easy task. Was the offender's rationality undermined by mental illness or extreme emotional distress? Was the criminal act an outcome of coercive influences? Was the action out of character? All of these questions factor into our ability to establish culpability. One observer suggests that the law, even when aided by social science research, cannot accurately determine who is culpable and who is not (Tullett, 2022).

The stark contrast between utilitarian and retributive approaches raises the more fundamental question of why we punish people. What are our motives for punishing others? Discovering how ordinary people think about this issue is important because those who draft and apply sentencing laws should know what the public prefers (Carlsmith & Darley, 2008).

Psychologists have taken different approaches to answering this question. Some have simply asked people which philosophy they prefer and have assumed that respondents can report their true beliefs. But in studies that measured people's agreement with various sentencing policies, people tended to agree with all of them (Anderson & MacCoun, 1999)! Furthermore, people are sometimes unaware of the factors that influence their preferences (Wilson, 2002). An alternative research design involves presenting vignettes to respondents, varying the nature of the crime and details about the offender, and then measuring respondents' sentencing preferences.

Public Preferences for Deterrence and Retribution.
In a now-classic study, Carlsmith, Darley, and Robinson (2002) used a **policy capturing** research technique to assess the punishment motives of ordinary people. The specific motives for punishment that they contrasted were deterrence and retribution. Using vignettes that described a variety of harmful actions, the researchers attempted to understand (or "capture") the policies underlying the punishments that people assigned. They varied different elements of the crimes described, elements that should or should not matter to respondents depending on which motive they preferred. For example, the magnitude of the harm should matter to people who are motivated by retribution, and the likelihood of reoffending should matter to those who are concerned with future deterrence. Carlsmith and his colleagues then measured the degree to which each respondent's sentence was influenced by these variables. The data showed a high

sensitivity to factors associated with retribution and relative insensitivity to factors associated with deterrence. In fact, people actively seek information relevant to retribution (e.g., the magnitude of the harm and the perpetrator's intent) when they know that a crime has been committed and are asked to assign punishments (Carlsmith, 2006). The magnitude of harm caused seems especially important, as it is also related to punishment preferences for low-level offenses such as theft when length of probation is considered (Vardsveen & Wiener, 2021).

But the offender's intentions matter too. People react differently to those who intended to cause harm than to those who were simply careless. People respond to the former with a sense of moral outrage and the desire for retribution. Their primary reaction to the latter is a preference for restitution (Darley & Pittman, 2003). Regardless of whether the crime affects one individual or a large group of victims, and whether it involves a serious or lower-level offense, people's preferences for punishment often focus on what they believe an offender deserves.

Interestingly, this is not what people *say* about their punishment beliefs. Responding to opinion polls, people are more likely to indicate support for punishment that deters criminals than punishment that exacts retribution (Carlsmith, 2008; Vardsveen & Wiener, 2021). This suggests that people do not have a good sense of their own motivations for punishing others and may explain why citizens enact legislation one year, then soon reject it as unjust and vote to repeal it shortly thereafter (Carlsmith & Darley, 2008).

Why do people say they support deterrence but act like they favor retribution? One possibility is that people have a limited awareness of their own reasons for their punishment preferences. As social psychologists have pointed out, when it comes to introspecting about why we behave in a particular way, "we are all strangers to ourselves" (Wilson, 2002). It may also be less socially acceptable to say that we favor a penalty based on reprisal and revenge than one based on notions of future good.

These findings appear to support the idea that many people actually favor punitive sanctions, and at least some politicians are happy to respond. Joe Arpaio, the controversial former sheriff of Maricopa County, Arizona (Phoenix), called himself "America's toughest sheriff." His philosophy, which garnered him national notoriety (as well as federal investigations into his management of funds), was to make jail so unpleasant that no one would want to come back—while simultaneously saving money. He sheltered prisoners in "leaky, dilapidated military-surplus tents set on gravel fields surrounded by barbed wire" and fed them "bologna streaked with green and blue packaging dye" (Morrison, 1995). He established the first women's and juveniles' chain gangs. His "air posse" of 30 private planes tracked illegal immigrants and drug smugglers and led to racial profiling lawsuits. Although people voted for Arpaio repeatedly—consistent with their preference for retribution—Arpaio was

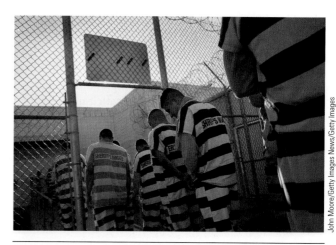

Inmates at a Maricopa County (AZ) jail run by former Sheriff Joe Arpaio.

eventually ousted from office in 2016 after 24 years as sheriff. Arizona taxpayers are still footing the bills from thousands of lawsuits stemming from his actions.

Another retributive goal—moral outrage—allows society the satisfaction of knowing that offenders have been made to pay for the harms they caused. Professor Dan Kahan (1996) argued that for a sentence to be acceptable to the public, it must reflect society's outrage. He maintained that the expressive dimension of punishment is not satisfied by "straight" probation, "mere" fines, or direct community service. According to Kahan, probation appears to be no punishment, a fine appears to be a means to "buy one's way out," and community service is something everyone ought to do. Kahan argued that imposing a **shaming penalty** would allow society to express its moral denunciation of criminal wrongdoers.

Shaming was a traditional means by which communities punished offenders. In colonial days, those who committed minor offenses were put in stocks in a public place for several hours for all to see and ridicule. Serious offenders were branded or otherwise marked so they would be "shamed" for life. In Williamsburg, Virginia, thieves were nailed to the stocks by the ear; after a period of time the sheriff would rip the offender from the stocks, thus "ear-marking" the offender for life (Book, 1999). Though shaming has not been used much since the early 1800s, by some accounts, it is making a comeback (Portman, 2019).

The modern version of shaming allows low-level offenders—shoplifters, trespassers, and traffic code violators—to avoid all or part of a jail sentence by publicly renouncing their crimes in a humiliating way. The impetus for these alternative sentences is twofold. First, judges have become frustrated with revolving-door justice: a large number of offenders who are released from prison eventually return, suggesting that their punishments had little long-term effectiveness. Second, judges are aware of the longstanding problem of prison overcrowding and the high costs of incarceration. The American Bar Association has urged judges to provide alternatives to incarceration for offenders who might benefit from them. Some judges have been happy to oblige, and some of the sentences they have imposed are truly ingenious. For example, men caught on surveillance cameras in the process of soliciting prostitutes in Oakland, California had their faces plastered on bus stop signs and billboards (Stryker, 2005). Another innovative sentence is described in Box 14.1.

As you might expect, sentences like these are highly controversial. Some lawyers—defense attorneys and prosecutors alike—applaud them, acknowledging that judges often have discretion in sentencing and that incarceration is costly and does not always work. But others worry that the shaming inherent in these sentences is extreme, morally repugnant, and unlikely to have its intended effect. They point out that shame tends to anger offenders and causes them to blame others ("that stupid judge," "those stupid laws") rather than accept responsibility themselves (Tangney & Dearing, 2002). Even Dan Kahan, the early proponent of shaming penalties, now shuns them (Kahan, 2006).

Restorative Approaches

Over the years, many people have become disenchanted with retributive justice. For one thing, punishing offenders in proportion to the severity of their offenses, although cathartic, has apparently done little to curb crime, reduce suffering, or address structural factors that lead to criminal behavior in the first place. For another, inflicting punishment on offenders who "deserve" to be punished provides little opportunity for victims to be involved in the process or to have their own needs met. As a result, victims are often dissatisfied with their experiences in the criminal justice system. Finally, some shamed people become defensive and escape that feeling by denying responsibility altogether (Tangney et al., 2011).

In the 1970s, an approach emerged that attempts to repair the damage caused by criminal offenses and encourage offenders to take responsibility. This approach, **restorative justice**, borrowed from features of indigenous justice systems including the First Nations people of Canada and the U.S. and the Maori of New Zealand. It views crime as a violation of the victim and the community, rather than the state. It uses open dialogue to gain consensus about responsibility-taking and dispute resolution. The goals of restorative justice are to repair the harm and restore the losses caused by offensive activity, reintegrate offenders into society, and empower victims and the community to move from feelings of vulnerability and loss to a sense of understanding and closure (Umbreit et al., 2005).

Restorative justice is based on the premise that those who are most affected by crime—victims and offenders—should have a prominent role to play in resolving the conflict and that the community has a stake in its outcome too. Thus, it expands the circle of participants beyond the offender and the state, and encourages participants to use some combination of apology, remorse, and forgiveness to move past the harms caused by crime.

Restorative justice policies are used throughout the world. The Truth and Reconciliation Commissions in South Africa and Rwanda were based on these principles and the entire youth justice system in New Zealand uses a restorative justice model. These practices are becoming more common in the criminal, civil, and juvenile justice systems in the United States, as well. Many jails and prisons now offer victim impact intervention training in which inmates interact with victims in order to understand how victimization has affected them. We provide an example of a restorative procedure in Box 14.2.

How do people feel about achieving justice through a restorative process? Given the public's strong desire to punish offenders, is there support for procedures that focus on

---

Box 14.1

The Case of the Poacher Forced to Watch *Bambi* Every Month for a Year

Nabbed in one of Missouri's largest-ever poaching investigations, David Berry Jr. pled guilty to the "illegal taking of deer" and violating his felony firearms prohibition. Berry, his brothers, and father had illegally killed hundreds of deer, sometimes taking the heads and leaving the bodies to decay. Berry was sentenced to a year imprisonment with an unusual twist: The judge ordered him to watch the cartoon movie *Bambi*, about hunters who kill the fawn Bambi's mother, every month during that period.

Critics point out that unusual sentences like this may do little more than endear judges, many of whom are elected state officials, to a segment of voters who delight in these "zany judicial stunts." Law Professor Jonathan Turley is one of them: "The judge cannot possibly believe that watching *Bambi* is going to produce an epiphany in this man's life. That leaves two possibilities: that the judge is trying to make a mockery of the defendant or is simply trying to use the defendant for a type of public joke" (Mak, 2018).

Critical Thought Question

Discuss the advantages and disadvantages of shaming as an approach to criminal sentencing in light of the goals of punishment discussed earlier in the chapter.

Box 14.2

The Case for Restorative Justice: Healing a Mother Wounded by Tragedy

On July 19, 2009, Sandy Eversole got the news that all parents fear and dread: Her son David Mueller, a star athlete and college student, had been killed in an automobile accident. David was riding in a car driven by his friend Dylan Salazar, travelling nearly 100 mph on a Colorado Springs city street before running off the road. As expected, Sandy and her family were overwhelmed by grief in the first few months after the accident and then angered and frustrated by the claims settlement and criminal justice responses. She wanted to know what had happened that night and why, but after the driver was sentenced to four years in a youth correctional facility, Sandy had no way to ask questions or seek solace. That changed when the District Attorney's office gave her an opportunity to meet with Dylan in a restorative justice session led by a trained mediator. Despite initial concerns

about whether she would be capable of controlling her rage, Sandy was able to tell Dylan what her family had endured. Also apprehensive, he apologized and took responsibility for the accident. Reflecting on the experience, Sandy recalled, "Right away I could tell that he was full of remorse and sadness. It was hard to find out some of the details but I was glad I did. It was easy to forgive him after I saw his tears" (www.restorativemediationproject.org).

Critical Thought Question

Historically, victims have had little say in how criminal offenders are punished. Why? The restorative justice approach seeks to empower victims by giving them a voice in this matter. In your opinion, should victims' perspectives influence the punishment meted out to offenders?

other justice goals? People apparently do value its role in repairing harm done to victims and communities. In fact, for less serious crimes, people prefer to respond with restorative measures, and even for more serious offenses, people prefer responses that combine restorative procedures and punitive sanctions (i.e., prison sentences), rather than either of these options alone (Gromet & Darley, 2006). Victim satisfaction seems to drive these reactions: When observers believe that victims have achieved satisfaction and closure via a restorative justice process, they are less likely to endorse additional retributive sanctions such as prison sentences for offenders (Gromet et al., 2012).

Also implicit in restorative justice practices is concern for the offender. The question arises whether, after the period of punishment is complete, an offender should be reintegrated in society. The idea of giving offenders a clean slate is relevant to a number of policy decisions concerning ex-offenders because having a criminal record can affect employment opportunities, housing options, and voting rights. A 2018 study assessed whether there was public support for the idea that, in addition to seeking retribution, punishments should also give offenders a clean slate (Brubacher, 2018). In concordance with previous studies, results showed that as crime severity increased, support for retribution increased, and—the novel finding—that support for a clean slate decreased. People tended to support a clean slate for minor crimes but not for serious crimes. These priorities are consistent with the mission statement of the U.S. Federal Bureau of Prisons which emphasizes retribution and rehabilitation and makes no mention of allowing offenders to be reintegrated into society.

So the public seems to prioritize retribution, rehabilitation, and restoration as a function of the context: When the criminal action has imposed significant harms on victims,

retributive sanctions are preferred. But for less serious crimes, rehabilitation and restorative approaches are valued as well. In light of this nuanced picture of punishment preferences, it is worthwhile examining how judges actually assign criminal punishments, to what extent their choices mirror public sentiments, and how psychological factors influence their decisions.

Judicial Discretion in Sentencing

Criminal sentencing lies at the heart of society's efforts to ensure public order. Hoffman and Stone-Meierhoefer (1979) go so far as to state, "Next to the determination of guilt or innocence…the sentencing decision is probably the most important decision made about the criminal defendant in the entire process" (p. 241).

Although sentencing is a judicial function, sentencing decisions are largely controlled by the legislative branch—Congress and state legislatures. The legislative branch dictates the extent of judges' discretion, and many legislators believe that judges should have little or no discretion. They emphasize retribution and argue that the punishment should fit the crime. Mandatory sentences, sentencing guidelines, and the abolition of parole in the federal system have been the primary ingredients in these "get tough" schemes.

Other legislators maintain that the sentence should also fit the offender—in essence, that judges should have discretion to make the sentence fit both the crime and the criminal. Those who advocate individually tailored sentences note that each offender's personal and external circumstances are different and that each deserves to be treated as an individual: "Theories [that] place primary emphasis on linking deserved punishments to the severity of crimes, in the interest of treating cases alike ... lead to disregard of other ethically relevant differences between offenders—like their personal backgrounds and the effects of punishments on them and their families" (Tonry, 1996, p. 15).

Sentencing Policies

Some states have indeterminate sentencing schemes, in which judges exercise their discretion by imposing a variable period of incarceration for a given offense (e.g., 6–20 years), and a parole board determines the actual date of release (Hritz, 2021). Such policies have been both hailed and criticized: hailed because they provide incentives for good behavior and encourage offenders to take advantage of available treatment programs to enhance the chances of earlier release, and criticized because they allow parole boards wide discretion in determining when the conditions of the sentence have been satisfied. When indeterminate sentencing works as it should, individuals are neither released early nor subjected to confinement beyond that necessary to ensure public protection.

In other states, the legislative branch has imposed a determinate sentencing system on the judiciary, effectively reducing judges' discretion. In these systems, those convicted are sentenced for a fixed length of time determined by statutes and guidelines, and there is no parole. The primary goals of these sentences are retribution and moral outrage. There is little concern for individuals' personal characteristics, apart from their criminal record, and less potential for arbitrary or discriminatory decisions about when an individual should be released.

In a further attempt to reduce discretion, some states and the federal government impose mandatory minimum sentences for certain offenses, including drug crimes. These policies require judges to sentence convicted individuals to a minimum number of years in prison regardless of any extenuating circumstances. They, too, have been criticized as unjust. Critics contend that prosecutors have a great deal of discretion in the ways they charge and that, as a result, people from marginalized communities face tougher sentencing than privileged individuals for the same crime. Mandatory minimum sentences have also resulted in lengthy terms of incarceration for those convicted of drug offenses. The American Psychological Association (APA) has spoken out against them: "[T]hey have done nothing to reduce crime or put big-time drug dealers out of business. What they have done ... is to fill prisons with young, nonviolent, low-level drug offenders serving long sentences at enormous and growing cost to taxpayers" (Hansen, 1999, p. 14).

Indeed, mandatory minimum penalties have significantly affected both the composition and size of the federal prison population. In late 2016, nearly half of all inmates had been convicted of drug offenses, and nearly three-quarters were convicted of offenses that carried minimum mandatory sentences. Their average sentence was 94 months, more than double the term for drug offenders not subjected to mandatory minimum penalties (U.S. Sentencing Commission, 2017). But in the most extensive prison reform legislation since the mid-1980s, the First Step Act of 2018, which we mentioned in the context of compassionate release, also reduced the length of automatic minimum sentences for federal inmates. Several states have also reduced minimum sentences for nonviolent drug offenses.

Sentencing Process

In most courts, sentencing procedures entail several components. The judge receives a file that contains information about the individual's personal history and prior convictions (if any), and a number of documents describing various details of the case (e.g., the date of the arraignment, the formal indictment). The judge reviews the file before the sentencing hearing.

At the hearing, recommendations for a sentence are presented, first by the prosecutor and then by the defense attorney. Statements are arranged in this order to give the defendant the final word before the judge makes a decision. But there may be an unexpected consequence of granting the prosecution the opportunity to make an initial recommendation. A large body of research has shown that initial numeric requests serve as powerful standards or "anchors" on subsequent judgments (Kahneman, 2011). In fact, judges' sentencing decisions are highly influenced by the prosecutor's request for a lengthy sentence (Englich & Mussweiler, 2001), a finding that can be explained by a judgment process called anchoring.

Defense attorneys also provide sentencing recommendations, though their positions are *also* influenced by the prosecutors' demands. When researchers asked lawyers to assume the role of defense attorneys in a simulated rape case, they found that although defense attorneys requested a lower punishment than prosecutors, they were still influenced by the level of the prosecutors' recommendations and assimilated their own sentencing demands to those of the prosecutor (Englich et al., 2005). This behavior, in turn, will affect judges' decisions. So rather than being aided by going last, the defense may be hindered by having to follow, and counter, the prosecution's demand—its "anchor."

In addition to demands from the prosecutor and defense attorney, the sentencing judge has a probation officer's report and recommendation. This report carries a good deal of weight with judges. In one study, the judge agreed with the probation officer's recommendation in 78% of cases that resulted in community sanctions and 62% of cases that resulted in incarceration (Leiber et al., 2017). The judge may ask the offender questions and will usually permit the offender to make a statement. In some cases, a forensic mental health professional may provide input on issues such as diminished capacity or coercion and duress (Krauss & Goldstein, 2007), addressing questions such as whether defendants were able to understand the wrongfulness of the crime, were able to conform their conduct to the requirements of the law, and had particular treatment or rehabilitation needs. On the basis of these sources of information and taking sentencing options into account, the judge then sentences the offender.

To this point, we have described a system of **front-end sentencing** by judges that marks the beginning of an offender's punishment. But another sanction, **back-end sentencing**, also merits attention. Back-end sentencing occurs when parolees are arrested for new crimes or violate the conditions of their parole and are returned to prison by state parole boards (Lin et al., 2010). Back-end sentencing has been responsible for approximately one-half of all prison admissions in California (Grattet, 2020). Examination of these parole revocations shows that parole board officials, eager to protect themselves from public scorn, are especially harsh on sex offenders and serious and violent offenders, regardless of what these offenders did to violate their parole. Parole boards also consider offenders' gender and race when they ratchet penalties up and down (Lin et al., 2010). We discuss these sorts of implicit biases more thoroughly in the next section.

Determinants of Sentencing: Relevant and Irrelevant

Sentencing decisions are based largely on two legally relevant factors: the severity of the offense and the offender's prior record (Ruback, 2015). Even in jurisdictions that grant judges wide latitude in sentencing, more serious crimes earn more severe punishments (Goodman-Delahunty & Sporer, 2010). And across all jurisdictions, offenders with a prior criminal record are sentenced more harshly. "Three strikes laws," also known as habitual offender laws, provide an example. Under these statutes, which exist in more than half the states, a third-time offender with two prior convictions for violent felonies can be sentenced to very lengthy prison terms.

But do judges consider *only* those legally relevant factors or do they also consider seemingly irrelevant factors like race, ethnicity, and gender? Moreover, *should* they consider other factors? For example, should an offender's experiences be taken into account? Should it matter that a convicted offender was deprived as a child, hungry, abused, and denied opportunities to go to school or look for work? Should it matter that an offender is male or female? Black or White? Gay or straight?

To examine whether these extra-legal factors affect judges' decisions, researchers have used a variety of procedures including observational studies, archival analyses of case records and sentencing statistics, and interviews. They have conducted experiments in which they manipulate various facts in simulated cases or vignettes and ask sentencers to respond.

What they have found is that many of these factors, including the offender's gender and race, influence sentencing decisions, often without conscious awareness of the judge. Women are less likely than men to be sentenced to prison (Freiberger & Hilinski, 2013) and when they are,

less likely to receive a lengthy sentence (Koons-Witt et al., 2014). These gender effects vary according to the type of crime. Males are more likely than females to be sentenced to secure confinement and serve longer sentences for property and drug offenses. But women are just as likely as men to be sentenced to prison for committing a violent offense (Rodriguez et al., 2006).

What accounts for gender disparities? Sentencing is a complex cognitive activity and there is some evidence that disparities arise because presentence reports provided to judges contain a great deal of difficult-to-process detail. To manage the information overload, judges may rely on well-honed stereotypes and attributions about the case and the defendant's characteristics to aid their decisions (Steffensmeier & Demuth, 2006). According to the **focal concerns theory** of judicial decision making, judges focus on three main concerns in reaching sentencing decisions: (1) the defendant's culpability, (2) protection of the community (emphasizing incapacitation and general deterrence), and (3) practical constraints and consequences of the sentence, including concerns about disrupting ties to children and other family members.

It is not exactly clear how judges evaluate these focal concerns. But evidence from sentencing hearings (Steffensmeier et al., 2017) suggests that judges may view most women as less likely to reoffend, understand women's crimes in the context of women's own victimization (e.g., by coercive men, alcohol or drug problems), and perceive the social costs of detaining women as higher. In fact though, judges now consider the social consequences of incarceration—particularly the effects on an offender's family—for both male and female offenders, and those who have familial caretaker roles are less likely to be incarcerated than those who are not caring for others (Freiburger, 2010; Holmes et al., 2022).

Another important demographic characteristic that influences sentencing decisions is the race of the offender. Decades of research show that Blacks and Latinos are sentenced more harshly than Whites (Spohn, 2015) and determinate sentencing and sentencing guidelines have not been able to eliminate those racial disparities. The discrepancy is larger for drug offenses (meaning that differences in sentence length for Blacks and Whites are larger for drug crimes than for other crimes). Although some of these disparities are related to diverse patterns of offending and criminal histories (Markowitz & Salvatore, 2012), those factors cannot fully account for racial effects in sentencing. Certainly, the war on drugs of the 1980s and 1990s and the moral panic over crack cocaine is a factor, as are higher arrest rates for Blacks who commit serious violent crimes than for other racial groups who commit those same crimes. Some of the disparity results from conscious or unconscious bias and discrimination (Spohn, 2015). As critic Michelle Alexander bluntly asserted, "The fact that more than half of the young black men in any large American city are currently under the control of the criminal justice system (or saddled with criminal records) is not—as many argue—just a symptom of poverty or poor choices, but rather evidence of a new racial caste system at work" (2010, p. 16).

Another factor that influences judicial sentencing patterns is the way a conviction came about: whether by guilty plea or trial. Defendants who plead guilty are typically given a reduced sentence, partly to encourage them to plead guilty and thereby reduce costs for court time and personnel. For example, using federal sentencing data for the years 2000–2002, Ulmer et al. (2010) determined that offenders who pled guilty received 15% shorter sentences than those convicted by trial. This pattern—called the plea discount—has been found in nearly all studies of state and federal court sentencing outcomes and observed for violent, drug, and white-collar crimes (Lehmann, 2021).

Obviously, judges are human. When they have latitude in the punishments they can give, their backgrounds, attitudes, and personal characteristics can play a role. They may be prejudiced for or against certain groups—such as immigrants, Black Lives Matter protestors, or anti-abortion activists. Judges may lack willingness or ability to analyze complex problems systematically and therefore impose sentences that include rounded, even numbers that are easier to manipulate mentally (Dhami et al., 2020). Judges may simply be uninformed. A Maryland judge acquitted an alleged assailant on domestic violence charges after the victim failed to testify. He stated that one can't simply assume that a woman who is being hit didn't consent to the attack. "Sadomasochists sometimes like to get beat up," he said (Houppert, 2007).

Sentencing Juvenile Offenders

The juvenile justice system differs from the adult system in some crucial ways. First, not all juveniles come into the system via arrests. Some are referred by school officials, social service agencies, or even by parents. Second, there is an emphasis on rehabilitating youthful offenders, rather than simply punishing them. Finally, early in a case, juvenile justice officials must decide whether to send it into the court system or divert the offender to alternative programs such as drug treatment, educational and recreational programs, or individual and group counseling.

If the choice is to involve the courts, then prosecutors may recommend, or juvenile court judges may decide, to transfer cases involving serious charges such as sexual assault and attempted murder from juvenile court to criminal court. Sentencing procedures and options vary depending on whether the child is adjudicated in juvenile court or transferred to adult criminal court. Judges' beliefs about the deterrent effects of transfer—the possibility that juveniles will refrain from committing crimes because they fear being tried as adults—affect these decisions (Redding & Hensl, 2011). More experienced judges see greater rehabilitative potential in juveniles and are less likely than inexperienced judges to transfer cases to criminal court. Some data suggest that youths transferred to criminal court receive sentences even longer than adult offenders (Jordan & McNeal, 2016).

Juvenile Court Dispositions

The majority of young people whose cases are adjudicated in juvenile court are found to be delinquent, the equivalent of an adult offender being found guilty (Puzzanchera et al., 2010). Their cases then move to the sentencing or **dispositional phase**. Dispositional hearings typically combine adversarial procedures and attention to the particular needs—social, psychological, physical—of the child. They include recommendations by probation officers and social workers, reports of social and school histories, and discussions with the offenders and their families, probation staff, and other professionals (Binder et al., 2001). Issues of substance abuse, family dysfunction, mental health needs, peer relationships, and school problems may be addressed.

The goals of juvenile court dispositions—ensuring public safety and addressing children's needs—are reflected in the options available to juvenile court judges. These include (1) commitment to a correctional facility that houses juveniles; (2) probation, sometimes with intensive supervision; (3) referral to a group home or other lower security residential placement; (4) referral to day treatment or a mental health program; or (5) imposition of a fine, community service, or restitution.

When determining the appropriate disposition for a juvenile, judges may consider whether the parents are able to supervise the offender at home, assist in rehabilitation efforts, and insist on school attendance. They may also consider the family's financial resources and the availability of community-based treatment programs and facilities (Campbell & Schmidt, 2000). Having a supportive family can be crucial: recidivism rates for violent juvenile offenders assigned to in-home probation were less than half those of youths assigned to secure settings (Ryan et al., 2014).

Juvenile court judges are also expected to assess offenders' rehabilitative needs and personal circumstances. Thus, one might expect that they would put considerable weight on individual factors, such as offenders' psychosocial functioning, developmental maturity, responsibility taking, and gang involvement. But researchers who examined the effects of these individual factors on dispositional outcomes (i.e., probation and confinement) in a sample of 1,355 juvenile offenders found that legal factors (e.g., seriousness of the offense, whether the offender had prior court referrals) had the strongest influence on dispositions. Individual factors were not strongly linked to dispositional decisions (Cauffman et al., 2007).

Blended Sentencing

Juveniles who meet the criteria for transfer to adult criminal court may be sentenced under **blended sentencing** statutes that combine the options available in juvenile court with those used in criminal court, in states that have such blended sentencing in statutes (Heilbrun et al., 2017). These sentencing laws attempt to simultaneously address rehabilitation concerns and impose a "get tough" accountability (Redding & Mrozoski, 2005). In practice, this means that serious and violent young offenders can stay under juvenile court jurisdiction and receive more lenient sentences than if they were transferred to adult court. But they can also be subjected to harsh sentences if they commit new offenses, violate probation, or fail to respond to rehabilitation efforts. Blended sentencing schemes provide incentives to offenders to avoid the more serious consequences of an adult sentence. Prosecutors often use the threat of transfer to adult criminal court to persuade juvenile offenders to plead guilty and accept a particular blended sentence (Podkopacz & Feld, 2001). But there are troubling questions about the effectiveness of blended sentencing, since roughly half of serious delinquents released early without continuing their sentence in adult prison were rearrested for a felony offense (Trulson et al., 2011).

Life Sentences for Juvenile Offenders

Judges can impose very lengthy prison sentences on offenders who were under 18 when they committed a serious offense. At the start of 2020, approximately 1,500 offenders were serving mandatory life without parole (LWOP) sentences in the U.S. for crimes they committed as juveniles (https://www.sentencingproject.org/publications/juvenile-life-without-parole/). The number of juvenile LWOP prisoners declined substantially as the result of a flurry of activity at the Supreme Court in the 2010s. In those cases, the Court invalidated LWOP sentences for juveniles convicted of non-homicide offenses (*Graham v. Florida*, 2010), deemed *mandatory* LWOP sentences for juveniles to be

unconstitutional (*Miller v. Alabama*, 2012), applied that rule to previously resolved cases (*Montgomery v. Louisiana*, 2016), and then reaffirmed *Miller* and *Montgomery* while also ruling that the youth in question need not be deemed "permanently incorrigible" to be sentenced to LWOP (*Jones v. Mississippi*, 2021). How this issue will fare in the more conservative Court of the mid-2020s is an open question.

These cases pit human rights and judicial reform advocates on the one hand against prosecutors and victims' rights groups on the other. Human rights groups argue that applying life-without-parole sentences to juveniles constitutes cruel and unusual punishment. Stephen Bright, director of the Southern Center for Human Rights, said, "It goes against human inclinations to give up completely on a young teenager. It's impossible for a court to say that any 14-year-old never has the possibility to live in society." Prosecutors and victims' groups say that such statutes are comforting to victims and make sense in their "adult-crime, adult-time" approach. But public sentiment is generally not supportive of life sentences for juveniles of any age (Greene et al., 2017). We delve further into the complexity of these issues by describing the case of Jacob Ind in Box 14.3.

Sentencing Those Convicted of Sexual Offenses

Many people believe that those convicted of sex crimes are especially likely to reoffend, and therefore require different kinds of punishment than those convicted of other crimes

---

Box 14.3

The Case of Jacob Ind: When a Kid Gets Life

On the morning of December 17, 1992, 15-year-old Jacob Ind went to school in Woodland Park, Colorado, planning to tell a friend that he had just murdered his mother and stepfather and that he was going to commit suicide. But the friend immediately went to the principal, who called the police. Eighteen months later, Jacob was convicted of two counts of first-degree murder and sentenced to life without parole. According to Jacob's older brother, Charles, the murders ended years of physical and sexual abuse of both boys at the hands of their stepfather and of emotional betrayal by their mother. At Jacob's trial, Charles testified that their stepfather would wait for the boys to get home from school, then drag them into the bathroom, tie them with ropes to the toilet, and sexually molest them. Jacob claimed that his mother made it absolutely clear that she hated him (Jacob) and "[to] a child, that is more hurtful than getting hit across the face or getting beaten."

Jacob Ind spent more than 25 years in prison, including eight years in solitary confinement. He was released in 2020 in light of the *Montgomery* case. Despite earning a bachelor's degree in biblical studies while incarcerated, Ind has

struggled on the outside. He claims that "door after door" has been slammed in his face as he tried to explain his criminal history to potential employers and landlords.

Critical Thought Question

Research on brain development shows that the adolescent brain is a work in progress, not fully mature with an intact frontal lobe—responsible for reasoning and judgment—until sometime between the ages of 25 and 30. Some psychologists (e.g., Steinberg, 2017) contend that this means adolescents are fundamentally different from adults and warrant differential treatment by the law. On the other hand, there is a great deal of variability in brain and behavioral development among same-aged teenagers, and some older adolescents are comparable to young adults in psychological maturity. Should these factors be considered in determining the appropriate punishment for a juvenile offender? For Jacob Ind? Would your decision be affected by learning that psychologists are not particularly good at predicting adult functioning from snapshots of teenage behavior?

(Knighton et al., 2014). But although recidivism is hard to measure—after all, sex crimes happen behind closed doors, they often go unreported, and researchers calculate recidivism in varying ways—the data tend to show otherwise. A meta-analysis of recidivism rates in approximately 4,900 treated and 5,400 untreated individuals convicted of sexual offenses showed low sexual recidivism rates overall, with just 10.1% of treated and 13.7% of untreated offenders recidivating sexually (Schmucker & Losel, 2015). So the majority of individuals convicted of sexual offenses were *not* rearrested for another sex crime. Further, the likelihood of sexual reoffending after 10–15 years in the community is equivalent to that of people who were convicted of nonsexual offenses (Hanson et al., 2018). A consistent finding across studies is that sex offenders who *do* reoffend are far more likely to commit a nonsexual rather than a sexual offense (U.S. Department of Justice, 2017).

But in a number of ways, judges and corrections professionals do treat individuals who offend sexually differently than other offenders. Prior to being sentenced, individuals convicted of sexual offenses undergo risk assessment evaluations that inform judges' decisions about the appropriate sentence, custody level, or community placement and help determine treatment needs, settings, and modalities. Upon release from prison, these individuals are required to register with state officials, who then publicly notify the community about the location of their residence. They are prohibited from living within certain distances of schools, day-care facilities, parks, and other locations frequented by children, and can be involuntarily committed to a mental health facility following the completion of their sentence. In addition, these individuals can be subjected to extraordinary sanctions, including enhanced sentences and mandatory treatments.

Many of these actions are guided by formal risk assessments in which evaluators provide important information about the risk to public safety that such individuals pose. Several specialized actuarial measures or structured professional judgment measures have now been validated on sex offender populations (Douglas & Otto, 2021; van den Berg et al., 2017) and show respectable levels of predictive accuracy (U.S. Department of Justice, 2017). Obviously, these instruments cannot predict with perfect accuracy that a given individual will behave in any particular way, but especially when combined with individualized clinical risk assessments, they can be quite useful in gauging the likelihood of future behavior (Slobogin, 2011).

Registration and Notification

All 50 states and the federal government have registration and notification laws in place for individuals convicted of sexual offenses. Such individuals are required to register with a local law enforcement agency after they are released from prison (registration) and officials can disseminate information about their whereabouts to the public (notification). The intent of these laws is to deter sexual offending, reduce recidivism, and increase public safety.

The period of required registration depends on the classification of the individual, which is a product of a formal risk assessment. In Kentucky, for example, high-risk individuals are required to register for life, whereas moderate- or low-risk individuals must register for 10 years after their formal sentence is completed. In the U.S., the federal government and approximately 40 states also require juveniles, including youth whose sexual offense charges were resolved in juvenile courts, to register as sex offenders, sometimes for life. Unfortunately, many do not register, and others fail to inform authorities when they move, and a lack of resources within jurisdictions hinders follow-up. One investigation revealed that California authorities lost track of more than 33,000 individuals convicted of sexual offenses who were registered at one point (Associated Press, 2003).

Notification is more controversial than registration. In the past, some states (New Jersey, for example) had police go door to door to notify neighbors that a high-risk individual convicted of a sexual offense had moved into the neighborhood (Witt & Barone, 2004). Now though, states and the federal government rely on the Internet as the primary means of notification. Typically, individuals' names are placed online for the period of their required registration, and law enforcement officials take no further steps to notify the community. But online notification appears to be plagued by the worst of two extremes. On the one hand, it is over-inclusive; the entire world can learn about the individual, even though only one or a few communities really need to know. On the other hand, online notification is under-inclusive; persons who cannot or do not regularly access the relevant website will not be made aware that such an individual is living in the neighborhood.

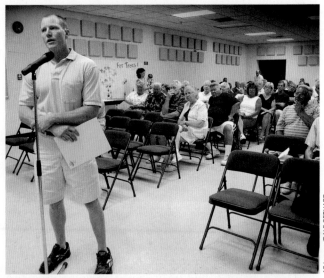

Steve Elwell, left, a registered sex offender in Cape May County, N.J., speaks during a council meeting, opposing local ordinance that bans sex offenders from residing or loitering within 2,500 feet of schools and public areas.

Internet posting also raises concerns about invasion of privacy. No matter how minor the offense, states and the federal government post individuals' personal information (sometimes including their photos) online for all to see. Those convicted of murder could move to a new community, safe in the knowledge that their past, although a matter of public record, is not readily accessible to friends and neighbors. But individuals registered as a sex offender will know that their past is available to anyone in the world at the touch of a screen.

How effective are sex offender registration and notification laws at meeting their objectives of deterrence and protection of the public? For adult offenders, the data are inconclusive: some studies show lower rates of sexual reoffending after implementation of registration and notification requirements, but others do not (U.S. Department of Justice, 2017). (As we describe in Box 14.4, registration and notification do nothing to restrain some from committing additional, horrific crimes.) The picture for juveniles is somewhat clearer: findings show no changes in recidivism or prevention measures from before to after the registry requirements were put in place (e.g., Sandler et al., 2017). Even so, the public tends to believe that the laws prevent reoffending (Schiavone & Jeglic, 2009). So paradoxically, community members *think* the laws make them safer, but data to support their beliefs are lacking.

Interestingly, according to Lasher and McGrath (2012), many offenders share the belief that registration and notification make communities safer, and that they deter offending. But there are discernible downsides to these laws for offenders, also documented by Lasher and McGrath. Offenders report feelings of stress and isolation, threats and harassment, property damage, and loss of jobs and housing.

Residency Restrictions

In the best-selling novel *Lost Memory of Skin*, the main character is a young man, recently released from prison and on probation for soliciting an underage female. He is shackled to a GPS device and forbidden from living within 2,500 feet of places where children congregate. Though fictional, the story takes place in the all-too-real community of people convicted of sexual offenses that sprang up under the Julia Tuttle Causeway in Miami.

To manage the risk posed by such individuals, residency restrictions were enacted by most states and hundreds of communities. They establish a "buffer zone" around schools, parks, and even bus stops in which those convicted of sexual offenses may not live. Though the laws vary with regard to the size of the area, the group of individuals to whom they apply, and whether they also restrict places of employment, all such laws are premised on the idea that such individuals are opportunistic and seek victims in public places. But an

---

Box 14.4

The Case of John Albert Gardner III: Registered as a Sex Offender and Confessed to Homicide

In 2000, 21-year-old John Albert Gardner III was convicted of luring a 13-year-old neighbor into his mother's home in an upscale community north of San Diego and punching and molesting the child. A psychiatrist who interviewed Gardner recommended a 30-year sentence, noting that Gardner lacked remorse and would continue to pose a danger to young women in the area. But prosecutors wanted to spare the victim from testifying and

John Albert Gardner III is a convicted sex offender.

accepted a plea bargain that landed Gardner behind bars for five years. He was released in 2008 and registered as a sex offender.

Registration did little to quell Gardner's urges. Later that year he attempted to rape a jogger in a park near Escondido, California. Two months later, he killed 14-year-old Amber Dubois, who vanished while walking to school, and 17-year-old Chelsea King, whom Gardner admitted to raping and strangling in the same park. To avoid the death penalty, Gardner pleaded guilty to all of these crimes. King's parents championed legislation, fittingly named "Chelsea's Law," that allows life without parole sentences for offenders who kidnap, drug, or use a weapon against a child and requires lifetime parole with GPS tracking for offenders who commit forcible sex crimes against children under age 14. Former Governor Arnold Schwarzenegger signed the law in 2010.

Critical Thought Question

Gardner registered as a sex offender. So why did registration have no apparent effect on his pattern of sexual offending?

estimated 79–93% of sexual offenses are committed by a person known to the victim (Mercado, 2009), typically in a private setting, which raises questions about the effectiveness of laws that focus solely on geographic proximity. Residency restrictions result in other problems: they seriously reduce housing options in communities where nearly all residential properties are within the buffer zones (Chajewski & Mercado, 2009), and result in the clustering of those convicted of sexual offenses in more rural areas, making access to jobs, education, and treatment more difficult and destabilizing to offenders. Furthermore, they do not deter recidivism (Socia, 2012).

Although residency restrictions may be a visible way for legislators to attempt to address sexual recidivism, empirical data suggest that they will have little impact. In fact, policies that entail registration, notification and residency restrictions, though well-intended, exemplify **crime control theater**, because they were enacted in response to a moral panic and inspired by fear and folk logic about crime, rather than by any research evidence to support their effectiveness (e.g., DeVault et al., 2016).

Involuntary Commitment

Another form of sanction imposed on individuals with a history of repeated sexual offenses is involuntary commitment to a mental health facility after the prison term has been completed. Whereas prison sentences are intended to punish an offender for past bad acts, involuntary commitment is intended to protect the public from future harms.

The leading case on this topic is *Kansas v. Hendricks* (1997). Leroy Hendricks was "every parent's nightmare" (Kolebuck, 1998, p. 537). He was in his 60s when, in 1994, he was scheduled to be released from a Kansas prison where he had served 10 years for child molestation, following a long history of sexually abusing children. But he told a Kansas judge that only his death would guarantee that he would never commit another sexual offense on a child. Kansas had recently passed a Sexually Violent Predator (SVP) Act, allowing for the involuntary commitment of offenders suffering a "mental abnormality" that would make them likely to commit predatory acts of sexual violence. A Kansas judge determined that Hendricks was an SVP and committed him to a psychiatric hospital where he stayed for ten years prior to release. In *Kansas v. Hendricks*, the U.S. Supreme Court deemed the SVP Act to be constitutional.

Court rulings on SVP laws make clear that selected individuals must have a "mental abnormality" or personality disorder that predisposes them to sexual violence and makes them undeterred by the prospect of further punishment (Slobogin, 2011). In making assessments of "mental abnormality," evaluators typically use the diagnostic criteria for pedophilia, paraphilia, or antisocial personality disorder set out in the *Diagnostic and Statistical Manual*. The U.S. Supreme Court has also said that individuals subjected to SVP laws must be unable to control their behavior and thus, likely to commit future sexually violent crimes (*Kansas v. Crane*, 2002).

Professor Stephen Morse has raised concerns about the role of the *Hendricks* case in striking a balance between the due process and crime control models of criminal justice (Morse, 1998). He asserted that in its quest for public safety, society is now willing to punish people who are merely *at risk for* reoffending, in essence punishing them more severely than they deserve.

Yet, predictably, other states passed statutes similar to the Kansas statute. Nearly half the states and the federal government have enacted some form of civil authorization for the involuntary commitment of sex offenders, though only a tiny fraction of sex offenders are designated as SVPs. Once an individual is committed, release is rare. By 2007, almost 2,700 persons had been committed as SVPs, but only about 250 had been released, half on technical or legal grounds unrelated to treatment (Davey & Goodnough, 2007). There are not yet sufficient numbers of released offenders to allow researchers to gauge the impact of this sanction (U.S. Department of Justice, 2017).

Mandated Treatments

Unlike other offenders, individuals convicted of sexual offenses are often required to undergo treatment designed to "cure" them of their antisocial tendencies. Those sentenced to prison are required to participate in offender treatment programs or give up hope of parole; those offered probation are required to participate in counseling sessions. These typically involve cognitive-behavioral interventions that require offenders to acknowledge wrongdoing and that challenge their rationalizations, minimizations (e.g., "no one was hurt"), and other erroneous beliefs that support the commission of the offense. Treatment may also include an assortment of behavior modification techniques, including aversive conditioning that pairs aversive stimuli such as mild electric shock with deviant sexual responses. Over time, the deviant behavior is expected to decrease. Treatment programs that combine cognitive behavioral therapy with relapse prevention and that focus on an offender's risk of reoffending and responsiveness to treatment have been successful in reducing recidivism (Hanson et al., 2009; Kim et al., 2016). These programs have more risk-reduction impact on high risk individuals (Lovins et al., 2009).

Some treatment programs have effectively reduced sexual offending by suppressing individuals' sex drive. This pharmacological approach, sometimes called **chemical castration**, involves administering hormones to reduce testosterone levels and thereby lower sex drive, sexual arousal, and sexual fantasizing. Therapists have also had some success using selective serotonin reuptake inhibitors (SSRIs) to reduce deviant sexual behavior. This class of drugs may reduce intrusive or obsessive thoughts associated with sexual offending (Marshall et al., 2006). In the past, judges have sometimes given convicted sex offenders a choice: prison or hormone treatment. It is not surprising that some men have opted for the drugs, even though the possible side effects include lethargy, hot flashes, nightmares, hypertension, and shortness of breath (Keene, 1997).

California was the first state to pass a law requiring those convicted of repeated child molestation to be treated with hormones as a condition of parole. The California statute requires that clinicians assess offenders to determine whether they display the symptoms of a condition (e.g., **pedophilia disorder**) that creates a substantial risk of reoffending. If so, the California legislature reasoned, it makes sense to deny parole unless the offender agrees to the treatment.

The Death Penalty: The Ultimate Punishment

The ultimate punishment, of course, is death. Unlike sentences imposed in nearly all other criminal cases (i.e., by judges), a decision to sentence someone to death is made by a jury, reflecting the enormous gravity of capital punishment.

Citizens of the United States can be executed by the governments of 27 states. (As of May 2022, three of those states and the federal government had a moratorium on executions.) A 2021 poll of approximately 5,000 Americans showed that 60% believe the death penalty is morally justified for people convicted of murder, though support for capital punishment, and the frequency of executions, have both waned since the late 1990s. A large share of the population also has serious concerns about the fairness of capital punishment and the possibility that an innocent person will be put to death (Pew Research Center, 2021).

The modern history of capital punishment in the United States began in 1972 when the U.S. Supreme Court effectively abolished the death penalty on the grounds that it constituted "cruel and unusual punishment" (*Furman v. Georgia*, 1972). After the *Furman* case, state legislatures revised their death penalty laws to address the Court's concern that capital punishment was being applied in an arbitrary and discriminatory fashion as a consequence of "unbridled discretion" given to juries resulting in biased death penalty outcomes.

To remedy this problem, states passed statutes that guided the sentencing choices of capital juries. First, only certain crimes became eligible for the death penalty. Second, the structure of capital trials changed. Now, if a defendant is charged with one of these crimes and the prosecutor seeks the death penalty, the trial is conducted in two phases. The jury decides the guilt or innocence of the defendant in the first phase (the "guilt phase"). If the defendant is found guilty, then the second phase, or "sentencing phase," of the trial is held. During this phase, the same jury hears evidence of **aggravating factors** (elements of the crime, such as killing in an especially brutal or heinous manner, that make the defendant more likely to receive a death sentence) and **mitigating factors** (elements of the defendant's background or the crime, such as experiencing mental illness or acting under duress at the time of the offense, that make life imprisonment the more appropriate verdict). Before

Pictured here is a gurney on which prisoners are executed by lethal injection.

reaching a sentencing decision, jurors hear instructions from the judge on how to weigh the aggravating and mitigating factors. Generally, a jury cannot vote for a death sentence unless it determines that the prosecution has proven at least one aggravating factor.

In 1976, in the case of *Gregg v. Georgia*, and in response to these newly enacted laws and procedures, the Supreme Court reinstated the death penalty. Following the *Gregg* decision, state after state began to execute those convicts who had been sentenced to die. Since the death penalty was reintroduced, approximately 1,550 people have been executed. The greatest number (98) were executed in 1999. In 2021, only 18 inmates were executed (Death Penalty Information Center, 2021), an historic low related, in part, to the pandemic. More than 80% of executions since the *Gregg* case have occurred in southern states, and Texas alone accounts for more than one-third of them.

Justifications for the Death Penalty

Many reasons have been advanced for endorsing the irrevocable penalty of death. While he was the mayor of New York City, Ed Koch contended that the death penalty "affirms life." By failing to execute those convicted of murder, he said, we "signal a lessened regard for the value of the victim's life" (quoted by Bruck, 1985, p. 20).

Most justifications for the death penalty reflect retributive beliefs (e.g., "an eye for an eye") and thus extend beyond the capacity of empirical research to prove or disprove. But a testable argument for capital punishment is the expectation that it will act as a deterrent to criminal activity. Proponents of this position suggest that (1) the death penalty accomplishes general, as well as specific, deterrence; (2) highly publicized executions have at least a short-term deterrent effect; and (3) murderers are such dangerous people that allowing them to live increases the risk of injury or death to other inmates and prison guards.

Using a variety of empirical approaches, social scientists have evaluated the deterrent effects of the death penalty, and their studies consistently lead to the conclusion that the death penalty does not affect the rate of crimes of violence (e.g., Zimring et al., 2010.) The American public is also skeptical of any deterrent effects (Pew Research Center, 2021). Evidence also contradicts the view that those convicted of murders are especially dangerous inmates. A good deal of data indicate that such individuals tend to commit fewer violent offenses and prison infractions than parole-eligible inmates (Cunningham, 2010).

Equality versus Discretion in Application of the Death Penalty

Does the death penalty further the goal of equal treatment before the law? Only about half of the states permit it, and remarkably, only 2% of U.S. counties have been responsible for the majority of executions since the penalty was reinstated (Death Penalty Information Center, 2021). Even in those states where the sentence is on the books,

only a small subset of eligible individuals is charged with capital murder, the crime punishable by death. So if equal treatment is the goal, it is safe to say that the death penalty has not furthered that goal. In the words of former Supreme Court Justice Potter Stewart, receiving a death sentence is like "being struck by lightning for a capriciously selected random handful" (*Furman v. Georgia*, 1972, p. 309).

Another concern is the issue of race, particularly of the victim. Although victims of intentional homicide are equally divided between Blacks and Whites, the chance of a death sentence is much greater for offenders who kill Whites than those who kill Blacks (though Devine and Kelly [2015] paint a more complex picture of the relationship). In fact, data from governmental and capital defense organizations show that between the late 1970s and the early 2000s, there was tremendous racial disparity in death sentences. So, for example, between 1990 and 1999, California offenders who killed Whites were more than three times more likely to receive the death penalty than offenders who killed Blacks, and more than four times more likely than offenders who killed Latinos (Pierce & Radelet, 2005).

The leading Supreme Court case on the issue of race and application of the death penalty, *McCleskey v. Kemp* (1987), considered this issue. The question was whether the death penalty discriminated against persons who murdered Whites. We describe McCleskey's case in Box 14.5.

Box 14.5

The Case of Warren McCleskey: Does Race Matter?

Warren McCleskey, a Black man, was convicted in 1978 of armed robbery and the murder of a White police officer who had responded to an alarm while the robbery was in progress. McCleskey was sentenced to die in Georgia's electric chair. He challenged the constitutionality of the death penalty on the ground that it was administered in a racially discriminatory manner in Georgia. In the words of one of his attorneys, "When you kill the organist at the Methodist Church, who is White, you're going to get the death penalty, but if you kill the Black Baptist organist, the likelihood is that it will be plea bargained down to a life sentence" (quoted by Noble, 1987, p. 7).

The foundation for McCleskey's appeal was a comprehensive study of race and capital sentencing in the state of Georgia conducted by David Baldus, a law professor at the University of Iowa, and his colleagues. They analyzed the race of the offender and the race of the victim for about 2,000 murder and manslaughter convictions from 1973 to 1979 and concluded that those who killed Whites were 11 times more likely to receive the death penalty than those who killed Blacks (Baldus et al., 1983). Anticipating the

argument that the heinousness of the murders may explain this finding, Baldus and colleagues eliminated cases in which extreme violence or other aggravating circumstances virtually ensured the death penalty and cases in which overwhelming mitigating circumstances almost guaranteed a life sentence. For the remaining cases—which permitted the greatest jury discretion—they found that defendants were about four times more likely to be sentenced to death if their victims were White.

Despite the mass of statistical evidence, the Supreme Court upheld McCleskey's death sentence. Because there was no evidence that individual jurors in his trial were biased, the Court was unwilling to assume that McCleskey's jury valued a White life more than a Black life. Interestingly, at the end of his career, Supreme Court Justice Lewis Powell, who authored the 5-4 decision, said it was the one ruling he regretted.

Critical Thought Question

What legally irrelevant factors in McCleskey's case—in addition to the race of the victim—may have increased the likelihood that he would be sentenced to die for his crime?

Psychologists have determined that not all Black offenders are equally likely to be sentenced to death for killing a White person. Professor Jennifer Eberhardt and her colleagues showed to Stanford undergraduates the photographs of 44 Black offenders whose trials advanced to the penalty phase in Philadelphia between 1979 and 1999, and asked them to rate the stereotypicality of each offender's appearance. Controlling for other factors that influence sentencing, such as the severity of the murder and the defendant's and victim's socioeconomic status, researchers found that offenders whose appearance was rated as more stereotypically Black were more likely to have received the death penalty than offenders whose appearance was less stereotypical (Eberhardt et al., 2006). Apparently, offenders' appearance can also lead to unequal treatment in the administration of capital punishment.

Capital Jury Decision Making

The *Furman* and *Gregg* cases, pivotal challenges to the constitutionality of the death penalty, focused on the role of the jury in capital cases. For this reason, it is not surprising that there has been intense public and scientific scrutiny of two aspects of capital jury decision making: the process of selecting jurors in capital cases, and the ability of those jurors to understand and apply the sentencing instructions they receive from the judge.

How Jurors are Selected in Capital Cases: "Death Qualification."
During jury selection in cases in which the prosecutor seeks a death penalty, prospective jurors are required to answer questions about their attitudes toward capital punishment. This procedure is called **death qualification**. If jurors indicate extreme opposition to the death penalty, they may be excused "for cause" and dismissed from that case. Prospective jurors dismissed for this reason are termed *excludables*, and those who remain are termed *death qualified*. (Another group of prospective jurors—those who would automatically impose the death penalty at every opportunity—so-called "automatic death penalty" jurors—are also dismissed for cause, although they are far fewer in number than "excludables.") Death-qualified jurors are qualified to impose the death penalty because they do not have strong scruples or reservations for or against it.

Death qualification raises some important issues. Recall that capital cases involve two phases but only one jury to decide both guilt and punishment. Although excludable jurors might be unwilling to impose the death penalty, many could fairly determine the guilt or innocence of the defendant. Yet death qualification procedures deny them the opportunity to make a decision. These procedures raise concerns about the leanings of jurors who *do* assess guilt, concerns that have grown over the years.

Intuitively, one might expect that death-qualified juries (those made up of people who are not opposed to the death penalty) would be somewhat more conviction prone than the general population. Indeed, research studies have

demonstrated the conviction-proneness of death-qualified juries (Cowan et al., 1984; Thompson et al., 1984).

Some social scientists have evaluated whether waning support for the death penalty, apparent in many polls, affects the composition and decision making of capital juries. Garrett et al. (2017) surveyed people reporting for jury duty in Orange County, California, one of the leading U.S. counties in terms of death sentences imposed. Remarkably, given the conservative political leanings of Orange County, 35% of prospective jurors met the criterion for "excludable" and roughly 25% said they would be reluctant to find a person guilty of capital murder if that meant the person might be executed. Compared with numbers from the 1980s, more people today would be dismissed because of their opposition to capital punishment. Who remains? An even narrower swath of the population, less racially diverse, and even less representative of their communities. Via in-depth telephone surveys with people who would be deemed "death qualified" in locations as diverse as California, New Hampshire, and Florida, another team of researchers found that, compared with "excludables," death qualified people were more punitive, less well-informed about capital sentencing, more willing to use aggravating factors, and less willing to use mitigating factors (Haney et al., 2022). As a result, prosecutors may be even more likely to obtain a conviction now than they were in the past.

Clearly, death-qualified juries are more disposed toward conviction than juries that include a cross-section of the community. In the mid-80s, lawyers for Ardia McCree made that argument before the U.S. Supreme Court (*Lockhart v. McCree*, 1986). At McCree's trial, an Arkansas judge excluded eight prospective jurors who said that they could not impose a death sentence. McCree was convicted and sentenced to death. He appealed his conviction by arguing that death qualification produced juries that were likely to be conviction prone and unrepresentative of the larger community.

In spite of the substantial body of empirical support for McCree's position, the Supreme Court held that his jury was not an improper one. An impartial jury, Chief Justice William Rehnquist wrote, "consists of nothing more than jurors who will conscientiously apply the law and find the facts." Because McCree conceded that each of the jurors who convicted him met that test, the Court upheld the state's use of a death-qualified jury for the guilt phase.

How Capital Jurors Use Instructions.
Jurors in capital cases receive a set of complex instructions that explain how to evaluate and weigh aggravating and mitigating circumstances to reach a sentencing decision. Several studies indicate that jurors do not adequately comprehend the instructions they receive about mitigating factors because, like other types of judicial instructions, they are couched in legal jargon and are lengthy and grammatically complex (Lynch & Haney, 2009; Smith & Haney, 2011).

If jurors do not understand the judge's instructions, they are more likely to rely on other, more familiar factors to guide their verdicts, such as the heinousness of the crime or extralegal considerations such as racial stereotypes, sympathy for victims, or the presumed expertise of the lawyers. For example, Lynch and Haney (2000) found that jury-eligible participants with poor comprehension of sentencing instructions recommended death 68% of the time for Black-defendant/White-victim cases versus 36% of the time for White-defendant/Black-victim cases. Among participants who comprehended instructions well, neither the race of the defendant nor that of the victim affected their sentences.

Would jurors fare better if these all-important instructions were presented in a different format? Richard Wiener and colleagues posed this question. They tested various methods of improving jurors' **declarative knowledge** (their understanding of legal concepts) and **procedural knowledge** (their ability to know what to do in order to reach a sentencing decision) in a highly realistic trial simulation that involved both the guilt and sentencing phases of a capital murder trial (Wiener et al., 2004). Modifications to the instructions involved (1) simplifying the language, (2) presenting instructions in a flowchart format, (3) giving jurors the chance to review and use the instructions in a mock case prior to the real trial, and (4) offering corrections to common misconceptions about aggravating and mitigating circumstances. Each of these modifications was helpful in enhancing some aspect of jurors' declarative and procedural knowledge.

Concerns about Innocence

David Protess, a Northwestern University journalism professor, drew attention to the possibility of "executing the innocent" when students under his supervision tracked down and obtained confessions from true killers, thereby exonerating two men on death row. We do not know exactly how many innocent people have been sentenced to death. One estimate is that 2.3% of those sentenced to death may actually be innocent (Gross & O'Brien, 2007). Another estimate puts the figure at 5% (Risinger, 2007). We also do not know exactly how many innocent people have been executed, though some have.

Since executions resumed after the *Gregg* case, 186 people have been freed from death rows upon proof of their innocence (Death Penalty Information Center, 2021). That number translates to one exoneration for every 8.3 executions. Some of these condemned individuals were cleared when new evidence came to light or when witnesses changed their stories. DNA evidence is credited with proving the innocence of scores of death row inmates (Gross et al., 2005). As a result of these widely publicized errors, some states give death row inmates the right to post-conviction DNA testing, though the Supreme Court has ruled that states are not required to provide such testing (*District Attorney's Office for Third Judicial District v. Osborne,* 2009).

What can account for so many errors? A study that analyzed every capital conviction in the United States between 1973 and 1995 revealed that serious mistakes were made in two-thirds of the cases, a startling indictment of the criminal justice system (Liebman, 2000). The most common problems included incompetent defense attorneys (37%), faulty jury instructions (20%), and misconduct on the part of prosecutors (19%).

Is the death penalty still justified if we know that innocent people have been executed? Some proponents insist that it is, invoking the analogy that administering a vaccine is justified even though a child might have an adverse—even lethal—reaction to it. Proponents of capital punishment suggest that even though innocent people are occasionally and mistakenly put to death, other compelling reasons justify maintaining this system of punishment.

Limiting Use of the Death Penalty

Another highly controversial aspect of the death penalty has been its use in cases where the defendant, for reasons of youth, intellectual disability, dementia, or mental illness, may not be fully culpable. The Supreme Court has deemed the death penalty unconstitutional for youthful offenders (*Roper v. Simmons,* 2005), so no one can be executed for crimes committed prior to age 18. But controversies linger regarding intellectual disabilities, dementia, and mental illness, primarily in terms of their diagnosis and assessment. Psychologists often play a vital role in these cases, evaluating and rendering expert opinions on questions concerning defendants' cognitive abilities and whether they meet diagnostic criteria for various psychiatric disorders.

Intellectual Disability. In 2002, the Supreme Court ruled that it was cruel and unusual punishment, in violation of the Eighth Amendment, to execute people with intellectual disabilities (*Atkins v. Virginia,* 2002). This landmark ruling reflected awareness that those with limited intellectual abilities often cannot understand the consequences of their actions, the complex and abstract concepts involved in criminal law, or the finality of a death sentence.

But the Court offered only general guidance about how intellectual abilities should be measured and left interpretation of their ruling to the states, which took different approaches (Taylor & Krauss, 2014). Florida, for example, took a "bright line approach," deeming an IQ score of 70 "subaverage." (An IQ score of 100 is considered average.) So, according to Florida law, an offender with an IQ score of 71 is not intellectually disabled.

Now consider the case of Freddie Hall, who was convicted and sentenced to death for murdering a 21-year-old pregnant woman and a deputy sheriff in 1978. After the *Atkins* decision, Hall's attorneys petitioned to have his death sentence reconsidered, arguing that his intellectual disability exempted him from the death penalty. At one point, he scored as low as 60. But when tested in the process of his appeal, Hall's IQ score was (you probably guessed) 71. His appeal to the Supreme Court contended that the 70-point

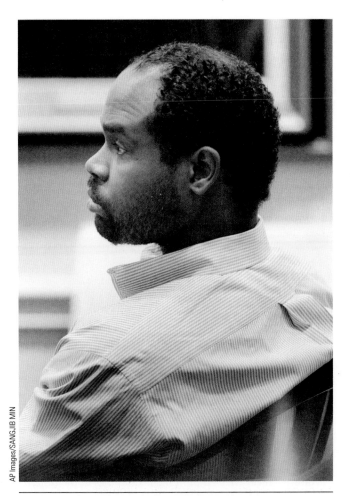

AP Images/SANGJIB MIN

Daryl Atkins's case led to the Supreme Court ruling that the execution of people with intellectual disability is unconstitutional and cruel.

cutoff was overly rigid and that IQ scores should be interpreted as part of a range. (Indeed, the manual that accompanies the IQ test interprets scores within confidence intervals to account for measurement error, and the 95 percent **confidence interval**—a range within which we can be 95% sure that the actual score rests—for an IQ score of 70 is between 67.5 and 72.5.) The Supreme Court agreed with Hall, noting that an IQ test has a standard error of measurement that should have been considered (*Hall v. Florida,* 2014).

This decision means that states with fixed cutoff scores must use a broader range of scores that take measurement error into account. This position squares with psychological research showing that IQ scores change over time (Trahan et al., 2014), and can be influenced by literacy skills (Marks, 2011), different levels of IQ (Spitz, 1989), and who administered the test (McDermott et al., 2014).

Dementia. A similar question—whether the Eighth Amendment prohibition of cruel and unusual punishment applies to people whose mental disability renders them unable to understand why they are being executed—arose in the case of *Madison v. Alabama* (2019). But in

this instance, the issue was the offender's vascular dementia. Vernon Madison had suffered several serious strokes during the 30 years he spent on death row in Alabama. He challenged his competency to be executed because the strokes resulted in brain damage, blindness, slurred speech, and memory loss. In a 5-3 decision (Justice Kavanaugh took no part), the Court ruled that the death penalty is unconstitutional if defendants' dementia robs them of the "capacity to understand why the state is exacting death as a punishment."

Mental Illness. Is it unconstitutional to execute an inmate who, because of a serious mental illness, lacks a rational understanding of why they are being put to death? That question was posed to the U.S. Supreme Court in the case of *Panetti v. Quarterman* (2007).

In 1992, Scott Panetti killed his estranged wife's parents, with whom his wife had been living in Fredericksburg, Texas, and held his wife and 3-year-old daughter hostage in a lengthy police standoff. Panetti had a history of psychiatric problems prior to his conviction, including 14 hospital stays over 11 years. During earlier stages of the case, four mental health professionals agreed that Panetti displayed symptoms of impaired cognitive processes and delusions consistent with schizoaffective disorder. Scott Panetti believed that the government was executing him to prevent him from preaching the Gospel, not because he murdered his in-laws.

The American Psychological Association (APA) teamed with the National Alliance on Mental Illness to assist the Court in developing standards for determining what level of mental illness should exempt an offender from execution. In its *amicus curiae* brief to the Supreme Court, the APA distinguished factual understanding from rational understanding. According to one of the authors of this book who consulted on the APA brief (Heilbrun), "factual understanding is about information. Rational understanding allows us to place that information in a meaningful context, without gross interference caused by certain symptoms of severe mental illness, or very serious impairment of intellectual functioning" (Medical News Today, 2007). The APA brief explained that some individuals who experience psychotic disorders have bizarre delusions that disrupt their understanding of reality and make it difficult or impossible for them to connect their criminal acts to punishment.

The Supreme Court ruled that Panetti's delusions may have prevented him from understanding the reason for his punishment. The decision effectively means that defendants with a mental illness may not be executed if they do not understand *why* they are being put to death.

The question of whether Dylann Roof, the young man who murdered nine Black parishioners in South Carolina in 2016, was also acting under delusional beliefs, may never be answered because Roof refused to allow mental health evidence to be used at his trial. We describe his case, including information about his mental health, in Box 14.6.

Box 14.6

The Case of Dylann Roof: (Lack of) Evidence about Mental Illness

In one of the many cold-blooded mass murders in recent history, White supremacist Dylann Roof walked into Emanuel African Methodist Episcopal Church in Charleston, South Carolina during Bible study on June 17, 2015. A Glock semiautomatic handgun was hidden in his clothing. Roof was offered a spot in the prayer circle where he sat for approximately 45 minutes before opening fire, shooting randomly at the twelve congregants and killing nine of them. Roof confessed immediately, saying that he chose churchgoers as his victims to gain notoriety. He stated that he committed the murders as a wake-up call to persecuted Whites, and that he hoped his attack would increase racial tensions and lead to a race war.

Was Roof's thinking delusional? We may never know because he refused to allow evidence of his mental health status to be used during his capital murder trial. (He also opted to represent himself without a lawyer in the penalty phase, which some would argue is either delusional or reflects extraordinarily poor judgment.) But in court documents unsealed after Roof's conviction and death sentence, a court-appointed psychiatrist who evaluated Roof a few months after the shooting concluded that he "suffers from Social Anxiety Disorder, a Mixed Substance Abuse Disorder, a Schizoid Personality Disorder, depression by history, and a possible Autistic Spectrum Disorder (Sack, 2017)." The document also stated that "the defendant's high IQ is compromised by a significant discrepancy between this ability to comprehend and to process information and a poor working memory." Did these disorders and discrepancies seriously impair Roof's thinking? Do they indicate a deep-seated psychosis or delusion? Since Roof was "steadfastly committed to preventing any public examination of his mental state or background" (Sack &

Charleston County Sheriff's Office Detention Center

0001518680   Name: ROOF, DYLANN STORM

Date of Birth: 04/03/94   Booking Date: 06/18/15

Race: W   Sex: M   Height: 0'0"

Dylan Roof

Blinder, 2017), no psychiatric or psychological expertise was introduced at his trial. In prominent headlines at the time, "Dylann Roof himself rejects best defense against execution" (Sack & Blinder).

Critical Thought Question

According to Supreme Court decisions concerning mental illness and the death penalty, what level of understanding must Dylann Roof possess in order to be put to death?

Summary

1. **What are the purposes of punishment?** Punishment is associated with seven purposes: general deterrence, individual deterrence, incapacitation, retribution, expression of moral outrage, rehabilitation, and restitution. Although many citizens favor the punitive approaches of retribution and incapacitation, recidivism data suggest that these approaches may not be effective. A different perspective on punishment, restorative justice, brings people together to repair the damage caused by wrongdoing.

2. **How are the values of discretion and fairness reflected in sentencing decisions?** The allocation of punishments is second only to the determination of guilt in importance to the criminal defendant. The sentencing process reflects many of the conflicts that permeate a psychological approach to the legal system. Historically, judges were given broad discretion in sentencing. Some judges were much more severe than the norm; others were more lenient. Concern over sentencing disparity led to greater use of determinate sentencing and tighter

controls over judicial discretion in sentencing. Now, sentencing guidelines are merely advisory, however.

3. **What factors influence sentencing decisions?** Determinants of sentencing can be divided into relevant and irrelevant factors. For example, the seriousness of the crime is a relevant factor, and there is a general relationship between it and the severity of punishment. An offender's criminal history is another relevant determinant, typically considered. But a number of other, less relevant factors such as the race and gender of the offender and victim, are also related to the severity of the sentence.

4. **What special factors are considered in the sentencing of juveniles? Of those convicted of sexual offenses?** Sentences for those adjudicated delinquent are influenced by the setting in which the minor is sentenced (juvenile court, criminal court), the seriousness of the offense, the offender's rehabilitative needs, and professionals' recommendations. Because they are believed to be at high risk for reoffending, those convicted of sexual offenses have been singled out for special punishment, including mandatory registration and community notification, residency restrictions, involuntary commitment, and enhanced sentences and pharmacological treatment.

5. **How is the death penalty decided by juries?** Jurors who oppose the death penalty regardless of the nature of the crime or the circumstances of the case are excluded from both the guilt phase and the sentencing phase of capital trials. Social science research has shown that the remaining so-called death-qualified jurors are conviction prone. But the Supreme Court has not been responsive to these findings. Capital juries tend to misunderstand their instructions, particularly regarding mitigating evidence.

6. **How has the Supreme Court limited the use of capital punishment, and what role have psychologists played in these decisions?** The Supreme Court has deemed the death penalty unconstitutional in cases in which the defendant was younger than 18 at the time of the crime, and in which the defendant is intellectually disabled (though assessing intellectual disability has been a challenge.) The Supreme Court has also indicated that executing those with dementia or mental illness may be limited if such defendants do not understand the reasons for their execution. Psychologists have been involved in these cases to assess offenders' cognitive abilities, diagnose mental illness, and provide data to the court about decision making and judgment.

Key Terms

aggravating factors

anchoring

assimilated

back-end sentencing

blended sentencing

chemical castration

confidence interval

crime control theater

culpability

death qualification

declarative knowledge

determinate sentencing

dispositional phase

evidence-based sentencing

focal concerns theory

front-end sentencing

indeterminate sentencing

mandatory minimum
  sentences

mitigating factors

pedophilia disorder

policy capturing

procedural knowledge

recidivism

restorative justice

retributive

sentencing disparities

shaming penalty

utilitarian

Chapter 15

Juvenile and Adult Corrections

Orienting Questions

1. What are the important considerations in assessing juveniles prior to placement decisions?

2. What is the evidence for the effectiveness of interventions with juveniles in the community?

3. What are some characteristics of an effective treatment program?

4. How can risk/need/responsivity help to provide effective rehabilitative services for adults?

5. How do specialized problem-solving courts compare to other correctional interventions?

6. What are the differences between jails and prisons and what roles do psychologists play in these settings?

7. What kinds of interventions are delivered in jails and prisons?

8. What are some of the psychological consequences of imprisonment?

9. What are the priorities in preparing individuals for the transition from incarceration to community living (the reentry process)?

At the end of 2019, there were about 6.3 million people under correctional supervision, meaning that 1 in 40 Americans was in prison, on probation, or on parole. Despite an annual average decline of 1.3% each year since 2009, this is still the highest per capita correctional rate in the world (Bureau of Justice Statistics, 2021). Correctional systems also disproportionately target young African American males, with Black men incarcerated in state prison at almost five times the rate of Whites (The Sentencing Project, 2021).

In this final chapter, we discuss the process following a defendant's conviction for a criminal offense. This discussion will include both **adjudication of delinquency** (for juveniles) and **criminal conviction** (for adults). It will address the traditional aspects of corrections—**probation** (community-based supervision instead of incarceration), commitment to juvenile programs, incarceration in jail and prison for adults, and **parole** (community-based supervision following release from incarceration). But there have been some important innovations in correctional practice since 2000—primarily in response to high rates of incarceration—which we will also discuss. In particular, there is now more emphasis on **diversion** and **reentry** (returning from incarceration to the community) as well as increased specialization in the nature of parole and probation and the rehabilitative services delivered. These efforts have resulted from lawmakers' receptiveness to new models of correctional interventions and from increasingly rigorous analyses by psychologists and others of the effectiveness of these programs.

Four major justifications for correctional intervention have been traditionally cited: incapacitation; deterrence (both general, as it applies to others, and specific to the individual convicted); retribution; and rehabilitation. The role of psychology in addressing these goals is focused largely on deterrence and rehabilitation. The question of whether individuals undergoing juvenile or correctional intervention are deterred from committing further offenses is an important topic that psychological research can help address. Deterrence is also related to the goal of rehabilitation. But the rehabilitative question is broader: Has the individual gained skills, changed patterns of thinking, and decreased deficits? Such changes facilitate a more responsible lifestyle. Much of the discussion in this chapter, as it relates to both juveniles and adults, will address how psychology contributes to the broad goals of deterring future crime, enhancing public safety, and rehabilitation.

Juvenile Corrections

Interventions for adjudicated delinquents involve delivering services designed to reduce the risk of future offending, and improve or eliminate deficits that are relevant to such risk. The goal of these interventions is to interrupt the criminal trajectories of young offenders before they become career criminals. This can be done in different settings, ranging from the community to secure residential programs. (In some states, these programs are simply called juvenile prisons.)

It is useful to consider what such interventions might have in common. In 2004, the National Institutes of Health assembled a "state of the science" conference entitled *Preventing Violence and Related Health-Risking Social Behaviors in Adolescents.* Summarizing the evidence presented at this conference, the organizers concluded that there are certain characteristics shared by programs that are successful in reducing the rates of violence, antisocial behavior, and risky health behavior in adolescents:

- They are derived from sound theoretical rationales.
- They address strong risk factors (such as substance abuse, family problems, and educational problems).
- They involve long-term treatments, often lasting a year and sometimes much longer.
- They work intensively with those targeted for treatment and often use a clinical approach.
- They follow a cognitive behavioral strategy.
- They are multimodal and multicontextual (they use different kinds of interventions and deliver them in different contexts, such as home and school).
- They focus on improving social competency and other skill development strategies for targeted youth and/or their families.
- They are developmentally appropriate.
- They are not delivered in coercive institutional settings.
- They have the capacity for delivery with fidelity (meaning that services are delivered as intended).

Likewise, there are common elements of programs that appear to be ineffective:

- They fail to address strong risk factors.
- They are of limited duration.
- They aggregate high-risk youth in ways that facilitate contagion (i.e., the incarcerated youth are influenced by the antisocial behavior modeled by their peers).
- Their implementation protocols are not clearly articulated.
- Their staff are not well supervised or held accountable for outcomes.
- They are limited to scare tactics (e.g., Scared Straight) or toughness strategies (e.g., classic boot camps).
- They consist largely of adults lecturing at youth (e.g., the classic drug abuse resistance education program D.A.R.E.).

This review of the science has promoted further efforts to prevent and reduce youth violence, spurred by national organizations such as the Centers for Disease Control and

Prevention and regional projects such as the Philadelphia Collaborative Violence Prevention Center (consider https://violence.chop.edu/research-and-programs/completed-and-foundational-projects/philadelphia-collaborative-violence). The elements of interventions described in this work have a good deal of applicability to juvenile corrections. Consider them as we discuss strategies, procedures, and outcomes, and try to distinguish between what will be effective and what will not.

Assessing Risk and Needs in Juveniles

There are two important considerations that recur in juvenile forensic assessment: public safety and treatment needs/amenability. The former means that courts, the juvenile system, and the larger society are rightly concerned with the question of whether the juvenile will reoffend following completion of the intervention. The second refers to the youth's deficits, problems, and symptoms, particularly those related to reoffense risk—and whether they can be improved or eliminated through intervention and within the time that is available until the youth "ages out" of eligibility for treatment as a juvenile (Grisso, 1998).

Social scientists have recognized that a number of influences are related to the risk of juvenile offending. For example, the Office of Juvenile Justice and Delinquency Prevention (1995) identified risk factors for future offending in arrested juveniles in a category they termed *serious, violent, and chronic* offenders. These risk factors included age at first justice involvement, number of prior justice involvements, current offense, drug/alcohol problems, school difficulties, negative peers, and family problems. These factors can be either static (with no potential to change through intervention) or dynamic (with the potential to change through intervention). There is evidence that using this classification can be valuable, as the risk and protective factors for youth in the serious/violent/chronic category differ from those in other justice-involved youth (Baglivio et al., 2014) and suggest the importance of earlier intervention in the community for the former group.

Focusing on both risk and risk-relevant needs is an approach that was formally conceptualized in the late 1980s. Andrews, Bonta, and Hoge (1990) described three separate considerations, which they termed **risk, need, and responsivity (RNR)**. Risk refers to the likelihood of committing future offenses, with those at highest risk receiving the most intensive interventions. Needs are the deficits (such as substance abuse, family problems, educational problems, and procriminal attitudes) that increase the risk of reoffending. These are sometimes called **criminogenic needs**. Responsivity involves the likelihood of a favorable reaction to the interventions, and the influences that may affect such responding. It is easy to understand the conceptual relationship between the juvenile priorities of public safety, treatment needs, and treatment amenability on one hand, and the Andrews, Bonta and Hoge concepts of risk, need, and responsivity on the other. Accordingly, the RNR model is a very useful foundation for the evaluation of juveniles (Andrews & Hoge, 2010).

There are two specialized tools in particular that focus on the measurement of juvenile risk and needs: the Structured Assessment of Violence Risk in Youth (SAVRY) (Borum et al., 2005) and the Youth Level of Service/Case Management Inventory (Hoge & Andrews, 2002). Both prompt the user to consider historical factors, such as the nature of current and previous offending, as well as contextual factors (e.g., family, school, peers) and personal factors (e.g., substance abuse, anger, impulsivity, callousness, attitudes toward intervention, offending, and authority). The SAVRY also considers protective influences such as social support, attachment, resilience, and commitment to positive activities. A similar tool, the Risk–Sophistication–Treatment Inventory (Salekin, 2004), also guides the evaluator in appraising influences related to risk and risk-relevant treatment needs. It includes "sophistication" (referring to the youth's adeptness and adult-like attitudes regarding offending), another factor that often appears in the law for decisions on juveniles.

Evaluating youth on the dimensions of risk and needs provides valuable information for several reasons. First, it structures the evaluation to require the psychologist to consider the influences that theory and research indicate are most strongly related to risk and needs. Second, it provides useful information for intervention planning. A specialized risk–needs tool could be used to help the court decide about placement, but could also be used by a program once the youth is placed to help determine what interventions should be provided to that individual. Third, it offers one approach to measuring progress and current status. A youth with deficits in certain areas who begins a program should be reevaluated at different times throughout the program to gauge whether they are making progress in important areas. This affects the assessment of current risk, as well as the needs for additional interventions following completion of the program. A careful evaluation of youth risk and needs is important for planning and future interventions at various levels in the juvenile system (Borum & Verhaagen, 2006; Heilbrun et al., 2017).

Community-Based Interventions

There are a number of approaches to the rehabilitation and management of adjudicated delinquent youth in the community. Youth may be placed on probation, involving a specified set of conditions for which compliance is monitored by the probation officer assigned to the case. A variation on the standard conditions of probation involves **school-based probation**, in which the youth's attendance, performance, and behavior in school are monitored through the probation officer's personal visits to the school. Probation conditions may also include drug use monitoring (through testing blood or urine); substance abuse treatment; mental health treatment; and skills-based training in particular areas (e.g., anger management, decision-making). Probation may also vary in intensity, with intensive probation involving more frequent monitoring contact. Juvenile probation can be guided by developmental and behavioral science in some important ways. For example, psychologist Naomi Goldstein (Stoneleigh Foundation, 2022) has worked on developing Graduated Response, a scientifically informed approach to probation case management for juveniles. It uses a range of responses—positive reinforcement, incentives, constructive feedback, and sanctions—to guide probation officers in assisting youth on their caseloads to comply with probation conditions. It uses the evidence discussed through this chapter indicating that monitoring and coercion alone are less effective than more graduated, developmentally consistent, and rehabilitatively oriented approaches to affecting human behavior in justice contexts. Refer to https://stoneleighfoundation.org/project/enhancing-juvenile-probation-through-graduated-response-implementation/.

Youths who are placed on probation typically live at home. Alternatively, a youth in a community-based placement might participate in a specific program or alternative school during the day but return home at night. Oakland's Evening Reporting Center for juvenile offenders is one such program. In order to remain in the community, adjudicated juveniles must report straight to the Center after school and remain there until 8 P.M. The program provides opportunities to participate in art, music, and sports; a sit-down dinner with caring adults; and a ride home at the end of each evening. Together, these components have contributed to reduced rates of incarceration, particularly for Oakland's minority youths (Porter, 2012).

There is a wide range of specific interventions and broader programs available in the community to youth adjudicated as delinquent. Rather than attempting to describe them all, we focus on three particular community-based interventions for delinquent youth that have been heavily researched: Multisystemic Therapy, Multidimensional Treatment Foster Care, and Functional Family Therapy. On the basis of this research, these interventions can be described as empirically supported, cost-effective, risk-reducing, and amenable to quality assurance monitoring (Henggeler, 2016).

Multisystemic Therapy (MST). As the name implies, Multisystemic Therapy (Henggeler et al., 1998) focuses on multiple "systems": the individual, family, peer, school, and social networks as they relate to identified problems and risk factors for offending. It delivers services based in the home, school, or elsewhere in the community, with three to four therapists working in a team. This increases the frequency of participation well beyond what would be expected from having juveniles and their families come to the program or individual therapist's office. The training of therapists and supervisors in MST is highly standardized (Henggeler & Schoenwald, 1999), and the MST procedures are very clearly specified (Henggeler et al., 1998), so those receiving MST services are likely to receive them as they were intended to be delivered. (Researchers call this "treatment integrity.") Therapists are available 24/7, working to prevent problems or crises in the youth's life from having a major impact. Consequently, the rate of engaging and retaining families in treatment is very high; over the three to six months of direct service usually needed for MST, the retention rates are as high as 98% (Henggeler et al., 1999).

As MST has become more popular, the amount of research on it has grown. The focus on treatment integrity has been important—particularly since studies have supported the link between adherence to MST treatment principles and favorable outcomes (Henggeler, 2016; Markham, 2018). In other words, there is a substantial "quality assurance" component built into MST; this intervention was being provided in more than 34 states and 15 nations as of 2014 (MST Services, 2014).

MST is one of the best-validated interventions for juveniles. A review of 12 studies in which participants were randomly assigned to either MST or individual counseling (the strongest kind of research design, with the random assignment to treatment versus control groups allowing the researcher to draw conclusions about the causal relationship between treatment and outcome) described efficacy of MST when compared with treatment as usual. These treatment effects included reduction of antisocial behavior, including delinquency; reduction of suicidal attempts in youths presenting with psychiatric emergencies; and lower cost (Tan & Fajardo, 2017). Four studies showed that MST was less costly than treatment as usual (TAU) in the short term, with further analysis required for long-term cost-effectiveness.

A long-term (22-year) follow-up of the differences between those who received MST and those who received another intervention (Sawyer & Borduin, 2011) included criminal and civil court outcomes for 176 serious and violent juvenile offenders who participated an average 21.9 years earlier (range = 18.3–23.8) in a clinical trial of MST, or who, alternatively, received individual therapy (IT). Results showed that felony recidivism rates were significantly lower for MST participants than for individual therapy participants (34.8% vs. 54.8%, respectively) and that the frequency of misdemeanor offending was five times lower for MST participants. Also, the odds of involvement in family related civil suits during adulthood were twice as high for IT participants as for MST participants.

There is also evidence that MST is effective with delinquent youth in Great Britain (Butler et al., 2011) and Dutch youth with severe and violent antisocial behavior (Asscher et al., 2013). In the former study, favorable outcomes observed 18 months after MST included reduced offenses (41% decrease), reduced placements (also a 41% decrease), fewer reported signs of delinquency, and improved parenting. The Dutch youth in the latter study showed decreased antisocial behavior and increased association with prosocial peers, with increased parental competence and positive discipline, observed six months after MST was delivered. An important finding in both studies involved the improvements in parenting, and in the relationship between the youth and their parents, reflecting the family as a prioritized aspect of MST.

In addition, there is evidence that MST is effective with juveniles with substance abuse or dependence. Another study using random assignment to MST versus "treatment as usual" for substance-abusing juveniles ($N = 118$) (Henggeler et al., 1999) showed a decrease in drug use, a 50% decrease in time in out-of-home placement, and a 26% decrease in recidivism over a one-year period, while a longer follow-up (four years) yielded significantly reduced violent offending and significantly increased drug use abstinence in the MST group (Henggeler et al., 2002). Finally, a study conducted by the Washington State Institute for Public Policy (Aos et al., 2006; Lieb, 2001) concluded that the MST intervention costs an average of $4,743 per family. Considering that cost, the evidence of its effectiveness, and the savings from not placing the juvenile outside the home, the study estimated cost savings of nearly $32,000 per youth and about $132,000 in additional savings from decreased costs to victims. We provide a case example in Box 15.1.

Treatment Foster Care Oregon (TFCO). Treatment Foster Care Oregon (formerly called Multisystemic Treatment Foster Care and Oregon Treatment Foster Care) is another treatment intervention based in the community, developed in the 1980s as an alternative to "treatment as usual" (typically out-of-home placement) for juveniles charged with serious offenses. The procedures for delivering this intervention are described in a treatment manual (Chamberlain & Mihalic, 1998), which increases TFCO's treatment integrity. It involves placing juveniles with specially trained foster parents rather than in residential placement. Like MST, this intervention uses a team approach. The TFCO team includes a case manager and therapists, as well as foster parents who are available 24/7 over the 6–12 months usually needed. TFCO is designed to provide close supervision (including supportive relationships with adult mentors and reduced exposure to negative peers) within consistent limits. A variety of treatment modalities (including individual and group counseling, family therapy, and interventions to improve specific skills such as anger control and decision-making) may be used. These are often conducted with the family, using both the foster parents and the biological parent(s), and in the school.

TFCO has been identified as a model treatment program by the U.S. Surgeon General (U.S. Public Health Service, 1999) and the *Blueprints for Violence Prevention* initiative (Mihalic et al., 2001). One study involving TFCO (Chamberlain, 1990) treated 13- to 18-year-olds ($N = 16$) matched with a comparison group of 16 other juveniles treated in community residential treatment. Those in the TFCO group were less likely to be incarcerated and more likely to complete treatment over a two-year follow-up period. A second TFCO study (Chamberlain & Reid, 1998) involved random placement of youth ($N = 79$) between the ages of 12 and 17 into TFCO or treatment as usual. Youth treated with TFCO were more likely to complete treatment, spent more time with biological relatives and less time in detention over the next year, and were arrested less often during this period. Subsequent analyses using this dataset showed decreased violent recidivism (by 45%; Eddy et al., 2004) and decreased substance use (Smith et al., 2010). Other evidence for the effectiveness of TFCO has also been reviewed (Moore et al., 2001).

TFCO is also a relatively cost-effective intervention. An analysis conducted by the Washington State Institute for Public Policy (Aos et al., 2001) estimated the cost per youth of about $2,000 (plus foster placement costs), which represents a savings of about $22,000 per youth relative to placement in group homes, and further savings of more than $87,000 in victim costs for each individual in TFCO.

Although TFCO has been described as promising, there has been relatively little research conducted on it in the last two decades. It is important for any such intervention to receive ongoing research attention to document its continued effectiveness, so this is somewhat problematic. In addition, TFCO has been the subject of fewer randomized controlled trials than has MST, making it more difficult to describe as strongly empirically supported. It does share some common features with MST, however (community-based, using a team approach and multiple intervention modalities, and often incorporating the family), suggesting shared influences for effective interventions with adolescents.

Functional Family Therapy (FFT). Functional Family Therapy is a third community-based intervention for juvenile offenders. It is somewhat older than either MST or TFCO, having been used for almost 35 years. It is provided by a single therapist, who has a caseload of 12–15 cases, with weekly sessions over an average period of three months. As the name implies, it is family focused and is often delivered in the home (Alexander et al., 1998). Quality assurance/treatment integrity is addressed by careful training of therapists, yearly on-site consultation, ongoing telephone consultation, feedback from families, and weekly supervision. As we have discussed, such quality assurance is a component that is common to FFT, MST, and TFCO—each ensures that services are delivered as intended.

The Office of Juvenile Justice and Delinquency Prevention identified FFT as a model treatment program (Mihalic et al., 2001). The effectiveness of FFT apparently depends

Box 15.1

The Case of Marcus: A Youth Treated in the Community with Multisystemic Therapy

Marcus was 15 years old when he was arrested for stealing a bicycle from a classmate. This was his second arrest. A year earlier he had been arrested for possession of marijuana and received a disposition of six months of school-based probation, which required him to attend school (his probation officer periodically came to his school and checked whether he was there) and undergo urine tests for drug use.

Marcus completed his six-month probation without violating any of his conditions. However, despite this, he continued to have a number of difficulties in his life that increased the risk that he would continue to offend. His father had been absent from the family since Marcus was very young. He and his four siblings lived with his mother and grandmother. Because his mother had serious substance abuse problems herself, she was often unemployed and sometimes absent. The burden for supervising the children and supporting the family financially fell mainly on Marcus's grandmother. As she became older, she began to develop significant medical problems, and could not be as attentive to all the children as she had been previously.

Marcus's grades and behavior in school improved during the first six months of the ninth grade, but after the probation was finished, he began missing a number of school days and falling behind in his work. Marcus was measured in the Average range on a standard IQ test (higher than most juveniles who are arrested), but he found it hard to pay attention to written materials and to his teachers when they were talking. He tended to avoid doing his homework as a result. He preferred playing basketball with his friends, talking with girls from his neighborhood, and hanging out with older boys who sold drugs.

After he was arrested for his present offense, Marcus was evaluated by a psychologist appointed by the juvenile court judge. The psychologist concluded that Marcus had potentially serious problems with family, school, substance abuse, and negative peers. However, he also had some strengths, including a close relationship with his grandmother who was a strong role model; average intelligence; and an interest in sports. He was recommended for a community disposition that involved treatment with MST.

The judge adjudicated Marcus delinquent on the charge of stealing the bicycle and sentenced him to one year of juvenile probation. One condition of probation involved treatment with MST. Marcus's MST team included a case manager, a family therapist, a substance abuse counselor, and two other staff members responsible for working with Marcus in school and in the neighborhood. The case manager immediately made an appointment with a child psychiatrist, who diagnosed Marcus with attention deficit disorder and prescribed medication for the symptoms. One of his MST team members helped Marcus to join a community basketball league; his team practiced every day after school, and the gym was open for casual play (with adult supervision) after the season ended. His family therapist met with Marcus twice a week in his home to address the issues facing his family, including helping his grandmother schedule her medical appointments more effectively, providing access to job training and substance abuse support for his mother, and arranging for a regular supervision schedule involving Marcus's grandmother, mother, and all the children. During the second week of scheduled appointments, the family therapist and case manager found nobody at home at the time of each appointment. Therefore, they came to the home at 6:00 A.M. on Sunday and held a make-up meeting at that time.

By the end of the six-month MST session, Marcus was doing much better. His school attendance and behavior were consistently improved, his after-school hours were almost always spent playing basketball, his mother and grandmother were much more attentive to him and the other children, and he was able to concentrate on his homework more easily. Much of this improvement resulted because MST was administered in the home, school, and gym rather than the office of a therapist or probation officer. In addition, those administering the MST were careful to do it precisely as intended, and were firm about making sure that appointments were kept.

Critical Thought Question

What are some of the features of MST that make it effective for Marcus?

on adherence to the model, however (Sexton & Turner, 2010). Researchers compared the effectiveness of FFT to that of probation services in a community juvenile justice setting 12 months after treatment. FFT was effective in reducing youth behavioral problems—but only when the therapists adhered to the treatment model. High-adherent therapists delivering FFT had a statistically significant reduction of felony reoffending (35%) and violent reoffending (30%) when compared to the control condition. The low-adherent therapists, however, had significantly higher recidivism rates than either the FFT high-adherent or the control groups.

There is some evidence that FFT is effective in reducing the risk of substance abuse (which itself is a risk factor for criminal offending). Runaway adolescents with alcohol problems receiving FFT showed decreased alcohol use when compared with others provided treatment as usual (Slesnick & Prestopnik, 2009). Other adolescents with substance abuse problems receiving either FFT or a combination of FFT and cognitive behavior therapy showed favorable outcomes for reduced marijuana use three months after treatment (Barrett et al., 2001). While neither of these studies included criminal offending as an outcome, the evidence that they improved problems with substance abuse is encouraging with respect to their potential to reduce reoffense risk by addressing drug and alcohol problems.

The same Washington State Institute for Public Policy report (Aos et al., 2001) noted earlier, which described the cost and savings associated with MST and TFCO, indicated that FFT had an average cost of $2,161 per participant. It also saved an average of $14,149 in costs for intervention compared with standard treatment in the juvenile justice system, and saved another $45,000 in victim costs per participant.

How would Marcus (Box 15.1) have done with TFCO or FFT? Consider the similarities in TFCO, FFT, and MST on the dimensions described earlier in this chapter. All three directly target important influences such as substance abuse, family problems, and educational deficits. All three involve intensive work, including clinical interventions, and protocols to ensure that the planned interventions are actually delivered. (Remember the unscheduled 6:00 A.M. Sunday meeting with Marcus's family after missed appointments? This kind of extreme but effective response is sometimes necessary.) All three approaches use different interventions delivered in more than one setting, such as at home and in the school. These interventions are delivered in the community rather than a residential placement, and include goals that are developmentally appropriate. Finally, the interventions are carefully planned and monitored for consistency with the plan. Marcus probably would have responded favorably to any of these three empirically supported interventions.

Secure Residential Interventions

The previous section described three interventions that appear effective, both in terms of reducing the risk of reoffending and in saving money. So why not deliver most or all of juvenile interventions in the community, using one of these interventions? There are two answers to this question. First, not all communities offer them. We cannot assume that because an effective intervention *could* be delivered in the community, it *will* be. Second, many judges would be inclined to place a youth in a secure residential facility as a consequence of a delinquency adjudication for a serious offense, even if that youth could possibly be treated in the community. Why? Community values (which judges

represent) may support such a placement. The publicly perceived risk to society is lower when a youth is placed in a secure residential program, even though the actual risk (gauged through outcome research) may not be. Unfortunately, the impact of different placements for juveniles who commit serious offenses is very difficult to judge through research. The ideal study to help understand the impact of a given program or placement involves random assignment to such a program, comparing the outcomes to "treatment as usual." Very few judges, juvenile system leaders, or legislators would support research that randomly placed serious offenders in the community (versus in residential placement) to determine the impact of each on subsequent reoffense risk.

Accordingly, we must describe residential placements and their effectiveness without the best kind of evidence. While this is inconvenient for researchers, it is probably appropriate for those who represent our society and are responsible for promoting its safety. It would be very helpful to have good evidence about program effectiveness, but certainly tragic if citizens were victimized by offending as a result of such research. This is the main reason why research with random assignment is difficult to conduct in the juvenile and criminal justice systems—and why researchers must be satisfied with comparing a given intervention to "treatment as usual" rather than "no treatment." In a study like this, no citizen is put at additional risk, which could occur when "no treatment" is provided to a group of serious offenders.

A meta-analysis of the predictors of general recidivism in juveniles (Cottle et al., 2001) suggested a number of "treatment targets" that may be addressed at any stage of the intervention process. However, since residential placement is typically longer and more intensive, these targets may be particularly relevant for residential placement. The treatment targets include, in order of their strength, non-severe pathology (such as conduct disorder); family problems; ineffective use of leisure time; delinquent peers; and substance abuse. A smaller meta-analysis, focusing on predictors of recidivism in violent juvenile offenders (Heilbrun et al., 2005), identified cognitive and family therapies as more effective in reducing recidivism rates than usual services (e.g., treatments with other orientations; standard case management). This underscores an important weakness in residential interventions: If the juvenile is isolated from their family because of the location of the program, it is much more difficult to involve the family in a meaningful way. Conversely, one of the common features of the effective community-based interventions discussed earlier in this chapter is the close involvement of families in the intervention.

One meta-analysis of 32 studies of juvenile and adult treatment programs, many of them residential, found a reduction in recidivism in 75% of the studies (Redondo et al., 1999). Behavioral and cognitive-behavioral treatments appear to be most effective in reducing recidivism. Lipsey's (1992) meta-analysis of the impact of intervention on general recidivism risk in juveniles included a large number of studies (443) and estimated a 10% decrease in delinquency rates for juveniles receiving some kind of intervention. More frequent contact and longer periods of treatment were associated with more favorable outcomes—but only to a certain extent. This suggests that there is a "drop-off" in effectiveness of the intervention after a certain time.

In a review of meta-analyses focusing on a broad sample of residential treatment programs for justice-involved youth, the estimated difference in reoffense rate involved reoffending in more than half (54.5%) of the control group, and less than half (45.5%) of the residential treatment group (Grietens & Hellinckx, 2004). More structured and multimodal treatments had a stronger impact. Lipsey and Wilson's (1998) meta-analysis of 83 treatment programs for institutionalized juvenile offenders found that the most effective treatments reduced violent recidivism risk by 15–20%. The most effective of the residential treatments involved interpersonal skills training and family centered interventions. As with MST, TFCO, and FFT, the most effective treatment programs were attentive to quality assurance, making them consistent with the treatment model. Individual characteristics of the juveniles being treated had little effect on these outcomes. The influence of program philosophy (e.g., rehabilitative vs. control/surveillance) and treatment integrity (adherence to the principles of risk, need, and responsivity) have been shown to vary independently, and each to affect recidivism reduction significantly (Lowenkamp et al., 2010).

This research tells us that residential placements for juveniles can be effective, particularly when they focus on skills training (in areas like anger control and decision-making), vocational training, and educational and mental health needs, and also employ a treatment model that is "checked" through quality assurance. They must also be safe. If residents do not feel safe, it is very unlikely that rehabilitation efforts will be effective.

There have also been studies of specific kinds of facilities, where youth are placed for mental health or substance abuse treatment—sometimes through court order (OJJDP, 2008). The OJJDP identified three residential programs supported by research. Two of the programs focused on the treatment of substance abuse and targeted both juveniles and other youths who were not involved in the juvenile justice system. Participation in either program resulted in reduced levels of drug and alcohol abuse, although one program did not show a reduced rate of offending after one year (Morral et al., 2004), and the second did not even consider reoffending as an outcome in the study (Morehouse & Tobler, 2000). The third effective residential program combined security with mental health treatment for adolescents who had not responded well to "treatment as usual" in Wisconsin's juvenile justice system (Caldwell & Van Rybroek, 2005). The goal was to interrupt the escalation of defiance and legal consequences. Individualized therapy, behavioral control, and motivational interviewing were among the approaches used in this program. Those treated in this program were significantly less likely to recidivate within two years when compared with other juveniles with similar offenses who had been assessed (but not treated) in this program. This may be a particularly useful approach for serious offenders who also have substantial mental health problems.

A primary goal of residential treatment for juveniles is to reduce the deficits that are associated with reoffending risk. One approach to addressing anger problems (Anger Replacement Training; Goldstein, 2004) can be delivered either in a residential or community setting. It involves meeting with a therapist three times weekly for 10 weeks, and focuses on the development of specific skills such as impulse control, anger control, and thinking ahead, as well as reasoning. Research has demonstrated reductions in anger problems in secure residential settings (Goldstein, 2004), although the impact on recidivism risk has not yet been studied (Heilbrun et al., 2011).

Another anger management program has been developed for girls in residential juvenile facilities. The Juvenile Justice Anger Management (JJAM) Treatment for Girls is an 8-week, 16-session group intervention that is delivered with careful attention to treatment integrity (through manuals and careful training of therapists) and intended to teach self-control, problem-solving, and anger management (Goldstein et al., 2007). A randomized controlled trial demonstrated significant reductions in anger, general aggression, verbal aggression, and indirect (relational) aggression for girls who completed the JJAM treatment in addition to treatment as usual, when compared with other girls who received only treatment as usual.

The field has increasingly recognized the potential impact of trauma and other adverse experience upon justice involvement and offending risk (Zelechoski, 2016). One program that promotes psychoeducation about trauma response and facilitates better current coping is Trauma Affect Regulation: Guide for Education and Therapy (TARGET; Ford & Russo, 2006). When delivered in a residential facility, this program has been associated with a substantial reduction in disciplinary incidents and related seclusion (Ford & Hawke, 2012). Program participation was not directly related to a reduction in recidivism risk—although overall risk for *all* residents did decline after TARGET was implemented for some.

Residential programs face specific challenges to effective rehabilitation of youth. These include *mental health disorders* (a number of youth may have particular treatment needs for mental health symptoms), *deviancy training* (the process by which deviant peers positively reinforce antisocial communication and behavior), *attitudes toward rehabilitation* (both youth and facility staff may be less than fully committed to rehabilitative goals), and *difficulty of involving families* due to more remote locations (Cruise et al., 2016). Residential programs that are more effective must recognize and address these challenges.

When should juveniles be placed in the community, and when should they be assigned to secure residential placements? This decision depends on several considerations.

Higher risk juveniles, often with a history of prior offenses, may require more secure placement. A judge may decide that a single offense, if it is very serious, merits a secure placement. Sometimes it can be important to remove a juvenile from extremely problematic circumstances (involving family, peers, gangs, and the like) that would continue with a community placement. However, there are substantial costs (both to the individual adolescent and to society) associated with secure placements. This was underscored during the COVID-19 pandemic, when there were significant medical risks to being confined in a secure residential placement. Juveniles very often respond better to correctional interventions when they are delivered in the community and can involve important influences such as family and school. The case described in Box 15.2 highlights some of the complexities of secure placement.

This story raises some important questions about where juvenile correctional interventions should be made. When there are no proper resources and procedures in the community, interventions can be ineffective and put the public at continued risk. When there are no proper resources and procedures in secure settings, interventions are also ineffective and conditions can be brutal and dangerous. How can the necessary resources be obtained? (Lawsuits are one approach, as this story demonstrates.) How can they be most efficiently invested, so that interventions are as effective as possible? Much of the discussion in this chapter centers on the most efficient ways to use resources to provide effective interventions.

Reentry

Behavioral treatments for delinquent youth provided in residential facilities frequently do not generalize to the community after discharge (Quinsey et al., 2006). The process of reentry into the community should include planning for aftercare services (in some states, called juvenile parole) that are important to ensure ongoing treatment in the community and reduced recidivism risk. There are six areas in particular that are important in the reentry planning process: family functioning, housing (if not living with the family), school or job, mental health and/or substance abuse services, monitoring, and social support. Addressing each of these areas can help provide a smoother, safer transition from the youth's placement back to the community. Promising approaches to such relevant aftercare include the intensive aftercare program, wraparound services, and several of the community interventions already discussed (MST, FFT).

Intensive aftercare was developed to address the needs of chronic and serious juvenile offenders who are returning from residential placement. It used a graduated sanctions approach involving three steps: (1) prerelease planning; (2) a structured transition involving institutional and aftercare staff prior to, and following, release; and (3) long-term reintegrative activities to facilitate service delivery and social control (Altschuler & Armstrong, 1997). Early studies addressing the impact of intensive aftercare (Altschuler, 1998) showed mixed results, and there has been little published research evidence on this intervention for the last two

Box 15.2

The Case of Thomas Harris: Imprisoned, Violent, and Skeptical

In the spring of 2008, 18-year-old Thomas Harris sat in a locked cell in an Ohio juvenile prison, where he'd been for 2.5 years. (This is longer than most juveniles are incarcerated, even for serious offenses.) In that time, he'd had group therapy approximately twice a month, had been beaten up 12 times, and had sustained a fractured leg and cut lip.

So when the agency that runs Ohio's juvenile prison agreed to improve the conditions for juvenile offenders—including offering better mental health and medical treatment and reducing violence—Harris was understandably skeptical. He said in a telephone interview from prison, "They tell us, 'We're going to hire more staff to make you feel safer and hire more social workers so we can get you on the road to success.' It never happens" (DeMartini, 2008).

Violence in the Ohio juvenile prison system had been escalating around this time. At the Marion County juvenile prison, juveniles attacked one another or a correctional officer 504 times in 2007, up one-third from 2006. Violence may result from incarcerated juveniles' perceptions that they

must fight to protect themselves. Violent acts may be used by juveniles to establish themselves in the hierarchy, or to get what they want. Violent behavior may also stem from a feeling of being disrespected. Whatever the reasons why Thomas Harris and others are involved in violence, such behavior must be controlled and minimized for rehabilitation to be effective.

The agreement settled a class-action lawsuit filed against the Ohio prison system by a group of child-advocacy lawyers who claimed that the system was violent and ineffective. The new plan restricted how often and when prison staff can put juvenile offenders in solitary confinement, provided more medical and mental health services, and addressed overcrowding issues by releasing inmates who served their minimum sentence and progressed in therapy.

Critical Thought Question

Why is it particularly important that juveniles be placed in a facility that is rehabilitatively oriented?

decades. Rather, it has moved conceptually into the realm of being consistent with the "risk" principle of the RNR model ("treat the highest risk individuals most intensely") and addressing RNR needs in a way that is consistent with the individual's responsivity, as being most individually suited to that person.

"Wraparound services" involve the delivery of individualized services in the context of collaboration between agencies such as those responsible for mental health care, educational services, and juvenile corrections. In this approach, funding follows the adolescent's treatment, rather than being allocated to particular programs (Brown et al., 2001). Such services are useful particularly for youths with serious mental or emotional problems. The contemporary focus of wraparound services is the delivery of individualized services in a family inclusive and culturally competent fashion.

The National Wraparound Initiative has developed ten guiding principles for the development, selection, and implementation of wraparound services (refer to https://nwi.pdx.edu/NWI-book/Chapters/Bruns-2.1-(10-principles-of-wrap).pdf). These include *family choice*, *team composition* drawing on *supportive networks*, *collaboration*, being *based in the community*, *cultural competence*, *individualized* and *strengths-based* services, *unconditional support*, and *observable outcomes*. These principles provide structure for wraparound services, but they could also be applied to other services delivered to justice-involved youth in the community—whether after or instead of residential placement.

Adult Corrections

The justifications for sentencing and intervening with adult offenders are somewhat different than for those with juveniles. Retribution has been strongly emphasized in the United States during the period from the 1970s through the early 2000s—and particularly since 9/11, when concerns about terrorism were added to societal attention to criminal offending. One commentator has called this era of harsh punishment the *mean season of corrections* (Haney, 2006).

But there has also been a growing interest in delivering (and studying) rehabilitative services delivered to both juveniles *and* adults, coinciding with more sophisticated assessment of risk and needs and with the development of various interventions linked to this assessment. Deterrence and rehabilitation as broad goals have long underscored the potential value in assessing risk and needs—but the improvement in the profession's skills in these areas has made their implementation more realistic.

Assessing and Diverting Offenders

The risk–need–responsivity (RNR) model, discussed earlier in this chapter, applies as well to adult corrections as it does to juveniles. Offenders who are convicted of criminal offenses (or charged with offenses but diverted from standard prosecution) will be assessed at some time, either as part of the legal proceeding or post-sentencing, to gauge their risk and rehabilitation needs. In the prison system, this is called **classification**. Following the offender's commitment to the state department of corrections, they typically are evaluated at a classification center before being placed in a particular prison. The "risk" assessed at that stage is typically the risk of escape or misconduct within the prison, as these have direct implications for the security level of the prison to which this individual is assigned.

The risk of reoffending and the needs related to such risk are important for the vast majority of offenders who will be released from prison and return to the community following completion of their sentences or on parole. Assessing risk and needs can be facilitated by using a specialized measure. One example of such a measure is the Level of Service/Case Management Inventory (LS/CMI; Andrews et al., 2004).

The LS/CMI is composed of 58 items in the following areas: Criminal History, Education/Employment, Family/Marital, Leisure/Recreation, Companions, Alcohol/Drug Problem, Procriminal Attitude/Orientation, and Antisocial Pattern (Andrews et al., 2004). It has been validated on both males and females. The males ($N = 956$), drawn from three Canadian correctional facilities, had a mean age of 26.9 years, mean sentence length of 325.6 days, and mean number of convictions of 3.7. The females ($N = 1,414$) were from the medium-security institution for adult women operated by Ontario Ministry of Correctional Services; they had a mean age of 30.2 years and a mean sentence length of 322 days. LS/CMI total scores have been associated with (1) propensity for rules violations and assigned levels of supervision; (2) outcomes such as program outcome status, recidivism, and self-reported criminal activity in probation settings; (3) parole outcome; (4) the success of halfway house placements; and (5) maladjustment (Bonta & Andrews, 2017). This tool is useful in appraising risk for a variety of outcomes, applying to those in prison, various community settings, and under parole supervision.

Community-Based Interventions

Probation for adult offenders remains a frequent form of disposition of criminal charges, with the court placing the convicted offender on community supervision in lieu of incarceration. An estimated 3.89 million adults in the United States (1 in every 66 adult residents) were on probation, parole, or some other post-incarceration supervision at the end of 2020. This represented a decline of 8.3% from the previous year, the largest such drop since 1980. It continued a two-decade trend in decreasing numbers in the community under correctional supervision—although the drop from 2019 to 2020 was also likely influenced by the COVID-19 pandemic. This decreasing number was clearly national in scope, as 42 states, the District of Columbia, and the federal system all had fewer individuals in the community under correctional jurisdiction. Those on probation accounted for the great majority of the adults under community supervision (Bureau of Justice Statistics, 2021).

Correctional supervision in the community involves monitoring adherence to specified conditions. This is true for both probation and parole. The number of conditions and the nature of the monitoring can vary, depending on the individual's needs. Standard conditions involve specifying how often individuals must meet with a parole or probation officer; where they will live; whether they will work (or receive another kind of financial support, such as Social Security disability); and certain activities that must be avoided (e.g., alcohol or drug use, weapon possession). Additional conditions can be added as needed. For example, if the individual had a serious drug abuse problem, they might be required to undergo urine screens and attend substance abuse treatment and Narcotics Anonymous meetings. An individual with a severe mental illness might be required to attend mental health treatment, take prescribed medication, and meet with a case manager.

Requiring adherence to specified conditions, and monitoring whether the individual actually does comply with these conditions, means that some individuals will violate the requirements of their probation or parole. If they do, there may be serious consequences, including the possibility of returning to a correctional facility. For some individuals, such as those with serious substance use problems, the dilemma between abstinence/adherence to probation conditions and relapse into substance use can be a thorny one. This was described in the story of Eric Daley (refer to https://www.inquirer.com/news/inq/probation-parole-pennsylvania-philadelphia-addiction-criminal-justice-system-20191024.html#loaded), who was on "addict supervision" that required him to balance demanding reporting requirements (including travel to testing sites that interfered with his job) against the possible consequences of violation and even prison incarceration he did not meet the required conditions. The "zero tolerance" approach to probation supervision failures made it exceedingly difficult for him to meet the basic demands of adult citizenship, particularly holding a job. Would a specialized drug court—a problem-solving court for individuals with substance abuse difficulties—help? Possibly—but adhering to the conditions of such a court can even increase the demands on those who participate.

Yet there is reason to hope for many individuals on probation or parole. Those who do manage to comply with the conditions of their probation or parole are more likely to be successful in returning, crime-free, to society. We describe one such defendant on probation in Box 15.3.

Some people are required to undergo mental health treatment as a condition of community supervision. To what extent are probation and parole effective interventions for these individuals? This question was considered in some detail by Skeem and Louden (2006), who concluded that specialty agencies, in which offenders are assigned to officers with smaller caseloads, are more effective than traditional agencies. They are also more effective in linking probationers with treatment services and reducing the risk of probation violation, and possibly in reducing the short-term

risk of parole violation. This was addressed further in a research-supported guide to interventions with individuals with mental illness who are also justice-involved (Prins & Draper, 2009). This guide identified specific research-supported clinical interventions (Acceptance and Commitment Therapy, integrated services for mental health and substance abuse) as well as overarching intervention categories (RNR, CBT, drug treatment in the community) and approaches ("firm but fair," problem-solving rather than coercive, boundary spanning).

We now turn to specialized interventions in the community—drug courts, mental health courts, and veterans courts—that are also outside the standard approach to prosecution and subsequent incarceration of those convicted of criminal offenses.

Drug Courts in Corrections. After 1980, in part because of the "War on Drugs" that began in the United States in the 1970s and expanded into the 1980s, the number of those charged with and convicted of drug offenses expanded dramatically. Jail and prison admissions more than tripled during this period (Harrison & Karberg, 2003), with drug offenses involved in about 60% of the federal cases and 30% of the state-level cases that were part of this increase (Harrison & Beck, 2002). But neither punishing drug offenders by incarcerating them for long periods (the *public safety* approach) nor providing treatment while conceptualizing drug addiction as a disease (the *public health* approach) has been particularly effective in reducing the prevalence of drug abuse and drug-related crime. A review of research on the effectiveness of substance abuse treatment at different points in the criminal justice system (diversion, jail, prison, community) noted that about 50% of drug offenders reoffend within a year of release from prison, with modest reductions in that percentage when incarcerated individuals are treated (Belenko et al., 2013).

A community-based intervention that is both more effective and less costly than incarceration and prison-based rehabilitation would be very useful. Drug courts appear to be such an alternative. They are one form of "problem-solving courts," which have been influenced both by public safety and public health considerations. Consistent with the legal philosophy of **therapeutic jurisprudence** (Wexler & Winick, 1996), such courts consider how laws and legal decision makers can improve lives and solve problems and are designed to promote rehabilitation. Like the effective juvenile interventions described earlier in this chapter, drug courts are intended to provide an intensive and specific intervention targeting a very strong risk factor (substance abuse) for reoffending. Theoretically, for offenders with a serious substance abuse problem and a history of offending related directly to this problem, treating this risk factor (and ensuring that the right kind of treatment is delivered) should substantially reduce the risk of criminal reoffending.

Drug courts provide judicially supervised drug abuse treatment and case management services to non-violent

Box 15.3

The Case of Louise Franklin: A Defendant on Probation

Louise Franklin was a 24-year-old mother of three who was arrested for assault following an argument with a neighbor whom she thought was stealing from her. Prior to the disposition of her case, Ms. Franklin was evaluated by a probation officer regarding her criminal history (she had no prior arrests), vocational status and financial circumstances (she was the sole source of support for her children), home and family circumstances, drug and alcohol use here, and medical/mental health history. Based on this evaluation (called a "presentence investigation"), and also using the results of a short actuarial tool to inform the court about reoffense risk level, Ms. Franklin was recommended for probation as a low-risk offender. The judge considered this recommendation and assigned a one-year period of probation following a plea bargain in which Ms. Franklin pled guilty to assault.

There were several "standard" conditions of probation imposed: having monthly meetings with her probation officer, obtaining permission from her probation officer prior to leaving the city, paying $250 in restitution to cover her victim's medical costs, and maintaining continued employment and her current residence. There was one additional condition specific to her probation: completing anger management group therapy. This condition was imposed because the judge observed that Ms. Franklin had been in two arguments (although not physical altercations) with other neighbors during the past year that resulted in police being contacted.

Ms. Franklin was glad that she was not incarcerated. She was also diligent about keeping her scheduled appointments with her probation officer. However, she insisted for the first three months that she had been unfairly treated, that her neighbor had started their dispute, and that she responded by slapping her neighbor (resulting in a fall and a trip to the emergency room) only to protect herself. She also had not paid the $250 in restitution by the six-month mark in her probationary year, when she was required to have done so.

Her probation officer indicated to her in their sixth monthly meeting that she must do so, or he would inform the court that she was in violation of the conditions of her probation. (This would result in a violation hearing and possible incarceration.) After this meeting, Ms. Franklin made arrangements to make this restitution payment within one week.

She attended weekly meetings of her anger management group for a total of 20 sessions, the scheduled duration of the group. She did not miss a meeting, and actively participated in the group. Her contributions reflected her initial feeling that she did not have a temper problem—she felt that others often provoked her, and she was justified in her reactions to such provocations. As the group progressed, however, Ms. Franklin began to understand that others with similar perspectives did seem harsh and impulsive in their responses during the group sessions. She learned and practiced alternatives to angry dispute resolution, including identifying her own feelings better, avoiding confrontation when she was already angry, avoiding "high-risk" situations, dealing more openly and assertively with conflict, and "pausing and counting" before responding in situations in which unexpected confrontation occurred. She reported a noticeable decrease in the number of times she lost her temper after four months of being involved in this group. She also described feeling more patient with her children. Her therapist reported to her probation officer that Ms. Franklin had satisfactorily completed anger management group therapy after six months. Ms. Franklin had satisfied all conditions of her probation after one year, so she was discharged from the supervision of the Department of Parole and Probation at that time.

Critical Thought Question

Some research has characterized the approach of probation officers who are particularly effective with clients with mental health problems as "firm but fair." How might this apply to Ms. Franklin's probation officer?

---

drug-involved offenders, taking them out of the standard "prosecution/conviction/incarceration" process. Participation is voluntary, and whether a defendant is eligible may be at the discretion of the prosecutor.

Diversion in drug courts comes in two forms. First, those charged with a crime may be diverted entirely from prosecution, with the stipulation that they successfully complete the requirements imposed in drug court or face reinstatement of prosecution. Second, those who are convicted of a crime may be diverted to drug court to avoid prison or modify their probation conditions.

How well do they work? The research conducted during the last 30 years gives reason for optimism about this

particular intervention. A review considering research in this area (Logan & Link, 2019) concluded that drug courts remain an empirically based practice for both reducing the rate of subsequent offending and the frequency of relapse into substance use, with about 3,100 drug courts in operation in the United States (Office of Justice Programs, 2018).

Four randomized controlled trials (the strongest kind of research design) indicate that drug court effectiveness is greater than standard criminal justice approaches to offenders with substance abuse. Drug court clients in one study (Turner et al., 1999) were rearrested within three years at a rate of 33%, compared with 47% of those with drug problems on probation as usual. A second study using random assignment to drug court (Gottfredson & Exum, 2002) reported that 48% of drug court clients, as compared with 64% of "treatment as usual" adjudicated control clients, were rearrested within one year, although the percentages of those arrested from each group were about the same by the end of the second year (Gottfredson et al., 2003). A third study (Eddy & Bellatty, 2014) focused on mandated post-adjudication intensive drug court services for medium- to high-risk property offenders using a multi-site randomized controlled trial study to evaluate the effectiveness of these drug courts compared with traditional probation. Those in the drug court group had a lower rate of new charges (20.6% lower) than the traditional probation group—and a 30.6% lower rate of new drug charges. All differences were statistically significant, or nearly so. In a fourth RCT (Kearley & Gottfredson, 2020), investigators compared 15-year recidivism and incarceration outcomes for participants ($N = 235$) in Baltimore City's Drug Treatment Court to participants in adjudication processing as usual. Participation in drug treatment court yielded significantly fewer arrests, charges, and convictions over 15 years, suggesting that drug courts can result in long term reduction of the risk of criminal offending for individuals with histories of offending and chronic substance use.

In addition, one meta-analysis (Wilson et al., 2006) of 50 studies representing 55 drug court program evaluations found that the majority of studies reported lower rates of reoffending among drug court participants, with the average difference being 26% across all studies. A second meta-analysis (Mitchell et al., 2012) included 154 independent studies (92 of adult drug courts, 34 of juvenile drug courts, and 28 of Driving While Intoxicated courts) and reported that the great majority of adult drug court evaluations report that participants have lower recidivism than nonparticipants. They described the "average effect" of participation as comparable to a decrease in recidivism from 50% to 38%, with effects lasting up to three years. DWI drug courts were associated with comparably sized effects. However, juvenile drug courts were associated with much smaller effects on recidivism. The strongest effects were reported in courts with high graduation rates that accepted only non-violent offenders. Taken together, this research provides strong evidence that drug courts are more effective at reducing the rates of both substance abuse and reoffending over outcome periods of one to three years, compared with more traditional forms of community supervision such as parole and probation. This effect is particularly striking when considering the outcomes of those who successfully complete treatment, but not those who attempt but do not complete such treatment, consistent with a more widely observed trend in criminal justice rehabilitation (McMurran & Theodosi, 2007).

Mental Health Courts in Corrections. Mental health courts handle both felony and misdemeanor offenders (Redlich et al., 2005), although some courts exclude those charged with felonies. Juvenile mental health courts have also been developed (Cocozza & Shufelt, 2006). Mental health services that include psychotropic medication, case management, and individual and group therapy are among those delivered through such specialized courts, with progress monitored by the court. Despite local differences, most mental health courts feature (1) a specialized docket for selected offenders, (2) judicial supervision of clients, (3) regularly scheduled hearings, and (4) specific criteria that must be met if an individual is to remain in, and complete, the program (Thompson et al., 2007).

Mental health courts provide adjudication and monitoring for a particular group of defendants. In the context of corrections, how well do they work? There is less empirical evidence for the effectiveness of mental health courts than for drug courts. There are also fewer well-designed studies (particularly randomized controlled trials), and the operation of mental health courts varies more widely across different courts. Consequently, it is more difficult to draw conclusions about the operation of mental health courts (Heilbrun et al., 2011).

But there is some relevant research. Boothroyd et al. (2003) compared mental health court offenders ($N = 121$) and criminal court offenders ($N = 101$). They reported that the percentage of individuals under mental health court jurisdiction who received behavioral health services increased from 36% to 53% after coming under mental health court jurisdiction, while only 28% of criminal court offenders received behavioral treatment. Another study compared mental health court clients charged with misdemeanors ($N = 368$) before and after coming under mental health court jurisdiction. It reported an increase in the hours of case management and medication management, and the days of outpatient service, as well as fewer crisis intervention services and inpatient days (Herinckx et al., 2005).

Several other studies have focused on whether greater access to clinical services actually results in improved clinical functioning. In one study using random assignment of offenders ($N = 235$) to mental health court versus "treatment as usual" (criminal court), investigators found that participants in both conditions improved in satisfaction and independent functioning, but mental health court individuals reduced their drug use more and developed more independent living skills (Cosden et al., 2003).

By contrast, another study comparing mental health court offenders ($N = 97$) with criminal court offenders ($N = 77$) did not find differences between the mental health functioning of these two groups, or the nature of the mental health services available to both groups (Boothroyd et al., 2005). The investigators suggested that one explanation for these results might be the fact that the mental health court judges did not have much control over whether the mental health services were actually delivered. If their explanation is correct, it underscores the importance of control over service delivery. It would not be particularly useful to develop a specialized mental health court and divert those with particular mental health needs into this court, unless there was some assurance that additional specialized mental health services were available to those under the jurisdiction of this specialized court.

Other research has focused on criminal recidivism as an outcome variable in studying the impact of mental health courts. There is also mixed evidence on this question. One study (Trupin & Richards, 2003) reported that mental health court clients had fewer arrests post-discharge than did criminal court clients, while another study (Christy et al., 2005) reported that the number of arrests decreased for mental health court clients—but not significantly more than it did for those in criminal court. A third study (Cosden et al., 2003) used random assignment of offenders ($N = 235$) to either assertive community treatment (a particular form of mental health case management involving additional services and small caseloads, sometimes used as part of mental health court) or the standard case management services associated with criminal court. After one year, mental health court clients had significantly fewer arrests and convictions. After two years, however, these differences were much smaller, and both groups showed an increased number of arrests when compared with the first year (Cosden et al., 2005).

One of the most important considerations in whether mental health court participation reduces criminal recidivism is whether the client actually completes the treatment required by the court; participants completing mental health court in one study were nearly four times less likely to reoffend than were those who did not graduate (Herinckx et al., 2005). Indeed, participants in mental health court who do not complete the program may not differ from those who are processed through traditional criminal court. For instance, Moore and Hiday (2006) reported that those who completed mental health court were rearrested at a rate about one-fourth that of those in criminal court after one year—and those who did *not* complete mental health court were rearrested at about the same rate as the criminal court clients. Other investigators (McNiel & Binder, 2007) also noted both the risk reduction impact of mental health court and the importance of successfully completing mental health court.

One meta-analysis of mental health court outcomes was conducted as part of a doctoral dissertation (Sarteschi, 2009). It was noted that there are over 150 mental health courts operating in the United States, but this was apparently the first meta-analysis (underscoring that there is less relevant research than with drug courts). This meta-analysis reviewed 23 studies conducted through May 2008, with over 11,000 mental health court participants. Aggregate effects included a large effect for recidivism and a medium effect for quality of life, representing the most stable estimate of how mental health courts reduce recidivism and increase quality of life in their participants. But this finding should be replicated, updated, and published to ensure more confidence in these results.

A subsequent meta-analysis (Lowder et al., 2017) involved 17 studies ($N = 16,129$ participants) published between 2004 and 2015. Results indicated a small effect of participating in mental health courts when compared with "processing as usual" in the criminal justice system. The greatest apparent impact of mental health courts was in outcomes involving reduced jail time.

A principle of effective intervention discussed earlier in this chapter is treatment integrity. In order to be effective, interventions need to be delivered the way they were intended, and need to be completed. The data from completers versus non-completers in mental health courts are consistent with this principle. If a defendant is processed through a mental health court and does not participate in the services required by the court, then we should not expect their outcome to be better than it would have been through standard prosecution and disposition. Indeed, there is strong evidence from meta-analysis that non-completers have higher rates of recidivism than those who do successfully complete interventions—and also higher than those who do not receive treatment at all (McMurran & Theodosi, 2007).

This research suggests that mental health courts, like drug courts, can have a favorable impact on both symptoms amelioration and reoffense risk reduction—provided that services are delivered and clients participate. Mental health courts vary more than drug courts in how they are administered across sites, however, and the supporting research is not as strong.

Veterans Courts in Corrections. Veterans courts are another kind of problem-solving court, developed using the same approach as drug courts and mental health courts: applying rehabilitative interventions under the jurisdiction of a specialized court (usually but not always on a pre-adjudication basis) for individuals who meet that court's criteria for inclusion. In this case, veterans court focuses on the problems that are experienced by justice-involved veterans of U.S. military service, including challenges such as substance abuse, PTSD, depression, anxiety, and related difficulties in adjusting to civilian life. The first veterans court opened in Anchorage, Alaska in 2004, followed four years later by the establishment of the Buffalo Veterans Treatment Court (Holbrook & Anderson, 2011). Veterans courts often work closely with Veterans Affairs facilities, particularly VA Veteran Justice Outreach (VJO) Specialists, in providing services to veterans who are VA-eligible.

In telephone surveys conducted in 2012, investigators (McGuire et al., 2013) sought to answer a number of questions about the current operation of veterans courts in the United States. They identified 168 veterans courts, dockets, and tracks in existence at the end of 2012. (The number of these courts has grown rapidly since 2008, but the empirical evidence tracking their operation and effectiveness is very limited—making this survey a welcome contribution to our understanding of veterans courts.) Two-thirds of the courts are specifically considered to be veteran treatment courts; they serve veterans of all eras. Nearly two-thirds (64%) of the courts provide services to veterans who are not VA-eligible, with these individuals comprising an average of 14% of the caseloads. The inclusion of volunteer veteran mentors is recognized as an important component of the veterans treatment court model, with more than half the courts having mentors. A total of 7,724 veterans had been part of veterans courts at the time of this survey, with court jurisdiction averaging 15–18 months. About two-thirds of veterans who were no longer under court jurisdiction successfully completed court and treatment requirements.

There are now over 400 veterans treatment courts in the United States. A national survey (Tsai et al., 2018) considered various outcomes of court participants: housing, employment, income, and criminal justice. A total of 14% were reincarcerated after completing an average of about one year in veterans court. There were increases in housing (10% more had their own housing), receipt of VA benefits (12% more), and employment (1% more were employed). A history of incarceration was the strongest predictor of poor outcomes in criminal justice, housing, and employment; having substance use disorders was also associated with poorer outcomes. Investigators highlighted the importance of substance abuse treatment as part of veterans courts and promoting successful outcomes.

Institutional Interventions

There are several important differences between jails and prisons, even though both are secure institutional facilities that incarcerate individuals who have been convicted of criminal offenses. A jail is a community-based facility that houses both individuals who are pretrial (those who have been charged with offenses, but not yet convicted) and others who have been convicted of relatively minor offenses, usually with sentences no longer than a year. By contrast, a prison is part of a correctional system that is operated either by the state (usually a state department of corrections will include a number of prisons) or the federal government (which operates the Federal Bureau of Prisons within the Department of Justice). Those who are incarcerated in prison have all been convicted of criminal offenses. They have also received sentences that are longer than the relatively short sentences associated with jail inmates. Prison sentences can range from slightly over one year to life, and prisons also house those who have received a death sentence.

The Federal Bureau of Prisons (2017) provides a range of programs for inmates. These include:

- Substance abuse treatment
- Sexual offending treatment
- Educational and vocational training
- Skills development
- Religious programs

The nature of this programming reflects the view that the important influences contributing to reoffending risk include deficits in skills, work training, and experience; they also include problems with drugs or alcohol. Religion may serve as a protective factor for some individuals, offering a structure and set of beliefs that are inconsistent

The United States Medical Center for Federal Prisoners in Springfield, Missouri

with criminal offending. Psychologists may play a role in the delivery of some of these services, particularly substance abuse treatment and skills development. Of course, psychologists may also be involved in the delivery of mental health services to inmates with mental and emotional disorders.

Many of the same kinds of services are provided in prisons operated by the states. For example, the New York Department of Corrections and Community Supervision (2022) has programs and services for inmates that include educational and vocational training, substance abuse treatment, parenting skills, anger management, domestic violence counseling, health education, sex offender treatment, religious services, and others. The substantial overlap between the kinds of rehabilitative services provided by federal and state facilities reflects the common views about the needs of offenders that would reduce their reoffense risk and promote the possibility that they will live responsible lives without offending, following their return to their communities.

Jails are somewhat different in providing rehabilitative services. While those in prison have been convicted of criminal offenses and are serving sentences, this is true for only a subgroup of individuals in jails. Some have been convicted of offenses that are less serious than those of individuals in state or federal prisons, so they serve shorter sentences in jail rather than prison. Others, however, are awaiting disposition of charges, and will be held in the jail for periods ranging from days (for those who have charges dismissed, for example, or who are able to post bond and are released from incarceration pending disposition of charges) to years (for some with serious charges which, for different reasons, take a longer time to resolve). Since jails cannot anticipate whether their pretrial inmates will remain in the jail, they provide services focusing on immediate needs (e.g., medical and mental health care) rather than longer-term rehabilitation. In addition to medical and mental health services, educational services are also provided. Psychologists are involved in delivering such services, but also in assessing inmates' needs and short-term risk for self-harm or violence toward others, as well as risk for perpetration or victimization of sexual assault (National Commission on Correctional Healthcare, 2022).

The functions carried out by psychologists also differ between jails and prisons. There are four broad purposes served by mental health professionals, particularly psychologists, in both jails and prisons: classification, consultation/crisis intervention, rehabilitation, and reentry planning. Because the nature of each function varies according to the facility, each will be discussed in terms of whether it is carried out in a jail or a prison.

The Role of Psychologists in Jails. There has been some fluctuation in the number of jail beds in the United States between the years 1999 and 2020. During this period, the number of individuals in local jails increased by 21%, from 605,943 to 734,500, and then dropped about 25% from the middle of 2019 to the middle of 2020 as the COVID-19 pandemic began.

There is a much higher rate of severe mental illness in jail than in the general population (Bureau of Justice Statistics, 2006). For example, using inmate self-report of experiencing symptoms of severe mental illness such as hallucinations or delusions during the last 12 months, 17.5% of jail inmates reported the former and 13.7% the latter. These percentages are substantially higher than the percentage of adults over the age of 18 who report having experienced either symptom (3.1%). Another study (Steadman et al., 2009) estimated prevalence rates of serious mental illness among adult male and female inmates in five jails during two time periods: 2002–2003 and 2005–2006. A total of 822 admitted inmates at two jails in Maryland and three jails in New York were selected to receive the Structured Clinical Interview for DSM-IV. Serious mental illness (defined as a major mood disorder or a psychotic disorder) was observed in 14.5% of male inmates and 31% of female inmates. More recently, the Bureau of Justice Statistics (2017) noted that 26% of jail inmates reported experiencing "serious psychological distress" in the last 30 days—a figure that is much higher than the rate reported in the general population (5%), with psychotropic medication the most common treatment for such symptoms.

Given these numbers, we might expect that many of the psychological services provided to jail inmates would focus on those with mental disorders. Such services include:

- Screening, evaluation, classification of incarcerated individuals

- Diversion (helping to determine whether a pretrial inmate might meet criteria for a community-based program such as drug court or mental health court)

- Suicide prevention

- Crisis intervention

- Case management services/reentry (liaison with community treatment providers, planning for release, assistance with housing and transportation)

- Teaching life skills

- Group therapy for incarcerated individuals and their families

- Treatment of incarcerated individuals with severe mental illness

- Quality assurance (International Association of Correctional and Forensic Psychology, 2010)

Larger jails with more resources might be able to offer most or all of these services, so a psychologist's role in such jails would be more varied. Smaller jails, by contrast, might be limited to screening, suicide prevention, and crisis intervention.

The Role of Psychologists in Prisons. The contemporary prison can trace its roots to London in the nineteenth century, when Jeremy Bentham developed the notion that

California Department of Corrections

Aerial view of Pelican Bay prison, California Department of Corrections.

incarceration could be considered part of punishment rather than just a means of holding an individual until trial (as jails do) or execution. Facilities at that time were sometimes called "penitentiaries," reflecting the goal of invoking penance from those who were confined in them.

Imprisoning offenders is not necessarily the most effective approach to reducing the risk of future offending. This is perhaps not a surprise. Among the goals of criminal sentencing and incarceration are retribution, incapacitation, and general deterrence. Although lengthy sentences and punitive prison conditions may be consistent with these goals, such conditions are not necessarily consistent with the goal of rehabilitation. A meta-analysis of over 100 studies (Smith et al., 2002) indicated that the rate of reoffending following release from prison was 7% higher than following the completion of nonresidential sanctions.

Some approaches to prison-based rehabilitation are more effective than others, however. Bonta (1997) classified rehabilitation programs as either "appropriate" or "inappropriate" by determining their consistency with risk/need/responsivity principles discussed earlier in the chapter. Appropriate (RNR-consistent) treatments reduced criminal reoffending by an average of 50% when compared with inappropriate approaches. Appropriate treatment approaches were those that systematically assessed offender risk and needs with specialized tools (e.g., the Level of Service/Case Management Inventory; Andrews et al., 2004), targeted the criminogenic needs of offenders in treatment, and used cognitive-behavioral approaches to change deficits and increase strengths. By contrast, programs classified as inappropriate provided intensive services for low-risk offenders or targeted noncriminogenic needs such as self-esteem. Such interventions were associated with slight *increases* in recidivism. RNR-consistent interventions, whether provided in prison or in the community, reduce recidivism risk and protect the public in the process. The exclusive use of punitive approaches, by contrast, does not reduce reoffending risk and is therefore less useful for public safety—at least via the rehabilitation of offenders (Bonta & Andrews, 2017).

One other approach that shows promise, particularly in treating drug offenders in prison, is the **therapeutic community** (TC). This is an approach in which the staff, other clients, and physical setting are all part of the therapeutic environment. Group therapy, individual counseling, "community meetings" involving all residents, and specialized interventions to build skills in areas such as anger control, decision-making, and recognizing high-risk situations are all used in the TC. Staff functions are not divided into those responsible for "security" versus those responsible for "treatment" (as is often the case in a secure hospital or correctional setting). Instead, all staff members are considered to be part of the rehabilitation process. All residents are likewise involved in maintaining an environment in which therapeutic goals are clear and important.

In correctional settings, the TC has most often been used to treat those with substance abuse problems. A systematic review of relevant studies (Malivert et al., 2012) focusing on abstinence from subsequent drug use reported that (a) most studies were poorly controlled; (b) completion rates ranged from 9% to 56%, with successful completion the best predictor of future abstinence; and (c) there were immediate benefits noted in the drop of consumption following completion, but longer-term benefits were less clear.

One of the questions concerning the impact of rehabilitation in prison concerns "how much is enough?" Criminal sentences are imposed for a specific amount of time, not necessarily with rehabilitation as a primary determinant. But one interesting study (Bourgon & Armstrong, 2005) asked precisely this question: How much treatment is needed to reduce criminal reoffending? Researchers considered the recidivism rates of offenders in a Canadian prison ($N = 620$) who were followed up for one year after their release. While incarcerated, they had received either (1) no treatment, (2) 100 hours of treatment over 5 weeks, (3) 200 hours of treatment over 10 weeks, or (4) 300 hours of treatment over 15 weeks. Treatment programs were cognitive-behavioral, and focused on substance abuse, criminal attitudes, aggression, and criminal peers. Offenders' risk and needs had also been assessed as part of their incarceration. A total of 31% of offenders who received treatment in any dosage recidivated, compared with 41% who received no treatment. Offenders with different risk–needs levels required different amounts of treatment for an effective "dosage." In high-risk offenders with many criminogenic needs, for example, 300 hours of treatment reduced the observed rate of recidivism from 59% to 38%. By contrast, for medium-risk offenders with few criminogenic needs, 100 hours of treatment was sufficient to reduce recidivism from 28% to 12%—but more treatment was not associated with a further reduction in recidivism. For high- and medium-risk offenders with a moderate number of criminogenic needs, 200 hours of treatment was associated with a recidivism rate of 30%, as compared to 44% for similar offenders who received no treatment.

These results have several implications for rehabilitation in prison. First, just as in correctional interventions with juveniles, it is useful to employ a formal, structured approach to assessing relevant needs and intervening according to those needs. Second, it is possible to identify a "dosage effect" for relevant treatment, and to administer such treatment according to who is likely to receive the most benefit. Third, it is feasible to have a favorable impact over a relatively short period of time. Long sentences are not necessary to rehabilitate many of those who are sentenced to prison—so the justification for keeping inmates in prison for a lengthy period must be drawn from other reasons, such as retribution and deterrence.

Psychological Consequences of Imprisonment

The psychological effects of institutional confinement are complex. Vast differences in prison conditions are undoubtedly important: Incarceration in a well-run minimum-security prison with adequate programming and treatment options will have different effects than imprisonment in an overcrowded, mismanaged facility where staff members use highly punitive practices such as excessive surveillance and isolation to control inmates. The psychological vulnerability and resilience of inmates and the length of their confinement matter as well.

For a number of reasons, high-quality empirical studies of the psychological consequences of imprisonment are limited. First, it has been difficult to develop a standard measure to quantify the effects of long-term incarceration because they are so variable and subjective. Second, because incarcerated individuals can adapt and attempt to achieve a tolerable existence *inside* the prison, the full psychological implications of long-term confinement may be apparent only after release (Haney, 2006). It is too simplistic to assert that violent offenders will be more likely to be violent toward others in prison. One study found that although inmates convicted of assault, robbery, and certain other violent offenses were more likely to commit serious rules infractions in prisons, inmates convicted of homicide were not—and those convicted of sexual offenses were even less likely to commit such infractions (Sorenson & Davis, 2011).

But social scientists have learned something about the consequences of long-term incarceration. Many inmates show a particular pattern of coping mechanisms in response to high levels of prison stress. They may become hypervigilant in order to deal with the significant risks to their personal safety, learn to project a "tough-guy veneer," socially isolate themselves and suppress any signs of emotion, and become generally distrustful of others (McCorkle, 1992). None of these characteristics will facilitate their reintegration into society. Indeed, some evidence suggests that assigning an individual to a higher-security prison actually increases that individual's risk for reoffending (Bench & Allen, 2003;

Chen & Shapiro, 2007). One study (Gaes & Camp, 2009) even used random assignment to prison security level to show that inmates with a randomly assigned higher security classification had a rate of returning to prison that was 31% higher than that of their counterparts who were assigned to a prison with a lower security level. There were no differences in the rates of serious institutional misconduct of these participants.

Inmates report that their initial period of confinement is the most difficult (Harding & Zimmerman, 1989). Over time, a gradual process takes place in which prisoners adjust to their environment. Sociologist Donald Clemmer called this process **prisonization** and defined it as "the taking on in greater or less degree of the folkways, mores, customs, and general culture of the penitentiary" (Clemmer, 1958). This tends to happen without conscious awareness in inmates as they gradually learn to give up control of choices and decisions, and to depend on institutional rule-makers to provide structure and routine to their lives. One commentator likened it to a kind of "behavioral deep freeze" (Zamble, 1992) from which it is difficult to emerge, especially into the unstructured and unpredictable world that awaits an inmate upon release.

One scholar of correctional systems raised the intriguing possibility that prisons themselves serve to further the maladaptive and dysfunctional behavioral patterns that resulted in confinement in the first place:

> [T]he long-term effects of exposure to powerful and destructive situations, contexts, and structures mean that prisons themselves also can act as criminogenic agents—in both their primary effects on prisoners and secondary effects on the lives of the persons who are connected to them…. Programs (focusing on) prisoner change cannot ignore the situations and social conditions that prisoners encounter after they are released if there is to be any real chance of sustaining whatever positive growth or personal gains were achieved during imprisonment. (Haney, 2006, p. 8)

Contemporary corrections face a number of challenges in working with those who are incarcerated. A comprehensive survey (Bureau of Justice Statistics, 2017) describing those in jails and prisons in the United States in 2011–2012 focused on two important indicators of mental health problems: severe psychological distress experienced within the last 30 days, and history of mental health problems. The proportion of incarcerated individuals reporting recent severe psychological distress was 26% in jails and 14% in prisons (for men) and even higher for women (32% of those in jails and 20% in prisons). Those with a history of mental health problems were estimated at 44% (jails) and 37% (prisons). These figures reflect the substantial proportion of contemporary jail and prison inmates with acute mental health crises, longstanding problems, or both. Treating such individuals in a secure correctional setting, addressing symptoms and adjustment problems, and minimizing the risk of self-harm, victimization by others, or aggression toward others must be high priorities, given these proportions. A comprehensive strategy for addressing the overrepresentation of behavioral health problems among incarcerated populations while prioritizing the correctional goal of reducing reoffense risk has been described (Council for State Governments Justice Center, 2012). This strategy focuses on addressing mental health and substance abuse problems, particularly when they co-occur, from the perspective of how each contributes to reoffending risk and affects responsiveness to interventions.

We now turn to the problems associated with reentry from prison back into the community.

Reentry

The process of reentry focuses on preparing inmates to move from incarceration back into the community and to face a world that is fundamentally different from the one to which they adapted while in prison. To be successful, they must adjust quickly. Fortunately, and appropriately, there has been more emphasis on this transition since 2000. In this chapter, we have highlighted the importance of services delivered in the community—and planning so that services are delivered as needed and intended. This means that services should focus on relevant risk factors, be delivered with the needed frequency and intensity, and address the problem of "competing demands" on individuals' time with the goal of avoiding missed sessions.

There were over 862,100 individuals on parole in the United States at the end of 2020, a modest increase of 1.3% over the previous year (Bureau of Justice Statistics, 2021). (This is a small part of the overall estimated 3.89 million justice-involved adults who were on some form of community supervision at this time, however.) About 22% of those on parole committed some kind of new offense or technical violation in 2020 leading to a revocation of parole, a considerable improvement over this figure (about 33%) in 2005 (Bureau of Justice Statistics, 2021). The important consideration here is that all incarcerated individuals returning to the community go through reentry—some with more support and more success than others.

Partly because of the developing emphasis on reentry in corrections, there is limited empirical research regarding the effectiveness of reentry programs. Existing research in this area has been summarized (Heilbrun et al., 2012).

The priorities for reentry begin with the goal of reducing the risk of reoffending. There are a number of ways to pursue this goal. Just as drug courts and mental health courts target specific constellations of clinical symptoms with the expectation that providing relevant services in these areas will reduce the symptoms, promote better adjustment, *and* reduce recidivism risk, the reentry process aims to target risk-relevant needs as the individual returns to the community. Released inmates account for a large proportion of the population with communicable health problems—for instance, HIV/AIDS and hepatitis B and C (Mellow et al., 2008). Reentry services can promote the provision of necessary health care services. Reentry services can also yield significant cost savings when provided effectively. This is always an important consideration for local and state governments dealing with crime.

Reentry can actually be considered broadly as including services provided during custody, in preparation for release, and during the period of community supervision and eventual discharge. The custody phase involves measuring offenders' risks, needs, and strengths upon entry to the correctional facility and providing interventions designed to reduce risk, address needs, and build strengths. The release phase includes *inmate release preparation*, with a parole plan for supervision, housing, employment, drug testing, and other considerations, and *release decision-making*, regarding the parole decision. The community supervision/discharge phase involves *supervision and services*, *revocation decision-making* (including graduated sanctions in response to infractions), and *discharge and aftercare*, when community correctional supervision is terminated. This section of the chapter focuses on the community supervision/discharge phase of reentry.

An inmate in the California Institute for Men, Dagoberto Noyola, 45, exemplifies both the benefit of reentry programs and the ease with which some inmates slip back into old patterns of behavior upon release. Noyola says that a program that taught him to provide drug counseling to high school students and land a job laying tile for a construction company enabled him to reintegrate into society during his parole. But the career criminal landed behind bars again after a burglary conviction. Still, he was hoping to return to tiling when released again. Looking over a sea of inmates in the prison's gym, Noyola said, "A lot of guys want to go out there and do good. Nobody wants to be in here" (Gould, 2011).

The "community classification center" is part of the trend toward greater structure in reentry. Such facilities accept inmates who are released from prison and returning to the community. However, rather than either placing them directly in the community or sending them home, the community classification centers provide a kind of "halfway back" setting, structuring the reentry process so that individuals receive housing and services that are consistent with their needs. Some limited evidence suggests that such centers do a good job in both providing treatment services and managing the risk of reoffending during the first 6–12 months in the community following prison (Wilkinson, 2001). Programs that target specific offender needs have also been associated with lower recidivism rates (Seiter & Kadela, 2003).

There have been other changes in practice consistent with contemporary approaches to reentry (Lowenkamp & Latessa, 2005). The Second Chance Act of 2007: Community Safety through Recidivism Prevention, which was signed into law by

Box 15.4

The Supervision to Aid Reentry (STAR) Program: Assisting Individuals Returning from Prison

This reentry program began in 2007. It is operated by the federal courts in Philadelphia and provides supervision and obtains services for individuals returning to the community following incarceration in federal prison. Targeting individuals with a significant risk of recidivism and history of violent crime, the STAR program uses a structured risk assessment score to identify those at medium risk or higher for reoffending—and offers them the opportunity to participate. The early focus was on employment, offering training and assistance in finding a job. But the goals expanded as the program matured, with services in housing, family functioning, and behavioral health subsequently being sought and obtained for participants. (One of the authors of this book, KH, has provided pro bono assessment and treatment services to STAR clients beginning in 2015, by developing a reentry program staffed by clinical doctoral trainees at Drexel University.)

At any given time, about 30–40 participants, divided in two separate courts, attend bimonthly sessions in open court before a judge for 52 weeks. Participants can graduate after 52 weeks of compliance. Credit is awarded weekly unless the participant fails to meet program requirements or is involved in new criminal activity. Representatives of the U.S. Attorney's Office, the Federal Public Defender's Office, the

Probation Office, the Department of Justice Reentry Coordinators, and judges are all a part of the STAR program. Among the highlights:

- Only 9.4% of 296 STAR graduates have been arrested or revoked, a rate that is significantly below the district's revocation rate for returning individuals who are not in STAR. This is particularly impressive since STAR participants are selected because they are at higher risk than many others returning from prison. This arrest/revocation rate has been stable for the 14 years of the program's operation.

- This reduction in revocation and reincarceration can save significant public funds, considering the estimated annual cost of federal prison ($38,000 per incarcerated individual).

- It also reduces the adverse consequences to the individuals and their families of return to prison.

- The program has been continuously evaluated by researchers from local universities, allowing program leaders to be clear about the outcomes of interest.

Critical Thought Question

What aspects of this program appear consistent with good practice in reentry programming described in this chapter?

President George W. Bush in April 2008, provides funding for improving reentry using approaches consistent with evidence-based policy (Burke & Tonry, 2006; Center for Effective Public Policy, 2007). Guidelines to assist in the reentry process have been published (Aos et al., 2006; International Association of Chiefs of Police, 2006). The interest in using empirical evidence to guide the practice of reentry is strong, as it is in contemporary medicine and mental health under the rubric "evidence-based practice."

There has been a limited amount of empirical research on parole services provided in the reentry process. In the early 1990s, California started a community-based program to facilitate parolee success for reintegration into society (Zhang et al., 2006). The investigators reported that those not participating in this program were 1.4 times more likely to be rearrested within 12 months on parole, and that meeting goals in four specified domains (which this program facilitated) was associated with the lowest risk for reincarceration. A second study (Martin et al., 2003) focused on a community-based supervision facility providing relevant services (e.g., life skills training, violence prevention, literacy classes, job skills training, job placement services, and

GED preparation) during the day. The findings of this study reflect the importance of sufficient time in a program. More clients remained arrest-free after a longer period in the program (70+ days) than after a shorter period (less than 10 days). This difference in the recidivism reduction between the two groups (25% reduction for the first versus 10% for the second) provides an estimate of the potential "dosage" impact of this program. A third study (Bouffard & Bergeron, 2006) described a small program targeting serious and violent offenders during reentry; the program provided more referrals to community-based services and increased drug testing frequency during parole. Participants were less likely to test positive for drug use while on parole, had similar parole revocation rates, and had a 60% lower likelihood of post-parole rearrest.

Research in this area reflects several trends for individuals with severe mental illness returning from prison to the community (Heilbrun et al., 2012). The available evidence does support better criminal justice outcomes (reductions in rates of rearrest or reincarceration) for participants in programs based upon either the Assertive Community Treatment (Lamberti et al., 2011) or Intensive Case Management

Incarcerated Individuals Preparing for Reentry.

(Steadman & Naples, 2005) models. Evidence on mental health outcomes is also generally favorable, although more mixed; some studies show consistently favorable mental health and community adjustment outcomes, while others suggest that certain health outcomes (e.g., hospital days) may actually be greater for those in specialized programs. The evidence in this area is generally promising, however, subject to the caveat that we clearly need more studies that are well-designed (including comparison/control groups and large samples) to support these conclusions with more confidence.

There is growing interest in providing relevant reentry services to individuals on parole returning to the community. In an overview of important needs (employment, behavioral health, housing, social support), a recent review (Green, 2019) observed that much of the available programming has not yet received empirical research support. Nonetheless, there are interventions in each of these areas that have received enough support to be considered promising—and the application of risk/need/responsivity theory (Bonta & Andrews, 2017) provides a helpful structure for the kinds of specific interventions that can be applied. It can also help to guide the kind of comprehensive reentry program that addresses multiple needs of returning individuals, as

witnessed in the Supervision to Aid Reentry (STAR) program, a federal reentry court in Philadelphia.

Somewhat more research has been done on specialized parole services to individuals with mental disorders. A "firm but fair" approach to working with clients seems to distinguish parole officers who are more effective with this population (Eno Louden et al., 2015; Skeem & Eno Louden, 2006). Both traditional and specialty parole/probation officers used graduated sanctions, but traditional officers generally responded to noncompliance with more punitive approaches (Eno Louden et al., 2008). This relates to the differences between specialty agencies and traditional parole services; the former are more likely to focus on monitoring medication and treatment attendance and to use problem-solving strategies, and less likely to use threats of incarceration (Skeem et al., 2006). This appears particularly valuable with parolees who have co-occurring mental illness and substance abuse, as these individuals generally have poor relationships with professionals and are more likely to feel coerced into treatment (Skeem et al., 2009).

If community reentry programs are to be effective, it is very important that they be committed to the "quality assurance" process described for effective juvenile programs—ensuring that intended services are actually delivered as planned. One consideration is whether such services are voluntary or required as part of parole. One would expect that required participation would increase the overall compliance rate. However, there is some evidence for a self-selection process in which reentry services are voluntary, with the more motivated individuals seeking out and receiving services—and benefiting more. In one California program, for example, services to parolees were provided on a voluntary basis and included employment, substance abuse recovery, math and literacy skills, and housing services. Participants in at least one of these areas had a recidivism rate of 33.6%, compared to a recidivism rate of 52.8% among those not participating in this program (Zhang et al., 2006).

Summary

1. **What are the important considerations in assessing juveniles prior to placement decisions?** The domains that are most often weighed by courts in making juvenile placements are public safety and offenders' treatment needs and amenability to treatment. These factors, often cited in the law, overlap considerably with components of risk/need/responsivity, a well-supported approach to assessing and treating both juveniles and adults who have committed criminal offenses.

2. **What is the evidence for the effectiveness of interventions with juveniles in the community?** There is strong evidence for the effectiveness of three particular approaches to the community-based treatment of juveniles: Multisystemic Therapy, Treatment Foster Care Oregon, and Functional Family Therapy. These approaches are successful in both providing needed services for offenders, and reducing the risk of reoffending in those who receive them.

3. **What are some characteristics of an effective program?** Research has identified a number of common elements in programs that are effective. They tend to use different treatment modalities, carefully train those who deliver services, use a team approach, monitor service delivery to ensure that services are actually being provided as intended and individuals do not drop out or miss appointments, and deliver services in family and school settings.

4. **How can risk/need/responsivity help to provide effective rehabilitative services for adults?** Assessment of risk helps determine who should be treated at a particular intensity (frequency of service) and dosage (total amount of service received). Assessment of needs helps to target the particular interventions that may be provided to individuals. Considering responsivity helps a program to decide on the most applicable kinds of interventions—those to which inmates are likely to respond best.

5. **How do specialized problem-solving courts compare to other correctional interventions?** These courts serve specific populations—individuals with particular problems (such as substance abuse or mental illness) or having a particular status (being a veteran, for example), for whom the provision of treatment services would both rehabilitate the individual and reduce the risk of reoffending. Service delivery and treatment participation are monitored by the court, giving participants a strong incentive to complete the planned course of treatment. These courts can either divert defendants from standard prosecution (unlike more conventional correctional dispositions) or function as a specialized form of community corrections similar to probation. In some jurisdictions, if a defendant does not satisfy the required conditions of the specialized problem-solving court, they may be returned to the traditional prosecution process.

6. **What are the differences between jails and prisons, and what role do psychologists play in these settings?** A jail is a community-based setting that houses both pretrial defendants and inmates who have been convicted of minor offenses and sentenced to terms of less than two years. A prison is part of a state- or federal-level correctional system, housing only individuals who have been convicted of more serious offenses. There are four particular functions served by psychologists who work in either a jail or a prison: classification, consultation/crisis intervention, rehabilitation, and reentry planning. The nature, scope, and distribution of these tasks vary according to whether the facility is a jail or a prison; they can also vary according to the size and resources of the facility.

7. **What kinds of interventions are delivered in jails and prisons?** Because of heterogeneity in jail populations, jails generally cannot provide rehabilitative services whose delivery requires individuals to remain in the facility for predictable periods of time. Accordingly, they focus on providing present-state services (e.g., medical, mental health, educational, substance abuse). Prisons, by contrast, can offer additional rehabilitative services that include more extensive educational and vocational training, skill building, and specialized interventions (e.g., for sexual offenders). Both kinds of facilities also offer religious services, which may have a protective influence for some individuals at risk of future offending.

8. **What are some of the psychological consequences of imprisonment?** Responses to imprisonment vary significantly as a function of the conditions of incarceration and inmates' psychological resilience and mental health. Many inmates experience adjustment problems early in their imprisonment; they may become hypervigilant, socially isolated, and emotionally constricted. Exposure to prison violence and sexual offending can have a serious impact on psychological well-being. Individuals who are incarcerated for offenses such as assault and robbery (but not homicide or sexual offenses) may be more likely to behave violently toward others in a jail or prison.

9. **What are the priorities in preparing individuals for the transition from incarceration to community living (the reentry process)?** There are six areas in particular that are important in the reentry planning process. How is the family functioning, and will the individual live within it; if not, where will they be housed? Will the individual return to school, have a job, or be actively receiving any kind of job training? What mental health and/or substance abuse services are needed, and how will they be delivered? How will the individual be monitored for adherence to conditions specified in the plan? Will there be particular intensity to this monitoring, or specialized aspects (e.g., case management)? Finally, what kind of social support is available, and what peers will the individual be around?

Key Terms

adjudication of delinquency

classification

criminal conviction

criminogenic needs

diversion

Functional Family Therapy

Graduated Response

intensive probation

Multisystemic Therapy

parole

prisonization

probation

reentry

risk, needs, and responsivity
    (RNR)

school-based probation

therapeutic community

therapeutic jurisprudence

Treatment Foster Care
    Oregon

Glossary

A

Active Bystandership for Law Enforcement An intervention developed to address police misconduct that involves teaching officers effective ways to step in when they witness such misconduct and help agencies create a culture that supports such intervention.

acute stress disorder The development of anxiety-related, dissociative, and other symptoms that occurs within one month after exposure to an extreme traumatic event and whose duration is between two days and four weeks.

adjudication of delinquency The legal determination that a juvenile is culpable of an offense. When responsible for offending, juveniles are adjudicated delinquent; adults are found guilty.

adjudicative competence The legal capacities necessary for a defendant to stand trial or otherwise resolve criminal charges (see "competence to stand trial" and "competence to plead guilty").

advance medical directives Legal documentation in which an individual indicates the kinds of future medical treatments she will accept should she be incapacitated (and therefore be unable to make treatment decisions) at the time the treatment is needed.

adversarial system A system of resolving disputes in which the parties, usually represented by counsel, argue and present evidence to a neutral fact finder, who makes a decision based on the evidence and arguments presented by the parties; as distinguished from an inquisitorial system, in which the fact finder takes an active part in determining what occurred.

adverse experience Human experience that is negative and influences people's lives, although not traumatic in an acutely life-threatening sense.

aggravating factors Conditions or components that make a criminal act more serious.

amicus curiae brief A "friend-of-the-court" brief filed by a person or organization not a party to the litigation, but with a strong view on the subject matter in the case.

anchoring A cognitive bias that describes the common human tendency of individuals to rely too heavily, or "anchor," on a suggested piece of information (e.g., a dollar value in the context of damage awards) when making decisions.

anomie A sense of alienation or meaninglessness.

antisocial personality disorder A pervasive pattern of disregard for, and violation of, the rights of others that begins in childhood or early adolescence and continues into adulthood.

applied scientist An individual whose research focuses on solving problems rather than acquiring knowledge for the sake of understanding (see "basic scientist").

arbitration A form of dispute resolution in which a neutral third party makes a decision that is binding on the two disputants.

archival analysis In psychology and law, a method of data collection that involves examination of previously decided issues and cases.

arraignment A formal statement of charges and an initial plea by the defendant to these charges.

artificial intelligence Computerized systems performing tasks generally associated with human intelligence, including prediction, decision-making, language translation, visual perception, and other areas.

assimilated Having completed the mental process in which an individual internalizes a current perception or conception into their preexisting representation.

attribution theory A theory in social psychology focusing on people's explanations for the causes of their behavior and the behavior of others.

authoritarianism A set of beliefs and characteristics that includes submissiveness to authority, demands for obedience from subordinates, intolerance of minorities and other outgroups, and endorsement of the use of power and punishment to ensure conformity to conventional norms.

autobiographical memory Memory for one's own life experiences.

aversive racism A description of those who believe in racial equality and view themselves as nonprejudiced, but have unconscious, negative beliefs about people of other races. In situations that elicit these negative beliefs, such individuals try to avoid acting on them or express them in subtle ways.

B

back-end sentencing Sentencing that occurs when parolees are arrested for new crimes or violate the conditions of their parole and are returned to prison by state parole boards as a consequence (as contrasted with front-end sentencing).

basic scientist A scientist who pursues knowledge motivated by scientific curiosity or interest in a scientific question, studying a phenomenon to better understand it rather than to solve a problem.

battered woman syndrome A collection of symptoms described in women who have experienced prolonged and extensive abuse from their partners.

behavioral confirmation An influence in which people's expectations cause them to act in ways that confirm those expectations.

behavioral confirmation processes Influences in which people's expectations cause them to act in ways that confirm those expectations.

bench trial A trial in which the outcome (verdict) is decided by a judge rather than a jury.

biological theory of crime An explanation for the causes of criminal behavior that uses heredity and constitutional characteristics of the lawbreaker.

bioterrorism A form of terrorism that uses biological "weapons," such as viruses and bacteria, to harm or threaten others.

black-letter law Basic principles of law generally accepted by courts and embodied in statutes.

black-sheep effect The tendency to be more punitive toward those members of one's group who violate the norms of the group.

blended sentencing A sentencing mechanism that allows judges, in sentencing juveniles tried as adults, to combine sanctions available in juvenile court with those used in criminal court.

borderline personality disorder A personality disorder characterized by impulsivity and instability in moods, behavior, self-image, and interpersonal relationships.

brain fingerprinting A procedure that involves the measurement of brain waves in response to a stimulus to assess whether the brain recognizes that stimulus.

Brawner rule This rule states that a defendant is not responsible for criminal conduct when, because of a mental disease or defect, he or she lacks substantial capacity either to appreciate the criminality (wrongfulness) of the conduct or to conform his or her conduct to the requirements of the law (also known as the American Law Institute, or ALI, rule).

breached duty   The violation, through either negligence or intentional wrongdoing, of a duty that one party legally owes to another party.

burnout   A process occurring in response to prolonged stress; manifestations may include detachment from work and personal relationships, exhaustion, cynicism, and reduced productivity.

C

case law   The body of previous legal decisions and legal principles developed from these earlier decisions, as contrasted with statutory laws (passed by the legislative branch and approved by the executive branch). Case law develops through the courts over time, based upon precedent, and tends to change slowly because of the legal principle of *stare decisis*.

casuistry   Fallacious reasoning in order to justify questionable behavior.

challenges for cause   Occurring during jury selection, such challenges can be made by an attorney seeking to excuse a potential juror on grounds of bias. In addition, a judge may excuse a prospective juror for cause without a request to do so from either attorney. There is no limit on the number of challenges for cause that an attorney can make (by contrast, see "peremptory challenges").

change of venue   Moving a trial to another locality, usually because extensive pretrial publicity has prevented the assembling of an unbiased jury.

charge bargaining   A form of plea bargaining in which a prosecutor reduces the number or severity of charges against a criminal defendant in exchange for a guilty plea.

chemical castration   The use of injections of a female hormone into male rapists as a method of reducing their sex drive.

civil commitment   The legal process involving the involuntary hospitalization of persons who are mentally ill and dangerous to themselves or others.

civil competencies   This term applies to civil (noncriminal) legal contexts in which the question of mental competence for a specific task (e.g., making a will) is raised.

classical conditioning   A procedure in which one learns to associate a new response with a stimulus.

classical school of criminology   The point of view, which evolved in the 1700s and 1800s, emphasizing the role of free will and cost-benefit analysis in determining criminal behavior.

classification   The evaluation of convicted offenders by a correctional facility or parole office to assess the level of risk of criminal recidivism, institutional misconduct, and escape or noncompliance.

closing argument   A summation of evidence, made by an attorney at the end of a trial.

coercive control   A pattern of behavior involving acts of assault, threats, humiliation and intimidation or other abuse that is used to harm, punish, or frighten others, often cited as part of domestic abuse.

cognitive interview   A procedure used to assist victims in recalling aspects of a crime or other traumatic event.

cognitive load   The demand placed on a person's thought processes.

cognizable groups   Specific groups of persons, usually defined by demographic characteristics such as race or gender.

coherence-based reasoning   As applied to jurors' cognitions, a theory that individuals form coherent representations of the evidence to reach a confident verdict.

commonsense justice   Ordinary citizens' basic notions of what is just and fair in contrast to the dictates of formal, statutory law.

community-based policing   A policy that increases direct police/citizen contacts within a neighborhood.

compensatory damages   The payment or restitution owed to a plaintiff for the damages and harm that have been determined to be caused by a civil defendant.

competence   An individual's capacity to understand and behave in a way specified by the particular legal question. There are numerous forms of legal competency.

competence to plead guilty   The ability of a defendant to understand the possible consequences of pleading guilty to criminal charges instead of going to trial, and to make a rational choice between the alternatives.

competence to stand trial   Sufficient present ability to understand the legal proceedings in which one is involved and to consult with one's attorney with a reasonable degree of rational understanding.

compliant false confessions   Confessions elicited when the suspect is induced to comply with the interrogator's demands to make an incriminating statement.

Concealed Information Test   An approach to interrogating criminal suspects focusing on relevant concealed knowledge in the suspect's mind, not the truthfulness of his/her statements. Such information is particularly important when only a guilty individual would know it.

concordance rate   The extent of similarity in a behavior or characteristic between twins.

confidence interval   The amount of uncertainty associated with a population estimate (e.g., the mean plus or minus the margin of error).

confirmation bias   A tendency to search for information that confirms one's preconceptions.

confrontation clause   Language in the Sixth Amendment of the United States Constitution that guarantees defendants the right to confront their accusers.

containment theory   The proposition that societal pressure controls the rate of crime.

Control Question Test   A polygraph technique in which the subject is asked a question that elicits an emotional response.

control theory   The proposition that people will act in an antisocial way unless they are prevented from doing so.

correctional psychology   Application of psychological assessment and intervention to those individuals involved in the correctional system, including those on probation, parole, incarcerated, or involved in alternative community-based dispositions to offending.

counseling   Verbal intervention by a trained professional focused on problem-solving, decision-making, and symptomatic improvement.

countermeasures   Techniques employed by a deceptive subject to "beat" the polygraph test in order to avoid detection (e.g., breathing strategies, complex mental calculations, thinking about something exciting or dangerous, self-inflicted pain).

crime control model   The model that emphasizes the reduction of crime rates and vindicating victims' rights by the efficient detection of suspects and the effective prosecution of defendants, to help ensure that criminal activity is being contained or reduced.

crime control theater Legal policies that appear to address crime, but that are reactionary and unsupported by empirical analysis.

criminal conviction The outcome of a criminal prosecution that concludes in a judgment that the adult defendant is guilty of the crime charged.

criminal profiling The use of psychological principles as a crime investigation technique to guide police toward suspects who possess certain personal characteristics as suggested by evidence from the crime scene.

criminalization hypothesis The idea that untreated symptoms of mental illness result in behavior that is criminal, or is treated as criminal.

criminogenic needs The deficits (such as substance abuse, family problems, educational problems, and pro-criminal attitudes) that increase the risk of reoffending.

criminology The study of crime and criminal behavior.

Crisis Intervention Team (CIT) A program designed by the Memphis Police Department (also known as the Memphis Model) to increase officer and public safety while attempting to redirect those with behavioral health problems from the judicial system to treatment-oriented alternatives. It involves training in more effective interactions with those experiencing behavioral health problems.

culpability Responsibility for a wrong; blameworthiness.

cyberterrorism Politically-motivated use of information technology to create disruption or widespread fear in society.

cycle of violence Behavior involving a pattern of periodic domestic violence, often exhibited by batterers, making their victims fearful of the battering they believe is inevitable.

D

damages Money awarded to a person injured by the unlawful act or negligence of another.

dangerousness A propensity to behavior that involves acts of physical violence or threats by one person against another. In some contexts, it is considered more broadly to include antisocial behavior of other kinds, including property damage, theft, and other illegal acts.

death qualification Questioning of prospective jurors during jury selection in death penalty cases regarding their attitudes toward capital punishment. Jurors endorsing extreme beliefs about the death penalty (such as an unwillingness to impose it under any circumstances) may be dismissed from consideration, leaving the remaining "death-qualified" pool of prospective jurors.

declarative knowledge In the context of jury behavior, jurors' understanding of legal concepts (as contrasted with procedural knowledge).

defensive attribution An explanation for behavior that enables people to deal with perceived inequities in others' lives and to avoid feelings of vulnerability.

deinstitutionalization The long-term trend of closing mental hospitals and transferring care to community-based mental health treatment facilities.

deliberative processes Thought processes that involve mental effort, concentration, motivation, and the application of learned rules.

determinate sentencing A sentence of confinement or probation for a fixed period of time specified by statute, as contrasted with an indeterminate sentence whose duration is determined by the offender's behavior.

diagnostic cues Cues that enable professionals to diagnose or distinguish among available alternatives (e.g., between psychopaths and nonpsychopaths, or between truth-tellers and liars).

diagnosticity A term used to denote the probability of identifying the suspect from a lineup depending on whether the suspect is the culprit or not.

differential association reinforcement theory A learning-theory approach that asserts that criminal behavior is the result of socialization into a system of values that is conducive to violations of the law.

diminished capacity A variation of the insanity defense that is applicable if the defendant (in the words of the law) lacks the ability to "meaningfully premeditate the crime."

discovery A procedure in which the attorney for one side seeks to become aware of the materials used by the other side to form its case.

discretion The ability to act according to one's own judgment and conscience. In judicial decisions, discretion refers to a judge's consideration of factors that may lead to appropriate *variations* in how the system responds to offenses, as opposed to a decision based on predefined legal guidelines or rules.

dispositional phase The sentencing phase of the case in which hearings typically combine adversarial procedures and attention to the particular needs of the defendant.

dissociation The act of "escaping" from a traumatic event by extreme detachment.

distributive justice Concerns about what is right or just with respect to the allocation of goods within a society.

diversion The practice of officially stopping or suspending a case prior to court adjudication (without a formal trial) and referring the defendant to a community education, treatment, or work program in lieu of adjudication or incarceration.

dizygotic twins (DZ) Commonly called fraternal twins, occurring when two eggs are fertilized.

domestic violent extremists A kind of terrorism inflicted on citizens of a country by others who are also citizens of that country.

double-blind testing procedures Experimental procedures in which both the participant and experimenter are unaware of the particular conditions being tested.

dual-process models Descriptions of two approaches to human information processing. Typically they propose both a rational, deliberate approach, and a quick, intuitive approach. The former requires motivation, effort, and ability; the latter does not.

due process model A perspective that emphasizes due process or procedural justice (fairness) under the law. In contrast to the crime control model, this model places stronger emphasis on defendants' rights.

duty The obligation that one party legally owes to another party.

E

ecological validity The extent to which the methods, materials, and setting of a research study resemble the real-life phenomena being investigated.

ecphoric similarity Match between a presented stimulus and the memory of that stimulus.

encoding The process of entering a perception into memory.

equality The principle that all who commit the same crime should receive the same consequences.

estimator variable The factors that are beyond the control of the justice system and whose impact on the reliability of the eyewitness can only be estimated (e.g., the lighting conditions at the time of the crime; whether the perpetrator was wearing a disguise).

euthanasia The act of killing an individual for reasons that are considered merciful.

evaluation apprehension Concern about the ways that others evaluate us.

evidence ploys Used in criminal interrogation, these are ruses that involve providing false information to suspects about their guilt, which can apparently cause them to doubt their memories and rely instead on external sources to infer what happened.

evidence-based sentencing The application of findings from risk reduction studies (including offenders' risks, needs, and responsivity) to sentencing practices.

evidence-driven deliberation A form of deliberation in which the jury thoroughly discusses the evidence before taking a vote.

evidentiary strength Refers to the nature of the evidence regarding guilt in a legal proceeding, and is probably the most important determinant of jurors' verdicts.

exculpatory Tending to clear a defendant of fault or guilt.

executive function The cognitive ability to plan and regulate behavior.

experiential inflammatory bias The notion that people who witness the use of virtual environments may be so swept up in the experience and persuaded by the lifelike nature of these scenes that they have difficulty imagining or visualizing a different point of view.

experimental methodology Experimental research studies that involve the manipulation of one or more factors (termed "independent variables"), observation of the effects of these factors on some behavior (termed "dependent variables"), and control of other relevant factors.

experimenter bias An experimenter's influence on the results of a research study.

expert witness A witness who has special knowledge beyond that of the ordinary lay person about a subject enabling him or her to give testimony regarding an issue that requires expertise to understand. Experts are permitted to give opinion testimony, while a nonexpert witness is typically limited to testimony about which he or she has direct knowledge through first-hand observation.

external validity A measure of whether the results of scientific research, conducted with a sample of the population, can be generalized to a larger group or that population.

extralegal factors Influences that are legally irrelevant in that they cannot serve as evidence in a legal proceeding (e.g., age, race, gender, and socioeconomic status).

extralegal information Information that is legally irrelevant in that it cannot serve as evidence in a legal proceeding (e.g., age, race, gender, and socioeconomic status).

extraversion The personality cluster characterized by outgoing orientation, enthusiasm, and optimism.

extrinsic motivation The desire to pursue goals that would please and impress others.

F

fabricated evidence False evidence presented by interrogators in order to elicit information from suspects.

false confession An admission of guilt to a crime for which the confessor is not culpable. False confessions occur for different reasons and they can be explained by different situational and dispositional factors.

false denial A guilty suspect's proclamation of innocence and denial of involvement in crimes for which he or she is actually responsible.

field studies Scientific research done in real-world settings, as contrasted with a more artificial environment. Field studies have more ecological validity (a greater resemblance to actual practice) but are more difficult to carefully control.

fitness-for-duty evaluation The psychological assessment of an employee conducted to determine whether that individual is mentally, emotionally, or behaviorally impaired, which might prevent the return to workplace duties. It is often used with those in dangerous occupations, such as police work, firefighters, and the military.

focal concerns perspective A viewpoint in criminology based on focal concerns theory.

focal concerns theory A theory that explains the criminal activities of lower-class adolescent gangs as an attempt to achieve the ends that are most valued in their culture through behaviors that appear best suited to obtain those ends.

forensic evaluator A professional role played by psychologists, psychiatrists, and social workers when providing forensic mental health assessments and expert testimony on a variety of topics related to legal questions involving mental and emotional disorder, intellectual functioning, substance abuse, and other clinical disorders, as well as capacities that are directly related to the legal question.

forensic mental health assessment Evaluations conducted by a variety of professionals including psychiatrists, psychologists, and social workers. The assessments address a wide range of questions in civil, criminal, and family law (e.g., competency to stand trial, child custody, civil commitment, capital sentencing).

forensic psychologists These psychologists apply scientific findings and knowledge to questions and issues related to the legal system. Their work may include conducting forensic mental health assessments for courts and attorneys, providing treatment to those under the supervision of the legal system, offering consultation to law enforcement agencies and personnel, and other related tasks.

forensic psychology The specialized sub-discipline involving the application of scientific findings and knowledge to questions and issues related to the legal system. It may include conducting forensic mental health assessments for courts and attorneys, providing treatment to those under the supervision of the legal system, offering consultation to law enforcement agencies and personnel, and other related tasks.

framing effects The way decision alternatives are presented (or framed)—as either gains or losses—can have a significant impact on a person's choice. Individuals are more willing to take chances when the decision alternatives are presented in terms of gains than in terms of losses.

front-end sentencing Sentencing imposed following conviction for a crime committed when the offender was not under correctional jurisdiction (as contrasted with back-end sentencing).

Functional Family Therapy A community-based intervention for juvenile offenders. It is provided weekly by a single therapist, over an average period of three months. It is family-focused, and is often delivered in the home.

functional magnetic resonance imaging A type of specialized neuroimaging that registers blood flow related to neural activity in the brain or spinal cord.

fundamental attribution error   The belief that behavior is caused by stable factors internal to a person rather than by situational factors external to a person.

future best interests of the child   The legal standard by which child custody decisions are made in the United States.

G

generalize   To move from specific evidence to broader groups or domains.

generic prejudice   Prejudice arising from media coverage of issues not specifically related to a particular case but thematically relevant to the issues at hand.

Good Lives Model   A correctional rehabilitation theory that is strengths-based and uses principles of risk, need, and responsivity to promote outcomes that are broader than recidivism (e.g., other aspects of "good lives").

Graduated Response   Approach used in a juvenile or correctional context involving the use of sanctions that are proportional to the violation, begin in a limited way, and increase with the number of violations.

grand jury   A group of citizens who hear evidence in closed proceedings and decide whether to issue an indictment.

grievance   A real or imagined wrong serving as the basis for complaint or protest, particularly focused on perceived unfair treatment.

ground truth   A clear and accurate measure of the outcome of interest in a study.

H

harm   The losses or adversities suffered by a person who is the victim of wrongdoing.

hate crimes   Criminal acts intended to harm or intimidate people because of their race, ethnicity, sexual orientation, religion or other minority group status.

heuristics   A mental shortcut, "rule of thumb," or educated guess used to help solve a problem. These methods typically utilize experimentation and trial-and-error techniques.

hostile workplace harassment   A form of workplace harassment that does not involve a specific response (see "*quid pro quo* harassment"), but instead involves gender harassment and unwanted sexual attention, resulting in an intimidating, hostile, or offensive working environment.

I

imagination inflation   A kind of distortion of memory involving the inaccurate recollection of an item seen or an action taken when it has only been imagined.

impeachment   During a trial, the cross-examination of a witness for the purpose of calling into question his or her credibility or reliability.

implicit bias   Unconscious beliefs that influence how people interpret and judge thoughts and actions.

implicit personality theory   A person's preconceptions about how certain attributes are related to one another and to behavior.

inadmissible evidence   Evidence in a legal proceeding that the court holds cannot be admitted, and therefore cannot be considered by the fact finder.

indeterminate sentencing   Sentencing scheme in which the judge imposes an indefinite period of incarceration for a given offense (e.g., 6–20 years) and the actual length of stay depends on the individual's behavior while incarcerated. Such behavior affects whether the individual will be released on parole or will serve the maximum sentence.

indictment   An accusation issued by a grand jury charging the defendant with criminal conduct.

informational social influence   A process in which people accept evidence provided by others and modify their opinions accordingly.

in-group/out-group differences   An in-group shares a common identity and sense of belonging, while an out-group lacks these things.

initial appearance   The constitutional right to be brought before a judge within 48 hours of arrest. The primary purpose is for the judge to review the evidence summarized by the prosecutor and determine whether there is sufficient reason to believe that the suspect may have committed the alleged offenses.

inquisitorial system   The legal system in which the judge plays a very active role in determining the accuracy of evidence before the court (as contrasted with the adversarial approach, in which the judge is a more passive evaluator of evidence presented in a trial).

insanity   The principal legal doctrine permitting consideration of mental abnormality in assessing criminal liability. Those acquitted of criminal charges because they are found not guilty by reason of insanity are typically required to spend an indeterminate period of treatment in a secure mental health facility until they are no longer dangerous to self or others.

intensive probation   Probation involving frequent monitoring and contact.

intention   The offender's frame of mind in committing a criminal act.

intentional behavior   Purposeful conduct in which a person meant the outcome of a given act to occur.

internalized false confessions   An inaccurate confession that is genuinely believed. Internalized false confessions can result when, after hours of being questioned, badgered, and told stories about what "must have happened," the suspect begins to develop a profound distrust of his or her own memory.

intrinsic motivation   The pursuit of goals that involve internal or personal desires rather than external incentives.

intuitive processes   Incidents of spontaneous mental processing that are often acted on but not given careful thought or effort.

J

jail diversion programs   Programs attempting to divert certain groups of criminal offenders from jail incarceration into a rehabilitative, community-based alternative.

joint custody   A legal outcome in which divorcing parents share or divide various decision-making and control responsibilities for their children.

judicial discretion   A judge's ability to make decisions guided by personal values and beliefs (e.g., juvenile court judges use discretion to decide whether a youth should be transferred to criminal court).

juror bias   The tendency of any juror to use irrelevant, inadmissible, or extralegal evidence or considerations in the course of legal decision-making.

jury nullification   An option allowing the jury to disregard both the law and the evidence, and acquit the defendant, if the jury believes that an acquittal is justified.

jury sentiments   Beliefs, opinions, and views of jurors that are unrelated to the evidence and the law in a trial.

L

learned helplessness A condition in which people come to believe that they have no personal influence over what happens to them; consequently, they passively endure aversive treatment rather than to try to control it.

learning theory A form of criminological theory that emphasizes how specific criminal behaviors are learned directly from reinforcement and modeling influences.

legal factors Variables related to the offense or the offender's legal history.

legal formalism The model holding (in contrast to legal realism) that legal decision makers dispassionately consider the relevant laws, precedents, and constitutional principles, and that personal bias has no part in decision-making.

legal realism The model holding (in contrast to legal formalism) that judges view the facts of cases in light of their attitudes and values, and make decisions accordingly.

liable Responsible or answerable for some action.

lie bias The assumption that most statements, even truthful statements, are lies and deceptions.

limiting instruction An instruction to the jury placing explicit limitations on how certain evidence can be considered. For example, a judge may limit the consideration of a defendant's prior record to gauging the defendant's credibility only.

M

M'Naghten rule One test for the insanity defense. Under this rule, defendants may be deemed insane by the court if, because of a "disease of the mind," they (1) did not know what they were doing or (2) did not know that what they were doing was wrong.

malingering The deliberate fabrication or exaggeration of physical or psychological symptoms in order to gain an advantage.

mandatory minimum sentences Sentencing schemes in which judges sentence offenders to a minimum number of years in prison following conviction for a given offense regardless of any extenuating circumstances or mitigating behavior while in prison.

mass murderer A person who kills four or more victims in one location during a period of time that lasts anywhere from a few minutes to several hours.

matching heuristic A process in which decision makers search through a subset of available case information and then make a decision based on only a small number of factors (e.g., offense severity and prior record), often ignoring other seemingly relevant information.

mediation A form of alternative dispute resolution in which a neutral third party helps the disputing parties agree on a resolution to their conflict.

mens rea A guilty mind. One of two elements that must be proven by the prosecution (the other being "a guilty act") in order to obtain a criminal conviction.

meta-analysis A statistical technique that combines the results of individual studies using similar variables and addressing similar questions.

Miranda rights Rights afforded to individuals in police custody in the United States. They include, among other things, the right to avoid self-incrimination (Fifth Amendment) and to have a lawyer present and be represented by counsel (Sixth Amendment), and stem from the case, *Miranda v. Arizona*.

mitigating factors Factors such as age, mental capacity, motivation, or duress that lessen the degree of guilt in a criminal offense and thus the nature of the punishment.

monozygotic twins Commonly called identical twins, multiple births that occur when a single egg is fertilized to form one zygote, which then divides into two embryos.

motion in *limine* A legal request for a judge to make a pretrial ruling on some matter of law expected to arise at the trial.

motivated reasoning A phenomenon in which one's reasoning is directed by the desire to reach a certain conclusion. This may involve seeking out information that confirms a pre-existing belief.

Multisystemic Therapy An empirically supported intervention for juvenile offenders implemented in multiple domains (e.g., family, school, structured activity) to reduce serious antisocial behavior and strengthen dysfunctional families.

myside bias A form of cognitive bias in which people evaluate information in a way influenced by their existing beliefs and attitudes.

N

Need for Cognition The inclination to engage in and enjoy effortful cognitive work.

negative incentives In the context of interrogations, tactics (such as accusations, attacks on the suspect's denials, and evidence fabrications) that interrogators use to convey that the suspect has no choice but to confess.

negligence Behavior that falls below a legal standard for protecting others from unreasonable risks; it is often measured by asking whether a "reasonable person" would have acted as the civil defendant acted in similar circumstances.

negotiation The process of conferring with another to attempt to settle a legal matter.

neuroticism A major dimension of personality involving the tendency to experience negative emotions such as anxiety, anger, and depression, often accompanied by distressed thinking and behavior.

normative social influence A process in which people conform to others' expectations, often to gain acceptance.

O

open-ended questions This type of question does not specify or restrict the answers to be given; rather, respondents are prompted to suggest their own ideas for answers.

opening statement Not part of the evidence, these comments made by the lawyers on each side give an overview of the evidence that will be presented.

operant learning A form of learning in which the consequences of a behavior influence the likelihood of its being performed in the future.

outcome severity The severity of an accident or injury.

overconfidence bias The tendency to hold an unrealistically optimistic view of the likelihood of a favorable outcome in litigation. It applies to defendants who believe (incorrectly) that they have a good chance to win at trial, sometimes leading to rejection of reasonable plea offers from prosecutors.

own-race bias The tendency for people to more accurately recognize faces of individuals of their own race.

P

parole   The conditional release from prison of a person convicted of a crime prior to the expiration of that person's term of imprisonment, subject to both the supervision of the correctional authorities during the remainder of the term and a resumption of the imprisonment upon violation of the conditions imposed.

pedophilia disorder   A disorder characterized by intense, recurrent sexual fantasies or behaviors involving pre-pubescent individuals.

peremptory challenges   Opportunities available to each attorney during jury selection to exclude potential jurors without having to give any reason. Their number, determined by the judge, varies from one jurisdiction to another.

perjury   Lying while under oath.

photographic lineup   A display of photographs of potential suspects that police often ask an eyewitness to examine to identify a suspect (also called a photospread).

photospread   A display of photographs of potential suspects that police often ask an eyewitness to examine to identify a suspect (also called a photographic lineup).

physiognomic variability   Perceived differences based on physical features.

plea bargains   In exchange for the defendant's promise to forgo a trial, the government may promise to charge the defendant with a lesser crime or ask the judge for a reduced sentence. When the "bargain" is reached, the defendant pleads guilty and no trial is held.

policy capturing   Research to determine (capture) policy preferences and inclinations (e.g., the punishment motives of ordinary people).

policy evaluator   A role in which psychologists who have methodological skills in assessing policy provide data regarding the impact of such policy (e.g., degree of change, degree of effectiveness, design recommendations, observed outcomes).

polygraph   (sometimes called "lie detector") An instrument for recording variations in several physiological functions that may indicate whether a person is telling the truth.

positive inducements   Tactics used by interrogators to motivate suspects to see that an admission of guilt is in their best interest. It involves conveying that the suspect will receive some benefit in exchange for his confession.

positivist school of criminology   A point of view that emphasized that criminal behavior by a person was determined, rather than a product of free will.

postdiction variable   In the context of eyewitness memory, a variable (such as the speed of an identification) that does not directly affect the reliability of identification, but instead is a measure of some process that correlates with reliability.

post-event information   Details about an event to which an eyewitness is exposed after the event has occurred.

posttraumatic stress disorder (PTSD)   An anxiety disorder in which the victim experiences a pattern of intense fear reactions after being exposed to a highly stressful event.

precedent   A ruling (or opinion) announced in a previous case that provides a framework in which to decide a current case. The expectation that a court should abide by precedent is called *stare decisis*.

predecisional distortion   A phenomenon by which jurors' initial inclinations influence the way they interpret evidence presented during a trial.

predictive validity   One form of psychometric validity, involving the accuracy with which a measure can predict something it should theoretically be able to predict.

preliminary hearing   The step between arrest and trial. At a preliminary hearing, the prosecution must offer some evidence on every element of the crime charged and the judge must decide whether the evidence is sufficient to pursue the case further.

preponderance of evidence   The standard of proof required in civil litigation, in which the evidence for one side must outweigh that on the other side by even a slight margin.

presence   When used in reference to virtual reality, the degree to which a user or observer has the impression of actually "being in another world" due to the presentation in the virtual environment.

President's Task Force on 21st Century Policing   Task force appointed by President Obama in 2014 to identify best practices in policing and make recommendations on how policing can both reduce crime and build public trust.

preventive detention   The detention of accused persons who pose a risk of flight or dangerousness.

primacy effect   The influence of information that is presented first, or early in a series.

primary deviance   Behavior that violates a law or norm for socially acceptable conduct.

principle of proportionality   The principle that the punishment should be consistently related to the magnitude of the offense.

prisonization   The gradual process in which prisoners adjust to their environment (i.e., assimilate to the customs and culture of the penitentiary).

probabilistic estimates   Predictions about outcomes, made far in advance of the known outcome. Attorneys make probabilistic estimates in deciding whether to accept a case.

probation   The conditional freedom from incarceration following criminal conviction. It involves a specified set of conditions for which compliance is monitored by the probation officer assigned to the case. Probation conditions may include drug use monitoring, substance abuse treatment, mental health treatment, and skills-based training in particular areas (e.g., anger management, decision-making).

probative value   Tending to prove or actually proving.

problem-solving court   A specialized kind of court focusing on the underlying behaviors of criminal defendants and seeking to rehabilitate them, thereby addressing the particular problems causing the offending. Examples include drug courts, mental health courts, domestic violence courts, homeless courts, and veterans' courts.

procedural justice   The consideration of the fairness of the methods for resolving a dispute and allocating resources.

procedural knowledge   Jurors' awareness of the correct process for reaching a decision (as contrasted with declarative knowledge).

propensity evidence   Evidence of a defendant's past wrongdoings that suggest the defendant had the propensity, or inclination, to commit a crime.

proportionality in sentencing   Proportionality in sentencing means that the nature and duration of the sentence should correspond to the seriousness of the offense.

prosecutorial discretion   The authority of prosecutors to make decisions about certain aspects of criminal proceedings. In the context of juvenile offenders, it involves deciding whether cases involving serious charges are filed initially in juvenile or adult court.

proximate cause   An obvious or substantially supported link between behavior and subsequent harm; a necessary element to establish in personal injury litigation.

psycholinguistics   The psychological study of how people use and understand language.

psychological autopsies   An attempt to determine the mode of death (whether an accident, suicide, homicide, or natural causes) by an examination of what was known about the behavior of the deceased.

psychological theories (of crime)   Scientific principles that are formulated and applied to the analysis and understanding of cognitive and behavioral phenomena. For example, psychological theories of crime emphasize individual differences in behavior and the approaches to thinking, feeling, and decision-making that make some people predisposed to committing criminal acts.

psychopathy   A personality disorder characterized by a long-term pattern of antisocial behavior and personal characteristics such as shallow emotion, limited capacities for guilt and empathy, and failure to learn from experience.

punitive damages   Financial compensation awarded to a prevailing party in civil litigation as a form of punishment for a specific act or omission.

Q

quid pro quo **harassment**   An implicit or explicit bargain in which the harasser promises a reward or threatens punishment in exchange for a specific response (often sexual in nature) from a workplace supervisee.

R

racial bias   When police officers, prosecutors, jurors, and judges use an individual's race as the primary determinant for discretionary decisions or judgments of his or her behavior.

racial profiling   The police practice of using race as a factor in determining actions such as traffic stops, arrests, and questioning of suspects.

randomized controlled trials (RCT)   A research methodology in which participants are randomly assigned either to control or treatment conditions and outcomes are compared.

rape trauma syndrome   A collection of behaviors or symptoms that are frequent aftereffects of having been raped.

reactance theory   A theory proposing that if something is denied or withheld from a person, the person's desire for it will increase.

reasonable suspicion standard   A standard that is below probable cause, involving the perception that a reasonable person would have that a crime has been, is being, or will be committed.

rebuttal evidence   Evidence presented to counter or disprove facts previously introduced by the adverse party.

recency effect   The influence on memory and decision-making of information that is presented last or later in a series.

recidivism   In the context of criminal behavior, the commission of a new crime resulting in re-arrest, reconviction, or reincarceration.

recross   To cross-examine a witness a second time, after redirect examination.

redirect questioning   Questioning by the original attorney that follows the opposing counsel's cross-examination.

reentry   The process of returning from incarceration to the community.

reflector variables   Variables that provide information about whether eyewitness identifications are accurate.

relative judgment   An eyewitness's process of deciding, when looking at a simultaneous lineup, which of the people shown in the lineup most closely resembles the perpetrator.

reminiscence effect   When recalling previous experience, people often report (reminisce) new information on each recall attempt, suggesting that recollection is often incomplete on the first telling and that it is normal to produce unrecalled information in later interviews.

repression   The process by which unpleasant thoughts or memories are moved outside of conscious awareness.

reservation price   In negotiations, a negotiator's bottom line. Defendants in settlement negotiations typically have maximum amounts they are willing to pay and plaintiffs have minimum amounts they are willing to accept.

restorative justice   An approach seeking to restore what has been lost through criminal offending. It includes programs designed to reconcile offenders with their victims, helping the offender appreciate the victim's pain and the victim to understand why the offender committed the crime.

retention interval   The period of time in which a memory is retained. In eyewitnesses, the retention interval occurs between viewing an event and being questioned about it.

retributive   The notion that punishment should be exacted on a person who has taken something from another.

retrieval   The process by which a memory is returned to consciousness.

reverse transfer   When juveniles initially placed in adult court are returned ("transferred back") to juvenile court.

risk assessment   The assessment of the probability that a person will behave violently, often accompanied by suggestions for how to reduce the likelihood of violent conduct.

risk averse   Seeking to minimize risk.

risk, needs, and responsivity (RNR)   A theory that describes three separate considerations (risk, need, and responsivity) involving interventions for criminal offenders. Risk means that the likelihood of committing future offenses should be evaluated; those at highest risk should receive the most intensive interventions. Needs are the deficits (such as substance abuse, family problems, educational problems, and procriminal attitudes) that increase the risk of reoffending. Responsivity involves the likelihood of a favorable response to the interventions, and the influences that may affect such responding.

S

schema   An individual's cognitive framework or set of preconceptions that helps that person attend to, organize, and interpret relevant information.

school-based probation   A variation on the standard conditions of probation in which the youth's attendance, performance, and behavior in school are monitored through the probation officer's personal visits to the school.

scientific jury selection   A process used by social scientists when acting as jury selection consultants. These consultants use empirically based procedures such as focus groups, shadow juries, systematic ratings of prospective jurors, and surveys of the community.

secondary deviance   Creating or increasing the deviant identity of a person using official labels or formal legal sanctions.

selection effects   A bias that occurs when random assignment is not achieved in a research study and results can be attributed to the selection of respondents.

selective attention   People have limited attentional capacity and cannot process all of the stimuli available at a given time, so they unconsciously select the information to which they will attend. The threatening aspect of a weapon is one example of something that would draw attention (see "weapon focus effect").

self-administered interview An investigative tool that can be used to obtain detailed initial statements from those witnessing an event.

self-defense A legal defense relied upon by criminal defendants typically charged with homicide; it asserts that the defendant's actions were justified by a reasonable belief that he or she was in imminent danger of death or bodily harm from an attacker.

self-determination theory of optimal motivation Theory describing situational and personality factors that cause positive and negative motivation and, eventually, changes in subjective well-being.

self-serving bias The tendency to interpret information or make decisions in ways that are consistent with one's own interests, rather than in an objective fashion.

sentence bargaining A form of plea bargaining in which a prosecutor recommends a reduced sentence in exchange for a guilty plea.

sentencing disparity The differences in the decisions of different judges in sentencing for the same crime.

Sequential Intercept Model The model assesses diversion needs for individuals with serious mental illness. It describes a number of points at which an intervention can be made to prevent further progress along the conventional criminal track. These points are (a) law enforcement and emergency services; (b) initial detention and initial hearings; (c) jail, courts, forensic evaluations, and forensic commitments; (d) reentry from jails, state prisons, and forensic hospitalization; and (e) community corrections and community support.

sequential presentation A lineup presentation in which the choices are shown one at a time.

serial killer A person who kills four or more victims on separate occasions, usually in different locations.

serial murder The deliberate killing of four or more victims on separate occasions, usually in different locations.

settlement negotiation Process used to resolve (settle) civil disputes without a trial, typically in private negotiations between attorneys representing the disputing parties.

shaming penalty A criminal sanction designed to embarrass an offender by publicizing the offense; shaming penalties are thought to express the community's moral outrage and to deter others from committing this type of crime.

similarity–leniency hypothesis The hypothesis that fact finders treat those similar to themselves more leniently than they treat those they perceive as different from themselves.

simultaneous presentation A lineup presentation in which all choices are shown at the same time.

social cognitive theory The theory that focuses on the role of cognitive processes in social interactions.

social desirability effect People's wishes to present themselves in a socially appropriate and favorable way and the influence of such wishes on their behavior.

social judgments Judgments incorporating information about social categories, such as race and gender.

social labeling theory The theory that the stigma of being branded deviant by society can influence an individual's belief about himself or herself.

social learning theory A theory of human behavior suggesting that social behavior is learned by observing and imitating others' behavior.

social-psychological theory (of crime) A group of theories that propose that crime is learned in a social context; they differ about what is learned and how it is learned.

sociological theories (of crime) A group of theories that maintain that crime results from social or cultural contexts (e.g., family, school/workplace, peer groups, community, and society). The various theories emphasize different social features and differ on the social causes of crime.

sole custody Awarding custody of a child to one parent only (as contrasted with joint custody, in which both parents have custodial involvement).

sophistication-maturity A legal construct often applied to youthful offenders in transfer and reverse transfer proceedings. It encompasses the domains of criminal sophistication and developmental maturity.

source confusion Confusion about the origin of a memory.

source monitoring The ability to accurately identify the source of one's memory.

specialized police responding Police conduct after receiving specialized training in recognizing behavioral health symptoms and interacting with individuals who display such symptoms in a way that deescalates conflict, making treatment alternative more likely and standard criminal prosecution less likely.

specific pretrial publicity Media coverage concerning the details of one specific case prior to trial.

spree killer A person who kills victims at two or more different locations with almost no time between the murders.

stare decisis The legal principle emphasizing the importance of decision-making that is consistent with precedent; literally, "let the decision stand."

statutory exclusion A statute stipulating that certain serious offenses allegedly committed by an adolescent must be filed directly in adult court.

stimulation-seeking theory Theory suggesting that the thrill-seeking and disruptive behaviors of a psychopath serve to increase sensory input and raise arousal to a more tolerable level. As a result, the psychopathic person seems "immune" to many social cues that govern behavior.

stipulate To agree about a fact in a legal proceeding without further argument or examination.

Stockholm syndrome Feelings of dependency and emotional closeness that hostages sometimes develop toward their kidnappers in prolonged hostage situations.

storage That phase of the memory process referring to the retention of information.

story model The notion that people construct a story or narrative summary of the events in a dispute.

structural explanations A key concept of structural approaches is that certain groups of people suffer fundamental inequalities in opportunities that impair their ability to achieve the goals valued by society.

structured interviews Interviews in which the wording, order, and content of the questions are standardized in order to improve the reliability of the information obtained by an interviewer.

subcultural explanations The subcultural version of sociological theory maintains that a conflict of norms held by different groups causes criminal behavior. This conflict arises when various groups endorse subcultural norms, pressuring their members to deviate from the norms underlying the criminal law.

suggestive questions Questions asked in a way that provides cues regarding possible answers.

suicide by cop A crisis situation in which a citizen precipitates his or her own death by behaving in such a fashion that a police officer is forced to use lethal force.

summary jury trial   An abbreviated, expedited form of a jury trial that is intended to be helpful in resolving simple, lower-value cases.

sunk-cost fallacy   Phenomenon in which there is reluctance to change a behavior or course of action because of prior heavy investment in it, even when changing would be beneficial.

sympathy hypothesis   The assumption that jurors' decisions will be influenced by feelings of sympathy.

system variable   In eyewitness identifications, a variable whose impact on an identification can be controlled by criminal justice system officials. Examples include the way a lineup is presented and the way a witness is questioned.

T

team policing   A policy of less centralized decision-making within police organizations.

terrorism   The use of threats of violence to achieve certain organizational goals.

testamentary capacity   Having the mental capacity to execute a will, including the capacity to resist the pressures or domination of any person who might use undue influence on the distribution of the estate of the person writing the will.

therapeutic community   A community-based approach in which all staff and participants are considered to be part of the treatment process. It has generally been used for drug offenders and domestic violence offenders. This approach may include group therapy, individual counseling, and drug testing with the objective of building skills in controlling anger, improving decision-making, and recognizing high-risk situations.

therapeutic jurisprudence   An approach to the law emphasizing the favorable mental health impact or otherwise "therapeutic" impact of the legal system upon its participants.

thought suppression   The attempt to avoid thinking about something specific.

threat assessment   A process that involves carefully considering the nature of the threat, the risk posed by the individual making it, and the indicated response to reduce the risk of harmful action.

tort   A private or civil wrong or injury other than breach of contract, subject to civil litigation.

transferred   The status of a juvenile charged with committing a serious offense when moved from juvenile court to criminal court.

trauma   An emotional response to a very threatening or stressful event (e.g., fatal accident, sexual assault, natural disaster).

Treatment Foster Care Oregon   An empirically supported juvenile intervention that involves placing juveniles with specially trained foster parents rather than in residential placement.

treatment needs and amenability   Rehabilitative needs and the likelihood of favorable response to interventions designed to reduce the risk of future criminal offending. It is an important consideration in decisions involving the transfer of juveniles.

trial consulting   The use of professionals trained in the social sciences to assist attorneys in preparing and presenting evidence in a trial.

truth bias   The assumption that most statements are honest and truthful. In the context of interrogations, people are better at detecting truthful denials than accurately judging deceptive elaborations.

U

ultimate opinion testimony   Testimony that offers a conclusion about the specific defendant or a specific witness, in contrast to testimony about a general phenomenon.

unconscious transference   Generation of a memory that is based on the recall of past interactions with a suspect, so that an innocent person may be confused with an offender.

utilitarian   The notion that criminal sentences should be designed to accomplish a useful outcome, such as compensating the victim or rehabilitating the offender.

V

validity scales   Measures of an individual's approach to a psychological test, typically including the underreporting or overreporting of symptoms, problems, and unusual experiences.

venire   A panel of prospective jurors drawn from a large list.

verdict-driven deliberation   A form of deliberation in which the jury takes an immediate vote and discussion focuses on reaching agreement on a verdict.

vicarious learning   Learning by observing the actions of another person and their outcomes.

victimology   The study of the process and consequences of victim's experiences, including recovery.

vividness effect   Information has a greater impact on judgments and decisions when it is vivid and attention-grabbing than when it is pallid and bland. Information presented in a highly imaginable way is more persuasive than simple verbal descriptions of the same material.

voir dire   The process by which the judge and/or attorneys ask potential jurors questions and attempt to uncover any biases.

voluntary false confessions   False confessions that arise because people seek notoriety, desire to cleanse themselves of guilt feelings from previous wrongdoings, want to protect the real criminal, or have difficulty distinguishing fact from fiction.

W

weapon focus effect   When confronted by an armed attacker, the victim's tendency to focus attention on the weapon and fail to notice other stimuli.

Z

zero-tolerance   An approach to law enforcement in which the police attempt to arrest all lawbreakers, even those who have committed petty or nuisance crimes.

References

Abram, K., Teplin, L. A., Charles, D., Longworth, S., McClelland, G., & Dulcan, M. (2004). Posttraumatic stress disorder and trauma in youth in juvenile detention. *Archives of General Psychiatry, 61*, 403–410. doi:10.1001/archpsych.61.4.403

Abram, K. M., Teplin, L. A., Charles, D. R., Longworth, S. L., McClelland, G. M. & Dulcan, M. K. (2004). Posttraumatic stress disorder and trauma in youth in juvenile detention. *Archives of General Psychiatry, 61*, 403–410.

Abram, K. M., Washburn, J. J., Teplin, L. A., Emanuel, K. M., Romero, E. G., & McClelland, G. M. (2007). Posttraumatic stress disorder and psychiatric comorbidity among detained youths. *Psychiatric Services, 58*, 1311–1316.

Abramson, A. (2021). Building mental health into emergency responses. *American Psychological Association Monitor on Psychology, 52*(5), 30-ff. Retrieved January 16, 2022, from https://www.apa.org/monitor/2021/07/emergency-responses.

Abramson, J. (1994). *We, the jury.* New York, NY: Basic Books.

Acharya, A. P., & Acharya, A. (2017). Cyberterrorism and biotechnology: When ISIS meets CRiSPR. *Snapshot.* Retrieved July 14, 2017, from https://www.foreignaffairs.com/articles/world/2017-06-01/cyberterrorism-and-biotechnology

Ackerman, M. J., & Ackerman, M. C. (1997). Child custody evaluation practices: A survey of experienced professionals (revisited). *Professional Psychology: Research and Practice, 28*, 137–145.

Ackerman, M. J., Bow, J. N., & Mathy, N. (2021). Child custody evaluation practices: Where we were, where we are, and where we are going. *Professional Psychology: Research and Practice, 52*(4), 406–417. doi.org/10.1037/pro0000380

Adams, R. E., Rohe, W. M., & Arcury, T. A. (2005). Awareness of community-oriented policing and neighborhood perceptions in five small to midsize cities. *Journal of Criminal Justice, 33*, 43–54.

Ainsworth, P. (2001). *Offender profiling and crime analysis.* Portland, OR: Willan.

Ajzen, I., and Fishbein, M. (1977). Attitude-behavior relations: A theoretical analysis and review of empirical literature. *Psychological Bulletin, 84*, 888–918.

Ake v. Oklahoma, 105 S.Ct. 977 (1985).

Akers, R. L., Krohn, M. D., Lanz-Kaduce, L., & Radosevich, M. (1996). Social learning and deviant behavior: A specific test of a general theory. In D. G. Rojek & G. F. Jensen (Eds.), *Exploring delinquency: Causes and control* (pp. 109–119). Los Angeles, CA: Roxbury.

Alceste, F., Jones, K., & Kassin, S. (2020). Facts only the perpetrator could have known? A study of contamination in mock crime interrogations. *Law and Human Behavior, 44*, 128–142.

Alexander, J., Barton, C., Gordon, D., Grotpeter, J., Hansson, K., Harrison, R., … Sexton, T. (1998). *Blueprints for violence prevention: Book three. Functional family therapy.* Boulder, CO: Center for the Study and Prevention of Violence.

Alexander, K., Quas, J., Goodman, G., Ghetti, S., Edelstein, R., Redlich, A., … Jones, D. (2005). Traumatic impact predicts long-term memory for documented child sexual abuse. *Psychological Science, 16*, 33–40.

Alexander, M. (2010). *The new Jim Crow: Incarceration in the age of colorblindness.* New York: New Press.

Alhabib, S., Nur, U., & Jones, R. (2010). Domestic violence against women: Systematic review of prevalence studies. *Journal of Family Violence, 25*, 369–382.

Alschuler, A. W. (2016). A nearly perfect system for convicting the innocent. *Albany Law Review, 79*, 919–940.

Alton, S. (2017). The strange case of Dr. Jekyll's will: A tale of testamentary capacity. *Tulsa Law Review, 5*(2), 263–287. Retrieved January 26, 2022, from https://digitalcommons.law.utulsa.edu/cgi/viewcontent.cgi?referer=https://www.google.com/&httpsredir=1&article=3048&context=tlr

Altschuler, D. (1998). Intermediate sanctions and community treatment for serious and violent juvenile offenders. In R. Loeber & D. Farrington (Eds.), *Serious and violent juvenile offenders: Risk factors and successful interventions* (pp. 367–388). Thousand Oaks, CA: Sage.

Altschuler, D., & Armstrong, T. (1997). Aftercare not afterthought: Testing the IAP model. *Juvenile Justice, 3*, 115–122.

Amato, P. (2001). Children of divorce in the 1990s: An update of the Amato and Keith (1991) meta-analysis. *Journal of Family Psychology, 15*, 335–370.

American Academy of Child and Adolescent Psychiatry (2017, January). *Children and divorce.* Retrieved January 27, 2022, from https://www.aacap.org/AACAP/Families_and_Youth/Facts_for_Families/FFF-Guide/Children-and-Divorce-001.aspx

American Bar Association. (1993). *ABA formal opinion 93–379.* Chicago, IL: Author.

American Medical Association. (2007). *Guides to the evaluation of permanent impairment* (6th ed.). Chicago, IL: Author.

American Psychiatric Association. (2013). *Diagnostic and statistical manual of mental disorders* (5th ed.). Arlington, VA: Author.

American Psychological Association. (2010). Guidelines for child custody evaluations in family law proceedings. *American Psychologist, 65*, 863–867. Retrieved January 28, 2022, from https://www.apa.org/practice/guidelines/child-custody.

American Psychological Association. (2012). *Miller v. Alabama and Jackson v. Hobbs.* Retrieved from http://www.apa.org/about/offices/ogc/amicus/miller-hobbs.aspx

American Psychological Association. (2013). Specialty guidelines for forensic psychology. *American Psychologist, 68*(1), 7–19.

American Psychological Association. (2017). *Ethical principles of psychologists and code of conduct.* Retrieved May 24, 2022, from https://www.apa.org/ethics/code.

American Psychological Association Task Force on Violent Media. (2015). *Technical report on the review of the violent video game literature.* Retrieved October 24, 2016, from www.apa.org/pi/families/review-video-games.pdf

American Society of Trial Consultants. (2017). *The ASTC professional code.* Retrieved from http://www.astcweb.org/astc-bylaws

The Andrea Yates case: Chronology of the Yates case. (2005, January 7). *Houston Chronicle*, p. A10.

Anakwah, N., Horselenberg, R., Hope, L., Amankwah, P. M., & van Koppen, P. J. (2020). Cross-cultural differences in eyewitness memory reports. *Applied Cognitive Psychology, 34*(2), 504–515. https://doi.org/10.1002/acp.3637

Anderson, J. (2014). The impact of family structure on the health of children: Effects of divorce. *Linacre Quarterly, 81*(4): 378–387. doi: 10.1179/0024363914Z.00000000087

Anderson, M., & MacCoun, R. (1999). Goal conflict in juror assessments of compensatory and punitive damages. *Law and Human Behavior, 23*, 313–330.

Anderson, N. E. & Kiehl, K. A. (2012). The psychopath magnetized: Insights from brain imaging. *Trends in Cognitive Science, 16*, 52–60.

Andrews, D. A., & Bonta, J. (2010). Rehabilitating criminal justice policy and practice. *Psychology, Public Policy, and Law, 16*, 39–55.

Andrews, D. A., & Hoge, R. (2010). *Evaluation for risk of violence in juveniles.* New York, NY: Oxford University Press.

Andrews, D. A., Bonta, J., & Hoge, R. D. (1990). Classification for effective rehabilitation: Rediscovering psychology. *Criminal Justice and Behavior, 17*, 19–52.

Andrews, D. A., Bonta, J., & Wormith, J. (2004). *The Level of Service/Case Management Inventory user's manual.* North Tonawanda, NY: Multi-Health Systems.

Angermeyer, M., van der Auwera, S., Carta, M., & Schomerus, G. (2017). Public attitudes towards psychiatry and psychiatric treatment at the beginning of the 21st century: A systematic review and meta-analysis of population surveys. *World Psychiatry, 16*(1), 50–61.

Antrobus, E., McKimmie, B., & Newcombe, P. (2016). Mode of children's testimony and the effect of assumptions about credibility. *Psychiatry, Psychology and Law, 23*, 922–940.

Aos, S., Miller, M., & Drake, E. (2006). *Evidence-based adult corrections programs: What works and what does not.* Olympia, WA: Washington State Institute for Public Policy.

Aos, S., Miller, M., & Drake, E. (2006). *Evidence-based public policy options to reduce future prison construction, criminal justice costs, and crime rates.* Olympia: Washington State Institute for Public Policy.

Aos, S., Phipps, P., Barnoski, R., & Lieb, R. (2001). *The comparative costs and benefits of programs to reduce crime.* Olympia, WA: Washington State Institute for Public Policy. (Document No. 01-05-1201).

Aos, S., Phipps, P., Barnoski, R., & Lieb, R. (2001). *The comparative costs and benefits of programs to reduce crime.* Olympia, WA: Washington State Institute for Public Policy. (Document No. 01-05-1201).

Appelbaum, P. (2005). Law & psychiatry: Behavioral genetics and the punishment of crime. *Psychiatric Services, 56*, 25–27.

Appelbaum, P. (2007). The new lie detectors: Neuroscience, deception, and the courts. *Psychiatric Services, 58*, 460–462.

Appelbaum, P. (2020). *Kahler v. Kansas*: The constitutionality of abolishing the insanity defense. *Psychiatric Services.* Retrieved February 22, 2022, from https://doi.org/10.1176/appi.ps.202000707

Appelbaum, P. S., & Grisso, T. (1995). The MacArthur Treatment Competence Study. I: Mental illness and competence to consent to treatment. *Law and Human Behavior, 19*, 105–126.

Appleby, S., & Kassin, S. (2016). When self-report trumps science: Effects of confessions, DNA, and prosecutorial theories on perceptions of guilt. *Psychology, Public Policy, and Law, 22*, 127–140.

Arkes, H., & Mellers, B. (2002). Do juries meet our expectations? *Law and Human Behavior, 26*, 625–639.

Aronson, J. (2010). The law's use of brain evidence. *Annual Review of Law and Social Science, 6*, 93–108.

Arrigo, B. (2006). *Criminal behavior: A systems approach.* New York, NY: Pearson.

Arseneault, L. (2017). The persistent and pervasive impact of being bullied in childhood and adolescence: Implications for policy and practice. *Journal of Child Psychology and Psychiatry, 59*(4), 405–421.

Asendorpf, J. B., Denissen, J. J. A., & van Aken, M. A. G. (2008). Inhibited and aggressive preschool children at 23 years of age: Personality and social transitions into adulthood. *Developmental Psychology, 44*, 997–1011.

Ashkenazi, T., & Fisher, R. P. (2022). Field test of the cognitive interview to enhance eyewitness and victim memory, in intelligence investigations of terrorist attacks. *Journal of Applied Research in Memory and Cognition, 11*(2), 200–208. //doi.org/10.1037/h0101871.supp (Supplemental)

Asscher, J., Dekovic, M., Manders, W., van der Laan, P., & Prins, P. (2013). A randomized controlled trial of the effectiveness of multisystemic therapy in the Netherlands: Post-treatment changes and moderator effects. *Journal of Experimental Criminology, 9*, 169–187. doi:10.1007/s11292-012-9165-9

Associated Press. (1988, January 13). Former Kansas woman identifies man in attack. *Kansas City Times*, p. B5.

Associated Press. (2003). State loses track of 33,000 sex offenders. Retrieved from http://articles.latimes.com/2003/jan/08/local/me-offender8

Association of Family and Conciliation Courts. (2000). *Model standards of practice for family and divorce mediation.* Madison, WI: Author. Retrieved December 26, 2016, from www.afccnet.org

Association of Family and Conciliation Courts. (2006). *Model standards of practice for child custody evaluation.* Madison, WI: Author. Retrieved December 26, 2016, from www.afccnet.org

Association of Family and Conciliation Courts. (2016). *Guidelines for examining intimate partner violence: A supplement to the AFCC model standards of practice for child custody evaluation.* Madison, WI: Author. Retrieved December 26, 2016, from www.afccnet.org

Atkins v. Virginia, 536 U.S. 304 (2002).

Axt, J., Ebersole, C., & Nosek, B. (2016). An unintentional, robust, and replicable pro-black bias in social judgment. *Social Cognition, 34*, 1–39.

Babcock, B. (1993). A place in the palladium: Women's rights and jury service. *University of Cincinnati Law Review, 61*, 1139–1180.

Baglivio, M. T., Epps, N., Swartz, K., Huq, M. S., Sheer, A., & Hardt, N. S. (2014). The prevalence of Adverse Childhood Experiences (ACE) in the lives of juvenile offenders. *Journal of Juvenile Justice, 3*(2), 1–23.

Baglivio, M., Jackowski, K., & Greenwald, M., & Howell, J. (2014). Serious, violent, and chronic juvenile offenders: A statewide analysis of prevalence and prediction of subsequent recidivism using risk and protective factors. *Criminology & Public Policy, 13*(1), 83–116. //doi.org/10.1111/1745-9133.12064

Baglivio, M, T,, Epps, N., Swartz, K., Huq, M. S., Sheer, A., & Hardt, N. S. (2014). The prevalence of Adverse Childhood Experiences (ACE) in the lives of juvenile offenders. *Journal of Juvenile Justice, 3*(2), 1–23.

Baguley, C., McKimmie, B. & Masser, B. (2020). Reevaluating how to measure jurors' comprehension and application of jury instructions, *Psychology, Crime & Law, 26*, 53–66.

Bailenson, J., Blascovich, J., Beall, A., & Noveck, B. (2006). Courtroom applications of virtual environments, immersive virtual environments, and collaborative virtual environments. *Law & Policy, 28*, 249–270.

Baker, L. (1983). *Miranda: Crime, law, and politics.* New York, NY: Atheneum.

Bakhshay, S., & Haney, C. (2018). The media's impact on the right to a fair trial: A content analysis of pretrial publicity in capital cases. *Psychology, Public Policy, and Law, 24*, 326–340.

Baldus, D. C., Pulaski, C., & Woodworth, G. (1983). Comparative review of death sentences: An empirical study of the Georgia experience. *Journal of Criminal Law and Criminology, 74*, 661–753.

Baldus, D., Woodworth, G., Zuckerman, D., Weiner, N., & Broffit, B. (2001). The use of peremptory challenges in capital murder trials: A legal and empirical analysis. *University of Pennsylvania Journal of Constitutional Law, 3*, 3–169.

Bali, A., Martire, K., & Edmond, G. (2021). Lay comprehension of statistical evidence: A novel measurement approach. *Law and Human Behavior, 45*, 370–390.

Ballard, R., Holtzworth-Munroe, A., Applegate, A., D'Onofrio, B., & Bates, J. (2013). A randomized controlled trial of child-informed mediation. *Psychology, Public Policy, and Law, 19*(3), 271–281.

Bandes, S., Pryor, M., Kerrison, E., & Goff, P. (2019). The mismeasure of Terry stops: Assessing the psychological and emotional harms of stop and frisk to individuals and communities. *Behavioral Sciences & the Law, 37*(2), 176–194.

Bandura, A. (1976). Social learning analysis of aggression. In E. Ribes-Inesta & A. Bandura (Eds.), *Analysis of delinquency and aggression* (pp. 203–232). Hillsdale, NJ: Erlbaum.

Bandura, A. (1986). *Social foundations of thought and action: A social cognitive theory.* Englewood Cliffs, NJ: Prentice Hall.

Banks v. Goodfellow, L. R. 5 Q. B. 549 (1870).

Barber, L., Grawitch, M., & Trares, S. (2009). Service-oriented and force-oriented emotion regulation strategies in police officers. *Applied Psychology in Criminal Justice, 5*, 182–202.

Baron, S. W. (2003). Self-control, social consequences, and criminal behavior: Street youth and the general theory of crime. *Journal of Research in Crime and Delinquency, 40*(4), 403.

Barovick, H. (1998, June). DWB: Driving while black. *Time*, p. 35.

Barr, W. (1992, March). *Comments by the attorney general of the United States.* Speech delivered at the University of Kansas, Lawrence.

Barrett, H., Slesnick, N., Brody, J., Turner, C., & Peterson, T. (2001). Treatment outcomes for adolescent substance abuse at 4- and 7-month assessments. *Journal of Consulting and Clinical Psychology, 69*, 802–813. doi:10.1037/0022-006X.69.5.802

Barth, J., & Huffman, S. (2015). Sentiment toward same-sex divorce. In M. Miller, J. Blumenthal, & J. Chamberlain (Eds.), *Handbook of community sentiment* (pp. 129–141). New York, NY: Springer.

Bartlett, F. C. (1932). *Remembering: A study of experimental and social psychology.* New York, NY: Cambridge University Press.

Bartlett, J., & Zottoli, T. (2021). Paradox of conviction probability: Mock defendant want better deals as risk of conviction increases. *Law and Human Behavior, 45*, 39–54.

Bartol, C. R. (1983). *Psychology and American law.* Belmont, CA: Wadsworth.

Bartol, C. R. (1991). Predictive validation of the MMPI for small-town police officers who fail. *Professional Psychology: Research and Practice, 22*, 127–132.

Bartol, C. R., & Bartol, A. (2006). *Current perspectives in forensic psychology and criminal justice.* Thousand Oaks, CA: Sage.

Batson v. Kentucky, 476 U.S. 79 (1986).

Bauserman, R. (2002). Child adjustment in joint-custody versus sole-custody arrangements: A meta-analytic review. *Journal of Family Psychology, 16*(1), 91–102. doi: 10.1037//0893-3200.16.1.91.

Bureau of Justice Statistics (2016). *National crime victimization survey.* Retrieved February 27, 2023 from https://bjs.ojp.gov/sites/g/files /xyckuh236/files/media/document/cv16_old.pdf

Bureau of Justice Statistics (2020). Crime victimization 2019. Retrieved February 27, 2023 from https://bjs.ojp.gov/library/publications /criminal-victimization-2019

Baxter, J., Weston, R., & Qu, L. (2011). Family structure, co-parental relationship quality, post-separation parental involvement and children's emotional wellbeing. *Journal of Family Studies, 17*, 86–109.

Bazelon, D. (1974). Psychiatrists and the adversary process. *Scientific American, 230*, 18–23.

Beattey, R., Matsuura, T., & Jeglic, E. (2014). Judicial bond-setting behavior: The perceived nature of the crime may matter more than how serious it is. *Psychology, Public Policy, and Law, 20*, 411–420.

Bechara, A., Damasio, H., Tranel, D., & Damasio, A. R. (1997). Deciding advantageously before knowing the advantageous strategy. *Science, 275*, 1293–1294.

Beech, A. R., Fisher, D. D., & Thornton, D. (2003). Risk assessment of sex offenders. *Professional Psychology: Research and Practice, 34*, 339–352.

Begam, R. (1977). Voir dire: The attorney's job. *Trial, 13*, 3.

Begany, J. J., & Milburn, M. A. (2002). Psychological predictors of sexual harassment: Authoritarianism, hostile sexism, and rape myths. *Psychology of Men and Masculinity, 3*, 119–126.

Beggs, S., & Grace, R. (2011). Treatment gains for sexual offenders against children predicts reduced recidivism: A comparative validity study. *Journal of Consulting and Clinical Psychology, 79*, 182–192.

Beiser, E. N. (1973). Are juries representative? *Judicature, 57*, 194–199.

Beland, L., & Kim, D. (2016). The effect of high school shootings on schools and student performance. *Educational Evaluation and Policy Analysis, 38*, 113–126. doi:10.3102/0162373715590683

Belanger, H., Curtiss, G., Demery, J., Lebowitz, B., & Vanderploeg, R. (2005). Factors moderating neuropsychological outcomes following mild traumatic brain injury: A meta-analysis. *Journal of the International Neuropsychological Society, 11*, 215–227.

Belenko, S., Hiller, M., & Hamilton, L. (2013). Treating substance use disorders in the criminal justice system. *Current Psychiatry Reports, 15*(11). doi: 10.1007/s11920-013-0414-z

Bellafante, G. (2017, June 1). Getting rid of bail is only the start. Retrieved from https://www.nytimes.com/2017/06/01/nyregion/getting-rid-of-bail-is-only -the-start.html?smprod=nytcore-iphone&smid=nytcore-iphone-share

Bench, L., & Allen, T. (2003). Investigating the stigma of prison classification: An experimental design. *The Prison Journal, 83*, 307–382.

Bennell, C., Jones, N., Taylor, P., & Snook, B. (2006). Validities and abilities in criminal profiling: A critique of the studies conducted by Richard Kocsis and his colleagues. *International Journal of Offender Therapy and Comparative Criminology, 50*, 344–360.

Benner, A. W. (1986). Psychological screening of police applicants. In J. T. Reese & H. A. Goldstein (Eds.), *Psychological services for law enforcement* (pp. 11–20). Washington, DC: U.S. Government Printing Office.

Ben-Porath, Y., Corey, D., & Terescavage, A. (2017). Using the MMPI-2-RF in preemployment evaluations of police officer candidates. In C. Mitchell & E. Dorian (Eds.), *Police psychology and its growing impact on modern law enforcement* (pp. 51–78). Hershey, PA: IGI Global.

Ben-Porath, Y., & Tellegen, A. (2020). *The Minnesota Multiphasic Personality Inventory-3 (MMPI-3) technical manual.* Minneapolis: University of Minnesota Press.

Bergold, A., & Kovera, M. (2021). Diversity's impact on the quality of deliberations. *Personality and Social Psychology Bulletin, 47*, 1–15.

Berkemer v. McCarty, 468 U.S. 420 (1984).

Bernstein, M. (2016, October 28). Oregon standoff prosecutors failed to prove 'intent' to impede federal workers. Retrieved June 20, 2022, from https://www.oregonlive.com/oregon-standoff/2016/10/juror_4 _prosecutors_in_oregon.html#incart_maj-story-1

Bertman, L., Thompson, J., Waters, W., Estupinan-Kane, L., Martin, J., & Russell, L. (2003). Effect of an individualized treatment protocol on restoration of competency in pretrial forensic inpatients. *Journal of the American Academy of Psychiatry and Law, 31*, 37–35.

Besemer, S., Farrington, D., & Bijleveld, C. (2017). Labeling and intergenerational transmission of crime: The interaction between criminal justice intervention and a convicted parent. *PLoS One, 12*(3), e0172419. doi: 10.1371/journal.pone.0172419

Betts v. Brady, 316 U.S. 455 (1942).

Beune, K., Giebels, E., Adair, W., Fennis, B., & Van Der Zee, K. (2011). Strategic sequences in police interviews and the importance of order and cultural fit. *Criminal Justice and Behavior, 38*(9), 934–954.

Beune, K., Giebels, E., & Sanders, K. (2009). Are you talking to me? Influencing behaviour and culture in police interviews. *Psychology, Crime & Law, 15*(7), 597–617.

Beune, K. Giebels, E., & Taylor, P.J. (2010). Patterns of interaction patterns in police interviews: The role of cultural dependency. *Criminal Justice and Behavior, 37*(8), 904–925.

Beyer, M. (1997). Experts for juveniles at risk of adult sentences. In P. Puritz, A. Capozello, & W. Shang (Eds.), *More than meets the eye: Rethinking assessment, competency, and sentencing for a harsher era of juvenile justice* (pp. 1–22). Washington, DC: American Bar Association, Juvenile Justice Center.

Bibas, S. (2004). Plea bargaining outside the shadow of trial. *Harvard Law Review, 117*, 2463–2547.

Bild, E., Redman, A., Newman, E., Muir, B., Tait, D., & Schwarz, N. (2021). Sound and credibility in the virtual court: Low audio quality leads to less favorable evaluations of witnesses and lower weighting of evidence. *Law and Human Behavior, 45*, 481–495.

Binder, A. (1988). Juvenile delinquency. In M. R. Rosenzweig & L. W. Porter (Eds.), *Annual review of psychology* (pp. 253–282). Palo Alto, CA: Annual Reviews.

Binder, A., Geis, G., & Bruce, D. D. (2001). *Juvenile delinquency: Historical, cultural & legal perspectives.* Cincinnati, OH: Anderson.

Binder, J. R., Desai, R. H., Graves, W. W., & Conant, L. L. (2009). Where is the semantic system? A critical review and meta-analysis of 120 functional neuroimaging studies. *Cerebral Cortex, 19*, 2767–2796.

Bing, N., Nelson, W., & Wesolowski, K. (2009). Comparing the effects of amount of conflict on children's adjustment following parental divorce. *Journal of Divorce and Remarriage, 50*, 159–171.

Bishop, D. M., Frazier, C. E., Lanza-Kaduce, L., & Winner, L. (1996). The transfer of juveniles to criminal court: Does it make a difference? *Crime and Delinquency, 42*, 171–191.

Bittle, J. (March 3, 2020). Lie detectors have always been suspect. AI has made the problem worse. Retrieved March 14, 2022, from https://www.technologyreview.com/2020/03/13/905323 /ai-lie-detectors-polygraph-silent-talker-iborderctrl-converus-neuroid/

Blair, I., Judd, C., & Chapleau, K. (2004). The influence of Afrocentric facial features in criminal sentencing. *Psychological Science, 15*, 674–679.

Blakely v. Washington, 124 S. Ct. 2348 (2004).

Blanchard, S., Carlson, K., & Meloy, M. (2014). Biased predecisional processing of leading and nonleading alternatives. *Psychological Science, 25*, 812–816.

Bloeser, A., McCurley, C., & Mondak, J. (2012). Jury service as civic engagement: Determinants of jury summons compliance. *American Politics Research, 40*, 179–204.

Blumenthal, J. A. (1998). The reasonable woman standard: A meta-analytic review of gender differences in perceptions of sexual harassment. *Law and Human Behavior, 22*, 33–58.

Boba, R., Weisburd, D., & Meeker, J. W. (2009). The limits of regional data sharing and regional problem solving: Observations from the East Valley, CA COMPASS Initiative. *Police Quarterly, 12*, 22–41.

Bock, M., & Schneider, D. (2017). The voice of lived experience: Mobile video narratives in the courtroom. *Information, Communication & Society, 20*, 335–350.

Boehnert, C. (1989). Characteristics of successful and unsuccessful insanity pleas. *Law and Human Behavior, 13*, 31–40.

Bolin, J. (2019). *Attitudes on legal insanity and the impact of race.* Dayton, OH: Doctoral Dissertation, Wright State University. Retrieved August 30, 2021, from https://etd.ohiolink.edu/apexprod/rws_etd/send_file/send?accession=wsupsych1564414182185381&disposition=inline

Bolin, J. (2020). Attitudes on legal insanity and the impact of race. Retrieved on February 27, 2023 from http://rave.ohiolink.edu/etdc/view?acc_num=wsupsych1564414182185381

Bond, C., & DePaulo, B. (2006). Accuracy of deception judgments. *Personality and Social Psychology Review, 10*, 214–234.

Bond, C. F., Jr., & DePaulo, B. M. (2008). Individual differences in judging deception: Accuracy and bias. *Psychological Bulletin, 134*, 477–492.

Bonnie, R. J. (1993). The competence of criminal defendants: Beyond *Dusky* and *Drope. University of Miami Law Review, 47*, 539–601.

Bonta, J. (1997). *Offender rehabilitation: From research to practice.* Ottawa, ON: Department of the Solicitor General of Canada. (User Report No. 1997-01).

Bonta, J., & Andrews, D. (2017). *The psychology of criminal conduct* (6th ed.). New York: Routledge.

Bonta, J., & Andrews, D. (2017). *The psychology of criminal conduct* (6th ed.). New York: Routledge.

Booij, L., Tremblay, R. E., Leyton, M., Seguin, J. R., Vitaro, F., Gravel, P., … Benkelfat, C. (2010). Brain serotonin synthesis in adult males characterized by physical aggression during childhood: A 21-year longitudinal study. *PLoS ONE, 5*, ArtID e11255.

Book, A. S. (1999). Shame on you: An analysis of modern shame punishment as an alternative to incarceration. *William and Mary Law Review, 40*, 653–686.

Boone, K., Lu, P., and Herzberg, D. S. (2002). *The b Test manual.* Los Angeles: Western Psychological Service.

Boothroyd, R., Mercado, C., Poythress, N., Christy, A., & Petrila, J. (2005). Clinical outcomes of defendants in mental health court. *Psychiatric Services, 56*, 829–834.

Boothroyd, R., Poythress, N., McGaha, A., & Petrila, J. (2003). The Broward mental health court: Process, outcomes, and service utilization. *International Journal of Law & Psychiatry, 26*, 55–71.

Bordenkircher v. Hayes, 434 U.S. 357 (1978).

Bordens, K. S., & Bassett, J. (1985). The plea bargaining process from the defendant's perspective: A field investigation. *Basic and Applied Social Psychology, 6*, 93–110.

Bornstein, B. (1994). David, Goliath, and Reverend Bayes: Prior beliefs about defendants' status in personal injury cases. *Applied Cognitive Psychology, 8*, 232–258.

Bornstein, B. H. (2017). Jury simulation research: Pros, cons, trends, and alternatives. In M. Kovera (Ed.), *The psychology of juries* (pp. 207–226). Washington DC: American Psychological Association.

Bornstein, B. H., & Greene, E. (2011a). Consulting on damage awards. In R. Wiener & B. Bornstein (Eds.), *Handbook of trial consulting* (pp. 281–296). New York, NY: Springer.

Bornstein, B. H., & Greene, E. (2011b). Jury decision making: Implications for and from psychology. *Current Directions in Psychological Science, 20*, 63–67.

Bornstein, B. H., & Greene, E. (2017). *The jury under fire: Myth, controversy, and reform.* New York, NY: Oxford University Press.

Bornstein, B. H., & Muller, S. (2001). The credibility of recovered memory testimony: Exploring the effects of alleged victim and perpetrator gender. *Child Abuse and Neglect, 25*, 1415–1426.

Borum, R., Bartels, P., & Forth, A. (2005). *Structured assessment of violence risk in youth.* Lutz, FL: PAR.

Borum, R., Cornell, D., Modjelewski, W., & Jimerson, S. (2010). What can be done about school shootings? A review of the evidence. *Educational Researcher, 39*(1), 27–37.

Borum, R., & Fulero, S. M. (1999). Empirical research and the insanity defense and attempted reforms: Evidence toward informed policy. *Law and Human Behavior, 23*, 375–394.

Borum, R., & Verhaagen, D. (2006). *Assessing and managing violence risk in youth.* New York, NY: Guilford.

Borum, R., Williams, M., Deans, M., Steadman, H. J., & Morrissey, J. (1998). Police perspectives on responding to mentally ill people in crisis: Perceptions of program effectiveness. *Behavioral Sciences & the Law, 16*, 393–405.

Boud, D. & Molloy, E. (2013). Rethinking models of feedback for learning: The challenge of design. *Assessment & Evaluation in Higher Education, 38*(6), 698–712, doi: 10.1080/02602938.2012.691462

Bouffard, J., & Bergeron, L. (2006). Reentry works: The implementation and effectiveness of a serious and violent offender reentry initiative. *Journal of Offender Rehabilitation, 44*, 1–29.

Bourgon, G., & Armstrong, B. (2005). Transferring the principles of effective treatment into a "Real World" prison setting. *Criminal Justice and Behavior, 32*, 3–25.

Boyer, P. J. (2000, January 17). DNA on trial. *The New Yorker*, pp. 42–53.

Brandenburg v. Ohio, 395 U.S. 444 (1969).

Brank, E., & Scott, L. (2012). Let's make a deal: The psychology of plea agreements. *APA Monitor, 43*(4), 31.

Brannen, D., Salekin, R., Zapf, P., Salekin, K., Kubak, F., & DeCoster, J. (2006). Transfer to adult court: A national study of how juvenile court judges weight pertinent *Kent* criteria. *Psychology, Public Policy, and Law, 12*, 332–355.

Braver, S., Ellman, I., & Fabricius, W. (2003). Relocation of children after divorce and children's best interests: New evidence and legal considerations. *Journal of Family Psychology, 17*, 206–219.

Bravo, G., Dubois, M., & Pâquet, M. (2003). Advance directives for health care and research. *Alzheimer Disease and Associated Disorders, 17*(4), 215–222.

Brayer, P. (2015). Hidden racial bias: Why we need to talk with jurors about Ferguson. *Northwestern University Law Review, 109*, 163–170.

Bregant, J. (2009). Let's give them something to talk about: An empirical evaluation of predeliberation discussions. *University of Illinois Law Review, 2009*(4), 1213–1241.

Brehm, S. S., & Brehm, J. (1981). *Psychological reactance.* New York, NY: Academic Press.

Brenan, M. (2018, May 31). *Americans' strong support for euthanasia persists.* Retrieved November 5, 2021, from https://news.gallup.com/poll/235145/americans-strong-support-euthanasia-persists.aspx

Brennan, P. A., & Raine, A. (1997). Biosocial bases of antisocial behavior: Psychophysiological, neurological, and cognitive factors. *Clinical Psychology Review, 17*, 589–604.

Breslau, N., Lucia, V., & Alvarado, G. (2006). Intelligence and other predisposing factors in exposure to trauma and posttraumatic stress disorder: A follow-up study to age 17 years. *Archives of General Psychiatry, 63*, 1238–1245.

Brewer, N., & Burke, A. (2002). Effects of testimonial inconsistencies and eyewitness confidence on mock-juror judgments. *Law and Human Behavior, 26*, 353–364.

Brewster, J., & Stoloff, M. (2003). Relationship between IQ and first-year overall performance as a police officer. *Applied H. R. M. Research, 8*, 49–50.

Brey, T. (2009). Child custody evaluation practices: A survey of psychologists. *Dissertation Abstracts International: Section B: The Sciences and Engineering, 69*(7-B), 4410.

Brigham, J. C., & Ready, D. J. (1985). Own-race bias in lineup construction. *Law and Human Behavior, 9*, 415–424. doi:10.1007/BF01044480

Brigham, J., & Wasserman, A. (1999). The impact of race, racial attitude, and gender on reactions to the criminal trial of O. J. Simpson. *Journal of Applied Social Psychology, 29*, 1333–1370.

Bright, D., & Goodman-Delahunty J. (2006). Gruesome evidence and emotion: Anger, blame, and jury decisionmaking. *Law and Human Behavior, 30,* 183–202.

Bright, D., & Goodman-Delahunty, J. (2011). Mock juror decision making in a civil negligence trial: The impact of gruesome evidence, injury severity, and information processing route. *Psychiatry, Psychology and Law, 18,* 439–459.

Brimbal, L., Meissner, C. A., Kleinman, S. M., Phillips, E. L., Atkinson, D. J., Dianiska, R. E., Rothweiler, J. N., Oleszkiewicz, S., & Jones, M. S. (2021). Evaluating the benefits of a rapport-based approach to investigative interviews: A training study with law enforcement investigators. *Law & Human Behavior, 45*(1), 55–67.

Broidy, L., Albright, D., & Denman, K. (2016). Deterring future incidents of intimate partner violence: Does type of formal intervention matter? *Violence Against Women, 22*(9), 1113–1133.

Broner, N., Lattimore, P., Cowell, A., & Schlenger, W. (2004). Effects of diversion on adults with co-occurring mental illness and substance use: Outcomes from a national multi-site study. *Behavioral Sciences & the Law, 22,* 519–541.

Broner, N., Mayrl, D., & Landsberg, G. (2005). Outcomes of mandated and nonmandated New York City diversion for offenders with alcohol, drug, and mental disorders. *The Prison Journal, 85,* 18–49.

Bronson, J., & Carson, E. A. (2019). *Prisoners in 2017.* Washington, DC: Bureau of Justice Statistics.

Brooks-Gunn, J., Duncan, G. J., Klebanow, P. K., & Sealand, N. (1993). Do neighborhoods influence child and adolescent development? *American Journal of Sociology, 99,* 353–395.

Brown, L. T. (2003). Racial discrimination in jury selection: Professional misconduct, not legitimate advocacy. *Review of Litigation, 22,* 209–317.

Brown, T., Borduin, C., & Henggeler, S. (2001). Treating juvenile offenders in community settings. In J. Ashford, B. Sales, & W. Reid (Eds.), *Treating adult and juvenile offenders with special needs* (pp. 445–464). Washington, DC: American Psychological Association.

Brown v. Board of Education, 347 U.S. 483 (1954).

Brown v. Entertainment Merchants Association, Case # 08-1448 U.S. Supreme Court (2011).

Brownmiller, S., & Alexander, D. (1992, January/February). *From Carmita Wood to Anita Hill.* Ms., pp. 70–71.

Brubacher, M. (2018). Third-party support for retribution, rehabilitation, and giving an offender a clean slate. *Psychology, Public Policy, and Law, 24,* 503–517.

Brubacher, M. R., Fondacaro, M. R., Brank, E. M., Brown, V. E., & Miller, S. A. (2009). Procedural justice in resolving family disputes: Implications for childhood bullying. *Psychology, Public Policy, and Law, 15,* 149–167.

Brubacher, S., Glisic, U., Roberts, K., & Powell, M. (2011). Children's ability to recall unique aspects of one occurrence of a repeated event. *Applied Cognitive Psychology, 25,* 351–358.

Brubacher, S. P., Shulman, E. P., Bearman, M. J., & Powell, M. B. (2022). Teaching child investigative interviewing skills: Long-term retention requires cumulative training. *Psychology, Public Policy, and Law, 28*(1), 123–136. doi.org/10.1037/law0000332

Bruck, D. (1985, May 20). The death penalty: An exchange. *New Republic,* pp. 20–21.

Bruck, M., Ceci, S., & Hembrooke, H. (2002). The nature of children's true and false narratives. *Developmental Review, 22,* 520–554.

Brunner, H., Nelen, M., Breakefield, X., Ropers, H., & van Oost, B. (1993). Abnormal behavior associated with a point mutation in the structural gene for monoamine oxidase A. *Science, 262,* 578–580.

Bryan, P. (2005). *Constructive divorce: Procedural justice and sociolegal reform.* Washington, DC: American Psychological Association.

Bryan, W. J. (1971). *The chosen ones.* New York, NY: Vantage Press.

Buades-Rotger, M., & Gallardo-Pujol, D. (2014). The role of the monoamine oxidase A gene in moderating the response to adversity and associated antisocial behavior: A review. *Psychological Research in Behavior Management, 7,* 185–200.

Buades-Rotger, M., & Gallardo-Pujol, D. (2014). The role of the monoamine oxidase A gene in moderating the response to adversity and associated antisocial behavior: A review. *Psychological Research in Behavior Management, 7,* 185–200.

Bureau of Justice Statistics. (2002). *Rape and sexual assault: Reporting to police and medical attention, 1992–2000.* Washington, DC: U.S. Department of Justice.

Bureau of Justice Statistics. (2006). *Special report: Mental health problems of prison and jail inmates.* Retrieved January 26, 2009, from http://www.ojp .usdoj.gov/bjs/pub/pdf/mhppji.pdf

Bureau of Justice Statistics. (2010a). *Criminal victimization, 2010.* Retrieved from http://bjs.ojp.usdoj.gov/index.cfm?ty=tp&tid=31

Bureau of Justice Statistics. (2015a). *Criminal victimization, 2014.* Washington, DC: United States Department of Justice. Retrieved October 29, 2016, from https://www.bjs.gov/content/pub/pdf/cv14.pdf

Bureau of Justice Statistics. (2017). *Indicators of mental health problems reported by prisoners and jail inmates, 2011–12.* Washington, D.C.: Department of Justice. Retrieved February 4, 2022, from https://bjs.ojp.gov/content/pub /pdf/imhprpji1112.pdf

Bureau of Justice Statistics. (2017). *Police response to domestic violence, 2006–2015.* Washington, D.C.: United States Department of Justice. Retrieved January 17, 2022, from https://bjs.ojp.gov/pub/pdf/prdv0615

Bureau of Justice Statistics. (2021). Correctional populations in the United States, 2019—Statistical tables. Washington, D.C.: U.S. Department of Justice. Retrieved January 30, 2022, from https://bjs.ojp.gov/sites/g/files /xyckuh236/files/media/document/cpus19st.pdf

Bureau of Justice Statistics. (2021). *Jail inmates in 2020—Statistical tables.* Washington, D.C.: Department of Justice. Retrieved February 4, 2022, from https://bjs.ojp.gov/library/publications/jail-inmates -2020-statistical-tables

Bureau of Justice Statistics. (2021). Official website. Washington, D.C.: U.S. Department of Justice. Retrieved October 11, 2021, from https://bjs.ojp .gov/library/publications/list?subtopic=8626

Bureau of Justice Statistics. (2021). *Probation and parole in the United States, 2020.* Washington, D.C.: Department of Justice. Retrieved January 31, 2022, from https://bjs.ojp.gov/library/publications /probation-and-parole-united-states-2020

Burke, P., & Tonry, M. (2006). *Successful transition and reentry for safer communities: A call to action for parole.* Silver Spring, MD: Center for Effective Public Policy.

Burnet v. Coronado Oil and Gas Co., 52 S.Ct. 443 (1932).

Burt, M. R. (1980). Cultural myths and supports for rape. *Journal of Personality and Social Psychology, 38,* 217–230.

Burt, R., & Morris, N. (1972). A proposal for the abolition of the incompetency plea. *University of Chicago Law Review, 40,* 66–95.

Buss, A. H. (1966). *Psychopathology.* New York, NY: Wiley.

Butler, B., & Moran, G. (2007). The impact of death qualification, belief in a just world, legal authoritarianism, and locus of control on venirepersons' evaluations of aggravating and mitigating circumstances in capital trials. *Behavioral Sciences and the Law, 25,* 57–68.

Butler, P. (2016, April 5). Jurors need to take the law into their own hands. Retrieved June 26, 2022, from https://www.washingtonpost.com/news /in-theory/wp/2016/04/05/jurors-need-to-take-the-law-into-their -own-hands/

Butler, S., Baruch, G., Hickley, N., & Fonagy, P. (2011). A randomized controlled trial of multisystemic therapy and a statutory therapeutic intervention for young offenders. *Journal of the American Academy of Child and Adolescent Psychiatry, 12,* 1220–1235. doi:10.1016/j.jaac.2011.09.017

Butler, S., Fonagy, P., Baruch, G., & Hickey, N. (2011). A randomized controlled trial of multisystemic therapy and a statutory therapeutic intervention for young offenders. *Journal of the American Academy of Child and Adolescent Psychiatry, 50*(12), 1220–1235.

Butler, W. M., Leitenberg, H., & Fuselier, D. G. (1993). The use of mental health consultants to police hostage negotiation teams. *Behavioral Sciences & the Law, 11,* 213–221.

Cacioppo, J. T., Petty, R. E., Feinstein, J. A., & Jarvis, W. B. G. (1996). Dispositional differences in cognitive motivation: The life and times of individuals varying in Need for Cognition. *Psychological Bulletin, 119*, 197–253.

Caldwell, M., & Van Rybroek, G. (2005). Reducing violence in serious juvenile offenders using intensive treatment. *International Journal of Psychiatry and Law, 28*, 622–636.

Callahan, L., & Pinals, D. (2020, April). Challenges to reforming the competence to stand trial and competence restoration system. *Psychiatric Services online.* Retrieved February 22, 2022, from *https://ps.psychiatryonline.org/doi/10.1176/appi.ps.201900483*

Callahan, L. A., & Silver, E. (1998). Factors associated with the conditional release of persons acquitted by reason of insanity: A decision tree approach. *Law and Human Behavior, 22*(2), 147–163.

Camp, N., Voigt, R., Jurafsky, D., & Eberhardt, J. (2021). The thin blue waveform: Racial disparities in officer prosody undermine institutional trust in the police. *Journal of Personality and Social Psychology: Attitudes and Social Cognition,* 1–21.

Campbell, A. (2015). Is there a therapeutic way to balance community sentiment, student mental health, and study safety to address campus related violence? In M. Miller, J. Blumenthal, & J. Chamberlain (Eds.), *Handbook of community sentiment* (pp. 199–211). New York, NY: Springer.

Campbell, M. A., & Schmidt, F. (2000). Comparison of mental health & legal factors in the disposition outcome of young offenders. *Criminal Justice & Behavior, 27*, 688–715.

Canter, D., Alison, L., Alison, E., & Wentink, N. (2004). The organized/disorganized typology of serial murder: Myth or model? *Psychology, Public Policy and Law, 10*, 293–320.

Carlsmith, K. (2006). The roles of retribution and utility in determining punishment. *Journal of Experimental Social Psychology, 42*, 437–451.

Carlsmith, K. (2008). On justifying punishment: The discrepancy between words and actions. *Social Justice Research, 21*, 119–137.

Carlsmith, K., & Darley, J. (2008). Psychological aspects of retributive justice. *Advances in Experimental Social Psychology, 40*, 193–236.

Carlsmith, K., Darley, J., & Robinson, P. (2002). Why do we punish? Deterrence and just deserts as motives for punishment. *Journal of Personality and Social Psychology, 83*, 284–299.

Carnevale, P. (2008). Positive affect and decision frame in negotiation. *Group Decision and Negotiation, 17*, 51–63.

Carr. P. et al. (2000). Faculty perceptions of gender discrimination and sexual harassment in academic medicine. *Annals of Internal Medicine; 132*(11), 889–896.

Carroll, J. S., Kerr, N. L., Alfini, J. J., Weaver, F. M., MacCoun, R. J., & Feldman, V. (1986). Free press and fair trial: The role of behavioral research. *Law and Human Behavior, 10*, 187–201.

Carter, T. (2004, June). Red Hook experiment. *American Bar Association Journal, 90*, 37–42.

Casey, P., & Rottman, D. (2005). Problem-solving courts: Models and trends. *The Justice System Journal, 26*, 35–56.

Casey, T. (2004). When good intentions are not enough: Problem-solving courts and the impending crisis of legitimacy. *Southern Methodist University Law Review, 57*, 1459–1519.

Caspi, A., McClay, J., Moffitt, T., Mill, J., Martin, J., Craig, I., … Poulton, R. (2002). Role of genotype in the cycle of violence by maltreated children. *Science, 297*, 851–854.

Castelli, P., Goodman, G., & Ghetti, S. (2005). Effects of interview style and witness age on perceptions of children's credibility in sexual abuse cases. *Journal of Applied Social Psychology, 35*, 297–319.

Cauffman, E., Piquero, A., Kimonis, E., Steinberg, L., Chassin, L., & Fagan, J. (2007). Legal, individual, and environmental predictors of court disposition in a sample of serious adolescent offenders. *Law and Human Behavior, 31*, 519–535.

Center for Court Innovation. (2012). *Community court.* Retrieved from http://www.courtinnovation.org/topic/community-court

Center for Effective Public Policy. (2007). *Increasing public safety through successful offender reentry: Evidence-based and emerging practices in corrections.* Washington, DC: Author.

Center for Health and Justice at TASC. (2013). No entry: A national survey of criminal justice diversion programs and initiatives. Retrieved from https://www.centerforhealthandjustice.org/tascblog/Images/documents/Publications/CHJ%20Diversion%20Report_web.pdf

Centers for Disease Control and Prevention. (2018). 1992–2016 School-Associated Violent Death Surveillance System (SAVD-SS). Retrieved January 10, 2022, from https://www.cdc.gov/violenceprevention/youthviolence/schoolviolence/SAVD.html

Chajewski, M., & Mercado, C. (2009). An evaluation of sex offender residency restriction functioning in town, county, and city-wide jurisdictions. *Criminal Justice Policy Review, 20,* 44–61.

Chamberlain, P. (1990). Comparative evaluation of specialized foster care for seriously delinquent youths: A first step. *Community Alternatives: International Journal of Family Care, 2*, 21–36.

Chamberlain, P., & Mihalic, S. (1998). *Blueprints for violence prevention: Book eight. Multidimensional treatment foster care.* Boulder, CO: Center for the Study and Prevention of Violence.

Chamberlain, P., & Reid, J. (1998). Comparison of two community alternatives to incarceration for chronic juvenile offenders. *Journal of Consulting and Clinical Psychology, 66*, 624–633.

Chan, J., & LaPaglia, J. (2011). The dark side of testing memory: Repeated retrieval can enhance eyewitness suggestibility. *Journal of Experimental Psychology: Applied, 17*, 418–432.

Chapple, C., & Hope, T. (2003). An analysis of the self-control and criminal versatility of gang and dating violence offenders. *Violence and Victims, 18*(6), 671–690.

Charman, S., Carlucci, M., Vallano, J., & Gregory, A. (2010). The selective cue integration framework: A theory of postidentification witness confidence assessment. *Journal of Experimental Psychology: Applied, 16*, 204–218.

Charman, S., & Wells, G. (2006). Applied lineup theory. In R. C. L. Lindsay, D. F. Ross, J. D. Read, & M. P. Toglia (Eds.), *The handbook of eyewitness psychology: Vol. 2. Memory for people* (pp. 219–254). Mahwah, NJ: Erlbaum.

Charman, S. D., & Quiroz, V. (2016). Blind sequential lineup administration reduces both false identifications and confidence in those false identifications. *Law and Human Behavior, 40*, 477–487.

Chen, M. K., & Shapiro, J. (2007). Do harsher prison conditions reduce recidivism? A discontinuity-based approach. *American Law and Economics Review, 9*, 1–29.

Chicago Community Policing Evaluation Consortium. (2004). *Longitudinal evaluation of Chicago's community policing program, 1993–2001.* Chicago, IL: Author.

Chifflet, P. (2015). Questioning the validity of criminal profiling: An evidence-based approach. *Australian & New Zealand Journal of Criminology, 48*, 238–255.

Chlistunoff, M. (2016). Expert testimony and the quest for reliability: The case for a methodology questionnaire. *Texas Law Review, 94*, 1055–1078.

Chmielewski, M., Zhu, J., Burchett, D., Bury, A., & Bagby, M. (2017). The comparative capacity of the Minnesota Multiphasic Personality Inventory-2 (MMPI-2) and MMPI-2 Restructured Form (MMPI-2-RF) validity scales to detect suspected malingering in a disability claimant sample. *Psychological Assessment, 29*(2), 199–208. doi: 10.1037/pas0000328.

Chorn, J., & Kovera, M. (2019). Variations in reliability and validity do not influence judge, attorney, and mock juror decisions about psychological expert evidence. *Law and Human Behavior, 43*, 542–557.

Christie, R. (1976). Probability v. precedence: The social psychology of jury selection. In G. Bermant, C. Nemeth, & N. Vidmar (Eds.), *Psychology and the law: Research frontiers* (pp. 265–281). Lexington, MA: Lexington Books.

Christy, A., Poythress, N., Boothroyd, R., Petrila, J., & Mehra, S. (2005). Evaluating the efficiency and community safety goals of the Broward County mental health court. *Behavioral Sciences & the Law, 23*, 1–17.

Cirincione, C., & Jacobs, C. (1999). Identifying insanity acquittals: Is it any easier? *Law and Human Behavior, 23*, 487–497.

CIT National Advisory Board. (2006). *Crisis intervention team core elements.* Memphis, TN: University of Memphis CIT Center.

Clark, S. (2012). Costs and benefits of eyewitness identification reform: Psychological science and public policy. *Perspectives on Psychological Science, 7,* 238–259.

Clark, S., & Davey, S. (2005). The target-to-fillers shift in simultaneous and sequential lineups. *Law and Human Behavior, 29,* 151–172.

Clavet, G. J. (1996, August). *Ironic effects of juror attempts to suppress inadmissible evidence.* Paper presented at the meeting of the American Psychological Association, Toronto, ON, Canada.

Cleary, H. (2014). Police interviewing and interrogation of juvenile suspects: A descriptive examination of actual cases. *Law and Human Behavior, 38,* 271–282.

Clemmer, D. (1958). *The prison community.* New York, NY: Rinehart.

Clermont, K., & Eisenberg, T. (1992). Trial by jury or judge: Transcending empiricism. *Cornell Law Review, 77,* 1124–1177.

Clow, K. A., Leach, A.-M., & Ricciardelli, R. (2012). Life after wrongful conviction. In B. L. Cutler (Ed.), *Conviction of the innocent: Lessons from psychological research.* (pp. 327–341). American Psychological Association. doi.org/10.1037/13085-015

Cloward, R. A., & Ohlin, L. E. (1960). *Delinquency and opportunity: A theory of delinquent gangs.* New York, NY: Free Press.

Cocozza, J., & Shufelt, J. (2006, June). *Juvenile mental health courts: An emerging strategy.* Retrieved July 3, 2008, from http://www.ncmhjj.com /pdfs/publications/JuvenileMentalHealthCourts.pdf

Cogin, J. A., & Fish, A. J. (2009). Gender, work engagement and sexual harassment: An empirical investigation. *Journal of Management and Organisation, 15,* 47–61. doi:10.5172/jmo.837.15.1.47

Cole, D. (2014). The difference prevention makes: Regulating preventive justice. *Criminal Law and Philosophy, 9,* 501–519.

Colquitt, J. (2001). Ad hoc plea bargaining. *Tulane Law Review, 75,* 695–776.

Commaroto, L., Jewell, T., & Wilder, A. (2011). *Rochester Veterans Court: An expanded service of the Rochester Drug Court: Evaluation summary report.* Rochester, NY: Coordinated Care Services, Inc.

Committee on Ethical Guidelines for Forensic Psychologists. (1991). Specialty guidelines for forensic psychologists. *Law and Human Behavior, 15,* 655–665.

Compton, M., Bahara, M., Watson, A., & Oliva, J. (2008). A comprehensive review of extant research on Crisis Intervention Team (CIT) programs. *Journal of the American Academy of Psychiatry and Law, 36,* 47–55.

Condie, L. O. (2003). *Parenting evaluations for the court: Care and protection matters.* New York, NY: Springer.

Conger, R. (1980). Juvenile delinquency: Behavior restraint or behavior facilitation? In T. Hirschi & M. Gottfredson (Eds.), *Understanding crime: Current theory and research* (pp. 131–142). Newbury Park, CA: Sage.

Congressional Research Service (2-5-21). Community oriented policing services. Retrieved October 5, 2021, from https://crsreports.congress.gov /product/pdf/IF/IF10922

Connell, A., Klostermann, S., & Dishion, T. (2012). Family Check Up effects on adolescent arrest trajectories: Variation by developmental subtype. *Journal of Research on Adolescence, 22,* 367–380. doi:10.1111/j.1532-7795.2011.00765.x

Connolly, D. A., & Read, J. D. (2006). Delayed prosecutions of historic child sexual abuse: Analyses of 2064 Canadian criminal complaints. *Law and Human Behavior, 30,* 409–434.

Connor, K., et al. (2012). The next generation of psychological autopsy studies—part two: Interview procedures. *Suicide and Life-Threatening Behavior, 42*(1), 86–103.

Cooper v. Oklahoma, 116 S.Ct. 1373 (1996).

Cooper, J., & Neuhaus, I. M. (2000). The hired gun effect: Assessing the effect of pay, frequency of testifying, and credentials on the perception of expert testimony. *Law and Human Behavior, 24,* 149–172.

Cooper, V., & Zapf, P. (2003). Predictor variables in competency to stand trial decisions. *Law and Human Behavior, 27,* 423–436.

Copson, G., Badcock, R., Boon, J., and Britton, P. (1997). Articulating a systematic approach to clinical crime profiling. *Criminal Behaviour and Mental Health, 7,* 13–17.

Cornell, D. (2006). *School violence: Fears versus facts.* New York, NY: Routledge.

Cornell, D. (2020). Threat assessment as a school violence prevention strategy. *Criminology & Public Policy, 19*(8), 235–252. doi:10.1111/1745-9133.12471

Corey, D., & Zelig, M. (2020). *Evaluations of police suitability and fitness for duty.* New York: Oxford.

Cornell, D. G., & Sheras, P. L. (2006). *Guidelines for responding to student threats of violence.* Dallas, TX: Sopris West Educational Services.

Corrado, R. R., Vincent, G. M., Hart, S. D., & Cohen, I. M. (2004). Predictive validity of the Psychopathy Checklist: Youth version for general and violent recidivism. *Behavioral Sciences & the Law, 22,* 5–22.

Cosden, M., Ellens, J., Schnell, J., & Yamini-Diouf, Y. (2005). Efficacy of a mental health treatment court with assertive community treatment. *Behavioral Sciences & the Law, 23,* 199–214.

Cosden, M., Ellens, J., Schnell, J., Yamini-Diouf, Y., & Wolfe, M. (2003). Evaluation of a mental health court with assertive community treatment. *Behavioral Sciences & the Law, 21,* 415–427.

Costanzo, M., Shaked-Schroer, N., & Vinson, K. (2010). Juror beliefs about police interrogations, false confessions, and expert testimony. *Journal of Empirical Legal Studies, 7,* 231–247.

Cottle, C., Lee, R., & Heilbrun, K. (2001). The prediction of criminal recidivism in juveniles: A meta-analysis. *Criminal Justice and Behavior, 28,* 367–394.

Coulton, C. J., Korbin, J. E., Su, M., & Chow, J. (1995). Community level factors and child maltreatment rates. *Child Development, 66,* 1262–1276.

Council for State Governments Justice Center. (2012). Adults with behavioral health needs under correctional supervision: A shared framework for reducing recidivism and promoting recovery. Retrieved July 13, 2017, from https://www.bja.gov/Publications/CSG_Behavioral_Framework.pdf

Cowan, C. L., Thompson, W. C., & Ellsworth, P. C. (1984). The effects of death qualification on jurors' predispositions to convict and on the quality of deliberation. *Law and Human Behavior, 8,* 53–79.

Coy v. Iowa, 487 U.S. 1012 (1988).

Crisp, R. & Turner, R. (2011). Cognitive adaptation to the experience of social and cultural diversity. *Psychological Bulletin, 137,* 242–266.

Crocker, C., & Kovera, M. (2010). The effects of rehabilitative voir dire on juror bias and decision making. *Law and Human Behavior, 34,* 212–226.

Cruise, K., Morin, S., & Affleck, K. (2016). Residential interventions with justice-involved youths. In K. Heilbrun, D. DeMatteo, & N. Goldstein (Eds.), *APA handbook of psychology and juvenile justice* (pp. 611–639). Washington, DC: American Psychological Association. doi:10.1037 /14643-028

Cruzan v. Director, Missouri Department of Health, 497 U.S. 261 (1990).

Culhane, C. E., Hosch, H. M., & Weaver, W. G. (2004). Crime victims serving as jurors: Is there bias present? *Law and Human Behavior, 28,* 649–659.

Cunningham, M. (2010). *Evaluation for capital sentencing.* New York, NY: Oxford University Press.

Cutler, B. (2011). *Conviction of the innocent: Lessons from psychological research.* Washington, DC: American Psychological Association.

Daftary-Kapur, T., Dumas, R., & Penrod, S. (2010). Jury decision-making biases and methods to counter them. *Legal and Criminological Psychology, 15,* 133–154.

Daftary-Kapur, T., & Zottoli, T. (2014). A first look at the plea deal experiences of juveniles tried in adult court. *The International Journal of Forensic Mental Health, 13,* 323–336.

Daftary-Kapur, T., Henderson, K., & Zottoli, T. (2021). COVID-19 exacerbates existing system factors that disadvantage defendants: Findings from a national survey of defense attorneys. *Law and Human Behavior, 45,* 81–96.

Daftary-Kapur, T., & Penrod, S. (2019). Pre-and midtrial publicity in the age of Internet and social media. In Najdowski, C., & Stevenson, M. (Eds.), *Criminal juries in the 21st century* (pp. 155–172). New York: Oxford University Press.

Daftary-Kapur, T., Penrod, S., O'Connor, M., & Wallace, B. (2014). Examining pretrial publicity in a shadow jury paradigm: Issues of slant, quantity, persistence and generalizability. *Law and Human Behavior, 38,* 462–477.

Dalenberg, C. J., Brand, B. L., Gleaves, D. H., Dorahy, M. J., Loewenstein, R. J., Cardeña, E., … Spiegel, D. (2012). Evaluation of the evidence for the trauma and fantasy models of dissociation. *Psychological Bulletin, 138,* 550–588.

Dantzker, M. (2010). Differences in pre-employment screening protocols used and reasons for their use between police and clinical psychologists. *Dissertation Abstracts International: Section B: The Sciences and Engineering, 71*(3-B), 2042.

Danzer, G., Wheeler, E., Alexander, A., & Wasser, T. (2019). Competency restoration for adult defendants in different treatment environments. *Journal of the American Academy of Psychiatry and the Law, 47,* 68–81 Online. doi.org/10.29158/JAAPL.003819-19

Danziger, S., Levav, J., & Avnaim-Pesso, L. (2011). Extraneous factors in judicial decisions. *Proceedings of the National Academy of Sciences of the United States of America, 108,* 6889–6892.

Darley, J., & Pittman, T. (2003). The psychology of compensatory and retributive justice. *Personality and Social Psychology Review, 7,* 324–336.

Darley, J., Sanderson, C., & LaMantha, P. (1996). Community standards for defining attempt: Inconsistencies with the Model Penal Code. *American Behavioral Scientist, 39,* 405–420.

Daubert v. Merrell Dow Pharmaceuticals, Inc., 113 S.Ct. 2786 (1993).

Davey, M., & Goodnough, A. (2007). *Doubts rise as states hold sex offenders after prison.* Retrieved March 24, 2009, from http://www.nytimes.com/2007/03/04/us/04civil.html

Davis v. Monroe County Board of Education (Davis), 526 U.S. 629 (1999).

Day, M., & Ross, M. (2011). The value of remorse: How drivers' responses to police predict fines for speeding. *Law and Human Behavior, 35,* 221–234.

De Tocqueville, A. (1900). *Democracy in America* (Vol. 1) (Henry Reeve, Trans.). New York, NY: Colonial.

Deadman, D., & MacDonald, Z. (2004). Offenders as victims of crime?: An investigation into the relationship between criminal behaviour and victimization. *Journal of the Royal Statistical Society. Series A* (Statistics in Society), *167,* 53–67.

Death Penalty Information Center. (2021). The death penalty in 2021: Year end report. Retrieved May 5, 2022, from deathpenaltyinfo.org/facts-and-research/dpic-reports/dpic-year-end-reports/the-death-penalty-in-2021-year-end-report

DeCamp, W., & DeCamp, E. (2020). It's still about race: Peremptory challenge use on black prospective jurors. *Journal of Research in Crime and Delinquency, 57,* 3–30.

DeCelles, K., Adams, G., Howe, H., & John, L. (2021). Anger damns the innocent. *Psychological Science, 32,* 1214–1226.

Deci, E. L., & Ryan, R. M. (2000). The "what" and "why" of goal pursuits: Human needs and the self-determination of behavior. *Psychological Inquiry, 11,* 227–268.

Deffenbacher, K., Bornstein, B., McGorty, E., & Penrod, S. (2008). Forgetting the once-seen face: Estimating the strength of an eyewitness's memory representation. *Journal of Experimental Psychology: Applied, 14,* 139–150.

Deffenbacher, K., Bornstein, B. H., & Penrod, S. D. (2006). Mugshot exposure effects: Retroactive interference, mugshot commitment, source confusion, and unconscious transference. *Law and Human Behavior, 30,* 287–307.

Deffenbacher, K., Bornstein, B. H., Penrod, S. D., & McGorty, E. (2004). A meta-analytic review of the effects of high stress on eyewitness memory. *Law and Human Behavior, 28,* 687–706.

Degoldi, B. (2008). Lawyers' emerging experiences of interdisciplinary collaborative separation and divorce. *Psychiatry, Psychology and Law, 15,* 396–414.

DeLisi, M., & Scherer, A. (2006). Multiple homicide offenders: Offense characteristics, social correlates, and criminal careers. *Criminal Justice and Behavior, 33,* 367–391.

DeMartini, A. (2008). *Juvenile prisons to make changes.* Retrieved April 15, 2009, from http://www.dispatch.com/live/content/local_news/stories/2008/04/04/Prisons_will_change.ART_ART_04–04–08_A1_579R1G7.html?sid=101

DeMatteo, D., Hart, S., Heilbrun, K., Boccaccini, M., Cunningham, M., Douglas, K., Dvoskin, J., Edens, J., Guy, L., Murrie, D., Otto, R., Packer, I., & Reidy, T. (2020). Statement of concerned experts on the use of the Hare Psychopathy Checklist-Revised in capital sentencing to assess risk for institutional violence. *Psychology, Public Policy, and Law, 26,* 133–144. Retrieved February 22, 2022, from http://dx.doi.org/10.1037/law0000223

DeMatteo, D., Hart, S., Heilbrun, K., Boccaccini, M., Cunningham, M., Douglas, K., Dvoskin, J., Edens, J., Guy, L., Murrie, D., Otto, R., Packer, I., & Reidy, T. Death is different: Reply to Olver et al. (2020). *Psychology, Public Policy, and Law, 26*(4), 511–518. doi.org/10.1037/law0000285

DeMatteo, D., Heilbrun, K., Thornewill, A., & Arnold, S. (2019). *Problem-solving courts and the criminal justice system.* New York: Oxford.

DeMatteo, D., Murrie, D., Anumba, N., & Keesler, M. (2011). *Forensic mental health assessments in death penalty cases.* New York, NY: Oxford University Press.

DeMatteo, D., Hart, S., Heilbrun, K., Boccaccini, M., Cunningham, M., Douglas, K., Dvoskin, J., Edens, J., Guy, L., Murrie, D., Otto, R., Packer, I., & Reidy, T. (2020). Statement of concerned experts on the use of the Hare Psychopathy Checklist-Revised in capital sentencing to assess risk for institutional violence. *Psychology, Public Policy, and Law, 26,* 133–144.

DeMatteo, D., Hart, S., Heilbrun, K., Boccaccini, M., Cunningham, M., Douglas, K., Dvoskin, J., Edens, J., Guy, L., Murrie, D., Otto, R., Packer, I., & Reidy, T. Death is different: Reply to Olver et al. (2020). *Psychology, Public Policy, and Law, 26*(4), 511–518. http://dx.doi.org/10.1037/law0000285

Dennis, D., & Monahan, J. (Eds.). (1996). *Coercion and aggressive community treatment: A new frontier in mental health law.* New York, NY: Plenum.

Department of Defense. (2004, April). *Task force report on care for victims of sexual assault.* Washington, DC: Author.

Department of Defense Inspector General. (2005). *Report on sexual harassment and assault at the U.S. Air Force Academy.* Washington, DC: Department of Defense.

Department of Justice. (1999). *Postconviction DNA testing: Recommendations for handling requests.* Retrieved December 19, 2001, from http://www.ncjrs.org/pdffiles1/nij/177626.pdf

Derzon, J. H. (2010). The correspondence of family features with problem, aggressive, criminal, and violent behavior: A meta-analysis. *Journal of Experimental Criminology, 6,* 263–292.

Desmarais, S. & Zottola, S. (2020). Violence risk assessment: Current status and contemporary issues. *Marquette Law Review, 103,* 793–817.

Desmarais, S., Zottola, S., Duhart Clarke, S., & Lowder, E. (2021). Predictive validity of pretrial risk assessments: A systematic review of the literature. *Criminal Justice and Behavior, 48,* 398–420.

Detrick, P., & Chibnall, J. T. (2002). Prediction of police officer performance with the Inwald Personality Inventory. *Journal of Police and Criminal Psychology, 17,* 9–17.

Detrick, P., & Chibnall, J. T. (2008). Positive response distortion by police officer applicants: Association of Paulhus Deception Scales with MMPI-2 and Inwald Personality Inventory Validity scales. *Assessment, 15,* 87–96.

Detrick, P., Chibnall, J. T., & Rosso, M. (2001). Minnesota Multiphasic Personality Inventory-2 in police officer selection: Normative data and relation to the Inwald Personality Inventory. *Professional Psychology: Research and Practice, 32,* 484–490.

Detullio, D., Messer, S., Kennedy, T., & Millen, D. (2019). A meta-analysis of the Miller Forensic Assessment of Symptoms Test (M-FAST). *Psychological Assessment, 31*(11), 1319–1328. doi.org/10.1037/pas0000753

DeVault, A., Miller, M. K., & Griffin, T. (2016). Crime control theater: Past, present, and future. *Psychology, Public Policy, and Law, 22,* 341–348.

Devenport, J., Stinson, V., Cutler, B., & Kravitz, D. (2002). How effective are the cross-examination and expert testimony safeguards? Jurors' perceptions of the suggestiveness and fairness of biased lineup procedures. *Journal of Applied Psychology, 87*, 1042–1054.

Devine, D. (2012). *Jury decision making: The state of the science.* New York, NY: New York University Press.

Devine, D., Buddenbaum, J., Houp, S., Studebaker, N., & Stolle, D. (2009). Strength of evidence, extraevidentiary influence, and the liberation hypothesis: Data from the field. *Law and Human Behavior, 33*, 136–148.

Devine, D., & Caughlin, D. (2014). Do they matter? A meta-analytic investigation of individual characteristics and guilt judgments. *Psychology, Public Policy, and Law, 20*, 109–134.

Devine, D., Clayton, L., Dunford, B., Seying, R., & Pryce, J. (2001). Jury decision making: 45 years of empirical research on deliberating groups. *Psychology, Public Policy, and Law, 7*, 622–727.

Devine, D., & Kelly, C. (2015). Life or death: An examination of jury sentencing with the capital jury project database. *Psychology, Public Policy, and Law, 21*, 393–406.

Devine, D., Krouse, P., Cavanaugh, C., & Basora, J. (2016). Evidentiary, extraevidentiary, and deliberation process predictors of real jury verdicts. *Law and Human Behavior, 40*, 670–682.

Devins, N., & Baum, L. (2016). Split definitive: How party polarization turned the Supreme Court into a partisan court. *The Supreme Court Review, 2016*, 301–365.

deVries, M., Holland, R., Corneille, O., Rondeel, E., & Whitteman, C. (2012). Mood effects on dominated choices: Positive mood induces departures from logical rules. *Journal of Behavioral Decision Making, 25*, 74–81.

DeWitt, J. S., Richardson, J. T., & Warner, L. G. (1997). Novel scientific evidence and controversial cases: A social psychological examination. *Law & Psychology Review, 21*, 1–28.

Dhami, M. (2003). Psychological models of professional decision making. *Psychological Science, 14*, 175–180.

Dhami, M. (2011). Psychological models of professional decision making. In G. Gigerenzer & T. Pachur (Eds.), *Heuristics: The foundations of adaptive behavior* (pp. 602–610). New York, NY: Oxford University Press.

Dhami, M., & Ayton, P. (2001). Bailing and jailing the fast and frugal way. *Journal of Behavioral Decision Making, 14*, 141–168.

Dhami, M., Belton, I., Merrall, E., McGrath, A., & Bird, S. (2020). Criminal sentencing by preferred numbers. *Journal of Empirical Legal Studies, 17*, 139–163.

Diamond, S. (2006). Beyond fantasy and nightmare: A portrait of the jury. *Buffalo Law Review, 54*, 717–763.

Diamond, S., Bowman, L., Wong, M., & Patton, M. (2010). Efficiency and cost: The impact of videoconferenced hearings on bail decisions. *Journal of Criminal Law & Criminology, 100*, 869–902.

Diamond, S., Murphy, B., & Rose, M. (2012). The "kettleful of law" in real jury deliberations: Successes, failures, and next steps. *Northwestern University Law Review, 106*, 1537–1608.

Diamond, S. & Rose, M. (2018). The contemporary American jury. *Annual Review of Law and Social Science, 14*, 239–258.

Diamond, S., Rose, M., Murphy, B., & Meixner, J. (2011). Damage anchors on real juries. *Journal of Empirical Legal Studies, 8*, 148–178.

Diamond, S., Rose, M., Murphy, B., & Smith, S. (2006). Juror questions during trial: A window into juror thinking. *Vanderbilt Law Review, 59*, 1925–1972.

Diamond, S., & Salerno, J. (2020). Reasons for the disappearing jury trial: Perspectives from attorneys and judges. *Louisiana Law Review, 81*, 1, 119–163.

Diamond, S., & Salerno, J. (2020). Reasons for the disappearing jury trial: Perspectives from attorneys and judges. *Louisiana Law Review, 81*, 1, 119–163. https://digitalcommons.law.lsu.edu/lalrev/vol81/iss1/9

Diamond, S., & Vidmar, N. (2001). Jury room ruminations on forbidden topics. *Virginia Law Review, 87*, 1857–1915.

Diamond, S., Vidmar, N., Rose, M., Ellis, L., & Murphy, B. (2003). Juror discussions in civil trials: Studying an Arizona innovation. *Arizona Law Review, 45*, 1–81.

Dichter, M., Thomas, K., Crits-Cristoph, P., Shannon, N., & Rhodes, K. (2018). Coercive control in intimate partner violence: Relationship with women's experience of violence, use of violence, and danger. *Psychology of Violence, 8*(5), 596–604.

Dickerson v. United States, 530 U.S. 428 (2000).

Dickinson, J., Poole, D., & Laimon, R. (2005). Children's recall and testimony. In N. Brewer & K. Williams (Eds.), *Psychology and Law: An empirical perspective* (pp. 151–175). New York, NY: Guilford.

Dierkhising, C., Ko, S., Woods-Jaeger, B., Briggs, E., Lee, R., & Pynoos, R. (2013). Trauma histories among justice-involved youth: Findings from the National Child Traumatic Stress Network. *European Journal of Psychotraumatology, 4*, 1–12. doi:10.3402/ejpt.v4i0.20274

Dietvorst, B., & Simonsohn, U. (2019). Intentionally "biased": People purposely use to-be-ignored information, but can be persuaded not to. *Journal of Experimental Psychology: General, 148*, 1228–1238.

Dietz v. Bouldin, 579 U.S. ____ (2016).

Dirks-Linhorst, P., & Kondrat, D. (2012). Tough on crime or beating the system: An evaluation of Missouri Department of Mental Health's Not Guilty by Reason of Insanity murder acquittees. *Homicide Studies, 16*(2), 129–150. doi: 10.1177/1088767912438711

Dishion, T., & Tipsord, J. (2011). Peer contagion in child and adolescent social and emotional development. *Annual Review of Psychology, 62*, 189–214. doi: 10.1146/annurev.psych.093008.100412

District Attorney's Office for the Third Judicial District v. Osborne, U.S. Supreme Court 08-6 (2009).

Ditto, P., Jacobson, J., Smucker, W., Danks, J., & Fagerlin, A. (2006). Context changes choices: A prospective study of the effects of hospitalization on life-sustaining treatment preferences. *Medical Decision Making, 26*, 313–322.

Ditto, P., Smucker, W., Danks, J., Jacobson, J., Houts, R., Fagerlin, A., … Gready, R. M. (2003). Stability of older adults' preferences for life-sustaining medical treatment. *Health Psychology, 22*, 605–615.

Dobbie, W., Goldin, J., & Yang, C. (2018). The effects of pretrial detention on conviction, future crime, and employment: evidence from randomly assigned judges. *American Economic Review, 108*, 201–240.

Domagalski, K., Gongola, J., Lyon, T. D., Clark, S. E., & Quas, J. A. (2020). Detecting children's true and false denials of wrongdoing: Effects of question type and base rate knowledge. *Behavioral Sciences & the Law.* doi.org/10.1002/bsl.2487

Domitrovich, S. (2016). Fulfilling Daubert's gatekeeping mandate through court-appointed experts. *Journal of Criminal Law and Criminology, 106*, 35–48.

Doppelt, J. (1991). Generic prejudice: How drug war fervor threatens the right to a fair trial. *American University Law Review, 40*, 821–836.

Dougall, A. L., Hayward, M. C., & Baum, A. (2005). Media exposure to bioterrorism: Stress and the anthrax attacks. *Psychiatry, 68*, 28–43.

Douglas, J., Burgess, A. W., Burgess, A. G., & Ressler, R. (2006). *Crime classification manual: A standard system for investigating and classifying violent crimes* (2nd ed.). New York, NY: Wiley.

Douglas, K., Hart, S., Webster, C., & Belfrage, H. (2013). *HCR-20V3.* Simon Fraser University: Mental Health, Law, and Policy Institute.

Douglas, J. E., Ressler, R. K., Burgess, A. W., & Hartman, C. R. (1986). Criminal profiling from crime scene analysis. *Behavioral Sciences & The Law, 4*, 401–421.

Douglas, K. & Otto, R.K. (Eds.) (2021). *Handbook of violence risk assessment* (2nd ed.) New York: Routledge.

Douglass, A. B., Neuschatz, J. S., Imrich, J., & Wilkinson, M. (2010). Does post-identification feedback affect evaluations of eyewitness testimony and identification procedures? *Law and Human Behavior, 34*(4), 282–294. doi-org.lprx.bates.edu/10.1007/s10979-009-9189-5

Douglass, A. B., & Smalarz, L. (2019). Post-identification feedback: State of the science. In B. H. Bornstein & M. K. Miller (Eds.). *Advances in Psychology and Law, vol 4*. (pp. 101–136). Springer.

Dowling, F., Moynihan, G., Genet, B., & Lewis, J. (2006). A peer-based assistance program for officers with the New York City Police Department: Report of the effects of Sept. 11 2001. *American Journal of Psychiatry, 163*, 151–153.

Dragowski, E., Halkitis, P., Grossman, A., & D'Augelli, A. (2011). Sexual orientation victimization and posttraumatic stress symptoms among lesbian, gay, and bisexual youth. *Journal of Gay & Lesbian Social Services: The Quarterly Journal of Community & Clinical Practice, 23*, 226–249.

Driscoll, D. M., Kelly, J. R., & Henderson, W. L. (1998). Can perceivers identify likelihood to sexually harass? *Sex Roles, 38*, 557–588.

Drizin, S., & Colgan, B. (2004). Tales from the juvenile confession front: A guide to how standard police interrogation tactics can produce coerced and false confessions from juvenile suspects. In G. D. Lassiter (Ed.), *Interrogations, confessions, and entrapment* (pp. 127–162). New York, NY: Kluwer Academic/Plenum.

Drizin, S., & Leo, R. (2004). The problem of false confessions in the post-DNA world. *North Carolina Law Review, 82*, 891–1007.

Drizin, S., & Riley, H. (2014, February 12). Knox and Sollecito: Victims of a prosecutor's 'conspiracy theories' to explain away DNA. Retrieved from http://www.huffingtonpost.com/steve-drizin/-amanda-knox-and -raffaele-_b_4757435.html

Drummond, M. (2017). Voir dire: Don't let the judge cut you out. *American Bar Association Litigation News*. Retrieved from https://apps.americanbar .org/litigation/litigationnews/articles-print/050412-practice-points -spring12.html

Duggan, M. (2017). Men, women experience and view online harassment differently. Pew Research Center. Retrieved February 21, 2022, from https://www.pewresearch.org/fact-tank/2017/07/14 /men-women-experience-and-view-online-harassment-differently/

Duncan v. Louisiana, 391 U.S. 145 (1968).

Durbin, J., Lin, E., & Zaslavska, N. (2010). Police-citizen encounters that involve mental health concerns: Results of an Ontario police services survey. *Canadian Journal of Community Mental Health, 29*, 53–71.

Dusky v. United States, 362 U.S. 402 (1960).

Dutton, D. G. (2000). *The domestic assault of women* (3rd ed.). Vancouver, BC: University of British Columbia Press.

Dutton, M. (2014). Critique of the "battered woman syndrome" model. *American Academy of Experts in Traumatic Stress*. Retrieved November 6, 2016, from http://www.aaets.org/article138.htm

Dvoskin, J., Knoll, J., & Silva, M. (2020). A brief history of the criminalization of mental illness. CNS Spectr., *25*(5), 638–650. Retrieved January 16, 2022, from https://pubmed.ncbi.nlm.nih.gov/32192554/

Dvoskin, J., Skeem, J., Novaco, R., & Douglas, K. (Eds.) (2011). *Using social science to reduce violent offending*. New York, NY: Oxford University Press.

Eagly, I. (2015). Remote adjudication in immigration. *Northwestern University Law Review, 109*, 933–1020.

Earnshaw, V. A., Pitpitan, E. V., & Chaudoir, S. R. (2011). Intended responses to rape as functions of attitudes, attributions of fault, and emotions. *Sex Roles, 64*, 382–393.

Earnshaw,, V., et al. (2016). Bullying among lesbian, gay, bisexual, and trans-gender youth. *Pediatric Clinics of North America, 63* (6), 999–1010.

Eaton, L., & Kaufman, L. (2005, April 26). In problem-solving courts, judges turn therapist. *The New York Times*, p. A1.

Eberhardt, J., Davies, P., Purdie-Vaughns, V., & Johnson, S. (2006). Looking deathworthy: Perceived stereotypicality of Black defendants predicts capital-sentencing outcomes. *Psychological Science, 17*, 383–386.

Ebreo, A., Linn, N., & Vining, J. (1996). The impact of procedural justice on opinions of public policy: Solid waste management as an example. *Journal of Applied Social Psychology, 26*, 1259–1285.

Eckholm, E. (1985, July 4). Stockholm syndrome: Hostages' reactions. *Lawrence Journal-World*, p. 6.

Eckholm, E. (2008, October 14). Courts give addicts a chance to straighten out. *The New York Times*. Retrieved October 15, 2008, from www. nytimes.com/2008/10/15/us/15drugs.html

Eddings v. Oklahoma, 436 U.S. 921 (1982).

Eddy, J., & Bellatty, P. (2014). *Randomized controlled trial of Measure 57 intensive drug court for medium to high risk property offenders*. Oregon Criminal Justice Commission. Retrieved December 22, 2016, from https://www.oregon.gov/cjc/SAC/Documents/M57_Intensive_Drug _Court_Evaluation.pdf

Eddy, J., Whaley, R., & Chamberlain, P. (2004). The prevention of violent behavior by chronic and serious male juvenile offenders: A 2-year follow-up of a randomized clinical trial. *Journal of Emotional and Behavioral Disorders, 12*, 2–8.

Edkins, V. (2011). Defense attorney plea recommendations and client race: Does zealous representation apply equally to all? *Law and Human Behavior, 35*, 413–425.

Edkins, V., & Dervan, L. (2018). Freedom now or a future later: Pitting the lasting implications of collateral consequences against pretrial detention in decisions to plead guilty. *Psychology, Public Policy, and Law, 24*, 204–215.

Eigen, Z., & Listokin, Y. (2012). Do lawyers really believe their own hype, and should they? A natural experiment. *Journal of Legal Studies, 41*, 239–267.

Eisenberg, T., Hannaford-Agor, P., Hans, V., Waters, N., Munsterman, T., Schwab, S., & Wells, M. T. (2005). Judge-jury agreement in criminal cases: A partial replication of Kalven and Zeisel's *The American Jury*. *Journal of Empirical Legal Studies, 2*, 171–207.

Eisenberg, T., & Hans, V. (2009). Taking a stand on taking the stand: The effect of prior criminal record on the decision to testify and on trial outcomes. *Cornell Law Review, 94*, 1353–1390.

Eisenberg, T., LaFountain, N., Ostrom, B., Rottman, D., & Wells, M. (2002). Juries, judges, and punitive damages: An empirical study. *Cornell Law Review, 87*, 743–782.

Ekman, P., & O'Sullivan, M. (1991). Who can catch a liar? *American Psychologist, 46*, 913–920.

Eldred, L., Gifford, E., McCutchan, S., & Sloan, F. (2016). Factors predicting prosecution in child maltreatment cases. *Child and Youth Services Review, 70*, 201–205.

Ellis, L., & Diamond, S. (2003). Race, diversity, and jury composition: Battering and bolstering legitimacy. *Chicago-Kent Law Review, 78*, 1033–1058.

Ellsworth, P. C., & Reifman, A. (2000). Juror comprehension and public policy: Perceived problems and proposed solutions. *Psychology, Public Policy, and Law, 6*, 788–821.

Elmi, M. H., Daignault, I. V., & Hébert, M. (2018). Child sexual abuse victims as witnesses: The influence of testifying on their recovery. *Child Abuse & Neglect, 86*, 22–32. doi.org/10.1016/j.chiabu.2018.09.001

Elwork, A., Sales, B. D., & Suggs, D. (1981). The trial: A research review. In B. D. Sales (Ed.), *The trial process* (pp. 1–68). New York, NY: Plenum.

Emery, R., Sbarra, D., & Grover, T. (2005). Divorce mediation: Research and reflections. *Family Court Review, 43*(1), 22–37. https://doi .org/10.1111/j.1744-1617.2005.00005.x

Emery, R. E., Laumann-Billings, L., Waldron, M., Sbarra, D., & Dillon, P. (2001). Child custody mediation and litigation: Custody, contact, and coparenting 12 years after initial dispute resolution. *Journal of Consulting and Clinical Psychology, 69*, 323–332.

Engelhard, I. M., McNally, R. J., & van Schie, K. (2019). Retrieving and modifying traumatic memories: Recent research relevant to three controversies. *Current Directions in Psychological Science, 28*(1), 91–96. doi.org/10.1177/0963721418807728

Englich, B., & Mussweiler, T. (2001). Sentencing under uncertainty: Anchoring effects in the courtroom. *Journal of Applied Social Psychology, 31*, 1535–1551.

Englich, B., Mussweiler, T., & Strack, F. (2005). The last word in court: A hidden disadvantage for the defense. *Law and Human Behavior, 29*, 705–722.

Eno Louden, J., Manchak, S., O'Connor, M., & Skeem, J. (2015). Applying the Sequential Intercept Model to reduce recidivism among probationers and parolees with mental illness. In P. Griffin, K. Heilbrun, E. Mulvey, D. DeMatteo, & C. Schubert, *The Sequential Intercept Model and criminal justice: Promoting community alternatives for individuals with serious mental illness* (pp. 118–136). New York, NY: Oxford.

Eno Louden, J., & Skeem, J. (2007). Constructing insanity: Jurors' prototypes, attitudes, and legal decision-making. *Behavioral Sciences & The Law, 25,* 449–470.

Eno Louden, J., Skeem, J., Camp, J., & Christensen, E. (2008). Supervising probationers with mental disorder: How do agencies respond to violations? *Criminal Justice and Behavior, 35,* 832–847.

Espelage, D., Aragon, S., & Birkett, M. (2008). Homophobic teasing, psychological outcomes, and sexual orientation among high school students: What influences do parents and schools have? *School Psychology Review, 37,* 202–216.

Estrada-Reynolds, V., Freng, S., Schweitzer, K., & Leki, E. (2022). Is all prejudice created equal? The role of modern and aversive racism in mock juror decisions. *Psychiatry, Psychology and Law,* in press.

Evans, J., Michael, S., Meissner, C., & Brandon, S. (2013). Validating a new assessment method for deception detection: Introducing a psychologically based credibility assessment tool. *Journal of Applied Research in Memory and Cognition, 2,* 33–41.

Evans, J., Pimentel, P., Pena, M., & Michael, S. (2017). The ability to detect false statements as a function of the type of statement and the language proficiency of the statement provider. *Psychology, Public Policy, and Law, 2*(3), 290–300.

Evans, J. R., Meissner, C. A. Brandon, S. E., Russano, M. B., & Kleinman, S. M. (2010). Criminal versus HUMINT interrogations: The importance of psychological science to improving interrogative practice. *Journal of Psychiatry and Law, 38,* 215–249.

Everington, C. T., & Luckasson, R. (1992). *Competence assessment for standing trial for defendants with mental retardation (CAST-MR) test manual.* Columbus, OH: International Diagnostic Systems.

Eysenck, H. J. (1964). *Crime and personality.* Boston, MA: Houghton Mifflin.

Fagan, J. (1996). The comparative advantage of juvenile versus criminal court sanctions on recidivism among adolescent felony offenders. *Law & Policy, 18,* 79–113.

Fagan, J., Kupchik, A., and Liberman, A. (2004). Be careful what you wish for: Comparative impacts of juvenile versus criminal court sanctions on recidivism among adolescent felony offenders. *Columbia Law School, Law Research Paper* No. 03-61.

Farah, M., Hutchinson, J. Phelps, E., & Wagner, A. (2014). Functional MRI-based lie detection: Scientific and societal challenges. *Nature Reviews: Neuroscience, 15,* 123–151.

Faretta v. California, 422 U.S. 806 (1975).

Farrington, D. (2019). The development of violence from age 8 to 61. *Aggressive Behavior, 45*(4), 365–376. https://doi.org/10.1002/ab.21831

Farrington, D. P. (1995). The development of offending and antisocial behavior from childhood: Key findings from the Cambridge Study in Delinquent Development. *Journal of Child Psychology and Psychiatry, 360,* 929–964.

Farwell, L. (2012). Brain fingerprinting: A comprehensive tutorial review of detection of concealed information with event-related brain potentials. *Cognitive Neurodynamics, 6,* 115–154.

Faust, D. (Ed.) (2012). *Coping with psychiatric and psychological testimony* (6th ed.). New York: Oxford.

Fawcett, J., Peace, K., & Greve, A. (2016). Looking down the barrel of a gun: What do we know about the weapon focus effect? *Journal of Applied Research in Memory and Cognition, 5,* 257–263.

FBI Academy. (2002). *Countering terrorism: Integration of practice and theory.* Retrieved July 22, 2005, from http://www.apa.org/releases/countering_terrorism.pdf

Federal Bureau of Investigation. (2011). *Crime in the United States 2010.* Retrieved from http://www.fbi.gov/about-us/cjis/ucr/crime-in-the-u.s/2010/crime-in-the-u.s.-2010/violent-crime/rapemain

Federal Bureau of Investigation. (2015a). *2014 law enforcement officers killed and assaulted.* Washington, DC: Department of Justice, Uniform Crime Reports. Retrieved October 31, 2016, from https://ucr.fbi.gov/leoka/2014/officers-feloniously-killed/main

Federal Bureau of Investigation. (2015b). *Crime in the United States.* Washington, DC: Author. Retrieved October 25, 2016, from https://ucr.fbi.gov/crime-in-the-u.s/2015/crime-in-the-u.s.-2015/offenses-known-to-law-enforcement/violent-crime

Federal Bureau of Investigation. (2016). *FBI releases 2015 preliminary statistics for law enforcement officers killed in the line of duty.* Washington, DC: FBI National Press Office. Retrieved October 31, 2016, from https://www.fbi.gov/news/pressrel/press-releases/fbi-releases-2015-preliminary-statistics-for-law-enforcement-officers-killed-in-the-line-of-duty

Federal Bureau of Investigation. (2011). *Crime in the United States 2010.* Retrieved from http://www.fbi.gov/about-us/cjis/ucr/crime-in-theu.s/2010/crime-in-the-u.s.-2010/violent-crime/rapemain

Federal Bureau of Investigation. (2015). *2014 law enforcement officers killed and assaulted.* Washington, DC: Department of Justice, Uniform Crime Reports. Retrieved October 31, 2016, from https://ucr.fbi.gov/leoka/2014/officers-feloniously-killed/main

Federal Bureau of Investigation. (2020). 2019 law enforcement officers killed & assaulted. *Uniform Crime Reports.* Washington, D.C.: Department of Justice. Retrieved October 4, 2021, from https://ucr.fbi.gov/leoka/2019

Federal Bureau of Prisons. (2017). *Directory of national programs.* Retrieved February 4, 2022, from https://www.bop.gov/inmates/custody_and_care/docs/20170518_BOPNationalProgramCatalog.pdf

Federal Rules of Evidence. (2009). *Federal Rules of Evidence.* St. Paul, MN: West.

Feige, D. (2006, June 7). *Witnessing guilt, ignoring innocence?* Retrieved July 28, 2008, from http://www.nytimes.com/2006/06/06/opinion/06feige.html?_r=1&scp=11&sq=david%20feige&st=cse&oref=slogin

Feigenson, N. (2016). Jurors' emotions and judgments of legal responsibility and blame: What does the experimental research tell us? *Emotion Review, 8,* 26–31.

Feigenson, N., Park, J., & Salovey, P. (2001). The role of emotions in comparative negligence judgments. *Journal of Applied Social Psychology, 31,* 576–603.

Feinblatt, J., & Berman, G. (2001). *Responding to the community: Principles for planning and creating a community court.* Washington, DC: U.S. Department of Justice.

Feldman, M. P. (1977). *Criminal behavior: A psychological analysis.* New York, NY: Wiley.

Feldmann, T. B. (2001). Characteristics of hostage and barricade incidents: Implications for negotiation strategies and training. *Journal of Police Crisis Negotiations, 1,* 3–33.

Felitti, V. J., Anda, R. F., Nordenberg, D., Williamson, D. F., Spitz, A. M., Edwards, V., … Marks, J. S. (1998). Relationship of childhood abuse and household dysfunction to many of the leading causes of death in adults: The adverse childhood experiences (ACE) study. *American Journal of Preventive Medicine, 14,* 245–258.

Ferguson, A. (2016). The big data jury. *Notre Dame Law Review, 91,* 935–1006.

Ferguson, D. P., Rhodes, G., Lee, K., & Sriram, N. (2001). "They all look alike to me": Prejudice and cross-race face recognition. *British Journal of Psychology, 92*(4), 567–577. https://doi.org/10.1348/000712601162347

Finkel, N. (1989). The Insanity Defense Reform Act of 1984: Much ado about nothing. *Behavioral Sciences & the Law, 7,* 403–419.

Finkel, N. (1995). *Commonsense justice: Jurors' notions of the law.* Cambridge, MA: Harvard University Press.

Finkel, N., & Groscup, J. L. (1997). When mistakes happen: Commonsense rules of culpability. *Psychology, Public Policy, and Law, 3,* 65–125.

Finkel, N., & Slobogin, C. (1995). Insanity, justification, and culpability toward a unifying theme. *Law and Human Behavior, 19,* 447–464.

Finnila, K., Mahlberga, N., Santtilaa, P., Sandnabbaa, K., & Niemib, P. (2003). Validity of a test of children's suggestibility for predicting responses to two interview situations differing in their degree of suggestiveness. *Journal of Experimental Child Psychology, 85*, 32–49.

Fisher, R. P., & Geiselman, R. E. (1992). *Memory enhancing techniques for investigative interviewing: The cognitive interview.* Springfield, IL: Thomas.

Fisher v. University of Texas, 579 U.S. ___ (2016).

Fiske, S., & Taylor, S. (1991). *Social cognition* (2nd ed.). New York, NY: McGraw-Hill.

Fitzgerald, R., & Price, H. (2015). Eyewitness identification across the life span: A meta-analysis of age differences. *Psychological Bulletin, 141*, 1228–1265.

Florence v. Board of Chosen Freeholders, 132 S.Ct. 1510 (2012).

Flowers v. Mississippi, 139 S.Ct. 2228 (2019).

Foa, E. B., & Kozak, M. J. (1986). Emotional processing of fear: Exposure to corrective information. *Psychological Bulletin, 99*, 20–35.

Foa, E. B., Hearst-Ikeda, D., & Perry, K. J. (1995). Evaluation of a brief cognitive behavioral program for the prevention of chronic PTSD in recent assault victims. *Journal of Consulting and Clinical Psychology, 63*, 948–955.

Foa, E. et al. (Eds.). (2009). *Effective treatments for PTSD: Practice guidelines from the International Society for Traumatic Stress Studies* (2nd ed.). Guilford Press.

Ford, J., & Hawke, J. (2012). Trauma affect regulation psychoeducation group and milieu intervention outcomes in juvenile detention facilities. *Journal of Aggression, Maltreatment, and Trauma, 21*, 365–384. doi:10.1080/1092 6771.2012.673538

Ford, J., & Russo, E. (2006). Trauma-focused, present-centered, emotional self-regulation approach to integrated treatment for posttraumatic stress and addiction: Trauma adaptive recovery group education and therapy (TARGET). *American Journal of Psychotherapy, 60*, 335–355.

Ford Motor Credit Co. v. Sheehan, 373 So. 2d 956 (Fla. App. 1979).

Ford v. Wainwright, 477 U.S. 399 (1986).

Forgas, J. (2011). Affective influences on self-disclosure: Mood effects on the intimacy and reciprocity of disclosing personal information. *Journal of Personality and Social Psychology, 100*, 449–461.

Forst, M., Fagan, J., & Vivona, T. S. (1989). Youth in prisons and training schools: Perceptions and consequences of the treatment-custody dichotomy. *Juvenile and Family Court Journal, 40*, 1–14.

Forster, M., Grigsby, T. J., Unger, J. B., & Sussman, S. (2015). Associations between gun violence exposure, gang associations, and youth aggression: Implications for prevention and intervention programs. *Journal of Criminology, 2015*, 1–8.

ForsterLee, L., & Horowitz, I. (2003). The effects of jury-aid innovations on juror performance in complex civil trials. *Judicature, 86*, 184–190.

Foster, T. (2011). Adverse life events proximal to adult suicide: A synthesis of findings from psychological autopsy studies. *Archives of Suicide Research, 15*, 1–15.

Foster v. Chatman, 578 U.S. ___ (2016).

Foucha v. Louisiana, 112 S.Ct. 1780 (1992).

Fountain, E. N., & Woolard, J. L. (2018). How defense attorneys consult with juvenile clients about plea bargains. *Psychology, Public Policy, and Law, 24*, 192–203.

Fox, B., & Farrington, D. (2015). An experimental evaluation of the utility of burglary profiles applied in active policy investigations. *Criminal Justice and Behavior, 42*, 156–175.

Fox, J. A., & Levin, J. (1998). Multiple homicide: Patterns of serial and mass murder. *Crime and Justice, 23*, 407–455.

Fox, J. A., & Levin, J. (2005). *Extreme killing: Understanding serial and mass murder.* Beverly Hills, CA: Sage.

Frantzen, D. (2015). *Evaluation of the Bexar County Veterans Treatment Court.* San Antonio: Texas A & M University. Retrieved on November 6, 2017, from https://www.bexar.org/1085/Veterans-Treatment-Court

Frazer, M. (2006). *The impact of the community court model on defendant perceptions of fairness: A case study at the Red Hook Community Justice Center.* New York, NY: Center for Court Innovation.

Frederick, R. (1997). *Validity Indicator Profile manual.* Minnetonka, MN: NSC Assessments.

Frederick, R. (2000). Mixed group validation: A method to address the limitations of criterion group validation in research on malingering detection. *Behavioral Sciences & the Law, 18*, 693–718.

Frederick, R., & Crosby, R. (2000). Development and validation of the Validity Indicator Profile. *Law and Human Behavior, 24*, 59–82.

Freedman, J., Martin, C., & Mota, V. (1998). Pretrial publicity: Effects of admonition and expression pretrial opinions. *Legal and Criminological Psychology, 3*, 255–270.

Freiburger, T. L., & Hilinski, C. M. (2013). An examination of the interactions of race and gender on sentencing using a trichotomous dependent variable. *Crime & Delinquency, 59*, 59–86.

Frendak v. United States, 408 A. 2d 364 (D.C. 1979).

Freiburger, T. (2010). The effects of gender, family status, and race on sentencing decisions. *Behavioral Sciences and the Law, 28*, 378–395.

Friedman, R., Anderson, C., Brett, J., Olekalns, M., Goates, N., & Lisco, C. (2004). The positive and negative effects of anger on dispute resolution: Evidence from electronically mediated disputes. *Journal of Applied Psychology, 89*, 369–376.

Frisell, T., Pawitan, Y., Langstrom, N., & Lichtenstein, P. (2012). Heritability, assortative mating and gender differences in violent crime: Results from a total population sample using twin, adoption, and sibling models. *Behavior Genetics, 42*, 3–18. doi:10.1007/S10519-011-9483-0

Frye v. United States, 293 F. 1013 (D.C. Cir. 1923)

Fryer, R. (2019). An empirical analysis of racial differences in police use of force. *Journal of Political Economy, 127*(3), 1210–1261.

Fulero, S. M., & Finkel, N. J. (1991). Barring ultimate issue testimony: An "insane" rule? *Law and Human Behavior, 15*, 495–508.

Funder, D. C. (2004). *The personality puzzle* (3rd ed.). New York, NY: Norton.

Furman v. Georgia, 408 U.S. 238 (1972).

Fuhrmann, G., & Zibbell, R. (2011). *Evaluation for child custody.* New York, NY: Oxford University Press.

Gabbert, F., Hope, L., & Fisher, R. P. (2009). Protecting eyewitness evidence: examining the efficacy of a self-administered interview tool. *Law and Human Behavior, 33*, 289–307. doi:10.1007/s10979-008-9146-8

Gaes, G., & Camp, S. (2009). Unintended consequences: Experimental evidence for the criminogenic effect of prison security level placement on post-release recidivism. *Journal of Experimental Criminology, 5*(2), 139–162.

Galanter, M. (2004). The vanishing trial: An examination of trials and related matters in state and federal courts. *Journal of Empirical Legal Studies, 1*, 459–570.

Galanter, M., & Frozena, M. (2014). A grin without a cat: The continuing decline & displacement of trials in American courts. *Daedalus, 143*, 115–128.

Garbarino, J. (1995). *Raising children in a toxic environment.* San Francisco, CA: Jossey-Bass.

Garofalo, R. (1914). *Criminology* (R. W. Millar, Trans.). Boston, MA: Little, Brown.

Garrett, B. (2008). Judging innocence. *Columbia Law Review, 108*, 55–142.

Garrett, B. (2011). *Convicting the innocent: Where criminal prosecutions go wrong.* Cambridge, MA: Harvard University Press.

Garrett, B., Krauss, D. A., & Scurich, N. (2017). Capital jurors in an era of death penalty decline. *Yale Law Journal Forum, 126*, 417–430.

Garrioch, L., & Brimacombe, C. A. E. (2001). Lineup administrators' expectations: Their impact on eyewitness confidence. *Law and Human Behavior, 25*, 299–315.

Garry, M., Manning, C. G., Loftus, E. F., & Sherman, S. J. (1996). Imagination inflation: Imagining a childhood event inflates confidence that it occurred. *Psychonomic Bulletin & Review, 3*(2), 208–214. https://doi.org/10.3758/BF03212420

Garvey, S., Hannaford-Agor, P., Hans, V., Mott, N., Munsterman, G. T., & Wells, M. (2004). Juror first votes in criminal trials. *Journal of Empirical Legal Studies, 1*, 371–399.

Gastil, J., Deess, E., Weiser, P., & Simmons, C. (2010). *The jury and democracy: How jury deliberation promotes civic engagement and political participation.* Oxford, UK: Oxford University Press.

Gates, P., Frederick, J., & Lisko, K. (2021). Virtual juries: We can, but should we? And if so, how? *Litigation, 47,* 12–17.

Gatowski, S. I., Dobbin, S. A., Richardson, J. T., Ginsburg, G. P., Merlino, M. L., & Dahir, V. (2001). Asking the gatekeepers: A national survey of judges of judging expert evidence in a post-*Daubert* world. *Law and Human Behavior, 25,* 433–458.

Gau, J. (2016). A jury of whose peers? The impact of selection procedures on racial composition and the prevalence of majority-white juries. *Journal of Crime and Justice, 39,* 75–87.

Gebser v. Lago Vista Independent School District (Gebser), 524 U.S. 274 (1998).

Geiselman, R. E., Fisher, R. P., MacKinnon, D. P., & Holland, H. L. (1985). Eyewitness memory enhancement in the police interview. *Journal of Applied Psychology, 70,* 401–412.

Gelman, A., Fagan, J., & Kiss, A. (2007). An analysis of the New York City Police Department's "stop-and-frisk" police in the context of claims of racial bias. *Journal of the American Statistical Association, 102,* 813–823.

Georges, L., Wiener, R., & Keller, S. (2013). The angry juror: Sentencing decisions in first-degree murder. *Applied Cognitive Psychology, 27,* 156–166.

Georgia v. McCollum, 505 U.S. 42 (1992).

Geraerts, E. (2012). Cognitive underpinnings of recovered memories of childhood abuse *Nebraska Symposium on Motivation, 58,* 175–191.

Geraerts, E., Bernstein, D., Merckelbach, H., Linders, C., Raymaekers, L., & Loftus, E. (2008). Lasting false beliefs and their behavioral consequences. *Psychological Science, 19,* 749–753.

Geraerts, E., Schooler, J., Merckelbach, H., Jelicic, M., Hauer, B., & Ambadar, Z. (2007). The reality of recovered memories: Corroborating continuous and discontinuous memories of childhood sexual abuse. *Psychological Science, 18,* 564–568.

Gibson, C. (2005, January 7). *Andrea Yates case interview with Andrea Yates's mother* [ABC News Transcript, Good Morning America]. Retrieved August 7, 2005, from http://www.lexisnexis.com/us /lnacademic/ results/docview/docview.do?docLinkInd=true&risb=21 _T8239962496&format=GNBFI&sort=RELEVANCE& -startDocNo=1&resultsUrlKey=29_T8239962499&cisb=22 _T8239962498&treeMax=true&treeWidth=0&csi=8277&docNo=7

Gideon v. Wainwright, 372 U.S. 335 (1963).

Gidycz, C., Rich, C., Orchowski, L., King, C., & Miller, A. (2006). The evaluation of a sexual assault self-defense and risk-reduction program for college women: A prospective study. *Psychology of Women Quarterly, 30,* 173–186.

Gilfoyle N., & Dvoskin, J. (2017). APA's amicus curiae program: Bringing psychological research to judicial decisions. *American Psychologist, 72*(8), 753–763.

Gilovich, T., Kerr, M., & Medvec, V. H. (1993). Effect of temporal perspective on subjective confidence. *Journal of Personality and Social Psychology, 64,* 552–560.

Givelber, D. (2001). The adversary system and historical accuracy: Can we do better? In S. Westervelt & J. Humphrey (Eds.), *Wrongly convicted: Perspectives on failed justice* (pp. 253–268). New Brunswick, NJ: Rutgers University Press.

Givelber, D., & Farrell, A. (2008). Judges and juries: The defense case and differences in acquittal rates. *Law and Social Inquiry, 33,* 31–52.

Glymour, B., Glymour, C., & Glymour, M. (2008). Watching social science: The debate about the effects of exposure to televised violence on aggressive behavior. *American Behavioral Scientist, 51,* 1231–1259.

Godinez v. Moran, 113 S.Ct. 2680 (1993).

Goh, K., Lu, M., & Jou, S. (2021). Childhood trauma and aggression in persons convicted for homicide: An exploratory study examines the role of plasma oxytocin. *Frontiers in Psychiatry.* doi.org/10.3389 /fpsyt.2021.719282

Golding, J. M., Bradshaw, G. S., Dunlap, E. E., & Hodell, E. C. (2007). The impact of mock jury gender composition on deliberations and conviction rates in a child sexual assault trial. *Child Maltreatment, 12,* 182–190.

Golding, S. L. (1993). *Interdisciplinary Fitness Interview-Revised: A training manual.* Salt Lake City, UT: State of Utah Division of Mental Health.

Golding, S. L., Roesch, R., & Schreiber, J. (1984). Assessment and conceptualization of competency to stand trial: Preliminary data on the Interdisciplinary Fitness Interview. *Law and Human Behavior, 8,* 321–334.

Goldinger, S., He, Y., & Papesh, M. (2009). Deficits in cross-race face learning: Insights from eye movements and pupillometry. *Journal of Experimental Psychology: Learning, Memory, and Cognition, 35,* 1105–1122.

Goldstein, A. P. (2004). Evaluations of effectiveness. In A. P. Goldstein, R. Nensen, B. Daleflod, & M. Kalt (Eds.), *New perspectives on aggression replacement training* (pp. 230–244). Chichester, UK: Wiley.

Goldstein, J. (2017, August 17). After backing alt-right in Charlottesville, A.C.L.U. wrestles with its role. *New York Times.* Retrieved from https:// www.nytimes.com/2017/08/17/nyregion/aclu-free-speech-rights -charlottesville-skokie-rally.html

Goldstein, N. E. S., Dovidio, A., Kalbeitzer, R., Weil, J., & Strachan, M. (2007). An anger management intervention for female juvenile offenders: Results of a pilot study. *Journal of Forensic Psychology Practice, 7,* 1–28.

Goldstein, R., Grant, B., Ruan, W., Smith, S., & Saha, T. (2006). Antisocial Personality Disorder with childhood- versus adolescence-onset conduct disorder: From the National Epidemiologic Survey on alcohol and related conditions. *Journal of Nervous and Mental Disease, 194,* 667–675.

Gollwitzer, M., & Keller, L. (2010). What you did only matters if you are one of us: Offenders' group membership moderates the effect of criminal history on punishment severity. *Social Psychology, 41,* 20–26.

Goodman, G. S., Pyle-Taub, E., Jones, D., England, P., Port, L., Rudy, L., … Melton, G. B. (1992). Testifying in criminal court: Emotional effects of criminal court testimony on child sexual assault victims. *Monographs of the Society for Research in Child Development, 57* (5, Serial No. 229), i, ii, v, 1–159.

Goodman, G. S., & Quas, J. A. (2008). Repeated interviews and children's memory. It's more than just how many. *Current Directions in Psychological Science, 17,* 386–390.

Goodman, G. S., Tobey, A., Batterman-Faunce, J., Orcutt, H., Thomas, S., & Shapiro, C. (1998). Face-to-face confrontation: Effects of closed-circuit technology on children's eyewitness testimony and jurors' decisions. *Law and Human Behavior, 22,* 265–203.

Goodman-Delahunty, J., & Foote, W. (2011). *Evaluation for workplace discrimination and harassment.* New York, NY: Oxford University Press.

Goodman-Delahunty, J., Granhag, P. A., Hartwig, M., & Loftus, E. F. (2010). Insightful or wishful: Lawyers' ability to predict case outcomes. *Psychology, Public Policy, and Law, 16,* 133–157.

Goodman-Delahunty, J., Greene, E., & Hsiao, W. (1998). Construing motive in videotaped killings: The role of jurors' attitudes toward the death penalty. *Law and Human Behavior, 22,* 257–271.

Goodman-Delahunty, J., & Martschuk, N. (2020). Mock jury and juror responses to uncharged acts of sexual misconduct. *Zeitschrift für Psychologie, 228,* 199–209.

Goodman-Delahunty, J., & Sporer, S. (2010). Unconscious influences in sentencing decisions: A research review of psychological sources of disparity. *Australian Journal of Forensic Sciences, 42,* 19–36.

Goodmark, L. (2020). Reimagining VAWA: Why criminalization is a failed policy and what a non-carceral VAWA could look like. *Violence Against Women,* 1–18. Retrieved January 17, 2022, from https://www.nyscasa.org /wp-content/uploads/2020/09/VAW-Crim-as-failed-policy-1.pdf.

Gordon, N. (2022). Embracing the gains of virtual trials. Retrieved February 27, 2023 from https://www.doar.com/author/ngordon/

Gothard, S., Rogers, R., & Sewell, K. W. (1995). Feigning incompetency to stand trial: An investigation of the Georgia Court Competency Test. *Law and Human Behavior, 19,* 363–374.

Gothard, S., Viglione, D. J., Meloy, J. R., & Sherman, M. (1995). Detection of malingering in competency to stand trial evaluations. *Law and Human Behavior, 19,* 493–506.

Gottfried, E. et al. (2015). Improving the detection of feigned knowledge deficits in defendants adjudicated incompetent to stand trial. *Assessment, 24*(2), 1–12.

Gottfredson, D., & Exum, M. (2002). The Baltimore city drug treatment court: One-year results from a randomized study. *Journal of Research in Crime and Delinquency, 39,* 337–356.

Gottfredson, D., Najaka, S., & Kearley, B. (2003). Effectiveness of drug courts: Evidence from a randomized trial. *Criminology & Public Policy, 2,* 171–196.

Gottfredson, M, & Hirschi, T. (1990). *A general theory of crime.* Stanford: Stanford University Press.

Gould, J. (2011). *As California fights prison overcrowding, some see a golden opportunity.* Retrieved June 12, 2012, from http://www.time.com/time /nation/article/0,8599,2094840,00.html

Grabman, J. H., Dobolyi, D. G., Berelovich, N. L., & Dodson, C. S. (2019). Predicting high confidence errors in eyewitness memory: The role of face recognition ability, decision-time, and justifications. *Journal of Applied Research in Memory and Cognition, 8*(2), 233–243. doi.org/10.1037 /h0101835.supp (Supplemental)

Graham, J., Haidt, J., & Nosek, B. (2009). Liberals and conservatives rely on different sets of moral foundations. *Journal of Personality and Social Psychology, 96,* 1029–1046.

Graham v. Florida, 130 S.Ct. 2011 (2010).

Gramlich, J. (2019, June 11). Only 2% of federal criminal defendants go to trial, and most who do are found guilty. Retrieved January 19, 2022, from https://www.pewresearch.org/fact-tank/2019/06/11/only-2-of-federal -criminal-defendants-go-to-trial-and-most-who-do-are-found-guilty/

Grattet, R. (2020). Back end sentencing and parole revocation. Retrieved April 20, 2022, from https://www.oxfordbibliographies.com/view /document/obo-9780195396607/obo-9780195396607-0277 .xml#:~:text=Back%2Dend%20sentencing%20refers%20to,to%20 prison%20for%20parole%20violations

Gray, E. (1993). *Unequal justice: The prosecution of child sexual abuse.* New York, NY: Macmillan.

Gready, R., Ditto, P., Danks, J., Coppola, K., Lockhart, L., & Smucker, W. (2000). Actual and perceived stability of preferences for life-sustaining treatment. *Journal of Clinical Ethics, 11,* 334–346.

Greathouse, S., & Kovera, M. (2009). Instruction bias and lineup presentation moderate the effects of administrator knowledge on eyewitness identification. *Law and Human Behavior, 33,* 70–82.

Greely, H., & Illes, J. (2007). Neuroscience-based lie detection: The urgent need for regulation. *American Journal of Law and Medicine, 33,* 377–421.

Green, A. (2004, August 30). The waiting room: August. *The New Yorker,* pp. 37–38.

Green, E. (2019). An overview of evidence-based practices and programs in prison reentry. *Illinois Criminal Justice Information Authority.* Retrieved February 4, 2022, from https://icjia.illinois.gov/researchhub /articles/an-overview-of-evidence-based-practices-and-programs-in -prison-reentry

Green, S. (2005, January 31). When justice is delayed. *National Law Journal,* p. 22.

Greene, E. (2002). How effective? Review of *Stack and sway: The new science of jury consulting. Judicature, 85,* 1–3.

Greene, E. (2008). "Can we talk?" Therapeutic jurisprudence, restorative justice, and tort litigation. In B. Bornstein & R. Wiener (Eds.), *Civil juries and civil justice: Empirical perspectives* (pp. 235–258). New York, NY: Springer.

Greene, E. (2009). Psychological issues in the civil trial. In J. Lieberman & D. Krauss (Eds.), *Jury psychology: Social aspects of trial processes. Vol. 1: Psychology of the Courtroom* (pp. 183–206). Burlington, VT: Ashgate.

Greene, E., & Bornstein, B. (2000). Precious little guidance: Jury instructions on damage awards. *Psychology, Public Policy, and Law, 6,* 743–768.

Greene, E., & Bornstein, B. (2003). *Determining damages: The psychology of jury awards.* Washington, DC: American Psychological Association.

Greene, E., Duke, L., & Woody, W. (2017). Stereotypes influence beliefs about transfer and sentencing of juvenile offenders. *Psychology, Crime, & Law, 23,* 841–858.

Greene, E., Goodman, J., & Loftus, E. (1991). Jurors' attitudes about civil litigation and the size of damage awards. *American University Law Review, 40,* 805–820.

Greene, E., & Gordon, N. (2016). Can the "hot tub" enhance jurors' understanding and use of expert testimony? *Wyoming Law Review, 16,* 359–385.

Greene, E., Hayman, K., & Motyl, M. (2008). "Shouldn't we consider …?" Jury discussions of forbidden topics and effects on damage awards. *Psychology, Public Policy, and Law, 14,* 194–222.

Greene, E., & Johns, M. (2001). Jurors' use of instructions on negligence. *Journal of Applied Social Psychology, 31,* 840–859.

Greene, E., Johns, M., & Smith, A. (2001). The effects of defendant conduct on jury damage awards. *Journal of Applied Psychology, 86,* 228–237.

Greene, E., & Loftus, E. (1985). When crimes are joined at trial. *Law and Human Behavior, 9,* 193–207.

Greene, E., Sturm, K. A., & Evelo, A. J. (2016). Affective forecasting about hedonic loss and adaptation: Implications for damage awards. *Law and Human Behavior, 40,* 244–256.

Greene, J. A. (1999). Zero tolerance: A case study of police policies and practices in New York City. *Crime and Delinquency, 45,* 171–187.

Greenhouse, L. (1994, April 20). High court bars sex as standard of picking jurors. *The New York Times,* pp. A1, A10.

Gregg v. Georgia, 428 U.S. 153 (1976).

Gregory, W. L., Mowen, J. C., & Linder, D. E. (1978). Social psychology and plea bargaining: Applications, methodology, and theory. *Journal of Personality and Social Psychology, 36,* 1521–1530.

Greiner, D. J., & Matthews, A. (2016). Randomized control trials in the United States legal profession. *Annual Review of Law and Social Science, 12,* 295–312.

Grietens, H., & Hellinckx, W. (2004). Evaluating effects of residential treatment for juvenile offenders by statistical meta-analysis: A review. *Aggression and Violent Behavior, 9,* 401–415. doi:10.1016 /S1359-1789(03)00043-0

Griffin, M. (2008, March). *Old dogs and new tricks: Demographic variables and interest in technology implementation in the courtroom.* Paper presented at the annual conference of American Psychology-Law Society, Jacksonville, FL.

Griffin, P. (2003). *Trying and sentencing juveniles as adults: An analysis of state transfer and blended sentencing laws.* Pittsburgh, PA: National Center for Juvenile Justice.

Griffin, P., Heilbrun, K., Mulvey, E., DeMatteo, D., & Schubert, C. (Eds.). (2015). *Criminal justice and the Sequential Intercept Model: Promoting community alternatives for people with severe mental illness.* New York, NY: Oxford University Press.

Grills-Taquechel, A., Littleton, H., & Axsom, D. (2011). Social support, world assumptions, and exposure as predictors of anxiety and quality of life following a mass trauma. *Journal of Anxiety Disorders, 25,* 498–506.

Grisso, T. (1998). *Forensic assessment of juveniles.* Sarasota, FL: Professional Resource Press.

Grisso, T. (2003). *Evaluating competencies: Forensic assessments and instruments* (2nd ed.). New York, NY: Kluwer/Plenum.

Grisso, T., & Appelbaum, P. (1998a). *Assessing competence to consent to treatment: A guide for physicians and other health professionals.* New York, NY: Oxford University Press.

Grisso, T., & Appelbaum, P. (1998b). *MacArthur competence assessment tool for treatment (MacCAT-T).* Sarasota, FL: Professional Resource Press.

Grisso, T., & Appelbaum, P. S. (1995). The MacArthur Treatment Competence Study. III: Abilities of patients to consent to psychiatric and medical treatments. *Law and Human Behavior, 19*, 149–174.

Grisso, T., Appelbaum, P. S., Mulvey, E. P., & Fletcher, K. (1995). The MacArthur Treatment Competence Study. II: Measures of abilities related to competence to consent to treatment. *Law and Human Behavior, 19*, 127–148.

Grisso, T. et al. (1994). The organization of pretrial forensic evaluation services: A national profile. *Law and Human Behavior, 18*, 377–393.

Grisso, T., & Kavanaugh, A. (2016). Prospects for developmental evidence in juvenile sentencing based on Miller v. Alabama. *Psychology, Public Policy, and Law, 22*, 235–249.

Grisso, T., Steinberg, L., Woolard, J., Cauffman, E., Scott, E., Graham, S., … Schwartz, R. (2003). Juveniles' competence to stand trial: A comparison of adolescents' and adults' capacities as trial defendants. *Law and Human Behavior, 27*, 333–363.

Gromet, D., & Darley, J. (2006). Restoration and retribution: How including retributive components affects the acceptability of restorative justice procedures. *Social Justice Research, 19*, 395–432.

Gromet, D., Okimoto, T., Wenzel, M., & Darley, J. (2012). A victim-centered approach to justice? Victim satisfaction effects on third-party punishments. *Law and Human Behavior, 36*, 375–389.

Grosso C. & O'Brien, B. (2011–2012). A stubborn legacy: the overwhelming importance of race in jury selection in 173 North Carolina capital trials. *Iowa Law Review, 97*, 1531–1559.

Gross, S., Jacoby, K., Matheson, D., Montgomery, N., & Patil, S. (2005). Exonerations in the United States 1989 through 2003. *Journal of Criminal Law and Criminology, 95*, 523–560.

Gross, S., & O'Brien, B. (2008). Frequency and predictors of false conviction: Why we know so little, and new data on capital cases. *Journal of Empirical Legal Studies, 5*, 927–962.

Grove, W. M., & Barden, R. C. (1999). Protecting the integrity of the legal system: The admissibility of testimony from mental health experts under *Daubert/Kumho* analyses. *Psychology, Public Policy, and Law, 5*, 224–242.

Grow, B. (2010). As jurors go online, U.S. trials go off track. Retrieved on June 9, 2022, from https://jp.reuters.com/article/us-internet-jurors/as-jurors-go-online-u-s-trials-go-off-track-idUKTRE6B74Z820101208

Grutter v. Bollinger, 539 U.S. 306 (2003).

Gubi-Kelm, S., Grolig, T., Strobel, B., Ohlig, S., & Schmidt, A. F. (2020). When do false accusations lead to false confessions? Preliminary evidence for a potentially overlooked alternative explanation. *Journal of Forensic Psychology Research and Practice, 20*(2), 114–133.

Gudjonsson, G.H. & Pearse, J. (2011). Suspect interviews and false confessions. *Current Directions in Psychological Science, 20*, 33–37.

Gudjonsson, G.H. & Copson, G. (1997). The role of the expert in criminal investigation. In J. L. Jackson & D. A. Bekerian (Eds.), *Offender profiling: Theory, research, and practice* (pp. 61–76). Chichester, UK: Wiley.

Gunnell, J., & Ceci, S. (2010). When emotionality trumps reason: A study of individual processing style and juror bias. *Behavioral Sciences and the Law, 28*, 850–877.

Gutek, B. A., & O'Connor, M. (1995). The empirical basis for the reasonable woman standard. *Journal of Social Issues, 51*, 151–166.

Guthrie, C., Rachlinski, J., & Wistrich, A. (2001). Inside the judicial mind. *Cornell Law Review, 86*, 777–830.

Guthrie, C., Rachlinski, J., & Wistrich, A. (2007). Blinking on the bench: How judges decide cases. *Cornell Law Review, 93*, 1–44.

Guthrie, C., Rachlinski, J. J., & Wistrich, A. J. (2009). The "hidden judiciary": An empirical examination of the executive branch of justice. *Duke Law Journal, 58*, 1477–1530.

Haby, J., & Brank, E. (2013). The role of anchoring in plea bargains. *APA Monitor, 44*, 30.

Hahn, R., & Kleist, D. (2000). Divorce mediation: Research and implications for family and couples counseling. *The Family Journal, 8*, 165–171.

Hakuta, J., Soroushian, V., & Kralstein. (2008). *Do community courts transform the justice response to misdemeanor crime? Testing the impact of the Midtown Community Court*. New York, NY: Center for Court Innovation.

Hall v. Florida, 134 S. Ct. 1986 (2014).

Haney, C. (2006). *Reforming punishment: Psychological limits to the pains of imprisonment*. Washington, DC: American Psychological Association.

Haney, C., Zurbriggen, E. L., & Weill, J. M. (2022). The continuing unfairness of death qualification: Changing death penalty attitudes and capital jury selection. *Psychology, Public Policy, and Law, 28*, 1–31.

Haney-Caron, E., & Heilbrun, K. (2014). Lesbian and gay parents and determination of child custody: The changing legal landscape and implications for policy and practice. *Psychology of Sexual Orientation and Gender Diversity, 1*, 19–29. doi:10.1037/sgd0000020

Hannaford-Agor, P., Hans, V., Mott, N., & Munsterman, G. (2002). *Are hung juries a problem?* Retrieved July 2, 2022, from www.ncsc-jurystudies.org

Hannaford-Agor, P., Rottman, D., & Waters, N. (2012). *Jurors and new media: A baseline exploration*. In Perspectives on State Court Leadership. Williamsburg, VA: National Center for State Courts.

Hannaford-Agor, P., Trochesset, A., Bailey, E., & Kelliher, C. (2021). *Jurors and new media: Filling knowledge gaps for judicial and legal policymakers*. Retrieved June 10, 2022, from https://ncsc.contentdm.oclc.org/digital/collection/juries/id/328

Hannaford, P., Hans, V., & Munsterman, G. T. (2000). Permitting jury discussions during trial: Impact of the Arizona reform. *Law and Human Behavior, 24*, 359–382.

Hans, V.P. (1986). An analysis of public attitudes toward the insanity defense. *Criminology, 24*(2), 393–414.

Hans, V.P. (1992). Judgments of justice. *Psychological Science, 3*, 218–220.

Hans, V.P. (1996). The contested role of the civil jury in business litigation. *Judicature, 79*, 242–248.

Hans, V.P., Blume, J. H, Eisenberg, T., Hritz, A. C., Johnson, S. L., Royer, C. E., & Wells, M. T. (2015). The death penalty: Should the judge or the jury decide who dies? *Journal of Empirical Legal Studies, 12*, 70–99.

Hans, V.P., Fukurai, H., Ivkovic, S., & Park, J. (2017). Global juries: A plan for research. In M. Kovera (Ed.), *The psychology of juries* (pp. 131–158). Washington, DC: APA.

Hans, V.P., Kaye, D., Dann, B., Farley, E., & Albertson, S. (2011). Science in the jury box: Jurors' comprehension of mitochondrial DNA evidence. *Law and Human Behavior, 35*, 60–71.

Hans, V.P., Reed, K., Reyna, V., Garavito, D., & Helm, R. (2022). Guiding jurors' damage award decisions: Experimental investigations of approaches based on theory and practice. *Psychology, Public Policy, and Law, 28*, 188–212.

Hans, V. P., & Reyna, V. F. (2011). To dollars from sense: Qualitative to quantitative translation in jury damage awards. *Journal of Empirical Legal Studies, 8*, 120–147.

Hans, V.P., & Saks, M. (2018). Improving judge and jury evaluation of scientific evidence. *Daedelus, 147*, 164–180.

Hans, V.P., & Vidmar, N. (1986). *Judging the jury*. New York, NY: Plenum.

Hans, V.P., & Vidmar, N. (1991). The American jury at twenty-five years. *Law and Social Inquiry, 16*, 323–351.

Hansen, M. (1999, April). Mandatories going, going … going. *American Bar Association Journal, 85*, 14.

Hanson, R., Bourgon, G., Helmus, L., & Hodgson, S. (2009). The principles of effective correctional treatment also apply to sexual offenders: A meta-analysis. *Criminal Justice and Behavior, 36*, 865–891.

Hanson, S. S. and Doukas, D. J. (2009). Advance directives. In V. Ravitsky, A. Fiester, & A. Caplan (Eds.), *The Penn Center Guide to Bioethics* (pp. 749–760). New York, NY: Springer.

Hanson, R. K., Harris, A. R., Letourneau, E., Helmus, L. M., & Thornton, D. (2018). Reductions in risk based on time offense-free in the community: Once a sexual offender, not always a sexual offender. *Psychology, Public Policy, And Law, 24*(1), 48–63.

Harding, T., & Zimmerman, E. (1989). Psychiatric symptoms, cognitive stress and vulnerability factors: A study in a remand prison. *British Journal of Psychiatry, 155*, 36–43.

Hare, R. D. (2003). *The Hare Psychopathy Checklist—Revised (PCL-R)* (2nd ed.). Toronto, ON: Multi-Health Systems.

Hare, R. D., & Neumann, C. (2008). Psychopathy as a clinical and empirical construct. *Annual Review of Clinical Psychology, 4*, 217–246.

Hare, T. A., O'Doherty, J., Camerer, C. F., Schultz, W., & Rangel, A. (2008). Dissociating the role of the orbitofrontal cortex and the striatum in the computation of goal values and prediction errors. *Journal of Neuroscience, 28*, 5623–5630.

Harpold, J. A., & Feemster, S. L. (2002). Negative influences of police stress. *FBI Law Enforcement Bulletin, 71*(9), 1–7. Retrieved July 18, 2005, from http://www.fbi.gov/publications/leb/2002/sept2002/sept02leb.htm#page_2

Harrington v. Iowa, 659 NW 2d 509 (Iowa, 2003).

Harris v. Forklift Systems, Inc., 510 U.S. 17 (1993).

Harris v. New York, 401 U.S. 222 (1971).

Harris, A., & Sen, M. (2019). Bias and judging. *Annual Review of Political Science, 22*, 241–259.

Harris, A., Walfield, S., Shields, R., & LeTourneau, E. (2016). Collateral consequences of juvenile sex offender registration and notification: Results from a survey of treatment providers. *Sexual Abuse: A Journal of Research and Treatment, 38*, 770–790.

Harris, G., Rice, M., & Quinsey, V. (2013). *Violence Risk Appraisal Guide-Revised.* https://hdl.handle.net/10864/12053

Harris, L., Block, S., Ogle, C., Goodman, G., Augusti, E., Larson, R., … Urquiza, A. (2016). Coping style and memory specificity in adolescents and adults with histories of child sexual abuse. *Memory, 24*, 1078–1090.

Harrison, P., & Beck, A. J. (2002). *Prisoners in 2001. Bureau of Justice Statistics Bulletin.* Washington, DC: U.S. Department of Justice.

Harrison, P. M., & Karberg, J. C. (2003, April). *Prison and jail inmates at midyear 2002. Bureau of Justice Statistics Bulletin.* Washington, DC: U.S. Department of Justice.

Hartley, R. (2008). Dedication for the special issue on problem-solving courts. *Criminal Justice Review, 33*, 289–290.

Hartwig, M. (2011). Methods in deception detection research. In B. Rosenfeld & S. Penrod (Eds.), *Research methods in forensic psychology* (pp. 136–155). Hoboken, NJ: Wiley.

Hartwig, M., Granhag, P. A., Strömwall, L., & Doering, N. (2010). Impression and information management: On the strategic

Hartwig, M., & Bond, C. (2014). Lie detection from multiple cues: A meta-analysis. *Applied Cognitive Psychology, 28*, 661–676.

Hartwig, M., & Bond, C. (2014). Lie detection from multiple cues: A meta-analysis. *Applied Cognitive Psychology, 28*, 661–676. self-regulation of innocent and guilty suspects. *The Open Criminology Journal, 3*, 10–16.

Hasel, L. E., & Kassin, S. M. (2009). On the presumption of evidentiary independence: Can confessions corrupt eyewitness identifications? *Psychological Science, 20*(1), 122–126. doi-org.lprx.bates.edu/10.1111/j.1467-9280.2008.02262.x

Hasemann, D. (1997). *Practices and findings of mental health professionals conducting workers' compensation evaluations.* Unpublished doctoral dissertation, University of Kentucky, Lexington, KY.

Hassell, K. D., & Brandl, S. G. (2009). An examination of the workplace experiences of police patrol officers: The role of race, sex, and sexual orientation. *Police Quarterly, 12*, 408–430. doi:10.1177/1098611109348473

Hastie, R. (1991). Is attorney-conducted voir dire an effective procedure for the selection of impartial juries? *American University Law Review, 40*, 703–726.

Hastie, R., Penrod, S. D., & Pennington, N. (1983). *Inside the jury.* Cambridge, MA: Harvard University Press.

Hatcher, C., Mohandie, K., Turner, J., & Gelles, M. G. (1998). The role of the psychologist in crisis/hostage negotiations. *Behavioral Sciences & the Law, 16*, 455–472.

Hauch, V., Sporer, S., Michael, S., & Meissner, C. (2016). Does training improve the detection of deception? A meta-analysis. *Communication Research, 43*, 283–343.

Haw, R., & Fisher, R. (2004). Effects of administrator—witness contact on eyewitness identification accuracy. *Journal of Applied Psychology, 89*, 1106–1112.

Hawkins, H. C. (2001). Police officer burnout: A partial replication of Maslach's burnout inventory. *Police Quarterly, 4*, 343–360.

Hazelwood, R. R., & Douglas, J. E. (1980). The lust murderer. *FBI Law Enforcement Bulletin, 49*, 18–22.

Hazelwood, R. R., & Michaud, S. (2001). *Dark dreams.* New York, NY: Macmillan.

Hazelwood, R. R., Ressler, R. K., Depue, R. L., & Douglas, J. C. (1995). Criminal investigative analysis: An overview. In A. W. Burgess & R. R. Hazelwood (Eds.), *Practical aspects of rape investigation: A multidisciplinary approach* (2nd ed., pp. 115–126). Boca Raton, FL: CRC.

Heilbrun, K. (1987). The assessment of competency for execution: An overview. *Behavioral Sciences & the Law, 5*, 383–396.

Heilbrun, K. (2001). *Principles of forensic mental health assessment.* New York, NY: Kluwer Academic/Plenum.

Heilbrun, K. (2009). *Evaluation for risk of violence in adults.* New York, NY: Oxford University Press.

Heilbrun, K., DeMatteo, D., King, C., & Filone, S. (2017). *Evaluating juvenile transfer and disposition: Law, science, and practice.* New York: Routledge.

Heilbrun, K., DeMatteo, D., King, C., Thornewill, A., & Phillips, S. (2016). Risk-reducing interventions for justice-involved individuals: A critical review. In B. Bornstein & M. Miller (Eds.), *Advances in law and psychology* (pp. 271–304). New York: Springer.

Heilbrun, K., DeMatteo, D., Yasuhara, K., Brooks Holliday, S., Shah, S., King, C., … Laduke, C. (2012). Community-based alternatives for justice-involved individuals with severe mental illness: Review of the relevant research. *Criminal Justice and Behavior, 39*, 351–419.

Heilbrun, K., Douglas, K., & Yasuhara, K. (2009). Violence risk assessment: Core controversies. In J. Skeem, K. Douglas, & S. Lilienfeld (Eds.), *Psychological science in the courtroom: Controversies and consensus* (pp. 333–357). New York, NY: Guilford.

Heilbrun, K., Fishel, S., Lankford, C., & Ratkalkar, M. (2020). Therapy with exonerated clients: Review and recommendations. *Journal of Forensic Practice, 22*, 123–135.

Heilbrun, K., Giallella, C., Wright, H. J., DeMatteo, D., Griffin, P. A., Gowensmith, N., Locklair, B., Ayers, D., Desai, A., & Pietruszka, V. (2021). Jackson-based restorability to competence to stand trial: Critical analysis and recommendations. *Psychology, Public Policy, and Law, 27*, 370–386. doi.org/10.1037/law0000307

Heilbrun, K., Giallella, C., Wright, H.J., DeMatteo, D., Griffin, P., Gowensmith, N., Locklair, B., Ayers, D., Desai, A., & Pietruszka, V. (in press). Appraising *Jackson*-based unrestorability to competence to stand trial: The Demonstration Model. *Psychological Services.*

Heilbrun, K., Goldstein, N., DeMatteo, D., Hart, A., Riggs Romaine, C., & Shah, S. (2011). Interventions in forensic settings: Juveniles in residential placement, defendants in drug courts or mental health courts, and defendants in forensic hospitals as Incompetent to Stand Trial. In Barlow, D. (Ed.), *Oxford handbook of clinical psychology* (pp. 649–679). New York, NY: Oxford University Press.

Heilbrun, K., Grisso, T., & Goldstein, A. (2009). *Foundations of forensic mental health assessment.* New York, NY: Oxford University Press.

Heilbrun, K., Heilbrun, P., & Griffin, N. (1988). Comparing females acquitted by reason of insanity, convicted, and civilly committed in Florida: 1977–1984. *Law and Human Behavior, 12*, 295–312.

Heilbrun, K., Lee, R., & Cottle, C. (2005). Risk factors and intervention outcomes: Meta-analyses of juvenile offending. In K. Heilbrun, N. Sevin-Goldstein, & R. Redding (Eds.), *Juvenile delinquency: Prevention, assessment, and intervention* (pp. 111–133). New York, NY: Oxford University Press.

Heilbrun, K., & McClaren, H. (1988). Assessment of competency for execution? A guide for mental health professionals. *Bulletin of the American Academy of Psychiatry and the Law, 16*, 206–216.

Heilbrun, K., Yasuhara, K., Shah, S., & Locklair, B. (2021). Approaches to violence risk assessment: Overview, critical analysis, and future directions. In K. Douglas & R.K. Otto (Eds.), *Handbook of violence risk assessment* (2nd ed.) (pp. 3–27). New York: Routledge.

Helm, R., Ceci, S., & Burd, K. (2016). Unpacking insanity defence standards: An experimental study of rationality and control tests in criminal law. *European Journal of Psychology Applied to Legal Context, 8*(2), 63–68.

Helm, R. K., & Reyna, V. F. (2017). Logical but incompetent plea decisions: A new approach to plea bargaining grounded in cognitive theory. *Psychology, Public Policy, and Law, 23*(3), 367–380.

Helm, R., Reyna, V., Franz, A., & Novick, R. (2018). Too young to plead? Risk, rationality, and plea bargaining's innocence problems with adolescents. *Psychology, Public Policy, and Law, 24*, 180–191.

Henderson, K., & Levett, L. (2016). Can expert testimony sensitize jurors to variations in confession evidence? *Law and Human Behavior, 40*, 638–649.

Henggeler, S. (2016). Community-based interventions for juvenile offenders. In K. Heilbrun, D. DeMatteo, & N. Goldstein (Eds.), *APA handbook of psychology and juvenile justice* (pp. 575–595). Washington, DC: American Psychological Association.

Henggeler, S., Clingempeel, W., Brondino, M., & Pickrel, S. (2002). Four-year follow-up of multi-systemic therapy with substance-abusing and substance-dependent juvenile offenders. *Journal of the American Academy of Child and Adolescent Psychiatry, 41*, 868–874.

Henggeler, S., Pickrel, S. G., & Brondino, M. J. (1999). Multisystemic treatment of substance abusing and dependent delinquents: Outcomes, treatment fidelity, and transportability. *Mental Health Services Research, 1*, 171–184.

Henggeler, S., Rowland, M., Randall, J., Ward, D., Pickrel, S., Cunningham, P., ... Santos, A. (1999). Home-based multisystemic therapy as an alternative to the hospitalization of youths in psychiatric crisis: Clinical outcomes. *Journal of the American Academy of Child and Adolescent Psychiatry, 38*, 1331–1339.

Henggeler, S., & Schoenwald, S. K. (1999). The role of quality assurance in achieving outcomes in MST programs. *Journal of Juvenile Justice and Detention Services, 14*, 1–17.

Henggeler, S., Schoenwald, S. K., Borduin, C. M., Rowland, M. D., & Cunningham, P. B. (1998). *Multisystemic treatment of antisocial behavior in children and adolescents*. New York, NY: Guilford.

Henry, M., & Rafilson, F. (1997). The temporal stability of the National Police Officer Selection Test. *Psychological Reports, 81*, 1259–1265.

Herbert, B. (2002 August 15). An imaginary homicide. *The New York Times*. Retrieved March 16, 2022, from www.nytimes.com/2002/08/15/opinion/an-imaginary-homicide.html

Herbert, B. (2010, March 2). *Watching certain people*. Retrieved July 13, 2012, from http://www.nytimes.com/2010/03/02/opinion/-02herbert.html

Herinckx, H., Swart, S., Ama, S., Dolezal, C., & King, S. (2005). Rearrest and linkage to mental health services among clients of the Clark County Mental Health Court Program. *Psychiatric Services, 56*, 853–857.

Heilbrun, K. et al. (2019). Treatment for restoration of competence to stand trial: Critical analysis and policy recommendations. *Psychology, Public Policy, and Law, 25*(4), 266–283. Advance online publication August 22, 2019.

Hersch, J., & Viscusi, W. (2004). Punitive damages: How judges and juries perform. *Journal of Legal Studies, 33*, 1–36.

Hershkowitz, I., Lamb, M., Orbach, Y., Katz, C., & Horowitz, D. (2012). The development of communicative and narrative skills among preschoolers: Lessons from forensic interviews about child abuse. *Child Development, 83*, 611–622.

Hetherington, E., & Kelly, J. (2002). *For better or worse: Divorce reconsidered*. New York, NY: Norton.

Hetherington, E. M., Cox, M., & Cox, R. (1982). Effects of divorce on parents and children. In M. Lamb (Ed.), *Non-traditional families* (pp. 223–288). Hillsdale, NJ: Erlbaum.

Hickey, E. (2009). *Serial murderers and their victims*. Belmont, CA: Wadsworth.

Hickman, M. J., & Reaves, B. A. (2001, revised March 27, 2003). *Community policing in local police departments, 1997 and 1999*. Special Report, U.S. Department of Justice, Office of Justice Programs, NCJ 184794, 1–11.

Hill, C., Memon, A., & McGeorge, P. (2008). The role of confirmation bias in suspect interviews: A systematic evaluation. *Legal and Criminological Psychology, 13*, 357–371.

Hille, C. A. (2010). Law enforcement-related stress and relationship satisfaction. *Dissertation Abstracts International Section A: Humanities and Social Sciences, 71*(2–A), 729.

Hillebrandt, A., & Barclay, L. (2017). Comparing integral and incidental emotions: Testing insights from emotions as social information theory and attribution theory. *Journal of Applied Psychology, 102*(5), 732–752.

Hilton, N., Harris, G., Rice, M., Lang, C., & Cormier, C. (2004). A brief actuarial assessment for the prediction of wife assault recidivism: The ODARA. *Psychological Assessment, 16*, 267–275.

Ho, B., & Liu, E. (2011). What's an apology worth? Decomposing the effect of apologies on medical malpractice payments using state apology laws. *Journal of Empirical Legal Studies, 8*, 179–199.

Hobbs, S., Goodman, G., Block, S., Oran, D., Quas, J., Park, A., ... Baumrind, N. (2014). Child maltreatment victims' attitudes about appearing in dependency and criminal courts. *Child and Youth Services Review, 44*, 407–416.

Hodell, E., Dunlap, E., Wasarhaley, N., & Golding, J. (2012). Factors impacting juror perceptions of battered women who kill their abusers: Delay and sleeping status. *Psychology, Public Policy, and Law, 18*(2), 338–359.

Hoetger, L., Devine, D., Brank, E., Drew, R., & Rees, R. (2022). The impact of pretrial publicity on mock juror and jury verdicts: A meta-analysis. *Law and Human Behavior, 46*, 121–139.

Hoff, R., Baranosky, M., Buchanan, J., Zonana, H., & Rosenheck, R. (1999). The effects of a jail diversion program on incarceration: A retrospective cohort study. *Journal of the American Academy of Psychiatry and the Law, 27*, 377–386.

Hoffberger, C. (2013, August 16). Seale and Balko visit peaceful streets. Police watchers aim to educate public on citizens' rights. *The Austin Chronicle*. Retrieved from http://www.austinchronicle.com/news/2013-08-16/seale-and-balko-visit-peaceful-streets/

Hoffman, J. (2014, October 13). In interrogations, teenagers are too young to know better. Retrieved from https://well.blogs.nytimes.com/2014/10/13/in-interrogations-teenagers-are-too-young-to-know-better/

Hoffman, P. B., & Stone-Meierhoefer, B. (1979). Application of guidelines to sentencing. In L. E. Abt & I. R. Stuart (Eds.), *Social psychology and discretionary law* (pp. 241–258). New York, NY: Van Nostrand Reinhold.

Hoffmeister, T., & Watts, A. (2018). Social media, the Internet, and trial by jury. *Annual Review of Law and Social Science, 14*, 259–270.

Hoge, R. (2016). Risk, need, and responsivity in juveniles. In K. Heilbrun, D. DeMatteo, & N. Goldstein (Eds.), *APA handbook of psychology and juvenile justice* (pp. 179–196). Washington, DC: American Psychological Association. doi:10.1037/14643-009

Hoge, R., & Andrews, D. (2002). *The Youth Level of Service/Case Management Inventory (YLS/CMI) user's manual*. North Tonawanda, NY: Multi-Health Systems.

Hoge, S., & Bonnie, R. (2021). A new commitment pathway for offenders with serious mental illness: Expedited diversion to court-order treatment. *Psychiatric Services, 72*, 969–971.

Hoge, S. K., Bonnie, R. J., Poythress, N., Monahan, J., Eisenberg, M., & Feucht-Haviar, T. (1997). The MacArthur adjudicative competence study: Development and validation of a research instrument. *Law and Human Behavior, 21*, 141–179.

Hoge, S. K., Poythress, N., Bonnie, R., Monahan, J., Eisenberg, M., & Feucht-Haviar, T. (1997). The MacArthur adjudicative competence study: Diagnosis, psychopathology, and competence-related abilities. *Behavioral Sciences & the Law, 15*, 329–345.

Hogg, A., & Wilson, C. (1995). *Is the psychological screening of police applicants a realistic goal? The successes and failures of psychological screening.* Payneham, Australia: National Police Research Unit. (National Police Research Unit Report Series No. 124).

Holbrook, J., & Anderson, S. (2011). *Veterans courts: Early outcomes and key indicators of success.* Widener Law School Legal Series Research Paper. Retrieved December 23, 2016, from http://ssrn.com/-abstract=1912655

Hollander-Blumoff, R., & Tyler, T. (2008). Procedural justice in negotiation: Procedural fairness, outcome acceptance, and integrative potential. *Law and Social Inquiry, 33*, 473–500.

Holloway, C., & Wiener, R. (2019). The role of emotion and motivation in jury decision-making. In C. Najdowski & M. Stevenson (Eds.), *Criminal juries in the 21st century* (pp. 247–270). New York: Oxford University Press.

Holmes, B., D'Amato, C., & Holmes, S. (2022). The offense-specific nature of gender and familial responsibility in United States Federal Sentencing, 2010–2016. *Criminal Justice Policy Review, 33*, 399-428.

Holmes, M. D., & Smith, B. W. (2008). *Race and police brutality.* Albany, NY: SUNY Press.

Holmes, O. (1881). *The common law.* Boston, MA: Little, Brown.

Holmes, R. M., & DeBurger, J. (1988). *Serial murder.* Newbury Park, CA: Sage.

Homant, R. J., & Kennedy, D. B. (1998). Psychological aspects of crime scene profiling. *Criminal Justice and Behavior, 25*, 319–343.

Honegger, L. (2015). Does the evidence support the case for mental health courts? A review of the literature. *Law and Human Behavior, 39*, 478–488.

Honts, C., & Kircher, J. (2011). Research methods for psychophysiological deception detection. In B. Rosenfeld & S. Penrod (Eds.), *Research methods in forensic psychology* (pp. 105–121). Hoboken, NJ: Wiley.

Honts, C., Thurber, S., & Handler, M. (2021). A comprehensive meta-analysis of the comparison question polygraph test. *Applied Cognitive Psychology, 35*, 411–427.

Hope, L., & Wright, D. (2007). Beyond unusual? Examining the role of attention in the weapon focus effect. *Applied Cognitive Psychology, 21*, 951–961.

Hopt v. Utah, 110 U.S. 574 (1884).

Horgan, J. (2011). Code rage: The "warrior gene" makes me mad! (Whether I have it or not.) *Scientific American.* Retrieved October 20, 2016, from https://blogs.scientificamerican.com/cross-check/code-rage-the-warrior-gene-makes-me-mad-whether-i-have-it-or-not/

Horan, J., & Maine, S. (2014). Criminal jury trials in 2030: A law odyssey. *Journal of Law and Society, 41*, 551–575.

Hornsey, M. (2020). Why facts are not enough: Understanding and managing the motivated rejection of science. *Current Directions in Psychological Science, 29*(6), 583–591.

Horrigan, D. (2002). Technology on trial: Operating in virtual reality. Retrieved February 27, 2023 from https://www.law.com/thelegalintelligencer/almID/900005373327/

Horry, R., Halford, P., Brewer, N., Milne, R., & Bull, R. (2014). Archival analyses of eyewitness identification test outcomes: What can they tell us about eyewitness memory? *Law and Human Behavior, 38*, 94–108.

Horwitz, A., Widom, C. S., McLaughlin, J., & White, H. (2001). The impact of childhood abuse and neglect on adult mental health: A prospective study. *Journal of Health and Social Behavior, 42*, 184–201.

Hotelling, K. (1991). Sexual harassment: A problem shielded by silence. *Journal of Counseling and Development, 69*, 497–501.

Houppert, K. (2007). *Deluded judge suggests domestic violence victim wanted to be hit.* Retrieved February 21, 2009, from http://www.alternet.org/blogs/peek/66153/

Howard, R. C., & Clark, C. R. (1985). When courts and experts disagree: Discordance between insanity recommendations and adjudications. *Law and Human Behavior, 9*, 385–395.

Hritz, A. (2021). Parole board decision making and constitutional rights. *Annual Review of Law and Social Science, 17*, 335–351.

Huber, G., & Gordon, S. (2004). Accountability and coercion: Is justice blind when it runs for office? *American Journal of Political Science, 48*, 247–263.

Huesmann, L. R., Moise-Titus, J., Podolski, C., & Eron, L. D. (2003). Longitudinal relations between children's exposure to TV violence and their aggressive and violent behavior in young adulthood: 1977–1992. *Developmental Psychology, 39*, 201–221.

Hunter, J. D. (1991). *Culture wars: The struggle to define America.* New York: Basic Books.

Hunt, J. (2015). Race, ethnicity, and culture in jury decision making. *Annual Review of Law and Social Science, 11*, 269–288.

Hunt, J. S. (2015). Race in the justice system. In B. L. Cutler & P. A. Zapf (Eds.), *APA Handbook of forensic psychology: Vol. 2. Criminal investigation, adjudication, and sentencing outcomes* (pp. 125–161). Washington, DC: APA.

Hunt, J. S., & Budesheim, T. L. (2004). How jurors use and misuse character evidence. *Journal of Applied Psychology, 89*, 347–361.

Iacono, W., & Ben-Shakhar, G. (2019). Current status of forensic lie detection with the comparison question technique: An update of the 2003 National Academy of Sciences report on polygraph testing. *Law and Human Behavior, 43*, 86–98.

Ilies, R., Hauserman, N., Schwochau, S., & Stibal, J. (2003). Reported incidence rates of work-related sexual harassment in the United States: using meta-analysis to explain reported rate disparities. *Personnel Psychology, 56*(3), 607–631.

Imwinkelried, E. J. (1994). The next step after *Daubert*: Developing a similarly epistemological approach to ensuring the reliability of nonscientific expert testimony. *Cardozo Law Review, 15*, 2271–2294.

In re Corrugated Container Antitrust Litigation, 614 F2d 958 (5th Circuit, 1980).

In re Gault, 387 U.S. 1 (1967).

Inbau, F. E., Reid, J. E., Buckley, J. P., & Jayne, B. C. (2013). *Criminal interrogation and confessions* (5th ed.). Burlington, MA: Jones & Bartlett Learning.

Indiana v. Edwards, 554 U.S. 164 (2008).

Ingram, P., & Ternes, M. (2016). The detection of content-based invalid responding: A meta-analysis of the MMPI-2-Restructured Form's (MMPI-2-RF) over-reporting validity scales. *Clinical Neuropsychology, 30*(4), 473–496. doi: 10.1080/13854046.2016.1187769.

Innocence Project, 2022 https://innocenceproject.org/

International Association of Chiefs of Police. (2006). *Building an offender reentry program: A guide for law enforcement.* Washington, DC: U.S. Bureau of Justice Assistance.

International Association of Chiefs of Police. (2013). *Psychological fitness-for-duty guidelines.* Retrieved March 24, 2017, from http://www.theiacp.org/portals/0/documents/pdfs/psych-fitnessfordutyevaluation.pdf

International Association of Chiefs of Police. (2016). *Discover policing.* Retrieved October 27, 2016, from http://discoverpolicing.org/

International Association of Chiefs of Police. (2016). *Officer-involved shootings: A guide for law enforcement leaders.* Washington, D.C.: Office of Community Oriented Policing Services. Retrieved February 17, 2022, from https://www.theiacp.org/sites/default/files/2018-08/e051602754_Officer_Involved_v8.pdf.

International Association of Chiefs of Police and the Urban Institute. (2017). *2016 law enforcement use of social media survey.* Retrieved January 17, 2022, from https://www.urban.org/sites/default/files/publication/88661/2016-law-enforcement-use-of-social-media-survey_5.pdf.

International Association of Correctional and Forensic Psychology. (2010). Standards for psychology services in jails, prisons, correctional facilities, and agencies (3rd ed.). *Criminal Justice and Behavior, 37*(7), 751–808.

Inwald, R. (1992). *Inwald Personality Inventory technical manual* (Rev. ed.). Kew Gardens, NY: Hilson Research.

Inwald, R. (2008). The Inwald Personality Inventory (IPI) and Hilson Research Inventories: Development and rationale. *Aggression and Violent Behavior, 13*, 298–327.

Inwald, R., Knatz, H., & Shusman, E. (1983). *Inwald Personality Inventory manual*. New York, NY: Hilson Research.

Irwin, J. (1970). *The felon*. Englewood Cliffs, NJ: Prentice Hall.

J.D.B. v. North Carolina, 131 S.Ct. 2394 (2011).

J.E.B. v. Alabama ex rel. T.B., 511 U.S. 127 (1994).

Jackson v. Indiana, 406 U.S. 715 (1972).

Jackson, B., Vermeer, M., Woods, D., Banks, D., Goodison, S., Russo, J., Barnum, J., Gourdet, C., Langton, L., Planty, M., Shelton, S., Sitar, S., & Witwer, A. (2021). How the criminal justice system's COVID-19 response has provided valuable lessons for broader reform: Looking to the future. Santa Monica, CA: RAND Corporation. https://www.rand.org/pubs/research_briefs/RBA108-6.html.

Jackson, S. (2018). Juvenile competency law and remediation programming: Santa Clara County's experience replicating the Virginia Model. *Journal of Applied Juvenile Justice Services*. Retrieved August 29, 2021, from http://npjs.org/jajjs/

Jacobs, J. (1-16-22). Our kinder, gentler, nobody-moves-out divorce. *New York Times*. Retrieved January 28, 2022, from https://www.nytimes.com/2022/01/14/style/modern-love-kinder-gentler-divorce.html

Jacobson, J., Dobbs-Marsh, J., Liberman, V., & Minson, J. (2011). Predicting civil jury verdicts: How attorneys use (and misuse) a second opinion. *Journal of Empirical Legal Studies, 8*, 99–119.

Jayne, B., & Buckley, J. (2017). *The investigator anthology* (2nd ed.) Chicago, IL: John E. Reid and Associates, Inc.

Jeffers, H. P. (1991). *Who killed Precious?* New York, NY: Pharos.

Jesness, C. (1996). The Jesness Inventory manual. Multi-Health Systems.

Johns, M., Lowry, R., Haderxhanaj, L., Rasberry, C., Robin, Scales, L., Storo, D., & Suarez, N. (2020). Trends in violence victimization and suicide risk by sexual identity among high school students—Youth Risk Behavior Survey, United States, 2015–2019. *MMMR, 69*(1), 19–27.

Johnson, A., & Hoover, S. (2015). The potential of sexual consent interventions on college campuses: A literature review on the barriers to establishing affirmative sexual consent. *PURE Insights, 4*(5). Available at https://digitalcommons.wou.edu/pure/vol4/iss1/5

Johnson v. Zerbst, 304 U.S. 458 (1938).

Johnson, R. (2006). Confounding influences on police detection of suspiciousness. *Journal of Criminal Justice, 34*, 435–442.

Johnson, R. S., Stolar, A. G., McGuire, J. F., Mittakanti, K., Clark, S., Coonan, L. A., & Graham, D. P. (2017). Predictors of incarceration of veterans participating in U.S. veterans' courts. *Psychiatric Services, 68*, 144–150.

Jones, A. M., Bergold, A. N., Dillon, M. K., & Penrod, S. D. (2017). Comparing the effectiveness of Henderson instructions and expert testimony: Which safeguard improves jurors' evaluations of eyewitness evidence? *Journal of Experimental Criminology, 13*, 29–52.

Jones, A. M., Bergold, A. N., & Penrod, S. (2020). Improving juror sensitivity to specific eyewitness factors: Judicial instructions fail the test. *Psychiatry, Psychology and Law, 27*, 366–385. doi.org/10.1080/13218719.2020.1719379

Jones, C., Stalker, K., Franklin, A., Fry, D., Cameron, A., & Taylor, J. (2017). Enablers of help-seeking for deaf and disabled children following abuse and barriers to protection: A qualitative study. *Child and Family Social Work, 22*, 762–771.

Jones, J. S., Wynn, B. N., Kroeze, B., Dunnuck, C., & Rossman, L. (2004). Comparison of sexual assaults by strangers versus known assailants in a community-based population. *American Journal of Emergency Medicine, 22*, 454–459.

Jones v. Mississippi, 593 U.S. ____ (2021).

Jordan, K. L., & McNeal, B. A. (2016). Juvenile penalty or leniency: Sentencing of juveniles in the criminal justice system. *Law and Human Behavior, 40*(4), 387–400.

Judicial Council of California. (2004). *Final report: Task force on jury system improvements*. San Francisco, CA: Author.

Junkin, T. (2004). *Bloodsworth: The true story of the first death row inmate exonerated by DNA*. Chapel Hill, N.C.: Algonquin Books of Chapel Hill.

Justice Education Center, Inc. (2002). *Evaluation of the Hartford Community Court*. Hartford, CT: Author.

Kaban, B., & Quinlan, J. C. (2004). Rethinking a "knowing, intelligent and voluntary waiver" in Massachusetts' juvenile courts. *Journal of the Center for Families, Children, and the Courts, 5*, 35–55.

Kadri, S. (2005). *The trial: A history, from Socrates to O. J. Simpson*. New York, NY: Random House.

Kahan, D. (1996). What do alternative sanctions mean? *University of Chicago Law Review, 63*, 591–653.

Kahan, D. (2006). What's really wrong with shaming sanctions. *Texas Law Review, 84*, 2075–2095.

Kahan, D., Hoffman, D., Braman, D., Evans, D., & Rachlinski, J. (2012). They saw a protest: Cognitive illiberalism and the speech-conduct distinction. *Stanford Law Review, 64*, 851–906.

Kahan, D., Hoffman, D., Evans, D., Devins, N., Lucci, E., & Cheng, K. (2016). "Ideology" or "situation sense"? An experimental investigation of motivated reasoning and professional judgment. *University of Pennsylvania Law Review, 164*, 349–439.

Kahler v. Kansas, 140 S.Ct. 1021 (2020).

Kahneman, D. (2011). *Thinking, fast and slow*. New York, NY: Farrar, Straus, & Giroux.

Kahneman, D. (2011). Thinking, fast and slow. New York, NY: Farrar, Straus, & Giroux.

Kairys, D. (1972). Juror selection: The law, a mathematical method of analysis, and a case study. *American Criminal Law Review, 10*, 771–806.

Kalven, H., & Zeisel, H. (1966). *The American jury*. Boston, MA: Little, Brown.

Kamisar, Y., LaFave, W. R., & Israel, J. (1999). *Basic criminal procedure: Cases, comments and questions*. St. Paul, MN: West.

Kane, A., & Dvoskin, J. (2011). *Evaluation for personal injury claims*. New York, NY: Oxford University Press.

Kang, M., & Shepherd, J. (2011). The partisan price of justice: An empirical analysis of campaign contributions and judicial decisions. *New York University Law Review, 86*, 69–130.

Kansas v. Crane, 534 U.S. 407 (2002).

Kansas v. Hendricks, 117 S. Ct. 2013 (1997).

Kaplan, J. (1996). *Criminal law*. Boston, MA: Little, Brown.

Kaplan, J., & Cutler, B. (2022). Co-occurrences among interrogation tactics in actual criminal investigations, *Psychology, Crime & Law, 28*, 1–19.

Kaplan, M. F., & Miller, C. E. (1987). Group decision making and normative v. informational influence: Effects of type of issue and decision rule. *Journal of Personality and Social Psychology, 53*, 306–313.

Kaplow, J., & Widom, C. S. (2007). Age of onset of child maltreatment predicts long-term mental health outcomes. *Journal of Abnormal Psychology, 116*, 176–187.

Kassin, S. (2005). On the psychology of confessions: Does innocence put innocents at risk? *American Psychologist, 60*, 215–228.

Kassin, S. (2012). Why confessions trump innocence. *American Psychologist, 67*, 431–445.

Kassin, S., Drizin, S., Grisso, T., Gudjonsson, G., Leo, R., & Redlich, A. (2009). Police-induced false confessions: Risk factors and recommendations. *Law and Human Behavior*. Published online July 15, 2009. doi:10.1007/s10979.009-9188-6

Kassin, S., Drizin, S., Grisso, T., Gudjonsson, G., Leo, R., & Redlich, A. (2010). Police-induced confessions: Risk factors and recommendations. *Law and Human Behavior, 34*, 3–38.

Kassin, S., & Gudjonsson, G. (2004). The psychology of confessions: A review of the literature and issues. *Psychological Science in the Public Interest, 5*, 33–67.

Kassin, S. (2005). On the psychology of confessions: Does innocence put innocents at risk? *American Psychologist, 60*, 215–228.

Kassin, S., Kukucka, J., Lawson, V., & DeCarlo, J. (2014). Does video recording alter the behavior of police during interrogation? A mock crime-and-investigation study. *Law and Human Behavior, 38*, 73–83.

Kassin, S., Kukucka, J., Lawson, V. Z., & DeCarlo, J. (2017). Police reports of mock suspect interrogations: A test of accuracy and perception. *Law and Human Behavior, 41*, 230–243.

Kassin, S., Leo, R., Meissner, C., Richman, K., Colwell, L., Leach, A., & La Fon, D. (2007). Police interviewing and interrogation: A self-report survey of police practices and beliefs. *Law and Human Behavior, 31*, 381–400.

Kassin, S., & Neumann, K. (1997). On the power of confession evidence: An experimental test of the "fundamental difference" hypothesis. *Law and Human Behavior, 21*, 469–484.

Kassin, S., & Norwick, R. (2004). Why suspects waive their *Miranda* rights: The power of innocence. *Law and Human Behavior, 28*, 211–221.

Kassin, S. M., Russano, M. B., Amrom, A. D., Hellgren, J., Kukucka, J., & Lawson, V. Z. (2019). Does video recording inhibit crime suspects? Evidence from a fully randomized field experiment. *Law and Human Behavior, 43*(1), 45–55.

Kassin, S., & Wrightsman, L. S. (1985). Confession evidence. In S. M. Kassin & L. S. Wrightsman (Eds.), *The psychology of evidence and trial procedure* (pp. 67–94). Newbury Park, CA: Sage.

Katzman, J., & Kovera, M. B. (2022). Evidence strength (insufficiently) affects police officers' decisions to place a suspect in a lineup. *Law and Human Behavior, 46*(1), 30–44. doi.org/10.1037/lhb0000476.supp (Supplemental)

Kearley, B., & Gottfredson, D. (2020). Long term effects of drug court participation: Evidence from a 15-year follow-up of a randomized controlled trial. *Journal of Experimental Criminology, 16*(3), 1–21. doi: 10.1007/s11292-019-09382-1

Kearl, H., Johns, N., & Raj. A. (2019). Measuring #MeToo: A national study on sexual harassment and assault. San Diego, CA: UC San Diego Center on Gender Equity and Health. Retrieved February 21, 2022, from https://gehweb.ucsd.edu/wp-content/uploads/2019/05/2019-metoo-national-sexual-harassment-and-assault-report.pdf

Keator, K. J., Callahan, L., Steadman, H. J., & Vesselinov, R. (2013). The impact of treatment on the public safety outcomes of mental health court participants. *American Behavioral Scientist, 57*, 231–243.

Kebbell, M., & Milne, R. (1998). Police officers' perception of eyewitness factors in forensic investigations. *Journal of Social Psychology, 138*, 323–330.

Keene, B. (1997). Chemical castration: An analysis of Florida's new "cutting-edge" policy towards sex criminals. *Florida Law Review, 49*, 803–820.

Keilitz, S. (2004). *Specialization of domestic violence case management in the courts: A national survey.* Washington, DC: United States Department of Justice. Retrieved from https://www.ncjrs.gov/pdffiles1/nij/199724.pdf

Kellough, G., & Wortley, S. (2002). Remand for plea: Bail decisions and plea bargaining as commensurate decisions. *British Journal of Criminology, 42*, 186–210.

Kelly, J., & Emery, R. (2003). Children's adjustment following divorce: Risk and resilience perspectives. *Family Relations, 52*, 352–362.

Kelly, C., Miller, J., & Redlich, A. (2016). The dynamic nature of interrogation. *Law and Human Behavior, 40*, 295–309.

Kelly, J. (1996). A decade of divorce mediation research. *Family Court Review, 34*, 373–385.

Kennard, J. B., Otis, C. C., Austin, J. L., Zimmerman, D. M., & Kovera, M. B. (2014). *Behavioral confirmation in voir dire: Effects on jury selection and verdict choices.* Unpublished manuscript.

Kennedy, D. (2018, February 22). I sent an innocent man to prison: A juror's regret. The Marshall Project. Retrieved July 27, 2022, from https://www.themarshallproject.org/2018/02/22/i-sent-an-innocent-man-to-prison

Kerr, N., Kramer, G. P., Carroll, J. S., & Alfini, J. J. (1991). On the effectiveness of voir dire in criminal cases with prejudicial pretrial publicity: An empirical study. *American Law Review, 40*, 665–701.

Kerr, N., & Jung, J. (2018). Should jurors be allowed to discuss trial evidence before deliberation?: New research evidence. *Law and Human Behavior, 42*, 413–426.

Key, K. N., Neuschatz, J. S., Bornstein, B. H., Wetmore, S. A., Luecht, K. M., Dellapaolera, K. S., & Quinlivan, D. S. (2018). Beliefs about secondary confession evidence: A survey of laypeople and defense attorneys. *Psychology, Crime & Law, 24*(1), 1–13.

Kim, B., Merlo, A. V. & Benekos, P. J. (2016). Sex offender recidivism revisited: Review of recent meta-analyses on the effects of sex offender treatment. *Trauma, Violence, & Abuse, 17*(1), 105–117.

King, C. (2017). The psychological factors for juvenile transfer and reverse transfer evaluations. *Behavioral Sciences & the Law, 36*(1), 46–64. doi-org.ezproxy2.library.drexel.edu/10.1002/bsl.2298

Kiser, R. (2010). *Beyond right and wrong.* Berlin, Germany: Springer-Verlag.

Kiser, R., Asher, M., & McShane, B. (2008). Let's not make a deal: An empirical study of decision making in unsuccessful settlement negotiations. *Journal of Empirical Legal Studies, 5*, 551–591.

Klein, D., & Mitchell, G. (Eds.). (2010). *The psychology of judicial decision making.* New York, NY: Oxford University Press.

Kleinberg, H. (1989, January 29). It's tough to have sympathy for Bundy. *Lawrence Journal-World*, p. 5A.

Klein, S. (2016). Sentencing reductions versus sentencing equality. *University of Toledo Law Review, 47*, 723–741.

Kleinmuntz, B., & Szucko, J. J. (1984). Lie detection in ancient and modern times: A call for contemporary scientific study. *American Psychologist, 39*, 766–776.

Knighton, J., Murrie, D., Boccaccini, M., & Turner, D. (2014). How likely is "likely to reoffend" in sex offender civil commitment trials? *Law and Human Behavior, 38*, 293–304.

Knudsen, K., & Wigenfeld, S. (2016). A specialized treatment court for veterans with trauma exposure: Implications for the field. *Community Mental Health Journal, 52*, 127–135.

Knutson, A., Gordon, N., & Greene, E. (2015). More than a feelin': Using small group research to inform settlement decisions in civil lawsuits. *Georgia State University Law Review, 31*, 685–714.

Knutson, A., Greene, E., & Durham, R. (2015). The Juror Internet Research Scale (JIRS): Identifying the jurors who won't stay offline. *The Jury Expert, 27*(4).

Kocsis, R. (2003). Criminal psychological profiling: Validities and abilities. *International Journal of Offender Therapy and Comparative Criminology, 42*, 126–144.

Kocsis, R. (2006). Validities and abilities in criminal profiling: The dilemma for David Canter's investigative psychology. *International Journal of Offender Therapy and Comparative Criminology, 50*, 458–477.

Kocsis, R., & Palermo, G. (2015). Disentangling criminal profiling: Accuracy, homology, and the myth of trait based profiling. *International Journal of Offender Therapy and Comparative Criminology, 59*, 313–332.

Koehler, J., Schweitzer, N., Saks, M., & McQuiston, D. (2016). Science, technology, or the expert witness: What influences jurors' judgments about forensic science testimony? *Psychology, Public Policy, and Law, 22*, 401–413.

Kolebuck, M. D. (1998). *Kansas v. Henricks*: Is it time to lock the door and throw away the key for sexual predators? *Journal of Contemporary Health and Law Policy, 14*, 537–561.

Koons-Witt, B. A., Sevigny, E. L., Burrow, J. D., & Hester, R. (2014). Gender and sentencing outcomes in South Carolina: Examining the interactions with race, age, and offense type. *Criminal Justice Policy Review, 25*, 299–324.

Kopelman, S., Rosette, A. S., & Thompson, L. (2006). The three faces of Eve: An examination of the strategic display of positive, negative, and neutral emotions in negotiations. *Organizational Behavior and Human Decision Processes, 99*, 81–101.

Kopfinger, S. (2007). *PTSD victim tells gripping story.* Retrieved May 15, 2009, from http://lancasteronline.com/article/local/208863_PTSD-victim-tells-gripping-story.html

Korobkin, R., & Doherty, J. (2009). Who wins in settlement negotiations? *American Law and Economics Review, 11*, 162–209.

Korre, M., Loh, K., Eshleman, E., Lessa, F., Porto, L., Christophi, C., & Kales, S. (2019). Recruit fitness and police academy performance: A prospective validation study. *Occupational Medicine, 69*(8–9), 541–548.

Kovera, M. (2002). The effects of general pretrial publicity on juror decisions: An examination of moderators and mediating mechanisms. *Law and Human Behavior, 26*, 43–72.

Kovera, M. (2019). Racial disparities in the criminal justice system: Prevalence, causes, and a search for solutions. *Journal of Social Issues, 75*, 1139–1164.

Kovera, M., & Austin, J. (2016). Identifying juror bias: Moving from assessment and prediction to a new generation of jury selection research. In C. W. Esqueda & B. H. Bornstein (Eds.), *The witness stand and Lawrence S. Wrightsman, Jr.* (pp. 75–94). New York, NY: Springer-Verlag.

Kovera, M., Dickinson, J., & Cutler, B. (2002). Voir dire and jury selection. In A. Goldstein (Ed.), *Comprehensive handbook of psychology: Forensic psychology* (Vol. 11, pp. 161–175). New York, NY: Wiley.

Kovera, M., Greathouse, S., Otis, C., Kennard, J., & Chorn, J. (2014). *Attorney expectations influence the voir dire process* (Unpublished manuscript). City University of New York.

Kraemer, G. W., Lord, W. D., & Heilbrun, K. (2004). Comparing single and serial homicide offenses. *Behavioral Sciences & the Law, 22*, 325–343.

Kraemer, H., Kazdin, A., Offord, D., Kessler, R., Jensen, P., & Kupfer, D. (1997). Coming to terms with the terms of risk. *Archives of General Psychiatry, 54*, 337–343.

Kralstein, D. (2005). *Community court research: A literature review*. New York, NY: Center for Court Innovation.

Kramer, G. M., Wolbransky, M., & Heilbrun, K. (2007). Plea bargaining recommendations by criminal defense attorneys: Evidence strength, potential sentence, and defendant preference. *Behavioral Sciences & the Law, 25*, 573–585.

Kramer, G. P., Kerr, N. L., & Carroll, J. S. (1990). Pretrial publicity, judicial remedies, and jury bias. *Law and Human Behavior, 14*, 409–438.

Krauss, D., Gongola, J., Scurich, N., & Busch, B. (2018). Mental state at time of offense in the hot tub: An empirical examination of concurrent expert testimony in an insanity case. *Behavioral Sciences and the Law, 36*, 358–372.

Krauss, D., & Goldstein, A. (2007). The role of forensic mental health experts in federal sentencing proceedings. In A. Goldstein (Ed.), *Forensic psychology: Emerging topics and expanding roles* (pp. 359–384). Hoboken, NJ: Wiley.

Krauss, D., McCabe, J., & Lieberman, J. (2012). Dangerously misunderstood: Representative jurors' reactions to expert testimony on future dangerousness in a sexually violent predator trial. *Psychology, Public Policy, and Law, 18*, 18–49.

Kravitz, H. M., & Kelly, J. (1999). An outpatient psychiatry program for offenders with mental disorders found Not Guilty by Reason of Insanity. *Psychiatric Services, 50*, 1597–1605.

Krebs, C., Lindquist, C., Warner, T., Fisher, B., & Martin, S. (2007). *Campus sexual assault study* (final report). Washington, DC: National Institute of Justice. Retrieved March 29, 2017, from https://www.ncjrs.gov/App /abstractdb/AbstractDBDetails.aspx?id=243011

Kreis, M., & Cooke, D. (2013). The manifestation of psychopathic traits in women: An exploration using case examples. *International Journal of Forensic Mental Health, 11*, 267–279.

Kressel, N., & Kressel, D. (2002). *Stack and sway: The new science of jury consulting*. Boulder, CO: Westview.

Krings, F., & Facchin, S. (2009). The moderating role of sexism and personality. *Journal of Applied Psychology, 94*, 501–510.

Kropp P. R., Hart S. D., & Belfrage H. (2010). *Brief Spousal Assault Form for the Evaluation of Risk (B-SAFER), version 2: User manual*. ProActive ReSolutions.

Kritzer, H., & Drechsel, R. (2012). Local news of civil litigation. All the litigation news that's fit to print or broadcast. *Judicature, 96*, 16–22.

Kroner, D. G., & Morgan, R. D. (2014). An overview of strategies for the assessment and treatment of criminal thinking. In R. C. Tafrate & D. Mitchell (Eds.), *Forensic CBT: A handbook for clinical practice* (pp. 87–103). Wiley Blackwell.

Kropp, R., Hart, S., Webster, C., & Eaves, D. (1994). *Manual for the Spousal Assault Risk Assessment Guide*. Vancouver, BC, Canada: The British Columbia Institute Against Family Violence.

Kropp, R., Hart, S., Webster, C., & Eaves, D. (1999). *Spousal Assault Risk Assessment: User's guide*. Toronto, ON, Canada: Multi-Health Systems, Inc.

Kropp P. R., Hart S. D., & Belfrage H. (2010). *Brief Spousal Assault Form for the Evaluation of Risk (B-SAFER), version 2: User manual*. ProActive ReSolutions.

Kuehnle, K., & Kirkpatrick, H.D. (2014). Mental health professionals' role in assisting the court in determining the veracity of allegations of child sexual abuse. In K. Heilbrun, D. DeMatteo, S. Brooks Holliday, & C. LaDuke (Eds.), *Forensic mental health assessment: A casebook* (2nd ed.) (pp. 395–396). New York: Oxford.

Kukucka, J., Applegarth, H. K., & Mello, A. L. (2020). Do exonerees face employment discrimination similar to actual offenders? *Legal and Criminological Psychology, 25*(1), 17–32. https://doi.org/10.1111/lcrp.12159

Kumho Tire Co. v. Carmichael, 526 U.S. 137 (1999).

Kunda, Z. (1990). The case for motivated reasoning. *Psychological Bulletin, 108*, 480–498.

Kuris, G. (2020, June 8). *What underrepresented law school applicants should know*. Retrieved December 27, 2021, from https://www .usnews.com/education/blogs/law-admissions-lowdown/articles /what-underrepresented-law-school-applicants-should-know

Kutateladze, B., & Andiloro, N. (2014). *Prosecution and racial justice in New York County-Technical Report*. New York, NY: Vera Institute of Justice.

Kutateladze, B. L., Andiloro, N. R., & Johnson, B. D. (2016). Opening Pandora's box: How does defendant race influence plea bargaining? *Justice Quarterly, 33*, 398–426.

Kwiatkowski, J., & Miller, M. (2015). How attitude functions, attitude change, and beliefs affect community sentiment toward the Facebook law. In M. Miller, J. Blumenthal, & J. Chamberlain (Eds.), *Handbook of community sentiment* (pp. 159–170). New York, NY: Springer.

La Fon, D. (2008). *Psychological autopsies: Science and practice*. Boca Raton, FL: CRC.

La Rooy, D., Katz, C., Malloy, L., & Lamb, M. (2010). Do we need to rethink guidance on repeated interviews? *Psychology, Public Policy, and Law, 16*, 373–392.

Labriola, M., Bradley, S., O'Sullivan, C., Rempel, M., & Moore, S. (2010). *A national portrait of domestic violence courts*. Washington, DC: United States Department of Justice. Retrieved from https://www.ncjrs.gov/pdffiles1/nij /grants/229659.pdf

Lafler v. Cooper, U.S. Supreme Court No. 10–209 (2012).

Lake, D. A. (2002, Spring). Rational extremism: Understanding terrorism in the twenty-first century. *Dialog-IQ*, 15–29.

Laliberete, E., Yim, H., Stone, B., & Dennis, S. (2021). The fallacy of an airtight alibi: Understanding human memory for "where" using experience sampling. *Psychological Science, 23*, 944–951.

Lamar, J. V. (1989, February 6). "I deserve punishment." *Time*, p. 34.

Lamb, M. E. (2015). Toward developmentally aware practices in the legal system: Progress, challenge, and promise. *American Psychologist, 70*(8), 686–693. doi.org/10.1037/a0039634

Lamberti, J., Deem, A., Weisman, R., & LaDuke, C. (2011). The role of probation in forensic assertive community treatment. *Psychiatric Services, 62*, 418–421.

Lamberti, J., Weisman, R., Schwarzkopf, S., Price, N., Ashton, R., & Trompeter, J. (2001). The mentally ill in jails and prisons: Towards an integrated model of prevention. *Psychiatric Quarterly, 72*, 63–77.

Lampinen, J., Judges, D., Odegard, T., & Hamilton, S. (2005). The reactions of mock jurors to the department of justice guidelines for the collection and preservation of eyewitness evidence. *Basic and Applied Social Psychology, 27*, 155–162.

Lander, T., & Heilbrun, K. (2009). The content and quality of forensic mental health assessment: Validation of a principles-based approach. *International Journal of Forensic Mental Health, 8,* 115–121.

Landstrom, S., & Granhag, P. (2010). In-court versus out-of-court testimonies: Children's experiences and adults' assessments. *Applied Cognitive Psychology, 24,* 941–955.

Langbein, J. (2012). The disappearance of civil trials in the United States. *Yale Law Journal, 122,* 522–572.

Langhout, R., Bergman, M., Cortina, L., Fitzgerald, L., Drasgow, F., & Hunter Williams, J. (2005). Sexual harassment severity: Assessing situational and personal determinants and outcomes. *Journal of Applied Social Psychology, 35,* 975–1007. doi:10.1111/j.1559-1816.2005.tb02156.x

Langleben, D., & Moriarty, J. (2013). Using brain imaging for lie detection: Where science, law, and policy collide. *Psychology, Public Policy, and Law, 19,* 222–234.

Lapierre, L., Spector, P., & Leck, J. (2005). Sexual versus nonsexual workplace aggression and victims' overall job satisfaction: A meta-analysis. *Journal of Occupational Health Psychology, 10,* 155–169. doi:10.1037/1076-8998.10.2.155

Larochelle, S., Diguer, L., Laverdiere, O., & Greenman, P. (2011). Predictors of psychological treatment noncompletion among sexual offenders. *Clinical Psychology Review, 31,* 554–562.

Larson, K., & Grisso, T. (2011). *Developing statutes for competence to stand trial in juvenile delinquency proceedings: A guide for lawmakers.* Chicago: National Youth Screening & Assessment Project, Models for Change, John D. and Catherine T. MacArthur Foundation. Retrieved November 29, 2016, from http://www.njjn.org/uploads/digital-library/Developing_Statutes_for_Competence_to_Stand_Trial_in_Juvenile_Delinquency_Proceedings_A_Guide_for_-Lawmakers-MfC-3_1.30.12_1.pdf

Lasher, M. & McGrath, R. J. (2012). The impact of community notification on sex offender reintegration: A quantitative review of the research literature. *International Journal of Offender Therapy and Comparative Criminology, 56*(1), 6–28.

Laub, C. E., Kimbrough, C. D., & Bornstein, B. H. (2016). Mock juror perceptions of eyewitnesses vs. earwitnesses: Do safeguards help? *American Journal of Forensic Psychology, 34,* 33–56.

Laumann-Billings, L., & Emery, R. (2000). Distress among young adults from divorced families. *Journal of Family Psychology, 14,* 671–87.

Lea, R., & Chambers, G. (2007). Monoamine oxidase, addiction, and the "Warrior" gene hypothesis. *Journal of the New Zealand Medical Association, 120,* U2441.

Lecci, L., & Myers, B. (2009). Predicting guilt judgments and verdict change using a measure of pretrial bias in a videotaped mock trial with deliberating jurors. *Psychology, Crime and Law, 15,* 619–634.

Lehmann, P. (2021). Trial penalties under Florida's sentencing guidelines: The moderating role of case seriousness. *Crime & Delinquency, 67,* 1728–1764.

Leiber, M., Beaudry-Cry, M., Peck, J., & Mack, K. (2017). Sentencing recommendations by probation officers and judges: An examination of adult offenders across genders. *Women & Criminal Justice,* advance online publication.

Leifman, S., & Coffey, T. (2015). Rethinking mental health legal policy and practice: History and needed reforms. In P. Griffin, K. Heilbrun, E. Mulvey, D. DeMatteo, & C. Schubert (Eds.), *The sequential intercept model and criminal justice: Promoting community alternatives for individuals with serious mental illness* (pp. 217–238). New York, NY: Oxford.

Leipold, A., & Abbasi, H. (2006). The impact of joinder and severance on federal criminal cases: An empirical study. *Vanderbilt Law Review, 59,* 347–404.

Leippe, M. R., Eisenstadt, D., Rauch, S. M., & Stambush, M. A. (2006). Effects of social-comparative memory feedback on eyewitnesses' identification confidence, suggestibility, and retrospective memory reports. *Basic and Applied Social Psychology, 28,* 201–220.

Leistico, A., Salekin, R., DeCoster, J., & Rogers, R. (2008). A large-scale meta-analysis relating the are measures of psychopathy to antisocial conduct. *Law and Human Behavior, 32,* 28–45.

Lemert, E. M. (1972). *Human deviance, social problems, and social control* (2nd ed.). Englewood Cliffs, NJ: Prentice Hall.

Lempert, R. (1993). Civil juries and complex cases: Taking stock after twelve years. In R. E. Litan (Ed.), *Verdict: Assessing the civil jury system* (pp. 181–247). Washington, DC: The Brookings Institution.

Leo, R. (2008). *Police interrogation and American justice.* Cambridge, MA: Harvard University Press.

Leo, R., & Ofshe, R. (1998). The consequences of false confessions: Deprivations of liberty and miscarriages of justice in the age of psychological interrogation. *Journal of Criminal Law and Criminology, 88,* 429–496.

Lerer, L., & Herndon, A. (2021, Nov. 12). *Menace enters the Republican mainstream.* Retrieved November 12, 2021, from https://www.nytimes.com/2021/11/12/us/politics/republican-violent-rhetoric.html

Lerner, M. J. (1980). *The belief in a just world.* New York, NY: Plenum.

Levenson, R., & Dwyer, L. (2003). Peer support in law enforcement: Past, present, and future. *International Journal of Emergency Mental Health, 5,* 147–152.

Levett, L, & Devine, D. (2017). Integrating individual and group models of juror decision making. In M. Kovera (Ed.), *The psychology of juries* (pp. 11–36). Washington DC: American Psychological Association.

Levett, L., & Kovera, M. (2008). The effectiveness of opposing expert witnesses for educating jurors about unreliable expert evidence. *Law and Human Behavior, 32,* 363–374.

Lewis, A. (1964). *Gideon's trumpet.* New York, NY: Knopf.

Lewis, M. (2017). *The undoing project.* New York, NY: W.W. Norton.

Lieberman, J. (2009). The psychology of the jury instruction process. In J. Lieberman & D. Krauss (Eds.), *Jury psychology: Social aspects of trial processes* (pp. 129–156). Burlington, VT: Ashgate.

Lieberman, J. (2011). The utility of scientific jury selection: Still murky after 30 years. *Current Directions in Psychological Science, 20,* 48–52.

Lieberman, J., & Arndt, J. (2000). Understanding the limits of limiting instructions: Social psychological explanations for the failures of instructions to disregard pretrial publicity and other inadmissible evidence. *Psychology, Public Policy, and Law, 6,* 677–711.

Lieberman, J., & Olson, J. (2016). The psychology of jury selection. In Lieberman, J., & Krauss, D. (Eds.), *Jury psychology: Social aspects of trial processes: Psychology in the courtroom, Vol. 1* (pp. 97–128).

Liebman, J. S. (2000). *A broken system: Error rates in capital cases, 1973—1995.* Retrieved October 1, 2005, from http://ccjr.policy.net/cjedfund/jpreport/

Lilly, J. R., Cullen, F. T., & Ball, R. A. (1989). *Criminological theory: Context and consequences.* Newbury Park, CA: Sage.

Lin, J., Grattet, R., & Petersilia, J. (2010). "Back-end sentencing" and reimprisonment: Individual, organizational, and community predictors of parole sanction decisions. *Criminology, 48,* 759–795.

Linares, L. O., Heeren, T., Bronfman, E., Zuckerman, B., Augustyn, M., & Tronick, E. (2001). A mediational model for the impact of exposure to community violence on early child behavioral problems. *Child Development, 72*(2), 639–653.

Lind, E. A. (1982). The psychology of courtroom procedure. In N. L. Kerr & R. M. Bray (Eds.), *Psychology in the courtroom* (pp. 13–37). Orlando, FL: Academic Press.

Lindsay, D., Hagen, L., Read, J., Wade, K., & Garry, M. (2004). True photographs and false memories. *Psychological Science, 15,* 149–154.

Lipsey, M. (1992). Juvenile delinquency treatment: A meta-analytic inquiry into the variability of effects. In T. Cook, H. Cooper, S. Cordray, H. Hartmann, L. Hedges, R. Light, et al. (Eds.), *Meta-analysis for explanation: A casebook* (pp. 83–128). New York, NY: Russell Sage Foundation.

Lipsey, M., & Wilson, D. (1998). Effective intervention for serious juvenile offenders: A synthesis of research. In R. Loeber & D. Farrington (Eds.), *Serious and violent juvenile offenders: Risk factors and successful interventions* (pp. 313–345). Thousand Oaks, CA: Sage.

Liptak, A. (2015, November 2). Supreme Court to decide if Georgia went too far in excluding black jurors. Retrieved from http://www.nytimes.com/2015/11/03/us/politics/supreme-court-to-decide-if-georgia-went-too-far-in-excluding-black-jurors.html

Liptak, A. (2016, May 23). Supreme Court finds racial bias in jury selection for death penalty case. Retrieved from https://www.nytimes.com/2016/05/24/us/supreme-court-black-jurors-death-penalty-georgia.html

Listwan, S., Van Voorhis, P., & Ritchey, P. (2006). Personality, criminal behavior, and risk assessment: Implications for theory and practice. *Criminal Justice and Behavior, 33*(5), 1–23.

Littleton, H., Axsom, D., & Grills-Taquechel, A. (2009). Sexual assault victims' acknowledgment status and revictimization risk. *Psychology of Women Quarterly, 33,* 34–42.

Livingston, J. (2016). Contact between police and people with mental disorders: A review of rates. *Psychiatric Services. 67,* 850–857. doi.org/10.1176/appi.ps.201500312

Lockett v. Ohio, 438 U.S. 604 (1978).

Lockhart v. McCree, 476 U.S. 162 (1986).

Loeber, R., & Stouthamer-Loeber, M. (1986). Family factors as correlates and predictors of juvenile conduct problems and delinquency. In M. Tonry & N. Morris (Eds.), *Crime and justice: An annual review of research* (Vol. 7, pp. 29–149). Chicago, IL: University of Chicago Press.

Loftus, E. F. (1974). Reconstructing memory: The incredible witness. *Psychology Today, 8,* 116–119.

Loftus, E. F. (1975). Leading questions and the eyewitness report. *Cognitive Psychology, 7,* 560–572.

Loftus, E. F. (1979). *Eyewitness testimony.* Cambridge, MA: Harvard University Press.

Loftus, E. F., & Pickrell, J. E. (1995). The formation of false memories. *Psychiatric Annals, 25,* 720–725.

Logan, M., & Link, N. (2019). Taking stock of drug courts: Do they work? *Victims & Offenders, 14,* 283–298. https://doi.org/10.1080/15564886.2019.1595249

Lombroso, C. (1876). *L' Uomo delinquente.* Milan: Hoepli.

London, K., Kulkofsky, S., & Perez, C. O. (2021). Factors affecting the reliability of children's forensic reports: An updated review. In J. Rummel (Ed.), *Current issues in memory: Memory research in the public interest.* (pp. 272–295). Routledge/Taylor & Francis Group.

London, K., & Nunez, N. (2000). The effect of jury deliberations on jurors' propensity to disregard inadmissible evidence. *Journal of Applied Psychology, 85,* 932–939.

Long, B., Rouse, S., Nelsen, R., & Butcher, J. (2004). The MMPI-2 in sexual harassment and discrimination litigants. *Journal of Clinical Psychology, 60,* 643–657.

Lovins, B., Lowenkamp, C.T. & Latessa, E. J. (2009). Applying the risk principle to sex offenders: Can treatment make some sex offenders worse? *The Prison Journal, 89,* 344–357.

Lowder, E., Rade, C., & Desmarais, S. (2017). Effectiveness of mental health courts in reducing recidivism: A meta-analysis. *Psychiatric Services., 69,* 15–22. doi:10.1176/appi.ps.201700107

Lowenkamp, C., Flores, A., Holsinger, A., Makarios, M., & Latessa, E. (2010). Intensive supervision programs: Does program philosophy and the principles of effective intervention matter? *Journal of Criminal Justice, 38,* 368–375.

Lowenkamp, C., & Latessa, E. (2005, April). Developing successful reentry programs: Lessons learned from the "what works" research. *Corrections Today, 67,* 72–77.

Ludwig, E. (2002). The changing role of the trial judge. *Judicature, 85,* 216–217.

Lui, J., & Li, X. (2019). Legal techniques for rationalizing biased judicial decisions: Evidence from experiments with real judges. *Journal of Empirical Legal Studies, 16,* 630–670.

Luna, K., & Migueles, M. (2008). Typicality and misinformation: Two sources of distortion. *Psicologica, 29,* 171–187.

Lurigio, A. J., & Skogan, W. G. (1994). Winning the hearts and minds of police officers: An assessment of staff perceptions of community policing in Chicago. *Crime and Delinquency, 40,* 315–330.

Luskin, M. L. (2013). More of the same? Treatment in mental health courts. *Law and Human Behavior, 37,* 255–266.

Luthar, S. S., & Goldstein, A. (2004). Children's exposure to community violence: Implications for understanding risk and resilience. *Journal of Clinical Child and Adolescent Psychology, 33,* 499–505.

Lynam, D., Moffitt, T., & Stouthamer-Loeber, M. (1993). Explaining the relation between IQ and delinquency: Class, race, test motivation, school failure, and self-control. *Journal of Abnormal Psychology, 102,* 187–196.

Lynch, M., & Haney, C. (2000). Discrimination and instructional comprehension: Guided discretion, racial bias, and the death penalty. *Law and Human Behavior, 24,* 337–358.

Lynch, M., & Haney, C. (2009). Capital jury deliberation: Effects on death sentencing, comprehension, and discrimination. *Law and Human Behavior, 33,* 481–496.

Lynch, T. (2003, Fall). The case against plea bargaining. *Regulation, 26,* 24–27.

Lynn, S. J., Lilienfeld, S. O., Merckelbach, H., Giesbrecht, T., McNally, R. J., Loftus, E. F., Bruck, M., Garry, M., & Malaktaris, A. (2014). The trauma model of dissociation: Inconvenient truths and stubborn fictions Comment on Dalenberg et al (2012). *Psychological Bulletin, 140*(3), 896–910. https://doi.org/10.1037/a0035570

Maddera, J. (2016). Batson in transition: Prohibiting peremptory challenges on the basis of gender identity or expression. *Columbia Law Review, 116,* 195–236.

Madison v. Alabama, 586 U.S. ____ (2019).

Madon, S., Guyll, M., Scherr, K., Greathouse, S., & Wells, G. (2011, March). *The differential impact of proximal and distal consequences on the elicitation of criminal confessions.* Paper presented at American Psychology-Law Society, Miami, FL.

Mador, J. (2010, March 22). *New veterans' court aims to help soldiers struggling at home.* Retrieved July 1, 2011, from www.minnesota.public.radio.org/display/web/2010/03/22/veterans-court/

Maeder, E., & Hunt, J. (2011). Talking about a black man: The influence of defendant and character witness race on jurors' use of character evidence. *Behavioral Sciences and the Law, 29,* 608–620.

Magdol, L., Moffitt, T. E., Caspi, A., & Silva, P. A. (1998). Developmental antecedents of partner abuse: A prospective-longitudinal study. *Journal of Abnormal Psychology, 107,* 373–389.

Magnussen, S., & Melinder, A. (2012). What psychologists know and believe about memory: A survey of practitioners. *Applied Cognitive Psychology, 26,* 54–60.

Magson, N., Freeman, J., Rapee, R., Richardson, C., Oar, E., & Fardouly, J. (2021). Risk and protective factors for prospective changes in adolescent mental health during the COVID-19 pandemic. *Journal of Youth and Adolescence, 50,* 44–57.

Mak, A. (2018, December 18). A judge sentenced a poacher to watch *Bambi* once a month for a year. Can he really do that? Retrieved May 3, 2022, from https://slate.com/news-and-politics/2018/12/bambi-judge-sentence-poacher-watch.html

Malivert, M., Fatseas, M., Denis, C., Langlois, E., & Auriacombe, M. (2012). Effectiveness of therapeutic communities: A systematic review. *European Addiction Research, 18,* 1–11. doi.org/10.1159/000331007

Malpass, R. S., & Devine, P. G. (1981). Eyewitness identification: Lineup instructions and the absence of the offender. *Journal of Applied Psychology, 66,* 482–489.

Mandracchia, J., & Morgan, R. (2011). Understanding criminals' thinking: Further examination of the measure of offender thinking styles-revised. *Assessment, 18,* 442–452.

Marcus, D. R., Lyons, P. M., & Guyton, M. R. (2000). Studying perceptions of juror influence *in vivo*: A social relations analysis. *Law and Human Behavior, 24,* 173–186.

Margulies, J. (2011). Deviance, risk, and law: Reflections on the demand for the preventive detention of suspected terrorists. *Journal of Criminal Law and Criminology, 101,* 729–780.

Markham, A. (2018). A review following systematic principles of Multisystemic Therapy for antisocial behavior in adolescents aged 10–17 years. *Adolescent Research Review, 3,* 67–93.

Markowitz, M. & Salvatore, C. (2012). Exploring race based differences in patterns of life-course criminality. *Deviant Behavior, 33,* 589–605.

Marks, D. (2011). IQ variations across time, race, and nationality: An artifact of differences in literacy skills. *Counselor Education and Supervision, 50,* 643–664.

Marlowe, D. B., Hardin, C. D., & Fox, C. L. (2016). *Painting the current picture: A national report on drug courts and other problem-solving courts in the United States.* Alexandria, VA: National Drug Court Institute.

Marquardt, E. (2006). *Between two worlds: The inner lives of children of divorce.* New York, NY: Three Rivers Press.

Marsee, M., Silverthorn, P., & Frick, P. (2005). The association of psychopathic traits with aggression and delinquency in non-referred boys and girls. *Behavioral Sciences & the Law, 23,* 803–817. doi:10.1002/bsl.662

Marshall, W. L., Fernandez, Y., Marshall, L., & Serran, G. (2006). *Sexual offender treatment: Controversial issues.* West Sussex, UK: Wiley.

Marshall, W., Marshall, L., Serran, G., & Fernandez, Y. (2006). *Treating sexual offenders: An integrated approach.* New York: Routledge.

Martin, C., Lurigio, A., & Olson, D. (2003). An examination of rearrests and reincarcerations among discharged day reporting center clients. *Federal Probation, 67,* 24–30.

Martinson, R. (1974). What works? Questions and answers about prison reform. *Public Interest, 35,* 22.

Martire, K. A., & Kemp, R. I. (2011). Can experts help jurors to evaluate eyewitness evidence? A review of eyewitness expert effects. *Legal and Criminological Psychology, 16,* 24–36.

Marvasti, J. (2010). Combat trauma and PTSD in veterans: Forensic aspect and 12-step program. *American Journal of Forensic Psychiatry, 31,* 5–30.

Maryland v. Craig, 110 S.Ct. 3157 (1990).

Maschi, T., Bradley, C., & Morgen, K. (2008). Unraveling the link between trauma and delinquency. *Youth Violence and Juvenile Justice, 6,* 136–157. doi:10.1177/1541204007305527

Maslach, C., & Jackson, S. E. (1984). Burnout in organizational settings. In S. Oskamp (Ed.), *Applied social psychology annual* (pp. 133–154). Newbury Park, CA: Sage.

Mason, C., & Cheng, S. (2001). *Re-arrest rates among youth sentenced in adult court.* Miami, FL: Miami-Dade County Public Defender's Office.

Matal v. Tam, 528 U.S. ___ (2017).

Matsumoto, D., & Hwang, H. (2015). Emotional reactions to crime across cultures. *International Journal of Psychology, 50,* 327–335.

Matsuo, K., & Miura, H. (2017). Effectiveness of the self-administered interview and drawing pictures for eliciting eyewitness memories. *Psychiatry, Psychology and Law, 24*(5), 643–654.

Maxfield, M. G., & Widom, C. S. (1996). The cycle of violence: Revisited 6 years later. *Archives of Pediatrics & Adolescent Medicine, 150,* 390–395.

Maxwell, C. D., Garner, J. H., & Fagan, J. A. (2002). The preventive effects of arrest on intimate partner violence: Research, policy and theory. *Criminology and Public Policy, 2,* 51–80.

Mazzoni, G., & Memon, A. (2003). Imagination can create false autobiographical memories. *Psychological Science, 14,* 186–188.

McAuliff, B. D., & Kovera, M. B. (2008). Juror need for cognition and sensitivity to methodological flaws in expert evidence. *Journal of Applied Social Psychology, 38,* 385–408.

McAuliff, B., Lapin, J., & Michel, S. (2015). Support person presence and child victim testimony: Believe it or not. *Behavioral Sciences and the Law, 33,* 508–527.

McCann, J. (1998). A conceptual framework for identifying various types of confessions. *Behavioral Sciences & the Law, 16,* 441–453.

McCann, T. (2004, August 21). *Jury consultants try to turn voir dire into a science.* Retrieved October 1, 2005, from http://www.zmf.com

McCleskey v. Kemp, 107 S. Ct. 1756 (1987).

McCorkle, R. (1992). Personal precautions to violence in prison. *Criminal Justice and Behavior, 19,* 160–173.

McCrae, R., & Costa, P. (1990). *Personality in adulthood.* New York, NY: Guilford.

McDermott, B., Scott, C., Busse, D., Andrade, F., Zozaya, M., & Quanbeck, C. (2008). The conditional release of insanity acquittees: Three decades of decision-making. *Journal of the American Academy of Psychiatry and the Law Online, 36*(3), 329–336.

McDermott, P., Watkins, M., & Rhoad, A. (2014). Whose IQ is it? Assessor bias variance in high-stakes psychological assessment. *Psychological Assessment, 26,* 207–214.

McDonough, M. (2004, October). Summary time blues. *American Bar Association Journal, 90,* 18.

Mcgorrery, P. (2016). "But I was so sure it was him": How Facebook could be making eyewitness identifications unreliable. *Internet Law Bulletin, 19,* 255.

McGuire, J., Clark, S., Blue-Howells, J., & Coe, C. (2013). *An inventory of VA involvement in Veterans courts, dockets and tracks.* VA Veterans Justice Programs. Retrieved December 23, 2016, from http://www.justiceforvets.org/sites/default/files/files/An%20Inventory%20of%20VA%20involvement%20in%20Veterans%20Courts.pdf

McIntyre, F., & Baradaran, S. (2013). Race, prediction, and pretrial detention. *Journal of Empirical Legal Studies, 10,* 741–770.

McKay v. Ashland Oil Inc., 120 F.R.D. 43 (E.D. Ky. 1988).

McKnight-Eily, L., Okoro, C., Strine, T. et al. (2021). Racial and ethnic disparities in the prevalence of stress and worry, mental health conditions, and increased substance use among adults during the COVID-19 pandemic — United States, April and May 2020. *Morbidity and Mortality Weekly Report, 70,* 162–166. doi.org/10.15585/mmwr.mm7005a3

McLaughlin, J., & Kan, L. (2014). Test usage in four common types of forensic mental health assessment. *Professional Psychology: Research and Practice, 45*(2), 128–135.

McLaurin v. Oklahoma State Regents for Higher Education, 339 U.S. 637 (1950).

McLean, C., & Foa, E. (2011). Prolonged exposure therapy for post-traumatic stress disorder: A review of evidence and dissemination. *Expert Review Neurotherapy, 11,* 1151–1163.

McLoughlin, N., Rucklidge, J. J., Grace, R. C., & McLean, A. P. (2010). Can callous unemotional traits and aggression identify children at high risk of anti-social behavior in a low socioeconomic group? *Journal of Family Violence, 25,* 701–712.

McMurran, M., & Theodosi, E. (2007). Is treatment non-completion associated with increased reconviction over no treatment? *Psychology, Crime & Law, 13*(4), 333–343. doi.org/10.1080/10683160601060374

McMurtrie, J. (2015). The unindicated co-ejaculator and necrophilia: Addressing prosecutors' logic-defying responses to exculpatory DNA results. *Journal of Criminal Law and Criminology, 105,* 853–879.

McNally, R. J. (2005). Debunking myths about trauma and memory. *The Canadian Journal of Psychiatry, 50,* 817–822.

McNatt, D. (2000). Ancient Pygmalion joins contemporary management: A meta-analysis of the result. *Journal of Applied Psychology, 85,* 314–322.

McNiel, D., & Binder, R. (2007). Effectiveness of a mental health court in reducing criminal recidivism and violence. *American Journal of Psychiatry, 164,* 1395–1403.

Medical News Today. (2007). *What level of mental illness should preclude execution and how to determine it?* Retrieved April 1, 2009, from www.medicalnewstoday.com

Medina, J., & Epstein, R. (2021, Nov. 19). *Republican celebrations and Democratic anger reveal a widening political divide.* Retrieved November 20, 2021, from https://www.nytimes.com/live/2021/11/19/us/kyle-rittenhouse-trial#rittenhouse-verdict-conservatives-liberals

Medina v. California, 112 S.Ct. 2572 (1992).

Meier, A., Arentsen, T. G., Pannell, L., & Putman, K. (2016). Attrition of police officers as predicted by peer evaluations during academy training. *Policing and Society, 28*(1), 1–10.

Meijer, E., Ben-Shakhar, G., Verschuere, B., & Donchin, E. (2013). A comment on Farwell (2012): Brain fingerprinting: a comprehensive tutorial review of detection of concealed information with even-related brain potentials. *Cognitive Neurodynamics, 7,* 155–158.

Meijer, E., Selle, N., Elber, L., & Ben-Shakhar, G. (2014). Memory detection with the Concealed Information Test: A meta-analysis of skin conductance, respiration, heart rate, and P300 data. *Psychophysiology, 51,* 879–904.

Meijer, E., & Verschuere, B. (2010). The polygraph and the detection of deception. *Journal of Forensic Psychology Practice, 10,* 325–338.

Meijer, E., & Verschuere, B. (2017). Deception detection based on neuroimaging: Better than the polygraph? *Journal of Forensic Radiology and Imaging, 8,* 17–21.

Meijer, E., Verschuere, B., Gamer, M., Merckelbach, H., & Ben-Shakhar, G. (2016). Deception detection with behavioral, autonomic, and neural measures: Conceptual and methodological considerations that warrant modesty. *Psychophysiology, 53,* 593–604.

Meissner, C., & Brigham, J. (2001). Thirty years of investigating the own-race bias in memory for faces: A meta-analytic review. *Psychology, Public Policy, and Law, 7,* 3–35.

Meissner, C., & Kassin, S. (2002). "He's guilty!": Investigator bias in judgments of truth and deception. *Law and Human Behavior, 5,* 469–480.

Meissner, C., & Kassin, S. (2004). "You're guilty, so just confess!" Cognitive and behavioral confirmation biases in the interrogation room. In G. D. Lassiter (Ed.), *Interrogations, confessions, and entrapment* (pp. 85–106). New York, NY: Kluwer Academic/Plenum.

Meissner, C., Redlich, A., Michael, S., Evans, J., Camilletti, C., Bhatt, S., & Brandon, S. (2014). Accusatorial and information-gathering interrogation methods and their effects on true and false confessions: A meta-analytic review. *Journal of Experimental Criminology, 10,* 459–486.

Melilli, K. (1996). *Batson* in practice: What we have learned about *Batson* and peremptory challenges. *Notre Dame Law Review, 71,* 447–503.

Mellow, J., Mukamal, D. A., LoBuglio, S. F., Solomon, A. L., & Osborne, J. W. L. (2008, May). *The jail administrator's toolkit for reentry.* Washington, DC: Urban Institute.

Meloy, J. R., & Felthous, A. R. (2004). Introduction to this issue: Serial and mass homicide. *Behavioral Sciences & the Law, 22*(3), 289–290.

Meloy, J. R., Hempel, A. G., Gray, B. T., Mohandie, K., Shiva, A., & Richards, T. C. (2004). A comparative analysis of North American adolescent and adult mass murderers. *Behavioral Sciences & the Law, 22*(3), 291–309.

Melton, G., Petrila, J., Poythress, N., Slobogin, C., Otto, R., Mossman, D., & Condie, L. (2018). *Psychological evaluations for the courts: A handbook for mental health professional and lawyers* (4th ed.). New York, NY: Guilford.

Memon, A., Meissner, C., & Fraser, J. (2010). The cognitive interview: A meta-analytic review and study space analysis of the past 25 years. *Psychology, Public Policy, and Law, 16,* 340–372.

Memon, A., & Wright, D. B. (1999). Eyewitness testimony and the Oklahoma bombing. *The Psychologist, 12*(6), 292–295.

Mercado, C. (2009, Summer). Are residence restrictions an effective way to reduce the risk posed by sex offenders? *AP-LS News.* Retrieved from http://www.ap-ls.org/publications/newsletters/aplsnews.sum2009.pdf

Meritor Savings Bank v. Vinson, 106 S.Ct. 2399 (1986).

Merton, R. K. (1968). *Social theory and social structure.* New York, NY: Free Press.

Metcalfe, C., & Chiricos, T. (2018). Race, plea, and charge reduction: An assessment of racial disparities in the plea process. *Justice Quarterly, 35,* 223–253.

Migueles, M., Garcia-Bajos, E., & Aizpurua, A. (2016). Initial testing does not necessarily affect eyewitness recall assessed by specific questioning. *Applied Cognitive Psychology, 30,* 294–300.

Mihalic, S., Irwin, K., Elliott, D., Fagan, A., & Hansen, D. (2001). *Blueprints for violence prevention.* Boulder, CO: Center for the Study and Prevention of Violence.

Milchman, M. (2012). From traumatic memory to traumatized remembering: Beyond the memory wars, Part 1: Agreement. *Psychological Injury and Law, 5,* 37–50.

Milgram, S. (1963). Behavioral study of obedience. *Journal of Abnormal and Social Psychology, 67,* 371–378.

Miller v. Alabama, 567 U.S. 460 (2012).

Miller, B., & Curry, B. (2017). Small-group dynamics, ideology, and decision making in the US Courts of Appeal. *Law and Policy, 39,* 48–72.

Miller, G. R., & Boster, F. J. (1977). Three images of a trial: Their implications for psychological research. In B. D. Sales (Ed.), *Psychology in the legal process* (pp. 19–38). New York, NY: Spectrum.

Miller, H. A. (2001). *M-FAST: Miller Forensic Assessment of Symptoms Test professional manual.* Odessa, FL: Psychological Assessment Resources.

Miller, H. A. (2004). Examining the use of the M-FAST with criminal defendants incompetent to stand trial. *International Journal of Offender Therapy and Comparative Criminology, 48,* 268–280.

Miller, J., & Lynam, D. (2001). Structural models of personality and their relation to antisocial behavior: A meta-analytic review. *Criminology, 39,* 765–798.

Miller, M., Blumenthal, J., & Chamberlain, J. (2015). *Handbook of community sentiment.* New York, NY: Springer.

Miller, S., Malone, P., Dodge, K., & Conduct Problems Prevention Research Group. (2010). Developmental trajectories of boys' and girls' delinquency: Sex differences and links to later adolescent outcomes. *Journal of Abnormal Child Psychology, 38,* 1021–1032. doi:10.1007/s10802-010-9430-1

Mills, R. B., McDevitt, R. J., & Tonkin, S. (1966). Situational tests in metropolitan police recruit selection. *Journal of Criminal Law, Criminology, and Police Science, 57,* 99–104.

Milstein, V. (1988). EEG topography in patients with aggressive violent behavior. In T. E. Moffitt & S. A. Mednick (Eds.), *Biological contributions to crime causation.* Dordrecht, Netherlands: Martinus Nijhoff.

Minton, T., Beatty, L., & Zeng, Z. (2021). *Correctional populations in the United Sates, 2019—Statistical Tables* (NCJ 300655). Washington, DC: U.S. Department of Justice, Bureau of Justice Statistics.

Minton, T., Zeng, Z., & Maruschak, L. (2021). *Impact of COVID-19 on the local jail population, January-June 2020* (NCJ 255888). Washington, DC: U.S. Department of Justice, Bureau of Justice Statistics.

Miraglia, R., & Hall, D. (2011). The effect of length of hospitalization on rearrest among insanity plea acquittees. *Journal of the American Academy of Psychiatry and the Law Online, 39*(4), 524–534.

Miranda v. Arizona, 384 U.S. 486 (1966).

Missouri v. Frye, 132 S.Ct. 1399 (2012).

Mitchell, O., Wilson, D., Eggers, A., & MacKenzie, D. (2012). Assessing the effectiveness of drug courts on recidivism: A meta-analytic review of traditional and non-traditional drug courts. *Journal of Criminal Justice, 40,* 60–71. doi:10.1016/j.jcrimjus.2011.11.009

Mitchell, P. (1976). *Act of love: The killing of George Zygmanik.* New York, NY: Knopf.

Mize, G. (1999, Spring). On better jury selection: Spotting UFO jurors before they enter the jury room. *Court Review, 36,* 10–15.

Mize, G., Hannaford-Agor, P., & Waters, N. (2007). *State of the States Survey of Jury Improvement Efforts.* Williamsburg, VA: National Center for State Courts.

Moffitt, T. (1993). Life-course-persistent and adolescence-limited antisocial behavior: A developmental taxonomy. *Psychological Review, 100,* 674–701.

Moffitt, T., & Lynam, D. (1994). The neuropsychology of conduct disorder and delinquency: Implications for understanding antisocial behavior. In D. Fowles, P. Sutker, & S. Goodman (Eds.), *Psychopathy and antisocial behavior: A developmental perspective* (pp. 233–262). New York, NY: Springer-Verlag.

Mohamed, F., Faro, S., Gordon, N., Platek, S., Ahmad, H., & Williams, J. (2006). Brain mapping of deception and truth telling about an ecologically valid situation: Functional MR imaging and polygraph investigation-initial experience. *Radiology, 238*, 679–688.

Monahan, J. (1984). The prediction of violent behavior: Toward a second generation of theory and practice. *American Journal of Psychiatry, 141*, 10–15.

Monahan, J. (2012). The individual risk assessment of terrorism: Conceptual and methodological challenges. *Psychology, Public Policy, and Law, 18*, 167–205. doi:10.10371a0025792

Monahan, J. (2012). The individual risk assessment of terrorism: Conceptual and methodological challenges. *Psychology, Public Policy, and Law, 18*, 167–205. doi:10.10371a0025792 Vecchi et al., 2005

Monahan, J. (2017). The individual risk assessment of terrorism. In G. LaFree & J. Freilich (Eds.), *The handbook of the criminology of terrorism* (pp. 520–534). Wiley.

Monahan, J., Metz, A., Garrett, B., & Jakubow, A. (2020). Risk assessment in sentencing and plea bargaining: The roles of prosecutors and defense attorneys. *Behavioral Sciences and the Law, 38*, 1–11. doi: 10.1002/bsl.2435

Monahan, J., & Walker, L. (2018). *Social science in law: Cases and materials.* Eagan, MN: West.

Monahan, K. C., Steinberg, L., & Cauffman, E. (2009). Affiliation with antisocial peers, susceptibility to peer influence, and antisocial behavior during the transition to adulthood. *Developmental Psychology, 45*, 1520–1530.

Montgomery v. Louisiana, 136 S.Ct. 718 (2016).

Moore, K., Sprengelmeyer, P., & Chamberlain, P. (2001). Community-based treatment for adjudicated delinquents: The Oregon Social Learning Center's "Monitor" Multidimensional Treatment Foster Care program. *Residential Treatment for Children & Youth, 18*(3), 87–97.

Moore, M. (2011). Psychological theories of crime and delinquency. *Journal of Human Behavior in the Social Environment, 21*, 226–239.

Moore, M., & Hiday, V. (2006). Mental health court outcomes: A comparison of re-arrest and re-arrest severity between mental health court and traditional court participants. *Law and Human Behavior, 30*, 659–674.

Moran, G., & Cutler, B. L. (1991). The prejudicial impact of pretrial publicity. *Journal of Applied Social Psychology, 21*, 345–367.

Morehouse, E., & Tobler, N. (2000). Preventing and reducing substance use among institutionalized adolescents. *Adolescence, 35*, 1–28.

Morgan, A. B., & Lilienfeld, S. O. (2000). A meta-analytic review of the relation between antisocial behavior and neuropsychological measures of executive function. *Clinical Psychology Review, 20*, 113–136.

Morgan, C., Hazlett, G., Doran, A., Garrett, S., Hoty, G., Thomas, P., … Southwick, S. M. (2004). Accuracy of eyewitness memory for persons encountered during exposure to highly intense stress. *International Journal of Law and Psychiatry, 27*, 265–279.

Morral, A., McCaffrey, D., & Ridgeway, G. (2004). Effectiveness of community-based treatment for substance abusing adolescents: 12-month outcomes from a case-control evaluation of a Phoenix academy. *Psychology of Addictive Behaviors, 18*, 257–268.

Morrison, P. (1995, August 21). The new chain gang. *National Law Journal*, pp. A1, A22.

Morris, P., McNiel, D., & Binder, R. (2021). Estimating annual numbers of competency to stand trial evaluations across the United States. *Journal of the American Academy of Psychiatry and the Law Online, 49*, 530–539. doi.org/10.29158/JAAPL.200129-20

Morse, S., & Bonnie, R. (2013). Abolition of the insanity defense violates due process. *Journal of the American Academy of Psychiatry and the Law, 41*, 488–495.

Morse, S. J. (1998). Fear of danger, flight from culpability. *Psychology, Public Policy, and Law, 4*, 250–267.

Morton, R., & Hilts, M. (Eds.) (2008). *Serial murder: Multidisciplinary perspectives for investigators.* Washington, DC: U.S. Department of Justice, Federal Bureau of Investigation.

Mossman, D. (1987). Assessing and restoring competency to be executed: Should psychiatrists participate? *Behavioral Sciences & the Law, 5*, 397–410.

MST Services (2014). Multisystemic Therapy (MST) overview. Retrieved January 30, 2022, from https://evidencebasedassociates.com/wp-content/uploads/2017/09/MST-Overview-long-2017.pdf

Mueller-Smith, M., & Schnepel, K. (2021). Diversion in the criminal justice system. *The Review of Economic Studies, 88*(2), 883–936.

Mullen, P. (2004). The autogenic (self-generated) massacre. *Behavioral Sciences & the Law, 22*, 311–323.

Mulvey, E. (2011). Highlights from Pathways to Desistance: A longitudinal study of serious adolescent offenders. *Pathways to Desistance Bulletin Series*, Office of Juvenile Justice and Delinquency Prevention. Washington, D.C.: Author.

Mulvey, E., & Cauffman, E. (2001). The inherent limits of predicting school violence. *American Psychologist, 56*, 797–802.

Munetz, M., & Griffin, P. (2006). Use of the sequential intercept model as an approach to decriminalization of people with serious mental illness. *Psychiatric Services, 57*, 544–549.

Muñoz Soro, J., & Serrano-Cinca, C. (2021). A model for predicting court decisions on child custody. *PLoS ONE, 16*(10): e0258993. doi.org/10.1371/journal.pone.0258993

Munson, L. J., Hulin, C., & Drasgow, F. (2000). Longitudinal analysis of dispositional influences and sexual harassment: Effects on job and psychological outcomes. *Personnel Psychology, 53*, 21–46. doi:10.1111/j.1744-6570.2000.tb00192.x

Murphy, E. R., Miller, M. K., Marsh, S. C., & Bornstein, B. H. (2021). Understanding the summary jury trial: Perspectives from the judiciary. *University of Illinois Law Review*, 2021, 113–129.

Murray, J. (2008). Media violence: The effects are both real and strong. *American Behavioral Scientist, 51*, 1212–1230.

Murray, J., & Farrington, D. (2010). Risk factors for conduct disorder and delinquency: Key findings from longitudinal studies. *The Canadian Journal of Psychiatry, 55*, 633–642.

Murrie, D., & Boccaccini, M. (2015). Adversarial allegiance among expert witnesses. *Annual Review of Law and Social Science, 11*, 37–55.

Murrie, D., Boccaccini, M., Guarnera, L., & Rufino, K. (2013). Are forensic experts biased by the side that retained them? *Psychological Science, 24*(10), 1889–1997. doi: 10.1177/0956797613481812

Myers, D. L. (2001). *Excluding violent youths from juvenile court: The effectiveness of legislative waiver.* New York, NY: LFB Scholarly.

Myers, D. L. (2003). The recidivism of violent youths in juvenile and adult court: A consideration of selection bias. *Youth Violence and Juvenile Justice, 1*, 79–101.

Naidoo, Y., Jackson, R., & Arfken, C. (2018). Comparing GBMI and non-GBMI female prisoners in Michigan. *Journal of the American Academy of Psychiatry and the Law Online, 46*(4), 480–485. doi.org/10.29158/JAAPL.003791-18

Nash, A. R., & Wade, K. A. (2009). Innocent but proven guilty: Eliciting internalized false confessions using doctored-video evidence. *Applied Cognitive Psychology, 23*, 357–371.

Nathan, D. & Snedeker, M. (1995). *Satan's silence.* New York: Basic Books.

Nathanson, R., & Saywitz, K. (2015). Preparing children for court: Effects of a model court education program on children's anticipatory anxiety. *Behavioral Sciences and the Law, 33*, 459–475.

National Academy of Sciences report. (2014). Identifying the Culprit: Assessing Eyewitness Identification. https://nap.nationalacademies.org/catalog/18891/identifying-the-culprit-assessing-eyewitness-identification

National Archive of Criminal Justice Data. (2010). *National criminal victimization survey, 2010.* Retrieved February 18, 2011, from http://www.icpsr.umich.edu/icpsrweb/NACJD/studies/31202/documentation

National Center for Education Statistics. (2021). *Violent deaths at school and away from school and school shootings.* Retrieved January 10, 2022, from https://nces.ed.gov/programs/coe/indicator/a01

National Center for State Courts. (2012). *Short, summary & expedited: The evolution of civil jury trials.* Retrieved April 9, 2012, from http://www.ncsc.org/~/media/Files/PDF/Information%20and%20Resources/Civil%20cover%20sheets/Monograph%20FINAL%20Electronic%20Version.ashx

National Commission on Correctional Healthcare. (2022). *Mental health screening and evaluation.* Retrieved February 4, 2022, from https://www.ncchc.org/mental-health-screening-evaluation

National Drug Court Resource Center. (2020). Interactive maps. Available at https://ndcrc.org/maps

National GAINS Center. (2002). *The Nathaniel Project: An alternative to incarceration program for people with serious mental illness who have committed felony offenses.* Delmar, NY: Author.

National Registry of Exonerations. (2021). *25,000 years lost to wrongful convictions.* Accessed July 26, 2022. https://www.law.umich.edu/special/exoneration/Documents/25000%20Years.pdf

National Research Council. (1989). *Improving risk communication.* Washington, DC: National Academy Press.

National Research Council. (2003). *The polygraph and lie detection.* Washington, DC: National Academy of Sciences.

National Research Council. (2009). *Strengthening forensic science in the United States: A path forward.* Washington, DC: Author.

National Research Council. (2014). *Identifying the culprit: Assessing eyewitness identification.* Washington, DC: The National Academies Press.

National Sexual Violence Resource Center. (2010). *The impact of sexual violence.* Enola, PA: Author. Retrieved November 9, 2016, from http://www.nsvrc.org/sites/default/files/Publications_NSVRC_-Factsheet_Impact-of-sexual-violence_0.pdf

Neal, T., & Brodsky, S. (2016). Forensic psychologists' perceptions of bias and potential correction strategies in forensic mental health evaluations. *Psychology, Public Policy, and Law, 22*(1), 58–76.

Neal, T., & Grisso, T. (2014). Assessment practices and expert judgment methods in forensic psychology and psychiatry: An international snapshot. *Criminal Justice and Behavior, 41,* 1406–1421.

Neal, T. M. S., Hight, M., Howatt, B. C., & Hamza, C. (2018). The cognitive and social psychological bases of bias in forensic mental health judgments. In M. K. Miller & B. H. Bornstein (Eds.), *Advances in psychology and law* (pp. 151–175). Springer International Publishing AG. doi.org/10.1007/978-3-319-75859-6_5

Neal, T., Slobogin, C., Saks, M., Faigman, D., & Geisinger, K. (2020). Psychological assessments in legal contexts: Are courts keeping "junk science" out of the courtroom? *Psychological Science in the Public Interest.* Advance online publication.

Neisser, U. (1976). *Cognition and reality: Principles and implications of cognitive psychology.* San Francisco, CA: Freeman.

Nekritz, A. (2022, January 5). Race in the jury selection procedure: Recent criminal cases. Retrieved June 10, 2022, from https://www.ncsc.org/information-and-resources/info-and-res-page-card-navigation/trending-topics/trending-topics-landing-pg/race-in-the-jury-selection-procedure-recent-criminal-cases

Nellis, A. (2016). *The color of justice: Racial and ethnic disparity in state prisons.* The Sentencing Project. Retrieved from www.sentencingproject.org

Nesbit-Bartsch, A., Mcdermott, B., & Warburton, K. (2021, March). Gender and malingering in defendants deemed incompetent to stand trial. *Journal of the American Academy of Psychiatry and the Law Online, 49*(2), 1–8. doi.org/10.29158/JAAPL.200083-20

New Jersey v. Henderson, 27 A.3d 872 (2011).

New York ACLU. (2016). Stop-and-frisk data. Retrieved October 31, 2016, from http://www.nyclu.org/content/stop-and-frisk-data

New York State Department of Corrections and Community Supervision. (2022). *Programs.* Retrieved February 4, 2022, from https://doccs.ny.gov/programs

Nicholls, T., Ogloff, J., Brink, J., & Spidel, A. (2005). Psychopathy in women: A review of its clinical usefulness for assessing risk for aggression and criminality. *Behavioral Sciences & the Law, 23,* 779–802. doi:10.1002/bsl.678

Nicholson, R. A., Norwood, S., & Enyart, C. (1991). Characteristics and outcomes of insanity acquittees in Oklahoma. *Behavioral Sciences & the Law, 9,* 487–500.

Nielsen, L. (2017). Re-examining the research on parental conflict, coparenting, and custody arrangements. *Psychology, Public Policy, and Law, 23,* 211–231. doi:10.1037/law0000109

Nietzel, M. T. (1979). *Crime and its modification: A social learning perspective.* New York, NY: Pergamon.

Nietzel, M. T., & Dillehay, R. C. (1986). *Psychological consultation in the courtroom.* New York, NY: Pergamon.

Nobile, P. (1989, July). The making of a monster. *Playboy,* 41–45.

Noble, K. B. (1987, March 23). High court to decide whether death penalty discriminates against blacks. *New York Times,* p. 7.

Nordheimer, J. (1989, January 25). Bundy is put to death in Florida, closing murder cases across U.S. *New York Times,* pp. A1, A11.

Norton, K., & Ryba, N. L. (2010). An investigation of the ECST-R as a measure of competence and feigning. *Journal of Forensic Psychology Practice, 10*(2), 91–106.

Nunez, N., Kehn, A., & Wright, D. (2011). When children are witnesses: The effects of context, age and gender on adults' perceptions of cognitive ability and honesty. *Applied Cognitive Psychology, 25,* 460–468.

Nunez, N., Myers, B., Wilkowski, B., & Schweitzer, K. (2017). The impact of angry versus sad victim impact statements on mock jurors' sentencing decisions in a capital trial. *Criminal Justice and Behavior, 44,* 862–886.

O'Connor v. Donaldson, 422 U.S. 563 (1975).

Obiakor, F., Merhing, T., & Schwenn, J. (1997). *Disruption, disaster, and death: Helping students deal with crises.* Reston, VA: Council for Exceptional Children.

O'Brien, B. (2009). A recipe for bias: An empirical look at the interplay between institutional incentives and bounded rationality in prosecutorial decision making. *Missouri Law Review, 74,* 999–1050.

O'Brien, B., & Grosso, C. (2019). Jury selection in the post-*Batson* era. In Najdowski, C., & Stevenson, M. (Eds.), *Criminal juries in the 21st century* (pp. 19–40). New York: Oxford University Press.

Odgers, C., Moffitt, T., Broadbent, J., Dickson, N., Hancox, R., Harrington, H., … Caspi, A. (2008). Female and male antisocial trajectories: From childhood origins to adult outcomes. *Development and Psychopathology, 20,* 673–716. doi:10.1017/S0954579408000333

Odgers, C., Reppucci, N. D., & Moretti, M. (2005). Nipping psychopathy in the bud: An examination of the convergent, predictive, and theoretical utility of the PCL-YV among adolescent girls. *Behavioral Sciences & the Law, 23,* 743–763. doi:10.1002/bsl.664

Odinot, G., & Wolters, G. (2006). Repeated recall, retention interval and the accuracy confidence relation in eyewitness memory. *Applied Cognitive Psychology, 20,* 973–985.

Odinot, G., Wolters, G., & Lavender, T. (2009). Repeated partial eyewitness questioning causes confidence inflation but not retrieval-induced forgetting. *Applied Cognitive Psychology, 23,* 90–97.

Office of Justice Programs. (2018). *Drug courts* (NCJ 238527). Washington, DC: U.S. Department of Justice.

Office of Justice Programs, U.S. Department of Justice. (2011). *Workplace violence, 1993–2009.* Retrieved from https://bjs.ojp.gov/content/pub/pdf/wv09.pdf.

Office of Juvenile Justice and Delinquency Prevention. (1995). *Guide for implementing the comprehensive strategy for serious, violent, and chronic juvenile offenders.* Washington, DC: Author.

Office of Juvenile Justice and Delinquency Prevention. (2008). *Model programs guide.* Retrieved June 11, 2008, from http://www.dsonline.com/mpg2.5/mpg_index.htm

Office of Juvenile Justice and Delinquency Prevention. (2018). *Statistical briefing book*. Retrieved January 22, 2022, from https://www.ojjdp.gov/ojstatbb/structure_process/qa04112.asp?qaDate=2018&text=yes&maplink=link1

Ogloff, J. R. P. (1991). A comparison of insanity defense standards on juror decision making. *Law and Human Behavior, 15*, 509–532.

Ogloff, J. R. P., & Otto, R. (1993). Psychological autopsy: Clinical and legal perspectives. *Saint Louis University Law Journal, 37*, 607–646.

OJJDP (2020, November). *OJJDP Statistical Briefing Book*. Retrieved January 10, 2022, from https://www.ojjdp.gov/ojstatbb/crime/qa05101.asp?qaDate=2019.

Oleszkiewicz, S. & Watson, S. (2021). A meta-analytic review of the timing for disclosing evidence when interviewing suspects. *Applied Cognitive Psychology, 35*, 342–359.

Olson, J., & Zanna, M. (1993). Attitudes and attitude change. *Annual Review of Psychology, 44*, 117–154.

Olver, M., Stockdale, K., Neumann, C., Hare, R., Mokros, A., Baskin-Sommers, A., ... Yoon, D. (2020). Reliability and validity of the Psychopathy Checklist-Revised in the assessment of risk for institutional violence: A cautionary note on DeMatteo et al. (2020). *Psychology, Public Policy, and Law, 26*(4), 490–510. doi.org/10.1037/law0000256

Oppel, R. (2011, September 26). *Sentencing shift gives new leverage to prosecutors*. Retrieved March 22, 2012, from http://www.nytimes.com/2011/09/26/us/tough-sentences-help-prosecutors-push-for-plea-bargains.html?pagewanted=all

Orchowski, L. M., Gidycz, C. A., & Raffle, H. (2008). Evaluation of a sexual assault risk reduction and self-defense program: A prospective analysis of a revised protocol. *Psychology of Women Quarterly, 32*, 204–218.

Osman, S. (2011). Predicting rape empathy based on victim, perpetrator, and participant gender, and history of sexual aggression. *Sex Roles, 64*, 506–515.

Ostrov, E. (1986). Police/law enforcement and psychology. *Behavioral Sciences & the Law, 4*, 353–370.

Otgaar, H., Howe, M. L., Dodier, O., Lilienfeld, S. O., Loftus, E. F., Lynn, S. J., Merckelbach, H., & Patihis, L. (2021). Belief in unconscious repressed memory persists. *Perspectives on Psychological Science, 16*(2), 454–460. doi.org/10.1177/1745691621990628

Otgaar, H., Howe, M. L., Merckelbach, H., & Muris, P. (2018). Who is the better eyewitness? Sometimes adults but at other times children. *Current Directions in Psychological Science, 27*(5), 378–385. doi.org/10.1177/0963721418770998

Otgaar, H., Howe, M. L., Patihis, L., Merckelbach, H., Lynn, S. J., Lilienfeld, S. O., & Loftus, E. F. (2019). The return of the repressed: The persistent and problematic claims of long-forgotten trauma. *Perspectives on Psychological Science, 14*(6), 1072–1095. doi.org/10.1177/1745691619862306

Otto, R., & Edens, J. (2003). Parenting capacity. In T. Grisso (Ed.), *Evaluating competencies* (2nd ed., pp. 229–308). New York, NY: Springer.

Otto, R., Poythress, N., Nicholson, R., Edens, J., Monahan, J., Bonnie, J. et al. (1998). Psychometric properties of the MacArthur Competence Assessment Tool-Criminal Adjudication (MacCAT-CA). *Psychological Assessment, 10*, 435–443.

Otto, R., Poythress, N., Starr, K., & Darkes, J. (1993). An empirical study of the reports of APA's peer review panel in the congressional review of the *USS Iowa* incident. *Journal of Personality Assessment, 61*, 425–442.

Owen, D. (2004). *Criminal minds: The science and psychology of profiling*. New York, NY: Barnes & Noble Books.

Packer, H. L. (1964). Two models of the criminal process. *University of Pennsylvania Law Review, 113*, 1–68.

Palmer, C., & Hazelrigg, M. (2000). The guilty but mentally ill verdict: A review and conceptual analysis of intent and impact. *Journal of the American Academy of Psychiatry and the Law, 28*(1), 47–54.

Panetti v. Quarterman, 551 U.S. 930 (2007).

Pantazi, M., Klein, O., & Kissine, M. (2020). Is justice blind or myopic? An examination of the effects of meta-cognitive myopia and truth bias on mock jurors and judges. *Judgment and Decision Making, 15*, 214–229.

Park, J., & Feigenson, N. (2013). Effects of visual technology on mock juror decision making. *Applied Cognitive Psychology, 27*, 235–246.

Patihis, L., Ho L. Y., Tingen, I. W., Lilienfeld, S. O., & Loftus, E. F. (2014). Are the "memory wars" over? A scientist-practitioner gap in beliefs about repressed memory. *Psychological Science, 25*, 519–530.

Patihis, L., Wood, R. S., Pendergrast, M. H., & Herrera, M. E. (2022). Reports of recovered memories in therapy in undergraduate students. *Psychological Reports, 125*(1), 129–147. doi.org/10.1177/0033294120971756

Patrick, C. (2008). Psychophysiological correlates of aggression and violence: An integrative review. *Philosophical Transactions of the Royal Society B: Biological Sciences, 363*, 2543–2555.

Patton v. Yount, 467 U.S. 1025 (1984).

Payne, B. K., & Button, D. M. (2009). Developing a citywide youth violence prevention plan. *International Journal of Offender Therapy and Comparative Criminology, 53*, 517–534.

Paz-Alonso, P., & Goodman, G. (2016). Developmental differences across middle childhood in memory and suggestibility for negative and positive events. *Behavioral Sciences and the Law, 34*, 30–54.

Pearson, A., Dovidio, J., & Gaertner, S. (2009). The nature of contemporary prejudice: Insights from aversive racism. *Social and Personality Psychology Compass, 3*, 314–338.

Pena-Rodriguez v. Colorado, 137 S. Ct. 855 (2017).

Pennington, N., & Hastie, R. (1986). Evidence evaluation in complex decision making. *Journal of Personality and Social Psychology, 51*, 242–258.

Pennington, N., & Hastie, R. (1988). Explanation-based decision making: Effects of memory structure on judgment. *Journal of Experimental Psychology: Learning, Memory, and Cognition, 14*, 521–533.

Pennington, N., & Hastie, R. (1993). The story model for juror decision making. In R. Hastie (Ed.), *Inside the juror: The psychology of juror decision making* (pp. 192–221). New York, NY: Cambridge University Press.

Penrod, S. D., Loftus, E. F., & Winkler, J. (1982). The reliability of eyewitness testimony: A psychological perspective. In N. L. Kerr & R. M. Bray (Eds.), *The psychology of the courtroom* (pp. 119–168). Orlando, FL: Academic Press.

People v. Taylor, 598 N.E.2d 693 (1992).

Peter-Hagene, L. (2019). Jurors' cognitive depletion and performance during jury deliberation as a function of jury diversity and defendant race. *Law and Human Behavior, 43*, 232–249.

Peter-Hagene, L. & Bottoms, B. (2017). Attitudes, anger, and nullification instructions influence jurors' verdicts in euthanasia cases, *Psychology, Crime & Law, 23*, 983–1009.

Petherick, W. (2005). *The science of criminal profiling*. New York, NY: Barnes & Noble.

Pew Research Center. (2020). Black imprisonment rate in the U.S. has fallen by a third since 2006. Retrieved August 26, 2021, from https://www.pewresearch.org/fact-tank/2020/05/06/share-of-black-white-hispanic-americans-in-prison-2018-vs-2006/

Pew Research Center. (2021, June 2). Most Americans favor the death penalty despite concerns about its administration. Retrieved May 5, 2022, from https://www.pewresearch.org/politics/2021/06/02/most-americans-favor-the-death-penalty-despite-concerns-about-its-administration/

Pfohl, S. J. (1984). Predicting dangerousness: A social deconstruction of psychiatric reality. In L. A. Teplin (Ed.), *Mental health and criminal justice* (pp. 201–225). Newbury Park, CA: Sage.

Phalen, H., Salerno, J., & Nadler, J. (2021). Emotional evidence in court. In S. Bandes, J.L. Madeira, K. Temple. & E.K. White (Eds.), *Research Handbook on Law and Emotion*. (pp. 288–311). Edward Elger Publishing.

Phelps, M. (2011). Rehabilitation in the punitive era: The gap between rhetoric and reality in U.S. Prison programs. *Law and Society Review, 45*, 33–68.

Phillips, C. (Producer). (2006, October 1). *Dexter* [Television Series]. Long Beach, CA: Showtime Network.

Phillips, D. A. (1979). *The great Texas murder trials: A compelling account of the sensational T. Cullen Davis case.* New York, NY: Macmillan.

Phillips, M. (2012). *Decade of bail research in New York City.* Bureau of Justice Statistics. Washington, DC: U.S. Department of Justice.

Phillips, M., McAuliff, B., Kovera, M., & Cutler, B. (1999). Double-blind photoarray administration as a safeguard against investigator bias. *Journal of Applied Psychology, 84,* 940–951.

Pickel, K., French, T., & Betts, J. (2003). A cross-modal weapon focus effect: The influence of a weapon's presence on memory for auditory information. *Memory, 11,* 277–292.

Piechowski, L. (2011). *Evaluation of workplace disability.* New York, NY: Oxford University Press.

Pienaar, J., Rothmann, S., & Van de Vijver, F. J. R. (2007). Occupational stress, personality traits, coping strategies, and suicide ideation in the South African Police Service. *Criminal Justice and Behavior, 34,* 246–258. doi:10.1177/0093854806288708

Pierce, G., & Radelet, M. (2005). The impact of legally inappropriate factors on death sentencing for California homicides, 1990–1999. *Santa Clara Law Review, 46,* 1–47.

Pierson, E., Simoiu, C., Overgoor, J., Corbett-Davies, S., Jenson, D., Shoemaker, A., Ramachandran, V., Barghouty P., Phillips, C., Shroff, R.,& Goel, S. (2020). A large-scale analysis of racial disparities in police stops across the United States. *Nature Human Behaviour, 4,* no pagination. Retrieved January 17, 2022, from https://openpolicing.stanford.edu/publications/.

Pinizzotto, A. J., & Finkel, N. J. (1990). Criminal personality profiling: An outcome and process study. *Law and Human Behavior, 14,* 215–234.

Piquero, A., MacDonald, J., Dobrin, A., Daigle, L., & Cullen, F. (2005). Self-control, violent offending, and homicide victimization: Assessing the general theory of crime. *Journal of Quantitative Criminology, 21*(1), 55–70.

Plessy v. Ferguson, 163 U.S. 537 (1896).

Podkopacz, M., & Feld, B. (2001). The back door to prison: Waiver reform, blended sentencing, and the law of unintended consequences. *Journal of Criminal Law & Criminology, 91,* 997–1071.

Police Executive Research Forum. (2013). *A National Survey of Eyewitness Identification Procedures in Law Enforcement Agencies.* Report submitted to the National Institute of Justice, March 8, 2013.

Politis, S., Sivasubramaniam, D., Klettke, B., Nolan, M., Horand, J., & Schuller, R. (2021). Juror motivations: Applying procedural justice theory to juror decision making. *Psychology, Crime, and Law, 27,* 606–629.

Pollack, D., McFarland, B., Mahler, J., & Kovas, A. (2005). Outcomes of patients in low-intensity, short-duration involuntary outpatient commitment program. *Psychiatric Services, 26,* 863–866.

Poole, D., Brubacher, S., & Dickinson, J. (2015). Children as witnesses. In B. Cutler & P. Zapf (Eds.), *APA Handbook of forensic psychology, Vol. 2. Criminal investigation, adjudication, and sentencing outcome* (pp. 3–31). Washington, DC: APA.

Porter, B. (1983). Mind hunters. *Psychology Today, 17,* 44–52.

Porter, R. (2012). *Giving juvenile offenders a second chance at Oakland's Youth UpRising.* Retrieved from http://oaklandlocal.com/posts/2012/03/giving -juvenile-offenders-second-chance-oaklands-youth-uprising-community-voices

Portland State University Criminology and Criminal Justice Senior Capstone. (2014). *Prevention and management of stress in policing: A review of the literature.* Criminology and Criminal Justice Senior Capstone Project. Paper 11. Retrieved from http://pdxscholar.library.pdx.edu/ccj_capstone/11

Portman, J. (2019, June 1). Shaming convicted criminal defendants. Retrieved April 19, 2022, from https://www.lawyers.com/legal-info/criminal /criminal-law-basics/shame-on-you-do-shaming-punishments-work.html

Posey, A. (2015). From war protestors to corporate litigants: The evolution of the profession of trial consulting. In C. W. Esqueda & B. H. Bornstein (Eds.), The witness stand and Lawrence S.

Posey, A. (2016). From war protestors to corporate litigants: The evolution of the profession of trial consulting. In C. W. Esqueda & B. H. Bornstein (Eds.), *The witness stand and Lawrence S. Wrightsman, Jr.* (pp. 129–151). New York, NY: Springer-Verlag.

Post, C. G. (1963). *An introduction to the law.* Englewood Cliffs, NJ: Prentice Hall.

Post, L. (2004a, June 7). Courts mix justice with social work. *National Law Journal,* p. 1.

Post, L. (2004b, November 8). *Spelling it out in plain English.* Retrieved November 11, 2004, from www.law.com/jsp/nlj

Powell, M. B., Brubacher, S. P., & Baugerud, G. A. (2022). An overview of mock interviews as a training tool for interviewers of children. *Child Abuse & Neglect, 129,* 1–11. doi-org.lprx.bates.edu/10.1016/j. chiabu.2022.105685

Powers v. Ohio, 499 U.S. 400 (1991).

Powers, M., Halpern, J., Ferenschak, M., Gillihan, S., & Foa, E. (2010). A meta-analytic review of prolonged exposure for Posttraumatic Stress Disorder. *Clinical Psychology Review, 30,* 635–641.

Poythress, N., Bonnie, R., Monahan, J., Otto, R., & Hoge, S. K. (2002). *Adjudicative competence: The MacArthur Studies.* New York, NY: Kluwer Academic/Plenum.

Poythress, N. G., Nicholson, R., Otto, R. K., Edens, J. F., Bonnie, R. J., Monahan, J., & Hoge, S. K. (1999). *The MacArthur Competence Assessment Tool—Criminal Adjudication: Professional Manual.* Odessa, FL: Psychological Assessment Resources.

Pozzulo, J. (2017). *The young eyewitness: How well do children and adolescents describe and identify perpetrators?* Washington, DC: American Psychological Association. doi.org/10.1037/14956-000

Pozzulo, J., & Dempsey, J. (2009). Witness factors and their influence on jurors' perceptions and verdicts. *Criminal Justice and Behavior, 36,* 923–934.

President's Task Force on 21st Century Policing. (2015). *Final report of the President's Task Force on 21st Century Policing.* Washington, DC: Office of Community Oriented Policing Services.

Prettyman, E. B. (1960). Jury instructions—First or last? *American Bar Association Journal, 46,* 10–66.

Price, H., & Fitzgerald, R. (2016). Face-off: A new identification procedure for child eyewitnesses. *Journal of Experimental Psychology. Applied, 22,* 366–380.

Priebe, G., & Svedin, C. G. (2008). Child sexual abuse is largely hidden from the adult society: An epidemiological study of adolescents' disclosures. *Child Abuse & Neglect, 32,* 1095–1108.

Prins, S., & Draper, L. (2009). *Improving outcomes for people with mental illnesses under community corrections supervision: A guide to research-informed policy and practice.* New York: Council of State Governments Justice Center. Retrieved January 31, 2022, from https://csgjusticecenter .org/wp-content/uploads/2020/02/Community-Corrections-Research -Guide.pdf

Pryor, J. B., Giedd, J. L., & Williams, K. B. (1995). A social psychological model for predicting sexual harassment. *Journal of Social Issues, 51,* 69–84.

Purkett v. Elem, 514 U.S. 765 (1995).

Puzzanchera, C., Adams, B., & Sickmund, M. (2010). *Juvenile Court Statistics, 2006–2007.* Pittsburgh, PA: National Center for Juvenile Justice.

Qualters, S. (2010, September 22). Two federal judges offer differing takes on declining trial numbers. *New York Law Journal.* Retrieved from http:// www.newyorklawjournal.com/PubArticleNY.jsp?id=1202472305785

Qualters, S. (2012, March 8). *Seventh Circuit gives plaintiff new trial in bias case.* Retrieved June 9, 2012, from http://www.law.com/jsp/law /LawArticleFriendly.jsp?id=1202545092993&slreturn=1

Quas, J. A., & Goodman, G. S. (2012). Consequences of criminal court involvement for child victims. *Psychology, Public Policy, and Law, 18*(3), 392–414. doi.org/10.1037/a0026146

Quas, J., Goodman, G., Ghetti, S., Alexander, K., Edelstein, R., Redlich, A., … Jones, D. (2005). Childhood sexual assault victims: Long-term outcomes after testifying in criminal court. *Monographs of the Society for Research in Child Development, 70*(2, Serial No. 280), 1–145.

Quas, J., Malloy, L., Melinder, A., Goodman, G., D'Mello, M., & Schaaf, J. (2007). Developmental differences in the effects of repeated interviews and interviewer bias on young children's event memory and false reports. *Developmental Psychology, 43,* 823–837.

Quas, J., & Schaaf, J. (2002). Children's memories of experienced and nonexperienced events following repeated interviews. *Journal of Experimental Child Psychology, 83*, 304–338.

Quay, H. C. (1965). Personality and delinquency. In H. C. Quay (Ed.), *Juvenile delinquency* (pp. 139–169). Princeton, NJ: Van Nostrand.

Quinlivan, D., Neuschatz, J., Cutler, B., Wells, G., McClung, J., & Harker, D. (2012). Do pre-admonition suggestions moderate the effect of unbiased lineup instructions? *Legal and Criminological Psychology, 17*, 165–176.

Quinn, J. (1996). "Attitudinal" decision making in the federal courts: A study of constitutional self-representation claims. *San Diego Law Review, 33*, 701–754.

Quinsey, V., Harris, G., Rice, M., & Cormier, C. (2006). *Violent offenders: Appraising and managing risk* (2nd ed.). Washington, DC: American Psychological Association.

Rachlinski, J., & Wistrich, A. (2017). Judging the judiciary by the numbers: Empirical research on judges. *Annual Review of Law and Social Science, 13*, 203–229.

Rachlinski, J., Wistrich, A., & Guthrie, C. (2017). Judicial politics and decision making: A new approach. *Vanderbilt Law Review, 70*, 2051–2103.

Radelet, M., Bedau, H., & Putnam, C. (1992). *In spite of innocence: Erroneous convictions in capital cases*. Boston, MA: Northeastern University Press.

Rafilson, F., & Sison, R. (1996). Seven criterion-related validity studies conducted with the National Police Officer Selection Test. *Psychological Reports, 78*, 163–176.

Raine, A. (2002). Annotation: The role of prefrontal deficits, low autonomic arousal, and early health factors in the development of antisocial and aggressive behavior in children. *Journal of Child Psychology & Psychiatry, 43*, 417–434.

Raine, A., Lencz, T., Bihrle, S., Lacasse, L., & Colletti, P. (2000). Reduced prefrontal gray matter volume and reduced autonomic activity in antisocial personality disorder. *Archives of General Psychiatry, 57*, 119–127.

Raine, A., Meloy, J., & Buchsbaum, M. (1998). Reduced prefrontal and increased subcortical brain functioning using positron emission tomography in predatory and affective murderers. *Behavioral Sciences & the Law, 16*, 319–332.

Rakoff, J. (2014, November 20). Why innocent people plead guilty. *The New York Review of Books*. Retrieved from http://www.nybooks.com/articles/2014/11/20/why-innocent-people-plead-guilty/

Rassin, E. (2016). Rational thinking promotes suspect-friendly legal decision making. *Applied Cognitive Psychology, 30*, 460–464.

Reaves, B. (2013). *Felony defendants in large urban counties, 2009*. Washington, DC: U.S. Department of Justice, Bureau of Justice Statistics.

Reckless, W. C. (1967). *The crime problem* (4th ed.). New York, NY: Meredith.

Redding, R. E., Floyd, M. Y., & Hawk, G. L. (2001). What judges and lawyers think about the testimony of mental health experts: A survey of the courts and bar. *Behavioral Sciences & the Law, 19*, 583–594.

Redding, R. E., & Hensl, K. B. (2011). Knowledgeable judges make a difference: Judicial beliefs affect juvenile court transfer decisions. *Juvenile and Family Court Journal, 62*, 15–24.

Redding, R., & Mrozoski, B. (2005). Adjudicatory and dispositional decision making in juvenile justice. In K. Heilbrun, N., Goldstein, & R. Redding (Eds.), *Juvenile delinquency: Prevention, assessment, and intervention* (pp. 232–256). New York, NY: Oxford University Press.

Redlich, A., Bibas, S., Edkins, V., & Madon, S. (2017). The psychology of defendant plea decision making. *American Psychologist, 72*, 339–352.

Redlich, A. D., Bushway, S., & Norris, R. J. (2016). Plea decision-making by attorneys and judges. *Journal of Experimental Criminology, 12*, 537–561.

Redlich, A. D., Hoover, S., Summers, A., & Steadman, H. J. (2010). Enrollment in mental health courts: Voluntariness, knowingness, and adjudicative competence. *Law and Human Behavior, 34*, 91–104.

Redlich, A., & Shteynberg, R. (2016). To plead or not to plead: A comparison of juvenile and adult true and false plea decisions. *Law and Human Behavior, 40*, 611–625.

Redondo, S., Sanchez-Meca, J., & Garrido, V. (1999). The influence of treatment programs on the recidivism of juvenile and adult offenders: A European meta-analytic review. *Psychology, Crime and Law, 5*, 251–278.

Reed, K. (2020). The experience of a legal career: Attorneys' impact on the system and the system's impact on attorneys. *Annual Review of Law and Social Sciences, 16*, 385–404.

Reed, K., & Bornstein, B. H. (2013). A stressful profession: The experience of attorneys. In M. K. Miller & B. H. Bornstein (Eds.), *Stress, trauma, and wellbeing in the legal system*. New York, NY: Oxford University Press.

Reed, K,, Bornstein, B. H., Jeon, A., & Wylie, L. (2016). Problem signs in law school: Fostering attorney well-being early in professional training. *International Journal of Law and Psychiatry, 47*, 148–156.

Reiber, M., & Weinberg, J. (2010). The complexity of complexity: An empirical study of juror competence in civil cases. *University of Cincinnati Law Review, 78*, 929–968.

Reichherzer, C., Cunningham, A., Coleman, T., et al. (2021). Bringing the jury to the scene of the crime: Memory and decision-making in a simulated crime scene. *Proceedings of the 2021 CHI Conference on Human Factors in Computing Systems*, Article No. 709, 1–12.

Reisner, A., Piel, J., & Makey, M. (2013). Competency to stand trial and defendants who lack insight into their mental illness. *Journal of the American Academy of Psychiatry and the Law Online, 41*(1), 85–91.

Resnick, H. et al. (1993). Prevalence of civilian trauma and posttraumatic stress disorder in a representative national sample of women. *Journal of Consulting and Clinical Psychology, 61*(6), 984–991.

Ressler, R. K., Burgess, A. W., & Douglas, J. E. (1988). *Sexual homicide: Patterns and motives*. Lexington, MA: Lexington Books.

Reuland, M., Schwarzfeld, M., & Draper, L. (2009). *Law enforcement responses to people with mental illness: A guide to research-informed policy and practice*. New York, NY: Justice Center, Council of State Governments. Retrieved July 14, 2017, from https://csgjusticecenter.org/wp-content/uploads/2012/12/le-research.pdf

Rhee, N. (2016, April 13). How Chicago police can rebuild trust. *Christian Science Monitor*. Retrieved November 21, 2017 from https://www.csmonitor.com/USA/Justice/2016/0413/How-Chicago-police-can-rebuild-trust

Rhee, S., & Waldman, I. (2002). Genetic and environmental influences on antisocial behavior: A meta-analysis of twin and adoption studies. *Psychological Bulletin, 128*, 490–529. doi:10.1037/0033-2909.128.3.490

Rhode, D. (2001). Access to justice. *Fordham Law Review, 69*, 1785–1819.

Rhode Island v. Innis, 446 U.S. 291 (1980).

Richeson, J., & Sommers, S. (2016). Toward a social psychology of race and race relations for the twenty-first century. *Annual Review of Psychology, 67*, 439–463.

Richeson, J., Trawalter, S. & Shelton, J. (2005). African Americans' implicit racial attitudes and the depletion of executive function after interracial interactions. *Social Cognition, 23*, 336–352.

Richter, E., & Humke, A. (2011). Demonstrative evidence: Evidence and technology in the courtroom. In R. Wiener & B. Bornstein (Eds.), *Handbook of trial consulting* (pp. 187–202). New York, NY: Springer.

Rickert, J. (2010). Denying defendants the benefit of a reasonable doubt: Federal rule of evidence 609 and past sex crime convictions. *Journal of Criminal Law and Criminology, 100*, 213–242.

Rideau v. Louisiana, 373 U.S. 723 (1963).

Rider, A. O. (1980). The firesetter: A psychological profile. *FBI Law Enforcement Bulletin, 49*, 123.

Ring v. Arizona, 536 U.S. 584 (2002).

Risinger, D. M. (2007). Innocents convicted: An empirically justified factual wrongful conviction rate. *Journal of Criminal Law and Criminology, 97*, 761–806.

Risinger, D. M., & Loop, J. (2002). Three card monte, Monty Hall, modus operandi, and "offender profiling": Some lessons of modern cognitive science for the law of evidence. *Cardozo Law Review, 24*, 193–253.

Robbennolt, J. K. (2000). Outcome severity and judgments of "responsibility": A meta-analytic review. *Journal of Applied Social Psychology, 30,* 2575–2609.

Robbennolt, J. K. (2002). Punitive damage decision making: The decisions of citizens and trial court judges. *Law and Human Behavior, 26,* 315–342.

Robbennolt, J. K. (2013). The effects of negotiated and delegated apologies in settlement negotiation. *Law and Human Behavior, 37*(2), 128–135.

Robbennolt, J. K., & Davidson, S. (2011). Legal research techniques for social scientists. In B. Rosenfeld & S. Penrod (Eds.), *Research methods in forensic psychology* (pp. 3–25). New York, NY: Wiley.

Robbennolt, J. K., & Hans, V. P. (2016). *The psychology of tort law.* New York, NY: New York University Press.

Robertiello, G., & Terry, K. (2007). Can we profile sex offenders? A review of sex offender typologies. *Aggression and Violent Behavior, 12,* 508–518.

Roberts, A. (2019). Implicit jury bias. Are informational interventions effective? In Najdowski, C., & Stevenson, M. (Eds.), *Criminal juries in the 21st century* (pp. 85–107). New York: Oxford University Press.

Roberts, A. L., Gillman, S. E., Breslau, J., Breslau, N., & Koenen, K. C. (2011). Race/ethnic differences in exposure to traumatic events, development of post-traumatic stress disorder, and treatment-seeking for post-traumatic stress disorder in the United States. *Psychological Medicine: A Journal of Research in Psychiatry and the Allied Sciences, 41,* 71–83.

Roberts, C. F., & Golding, S. L. (1991). The social construction of criminal responsibility and insanity. *Law and Human Behavior, 15,* 349–376.

Roberts, R., Tarescavage, A., Ben-Porath, Y., & Roberts, M. (2019). Predicting postprobationary job performance of police officers using CPI and MMPI-2-RF test data obtained during preemployment psychological screening. *Journal of Personality Assessment, 101*(5), 544–555.

Robertson, C. T. (2010). Blind expertise. *New York University Law Review, 85,* 175–257.

Robertson, C., & Yokum, D. (2011). *Effect of blinded experts on mock jurors' assessments of credibility and verdicts in civil trials.* Arizona Legal Studies Discussion Paper No. 11–30. Retrieved July 17, 2012, from http://papers .ssrn.com/sol3/papers.cfm?abstract_id=1884765

Robinson, E. (2011). Jury instructions for the modern age: A 50-state survey of jury instructions on Internet and social media. *Reynolds Courts & Media Law Journal, 1,* 307–415.

Rodriguez, F., Curry, T., & Lee, G. (2006). Gender differences in criminal sentencing: Do effects vary across violent, property, and drug offenses? *Social Sciences Quarterly, 87,* 318–339.

Roe v. Wade, 410 U.S. 113 (1973).

Roesch, R., Zapf, P., & Eaves, D. (2006). *Fitness Interview Test-Revised (FIT-R): A structured interview for assessing competency to stand trial.* Sarasota, FL: Professional Resource Press.

Rogers, C., & Guillon, S. (2019). *Giving Up on Impartiality: The Threat of Public Capitulation to Contemporary Attacks on the Rule of Law,* Denver, CO: Institute for the Advancement of the American Legal System.

Rogers, R. (1986). *Conducting insanity evaluations.* New York, NY: Van Nostrand.

Rogers, R. (2001). *Handbook of diagnostic and structured interviewing* (2nd ed.). New York, NY: Guilford.

Rogers, R., & Bender, S. (2008). *Clinical assessment of malingering and deception* (4th ed) Guilford. Conner et al., 2012

Rogers, R., & Bender, S. (Eds.) (2018). *Clinical assessment of malingering and deception* (4th ed.). New York: Guilford.

Rogers, R., & Ewing, C. P. (1989). Ultimate opinion proscriptions: A cosmetic fix and a plea for empiricism. *Law and Human Behavior, 13,* 357–374.

Rogers, R., & Ewing C. P. (2003). The prohibition of ultimate opinions: A misguided enterprise. *Journal of Forensic Psychology Practice, 3,* 65–75.

Rogers, R., Grandjean, N., Tillbrook, C., Vitacco, M., & Sewell, K. (2001). Recent interview-based measures of competency to stand trial: A critical review augmented with research data. *Behavioral Sciences & the Law, 19,* 503–518.

Rogers, R., & Johansson-Love, J. (2009). Evaluating competency to stand trial with evidence-based practice. *Journal of the American Academy of Psychiatry and Law Online, 37*(4), 450–460.

Rogers, R., Otal, T., Drogin, E., & Dean, B. (2020). Effectiveness of the Miranda acquiescence questionnaire for investigating impaired Miranda reasoning. *Journal of the American Academy of Psychiatry and the Law, 48,* 226–236.

Rogers, R., Rogstad, J., Steadham, J., & Drogin, E. (2011). In plain English: Avoiding recognized problems with *Miranda* comprehension. *Psychology, Public Policy, & Law, 17,* 264–285.

Rogers, R., & Sewell, K. (1999). The R-CRAS and insanity evaluations: A re-examination of construct validity. *Behavioral Sciences & the Law, 17*(2), 181–194. doi: 10.1002/(sici)1099-0798(199904/06) 17:2<181::aid-bsl338>3.0.co;2-4.

Rogers, R., Steadham, J. A., Carter, R. M., Henry, S. A., Drogin, E. Y., & Robinson, E. V. (2016). An examination of juveniles' Miranda abilities: Investigating differences in Miranda recall and reasoning. *Behavioral Sciences & the Law, 34,* 515–538.

Rogers, R., Tillbrook, C., & Sewell, K. (2004). *Evaluation of Competency to Stand Trial-Revised (ECST-R) and professional manual.* Odessa, FL: Psychological Assessment Resources.

Rohling, M. L., Binder, L. M., & Langhrinrichsen-Rohling, J. (1995). Money matters: A meta-analytic review of the association between financial compensation and the experience and treatment of chronic pain. *Health Psychology, 14,* 537–547.

Roofeh, A. (2019). The one big predictor of sexual harassment in the workplace (and what individuals can do about it). *The Startup.* Retrieved February 21, 2022, from https://medium.com/swlh/the-one-big-predictor -of-sexual-harassment-in-the-workplace-and-what-individuals-can-do -about-it-1104c141755e#_ftn1

Roper v. Simmons, 543 U.S. 551 (2005).

Rose, M. R., Casarez, R., & Gutierrez, C. (2018). Jury pool underrepresentation in the modern era: Evidence from the federal courts. *Journal of Empirical Legal Studies, 15,* 378–405.

Rose, M. R., & Diamond, S. (2008). Judging bias: Juror confidence and judicial rulings on challenges for cause. *Law and Society Review, 42,* 513–548.

Rose, M. R., Diamond, S. S., & Musick, M. A. (2012). Selected to serve: An analysis of lifetime jury participation. *Journal of Empirical Legal Studies, 9,* 33–55.

Rose, M. R., Ellison, C., & Diamond, S. (2008). Preferences for juries over judges across racial and ethnic groups. *Social Science Quarterly, 89,* 372–391.

Rosen, G. M. (1995). The *Aleutian Enterprise* sinking and posttraumatic stress disorder: Misdiagnosis in clinical and forensic settings. *Professional Psychology: Research and Practice, 26,* 82–87.

Rosenbaum, A., & Gearan, P. J. (1999). Relationship aggression between partners. In V. B. Van Hasselt & M. Hersen (Eds.), *Handbook of psychological approaches with violent offenders: Contemporary strategies and issues* (pp. 357–372). New York: Kluver Academic/Plenum.

Rosenfeld, J., Soskins, M., Bosh, G., & Ryan, A. (2004). Simple effective countermeasures to P300-based tests of detection of concealed information. *Psychophysiology, 41,* 205–219.

Rosenmerkel, M., Durose, M., & Farole, D. (2009). *Felony sentences in state courts, 2006.* Bureau of Justice Statistics Report NCJ 226846. Washington, DC: Department of Justice.

Rosenthal, H., & Crisp, R. (2006). Reducing stereotype threat by blurring intergroup boundaries. *Personality and Social Psychology Bulletin, 32,* 501–511.

Rosenthal, R., & Jacobson, L. (1968). *Pygmalion in the classroom: Teacher expectation and pupils' intellectual development.* New York, NY: Holt.

Rotundo, M., Nguyen, D., & Sackett, P. (2001). A meta-analytic review of gender differences in perceptions of sexual harassment. *Journal of Applied Psychology, 86*, 914–922.

Rowhani-Rabhar, A., & Moe, C. (2019). School shootings in the U.S.: What is the state of the evidence? *Journal of Adolescent Health, 64*, 693–694.

Ruback, R. B. (2015). Sentencing. In B. Cutler & P. Zapf (Eds.), *APA handbook of forensic psychology: Vol. 2. Criminal investigation, adjudication, and sentencing outcomes* (pp. 385–414). Washington, DC: APA.

Rubin, D., & Boals, A. (2010). People who expect to enter psychotherapy are prone to believing that they have forgotten memories of childhood trauma and abuse. *Memory, 18*, 556–562.

Russell, B., & Melillo, L. (2006). Attitudes toward battered women who kill: Defendant typicality and judgments of culpability. *Criminal Justice and Behavior, 33*, 219–241.

Russell, M., & Odgers, C. (2016). Desistance and life-course persistence: Findings from longitudinal studies using group-based trajectory modeling of antisocial behavior. In K. Heilbrun, D. DeMatteo, & N. Goldstein (Eds.), *APA handbook of psychology and juvenile justice* (pp. 159–175). Washington, DC: American Psychological Association. doi:10.1037/14643-015

Ruva, C., Diaz Ortega, S., & O'Grady, K. (2022). What drives a jury's deliberation? The influence of pretrial publicity and jury composition on deliberation slant and content. *Psychology, Public Policy, and Law, 28*, 32–52.

Ruva, C., & Guenther, C. (2015). From the shadows into the light: How pretrial publicity and deliberation affect mock jurors' decisions, impressions, and memory. *Law and Human Behavior, 39*, 294–310.

Ruva, C., & Guenther, C. (2017). Keep your bias to yourself: How deliberating with differently biased others affects mock-jurors' guilt decisions, perceptions of the defendant, memories, and evidence interpretation. *Law and Human Behavior, 41*, 478–493.

Ruva, C., McEvoy, C., & Bryant, J. (2007). Effects of pretrial publicity and collaboration on juror bias and source monitoring errors. *Applied Cognitive Psychology, 21*, 45–67.

Ryan, J., Abrams, L., & Huang, H. (2014). First-time violent juvenile offenders: Probation, placement, and recidivism. *Social Work Research, 38*, 7–18.

Ryan, W. (1970). *Blaming the victim.* New York, NY: Vintage.

Sable, M., Danis, F., Mauzy, D., & Gallagher, S. (2006). Barriers to reporting sexual assault for women and men: Perspectives of college students. *Journal of American College Health, 55*(3), 157–162.

Sack, E. (2002). *Creating a domestic violence court: Guidelines and best practices.* San Francisco, CA: Family Violence Prevention Fund.

Sack, K. (2017, February 2). Trial documents show Dylann Roof had mental disorders. Retrieved May 29, 2022, from https://www.nytimes.com/2017/02/02/us/dylann-roof-charleston-killing-mental.html

Sack, K., & Blinder, A. (2017, January 1). Dylann Roof himself rejects best defense against execution. *New York Times.* Retrieved from https://www.nytimes.com/2017/01/01/us/dylann-roof-execution-defense-charleston-church-shooting.html

Saks, M. (1997). What do jury experiments tell us about how juries (should) make decisions? *Southern California Interdisciplinary Law Journal, 6*, 1–53.

Saks, M., Hollinger, L., Wissler, R., Evans, D., & Hart, A. (1997). Reducing variability in civil jury awards. *Law and Human Behavior, 21*, 243–256.

Salekin, R. (2004). *The Risk-Sophistication-Treatment Inventory.* Lutz, FL: Psychological Assessment Resources.

Salekin, R., Trobst, K., & Krioukova, M. (2001). Construct validity of psychopathy in a community sample: A nomological net approach. *Journal of Personality Disorders, 15*, 425–441.

Salerno, J. (2021). The impact of experienced and expressed emotion on legal factfinding. *Annual Review of Law and Social Science, 17*, 181–203.

Salerno, J., Bottoms, B., & Peter-Hagene, L. (2017). Individual versus group decision making: Jurors' reliance on central and peripheral information to evaluate expert testimony. *PLoS ONE, 12*, e0183580.

Salerno, J., Campbell, J., Phalen, H., Bean, S., Hans, V., Spivack, D., & Ross, L. (2021). The impact of minimal versus extended voir dire and judicial rehabilitation on mock jurors' decisions in civil cases. *Law and Human Behavior, 45*, 336–355.

Salerno, J., & Phalen, H. (2019). The impact of gruesome photographs on mock jurors' emotional responses and decision making in a civil case. *DePaul Law Review, 69*, 633–56.

Salfati, C. G., & Canter, D. V. (1999). Differentiating stranger murders: Profiling offender characteristics from behavioral styles. *Behavioral Sciences & the Law, 17*, 391–406.

Sample, J., Skaggs, A., Blitzer, J., & Casey, L. (2010). The new politics of judicial elections 2000–2009: Decade of change. Retrieved from www.justiceatstake.org/media/cms/JASNPJEDecadeONLINE_EC9663F6F7865.pdf

Sampson, R., & Groves, W. B. (1989). Community structure and crime: Testing social disorganization theory. *American Journal of Sociology, 94*(4), 774–802.

Sanborn, H. (2002, October). The vanishing trial. *American Bar Association Journal, 87*, 24–27.

Sanders, J. (1993). The jury decision in a complex case: *Havener v. Merrell Dow Pharmaceuticals. The Justice System Journal, 16*, 45.

Sandler, J. C., Letourneau, E. J., Vandiver, D. M., Shields, R. T., & Chaffin, M. (2017). Juvenile sexual crime reporting rates are not influenced by juvenile sex offender registration policies. *Psychology, Public Policy, and Law, 23*(2), 131–140.

Sanschagrin, K., Stevens, T., Bove, A., & Heilbrun, K. (2006, March). *Quality of forensic mental health assessment of juvenile offenders: An empirical investigation.* Paper presented at the annual conference of the American Psychology-Law Society, Tampa, Florida.

Santobello v. New York, 404 U.S. 257 (1971).

Sarteschi, C. (2009). *Assessing the effectiveness of mental health courts: A meta-analysis of clinical and recidivism outcomes.* Doctoral Dissertation, University of Pittsburgh. Retrieved December 22, 2016, from http://d-scholarship.pitt.edu/9275/

Sarteschi, C. M., Vaughn, M. G., & Kim, K. (2011). Assessing the effectiveness of mental health courts: A quantitative review. *Journal of Criminal Justice, 39*, 12–20.

Satterwhite v. Texas, 108 S. Ct. 1792 (1988).

Sawyer, A., & Borduin, C. (2011). Effects of multisystemic therapy through midlife: A 21.9-year follow-up to a randomized clinical trial with serious and violent juvenile offenders. *Journal of Consulting and Clinical Psychology, 79*, 634–652.

Scherr, K., & Madon, S. (2012). You have the right to understand: The deleterious effect of stress on *Miranda* comprehension. *Law and Human Behavior, 36*, 275–282.

Scherr, K., Redlich, A., & Kassin, S. (2020). Cumulative disadvantage: A psychological framework for understanding how innocence can lead to confession, wrongful conviction, and beyond. *Perspectives on Psychological Science, 15*, 353–383.

Schiavone, S. K. & Jeglic, E. L. (2009). Public perception of sex offender social policies and the impact on sex offenders. *International Journal of Offender Therapy and Comparative Criminology, 53*(6), 679–695.

Schindler, A. (2020, February, 14). https://www.firstcoastnews.com/article/news/crime/hold-til-friday-1145-am-innocent-man-not-innocent-enough-to-qualify-for-compensation/77-21a809d1-81dd-4193-8e66-d4c5169d1a05 Downloaded August 28, 2022

Schmucker, M., & Losel, F. (2015). The effects of sexual offender treatment on recidivism: An international meta-analysis of sound quality evaluations. *Journal of Experimental Criminology, 11*, 597–630.

Schreiber, J., Green, D., Kunz, M., Belfi, B., & Pequeno, G. (2015). Offense characteristics of Incompetent to Stand Trial defendants charged with violent offenses. *Behavioral Sciences & the Law, 33*, 257–278. doi:10.1002/bsl.2174.

Schreiber, N., Bellah, L. D., Martinez, Y., McLaurin, K. A., Strok, R., Garven, S., & Wood, J. M. (2006). Suggestive interviewing in the McMartin Preschool and Kelly Michaels Daycare abuse cases: A case study. *Social Influence, 1*(1), 16–47. https://doi.org/10.1080/15534510500361739

Schroeder, L. (2014). Cracks in the ivory tower: How the Campus Sexual Violence Elimination Act can protect students from sexual assault. *Loyola University Chicago Law Journal, 45*, 1195–1243.

Schuller, R., McKimmie, B., & Janz, T. (2004). The impact of expert testimony in trials of battered women who kill. *Psychiatry, Psychology and Law, 11*, 1–12.

Schwaeble, K., & Sundt, J. (2020). Attitudes and public opinion about punishment. Retrieved April 29, 2022, from *Oxford Research Encyclopedia of Criminology and Criminal Justice,* https://oxfordre.com/criminology/view/10.1093/acrefore/9780190264079.001.0001/acrefore-9780190264079-e-222

Schwartzapfel, B. (2020, May 13). More and more states are finally confronting unconscious racism in jury selection. Retrieved June 1, 2020, from https://www.motherjones.com/crime-justice/2020/05/more-and-more-states-are-finally-confronting-unconscious-racism-in-jury-selection/

Schwartz, F., Djeriouat, H., & Tremoliere, B. (2022). Judging accidental harm: Reasoning style modulates the weight of intention and harm severity. *Quarterly Journal of Experimental Psychology,* in press.

Science Daily. (2007, June 28). New study shows how often juries get it wrong. *Science Daily.* Retrieved June 5, 2012, from http://www.sciencedaily.com/releases/2007/06/070628161330.htm

Scoboria, A., Wade, K., Lindsay, D., Azad, T., Strange, D., Ost, J., & Hyman, I. (2017). A mega-analysis of memory reports from eight peer-reviewed false memory implantation studies. *Memory, 25*, 146–163.

Scott, R., & Stuntz, W. (1992). Plea bargaining as contract. *The Yale Law Journal, 101*, 1909–1968.

Scott, Y. M. (2004). Stress among rural and small-town patrol officers: A survey of Pennsylvania municipal agencies. *Police Quarterly, 7*, 237–261. doi:10.1177/1098611103258958

Scurich, N., & Krauss, D. (2020). Public's views of risk assessment algorithms and pretrial decision making. *Psychology, Public Policy, and Law, 26*, 1–9.

Scurich, N., Krauss, D., Reiser, L., Garcia, R., & Deer, L. (2015). Venire jurors' perceptions of adversarial allegiance. *Psychology, Public Policy, and Law, 21*, 161–168.

Scurich, N., & Monahan, J. (2016). Evidence-based sentencing: Public openness and opposition to using gender, age, and race as risk factors for recidivism. *Law and Human Behavior, 40*, 36–41.

Seamon, J., Philbin, M., & Harrison, L. (2006). Do you remember proposing marriage to the Pepsi machine? False recollections from a college walk. *Psychonomic Bulletin & Review, 13*, 752–756.

Seiter, R. P., & Kadela, K. R. (2003). Prisoner reentry: What works, what does not, and what is promising. *Crime & Delinquency, 49*, 360–388.

Sellier, A.-L., Scopelliti, I., and Morewedge, C. K. (2019). Debiasing training improves decision making in the field. *Psychological Science, 30*, 1371–1379.

Sell v. United States, 539 U.S. 166 (2003).

Semmler, C., Brewer, N., & Douglass, A. (2012). Jurors believe eyewitnesses. In B. Cutler (Ed.), *Conviction of the innocent: Lessons from psychological research* (pp. 185–209). Washington, DC: American Psychological Association.

The Sentencing Project. (2016). Incarcerated women and girls. Retrieved October 19, 2016, from www.sentencingproject.org/wp/content/uploads/2016/02/Incarcerated-Women-and-Girls.pdf

The Sentencing Project. (2018). *Report to the United Nations on racial disparities in the U.S. criminal justice system.* Retrieved March 1, 2022, from https://www.sentencingproject.org/publications/un-report-on-racial-disparities/

The Sentencing Project. (2020). Retrieved August 4, 2021, from https://www.sentencingproject.org/publications/incarcerated-women-and-girls/

The Sentencing Project. (2021). The color of justice: Racial and ethnic disparity in state prisons. Retrieved January 30, 2022, from https://www.sentencingproject.org/publications/color-of-justice-racial-and-ethnic-disparity-in-state-prisons/

Settles, I., Buchanan, N., Yap, S., & Harrell, Z. (2014). Sex differences in outcomes and harasser characteristics associated with frightening sexual harassment appraisals. *Journal of Occupational Health Psychology, 19*(2), 133–142. doi:10.1037/a0035449

Seventh Circuit American Jury Project. (2008). Retrieved January 30, 2009, from www.7thcircuitbar.org/associations/1507/files/7th%20Circuit%20American%20Jury%20Project%20Final%20Report.pdf

Sevier, J. (2014). The truth-justice tradeoff: Perceptions of decisional accuracy and procedural justice in adversarial and inquisitorial legal system. *Psychology, Public Policy, and Law, 20*, 212–224.

Sexton, T., & Turner, C. (2010). The effectiveness of functional family therapy for youth with behavioral problems in a community practice setting. *Journal of Family Psychology, 24*, 339–348.

Shafer, M., Arthur, B., & Franczak, M. (2004). An analysis of post-booking jail diversion programming for persons with co-occurring disorders. *Behavioral Sciences and the Law, 22*, 771–785.

Shaffer, D. K. (2011). Looking inside the black box of drug courts: A meta-analytic review. *Justice Quarterly, 28*, 493–521.

Shaw, J., Appio, L., Zerr, T., & Pontoski, K. (2007). Public eyewitness confidence can be influenced by the presence of other witnesses. *Law and Human Behavior, 31*, 629–652.

Shaw, J., & Porter, S. (2015). Constructing rich false memories of committing crime. *Psychological Science, 26*, 291–301.

Shaw, L. A. (2010). Divorce mediation outcome research: A meta-analysis. *Conflict Resolution Quarterly, 27*, 447–467.

Sheldon, K., & Krieger, L. (2004). Does legal education have undermining effects on law students? Evaluating changes in motivation, values, and well being. *Behavioral Sciences & the Law, 22*, 261–286.

Sheldon, K., & Krieger, L. (2007). Understanding the negative effects of legal education on law students: A longitudinal test of self-determination theory. *Personality and Social Psychology Bulletin, 33*, 883–897.

Sherman, L. W., & Berk, R. A. (1984). *The Minneapolis domestic violence experiment.* Washington, DC: Police Foundation.

Shestowsky, D. (2014). The psychology of procedural preference: How litigants evaluate legal procedures ex ante. *Iowa Law Review, 99*, 637–710.

Shulman, K. I., Cohen, C. A., & Hull, I. (2004). Psychiatric issues in retrospective challenges of testamentary capacity. *International Journal of Geriatric Psychiatry, 20*, 63–69.

Shuman, D. W., & Champagne, A. (1997). Removing the people from the legal process: The rhetoric and research on judicial selection and juries. *Psychology, Public Policy, and Law, 3*, 242–258.

Siegel, A. M., & Elwork, A. (1990). Treating incompetence to stand trial. *Law and Human Behavior, 14*, 57–65.

Siegel, L. J., & McCormick, C. (2006). *Criminology in Canada: Theories, patterns, and typologies* (3rd ed.). Toronto: Thompson.

Sigillo, A. (2015). Promoting positive perceptions of justice by listening to children's sentiment in custody decisions. In M. Miller, J. Blumenthal, & J. Chamberlain (Eds.), *Handbook of community sentiment* (pp. 173–182). New York, NY: Springer.

Silver, E. (1995). Punishment or treatment? Comparing the lengths of confinement of successful and unsuccessful insanity defendants. *Law and Human Behavior, 19*, 375–388.

Silver, E., Cirincione, C., & Steadman, H. J. (1994). Demythologizing inaccurate perceptions of the insanity defense. *Law and Human Behavior, 18*, 63–70.

Silver, R. B., & Silver, D. B. (2009). The Sieve Model: An innovative process for identifying alternatives to custody evaluations. *Conflict Resolution Quarterly, 26*, 333–348.

Simon, D. (2004). Third view of the black box: Cognitive coherence in legal decision making. *University of Chicago Law Review, 71*, 511–586.

Simon, D. (2012). *In doubt: The psychology of the criminal justice process.* Cambridge, MA: Harvard University Press.

Simon, D., Ahn, M., Stenstrom, D. M., & Read, S. J. (2020). The adversarial mindset. *Psychology, Public Policy, and Law, 26*, 353–377.

Simon, D., Snow, C., & Read, S. (2004). The redux of cognitive consistency theories: Evidence judgments by constraint satisfaction. *Journal of Personality and Social Psychology, 86*, 814–837.

Simons, D. J., & Chabris, C. F. (1999). Gorillas in our midst: Sustained inattentional blindness for dynamic events. *Perception, 28*(9), 1059–1074. https://doi.org/10.1068/p2952

Singleton, J. V., & Kass, M. (1986). Helping the jury understand complex cases. *Litigation, 12*, 11–13, 59.

Skagerberg, E., & Wright, D. (2008). Co-witness feedback in lineups. *Applied Cognitive Psychology, 21*, 489–497.

Skeem, J., & Bibeau, L. (2008). How does violence potential relate to Crisis Intervention Team responses to emergencies? *Psychiatric Services, 59*, 201–204.

Skeem, J., Emke-Francis, P., & Eno Louden, J. (2006). Probation, mental health, and mandated treatment: A national survey. *Criminal Justice and Behavior, 33*, 158–184.

Skeem, J., & Eno Louden, J. (2006). Toward evidence-based practice for probationers and parolees mandated to mental health treatment. *Psychiatric Services, 57*, 333–342.

Skeem, J., Eno Louden, J., Manchak, S., Vidal, S., & Haddad, E. (2009). Social networks and social control of probationers with co-occurring mental and substance abuse problems. *Law and Human Behavior, 33*, 122–135.

Skeem, J., & Golding, S. L. (2001). Describing jurors' personal conceptions of insanity and their relationship to case judgments. *Psychology, Public Policy, and Law, 7*, 561–621.

Skeem, J., & Lowenkamp, C. (2016). Risk, race, and recidivism: Predictive bias and disparate impact. *Criminology, 54*, 680–712.

Skipper v. South Carolina, 476 U.S. 1 (1986).

Skogan, W. G., Steiner, L., DuBois, J., Gudell, J. E., & Fagan, A. (2002). *Community policing and "the new immigrants": Latinos in Chicago* (NCJ 189908). Washington, DC: U.S. Department of Justice, Office of Justice Programs, National Institute of Justice.

Slater, D., & Hans, V. P. (1984). Public opinion of forensic psychiatry following the *Hinckley* verdict. *American Journal of Psychiatry, 141*, 675–679.

Slattery, M., Dugger, M. T., Lamb, T. A., & Williams, L. (2013). Catch, treat, and release: Veteran treatment courts address the challenges of returning home. *Substance Use and Misuse, 48*, 922–932.

Slesnick, N., & Prestopnik, J. (2009). Comparison of family therapy outcome with alcohol-abusing, runaway adolescents. *Journal of Marital and Family Therapy, 35*, 255–277. doi:10.1111/j.1752-0606.2009.00121.x

Sloat, L. M., & Frierson, R. L. (2005). Juror knowledge and attitudes regarding mental illness verdicts. *Journal of the American Academy of Psychiatry and Law, 33*, 208–213.

Slobogin, C. (2011). Prevention of sexual violence by those who have been sexually violent. *International Journal of Law and Psychiatry, 34*, 210–216.

Slobogin, C. (2014). Lessons from inquisitorialism. *Southern California Law Review, 87*, 699–731.

Slobogin, C., & Fondacaro, M. (2011). *Juveniles at risk: A plea for preventive justice.* New York, NY: Oxford University Press.

Slobogin, C., Melton, G., & Showalter, S. R. (1984). The feasibility of a brief evaluation of mental state at the time of the offense. *Law and Human Behavior, 8*, 305–321.

Smalarz, L., Ireri, H., & Fink, J. A. (2021). Presumed-blind lineup administrators can influence eyewitnesses' identification decisions and confidence. *Psychology, Public Policy, and Law, 27*(4), 466–478. https://doi.org/10.1037/law0000317

Smalarz, L., & Wells, G. (2015). Contamination of eyewitness self-reports and the mistaken-identification problem. *Current Directions in Psychological Science, 24*, 120–124.

Smith, A. (2008). *Case of a lifetime: A criminal defense lawyer's story.* New York, NY: Palgrave Macmillan.

Smith, A. (2021, July 29). There are more women lawyers than ever, and they're not pleased with the legal industry. Retrieved December 27, 2021, from https://www.law.com/americanlawyer/2021/07/29/there-are-more-women-lawyers-than-ever-and-theyre-not-pleased-with-legal-industry-norms/?slreturn=20211127134606

Smith, A., & Haney, C. (2011). Getting to the point: Attempting to improve juror comprehension of capital penalty phase instructions. *Law and Human Behavior, 35*, 339–350.

Smith, D., Chamberlain, P., & Eddy, J. (2010). Preliminary support for multidimensional treatment foster care in reducing substance use in delinquent boys. *Journal of Child and Adolescent Substance Abuse, 19*, 343–358. doi:10.1080/1067828X.2010.511986

Smith, J., & MacQueen, G. (2017). Going, going, but not quite gone: Trials continue to decline in federal and state courts. Does it matter? *Judicature, 101*(4), 27–39.

Smith, P., Goggin, C., & Gendreau, P. (2002). *The effects of prison sentences and intermediate sanctions on recidivism: General effects and individual differences.* Ottawa, ON: Public Safety Canada. (User Report 2002-01).

Smith, S. (1989). Mental health expert witnesses: Of science and crystal balls. *Behavioral Sciences & the Law, 7*, 145–180.

Snook, B., Cullen, R., Bennell, C., Taylor, P., & Gendreau, P. (2008). The criminal profiling illusion: What's behind the smoke and mirrors? *Criminal Justice and Behavior, 35*, 1257–1276.

Snook, B., Eastwood, J., Gendreau, P., Goggin, C., & Cullen, R. (2007). Taking stock of criminal profiling: A narrative review and meta-analysis. *Criminal Justice and Behavior, 34*, 437–453.

Snyder, H., & Sickmund, M. (2006). *Juvenile offenders and victims: 2006 national report.* Washington, DC: U.S. Department of Justice, Office of Justice Programs, Office of Juvenile Justice and Delinquency Prevention. (NCJ No. 212906).

Socia, K. M., 2012. The efficacy of county-level sex offender residence restrictions in New York. *Crime & Delinquency, 58*, 612–642.

Sojo, V., Wood, R., & Genat, A. (2016). Harmful workplace experiences and women's occupational well-being: A meta-analysis. *Psychology of Women Quarterly, 40*(1), 10–40.

Solomon, R. C. (1990). *A passion for justice.* Reading, MA: Addison-Wesley.

Sommers, S. (2006). On racial diversity and group decision making: Identifying multiple effects of racial composition on jury deliberations. *Journal of Personality and Social Psychology, 90*, 597–612.

Sommers, S. (2008). Determinants and consequences of jury racial diversity: Empirical findings, implications, and directions for future research. *Social Issues and Policy Review, 2*, 65–102.

Sommers, S., & Kassin, S. (2001). On the many impacts of inadmissible testimony: Selective compliance, need for cognition, and the overcorrection bias. *Personality and Social Psychology Bulletin, 27*, 1368–1377.

Sommers, S., & Norton, M. (2007). Race-based judgments, race-neutral justifications: Experimental examination of peremptory use and the *Batson* challenge procedure. *Law and Human Behavior, 31*, 261–273.

Sommers, S., Warp, L., & Mahoney, C. (2008). Cognitive effects of racial diversity: White individuals' information processing in heterogeneous groups. *Journal of Experimental Social Psychology, 44*, 1129–1136.

Sommers, S., & Ellsworth, P. C. (2000). Race in the courtroom: Perceptions of guilt and dispositional attributions. *Personality and Social Psychology Bulletin, 26*, 1367–1379.

Sorby, M., & Kehn, A. (2021). Juror perceptions of the stereotypical violent crime defendant. *Psychiatry, Psychology and Law, 28*, 645–664.

Sorenson, J., & Davis, J. (2011). Violent criminals locked up: Examining the effect of incarceration on behavioral continuity. *Journal of Criminal Science, 39*, 151–158.

Sowell v. Walker, 755 A. 2d 438 (2000).

Spano, L., Daftary-Kapur, T., & Penrod, S. (2011). Trial consulting in high-publicity cases. In B. Rosenfeld & S. Penrod (Eds.), *Research methods in forensic psychology* (pp. 215–236). New York, NY: Wiley.

Spence, S. A., Kaylor-Hughes, C., Brook, M., Lankappa, S. T., & Wilkinson, I. D. (2008). "Munchausen's syndrome by proxy" or a "miscarriage of justice"? An initial application of functional neuroimaging to the question of guilt versus innocence. *European Psychiatry, 23*, 309–314.

Spencer, B. (2007). Estimating the accuracy of jury verdicts. *Journal of Empirical Legal Studies, 4*, 305–329.

Spencer, S. (2013, August 30). NFL concussion class-action lawsuit settles for $765 mil. *The Legal Intelligencer*. Retrieved from http://www.thelegalintelligencer.com/id=1202617468396/NFL-Concussion-Class-Action-Lawsuit-Settles-for-$765-Mil

Spengler, P., Walters, N., Bruan, E., & Millspaugh, B. (2020). Attorneys' attitudes toward coaching forensic clients on the MMPI-2: Replication and extension of attorney survey by Wetter and Corrigan (1995). *Journal of Personality Assessment, 102*(1), 56–65.

Spitz, H. (1989). Variations in Wechsler interscale IQ disparities at different levels of IQ. *Intelligence, 13*, 157–167.

Spivak, B., Ogloff, J., Clough, J., Tinsley, Y., & Young, W. (2020). The impact of fact-based instructions on juror application of the law: Results from a trans-Tasman field study. *Social Science Quarterly, 101*, 346–361.

Spohn, C. (2015). Race, crime, and punishment in the twentieth and twenty-first centuries. *Crime & Justice, 44*, 49–97.

Sporer, S. (2001). Recognizing faces of other ethnic groups: An integration of theories. *Psychology, Public Policy, and Law, 7*, 170–200.

Stanovich, K. E., West, R. F., & Toplak, M. E. (2013). Myside bias, rational thinking, and intelligence. *Current Directions in Psychological Science, 22*, 259–264.

State of North Carolina v. Jackson, No. COA10-1135 (N.C. Ct. App. Oct. 1, 2011).

State v. Henderson (No. 062218), (N.J. Supreme Court 2011).

State v. Lawson. 352 Or. 724, 291 P.3d 673 (2012).

State v. Lozano, 616 So. 2d 73 (Fla. App. 1993).

Steadman, H. (1979). *Beating a rap? Defendants found incompetent to stand trial.* University of Chicago Press.

Steadman, H. J., & Braff, J. (1983). Defendants not guilty by reason of insanity. In J. Monahan & H. J. Steadman (Eds.), *Mentally disordered offenders: Perspectives from law and social science* (pp. 109–132). New York, NY: Plenum.

Steadman, H. J., McGreevy, M., Morrissey, J., Callahan, L., Robbin, P., & Cirincione, C. (1993). *Before and after Hinckley: Evaluating insanity defense reform.* New York, NY: Guilford.

Steadman, H. J., & Naples, M. (2005). Assessing the effectiveness of jail diversion programs for persons with serious mental illness and co-occurring substance use disorders. *Behavioral Sciences & the Law, 23*, 163–170.

Steadman, H. J., Osher, F. C., Robbins, P. C., Case, B., Samuels, S. (2009). Prevalence of serious mental illness among jail inmates. *Psychiatric Services, 60*, 761–765.

Steblay, N. (2015). Eyewitness memory. In B. Cutler & P. Zapf (Eds.), *APA Handbook of forensic psychology, Vol. 2. Criminal investigation, adjudication, and sentencing outcomes* (pp. 187–224). Washington, DC: APA.

Steblay, N., Besirevic, J., Fulero, S., & Jiminez-Lorente, B. (1999). The effects of pretrial publicity on jury verdicts: A meta-analytic review. *Law and Human Behavior, 23*, 219–235.

Steblay, N., Dysart, J., & Wells, G. (2011). Seventy-two tests of the sequential lineup superiority effect: A meta-analysis and policy discussion. *Psychology, Public Policy, and Law, 17*, 99–139.

Steblay, N., Hosch, H., Culhane, S., & McWerthy, A. (2006). The impact on juror verdicts of judicial instruction to disregard inadmissible evidence: A meta-analysis. *Law and Human Behavior, 30*, 469–492.

Steblay, N. (2013). Lineup instructions. In B. Cutler (Ed.), *Reform of eyewitness identification procedures* (pp. 65–81). Washington, DC: APA.

Steblay, N., Wells, G., & Douglass, A. B. (2014). The eyewitness post-identification feedback effect 15 years later: Theoretical and policy implications. *Psychology, Public Policy, and Law, 20*, 1–18.

Steffensmeier, D., & Demuth, S. (2006). Does gender modify the effects of race-ethnicity on criminal sanctioning? Sentences for male and female White, Black, and Hispanic defendants. *Journal of Quantitative Criminology, 22*, 241–261.

Steffensmeier, D., Painter-Davis, N., & Ulmer, J. (2017). Intersectionality of race, ethnicity, gender, and age on criminal punishment. *Sociological Perspectives, 60*, 810–833.

Steinberg, L. (2017). Adolescent brain science and juvenile justice policymaking. *Psychology, Public Policy, and Law, 23*, 410–420.

Steiner, B., Hemmens, C., and Bell, V. (2006). Legislative waiver reconsidered: General deterrent effects of statutory exclusion laws enacted post-1979. *Justice Quarterly, 23*, 33–59.

Steiner, B., & Wright, E. (2006). Assessing the relative effects of state direct file waiver laws on violent juvenile crime: Deterrence or irrelevance? *The Journal of Criminal Law and Criminology, 96*, 1451–1477.

Sternlight, J., & Robbennolt, J. (2015). Psychology and effective lawyering: Insights for legal educators. *Journal of Legal Education, 64*, 365–384.

Stevens, R. (1983). *Law school: Legal education in America from the 1850s to the 1980s.* Chapel Hill, NC: University of North Carolina Press.

Stevenson, R. L. (1886). *The strange case of Dr. Jekyll and Mr. Hyde.* London: Longmans, Green & Co.

St. George, S., Garcia-Johnson, A., Denne, E., & Stolzenberg, S. (2020). "Did you ever fight back?" Jurors' questions to children testifying in criminal trials about alleged sexual abuse. *Criminal Justice & Behavior, 47*, 1032–1054.

Stinchcomb, J. (2004). Searching for stress in all the wrong places: Combating chronic organizational stressors in policing. *Police Practice and Research, 5*, 259–277.

Stinson, V., & Cutler, B. (2011). Training of trial consultants. In R. Wiener & B. Bornstein (Eds.), *Handbook of trial consulting* (pp. 331–350). New York, NY: Springer.

Stinson, V., Devenport, J. L., Cutler, B. L., & Kravitz, D. A. (1997). How effective is the motion-to-suppress safeguard? Judges' perceptions of the suggestiveness and fairness of biased lineup procedures. *Journal of Applied Psychology, 82*(2), 211–220. https://doi.org/10.1037/0021-9010.82.2.211

Stipanowich, T. (2010). Arbitration: The "new litigation." *University of Illinois Law Review, 2010*, 1–58.

Stolle, D., & Studebaker, C. (2011). Trial consulting and conflicts of interest: An introduction. In R. Wiener & B. Bornstein (Eds.), *Handbook of trial consulting* (pp. 351–370). New York, NY: Springer.

Stoneleigh Foundation (2022). *Enhancing juvenile probation through Graduated Response implementation.* Retrieved February 5, 2022, from https://stoneleighfoundation.org/project/enhancing-juvenile-probation-through-graduated-response-implementation/

Storm, J., & Graham, J. (2000). Detection of coached general malingering on the MMPI-2. *Psychological Assessment, 12*, 158–165.

Storm, K., & Rothmann, S. (2003). A psychometric analysis of the Maslach Burnout Inventory-General Survey in the South African Police Service. *South African Journal of Psychology, 33*, 219–226.

Strauder v. West Virginia, 100 U.S. 303 (1880).

Straus, M. (2011). Gender symmetry and mutuality in perpetration of clinical-level partner violence: Empirical evidence and implications for prevention and treatment. *Aggression and Violent Behavior, 16*, 279–288.

Strier, F. (1999). Whither trial consulting? Issues and projections. *Law and Human Behavior, 23*, 93–115.

Strier, F. (2011). Reform proposals. In R. Wiener & B. Bornstein (Eds.), *Handbook of trial consulting* (pp. 371–392). New York, NY: Springer.

Strömwall, L., & Granhag, P. (2003). How to detect deception? Arresting the beliefs of police officers, prosecutors and judges. *Psychology, Crime and Law, 9*,19–36.

Strömwall, L., & Willen, R. (2011). Inside criminal minds: Offenders' strategies when lying. *Journal of Investigative Psychology and Offender Profiling, 8, 271–281.*

Stryker, J. (2005). *Using shame as punishment. Have sex, get infamous.* Retrieved from http://articles.sfgate.com/2005-03-13/-opinion/17365359_1_shame -prostitution-legal-system

Studebaker, C., Robbennolt, J., Penrod, S., Pathak-Sharma, M., Groscup, J., & Devenport, J. (2002). Studying pretrial publicity effects: New methods for improving ecological validity and testing external validity. *Law and Human Behavior, 26*, 19–42.

Stukas, A., & Snyder, M. (2002). Targets' awareness of expectations and behavioral confirmation in ongoing interactions. *Journal of Experimental Social Psychology, 38*, 31–40.

Suarez, E., & Gadalla, T. (2010). Stop blaming the victim: A meta-analysis on rape myths. *Journal of Interpersonal Violence, 25*, 2010–2035.

Suchotzki, K., Verschuere, B., Bockstaele, B., Ben-Shakhar, G., & Crombez, G. (2017). Lying takes time: A meta-analysis on reaction time measures of deception. *Psychological Bulletin, 143*, 428–453.

Sullivan, T. P. (2008). Recording federal custodial interviews. *American Criminal Law Review, 45*, 1297–1345.

Sunstein, C., Hastie, R., Payne, J., Schkade, D., & Viscusi, W. (2002). *Punitive damages: How juries decide.* Chicago, IL: University of Chicago Press.

Sutherland, E. H., & Cressey, D. R. (1974). *Principles of criminology* (9th ed.). New York, NY: Lippincott.

Swahn, M. H., Whitaker, D. J., Pippen, C. B., Leeb, R. T., Teplin, L. A., Abram, K. M., & McClelland, G. M. (2006). Concordance between self-reported maltreatment and court records of abuse or neglect among high-risk youths. *American Journal of Public Health: Mental Health for Individuals and Communities, 96*, 1849–1853.

Swain v. Alabama, 380 U.S. 202 (1965).

Swartz, M., Bhattacharya, S., Robertson, A., & Swanson, J. (2017). Involuntary outpatient commitment and the elusive pursuit of violence prevention: A view from the United States. *Canadian Journal of Psychiatry, 62*(2): 102–108. doi: 10.1177/0706743716675857

Sydeman, S. J., Cascardi, M., Poythress, N. G., & Ritterband, L. M. (1997). Procedural justice in the context of civil commitment: A critique of Tyler's analysis. *Psychology, Public Policy, and Law, 3*, 207–221.

Tanay, E. (2010). *American legal injustice: Behind the scenes with an expert witness.* Lanham, MD: Jason Aronson.

Tangney, J., & Dearing, R. (2002). *Shame and guilt.* New York: The Guilford Press.

Tangney, J. P., Stuewig, J., & Hafez, L. (2011). Shame, guilt, and remorse: Implications for offender populations. *Journal of Forensic Psychiatry & Psychology, 22*, 706–723.

Tanha, M., Beck, C., Figueredo, A., & Raghavan, C. (2010). Sex differences in intimate partner violence and the use of coercive control as a motivational factor for intimate partner violence. *Journal of Interpersonal Violence, 25*, 1836–1854.

Tan, J., & Fajardo, M. (2017). Efficacy of Multisystemic Therapy in youths aged 10–17 with severe antisocial behavior and emotional disorders: Systematic review. *London Journal of Primary Care (Abingdon), 9*(6), 95–103.

Tanielian, T., & Jayco, L., (Eds.) (2008). *Invisible wounds of war: Psychological and cognitive injuries, their consequences, and services to assist recovery.* Santa Monica, CA: RAND Corporation.

Tarasoff v. Regents of the University of California, 529 P. 2d 553 (1974), 551 P. 2d 334 (1976).

Tarescavage, A., Brewster, J., Corey, D., & Ben-Porath, Y. (2015). Use of pre-hire MMPI-2-RF police candidate scores to predict supervisor ratings of post-hire performance. Assessment, 22(4), 411–428. doi:10.1177/1073191114548445ß

Taylor, G. (1992, March 2). Justice overlooked. *National Law Journal*, p. 43.

Taylor, J., & Krauss, D. (2014). Revisiting intellectual disability and the death penalty. *APA Monitor, 45*, 26.

Taylor, S. E., Klein, L. C., Lewis, B. P., Gruenewald, T. L., Gurung, R. A. R., & Updegraff, J. A. (2000). Biobehavioral responses to stress in females: Tend-and-befriend, not fight-or-flight. *Psychological Review, 107*, 411–429.

Tedder-King, A., & Marinakis, C. (2016, October 3). Cut the bull: What can trial consultants really do? Retrieved from http://litigationinsights.com /jury-consulting/bull-cbs-trial-consultants-really-do/

Teller, J., Munetz, M., Gil, K., & Ritter, C. (2006). Crisis Intervention Team training for police officers responding to mental disturbance calls. *Psychiatric Services, 57*, 232–237.

Temcheff, C. E., Serbin, L. A., Martin-Storey, A. Stack, D. M., Hodgins, S., Ledingham, J., & Schwartzman, A. E. (2008). Continuity and pathways from aggression in childhood to family violence in adulthood: A 30-year longitudinal study. *Journal of Family Violence, 23*(4), 231–242.

Tennessee v. Garner, 471 U.S. 1 (1985).

Teplin, L. A. (1984). The criminalization of the mentally ill: Speculation in search of data. In L. A. Teplin (Ed.), *Mental health and criminal justice* (pp. 63–85). Newbury Park, CA: Sage.

Terman, L. M. (1917). A trial of mental and pedagogical tests in a civil service examination for policemen and firemen. *Journal of Applied Psychology, 1*, 17–29.

Terpstra, J., & Schaap, D. (2013). Police culture, stress conditions, and working styles. *European Journal of Criminology, 10*, 59–73. doi:10.1177/1477370812456343

Thibaut, J., & Walker, L. (1978). A theory of procedure. *California Law Review, 66*, 541–566.

Thibaut, J.W. and Walker, L. (1975). *Procedural justice: A psychological analysis.* L. Erlbaum Associates.

Thiele, J., & Martinez, R. (2016). Ability to waive the right to counsel when competency is questioned. *Journal of the American Academy of Psychiatry and the Law Online, 44*(4), 507–509.

Thomas, C. (1996, April 8). *Judging.* Invited address, School of Law, University of Kansas, Lawrence, KS.

Thomas, S. (2017). What happened to the American jury? Proposals for revamping plea bargaining and summary judgment. *Litigation, 43.* Retrieved from https://ssrn.com/abstract=2974069

Thompson, M., Osher, F., & Tomasini-Joshi, D. (2007). *Improving responses to people with mental illnesses: The essential elements of a mental health court.* New York, NY: Council of State Governments Justice Center.

Thompson, W. C., Cowan, C. L., Ellsworth, P. C., & Harrington, J. C. (1984). Death penalty attitudes and conviction proneness: The translation of attitudes into verdicts. *Law and Human Behavior, 8*, 95–113.

Thorley, C., Beaton, L. Deguara, P., Jerome, B., Khan, D., & Schopp, K. (2020). Misinformation encountered during a simulated jury deliberation can distort jurors' memory of a trial and bias their verdicts. *Legal and Criminological Psychology, 25*, 150–164.

Tillbrook, C., Mumley, D., & Grisso, T. (2003). Avoiding expert opinions on the ultimate legal question: The case for integrity. *Journal of Forensic Psychology Practice, 3*, 77–87.

Tjaden, P., & Thoennes, N. (2006). *Extent, nature, and consequences of rape victimization: Findings from the National Violence Against Women Survey.* Washington, DC: National Institute of Justice, Office of Justice Programs.

Tombaugh, T. (1997). *TOMM: Test of Memory Malingering manual.* Toronto, ON: Multi-Health Systems.

Tonry, M. (1996). *Sentencing matters.* New York, NY: Oxford University Press.

Tonry, M., & Melewski, M. (2008). The malign effects of drug and crime control policies on Black Americans. *Crime and Justice, 37*, 1–44.

Toot, J., Dunphy, G., Turner, M., & Ely, D. (2004). The SHR Y-chromosome increases testosterone and aggression, but decreases serotonin as compared to the WKY Y-chromosome in the rat model. *Behavioral Genetics, 34*, 515–524.

Tor, A., Gazal-Ayal, O., & Garcia, S. (2010). Fairness and willingness to accept plea bargain offers. *Journal of Empirical Legal Studies, 7*, 97–116.

Torres, A., Boccaccini, M., & Miller, H. (2006). Perceptions of the validity and utility of criminal profiling among forensic psychologists and psychiatrists. *Professional Psychology: Research and Practice, 37*, 51–58.

Trahan, L., Stuebing, K., Fletcher, J., & Hiscock, M. (2014). The Flynn effect: A meta-analysis. *Psychological Bulletin, 140*, 1332–1360.

Trickner, R., Jackson, J. & Tyler, T. (2018). Bounded authority: Expanding "appropriate" police behavior beyond procedural justice. *Law and Human Behavior, 42*, 280–293.

Trinkner, R., Tyler, T., & Goff, P. (2016). Justice from within: The relations between a procedurally just organizational climate and police organizational efficiency, endorsement of democratic policing, and officer well-being. *Psychology, Public Policy, and Law, 22*, 158–172.

Trivedi, S. B. (2011). Intellectual differences between violent and nonviolent juveniles: Utilizing the Wechsler Abbreviated Scale of Intelligence: A study of three ethnic groups. *Dissertation Abstracts International: Section B: The Sciences and Engineering, 71*(10-B), 6454.

Trop v. Dulles, 356 U.S. 86 (1958).

Trope, Y., & Liberman, N. (2003). Temporal construal. *Psychological Review, 110*, 403–421.

Trulson, C., Caudill, J., Belshaw, S., & DeLisi, M. (2011). A problem of fit: Extreme delinquents, blended sentencing, and the determinants of continued adult sanctions. *Criminal Justice Policy Review, 22*, 263–284.

Trulson, C., Haerle, D., DeLisi, M., & Marquart, J. (2011). Blended sentencing, early release, and recidivism of violent institutionalized delinquents. *Prison Journal, 92*, 255–278.

Trupin, E., & Richards, H. (2003). Seattle's mental health courts: Early indicators of effectiveness. *International Journal of Law & Psychiatry, 26*, 33–53.

Tsai, J., Finlay, A., Flatley, B., Kasprow, W., & Clark, S. (2018). A national study of veterans treatment court participants: Who benefits and who recidivates. *Administration and Policy in Mental Health and Mental Health Services Research, 45*(2), 236–244.

Tsao, E. (2014). The impact of jury instruction formatting and insanity defense consistency on juror knowledge and decision-making. Scripps Senior Theses, Paper 549. http://scholarship.claremont.edu/scripps_theses/549

Tullett, A. (2022). The limitations of social science as the arbiter of blame: An argument for abandoning retribution. *Perspectives on Psychological Science. 17*(4), 995–1007. doi.org/10.1177/17456916211033284

Tulving, E. (1981). Similarity relations in recognition. *Journal of Verbal Learning and Verbal Behavior, 20*, 479–496.

Turner, J. (2021). Transparency in plea bargaining. *Notre Dame Law Review, 96*, 973–1024.

Turner, J., & Sexton, C. (2020, June 9). https://www.news4jax.com/news/local/2020/06/09/gov-approves-21-million-for-jacksonville-man-wrongfully-imprisoned/ Downloaded August 28, 2022.

Turner, S., Greenwood, P., Fain, T., & Deschenes, E. (1999). Perceptions of drug court: How offenders view ease of program completion, strengths and weaknesses, and the impact on their lives. *National Drug Court Institute Review, 2*, 61–85.

Turvey, B. (2012). *Criminal profiling: An introduction to behavioral evidence analysis* (4th ed.). Burlington, MA: Elsevier.

Tyler, T. (1990). *Why people obey the law.* New Haven, CT: Yale University Press.

Tyler, T., & Huo, Y. (2002). *Trust in the law: Encouraging public cooperation with the police and court.* New York, NY: Russell Sage Foundation.

Tyler, T. R., & Jackson, J. (2014). Popular legitimacy and the exercise of legal authority: Motivating compliance, cooperation and engagement. *Psychology, Public Policy, and Law, 20*, 78–95.

U.S. Department of Education, Office for Civil Rights. (2001). *Revised sexual harassment guidance: Harassment of students by school employees, other students, or third parties.* Washington, DC: Author. Retrieved November 10, 2016, from http://www2.ed.gov/about/offices/list/ocr/docs/shguide.pdf

U.S. Department of Justice. (1999). *Eyewitness evidence: A guide for law enforcement.* Washington, DC: Author.

U.S. Department of Justice. (2017). *Sex Offender Management Assessment and Planning Initiative.* Retrieved May 3, 2022, from https://smart.ojp.gov/somapi/initiative-home

U.S. Equal Employment Opportunity Commission. (2016). *Select task force on the study of harassment in the workforce: Report of co-chairs.* Washington, DC: Author. Retrieved November 10, 2016, from https://www.eeoc.gov/eeoc/task_force/harassment/upload/report.pdf

U.S. Public Health Service. (1999). *Mental health: A report of the Surgeon General.* Rockville, MD: U.S. Department of Health and Human Services, National Institutes of Health, National Institute of Mental Health.

U.S. Sentencing Commission. (2017). *Mandatory minimum penalties for drug offenses in the federal system.* Washington DC: U.S. Sentencing Commission.

U.S. Sentencing Commission. (2022). *Compassionate release. The impact of the First Step Act and COVID-19 Pandemic.* Washington DC: U.S. Sentencing Commission.

U.S. v. Tsarnaev. Oyez. Retrieved July 1, 2022, from www.oyez.org/cases/2021/20-443

Ulmer, J., Eisenstein, J., & Johnson, B. (2010). Trial penalties in federal sentencing: Extra-guidelines factors and district variation. *Justice Quarterly, 27*, 560–592.

Umbreit, M., Vos, G., Coates, R., & Lightfoot, E. (2005). Restorative justice in the 21st century: A social movement full of opportunities and pitfalls. *Marquette Law Review, 89*, 251–304.

United States Department of Justice, Community Oriented Policing Services. (2016). *Grants and funding.* Retrieved December 17, 2016, from http://cops.usdoj.gov

United States Office of Personnel Management. (2008). *Structured interviews: A practical guide.* Washington, DC: Author. Retrieved October 27, 2016, from https://www.opm.gov/policy-data-oversight/-assessment-and-selection/structured-interviews/guide.pdf

United States v. Booker, 125 S. Ct. 735 (2005).

United States v. Kowalczyk, 805 F.3d 847 (9th Cir. 2015).

United States v. Salerno, 481 U.S. 739 (1987).

van den Berg, J. W., Smid, W., Schepers, K., Wever, E., van Beek, D., Janssen, E., & Gijs, L. (2017). The predictive properties of dynamic sex offender risk assessment instruments: A meta-analysis. *Psychological Assessment. 30*(2), 179–191.

Vardsveen, T. C., & Wiener, R. L. (2021). Public support for sentencing reform: A policy-capturing experiment. *Journal of Experimental Psychology: Applied, 27*(2), 430–446.

Vecchi, G. (2009). Conflict and crisis communication: A methodology for influencing and persuading behavioral change. *Annals of the American Psychotherapy Association, 12*, 34–42.

Velopulos, C., Carmichael, H., Zakrison, T., & Crandall, M. (2019). Comparison of male and female victims of intimate partner homicide and bidirectionality: An analysis of the national violent death reporting system. *Journal of Trauma and Acute Care Surgery, 87*(2), 331–336.

Verlinden, S., Hersen, M., & Thomas, J. (2000). Risk factors in school shootings. *Clinical Psychology Review, 20*, 3–56.

Verona, E., & Vitale, J. (2018). Psychopathy in women: Assessment, manifestations, and etiology. In C. J. Patrick (Ed.), *Handbook of psychopathy* (pp. 509–528). New York: Guilford Press.

Verschuere, B., Bogaard, G., & Meijer, E. (2021). Discriminating deceptive from truthful statements using the verifiability approach: A meta-analysis. *Applied Cognitive Psychology 35*, 374–384.

Veysey, B. (2015). Gender role incongruence and the adjudication of criminal responsibility. *Albany Law Review, 78*(3), 1087–1107.

Victor, T. L., & Abeles, N. (2004). Coaching clients to take psychological and neuropsychological tests: A clash of ethical obligations. *Practice Issues in Forensic Psychology, 35*, 373–379.

Vidmar, N. (2002). Case studies of pre- and midtrial prejudice in criminal and civil litigation. *Law and Human Behavior, 26*, 73–106.

Vidmar, N. (2005). Expert evidence, the adversary system, and the jury. *American Journal of Public Health, 95*, S137–S143.

Vidmar, N. (2011). The psychology of trial judging. *Current Directions in Psychological Science, 20*, 58–62.

Vidmar, N., & Hans, V. P. (2007). *American juries. The verdict.* Amherst, NY: Prometheus.

Viglione, J., Hannon, L., & DeFina, R. (2011). The impact of light skin on prison time for Black female offenders. *Social Science Journal, 48*, 250–258.

Viljoen, J. L., Roesch, R., Ogloff, J. R. P., & Zapf, P. A. (2003). The role of Canadian psychologists in conducting fitness and criminal responsibility evaluations. *Canadian Psychology, 44*, 369–381.

Viljoen, J., Wingrove, T., & Ryba, N. (2008). Adjudicative competence evaluations of juvenile and adult defendants: Judges' views regarding essential components of competence reports. *The International Journal of Forensic Mental Health, 7*, 107–119.

Vinson, K. V., Costanzo, M. A., & Berger, D. E. (2008). Predictors of verdict and punitive damages in high-stakes civil litigation. *Behavioral Sciences & the Law, 26*, 167–186.

Violanti, J. M., Fekedulegn, D., Hartley, T., Charles, L., Andrew, M., Ma, C., & Burchfiel, C. (2016). Highly rated and most frequent stressors among police officers: Gender differences. *American Journal of Criminal Justice, 43*(4), 645–662.

Vitacco, M. J., Rogers, R., & Gabel, J. (2009). An investigation of the ECST-R in male pretrial patients: Evaluating the effects of feigning on competency evaluations. *Assessment, 16*, 249–257.

Vitale, J. E., & Newman, J. P. (2001). Using the Psychopathy Checklist—Revised with female samples: Reliability, validity, and implications for clinical utility. *Clinical Psychology: Science & Practice, 8*, 117–132.

Vorms, M., & Lagnado, D. (2022). Evidential reasoning and story building: A critical examination of the story model. *Droit et Societe, 110*, 87–105.

Vossekuil, B., Fein, R., Reddy, M., Borum, R., & Modzeleski, W. (2004). *The final report and findings of the safe school initiative: Implications for the prevention of school attacks in the United States.* Washington, DC: United States Secret Service and United States Department of Education.

Vrij, A. (2015). Deception detection. In B. Cutler & P. Zapf (Eds.), *APA handbook of forensic psychology: Vol 2. Criminal investigation, adjudication, and sentencing outcomes* (pp. 225–244). Washington, DC: APA.

Vrij, A. (2019). Deception and truth detection when analyzing nonverbal and verbal cues. *Applied Cognitive Psychology, 33*, 160–167.

Vrij, A., Granhag, P., & Porter, S. (2010). Pitfalls and opportunities in nonverbal and verbal lie detection. *Psychological Science in the Public Interest, 11*, 89–121.

Vrij, A., Leal, S., Granhag, P. A., Mann, S., Fisher, R. P., Hillman, J., & Spery, K. (2009). Outsmarting the liars: The benefit of asking unanticipated questions. *Law and Human Behavior, 33*, 159–166.

Vrij, A., Mann, S., Fisher, R., Leal, S., Milne, B., & Bull, R. (2008). Increasing cognitive load to facilitate lie detection: The benefit of recalling an event in reverse order. *Law and Human Behavior, 32*, 253–265.

Wade, K., Garry, M., Read, J., & Lindsay, D. (2002). A picture is worth a thousand lies: Using false photographs to create false childhood memories. *Psychonomic Bulletin & Review, 9*, 597–603.

Walker, L. E. (1979). *The battered woman.* New York, NY: Harper & Row.

Walker, L. E. (2009). *The battered woman syndrome* (3rd ed.). New York, NY: Springer.

Wallerstein, J., & Blakeslee, S. (2003). *What about the kids? Raising your children before, during, and after divorce.* New York, NY: Hyperion.

Wallerstein, J., & Kelly, J. (1980). *Surviving the breakup*: New York, NY: Basic Books.

Walsh, B. (2012). *Oil spill: Why the BP settlement is just the beginning of the end.* Retrieved April 3, 2012, from http://ecocentric.blogs.time.com/2012/03/03/oil-spill-why-the-bp-settlement-is-just-the-beginning-of-the-end/

Walters, G. (2002). The Psychological Inventory of Criminal Thinking Styles (PICTS): A review and meta-analysis. *Assessment, 9*, 278–291.

Walters, G. D., & Mandell, W. (2007). Assessing the incremental validity of the Psychological Inventory of Criminal Thinking Styles (PICTS) and Psychopathy Checklist: Screening Version (PCL: SV) with disciplinary report count data. *Law and Human Behavior, 31*, 141–157.

Waltz, J., Babcock, J. C., Jacobson, N. S., & Gottman, J. M. (2000). Testing a typology of batterers. *Journal of Consulting and Clinical Psychology, 68*, 658–669.

Wang, J., Iannotti, R., Luk, J., & Nansel, T. (2010). Co-occurrence of victimization from five subtypes of bullying: Physical, verbal, social exclusion, spreading rumors, and cyber. *Journal of Pediatric Psychology, 35*, 1103–1112.

Ward, T., & Brown, M. (2004). The good lives model and conceptual issues in offender rehabilitation. *Psychology, Crime, & Law, 13*(3), 243–257.

Warren, E. (1977). *The memoirs of Earl Warren.* Garden City, NY: Doubleday.

Waterhouse, G., Ridley, A., Bull, R., La Rooy, D., & Wilcock, R. (2016). Dynamics of repeated interviews with children. *Applied Cognitive Psychology, 30*, 713–721.

Waterman, A., Blades, M., & Spencer, C. (2001). Interviewing children and adults: The effect of question format on the tendency to speculate. *Applied Cognitive Psychology, 15*, 521–531.

Watson, A., Ottati, V., Morabito, M., Draine, J., Kerr, A., & Angell, B. (2010). Outcomes of police contacts with persons with mental illness: The impact of CIT. *Administration and Policy in Mental Health and Mental Health Services Research, 37*, 302–317.

Watson, P. (1996). The search for justice—A case for reform in the civil justice system in Britain. *ILSA Journal of International and Comparative Law, 2*, 453.

Wegner, D. M. (1994). Ironic processes of mental control. *Psychological Review, 101*, 34–52.

Weiss, W., Davis, R., Rostow, C., & Kinsman, S. (2003). The MMPI-2 L scale as a tool in police selection. *Journal of Police and Criminal Psychology, 18*, 57–60.

Wells, G. (1978). Applied eyewitness testimony research: System variables and estimator variables. *Journal of Personality and Social Psychology, 36*, 1546–1557.

Wells, G. (1993). What do we know about eyewitness identification? *American Psychologist, 48*, 553–571.

Wells, G. L. (2020). Psychological science on eyewitness identification and its impact on police practices and policies. *American Psychologist, 75*, 1316–1329.

Wells, G. L., & Bradfield, A. L. (1998). "Good, you identified the suspect": Feedback to eyewitnesses distorts their reports of the witnessing experience. *Journal of Applied Psychology, 83*(3), 360–376. https://doi.org/10.1037/0021-9010.83.3.360

Wells, G. L., Kovera, M. B., Douglass, A. B., Brewer, N., Meissner, C., & Wixted, J. (2020). Policy and procedure recommendations for the collection and preservation of eyewitness identification evidence. *Law and Human Behavior, 44*, 3–36. https://doi-org.lprx.bates.edu/10.1037/lhb0000359

Wells, G. L., Yang, Y., & Smalarz, L. (2015). Eyewitness identification: Bayesian information gain, base-rate effect equivalency curves, and reasonable suspicion. *Law and Human Behavior, 39*(2), 99–122. https://doi.org/10.1037/lhb0000125

Wells, G., & Luus, C. (1990). Police lineups as experiments: Social methodology as a framework for properly conducted lineups. *Personality and Social Psychology Bulletin, 16*, 106–117.

Wells, G., & Quinlivan, D. (2009). Suggestive eyewitness identification procedures and the Supreme Court's reliability test in light of eyewitness science: 30 years later. *Law and Human Behavior, 33*, 1–24.

Wells, G., Small, M., Penrod, S., Malpass, R., Fulero, S., & Brimacombe, C. (1998). Eyewitness identification procedures: Recommendations for lineups and photospreads. *Law and Human Behavior, 22*, 603–647.

Wells, G., Steblay, N., & Dysart, J. (2015). Double-blind lineup procedures using actual eyewitnesses: An experimental test of the sequential versus simultaneous lineup procedure. *Law and Human Behavior, 39*, 1–14.

Wells, G., Wrightsman, L., & Miene, P. (1985). The timing of the defense opening statement: Don't wait until the evidence is in. *Journal of Applied Social Psychology, 15*, 758–772.

Wells, G., Small, M., Penrod, S., Malpass, R. S., Fulero, S. M., & Brimacombe, C. A. E. (1998). Eyewitness identification procedures: Recommendations for lineups and photospreads. *Law and Human Behavior, 22*, 603–647.

Wendzel, B. (2020). Not guilty, yet continuously confined: Reforming the insanity defense. *American Criminal Law Review, 57*(2), 391–411.

Wertz, J., Caspi, A., Belshy, D., Beckley, A., Arseneault, L., Barnes, J., Corcoran, D., Hogan, S., Houts, R., Morgan, N., Odgers, C., Prinz, J., Sugden, K., Williams, B., Poulton, R., & Moffitt, T. (2018). Genetics and crime: Integrating new genomic discoveries into psychological research about antisocial behavior. *Psychological Science, 29*(5), 791–803.

Wexler, D., & Winick, B. (Eds.). (1996). *Law in a therapeutic key: Developments in therapeutic jurisprudence.* Durham, NC: Carolina Academic Press.

Wexler, D. (1992). Putting mental health into mental health law: Therapeutic jurisprudence. *Law and Human Behavior, 16*, 27–38.

Whalen v. United States, 346 F. 2d 812 (1965).

Whren et al. v. United States, 517 U.S. 806 (1996).

Widman, L., & Olson, M. (2013). On the relationship between automatic attitudes and self-reported sexual assault in men. *Archives of Sex Behavior, 42*, 813–823.

Widom, C. S. (1989). Child abuse, neglect, and adult behavior: Research design and findings on criminality, violence, and child abuse. *American Journal of Orthopsychiatry, 59*, 355–367.

Widom, C. S. (1992). *The cycle of violence: National Institute of Justice Research in brief.* Washington, DC: U.S. Department of Justice.

Widom, C. S., Schuck, A., & White, H. (2006). An examination of pathways from childhood victimization to violence: The role of early aggression and problematic alcohol use. *Violence and Victims, 21*, 675–690.

Wiener, R., Arnot, L., Winter, R., & Redmond, B. (2006). Generic prejudice in the law: Sexual assault and homicide. *Basic and Applied Social Psychology, 28*, 145–155.

Wiener, R., Bornstein, B., & Voss, A. (2006). Emotion and the law: A framework for inquiry. *Law and Human Behavior, 30*, 231–248.

Wiener, R., & Gutek, B. (1999). Advances in sexual harassment research, theory, and policy. *Psychology, Public Policy, and Law, 5*, 507–518.

Wiener, R., Hurt, L., Russell, B., Mannen, K., & Gasper, C. (1997). Perceptions of sexual harassment: The effects of gender, legal standard, and ambivalent sexism. *Law and Human Behavior, 21*, 71–94.

Wiener, R., Rogers, M., Winter, R., Hurt, L., Hackney, A., Kadela, K., … Morasco, B. (2004). Guided jury discretion in capital murder cases: The role of declarative and procedural knowledge. *Psychology, Public Policy, and Law, 10*, 516–576.

Wiener, R., Winick, B., Georges, L., & Castro, A. (2010). A testable theory of problem-solving courts: Avoiding past empirical and legal failures. *International Journal of Law and Psychiatry, 33*, 417–427.

Wikstrom, P., Ceccato, V., Hardie, B., & Treiber, K. (2010). Activity fields and the dynamics of crime: Advancing knowledge about the role of the environment in crime causation. *Journal of Quantitative Criminology, 26*, 55–87.

Wikstrom, P. H., & Loeber, R. (2000). Do disadvantaged neighborhoods cause well-adjusted children to become adolescent delinquents? A study of male juvenile serious offending, individual risk and protective factors, and neighborhood context. *Criminology, 38*(4), 1109–1142.

Wilcox, P., Sullivan, L., Jones, S., & van Gelder, J. (2014). Personality and opportunity: An integrated approach to offending and victimization. *Criminal Justice and Behavior, 41*, 880–901.

Wilcox, P., Sullivan, L., Jones, S., & van Gelder, J. (2014). Personality and opportunity: An integrated approach to offending and victimization. *Criminal Justice and Behavior, 41*, 880–901.

Wilford, M., & Bornstein, B. (2021). The disappearing trial: How social scientists can help save the jury from extinction. *Psychology, Crime & Law*, in press.

Wilford, M., Van Horn, M., Penrod, S., & Greathouse, S. (2018). Not separate but equal? The impact of multiple-defendant trials on juror decision-making. *Psychology, Crime, and Law, 24*, 14–37.

Wilkenfeld, J. (2004). Newly compelling: Reexamining judicial construction of juries in the aftermath of *Grutter v. Bollinger. Columbia Law Review, 104*, 2291–2327.

Wilkinson, R. (2001). Offender reentry: A storm overdue. *Corrections Management Quarterly, 5*, 46–51.

Williams, K., & Houghton, A. (2004). Assessing the risk of domestic violence reoffending: A validation study. *Law and Human Behavior, 24*, 437–455.

Williams, M. (2016). From bail to jail: The effect of jail capacity on bail decisions. *American Journal of Criminal Justice, 41*, 484–497.

Willness, C. R., Steel, P., & Lee, K. (2007). A meta-analysis of the antecedents and consequences of workplace sexual harassment. *Personnel Psychology, 60*, 127–162. doi:10.1111/j.1744-6570.2007.00067.x

Wilson, D., Mitchell, O., & Mackenzie, D. (2006). A systematic review of drug court effects on recidivism. *Journal of Experimental Criminology, 2*, 459–487.

Wilson, J. L., Bandyopadhyay, S., Yang, H., Cerulli, C., & Morse, D. S. (2018). Identifying predictors of substance use and recidivism outcome trajectories among drug treatment court clients. *Criminal Justice and Behavior, 45*, 447–467.

Wilson, J. Q. (1975). *Thinking about crime.* New York, NY: Basic Books.

Wilson, J. Q., & Herrnstein, R. (1985). *Crime and human nature.* New York, NY: Simon & Schuster.

Wilson, T. (2002). *Strangers to ourselves: Discovering the adaptive unconscious.* Cambridge, MA: Harvard University Press.

Winick, B. (1996). Incompetency to proceed in the criminal process: Past, present, and future. In B. D. Sales & D. W. Shulman (Eds.), *Law, mental health, and mental disorder* (pp. 310–340). Pacific Grove, CA: Brooks/Cole.

Winick, B., Wiener, R., Castro, A., Emmert, A., & Georges, L. (2010). Dealing with mentally ill domestic violence perpetrators: A therapeutic jurisprudence judicial model. *International Journal of Law and Psychiatry 33*, 428–439.

Winslade, W. J., & Ross, J. W. (1983). *The insanity plea.* New York, NY: Scribners.

Winters, G. M., Colombino, N., Schaaf, S., Laake, A. L. W., Jeglic, E. L., & Calkins, C. (2020). Why do child sexual abuse victims not tell anyone about their abuse? An exploration of factors that prevent and promote disclosure. *Behavioral Sciences & the Law.* http://dx.doi.org/10.1002/bsl.2492

Wissler, R., & Dauber, B. (2007). Court-connected arbitration in the Superior Court of Arizona: A study of its performance and proposed rule changes. *Journal of Dispute Resolution, 2007*, 65–99.

Wistrich, A., Guthrie, C., & Rachlinski, J. (2005). Can judges ignore inadmissible information? The difficulty of deliberately disregarding. *University of Pennsylvania Law Review, 153*, 1251–1345.

Wistrich, A., & Rachlinski, J. (2013). How lawyers' intuitions prolong litigation. *Southern California Law Review, 86*, 571–636.

Wistrich, A., Rachlinski, J., & Guthrie, C. (2015). Heart versus head: Do judges follow the law or follow their feelings? *Texas Law Review, 93*, 855–923.

Witt, P., & Barone, N. (2004). Assessing sex offender risk: New Jersey's methods. *Federal Sentencing Reporter, 16*, 170.

Wixted, J. T., & Wells, G. (2017). The relationship between eyewitness confidence and identification accuracy: A new synthesis. *Psychological Science in the Public Interest, 18*, 10–65.

Woestehoff, S. A., & Meissner, C. A. (2016). Juror sensitivity to false confession risk factors: Dispositional vs. situational attributions for a confession. *Law and Human Behavior, 40*, 564–579.

Wogalter, M., Malpass, R., & McQuiston, D. (2004). A national survey of U.S. police on preparation and conduction of identification lineups. *Psychology, Crime, and Law, 10*, 69–82.

Wolf, S. M. (2009). A study of the differences in trauma related symptoms in adult female rape victims across levels of support systems. *Dissertation Abstracts International: Section B: The Sciences and Engineering, 69*(12-B), 7828.

Wolff, N., Fabrikant, N., & Belenko, S. (2011). Mental health courts and their selection processes: Modeling variation for consistency. *Law and Human Behavior, 35*, 402–412.

Woodworth, M., & Porter, S. (2000). Historical foundations and current applications of criminal profiling in violent crime investigations. *Expert Evidence, 7*, 241–264.

Woody, W. & Forrest, K. (2020). *Understanding police interrogation: Confessions and consequences.* New York: New York University Press.

Woolard, J., & Fountain, E. (2016). Serious questions about serious juvenile offenders: Patterns of offending and offenses. In K. Heilbrun, D. DeMatteo, & N. Goldstein (Eds.), *APA handbook of psychology and juvenile justice* (pp. 141–157). Washington, DC: American Psychological Association. doi:10.1037/14643-015

Wordsworth, A. (2005, January 7). Child-killer unfairly convicted, court rules: Expert witness misled jury in Andrea Yates trial. *National Post, Toronto Edition*, p. A13.

Wright, D. B., Boyd, C. E., & Tredoux, C. G. (2003). Inter-racial contact and the own-race bias for face recognition in South Africa and England. *Applied Cognitive Psychology, 17*(3), 365–373. https://doi.org/10.1002/acp.898

Wright, D. B., Self, G., & Justice, C. (2000). Memory conformity: Exploring misinformation effects when presented by another person. *British Journal of Psychology, 91*(2), 189–202. https://doi.org/10.1348/000712600161781

Wrightsman, Jr.(pp. 129–151). New York, NY: Springer-Verlag.

Wrightsman, L. (1999). *Judicial decision making: Is psychology relevant?* New York, NY: Kluwer Academic/Plenum Publishers.

Wrightsman, L. (2010). The Supreme Court on Miranda rights and interrogations: The past, the present, and the future. In G. D. Lassiter & C. Meissner (Eds.), *Police interrogations and false confessions* (pp. 161–178). Washington, DC: American Psychological Association.

Wrightsman, L., & Kassin, S. (1993). *Confessions in the courtroom.* Thousand Oaks, CA: Sage.

Wylie, L., Knutson, A., & Greene, E. (2017). Extraordinary and compelling: The use of compassionate release laws in the United States. *Psychology, Public Policy, and Law.*

Yip, J., & Schweitzer, M. (2016). Mad and misleading: Incidental anger promotes deception. *Organizational Behavior and Human Decision Processes, 137*, 207–217.

Yokum, D., Robertson, C. T., & Palmer, M. (2019). The inability to self-diagnose bias. *Denver University Law Review, 96*(4), 869–916.

York, E., & Cornwell, B. (2006). Status on trial: Social characteristics and influence in the jury room. *Social Forces, 85*, 455–477.

Yoshi, N., Ishiwara, T., & Tani, K. (2008). Juvenile delinquents and their abnormal EEG's (2) continuous theta waves. *Psychiatric and Clinical Neurosciences, 18*(2), 161–167. doi: 10.1111/j.1440-1819.1964.tb00021.x

Young, C. (2014). Employing virtual reality technology at trial: New issues posed by rapid technological advances and their effects on jurors' search for "the truth." *Texas Law Review, 93*, 257–274.

Zamble, E. (1992). Behavior and adaptation in long-term prison inmates. *Criminal Justice and Behavior, 19*, 409–425.

Zapf, P. A., & Roesch, R. (2011). Future directions in the restoration of competency to stand trial. *Current Directions in Psychological Science, 20*, 43–47.

Zapf, P., Boccaccini, M., & Brodsky, S. (2003). Assessment of competency for execution: Professional guidelines and an evaluation checklist. *Behavioral Sciences & the Law, 21*, 102–120.

Zapf, P., & Roesch, R. (2009). *Evaluation of competence to stand trial.* New York, NY: Oxford University Press.

Zapf, P., & Roesch, R. (2011). *Evaluation of competence to stand trial.* New York, NY: Oxford.

Zapf, P., Roesch, R., & Viljoen, J. (2001). Assessing fitness to stand trial: The utility of the Fitness Interview Test (revised edition). *Canadian Journal of Psychology, 46*(5), 426–432. doi: 10.1177/070674370104600508

Zaragoza, M., Hyman, I., & Chrobak, Q. M. (2019). False memory. In N. Brewer and A. B. Douglass (Eds.) *Psychological Science and the Law*, pp. 182–207. New York, NY: Guilford Press.

Zelechoski, A. (2016). Trauma, adverse experience, and offending. In K. Heilbrun, D. DeMatteo, & N. Goldstein (Eds.), *APA handbook of psychology and juvenile justice* (pp. 325–342). Washington, DC: American Psychological Association. doi:10.1037/-14643-007

Zelle, H., Romaine, C., & Goldstein, N. (2015). Juveniles' *Miranda* comprehension: Understanding, appreciation, and totality of circumstances factors. *Law and Human Behavior, 30*, 281–293.

Zembrowski, D. (2011). Sociological theories of crime and delinquency. *Journal of Human Behavior in the Social Environment, 21*, 240–254.

Zhang, S., Roberts, R., & Callanan, V. (2006). Preventing parolees from returning to prison through community-based reintegration. *Crime & Delinquency, 52*, 551–571.

Zimring, F., Fagan, J., & Johnson, D. (2010). Executions, deterrence, and homicide: A tale of two cities. *Journal of Empirical Legal Studies, 7*, 1–29.

Zirpolo, K. (2005, October 30). I'm sorry. *Los Angeles Times.* Retrieved July 27, 2022, from https://www.latimes.com/archives/la-xpm-2005-oct-30-tm-mcmartin44-story.html

Zottoli, T., Daftary-Kapur, T., Edkins, V., Redlich, A., King, C., Dervan, L., & Tahan, E. (2019). State of the states: A survey of statutory law, regulations and court rules pertaining to guilty pleas across the United States. *Behavioral Sciences and the Law, 37*, 388–434.

Zottoli, T., Daftary-Kapur, T., Winters, G., & Hogan, C. (2016). Plea discounts, time pressures, and false-guilty pleas in youth and adults who pleaded guilty to felonies in New York City. *Psychology, Public Policy, and Law, 22*, 250–259.

Zukov, I., Ptacek, R., & Fischer, S. (2008). EEG abnormalities in different types of criminal behavior. *Activitas Nervosa Superior, 50*, 110–113.

Name Index

A

Abbasi, H., 152
Abbott, Greg, 6, 11
Abeles, N., 217
Abram, K. M., 110, 122
Abrams, L., 284
Abramson, A., 69
Abramson, J., 255, 263, 273
Acharya, A., 73
Acharya, A. P., 73
Ackerman, M. C., 227
Ackerman, M. J., 227
Adams, B., 284
Adams, G., 134
Adams, R. E., 79
Affleck, K., 303
Ahmad, H., 136
Ahn, M., 23, 36, 161
Ailes, Roger, 119
Ainsworth, P., 126
Aizpurua, A., 86
Ajzen, I., 245
Akers, R. L., 52
Ake v. Oklahoma, 204
Albertson, S., 271
Albright, D., 71
Alceste, F., 143
Alexander, A., 191
Alexander, D., 118
Alexander, J., 300
Alexander, K., 99
Alexander, Travis, 122
Alfini, J. J., 245, 250
Alhabib, S., 110
Alison, E., 131
Alison, L., 131
Alito, Samuel, 7
Allen, T., 313
Alschuler, A. W., 145
Alton, S., 221
Altschuler, D., 304
Alvarado, G., 110
Amankwah, P. M., 86
Ama, S., 308, 309
Amato, P., 225
Ambadar, Z., 101
American Academy of Child and Adolescent
    Psychiatry, 225
American Bar Association, 33, 158
American Medical Association, 217
American Psychiatric Association, 50, 114
American Psychological Association (APA), 10,
    15, 19, 53–54, 58–59, 187, 226
American Psychological Association Task Force on
    Violent Media, 53
American Society of Trial Consultants, 20
Amrom, A. D., 146
Anakwah, N., 86
Anda, R. F., 106, 107, 110
Anderson, C., 161
Anderson, J., 225
Anderson, M., 278

Anderson, N. E., 136
Anderson, S., 183, 309
Andiloro, N., 154, 159
Andiloro, N. R., 159
Andrade, F., 204
Andrew, M., 75
Andrews, D., 53, 54, 59, 207, 298, 305, 312, 316
Andrews, D. A., 207, 278, 298, 305, 312
Angell, B., 177
Angermeyer, M., 205
Antrobus, E., 100
Anumba, N., 207
Aos, S., 300, 302, 315
Appelbaum, P., 47, 136, 206, 221
Appelbaum, P. S., 220, 221
Appio, L., 94
Appleby, S., 141
Applegarth, H. K.,
Applegate, A., 173
Arbery, Ahmaud, 105
Arcury, T. A., 79
Arentsen, T. G., 67
Arfken, C., 206
Arias, Jodi, 122
Aristotle, 44
Arkes, H., 258
Armstrong, B., 312
Armstrong, T., 304
Arndt, J., 268
Arnold, S., 178, 179
Arnot, L., 248, 267
Aronson, J., 138
Arrigo, B., 46
Arseneault, L., 47, 107
Artan, Abdul Razak Ali, 199
Arthur, B., 177
Asendorpf, J. B., 58
Asher, M., 161
Ashkenazi, T., 91
Ashton, R., 177
Asscher, J., 300
Associated Press, 88, 286
Association of Family and Conciliation Courts, 226
Atkins, Daryl, 293
Atkinson, D. J., 134
Atkins v. Virginia, 207, 292
Augustyn, M., 46
Auriacombe, M., 312
Austin, J., 245
Austin, J. L., 245
Avnaim-Pesso, L., 32
Axsom, D., 109, 115
Axt, J., 241
Ayton, P., 154
Azad, T., 102

B

Babcock, B., 242
Babcock, J. C., 110
Bacon, Francis, 44
Badcock, R., 125

Bagby, M., 219
Baglivio, M., 55, 298
Baglivio, M. T., 55
Baguley, C., 261
Bahara, M., 69, 175, 176
Bailenson, J., 167
Bailey, E., 250, 251
Baker, L., 139
Bakhshay, S., 250
Baldus, D., 240, 290
Baldus, D. C., 290
Bali, A., 259
Ballard, R., 173
Ball, R. A., 55
Bandes, S., 9
Bandura, Albert, 53
Bandyopadhyay, S., 179
Banks, Brian, 159
Banks, D., 174
Banks v. Goodfellow, 222
Banon, Tristane, 113
Baradaran, S., 154
Baranosky, M., 177
Barber, L., 65
Barclay, L., 161
Barden, R. C., 211
Barghouty, P., 77
Barnes, J., 47
Barnoski, R., 300, 302
Barnum, J., 174
Barone, N., 286
Baron, S. W., 52
Barovick, H., 8–9
Barrett, Amy Coney, 31
Barrett, H., 302
Barr, William, 6
Bartels, P., 207, 298
Barth, J., 29
Bartlett, F. C., 262
Bartlett, J., 156
Bartol, A., 65, 73
Bartol, C. R., 65, 66, 73
Barton, C., 300
Baruch, G., 299
Baskin-Sommers, A., 51, 207
Basora, J., 243, 244, 258
Bassett, J., 157
Batterman-Faunce, J., 100
Baugerud, G. A., 98
Baum, A., 73
Baum, L., 31
Baum, Rex, 54
Baumrind, N., 99
Bauserman, R., 224, 225
Baxter, J., 172
Bazelon, D., 212
Beall, A., 167
Bearman, M. J., 98
Beaton, L. 271
Beattey, R., 153
Beatty, L., 276
Beaudry-Cry, M., 282
Beccaria, Cesare, 44

Subject Index